LEGAL PROBLEMS OF
INTERNATIONAL
ECONOMIC
RELATIONS

CASES, MATERIALS AND TEXT ON THE NATIONAL AND INTERNATIONAL REGULATION OF TRANSNATIONAL ECONOMIC RELATIONS

Fourth Edition

By

John H. Jackson
University Professor,
Georgetown Law Center

William J. Davey
Edwin M. Adams Professor of Law,
University of Illinois College of Law

Alan O. Sykes, Jr.
Frank and Bernice Greenberg Professor of Law,
University of Chicago Law School

AMERICAN CASEBOOK SERIES®

WEST
GROUP

A THOMSON COMPANY

ST. PAUL, MINN., 2002

American Casebook Series, and the West Group symbol are registered trademarks used herein under license.

ISBN 0–314–24660–6

TEXT IS PRINTED ON 10% POST
CONSUMER RECYCLED PAPER

1st Reprint — 2003

Preface to the Fourth Edition

In the preface to the First Edition of this Casebook, we said that "preparing a book on the subject of international economic regulation is like trying to describe the landscape by looking out the window of a moving train—events tend to move faster than one can describe them." Nothing could be more true in our experience as we prepared the Fourth Edition. Indeed, we had to add a final chapter—Chapter 27—at the last minute to reflect developments at the WTO's Doha ministerial that will lead to a new series of multilateral negotiations.

The breadth and scope of the subject matter has become almost overwhelming, and has posed great challenges to us, as well as our many colleagues in law teaching who teach from this book, and all of our students. The treaty framework of our subject has not greatly changed since the Third Edition—which described in detail the full results of the Uruguay Round and the creation of the World Trade Organization (WTO). However, since 1996 an amazingly rich and detailed jurisprudence has developed in the WTO, particularly through the more than 40 decisions of the new Appellate Body, which has put its stamp on the interpretation of a number of important GATT provisions (especially Articles III and XX), as well as several of the other WTO agreements (particularly, the Safeguards, SPS and Subsidies Agreements). It has been the goal of our work on the Fourth Edition to incorporate this jurisprudence into these teaching materials to the fullest extent possible.

The basic theme of the previous editions—the impact of international economic interdependence and the struggle of legal institutions to cope with that circumstance—has been confirmed many times over, and is carried forward in this edition.

We have benefited from our own experiences in teaching with the previous editions. We have also benefited from the suggestions and criticisms of the many student and other faculty users. The Uruguay Round expanded the subject, and to keep the book manageable, it will be easily seen that both the subtractions and the additions for this edition have been substantial. We do not claim the perfect balance between the myriad of competing desires of teachers and students of this subject, but we hope and expect that we have considerably improved the book with our efforts.

An important basic goal of all editions, however, needs to be repeated. It is very easy to tally up multiple dozens of subjects which a potential international legal practitioner would find useful when he or she begins to grapple with real world problems. We do not intend to offer a complete coverage of these dozens of subjects, nor even a substantial portion of them. We aim, instead, to offer the student, professor, or current practitioner, the means to achieve a basic understanding of the international economic system as it operates in real life, and as it is constrained or aided by a number of fundamental legal institutions, including national and international constitutional documents and processes. In doing this adequately, we have necessarily had to minimize the coverage of many other practical topics. In a number of cases, however, many of those topics have been covered in other courses in the curriculum.

Our goal for this book, and courses based upon it, is to penetrate deeply into subjects which can have great importance to the government or private practitioner, but which are essentially not covered in other law courses. In addition our goal is to build for the student a knowledge of the "foundations" of the legal system and institutions of international economic relations. This implies knowledge of the constituent international instruments and processes, and the ways those interact with the important national constituent instruments and processes.

The objective of this book is to look at the legal principles and processes as they affect decisions regarding international economic relations, whether the decisions be those of private citizens or enterprises, or government officials. Thus there is an integration of national regulation and international law, and to a lesser extent private transaction law (which however is not emphasized in this course because it is often a part of or at least analogous to material learned in other courses). For example, United States constitutional and regulatory rules have an intimate and weighty connection and influence on the international rules of the WTO. One must study both to fully understand how they operate, because they interact.

Secondly, the emphasis is on trade in goods because this is generally at the center of international economic relations. However, we have expanded our treatment of the new topics added in the Uruguay Round negotiations, with particular focus on dispute settlement decisions in the intellectual property area, and we have included chapters as well on the so-called post-Uruguay Round new issues—competition and investment. Nonetheless, it is our view that the principles learned in discussing trade in goods are almost always transferable to other economic relation subjects, e.g. the constitutional problems of division of governmental authority within a nation, the practicalities of negotiating new international rules, the "constitutional" status of international norms, the difficulties of international dispute settlement procedures, the particular weight of special interest groups and their influence compared with broader but more diffuse foreign policy objectives or the interests of the consumers, the operation of legislative bodies, the decision and voting processes of international organizations, the economic complexity of some of the rules and the difficulty of fact finding.

Thirdly, the emphasis of this book is on the legal processes in *context*, but the emphasis is on *law*. The context obviously includes difficult conceptional and empirical questions of economics and political science, of sociology, history and especially overall foreign policy. But the emphasis here is on those subjects which have developed relatively sophisticated *rule* systems. There are many important subjects which have not yet developed such rule systems, and while touched upon they have not been selected for extensive treatment. (A course in economics, or world politics, therefore, might involve quite a different selection.) For example, both export controls and problems of developing countries merit considerable policy attention. But rule systems or the influence of law on those subjects is not (yet) weighty. Both subjects are dealt with in this book, but the focus on the primary goal of understanding the operation of *law*, means that it is necessary to eschew some tempting elaborations of policy questions when they, as yet, depend so little on law. This does not foreclose, of course, the opportunity for a particular teacher to construct for his or her class a rule formulating exercise based on the current and temporary materials bearing on the policy issues. Nor does this reflect any view of the authors regarding the relative importance in a broader context of nonlegal materials or information. It reflects our view that it is useful for law students to examine closely to what extent their particular skills and knowledge could contribute to solution of the myriad international economic problems.

Fourthly, a basic goal of these materials is to be sensitive to their use in the setting of the American law school curricula, so as to avoid unnecessary duplication of other courses, and to present to the student a coherent subject matter that is not likely to be obtained elsewhere. This is the reason, for example, for de-emphasizing private transaction law in this book, while focusing on government regulation. It is also a reason for minimizing duplication of material often included in either public or private (conflicts) international law. To a certain degree we see this course as a logical sequel to the course in public international law. However, this book is designed to accommodate the many students who take it without first having taken international law.

Fifthly, closely related to the previous "premise," is the notion that this course should be sensitive to the problems faced by practitioners—lawyers or officials, but should also offer the student something which he or she may never again (in practice) have the opportunity to get—namely, an opportunity to examine at length and in depth the overall operation of the "legal system" governing international economic affairs. The day to day problems faced by practitioners will quickly give the young lawyer experience in "how to do it," and great expertise on rather precise narrow topics. What is hard to obtain after leaving law school is the opportunity to spend a considerable amount of time achieving a comprehensive understanding of the total system and the interrelationships of its parts. This book emphasizes this comprehensive viewpoint.

Finally, so as to minimize the otherwise rapid obsolescence of both this book and students' learning, attention has been directed more toward the "constitutional" or fundamental aspects of the subject, eschewing too much concern with very recent "current events."

One last note. Many non-case materials are included. In particular, documents are important, and the supplement contains the text of key documents. Most chapters contain many queries or problems, and often these must be discussed in the context of the documents in the supplement. Consequently the class time needed for such discussion may be greater than would appear from the number of pages devoted to a topic. Often class discussion can center around the problems in the light of the material furnished, including the documents.

This book is designed primarily for a three-semester-hour course (45 classroom hours) although it is clear that a course of such length cannot cover all of this book. A four-hour (60 classes) course would likely be both necessary (and sufficient) to complete all of this book. A shorter course is feasible with careful selection, as many of our users know.

JOHN H. JACKSON
WILLIAM J. DAVEY
ALAN O. SYKES

Washington, D.C.
Champaign, Illinois
Chicago, Illinois
December 2001

Acknowledgments

The fourth edition of this book has built considerably on the first three, and thus we continue to be in the debt of all those who contributed so much to them. As the book evolved into its fourth edition, we were particularly indebted to the comments and reactions received from teachers and students who used prior editions, in particular those who have taken our courses in international trade law at the University of Michigan Law School, the Georgetown University Law Center, the University of Illinois College of Law and the University of Chicago Law School. In addition, we are much indebted to our friends and colleagues, both within and without the legal profession, both here and abroad, who have patiently engaged in discussions with us and/or reviewed drafts of the manuscript covering some of the difficult issues raised in a book with such a broad scope as this one.

While it is not possible to name all of those who contributed significantly to our work and thinking in preparing this edition, a few individuals who have worked with us closely are particularly worthy of recognition. These include Professor Jackson's administrative assistant, Joanna Sokolow, and his research assistant, Matthew Dunne; Professor Davey's administrative assistant, Ruth Manint; and Professor Sykes' administrative assistants, Shirley Evans and Kristy Skurauskis, and his research assistant Michael Mullican.

*

Summary of Contents

Chapter 1. The Policies Underlying International Economic Relations

Sec.

Chapter 2. International Sales Transactions

Chapter 3. The United States Constitution and Regulation of International Economic Affairs

Chapter 4. International Economic Regulation in the European Union and Japan

*

Table of Contents

———

Chapter 1.   The Policies Underlying International Economic Relations

Chapter 7.   Dispute Settlement

Chapter 16. The Regulation of Dumping

Chapter 23.   Competition Rules and the WTO

*

Table of Cases

The principal cases are in bold type. Cases cited or discussed in the text
are roman type. References are to pages. Cases cited in principal
cases and within other quoted materials are not included.

Court Decisions (U.S. and European)

*

Table of U.S. Administrative Decisions

(Principal cases are in bold)

*

Table of WTO, GATT, NAFTA and CUSFTA DECISIONS

(Principal cases are in bold)

GATT DECISIONS

*

A Note on Style and Abbreviations

We have indicated deletions from quoted materials by asterisks, except that we have not indicated deletions of footnotes, citations or internal cross references. The following is a list of common abbreviations used in the book:

List of Common Abbreviations

AB	Appellate Body
AD	Antidumping
ASP	American Selling Price
BNA ITR	Bureau of National Affairs, International Trade Reporter—Current Reports
BOP	Balance of Payments
BTN	Brussels Tariff Nomenclature
CAP	Common Agricultural Policy of the EU
CIF	Cost, Insurance and Freight
CIT	Court of International Trade
Comecon	Council for Mutual Economic Assistance (Communist countries)
COREPER	Committee of Permanent Representatives
CUSFTA	Canada-United States Free Trade Area
CVD	Countervailing duty(ies)
DSU	Dispute Settlement Understanding
EC	European Community or European Communities
E.C.R.	European Court Reports; Official Reports of the Court of Justice of the EC
ECSC	European Coal and Steel Community
EEA	European Economic Area
EEC	European Economic Community
EFTA	European Free Trade Association
Euratom	European Atomic Energy Community
EU	European Union
FCN	Friendship Commerce and Navigation
FOB	Free on Board
GATS	General Agreement on Trade in Services
GATT	General Agreement on Tariffs and Trade
GSP	Generalized System of Preferences
HTS	Harmonized Tariff System
IBRD	International Bank for Reconstruction and Development ("World Bank")
IMF	International Monetary Fund
ITA	International Trade Administration, U.S. Department of Commerce
ITC	International Trade Commission (U.S. independent agency)
ITO	International Trade Organization
ITRD	Bureau of National Affairs International Trade Reporter—Decisions
LDC	Less Developed or Developing Countries
MAI	Multilateral Agreement on Investment (failed proposal)
MFN	Most-Favored-Nation clause or treatment
MTN	Multilateral Trade Negotiations
NAFTA	North American Free Trade Area

NMEs	Nonmarket Economies
NTB	Nontariff Barrier
OECD	Organization for Economic Cooperation and Development
OMA	Orderly Marketing Agreement
OTC	Organization for Trade Cooperation
PPA	Protocol of Provisional Application of GATT
SPS	Sanitary and Phytosanitary
SDR	Special Drawing Rights (in the IMF)
STC	State Trading Corporations
STR	Special Trade Representative (U.S. Government)
TEA	Trade Expansion Act of 1962 (U.S.)
TRIPS	Trade-Related Intellectual Property Rights
TRIMs	Trade-Related Investment Measures
TEU	Treaty on European Union (known also as the Maastricht Treaty)
UNCITRAL	United Nations Commission on International Trade Law
UNIDROIT	International Institute for the Unification of Private Law
UNSITC	United Nations Standard International Trade Classification
USITC	United States International Trade Commission (see ITC)
USTR	United States Trade Representative (ex. Special Trade Representative (STR))
VER	Voluntary Export Restraint
VRA	Voluntary Restraint Agreement
WTO	World Trade Organization

LEGAL PROBLEMS OF
INTERNATIONAL ECONOMIC RELATIONS

CASES, MATERIALS AND TEXT ON THE NATIONAL AND INTERNATIONAL REGULATION OF TRANSNATIONAL ECONOMIC RELATIONS

Fourth Edition

*

Chapter 1

THE POLICIES UNDERLYING INTERNATIONAL ECONOMIC RELATIONS

SECTION 1.1 INTERNATIONAL ECONOMIC RELATIONS AND THE LAW

(A) INTERDEPENDENCE AND THE BRETTON WOODS SYSTEM

"Interdependence" may be overused, but it accurately describes our world today. Economic forces flow with great rapidity from one country to the next. Despite all the talk about sovereignty and independence, these concepts can mislead when applied to today's world economy. How "sovereign" is a country with an economy so dependent on trade with other countries that its government cannot readily affect the real domestic interest rate, implement its preferred tax policy, or establish an effective program of incentives for business or talented individuals? Many governments face such constraints today including, increasingly and inevitably, the government of the United States.

To a great extent, contemporary international economic interdependence can be attributed to the success of the institutions put in place just after World War II, what we call in this book the Bretton Woods System, which includes the IMF (International Monetary Fund) and GATT (the General Agreement on Tariffs and Trade). GATT was the engine for reducing tariff barriers to trade in goods, at least among the democratic market-oriented industrial countries. With the successful conclusion of the Uruguay Round of trade negotiations, the World Trade Organization (WTO) was created to replace the GATT. The WTO system goes beyond the old GATT system to address trade in services, intellectual property, and other important areas previously outside its purview. Decreasing costs of transportation and communication have also played a profound role in increasing levels of trade and interdependence during the years since World War II.

With the decline of tariffs to near de minimis levels in developed countries, other much more complex barriers or distortions of trade have become relatively more important. Nontariff barriers are myriad, and the ingenuity of man to invent new ones assures us that the problem of trade barriers will never go away.

Of particular interest to us in this book, and to practicing trade lawyers, are laws against "unfair" trade practices. In some cases trade may indeed be "unfair" by some intelligible standard, but in others the suspicion arises that practices are unfair only in the eyes of the import-competing industries that would like freedom from the challenges that competition can bring. Further, an increasing number of situations involve conflicts among contradictory economic, cultural and political goals across nations. Disputes about what is "unfair," therefore, often go to deep and fundamental differences of opinion about the appropriate economic role of governments.

Recent years have seen other issues bubble to the surface. The protestors at world economic summits of late, such as the WTO ministerial meeting in Seattle, urge that the globalization associated with the rise of the WTO poses a threat to the environment, to food safety, and even to human rights. Others complain that the governing bodies of the global economy—again most especially the WTO—are undemocratic and lacking in transparency. Whether or not these arguments have merit, they have clearly had an impact on political support for the WTO system, and on its likely agenda going forward.

There are innumerable other important and perplexing issues in international economic relations. Monetary issues take a central place among them. With fundamental shifts in the Bretton Woods System, the world has experienced considerable volatility in its exchange rates. When an exchange rate changes by 20 or 30 percent within even one year, the effects on trade can swamp those of the conventional instruments of commercial policy such as tariffs and quotas. Additional topics such as trade in services, competition policy, the environment and intellectual property, have become increasingly important to economic relations between nations.

We are also concerned in this book with the way that national legal systems interact with international legal rules and institutions. The process by which nations bind themselves to international agreements, for example, and the institutional structure of domestic institutions that implement rights and responsibilities under international law, is of deep practical and intellectual significance.

(B) OVERVIEW AND STRUCTURE OF THE BOOK

The law of international transactions has three components. The first involves the private law of the transaction, which includes the contract and sales laws of the two nations involved, conflict of laws rules ("private international law"), insurance law, corporate law, maritime law and options for dispute resolution involving such matters. Because these subjects are treated in other basic law school courses, this book does not emphasize the private law of international transactions, but it does provide some introduction to the issues.

The second component of the law of international transactions involves national government regulation of the transaction. By this we mean the law of customs tariffs, export and import controls, quality and packaging standards, internal taxes (which may discriminate against foreign goods), special mixing or purchasing requirements (such as "Buy American" laws) and other regulatory matters. The purposes to be achieved by these laws are varied, often contradictory, and sometimes related to political pressures from special-interest groups at the expense of the nation as a whole.

The third and last component of the law of international transactions is the international law, or law of international economic institutions. Typically, this body of law binds governments rather than private actors, yet its effects on private transactions can be profound, as much national legislation springs from it.

Chapters 1 through 7 of this book are designed to introduce these three components of the law of international transactions, and to present an overall view of the "constitutional" working of the international legal system as it applies to international economic relations. In the remainder of this first chapter, we focus on the basic economic and other policies which motivate national and international governmental institutions in their development and application of the rules. Chapter 2 provides a brief introduction to the private law of the underlying transactions, emphasizing the ways in which international transactions differ from domestic ones. Chapters 3 and 4 then turn to national government legal systems. The United States is the focus of a rather extended treatment in Chapter 3, partly because the book is designed for courses in that country, and also because the U.S. economy is so important to the trading system. The European Union is the focus of Chapter 4, although we include some materials on Japan as well. Chapters 5 through 7 then introduce the ground work for an understanding of the "international constitution" of the world trading system, with special attention to the WTO/GATT treaty structure and its dispute settlement system.

Chapters 8 through 18 take up the core subjects involved in the regulation of imports. Each chapter discusses one central regulatory technique or principle, relating the national law to the international rules and institutions. These chapters cover basic import restrictions—tariffs and quotas, most-favored-nation obligations and the free trade area exception to them, national treatment rules, the basic GATT exceptions for health and environment, the rules on product standards, safeguards and escape clauses, and finally laws designed to permit responses to "unfair" actions of governments or firms engaged in exporting.

These chapters should be viewed not only as an introduction to important trade policy issues, but as case studies of contemporary national and international legal rules relating to economic relations among nations. The legal principles explored in these chapters are possibly the most complex and refined of any international rules in existence today. How they operate (or fail to operate) in the face of modern economic, constitutional and other legal constraints is instructive beyond the details of the particular rules themselves.

We next turn to a series of other increasingly important subjects. In Chapters 19 and 20 we examine two new subjects of regulation in the WTO/GATT system—intellectual property and services. Thereafter, we provide overview chapters concerning linkages between trade rules and other policies (environment, human rights, labor standards and national security), monetary affairs, competition and investment policies. The list could easily be longer, but space constraints preclude expanding it any further. Chapter 25 considers the special issues that arise for developing countries.

Finally, in Chapter 26, we step back from the mosaic of detail and try to develop some preliminary conclusions about the various national and international rules and institutions that can have such an important effect on the economic and even geo-political future of the world. Some readers may find that this chapter serves as much as an introduction as a conclusion, and may wish to review it now.

SECTION 1.2   THE GROWTH AND IMPORTANCE OF INTERNATIONAL TRADE

Trade between different areas of the world has occurred throughout history. Indeed, much of the world was discovered and explored by those seeking new trading opportunities—from the Phoenicians to Marco Polo to the Portuguese and Spanish explorers of the fifteenth and sixteenth centuries. The risks of trading expeditions in these times were great but they were viewed as worth taking in light of the potential profits.

In the "Mercantilist" era, nations valued trade for the gold that it earned for the exporting nation and its citizens. To expand those earnings by gaining control of the sources of export commodities, as well as to secure export markets, European nations established colonies throughout the world. To maximize their earnings from trade, they often severely restricted imports. In the nineteenth century, however, in part due to economists who argued that gains from trade would be maximized if trade occurred without restrictions, nations began to reduce their import restrictions. The trend toward reduction was reversed in the 1870's, but the volume of trade continued to grow until World War I.

The period between World War I and World War II was a difficult time in the international economy. Increasing tariffs, particularly those enacted in the early 1930's by the Smoot–Hawley Tariff Act in the United States and comparable measures elsewhere, led to sharp declines in imports and exports. Many economic historians believe that these trade restrictions deepened the Great Depression significantly, although such claims are controversial and the effects of trade restrictions from country to country no doubt varied.[1]

Following World War II, many national leaders were convinced that it would be mutually advantageous—economically and otherwise—to promote international trade. This book is essentially a study of the institutions and structure that were put in place immediately after the war, as they have evolved to the present day. The focus will be on the central agreements of that structure—the World Trade Organization (WTO) charter and the General Agreement on Tariffs and Trade which it subsumed, better known as GATT. The principal goal of GATT, first signed in 1947, was to establish limitations on tariffs and to control the use of certain non-tariff barriers to trade. As a result of eight series of negotiations (called "rounds"), such as the Kennedy Round in the 1960's, the Tokyo Round in the 1970's, and the Uruguay Round in the 1980's and 1990's, significant reductions in tariffs have occurred. The history of tariff rates in the United States is shown in Table 1.1:[2]

Table 1.1

Ratio of Duties Collected to Dutiable
Imports—United States

1821		45.0%
1831	(after Tariff of Abominations)	47.4
1841	(after Compromise Tariff)	34.6
1851	(after Walker Tariff)	26.6
1861	(after Tariff of 1857)	18.8
1871	(after Morrill and War tariffs)	44.0
1881		43.2
1891	(after McKinley Tariff)	46.5
1901	(after Wilson–Gorman and Dingley tariffs)	49.8
1911	(after Payne–Aldrich Tariff)	41.3
1921	(after Underwood Tariff)	29.5
1931	(after Fordney–McCumber and Smoot–Hawley tariffs)	53.2
1941	(after Trade Agreements Act of 1934)	36.8
1951	(after formation of GATT)	12.3
1961		12.1
1971	(after Kennedy Round)	9.0
1981	(after Tokyo Round)	4.9
1991		5.1
2000		4.8

1. The excerpt in Section 1.4 from Richard Cooper makes the argument that the Depression was compounded by trade wars. For a contrary view, see Barry J. Eichengreen, The Origins and Nature of the Great Slump Revisited, 45 Econ.Hist.Rev. 213 (1992); Barry J. Eichengreen, Did International Economic Forces Cause the Great Depression?, 6 Contemp.Pol. Issues 90 (1988).

2. Source: Bureau of the Census, Historical Statistics of the United States (various issues); and Department of Commerce, Statistical Abstract of the United States (1992); Peter Kenen, The International Economy 226 (1985); U.S. International Trade Commission, Value of U.S. Imports for Consumption, Duties Collected, and Ratio of Duties to Values, www.usitc.gov.

From 1934 to 1952, i.e. from the time of the Smoot–Hawley tariff through the Reciprocal Trade Agreements Program to the initial implementation of GATT, average U.S. tariffs on dutiable imports fell from 53% to 12.8%. Little reduction occurred in the next decade, but considerable further reductions occurred as a result of the Kennedy and Tokyo Rounds. Similar reductions have occurred in the tariff rates of other industrialized countries. The tariff cuts of the Uruguay Round reduce average tariffs for developed countries by another 38% and for developing countries by 24%.[3] In the year 2000, the average tariff rate in the United States on dutiable imports was 4.8% as the Table indicates—if the average is calculated to include duty free imports as well, the average tariff is a mere 1.6%.

Given the decline in protection that GATT initiated, it is no surprise that the period since the formation of GATT has witnessed significant increases in the volume of world trade. Between 1963 and 1973, world exports grew at a rate of approximately 8½% per year in volume. Even with the economic slowdown of the early 1980's, world exports grew at a rate of about 3% per year between 1973 and 1983. And, between 1983 and 1990, exports grew at a 6% rate. In each case, the growth in export volumes was at least 50% greater than the growth in total production during the same period.[4] That pattern continued and accelerated through the 1990's, with merchandise exports growing at a rate more than triple the rate of growth in merchandise production.[5] As a consequence, international trade has continued to grow more important to national economies. For the United States, the International Monetary Fund reported in 1992 that the combined total of imports and exports exceeded one trillion dollars for the first time. In the year 2000, that total was approaching $2 trillion.

The degree of importance of trade to each country varies, of course, and one way to measure it is to compare the value of a country's exports with its total gross domestic product, as is done in Table 1.2.[6]

Table 1.2

Exports of Goods and Services as a Percentage of Gross Domestic Product

(Measured at Current Prices)

Country	1960	2000
Canada	17.2	45.8
France	14.5	28.7
Germany	19.0	33.4

3. 11 BNA ITR 564 (1994); GATT, GATT Focus Newsletter, December 1993, at 6.

4. GATT, International Trade 1983/84, at 2 (Table 1) (1984); GATT, International Trade 1990/91, at 6 (Table 2) (1991).

5. WTO, International Trade Statistics 2000, available online at *www.wto.org*.

6. The OECD National Accounts 1960–97, Vol. 1, "Main aggregates" table for each country, plus OECD National Accounts, 2001 Quarterly Report, Vol. 1 (for 2000 data).

Country	1960	2000
Japan	10.7	10.8
Netherlands	47.7	67.1
Sweden	22.8	47.4
Switzerland	29.3	45.1
United Kingdom	20.9	27.2
United States	5.2	11.0

The increasing relative importance of world trade has meant that the economic welfare of one country is often tied closely to that of another. As we will see, this increasing interdependence of national economies has put strains on the WTO/GATT system, particularly during times of recession and slow economic growth.

SECTION 1.3   ECONOMIC THEORY AND INTERNATIONAL ECONOMIC POLICY

While an understanding of the basic economic principles relating to international trade is not essential to a study of the law of international economic relations, some general exposure to those principles is helpful. Economists are not always in agreement on how these basic principles should be translated into policy, and their views are not always accepted in any event. Nonetheless, their views on the desirability of international trade and the effects of interferences with trade have played an important role in shaping the legal framework in which trade occurs. While much of the economics literature is too theoretical and technical for our purposes, the basic principles can be grasped by non-economists.[1] This section introduces a few of those principles, to which we will refer throughout the book, as well as a sampling of more advanced economic thought in the field of international trade. Here we consider 1) comparative advantage and gains from trade; 2) the effect of restraints on trade; 3) the validity of arguments in favor of trade restraints; and 4) the reasons for, or "political economy" of, trade restraints.

(A) COMPARATIVE ADVANTAGE AND GAINS FROM TRADE

Early economists embraced the "labor theory of value" as a way of understanding how prices are determined. The concept of comparative

---

1. There are a number of useful textbooks and reference works on international trade. Less technically inclined readers may wish to consult the books excerpted in this chapter by Kindleberger and Kenen, as well as Peter H. Lindert, International Economics (9th ed. 1991) and Paul R. Krugman & Maurice Obstfeld, International Economics: Theory and Policy (5th ed. 2000). More advanced treatments may be found in Avinash K. Dixit & Victor D. Norman, Theory of International Trade (1980); Jagdish N. Bhagwati, Arvind Panagariya, & T.N. Srinivasan, Lectures on International Trade (2d ed. 1998); the Handbook of International Economics, Volumes I, II (Ronald W. Jones & Peter B. Kenen eds., 1984); and the Handbook of International Economics, Volume III (Gene Grossman and Kenneth Rogoff eds., 1995). The "new trade theory," emphasizing imperfect competition and increasing returns, is discussed in Elhanan Helpman & Paul R. Krugman, Market Structure and Foreign Trade (1985), Elhanan Helpman & Paul R. Krugman, Trade Policy and Market Structure (1989); and in Paul R. Krugman, Rethinking International Trade (1990).

advantage developed during this early period, and thus relied at first on this now discarded theory of value. Nevertheless, the basic idea of comparative advantage survived, and is most easily exposited using the simplifying assumptions of these early economists. The following excerpt from Kindleberger recounts the development of the theory of comparative advantage, and indicates how it has survived into the modern period under more general assumptions.

CHARLES P. KINDLEBERGER, INTERNATIONAL ECONOMICS 17–21, 27, 33 (5th Ed. 1973)[2]

LAW OF COMPARATIVE ADVANTAGE

The classical economists asked what goods would be traded between two countries because they thought the answer for trade between countries was different from that for trade within a country. Within a country, a region produces the goods it can make cheaper than other regions. The value of a commodity within a country, moreover, is determined by its labor content. If the product of a certain industry can be sold for more than the value of the labor it contains, additional labor will transfer into that industry from other occupations to earn the abnormal profits available there. Supply will expand until the price is brought down to the value of the labor it contains. Similarly, if a commodity sells for less than the worth of its labor, labor will move away into other lines until the gap is closed. The tendency of wages toward equality within a country results in prices of goods equal to their labor such as to equalize the return to labor in all occupations and regions. If wages are higher in California than in Massachusetts, labor will migrate to California. This will lower wages in California and raise them in Massachusetts, and the movement will continue until the return to labor is equated in the two regions. After labor has spread itself among several regions to equalize wages, these regions will produce and sell to each other what each region can make the cheapest. Its advantage in such commodities over other regions will be absolute. Therefore the theory of trade applicable to regions of a country is the theory of absolute advantage.

Classical economists thought that the labor theory of value valid in trade within a country cannot be applied between nations, since factors of production are immobile internationally. If wages are higher in the United States than in Britain, they stay higher, for migration cannot take place on a scale sufficient to eliminate discrepancies. Under these circumstances, the classical economists asked, what will the United States sell to Britain and Britain to America?

Let us assume two countries and two commodities. If each country can produce one good cheaper (i.e., with less labor) than it can be produced in the other, as in the case of domestic trade, each will have an

2. Reprinted by permission from International Economics, Fifth Edition, by Kindleberger (Homewood, IL: Richard D. Irwin, Inc., 1973).

advantage in the production of one commodity and a disadvantage in the production of the other. Each country will then be anxious to export the commodity in which it has an advantage and import the commodity in which it has a disadvantage. The position is suggested in the following table, where wheat can be produced more cheaply in the United States and cloth more cheaply in Britain. The United States has an absolute advantage in wheat and an absolute disadvantage in cloth. It will export wheat and import cloth, which, with the numerical values given, may be assumed to exchange one for the other at something like the rate of one yard of cloth for one bushel of wheat:

Production of One Man in One Week

Product	In United States	In United Kingdom
Wheat	6 bushels	2 bushels
Cloth	2 yards	6 yards

But suppose that the labor content of both wheat and cloth is less in the United States than in Britain. Suppose that instead of merely 2 yards of cloth per week a man in the United States can produce 10. The position is then as follows:

Production of One Man in One Week

Product	In United States	In United Kingdom
Wheat	6 bushels	2 bushels
Cloth	10 yards	6 yards

It is evident that labor is more efficient in the United States than in the United Kingdom, and wages in the United States will be higher on that account. By assumption, however, migration will not take place to equalize wage rates.

Trade cannot now follow the decree of absolute advantage and a new principle is needed to take its place. This was developed by David Ricardo more than 150 years ago, in the law of comparative advantage. Ricardo observed that in cases similar to ours, while the United States had an absolute advantage over Britain in both wheat and cloth, it had a greater advantage in wheat than in cloth. He concluded that a country would export the product in which it had the greater advantage, or a comparative advantage, and import the commodity in which its advantage was less, or in which it had a comparative disadvantage. In this example the United States would export wheat and import cloth, even though it could produce cloth more efficiently than Britain.

The reasoning underlying this conclusion may be demonstrated arithmetically. Without international trade, wheat and cloth would exchange for one another in each country at their respective labor contents, which would differ as between the two countries. In the United States, 6 bushels of wheat, or one week's labor, would buy 10 yards of cloth. In Britain, by the same token, 6 bushels of wheat—three weeks' labor in the less productive country—would buy 18 yards of cloth. If the United States through trade can get more than 10 yards of cloth for 6 bushels of wheat (or more than 1⅔ yards of cloth per bushel of wheat), it will pay it to do so. It cannot hope to get more than 18 yards of cloth for 6 bushels of wheat (3 yards of cloth for a single bushel). This is the price which cloth producers in Britain can get without trade, and there is no reason for them to enter into foreign trade and be worse off.

Similarly, if Britain can get more than 2 bushels of wheat for 6 yards of cloth (more than one third of a bushel of wheat per yard of cloth), it will pay it to export cloth and buy wheat. But it cannot hope to get more than six tenths or three fifths of a bushel per yard—the American wheat farmers' price without trade.

For effective comparison, the prices should be quoted the same way. At any price for cloth cheaper than 10 yards (of cloth) for 6 bushels (of wheat), that is, for any more than 10 yards for 6 bushels, the United States will gain by shifting resources out of cloth into wheat and importing cloth. Similarly, at a price of cloth which would involve Britain giving up less than 18 yards for 6 bushels (equal to 6 yards for 2 bushels), it will pay Britain to move its labor out of wheat into cloth and import wheat in exchange for cloth rather than grow grain itself. Trade raises the price of wheat and lowers the price of cloth in the United States; it raises the price of cloth and lowers the price of wheat in Britain. Even when one country can produce both commodities more efficiently than another country, both can gain from specialization and exchange, provided that the efficiency advantage is greater in some commodity or commodities than in others.

On the basis of this type of demonstration, the classical economists concluded that international trade does not require offsetting absolute advantages but is possible where a comparative advantage exists. It goes without saying but must be said, as it is frequently forgotten, that a comparative advantage is always (and by definition) accompanied by a comparative disadvantage.

Production Possibilities Curves

The labor theory of value on which this analysis rested was subsequently rejected as invalid. The tendency for the return to labor to be equal throughout a country was seen by observation to be weak and faltering. Labor is not homogeneous. If there is an increase in the demand for barrels, the wages of coopers will rise above those of smiths, with whom they are not interchangeable. It became recognized that there is not one great class of labor with a single wage but a series of noncompeting groups among which the tendency to equalization of wages, at least in the short run, is weak or nonexistent.

A more fundamental objection, however, which would apply even if labor were homogeneous and commanded one price in a perfectly competitive market, is that goods are not produced by labor alone but by various combinations of all the factors of production: land, labor, and capital. To compare the labor content of two commodities—say, gasoline and textiles, or meat and shoes—gives an erroneous view of relative values. Gasoline production requires far more capital per unit of labor than textiles, and meat output more land than shoes. Variable proportions of factors in the production of different commodities make it impossible to use the labor theory of value, however qualified.

An escape from this impasse has been provided by Gottfried Haberler in the theory of opportunity costs. The cost of wheat in the long run is how much cloth a country has to give up to get additional units of wheat. It makes little difference whether the factors which leave the production of cloth are all suited to the output of wheat or not. The question is simply how much of one commodity must be given up to get more of the other.

The notion of opportunity cost is illustrated in international trade theory with production possibilities or transformation curves. Instead of saying that a week's labor will produce either 6 bushels of wheat or 10 yards of cloth, one says that all the factors of production can produce either 6 bushels of wheat or 10 yards of cloth per some appropriate unit of time, or some intermediate combination of them. In figure 2.1, where the vertical axis represents wheat and the horizontal axis cloth, the U.S. curve means that the resources of the United States, in the absence of foreign trade, can be used entirely to produce wheat, in which case 6 bushels (per capita per week) can be produced, exclusively for cloth, in which case output will consist of 10 yards per man-week, or some appropriate intermediate combination, such as 3 bushels of wheat and 5 yards of cloth. The production possibilities curve does not tell what will in fact be produced. More information is needed for this purpose, on the side of demand. It merely sets out what the possibilities are.

FIGURE 2.1. Production Possibilities Curves, Constant Opportunity Costs

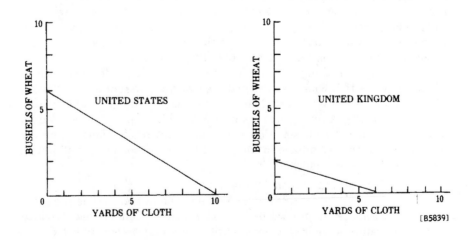

[B5839]

* * *

Factor Proportions

If international trade is based on differences in comparative costs, the curious student will proceed to the next question: What makes for differences in comparative costs? Why do the transformation curves of various countries differ?

The answer given to this question by Swedish economist Bertil Ohlin is two-fold: Different goods, he stated, require different factor inputs; and different countries have different factor endowments. If wheat is technologically best produced with lots of land relative to labor and capital, countries that have an abundance of land will be able to produce wheat cheaply. This is why Australia, Argentina, Canada, Minnesota, and the Ukraine export wheat. On the other hand, if cloth requires much labor relative to capital and land, countries that have an abundance of labor—Hong Kong, Japan, India—will have a comparative advantage in cloth manufacture and be able to export it.

* * *

Differences in comparative costs come about not only because of differences in factor endowments but also through specialization in different commodities. To a degree the choice of whether the United States or Britain specializes in one kind of an automobile or another, or this tractor or that, may be determined by historical accident. The fact is that, with each country specialized, a basis for trade exists, since each can produce one good cheaper than the other.

Notes

(1) As the reading from Kindleberger suggests, the principle of comparative advantage holds that nations trade because the amount of a good that must be sacrificed internally to produce a unit of another good varies across countries. The question as to why this tradeoff in production should vary need not be answered confidently before we can know that there are gains from trade. Nevertheless, the Kindleberger reading does suggest two of the traditional hypotheses about the sources of comparative advantage. Implicit in the old Ricardian model with labor as the only factor of production is one of them—some nations have access to superior technology, at least for the production of some things. The other hypothesis, mentioned explicitly by Kindleberger, is that countries are endowed with a different mix of "factors of production," such as unskilled labor, skilled labor, land and other natural resources. Because some goods require relatively more of these various factors to produce them, a nation that has them in abundant supply can have a comparative advantage in the production of a good even if all nations have access to the same technology.

A more recent and related idea is the "technology-gap" model of trade, often attributed to the late Raymond Vernon. The notion here is that some countries specialize in innovation and the introduction of new products, probably because of their greater scientific base and better educated work force (a factor endowment differential, although the "endowment" may be affected by social policy over time). Other nations specialize in imitation and mass production, which becomes possible after the production process is standardized and routinized: "The technological-gap theory makes use of the sequence of innovation and imitation, particularly as they affect exports. As a new product is developed in a country and becomes profitable in the domestic market, the innovating firm, which enjoys a temporary monopoly, has initially an easy access to foreign markets. * * * Later on, however, the profits of the innovating firm prompt imitation in other countries which may actually prove to have a comparative advantage in the production of the new commodity after the innovation is disseminated. * * * But as the innovating country loses, through imitation, its absolute advantage in one commodity, a new cycle of innovation imitation begins in another. Thus, the innovating country may continue to develop new products and may continue to have a temporary absolute advantage in products which are eventually more efficiently produced by other countries." Miltiades Chacoliades, International Trade Theory and Policy 305–06 (1978).[3]

(2) A rather different kind of argument to explain the pattern of trade relates to the possibility that trade may be driven by economies of scale. Suppose, for example, that two nations are identical in all relevant respects, but one of them somehow gets a "head start" in the production of a good that has substantial learning-by-doing economies. The nation with the head start may retain a cost advantage for a long time, or even indefinitely, and thus specialize in the production of the good for export. See Paul R. Krugman, Rethinking International Trade 152–82 (1990). Kindleberger hints at the possibility in the last paragraph of the excerpt, where he refers to patterns of trade that result from historical accident.

(3) The older theories of trade left little room for government action to affect comparative advantage or the pattern of specialization. The more modern theories, by contrast, suggest that the concept of "comparative advantage" itself may be fraught with confusion, because the pattern of trade that results in the end will reflect not only pre-existing "exogenous" differences among countries but also the results of governmental policies or chance. Likewise, they raise the possibility that government can deliberately create "comparative advantage" through subsidies for research and development, for specialized education, or for the establishment of particular industries subject to increasing returns to scale. The popular term for such government measures is "industrial policy." To be sure, the wisdom and efficacy of those policies is hotly disputed. We will not enter the fray, but will later consider whether industrial policy is somehow "unfair" and whether countries that do not employ it should want to and be able to restrict trade with those that do.

(4) The theory of comparative advantage developed under assumptions of perfect competition. Some of the implications of relaxing that assumption are explored below in the materials on strategic trade policy. If firms have monopoly power in a domestic market, however, one obvious consequence of trade is to constrain the ability of those firms to charge monopoly prices. Recent empirical evidence suggests that this effect can be quite important at

---

3. See also Edward Leamer, Sources of   (1984).
International   Comparative   Advantage

times. See Levinson, Testing the Imports-as-Market-Discipline Hypothesis, 35 J.Intl.Econ. 1 (1993).

(5) The readings and comments to this point make no mention of exchange rates. In traditional economic models of trade, trade is always in balance and the exchange rate is an afterthought—indeed, money is not included formally, on the premise that exchange rates simply adjust to clear the market by balancing import expenditures with export earnings. Further, because the simple models are "static," there is no reason for the terms of the exchange between countries to fluctuate once trade has been opened and an equilibrium has been reached.

In reality, however, trade occurs with money, and the price of that money in terms of other currencies is variable. The fluctuation of exchange rates can have important effects upon the competitiveness of firms in international markets. For some time, for example, the suggestion was made that the U.S. dollar was "overvalued."[4] That is, it was asserted that the price of dollars relative to, say, yen, caused American goods to be "too expensive" in Japan and Japanese goods to be "too cheap" in the United States, resulting in a trade imbalance in favor of Japan. Such an imbalance is possible because when Americans buy yen in order to import from Japan, those abroad who sell the yen for dollars do not always use the dollars to buy goods and services from the United States. Instead, they may buy real estate, shares of stock, or other capital assets, among other things.

Turning the point on its head, when a country such as the United States becomes a relatively attractive place to invest—presumably because the real returns to those investments are expected to be relatively high—U.S. exporters will suffer because the dollar will appreciate due to the demand for dollars for investment purposes. The same thing may happen because a trading partner has a comparatively high savings rate (like Japan). The United States then finances some of its imports by selling claims on capital assets rather than by selling its own goods and services in foreign markets. We will return in a later chapter to the question whether this deficit in the balance of trade should be viewed as a "problem" when we consider trade intervention for balance of payments purposes. At present, however, it suffices to note that because exchange rates do not automatically adjust to balance imports and exports, the teachings of comparative advantage models must be tempered by the realization that, putting it loosely, "comparative advantage" may lie in part in the export of claims on capital assets. Likewise, nations may at times find that comparative advantage in the production of goods and services erodes due to the appreciation of their currency.

(B) INTERFERENCE WITH FREE TRADE

Economist and Nobel Laureate Paul Samuelson once wrote, "[T]here is essentially only one argument for free trade or freer trade, but it is an exceedingly powerful one, namely: Free trade promotes a

---

4. See, e.g., Rudiger Dornbusch, The Overvalued Dollar, Lloyds Bank Review, April, 1984, at 1–12; C. Fred Bergsten, The Villain is an Overvalued Dollar, *in* The United States in the World Economy: Selected Papers of C. Fred Bergsten 799–91 (1983).

mutually profitable division of labor, greatly enhances the potential real national product of all nations, and makes possible higher standards of living all over the globe."[5] Put differently, Samuelson's claim is that free trade increases economic welfare, both for the world as a whole, and for each nation. In this section, we explore this claim in greater detail, including some of the new challenges to its correctness.

(1) Efficiency vs. Distribution

The gains from free trade to which Samuelson adverts, whether national or international, are *aggregate* gains. In other words, if one adds up the effect of a movement toward free trade on all affected parties—consumers, producers and government (the latter through its revenues)—the claim is that the net effect of a movement toward free trade is positive. For those familiar with concepts of producer and consumer surplus, the claim more precisely is that a movement toward free trade increases the sum of producer and consumer surplus in the economy, plus government revenue if it is not already redistributed and otherwise counted. These aggregate effects we term the "efficiency" consequences of trade policy.

Even if freer trade produces efficiency gains, that fact is entirely compatible with the possibility that a movement toward free trade may harm some individuals greatly. If the U.S. textile, footwear or sugar markets were opened overnight to unfettered international competition, for example, many producers in those industries would no doubt soon go bankrupt, and many workers would lose their jobs. This has two important implications for thoughtful reflection about trade policy.

First, as a normative matter, the economist's argument for free trade is persuasive only if one supposes (a) that aggregate efficiency gains are a proper basis for evaluating the wisdom of policy irrespective of the changes in income distribution that may accompany them, or (b) that any unacceptable consequences of free trade for the income distribution are better addressed through alternative policy instruments. Even for those skeptical of the former position, the latter position may have much to commend it, though we are not able to dwell on it here.[6]

Second, as a positive matter, the fact that changes in trade policy produce gainers and losers explains the existence of political opposition to free trade. We return to these issues later.

5. Paul A. Samuelson, Economics 692 (9th ed. 1973).

6. One of us has discussed the efficiency/distribution tension at length elsewhere, disputing many of the distribution arguments on their merits and developing the further argument that trade policy is a poor tool for redistribution in any event. See Alan O. Sykes, Countervailing Duty Law: An Economic Perspective, 89 Colum.L.Rev. 199, 209–13 (1989); Alan O. Sykes, Protectionism as a Safeguard: A Positive Analysis of the GATT Escape Clause with Normative Speculations, 58 U.Chi.L.Rev. 255, 269–72 (1991). See also Gary C. Hufbauer & Kimberly A. Elliot, Measuring the Costs of Protection in the United States (1993).

(2) The Efficiency Case for Free Trade and the Consequences of Tariffs and Quotas

The two most common types of restraints on imports are tariffs (a tax levied on imports at the time of importation, which usually has the effect of increasing the prices at which the imports are sold) and quotas (an upper limit on the quantity or value of imports allowed during a given time period). The effects of tariffs and quotas are analyzed with the aid of diagrams in the Appendix to this Chapter. Here, we will discuss their effects verbally.

Samuelson's argument above for free trade, and thus against the use of tariffs and quotas, is actually a trivial corollary of a well-know proposition in price theory often termed the first theorem of welfare economics: competitive markets, without externalities, are efficient, and interference with them is inefficient. To elaborate the idea with particular reference to trade, consider first the effects of a tariff. A tariff typically raises the price of an imported good because domestic sellers of that good now have an additional cost of production (the tariff) that must be recouped. Domestic producers of goods that compete with the imported good will often be able to raise their prices as well because import competition is less of a constraint on their pricing policies. If so, domestic producers gain from the tariff. Just as clearly, domestic consumers lose from the need to pay higher prices. The government gains some revenue from the tariff. Samuelson's proposition can be restated as a claim that the sum of these effects is negative, and a geometric "proof" for a single market in a single importing country can be found in the Appendix. Roughly speaking, the proof identifies two sources of net loss to an importing nation from a tariff: (1) the fact that some "marginal consumers" are priced out of the market by the higher price, so that their loss of consumer surplus is not recouped by any producer in the form of a higher price charged to them; and (2) the fact that the tariff induces domestic producers to expand their production of goods that compete with the imported good, consuming resources in the import-competing industry that could better be deployed elsewhere. The proof does rely implicitly on assumptions about the competitiveness of markets and the absence of externalities, and the implications of relaxing those assumptions are explored in the materials that follow.

The complete argument against tariffs in the competitive case is in fact more complicated, because we have discussed only the effects on the market directly affected by the tariff (as does the Appendix). In reality, a tariff reduces the demand for imports, and thus for the foreign exchange to buy them. The home currency appreciates as a consequence, and exports become more expensive to foreign purchasers. These effects must also be considered in a complete "general equilibrium" analysis of tariffs in an importing country. Attention to them, however, does not alter the conclusion that the sum of all the effects is adverse.[7] Likewise, it should come as no surprise that consideration of the welfare effects of tariffs on trading partners can only strengthen the argument against them.

---

7. An accessible treatment of the general equilibrium result for the two-country, two-good competitive case may be found in David D. Friedman, Price Theory 537–41 (2d ed. 1990).

Various implications of a departure from the assumption of competition will follow, but one of them bears mention here and can significantly strengthen the case against tariffs. If a domestic industry is highly concentrated and able to exercise market power in the absence of free international competition, the elimination of tariffs can eliminate the distortions attributable to monopoly/oligopoly pricing. The major caveat relates to the strategic trade ideas in the next section.

A further consideration is that significant resources may be expended in the pursuit of tariffs through the political process. Governments that are receptive to protectionist pressures, at least some of the time, encourage import-competing interests to lobby for protection. Likewise, interests that may be injured by protection will mobilize to resist it. These lobbying efforts are not costless, as anyone who has hired a Washington lobbying firm or who has bought a ticket to a Washington fund raiser can attest. An adamant commitment to free trade by a government, therefore, may have the additional benefit of discouraging such "rent-seeking behavior." (Of course, an adamant and credible commitment to *any* policy may do much the same thing, and the observation that the level of rent-seeking may be influenced by the prevailing policy in fact raises a host of subtle complications.)

Regarding quotas, their effects are in one sense equivalent to the effects of tariffs under conditions of competition. The equivalence idea can be seen as follows: For any tariff, observe the quantity of imports that enters the country. Then, abolish the tariff and replace it by a quota equal to that quantity of imports. Nothing should change in the market as far as equilibrium price, domestic production, and the quantity of imports is concerned, because total supply and demand at the original equilibrium price will still balance. But what about government revenue? Herein lies the distinction—under a tariff, the government collects revenue equal to the difference between the world market price for the imported goods and the price charged for imports in the domestic market. A quota, however, yields no revenue to the government unless the rights to import under the quota are sold. Typically, they are not, and then some private entrepreneur will capture the difference between the price at which imported goods can be bought on world markets and the price in the domestic market that results from the restriction of import competition. This difference is termed the "quota rent." In many cases, the quota rent is captured by foreign sellers, who are given rights to sell under the quota for free. In that event, from the perspective of the importing country, the economic effects of a quota may be much worse than the effect of a tariff that results in an equivalent volume of imports. Everything is the same except that what would be government revenue under a tariff is captured by foreign sellers as a kind of monopoly profit. From the international perspective, however, this difference is a wash— the importing country's loss is someone else's gain.

There are numerous other considerations that may influence the choice between tariffs and quotas. For example, it is sometimes argued that quotas tend to conceal from the public the degree of protection being afforded domestic producers—the price effect of tariffs is more obvious. On the other hand, economic planning may be easier if the precise amount of imports can be predicted. Quotas may allow this, while tariffs make such prediction more difficult.

(3) Arguments for Trade Restrictions

The arguments for trade restrictions raised by the potential beneficiaries of them are numerous and varied. Most of the arguments have no foundation in economic analysis, although some are based on a belief that certain unrealistic assumptions underlie the economic analysis above. Interestingly, the arguments most often advanced in the press and in political circles tend to be the less persuasive, at least from the economic perspective. We begin with the arguments that, at least to us, appear quite unconvincing in general, and proceed to those that require more serious attention.

(a) Some Popular But Dubious Arguments

ALAN O. SYKES, COMPARATIVE ADVANTAGE AND THE NORMATIVE ECONOMICS OF INTERNATIONAL TRADE POLICY

1 J. Int'l Econ. L. 49, 68–70 (1998)[8]

SOME MISCONCEPTIONS ABOUT FREE TRADE

1. Trade and Jobs

Ross Perot's recent Presidential campaign in the United States devoted much energy to pressing the claim that trade liberalization—NAFTA in particular—would reduce the number of jobs in the American economy. NAFTA proponents responded with the claim that NAFTA would increase the number of jobs. This debate over the impact of trade on the number of jobs seems to resurface every time an important trade initiative arises.

To an economist, both sides of the debate ring hollow. Supply and demand in the labor market may be expected to balance in the long run just as it does in any other market, although transitory periods of disequilibrium may occur. The number of jobs in an economy will be determined by the labor supply and by the reservation wages of workers. A general decline in real wages may be expected to reduce the labor force somewhat as some workers exit to work in the home or to pursue leisure activities, and the reverse phenomenon may be expected if real wages rise. But absent a significant change in real wages economy wide, there is little reason to expect any significant change in the number of workers or jobs.

Incremental trade liberalization (such as that associated with NAFTA or the recent Uruguay Round) should not have much effect on real

8. Reprinted with permission.

wages *on average*. To be sure, workers with specific human capital investments in import-competing industries can anticipate that their wages will fall with increased import competition, and the number of jobs in those industries will thus tend to decline. But workers in the export side of the economy will see increasing wages and employment opportunities as production shifts toward areas of greater comparative advantage. As a first order approximation, these effects may be expected to cancel out on average. Trade-related changes in the number of jobs, therefore, if any, are likely to be vastly smaller than other forces affecting job growth or loss such as the business cycle.

2. *Low Wage Competition*

Related to the argument that trade will reduce the number of jobs is the claim that trade between high wage, developed countries and low wage countries will tend to impoverish workers in the higher wage countries. In its popular form this argument is also flawed for much the same reasons as above—there is little reason to expect significant change in *average* real wages from the incremental trade liberalization that we have seen in recent years once the economy has fully adjusted to changes in trade patterns.

Further, if we shift the focus from wages to the overall standard of living, the effect of trade liberalization on the real *incomes* of citizens should be positive. The exploitation of comparative advantage enhances consumption possibilities for trading nations, as indicated earlier. The real purchasing power of citizens as a whole will rise, through an increase in the combined real returns to all factors of production.

These propositions do not rest on any assumptions about wage parity at the outset across trading nations. Low wages in developing countries should not be viewed as a threat to developed nations, but rather as a source of comparative advantage for developing nations that can usefully be exploited through trade.

To be sure, it is well known in the economics literature that an increase in the price of a good caused by trade will tend to increase the prices of the factors of production used intensively in the production of that good, while a decrease in the price of a good will tend to reduce the prices of factors of production used intensively in the production of that good (the Stolper–Samuelson theorem). Thus, workers whose skills are used intensively in the production of import-competing goods will tend to find their wages reduced by greater import competition. Further, if low wage workers abroad are relatively unskilled and produce goods that tend to compete with goods produced by relatively low wage, unskilled domestic workers, then these comparatively less affluent domestic workers may bear the brunt of the effects of greater import competition. But this problem is really just a corollary of the distributional concerns noted previously, raising again the tension between efficiency and distribution. We then come full circle to the question whether protectionist trade policies are ever the best way to promote a more equitable income distribution. For the reasons given above, the answer seems likely to be no.

3. National Security and Self Sufficiency

Proponents of protectionist policies also appeal with some regularity to concerns about national security. Industries from steel to textiles to mining to agriculture can be heard to argue that their presence and prosperity is essential to the ability of the nation to prosecute a war effort successfully.

To be sure, war does require armaments and munitions, the soldiers must have uniforms and they must somehow be fed. But it hardly follows that a nation which may confront conditions of war must protect the industries that produce such items from decline in the face of foreign competition. Before arguments for protectionist policies based on national security can be taken seriously, a number of conditions must exist and a number of alternatives must be ruled out.

Many of the most important domestic productive facilities for national defense purposes will be supported in peacetime by government defense procurement—only where peacetime procurement is insufficient to support vital productive facilities do potential concerns about the contraction of domestic producers become important. Even then, the quantity of production of any particular good necessary to sustain a war effort and the domestic population during wartime may be considerably smaller than existing levels of domestic production. To take the case of steel in the United States, for example, the amount of production required for tanks, battleships and so on may be only a fraction of domestic capacity, and during large scale conflict other uses for steel such as new automobiles and new building construction can be put on hold. Only where import dependence would still exist at those reduced levels of domestic consumption need the analysis proceed any further.

The likelihood of imports becoming unavailable in wartime must then be carefully considered. For a nation like the United States, serious interruption of seaborne commercial traffic seems unlikely to occur for most goods or commodities in any scenario short of global conventional conflict on the scale of World War II. The probability of such conflict seems small at best in the nuclear age. Further, in the event of an interruption in seaborne traffic, adjacent trading partners may be able to take up much of the slack on many items (in the case of the United States, Canada to the North and Mexico to the South).

Where interruption of necessary imports seems a serious risk, the next issue is whether domestic capacity can be restored with reasonable dispatch. Even if an industry has closed down certain productive facilities that might be needed in wartime, it does not follow that those facilities cannot be reopened or rebuilt quickly enough to satisfy essential needs.

Finally, stockpiling during peacetime may well be a superior alternative to the protection of domestic capacity. Where the item in question is not perishable, a nation might be better off by buying up a supply of vital material at low prices in an open trading system than to burden itself over time with the high prices attendant on protectionism as a hedge against armed conflict. The funds tied up in a stockpile have some opportunity cost to be sure, but this cost can easily be smaller than the costs of excluding efficient foreign suppliers from the domestic market. In the end, therefore, arguments for protectionism from the national security perspective require careful scrutiny and will rarely hold up to it.

(b) Trade Restrictions to Address Domestic Distortions

The efficiency argument for free trade, as noted, is a corollary of the principle that competitive markets, without externalities, are efficient. What if there are externalities?

ALAN V. DEARDORFF & ROBERT M. STERN, CURRENT ISSUES IN U.S. TRADE POLICIES: AN OVERVIEW[9]

"Second-Best" Arguments for Intervention

A crucial assumption underlying the classic gains-from-trade proposition is that everything within the domestic economy is working properly: all domestic markets are perfectly competitive, prices and wages adjust freely so that markets clear, and there are no externalities in production or consumption. If any of these conditions fails to hold, then there exists a domestic distortion and the first-best optimal results of free trade are no longer assured. Instead, the very distortionary effects that trade interventions are known to have could conceivably be used to offset the domestic distortion and make the economy better off.

* * *

Such use of trade intervention is said to be second best * * *. Because a tariff always distorts both producer and consumer behavior, while the externality in question concerns only one of these groups, a better policy is possible that addresses the original distortion more directly. * * *

The general principle is that trade intervention, by introducing two distortions rather than one, may succeed in solving one problem but only at the same time that it causes another. Trade policy is like doing acupuncture with a fork. No matter how carefully you insert one prong, the other is likely to do damage.

Such examples are rife in the theory of protection. The classic example is the infant-industry argument, where a tariff is said to protect a young industry while it learns to be efficient. The assumption here is that some market failure—such as an imperfection in the loan market or the impossibility of keeping new technical knowledge from being cop-

9. U.S. Trade Policies in a Changing World Economy 15, 38–40 (Robert Stern ed., 1987). © 1987 by The Massachusetts Institute of Technology. Reprinted by permission of The MIT Press.

ied—makes it impossible for competitive firms to take advantage of what would otherwise be a profitable opportunity. A tariff or other import restriction can therefore be used temporarily to make the operation profitable even in the short run while the learning process is under way. Naturally, though, the success of such a policy depends crucially on a correct diagnosis of which industries really do offer the potential for such improvement over time. Also it may be difficult politically to remove protection once it has been put in place, even though this particular rationale for protection is explicitly temporary.

As in the case of the externality discussed above, the infant industry argument may be valid in the sense that a tariff may indeed be beneficial. But it is also true that some other policy would be superior. Once again a production subsidy, equal in size to the tariff, would yield exactly the same benefits to producers as the tariff, without causing the additional costly distortion of consumer choice. And even better might be a policy that subsidizes or guarantees loans to the industry, if the capital market was the real source of the distortion, or a policy that permits firms to appropriate technology if that was the problem. The general principle is simply that first best policies deal directly with the distortions involved, and distortions rarely involve the double effect on both producer and consumer choice that would be best addressed with trade intervention.

Many other arguments for intervention can similarly be traced to the presumption of a distortion somewhere in the domestic economy. Tariffs to protect "essential" industries, for example, depend on the private sector being unable to perceive or take advantage of the fact that these industries are essential, which often means that they confer social benefits on others in society. Tariffs to discourage consumption of undesirable goods similarly assume an undesirable social effect of such consumption, or else that consumers themselves have a distorted view of their own welfare. And finally, tariffs for employment and balance-of-payments purposes assume rather obviously that certain markets—labor and foreign exchange—are for some reason failing to adjust to equilibrium.

All of these arguments may be valid if the distortions on which they rest are correctly diagnosed, but once again they could be better dealt with by means of some other policies that deal more directly with the distortions in question.

(c) The "Optimal Tariff" Argument

The "proof" that tariffs and quotas reduce aggregate efficiency in an importing country, as noted, relied on "competitive assumptions." One of these assumptions is that the importing nation is a "price taker" in international markets, and cannot hope to lower the price that it pays for imports by restricting its purchases of them. If it can, it may be able to extract profits from foreign producers through appropriate tariff intervention.

ALAN V. DEARDORFF & ROBERT M. STERN,
CURRENT ISSUES IN U.S. TRADE
POLICIES: AN OVERVIEW[10]

NATIONAL MONOPOLY POWER AND THE OPTIMAL TARIFF

The idealized assumptions of the classic argument for free trade imply the optimality of free trade only for the world as a whole. For individual countries the optimality of free trade requires the additional assumption that the country is too small to have any influence, through its policies, over the prices at which it trades. Without that assumption it is well known that free trade is not optimal from a national perspective, and instead that there exists an optimal degree of trade intervention, known as the optimal tariff, that works by turning the country's terms of trade in its favor.

* * *

This argument is sometimes thought to require that the country in question be large, and therefore to apply only to such large industrialized countries as the U.S. However, the argument really applies to some extent to any country that is not insignificantly small. Furthermore, the size that is important is not the size of the country as a whole, but rather its share of world trade in markets in which it exports and imports. Since many countries tend to specialize their exports in a fairly small range of goods—exactly as trade theory predicts they should, incidentally—even quite small countries may have enough market power over the prices of their exports for the optimal tariff argument to apply.

The optimal tariff argument has the important feature that it involves a benefit for the intervening country only at the expense of the country's trading partners. Indeed, since free trade is known to be optimal for the world as a whole, it must be true that the rest of the world loses more than the tariff-levying country gains. Furthermore, the rest of the world, were it able to act collectively, would have the same sort of power over the terms of trade as does the original country and it is therefore quite inappropriate to think of a single country as levying an optimal tariff in isolation. The possibility that other countries may do the same, either in retaliation or simply because they too think they recognize an opportunity for gain, must surely be considered.

This feature of the optimal tariff argument—that it involves gain by one country at other countries' expense—is one that [is found] in some of the newer arguments for trade intervention. To address such arguments in a common framework, we will refer to such trade policies as being "exploitative intervention." Such policies typically are available to more than one, if not many, countries, each of which can have adverse

10. U.S. Trade Policies in a Changing World Economy 37–38 (Robert Stern ed., 1987). © 1987 by The Massachusetts Insti- tute of Technology. Reprinted by permission of The MIT Press.

effects on the others, and therefore require that strategic issues be considered. Like other forms of exploitative intervention to be considered below, the optimal tariff argument is likely to find countries in the classic position of the Prisoners' Dilemma. That is, each country has available a policy that will benefit itself at the expense of others, but, if all countries simultaneously pursue that policy, all are likely to lose.

* * *

The appropriate policy * * * depends on what policies will be undertaken abroad, on how those policies may depend on the policies that we ourselves pursue or claim that we will pursue, and so forth. Thus exploitative intervention policies, even without the complications of imperfect competition, inevitably raise the complicated and perhaps unsolvable strategic issues.

Notes and Questions

(1) Just as nations may have market power with respect to their imports, so may they have market power in export markets. Governments can then assist their domestic industries in capturing monopoly profits from their foreign sales by limiting the quantity of exports with an export quota. Alternatively, the government can capture monopoly profits for itself through export taxes.

(2) There is little doubt that the United States has more monopoly power over its imports on average than any other country because of the size of its market. Likewise, small nations have little or no monopoly power, and cannot retaliate through their own optimal tariff measures if the United States tries to exploit its position. Are there other forms of "retaliation" that must be considered?

(d) Strategic Trade Policy and Its Extensions

The domestic distortion and optimal tariff analysis invokes national monopoly power and externalities to qualify, or at least refine, the efficiency case for free trade. The modern literature on "strategic trade policy" also relies on imperfect competition and externalities, but of a different sort.

PAUL R. KRUGMAN, IS FREE TRADE PASSÉ?[11]

The new view of international trade holds that trade is to an important degree driven by economies of scale rather than comparative advantage, and that international markets are typically imperfectly competitive. This new view has suggested two arguments against free trade, one of which is a wholly new idea, the other of which is an old idea given new force. The new idea is the *strategic trade policy* argument, which holds that government policy can tilt the terms of oligopolistic competition to shift excess returns from foreign to domestic firms. The old idea is that

11. Journal of Economic Perspectives, Fall 1987, at 131–44. Reprinted with per-   mission of the American Economic Association.

government policy should favor industries that yield *externalities,* especially generation of knowledge that firms cannot fully appropriate.

Strategic Trade Policy

The strategic trade policy argument begins with the observation that in a world of increasing returns and imperfect competition, lucky firms in some industries may be able to earn returns higher than the opportunity costs of the resources they employ. For example, suppose that economies of scale are sufficiently large in some industry that there is only room for one profitable entrant in the world market as a whole; that is, if two firms were to enter they would both incur losses. Then whichever firm manages to establish itself in the industry will earn super-normal returns that will not be competed away.

A country can raise its national income at other countries' expense if it can somehow ensure that the lucky firm that gets to earn excess returns is domestic rather than foreign.

Suppose, then, that two countries are capable of producing a good. For concreteness, let the good be a 150–seat passenger aircraft, and call the "countries" America and Europe. Also, let there be one firm in each country that could produce the good: Boeing and Airbus, respectively.

To focus attention on the competition for excess returns, assume that neither America nor Europe has any domestic demand for the good, so that the good is intended solely for export; this allows us to identify producer surplus with the national interest. Also, assume that each firm faces only a binary choice, to produce or not to produce. Finally, assume that the market is profitable for either firm if it enters alone, unprofitable for both if both enter.

Given these assumptions, the game between Boeing and Airbus may be represented by a matrix like that shown in Table 1. Boeing's choices to produce (P) or not to produce (N) are represented by upper case letters, Airbus's corresponding choices by lower case letters. In each cell of the matrix, the lower left number represents Boeing's profit (over and above the normal return on capital), the upper right number represents Airbus's profit.

As the game is set up here, it does not have a unique outcome. To give it one, let us assume that Boeing has some kind of head start that allows it to commit itself to produce before Airbus's decision. Then in the absence of government intervention, the outcome will be Pn, in the upper right cell: Boeing will earn large profits, while deterring entry by Airbus.

Clearly Europe's government would like to change this outcome. The strategic trade policy point is that it can change the outcome if it is able to commit itself to subsidize Airbus, at a point before Boeing is committed to produce. Suppose that Europe's government can commit itself in advance to pay a subsidy of 10 to Airbus if it produces the plane, regardless of what Boeing does. Then the payoff matrix is shifted to that represented by Table 2. The result is to reverse the game's outcome.

Table 1

Hypothetical payoff matrix

Airbus

		p	n
Boeing	P	−5 −5	0 100
	N	100 0	0 0

Table 2

Hypothetical payoff matrix after European subsidy

Airbus

		p	n
Boeing	P	5 −5	0 100
	N	110 0	0 0

Boeing now knows that even it if commits itself to produce, Airbus will still produce as well, and it will make losses. Thus Boeing will be induced not to produce, and the outcome will be Np instead of Pn. The surprising result will be that a subsidy of only 10 raises Airbus's profits from 0 to 110! Of this, 100 represents a transfer of excess returns from America to Europe, a gain in Europe's national income at America's expense.

The strategic trade policy argument thus shows that at least under some circumstances a government, by supporting its firms in international competition, can raise national welfare at another country's expense. The example just presented showed this goal being achieved via a subsidy, but other policies might also serve this purpose. In particular, when there is a significant domestic market for a good, protection of this market raises the profits of the domestic firm and lowers the profits of the foreign firm in the case where both enter; like an export subsidy, this can deter foreign entry and allow the domestic firm to capture the excess returns. As businessmen have always said, and as economists have usually denied, a protected domestic market can—under some circumstances!—promote rather than discourage exports, and possibly raise national income.

External Economies

There is nothing new about the idea that it may be desirable to deviate from free trade to encourage activities that yield positive external economies. The proposition that protection can be beneficial when an industry generates external economies is part of the conventional theory of trade policy. However, the rethinking of international trade theory has given at least the appearance of greater concreteness to the theoretical case for government intervention to promote external benefits.

It is possible to imagine bees-and-flowers examples in which externalities arise from some physical spillover between firms, but empirically the most plausible source of positive externalities is the inability of innovative firms to appropriate fully the knowledge they create. The presence of problems of appropriability is unmistakable in industries experiencing rapid technological progress, where firms routinely take each others' products apart to see how they work and how they were made.

* * *

External economies can now be identified with incomplete appropriability of the results of R & D, which immediately suggests that they are most likely to be found in industries where R & D is an especially large part of firms' costs. So by making tractable the modeling of a specific mechanism generating externalities, the new trade theory also seems to offer guidance on where these externalities are likely to be important.

The emphasis on external economies suggested by new trade theory is similar to the strategic trade policy argument in offering a reason for government targeting of particular sectors. However, the external economies argument differs in one important respect; policies to promote sectors yielding external economies need not affect other countries adversely. Whether the effect of one country's targeting of high-externality sectors on other countries is positive or negative depends on whether the scope of the externalities is national or international. There is a conflict of interest if knowledge spills over within a country but not between countries.

Critique of the New Interventionism

The positive economics of the new trade theory, with its conclusion that much trade reflects increasing returns and that many international markets are imperfectly competitive, has met with remarkably quick acceptance in the profession. The normative conclusion that this justifies a greater degree of government intervention in trade, however, has met with sharp criticism and opposition—not least from some of the creators of the new theory themselves.

Empirical Difficulties

The previous numerical example assumed that the European government knew the payoff matrix and knew how Boeing would respond to its policy. In reality, of course, even the best informed of governments will not know this much. Uncertainty is a feature of all economic policy, of course, but it is even greater when the key issue is how a policy will affect oligopolistic competition. The simple fact is that economists do not have reliable models of how oligopolists behave.

The externality argument for intervention runs up against the empirical problem of measuring external economies. By their nature, spillovers of knowledge are elusive and difficult to calculate; because they represent non-market linkages between firms, they do not leave a "paper trail" by which their spread can be traced. A combination of careful case study work and econometrics on the history of an industry may be able to identify significant external economies, but what we need for trade policy is an estimate of the future rather than the past. Will a dollar of R & D in the semiconductor industry convey ten cents worth of external benefits, or ten dollars? Nobody really knows.

By itself, the argument that making policy based on the new trade theory is an uncertain enterprise would only dictate caution and hard study, not inaction. When it is linked with the political economy concerns described below, however, it raises the question of whether the political risks associated with action outweigh any likely gains.

Entry

Suppose that a government is somehow able to overcome the empirical difficulties in formulating an interventionist trade policy. It may still not be able to raise national income if the benefits of its intervention are dissipated by entry of additional firms.

* * *

Suppose that external economies are associated with the manufacture of semiconductor chips, seemingly justifying a subsidy to chips production. If additional resources of labor and capital are supplied elastically to the industry, the external benefits of larger production will not be confined to the promoting country. Instead, they will be passed on to consumers around the world in the form of cheaper chips.

General Equilibrium

Even in a world characterized by increasing returns and imperfect competition, budget constraints still hold. A country cannot protect everything and subsidize everything. Thus interventionist policies to promote particular sectors, whether for strategic or externality reasons, must draw resources away from other sectors. This substantially raises the knowledge that a government must have to formulate interventions that do more good than harm.

Consider first the case of strategic trade policy. When a particular sector receives a subsidy, this gives firms in that sector a strategic advantage against foreign competitors. However, the resulting expansion of that sector will bid up the price of domestic resources to other sectors, putting home firms in these other sectors at a strategic disadvantage. Excess returns gained in the favored sector will thus be offset to at least some extent by returns lost elsewhere. If the government supports the wrong sector, the gain there will conceal a loss in overall national income. * * *

A similar point applies to externalities. Promoting one sector believed to yield valuable spillovers means drawing resources out of other sectors. Suppose that glamorous high-technology sectors yield less external benefit than the government thinks, and boring sectors more. Then a policy aimed at encouraging external economies may actually prove counterproductive. Again, the government needs to understand not only the targeted sector but the rest of the economy to know if a policy is justified.

* * *

Retaliation and Trade War

Strategic trade policy aimed at securing excess returns for domestic firms and support for industries that are believed to yield national benefits are both beggar-thy neighbor policies that raise income at the expense of other countries. A country that attempts to use such policies will probably provoke retaliation. In many (though not all) cases, a trade war between two interventionist governments will leave both countries worse off than if a hands-off approach were adopted by both.

Domestic Politics

Governments do not necessarily act in the national interest, especially when making detailed microeconomic interventions. Instead, they are influenced by interest group pressures. The kinds of interventions that new trade theory suggests can raise national income will typically raise the welfare of small, fortunate groups by large amounts, while imposing costs on larger, more diffuse groups. The result, as with any microeconomic policy, can easily be that excessive or misguided intervention takes place because the beneficiaries have more knowledge and influence than the losers.

LAURA D'ANDREA TYSON, WHO'S BASHING WHOM? TRADE CONFLICT IN HIGH TECHNOLOGY INDUSTRIES 10–11, 13 (1992)[18]

A dwindling number of economists and very few policymakers espouse the traditional free trade arguments as an overall prescription for US trade policy. Instead, a growing number of academic and policy economists are best described as moderate free traders: although they support the free trade ideal, they grudgingly concede that it is a long way

---

18. Reprinted by permission of the In- ington, DC.
stitute for International Economics, Wash-

off and conclude that unilateral measures to serve the national interest may be justified under some circumstances. * * *

Although I could easily hide behind the moderate free trade disguises described here, it would be disingenuous for me to do so. Unlike most free traders unilateral and moderate alike, I believe that what we as a nation make and what we trade matter. The composition of our production and trade does influence our economic well-being. Technology-intensive industries, in particular, make special contributions to the long-term health of the American economy. A dollar's worth of shoes may have the same effect on the trade balance as a dollar's worth of computers. But * * * the two do not have the same effect on employment, wages, labor skills, productivity, and research—all major determinants of our long-term economic health. In addition, because technology-intensive industries finance a disproportionate share of the nation's R & D spending, there is a strong presumption—supported by the evidence and the arguments * * * that they generate positive externalities for the rest of the economy. * * *

My trade policy agenda is a defensive one. I recommend that the nation's trade laws be used to deter or compensate for foreign practices that are not adequately regulated by existing multilateral rules. Unlike most traditional and even many moderate free traders, I am convinced that such practices can inflict substantial long-term injury on American producers. The case studies [in this book] provide compelling evidence of such injury. In addition I believe that, in pursuit of defensive objectives, US policymakers should be guided by the principle of selective reciprocity and motivated by the goal of opening foreign markets. Wherever possible, they should favor approaches that encourage trade and competition over those that discourage them.

As the case studies demonstrate, cautious activism in trade policy is not synonymous with protectionism. Indeed, both the cases and the global logic of high-technology industries indicate that protectionist measures, such as voluntary restraint agreements and price floors on imports, are at least as ineffective or counterproductive in such industries as they have proven to be elsewhere in the economy. * * * But cautious activism does sometimes violate the principles of nondiscrimination and diffuse reciprocity that remain the mainstays of US trade policy. Moreover, cautious activism does sometimes involve forceful unilateralism. And, as Moran notes, "Armtwisting is hardly an attractive remedy compared to multilateral agreements founded upon mutual concessions."

All too often, however, the choice between self-serving unilateralism and cooperative multilateralism does not exist. Sometimes the only real choice is between inaction on the one hand and bilateral deals or unilateral action on the other. Under some circumstances the costs of inaction for American economic welfare are unacceptably high. We must not be hoodwinked by the soothing notion that, in the absence of US intervention, the fate of America's high-technology industries will be determined by market forces. Instead, they will be manipulated by the trade, regulatory, and industrial policies of our trading partners. Cautious activism has implications for domestic economic policy as well as for trade policy. A cautious activist supports general policy measures such as a more generous R & D tax credit and increases in public funding for civilian R & D and education—initiatives that would promote all of the nation's high-technology producers without singling out any one of them for special favor. But a cautious activist is willing to go further, recognizing that measures to support particular technologies or industries are sometimes warranted. To determine when such measures are required and what form they should take, the government needs an institutional capacity to monitor and respond to trends in global competition. Without such a capacity, America's policy has often been too little, too late. While we scramble to help our producers address crises that have been long in the making, both Japan and the European Community have forward-looking policies to nurture their high-technology industries. The American approach is no longer adequate, particularly at a time when cutbacks in defense R & D programs threaten to decimate public funding for science and technology unless new civilian programs are established to replace them.

Notes and Questions

(1) Laura Tyson, of course, was chair of the Council of Economic Advisors for a time during the Clinton administration. Her excerpt makes clear, as does Krugman's, that proponents of strategic trade policy advocate measures like subsidies and tax credits as often or more often than trade protection. This should remind you of the domestic distortions debate, and the problem of selecting the most efficient policy instrument for the job.

(2) Does Tyson have an adequate answer to Krugman's concerns about interventionism, such as the inability of government to know where to intervene, and the problem of capture by special interest groups?

(3) If high technology industries generate important positive externalities because of the research and development that goes on in them, why not let other countries subsidize it, and then free ride on the results? Is there any tension between the arguments above for the promotion of high-technology industries, and the popular sense that America does the research and Japan does the production?

(4) An important distinction to draw in thinking about trade intervention is between measures that benefit one country even though they reduce economic welfare globally, and measures that may enhance global as well as national welfare. Are you clear from the above materials as to which measures fall into each category? Would you expect nations acting together through a regime such as the WTO/GATT system to try and promise each other not to engage in the former sort of behavior, but to permit the latter? This issue, which raises at bottom the question whether governments are out to pursue national economic welfare or something else, leads us to the next set of materials.

(e) Distributional Considerations Again

DANI RODRIK, HAS GLOBALIZATION
GONE TOO FAR? 4–7 (1997)[13]

I focus on three sources of tension between the global market and social stability and offer a brief overview of them here.

First, reduced barriers to trade and investment accentuate the asymmetry between groups that can cross international borders (either directly or indirectly, say through outsourcing) and those that cannot. In the first category are owners of capital, highly skilled workers, and many professionals, who are free to take their resources where they are most in demand. Unskilled and semiskilled workers and most middle managers belong in the second category. Putting the same point in more technical terms, globalization makes the demand for the services of individuals in the second category *more elastic*—that is, the services of large segments of the working population can be more easily substituted by the services of other people across national boundaries. Globalization therefore fundamentally transforms the employment relationship.

The fact that "workers" can be more easily substituted for each other across national boundaries undermines what many conceive to be a post-war social bargain between workers and employers, under which the former would receive a steady increase in wages and benefits in return for labor peace. This is because increased substitutability results in the following concrete consequences:

— Workers now have to pay a larger share of the cost of improvements in work conditions and benefits (that is, they bear a greater incidence of nonwage costs).

— They have to incur greater instability in earnings and hours worked in response to shocks to labor demand or labor productivity (that is, volatility and insecurity increase).

— Their bargaining power erodes, so they receive lower wages and benefits whenever bargaining is an element in setting the terms of employment.

These considerations have received insufficient attention in the recent academic literature on trade and wages, which has focused on the downward shift in demand for unskilled workers rather than the increase in the elasticity of that demand.

Second, globalization engenders conflicts within and between nations over domestic norms and the social institutions that embody them. As the technology for manufactured goods becomes standardized and diffused internationally, nations with very different sets of values, norms, institutions, and collective preferences begin to compete head on in markets for similar goods. And the spread of globalization creates opportunities for trade between countries at very different levels of development.

This is of no consequence under traditional multilateral trade policy of the WTO and the General Agreement on Tariffs and Trade (GATT): the "process" or "technology" through which goods are produced is immaterial, and so are the social institutions of the trading partners. Differences in national practices are treated just like differences in factor endowments or any other determinant of comparative advantage. However, introspection and empirical evidence both reveal that most people attach values to processes as well as outcomes. This is reflected in the norms that shape and constrain the domestic environment in which goods and services are produced—for example, workplace practices, legal rules, and social safety nets.

Trade becomes contentious when it unleashes forces that undermine the norms implicit in domestic practices. Many residents of advanced industrial countries are uncomfortable with the weakening of domestic institutions through the forces of trade, as when, for example, child labor in Honduras displaces workers in South Carolina or when pension benefits are cut in Europe in response to the requirements of the Maastricht treaty. This sense of unease is one way of interpreting the demands for "fair trade." Much of the discussion surrounding the "new" issues in trade policy—that is, labor standards, environment, competition policy, corruption—can be cast in this light of procedural fairness.

We cannot understand what is happening in these new areas until we take individual preferences for processes and the social arrangements that embody them seriously. In particular, by doing so we can start to make sense of people's uneasiness about the consequences of international economic integration and avoid the trap of automatically branding all concerned groups as self-interested protectionists. Indeed, since trade policy almost always has redistributive consequences (among sectors, income groups, and individuals), one cannot produce a principled defense of free trade without confronting the question of the fairness and legitimacy of the practices that generate these consequences. By the same token, one should not expect broad popular support for trade when trade involves exchanges that clash with (and erode) prevailing domestic social arrangements.

Third, globalization has made it exceedingly difficult for governments to provide social insurance—one of their central functions and one that has helped maintain social cohesion and domestic political support for ongoing liberalization throughout the postwar period. In essence, governments have used their fiscal powers to insulate domestic groups from excessive market risks, particularly those having an external origin. In fact, there is a striking correlation between an economy's exposure to foreign trade and the size of its welfare state. It is in the most open countries, such as Sweden, Denmark, and the Netherlands, that spending on income transfers has expanded the most. This is not to say that the government is the sole, or the best, provider of social insurance. The extended family, religious groups, and local communities often play similar roles. My point is that it is a hallmark of postwar period that governments in the advanced countries have been expected to provide such insurance.

At the present, however, international economic integration is taking place against the background of receding governments and diminished social obligations. The welfare state has been under attack for two decades. Moreover, the increasing mobility of capital has rendered an important segment of the tax base footloose, leaving governments with the unappetizing option of increasing tax rates disproportionately on labor income. Yet the need for social insurance for the vast majority of the population that remains internationally immobile has not diminished. If anything, this need has become greater as a consequence of increased integration. The question therefore is how the tension between globalization and the pressures for socialization of risk can be eased. If the tension is not managed intelligently and creatively, the danger is that the domestic consensus in favor of open markets will ultimately erode to the point where a generalized resurgence of protectionism becomes a serious possibility.

Each of these arguments points to an important weakness in the manner in which advanced societies are handling—or are equipped to handle–the consequences of globalization. Collectively, they point to what is perhaps the greatest risk of all, namely that the cumulative consequence of the tensions mentioned above will be the solidifying of a new set of class divisions—between those who prosper in the globalized economy and those who do not, between those who share its values, and those who would rather not, and between those who can diversify away its risks and those who cannot. This is not a pleasing prospect, even for individuals on the winning side of the divide who have little empathy for the other side. Social disintegration is not a spectator sport—those on the sidelines also get splashed with mud from the field. Ultimately, the deepening of social fissures can harm all.

(C) THE POLITICAL ECONOMY OF TRADE POLICY

The preceding materials are largely normative in their focus, addressing the question whether intervention is a good idea as a matter of economic policy. Another impressive body of economic thought addresses the positive aspects of trade policy, trying to explain the pattern of intervention that we actually observe, and to explain the extent of international cooperation over trade matters. We can only touch on these matters briefly.

The questions that one can address in this framework are virtually unlimited and, not surprisingly, many do not have satisfactory answers as yet. An essentially random sample of possible queries is: If all import-competing industries would like protection, other things being equal, why do only some industries get significant protection? If high technology industries are the ones that economic theory suggests *might* be appropriate to promote, why is protection usually greatest in declining industries such as steel and textiles? Are pressures for protection linked to the business cycle? Why did the European Common Market form when it did, and what explains who joined and who did not? Why does the WTO/GATT system have an unconditional most-favored-nation obligation built into much of it? Why do antidumping laws exist, and why does GATT tolerate them?

To answer such questions, one must have a convincing explanation for how the political process operates in the trade policy arena. Our point of departure is an older perspective on the matter from a distinguished trade theorist, Max Corden.

W. M. CORDEN, TRADE POLICY AND ECONOMIC WELFARE 107–08 (1974)[14]

Let us now introduce the conservative social welfare function, a concept which seems particularly helpful for understanding actual trade policies of many countries. Put in its simplest form it includes the following income distribution target: any significant absolute reductions in real incomes of any significant section of the community should be avoided. This is not quite the same as setting up the existing income distribution as the best, but comes close to it, and so can indeed be described as "conservative." In terms of welfare weights, increases in income are given relatively low weights and decreases very high weights.

The conservative social welfare function helps to explain the income maintenance motivation of so many tariffs in the past and the reluctance to reduce income maintenance tariffs even when it has become clear that the need for them is more than temporary. It can be regarded as expressing a number of ideas.

Firstly, it is "unfair" to allow anyone's real income to be reduced significantly—and especially if this is the result of deliberate policy decisions—unless there are very good reasons for this and it is more or less unavoidable.

Secondly, insofar as people are risk averters, everyone's real income is increased when it is known that a government will generally intervene to prevent sudden or large and unexpected income losses. The conservative social welfare function is part of a social insurance system.

Thirdly, social peace requires that no significant group's income shall fall if that of others is rising. Social peace might be regarded as a social good in itself or as a basis for political stability and hence perhaps economic development. And even if social peace does not depend on the maintenance of the incomes of the major classes in the community, the survival of a government may.

Finally, if a policy is directed at a certain target, such as protection of an industry or improving the balance of payments, most governments

---

14. Reprinted by permission of Oxford University Press.

want to minimize the adverse by-product effects on sectional incomes so as not to be involved in political battles incidental to their main purpose.

Notes and Questions

(1) Does the "conservative social welfare function" have any ethical appeal, or is it simply an effort to construct a positive explanation for observed policies? Is Corden implicitly saying that whatever we observe governments to be doing, it must be *defined* to be the maximization of social welfare? If Corden's construct is really just an attempt at explanation without normative overlay, how well does it work? Are all citizens treated equally in the degree of protection afforded against shocks to their incomes from import competition? Is comparable government protection afforded against loss of income due to domestic developments that lead companies to liquidate or to lay off workers? If not, can the conservative social welfare function provide an explanation?

(2) Corden wrote at a time when the modern theory of public choice was still relatively young. One of the central ideas of public choice is that political officials pursue their self interest, which often includes maximizing chances of reelection, maximizing campaign contributions, and the like (the theory has a distinct American bias given its origins, and detailed elaborations of how it would apply to non-democratic regimes are rare). As a general matter, this leads to the prediction that public officials will be more responsive to well-organized and well-financed interest groups that can mobilize votes, money, or both. It also suggests that governments will not maximize "social welfare" in any independent ethical sense.

With reference to trade policy, an immediate corollary is that consumer interests will often be poorly represented in policy formulation. The effects of most protectionist measures on the average consumer are quite modest, even though the aggregate effects are sizeable. Rarely will consumers mobilize to become involved with particular protectionist initiatives, therefore, because the gains to any one consumer are not worth the costs, and because each would like to free ride on the efforts of others. Producer groups, by contrast, will tend to organize quite well—the right government policy can be worth millions in profits.

Does this proposition lead to the prediction that all import-competing industries will receive considerable protection? The answer is no. Many industries are consumers of imported goods—the auto industry, for example, may utilize imported steel, imported electronics products, imported plastics, and so on. Such industries are hurt by protectionist measures that raise the costs of their inputs. Similarly, international capital is highly mobile. Many domestic companies earn substantial returns from their overseas operations. Protectionist initiatives can only damage those operations.

Moreover, the international consequences of protection must be considered. When nations act alone, it is still possible that a new protectionist initiative in one country will provoke retaliation in others—the response of other nations to the Smoot–Hawley tariff of the United States is illustrative. Hence, industries that rely on exports for much of their profits will have an incentive to oppose protectionist initiatives (the U.S. agriculture lobby, for example, often testifies about fears of retaliation before Congress). The interests of exporters can be mobilized even more effectively when an opportunity arises for international cooperation to reduce trade barriers. Then, the failure to liberalize trade at home has immediate and certain consequences in scuttling an agreement that would give exporters greater access to foreign markets.

According to the public choice perspective, the battle over protectionist measures will be fought mainly between these competing producer interests. Those that buy the most tickets to fund raisers and are most persuasive in their promises to mobilize the vote will win out. This is not to say that consumer interests have no say in the matter whatsoever, or that every politician is a fully selfish individual with no high-minded principles on her agenda. But the basic producer-interest model has had considerable success as a positive matter, and is at least a useful starting point in answering questions about why things are the way they are.[15]

(3) A further implication of the public choice perspective is that international agreements such as GATT (now WTO), the Treaty of Rome (which created the European Economic Community), and the North American Free Trade Agreement exist because they are politically beneficial to officials in their signatory governments, both initially and over time (otherwise, officials would benefit by causing their nations to drop out of them). To an extent, the detailed provisions of such agreements ought also to be explicable from this perspective, if indeed it is correct. Thus, the failure of the WTO to eliminate all tariffs could be attributed to the fact that the elimination of some tariffs would be very costly politically to officials in importing countries, and no country has offered a concession in return for their elimination that would yield sufficient political benefits to offset these costs.

(4) With regard to international agreements, an interesting question arises as to what holds them together. If a nation decides to ignore its WTO obligations, for example, no army will attack it, and the most that aggrieved nations can do realistically is to ignore their own obligations in response. Thus, to the extent that WTO agreements are respected by their signatories, and we shall see that compliance with those obligations is remarkably high, it must be because nations (or, more accurately, the officials in power) could not benefit politically from cheating, or that they refrain out of fear that cheating will provoke retaliation that will more than wipe out the gains. The former possibility seems implausible as it is likely that many nations would find it advantageous to renege on some of their trade concessions if they thought other nations would ignore it. The second hypothesis thus has more promise, and we will indeed focus intently on the retaliatory dimension in our studies of the WTO dispute resolution system.[16]

---

15. Readers who wish to pursue the matter further might wish to consult Robert E. Baldwin, The Economics of the GATT, *in* Issues in International Economics (Peter Oppenheimer ed., 1980); Robert E. Baldwin, The Political Economy of Protectionism, *in* Import Competition and Response (Jagdish N. Bhagwati ed., 1982); Jagdish N. Bhagwati, Protectionism (1988); The Political Economy of International Trade (Ronald W. Jones & Anne O. Krueger eds., 1990); Political Economy and International Economics (Jagdish N. Bhagwati & Douglas A. Irwin eds., 1991); The Political Economy of Trade Policy: Papers in Honor of Jagdish Bhagwati (Robert Feenstra, Gene Grossman & Douglas Irwin eds., 1996).

16. For a game theoretic take on what holds trade agreements together, see, Alan O. Sykes, Mandatory Retaliation for Breach

SECTION 1.4 FOREIGN POLICY GOALS AND INTERNATIONAL TRADE POLICY

As economists will quickly tell you, economic analysis is capable in principle of incorporating any consideration that affects the well being of any nation or the citizens of any nation. In practice, however, the economic perspective to emphasize issues that economic models can address readily. Other issues, however, may at times prove equally or more important.

(A) WAR AND PEACE

Probably the most important foreign policy goal related to international economic policy is the prevention of war. Many statesmen and scholars believe that modern history establishes a clear relationship between implementation of certain international economic policies and war. The importance of this relationship was particularly evident in the case of World War II.

RICHARD N. COOPER, TRADE POLICY AND FOREIGN POLICY[1]

The most disastrous single mistake any U.S. president has made in international relations was Herbert Hoover's signing of the Smoot–Hawley Tariff Act into law in June 1930. The sharp increase in U.S. tariffs, the apparent indifference of the U.S. authorities to the implications of their actions for foreigners, and the foreign retaliation that quickly followed, as threatened, helped convert what would have been otherwise a normal economic downturn into a major world depression. The sharp decline in foreign trade and economic activity in turn undermined the position of the moderates with respect to the nationalists in Japanese politics and paved the way for the electoral victory of the Nazis in Germany in 1932. Japan promptly invaded China in 1931, and the basis for World War II was laid.

Valuable lessons were learned from the Smoot–Hawley tariff experience by the foreign policy community: the threat of tariff retaliation is not always merely a bluff; tariffs do influence trade flows negatively; a decline in trade can depress national economies; economic depression provides fertile ground for politically radical nostrums; and political radicals often seek foreign (military) adventures to distract domestic attention away from their domestic economic failures. The seeds of World War II, in both the Far East and in Europe, were sown by Hoover's signing of the Smoot–Hawley tariff. * * *

---

of Trade Agreements: Some Thoughts on the Strategic Design of Section 301, 8 Bos. U.Intl.L.J. 301 (1990).

1. U.S. Trade Policies in a Changing World Economy 291–92 (Robert M. Stern ed., 1987). © 1987 by The Massachusetts Institute of Technology. Reprinted by permission of The MIT Press. See also John H. Jackson, World Trade and the Law of GATT ch. 2 (1969), particularly at 38ff.

This close relationship between the causes of the war and international economic policies was recognized by U.S. wartime leaders. For example, Harry Hawkins, then Director of the Office of Economic Affairs of the Department of State, said in a 1944 speech:[2]

"We've seen that when a country gets starved out economically, its people are all too ready to follow the first dictator who may rise up and promise them all jobs. Trade conflict breeds noncooperation, suspicion, bitterness. Nations which are economic enemies are not likely to remain political friends for long.

At the end of the war, the United States government, in suggesting a draft charter for an international trade organization, stated:[3]

The fundamental choice is whether countries will struggle against each other for wealth and power, or work together for security and mutual advantage. * * * The experience of cooperation in the task of earning a living promotes both the habit and the techniques of common effort and helps make permanent the mutual confidence on which the peace depends."

(B) OTHER FOREIGN POLICY GOALS

Not all foreign policy goals are aimed at, or even consistent with, promoting peace. Indeed, among the principal general foreign policy goals that affect international economic policies are the desire of one nation to strengthen its allies and to avoid strengthening its potential enemies and to convince (or to attempt to force) foreign countries to change their behavior or policies. For example, the United States has no doubt followed policies inconsistent with its economic self-interest, narrowly defined, in order to promote growth and economic strength in Western Europe and Japan. On the other hand, the United States maintains trade restrictions in respect of trade and other economic relations with countries such as North Korea and Iraq, that are viewed at this writing as actual or potential enemies. In the recent past use of trade restrictions designed to force policy changes has become more common. They are viewed as an acceptable alternative to the use of force, and while their effectiveness may often be questioned, they serve as a symbolic objection to the policies of the foreign state, thereby satisfying the domestic political need to do something to register such objections. These kinds of restraints and their effectiveness will be considered in detail in Chapter 21.

2. U.S. Dept. of State, Commercial Policy Series 74, at 3 (Pub. No. 2104, 1944).

3. United States Proposals, Dept. of State Pub. No. 2411, at 1–2 (1946).

APPENDIX. AN ECONOMIC ANALYSIS OF TARIFFS, QUOTAS AND SUBSIDIES

PETER B. KENEN, THE INTERNATIONAL ECONOMY 17–19, 175–77 (1985)[4]

PRODUCTION, CONSUMPTION, AND TRADE IN A SINGLE COMMODITY

The effects of differences in relative costs cannot be examined by looking at markets one at a time. It is necessary to look at an entire national economy, and then compare it with another. Therefore, international economic analysis cannot make much use of standard partial-equilibrium price theory—of ordinary demand and supply curves. It must use general-equilibrium theory most of the time. Demand and supply curves can be used, however, to show how the opening of trade in a single commodity affects production and consumption in the domestic market, and they can be used to quantify the gains from trade.

Equilibrium Before Trade Is Opened

In Figure 2–1, the domestic demand curve for cameras is D_H, and the domestic supply curve is S_H. When there is no international trade in cameras, equilibrium will be established at E. The domestic price of a camera will be OP, domestic production will be OQ, and production will necessarily equal consumption. The diagram, however, says much more.

4. © 1985. Reprinted by permission of Prentice–Hall, Englewood Cliffs, New Jersey.

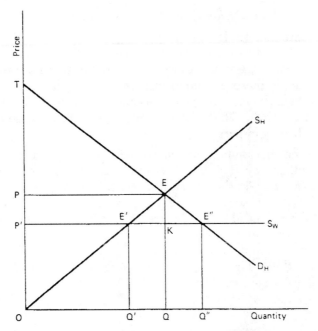

FIGURE   2-1

Effects of the Opening of Trade in the Market for a Single Good

Before trade is opened, the domestic price is OP, and the quantity OQ is produced
to satisfy domestic demand. When trade is opened at the world price OP', domestic
production falls to OQ', domestic consumption rises to OQ", and the quantity Q'Q"
is imported to close the gap. The production effect is Q'Q, and the corresponding
welfare gain is E'KE. The consumption effect is QQ", and the corresponding welfare
gain is KE"E.

When domestic markets are perfectly competitive, the supply curve
is the sum of the marginal cost curves of domestic firms. Accordingly,
the area under the supply curve measures the total cost of camera
production. (Strictly speaking, it measures the total variable cost, but
fixed cost plays no role in this analysis.) If OQ cameras are produced,
total cost is given by the area of the triangle OQE. But total payments to
producers (revenues) are given by the area of the rectangle $OQEP$.
Therefore, the area of the triangle OEP serves as a measure of profit or
producer surplus.

The area under the demand curve is meaningful, too. Under somewhat restrictive assumptions that need not detain us here, it measures
the cash equivalent of the utility that consumers derive from their
purchases of cameras. If OQ cameras are consumed, that cash equivalent
is the area $OQET$. But consumers pay $OQEP$ for their cameras. Therefore, the area of the triangle PET serves as a measure of net benefit or
consumer surplus.

Equilibrium After Trade Is Opened

Suppose now that trade in cameras is opened and that the world's supply curve is S_W. The world price of cameras, OP', is lower than the old domestic price, OP, and the world price must come to prevail in the domestic market if there are no transport costs or tariffs. Domestic firms will cut back production to OQ'. Domestic consumers will step up their purchases to OQ''. The gap between domestic demand and supply, $Q'Q''$, will be filled by imports.

What are the effects on economic welfare? Producer surplus will be $[OE'P']$. It will fall by $P'E'EP$. Consumer surplus will be $P'E''T$. It will rise by $P'E''EP$. As the increase in consumer surplus exceeds the decrease in producer surplus by $E'E''E$, consumers can compensate producers and come out ahead. The area $E'E''E$ measures the gain from the opening of trade in cameras. Note that it can be divided into two parts. The decrease in domestic output, $Q'Q$, contributes $E'KE$. This is the *production effect*. The increase in domestic purchases, QQ'', contributes $KE''E$. This is the *consumption effect*.

* * *

EFFECTS OF A TARIFF WITH A CONSTANT WORLD PRICE

At the start of Chapter 2 [*see above*], we used a simple diagram to study the effects of trade in a single market. The same diagram can be used to study the principal effects of a tariff.

Effects in a Single Market

In Figure 8–1, the demand curve for cameras is D_H, and the domestic supply curve is S_H. If there is no trade at all, equilibrium will be established at E. If there is free trade and the foreign supply curve is S_W, equilibrium will be established at F. The domestic price will equal the world price, OP_1. Domestic consumption will be OC_1, domestic production will be OQ_1, and imports will be Q_1C_1 (equal to $F'F$).

Suppose that the importing country imposes a tariff at an ad valorem rate equal to P_1P_2/OP_1. As the foreign supply curve is perfectly elastic, the world price will stay at OP_1. But the domestic price will rise to OP_2. Domestic consumption will fall to OC_2, domestic production will rise to OQ_2, and imports will fall to Q_2C_2 (equal to $G'G$). The *consumption effect* of the tariff is C_1C_2. The *production effect* is Q_1Q_2 and is also called the *protective effect*. The two together measure the *restrictive effect*, the amount by which the tariff reduces import volume. The government collects P_1P_2 of tariff revenue on each imported camera, which means that it collects $G'GTT'$ in total tariff revenue. At this point in our work, we will assume that all such revenue is returned to households; the government reduces other taxes or raises transfer payments, so tariffs do not cut consumers' incomes.

What are the effects on economic welfare? Consumer surplus falls by P_1FTP_2. Producer surplus rises by $P_1F'T'P_2$. The difference is

$F'FTT'$. But $G'GTT'$ of this loss is offset by returning tariff revenue to households, so the net loss is reduced to $F'G'T'$ *plus* FGT. The area $F'G'T'$ is the welfare loss associated with the protective effect; the area FGT is the loss associated with the consumption effect. The total welfare loss is related to the restrictive effect of the tariff.   * * *

Comparing Tariffs and Quotas

Figure 8–1 can be used to compare an import quota with an import tariff. Start again with free trade and suppose that the government imposes a quota that has the same restrictive effect as the tariff analyzed in Figure 8–1. It limits the volume of imports to Q_2C_2. The domestic price must rise to OP_2 to clear the domestic market. Domestic production will rise to OQ_2, imports will be Q_2C_2, and the two together will equal domestic consumption, which falls to OC_2. The consumption and protective effects of the quota are identical to those of the tariff when the two devices have identical restrictive effects.

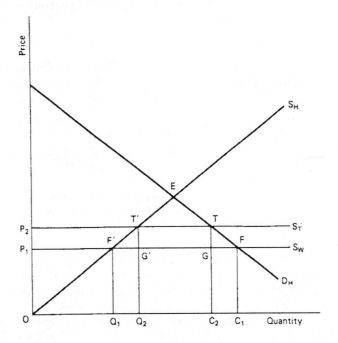

FIGURE 8-1

Effects of a Tariff in a Single Market

In the initial free-trade equilibrium, domestic consumers buy OC_1 at the price OP_1 determined by the foreign supply curve, S_W. Domestic producers supply OQ_1, and imports are Q_1C_1. An import tariff raises the domestic price to OP_2, so domestic consumers buy OC_2, domestic producers supply OQ_2, and imports are reduced to Q_2C_2. The consumption effect of the tariff is C_1C_2. The production (protective) effect is Q_1Q_2. The two together measure the restrictive effect. The government collects P_1P_2 of tariff revenue on each imported unit, or $G'GTT'$ in total tariff revenue.

There is, of course, one difference between the quota and the tariff. The tariff yields $G'GTT'$ in tariff revenue. The quota does not yield any. The revenue equivalent $G'GTT'$ goes as a windfall profit to importers standing at the head of the line when tickets are handed out. Under the assumption adopted previously, however, this difference is relatively unimportant. When the government returns its tariff revenue, consumers as a group get back what they pay out. When a quota is used instead of a tariff, importers collect what consumers pay out, but importers are consumers, too. Therefore, the welfare loss with the quota is $F'G'T'$ *plus* FGT, just as it was with the tariff.

The equivalence between a quota and a tariff can break down in two instances: when markets are not perfectly competitive and when the various demand and supply curves are subject to random shifts. Such random shifts need not affect the *expected* levels of production and consumption. Under a tariff, however, shifts in the foreign supply curve cause fluctuations in domestic output. Under a quota, they do not. (Furthermore, random fluctuations have different consequences for expected welfare under a tariff and under a quota.)

Notes

(1) The losses symbolized by $F'G'T'$ and FGT are sometimes referred to as "deadweight losses" of tariffs.

(2) In the case of quotas, it would be possible for the government establishing the quota to charge a fee for a license to use the quota, in which case it could recover some or all of the windfall profits of the importers.

(3) If a domestic industry is relatively concentrated, i.e. if only a few firms dominate the market, a quota could enable them to charge oligopolistic prices because no matter how high domestic prices rise, only a specified quantity of imports will be allowed to enter the country. More generally, there are other potentially important differences between tariffs and quotas in imperfectly competitive industries.

(4) If the aim of a quota or tariff is to protect the domestic industry, and it usually is, there is at least one other government action that could accomplish that result as well. If the government granted a subsidy to the domestic industry for each camera produced equal to P_2P_1, the domestic producers could afford to produce a quantity of cameras equal to Q_2 the same as if the P_1P_2/OP_1 tariff had been imposed. This would be true because their revenues would be the same as if the price were P_2 and they would therefore produce the amount associated with that price. Consumers would have the benefits of the free trade price of P_1. The government (and through taxes all citizens), of course, would have to pay for the subsidy. The taxes to raise the money for it would have their own distortions associated with them, and it is then an empirical question whether the subsidy would be better or worse from an efficiency standpoint. An argument for subsidy instead of protection, however, is that there are many ways to raise a given amount of revenue, and there is a decent chance that some method can be found that will be less damaging to the economy than trade protection. Whether the government would have any incentive to find that less-distorting method if it exists, of course, is another matter.

Chapter 2

INTERNATIONAL SALES TRANSACTIONS

SECTION 2.1 INTRODUCTION

This book focuses on national and international regulation of cross-border economic transactions, particularly sales of goods. It is consequently beyond the scope of the book to treat in any detail the private law of these transactions, but we will highlight in this chapter some of the major legal problems faced by private parties in structuring those transactions.[1]

Many of the legal issues that parties to international transactions must confront do not differ significantly from those facing parties to domestic transactions, and as such are well known to lawyers and law students. There are, however, some features of international transactions that are likely to raise legal problems. The additional risks and problems involved in an international transaction include: (1) a seller may hesitate to ship goods to a distant buyer without assurance of payment, and a buyer may hesitate to pay a distant seller before it has inspected the goods or at least knows that the goods have been shipped; (2) at least one of the parties will likely have to deal in a foreign currency; (3) often the parties will not share a common language, increasing the risk of a misunderstanding over the basic terms of the transaction; (4) the transaction will typically be subject to more government regulation than a domestic transaction and in addition will be subject to the regulation of more than one government; (5) more than one legal system and one set of business customs will be involved, which raises difficult questions of which law and which customs are to be applied in event of a dispute; and (6) if a dispute arises or a contract is breached, the determination and enforcement of contract obligations will be more difficult since foreign courts and foreign legal rules may be involved.

---

1. Additional and more detailed materials on international sales transactions can be found in: John A. Spanogle & Peter Winship, International Sales Law: A Prob- lem–Oriented Coursebook (2000); Andreas F. Lowenfeld, International Private Trade (3d ed. 1996).

Some of these problems can be reduced or even eliminated through the harmonization of disparate laws and practices around the world. Many efforts have been made toward unification of laws and standardization of customs. These efforts have typically taken three forms: international conventions or agreements in which governments agree to apply specific rules in certain situations; model laws that are proposed by international organizations for adoption into national law; and statements of customs or practice that parties may incorporate into their agreements.[2]

SECTION 2.2 INTERNATIONAL SALES TRANSACTIONS

(A) OUTLINE OF THE INTERNATIONAL SALES TRANSACTION

When a seller sells to a buyer located in the same country, the transaction is often quite simple, especially if the seller delivers the goods or the buyer picks them up and the price is then paid immediately. In a sale across national boundaries, however, a number of factors usually complicate the transaction, which typically involves a cluster of contracts. For example, when a buyer in New York purchases shirts from a seller in Sri Lanka, a simultaneous exchange is unlikely to be practicable and there may be doubts about the viability of a court action to enforce the contract. Consequently, the seller may be afraid to ship before getting paid, and the buyer may be afraid to pay before the goods are shipped. To rescue the transaction, international business has evolved the letter of credit, requiring the seller to ship before payment, but then assuring the seller of payment by a local bank immediately on presentation of acceptable proof of shipment. Such a typical international sales transaction might be diagrammed as follows:

S = Seller

B = Buyer

SB = Seller's Bank

BB = Buyer's Bank

C = Carrier

I = Insurer

---

2. A number of organizations play an active role in these efforts and have useful and informative websites. The International Chamber of Commerce (ICC) [www.iccwbo.org] has published widely used definitions of trade terms (Incoterms 2000) and rules regarding letters of credit (Uniform Customs and Practice for Documentary Credits 1993). It also provides arbitration services. The United Nations Commission on International Trade Law (UNCITRAL) [www.unicitral.org] was formed in 1966 by the United Nations General Assembly for the specific purpose of promoting the unification and harmonization of international trade law. It has sponsored the Convention on Contracts for the International Sale of Goods, as well as rules for arbitration. It also is now responsible for the 1958 UN Convention on the Recognition and Enforcement of Foreign Arbitral Awards (known as the "New York Convention"). Two other organizations active in this area are the Hague Conference on Private International Law [www.hcch.net] and the International Institute for the Unification of Private Law (UNIDROIT) [www.unidroit.org].

Solid lines indicate direct contractual relationships, dotted lines indicate beneficiaries of a contract.

[B5840]

Here we see at least six separate contracts:

(1) The basic sales agreement between Seller in Country A and Buyer in Country B;

(2) The agreement between Buyer and Buyer's Bank for the issuance of a letter of credit on Buyer's behalf;

(3) The letter of credit itself, whereby Buyer's Bank commits itself to pay Seller for the goods upon certain conditions; this letter is probably forwarded through Seller's Bank (or a bank near Seller) which will act as the agent of Buyer's bank;

(4) Seller's contract with Carrier for shipping the goods to Buyer, which is usually in the form of a bill of lading;

(5) Seller's contract with Insurer for insurance of the cargo;

(6) Perhaps a loan agreement between Buyer and Buyer's bank to provide Buyer with the funds to pay for the goods, which likely gives a security interest in the goods Buyer is buying to the bank.

In addition to the arrangements depicted in the diagram, Seller will forward a "draft" (bill of exchange) with the bill of lading, which will create further contractual obligations when accepted by Buyer or Buyer's Bank. Furthermore, Seller may have its own financing arrangements related to the transaction (e.g., Seller may have borrowed money on the strength of Buyer's order in order to process and ship the goods). Buyer may have contracted for an independent inspection company to certify the quality of the goods at the time they are shipped. Finally, several carriers or intermediaries such as freight forwarders may be involved in shipping the goods. Each additional participant raises the possibility of additional contractual relations.

To add to the complexity of the transaction, there may be governmental requirements and regulations that affect the various contracts mentioned above. For instance, tariff levels obviously affect Buyer's purchase decision. But in addition, government quotas may prohibit Buyer from importing, or Seller from exporting. Laws may affect the shipping contract and the power of banks to issue letters of credit and to finance international trade. Exchange controls may limit Buyer's ability to pay for the goods. Special certificates may be required by customs authorities to enable them to enforce applicable laws, such as health and safety regulations. Finally, it should be obvious that conflict of laws questions arise with respect to many potential areas of dispute. In the materials that follow, we can only touch on some of the difficult issues that parties may encounter.

(B) THE SALES CONTRACT

(1) General Considerations

In analyzing an international sales transaction, it is important to begin as with any other transaction with the question whether the parties have concluded an enforceable contract. Although there are variations among legal systems in respect of contract formation, they are generally not of great importance.[1] The precise scope of a party's rights and obligations, particularly rights in the event of breach by the other party, are more likely to vary under different legal systems. These problems may be minimized if the parties choose a governing law known to and acceptable to both of them since most courts accept the parties' right to choose the law applicable to their agreement. The parties' choice of law may not be enough to protect their expectations, however, if the chosen law has to be interpreted in a court that is unfamiliar with it. Thus, consideration must also be given to specifying the forum (whether a court or arbitral panel) that the parties want to interpret the contract. More and more, courts seem willing to accept the choice of forum made by the parties.[2] Of course, even a "favorable" choice of law and choice of forum provision may be negated if it is not possible to enforce any

---

1. For example, while civil law systems do not require consideration to be found in order to have a valid contract, the presence of consideration is not usually an issue in a commercial transaction anyway. Some of the differences in contract formation law between the UCC and civil law, and the way those differences were resolved in the Vienna Convention on Contracts for the International Sale of Goods are highlighted in Peter Winship, Formation of International Sales Contracts under the 1980 Vienna Convention, 17 Intl.Law. 1 (1983), and in

Burte A. Leete, Contract Formation Under the United Nations Convention on Contracts for the Sale of Goods and the Uniform Commercial Code: Pitfalls for the Unwary, 6 Temple Intl. & Comp.L.J. 193 (1992).

2. On party choice of law and fora, see generally Eugene F. Scoles, Peter Hay, Patrick J. Borchers & Symeon Symeonides, Hornbook on Conflict of Laws 343–352, 856–884 (3d ed. 2000).

judgment obtained in that forum without relitigating the issues in dispute in the court that is called upon for enforcement purposes.[3]

In choosing applicable law it is important to bear in mind that in some countries special rules apply to international sales transactions. In late 1986, the United States ratified the Vienna [sometimes called the United Nations] Convention on Contracts for the International Sale of Goods, which entered into force on January 1, 1988. The official English text is reproduced in 52 Fed.Reg. 6262 (1987). As of November 2000, 57 countries had ratified the Convention including Argentina, Australia, Canada, Chile, China, Egypt, Mexico, New Zealand, Russia, Singapore, Uruguay, Venezuela and most European countries.

The Convention is an important development in international sales law for U.S. companies. It applies automatically to all contracts for the sale of goods between two countries that are parties to the Convention unless the parties to the contract expressly opt out of having it apply or choose another applicable law. Among the important differences between the Convention and the UCC are (i) a contract is formed at the time the acceptance is received by the offeror, not when it is transmitted by the offeree; (ii) if the price is not specified, no contract is formed; (iii) an acceptance must mirror the terms of the offer for a contract to be formed, otherwise the acceptance will be viewed as a counteroffer; (iv) the extent and conditions under which an offer may be treated as irrevocable differ; (v) certain provisions regarding risk of loss when goods are changing hands differ; and (vi) certain aspects of the seller's right to cure differ. Article 6 of the Convention permits the parties to a contract subject to the Convention's rules to agree to vary any particular provision of the Convention.[4]

(2) The CIF Contract

The International Sale of Goods Convention is an effort to standardize the basic rules of contract law for international transactions, thereby to increase the predictability of dispute outcomes and to reduce the costs to parties of negotiating and drafting international contracts. Similar efforts have been undertaken to standardize the *terms* of international contracts, so that parties can without great ado invoke a sensible allocation of risks and responsibilities between them simply by referring to a standardized terminology. The International Chamber of Commerce (ICC) has been at the forefront of this effort, publishing detailed definitions of some of the principal terms used in these transactions, most recently as Incoterms 2000. They may be adopted expressly by the parties, and are often accepted in any event by courts in diverse countries as representing the common meaning of a particular term. Perhaps the best known, if not the most common, type of sales contract is the CIF contract.

---

3. See Section 2.3 infra.

4. See generally John Honnold, Uniform Law for International Sales under the 1980 United Nations Convention (2d ed. 1990).

A CIF contract is a shipment contract, not a destination contract. As the Incoterms definition makes clear, the seller's obligation under a CIF contract is to arrange for insurance and freight and to deliver the goods to the carrier. The seller takes the risk that shipping or insurance costs will be higher than anticipated, but the seller is not responsible for seeing that the goods actually reach their intended destination. If they are lost, the risk of loss falls on the buyer (and is hopefully covered by the insurance arranged by seller). A CIF contract is often framed as a contract for the delivery of documents rather than one for the delivery of goods. When the seller presents to the buyer or the buyer's agent evidence of insurance and a document of title from the carrier covering the goods,[5] the buyer is normally obligated to pay for the goods even though they have not arrived and the buyer has had no opportunity to inspect them. If non-conforming goods are shipped, the buyer will be out-of-pocket until a settlement is reached. Buyers sometimes try to reduce this risk by requiring, as a condition to payment, a certificate from an independent inspection agency that the goods conform to the contract. In light of the many events—wars, embargoes, etc.—that may prevent delivery of goods after shipment in an international transaction, the risk-of-loss allocation to the buyer may be significant. These risks occur not infrequently. Indeed many of the classic cases in contract law on impossibility or frustration involve international sales contracts.

The Incoterms definition of a CIF contract is made operational by specifying whether the seller or buyer is obligated to perform certain tasks essential to the international sale and delivery of goods. The CIF term is only one possible way of allocating these tasks. Other Incoterms either increase or decrease the respective duties of seller and buyer. If a seller sells "ex-works," the seller's only duty is to put the goods at the buyer's disposal at the seller's factory or other named place. At the other extreme, if the sale is made "delivered duty paid", the seller has to bear all the costs and risks involved in bringing the goods to the named destination, including import duties. The most common Incoterm other than CIF is probably "FOB—Free on Board (named port of shipment)." Under an FOB contract, the seller must arrange for the goods to be loaded on board a ship named by the buyer at the place of shipment. The seller has no responsibility for arranging carriage or insurance; its responsibilities end when the goods cross the ship's rail. Because of their comprehensive consideration of the tasks that must be performed by someone in an international sales transaction, the Incoterms definitions provide a handy planning checklist, even if they are not used in a given transaction.

---

5. This document may be a bill of lading, which is (a) a formal receipt by the shipowner acknowledging that goods alleged to be of the stated description are shipped to a stated destination in a certain ship, (b) a memorandum of the contract of carriage, and (c) a document of title to the goods enabling the consignee to dispose of the goods by endorsement and delivery of the bill of lading. There are international rules on bills of lading, which in the US are implemented in the Carriage of Goods by Sea Act (known as "COGSA"), 46 Appendix U.S.C.A. secs. 1300–1315.

(C) FINANCING EXPORTS—THE LETTER OF CREDIT[6]

If a seller of goods trusts the buyer, the seller may ship the goods to the buyer and bill the buyer on open account. Within the United States most ordinary sales are made this way. But in the international trade transaction this mode of business is much riskier because of the various factors discussed in Section 2.1. A seller can minimize those risks in a number of ways: (1) require the buyer to pay in advance, although the buyer may refuse to pay before evidence of shipment is presented; (2) send an agent (or hire one already in the buyer's locale) to collect from the buyer at the time the shipment arrives and is turned over to the buyer, although if the buyer doesn't pay, the goods will have to be resold in a foreign country, perhaps at a loss; (3) require the buyer to deposit money with an acceptable bank with instructions to pay the amount to the seller on presentation of acceptable shipping documents, although this may be inconvenient and expensive for the buyer; or (4) require the buyer to arrange for a bank, which the seller is willing to trust, to promise the seller that the bank, on its own account, will pay the seller when the seller presents acceptable shipping documents. The last alternative describes the typical letter of credit transaction. It is easy to see how the letter of credit enables the parties to overcome their fears about dealing with each other in an environment where a lawsuit against one by the other is impractical—the buyer does not have to worry that the foreign seller will take the money and ship nothing because the obligation to ship is a condition precedent to payment; the seller does not have to worry that the buyer will refuse to pay after the goods have been shipped because the letter of credit represents a promise of payment enforceable against a local bank. The convenience and relative safety of this mode of dealing has made it the backbone of international commerce.

The steps involved in the typical letter of credit transaction are as follows: Seller (S) and Buyer (B) contract for S to ship widgets, and B to pay for them, and as part of this contract B promises to open an irrevocable letter of credit (L/C) in S's favor. The following occurs:

(1) B goes to its bank in Paris and asks it to open the L/C. If the bank does not trust B it may ask for a deposit, but usually B is a regular customer of the bank. The bank will then open the L/C and advise S that the credit is open.

(2) S, thus assured, ships the goods and prepares the documents.

(3) S will want to present the documents in its own locale. If B's bank has a branch there, fine. If not, B's bank can send the L/C to a correspondent bank in S's locale to handle the presentment. In this case only B's bank in Paris stands behind the L/C.

---

6. See generally John F. Dolan, The Law of Letters of Credit (2d ed. 1990); Henry Harfield, Letters of Credit (1979).

(4) If S prefers to trust only its local bank, B may open the L/C at a distance with S's bank. But often, S's bank doesn't know B. So B opens the L/C at its own bank, and then B's bank opens a new L/C with S's bank, in favor of S. This is a "confirmed" letter of credit.

(5) S is called the "beneficiary" in this transaction.

(6) The banks involved charge a modest commission for their various services. The higher the risk that the bank assumes, the higher the commission (e.g., to confirm an L/C is riskier than merely transmitting an advice of credit.)

In an effort to standardize practices in the letter of credit area, the International Chamber of Commerce has published and from time to time updates the Uniform Customs and Practice for Documentary Credits ("UCP"). The most recent edition was published in 1993. The vast majority of letters of credit incorporate the UCP.

SECTION 2.3   RESOLVING INTERNATIONAL COMMERCIAL DISPUTES[1]

Some of the most troublesome aspects of international transactions concern dispute resolution. The dispute, if serious enough, may require litigation in a foreign country with a different legal system. If the party is lucky enough to be able to obtain jurisdiction and receive a court judgment in its favor in its "home territory," then it may be faced with enforcing that judgment in a foreign country. To avoid the difficulties associated with the use of national legal systems, many parties elect international arbitral procedures as an alternative. This section will briefly survey both arbitration and some of the complexities of litigation and the enforcement of judgments in national courts.

(A) ARBITRATION AND ENFORCEMENT OF ARBITRAL AWARDS

Arbitration has generally been favored as a dispute settlement mechanism in international transactions, although it is not without hazards. There are many arbitration procedures in use today. They range from those sponsored by trade associations for resolving disputes involving particular commodities to those sponsored by national arbitration associations to those sponsored by international bodies. Among the best known national associations are the American Arbitration Association, the London Court of International Arbitration and the Stockholm Chamber of Commerce. The International Chamber of Commerce [www.iccwbo.org] and the International Centre for Settlement of Investment Disputes [www.worldbank.org/icsid] are the two principal interna-

---

1. See generally Andreas F. Lowenfeld, International Litigation and Arbitration (1993); W. Michael Reisman, Jan Paulsson & William Park, International Commercial Arbitration, Materials and Notes on the Resolution of International Business Disputes (1997); The American Review of International Arbitration.

tional bodies providing arbitration services.[2] In an effort to provide more uniformity in arbitral practices, UNCITRAL [www.uncitral.org] has developed a set of procedural rules and a model national law to be applicable to international arbitration. There is an immense volume of material available on arbitration. Here we will consider only the problems of enforcing arbitral awards.

CHARLES L. EVANS & ROBERT W. ELLIS, INTERNATIONAL COMMERCIAL ARBITRATION: A COMPARISON OF LEGAL REGIMES[3]

C.   THE UNITED NATIONS CONVENTION

Against the background of very limited success with both bilateral and multilateral attempts to establish an international regime for the uniform enforcement of transnational arbitral agreements and awards came the 1958 United Nations Convention on the Recognition and Enforcement of Foreign Arbitral Awards.

The "New York" Convention, as it is commonly referred to, begins in article I by establishing a broad coverage applicable to all awards made in the territory of a State "other than the State where the recognition and enforcement of such awards are sought." The breadth of coverage, however, may be limited by two reservations contained in article I(3). These provide that any country may "on the basis of reciprocity declare that it will apply the Convention to * * * awards made only in the territory of another contracting State," or that it "will apply the Convention only to differences arising out of legal relationships * * * which are considered as commercial under the national law of the state making such declaration."

Arbitration agreements are given transnational validity by article II. Each state is required to "recognize" written agreements in which the parties agree to submit to arbitration their present or future differences on "a defined legal relationship * * * concerning a subject matter capable of settlement by arbitration."

The term "recognize" is not further clarified, but "it seems clear that it does not require a Contracting State to grant specific performance of the agreement by ordering a recalcitrant party to arbitrate." Furthermore, the courts of the forum state are empowered to decide whether the subject matter of the agreement is "capable of settlement by arbitration." This latitude in determining arbitrability impairs predictability and to that extent may weaken the Convention. Nonetheless, article II(3) addresses itself to the enforcement of an agreement and commands a court of a contracting state, "when seized of an action in a matter" to

2. On ICC arbitration generally, see ICC, ICC Rules of Conciliation and Arbitration (Pub. No. 581, 1998 edition); W. Laurence Craig, William W. Park & Jan Paulsson, International Chamber of Commerce Arbitration (3d ed. 2000). ICSID is available only to resolve investment disputes between nationals of one state and another state.

3. 8 Texas Intl.L.J. 17, 53–54 (1973). Reprinted by permission of the Texas International Law Journal.

which the parties have agreed to arbitrate, to refer the parties to arbitration, "unless it finds that the said agreement is null and void, inoperative or incapable of being performed."

Article III is the heart of the Convention, for it requires that each contracting state "recognize arbitral awards as binding and enforce them in accordance with the rules of procedure * * *" of the forum state. In addition, the forum state may not impose "substantially more onerous conditions or higher fees or charges on the recognition or enforcement of arbitral awards to which this Convention applies than are imposed on * * * domestic awards." Hence principles of national treatment and non-discrimination are provided for in the enforcement of foreign awards. Article IV supplements article III in providing that to obtain recognition and enforcement pursuant to article III, the party must, at the time of application, supply the original arbitration agreement and award, or duly certified copies thereof, in the official language of the forum state.

Article V establishes five grounds upon which recognition and enforcement of the award may be refused by the court upon request and proof by the party defendant. Two additional grounds permit the enforcing court on its own motion to refuse recognition and enforcement of a foreign award. The grounds requiring a motion and supporting evidence by the defendant are, briefly, the absence of a valid arbitration agreement, deprival of a fair opportunity to be heard, that the award or an inseverable part of it exceeds the submission to arbitration, improper composition of the arbitral tribunal or improper arbitral procedure, and that the award is not binding or has been set aside or suspended in the country of origin. The two further grounds invocable by the court on its own motion are that "[t]he subject matter of the difference is not capable of settlement by arbitration under the law of that country" and that "[t]he recognition or enforcement of the award would be contrary to the public policy of that country."

Note

After reviewing the court decisions under the New York Convention, Pieter Sanders concluded that courts generally enforce awards. Sanders, A Twenty Years' Review of the Convention on the Recognition and Enforcement of Foreign Arbitral Awards, 13 International Lawyer 269 (1979).

(B) LITIGATION AND ENFORCEMENT OF JUDGMENTS[4]

Litigation of international commercial disputes is often fraught with difficulties. It may be difficult to obtain jurisdiction over the defendant, to obtain evidence from outside the court's jurisdiction and to enforce any judgment ultimately obtained. Courts in the United States will exercise jurisdiction over a foreign defendant who has not consented to jurisdiction only if adequate notice of the lawsuit has been given and

---

4. See generally Lowenfeld, supra note 1, chapters II & III (jurisdiction), V (enforcement of foreign judgments) and VIII (discovery).

sufficient minimum contacts exist between the defendant and the forum. Obtaining evidence from abroad is often very difficult if the witness is uncooperative, although there are international agreements that establish procedures for doing so. Finally, once a judgment is obtained, there is the difficulty of enforcing it. In the absence of an international agreement on enforceability, foreign judgments may be enforced by a court as a matter of comity. However, the rules applicable to the enforcement of foreign judgments vary considerably from jurisdiction to jurisdiction.

Chapter 3

THE UNITED STATES CONSTI-TUTION AND REGULATION OF INTERNATIONAL ECONOMIC AFFAIRS

SECTION 3.1 INTRODUCTION TO CHAPTERS 3 AND 4

In this and the next chapter, we begin our study of national governmental regulation of international trade. In addition to regulations that apply to purely domestic affairs, governments traditionally have exercised an additional measure of control, for a variety of political and economic policy reasons, over transactions with persons in foreign nations. Objectives of these controls could be the following: protecting the balance of payments and national reserves, influencing international political alignments, protecting domestic business from competition of foreign goods, preserving natural resources, enhancing national security, protecting the environment, etc. Chapter 3 and 4 examine some of the basic national constitutional problems that impinge on the way nations regulate their international trade. Later, we will examine in some detail the specifics of various regulations, such as tariffs, antidumping and countervailing duties, and a plethora of non-tariff barriers.

This chapter focuses on the problems faced in regulating international economic transactions under the U.S. Constitution. The materials in this chapter are divided into five additional sections. Section 3.2 provides an overview of the constitutional division of powers in the United States between the President and Congress. Section 3.3 looks at the delegation of powers by Congress to the President and at the mosaic of legislation in the United States by which Congress has delegated extensive authority to the President in respect of international economic affairs, focusing especially on the series of trade acts which began with the 1934 Reciprocal Trade Agreements Act. In Section 3.4, we focus on U.S. constitutional provisions that affect the negotiation and implementation of international agreements. We then turn in Section 3.5 to the role of the courts in reviewing Executive Branch action in this area.

Finally, in Section 3.6, we consider problems related to the federal structure of the United States.

There are a number of very perplexing and relatively unanswered questions in U.S. constitutional law relating to international affairs generally and international economic affairs in particular. Some introductory comments at the beginning of the sections below pose some of these questions. The following excerpt should assist the reader to appreciate the relationship of various questions to each other and help focus attention on how issues concerning international constitutional divisions of regulatory power have important impacts on practical day-to-day affairs.

JOHN H. JACKSON, JEAN–VICTOR LOUIS & MITSUO MATSUSHITA, LAW AND WORLD ECONOMIC INTERDEPENDENCE[1]

* * * Immediately after World War II, several initiatives converged into a proposal to establish an International Trade Organization (ITO). After years of international negotiations, the 1948 draft Havana Charter was completed. This charter would have established an ITO to become the framework for international rules designed to prevent the kind of destructive national government "beggar-thy-neighbor" policies many thought had contributed to the causes of the war. Despite these elaborate preparations, the effort to create an ITO ultimately failed (although an earlier effort to create monetary rules and a monetary fund—the IMF—had succeeded). The ITO effort failed largely because of the domestic constitutional and political structure of the country then economically preeminent—the United States. It failed despite the fact that the major leadership for the effort to create it had come from the United States itself. But this leadership was that of the executive branch or presidency in the United States. Under the U.S. constitutional and legal requirements, for the government to formally accept the ITO charter, the executive branch had to get the approval of the U.S. Congress, and this the Congress refused to give. In 1950 it was clear that it would be futile to continue trying to obtain this approval, and the ITO was stillborn.

At the same time as the efforts to create an ITO were occurring, another set of international economic rules was being drafted. These were embodied in an agreement entitled The General Agreement on Tariffs and Trade, commonly called the GATT. Unlike the ITO, the GATT did come into force, largely because particular laws at that time allowed the executive branch to commit the United States to the GATT obligations without further approval of Congress. In fact the GATT gradually had to fill the vacuum created by the ITO failure, and today it has come to play the central role in the international economic system as

1. From John H. Jackson, Jean–Victor Louis & Mitsuo Matsushita, Implementing the Tokyo Round: National Constitutions and International Economic Rules 1–2 (1984). Reprinted by permission of the authors.

it relates to trade in goods. It plays this role uneasily, however, with a defective constitutional structure not designed to support it.

This sequence of events amply demonstrates the importance of national constitutional and legal constraints on the process of formulating, implementing, or changing international rules. The compartmentalization of legal processes into international on one hand and national on the other can lead to serious misunderstandings of the world today. In fact, that world is a complex intertwining of national and international legal, economic, and other constraints and forces. The current expression *international interdependence,* so apt and yet so trite, often conjures up an image of economic forces and influences, but the legal systems of nations have also become interdependent, not only among themselves but also with the international legal systems that now are influencing daily events.

* * *

The constitutional, governmental policy and structural questions considered here need not be viewed as unique to international economic relations. Many of the issues discussed come up in a large variety of subject areas, including many domestic subjects. The constant struggle between the President and Congress in the U.S. Government conditions much of the national political life of the United States. The study of this struggle in this book can, therefore, also be viewed as sort of a "case study" of constitutional law and politics. One of the interesting (and for lawyers perplexing) aspects of this struggle is that relatively little of it gets to the courts, especially the Supreme Court. This is more so for international affairs, but the fact is that the daily strife often ends in accommodations and compromises, or stand-offs, which none of the parties to a particular contest want to test in the courts. * * * Fortunately, we have a few court opinions to help us find our way into the foyer of the subject, but often these opinions raise more questions than they resolve. The rest of the way is relatively uncharted, and recourse must be had to a variety of historical and legal documents as well as to general reporting about various incidents that are relevant.

CONSTITUTION OF THE UNITED STATES OF AMERICA

Excerpts Relevant to International Economic Relations

ARTICLE I

SECTION 8. The Congress shall have Power To lay and collect Taxes, Duties, Imposts and Excises, to pay the Debts and provide for the common Defence and general Welfare of the United States; but all Duties, Imposts and Excises shall be uniform throughout the United States;

To borrow Money on the credit of the United States;

To regulate Commerce with foreign Nations, and among the several States, and with the Indian Tribes;

* * *

To make all Laws which shall be necessary and proper for carrying into Execution the foregoing Powers, and all other Powers vested by this Constitution in the Government of the United States, or in any Department or Officer thereof.

* * *

SECTION 10. No State shall enter into any Treaty, Alliance, or Confederation; grant Letters of Marque and Reprisal; coin Money; emit Bills of Credit; make any Thing but gold and silver Coin a Tender in Payment of Debts; pass any Bill of Attainder, ex post facto Law, or Law impairing the Obligation of Contracts, or grant any Title of Nobility.

No State shall, without the Consent of the Congress, lay any Imposts or Duties on Imports or Exports, except what may be absolutely necessary for executing its inspection Laws: and the net Produce of all Duties and Imposts, laid by any State on Imports or Exports, shall be for the Use of the Treasury of the United States; and all such Laws shall be subject to the Revision and Control of the Congress.

No State shall, without the Consent of Congress, lay any Duty of Tonnage, keep Troops, or Ships of War in time of Peace, enter into any Agreement or Compact with another State, or with a foreign Power, or engage in War, unless actually invaded, or in such imminent Danger as will not admit of delay.

ARTICLE II

SECTION 1. The executive Power shall be vested in a President of the United States of America. He shall hold his Office during the Term of four Years * * *

* * *

SECTION 2. The President shall be Commander in Chief of the Army and Navy of the United States, and of the Militia of the several States. * * *

He shall have Power, by and with the Advice and Consent of the Senate, to make Treaties, provided two thirds of the Senators present concur; and he shall nominate, and by and with the Advice and Consent of the Senate, shall appoint Ambassadors, other public Ministers and Consuls, Judges of the supreme Court, and all other Officers of the United States, whose Appointments are not herein otherwise provided for, and which shall be established by Law; but the Congress may by Law vest the Appointment of such inferior Officers, as they think proper, in the President alone, in the Courts of Law, or in the Heads of Departments.

* * *

SECTION 3. He shall * * * receive Ambassadors and other public Ministers; he shall take care that the laws be faithfully executed.

* * *

ARTICLE III

* * *

SECTION 2. The judicial Power shall extend to all Cases, in Law and Equity, arising under this Constitution, and Laws of the United States, and Treaties made, or which shall be made, under their Authority;—to all Cases affecting Ambassadors, other public ministers and Consuls;—to all Cases of admiralty and maritime Jurisdiction. * * *

In all Cases affecting Ambassadors, other public Ministers and Consuls, and those in which a State shall be Party, the supreme Court shall have original Jurisdiction. In all the other Cases before mentioned, the supreme Court shall have appellate Jurisdiction, both as to Law and Fact, with such Exceptions, and under such Regulations as the Congress shall make.

* * *

ARTICLE VI

* * *

This Constitution, and the Laws of the United States which shall be made in Pursuance thereof; and all Treaties made, or which shall be made, under the Authority of the United States, shall be the supreme Law of the Land; and the Judges in every State shall be bound thereby, any Thing in the Constitution or Laws of any State to the Contrary notwithstanding.

SECTION 3.2   THE UNITED STATES CON-STITUTION AND INTERNATIONAL ECONOMIC RELATIONS

(A) INTRODUCTION

It is impossible to extricate the question of distribution of powers over foreign economic affairs from the general problem of distribution of powers over foreign affairs in United States governmental and constitutional practice. The reader is probably familiar with the broad themes of this story:[1] The great increase in Executive power during the 1930's and

---

1. See John E. Nowak & Ronald D. Rotunda, Constitutional Law 229–259 (6th ed. 2000); Louis Henkin, Constitutionalism, Democracy, and Foreign Affairs (1990); Laurence H. Tribe, American Constitutional Law 637–657 (3rd ed. 2000); The Tethered Presidency: Congressional Restraints on Executive Power (Thomas H. Franck ed., 1981); Thomas H. Franck & Edward Weisband, Foreign Policy by Congress (1979); Arthur M. Schlesinger, The Imperial Presidency (1973); Louis Henkin, Foreign Affairs and the Constitution (2nd ed. 1975); Francis O. Wilcox, Congress, the Executive during and after World War II; the concern in the 1960's and early 1970's (particularly in relationship to the Vietnam War) that the Executive had become too strong; the revulsion at the disclosures of misuse of Executive power during the "Watergate" episode; and the ensuing struggle of Congress to restore some of its power in the international affairs area. However, in this book, and particularly this chapter, we endeavor to focus on the problem of international economic affairs, as opposed to foreign affairs generally.

There are some puzzling and very important questions involved in the issue of distribution of powers. For example, how can international negotiations, especially economic or trade negotiations, be carried on by a democracy such as the United States? Particularly when the Executive Branch is theoretically separate from the Legislative Branch, some important difficulties occur. It is perhaps impossible for Congress, as such, to negotiate economic subjects; its members are usually too beholden to particular parochial constituencies, and consequently have difficulty formulating overall negotiating positions and objectives that are in the broader national interest. In addition, who speaks for Congress? It is doubtful that even the duly constituted leadership of either House of Congress can speak for that House, much less for Congress as a whole, on international trade matters. Consequently, a foreign negotiator will not negotiate seriously with someone whom he feels cannot "deliver" on the commitments made. The Executive Branch is not quite in the same position. Generally, at least within the scope of the authority contained in the Executive Branch, whether by constitutional right or through statutory delegation by previous Act of Congress, the commitments of high officials negotiating on behalf of the United States can be formulated so as to represent the commitments of the President and the Executive Branch. Insofar as further legislation is necessary, however, there is a realm of uncertainty about the commitments, comparable to that described above for the Legislative Branch. Trading partners of the United States remember all too well commitments made during the course of the Kennedy Round of negotiations on tariffs and trade, which never came into effect because Congress never enacted the legislation required to implement them.

Consequently, the dilemma facing thoughtful students of international economic affairs in the United States today is that, on the one hand, there appears to be a need to limit or circumscribe the very extensive authority that has grown up in the Executive Branch over international economic affairs; on the other hand, it is not clear that the United States will be able to bargain effectively in international economic negotiations if such limitations are imposed. The Executive Branch appears to be the only viable agent for such negotiations, and the feebler

and Foreign Policy (1971); Symposium on   Prob. Nos. 2 & 3 (1976).
Presidential Power, 40 Law & Contemp.

its power, the less effective will be its negotiating ability, unless it can somehow persuade its trading partners that Congress is prepared to deliver on those commitments that require congressional action. We discuss how the United States has tried to address this problem in Section 3.3 below.

The materials of this section are divided into two substantive subsections. In Section 3.2(B), the President's "inherent" powers are examined. In Section 3.3, we return to presidential powers, but there in the context of the President's delegated powers under various statutes. There is not an easily defined distinction between the President's inherent powers and his delegated powers. The approach of the courts, or for that matter of Congress and the Presidency itself, towards delegated powers can be either broad or narrow. The philosophy of the *Curtiss-Wright* case, giving broad leeway to presidential inherent powers, would also lead to a broad approach with respect to statutory delegations. In Section 3.3(B) we give a brief overview of congressional powers, again a subject that recurs in later sections.

One broad question this leads to (probably unanswerable) is whether the President or Congress has generally implemented those policies that are in the best interests of the United States as a whole. For those who, like many economists (see Chapter 1), believe that a "liberal" or "freer" trade policy (allowing more imports) is in the best long-run interest of the United States as a whole, the question can be more specifically phrased: In general is the Presidency or Congress likely to be more protectionist?

More specifically, in considering the materials one can ask the following question: Was the *Curtiss-Wright* case correct (and was Justice Sutherland's dicta correct)? What is the impact of *Youngstown* and *Dames & Moore* on Sutherland's view of presidential foreign affairs powers?

What exactly did the *Guy Capps* case stand for? Does the Court of Appeals opinion have any viability today? What could we expect federal courts to do today in the event of a court challenge to an international agreement entered into by the President concerning economic matters but without congressional participation? How far will the courts likely go to limit the President's foreign affairs activities because of a lack of statutory delegated powers? How viable today would a challenge to presidential actions be under the arguments used in the *Consumers Union* case?

Finally, there are some other questions: How does the existence of legislation make a difference to presidential power when the legislation does not explicitly authorize what the President wants to do? What is "preemption" by Congress? And, as to all these questions, should the answers differ in the context of foreign affairs as opposed to domestic affairs?

(B) THE PRESIDENT'S INHERENT FOREIGN AFFAIRS POWERS

UNITED STATES v. CURTISS–WRIGHT EXPORT CORP.

Supreme Court of the United States, 1936.
299 U.S. 304, 57 S.Ct. 216, 81 L.Ed. 255.

MR. JUSTICE SUTHERLAND delivered the opinion of the Court.

On January 27, 1936, an indictment was returned in the court below, the first count of which charges that appellees, beginning with the 29th day of May, 1934, conspired to sell in the United States certain arms of war, namely fifteen machine guns, to Bolivia, a country then engaged in armed conflict in the Chaco, in violation of the Joint Resolution of Congress approved May 28, 1934, and the provisions of a proclamation issued on the same day by the President of the United States pursuant to authority conferred by § 1 of the resolution. In pursuance of the conspiracy, the commission of certain overt acts was alleged, details of which need not be stated. The Joint Resolution (c. 365, 48 Stat. 811) follows:

Resolved by the Senate and House of Representatives of the United States of America in Congress assembled, That if the President finds that the prohibition of the sale of arms and munitions of war in the United States to those countries now engaged in armed conflict in the Chaco may contribute to the reestablishment of peace between those countries, and if after consultation with the governments of other American Republics and with their cooperation, as well as that of such other governments as he may deem necessary, he makes proclamation to that effect, it shall be unlawful to sell, except under such limitations and exceptions as the President prescribes, any arms or munitions of war in any place in the United States to the countries now engaged in that armed conflict, or to any person, company, or association acting in the interest of either country, until otherwise ordered by the President or by Congress.

[The President proclaimed a prohibition on arms sales and the defendant violated the prohibition and was indicted. The lower court quashed the indictment and the United States appealed.]

Whether, if the Joint Resolution had related solely to internal affairs it would be open to the challenge that it constituted an unlawful delegation of legislative power to the Executive, we find it unnecessary to determine. The whole aim of the resolution is to affect a situation entirely external to the United States, and falling within the category of foreign affairs. The determination which we are called to make, therefore, is whether the Joint Resolution, as applied to that situation, is vulnerable to attack under the rule that forbids a delegation of the lawmaking power. * * *

It will contribute to the elucidation of the question if we first consider the differences between the powers of the federal government in respect of foreign or external affairs and those in respect of domestic or internal affairs. That there are differences between them, and that these differences are fundamental, may not be doubted.

The two classes of powers are different, both in respect of their origin and their nature. The broad statement that the federal government can exercise no powers except those specifically enumerated in the Constitution, and such implied powers as are necessary and proper to carry into effect the enumerated powers, is categorically true only in respect of our internal affairs. In that field, the primary purpose of the Constitution was to carve from the general mass of legislative powers *then possessed by the states* such portions as it was thought desirable to vest in the federal government, leaving those not included in the enumeration still in the states. Carter v. Carter Coal Co., 298 U.S. 238, 294, 56 S.Ct. 855, 865, 80 L.Ed. 1160. That this doctrine applies only to powers which the states had, is self evident. And since the states severally never possessed international powers, such powers could not have been carved from the mass of state powers but obviously were transmitted to the United States from some other source. During the colonial period, those powers were possessed exclusively by and were entirely under the control of the Crown. By the Declaration of Independence, "the Representatives of the United States of America" declared the United [not the several] Colonies to be free and independent states, and as such to have "full Power to levy War, conclude Peace, contract Alliances, establish Commerce and to do all other Acts and Things which Independent States may of right do."

As a result of the separation from Great Britain by the colonies acting as a unit, the powers of external sovereignty passed from the Crown not to the colonies severally, but to the colonies in their collective and corporate capacity as the United States of America. Even before the Declaration, the colonies were a unit in foreign affairs, acting through a common agency—namely the Continental Congress, composed of delegates from the thirteen colonies. That agency exercised the powers of war and peace, raised an army, created a navy, and finally adopted the Declaration of Independence. Rulers come and go; governments end and forms of government change; but sovereignty survives. A political society cannot endure without a supreme will somewhere. Sovereignty is never held in suspense. When, therefore, the external sovereignty of Great Britain in respect of the colonies ceased, it immediately passed to the Union.

* * *

It results that the investment of the federal government with the powers of external sovereignty did not depend upon the affirmative grants of the Constitution. The powers to declare and wage war, to conclude peace, to make treaties, to maintain diplomatic relations with other sovereignties, if they had never been mentioned in the Constitution, would have vested in the federal government as necessary concomitants of nationality. * * * As a member of the family of nations, the right and power of the United States in that field are equal to the right and power of the other members of the international family. Otherwise, the United States is not completely sovereign. * * *

* * *

* * * In this vast external realm, with its important, complicated, delicate and manifold problems, the President alone has the power to speak or listen as a representative of the nation. He *makes* treaties with the advice and consent of the Senate; but he alone negotiates. Into the field of negotiation the Senate cannot intrude; and Congress itself is powerless to invade it. As Marshall said in his great argument of March 7, 1800, in the House of Representatives, "The President is the sole organ of the nation in its external relations, and its sole representative with foreign nations." Annals, 6th Cong., col. 613. The Senate Committee on Foreign Relations at a very early day in our history (February 15, 1816), reported to the Senate, among other things, as follows:

> The President is the constitutional representative of the United States with regard to foreign nations. He manages our concerns with foreign nations and must necessarily be most competent to determine when, how, and upon what subjects negotiation may be urged with the greatest prospect of success. For his conduct he is responsible to the Constitution. The committee consider this responsibility the surest pledge for the faithful discharge of his duty. They think the interference of the Senate in the direction of foreign negotiations calculated to diminish that responsibility and thereby to impair the best security for the national safety. The nature of transactions with foreign nations, moreover, requires caution and unity of design, and their success frequently depends on secrecy and dispatch.

U.S. Senate Reports, Committee on Foreign Relations, vol. 8, p. 24.

It is important to bear in mind that we are here dealing not alone with an authority vested in the President by an exertion of legislative power, but with such an authority plus the very delicate, plenary and exclusive power of the President as the sole organ of the federal government in the field of international relations—a power which does not require as a basis for its exercise an act of Congress, but which, of course, like every other governmental power, must be exercised in subordination to the applicable provisions of the Constitution. It is quite apparent that if, in the maintenance of our international relations, embarrassment—perhaps serious embarrassment—is to be avoided and success for our aims achieved, congressional legislation which is to be made effective through negotiation and inquiry within the international field must often accord to the President a degree of discretion and freedom from statutory restriction which would not be admissible were domestic affairs alone involved. Moreover, he, not Congress, has the better opportunity of knowing the conditions which prevail in foreign countries, and especially is this true in time of war. He has his confidential sources of information. He has his agents in the form of diplomatic, consular and other officials. Secrecy in respect of information gathered by them may be highly necessary, and the premature disclosure of it productive of harmful results. Indeed, so clearly is this true that the first President refused to accede to a request to lay before the House of Representatives the instructions, correspondence and documents relating to the negotiation of the Jay Treaty—a refusal the wisdom of which was recognized by the House itself and has never since been doubted. * * *

The marked difference between foreign affairs and domestic affairs in this respect is recognized by both houses of Congress in the very form of their requisitions for information from the executive departments. In the case of every department except the Department of State, the resolution *directs* the official to furnish the information. In the case of the State Department, dealing with foreign affairs, the President is *requested* to furnish the information "if not incompatible with the public interest." A statement that to furnish the information is not compatible with the public interest rarely, if ever, is questioned.

* * *

* * * A legislative practice such as we have here, evidenced not by only occasional instances, but marked by the movement of a steady stream for a century and a half of time, goes a long way in the direction of proving the presence of unassailable ground for the constitutionality of the practice, to be found in the origin and history of the power involved, or in its nature, or in both combined.

* * *

The judgment of the court below must be reversed and the cause remanded for further proceedings in accordance with the foregoing opinion.

Reversed.

MR. JUSTICE MCREYNOLDS does not agree. He is of the opinion that the court below reached the right conclusion and its judgment ought to be affirmed.

MR. JUSTICE STONE took no part in the consideration or decision of this case.

Notes

(1) A particularly strong criticism of the Sutherland view of history is found in Raoul Berger, The Presidential Monopoly of Foreign Relations, 71 Mich.L.Rev. 1 (1972), who states at 26–28:[2]

> * * * The sole issue was whether this was an improper delegation, a question that might adequately have been answered under the *Field v. Clark* line of cases. But the aims of Justice Sutherland

---

2. Reprinted by permission of Raoul Berger.

soared beyond this modest goal; he would launch a theory of inherent presidential power over foreign relations. To this end he confined the enumeration of powers doctrine to "domestic or internal affairs"; in foreign affairs, he explained, in terms recalling the descent of the Holy Ghost, "the external sovereignty of Great Britain * * * immediately passed to the Union." In this he was deceived. It hardly needs more than Madison's statement in *The Federalist No. 45,* that "[t]he powers delegated by the proposed Constitution are *few and defined* * * * [they] will be exercised principally on *external* objects, as war, peace, negotiation, and foreign commerce," to prove that the powers over *foreign relations* were enumerated and "defined." Deferring for a moment further comment on Sutherland's aberrant theory, let it be assumed that somehow the *nation* or Union obtained "inherent" powers over foreign relations, and it still needs to be shown how the power came to be vested *in the President.* For, as Justice Frankfurter pointed out, "the fact that power exists in the Government does not vest it in the President." * * *

McDougal and Lans, who relied heavily on these dicta, acknowledged that Sutherland's analysis "unquestionably involves certain metaphorical elements and considerable differences of opinion about historical facts," but concluded that he "may have been expressing a thought more profound than any involved in quarrels about the naming of powers." This is to conclude that Sutherland was right for the wrong reasons. Apparently the "profound" thought was the "important fact * * * that the imperatives of survival have required the Federal Government to exercise certain powers."

(2) In YOUNGSTOWN SHEET & TUBE CO. v. SAWYER, 343 U.S. 579, 72 S.Ct. 863, 96 L.Ed. 1153 (1952), the Supreme Court faced a challenge to the decision, during the Korean War, by President Truman to seize American steel mills in order to keep them open in face of a labor strike. In the majority opinion, Justice Black noted that "[t]he President's power, if any, to issue the order must stem either from an act of Congress or from the Constitution itself." 343 U.S. at 585, 72 S.Ct. at 866. Since the Government did not rely on statutory authorization for the seizure, the issue was whether authority for the President's order could be found in some provisions of the Constitution. The Government argued that while there was no express power on which the President could rely, "presidential power should be implied from the aggregate of his powers under Article II of the Constitution. Particular reliance is placed on provisions in Article II which say that 'The executive Power shall be vested in a President...'; that 'he shall take Care that the Laws be faithfully executed'; and that he 'shall be Commander in Chief of the Army and Navy of the United States.'" 343 U.S. at 587, 72 S.Ct. at 867. Justice Black concluded that none of these general provisions could justify the seizure of steel mills in the United States.

Justice Jackson wrote a concurring opinion which contained the following often-quoted passage (343 U.S. at 635–638, 72 S.Ct. at 870–871):

> 1) When the President acts pursuant to an express or implied authorization of Congress, his authority is at its maximum. * * *

> 2) When the President acts in absence of either a congressional grant or denial of authority, he can only rely upon his own independent powers, but there is a zone of twilight in which he and Congress may have concurrent authority, or in which its distribution is uncertain. Therefore, congressional inertia, indifference or quiescence may sometimes, at least as a practical matter, enable, if not invite, measures on independent presidential responsibility. * * *

> 3) When the President takes measures incompatible with the expressed or implied will of Congress, his power is at its lowest ebb, for then he can rely only upon his own constitutional powers minus any constitutional powers of Congress over the matter. Courts can sustain exclusive Presidential control in such a case only by disabling the Congress from acting upon the subject. Presidential claim to a power at once so conclusive and preclusive must be scrutinized with caution, for what is at stake is the equilibrium established by our constitutional system.

DAMES & MOORE v. REGAN, 453 U.S. 654, 101 S.Ct. 2972, 69 L.Ed.2d 918 (1981), is one of the few Supreme Court cases since the end of World War II that has touched on the question of inherent presidential powers in foreign affairs. It involved a challenge to President Carter's orders transferring certain blocked Iranian assets under U.S. jurisdiction, nullifying attachment orders previously obtained thereon and suspending claims against Iran pending in U.S. courts. The orders were issued as part of the agreement by which American hostages held in Iran were released. In upholding the transfer and nullification orders, Justice Rehnquist gave a broad reading to the scope of the authority delegated to the President by Congress. After reviewing what he considered to be congressional acquiescence in past cases where a President had negotiated the settlement of international claims, Justice Rehnquist concluded: "In light of all of the foregoing—the inferences to be drawn from the character of the legislation Congress has enacted in the area, such as the International Emergency Economic Power Act (IEEPA) and the Hostage Act, and from the history of acquiescence in executive claims settlement—we conclude that the President was authorized to suspend pending claims." 453 U.S. at 686, 101 S.Ct. at 2990. The significance of this case is colored by the special factual setting in which it arose. The orders were necessary to implement the agreement under which the hostages were to be released. Given a more pedestrian factual situation, the Court might not have been so accommodating to the President.

(3) In UNITED STATES v. GUY W. CAPPS, INC., 204 F.2d 655 (4th Cir.1953), Chief Judge Parker refused to allow the United States to sue a company that had imported seed potatoes for planting purposes into the United States from Canada and had apparently resold them for food purposes. At the time, the U.S. and Canadian governments had agreed that Canada would limit its potato exports to the U.S. to seed potatoes and require all Canadian exporters to sign a contract to this effect. The suit by the United States government for damages as a third party beneficiary of the sales contract was based on this U.S.–Canada agreement. Judge Parker concluded that the agreement between the U.S. and Canada was improper because the President had not followed the statutory provisions established by Congress for imposing limits on agricultural imports. Those provisions included an investigation by the Tariff Commission. In Judge Parker's view (204 F.2d at 658–659):

> * * * We have little difficulty in seeing in the evidence breach of contract on the part of defendant and damage resulting to the United States from the breach. We think, however, that the executive agreement was void because it was not authorized by Congress and contravened provisions of a statute dealing with the very matter to which it related and * * * the contract relied on, which was based on the executive agreement, was unenforceable in the courts of the United States for like reason. We think, also, that no action can be maintained by the government to recover damages on account of what is essentially a breach of a trade regulation, in the absence of express authorization by Congress. The power to regulate foreign commerce is vested in Congress, not in the executive or the courts; and the executive may not exercise the power by entering into executive agreements and suing in the courts for damages resulting from breaches of contracts made on the basis of such agreements.

> In the Agricultural Act of 1948, Congress had legislated specifically with respect to the limitations which might be imposed on imports if it was thought that they would render ineffective or materially interfere with any program or operation undertaken pursuant to that act. * * *

> There was no pretense of complying with the requirements of this statute. * * *

> It is argued, however, that the validity of the executive agreement was not dependent upon the Act of Congress but was made pursuant to the inherent powers of the President under the Constitution. The answer is that * * * the power to regulate interstate and foreign commerce is not among the powers incident to the presidential office, but is expressly vested by the Constitution in the Congress. * * * In the recent case of Youngstown Sheet & Tube Co. v. Sawyer, 343 U.S. 579, 72 S.Ct. 863, 867, 96 L.Ed. 1153, * * * [t]he rule was well stated by Mr. Justice Jackson in his concurring opinion * * * as follows: [quoting the third numbered paragraph of the concurrence, see note (2) above].

We think that whatever the power of the executive with respect to making executive trade agreements regulating foreign commerce in the absence of action by Congress, it is clear that the executive may not through entering into such an agreement avoid complying with a regulation prescribed by Congress. Imports from a foreign country are foreign commerce subject to regulation, so far as this country is concerned, by Congress alone. * * *

The case was affirmed by the U.S. Supreme Court at 348 U.S. 296, 75 S.Ct. 326, 99 L.Ed. 329 (1955), but on completely different grounds. It dismissed the U.S. complaint against the defendant, noting that there was no showing of bad faith, neglect or carelessness on the part of defendant, since its purchaser, the A & P grocery chain, also sold potatoes for seed purposes. In his book, SUPER CHIEF—Earl Warren and His Supreme Court—A Judicial Biography 165–66 (1983), Bernard Schwartz described the Supreme Court's approach in the *Guy Capps* case. According to Schwartz, it appears that most of the Court agreed with Chief Justice Warren that the President had the power to do what he did, but the Court apparently wanted to avoid a decision on that issue, which was a controversial one in Congress at the time. Schwartz quotes a memorandum from Justice Frankfurter to his colleagues that stated: "In order to avoid entanglement in the explosive issue * * * the whole Court exercised not a little astuteness to have the case go off on a different ground to such an extent that the fact that the power to make treaties and executive agreements was in issue was not even mentioned but was discreetly covered up by reference to 'other questions' which we said there was no occasion to consider."

CONSUMERS UNION OF U.S., INC. v. KISSINGER

United States Court of Appeals, District of Columbia, 1974.
506 F.2d 136, cert. denied, 421 U.S. 1004, 95 S.Ct. 2406, 44 L.Ed.2d 673 (1975).

[The U.S. Court of Appeals upheld a judgment of the District Court that in negotiating voluntary export restraints undertaken by foreign producers to alleviate the domestic steel industry's problems in the 1960 and early 1970s, the Executive did not act in violation of Congress's foreign commerce powers under Article 1, Section 8, Clause 3 of the Constitution and of the laws relating to the regulation of foreign trade set forth in Title 19 of the U.S. Code, including Sections 301 and 352 of the Trade Expansion Act of 1962. In his opinion, Judge McGowan wrote:]

* * * State Department officials [had] entered into discussions that lasted from June to December, 1968, and resulted in letters being sent to the Secretary in which the Japanese and European producer associations stated their intentions to limit steel shipments to the United States to specified maximum tonnages for each of the years 1969, 1970 and 1971.[3]

3. [original note 4] The letters to the Secretary, dated December 23, 1968, were approvingly read by President Johnson after their receipt, and were transmitted by

* * * [E]xtensions, covering 1972 through 1974, were forthcoming in letters dated early in May, 1972, and announced by the President on May 6.

The two 1972 letters are substantially alike. Each states the signatories' intention to limit exports of steel products to the United States both in aggregate tonnages and, within such limits, in terms of product mix. Each represents that the signatories "hold themselves [itself] ready to consult with representatives of the United States Government on any problem or question that may arise with respect to this voluntary restraint undertaking" and expect the United States Government so to hold itself ready.[4] In addition, each states that its undertaking is based on the assumptions that (1) the effect will not be to place the signatories at a disadvantage relative to each other, (2) the United States will take no unilateral actions to restrict imports by the signatories to the United States, and (3) the representations do not violate United States or international laws.

* * *

* * * [N]othing in the process leading up to the voluntary undertaking or in the process of consultation under them differentiates what the Executive has done here from what all Presidents, and to a lesser extent all high executive officers, do when they admonish an industry with the express or implicit warning that action within their existing powers or enlarged powers to be sought, will be taken if a desired course is not followed voluntarily.

* * * From the comprehensive pattern of its legislation regulating trade and governing the circumstances under and procedures by which the President is authorized to act to limit imports, it appears quite likely that Congress has by statute occupied the field of *enforceable* import restrictions, if it did not, indeed, have exclusive possession thereof by the terms of Article 1 of the Constitution. There is no potential for conflict, however, between exclusive congressional regulation of foreign commerce—regulation enforced ultimately by halting violative importations at the border—and assurances of voluntary restraint given to the Executive. Nor is there any warrant for creating such a conflict by straining to endow the voluntary undertakings with legally binding effect, contrary to the manifest understanding of all concerned and indeed, to the manner in which departures from them have been treated.[5]

the Secretary on January 14, 1969, to the respective Chairmen of the Senate Finance Committee and the House Ways and Means Committee. The recipients thereupon issued a joint announcement welcoming the voluntary restraints and releasing the texts of the producers' and the Secretary's letters. No mandatory import quota legislation was recommended by the committee thereafter.

4. [original note 6] It is undisputed that "[i]n negotiating the arrangements and all

of their specific terms, the State Department officers explained to the foreign producers that they were being asked to make the requested commitments by the Executive Branch of the United States Government on the ground that they were in the national interest of the United States." JA 155a.

5. [original note 12] In 1969 the Japanese, and in 1972 all foreign producers, exported to the United States more steel or

Notes and Questions

(1) In his dissenting opinion in Consumers Union v. Kissinger, Judge Leventhal points at the economic effect of the voluntary restraints, "that parallels that of import quotas proclaimed by the President." Furthermore, he says, "(t)he arrangements are not unilateral announcements but the culmination of bilateral discussions that were not only participated in, but initiated by State Department officials. Although the final letters that embody the specific limitations are astutely couched in a litany of a 'voluntary restraint undertaking' on the part of the foreign steel producers, the circumstances are instinct with bilateral undertaking. * * * To say, as the majority opinion does, that the steel arrangements worked out by the President fall within inherent Presidential authority not preempted by Congress is to allow the circumvention of these procedural safeguards whenever that suits the Executive."

(2) Section 607 of the Trade Act of 1974 (Documents Supplement) contains a congressional grant of immunity from antitrust laws with respect to the voluntary arrangements on steel examined in this case. An interesting question is whether the procedures followed in this case could be used today in light of the escape clause provisions in the 1974 Act (Sections 201–204).

(3) So-called "voluntary export restraints" seemed to spread rapidly in the 1980's. There was considerable worry that these "grey area" measures were undermining the international regime of liberal trade. We will examine how the WTO Safeguards Agreement dealt with such measures in Chapter 15 infra.

SECTION 3.3   TRADE LEGISLATION IN THE UNITED STATES: PRESIDENT AND CONGRESS ACCOMMODATE

(A) INTRODUCTION

Although the President of the United States has only limited constitutional powers regarding the conduct of international economic relations, over the years Congress has delegated vast authorities to the President. These delegations, embodied in numerous statutes enacted over decades, often are so general or ambiguous as to give the President considerable freedom to act.

Subsection B will discuss delegation of international economic powers by Congress and the constitutional limitations on Congressional supervision of those delegated powers. Subsection C will discuss generally the delegated powers of the President and how they have been interpreted by the courts. Subsection D will briefly survey the history and substantive provisions of the "core" international trade legislation of the United States. Subsection E will then survey the U.S. government agencies that conduct international economic relations.

particular types of steel product than their undertakings contemplated. In no case were the "excess" goods denied entry into the United States. Rather, consultations were sought and the next year's voluntary quota reduced by the amount of the excess.

(B) CONGRESS AND CONTROL OF INTERNATIONAL ECONOMIC RELATIONS

The United States Constitution grants Congress the power "to lay and collect taxes, duties, imposts and excises," and "to regulate commerce with foreign nations and among the several states."[1] Congress is very conscious of its special role in international economic policy,[2] and even though the conduct of general foreign policy, particularly political and defense matters, may rest largely in the Executive Branch, when it comes to economic foreign policy, Congress does not hesitate to assert itself.

The basic dilemma, as stated before, is the problem of Congress exercising its power and control over international economic policy while accommodating the necessity of the United States acting and negotiating through spokesmen who have the authority to commit the United States.

Here we will look briefly at two constitutional issues that Congress must bear in mind in resolving its dilemma—the constitutional limits on delegation of legislative authority and the unconstitutionality of such congressional oversight devices as the legislative veto.

(1) The Constitution and Delegation of Authority by Congress

The general issue of the extent to which Congress may delegate its authority is sometimes thought to be largely an issue of the past. In the 1930's, several "New Deal" statutes were declared unconstitutional on these grounds.[3] Since that time, however, no statute has been invalidated for this reason by the Supreme Court, although Justice Brennan, in a concurring opinion dealing with the Subversive Activities Control Act of 1967, noted the danger of congressional delegation of power which allows "overbroad, unauthorized, and arbitrary application of criminal sanctions in an area of protected freedoms." In that opinion Justice Brennan felt that the statute was constitutionally insufficient because it "contains no meaningful standard" and no procedures to contest administrative designations under it.[4]

In the cases litigating the validity of the 1971 wage-price freeze, the courts sustained a broad congressional delegation of authority to the President to impose such controls. The challenged statute provided simply, "The President is authorized to issue such orders and regulations as he may deem appropriate to stabilize prices, rents, wages, and salaries at levels not less than those prevailing on May 25, 1970." In AMALGAMATED MEAT CUTTERS & BUTCHER WORKMEN OF NORTH AMERICA, AFL–CIO v. CONNALLY, 337 F.Supp. 737 (D.D.C. 1971), Judge Leventhal said (at 745):

1. U.S. Const. Art. I sec. 8, cls. 1, 3.

2. Senate Comm. on Finance, Trade Reform Act of 1974, S. Rep. No. 1298, 93d Cong., 2d Sess. 14 (1974).

3. John E. Nowak & Ronald D. Rotunda, Constitutional Law 150–154 (6th ed. 2000).

4. United States v. Robel, 389 U.S. 258, 272–73, 88 S.Ct. 419, 428, 19 L.Ed.2d 508 (1967).

* * * That officials may lawfully be given far greater authority than the power to recognize a triggering condition was recognized * * * in the famous *Grimaud* case where a unanimous Court "admitted that it is difficult to define the line which separates legislative power to make laws, from administrative authority to make regulations." There is no analytical difference, no difference in kind, between the legislative function—of prescribing rules for the future—that is exercised by the legislature or by the agency implementing the authority conferred by the legislature. The problem is one of limits.

* * * Congress is free to delegate legislative authority provided it has exercised "the essentials of the legislative function"—of determining the basic legislative policy and formulating a rule of conduct—held satisfied by "the rule, with penal sanctions, that prices shall not be greater than those fixed by maximum price regulations which conform to standards and will tend to further the policy which Congress has established." * * * The issue is whether the legislative description of the task assigned "sufficiently marks the field within which the Administrator is to act so that it may be known whether he has kept within it in compliance with the legislative will."

Note

The delegation issue has often arisen in the context of tariff and trade legislation, the classic case being Field v. Clark, 143 U.S. 649, 12 S.Ct. 495, 36 L.Ed. 294 (1892). In J.W. HAMPTON, JR., & CO. v. UNITED STATES, 276 U.S. 394, 48 S.Ct. 348, 72 L.Ed. 624 (1928), for instance, the Court upheld a statute saying, (at 409):

* * * If Congress shall lay down by legislative act an intelligible principle to which the person or body authorized to fix [customs duties on imported merchandise] is directed to conform, such legislative action is not a forbidden delegation of legislative power. If it is thought wise to vary the customs duties according to changing conditions of production at home and abroad, it may authorize the Chief Executive to carry out this purpose, with the advisory assistance of a Tariff Commission appointed under Congressional authority.

(2) Constitutional Limitations on Congressional Supervision of Delegated Powers

The fact that Congress has delegated power to act in an area to the President does not indicate that Congress has no interest in what the President does. Indeed, Congress carefully monitors presidential action through hearings and other means. One method developed by Congress to increase the effectiveness of its oversight procedures was the legislative or congressional veto. A typical congressional veto provision requires the President to report to Congress action taken pursuant to a delegated authority and permits Congress or one House thereof to veto or disallow the action within a certain time period. The use of such provisions was challenged in IMMIGRATION & NATURALIZATION SERVICE v. CHADHA, 462 U.S. 919, 103 S.Ct. 2764, 77 L.Ed.2d 317 (1983), where the U.S. Supreme Court, in an opinion by Chief Justice Burger, struck down a provision that authorized either House of Congress, by resolution, to invalidate a decision by the Attorney General, made pursuant to authority delegated by Congress, to allow a particular deportable alien to remain in the United States.

Such a "veto power", said the Court, is invalid because the decision is not taken by both Houses and is not presented to the President (thereby depriving him of his right to veto Congressional action, in which case a two-thirds vote in each House is required to enact the legislation). "Congress must abide by its delegation of authority until that delegation is legislatively altered or revoked." 462 U.S. at 955, 103 S.Ct. at 2786. In a dissenting opinion, Justice White stated that it was hard to understand why Congress may delegate legislative power, but may not reserve a check on that "legislative" power for itself. 462 U.S. at 986, 103 S.Ct. at 2802.

One particularly interesting alternative to the legislative veto is the so-called "fast track" procedure (described in Section (D) below), which has been used since 1979 to implement trade agreements into U.S. law. Under this procedure the President is authorized to take a particular action (e.g., negotiate an agreement), but congressional approval is required to implement the results of the negotiation. Since the form of congressional approval is a statute that could be vetoed by the President, the concerns of *Chadha* would seem to be met. The fast track procedure resembles the legislative veto in that the President is delegated power to negotiate an agreement, but either House can "veto" the President's proposed agreement by not passing the nonamendable implementing legislation proposed by the President.

(C) THE PRESIDENT AND DELEGATED INTERNATIONAL ECONOMIC POWERS

The President has been delegated a considerable amount of "emergency" power over international economic affairs. Congress has struggled to find the appropriate line between giving the President too much discretion and yet giving him enough authority so he can be effective when necessary. In this brief overview we look first at some of these delegations, and then turn to powers contained in non-emergency trade legislation.

(1) The President's Emergency Powers

The National Emergencies Act, adopted by Congress in 1976, provided for the termination of most of the President's emergency powers.[5] Exempted from these termination provisions was the Trading With the

5. Pub.L. No. 94–412, 90 Stat. 1255 (codified at 50 U.S.C.A. sec. 1601 et seq.). The Act contained legislative veto provisions that are probably unconstitutional in light of the *Chadha* decision discussed in Section 3.3(B) supra.

Enemy Act (TWEA), originally enacted in 1917.[6] This Act has been used to regulate economic relations between the United States and a number of countries considered to be unfriendly, such as Cuba, North Korea, and Vietnam. It was also used from 1968 to 1974 to regulate foreign direct investment by U.S. citizens.

In 1977, Congress adopted the International Emergency Economic Powers Act (IEEPA).[7] IEEPA restricted use of TWEA to time of war, and thus IEEPA is now the principal peacetime source of presidential emergency authority in international economic affairs.

IEEPA authorizes the President, if he declares a national emergency, inter alia, to regulate (a) foreign exchange transactions, (b) transfers or payments involving interests of a foreign country or national, and (c) property in which a foreign country or national has any interest, in order to deal with an unusual or extraordinary external threat to the national security, foreign policy or economy of the United States.[8]

(2) *The President's Specific Delegated Powers*

In addition to the "emergency" authority discussed above, there is a plethora of statutes that authorize regulation by the President of international economic relations.

Many of these that relate to trade will be mentioned or discussed in later chapters. They include subjects such as antidumping and countervailing duty legislation, Section 301 procedures, unfair trade practices, national security exceptions, and the Export Administration Act.

(3) *Judicial Control of Delegated Authorities*

The courts have generally treated the President kindly when interpreting his statutory powers. Since 1945, the U.S. Supreme Court has never found the President to have exceeded his powers in the area of international economic relations (but only a few cases of this type have been considered by the Supreme Court). The Executive Branch has not fared as well in the lower federal courts, but, as is discussed in Section 3.5(C) infra, that is usually because the contested action involved application by lower ranking government officials of specific statutory standards established by Congress in a detailed regulatory scheme such as

---

6. 50 U.S.C.A.App. sec. 1 et seq.

7. Pub.L. No. 95–223, title II, 91 Stat. 1626 (codified at 50 U.S.C.A. sec. 1701 et seq.). Congress permitted certain actions taken under TWEA—such as the regulations dealing with Cuba—to be renewed from time to time by the President. 50 U.S.C.A. sec. 1706(a)(2). The so-called grandfather powers under the TWEA were interpreted by the U.S. Supreme Court in Regan v. Wald, 468 U.S. 222, 104 S.Ct. 3026, 82 L.Ed.2d 171 (1984) (upholding President's right to revise regulations under grandfather powers). On IEEPA generally, see Lee R. Marks & John C. Grabow, The President's Foreign Economic Powers after Dames & Moore v. Regan: Legislation by Acquiescence, 68 Cornell L.Rev. 68 (1982); Note, The International Emergency Economic Powers Act: A Congressional Attempt to Control Presidential Emergency Power, 96 Harv.L.Rev. 1102 (1982).

8. 50 U.S.C.A. secs. 1701, 1702(a)(1).

the antidumping legislation, as opposed to the exercise by the President or his officers of a more discretionary power.[9]

A few significant cases which have struggled with delegated authorities to the President, and the degree of discretion or scope which would be allowed the President in implementing those authorities, include the following:

1) UNITED STATES v. SCHMIDT PRITCHARD & CO., 47 C.C.P.A. 152 (1960), cert. denied, 364 U.S. 919, 81 S.Ct. 283, 5 L.Ed.2d 259 (1960), this is one of the few cases that refused to uphold a Presidential trade action increasing duties. It held that the President was not authorized to increase duties on bicycles in an amount differing from that recommended by the Tariff Commission.

2) AIMCEE WHOLESALE CORP. v. UNITED STATES, 468 F.2d 202 (C.C.P.A.1972), upheld Presidential action increasing duties on bicycles, accepting that it was done pursuant to "renegotiation authority" under GATT Article XXVIII.

3) UNITED STATES v. YOSHIDA INTERNATIONAL, INC., 526 F.2d 560 (C.C.P.A.1975), reversing, 378 F.Supp. 1155 (C.C.P.A.1974), upheld the Presidential imposition of a "tariff surcharge" (generalized increase of tariffs on imported products) for balance of payments reasons, referring the broad wording of the Trading With The Enemy Act.

4) FEDERAL ENERGY ADMINISTRATION v. ALGONQUIN SNG, INC., 426 U.S. 548, 96 S.Ct. 2295, 49 L.Ed.2d 49 (1976). The Supreme Court upheld the Treasury Secretary's decision (under Presidential authority) to impose a substantial fee on oil product imports, because of broad statutory language authorizing the President to "adjust imports."

5) ZENITH RADIO CORP. v. UNITED STATES, 437 U.S. 443, 98 S.Ct. 2441, 57 L.Ed.2d 337 (1978). The Supreme Court upheld Treasury determinations not to assess countervailing duties to off-set certain alleged "subsidy practices" by the Japanese government on products shipped to the United States. The practice was remission of internal Japanese taxes on the products when they were exported, and the Supreme Court noted the historical interpretation of the countervailing duty law and the GATT rules which allowed such remission.

(4) Note: Statutes Governing the Administrative Process as It Relates to International Economic Relations

The extensive control over private transactions resulting from regulation of international economic affairs involves a number of questions also found in other areas of government economic regulation. There are several issues that promise to be peculiarly significant for the conduct of foreign affairs generally, and the problems of international economic regulation particularly. Essentially the question is whether foreign affairs issues should be exempted from "fair procedure" or similar statutes. Most significant are:

---

9. The major exceptions to this statement are the *Guy Capps* case, discussed in Section 3.2(B) supra, and the *Schmidt, Pritchard* case, discussed in this subsection.

(a) *The Administrative Procedure Act (APA),* exempting "military and foreign affairs functions" from certain procedures;[10]

(b) *The National Environmental Policy Act (NEPA)* for which the courts have held that the failure of the USTR to prepare the required environmental impact statements cannot be challenged because under the trade laws there is no reviewable final agency action under the APA until the President submits the agreement to Congress for approval (since Presidential actions are not reviewable under the APA, this effectively precludes review of a decision not to prepare an impact statement);[11]

(c) *The Freedom of Information Act (FOIA)* (5 U.S.C.A. sec. 552(b)) that exempts certain matters to be kept secret in the interest of national defense or foreign policy, as well as trade secrets and commercial or financial information obtained from a person and designated privileged or confidential; and

(d) *The Federal Advisory Committee Act* (5 U.S.C.A. App. secs. 1–15, that contains elaborate provisions with respect to public access to meetings, minutes and documents of federal "advisory committees." In the area of international economic relations many advisory committees operate.[12] Certain provisions of the Act do not apply to trade advisory committees established under Section 135 of the Trade Act of 1974. 21 U.S.C.A. sec. 2155(f).

(D) THE UNITED STATES TRADE ACTS AND THE RECIPROCAL TRADE AGREEMENTS PROGRAM

(1) History of U.S. Tariff Legislation

Professor F.W. Taussig, in his classic "The Tariff History of the United States" notes:[13]

> The early economic history of the United States may be divided into two periods. The first, which is in the main a continuation of the colonial period, lasted till about the year 1808; the embargo marks the beginning of the series of events which closed it. The second began in 1808, and lasted through the generation following. It was during the second period that the most decided attempt was made to apply protection to young industries in the United States.

10. See specifically Section 4 APA, 5 U.S.C.A. sec. 553(a)(1) (rule-making procedures); Section 5 APA, 5 U.S.C.A. sec. 554(a)(4) (adjudicatory procedures); Section 3 APA, 5 U.S.C.A. sec. 552(b)(1) (information supplying requirements). See also Mast Industries, Inc. v. Regan, 596 F.Supp. 1567 (CIT 1984).

11. Public Citizen v. USTR, 5 F.3d 549 (D.C.Cir.1993). In November 1999, President Clinton directed that a careful assessment and written review be made of the potential environmental impacts of major trade agreements. Executive Order 13141, 64 Fed.Reg. 63169 (implementing guidelines in 65 Fed.Reg. 77942).

12. S.Rep. No. 93–1298, 93d Cong., 2d Sess. (1974).

13. F. Taussig, The Tariff History of the United States 8 (8th ed. 1931). For other works on U.S. tariff history, see U.S. Senate, History of the Committee on Finance, 91st Cong., 2d Sess. 49 (S.Doc. No. 91–57, 1970).

From a time in the 18th century, when the British colonies in North America were essentially required to import virtually all manufactured items, to the 1930's, the history of U.S. tariffs is one of ups and downs, often related to domestic problems (such as the Civil War and the need for federal government revenues, a party overturn or some economic stress).

In describing the passage of the Tariff Act of 1930, the infamous Smoot–Hawley Tariff, Taussig goes on to note:[14]

> The difficulty, as already intimated, was mainly in our political system. The accepted procedure, not new in 1930 but then more firmly established than in previous years, deserves description. In each of the two committees which deal with the tariff—that on Ways and Means in the House and that on Finance in the Senate—the traditions and methods are ideal for log-rolling.

Since the Smoot–Hawley Tariff Act of 1930, thoughtful persons in Congress have recognized the difficulty of Congress' developing a tariff in the national interest. As one senator stated in 1934:[15]

> [O]ur experience in writing tariff legislation * * * has been discouraging. Trading between groups and sections is inevitable. Log-rolling is inevitable, and in its most pernicious form. We do not write a national tariff law. We jam together, through various unholy alliances and combinations, a potpourri or hodgepodge of section and local tariff rates, which often add to our troubles and increase world misery.

(2) The Reciprocal Trade Agreements Act of 1934

From this experience, and the leadership of Secretary of State Cordell Hull, Congress enacted the Reciprocal Trade Agreements Act of 1934, by which it delegated to the President the authority to negotiate international trade agreements for the reciprocal reduction of tariffs.

The language of the 1934 Act not only delegated negotiating authority to the President, but also gave the President authority to "proclaim" the resulting modifications of tariff and import restrictions, i.e. an implementing authority. This language, which has been included in every trade negotiating authority enacted since, was probably chosen for the original act more as a result of tradition and precedent than for any calculated purpose. As one of the authors has noted:[16]

> As early as 1798, an act empowered the President to undertake commercial intercourse with a foreign country (France) and "to make proclamation thereof." This terminology was followed in a series of other international trade statutes during the ensuing century. The Supreme Court, in passing on the constitutionality of

14. Id. at 491.

15. 78 Cong.Rec. 10379 (1934) (remarks of Senator Cooper).

16. John H. Jackson, The General Agreement on Tariffs and Trade in United States Domestic Law, 66 Mich.L.Rev. 249, 283 (1967). Reprinted by permission of the Michigan Law Review Association.

the delegation of power to the President under the Tariff Act of 1890, held that no "legislative power" was delegated because the President could only issue a proclamation based on particular findings of fact specified in the statute. Later tariff statutes reinforced this practice of establishing a proclamation power as the normal means for the President to implement tariff changes.

The Senate Report on the 1943 Act stated:[17]

> Under the Trade Agreements Act changes in our tariff rates are made, so far as our domestic law is concerned, by the President's proclamation under the authority of the Trade Agreement Act. Changes in the tariff rates are not made by the agreements, per se.

The authority granted in the 1934 Act extended for a period of three years, and this authority was renewed for various periods in a series of subsequent acts.[18] The 1945 renewal of the Act was crucial because it was the foundation of the United States' acceptance of membership in GATT (discussed in Chapter 6). By the time of the 1945 Act, the United States had entered into 32 reciprocal trade agreements, all of them bilateral in nature.[19]

(3) The Trade Act of 1974

After the completion of the Kennedy Round of negotiations in 1967, there was considerable criticism in Congress of the results of that negotiation from the point of view of U.S. domestic producers. When the trade agreements authority ran out on June 30, 1967, it was anticipated that it would be promptly renewed. However, protectionist pressure in the United States, reinforced by international economic problems that had arisen partly because of the Vietnam War, and partly because of the inflexibility of the Bretton Woods System (particularly as it involved fixed exchange rates), made the political climate difficult, to say the least, for a trade bill. It was not until the end of 1974 that it was renewed—the first significant gap in that authority since the original 1934 Act was passed.

17. S.Rep.No. 258, 78th Cong., 1st Sess. 47, 48 (1943).

18. Act of June 12, 1934, c. 474, 48 Stat. 943 (codified at 19 U.S.C.A. sec. 1351), as amended, Joint Resolution of March 1, 1937, c. 24, 50 Stat. 24 (three-year extension); Joint Resolution of April 12, 1940, c. 96, 54 Stat. 107 (three-year extension); Joint Resolution of June 7, 1943, c. 118, 57 Stat. 125 (two-year extension); Act of July 5, 1945, c. 269, sec. 1, 59 Stat. 410 (three-year extension); Act of June 26, 1948, c. 678, sec. 2, 62 Stat. 1053 (one-year extension); Act of September 26, 1949, c. 585, sec. 3, 63 Stat. 697 (three-year extension); Act of June 15, 1951, c. 141, sec. 2, 65 Stat. 72 (two-year extension); Act of August 7, 1953, c. 348, title I, sec. 101, 67 Stat. 472 (one-year extension); Act of July 1, 1954, c. 445, sec. 1, 68 Stat. 360 (one-year extension); Act of June 21, 1955, c. 169, sec. 2, 69 Stat. 162 (three-year extension); Act of August 20, 1958, Pub.L. No. 85–686, sec. 2, 72 Stat. 672 (four-year extension). Act of October 11, 1962, Pub. L. No. 87–794, 76 Stat. 872 (five-year extension and setting up also the provision of "Special Trade Representative"; further discussed in Subsection E below).

19. See Hearings on Extension of the Reciprocal Trade Agreements Act Before the House Comm. on Ways and Means, 79th Cong., 1st Sess. 38, 636, 932 (1948).

Meanwhile, in May 1970, the President had established a Commission on International Trade and Investment Policy, known as the Williams Commission.[20] The Commission was composed of a number of businessmen, labor leaders and academics, and had a professional staff headed by an economist as executive director, Professor Isaiah Frank. It was perhaps the most comprehensive official commission for the study of United States international trade policy that had ever been organized. The Williams Commission reported in 1971, avoiding extremes, but generally reporting a need for further liberalization of United States trade, while protecting U.S. trading interests from the shocks of surging imports and unfair activities from abroad. Most notable of its recommendations were probably those which advocated the renewal of tariff and trade agreements authority, and those which recommended a revision of the escape clause and adjustment assistance program so as to make these remedies more available.

The great significance of the Trade Act of 1974 existed not only in its renewal and revision of the traditional trade agreements authority, but also in a series of other titles dealing more or less comprehensively with United States relations with Communist countries, establishing a preferential tariff system for developing countries, and revising the rules bearing on United States law regarding imports affected by unfair foreign actions and portions of the law dealing with the escape clause and adjustment assistance. To a large extent it has been the framework for U.S. trade policy since, although often amended.

(4) The 1974 Trade Act and the Fast Track

It is difficult to negotiate agreements on non-tariff barriers (NTBs). The problem facing Congress is how to place limitations on the authority to negotiate such agreements, without at the same time destroying the credibility of United States negotiators. In 1973 a trade bill allowing Congress to "veto" trade agreements within a 90 day period, was introduced by the administration and was basically accepted by the House. The Senate, however, at the height of the Watergate presidential crisis, was not willing to go this far. Recognizing, however, that the usual process of adoption of a statute had failed in previous attempts to implement international NTB agreements, it was willing to go along with a special set of rules, the key ingredients of which, in the eyes of some observers, were threefold: 1) preventing a committee or committee chairman from "bottling up" legislation so that it could not come to the floor for a vote; 2) providing for consideration in each House of the NTB agreement and implementing legislation without the possibility of amendment, since amendment would require returning to the international bargaining table and redoing the bargain which had already been agreed internationally; and 3) providing for limitation of debate on the floor of both Houses (to prevent a Senate filibuster, for example). This is called the "Fast Track".

---

20. Commission on International Trade and Investment Policy, United States International Economic Policy in an Interdependent World, Report (1971).

The version adopted by the Senate was accepted by the House, and basically provided that NTB agreements and implementing statutes be rapidly considered by both Houses of Congress (within an overall time limit which is usually 90 days) under special procedures that satisfy the three criteria mentioned above.[21]

Other provisions of the 1974 Trade Act provided for extensive "pre-negotiation procedures" by which various sets of public hearings are to be held so that American citizens can comment on the possible effect of tariff reductions or NTB agreements before American negotiators are authorized to make concrete offers at the international bargaining table. Many of these procedures follow those which had been in effect for previous trade rounds, but in the 1974 Act there was an additional set of procedures relating to the establishment of particular economic sector negotiating advisory committees of private citizens or business representatives, having to do with major fields of manufacturing or agricultural endeavor (e.g., steel, chemicals, electronics, etc.)[22]

(5) The Trade Agreements Act of 1979

JOHN H. JACKSON, UNITED STATES LAW AND IMPLEMENTATION OF THE TOKYO ROUND NEGOTIATION[23]

For the United States to both accept and implement the major non-tariff agreements of the [Tokyo Round—MTN] required congressional approval, and under the Trade Act of 1974 this was to be accomplished by normal legislation, which, however, was to be considered by the Congress under the "fast-track" procedure described earlier. The interesting fashion in which the procedure turned out to operate is revealing for the United States governmental and confidential processes.

Under the "fast-track" procedure, the President was required to notify the Congress ninety days before he signed any NTB agreements, and to consult with key congressional committees during that time. Congress had been kept informed generally throughout the course of the Tokyo Round negotiations, and key congressional committees had developed professional staff whose full time was devoted to following the course of the negotiations. When the President notified the Congress in early January 1979, about the tentative NTB agreements, his officials sent to the Congress detailed information about the status of the negotiations, including the tentative drafts of the various agreements that were contemplated. Anticipating this, congressional staff, in consultation with key senators and congressmen, had designed a procedure

---

21. Trade Act of 1974, secs. 102, 151; 19 U.S.C.A. secs. 2112, 2191.

22. Id., secs. 131–35, 19 U.S.C.A. secs. 2151–2155.

23. From John H. Jackson, Jean–Victor Louis & Mitsuo Matsushita, Implementing the Tokyo Round: National Constitutions and International Economic Rules 162–168 (1984). Reprinted by permission of the author.

that closely paralleled the normal procedure followed in work on bills, except that in this case no bill had yet been introduced in the Congress.

When a committee of Congress begins to formally consider a bill that has been introduced and prepares that bill for report to the floor of the whole House, its session is often called a *markup,* indicating that the committee is marking up the bill with its proposed changes. The consultations with the executive branch during the ninety days before completion of the international agreements were called *non-markup* sessions, and followed very closely this type of procedure. One important difference was that the sessions were not open to the public.

The principal committees devoting time to this subject were the Senate Finance Committee and the House Ways and Means Committee (particularly the latter's Subcommittee on Trade). These committees met extensively with executive branch officials, including the trade negotiators, and on some subjects entered into detailed negotiations about the matters that should be included in a statute implementing the international agreements. Particularly close attention was given to antidumping and countervailing duty laws. Perhaps most surprising, the members of Congress informed the executive branch that they desired to have their own staff (including the legal staff of the House and the Senate), develop the actual text of the bill the President would introduce.

Further procedures also indicated the parallel with normal legislative processes. On certain issues the Ways and Means Committee and the Finance Committee did not agree, so they held a "non-conference" joint session at which they resolved their differences in order to present a united front to the executive branch. Throughout this process the executive branch officials participated, influenced the deliberations, and were in a position of some bargaining power, since it was understood that it was the President's bill that would be ultimately introduced and that could not be amended afterward.

After the international agreements were initialed in Geneva, the executive branch prepared the bill that the President introduced to the Congress. Understanding the political realities, the President's officials took almost the exact text of the draft bill that had been prepared by the congressional committees and staff. The President then arranged to have the bill introduced in June 1979.

Once the bill had been introduced, the basic substantive work was over, since it could not be amended. Thus, from the point of view of the Congress, the consultation period, including the non-markup and the non-conference, that went on before the bill was introduced was crucial in shaping the bill so that it would gain enough support in both houses of Congress to be able to pass. Thus, after the bill was introduced the normal procedures for enacting legislation were a formality. To no one's surprise, the bill passed. What was surprising was the overwhelming vote in favor of the bill: 90 to 4 in the Senate, and 395 to 7 in the House.

One interesting development in these congressional procedures for approval of the MTN agreements was the involvement of foreign nation interests. Early in the ninety-day consultation procedures, * * * officials of the EEC realized * * * that the shape of the statute the Congress was formulating would have a profound effect on the practical implementation of the MTN agreements. Once the statute became U.S. law, it would be hard to persuade the Congress to change it. * * * The fact that the United States procedures were moving faster than those of any other country would also be highly influential. Consequently, the EEC took the logical step: they hired professional (legal and economic) representation in Washington, D.C. to monitor as closely as possible what was going on in the congressional consultation with the executive branch officials. These representatives reported quickly and frequently to the EEC officials, and thus on certain issues EEC negotiators could raise questions with their American counterparts. If the EEC objected to a direction they saw the congressional-executive sessions taking, it could and did make it known that it would deem certain statutory formulations a breach of the international obligations assumed by both the EEC and the United States.

* * *

In all this extensive consultation between the executive branch and the Congress, with the tugging and compromising that inevitably goes on in the legislative process, the testimony of participants was that the congressional committees were responsive to executive branch objectives that nothing be included in the U.S. statute that would require the United States to be in default of any of its international obligations under the MTN results. To confirm this observation, after the bill was forwarded to the Congress in final form there was an official statement by the EEC Commission to the effect that in the opinion of the EEC officials, on the whole, the bill reflected the spirit and the letter of the MTN agreements.

Several aspects of this procedure for enacting the Trade Agreements Act of 1979 are particularly interesting and potentially significant. First, the Congress was evidently pleased with the procedure. The heavy involvement of the congressional committees in the drafting process gave the Congress confidence and a feeling of security that the executive branch was not trying to foist something upon Congress without giving it an opportunity to influence the results. * * *

The Congress' satisfaction with the procedure is evidenced not only by statements in the committee reports and other legislative history, but more concretely by the fact that it extended by eight years the period prescribed for the procedure under the 1974 act. In addition, in Section 3(c) of the 1979 act the Congress adopted virtually the same procedure for amending U.S. law implementing the MTN agreements when such amendments are necessary to fulfill a "requirement of, amendment to, or recommendation under such an agreement." * * * Thus, if an international disputes panel rules against the United States on a question of interpretation of an MTN agreement, and U.S. law prevented the executive branch from implementing the international interpretation, this procedure could be followed to change U.S. law.

The second interesting aspect of the procedures for enacting the 1979 act is a somewhat unusual problem concerning the techniques of interpreting it. Normally U.S. courts are influenced in their interpretation of a statute by its legislative history. This history consists of, among other things, the committee hearings and debates, the committee reports, and statements on the floor of both houses while the bill was being considered. * * * Under the "fast-track" procedure, however, a bill was introduced by the executive branch and could not be amended. Thus the executive branch was in theory the draftsman, and its intent was arguably the intent of the draftsman. The executive branch sent to Congress, along with the drafted bill, a Statement of Administrative Action indicating its intentions in administering the new legislation. Thus this statement is an important part of the legislative history, and arguably is the definitive source of legislative intent. However, [the House Report] * * * stakes out a claim to be considered as a prime source of legislative history, just as it would normally be for other legislation. Moreover it also presents a view of the role of the Statement of Administrative Action, and notes that those statements "are not part of the bill and will not become part of U.S. statutes. * * * They will not provide any new, independent legal authority for executive action."

Finally, the role of the MTN agreements themselves in the legislative history must be considered. As will be seen below, it is clear that the agreements do not themselves become U.S. law, but the committee reports state, "This bill is drafted with the intent to permit U.S. practice to be consistent with the obligations of the agreements, as the United States understands those obligations." Thus it seems fair to conclude that the trade agreements (and presumably *their* preparatory work) can be used as at least a secondary source of legislative history of the 1979 act when other sources fail to resolve an issue.

(6) The 1988 Trade Act and Fast Track

During the 1980's and early 1990's, there were two relatively major, general trade acts (1984 and 1988). The second of these addressed the participation of the United States in the Uruguay Round, and it provided for the use of fast track procedures to implement the result of the negotiations. As before, the tendency of Congress continued to be to specify that the international agreements that were ratified were not themselves "self-executing." In the implementing bills for the United States–Israel, United States–Canada and the North American Free Trade Agreements, the last of which was negotiated under the 1988 Act, there were clauses in the implementing statutes addressing this issue and legislative history that reinforced that the statute itself would implement the international obligations, but the treaties would not be directly applicable as "statute-like" laws in U.S. jurisprudence. In the United States–Canada and the North American Free Trade Agreement implementing statutes, additional attention was given to the role of the

States and State law in a federal system (which will be examined in Section 3.6). The same was true for the Uruguay Round.

Notes and Question

(1) The fast track procedures have now been used to implement a number of trade agreements, including the United States–Israel, United States–Canada and North American Free Trade Agreements and the Uruguay Round agreements. These procedures have been criticized by some, who argue that they are undemocratic. How could such an argument be constructed? Do you agree with it?

(7) Fast Track and the Uruguay Round Implementing Legislation

The following is an outline of the fast track procedure as applied to the Uruguay Round:[24]

1.   General Authority: Usually in its authority for non-tariff barrier negotiations, the Congress specifies the possibility of using the fast track procedure, with a deadline date before which the proposed agreement must be signed for it to qualify for the fast track. There is also a procedure for notifying the Congress when the President intends to begin negotiations that would utilize the fast track.

2.   Consultations with Congress: Generally, at least 90 calendar days before signing an international agreement (120 calendar days for the Uruguay Round under the 1993 extension of the fast track), the Executive must notify Congress of his intention to enter into an agreement. Usually the Executive will submit a reasonably complete draft of the agreement, so that Congress can appraise it and have its inputs. Congress will have hearings during this period. At the same time, or a little bit after the notification, various advisory committees to the negotiation must report.

3.   The signing of the agreement must be before the statutory deadline date in order for the fast track to be available for the adoption of the implementing legislation.

4.   After the signing, there has not in the past been any time limit within which the President must submit a Bill to the House and Senate. The practice has been for the Executive to consult extensively with Congress and then formulate a draft Bill. When the President finally submits the Bill, he can submit his own version recognizing that to deviate from the congressional desires will lose him votes in the process. Along with the implementing Bill, the President submits a "statement of administrative intent" which describes how he expects the legislation to be administered. This is an important part of the "legislative history" under this procedure.

---

24.   Trade Act of 1974, sec. 151, 19 U.S.C.A. 2191, as amended, Omnibus Trade and Competitiveness Act of 1988, secs. 1102–1103, 19 U.S.C.A. secs. 2902–2903; Pub.L.No. 103–49, sec. 1, 107 Stat. 239 (1993) (adding 19 U.S.C.A. 2902(e)(Special Provisions Regarding Uruguay Round Trade Negotiations)).

5. As part of the rules of procedure of the House and Senate, the Bill is sometimes considered simultaneously and sometimes completing the House first (as the Constitution requires for a revenue Bill). The key characteristics of the procedure are as follows:

1) The Bill may not be amended (this is perhaps the most important).

2) Committees must discharge the Bill within 45 days, so they cannot bottle up the process.

3) There must be a vote on the floor of each House within a certain number of days (e.g., 15 days after the Bill is reported) with limited debate in both Houses. (Thus, there can be no filibuster in the Senate.)

In general, there is a total time period of 60 legislative days unless a revenue Bill is involved, in which case it is 90 days. However, calendar days can amount to almost twice the amount of legislative days.

In the case of the Uruguay Round, the fast track authority in the 1988 Act expired in the summer of 1993 and had to be extended. Under the extension, notification had to be made to Congress under the required consultation period 120 days in advance of signing the agreement. The last date for signing the agreement was set at April 15, 1994. This meant that the Uruguay Round agreements needed to be sufficiently completed for notification to Congress (which is not a complete final draft) on December 15, 1993. This was achieved sufficiently for purposes of the statute and the congressional consultation period. Congress conducted hearings and extensive consultations during the first few months of 1994, and the Final Act of the Uruguay Round was signed in Morocco on April 15, 1994, thus qualifying for the fast track procedure.

After extensive discussions, the implementing legislation was introduced in September and adopted in December 1994. The Uruguay Round Agreements Act specifically provides that the agreements themselves do not prevail over any other U.S. statute, and that they do not create private rights of action, and special provisions are made for the relationship of the Treaty text to state law. See the Document Supplement for Uruguay Round Agreements Act, sec. 102; 19 U.S.C.A. sec. 3532.

The text of Section 102 (a) (1), declaring that the Uruguay Round agreements do not themselves prevail over another U.S. statute, is broadly identical to that of Section 3(a) of the 1979 Trade Agreements Act. Section 102(c)(1), limiting private rights of action, is broader than the corresponding provision of the 1979 Act (Section 3(f), 19 U.S.C.A. sec. 2504), but, since in both cases the agreements are non-self-executing, the effect is likely to be the same.[25]

In Section 6.7 we discuss the domestic law effect of the Uruguay Round agreements. Other notes regarding the 1994 Act occur through-

---

25. David Leebron, Implementation of the Uruguay Round Results in the United States, *in* John H. Jackson & Alan O. Sykes, Implementing the Uruguay Round 212 (1997).

out this book, and of course, the same is true for the effects of the agreement itself.

(E) THE STRUCTURE OF U.S. GOVERNMENT FOR CONDUCT OF FOREIGN ECONOMIC RELATIONS

It is impossible to give the reader any fixed or precise "road-map" of decision-making and exercises of regulatory power in the Executive Branch of the United States, because these functions are constantly shifting and changing.[26] At the apex, of course, is the White House and the aides and assistants immediately surrounding the President. Each President tends to operate with these individuals in a different way, and so the lines of authority tend to shift from one President to the next, and indeed even during the term of office of a particular President. Some Presidents have designated one particular "assistant" through which all international economic matters will funnel to the President. Other Presidents have even designated a small "agency" in the White House to perform this coordinating function. Most Presidents have also utilized "Cabinet Committees" of various types, which meet and make recommendations to the President. The most significant agency for trade matters affiliated with the Office of the President is that of the U.S. Trade Representative (USTR), which is described below.

When one moves down from the apex of United States government policy formation and coordination, going beyond the borders of the Executive Office of the President, one finds considerably more stability in the allocation of functions relating to various statutory delegations of authority over international economic policy. These functions are widely dispersed among various governmental agencies or departments. Many of these agencies or departments have developed particular constituencies, with special interest in the regulatory measures, that lead the departments to guard their jurisdictions jealously. It is not surprising, therefore, that occasions will arise when the United States government will be taking actions through one department which are, or at least appear to be, inconsistent with actions taken by another department. Overall, it is quite easy to count over four dozen agencies in the Executive Branch with jurisdiction touching on international economic matters and over a dozen independent agencies or authorities with such concerns. Obviously included among these departments are the Department of State, the Department of Treasury, the Department of Commerce, the Department of Defense, and important sections of the Department of Agriculture and Department of Labor. One of the most important independent agencies is the United States International

---

26. A description of trade policy functions as of June 1997, as well as a summary of U.S. trade laws, is found in House Comm. on Ways & Means, Overview and Compilation of U.S. Trade Statutes 221–229 105th Cong., 1st Sess. Comm. Print: WMCP: 105–6, (1997). Much of the information of this sub-section can also be found in the United States Government Manual. Other information has been obtained from interviews or from one of the author's general knowledge obtained from his work in Washington. In addition, there are many informative US Government agency websites, e.g. *www.ustr.gov, www.usitc.gov*, etc.

Trade Commission (ITC), formerly the United States Tariff Commission. Add to these the dozen and a half congressional committees and subcommittees giving attention to these matters and one can begin to appreciate the difficulty of originating and implementing a consistent overall international economic policy for the United States.

In the 1980's and early 1990's there have been a number of proposals to centralize and unify executive branch authority over international trade into a single department, sometimes called the "DITI" (Department of International Trade and Industry). These proposals have been very controversial. Some of them would merge the USTR with most of the current Commerce Department to create such new department. Some would even include the International Trade Commission in this department.[27]

As noted above, the most significant agency on trade matters in the Executive Branch is the office of the United States Trade Representative (USTR). Originally entitled the Special Trade Representative (STR) in the 1962 Act which created this agency, its permanence was recognized by a change of name in a 1980 Presidential reorganization order. The 1974 Act had already elevated the head of this agency (always called the Trade Representative, with status of Ambassador Extraordinary and Plenipotentiary) to cabinet level.[28]

This agency is charged with negotiations with foreign nations on trade and a number of other economic matters, and coordinates much of the United States government policy formulation on such matters. Statutes have set up a group of inter-agency committees, and USTR officials are often charged, either by statute or presidential order, to chair such committees. The agency has always been small, however, usually numbering only slightly more than 100 professional level staff persons. It often relies on other agencies or departments for staff work, and receives help from persons detailed from other agencies.

The U.S. government often works through inter-agency committees, and trade policy is no exception. There have been a series of trade committees at different levels, set up in statutes or regulations in connection with USTR, including the Trade Policy Staff Committee and the Trade Policy Committee (a Cabinet level committee). Sometimes, Presidents have also utilized other White House coordinating committees or cabinet level groups for coordination.

Usually, a committee composed of mid-level officials of many departments and agencies drafts instructions and cables for U.S. representatives abroad, prepares testimony and bills for Congress, etc. When agreement is not possible at this level, matters tend to be considered by

27. See 2 BNA Intl. Trade Rptr. 88, 421 (1985).

28. See Trade Expansion Act of 1962, Pub.L. No. 87–794, secs. 241–42, 76 Stat. 878 (codified in part at 19 U.S.C.A. sec. 1872); Trade Act of 1974, Pub.L. No. 93– 618, sec. 141, 88 Stat. 1999 (codified at 19 U.S.C.A. sec. 2171); Reorganization Plan No. 3 of 1979, 93 Stat. 1381; Executive Order No. 12188 of Jan. 2, 1980, 45 Fed. Reg. 989.

an intermediate level supervising committee, on which representatives are usually from the Assistant Secretary level. Subsequently, the matter can go to a cabinet level committee, and finally they can be referred to the President for his decision.

SECTION 3.4 INTERNATIONAL AGREEMENTS AND U.S. LAW

(A) INTRODUCTION—THE RELEVANT QUESTIONS

We turn in this section to an exploration of a series of key legal questions relating to international agreements in United States law, namely: (1) What is the legal authority of U.S. officials, such as the President or his officers, to negotiate internationally with a view to entering into an international agreement? (2) What is the legal authority and procedure for U.S. officials to accept an international agreement as a binding obligation of the United States under international law? and (3) What is the legal authority and procedure for implementing an international agreement in the domestic law of the United States? The second of these questions relates to so-called "treaty making" authority, although in the United States there are international agreements that are not called treaties. In the United States, the third question involves consideration of whether the agreement is "self-executing." In some other countries, the question is whether it has "direct effects" or is "directly applicable."[1]

As to the first of these questions, the generally accepted viewpoint is that the President and his officers can negotiate on any subject at any time. This does not necessarily imply the authority to accept as binding the results of the negotiation. The negotiation will often be "ad referendum," with the understanding that the President will have to obtain authority to accept the agreement which results from the negotiation. The limits of this "pure negotiating" authority have not often been probed by the Courts or by Congress; the *Consumers Union* case, Section 3.2 supra, is perhaps the best available judicial discussion of this topic.

Of course, the authority to "negotiate" may be relatively useless if representatives of other countries feel that the President or his officers will not be able to obtain authority to accept the results of the negotiation. This is a question of "negotiation credibility" to which we have alluded and which we will discuss again. It should be noted that in other countries or legal systems, such as the European Union, executive officials may not even have the authority to negotiate. That is to say, before any discussions with foreign representatives that could be characterized as potentially leading to an international agreement can occur, there must be some sort of authorization procedure.[2]

It is useful to set the questions mentioned above and explored in this section in some depth, in the context of a series of questions more

---

1. See Section 4.2(C) infra.   **2.** See Section 4.2(C) infra.

generally concerning making and implementing treaties. The following is one "inventory" of those questions, some of which do not trouble U.S. law much; but others of which are very troublesome. The questions with an asterisk are those which arguably most concern U.S. law but not all of those are discussed in this course (these questions are usually a central subject for general international law courses). Question 4 is the subject of sub-section B of this section; questions 6, 7 and 8 are dealt with in sub-section C.

VALIDITY UNDER U.S. CONSTITUTIONAL LAW

1. The power to negotiate

2. The power to "sign" (usually ad referendum, only to certify the text.)

*3. The power to "accept" as binding international law obligation (often termed ratification)

*4. The "validity" of the treaty under national (municipal) constitutional law. Cf. The validity under international law as a binding obligation.

IMPLEMENTING

*5. The power to implement, carry out, the treaty obligations

*6. Direct application of the treaty in domestic (municipal) law (or in the US "self-executing" or "statute like")

*7. Invocability in municipal law (contrasted with "direct effect")

*8. Hierarchy of norms in domestic law when treaty norm conflicts with other norms of municipal law.

ADMINISTERING

*9. The power to administer a treaty, which includes a series of issues such as:

— procedure to formally "ratify"

— power to interpret for domestic application and as a matter of international law

— power to represent the nation-state in treaty institutional procedures (bilateral or multilateral meetings, etc.)

— the power to "vote" in such procedures, the power to amend the treaty

— the power to terminate the treaty (on various grounds including the exercise of a treaty termination clause)

(B) POWER TO ENTER INTO INTERNATIONAL AGREEMENTS—EXECUTIVE AGREEMENTS AND THE PRESIDENT'S POWER

In U.S. law a distinction is made between treaties and executive agreements. The Constitution requires the Senate to advise and consent by a two-thirds vote to the ratification of a treaty, but it makes no mention of executive agreements. In international law, no such distinction is made—both "treaties" and "executive agreements" are considered to be treaties as that term is used in international law. The use of this different terminology in the United States—unfortunately unavoidable now—is a source of some confusion.

In fact one can discern the following different types of international agreements under U.S. law:

(1) Treaties, in the U.S. constitutional sense, requiring advice and consent of two-thirds of the Senate.

(2) Congressional Executive Agreements previously authorized, where Congress has enacted legislation delegating to the President the authority to enter into an international agreement (example: typical trade agreements authority, such as section 101 of the Trade Act of 1974).

(3) Congressional Executive Agreements subsequently authorized, where after an agreement is negotiated, the President seeks authority from Congress to accept the agreement as a binding international obligation of the United States (example: Bretton Woods Agreements Act, 22 U.S.C.A. §§ 286–86x).

(4) Presidential Executive Agreements, sometimes termed "inherent" presidential agreements, where the President accepts an agreement as a binding obligation of the United States without any participation by Congress, on the basis of his "inherent" or constitutional authority (examples: agreements on the disposition of armed forces in foreign countries under the Commander-in-Chief Clause).

(5) Treaty Executive Agreements, where a treaty approved by the Senate leaves certain details of implementation to be worked out by various governments at a later time, and may thus explicitly or implicitly authorize the President to enter into international agreements to accomplish such implementation. (The same could be said of authorizations contained in Congressional Executive Agreements.)

From the Executive Branch's point of view executive agreements are speedier and easier, and avoid the minority Senate veto (of one third, plus one) that could block a treaty. But from the point of view of Congress, of course, the presidential executive agreement threatens to diminish the congressional role in foreign affairs, thus risking direct domestic legal effects of self-executing agreements without congressional participation.

Some, like McDougal[3] argue that the broad powers of control over external relations that the Constitution has granted both to the President and to Congress would be meaningless if they did not "include the

3. Myres McDougal and Asher Lans, Treaties and Congressional—Executive or Presidential Agreements: Interchangeable Instruments of National Policy, 54 Yale L.J. 181, 534 (1945), at 187–89.

instrumental powers, first, to authorize the making of intergovernmental agreements and, secondly, to make these agreements the law of the land." McDougal argues that the practices of successive administrations have made executive agreements "appropriate instruments for handling many important aspects of our foreign relations." Resistance, he says, comes either from those who "fear what majority control may be able to achieve in an integrated, responsible foreign policy," from those defending the Senatorial prerogative, "upon an assumption often none too unconscious that the safety of the nation and the sanctity of the Constitution would be imperiled if one third of the Senate could not dictate the nation's foreign policy," or from those claiming that majority control would imperil minority interests.

On the other hand, the great increase in the use of executive agreements since the beginning of the Twentieth Century has been very worrisome to others who criticize unchecked Executive Branch power, particularly in light of Supreme Court decisions that held that executive agreements, as federal law, prevailed over inconsistent state law by reason of the Supremacy Clause. Raoul Berger points at the fact that executive agreements are not mentioned in the Constitution and at how the Framers "made clear beyond doubt that the specific objective of the treaty clause was to preclude the President, acting alone, from entering into international agreements."[4] Berger also points at the relatively recent nature of executive agreements and at the fact that in some cases they are even kept secret from the Senate and the general public. Citing Kurland he asks: "Should the Constitution really be read to mean that by calling an agreement an executive agreement rather than a treaty, the obligation to secure Senate approval is dissolved?"

During the 1994 Congressional debate over the adoption of the Uruguay Round Agreements Act (to authorize the President to ratify and to implement the Uruguay Round treaty)[5] a challenge was raised to the constitutionality of the fast track procedure used for Congressional approval of the Act. The challenge argued that Senate advice and consent pursuant to the treaty clause was the only proper procedure for approval. This was refuted by a group of eminent scholars, and the Congress, including the Senate, overwhelmingly approved the Act in 1994 (in a post election "lame-duck" special session at the end of the year). In fact, the Senate vote was more than two-thirds, but the process used was the fast track procedure described earlier.[6]

4. Raoul Berger, The Presidential Monopoly of Foreign Relations, 71 Mich. L.Rev. 1, 33–37 (1972).

5. Interested students can find more detail on some of this congressional action in John H. Jackson, The World Trading System ch. 3 (2nd ed. 1997); and "The Great 1994 Sovereignty Debate" in John H. Jackson, The Jurisprudence of the GATT and the WTO: Insights on Treaty Law and Economic Relations (2000) (also published as: John H. Jackson, The Great 1994 Sover-

eignty Debate: United States Acceptance and Implementation of the Uruguay Round Results, 36 Colum.J.Transnatl.L. 157–88 (1997)).

6. Letter from Laurence Tribe to Senator Robert Byrd, July 19, 1994, and Memorandum of Law Re: Statutory Procedure for Approval of the Uruguay Round Trade Negotiations and the WTO, November 11, 1994. See the account of the 1994 Congressional action on the Uruguay Round Agreements in David W. Leebron, Implementa-

The following is a U.S. Department of State document that was created to assist officials in deciding which "treaty making" procedure to use. Consider several questions: 1) Does this document really help? 2) Is this document really consistent with U.S. constitutional practice? 3) Is there *any* constitutional constraint on the President when he or his officials are choosing between the Senate Treaty process, or the Congressional statutory procedure?

U.S. DEPT. OF STATE, FOREIGN AFFAIRS MANUAL CIRCULAR NO. 175 (2D ED. 1985)

Section 720.2 *General Objectives*

The objectives [of these procedures] are:

a. That the making of treaties and other international agreements for the United States is carried out within constitutional and other appropriate limits;

* * *

c. That timely and appropriate consultation is had with congressional leaders and committees on treaties and other international agreements;

* * *

Section 721.3 *Considerations for Selecting Among Constitutionally Authorized Procedures*

In determining a question as to the procedure which should be followed for any particular international agreement, due consideration is given to the following factors along with [constitutional requirements]:

a. The extent to which the agreement involves commitments or risks affecting the nation as a whole;

b. Whether the agreement is intended to affect State laws;

c. Whether the agreement can be given effect without the enactment of subsequent legislation by the Congress;

d. Past U.S. practice with respect to similar agreements;

e. The preference of the Congress with respect to a particular type of agreement;

f. The degree of formality desired for an agreement;

g. The proposed duration of the agreement, the need for prompt conclusion of an agreement, and the desirability of concluding a routine or short-term agreement; and

h. The general international practice with respect to similar agreements.

tion of the Uruguay Round Results in the United States, *in* Implementing the Uruguay Round (John H. Jackson & Alan Sykes eds. 1997), at 175–242 (especially pp. 179, 180, 204, and 205). See also Jackson, supra note 5, at Section 3.2.

In determining whether any international agreement should be brought into force as a treaty or as an international agreement other than a treaty, the utmost care is to be exercised to avoid any invasion or compromise of the constitutional powers of the Senate, the Congress as a whole, or the President.

Section 721.4 *Questions as to Type of Agreement to Be Used; Consultation With Congress*

* * *

c.   Consultations on such questions will be held with congressional leaders and committees as may be appropriate.

Notes and Questions

Like two gladiators in a constitutional arena, Congress and the President are currently circling each other and probing to try to define what will be the appropriate relationship between them. Exactly what the division of power will ultimately be, or should be, is difficult to say. Consider some of the following problems.

(1) The General Agreement on Tariffs and Trade is an executive agreement which was accepted for the United States by the President in 1947 under the then existing Trade Agreements Act authority, which authorized the President

(1) To enter into foreign trade agreements * * *; and

(2) To proclaim such modifications of existing duties and other import restrictions * * * as are required or appropriate to carry out any [such] foreign trade agreement.[7]

Ever since, there have been questions raised whether the foregoing language authorized the President to enter into the General Agreement. We explore this issue in more detail in Section 6.7 infra.

(2) The 1967 Anti–Dumping Code, an agreement negotiated under GATT auspices in the Kennedy Round, was accepted by the President without explicit statutory authority, on the argument that it required changes only in administrative practices of the Executive Branch, which were within the delegated authority of that Branch. Is this an appropriate use of executive agreements? Does it matter whether the agreement requires changes in long established administrative practices, although the changes would not be inconsistent with any statute? Members of Congress have complained about Executive Branch changes in long established administrative practices, particularly when done to fulfill an executive agreement not approved by Congress. Indeed, as noted in Section 16.3 infra, Congress effectively forbade implementation of the Code. Later, under the Trade Act of 1974, a special procedure was set up for the approval of non-tariff barrier agreements, and in commenting on that procedure, the congressional reports make it abundantly clear that when such agreements change an established

---

7. Reciprocal Trade Agreements Act, sec. 350, 59 Stat. 410 (1945).

administrative practice (or regulation), they should be submitted for congressional approval.[8]

(3) The Organization for Economic Cooperation and Development is governed by a 1960 convention to which the United States is obligated as a treaty. Article 5 of that convention authorizes the Organization to take decisions that are binding on its members. It has been argued that, since the executive branch will be representing the United States in the Organization, the convention will operate to give the Executive power to agree on decisions in certain substantive fields. Abram Chayes, then Legal Adviser of the United States Department of State, however, stated: "This argument is based on the erroneous assumption that the convention in any way concerns itself with the distribution of powers within the United States or any other member state. * * * Under article 5 the Organization may take decisions, but the convention is silent as to the process by which a member nation, within its own internal system, arrives at the point where it may cast an effective vote in favor of a particular decision." A statement for the record added that "the power of the United States to cast a favorable vote and bind the United States in any particular case must be sought in a source outside the convention."[9] When the United States representative does not have the authority, under United States law, to bind the United States, he will either veto the decision, or abstain (thus permitting the decision to become binding as to other member countries) or approve, subject to compliance with U.S. constitutional procedures.

(C) DOMESTIC LEGAL EFFECT AND IMPLEMENTATION OF INTERNATIONAL AGREEMENTS IN U.S. LAW[10]

The question of whether and to what extent a valid international agreement has domestic legal effects involves at least three sub-questions that courts and officials do not always clearly distinguish. (Note: If the agreement is not valid under U.S. law, the next questions are irrelevant.) First, does the international agreement, or any part of it, have "direct applicability" or a "self-executing effect" in U.S. law, so that at least some litigants in U.S. courts are entitled to rely on its provisions, and courts must accept those provisions as applicable law?

The second question is whether a particular party to litigation can rely on a provision of an international agreement. This question is closely related to the first and often courts do not distinguish these two questions, but there can be a distinct difference between them. The second question concerns the "standing" of the party. Even if a provision of an international agreement is self-executing, is the particular

---

8. See, e.g., Senate Comm. on Finance, Trade Reform Act of 1974, S.Rep. No. 93–1298, 93d Cong., 2d Sess. 75 (1974).

9. 107 Cong.Rec. 4157 (1961); John H. Jackson, Status of Treaties in Domestic Legal Systems: A Policy Analysis, 96 Am. J.Intl.L. 310 (1992).

10. John H. Jackson, The Jurisprudence of GATT & the WTO 310–340 (2000); John

H. Jackson, United States of America, *in* The Effect of Treaties in Domestic Law 141 (Francis G. Jacobs & Shelley Roberts eds., 1987); Thomas Buergenthal, Self–Executing and Non–Self–Executing Treaties in National and International Law, 235 Recueil des Cours (1992–IV).

party who claims the benefit of that provision a party entitled to make such a claim under that provision?

Third, there is a separate question of "hierarchy of norms." If the international agreement is inconsistent with a prior or subsequent federal or state statute or constitutional provision, which prevails?

JOHN H. JACKSON, STATUS OF TREATIES IN DOMESTIC LEGAL SYSTEMS[11]

For those who have not had contact with the literature and practice of treaty effects in domestic law, let us first examine the broad outlines of the existing international situation with respect to the direct applicability of a treaty, using a simple paradigmatic hypothetical to illustrate it. Suppose nations M and D have entered into an international treaty that includes the following obligation:

> With respect to the right to own property within the territory of either contracting party (nation M or D), the citizens of the other contracting party shall have equal and nondiscriminatory treatment as compared to treatment received by the citizens of that contracting party within which the property is located.

The intent of this language is to equalize the property ownership rights of both countries' citizens within the territory of each contracting party, a traditional expression of "national treatment" obligations found in many bilateral and multilateral[12] treaties, although the subject of the obligation may differ widely.

In traditional explanations of the effect of treaties (going back a century or more), a distinction is made between "monist" and "dualist" states.[13] This terminology has been criticized, and clearly it is too "dichotomous" in flavor, since there are various degrees of direct application of treaties, to say nothing of the considerable confusion about it. Nevertheless, even though not precise, these terms are used and may help to demonstrate the major alternative approaches.

Let us assume that State M is considered "monist" and state D is considered "dualist," and in each state a citizen of the other has been refused rights to own property by the national government even though

---

11. Reproduced with permission from 86 AJIL 310, 313–315 (1992), © The American Society of International Law.

12. [original note 16] For example, The General Agreement on Tariffs and Trade (GATT), Article III; and many treaties of friendship, commerce, and navigation. * * *

13. [original note 18] [See, e.g., I. Brownlie, Principles of Public International Law (5th ed. 1990); Sasse, The Common Market: Between International & Municipal Law, 75 Yale L.J. 695 (1966).] The author is aware that some writers tend to down play this terminology, or feel that it is unnecessary. See, e.g., the descriptions of such views in McDougal, The Impact of International Law upon National Law: A Policy–Oriented Perspective, 4 S. Dakota L.Rev. 25, 28, 31 (1959). Nevertheless, as a matter of empirical observation, court opinions, national officials and authors do use this terminology, at least in some jurisdictions. See, e.g., I. Brownlie, supra, Chapter II; Meinhard Hilf, Rights, Institutions and Impact of International Law According to the German Basic Law 177 (1987).

that state's citizens possess those rights. What is the *national* legal situation?

Traditionally, the "monist" state's legal system is considered to include international treaties to which M is obligated. Thus, a citizen of D can sue as an individual in the courts of M to require that he be treated in accordance with the treaty standard.[14]

On the other hand, the term "dualist" has been used to describe the contrary result in state D. In a dualist state, international treaties are part of a separate legal system from that of the domestic law (hence a "dual" system). Therefore, a treaty is not part of the domestic law, at least not directly. Without further facts, a citizen of M who is refused the property ownership privilege in D that D's citizen has there, has no way to sue in the courts of D because those courts apply the law of D, which does not include the rule expressed in the treaty (at least not yet). The citizen of M's only recourse is to persuade his own government to use diplomatic means to encourage D to honor its obligation and assure him equal property ownership rights.

It is generally said that for the treaty rule to operate in the domestic legal system of a dualist state, there must be an "act of transformation," that is, a government action by that state incorporating the treaty norm into its domestic law.[15] This may be a statute duly enacted by the parliament that uses all or part of the treaty language and incorporates it as a statutory matter into domestic law.[16] Sometimes such a statute may paraphrase the treaty language, or "clarify" or elaborate the treaty language. In all these cases, the domestic law is that of the act of transformation, but the treaty language usually has "relevance" in interpreting the statutory language, under various theories of the domestic jurisprudence.[17] Other legal instruments can also serve as an act of

14. [original note 19] It is assumed in this article that aliens *or* citizens of the relevant foreign nation have access to the courts of a domestic legal system.

15. [original note 20] When an international treaty does not have direct effect in the domestic law system, but it is necessary to provide domestic rules to carry out the international treaty, in many cases such rules can be provided by an "act of transformation," such as a statute, which incorporates the treaty, or most of the treaty language, and makes that language through this statute a part of the domestic legal system.

16. [original note 21] In many cases, the statute which operates as the act of transformation also authorizes the appropriate government officials to "accept" or ratify the treaty itself. For example, see the U.S. Trade Agreements Act of 1979, Pub. L. No. 96–39, 93 Stat. 144 (1979), especially § 3 Relationship of Trade Agreements to Unit-

ed States Law, and relevant legislative history. See J. Jackson, The World Trading System: Law and Policy of International Economic Relations 97 (2nd ed. 1997); Frowein, Federal Republic of Germany, *in* The Effect of Treaties in Domestic Law 63, 66 (F. Jacobs & S. Roberts eds., 1987).

17. [original note 22] See e.g., American Law Institute, Restatement of the Law (Third), Foreign Relations Law of the United States § 114 (1987) (which reads, "Where fairly possible, a United States statute is to be construed so as not to conflict with international law, or with an international agreement of the United States"). See also J. Jackson, The World Trading System: Law and Policy of International Economic Relations 95–96 (2nd. Ed 1997); J. Jackson, J.-V. Louis & M. Matsushita, Implementing the Tokyo Round: National Constitutions and International Economic Rules 167 (1984). See generally The Effect of Treaties in Domestic Law (F. Jacobs & S. Roberts eds., 1987).

transformation, including a regulation of an administrative body (if its authority so permits), and possibly even an action or decision of a court or tribunal (again, depending on the authority of the tribunal.)[18]

(1) Self-Executing International Agreements

The question of whether a treaty has direct domestic law effect is, under United States law (in contrast to the law of a number of foreign nations), a question of whether the treaty is "self-executing" and purports directly by its own terms to give rights to individual citizens, rather than simply imposing the international legal obligation upon the national government to effectuate those rights. One classic case is Sei Fujii v. State of California, 38 Cal.2d 718, 242 P.2d 617 (1952), which held that certain provisions of the United Nations Charter were not self-executing. The California court said (242 P.2d at 620–22), "it must appear that the framers of the treaty intended to prescribe a rule that, standing alone, would be enforceable in the courts" and concluded that the United Nations Charter "pledges the various countries to cooperate" and "represents a moral commitment," but that the provisions at issue "were not intended to supersede existing domestic legislation."

If the provisions of an international agreement are not self-executing, and if implementation of the agreement requires some changes in domestic U.S. law (not always the case), then some additional action by government bodies will be necessary. This raises the question of authority to implement an agreement. A number of different forms of implementation are possible. Congress may enact a statute that will implement the agreement or the President or other officials may have authority to implement the agreement by issuing or changing regulations.

Sometimes the question of "self-executing" is made a subject of understanding between the Executive Branch and the Senate during the treaty ratification process. For example, the 1962 International Coffee Agreement was ratified after Senate approval,[19] but the Senate record notes understandings between the Senate and the Executive Branch (which were crucial for obtaining Senate approval) that the treaty would not be self-executing.[20]

How does a court determine when an international agreement is self-executing? What sort of language in the agreement itself does it look to? If the language of the agreement is ambiguous, what other sources will a court address? Intent of the draftsmen as expressed in the "preparatory work" for the agreement? Is the issue of any appropriate concern to the foreign parties, or is it solely a U.S. constitutional law

---

18. [original note 23] For example, (although probably rare) a court might be delegated authority to issue a device that would apply a treaty, perhaps on a petition for mandamus. This situation is to be distinguished from a court's deciding that a treaty is directly applicable in a particular case.

19. International Coffee Agreement Act of 1965, Pub. L. No. 89–23, 79 Stat. 112 (codified at 19 U.S.C.A. sec. 1356a et seq.)

20. 109 Cong. Rec. 1926 (1963).

question? If the latter, would U.S. courts look primarily or solely to the intentions expressed by the U.S. negotiators? Would that category be deemed to include Congressmen or Senators? Suppose the Senate, in its advice and consent, expressed its view that an international agreement was not self-executing as drafted, should that view prevail? Suppose it is clear from the record that the Senate advice to favor ratification was premised on the belief that the agreement was not self-executing, is that determinative? (We will have occasion to consider in Chapter 6 the question of whether the General Agreement on Tariffs and Trade is a self-executing agreement.)[21]

DETLEV F. VAGTS, THE UNITED STATES AND ITS TREATIES: OBSERVANCE AND BREACH[22]

It is generally agreed that some treaties of the United States are not self-executing, that is, that they cannot be enforced by the courts without further action by Congress. Which treaties are and which treaties are not self-executing is less clear.[23] Constitutionally, some treaties cannot be self-executing, most notably those that obligate the United States to pay money to a foreign state or to foreign parties, an obligation that cannot be carried out save by statute.[24] It has also been stated, though with less clear foundation, that a treaty cannot create criminal law.[25] Certain treaties have been found to be non-self-executing because the Senate clearly expressed such an intention or it can be implied. For present purposes, it suffices that there is a category of treaties that the United States is obligated to make domestically effective, although it has not done so.

CARLOS MANUEL VÁZQUEZ, THE FOUR DOCTRINES OF SELF-EXECUTING TREATIES[26]

The distinction between self-executing and non-self-executing treaties has particularly confounded the lower courts, whose decisions on the issue have produced a body of law that can only be described as being in a state of disarray. Much of the problem is the result of sloppy reasoning

---

21. Regarding how U.S. courts have evaluated whether a treaty is to be treated as self-executing, as described in John H. Jackson, The Jurisprudence of the GATT and the WTO: Insights on Treaty Law and Economic Relations ch. 17 (2000), based on John H. Jackson, United States, *in* Francis G. Jacobs & Shelley Roberts (eds.), The Effect of Treaties in Domestic Law ch. 8 (1987).

22. 95 Am.J.Intl.L. 313, 321 (April 2001).

23. [original note 66] For recent controversial writing on the topic, see John C. Yoo, "Globalism and the Constitution: Treaties, Non–Self–Execution, and the

Original Understanding," 99 Colum. L. Rev. 1955 (1999); Martin S. Flaherty, "History Right? Historical Scholarship, Original Understanding, and Treaties as 'Supreme Law of the Land,' " id., at 2095; Carlos Manuel Vázquez, "Laughing at Treaties," id. At 2154; John C. Yoo, "Treaties and Public Lawmaking: A Textual and Structural Defense of Non–Self–Execution," id. At 2218.

24. [original note 67] U.S. Const. Art. I, sec. 9.

25. [original note 68] The Over the Top, 5 F.2d 838, 843 (D.Conn.1925).

26. 89 Am.J.Intl.L. 695, 722–23 (October 1995).

and careless use of precedent. For example, the Ninth Circuit recently dismissed a treaty argument out of hand with a simply citation to a Supreme Court footnote stating that a different provision of the treaty was not "self-executing."[27] (As noted, it is well accepted that certain provisions of a treaty may be self-executing while others are not.) But even the courts that have been somewhat more conscientious in attempting to classify treaties according to Chief Justice Marshall's distinction have been confounded by the unusual hybrid domestic/international nature of the distinction. Unfortunately, they have had little guidance from the Supreme Court, which has not said more than a sentence or two about the distinction in any case for nearly a century.

* * *

If integrity is to be restored in to this area of the law, the courts must recognize that the terms "self-executing" and "non-self-executing" do not have a unique meaning with respect to treaties. In examining "self-execution" arguments, the courts should therefore carefully consider the precise reason that the particular treaties before them are claimed to be judicially unenforceable, and in deciding the issue they should rely only on precedents involving that issue. Finally, and most importantly, the courts should decide the issue in full cognizance of the central role that the Constitution assigns to them in the enforcement of treaties.

In connection with trade agreements, the U.S. Congress has been increasingly explicit about its desire that the agreements themselves not be self-executing. Section 102 of the implementing legislation for the Uruguay Round Agreements is a clear example of this.[28] Similar language can be found in implementing statutes relating to U.S. free trade agreements with Israel, Canada and Canada/Mexico in the North American Free Trade Agreement.[29] See Section 6.7 infra.

Although a treaty is sometimes not self-executing or "directly applicable," it is a serious mistake to assume that the treaty is therefore irrelevant. Such a treaty does not have "statute-like" status and will not have its own text directly applied in a case, but the treaty nevertheless has some serious impacts and effects (despite some misguided federal

---

27. [original note 136] See United States v. Aguilar, 883 F.2d 662, 680 (9th Cir.1989), cert. denied, 111 S.Ct. 751 (1991).

28. Uruguay Round Agreements Act, sec. 102; Pub. L. No. 103–182, § 102, 107 Stat. 2057, 2062 (1993) (codified at 19 U.S.C.A. sec. 3312); David W. Leebron, Implementation of the Uruguay Round Results in the United States, *in* John H. Jackson & Alan O. Sykes (eds.), Implementing the Uruguay Round 175, 211–218 (1997).

29. Uruguay Round Agreements Act, sec. 102; Pub.L.No. 103–182, sec. 102, 107 Stat. 2057, 2062 (1993) (codified at 19 U.S.C.A. sec. 3312) (NAFTA); Pub.L.No. 100–449, sec. 102, 102 Stat. 1851, 1853 (1988) (codified in note to 19 U.S.C.A. sec. 2112) (Canada); Pub.L.No. 99–47, sec. 5, 99 Stat. 82, 83 (1985) (codified in note to 19 U.S.C.A. sec. 2112) (Israel).

court opinion language in that regard). The following are some (but not all) of those effects:

1) The jurisprudence of the U.S. courts generally follows the idea that if any ambiguity exists in a statute which a court is interpreting, and one option is consistent with U.S. international obligations and others are not, the court should choose the option which makes the U.S. statute consistent (thus avoiding a U.S. breach of its treaty obligations.) This was established by the *Charming Betsy* case early in U.S. constitutional history, and is a principle enunciated in the Restatement of Foreign Relations Law.[30]

2) Sometimes a statute incorporates treaty language by reference, e.g., the statute says "the provisions of article X of the Treaty of Y shall apply in this case."

3) Sometimes a statute requires U.S. officials or others to do their duty "consistent with Treaty X" or "consistent with Article 5 of Treaty X."

4) The legislative history of the Statute may clearly or impliedly indicate that the purpose of the statute is to implement U.S. obligations under a treaty. This gives legislative history weight to an interpretation choice which pursues this goal. In the 1994 Act implementing the Uruguay Round agreement, the statute itself says that the Congress "approves" the Statement of Administrative Action made by the President as required by the Fast Track procedure, and this seems to even strengthen the concept of choosing treaty consistency in some cases.

5) Treaty language may be deemed to articulate policies which the treaty parties including the United States have accepted, and those policies maybe used to help interpret a statute.

6) The existence of treaties accepted by the U.S. may be indication of "federal preemption" of a subject matter, preventing state contrary action.[31]

(2) An Individual's Right to Invoke International Agreements; Standing

Even if an international agreement is self-executing, it remains to determine if a particular individual is entitled to invoke the agreement's provisions.[32] In other words, does that individual have "standing?" For example, an international agreement may be self-executing in that federal government officials have authority to implement its provisions in their daily official tasks (e.g., apply a particular tariff to Company A, or restrain the exports of Company B). On the other hand, a particular

---

30. See American Law Institute, Restatement of the Law 3rd, Foreign Relations Law of the United States, Section 114 (1986). That section's notes cite the case of Murray v. Schooner Charming Betsy, 6 U.S. (2 Cranch) 64, 2 L.Ed. 208 (1804). See also the discussion above in this section 3.4 (C).

31. See Bethlehem Steel Corp. v. Board of Commissions, described in Note 2 following the *Crosby* case in Section 3.6.

32. See generally Lori F. Damrosch, Louis Henkin, Richard C. Pugh, Oscar Schachter & Hans Smit, International Law: Cases and Materials 396–401 (4th ed. 2001).

challenger (e.g., Company X) may not be sufficiently affected by the provision for the courts to grant it the right to invoke it.

A case that touches on these subjects is Diggs v. Richardson, 555 F.2d 848 (D.C.Cir.1976). This case concerned a United Nations Security Council Resolution calling upon U.N. Members to have no dealings with South Africa that impliedly recognized the legality of its continued occupation of Namibia. Plaintiffs argued that the resolution was self-executing and that U.S. government officials had violated its terms. The U.S. government argued that Security Council resolutions are not legally binding, that the resolution at issue was not self-executing, that plaintiffs lacked standing and that the case concerned a political question not appropriate for judicial resolution. The Court of Appeals affirmed the dismissal of the case by the lower court (555 F.2d at 851), "on the ground, related to the issue of standing, but analytically distinct, that even assuming there is an international obligation that is binding on the United States—a point we do not in any way reach on the merits—the U.N. resolution underlying that obligation does not confer rights on the citizens of the United States that are enforceable in court in the absence of implementing legislation."

(3) *Hierarchy of Norms: Which Rules Take Precedence?*

If faced with a conflict between state and federal law or between an international agreement and a statute, a court must try to reconcile the opposing provisions. In doing so, a court should normally try to construe a statute so it does not conflict with international law or an international agreement of the United States.[33] If it is unable to do so, then it must decide which is superior. In the United States, federal law prevails over state law (see Section 3.6 below). Federal statutes and international agreements are deemed to be of the same rank, and thus generally it is considered that the later in time will prevail, at least in the case of treaties.[34]

In an interesting case concerning a U.S. statute which prohibited certain foreign organizations (such as the Palestine Liberation Organization) from having offices in the U.S., including prohibition of an office permitted by the United Nations and thus arguably falling under a treaty provision binding the U.S., a federal district court "reconciled" the treaty provision with the statute by saying in effect that the statute did not explicitly say the Congress intended to violate its treaty obligations so the words of the statute which seemed clearly to mandate closing the PLO office, were not applied to do so. The case was not appealed by the Executive Branch (which had originally opposed the statutory clause). Thus it is not likely that this approach will be deemed

---

33. American Law Institute, Restatement of the Law (Third), Foreign Relations Law of the United States sec. 114 (1987) [hereinafter Restatement].

34. Restatement, supra note 33, sec. 115. See, e.g. the *Guy Capps* case discussed

in Section 3.2 supra; Swearingen v. United States, 565 F.Supp. 1019 (D.Colo.1983); Note, Superceding Statutory Law by Sole Executive Agreement: An Analysis of the American Law Institute's Shift in Position, 23 Va.J.Intl.L 671 (1983).

to significantly influence future court cases, but the principle of requiring the Congress to be "super explicit" when they intend to act inconsistently with an international agreement, is an interesting approach with some merit.[35]

The following materials consider (a) whether the Treaty–Making Power expands federal constitutional authority and (b) the position of executive agreements vis-à-vis state law.

(a) The Treaty Power and Domestic Legal Effect

The reader probably recalls the United States Supreme Court case of MISSOURI v. HOLLAND, 252 U.S. 416, 40 S.Ct. 382, 64 L.Ed. 641 (1920), which held that a valid treaty (with Canada relating to migratory birds) must prevail over state law, even if a United States federal statute on the subject might be considered an unconstitutional interference with state power in the absence of a treaty. Justice Holmes said in this case:[36]

> * * * Acts of Congress are the supreme law of the land only when made in pursuance of the Constitution, while treaties are declared to be so when made under the authority of the United States. It is open to question whether the authority of the United States means more than the formal acts prescribed to make the convention. We do not mean to imply that there are no qualifications to the treaty-making power; but they must be ascertained in a different way. It is obvious that there may be matters of the sharpest exigency for the national well-being that an act of Congress could not deal with but that a treaty followed by such an act could, and it is not lightly to be assumed that, in matters requiring national action, "a power which must belong to and somewhere reside in every civilized government" is not to be found.

Subsequent cases suggest some limitations on the treaty-making power, such as constitutional civil liberties limitations (see Reid v. Covert, 354 U.S. 1, 77 S.Ct. 1222, 1 L.Ed.2d 1148 (1957)), and matters of "purely domestic concern," such as the right to provide for the development of the United States share of the waters of the Niagara River, reserved to Congress in a 1950 Treaty with Canada. Power Authority of New York v. Federal Power Commission, 247 F.2d 538 (D.C.Cir.1957).

(b) Executive Agreements and Domestic Legal Effect

In UNITED STATES v. BELMONT, 301 U.S. 324, 57 S.Ct. 758, 81 L.Ed. 1134 (1937), the United States Supreme Court was confronted with President Roosevelt's decision to grant diplomatic recognition to the Union of Soviet Socialist Republics in exchange for, inter alia, the assignment to the U.S. government of assets owned by a Russian corporation and located in the United States. The corporation had been

35. United States v. Palestine Liberation Organization, 695 F.Supp. 1456 (S.D.N.Y.1988). See reference at John H. Jackson, Status of Treaties in Domestic Legal Systems, *in* The Jurisprudence of the GATT and the WTO: Insights on Treaty Law and Economic Relations ch. 18 (esp. p. 357 n. 118) (2000).

36. 252 U.S. at 433, 40 S.Ct. at 383.

nationalized by the Soviet government. In a challenge to the title of the United States to the assets, the Court stated that "(t)he recognition, establishment of diplomatic relations, the assignment, and agreements with respect thereto, were all parts of one transaction, resulting in an international compact between the two governments." It continued by affirming that the actions fell within the President's powers over external affairs and that the advice and consent of the Senate was not required as in the case of treaties.

The Court then observed that, "although this might not be a treaty requiring ratification by the Senate, it was a compact negotiated and proclaimed under the authority of the President, and as such was a 'treaty' within the meaning of the Circuit Court of Appeals Act, the construction of which might be reviewed upon direct appeal to this court."

"Plainly," continued the Court, "the external powers of the United States are to be exercised without regard to state laws or policies. The supremacy of a treaty in this respect has been recognized from the beginning. Mr. Madison, in the Virginia Convention, said that if a treaty does not supersede existing state laws, as far as they contravene its operation, the treaty would be ineffective. 'To counteract it by the supremacy of the state laws, would bring on the Union the just charge of national perfidy, and involve us in war.' * * * And while this rule in respect of treaties is established by the express language of cl. 2, Art. VI, of the Constitution, the same rule would result in the case of all international compacts and agreements from the very fact that complete power over international affairs is in the national government and is not and cannot be subject to any curtailment or interference on the part of the several states. Compare United States v. Curtiss–Wright Export Corp., 299 U.S. 304, 316, et seq., 57 S.Ct. 216, 219, 81 L.Ed. 255."

Note

See also United States v. Pink, 315 U.S. 203, 62 S.Ct. 552, 86 L.Ed. 796 (1942).

SECTION 3.5   THE COURTS AND FOREIGN RELATIONS

(A) INTRODUCTION

The cases in the previous sections of this chapter suggest considerable hesitancy on the part of the courts to "second-guess" the President in his conduct of foreign affairs. As Professor Henkin has written "[F]oreign affairs make a difference. The courts are less willing to curb the political branches and have even developed doctrines of special deference to them. They have asserted judicial power to develop doctrines to safeguard the national interest in international relations against both judicial interference and invasion by the States."[1]

1. Louis Henkin, Foreign Affairs and the Constitution 206 (2nd ed. 1975).

One example of hesitancy by the federal courts to intrude into foreign affairs is the Act of State doctrine under which courts in the United States generally decline to examine the validity of acts of a governmental nature taken by a foreign sovereign government within its own territory. This doctrine has been held by the Supreme Court to be a matter of federal law, and therefore must be applied by state courts.[2] Although the Supreme Court has recognized that there may be exceptions to the doctrine, its hesitancy to intrude into foreign affairs is highlighted by the fact that the principal exception to the Act of State doctrine was created by Congress in reaction to the *Sabbatino* decision.[3] Similarly in the area of sovereign immunity (the general principle that a sovereign government cannot be sued without its consent), it has been Congress and not the courts that has taken the lead in expanding the jurisdiction of U.S. courts into areas that those courts had been hesitant to enter.[4] These two topics are treated extensively in most international law casebooks and will not be examined here.[5]

In this section, we will look first at a leading Supreme Court case, where the Court goes out of its way to avoid reviewing action taken by a regulatory agency because the President had the final say over the agency's ultimate decision. We will then briefly look at how federal courts have reviewed a variety of executive decisions taken under the various statutes regulating international trade.

(B) JUDICIAL REVIEW AND FOREIGN AFFAIRS

CHICAGO & SOUTHERN AIR LINES, INC. v. WATERMAN S.S. CORP.

Supreme Court of the United States, 1948.
333 U.S. 103, 68 S.Ct. 431, 92 L.Ed. 568.

MR. JUSTICE JACKSON delivered the opinion of the Court.

[By a five to four decision, the Supreme Court reversed a Court of Appeals decision and dismissed the petition of an airline company (Waterman) which was protesting the award of an international air route (between the U.S. and a foreign country) to Chicago and Southern.]

Congress has set up a comprehensive scheme for regulation of common carriers by air. Many statutory provisions apply indifferently

---

2. Banco Nacional de Cuba v. Sabbatino, 376 U.S. 398, 84 S.Ct. 923, 11 L.E.2d 804 (1964).

3. 22 U.S.C.A. sec. 2370(e)(2). This exception, created by the so-called Second Hickenlooper Amendment, provides that a U.S. court shall not invoke the Act of State doctrine in cases of expropriation that are illegal under principles of international law unless the President suggests to the court that the doctrine should be applied.

4. See Foreign Sovereign Immunities Act of 1976, Pub.L.No. 94–583, 90 Stat. 2891.

5. See, e.g., William W. Bishop, International Law 659–700, 876–99 (3rd ed. 1971); Barry E. Carter & Phillip R. Trimble, International Law 595–708 (1999); Henry J. Steiner, Detlev F. Vagts & Harold H. Koh, Transnational Legal Problems: Material and Text 753–819 (4th ed. 1994).

whether the carrier is a foreign air carrier or a citizen air carrier, and whether the carriage involved is "interstate air commerce," "overseas air commerce" or "foreign air commerce," each being appropriately defined. 49 U.S.C. § 401(20), 49 U.S.C.A. § 401(20). All air carriers by similar procedures must obtain from the [Civil Aeronautics Board (CAB)] certificates of convenience and necessity by showing a public interest in establishment of the route and the applicant's ability to serve it. But when a foreign carrier asks for any permit, or a citizen carrier applies for a certificate to engage in any overseas or foreign air transportation, a copy of the application must be transmitted to the President before hearing; and any decision, either to grant or to deny, must be submitted to the President before publication and is unconditionally subject to the President's approval. Also the statute subjects to judicial review "any order, affirmative or negative, issued by the Board under this Act, except any order in respect of any foreign air carrier subject to the approval of the President as provided in section 801 of this Act." It grants no express exemption to an order such as the one before us, which concerns a citizen carrier but which must have Presidential approval because it involves overseas and foreign air transportation. The question is whether an exemption is to be implied.

This Court long has held that statutes which employ broad terms to confer power of judicial review are not always to be read literally. Where Congress has authorized review of "any order" or used other equally inclusive terms, courts have declined the opportunity to magnify their jurisdiction, by self-denying constructions which do not subject to judicial control orders which, from their nature, from the context of the Act, or from the relation of judicial power to the subject-matter, are inappropriate for review.

* * *

* * * That aerial navigation routes and bases should be prudently correlated with facilities and plans for our own national defenses and raise new problems in conduct of foreign relations, is a fact of common knowledge. Congressional hearings and debates extending over several sessions and departmental studies of many years show that the legislative and administrative processes have proceeded in full recognition of these facts.

* * *

[W]hen a foreign carrier seeks to engage in public carriage over the territory or waters of this country, or any carrier seeks the sponsorship of this Government to engage in overseas or foreign air transportation, Congress has completely inverted the usual administrative process. Instead of acting independently of executive control, the agency is then subordinated to it. Instead of its order serving as a final disposition of the application, its force is exhausted when it serves as a recommendation to the President. Instead of being handed down to the parties as the conclusion of the administrative process, it must be submitted to the

President, before publication even can take place. Nor is the President's control of the ultimate decision a mere right of veto. It is not alone issuance of such authorizations that are subject to his approval, but denial, transfer, amendment, cancellation or suspension, as well. And likewise subject to his approval are the terms, conditions and limitations of the order. 49 U.S.C. § 601, 49 U.S.C.A. § 601. Thus, Presidential control is not limited to a negative but is a positive and detailed control over the Board's decisions, unparalleled in the history of American administrative bodies.

Congress may of course delegate very large grants of its power over foreign commerce to the President. The President also possesses in his own right certain powers conferred by the Constitution on him as Commander-in-Chief and as the Nation's organ in foreign affairs. For present purposes, the order draws vitality from either or both sources. Legislative and Executive powers are pooled obviously to the end that commercial strategic and diplomatic interests of the country may be coordinated and advanced without collision or deadlock between agencies.

* * *

In this case, submission of the Board's decision was made to the President, who disapproved certain portions of it and advised the Board of the changes which he required. The Board complied and submitted a revised order and opinion which the President approved. Only then were they made public, and that which was made public and which is before us is only the final order and opinion containing the President's amendments and bearing his approval. Only at that stage was review sought and only then could it be pursued * * *.

While the changes made at direction of the President may be identified, the reasons therefore are not disclosed beyond the statement that "because of certain factors relating to our broad national welfare and other matters for which the Chief Executive has special responsibility, he has reached conclusions which require" changes in the Board's opinion.

The court below considered, and we think quite rightly, that it could not review such provisions of the order as resulted from Presidential direction. The President, both as Commander-in-Chief and as the Nation's organ for foreign affairs, has available intelligence services whose reports neither are nor ought to be published to the world. It would be intolerable that courts, without the relevant information, should review and perhaps nullify actions of the Executive taken on information properly held secret. Nor can courts sit in camera in order to be taken into executive confidences. But even if courts could require full disclosure, the very nature of executive decisions as to foreign policy is political, not judicial. Such decisions are wholly confided by our Constitution to the political departments of the government, Executive and Legislative. They are delicate, complex and involve large elements of prophecy. They are and should be undertaken only by those directly responsible to the people whose welfare they advance or imperil. They are decisions of a kind for which the Judiciary has neither aptitude, facilities nor responsibility and have long been held to belong in the domain of political power not subject to judicial intrusion or inquiry. We therefore agree that whatever of this order emanates from the President is not susceptible of review by the Judicial Department.

* * *

* * * The dilemma faced by those who demand judicial review of the Board's order is that, before Presidential approval, it is not a final determination even of the Board's ultimate action, and after Presidential approval, the whole order, both in what is approved without change, as well as in amendments which he directs, derives its vitality from the exercise of unreviewable Presidential discretion.

* * *

MR. JUSTICE DOUGLAS, with whom MR. JUSTICE BLACK, MR. JUSTICE REED and MR. JUSTICE RUTLEDGE concur, dissenting.

Notes and Questions

(1) The dissent in the foregoing case did not question the non-reviewability of the President's action. Rather, it argued that orders of the Board should be reviewable, because "[t]hose orders can be reviewed without any reference to any conduct by the President, for that part of the orders which is the work of the Board is plainly identifiable." The dissenters believed that such limited review would ensure that the Board had acted within the limits of its authority.

(2) In HAIG v. AGEE, 453 U.S. 280, 101 S.Ct. 2766, 69 L.Ed.2d 640 (1981), the Supreme Court upheld State Department regulations applied to revoke the passport of an American citizen who was engaged in a campaign to expose the identities of agents of the Central Intelligence Agency. In so doing, it stated (453 U.S. at 290–292, 101 S.Ct. at 2773–74):

> The [1926] Passport Act does not in so many words confer upon the Secretary a power to revoke a passport. Nor, for that matter, does it expressly authorize denials of passport applications. Neither, however, does any statute expressly limit those powers. It is beyond dispute that the Secretary has the power to deny a passport for reasons not specified in the statutes. * * * Particularly in light of the "broad rule-making authority granted in the [1926] Act," *Zemel* [v. Rusk], 381 U.S., at 12, 85 S.Ct., at 1278 [1965], a consistent administrative construction of that statute must be followed by the courts "'unless there are compelling indications that it is wrong.'" This is especially so in the areas of foreign policy and national security, where congressional silence is not to be equated with congressional disapproval. * * * Applying these considerations to statutory construction, the *Zemel* Court observed:
>
> > [B]ecause of the changeable and explosive nature of contemporary international relations, and the fact that the Executive is immediately privy to information which cannot be swiftly presented to, evaluated by, and acted upon by the legislature, Congress—in giving

the Executive authority over matters of foreign affairs—must of necessity paint with a brush broader than that it customarily wields in domestic areas.

The opinion by Chief Justice Burger in this 7–2 decision was issued three days before *Dames & Moore v. Regan*, discussed in Section 3.2(B) supra.

(3) Are the policy reasons for deference to presidential discretion when exercised in the area of foreign affairs persuasive? Do these reasons adequately provide a rationale for distinguishing between foreign and domestic affairs as to the degree of judicial review that is appropriate? Do any of the reasons stated as applying to foreign affairs also apply to domestic affairs? If the world continues on a course of greater and greater economic (and other) interdependence, and more of everyone's affairs become intertwined with international transactions or policies, will a policy of greater deference to executive prerogative in foreign affairs cause serious inroads into the U.S. constitutional system of checks and balances? Of protection of individual citizen rights?

(4) The February 1, 1977 issue of Forbes magazine at page 23, described the procedure for presidential determinations under § 801 of the Federal Aviation Act as "a political cesspool," in reporting on an application by Delta Airlines for a transatlantic route from London to Atlanta and Texas which had been recommended by the CAB, but sent back by President Ford for a new analysis. The Forbes article suggested that the President's action may have been politically motivated because the outgoing administration was "piqued at the South, which voted for Carter." The article concludes: "If there is a moral to this, it is that Section 801 causes more trouble than it is worth. The State Department negotiates landing rights with other countries; by itself the CAB should decide which U.S. carriers fly under them. Other regulators—in international banking and telecommunications, for example— deal with foreign policy issues." (The CAB no longer exists; its functions were taken over by the Department of Transportation.)

(5) In UNITED STATES v. ALVAREZ–MACHAIN, 504 U.S. 655, 112 S.Ct. 2188, 119 L.Ed.2d 441 (1992), the Court refused to deny U.S. courts jurisdiction to try a Mexican citizen who was kidnapped in Mexico through activity allegedly induced by the United States government officials and brought to the United States and arrested for conspiracy to murder a U.S. Drug Enforcement Agent. The Supreme Court, with three dissents, upheld the arrest and concluded that an extradition treaty did not prevent it. At one point in the majority opinion, the Court said (112 S.Ct. at 2196):

> Respondent and his *amici* may be correct that respondent's abduction was "shocking," Tr. of Oral Arg. 40, and that it may be in violation of general international law principles. Mexico has protested the abduction of respondent through diplomatic notes, App. 33–38, and the decision of whether respondent should be returned to Mexico, as a matter outside of the Treaty, is a matter for the Executive Branch.

In a footnote the Court comments on "the advantage of the diplomatic approach to the resolution of difficulties between two sovereign nations, as opposed to unilateral action by the Courts of one nation." 504 U.S. at 669, 112 S.Ct. at 2196 n.16.

(C) JUDICIAL REVIEW OF ADMINISTRATIVE ACTION: THE PROBLEM OF STANDARD OF REVIEW

STEPHEN P. CROLEY & JOHN H. JACKSON, WTO DISPUTE PROCEDURES, STANDARD OF REVIEW, AND DEFERENCE TO NATIONAL GOVERNMENTS[6]

Until fairly recently, and broadly speaking, reviewing courts exercised considerable deference with respect to agencies' "factual" determinations, and accorded less deference to agencies' "legal" decisions.[7] This two-tiered approach reflected a familiar division of function between the separate branches of government, according to which agencies were to handle the more or less "technical" aspects of statutory implementation, while courts were to ensure that agencies exercised their authority within the boundaries of the law. This bifurcated approach also followed the U.S. Administrative Procedure Act's direction for courts to "decide all relevant questions of law,"[8] which itself reflected traditional understandings of the proper roles of courts and agencies. Traditionally, judicial deference to agencies' legal determinations required special justification, whereas deference to factual determinations did not. That general rule was altered, however, in 1984, when the U.S. Supreme Court handed its decision in Chevron U.S.A. v. Natural Resources Defense Council, Inc.,[9] in which the Court articulated a new standard of review for agencies' interpretations of law—the Chevron doctrine.

THE CHEVRON DOCTRINE

Courts applying the Chevron doctrine face to sequential questions, often referred to as "step one" and "step two" of Chevron. First: Has Congress "directly spoken to the precise question at issue,"[10] or is the statute interpreted by the agency "silent or ambiguous"?[11] To answer this question, the reviewing court applies the "traditional tools of statutory construction."[12] If upon applying those traditional tools, the reviewing court concluded that Congress has indeed spoken to the precise issue in question, then "that is the end of the matter";[13] the court will hold the agency faithful to Congress's will, as unambiguously expressed in the statute.[14]

---

6. Reproduced with permission from 90 AJIL 193, 202–204 (1996) (c) The American Society of International Law.

7. [original note 38] See, e.g., FTC v. Gratz, 253 U.S. 421, 427 (1920).

8. [original note 39] 5 U.S.C. § 706 (1988).

9. [original note 40] 467 U.S. 837 (1984).

10. [original note 42] Id. at 842.

11. [original note 43] Id. at 843.

12. [original note 44] Id. n.9; see also Kmart Corp. v. Cartier, Inc., 486 U.S. 281, 300 (1988) (Brennan, J. concurring); NLRB v. United Food & Commercial Workers Union, Local 23, 484 U.S. 112, 123 (1987); INS v. Cardoza–Fonseca, 480 U.S. 421, 446 (1987).

13. [original note 45] Chevron, 467 U.S. at 842.

14. [original note 46] For examples of lower courts' invocation of step one of the Chevron doctrine, see, e.g., Skandalis v. Rowe, 14 F.3d 173, 178–79 (2d Cir.1994); Sweet Home Chapter of Communities for a Great Oregon v. Babbitt, 17 F.3d 1463, 1464 (D.C.Cir.1994), rev'd on other grounds, 115 S.Ct. 2407 (1995); Satellite Broadcasting & Communications Ass'n of

If the court concluded instead that the statute is "silent or ambiguous" with respect to the interpretive question at issue, then the reviewing court proceeds to a second question—step two: Is the agency's interpretation of the statute a "reasonable" or "permissible" one?[15] If the court determines that the agency's interpretation is not reasonable, then the court will defer to the agency's interpretation, even if—and this is the bite of the Chevron doctrine—the agency's interpretation is not one the court would have adopted had it considered the question on its own.[16]

* * *

According to many U.S. administrative law scholars, the Chevron doctrine constituted a significant shift of power from courts to the agencies.[17] * * * (T)he shift is commonly justified by reference to some of the most important principles underlying U.S. administrative government— expertise, accountability and administrative efficiency.

Note

Professor Thomas Merrill has observed that in practice, the effects of the Chevron decision on judicial treatment of administrative decisions appears to have been limited:[18]

* * * First, it is clear that Chevron [was] often ignored by the Supreme Court [in the years following the decision].

* * *

Second, although Chevron is generally regarded as directing that courts give greater deference to executive interpretations, there is no discernible relationship between the application of the Chevron framework and greater acceptance of the executive view. Indeed, cases applying Chevron have on the whole produced fewer affirmances of executive interpretations than those that do not follow Chevron.

* * *

Third, * * * the emergence of Chevron has caused a decline in reliance on the traditional contextual factors for determining whether deference is appropriate.

Am. v. Oman, 17 F.3d 344, 348 (11th Cir.), cert. denied, 115 S.Ct. 88 (1994).

15. [original note 47] Chevron, 467 U.S. at 842–44.

16. [original note 48] Id. At 843 n. 11 ("The court need not conclude that the agency construction was the only one it permissibly could have adopted to uphold the construction, or even the reading the court would have reached if the question initially had arisen in a judicial proceeding.") (citations omitted).

17. [original note 51] See, e.g., Davis & Pierce, [Administrative Law Treatise], sec. 3.3 [3d ed. 1984].

18. Thomas W. Merrill, Judicial Deference to Executive Precedent, 101 Yale L.J. 969, 982–985 (1992). Reprinted by permission of the Yale Law Journal and Fred B. Rothman & Company from The Yale Law Journal, vol. 101, pp. 969–1041.

(D) FEDERAL COURT REVIEW OF ADMINISTRATIVE TRADE ACTIONS

(1) *The Court of International Trade* [19]

Most litigation involving international trade statutes in the United States now occurs in the Court of International Trade (CIT). The CIT was formerly known as the Customs Court. It received its new name in a 1980 statute that also significantly expanded its jurisdiction.[20] The CIT is a court of nine judges, no more than five of whom may belong to any one political party. It is based in New York City. Its decisions are appealable to the U.S. Court of Appeals for the Federal Circuit and ultimately to the Supreme Court.

The CIT has exclusive jurisdiction under 28 U.S.C.A. section 1581 over appeals or actions involving (a) denials of protests by the U.S. Customs Service, (b) challenges by U.S. competitors of import classification decisions, (c) antidumping and countervailing duty cases, (d) trade adjustment assistance to workers, firms and communities, (e) country of origin determinations, (f) disputes over the confidentiality of information submitted to the International Trade Commission, (g) customshouse brokers' licenses, (h) challenges by importers of classification decisions and (i) the United States as a defendant that arise out of any law providing for revenues from imports; tariffs, duties, fees or other taxes on imports; and embargoes or quantitative restrictions on imports (other than those imposed for public health and safety reasons).[21] It also has jurisdiction under 28 U.S.C.A. section 1582 over civil actions by the United States to recover duties, penalties and customs bonds. The 1980 Act in general greatly expanded access to the CIT to include most persons with a real interest in challenging or defending a trade-related action.[22]

The scope of review in the CIT depends on the type of action brought. A trial "de novo" is held in actions brought by the United States under section 1582 and in cases where jurisdiction is based on section 1581, category (a), (b), (e), (f) or (g) of the preceding paragraph.[23] In antidumping and countervailing duty cases, certain government actions are reviewed to determine if they were arbitrary, capricious, an

19. See generally William J. Davey, The United States Court of International Trade and the Court of Appeals for the Federal Circuit, *in* Adjudication of International Trade Disputes in International and National Economic Law 297–322 (Ernst–Ulrich Petersmann & Günther Jaenicke eds., 1992).

20. Customs Courts Act of 1980, Pub.L. No. 96–417, 94 Stat. 1727. The exclusive jurisdiction of the Court of International Trade was made broader in 1980 in part to avoid the problem of conflicting decisions on trade issues arising in the District Courts. Prior to the 1980 Act, there was confusion as to the extent of the Customs Court's exclusive jurisdiction and some par-

ties preferred to litigate in District Courts because the limited powers of the Customs Court often meant they could not obtain what they viewed as appropriate relief (e.g., injunctions). See H.Rep. No. 96–1235, 96th Cong., 2d Sess. 19 (1980). See generally Recent Developments, The Customs Courts Act of 1980, 13 Law & Poly.Intl.Bus. 281 (1981).

21. There is an exception to the CIT's jurisdiction for imports of obscene materials.

22. See 28 U.S.C.A. sec. 2631.

23. 28 U.S.C.A. sec. 2640(a).

abuse of discretion or unlawful; while others are reviewed to determine if they were supported by substantial evidence in the agency record or unlawful.[24] In some antidumping or countervailing duty cases, the courts have been very intrusive in altering administrative actions. In trade adjustment assistance cases, the determinations of the agency are considered conclusive if supported by substantial evidence in the record, but the CIT has the authority for good cause shown to order the agency to take further evidence.[25] In other actions, the CIT's review is made pursuant to the Administrative Procedure Act, which generally establishes a substantial-evidence standard for agency action taken on a record and an arbitrary-capricious standard for other agency action.[26]

(2) Judicial Review in International Trade Cases

This somewhat complex structure of review for international trade actions taken by the Executive Branch largely reflects a desire by Congress to limit Executive discretion under certain trade statutes. Given the opportunity, private litigants quickly began to challenge Executive action more frequently. Indeed, challenges of preliminary decisions in antidumping and countervailing duty cases became so burdensome that Congress limited them in 1984.[27] We will consider recent CIT and Federal Circuit decisions in some detail when we examine the various U.S. trade statutes in later parts of this book. Here we will only try to give a flavor of the scrutiny provided by the CIT and the Federal Circuit and of how it seems to vary depending on the nature of the challenged action.

Escape Clause. MAPLE LEAF FISH CO. v. UNITED STATES, 762 F.2d 86 (Fed.Cir.1985), arose under the so-called Escape Clause. The issue was the standard of review to be applied to a challenge to the President's decision to order import relief measures after the International Trade Commission (ITC) had found that the U.S. prepared and preserved mushroom industry was being injured by imports of those products. The Court ruled (762 F.2d at 89):

> The critical element is that the area of the "escape clause" legislation undoubtedly involves the President and his close relationship to foreign affairs, our nation's connections with other countries, and the external ramifications of international trade. More than that, Congress has vested the President with very broad discretion and choice as to what he decides to do affirmatively, or even whether he should do anything. * * *
>
> In international trade controversies of this highly discretionary kind—involving the President and foreign affairs—this court and its predecessors have often reiterated the very limited role of reviewing

---

24. 28 U.S.C.A. sec. 2640(b); 19 U.S.C.A. sec. 1516a.

25. 28 U.S.C.A. sec. 2640(c); 19 U.S.C.A. sec. 2395(b).

26. 28 U.S.C.A. sec. 2640(d); 5 U.S.C.A. sec. 706.

27. Trade and Tariff Act of 1984, sec. 623 (elimination of interlocutory appeals), Pub.L. No. 98–573, 98 Stat. 2948, amending 19 U.S.C.A. sec. 1516a.

courts. For a court to interpose, there has to be clear misconstruction of the governing statute, a significant procedural violation, or action outside delegated authority. On the other hand, "[t]he President's findings of fact and the motivations for his action are not subject to review."

Multifiber Arrangement. In upholding action taken by the Executive Branch in respect of limitations on textile imports against challenges alleging statutory, administrative and constitutional defects, the Court of Appeals for the Federal Circuit stated:

> We accentuate, again, that legislation conferring upon the President discretion to regulate foreign commerce involves, and is reinforced and augmented by, the President's constitutional power to oversee the political side of foreign affairs. In the area of international trade, "intimately involved in foreign affairs," "congressional authorizations of presidential power should be given a broad construction and not 'hemmed in' or 'cabined, cribbed, confined' by anxious judicial blinders."

AMERICAN ASSN. OF EXPORTERS & IMPORTERS—TEXTILE & APPAREL GROUP v. UNITED STATES, 751 F.2d 1239, 1248 (Fed.Cir. 1985).

Adjustment Assistance. In KATUNICH v. DONOVAN, 594 F.Supp. 744 (CIT 1984), an appeal of the Secretary of Labor's decision to refuse to grant benefits under the Trade Act of 1974, the CIT stated (594 F.Supp. at 753):

> In light of the Secretary's admission that "1980 would have been a better year for the present analysis," it was incumbent upon the Secretary to make a greater effort to obtain the required information. The record does not reveal any efforts made by the Secretary to obtain the necessary information for a meaningful evaluation of plaintiffs' petition.

Summary. If any conclusion can be drawn from the foregoing, it would seem to be that where courts are dealing with detailed statutory provisions, with legislative history that indicates dissatisfaction with past administration of those laws, such as the antidumping and countervailing duty laws, they are willing to exercise serious oversight of Executive Branch actions on the grounds that Congress has specified in some detail what rights it wishes to be protected. On the other hand, where courts are dealing with broad grants of power to the President or ministerial actions involving Customs administration, they are unlikely to second guess the Executive Branch.

(3) Costs of Judicial Review

The large increase in trade-related cases brought in the federal courts in the last few years has caused some to wonder if the costs of judicial review of complex administrative procedures are too high. One of the authors of this book has contrasted the benefits of the present system—promotion of open, informed, consistent decision-making by trade officials, giving every interested party a "day in court" and thereby promoting acceptance of decisions—with the costs—the risk of creating inflexible rules, unjustified harassment of weaker parties, large fees payable to lawyers and economists. His conclusions are set out in Chapter 26. As we analyze the operation of the many U.S. trade laws, the reader should attempt to form a view of whether the costs would seem to outweigh the apparent benefits.

(4) Scope of International "Judicial" Review

In recent years the question of the standard of review for an international dispute settlement panel, such as those in the GATT or the new WTO dispute settlement systems, has been more prominent. It was even a major issue in the final weeks of negotiation of the Uruguay Round in December 1993. This matter will be taken up in Chapter 7 when we deal with international dispute settlement.

SECTION 3.6   FEDERAL–STATE RELATIONS AND INTERNATIONAL ECONOMIC REGULATION

(A) INTRODUCTION

The United States has a federal form of government under its Constitution. A constitutional U.S. federal law overrides an inconsistent state law, although the Constitution places some limits on the powers of Congress and the federal government. The division of powers between the federal government and the state governments involves several important questions involved here.

First, what constitutional limits are there on the federal government, due to the federal structure of the United States? (It can plausibly be argued there are none, at least as to foreign affairs, although there clearly are political constraints resulting from a federal structure.) Second, the reverse question is what constitutional constraints are there on state government exercise of power, especially when that exercise affects international economic affairs (as almost everything does today)? This requires examination of several subordinate situations, such as: a) the case where the federal government has established a rule that conflicts with state law, and b) the case where there is no federal rule. Finally, it is useful to examine the evolution of cooperative mechanisms for state participation in federal activities regarding international economic relations.

The questions that remain troublesome in the area of Federal–State relations concern the power of the states to regulate and tax foreign commerce. The Constitution authorizes the federal government to regulate such commerce, but what state power exists when the federal government has not acted or prohibited state action? The cases in this section have been selected to highlight important issues of Federal–State relations as applied to international trade, such as:

(A) Can states ever regulate goods imported from a foreign country? Or exports to be sent to a foreign country? If they are not preempted, how far can they go? Are the tests of the limits on state power over interstate commerce also to be applied to foreign commerce, or will those tests be different?

(B) To what degree can states tax imports from another country? Tax foreign companies?

(C) Is there any limit on what the federal government can do by way of preventing state government actions which affect foreign commerce? Do these limits vary depending on whether imports or exports are involved? Do they apply to services as well as goods?

These questions cannot all be answered definitively, but the materials in the following sub-sections will provide some insights. We will return to some of these issues later in the book.

(B) FEDERAL CONSTRAINTS ON FEDERAL POWERS TO REGULATE AND MAKE TREATIES CONCERNING INTERNATIONAL ECONOMIC RELATIONS

JOHN H. JACKSON, UNITED STATES LAW AND IMPLEMENTATION OF THE TOKYO ROUND NEGOTIATION[1]

Since the structure of the U.S. government under its Constitution is federal in nature—that is, it consists not only of a central government but also of state governments that have considerable independent authority and sovereignty—it might be thought that the division of powers between the federal and state governments would be an important constraint on the scope of federal government action in the area of foreign affairs.

There has been a long and extraordinarily detailed history of constitutional evolution and accommodation between state powers and the federal powers. * * * Furthermore, in domestic affairs, the evolution of U.S. constitutional law has been generally in the direction of concentrating power in the federal government. It is reasonably well established today that the federal government has supremacy, if it chooses to exercise it, over almost all issues that have any commercial overtones.

* * *

In foreign affairs, there is virtually no Supreme Court opinion that rules against the exercise of federal power on the grounds that it conflicts with state power, as long as the exercise of federal power was

1. From John H. Jackson, Jean—Victor Louis & Mitsuo Matsushita, Implementing the Tokyo Round: National Constitutions and International Economic Rules 142–143 (1984). Reprinted by permission of the author.

itself otherwise constitutional. Thus, although the Supreme Court has held that state powers sometimes prevail over international treaties (such as in the offshore oil cases), the basis for this decision was itself an exercise of federal power, namely an act of Congress.

The courts and federal authorities can rely on a number of clauses in the Constitution in arguing that the exercise of federal power will prevail over state power in the areas of foreign relations. Such clauses include the commerce clause, the supremacy clause, the treaty clause, and clauses on presidential power, including his power to receive ambassadors, and his authority as Commander in Chief.

Notes and Questions

(1) In 1976, the Supreme Court (in a 5–4 decision) placed some limits on the power of the federal government to regulate state and local governments in National League of Cities v. Usery, 426 U.S. 833, 96 S.Ct. 2465, 49 L.Ed.2d 245 (1976), where it held that certain provisions of the Fair Labor Standards Act could not be applied to state and local government employees. The Court ruled essentially that the federal government could not impair the attributes of state sovereignty by regulating the wages of state employees and thereby interfering with the integral governmental functions of states. That case was overruled in a 5–4 decision in 1985. Garcia v. San Antonio Metropolitan Transit Authority, 469 U.S. 528, 105 S.Ct. 1005, 83 L.Ed.2d 1016 (1985). It remains to be seen whether the Court, as predicted by one dissenter, will reverse itself again soon.

In NEW YORK v. UNITED STATES, 505 U.S. 144, 112 S.Ct. 2408, 120 L.Ed.2d 120 (1992), the Supreme Court expressly declined to reconsider the holding in *Garcia*. In discussing the ability of the federal government to influence State regulatory decisions, the court wrote (505 U.S. at 167, 112 S.Ct. at 2423–2424):

> First, under Congress' spending power, "Congress may attach conditions on the receipt of federal funds." * * *

> Second, where Congress has the authority to regulate private activity under the Commerce Clause, we have recognized Congress' power to offer States the choice of regulating that activity according to federal standards or having state law preempted by federal regulation. * * *

> * * *

> By contrast, where the Federal Government compels States to regulate, [such compulsion is invalid].

(2) In Section 3.3(C)(3) we previously noted the case of Missouri v. Holland, 252 U.S. 416, 40 S.Ct. 382, 64 L.Ed. 641 (1920), in which the Court held that the federal government's powers vis-a-vis the states could be *enlarged* by the conclusion of an international agreement or treaty. Does this mean that the federal government can effectively regulate on matters (if any) otherwise reserved to states if it first enters into a treaty on the subject?

(C) STATE REGULATION AND FOREIGN COMMERCE

(1) Introduction

Considerably more U.S. federal court activity has concerned constitutional limits on state regulation which affects foreign commerce. First, where the federal government has acted in a particular area, by a statute, treaty or otherwise, several different situations can be analyzed: the case of a direct and explicit clash between the federal and the state law; and a situation where the federal government has acted but the clash between federal and state law is only implicit (a situation analyzed under the "preemption doctrine"). Second, where the federal government has not acted at all, the "dormant commerce clause" and related questions are raised.

(2) Federal Action and Federal Rules that Clash With State Rules

Notes and Questions

(1) In Section 3.4(C)(3), we discussed the general problems of "hierarchy of norms," i.e. which of two clashing rules should prevail. Here we face that question in the context of a federal-state conflict, but regarding not only international agreements but other federal law making (statute, regulation, etc.). The Restatement notes, "Since any treaty or other international agreement of the United States, and any rule of customary international law, is federal law * * *, it supersedes inconsistent State law or policy whether adopted earlier or later."[2]

(2) The issue of preemption is usually framed as follows: Although there may not be a direct clash between some federal rule and a state rule, if there is sufficient federal government regulatory and rule making activity that a court could imply that the federal government intended to exclude state action, i.e., to "preempt the field," then no state action concerning the particular subject matters would be valid. The most important case in this respect is Crosby v. National Foreign Trade Council.

CROSBY v. NATIONAL FOREIGN TRADE COUNCIL

Supreme Court of the United States, 2000.
530 U.S. 363, 120 S.Ct. 2288, 147 L.Ed.2d 352.

JUSTICE SOUTER delivered the opinion of the Court.

* * *

In June 1996, Massachusetts adopted an "Act Regulating State Contracts with Companies Doing Business with or in Burma (Myanmar)," 1996 Mass. Acts 239, ch. 130 (codified at Mass. Gen. Laws secs. 7:22G–7:22M, 40 F. 1/2 (1997)). The Statute generally bars state entities

2. American Law Institute, Restatement of the Law (Third), Foreign Relations Law of the United States, sec. 115 comment e (1987).

from buying goods or services from any person (defined to include a business organization) identified on a "restricted purchase list" of those doing business with Burma. * * *

* * *

[Three months later,] Congress passed a statute imposing a set of mandatory and conditional sanctions on Burma. See Foreign Operations, Export Financing, and Related Programs Appropriations Act, 1997, sec. 570, 110 Stat. 3009–166 to 3009–167 (enacted by the Omnibus Consolidated Appropriations Act, 1997, sec. 101(c), 110 Stat. 3009–121 to 3009–172). * * *

[The federal Act] imposes three sanctions directly on Burma. [First,] it bans all aid to the Burmese government except for humanitarian assistance, counternarcotics efforts, and promotion of human rights and democracy. The statute instructs United States representatives to international financial institutions to vote against loans or other assistance to or from Burma, and it provides that no entry visa shall be issued to any Burmese government official unless required by treaty or to staff the Burmese mission to the United Nations. These restrictions are to remain in effect "[u]ntil such time as the President determines and certifies to Congress that Burma has made measurable and substantial progress in improving human rights practices and implementing democratic government." Sec. 570(a).

Second, the federal Act authorizes the President to impose further sanctions subject to certain conditions. Sec. 570(b). * * *

Third, the statute directs the President to work to develop "a comprehensive, multilateral strategy to bring democracy to and improve human rights practices and the quality of life in Burma." Sec. 570(c). * * *

[A] fourth section requires the President to report periodically to certain congressional committee chairmen on the progress toward democratization and better living conditions in Burma as well as on the development of the required strategy. Sec. 570(d). And [a] fifth part * * * authorizes the President "to waive, temporarily or permanently, any sanction [under the federal act]... if he determines and certifies to Congress that the application of such sanction would be contrary to the national security interests of the United States." Sec. 570(e).

* * *

Respondent National Foreign Trade Council is a nonprofit corporation representing companies engaged in foreign commerce; 34 of its members were on the Massachusetts restricted purchase list in 1998. Three withdrew from Burma after the passage of the state Act, and one member had its bid for a procurement contract increased by 10 percent under the provision of the state law allowing acceptance of a low bid from a listed bidder only if the next-to-lowest bid is more than 10 percent higher.

[Previously,] the Council filed suit in the United States District Court for the District of Massachusetts, seeking declaratory and injunctive relief against the petitioner state officials charged with administering and enforcing the state Act. The Council argued that the state law unconstitutionally infringed on the federal foreign affairs power, violated the Foreign Commerce Clause, and was preempted by the federal Act. * * * [T]he District Court permanently enjoined enforcement of the state Act, holding that it "unconstitutionally impinge[d] on the federal government's exclusive authority to regulate foreign affairs."

The United States Court of Appeals for the First Circuit affirmed on three independent grounds. It found the state Act unconstitutionally interfered with the foreign affairs power of the National Government under Zschernig v. Miller, 389 U.S. 429, 88 S.Ct. 664, 19 L.Ed.2d 683 (1968); violated the dormant Foreign Commerce Clause, U.S. Const. Art. I, sec. 8, cl. 3; and was preempted by the congressional Burma Act.

* * *

A fundamental principle of the Constitution is that Congress has the power to preempt state law. Even without an express provision for preemption, we have found that state law must yield to a congressional Act in at least two circumstances. When Congress intends federal law to "occupy the field," state law in that area is preempted. And even if Congress has not occupied the field, state law is naturally preempted to the extent of any conflict with a federal statute. We will find preemption where it is impossible for a private party to comply with both state law and federal law, and where "under the circumstances of [a] particular case, [the challenged state law] stands as an obstacle to the accomplishment and execution of the full purposes and objectives of Congress." Hines v. Davidowitz, 312 U.S. 52, at 67, 61 S.Ct. 399, 85 L.Ed. 581 (1941). What is a sufficient obstacle is a matter of judgment, to be informed by examining the federal statute as a whole and identifying its purpose and intended effects. * * *

[W]e see the state Burma law as an obstacle to the accomplishment of Congress's full objectives under the federal Act. We find that the state law undermines the intended purpose and "natural effect" of at least three provisions of the federal Act. * * *

First, Congress clearly intended the federal act to provide the President with flexible and effective authority over economic sanctions against Burma. Although Congress immediately put in place a set of initial sanctions, * * * it authorized the President to terminate any and all of those measures upon determining and certifying that there had been progress in human rights and democracy in Burma. It invested the President with the further power to ban new investment by United States persons, dependent only on specific Presidential findings of repression in Burma. And, most significantly, Congress empowered the President "to waive, temporarily or permanently, any sanction [under the federal act] ... if he determines and certifies to Congress that the application of such sanction would be contrary to the national security interests of the United States."

* * * [T]he statute has placed the President in a position with as much discretion to exercise economic leverage against Burma, with an eye toward national security, as our law will admit. And it is just this plenitude of Executive authority that we think controls the issue of preemption here. The President has been given this authority not just to make a political statement but to achieve a political result. It is simply implausible that Congress would have gone to such lengths to empower the President if it had been willing to compromise his effectiveness by deference to every provision of state statute or local ordinance that might, if enforced, blunt the consequences of discretionary Presidential action.

And that is just what the Massachusetts Burma law would do in imposing a different system of economic pressure against the Burmese political regime. * * * [T]he state statute penalizes some private action that the federal Act * * * may allow, and pulls levers of influence that the federal Act does not reach. But the point here is that the state sanctions are immediate and perpetual, there being no termination provision. This unyielding application undermines the President's intended statutory authority by making it impossible for him to restrain fully the coercive power of the national economy when he may choose to take the discretionary action open to him * * *. Quite simply, if the Massachusetts law is enforceable the President has less to offer and less economic and diplomatic leverage as a consequence. * * * It thus "stands as an obstacle to the accomplishment and execution of the full purposes and objectives of Congress."

[Second,] Congress manifestly intended to limit economic pressure against the Burmese Government to a specific range. * * * Congress's calibrated Burma policy is a deliberate effort "to steer a middle path."

The State has set a different course, and its statute conflicts with federal law at a number of points by penalizing individuals and conduct that Congress has explicitly exempted or excluded from sanctions. [The Court furthermore points at differences in the scope of subject matter addressed by the ban and the class of companies at which the acts are aimed.]

The conflicts are not rendered irrelevant by the State's argument that there is no real conflict between the statutes because they share the same goals and because some companies may comply with both sets of restrictions. The fact of a common end hardly neutralizes conflicting means, and the fact that some companies may be able to comply with both sets of sanctions does not mean that the state Act is not at odds with achievement of the federal decision about the right degree of pressure to employ. * * * Sanctions are drawn not only to bar what they prohibit but to allow what they permit, and the inconsistency of sanctions here undermines the congressional calibration of force.

Finally, the state Act is at odds with the President's intended authority to speak for the United States among the world's nations in developing a "comprehensive, multilateral strategy to bring democracy to and improve human rights practices and the quality of life in Burma." * * * As with Congress's explicit delegation to the President of power over economic sanctions, Congress's express command to the President to take the initiative for the United States among the international community invested him with the maximum authority of the National Government, cf. Youngstown Sheet & Tube Co., 343 U.S., at 635, 72 S.Ct. 863, in harmony with the President's own constitutional powers. * * *

Again, the state Act undermines the President's capacity, in this instance for effective diplomacy. It is not merely that the differences between the state and federal Acts in scope and type of sanctions threaten to complicate discussions; they compromise the very capacity of the President to speak for the Nation with one voice in dealing with other governments. * * *

* * *

The State's remaining argument * * * contends that the failure of Congress to preempt the state Act demonstrates implicit permission. * * *

The argument is unconvincing on more than one level. A failure to provide preemption expressly may reflect nothing more than the settled character of implied preemption doctrine that courts will dependably apply, and in any event, the existence of conflict cognizable under the Supremacy Clause does not depend on express congressional recognition that federal and state law may conflict. Hines, 312 U.S., at 67, 61 S.Ct. 399. The State's interference of congressional intent is unwarranted here, therefore, simply because the silence of Congress is ambiguous.

Notes

(1) Although the Supreme Court affirmed the judgment of the Court of Appeals, we will see in the following note that it did so not on the same broad grounds used by that court, but limited itself to applying ordinary preemption rules. This narrow scope has been read by many to be at least a partial victory over the exceptional and much broader approach of the so-called dormant foreign affairs doctrine. Professor Vázquez, on the other hand, has argued that the case was in fact not a narrow decision.[3] "(E)ven though the Court said that its decision was based on a straightforward application of 'settled ... implied preemption doctrine,' the brand of preemption analysis the Court engaged in was anything but ordinary. Indeed, the Crosby version of preemption analysis is subject to the very same sorts of objections that Zschernig's critics have leveled at the Dormant Foreign Affairs doctrine. Moreover, if the case were taken as a model for deciding

3. Carlos Manuel Vázquez, Whither Zschernig?, Forthcoming in Villanova Law Review (Autumn 2001).

issues of preemption in purely domestic cases, it would be anything but narrow. The decision would be narrow only if it its approach to preemption were confined to suits implicating foreign relations. But then the Court's holding would begin to resemble a decision on dormant foreign affairs grounds." And in fact Professor Vázquez argues that Crosby's approach to preemption would have yielded the same conclusion even if there had been no federal Burma law.

(2) As noted above, the Court of Appeals in the *Crosby* case, in National Foreign Trade Council v. Natsios, 181 F.3d 38 (1st Cir. 1999), delivered a much more elaborate opinion, which included inter alia the following language:

> The Constitution's foreign affairs provisions have been long understood to stand for the principle that power over foreign affairs is vested exclusively in the federal government. James Madison commented that "if we are to be one nation in any respect, it clearly ought to be in respect to other nations." The Federalist No. 42, at 302 (James Madison); see also id. at 303 (noting that the Articles of Confederation, by failing to contain any "provision for the case of offences against the law of nations," left "it in the power of any indiscreet member to embroil the Confederacy with foreign nations"). Alexander Hamilton, discussing state regulation of foreign commerce, noted that
>
>> the interfering and unneighborly regulations of some States, contrary to the true spirit of the Union, have, in different instances, given just cause of umbrage and complaint to others, and it is to be feared that examples of this nature, if not restrained by a national control, would be multiplied and extended till they became not less serious sources of animosity and discord than injurious impediments to the intercourse between the different parts of the Confederacy.
>
> Id. No. 22, at 192 (Alexander Hamilton); see also id. No. 45, at 328 (James Madison) (stating that "the powers delegated by the proposed Constitution to the federal government are few and defined," and "will be exercised principally on external objects, as war, peace, negotiation, and foreign commerce"). Justice Taney echoed Madison's and Hamilton's views in Holmes v. Jennison, 39 U.S. (14 Pet.) 540, 10 L.Ed. 579 (1840), commenting that "it was one of the main objects of the Constitution to make us, so far as regarded our foreign relations, one people, and one nation." Id. at 575 (opinion of Taney, J.).
>
> Indeed, the Supreme Court has long held that "power over external affairs is not shared by the States; it is vested in the national government exclusively." United States v. Pink, 315 U.S. 203, 233, 62 S.Ct. 552, 86 L.Ed. 796 (1942). In The Chinese Exclusion Case, for example, the Court commented that "for local interests the several States of the Union exist, but for national purposes, embracing our relations with foreign nationals, we are but one people, one nation, one power." Chae Chan Ping v. United States, 130 U.S. 581, 606, 9 S.Ct. 623, 32 L.Ed. 1068 (1889). In Hines v. Davidowitz, 312 U.S. 52, 85 L.Ed. 581, 61 S.Ct. 399 (1941), the Court stated that "our system of government is such that the interest of the cities, counties and states, no less than the

interest of the people of the whole nation, imperatively requires that federal power in the field affecting foreign relations be left entirely free from local interference." Id. at 63; see also United States v. Belmont, 301 U.S. 324, 57 S.Ct. 758, 331, 81 L.Ed. 1134 (1937). ("In respect of our foreign relations generally, state lines disappear."). As the Court explained in United States v. Curtiss–Wright Export Corp., 299 U.S. 304, 57 S.Ct. 216, 81 L.Ed. 255, (1936), when it comes to foreign affairs, the powers of the federal government are not limited: "the broad statement that the federal government can exercise no powers except those specifically enumerated in the Constitution, and such implied powers as are necessary and proper to carry into effect the enumerated powers, is categorically true only in respect of our internal affairs." Id. at 315–16.

Federal dominion over foreign affairs does not mean that there is no role for the states. A limited role is granted by the Constitution. See Restatement (Third) of Foreign Relations Law of the United States sec. 201 reporters' note 9 (commenting that "under the United States Constitution, a State of the United States may make compacts or agreements with a foreign power with the consent of Congress (Article I, Section 10, clause 2), but such agreements are limited in scope and subject matter" and that "[a] State may make some agreements with foreign governments without the consent of Congress so long as they do not impinge upon the authority or the foreign relations of the United States"). * * * As one learned commentator explains, some degree of state involvement in foreign affairs is inevitable: "in the governance of their affairs, states have variously and inevitably impinged on U.S. foreign relations." L. Henkin, Foreign Affairs and the United States Constitution 162 (2d ed. 1996).

* * *

* * * There is a threshold level of involvement in and impact on foreign affairs which the states may not exceed. As Zschernig stated:

> The several States, of course, have traditionally regulated the descent and distribution of estates. But those regulations must give way if they impair the effective exercise of the Nation's foreign policy. Where those laws conflict with a treaty, they must bow to the superior federal policy. Yet, even in absence of a treaty, a State's policy may disturb foreign relations.

389 U.S. at 440–41 (emphasis added) (citations omitted). Zschernig did not hold, as Massachusetts argues, that a sufficiently strong state interest could make lawful an otherwise impermissible intrusion into the federal government's foreign affairs power.

* * *

* * * The Massachusetts law presents a threat of embarrassment to the country's conduct of foreign relations regarding Burma, and in particular to the strategy that the Congress and the President have chosen to exercise. That significant potential for embarrassment, together with the other factors [discussed previously], drives the conclusion that the Massachusetts Burma Law has more than an "incidental or

indirect effect" and so is an impermissible intrusion into the foreign affairs power of the national government.

* * *

* * * The importance of the federal government's ability to speak with one voice on foreign affairs does not mean that Congress must act, or that the states can never act, in a particular area. See 512 U.S. at 329. As the Court commented in Wardair Canada, Inc. v. Florida Department of Revenue, 477 U.S. 1, 106 S.Ct. 2369, 91 L.Ed.2d 1 (1986), * * * "the Federal Government is entitled in its wisdom to act to permit the States varying degrees of regulatory authority.... We never suggested in [*Japan Line*] or in any other [case] that the Foreign Commerce Clause insists that the Federal Government speak with any particular voice." Id. at 12–13 (emphasis in original).

* * *

The Supreme Court has repeatedly suggested that state regulations that touch on foreign commerce receive a greater degree of scrutiny than do regulations that affect only domestic commerce. See South–Central Timber, 467 U.S. at 96; Reeves, 447 U.S. at 437 n.9; Japan Line, 441 U.S. at 448 (noting that "there is evidence that the Founders intended the scope of the foreign commerce power to be ... greater" than that of the domestic commerce power). * * *

* * *

* * * Supreme Court decisions under the Foreign Commerce Clause have made it clear that state laws that are designed to limit trade with a specific foreign nation are precisely one type of law that the Foreign Commerce Clause is designed to prevent. In *Container Corp.*, the Supreme Court stated that state legislation that relates to foreign policy questions violates the Foreign Commerce Clause "if it either implicates foreign policy issues which must be left to the Federal Government or violates a clear federal directive." Container Corp., 463 U.S. at 194 (emphasis in original); see also Japan Line, 441 U.S. at 448–49 (stating that "foreign commerce is preeminently a matter of national concern" and noting that "the need for federal uniformity is no less paramount in ascertaining the negative implication of Congress' power to 'regulate Commerce with foreign Nations' under the Commerce Clause"). "If state action touching foreign commerce is to be allowed, it must be shown not to affect national concerns to any significant degree, a far more difficult task than in the case of interstate commerce." Tribe, American Constitutional Law sec. 6–21, at 469. * * *

* * *

* * * Supreme Court decisions * * * make clear that a state law can violate the dormant Foreign Commerce Clause by impeding the federal government's ability to "speak with one voice" in foreign affairs, because such state action harms "federal uniformity in an area where federal uniformity is essential." Japan Line, 441 U.S. at 448–49; see also Container Corp., 463 U.S. at 193.

* * *

* * * Where, as here, the federal government has acted in an area of unique federal concern and has crafted a balanced, tailored approach to an issue, and the state law threatens to upset that balance, the state law is preempted. Under the Supremacy Clause, the Massachusetts Burma Law is unconstitutional. Cf. Missouri v. Holland, 252 U.S. 416, 64 L. Ed. 641, 40 S. Ct. 382 (1920).

* * * The conduct of this nation's foreign affairs cannot be effectively managed on behalf of all of the nation's citizens if each of the many state and local governments pursues its own foreign policy. Absent express congressional authorization, Massachusetts cannot set the nation's foreign policy.

Consider the differences in approach of the Court of Appeals and of the U.S. Supreme Court. What is the significance of this difference in terms of future impact on the issues of allocating state and federal powers concerning foreign affairs activity? Why do you suppose the U.S. Supreme Court (unanimous opinion but two justices concurring) was so terse and constrained in its opinion?

(3) In Bethlehem Steel Corporation. v. Board of Commissioners, 276 Cal.App.2d 221, 80 Cal.Rptr. 800 (1969), the Court of Appeals of the Second District reviewed the California Buy American Act (Govt. Code secs. 4300–4305), requiring that contracts for the construction of public works or the purchase of materials for public use be awarded only to persons who will agree to use or supply materials which have been manufactured in the United States, substantially all from materials produced in the United States.

Citing United States v. Pink, 315 U.S. 203, 232, 62 S.Ct. 552, 566, 86 L.Ed. 796, the court noted that "these are delicate matters. If state action could defeat or alter our foreign policy, serious consequences might ensue. The nation as a whole would be held to answer if a State created difficulties with a foreign power."

As to the argument that until such time as the federal government acts, either by conflicting legislation or international agreement, state legislation is unobjectionable, the court replied, citing Hines v. Davidowitz, 312 U.S. 52, 63, 61 S.Ct. 399, 402, 85 L.Ed. 581, that

[o]ur system of government is such that the interest of the cities, counties and states, no less than the interest of the people of the whole nation, "imperatively requires that federal power in the field affecting foreign relations be left entirely free from local interference." To permit state legislation to concurrently operate in this sphere would very certainly "imperil the amicable relations between governments and vex the peace of nations." (Oetjen v. Central Leather Co., 246 U.S. 297, 304, 38 S.Ct. 309, 311, 62 L.Ed. 726; see Ricaud v. American Metal Co., 246 U.S. 304, 308–310, 38 S.Ct. 312, 62 L.Ed. 733.)

The court had stated earlier in its opinion:

Only the federal government can fix the rules of fair competition when such competition is on an international basis. Foreign trade is properly a subject of national concern, not state regulation. State regulation can only impede, not foster, national trade policies. The problems of trade expansion or non-expansion are national in scope, and properly should be national in scope in their resolution. The fact that international trade forms the basis of this country's foreign relations is amply demonstrated by the following. At the present time the United States is a party to commercial treaties with 38 foreign nations. In addition, there are tax treaties presently in effect between the United States and 31 countries. The United States is a party to many other international treaties and agreements regulating, directly and indirectly, its commercial relations with the rest of the world. See, for example, the General Agreement on Tariffs and Trade; The United Nations Charter; The International Monetary Fund Agreement of 1945. * * * Certainly, such problems are beyond the purview of the State of California. As stated in United States v. Pink, supra, 315 U.S. 203, 232, 62 S.Ct. 552, 566, 86 L.Ed. 796: "These are delicate matters. If state action could defeat or alter our foreign policy, serious consequences might ensue. The nation as a whole would be held to answer if a State created difficulties with a foreign power."

The court concluded that the California Buy American Act was an unconstitutional intrusion into an exclusive federal domain. The case was not appealed to the California Supreme Court.

(4) In U.S. v. Locke, 529 U.S. 89, 120 S.Ct. 1135, 146 L.Ed.2d 69 (2000) the Supreme Court unanimously struck down several state regulations governing Washington state waters used by oil tankers coming from the Pacific Ocean and either destined to American or Canadian ports. The Court acknowledged the international aspects of the case, noting also the United States' argument that international agreements would have "pre-emptive force over the state regulations in question." The Court, however, concluded that it was not necessary to deal with that issue, "because the state regulations * * * are pre-empted by federal statute and regulations." At 102. Later, the Court does bring back international obligations through a back door by stating that "(a) state law in this area [in which Congress had acted] * * * would frustrate the congressional desire of achieving uniform, international standards." At 110.

(5) In Gerling Global Reinsurance Corp. of America v. Harry W. Low, Commissioner of Insurance of the State of California, 240 F.3d 739 (9th Cir. 2001). The Court of Appeals found that, although California's Holocaust Victim Insurance Relief Act (HVIRA) indirectly affected foreign commerce by possibly requiring a company related to a Californian company to search for information, it did not impede the federal government's ability to speak with "one voice" in matters affecting foreign commerce. West's Ann. Cal. Ins. Code secs. 13800–13807. In fact, Congress had spoken affirmatively in the domain of Holocaust-era insurance policies by issuing the Holocaust Assets Commission Act and had therefore, at least implicitly, encouraged state laws such as the HVIRA. U.S. Holocaust Assets Commission Act of 1998, sec. 2, 22 U.S.C.A. sec. 1621 note. The federal government's power in the domain of foreign affairs, said the court, is not mentioned in the text of the Constitu-

tion, but can be derived from the structure of the Constitution and the nature of federalism.

(3) When the Federal Government Has Not Acted or Almost Not Acted (Dormant Commerce Clause)

TUPMAN THURLOW COMPANY v. MOSS

United States District Court, M.D. Tennessee, Nashville Division, 1966.
252 F.Supp. 641.

PER CURIAM.

[The Tennessee Labeling Act] challenged in this proceeding * * * requires that any person selling or offering for sale in the State of Tennessee any meats or meat foods which are the products of any foreign country to the United States "shall so identify each product and its foreign origin." If * * * labeling is not feasible, it is provided that "a conspicuous sign in lieu of the label shall be displayed near the stock or display of the product." If foreign meats are combined with domestically produced meat into one product, the product shall be so labeled. In the event preservatives of any kind are used in any packaged meat product, the preservative shall be identified, along with the quantity used, and clearly displayed on any such package.

* * *

The Plaintiff, a New York board meat importer, alleges that the passage of the Labeling Act has caused plaintiff's Tennessee customers to refuse to purchase its imported meat, thus for all practical purposes destroying the Tennessee market for its direct sales.

* * * While the Commerce Clause as construed by the Supreme Court does not prohibit all state regulatory measures affecting interstate commerce, the Supreme Court has invariably outlawed those state restrictions which unduly and unreasonably burden or restrain interstate commerce when evaluated in terms of legitimate state or local interests, or those state restrictions and regulations which unreasonably discriminate against such commerce. * * *

The burdensome and discriminatory character of the present legislation can scarcely admit of doubt when it is considered in the light of the pertinent facts. In sweeping terms the Labeling Act requires that "each quarter of each carcass, each carton, each retail package, or individually packaged item shall be plainly identified with a brand or label stating that it is a foreign product and naming the country of its origin." * * * The evidence discloses that manufacturers and processors of meatfoods and products, such as weiners, bologna, hamburgers, baby foods, and other products, customarily, use foreign and domestic meats indiscriminately without any effort to keep the one separate from the other. The Labeling Act would require such products to be labeled to show the fact of co-mingling and the country in which the foreign meat had its origin. It would be necessary for Tennessee handlers of plaintiff's meat or meat products to keep track of or trace the origin of such meat, purchased either directly or through wholesalers or manufacturers, in order that the ultimate product sold to consumers in the State of Tennessee could be identified and labeled with the country of origin, or labeled in such way as to indicate that foreign and domestic meats both had been used. That these requirements of labeling are exceedingly burdensome is self-evident. * * *

* * * It is insisted that for almost a century states have been enacting legislation pursuant to their police power, with the approval of the Supreme Court, to protect citizens from being deceived or misled in their purchase of commodities, especially foods and food products, at retail.

In seeking to answer the question how consumers in Tennessee are misled by the sale of meat in that state which was originally imported, defendants point to the fact that the plaintiff's imported meat is frozen in the country of origin[, but usually sold as a fresh processed product, thereby deceiving consumers into believing the product was never frozen].

[However] there is no evidence that food products, such as those referred to by the defendants, are supposed by a consumer to be a fresh product, in the sense that the meat content has never been frozen. Nor is there any evidence that such products are generally offered for sale or represented to the public as fresh products. But whether these assumptions by the defendants are correct or not, it is difficult to see how the Labeling Act could have been designed to protect the consumer from deception, when the same protection is not afforded him in purchasing the same products which have been manufactured from frozen domestic meat. * * *

* * * The present labeling requirement, in contrast, would do nothing except inform the public that a meat product had its origin in a foreign country without conveying any information as to its nature, quality or quantity. In addition, as noted, it imposes substantial burdens upon meat and meat products of foreign origin without imposing the same burdens upon meat and meat products of domestic origin.

It is further insisted by the defendants that the present legislation does not offend the Commerce Clause because it operates only on goods which have come to rest in Tennessee so as to become part of the common property of the state. The cases cited by the defendants involving the "come to rest" and original package doctrines, merely recognize, because of the nexus with the state thus established, the power of the state to impose taxes or regulations upon those foreign goods which are designed to compete in the domestic market. Conceding that the imported meats in the present case are designed to compete in the domestic market, and that the state therefore has the power to regulate, it remains evident that the state may do so only if the regulations apply equally to foreign and domestic meats, and thus make possible equal competition in the domestic market.

* * *

In accordance with this opinion a form of judgment will be submitted declaring the Labeling Act * * * to be in conflict with the Commerce Clause and therefore void, and permanently enjoining the State Commissioner of Agriculture and the State Chemist and Director of Foods Division, Department of Agriculture, from enforcing the provisions of [the Act].

Note

In PORTLAND PIPE LINE CORP. v. ENVIRONMENTAL IMPROVEMENT COMMISSION, 307 A.2d 1 (Me.1973), the Supreme Court of Maine upheld a complex state regulatory enactment designed to fix responsibility and compensation for oil spills occurring in Maine waters. The State regulation imposed an annual license fee per barrel of oil transferred over coastal waters of the state. This fee was used to create a revolving fund to cover clean-up costs of spills, and research and development concerning environmental damage due to the transfer of oil in those waters.

Among the many challenges to the state regulation were a challenge based on the U.S. constitutional clause (Article I, Section 10, Clause 2) that prohibits states (without consent of Congress) from laying imposts or duties on imports or exports, "except what may be absolutely necessary for executing * * * Inspection Laws," and a challenge based on the Commerce Clause.

The Court rejected the Import–Export Clause challenge on two grounds (307 A.2d at 36):

> * * * First, the license fee is not imposed *"on Imports or Exports."* Because the transfer fee is imposed on an *activity* related to the importation of oil [i.e., off-loading] *rather than on the property imported*, the fee is not sufficiently direct to be "on Imports" under Article I, Section 10, Clause 2.

> Second, the license fee is not a duty or impost since the overall effect of the Act is the establishment of a regulatory scheme for controlling oil pollution which is essentially to protect the public interest and affords benefits to those subject to the license fee.

The plaintiff's Commerce Clause challenge included the argument that this state regulation imposed excessive burdens on interstate commerce. In rejecting to this argument, the Court wrote (307 A.2d at 37–39):

> Included in the "just share" of state tax burdens imposed on interstate commerce is the cost of preventing and remedying harm caused by a danger inherent in the interstate commerce being taxed.

[The Court then applies a three-part test concluding (1) that the tax does not discriminate against interstate and foreign commerce because the fee is also imposed upon transfers resulting from intrastate shipment; (2) that the license fee reflects "a fair if imperfect approximation" of the conduct which gives rise to the danger against which the Act seeks to guard and (3) that plaintiffs have failed to sustain their burden of proving that the license fees collected are "excessive" in relation to the costs incurred by the taxing authorities. The Court therefore concludes that it cannot find that the $4,000,000 limit of the Fund is irrational in light of the catastrophic damages which may be cause by an oil spill.]

(4) Some Specific Subjects

(a) State Taxation of Foreign Commerce

In JAPAN LINE, LTD. v. COUNTY OF LOS ANGELES, 441 U.S. 434, 99 S.Ct. 1813, 60 L.Ed.2d 336 (1979), the Supreme Court considered whether the Commerce Clause permitted a State to impose a nondiscriminatory ad valorem tax on foreign-owned instrumentalities of international commerce.

Six Japanese shipping companies objected to taxation by Los Angeles County of cargo containers that were used exclusively for the transportation of cargo in foreign commerce. The containers were registered in Japan and were in constant transit, except for time spent undergoing repair or awaiting loading or unloading. Under California law, property present in California on March 1 of any year was subject to an ad valorem property tax. The Japanese containers also were subject to property taxation in Japan.

The California Supreme Court upheld the imposition of the tax. In reversing that decision, the U.S. Supreme Court wrote (441 U.S. at 444–451, 99 S.Ct. at 1819–1823):

> * * * In construing Congress' power to "regulate Commerce * * * among the several States," the Court recently affirmed that the Constitution confers no immunity from state taxation, and that "interstate commerce must bear its fair share of the state tax burden." If the states tax "is applied to an activity with a substantial nexus with the taxing State, is fairly apportioned, does not discriminate against interstate commerce, and is fairly related to the services provided by the State," no impermissible burden on interstate commerce will be found. Complete Auto Transit, Inc. v. Brady, 430 U.S. 274, 279, 97 S.Ct. 1076, 1079, 51 L.Ed.2d 326 (1977).

> * * *

> * * * [I]f the containers at issue here were instrumentalities of purely interstate commerce, *Complete Auto* would apply and be satisfied, and our Commerce Clause inquiry would be at an end. Appellants' containers, however, are instrumentalities of foreign commerce, both as a matter of fact and as a matter of law. * * *

> When a state seeks to tax the instrumentalities of foreign commerce, two additional considerations beyond those articulated in *Complete Auto*, come into play. * * *

> * * * [First, a] state tax, even though "fairly apportioned" to reflect an instrumentality's presence within the State, may subject foreign commerce " 'to the risk of a double tax burden to which

[domestic] commerce is not exposed, and which the commerce clause forbids.' "

Second, a state tax on the instrumentalities of foreign commerce may impair federal uniformity in an area where federal uniformity is essential. Foreign commerce is preeminently a matter of national concern.

Notes and Questions

(1) In Itel Containers Intl. Corp. v. Huddleston, 507 U.S. 60, 113 S.Ct. 1095, 122 L.Ed.2d 421 (1993), the Supreme Court upheld the application of a Tennessee sales tax on proceeds from the lease of shipping containers delivered in Tennessee. The Court rejected arguments that the tax was preempted by international agreements, violated the *Japan Line* tests and violated the Import–Export Clause. Justice Blackmun, the author of the *Japan Line*, was the only dissenter. The United States filed an amicus brief in favor of upholding the tax. How can the *Itel* case be distinguished from *Japan Line*? In Wardair Canada, Inc. v. Florida Dept. of Revenue, 477 U.S. 1, 106 S.Ct. 2369, 91 L.Ed.2d 1 (1986), the Court gave a narrow reading to *Japan Line* and permitted Florida to impose a tax on aviation fuel used by an air carrier engaged exclusively in international commerce, over the dissent of Justice Blackmun and the opposition of the Solicitor General. The Court found no explicit federal policy to preempt such state taxation, which was not expressly prohibited by the applicable international agreements. Is that decision consistent with *Japan Line*?

(2) Container Corp. of America v. Franchise Tax Board, 463 U.S. 159, 103 S.Ct. 2933, 77 L.Ed.2d 545 (1983), involved a Delaware corporation headquartered in Illinois and doing business in California and elsewhere. The Supreme Court upheld the so-called unitary tax applied by California to the income of corporations doing business in the state. The tax was based on the proportion of a corporation's total payroll, property and sales that are in California, a formula that many businesses believe unfairly inflates that part of their income subject to California tax. In June 1994, the Supreme Court rejected a challenge to the California tax by a *foreign*-based corporation. Barclays Bank, PLC v. Franchise Tax Board, 512 U.S. 298, 114 S.Ct. 2268, 129 L.Ed.2d 244 (1994). In respect of the multiple taxation, the Court noted that the alternative method—use of arms' length transfer prices—involved similar dangers of multiple taxation because of varying allocation rules. As to federal uniformity, the Court noted that it was for Congress to act if such uniformity was desired and that it had not done so despite many proposals since the *Container Corp.* case. As to past Executive Branch pronouncements on the tax, the Court noted, "Executive Branch communications that express federal policy but lack the force of law cannot render unconstitutional California's otherwise valid congressionally condoned [tax]."

(3) In Xerox Corp. v. Harris County, 459 U.S. 145, 103 S.Ct. 523, 74 L.Ed.2d 323 (1982), the Court relied on the Supremacy Clause to disallow local property taxation of goods manufactured in Mexico, shipped to the United States and held in a customs bonded warehouse while awaiting

shipment to Latin America. In R.J. Reynolds Tobacco Co. v. Durham County, 479 U.S. 130, 107 S.Ct. 499, 93 L.Ed.2d 449 (1986), the Court upheld a state property tax applied to tobacco imported by Reynolds and held in customs bond for two years for aging before processing by Reynolds in North Carolina. How can this case be distinguished from *Harris County*? Earlier, in Michelin Tire Corp. v. Wages, 423 U.S. 276, 96 S.Ct. 535, 46 L.Ed.2d 495 (1976), the Court had ruled that imports could be taxed once they were no longer in transit (e.g., stored in a warehouse awaiting further distribution within the United States).

(b) State Government Purchasers and Other Proprietary Action

In SOUTH–CENTRAL TIMBER DEVELOPMENT INC. v. WUN-NICKE, 467 U.S. 82, 104 S.Ct. 2237, 81 L.Ed.2d 71 (1984), the Supreme Court discussed the market participant doctrine at length. If a state is acting as a market participant, rather than as a market regulator, then the dormant Commerce Clause places no limitation on its activities.

The Alaska Department of Natural Resources proposed to sell a substantial amount of timber from state lands. The proposed contract required, as a condition of the sale, the purchaser to process partially the timber prior to shipping it out of Alaska. The stated purpose of the provision was to "protect existing industries, provide for the establishment of new industries, derive revenue from all timber resources, and manage the State's forests on a sustained yield basis." Alaska charged a significantly lower price for timber subject to this provision.

The plaintiff contended that the contract restrictions imposed by the Alaskan government were improper restrictions on foreign commerce.

The Alaskan government's defense rested heavily on the market participant doctrine. In rejecting Alaska's argument (and invalidating the contract provision), Justice White wrote for four of the eight Justices as follows (467 U.S. at 97–99):

> The limit of the market-participant doctrine must be that it allows a State to impose burdens on commerce within the market in which it is a participant, but allows it to go no further. The State may not impose conditions, whether by statute, regulation, or contract, that have a substantial regulatory effect outside of that particular market. Unless the "market" is relatively narrowly defined, the doctrine has the potential of swallowing up the rule that States may not impose substantial burdens on interstate commerce even if they act with the permissible state purpose of fostering local industry.

* * *

> There are sound reasons for distinguishing between a State's preferring its own residents in the initial disposition of goods when it is a market participant and a State's attachment of restrictions on dispositions subsequent to the goods coming to rest in private hands.

First, simply as a matter of intuition a State market participant has a greater interest as a "private trader" in the immediate transaction than it has in what its purchaser does with the goods after the State no longer has an interest in them. The common law recognized such a notion in the doctrine of restraints on alienation. * * *

Second, downstream restrictions have a greater regulatory effect than do limitations on the immediate transaction. Instead of merely choosing its own trading partners, the State is attempting to govern the private, separate economic relationships of its trading partners; that is, it restricts the post-purchase activity of the purchaser, rather than merely the purchasing activity. * * * In sum, the State may not avail itself of the market-participant doctrine to immunize its downstream regulation of the timber-processing market in which it is not a participant.

Notes and Questions

The reader should compare these note cases to the previous case and to the *Bethlehem Steel* case excerpted earlier in this section, and to Crosby v. National Foreign Trade Council.

(1) In K.S.B. Technical Sales Corp. v. North Jersey District Water Supply Commn., 75 N.J. 272, 381 A.2d 774 (1977), the New Jersey Supreme Court upheld a state "Buy American" statute which applied to purchases of equipment for a government water supply service, noting that although GATT applies with as much vigor as a treaty and is deemed supreme over state law under the U.S. Constitution, the specific exception in GATT Article III, paragraph 8, for government purchases exempted from the GATT national treatment obligation the purchases involved in the case.

On the question of whether the state statute was an impermissible intrusion by New Jersey into the field of foreign affairs, the court distinguished the *Zschernig* case on the grounds that the New Jersey statute was nondiscriminatory (thus state officials would not need to evaluate or differentiate between foreign countries or their policies) and distinguished the *Bethlehem* case itself on the grounds that the New Jersey statute was narrower than the California one in that it provided that domestic materials did not need to be used if their cost was unreasonable or if it would be impractical or inconsistent with the public interest to do so.

Finally, the New Jersey court noted U.S. Supreme Court authority to the effect that a state can discriminate against non-residents when it acts in a proprietary capacity as a buyer or a seller. (See the *South-Central Timber* case above.)

(2) An interesting opinion is Trojan Technologies, Inc. v. Pennsylvania, 916 F.2d 903 (3d Cir.1990), cert. denied, 501 U.S. 1212, 111 S.Ct. 2814, 115 L.Ed.2d 986 (1991) in which the Third Circuit upheld the Pennsylvania Steel Products Procurement Act, which directed Pennsylvania state agencies to require use of only U.S.-made steel in public works projects. The court concluded that the act (i) was not preempted by the U.S.-Canada Free Trade

Agreement, the GATT Government Procurement Code and federal statutes, (ii) did not violate the Commerce Clause in light of the market participant doctrine and (iii) did not interfere with the federal foreign affairs power. The U.S. government argued in favor of these conclusions as amicus.

(3) In LUCCHINO v. BRAZIL, 82 Pa.Cmwlth. 406, 476 A.2d 1369 (1984), the court upheld a state statute that banned the purchase by state government agencies of steel, iron and aluminum products imported from countries which in turn discriminate against such products made in Pennsylvania. The court found that the matter being commercial, neither sovereign immunity nor the Act of State Doctrine applied, and also found evidence that the defendant countries had discriminated against the relevant Pennsylvania products. The state court concluded (476 A.2d at 1376–77):

> 6.   The statutes, regulations, policies, procedures and practices of the respondent foreign countries Brazil, South Korea, Spain, Mexico and Argentina, as set forth in the Findings of Fact, have the practical effect of granting and/or bestowing a preference, discount or other competitive advantage to steel, iron or aluminum products manufactured in said respondent foreign countries, the effect whereof discriminates against the same or substantially similar steel, iron and aluminum products manufactured in this Commonwealth and furthermore places said products manufactured in this Commonwealth at a competitive disadvantage.

* * *

> 11.   The violations of the Pennsylvania Trade Practices Act by each of the respondent foreign countries * * * entitles petitioner to the relief he seeks and thereby makes it unlawful for any public agency to specify, purchase, or permit to be furnished or used, in any public works, steel, iron and aluminum products made in any of the respondent foreign countries which have been determined by this Court to discriminate pursuant to the Act.

The *Lucchino* case was subsequently removed to federal court and later dismissed on procedural grounds. 50 BNA Antitrust & Trade Reg.Rptr. 921 (1986).

(4) From the foregoing cases, how far would you say that the states may go in regulating matters affecting international trade? To what extent can their actions be overruled by federal action—either by Congress in enacting legislation or by the President in entering into a trade agreement on nontariff barriers to trade? Do you think the court would have ruled differently in any of these cases after Crosby v. National Foreign Trade Council?

(5) The relation of government purchases to imports is taken up in Section 12.5 infra. Could the U.S. federal government enter into and implement an international agreement regulating government procurement by state and municipal governments?

(D) STATE COOPERATION AND CONSULTATION IN U.S. INTERNATIONAL ECONOMIC AFFAIRS

MATTHEW SCHAEFER, NOTE ON STATE INVOLVEMENT IN TRADE NEGOTIATIONS, THE DEVELOPMENT OF TRADE AGREEMENT IMPLEMENTING LEGISLATION, AND THE ADMINISTRATION OF TRADE AGREEMENTS (JANUARY 18, 1994)[4]

Trade agreements are increasingly impacting sub-national governments. The reason for the increased impact is at least two-fold. First, there is an increased emphasis on binding sub-national governments to obligations within international trade agreements. Second, the enlarged scope of trade agreements includes areas in which sub-national governments exercise jurisdiction. For instance, the Uruguay Round negotiations will bring trade-in-services under rules of the world trading system for the first time. The U.S. states as well as sub-national governments in other nations are very active in regulating service industries, including professional and financial services. With this stated, it is important to note that devices are still used by which some existing practices of sub-national governments are exempted from international trade obligations. The North American Free Trade Agreement (NAFTA), for example, allows existing state and provincial measures that would otherwise violate the obligations of the services, financial services and investment chapters to be "grandfathered" if the measures are identified within a year or two.

While U.S. state government policy-makers have long realized the importance of trade agreements in economic terms, they have recently placed an enhanced emphasis on understanding, and sometimes attempting to limit, the potential legislative and regulatory constraints of such agreements. In response to these potential constraints, the U.S. states have sought continued input into U.S. trade negotiations, increased involvement in the development of implementing legislation for trade agreements, and a larger role in the administration of trade agreements for state-related matters.

The mechanism by which states give formal input in the negotiation of trade agreements is the Intergovernmental Policy Advisory Committee (IGPAC). IGPAC has a statutory basis originally dating to the 1974 Trade Act. Currently, IGPAC has 30 members, including 14 State Governors, 5 state legislative representatives, a state environmental secretary and a state agriculture commissioner. The IGPAC meets periodically throughout trade negotiations with U.S. trade negotiators to receive updates on the status of negotiations and to give advice on how negotiations should proceed. The IGPAC is required to submit a report

---

4. Matthew Schaefer, International Trade Consultant to the National Governor's Association and the Western Governor's Association (1994). This note was prepared at the request of Professor Jackson for inclusion in this book.

on negotiations thirty days after the President notifies Congress of his intent to enter into a trade agreement. Such reports give an assessment by IGPAC of the proposed agreement.

The large number of component units within the U.S. federation makes participation of all 50 states within the IGPAC forum difficult as a practical matter. Thus, many state associations in which all 50 states are represented, such as the National Governors' Association and the National Council of State Legislatures, have adopted policy resolutions on trade negotiations and transmitted the policy to the Administration. In some instances, however, state input has been given on a more ad hoc basis. For instance, IGPAC was not reconvened for the NAFTA supplemental negotiations on labor and environment. Instead, interested state Governors monitored the negotiations and sent letters expressing their views on the negotiations.

Therefore, state input in trade negotiations is generally limited to advice (i.e. the states have no veto power or binding advisory capacity). The one exception lies in the area of government procurement negotiations. The U.S. approach has been to bind the states to obligations within the renegotiated GATT Government Procurement Code on a voluntary basis only (despite the fact that U.S. negotiators believed as early as the Tokyo Round that they would have the constitutional authority to bind the states without their consent). While the U.S. is strongly seeking commitments from all 50 states to bind some of their procurement to the rules of the renegotiated Code, the final decision on whether to make a commitment and the extent of the commitment is a decision for each state to make on a voluntary basis. As of December 15, 1993, the United States Trade Representative had received voluntary commitments from 24 states to bind some or all of their procurement.

IGPAC reports and policy resolutions of the state associations contain recommendations for the implementing legislation of trade agreements as well. The number and depth of state recommendations for implementing legislation was greater than ever before for the implementing package of the NAFTA. One central element of the National Governors' Association and Western Governors' Association policy resolutions was a recommendation to ensure meaningful state participation in future dispute settlement cases and in the activities of committees established by NAFTA for the purpose of harmonizing standards. Additionally, the Governors sought to improve communications between the federal and state governments on trade matters.

Dispute settlement became a concern because of a 1992 GATT panel decision ruling that measures in over 40 states relating to alcoholic and malt beverages violated the GATT. The states believed that the informal consultation process during that dispute was insufficient. The states were interested in the work of the committees established under NAFTA because of a concern that harmonization efforts between the three countries would diminish the flexibility of states to set different standards. While any recommendations of the committees would be non-binding in the sense that further Congressional or Executive action would be necessary to implement them, such recommendations could provide the impetus for preemptive federal action.

The exact nature and extent of state participation and federal-state consultations with respect to the administration of NAFTA was worked out over many months of discussion between representatives of the Governors, the Congress, and the Office of the United States Trade Representative (USTR). The final results of the NAFTA implementing package established a new process for federal-state communication on trade. As directed by the NAFTA package, the USTR has named a "NAFTA Coordinator for State Matters." The coordinator is responsible for disseminating information to the states on relevant matters including dispute settlement cases affecting the states and committee activities addressing matters within the concurrent or exclusive jurisdiction of the states. The coordinator will cooperate with other federal agencies to ensure all relevant information is transmitted to the states. In return, the Governors have agreed to select a single point of contact within each of their states for NAFTA trade matters. The new communication system will reduce problems that have occurred in the past, such as the federal government sending surveys on trade related matters to the wrong state agency or official.

The NAFTA implementing legislation also requires the USTR to involve states "to the greatest extent practicable at each stage of the development of U.S. positions regarding [state-related] matters that will be addressed by committees, subcommittees or working groups established under the Agreement or through dispute settlement processes provided for under the Agreement." The legislation notes that the state involvement will include involvement through appropriate representatives of the States. The accompanying statement of administrative action clarifies that state representatives will be allowed to participate in federal agency preparations for committee activities and dispute settlement cases affecting their interests but will act only as observers at actual committee meetings and panel hearings, unless a more active role is determined to be appropriate.

The NAFTA implementing bill is the first time states have been granted a guaranteed right to be informed and participate in trade matters affecting the states. It represents an accommodation to the new realities of trade agreements, specifically the increased impact that trade agreements have on the states. It is likely that the NAFTA implementing package will serve as a model with appropriate modifications and additions for the Uruguay Round implementing package and future trade agreement implementing bills.

Notes and Questions

(1) The NAFTA implementing legislation referred to in the foregoing excerpt is section 102(b)(2) of the North America Free Trade Agreement Implementation Act, Pub. L. No. 103–182, 107 Stat. 2057 (1993) (codified at U.S.C.A. sec. 3312).

(2) Are the procedures described in the foregoing note adequate? If you were a Governor, would you want additional rights for States? Of what kind?

Chapter 4

INTERNATIONAL ECONOMIC REGULATION IN THE EUROPEAN UNION AND JAPAN

SECTION 4.1   INTRODUCTION

This book emphasizes problems of U.S. law, partly because of its expected audience but also because the United States plays such a major role in the world trading regime. Although space and time prevent exploring the legal systems of other major trading nations in any great depth, this chapter should assist the reader in understanding how some of the problems we explored in Chapter 3 are handled in the European Union (EU). We also look very briefly at Japan. Further, detailed information on how other WTO members formulate and implement trade policy can be found in the Trade Policy Reviews conducted of all WTO members by the WTO Trade Policy Review Body.

Some knowledge of the legal framework for international trade in the EU is crucial for obtaining an overall sound understanding of the operation of the international economic system. In 1999, the EU was the world's largest single trading entity, accounting for almost 39% of world merchandise trade (63.5% of which was internal EU trade), while the United States accounted for 12.4% and Japan for 7.5%.[1] For commercial service exports, the comparable statistics were EU: 42.5%; US: 18.8% and Japan: 4.5%.[2] In terms of economic power, the United States, the European Union and Japan have the overwhelmingly dominant role to play in the development of international economic policy. With addition of Canada, they are often referred to as the "quad" (from quadrilateral). Both the United States and the European Union probably have an effective veto over most proposals for international economic policy, and together they almost certainly have such a veto. Likewise, together they often have the power of initiative, in the sense that if they are agreed that a certain policy should be followed to promote certain international

---

1. World Trade Organization, International Trade Statistics 2000, Table I–4 (2000) (based on exports). Excluding internal EU trade, the statistics would be EU— 18.8%, U.S.—16.4% and Japan—9.9%. Id., Table I–5.

2. Id., Table I–7.

economic goals, on many issues (but certainly not all issues) this agreed position will prevail.

In Chapter 3, we saw that the ability of the United States to engage effectively in trade negotiations was very much affected by the constitutional division of powers between the President and Congress and between the federal government and the states. It may also be affected by the relative openness of the U.S. legislative process and the degree to which individuals have access to the courts to challenge state or federal actions that are allegedly inconsistent with U.S. international obligations. The other members of the world trading system also must deal with splits in authority between different constituent elements of their governments and with judicial systems with rules that differ from those applicable in U.S. courts.

In studying the materials in this chapter, the reader should focus on the following questions:

(1) How have the different institutional conflicts present in the United States, the EU and Japan affected the formation of international economic law in the past and how might they affect the scope and results of future negotiations on changes in such law?

(2) Does the possibility of an individual challenging government acts as inconsistent with international economic law (or the lack of such a possibility) mean that international agreements will be adhered to more (or less) faithfully?

(3) What implications should the answers to these questions have in constructing institutions and norms of international economic law?

(4) Which entities of the government structure have the authority to regulate international trade?

(5) What is the relationship between parliamentary institutions, executive organizations, and the judiciary, in this regard?

(6) What special problems do federal states or customs unions have with the authority of the central government over external trade matters?

(7) What bodies in a country or union have the power to enter into an international agreement?

(8) What is the legal effect of such an agreement in the country or union?

(9) In which cases does such an agreement prevail over other internal law, or not?

The materials in this chapter will not answer all these questions, but these questions have motivated the selection and emphasis of those materials.

SECTION 4.2   THE EUROPEAN UNION[1]

We study the European Union in part because it is one of the key players in international trade negotiations. As important, we examine it because it is a fascinating exercise in "nation" building, two aspects of which have considerable importance for the international system. The first is the way in which it has removed barriers to trade among its member states; the second is the role of effective dispute settlement and treaty enforcement in the process of economic integration. The international community is not about to engage in the degree of economic integration that characterizes the EU today, but the EU's experience in reducing trade barriers and improving compliance with agreements through dispute settlement mechanisms provides lessons of obvious relevance and importance. We begin this section by describing the activities and sketching the institutions of the EU. Then, we consider the relationship of EC law to member state law, followed by a examination of the respective external relations powers of the Union and its member states and the position of international agreements under EC law. We conclude with a broad perspective on the economic integration of Europe generally.

(A) THE ACTIVITIES AND INSTITUTIONS OF THE EUROPEAN UNION

The genesis of the European Union (EU) was the European Coal and Steel Community (ECSC), which was established in 1952. It was followed by the 1957 Treaty of Rome, which established the European Economic Community (EEC).[2] The EEC was often referred to initially as the European Common Market and more recently as the European Community or EC. As of November 1993, the Maastricht Treaty on European Union (TEU) came into force, creating a European Union, one component of which is the EC. From that point on, it became common to use the terms European Union or EU generally, even when referring to matters that technically concerned the EC. We will follow that usage for the most part, although we will use phrases such as "EC law" when discussing the EC Treaty and legislation adopted under it.[3] It is worth noting that almost all of the activities of the EU (as used in the foregoing broad sense) are in fact conducted pursuant to the EC Treaty and it is the EC that is a member of the WTO.

1. For further references on the European Union and the issues treated in this section, see George A. Bermann, Roger J. Goebel, William J. Davey & Eleanor M. Fox, Cases and Materials on European Union Law (2d ed. 2002).

2. There have been a number of significant amendments to the original EEC Treaty (now formally the EC Treaty), and its provisions have been renumbered. The most convenient source for the currently effective version of the treaty is the Europa

website: *www.europa.eu.int*. A third community—the European Atomic Energy Community, known as Euratom—was also established at Rome in 1957.

3. Our distinction may seem overly technical, however, the major English language publisher of European court decisions took four pages to explain the terminology it would use in respect of the EU following the TEU's entry into force! See Note on Post–Maastricht Terminology, [1994] 1 C.M.L.R. 4–7.

The original members of the EEC were Belgium, France, Italy, Luxembourg, the Netherlands and West Germany. They were joined in 1973 by Denmark, Ireland and the United Kingdom, in 1981 by Greece, in 1986 by Portugal and Spain, and in 1995 by Austria, Finland and Sweden. The EU is currently negotiating accession with Bulgaria, Cyprus, the Czech Republic, Estonia, Hungary, Latvia, Lithuania, Malta, Poland, Romania, the Slovak Republic and Slovenia. EU leaders have expressed the hope of completing negotiations with the best-prepared applicants by the end of 2002. Turkey has also applied for membership. In non-Soviet Europe only Iceland, Norway (where voters have twice rejected accession proposals), Switzerland and the Balkan states (except Slovenia) are not now negotiating accession.

The principal objective of the Treaty of Rome was the creation of a common market among its member states. More specifically, the Treaty provided for the elimination of barriers to the free movement of goods, workers, services and capital among the member states and the establishment of a common tariff and commercial policy towards non-members. To facilitate these measures, the Treaty also provided for common policies in agriculture, competition (antitrust matters) and transportation and for the harmonization of member state laws generally to the extent required for the proper functioning of the common market. As a result, there is important EC legislation in such fields as the environment, worker and consumer protection, gender equality, corporate law and securities regulation, and taxation. We will make reference to EC rules and policies throughout the book.

WILLIAM J. DAVEY, EUROPEAN INTEGRATION: REFLECTIONS ON ITS LIMITS AND EFFECTS[4]

The EC has largely succeeded in creating a true internal market in goods, labor, services and capital. By 1968, duties on trade in goods between the member states had been eliminated. Since then the Community has taken great strides to remove other barriers to free movement and in harmonizing laws to promote cross-border commerce. Its march toward the creation of an internal market has not been a steady one, however. For much of the late 1970s and early 1980s, relatively little progress was made at the legislative level because of the inability of the Council to reach consensus on many Commission proposals. Indeed, during this period it was largely through expansive Court of Justice decisions that continued progress was made towards realizing the internal market goal. The Court ruled, for example, that normally a good lawfully marketed in one member state could be marketed in the others, notwithstanding local restrictions that purported to limit such marketing possibilities [the *Cassis de Dijon* case, excerpted in Section 14.4

---

4. 1 Ind. J. Global Leg. Studies 185, 190–193 (1993). This and other excerpts from this publication in this chapter are reprinted with the permission of the Indiana Journal of Global Legal Studies.

infra]. While this ruling could be used by individuals to challenge many indirect member state restrictions on intra-Community trade, it was not a panacea for the creation of the internal market. By its nature, the Court's role was limited to striking down member state barriers to trade. It could not force adoption of positive legislation needed to complete the internal market.

In 1985, inspired by a Commission White Paper on the completion of the internal market, the member states agreed upon amendments to the basic treaties in the Single European Act, which came into force in 1987. The Single European Act set December 31, 1992, as a goal for completion of the internal market. The Act helped make that goal realistic by amending the legislative process so that a form of super ("qualified") majority voting, instead of unanimity, was made the rule for most measures necessary to complete the internal market. Spurred on by studies showing the great economic costs imposed on the EC by the lack of an internal market, the vast majority [95%] of the 1992 internal market program was agreed to on schedule [at the Community level, with 80% implementation at the member state level].

As a result, the EC has come close to creating a completely free and open internal market amongst its member states. Goods move freely, and so do workers. Where professional qualifications are an issue, there are rules on recognition of diplomas and so on. Services can be provided freely throughout the Community. Where they are regulated (such as insurance and banking), there are Community rules indicating which member state is allowed to regulate which service providers and on what types of substantive regulations may be imposed. As importantly, where divergent member state laws could have impeded the flow of goods from one member to another (e.g., different rules on labeling), the Community has often acted to adopt a single, community-wide rule. From the outset, the treaty established rules on competition, which are enforced by the Commission.

* * *

In addition to removing trade barriers, there are several other significant trade-related aspects of Community integration. First, market integration sharply highlights disparities in regional wealth and the trade-related consequences that may result therefrom. Richer countries will be concerned about possible job losses to poorer regions where wage rates are lower and environmental rules less strictly enforced; poorer countries will feel entitled to assistance in implementing common policies proposed by richer countries or may simply insist on such help as a price for supporting new Community initiatives. Accordingly, the Community has adopted mechanisms to reduce these disparities by transferring wealth from the richer member states to the poorer ones. * * *

Second, market integration necessitates [the adoption of joint policies] with respect to subsidization of industry. These policies include (i) limits on the rights of individual member states to subsidize local producers, which would distort trade patterns in the internal market and lead to wasteful competitive subsidization, and (ii) adoption of common strategies of increasing overall community wealth through government action, whether this be coordinated infrastructure developments or joint aid to specific industries. The Community over time has become more and more active in pursuing such policies.

Third, as economies become more closely entwined, economic conditions in one country inevitably have more of an effect in the others that are most closely connected to it. Economic policy decisions taken by one government affect others, sometimes in fundamental ways. Consequently, market integration increases pressures for coordination of economic policies. To date, the extent of such economic policy coordination in the EC has been rather limited, but under the Maastricht Treaty, ten of the member states [all but Denmark and the U.K.] have committed themselves to move toward a common currency and a European central bank. If that occurs, then those member states' economies will clearly be closely intertwined on other economic policy matters as well (particularly fiscal policy and budget deficits). [European Monetary Union is discussed in Chapter 22 infra.]

The success of the EU is explained in part by its institutional structure. There are five important institutions: The Commission, the Council, the European Council, the European Parliament and the Court of Justice. The *Commission,* which is based in Brussels, was designed to be the most "European" of the institutions. It consists of 20 commissioners who are appointed for five-year terms as independent persons and not as representatives of particular governments. Each member state has the right in practice to choose one (two in the case of the five most populous member states) of the commissioners to be appointed.

The Commission is the executive arm of the EC. It is charged with ensuring that the treaties are observed and that the decisions of the institutions are faithfully implemented. The Council has delegated extensive powers to the Commission to enable it to administer programs and enforce rules. The Commission also plays an important role in the legislative process. Generally, the Council may act only on a Commission proposal and may amend it only by unanimous vote, even if adoption of the proposal would normally require only a "qualified majority." (This power has been reduced in the later stages of the codecision procedure described below.) The Commission is headed by a President (chosen by the member states, but subject to approval by Parliament), with each commissioner being responsible for a particular part of the Commission's work. The Commission has some 20,000 employees. To finance its numerous programs, which in 2001 necessitated a budget of over 90 billion euros (approximately $80 billion), the EU relies mainly on its share of member state value added tax revenue, an amount from each member state based upon it gross domestic product, customs revenue and agricultural levies.

The *Council,* also based in Brussels, is composed of one representative from each member state. The actual membership of the Council varies depending on the issue before it—national transport ministers discuss transport issues; national agricultural ministers consider agricultural questions. The more important issues are handled by the general affairs council, which consists of the foreign ministers of the member states. The Council is the principal legislative body of the EU, although as noted below, the power of the European Parliament over legislation has grown significantly in the last decade or so.

Each member state has a permanent representative to the EU. These permanent representatives, who meet as a group known as the Committee of Permanent Representatives (COREPER), have an extensive staff (over 2500 employees). The representatives and their staff look after the interests of the member states between Council meetings and play an important role in preparing for Council meetings, a role that gives them considerable influence on actions ultimately taken by the Council.

The Council voting structure depends on which particular power under which of the treaties it is exercising. In some cases each member state has one vote and a simple majority prevails; in other cases a "qualified majority" is required (62 of 87 votes, with a state's votes roughly weighted by population; Luxembourg has two, the four largest member states each have ten); and in still other cases, unanimity is required.

The *European Council* is the name given to summit meetings of member state leaders. Although there was no treaty basis for these meetings until the adoption of the SEA, these meetings have long played a critical role in the operation of the Union. At meetings of the European Council, the leaders discuss and often decide upon the direction of EU policy. Their decisions are later implemented by member state representatives in the Council. These meetings occur at least twice a year.

The *European Parliament* is based in Strasbourg. Its members are directly elected by the voters of the various EU states, with the number of each state's seats allocated in rough proportion to the state's population. With respect to the Union legislative process, the Parliament initially had only the right to give non-binding advice on proposed legislation. More recently, it has gained considerable additional powers. In 1987, pursuant to the Single European Act, the consultation requirement was considerably strengthened by the addition of the so-called cooperation procedure. Although the Parliament's views could ultimately be ignored, the voting rules made it more difficult to do so in some cases. Under the Treaty of European Union, effective in 1993, Parliament gained so-called codecision powers in certain areas. These powers mean that Parliament can effectively veto adoption of legislation, although it still lacks the power to initiate legislation. The range of legislation subject to the codecision procedure was significantly expanded by the 1998 Amsterdam Treaty and will be further expanded by 2000 Nice

Treaty. As a result, codecision has become the process applicable to most legislation, although the Parliament's powers in some areas—particularly agriculture and the common commercial policy—remain relatively limited. However, under these recent amendments, Parliament has also gained powers in the field of external relations, where its approval is needed for certain types of international agreements (although not for simple commercial policy agreements). Parliament constantly seeks to expand its powers and influence, and it is likely that there will be further expansions of its power in the future, although some member states are leery of giving Parliament power at their expense. Others, however, feel that the Union suffers from a "democracy deficit" because Union institutions are too isolated from Union citizens. In their view, expanding the powers of Parliament would help to solve this problem. In the end, the struggle for power between the Council, on the one hand, and Commission (and Parliament), on the other, basically reflects the desire of the member states to retain their national sovereignty vis-à-vis the EU.

The *Court of Justice* (sitting at Luxembourg) is one of the most interesting, and from a juridical point of view, most impressive institutions of the European Union. Fifteen judges, assisted by six Advocates General, one of whom recommends a decision to the court in each case, form a judicial institution which has established a remarkable record over the last half century. The Court's work has on the whole enhanced both the unity and the central powers of the EU institutions. An American lawyer is struck by some of the parallels between Court of Justice case developments and those of the United States Supreme Court.[5] In effect, the European Community operates within a system of judicial review (court power to annul unconstitutional acts) which is both very similar to that of the United States and very different from the judicial systems in some of the major EU member states. Given the relatively subordinate role of the judiciary in many European government systems, it is striking to find such a strong judicial role played in the EU structure.

Under the provisions of the EC Treaty, the Commission or a member state may sue another member state in the Court for failing to fulfil an EC obligation. Likewise, the Commission, the Council or a member state can ask the Court to review acts of the Council or Commission for violations of the Treaty or EC rules, for lack of competence, for infringement of essential procedural requirements or for misuse of powers. They may also sue the Commission or Council for failure to act when required. In addition, when certain Community acts that are of direct and individual concern to a person are at issue, that person may bring an action challenging such acts. In addition, and of particular importance, a party litigant in the court of a member state may be able, in asserting the applicability of EC law, to obtain a Court of

5. For an informed discussion of such parallels, see Courts and Free Markets (T. Sandalow & E. Stein eds., 1982).

Justice ruling on that issue by requesting the member state court to refer the EC law issue to the Court of Justice. If there is no appeal of the member state court's decision in the case, that court is required to refer the EC law issue to the Court of Justice.

Pursuant to the SEA, a Court of First Instance was created. It initially was given jurisdiction over appeals of Commission competition law decisions and labor cases, with a right of appeal to the Court of Justice. As of 1994, it was given initial jurisdiction of all claims by individuals challenging EC acts.

Often, issues of EC law, whether they be interpretation of the basic treaties themselves or of "secondary legislation" (as regulations and other actions of the Commission and Council are called), can and will be brought to the Court of Justice. To a remarkable degree, then, one observes that much activity in the EU is conducted with reference to the fact of its ultimate challengeability in the Court. In short, lawyers are important, their expertise is growing, and possibly so also is their influence (although Europe, especially the Continent, has traditionally been less influenced by lawyers, private or public, than the United States has been). In connection with the EU's exercise of powers relating to international economic power, then, EC law can be expected to have considerable importance.

The wide range of EU activities has inevitably raised questions of how closely integrated politically the EU should become. Although the EU treaties focus on economic matters, it has been understood from the beginning that some of their framers viewed them as having the longer range objective of European political union. Indeed, the very title of the Treaty on European Union indicates that the EU member states are moving toward a closer political relationship. Under the SEA, a coordinated foreign policy apparatus—European Political Cooperation—was established under the auspices of the European Council, and it was expanded in the TEU into a common foreign and security policy. The TEU also introduced, in the EC Treaty, the idea of Union citizenship, and, outside of the EC Treaty, provided for cooperation in the fields of justice and home affairs (e.g., police matters). For years one of the major issues in the EU has been the question of how much and how fast the EU should evolve toward political union. The TEU represents another step toward such a union, but debate on this issue will undoubtedly continue as some argue that the current EU member states should "deepen" their relationship, while others argue that the Union should first "widen" itself and bring in new member states, something that might make deepening more difficult.

From the perspective of international economic relations, two questions concerning the EU are of particular importance: (1) To what extent is legislation or other action taken by the EU enforced in the individual member states, i.e. the relation of EC law to national law? (2) What powers does the EU have in the realm of international economic affairs and to what extent does it share them with the member states? We will look at each of these issues in turn.

(B) THE FORCE OF EC LAW IN THE MEMBER STATES

One of the more interesting questions presented by the European Union is the relationship of EC law to member state law. What is the status of the EC Treaty under member state law? Of other EC acts? What happens when there is a conflict? Who decides which law prevails? In reviewing the following material the student should consider how the issues discussed in Sections 3.4 (International Agreements and U.S. Law) and 3.6 (Federal–State Relations) would be resolved in the EU.

VAN GEND & LOOS v. NEDERLANDSE ADMINISTRATIE DER BELASTINGEN

Court of Justice of the European Communities, Case 26/62.
[1963] ECR 1.

[The Court of Justice was asked in an Article 234 reference whether former Article 12[6] of the EC Treaty had direct effects within the territory of a Member State, i.e. whether nationals of a State could, on the basis of Article 12, lay claim to individual rights that national courts had to protect. In this particular case, the issue was whether they could challenge in national court an alleged tariff increase on the ground that it violated Article 12. The Court responded as follows:]

To ascertain whether the provisions of an international treaty extend so far in their effects it is necessary to consider the spirit, the general scheme and the wording of those provisions.

The objective of the EEC Treaty, which is to establish a Common Market, the functioning of which is of direct concern to interested parties in the Community, implies that this Treaty is more than an agreement which merely creates mutual obligations between the contracting states. This view is confirmed by the preamble to the Treaty which refers not only to governments but to peoples. It is also confirmed more specifically by the establishment of institutions endowed with sovereign rights, the exercise of which affects Member States and also their citizens. * * *

In addition the task assigned to the Court of Justice under Article [234], the object of which is to secure uniform interpretation of the Treaty by national courts and tribunals, confirms that the states have acknowledged that Community law has an authority which can be invoked by their nationals before those courts and tribunals.

---

6. Article 12 was a transitional provision designed to prevent tariff increases of any kind during the period when tariffs between the member states were being phased out. It provided: "Member States shall refrain from introducing between themselves any new customs duties on imports or exports or any charges having equivalent effect, and from increasing those which they already apply in their trade with each other."

The conclusion to be drawn from this is that the Community constitutes a new legal order of international law for the benefit of which the states have limited their sovereign rights, albeit within limited fields, and the subjects of which comprise not only Member States but also their nationals. Independently of the legislation of Member States, Community law therefore not only imposes obligations on individuals but is also intended to confer upon them rights which become part of their legal heritage. These rights arise not only where they are expressly granted by the Treaty, but also by reason of obligations which the Treaty imposes in a clearly defined way upon individuals as well as upon the Member States and upon the institutions of the Community.

* * *

The wording of Article 12 contains a clear and unconditional prohibition which is not a positive but a negative obligation. This obligation, moreover, is not qualified by a reservation on the part of states which would make its implementation conditional upon a positive legislative measure enacted under national law. The very nature of this prohibition makes it ideally adapted to produce direct effects in the legal relationship between Member States and their subjects.

* * *

It follows from the foregoing considerations that, according to the spirit, the general scheme and the wording of the Treaty, Article 12 must be interpreted as producing direct effects and creating individual rights which national courts must protect.

AMMINISTRAZIONE DELLE FINANZE DELLO STATO v. SIMMENTHAL S.P.A.

Court of Justice of the European Communities,
Case 106/77.
[1978] ECR 629.

[An Italian beef importer brought an action in Italian court to recover certain veterinary and public health inspection fees it had been required to pay when importing beef from France. The Court of Justice had previously ruled that the fees violated Article [28] on the free movement of goods. Under Italian law only the Italian Constitutional Court could declare an Italian statute invalid. One of the questions asked by the lower Italian court in this Article [234] reference was whether Community law required that the lower court be able to take such action and order repayment of the fees. The Court of Justice answered:]

[I]n accordance with the principle of the precedence of Community law, the relationship between provisions of the Treaty and directly applicable measures of the institutions on the one hand and the national law of the Member States on the other is such that those provisions and measures not only by their entry into force render automatically inapplicable any conflicting provision of current national law but—in so far as they are an integral part of, and take precedence in, the legal order applicable in the territory of each of the Member States—also preclude the valid adoption of new national legislative measures to the extent to which they would be incompatible with Community provisions.

Indeed any recognition that national legislative measures which encroach upon the field within which the Community exercises its legislative power or which are otherwise incompatible with the provisions of Community law had any legal effect would amount to a corresponding denial of the effectiveness of obligations undertaken unconditionally and irrevocably by Member States pursuant to the Treaty and would thus imperil the very foundations of the Community.

The same conclusion emerges from the structure of Article [234]. * * *

The effectiveness of that provision would be impaired if the national court were prevented from forthwith applying Community law in accordance with the decision or the case-law of the Court.

It follows from the foregoing that every national court must, in a case within its jurisdiction, apply Community law in its entirety and protect rights which the latter confers on individuals and must accordingly set aside any provision of national law which may conflict with it, whether prior or subsequent to the Community rule.

Accordingly any provision of a national legal system and any legislative, administrative or judicial practice which might impair the effectiveness of Community law by withholding from the national court having jurisdiction to apply such law the power to do everything necessary at the moment of its application to set aside national legislative provisions which might prevent Community rules from having full force and effect are incompatible with those requirements which are the very essence of Community law.

Notes and Questions

(1) *Van Gend & Loos* sets forth the Court of Justice's classic formulation of the nature of the EC: "A new legal order * * * for the benefit of which the states have limited their sovereign rights * * * and the subjects of which comprise not only Member States but also their nationals." This viewpoint gives the Court great power and discretion since a new legal order may well require the Court to formulate new legal principles and rules.

(2) An issue similar to that in *Simmenthal II* arose in The Queen v. Secretary of State for Transport ex parte Factortame Ltd., Case C–213/89, [1990] ECR I–2433. In a case challenging an Act of Parliament as violating the EC Treaty, a U.K. trial court concluded that the plaintiffs would prevail on the merits and would suffer irreparable damage if interim relief were denied. It thereupon issued a preliminary injunction enjoining enforcement of the Act. The appeals court reversed on the ground that under U.K. constitutional tradition, a court may not enjoin an Act of Parliament. The House of Lords then asked the Court of Justice whether Community law required an English court to grant preliminary injunctive relief in such a

case. Relying on *Simmenthal II*, the Court answered that "Community law must be interpreted as meaning that a national court which, in a case before it concerning Community law, considers that the sole obstacle which precludes it from granting interim relief is a rule of national law must set aside that rule."

(3) One of the legal instruments used by the EC is the directive. A directive requires the member states to adopt legislation that conforms to the terms of the directive within a certain period of time. Directives have been used frequently, particularly to require harmonization of member state rules on matters affecting trade among the member states (e.g., environmental and consumer protection measures). In cases where a member state has failed to act within the specified time limit, the Court of Justice has ruled that provisions of the directive may have direct effect if the conditions specified in *van Gend & Loos* are met. See, e.g., Van Duyn v. Home Office, Case 41/74, [1974] ECR 1337. It has also ruled that individuals harmed by the failure of a member state to implement a directive have to be given a right of action for damages against the member state in certain circumstances. Francovich v. Italy, Case C–6/90, [1991] ECR I–5357. Such rulings obviously put pressure on the member states to implement directives promptly.

(4) The conclusion that EC law is supreme raises many of the same questions that arise in the U.S. in respect of federal-state relations. For example, to what extent does EC legislation preempt a field, so as to preclude member state legislation? The Court of Justice has not hesitated to find that member state legislation has been preempted. However, the recent amendments to the EC Treaty (the SEA and TEU) introduced the concept of "subsidiarity" to EC law:

> In areas which do not fall within its exclusive competence, the Community shall take action, in accordance with the principle of subsidiarity, only if and insofar as the objectives of the proposed action cannot be sufficiently achieved by the Member States and can therefore, by reason of the scale or effects of the proposed action, be better achieved by the Community.

EC Treaty, art. 5. This concept, combined with new provisions explicitly authorizing member states to impose stricter rules in certain areas (e.g., environment, consumer protection), so long as they are not otherwise inconsistent with the Treaty (EC Treaty, arts. 176, 153(f)), represents an interesting attempt to take local concerns into account in a federal system. Whether it will be given meaningful content remains to be seen.

A second example of preemption is raised by the following question: To what extent are member states prevented from applying local standards (e.g., health, safety, etc.) to bar entry of goods from other member states, assuming that those standards do not conflict with positive EC legislation? This question raises issues such as those found in so-called Dormant Commerce Clause cases under the U.S. Constitution. We touched on this issue in Section 3.6, and we will examine both the EU and U.S. approach to these problems in Chapter 14.

(5) Consider to what extent the supremacy of EC law over national law might allow member state governments to implement unpopular programs

opposed by national legislatures by not vigorously opposing such programs in EU institutions. What could a national legislature do to prevent this? This lack of accountability has given rise to discussion of whether there is a "democracy deficit" in the EU and, as noted in the prior subsection, motivates many of those who want to give more power to the European Parliament, so that there will be more popular control of EU institutions.

(6) Generally, over time the courts of the EU member states have accepted that EC law prevails over inconsistent national law, although German courts continue to claim that they could rule otherwise in certain circumstances. More specifically, the German Constitutional Court indicated early on that it reserved the right to review EC acts for consistency with the basic rights guaranteed in the German Constitution, but more recently it has decided that so long as the Court of Justice recognizes the existence of fundamental basic rights as a component of EC law, which it does,[7] the German court will not undertake such a review. The German court expressly reserves the right to do so, however, and it expressed a variant of this view most recently in 1993 in upholding the TEU against a claim that it violated the German Constitution. Brunner v. European Union Treaty, [1994] 1 CMLR 57, 89. It was initially expected that the United Kingdom would have difficulty accepting the primacy of EC law because of the traditional sovereign rights of Parliament. But to date, that has not seemed to be a problem. See generally George A. Bermann, Roger J. Goebel, William J. Davey & Eleanor M. Fox, European Community Law ch. 8 (2d ed. 2002).

(C) THE UNION'S POWER IN EXTERNAL COMMERCIAL RELATIONS

In this section we focus on the Union's power in external commercial relations. This power derives from Article 133 of the EC Treaty, which provides in part:

> 1.   The common commercial policy shall be based on uniform principles, particularly in regard to changes in tariff rates, the conclusion of tariff and trade agreements, the achievement of uniformity in measures of liberalization, export policy and measures to protect trade such as those to be taken in event of dumping or subsidies.

> 2.   The Commission shall submit proposals to the Council for implementing the common commercial policy.

> 3.   Where agreements with one or more States or international organizations need to be negotiated, the Commission shall make recommendations to the Council, which shall authorize the Commission to open the necessary negotiations.

---

7. Hauer   v.   Land   Rheinland–Pfalz, [1979] ECR 3727, 3745 ("[T]he Court is bound to draw inspiration from constitutional traditions common to Member States, so that measures which are incompatible with the fundamental rights recognized by the constitutions of those States are unacceptable in the Community * * * "). See also TEU, art. 6(2); Charter of Fundamental Rights of the European Union, approved at Nice, December 2000.

The Commission shall conduct these negotiations in consultation with a special committee appointed by the Council to assist the Commission in this task and within the framework of such directives as the Council may issue to it.

The EU negotiates trade agreements with third countries as follows: First, the Commission holds preliminary talks with the country concerned. If successful, the Commission recommends to the Council that formal negotiations be opened. If the Council agrees, it authorizes the Commission to negotiate along the lines of a specific mandate. The Commission then proceeds to negotiate the agreement under the watchful eye of a special committee composed of member state representatives (called the Article 133 Committee). If the negotiations succeed, the Commission initials the results on behalf of the EU and presents the results to the Council, which has the ultimate authority to approve or reject any agreement. The Council acts by qualified majority under Article 133. Parliamentary approval of Article 133 agreements is not required.

(1) Scope and Exclusivity of the Common Commercial Policy

OPINION 1/94

[1994]   ECR–I 5267
(World Trade Organization—WTO).

[The Community's Explicit External Powers]

The Commission's main contention is that the conclusion of both GATS [the WTO's General Agreement on Trade in Services] and TRIPs [the WTO Agreement on Trade–Related Aspects of Intellectual Property] falls within the exclusive competence conferred on the Community in commercial policy matters by Article [133] of the EC Treaty. That point of view has been vigorously disputed * * * by the Council, by the Member States * * * and by the European Parliament. * * *

As regards [services other than transport], it should be recalled at the outset that in Opinion 1/75 the Court * * * held that "the field of common commercial policy, and more particularly that of export policy, necessarily covers systems of aid for exports and more particularly measures concerning credits for the financing of local costs linked to export operations." The local costs in question concerned expenses incurred for the supply of both goods and services. Nevertheless, the Court recognized the exclusive competence of the Community, without drawing a distinction between goods and services.

In its Opinion 1/78, the Court rejected an interpretation of Article [133] "the effect of which would be to restrict the common commercial policy to the use of instruments intended to have an effect only on the traditional aspects of external trade." On the contrary, it considered that "the question of external trade must be governed from a wide point of view," as is confirmed by "the fact that the enumeration in Article [133] of the subjects covered by commercial policy . . . is conceived as a non-exhaustive enumeration.''

The Commission points out in its request for an opinion that in certain developed countries the services sector has become the dominant sector of the economy and that the global economy has been undergoing fundamental structural changes. The trend is for basic industry to be transferred to developing countries, whilst the developed economies have tended to become, in the main, exporters of services and of goods with a high value-added content. The Court notes that this trend is borne out by the WTO Agreement and its annexes, which were the subject of a single process of negotiation covering both goods and services.

Having regard to this trend in international trade, it follows from the open nature of the common commercial policy, within the meaning of the Treaty, that trade in services cannot immediately, and as a matter of principle, be excluded from the scope of Article [133], as some of the Governments which have submitted observations contend.

In order to make that conclusion more specific, however, one must take into account the definition of trade in services given in GATS in order to see whether the overall scheme of the Treaty is not such as to limit the extent to which trade in services can be included within Article [133].

Under Article I(2) of GATS trade in services is defined, for the purposes of that agreement, as comprising four modes of supply of services: (1) cross-frontier supplies not involving any movement of persons; (2) consumption abroad, which entails the movement of the consumer into the territory of the WTO member country in which the supplier is established; (3) commercial presence, i.e. the presence of a subsidiary or branch in the territory of the WTO member country in which the service is to be rendered; (4) the presence of natural persons from a WTO member country, enabling a supplier from one member country to supply services within the territory of any other member country.

As regards cross-frontier supplies, the service is rendered by a supplier established in one country to a consumer residing in another. The supplier does not move to the consumer's country; nor, conversely, does the consumer move to the supplier's country. That situation is, therefore, not unlike trade in goods, which is unquestionably covered by the common commercial policy within the meaning of the Treaty. There is thus no particular reason why such a supply should not fall within the concept of the common commercial policy.

The same cannot be said of the other three modes of supply of services covered by GATS, namely, consumption abroad, commercial presence and the presence of natural persons.

As regards natural persons, it is clear from Article 3 of the Treaty, which distinguishes between ''a common commercial policy'' in paragraph (b) and ''measures concerning the entry and movement of persons" in paragraph (d), that the treatment of nationals of non-member countries on crossing the external frontiers of Member States cannot be regarded as falling within the common commercial policy. More generally, the existence in the Treaty of specific chapters on the free movement of natural and legal persons shows that those matters do not fall within the common commercial policy.

It follows that the modes of supply of services referred to by GATS as "consumption abroad," "commercial presence" and the "presence of natural persons" are not covered by the common commercial policy.

* * *

The Commission's argument in support of its contention that the Community has exclusive competence under Article [133] is essentially that the rules concerning intellectual property rights are closely linked to trade in the products and services to which they apply.

It should be noted, first that Section 4 of Part III of TRIPs, which concerns the means of enforcement of intellectual property rights, contains specific rules as to measures to be applied at border crossing points. * * * Since measures of that type can be adopted autonomously by the Community institutions on the basis of Article [133] of the EC Treaty, it is for the Community alone to conclude international agreements on such matters.

However, as regards matters other than the provisions of TRIPs on the release into free circulation of counterfeit goods, the Commission's arguments cannot be accepted. [Although the Court conceded that there is a connection between intellectual property rights and trade in goods, it noted that is not enough to bring such rights them within the scope of Article 133, especially since they affect internal trade just as much as, if not more than, international trade. Moreover, the Court noted that while Articles 94, 95 and 308 provide a basis for harmonizing national laws on intellectual property, the decision-making rules under those articles differ from those applicable under Article 133.]

If the Community were to be recognized as having exclusive competence to enter into agreements with non-member countries to harmonize the protection of intellectual property and, at the same time, to achieve harmonization at Community level, the Community institutions would be able to escape the internal constraints to which they are subject in relation to procedures and to rules as to voting.

* * *

[The Community's Implied External Powers]

In the event of the Court rejecting its main contention that the Community has exclusive competence pursuant to Article [133], the Commission maintains in the alternative that the Community's exclusive competence to conclude GATS and TRIPs flows implicitly from the provisions of the Treaty establishing its internal competence, or from the existence of legislative acts of the institutions giving effect to that internal competence, or else from the need to enter into international commitments with a view to achieving an internal Community objective. The Commission also argues that, even if the Community does not have adequate powers on the basis of specific provisions of the Treaty or legislative acts of the institutions, it has exclusive competence by virtue of Articles [95 and 308] of the Treaty. The Council and the Member States which have submitted observations acknowledge that the Community has certain powers, but deny that they are exclusive.

With particular regard to GATS, the Commission cites three possible sources for exclusive external competence on the part of the Community: the powers conferred on the Community institutions by the Treaty at internal level, the need to conclude the agreement in order to achieve a Community objective, and, lastly, Articles [95 and 308].

The Commission argues, first, that there is no area or specific provision in GATS in respect of which the Community does not have corresponding powers to adopt measures at internal level. According to the Commission, those powers are set out in the chapters on the right of establishment, freedom to provide services and transport. Exclusive external competence flows from those internal powers.

That argument must be rejected.

It was on the basis of Article [71(1)(a)] which, as regards that part of a journey which takes place on Community territory, also concerns transport from or to non-member countries, that the Court held in *ERTA* that the "powers of the Community extend to relationships arising from international law, and hence involve the need in the sphere in question for agreements with the third countries concerned."

However, even in the field of transport, the Community's exclusive external competence does not automatically flow from its power to lay down rules at internal level. As the Court pointed out in *ERTA*, the Member States, whether acting individually or collectively, only lose their right to assume obligations with non-member countries as and when common rules which could be affected by those obligations come into being. Only insofar as common rules have been established at internal level does the external competence of the Community become exclusive. However, not all transport matters are already covered by common rules.

The Commission asserted at the hearing that the Member States' continuing freedom to conduct an external policy based on bilateral agreements with nonmember countries will inevitably lead to distortions in the flow of services and will progressively undermine the internal market. * * *

In reply to that argument, suffice it to say that there is nothing in the Treaty which prevents the institutions from arranging, in the common rules laid down by them, concerted action in relation to non-member countries or from prescribing the approach to be taken by the Member States in their external dealings. * * *

* * *

Unlike the chapter on transport, the chapters on the right of establishment and on freedom to provide services do not contain any provision expressly extending the competence of the Community to "relationships arising from international law." As has rightly been observed by the Council and most of the Member States which have submitted observations, the sole objective of those chapters is to secure the right of establishment and freedom to provide services for nationals of Member States. They contain no provisions on the problem of the first establishment of nationals of non-member countries and the rules governing their access to self-employed activities. One cannot therefore infer from those chapters that the Community has exclusive competence to conclude an agreement with non-member countries to liberalize first establishment and access to service markets, other than those which are the subject of cross-border supplies within the meaning of GATS, which are covered by Article [133].

Referring to Opinion 1/76, the Commission submits, second, that the Community's exclusive external competence is not confined to cases in which use has already been made of internal powers to adopt measures for the attainment of common policies. Whenever Community law has conferred on the institutions internal powers for the purposes of attaining specific objectives, the international competence of the Community implicitly flows, according to the Commission, from those provisions. It is enough that the Community's participation in the international agreement is necessary for the attainment of one of the objectives of the Community.

The Commission puts forward here both internal and external reasons to justify participation by the Community, and by the Community alone, in the conclusion of GATS and TRIPs. At [the] internal level, the Commission maintains that, without such participation, the coherence of the internal market would be impaired. At [the] external level, the European Community cannot allow itself to remain inactive on the international stage: the need for the conclusion of the WTO Agreement and its annexes, reflecting a global approach to international trade (embracing goods, services and intellectual property), is not in dispute.

That application of Opinion 1/76 to GATS cannot be accepted.

Opinion 1/76 related to an issue different from that arising from GATS. It concerned rationalization of the economic situation in the inland waterways sector in the Rhine and Moselle basins, and throughout all the Netherlands inland waterways and the German inland waterways linked to the Rhine basin, by elimination of short-term overcapacity. It was not possible to achieve that objective by the establishment of autonomous common rules, because of the traditional participation of vessels from Switzerland in navigation on the waterways in question. It was necessary, therefore, to bring Switzerland into the scheme envisaged by means of an international agreement. Similarly, in the context of conservation of the resources of the seas, the restriction, by means of internal legislative measures, of fishing on the high seas by vessels flying the flag of a Member State would hardly be effective if the same restrictions were not to apply to vessels flying the flag of a nonmember country bordering on the same seas. It is understandable, therefore, that external powers may be exercised, and thus become exclusive, without any internal legislation having first been adopted.

That is not the situation in the sphere of services: attainment of freedom of establishment and freedom to provide services for nationals of the Member States is not inextricably linked to the treatment to be afforded in the Community to nationals of non-member countries or in non-member countries to nationals of Member States of the Community.

Third, the Commission refers to Articles [95 and 308] of the Treaty as the basis of exclusive external competence.

As regards Article [95], it is undeniable that, where harmonizing powers have been exercised, the harmonization measures thus adopted may limit, or even remove, the freedom of the Member States to negotiate with non-member countries. However, an internal power to harmonize which has not been exercised in a specific field cannot confer exclusive external competence in that field on the Community.

Article [308], which enables the Community to cope with any insufficiency in the powers conferred on it, expressly or by implication, for the achievement of its objectives, cannot in itself vest exclusive competence in the Community at international level. Save where internal powers can only be effectively exercised at the same time as external powers, internal competence can give rise to exclusive external competence only if it is exercised. This applies a fortiori to Article [308].

* * *

Whenever the Community has included in its internal legislative acts provisions relating to the treatment of nationals of non-member countries or expressly conferred on its institutions powers to negotiate with non-member countries, it acquires exclusive external competence in the spheres covered by those acts.

The same applies in any event, even in the absence of any express provision authorizing its institutions to negotiate with non-member countries, where the Community has achieved complete harmonization of the rules governing access to a self-employed activity, because the common rules thus adopted could be affected within the meaning of *ERTA* if the Member States retained freedom to negotiate with non-member countries.

That is not the case in all service sectors, however, as the Commission has itself acknowledged.

It follows that competence to conclude GATS is shared between the Community and the Member States.

[The Commission raised arguments similar to the foregoing in respect of the TRIPS Agreement. The Court rejected them for the same reasons set out above in respect of GATS.]

At the hearing, the Commission drew the Court's attention to the problems which would arise, as regards the administration of the agreements, if the Community and the Member States were recognized as sharing competence to participate in the conclusion of the GATS and TRIPs agreements. While it is true that, in the negotiation of the agreements, the procedure under Article [133] of the Treaty prevailed subject to certain very minor adjustments, the Member States will, in the context of the WTO, undoubtedly seek to express their views individually on matters falling within their competence whenever no consensus has been found. Furthermore, interminable discussions will ensue to determine whether a given matter falls within the competence of the Community, so that the Community mechanisms laid down by the relevant provisions of the Treaty will apply, or whether it is within the competence of the Member States, in which case the consensus rule will operate. The Community's unity of action *vis-à-vis* the rest of the world will thus be undermined and its negotiating power greatly weakened.

In response to that concern, which is quite legitimate, it must be stressed, first, that any problems which may arise in implementation of the WTO Agreement and its annexes as regards the coordination necessary to ensure unity of action where the Community and the Member States participate jointly cannot modify the answer to the question of competence, that being a prior issue. As the Council has pointed out, resolution of the issue of the allocation of competence cannot depend on problems which may possibly arise in administration of the agreements.

Next, where it is apparent that the subject-matter of an agreement or convention falls in part within the competence of the Community and in part within that of the Member States, it is essential to ensure close cooperation between the Member States and the Community institutions, both in the process of negotiation and conclusion and in the fulfilment of the commitments entered into. That obligation to cooperate flows from the requirement of unity in the international representation of the Community.

The duty to cooperate is all the more imperative in the case of agreements such as those annexed to the WTO Agreement, which are inextricably interlinked, and in view of the cross-retaliation measures established by the [WTO] Dispute Settlement Understanding. Thus, in the absence of close cooperation, where a Member State, duly authorized within its sphere of competence to take cross-retaliation measures, considered that they would be ineffective if taken in the fields covered by GATS or TRIPs, it would not, under Community law, be empowered to retaliate in the area of trade in goods, since that is an area which on any view falls within the exclusive competence of the Community under

Article [133] of the Treaty. Conversely, if the Community were given the right to retaliate in the sector of goods but found itself incapable of exercising that right, it would, in the absence of close cooperation, find itself unable, in law, to retaliate in the areas covered by GATS or TRIPs, those being within the competence of the Member States.

Notes and Questions

1. The Court also ruled that the EC had the exclusive power to conclude the GATT-related agreements on trade in goods, including products subject to the ECSC and Euratom Treaties, and that Article 133 was a sufficient basis for such action, even in respect of the agreements on agriculture and sanitary and phytosanitary measures. In this regard, the Court stated: "The objective of the [WTO] Agreement on Agriculture is to establish, on a worldwide basis, a fair and market-oriented agricultural trading system (see the preamble to that Agreement). The fact that commitments entered into under that Agreement require internal measures to be adopted on the basis of Article [37] of the Treaty does not prevent the international commitments themselves from being entered into pursuant to Article [133] alone." When ratified, the 2000 Nice Treaty will expand the scope of Article 133.

(2) How does the general foreign relations power of the European Union compare with that of the United States federal government? How do its foreign commercial powers compare? Is there an "implied powers doctrine" in the European Union?

(2) Implementation of the Common Commercial Policy

At the base of the common commercial policy is the common tariff, known as the Combined Nomenclature (CN), that classifies and establishes tariff rates for all products imported into the EU. It is supplemented by the Taric, the integrated EU tariff, which is used for statistical reporting and which incorporates special import provisions not included in the CN. Generally speaking there are two tariff rates for each product: the autonomous rate applicable to those countries not accorded most-favored-nation treatment and the conventional rate applicable, inter alia, to goods from GATT members. (In practice, all countries generally receive the MFN (or a lower) rate.) In addition, the EU has entered into numerous preferential agreements that provide for duty-free entry of (or reduced duties on) goods originating in a country entitled to the preference and otherwise satisfying the terms of the applicable agreement. The EU has such agreements with most European and Mediterranean countries and most developing countries, some of which are described in the next subsection and others in Chapter 11 infra.

Pursuant to Article 133, rules for imports have been adopted, under which restrictions may be imposed on imports causing injury to an EU industry. In addition, the EU has adopted procedures pursuant to which antidumping duties may be imposed upon dumped products and countervailing duties may be imposed upon subsidized products. See Chapters 16–18 infra. It has also adopted procedures allowing imposition of duties or quotas or the suspension or withdrawal of trade concessions in response to injurious illicit commercial practices of other nations.

Notes and Questions

(1) As a negotiator for the United States, how would you satisfy yourself that an EU negotiating team consisting of Commission officials was authorized to negotiate pursuant to Article 133(3)? To enter into a particular agreement? Is the involvement of the Article 133 Committee sufficient protection? One of the French objections to the 1992 EU–U.S. agreement on agricultural trade matters was that the Commission had exceeded its negotiating mandate. The French objections ultimately led to changes in the agreement.

(2) If the Council (consisting of member state representatives) has to approve any agreement negotiated by the Commission, and if the Article 133 Committee (also consisting of member state representatives) oversees negotiations, why does it matter whether the member states participate directly in negotiations?

(3) In terms of implementing controversial international trade policies, would you say that it is easier, harder, or no different, to do in the EU than in the United States?

(3) Internal Legal Effect of International Agreements Under EC Law

The Court of Justice has held that international agreements form part of the EU legal system and that, in some cases, they may be invoked by individuals in member state courts, just as provisions of the EC Treaty may be invoked under *van Gend & Loos*. Under the Court's cases, a provision of an international agreement concluded by the EU may have direct effect if the provision sets forth an unconditional obligation that is central to the purpose of the agreement. In HAUPT-ZOLLAMT MAINZ v. C.A. KUPFERBERG & CIE., Case 104/81, [1982] ECR 3641, the Court stated (at 3665):

> * * * In order to reply to the question on the direct effect of the first paragraph of Article 21 of the Agreement between the Community and Portugal [then not a member state] it is necessary to analyze the provision in light of both the object and purpose of the Agreement and its context.
>
> The purpose of the Agreement is to create a system of free trade in which rules restricting commerce are eliminated in respect of virtually all trade in products originating in the territory of the parties, in particular by abolishing customs duties and charges having equivalent effect and eliminating quantitative restrictions and measures having equivalent effect.
>
> Seen in that context the first paragraph of Article 21 of the Agreement seeks to prevent the liberalization of the trade in goods through the abolition of customs duties and charges having equivalent effect and quantitative restrictions and measures having equiva-

lent effect from being rendered nugatory by fiscal practices of the Contracting Parties. That would be so if the product imported of one party were taxed more heavily than the similar domestic products which it encounters on the market of the other party.

It appears from the foregoing that the first paragraph of Article 21 of the Agreement imposes on the Contracting Parties an unconditional rule against discrimination in matters of taxation, which is dependent only on a finding that the products affected by a particular system of taxation are of like nature, and the limits of which are the direct consequence of the purpose of the Agreement. As such this provision may be applied by a court and thus produce direct effects throughout the Community.

The Court has limited the scope of the *Kupferberg* holding for trade agreements, however, by also ruling that even if a provision in an EU trade agreement is identical to one in the EC Treaty, the provision in the trade agreement may not be interpreted as broadly as the EC Treaty provision because the purposes of the two treaties are different. See, e.g, Polydor Ltd. v. Harlequin Records Shop Ltd., Case 270/80, [1982] ECR 329; European Economic Area, Opinion 1/91, [1991] ECR I–6079.

In INTERNATIONAL FRUIT CO. v. PRODUKTSCHAP, Cases 21–24/72, [1972] ECR 1219, 1227–1228, the Court of Justice considered whether GATT Article XI, which bans the use of quotas, had direct effect. It concluded that it did not because of what might be called the various loopholes in GATT. With the creation of the WTO and its stricter disciplines and binding dispute settlement system, the question arose again. In PORTUGUESE REPUBLIC v. COUNCIL, Case C–149/96, [1998] ECR I-7379, Portugal challenged the decision implementing a textiles agreement with India and Pakistan on grounds that it violated WTO rules, as well as certain rules and principles of Community law. As to the possibility of giving direct effect to WTO rules, the Court stated (paras. 36–48):]

While it is true that the WTO agreements, as the Portuguese Government observes, differ significantly from the provisions of GATT 1947, in particular by reason of the strengthening of the system of safeguards and the mechanism for resolving disputes, the system resulting from those agreements nevertheless accords considerable importance to negotiation between the parties.

[Noting WTO provisions dealing with failures to implement dispute settlement rulings, which include the possibility of negotiations over compensation on a temporary basis pending implementation, the Court stated that] to require the judicial organs to refrain from applying the rules of domestic law which are inconsistent with the WTO agreements would have the consequence of depriving the legislative or executive organs of the contracting parties of the possibility afforded by Article 22 of [the Dispute Settlement Understanding] of entering into negotiated arrangements even on a temporary basis.

* * *

As regards, more particularly, the application of the WTO agreements in the Community legal order, it must be noted that, according to its preamble, the agreement establishing the WTO, including the annexes, is still founded, like GATT 1947, on the principle of negotiations with a view to "entering into reciprocal and mutually advantageous arrangements" and is thus distinguished, from the viewpoint of the Community, from the agreements concluded between the Community and non-member countries which introduce a certain asymmetry of obligations, or create special relations of integration with the Community, such as the agreement which the Court was required to interpret in *Kupferberg*.

It is common ground, moreover, that some of the contracting parties, which are among the most important commercial partners of the Community, have concluded from the subject-matter and purpose of the WTO agreements that they are not among the rules applicable by their judicial organs when reviewing the legality of their rules of domestic law.

Admittedly, the fact that the courts of one of the parties consider that some of the provisions of the agreement concluded by the Community are of direct application whereas the courts of the other party do not recognize such direct application is not in itself such as to constitute a lack of reciprocity in the implementation of the agreement.

However, the lack of reciprocity in that regard on the part of the Community's trading partners, in relation to the WTO agreements which are based on reciprocal and mutually advantageous arrangements and which must *ipso facto* be distinguished from agreements concluded by the Community, * * * may lead to disuniform application of the WTO rules.

To accept that the role of ensuring that those rules comply with Community law devolves directly on the Community judicature would deprive the legislative or executive organs of the Community of the scope for maneuver enjoyed by their counterparts in the Community's trading partners.

It follows from all those considerations that, having regard to their nature and structure, the WTO agreements are not in principle among the rules in the light of which the Court is to review the legality of measures adopted by the Community institutions.

Notes and Questions

(1) The foregoing opinion is of particular interest because of its characterization of the General Agreement on Tariffs and Trade and the WTO Dispute Settlement Understanding, which are a major focus of this book. As

you read the rest of the materials in the book, consider whether the Court's characterization is apt. The Court of Justice did recognize in the *Portuguese Republic* case, at paragraph 49, as it has elsewhere that:

> [W]here the Community intended to implement a particular obligation assumed in the context of the WTO, or where the Community measure refers expressly to the precise provisions of the WTO agreements, [then] it is [appropriate] for the Court to review the legality of the Community measure in question in the light of the WTO rules.

In a subsequent case, the Court elaborated on this point as follows:

> 2. The procedural requirements of Article 50 of the TRIPS Agreement, and in particular Article 50(6), are not such as to create rights upon which individuals may rely directly before the Community courts and the courts of the Member States. Nevertheless, where the judicial authorities are called upon to apply national rules with a view to ordering provisional measures for the protection of intellectual property rights falling within a field to which the TRIPs Agreement applies and in respect of which the Community has already legislated, they are required to do so as far as possible in the light of the wording and purpose of Article 50(6) of the TRIPs Agreement, taking account, more particularly, of all the circumstances of the case before them, so as to ensure that a balance is struck between the competing rights and obligations of the intellectual property right holder and of the defendant.

Schieving–Nijstad v. Groeneveld, Case C–89–99, [2001] ECR I — (September 13, 2001) (answer to question 2).

(2) How do the decisions in *International Fruit* and *Portuguese Republic* on the direct effect of the General Agreement compare to the decisions discussed in Section 3.4 supra on self-executing international agreements and standing?

(3) Assuming that a treaty concluded by the EU was found to have direct effects, how would a conflict between the treaty and the Treaty of Rome be resolved? The treaty and prior EC legislation? The treaty and subsequent EC legislation? The treaty and a member state constitution? The treaty and prior member state legislation? The treaty and subsequent member state legislation?

(D) THE ECONOMIC INTEGRATION OF EUROPE

WILLIAM J. DAVEY, EUROPEAN INTEGRATION: REFLECTIONS ON ITS LIMITS AND EFFECTS[8]

E. Lessons From European Economic Integration

The recent history of Europe presents a textbook study of how economic integration proceeds. In particular, it suggests (i) that there are certain criteria that must be met before it is possible to move from

---

8. Supra note 4, at 194–203.

one level of economic integration to the next and (ii) that there may be basic sociopolitical factors that limit the economic integration process.

1.   Requirements for Integration

The experience of the EC suggests that there are at least two basic requirements for successful market integration to occur. First, there must be institutions with meaningful powers that have integration as one of their fundamental goals. In this connection, there needs to be both an institution that affirmatively promotes market integration and one that effectively enforces the integrating rules that are adopted. Second, there must be some minimum degree of commonality of interests (economic, environmental, social, etc.) among the countries that are attempting to integrate their markets. In the case of the EC, both of these requirements have been met.

Much of the success of the EC can be attributed to the existence of formal institutions at the European level that have pressed the case for further integration and that have taken steps to encourage and enforce integration. In particular, the Commission has served throughout most of the EC's history as a pro-market-integration force. Even when progress toward the single market was slow, the Commission continued to push for it. The actions of the Commission must be compared to the actions of the member states, acting individually or through the Council. By and large, the member states have often opposed expansive interpretations of the EC Treaty, and in particular the powers of the Community and the supremacy of Community law. They also tend to reflect parochial national interests in decisionmaking. This has not been true of all member states all of the time, but even the member states that on a general level have endorsed a strong and expanding Community have often opposed strength in the Community in specific cases when issues of particular concern to them were at stake. Thus, the existence of an institution like the Commission that has integration as a primary goal would seem to be a virtual prerequisite to market integration. Without such an institution, the natural tendencies of nations to resist incursions on their sovereignty (or detriments to groups in their populations) will greatly retard progress toward integration. This conclusion is underlined by the EC–EFTA experience, where the lack of meaningful institutions was viewed as a hindrance to integration. The EEA Agreement represents an improvement over the cooperation based on the EC–EFTA free trade agreements, but it does not provide for the transfer of any sovereign powers to EEA institutions and does not limit the power of decision of the parties. Intensification of integration in simple free trade areas may be expected to proceed slowly.

As important as effective institutions are as a driving force for integration, there is also a need for an institution to ensure that the rules providing for integration are enforced. In the case of the EC, the European Court of Justice (ECJ) has played a critical role in that regard. From its early decisions that established the right of individuals to invoke Community law in national courts, and the supremacy of Community rules over national rules, to far-reaching decisions striking down disguised barriers to trade, the ECJ has played a critical role in the integration process. It seems clear that integration would have proceeded at a much slower pace, but for the ECJ. In most of its path-breaking decisions, the member states (or some of them) were opposed to the position taken by the ECJ. Yet, they ultimately accepted the decisions, suggesting that their opposition was not fundamental, but that some institutional mechanism to overcome it was required. The ECJ has proved to be effective in that role.

The second requirement for market integration is a certain degree of commonality between participants in the market. This is not to say that countries have to be at identical levels of economic development with similar views on economic, environmental and social issues generally. But there is a need to have some degree of congruence. In the case of the EC, there is variance in the levels of development of the various member states which has caused problems. But, as noted above, they have been reduced through the provision of substantial aid from the richer countries to the poorer ones. Without such a process, one can wonder whether the Community would have integrated to the extent that it has, since there probably would have been more serious disputes over many issues. In particular, the use of mutual recognition as a market-unifying principle, both by the Court and in Community legislation, would have been much more restricted if the member states varied too widely in their approaches to regulating markets. As important, the free movement of workers, which is a fundamental part of an integrated market, is unlikely to be accepted if there are significant variations in the wealth of the constituent members since such variation will likely lead to significant, and potentially socially destabilizing, migration.

2.   *The Limitations on Integration*

The EC is already having to confront the question of whether there are natural limits on economic or market integration. In essence these potential limits seem to stem from a lack of a commonly accepted agreement between the various member states as to what policies need to be integrated in order to achieve an optimal level of market integration, while respecting national sovereignty. The lack of agreement appears at two levels: disagreements over the need to harmonize certain policies at all; and disagreements about what is the proper balance between harmonization and the rights of individual member states (or subdivisions thereof) to make their own, independent decisions on matters directly affecting them.

An example of a basic policy disagreement over the need for integration of a specific policy would be the UK decision to eschew monetary union and the social policy provisions to which others agreed at Maastricht. As the number of member states expands, such differences may be expected to occur more often. Fear of such a result has animated those who argue that the current Community should be "deepened" before it is "widened." In light of the decision to open accession negotiations with Austria, Finland, Norway and Sweden, it seems that the forces in favor of widening the Community first have won. Time will tell whether in fact a widened Community will be a less integrated one.

The second type of disagreement presents more fundamental problems and may arise even if there is fairly broad agreement on the general outlines of all major policies among the member states. This type of disagreement stems from the desire of local communities to have some say over matters that effect their quality of life directly. It is not about the desirability of eliminating "red tape" at borders or standardizing essentially mechanical details, such as the characteristics of basic products, but rather about such topics as the appropriate level of environmental protection. For example, all member states may agree on the need to regulate air pollution, but one or more may feel that it wants stricter standards than the ones to which the others are willing to agree. The current debate over "subsidiarity" highlights this problem. As discussed below, drawing the line between what should be regulated at the Community level and what may be done at the local level will probably preoccupy the Community in the coming years and will serve as a limit on further integration.

The process of European integration is instructive for those thinking about the future of the globalization process in the world at large, both economically and otherwise. Much of the globalization process is driven by factors beyond the control of governments, but the European experience suggests that such factors alone are not enough to maintain momentum toward a truly integrated global economy. It suggests, in particular, that the process needs institutions to push it forward and that even with relatively strong institutions, there are fundamental limits on the process imposed by desires for local autonomy over certain issues. On a practical level, it suggests that further integration of the world economy of the sort epitomized by GATT's Uruguay Round agenda may only be practical if combined with stronger institutions for rulemaking and improved dispute settlement procedures for rule enforcement. But such changes are precisely those that are strenuously opposed by groups seeking local autonomy. These factors suggest that the process of globalization may proceed more slowly in the near future than it has in the recent past.

SECTION 4.3 JAPAN

Japan is a key player on the world economic scene. Compared to the United States and the EU, however, Japan is often said to have played a relatively minor role in the GATT system and in the Uruguay Round negotiations. Why might this be so? Is it due to differences in governmental structure? To societal differences? To a desire not to aggravate trading partners upset with Japan's long-running large trade surplus (estimated at $90 billion for the 12 months ending June 2001)?[1]

---

1. The Economist, Sept. 1, 2001, at 87.

In the short space available, we highlight two aspects of the operation and formation of trade policy in Japan that are important in the WTO context. We first consider a practice relating to the operation of trade policies and measures known as administrative guidance. This term refers to the practice of government agencies giving written or oral advice, requests or instructions to the private sector. While this practice is generally not based on any statutory provisions and the advice, etc. is not legally enforceable, it is in fact typically followed. As such, the question is raised whether it should be viewed as a legally binding regulation would be in another country. In particular, should administrative guidance be assimilated to a measure or requirement that might be challenged for violating WTO rules. The fact that such guidance is informal means, of course, that its existence may be difficult to discover.

Second, as to trade policy formation, it is commonly believed that the various government ministries play a critical role, one that is much more important that of the Diet (Japan's parliament). These ministries are advised by various advisory councils, committees and study groups, whose members include business leaders, scholars and others. Reportedly, there is often tension and conflict among the various agencies and ministries in charge of formulating and executing trade policy. As two commentators have noted, "Even though the Cabinet is the forum in which such disagreements are to be reconciled, sometimes such conflicts persist and are difficult to resolve. In these cases, the [long-time dominant party—the Liberal Democratic Party] may act as a mediator and may try to reconcile the different points of view by suggesting a compromise. In any event, the bureaucracy plays a vital role in politics and also in economic policy because it is the key ministries where the best human resources and information about industries are pooled together. It is natural, then, that the real struggles take place there, in the very heart of the power structure. In this sense, something comparable to the conflict and tension between the Congress and the executive branch in the United States is present in the relationship among the key ministries." Mitsuo Matsushita & Thomas J. Schoenbaum, Japanese International Trade and Investment 25 (1989).

How does the role of the bureaucracy simplify or complicate trade negotiations with Japan? Does it call into question the power of the Prime Minister to carry out commitments made in international negotiations? How does this problem compare to similar problems noted earlier in respect of the United States (President vs. Congress—Section 3.2 supra) and of the EU (Commission vs. member states—Section 4.2 supra)? Given their respective systems, would you expect trade negotiators for the U.S., the EU or Japan to be more organized and coordinated? In terms of implementing controversial international trade policies, would you say that it is easier, harder or no different, to do in Japan as compared to the United States and the EU?

Chapter 5

INTERNATIONAL LAW AND IN-TERNATIONAL ECONOMIC RELATIONS

SECTION 5.1 INTRODUCTION: WHAT IS INTERNATIONAL LAW AND WHY DO NATIONS UTILIZE IT?

(A) INTERNATIONAL LAW AND INTERNATIONAL ECONOMIC LAW

Previous chapters have developed fundamental economic concepts, presented the basics of international sales transactions and explored important aspects of national government regulation. In this and the next two chapters, we introduce the basics of international law, which operates as the "constitution" for international economic relations.[1] To better understand this law, it is important to become acquainted with some of the fundamental concepts of international law and to understand the context of the more specialized international law relating to economic affairs. The latter topic includes both "international economic law" and "international economic organizations." These topics are discussed in the present chapter. In the next two chapters, we introduce other crucial aspects of this "constitution." Chapter 6 examines the most important institution in the world trading system, the World Trade Organization (WTO). Chapter 7 discusses the dispute settlement system that is so significant and so central to this international "constitution."

(B) INTERNATIONAL LAW

This book cannot, of course, consider very deeply the many aspects and complex facets of international law.[2] Some readers will have developed knowledge of that subject elsewhere. However, for readers who

---

1. See generally John H. Jackson, The World Trading System (2nd ed. 1997).

2. For additional materials, see Lori F. Damrosch et al, International Law: Cases and Materials (4th ed. 2001); Barry E. Carter & Phillip R. Trimble, International Law (3rd ed. 1999); Ian Brownlie, Principles of Public International Law (5th ed. 1998); Henry J. Steiner, Detlev F. Vagts & Harold H. Koh, Transnational Legal Problems: Materials and Text (4th ed. 1994).

have not had such opportunity, the next section has been designed to introduce some of the basic concepts of international law. The later sections will focus more particularly on international economic law and the landscape of international economic institutions and organizations.

When considering international law, the reader might reflect on the following questions or propositions:

1) What is the theoretical basis for international law rules and the obligation to follow them?

2) Sources of international law have often been divided into so-called "customary international law" norms, and "conventional" or "treaty" norms (treaties are sometimes called "conventions"). It is important to understand the distinction between these and the interplay between them. International economic law tends to focus on treaty law, since arguably there are very few substantive customary international law norms for economic behavior.

3) What are the important aspects of treaty law? The Vienna Convention on the Law of Treaties (1980), parts of which reflect rules of customary international law, is particularly relevant. For example, its treaty interpretation rules are very important.

4) An important question is the relationship of international treaties to domestic law. This question was taken up for the United States in Chapter 3 and for the EU in Chapter 4, but the relationship varies from country to country and constitution to constitution. We can only touch on that relation in this chapter, but in considering trade policy questions in later chapters, we often encounter issues about this relationship.

5) Sometimes it is hard for common law students and practitioners to understand that international law does not have a strict "stare decisis" precedent system. Like in many other legal systems in the world, courts or tribunals do not feel as strongly obligated to follow prior precedent as would be the case in common law systems. Nevertheless, precedent plays an important persuasive role, as will be seen throughout this book.

6) Traditional international law has been deemed to provide rules that govern relationships between governments. Thus, the basic origin of international law suggests a very small role for individuals or private firms. Governments enter into a treaty, or invoke a dispute settlement process. When individuals or private firms have a grievance against a foreign government, typically they must go to their own government and try to persuade their government to provide "diplomatic protection" in the sense of carrying their case forward to an international forum. This can be quite confusing at times. Increasingly this different legal status for governments as compared to individuals or firms is being broken down.

7) The role of the individual under international law, both as a legal entity obligated to obey international law norms and as a legal entity benefited by international law norms (such as human rights rules), has

been evolving. This evolution has been particularly rapid since World War II and it is now generally accepted that individuals do have a certain international legal status.

8) These various trends also relate to the question of "public participation" in international law processes. With the increasing attention for globalization and its impact on society, many international procedures and organizations have been criticized because they operate under diplomatic practices where only governments have access to information, the right to bring procedures or the right to participate in meetings. This is being strongly challenged in a number of countries by interest groups and academics who criticize the antidemocratic character of globalization and of these diplomatic traditions in international organizations.

(C) BASIC THEORY OF INTERNATIONAL OBLIGATIONS AND POLICIES SUPPORTING A "RULE BASED" SYSTEM

Why do or should nations follow international obligations? The "theory of international law" has long been a subject for extensive discussion and writings. A few extracts should suggest the flavor:

LOUIS HENKIN, HOW NATIONS BEHAVE, LAW AND FOREIGN POLICY 47 (2d ed. 1979)

It is probably the case that almost all nations observe almost all principles of international law and almost all of their obligations almost all of the time.

OSCAR SCHACHTER, TOWARDS A THEORY OF INTERNATIONAL OBLIGATION [3]

* * * As a subject, the "foundation of obligation" is as old as international law itself; it had a prominent place in the seminal treatises of the founding fathers—Suarez, Vittoria, Grotius, Pufendorf et al—and it remained a central issue in the great controversies of the nineteenth century. In our century it has had a lesser place; it was largely overtaken by the discussion of "sources" and evidence, centered around Article 38 of the Statute of the International Court. Although subordinated, it was not neglected and each of the leading scholars of the twentieth century found himself impelled to advance a fresh analysis. No single theory has received general agreement and sometimes it seems as though there are

---

3. From The Effectiveness of International Decisions (Papers and proceedings of a conference of the American Society of International Law) 9, 9–12, 30–31 (Steven M. Schwebel ed., 1971). Reprinted by permission of A.W. Sijthoff International Publishing Co. N.V., Leyden. Interested readers may also want to see: Thomas M. Franck, Fairness in International Law and Institu- tions (1995); Rosalyn Higgins, Problems & Process: International Law and How We Use It (1994); Abram Chayes and Antonia Handler Chayes, The New Sovereignty: Compliance With International Regulatory Agreements (1995); Louis Henkin, International Law: Politics and Values (1995); Oscar Schachter, International Law in Theory and Practice (1991).

as many theories or at least formulations as there are scholars. We can list at least a baker's dozen of "candidates" which have been put forward as the basis (or as one of the bases) of obligation in international law:

(i) Consent of states

(ii) Customary practice

(iii) A sense of "rightness"—the juridical conscience

(iv) Natural law or natural reason

(v) Social necessity

(vi) The will of the international community (the "consensus" of the international community)

(vii) Direct (or "stigmatic") intuition

(viii) Common purposes of the participants

(ix) Effectiveness

(x) Sanctions

(xi) "Systemic" goals

xii) Shared expectations as to authority

(xiii) Rules of recognition

On looking at this wide array of ideas concerning the "true" or "correct" basis of obligation in international law it may be wondered, on the one hand, whether the choice of a "basis" has any great practical significance and, on the other, whether the diversity of opinion does not reveal a radical weakness in the conceptual structure of international law.

For some pragmatically-inclined international lawyers, the issue is not likely to be regarded as important. As long as the obligation itself—the legal norm or prescription—can be identified in one of the so-called formal sources—treaty or custom or in general principles of law—it seems to matter little what the underlying basis of the obligation may be. It is, therefore, understandable that most contemporary treatises and textbooks on international law pass quickly and lightly over the problem of the "foundation." Like the chaplain's opening prayer at public meetings, it has little effect on what is said afterwards. The practical international lawyer is supposed to be concerned not with the foundation of obligation but with the so-called "sources," formal and material.

But this is more easily said than done. Somehow conceptions as to the basis of obligation arise time and again, and not only in theoretical discussion about the binding force of international law. They come up in concrete controversies as to whether a rule of law has emerged or has been terminated; whether an event is a violation or a precedent; and whether practice under a treaty is accepted as law. They are involved in dealing with situations in which solemn declarations, couched in legal terminology, are adopted by official bodies which have no formal authority to lay down prescriptive rules. They come up when there is substantial variance between what is preached and what is practiced; or when consensus (or expectations) are limited in geographical terms or in duration. These are not, of course, new problems and over the years they have been the subject of much jurisprudential writing. But in the last few years the general problem has assumed a new dimension. The peculiar features of contemporary international society have generated considerable normative activity without at the same time involving commensurate use of the formal procedures for international "legislation" and adjudication.

It may be useful to recall the main factors which have emerged in international life in the last few years to give enhanced importance to problems of indeterminacy of obligation.

First, there has been the much-discussed "quasi-legislative" activity by the General Assembly and other United Nations bodies purporting to lay down, expressly or by implication, requirements of State conduct or to terminate or modify existing requirements.

Second, there has been a recognition of so-called "rules of the game," based on implicit understandings or unilateral actions and acquiescence. This has been a notable feature of Great Power behavior in regard to their use of armed force.

Third, there have been the social revolutions which have overturned traditional orders and have challenged the assumptions on which prior conceptions of authority were based.

Fourth, the growing interdependence of States—especially in economic and technological activities—has vastly increased patterns of cooperation and reciprocal behavior which have not been institutionalized in the traditional modes of lawmaking.

Fifth, the increased "permeability" of national States has resulted in a diminishing barrier between matters of international concern and those of domestic jurisdiction. Related to this is the fact that the United Nations Charter—particularly its articles relating to respect for human rights and self-determination of peoples—has brought domestic activities before collective organs for appraisal on the basis of international criteria.

Sixth, the expansion of science and technology with international impact both beneficial and harmful has given rise to informal means of setting standards and exercising supervision without entering into tight and tidy legal instruments.

The mere statement of these trends indicates how extensive and far-reaching are normative processes which cannot easily be placed into the categories of treaty and customary law, at least as these terms have been applied traditionally. Lawyers are made uncomfortable by this and they ceaselessly endeavor to pour the new wine into the old bottles and to market it under the time-honored labels. They will treat many of the cases as problems of treaty interpretation; others will be dealt with on the assumptions applicable to traditional customary law. But when we examine the arguments and the grounds for decision, we find more frequently than not that the test of whether a "binding" rule exists or should be applied will involve basic jurisprudential assumptions. Even the International Court of Justice, which is governed expressly by Article 38 of its Statute as to the sources of law, has demonstrated time and again that in their deliberative process the judges have had to look to theory to evaluate practice.

* * *

By way of conclusion I shall anticipate some objections to the main tenor of my thesis and offer a brief defense.

First there is the criticism of those who will consider that "legal obligation" may be dissolved by having it depend on expectations, perceptions and probable compliance. In their view "legality like virtue is not a matter of degree" and while we may have compassion we should have no uncertainty when the fallen damsel has indeed fallen. But actually most of us will view virtue as a matter of degree and we should recognize that legal obligation—whether national or international—also may involve "degrees" and that it will depend on attitudes, expectations and compliance. True, these factors will in turn depend on law. The circularity is there, but it is not vicious; it simply takes account of interactions and influences. To be sure, at a given point one may have to decide in a concrete context whether or not an obligation exists (this can also be stated in operational terms) and that judgment will have to be made on the basis of the relevant variables. The more serious risk is to live in a "make-believe" world where the "law is always the law" and as a consequence in cynical reaction to reject a large body of normative phenomena that are actually operative in international behavior. To impose hard-and-fast categories on a world filled with indeterminancies and circularities can only result in a pseudo-realism which does justice neither to our experience nor to our higher purposes.

A second objection may come from those who believe that diverse political and cultural determinants preclude any truly international obligations in today's world. But this is a question of empirical fact, not of *a priori* judgment, and, as we indicated above, our experience provides enough evidence to indicate that divergent systems and beliefs exhibit concordances on a wide array of international norms. We have ample proof that mankind shares common characteristics and needs and its efforts to satisfy those needs provide a realistic basis for an international normative structure. In our view the specific features of that structure must be identified and validated in terms of shared expectations and attitudes, rather than in trans-empirical terms.

JOHN H. JACKSON, WORLD TRADE AND THE
LAW OF GATT 757, 760, 763 (1969)[4]

Departures from legal norms always occur in a legal system, to one degree or another. There is nothing unique about GATT or international legal norms in this respect. Many domestic laws fall into disuse or are abused. There is usually a price to be paid, however, for the widespread existence of practice that is inconsistent with the legal obligations. The price is not always easy to measure, but often the phrase "disrespect for the law" is used as a shorthand expression for it. The existence of practice that is inconsistent with legal rules, particularly when such divergent practice results in profit of one kind or another, usually increases the incentive for other departures from the rule and, therefore, the number of other departures. Consequently, one of the values of a legal rule—the enhancement of stability and predictability—is lost. Of course the practice of departing from legal rules can be limited to specific types of rules, and this can support an argument that the "custom" is itself a norm that now assists attainment of the goals of the legal system. But there are two detriments associated with such "customary" norms. First, the customary norms are usually less well-defined than legislated or agreed norms and therefore promote activity that is less stable and less predictable. Secondly, and perhaps more serious, when the customary activity is directly inconsistent with the legal norm, there are conflicting signals emitted in the prediction process and there is a danger that the custom of departing from the legal rule will encourage (or at least not discourage) departures from other legal rules.

* * *

Thus it can be seen that a variety of techniques have been utilized in GATT to achieve some of the basic objectives of the international community with respect to international trade and commerce. The four mentioned above can be summarized as: (1) legal norms, backed by a complaint or a dispute-settling procedure; (2) elaborate discussion and consultation, with a view to alerting other nations to future national policies; (3) the use of Working Parties, subcommittees, and discussions in plenary sessions to bring moral force upon countries to conform their individual national policies and practices to either the legal norms or the stated objectives of GATT; and (4) the use of negotiation and bargaining as a means to formulate new obligations and to settle differences about old obligations.

One of the features in GATT—and most likely a feature in many international organizations and institutions today—that makes it more complex to evaluate the degree of "compliance" with the existing legal norms is the confusion and ambiguity that exists about the nature of some of those norms. Some of these norms can be separated into two

---

4. From World Trade and the Law of GATT by John H. Jackson, copyright 1969, by the Bobbs Merrill Company, Inc. Reprinted by permission. All rights reserved.

groups. One group might be labeled "norms of obligations" while another group may be labeled "norms of aspiration." This dichotomy touches a basic problem of legal philosophy that exists in domestic law also. It requires elaboration.

Norms of obligations can be used to designate those legal norms toward which the attitude is that a person or country should feel obligated to follow. This feeling of obligation may stem from an idea of moral duty or a pragmatic recognition of consequences that might follow if the norm is broken but, in either case, the term designates more than just a "statement of purpose or objective."

A "norm of aspiration," on the other hand, can be used to designate a mode of conduct that everyone thinks is desirable, but toward which there is no feeling of obligation. Nations generally feel obligated to fulfill their treaty agreements. But when an international body votes a "recommendation," even if a nation voted in favor of the recommendation, it may not feel obligated to carry out that recommendation.

* * *

This somewhat elaborate discussion leads to the following point: there is a danger in mixing "norms of obligation" in the same instrument with "norms of aspiration," when the distinction between the two is not clearly signaled to the participants of that instrument. The danger is that some countries will consider a particular phrase to be a "norm of obligation" while others will consider the same phrase to be a "norm of aspiration." This can lead to tensions and disputes in international affairs and it can also be very misleading to particular participants in the institution. When many countries follow certain international obligations, the premium (in terms of economic reward) to a country that decides to depart from that obligation may be even greater than it would have been had there been no obligation at all. Just as in domestic society when the production or sale of an opiate drug is prohibited, the profit to be realized by successful evasion of that prohibition is immensely greater than would be the case if there were no prohibition at all. In certain circumstances, the same may be true in international economic relations. Another side of the same coin is the fact that certain activities that are inconsistent with an international legal norm have a greater chance of succeeding when other nations are inhibited from retaliation by the existence of that or other similar norms.

STATEMENT OF GATT DIRECTOR– GENERAL ARTHUR DUNKEL[5]

[I]nternational economic policy commitments, in the form of agreed rules, have far-reaching domestic effects, indeed effects so important that they are indispensable for democratic governance. They are the

---

5. Address in Hamburg, West Germany.   1982.
GATT Press Release No. 1312, March 5,

element which secures the ultimate coordination and mutual compatibility of the purely domestic economic policies. They form the basis from which the government can arbitrate and secure an equitable and efficient balance between the diverse domestic interests: producers vs consumers, export industries vs import-competing industries, between particular narrowly defined industries. Last but not least, only a firm commitment to international rules makes possible the all-important reconciliation, which I have already alluded to, of the necessary balance on the production side and on the financial side of the national economy.

I am still convinced that it is in the national interest of every trading nation to abide by the rules, which were accepted as valid for good times and bad, and to frame their internal policies accordingly. One of the major benefits of international disciplines is that they offer equal opportunities and require comparable sacrifices from all the countries involved in international competition. Those who believe in the open trading system must recognize and accept the need to correct those rigidities in their economic and social systems which obstruct the process of continuing adjustment on which economic growth depends. * * *

SECTION 5.2 CERTAIN FUNDAMENTALS OF INTERNATIONAL LAW

(A) SOURCES: CUSTOM OR TREATIES?

Traditionally, the sources of international law have been enumerated similarly to the list found in Article 38 of the Statute of the International Court of Justice:[1]

Article 38.—1. The Court, whose function is to decide in accordance with international law such disputes as are submitted to it, shall apply:

   a. international conventions, whether general or particular, establishing rules expressly recognized by the contesting states;

   b. international custom, as evidence of a general practice accepted as law;

   c. the general principles of law recognized by civilized nations;

   d. subject to the provisions of Article 59, judicial decisions and the teachings of the most highly qualified publicists of the various nations, as subsidiary means for the determination of rules of law.

   2. This provision shall not prejudice the power of the Court to decide a case ex aequo et bono, if the parties agree thereto.

---

1. Statute of the International Court of Justice, annexed to the Charter of the United Nations; signed at San Francisco, June 26, 1945; entered into force for the United States on Oct. 24, 1945 (59 Stat. 1031, 1055; TS 993; 3 Bevans 1153).

Yet it is generally recognized that rules or standards which effectively influence international action do not always fall within the above categories. The problem of recognizing the development of a new rule from the sources listed is often formidable.

JOHN H. JACKSON, THE WORLD TRADING SYSTEM 26–27 (2nd ed. 1997)[2]

Sources of international law can generally be divided into "customary" or "conventional." The latter term refers to treaties, which are often termed "conventions." Customary international law is defined as rules of national behavior that can be ascertained from the practice of nations when such practice reveals that nations are acting under a sense of legal obligation (opinio juris). Unfortunately, customary international law norms are quite often ambiguous and controversial. On many propositions of customary international law, scholars and practitioners disagree not only about their meaning but even about their existence. The traditional doctrines of establishing a norm of customary international law leave a great deal of room for such controversy.

(B) CUSTOMARY NORMS OF INTERNATIONAL LAW: WHAT ARE THEY?

AMERICAN LAW INSTITUTE, RESTATEMENT OF THE LAW (THIRD), FOREIGN RELATIONS LAW OF THE UNITED STATES, § 102 COMMENT B (1987)[3]

* * * "Practice of states" * * * includes diplomatic acts and instructions as well as public measures and other governmental acts and official statements of policy, whether they are unilateral or undertaken in cooperation with other states * * *. Inaction may constitute state practice, as when a state acquiesces in acts of another state that affect its legal rights. The practice necessary to create customary law may be of comparatively short duration, but * * * it must be "general and consistent." A practice can be general even if it is not universally followed; there is no precise formula to indicate how widespread a practice must be, but it should reflect wide acceptance among the states particularly involved in the relevant activity. Failure of a significant number of important states to adopt a practice can prevent a principle from becoming general customary law though it might become "particular customary law" for the participating states. * * * A principle of customary law is not binding on a state that declares its dissent from the principle during its development.

---

2. © 1997 by The Massachusetts Institute of Technology. Reprinted with permission of The MIT Press.

3. This and other excerpts from this publication in this chapter are reprinted by permission of the American Law Institute. Copyright 1987 by The American Law Institute.

In a book entitled "The Concept of Custom in International Law," Professor D'Amato notes the "tremendous amount of disagreement among scholars and publicists over the rules of customary international law,"[4] and Professor Byers has written that,[5]

> Unlike treaty rules, which result from formal negotiation and explicit acceptance, rules of customary international law arise out of frequently ambiguous combinations of behavioural regularity and expressed or inferred acknowledgments of legality. Despite (or perhaps because of) their informal origins, rules of customary international law provide substantive content to many areas of international law, as well as the procedural framework within which most rules of international law, including treaty rules, develop, exist and change.

Villiger notes:[6]

> Customary and treaty rules may exert a strong influence on each other. Non-identical rules of one source can modify rules of the other, or cause them to pass from use. Identical rules can parallel each other and assist in their mutual interpretation and ascertainment. * * * Clearly, if the rules of one source may bear in such a manner on the other, this results in a considerable *relativization* of the sources with regard to one another * * * Nevertheless, a relativization does not mean that customary law and treaties lose their independence or individuality, because otherwise such interactions as the customary modification of treaties would not be conceivable in the first place. The different conditions of the formation and existence of each source are the very cause for these processes.

IAN BROWNLIE, PRINCIPLES OF PUBLIC INTERNATIONAL LAW 7 (5th ed. 1998)[7]

Opinio juris et necessitatis. The Statute of the International Court refers to "a general practice *accepted as law.*" Brierly speaks of recognition by states of a certain practice "as obligatory," and Hudson requires a "conception that the practice is required by, or consistent with, prevailing international law." Some writers do not consider this psychological element to be a requirement for the formation of custom, but it is in fact a necessary ingredient. The sense of legal obligation, as opposed to motives of courtesy, fairness, or morality, is real enough, and the practice of states recognizes a distinction between obligation and usage. The essential problem is surely one of proof, and especially the incidence of the burden of proof.

4. Anthony A. D'Amato, The Concept of Custom in International Law 5 (1971).

5. Michael Byers, Custom, Power and the Power of Rules 3 (1999).

6. Mark E. Villiger, Customary International Law and Treaties: A Manual on the Theory and Practice of the Interpretation of Sources (2nd ed. 1997).

7. This and other excerpts from this publication in this chapter are reprinted with permission of the Clarendon Press, Oxford.

(C) TREATIES

MARK E. VILLIGER, CUSTOMARY INTERNATIONAL LAW AND TREATIES 57–58 (2nd ed. 1997)

Does international law provide for any superiority of rules of one source, namely customary law or treaties, which necessarily override rules of the other, regardless of origin, content, or duration of validity? * * * The silence in Article 38 [Statute of the International Court of Justice] as to a hierarchy of sources accurately reflects the structure of the international legal order to which an *a priori* hierarchy of the sources is an alien concept. The reason for this is that customary law and treaties are autonomous sources. * * * Some authors have given the different explanation that customary law and treaties must be independent because they can stimulate and influence each other.

———

Perhaps the most important source of international obligation and the one which writers tend to think is most often followed, treaties, nevertheless, pose a series of difficult questions. The basic "core" principle is "pacta sunt servanda." But how are treaties formed? Who do they bind? How are they changed? What effect do they have on domestic law of nations that are parties to the treaty? How are treaties terminated? How are they interpreted? Various attempts have been made to codify or systematize rules relating to these questions, the most prominent for the United States being the American Law Institute 1987 Restatement (Third) of the Foreign Relations Law of the United States, and the U.N. International Law Commission Convention on the Law of Treaties, put in final form at a conference at Vienna in 1969.[8] The Convention came into force in 1980. The United States has not ratified it, but considers many of its provisions to be rules of customary international law.

VIENNA CONVENTION ON THE LAW OF TREATIES

ARTICLE 26. PACTA SUNT SERVANDA

Every treaty in force is binding upon the parties to it and must be performed by them in good faith.

8. The Vienna Convention on the Law of Treaties, with annex, done at Vienna, 23 May, 1969 (text: UNGA U.N. Doc. A/Conf. 39/27, May 23, 1969; see also U.N. Conf. on the Law of Treaties, UNGA U.N. Docs. A/Conf. 39/1–28). See also Ian M. Sinclair, The Vienna Convention on the Law of Treaties (2d ed. 1984); T.O. Elias, The Modern Law of Treaties (1974); Shabtai Rosenne, The Law of Treaties: A Guide to the Legislative History of the Vienna Convention (1970). The Restatement (Third) closely follows the Vienna Convention. See American Law Institute, Restatement of the Law (Third), Foreign Relations of the United States, secs. 301–339 (1987).

ARTICLE 27. INTERNAL LAW AND OBSERVANCE OF TREATIES

A party may not invoke the provisions of its internal law as justification for its failure to perform a treaty. This rule is without prejudice to article 46.

* * *

ARTICLE 31. GENERAL RULE OF INTERPRETATION

1. A treaty shall be interpreted in good faith in accordance with the ordinary meaning to be given to the terms of the treaty in their context and in the light of its object and purpose.

2. The context for the purpose of the interpretation of a treaty shall comprise, in addition to the text, including its preamble and annexes:

(a) any agreement relating to the treaty which was made between all the parties in connection with the conclusion of the treaty;

(b) any instrument which was made by one or more parties in connection with the conclusion of the treaty and accepted by the other parties as an instrument related to the treaty.

3. There shall be taken into account, together with the context:

(a) any subsequent agreement between the parties regarding the interpretation of the treaty or the application of its provisions;

(b) any subsequent practice in the application of the treaty which establishes the agreement of the parties regarding its interpretation;

(c) any relevant rules of international law applicable in the relations between the parties.

4. A special meaning shall be given to a term if it is established that the parties so intended.

ARTICLE 32. SUPPLEMENTARY MEANS OF INTERPRETATION

Recourse may be had to supplementary means of interpretation, including the preparatory work of the treaty and the circumstances of its conclusion, in order to confirm the meaning resulting from the application of article 31, or to determine the meaning when the interpretation according to article 31:

(a) leaves the meaning ambiguous or obscure; or

(b) leads to a result which is manifestly absurd or unreasonable.

ARTICLE 33. INTERPRETATION OF TREATIES AUTHENTICATED
IN TWO OR MORE LANGUAGES

1. When a treaty has been authenticated in two or more languages, the text is equally authoritative in each language, unless the treaty

provides or the parties agree that, in case of divergence, a particular text shall prevail.

* * *

ARTICLE 34. GENERAL RULE REGARDING THIRD STATES

A treaty does not create either obligations or rights for a third State without its consent.

* * *

ARTICLE 46. PROVISIONS OF INTERNAL LAW REGARDING COMPETENCE TO CONCLUDE TREATIES

1.   A State may not invoke the fact that its consent to be bound by a treaty has been expressed in violation of a provision of its internal law regarding competence to conclude treaties as invalidating its consent unless that violation was manifest and concerned a rule of its internal law of fundamental importance.

2.   A violation is manifest if it would be objectively evident to any State conducting itself in the matter in accordance with normal practice and in good faith.

* * *

ARTICLE 60. TERMINATION OR SUSPENSION OF THE OPERATION OF A TREATY AS A CONSEQUENCE OF ITS BREACH

1.   A material breach of a bilateral treaty by one of the parties entitles the other to invoke the breach as a ground for terminating the treaty or suspending its operation in whole or in part.

2.   A material breach of a multilateral treaty by one of the parties entitles:

(a) the other parties by unanimous agreement to suspend the operation of the treaty in whole or in part or to terminate it either:

(i) in the relations between themselves and the defaulting State, or

(ii) as between all the parties;

(b) a party specially affected by the breach to invoke it as a ground for suspending the operation of the treaty in whole or in part in the relations between itself and the defaulting State;

(c) any party other than the defaulting State to invoke the breach as a ground for suspending the operation of the treaty in whole or in part with respect to itself if the treaty is of such a character that a material breach of its provisions by one party radically changes the position of every party with respect to the further performance of its obligations under the treaty.

3. A material breach of a treaty, for the purposes of this article, consists in:

(a) a repudiation of the treaty not sanctioned by the present Convention; or

(b) the violation of a provision essential to the accomplishment of the object or purpose of the treaty.

* * *

ARTICLE 62. FUNDAMENTAL CHANGE OF CIRCUMSTANCES

1. A fundamental change of circumstances which has occurred with regard to those existing at the time of the conclusion of a treaty, and which was not foreseen by the parties, may not be invoked as a ground for terminating or withdrawing from the treaty unless:

(a) the existence of those circumstances constituted an essential basis of the consent of the parties to be bound by the treaty; and

(b) the effect of the change is radically to transform the extent of obligations still to be performed under the treaty.

* * *

ARTICLE 64. EMERGENCE OF A NEW PEREMPTORY NORM OF GENERAL INTERNATIONAL LAW (JUS COGENS)

If a new peremptory norm of general international law emerges, any existing treaty which is in conflict with that norm becomes void and terminates.

(D) SOVEREIGNTY, SOVEREIGN EQUALITY AND THE PROBLEM OF VOTING

IAN BROWNLIE, PRINCIPLES OF PUBLIC INTERNATIONAL LAW 289 (5TH ED. 1998)

The sovereignty and equality of states represent the basic constitutional doctrine of the law of nations, which governs a community consisting primarily of states having a uniform legal personality. If international law exists, then the dynamics of state sovereignty can be expressed in terms of law, and, as states are equal and have legal personality, sovereignty is in a major aspect a relation to other states (and to organizations of states) defined by law. The principal corollaries of the sovereignty and equality of states are: (1) a jurisdiction, prima facie exclusive, over a territory and the permanent population living there; (2) a duty of non-intervention in the area of exclusive jurisdiction of other states; and (3) the dependence of obligations arising from customary law and treaties on the consent of the obligor.

LOUIS HENKIN, THE MYTHOLOGY OF SOVEREIGNTY[9]

1. Talk of "sovereignty" is heavy in the political air, often polluting it.

2. "Sovereignty" sometimes subsumes—and conceals—important values. It is used to express the essential quality of a state, the basic entity, abstract but real, of the international political systems. "Sovereignty" is used to describe the autonomy of states and the need for state consent to make law and build institutions. "Sovereignty" is used to justify and define the "privacy" of states, their political independence and territorial integrity; their right and the rights of their peoples to be let alone and to go their own way.

But sovereignty has also grown a mythology of state grandeur and aggrandizement that misconceives the concept and clouds what is authentic and worthy in it, a mythology that is often empty and sometimes destructive of human values.

3. For example: Sometimes—a half century after the UN Charter!—we still hear that a sovereign state cannot give up its sovereignty right to go to war, or to act in self-defense or in defense of other "vital interests," *as it sees them*. Often we still hear that a sovereign state cannot agree to be bound by particular international norms—e.g., on human rights, or on economic integration (as in Europe). Even more often, sovereignty has been invoked to resist "intrusive" measures to monitor compliance with international obligations—human rights commitments or arms control agreements.

4. It is time to bring sovereignty down to earth; to examine, analyze, reconceive the concept, cut it down to size, break out its normative content, repackage it, perhaps even rename it.

* * *

9. I do not insist that in international life there should necessarily be more rather than less governance. Minimal international governance means greater autonomy and privacy for states and societies, which are important values in international as in national life. But excessive international governance does not loom as a great threat; international law and institutions are still primitive. More international regulation generally and stronger international institutions may come with the enlightenment that comes with democracy in national societies, but for now, surely, there is need for effective international governance at least for maintaining international peace and to prevent genocide and other massive, gross violations of human rights.

* * *

11. Away with the "S" word!

9. Reproduced with permission from *ASIL Newsletter* (March–May 1993), at 1 & 6, (c) The American Society of International Law.

STEPHEN D. KRASNER, SOVEREIGNTY: ORGANIZED HYPOCRISY[10]

This muddle in part reflects the fact that the term "sovereignty" has been used in different ways, and in part it reveals the failure to recognize that the norms and rules of any international institutional system, including the sovereign state system, will have limited influence and always be subject to challenge because of logical contradictions (nonintervention versus promoting democracy, for instance), the absence of any institutional arrangement for authoritatively resolving conflicts (the definition of an international system), power asymmetries among principal actors, notably states, and the differing incentives confronting individual rulers.

* * *

The term sovereignty has been used in four different ways—international legal sovereignty, Westphalian sovereignty, domestic sovereignty, and interdependence sovereignty. International legal sovereignty refers to the practices associated with mutual recognition, usually between territorial entities that have formal juridical independence. Wesphalian sovereignty refers to political organization based on the exclusion of external actors from authority structures within a given territory. Domestic sovereignty refers to the formal organization of political authority within the state and the ability of public authorities to regulate the flow of information, ideas, goods, people, pollutants, or capital across the borders of their state. * * *

Organized hypocrisy is the normal state of affairs.

———

Readers may find it interesting and amusing to read the 1648 Treaty of Westphalia (often said to be the origin of nation-state sovereignty concepts). This can be found on the World Wide Web by searching for "Treaty Of Westphalia."

Question

A question to consider in relation to the WTO: Is full nation-state sovereignty a requirement of membership in the WTO? See Section 6.6 and WTO Articles XI, XII, and XIII.

One of the more perplexing questions of current international economic affairs is the problem of the appropriate structure for voting in international organizations. There are strong proponents for equal voting, "one nation— one vote," and equally strong proponents for other systems. The following excerpts may suggest some of the policies involved in connection with this

---

10. Reprinted from: Krasner, Stephen D. *Sovereignty: Organized Hypocrisy.*   Princeton: Princeton University Press, 1999 pp.3–9.

question, but they do not convey the intensity with which various views are held.

ROBERT A. KLEIN, SOVEREIGN EQUALITY AMONG STATES: THE HISTORY OF AN IDEA[11]

The resolutions of the United Nations are theoretically capable of expressing the general will of its members. The claim to legitimacy, however, is wide open to question. There is a gross disproportion between voting power and real power. The smallest and financially weakest states, representing a minority of the total population in the organization, possess a majority of the votes. Paying a fractional share of the assessments of the organization, they are able to outvote those paying the highest rates. At budget time, when expenditures for the coming year come up for approval, the major powers, paying two-thirds of all UN costs, feel the full impact of majority rule. They find themselves chosen to foot the bill for projects which they voted against and which the majority, by themselves could never afford.

[According to Klein, this often leads to injustices and irresponsible behavior. As an example he points at the reasoning of the General Assembly with regard to Gibraltar.] In 1713 Spain transferred the rock to Britain under the terms of the Treaty of Utrecht. In recent years Spain has contested before the appropriate organs of the United Nations the ancient cession of its territory. A 1966 resolution of the General Assembly invited the two parties to start negotiations and both accepted. [Great Britain, however, found that it] could not simply transfer one population to the rule of another country without regard to the opinions and desires of the people concerned. [The British Government therefore organized a referendum. According to the United Nations and Spain, however] the matter did not involve a colonial situation but the territorial integrity of Spain. The fate of the Gibraltarians was a matter to be determined solely by bilateral negotiations between the British and Spanish governments.

Britain, nevertheless, held the referendum. Forty-four voters chose to be affiliated with Spain; over 12,000 elected to remain under British rule. In spite of this overwhelming expression the General Assembly sought to nullify the result. Resolution 2429 XXIII declared the continuation of the colonial situation in Gibraltar incompatible with the purposes of the Charter and previous Assembly resolutions. Britain was given a deadline: to end its rule by 1 October 1969.

That day has long since come and gone. Neither Spain nor Britain has changed its position. The UN is powerless to enforce its resolution. Spain and Britain have resumed bilateral talks. But the contradictory levels of meaning embodied in the idea of equality and its corollary, the principle of self-determination, stand exposed.

11. Reprinted from Sovereign Equality Among States: The History of an Idea, at 148–149, by Robert A. Klein, by permission of the University of Toronto Press. © University of Toronto Press 1974.

Question

How do these issues relate to the question which States should have a permanent seat on the U.N. Security Council, or how the relative size of the Member States of the European Union should be reflected in the weight of their vote in the EU Council and the number of seats they have in the European Parliament? Are these issues also comparable to those related to the representational characters of the House of Representatives and the Senate in the American constitutional system? How should these issues affect governing principles of international economic organizations?

HENRY G. SCHERMERS & NIELS BLOKKER, INTERNATIONAL INSTITUTIONAL LAW: UNITY WITHIN DIVERSITY 795–797 (3rd rev. ed. 1995)[12]

B.   WEIGHTED VOTING

(i) Desirability

Several systems of weighted voting have been considered in order to compensate the inequality of Members.[13] The main argument in favor of this procedure is one of equality. It is unfair for the interests of a large population to be set aside in favor of the interests of two or three other populations which, even when combined, are smaller.

Another argument for weighted voting is its mitigating effect on "trading" with votes. In systems where votes are not weighted, states which have votes but no substantial interests may vote in favor of a proposal in order to gain support for other proposals instead of basing their vote on the issue involved. The effect of such abuses is decreased by giving States relatively fewer votes in matters in which they are not directly interested.

The main problem of weighted voting is the criterion on which extra weight should be given. Should it be population, national income, power, or some other criterion?

As a rule, the size of the population seems the most suitable factor, but in several fields this does not seem appropriate. States like China and India, which would thus obtain the greatest voting strength, have limited interest in foreign trade, air navigation, or safety at sea, which are of great importance to smaller States such as the Netherlands and Norway.

Several other criteria have also been considered. Voting power proportional to financial contribution unduly favors the richer States (contributions are based on financial capacity, rather than on the inter-

---

12. (c) 1995, 1997, 1999 Kluwer Law International. This and other excerpts from this work in this chapter are reprinted with the kind permission from Kluwer Law International.

13. [original note 135] Catharine Senf Manno, Selective Weighted Voting in the UN General Assembly, 20 Int.Org. (1966), pp. 37–62, and further literature quoted there (p. 37); Carol Barret and Hanna Newcombe, Weighted Voting in International Organizations, Peace Research Reviews, April 1968; Joseph Gold, Weighted Voting Power: Some Limits and Some Problems, 68 AJIL (1974), pp. 687–708; F.K. Listerm Decision–Making Strategies for International Organizations: The IMF Model (1989).

ests involved). Furthermore, this weighting may create problems if the decisions are so important that States would be prepared to pay larger contributions in order to obtain extra votes.

* * *

Only when the interests involved are specific and isolated from other interests is it relatively easy to find a key for a weighted voting system. If an organization covers many different interests, the use of a weighted voting formula might be considered only for some isolated subject matters and either a non-weighted or a differently weighted voting system for other subjects. This will inevitably lead to problems in defining to which category a particular question belongs, and although clear preliminary definitions may limit such problems, they can never be entirely excluded.

(E) ROLE OF PRECEDENT

STATUTE OF THE INTERNATIONAL COURT OF JUSTICE (1945)

ARTICLE 59

The decision of the Court has no binding force except between the parties and in respect of that particular case.

IAN BROWNLIE, PRINCIPLES OF PUBLIC INTERNATIONAL LAW 21 (5th ed. 1998)

* * * Strictly speaking, the Court does not observe a doctrine of precedent, but strives nevertheless to maintain judicial consistency.

(F) STATE RESPONSIBILITY

INTERNATIONAL LAW COMMISSION REPORT, 2000, DRAFT ARTICLES ON STATE RESPONSIBILITY[14]

ARTICLE 1—RESPONSIBILITY OF A STATE FOR ITS INTERNATIONALLY WRONGFUL ACTS

Every internationally wrongful act of a State entails the international responsibility of that State.

ARTICLE 31—REPARATION

1. The responsible State is under an obligation to make full repatriation for the injury caused by the internationally wrongful act.

ARTICLE 35—FORMS OF REPARATION

Full reparation for the injury caused by the internationally wrongful act shall take the form of restitution, compensation and satisfaction,

---

14. ILC Draft on State Responsibility in Third Report on State Responsibility by James Crawford, Special Rapporteur, UN GA Doc. A/CN.4/507 of 15 March 2000.

either singly or in combination, in accordance with the provisions of the present Chapter.

HENRY J. STEINER, DETLEV F. VAGTS & HAROLD H. KOH, TRANSNATIONAL LEGAL PROBLEMS: MATERIALS AND TEXT 338 (4th ed. 1994)

The growth of the law of state responsibility reflected the more intense identification of the individual (or later, the corporation) with his country that accompanied the nationalistic trends of the 18th to early 20th centuries. That growth would not have taken place but for Western colonialism and economic imperialism which reached their zenith during this period. Transnational business operations centered in Europe, and later in the United States as well, penetrated Asia, Africa and Latin America. Thus security of the person and property of a national inevitably became a concern of his government. That concern manifested itself in the vigorous assertion of diplomatic protection and in the enhanced activity of arbitral tribunals. Often the arbitrations occurred under the pressure of actual or threatened military force by the aggrieved nations particularly in Latin America.

WILLIAM W. BISHOP, JR., INTERNATIONAL LAW: CASES AND MATERIALS 742 (3rd ed. 1971)

What happens procedurally is that a national of state A who feels himself wronged by state B takes the matter up with the foreign office of his own country. If state A, the claimant's government, believes there has been a violation of international law by state B, it may, if it considers it desirable to do so, take the matter up through diplomatic channels with the foreign office of state B. A settlement may be reached at this stage, after presentation of the claim internationally and some negotiation; both foreign offices may agree that the claim is not good under international legal standards, or the respondent state may admit liability and make reparation. If the two states cannot agree, the claim may be submitted to arbitration, or held until enough claims have accumulated between the two states for them to create an arbitral claims commission, or dealt with as part of a lump sum settlement, often followed by adjudication before a national tribunal such as the Foreign Claims Settlement Commission of the United States.

(G) THE INDIVIDUAL AND INTERNATIONAL LAW

IAN BROWNLIE, PRINCIPLES OF PUBLIC INTERNATIONAL LAW 584–585 (5th ed. 1998)

* * * [T]o say the individual is, or is not, a 'subject' of international law is, in either case, to say too much and to beg a great many questions. The individual does not bear responsibility for breaches of obligations

imposed by the customary law of nations because most of these obligations can only rest on states and governments, and, further, he cannot bring international claims. Yet there is no rule that the individual cannot have some degree of legal personality, and he has such personality for certain purposes. Thus the individual as such is responsible for crimes against peace and humanity and for war crimes. Treaties may confer procedural capacity on individuals before international tribunals. It is not helpful therefore to pose the question as one of legal personality in all aspects or not at all. The problem, it is suggested, responds to an empirical approach. Although there is no rule that individuals cannot have procedural capacity before international jurisdictions, the assumption of the classical law that only states have procedural capacity is still dominant and affects the content of most treaties providing for the settlement of disputes which raise questions of state responsibility, in spite of the fact that frequently claims presented are in respect of the losses suffered by individuals and private corporations.

NORTH AMERICAN FREE TRADE AGREEMENT, CHAPTER ELEVEN: INVESTMENT

ARTICLE 1101

Scope and Coverage

1.   This Chapter applies to measures adopted or maintained by a Party relating to: (a) investors of another Party; (b) investments of investors of another Party in the Territory of the Party; and (c) with respect to Articles 1106 and 1114, all investments in the Territory of the Party.

* * *

ARTICLE 1116

Claim by an Investor of a Party on Its Own Behalf

1.   An investor of a Party may submit to arbitration under this Section a claim that another Party has breached an obligation under: (a) Section A or Article 1503(2) (State Enterprises), or (b) Article 1502(3)(a) (Monopolies and State Enterprises) where the monopoly has acted in a manner inconsistent with the Party's obligations under Section A, and that the investor has incurred a loss or damage by reason of, or arising out of, that breach.

———

Furthermore, individual states have substantial discretion in defining the rights of individuals to enforce international law. For example, states may grant rights to individuals which they may enforce directly. Alternatively, a state may provide a remedy under its domestic law to give effect to a rule of international law. In some cases, an individual or corporation may enter into an agreement with a foreign state by the terms of which disputes arising out of the agreement are to be decided according to principles of international law.

(H) EFFECTIVENESS AND SANCTIONS

HENRY G. SCHERMERS & NIELS BLOKKER, INTERNATIONAL INSTITUTIONAL LAW
1451–1517, 1549–1550 (3rd rev. ed. 1995)

The constitutions of most international organizations provide for some degree of coercion, but not for severe sanctions. This coercion can be introduced in cases where there is a major breach of obligations, but sometimes its use is restricted to particular situations, such as the non-payment of contributions. * * *

In some cases, the general congress may only impose specific sanctions. These sanctions usually deprive members of rights or privileges which result from their participation in the organization. * * * In other organizations, possible sanctions are not specified: the organization is empowered to take any coercive measures which it deems appropriate. * * *

Two general questions are relevant: (1) May international organizations impose sanctions on members which have violated obligations other than those contained in the constitutions of the organization? (2) May sanctions be taken which are not provided for in the constitution of the organization? A strict interpretation of powers would suggest a negative answer to both questions. An international organization's task is limited. It has no power to act beyond the field attributed to it. Expediency would also suggest a negative answer, at least to the first question. A delegation of meteorologists to a meeting of the WMO, for example, must decide whether WMO members fulfill their obligations under the WMO constitution. They may not be the most suitable people to judge whether a certain state is an aggressor or has violated basic principles of international law. On the other hand, international organizations are not isolated units: they form part of a general international structure and therefore should abide by the rules of that structure.

[Professors Schermers and Blokker discuss a number of possible sanctions, including:]

(a) Suspension of voting rights, which they say "is mainly used as sanction for the non-payment of financial contributions."

(b) Suspension of representation.

(c) Suspension of services of the organization: they cite particularly cases where the International Monetary Fund may declare a member ineligible to use its resources noting the following cases:

  (1) If a Member fails to fulfill any of its obligations under the constitution.

(2) When the Fund is of the opinion that a Member is using its resources in a manner contrary to its purposes.

(3) If a Member fails to exercise appropriate control to prevent the use of the Fund's resources to meet a large or sustained outflow of capital.

(d) Suspension of rights and privileges of membership.

(e) Expulsion from specific organs: They note: "(n)o constitutions provide for expulsion from particular organs as a sanction, but a member normally has no constitutional right to participate in an organ, apart from the general congress."

(f) Expulsion from the organization.

(g) Sanctions through other organizations:

Expulsion from some organizations automatically leads to ejection from others. Thus, states expelled from the UN cease to be members of UNESCO, states expelled from the International Monetary Fund cease to be members of the World Bank, states that are no longer members of the World Bank cease to be members of the IFC (International Finance Corporation) and the IDA (International Development Organization).

(h) Economic sanctions.

(i) Forces of international organizations and military enforcement: they note principally the practice of the United Nations.

(j) Other sanctions.

(k) Sanctions against individuals: publicity, warning, withdrawal of support and, most importantly, fines.

Note

We will explore some of the foregoing issues raised in this section—such as voting and sanctions—in the remainder of this chapter and in the two following chapters in the context of the International Monetary Fund and the WTO/GATT system.

SECTION 5.3 INTERNATIONAL ECONOMIC LAW

(A) INTRODUCTION

JOHN H. JACKSON, THE WORLD TRADING SYSTEM 25–26 (2d ed. 1997)[1]

In recent years one has increasingly heard references to "international economic law."[2] Unfortunately, this phrase is not well defined.

Scholars and practitioners have differing ideas about the meaning of this term. Some would have it cast a very wide net, and embrace almost any aspect of international law that relates to any sort of economic matter. Considered broadly, almost all international law could be called international economic law, because almost every aspect of international relations touches in one way or another on economics. Indeed, it can be argued from the latter observation that there cannot be any separate subject denominated as international economic law. A more restrained definition of international economic law, however, would embrace trade, investment, and services when they are involved in transactions that cross national borders, and those subjects that involve the establishment on national territory of economic activity of persons or firms originating from outside that territory.

* * *

Two unfortunate bifurcations of the subject of international economic law exist, however. One is the distinction between monetary and trade affairs. Given that both are, in a sense, "two sides of the same coin," a degree of artificiality separates them as topics. Yet international organizations, national governments, and even university departments tend to indulge in the same separation; and given that the whole world cannot be studied at once, there is great practical value in taking up the trade questions separately.

An even less fortunate distinction of subject matter is often made between international and domestic rules. This book will not indulge in that separation. In fact, the domestic and international rules and legal institutions of economic affairs are inextricably intertwined. It is not possible to understand the real operation of either of these sets of rules in isolation from the other. The national rules (especially constitutional rules) have had enormous influence on the international institutions and rules. Likewise the reverse influence can often be observed.

(B) INTERNATIONAL CUSTOMARY LAW AND ECONOMIC BEHAVIOR

When we search for customary norms of international law that relate to economic transactions, there is precious little to be found apart from the extensive developments on expropriation of property. There are, however, many international law norms that, although not focused on economic affairs, nevertheless have considerable importance to them. The basic norm of "Pacta Sunt Servanda"—the rule that treaties must be followed in good faith—is a foundation for treaty-based law (which is

---

2. [original note 43] See Pieter VerLoren van Themaat, The Changing Structure of International Economic Law (1981). See also John H. Jackson, "Economic Law, International" in Encyclopedia of Public International Law (1985); Dominique Carreau et al, Droit International Economique (1990); Paolo Picone and Giorgio Sacerdoti, Diritto Internatzionale Della Economia (1982); John H. Jackson, International Economic Law: Reflections on the "Boiler Room" of International Relations, 10 American University Journal of International Law and Policy, no. 2 (winter 1995), 595.

very important to economic regulation). The general subject of treatment of aliens, of which expropriation of property is a part, is also highly relevant to economic interaction among nations. Even international norms on human rights have been increasingly injected into discussions and negotiations on economic affairs. But let us try to ascertain what, if any, customary international norms exist specifically for economic affairs.

GEORG SCHWARZENBERGER, THE PRINCIPLES AND STANDARDS OF INTERNATIONAL ECONOMIC LAW [3]

I. THE FORMS OF INTERNATIONAL ECONOMIC LAW

Compared with the other two law-creating processes of international law—international customary law and the general principles of law recognized by civilized nations—the emphasis in International Economic Law is on treaties.

a. Treaties

The economic interest of States made short work of natural-law fallacies. Writers have asserted freedom of commerce or navigation as natural rights and deduced such rights from any first principles they cared to adopt as the starting points of their arguments. Yet, unless they were quick to reduce their claims to imperfect rights, they merely served to lend a spurious respectability to untenable claims. This was what happened when, in 1824, an ill-advised United States Secretary of State relied for evidence of the absolute right of freedom of navigation on the River St. Lawrence, on natural law in general and Grotius, Pufendorf, Wolff and Vattel, in particular. All that his British counterpart had to do was to take him at his word and raise the issue of reciprocal British privileges on navigable rivers in the United States not covered by British treaty rights.

* * *

b. International Customary Law

In relative significance, international customary law lags behind treaties in International Economic Law. Even so, it fulfills three important functions:

1. It provides the background against which consensual international economic law must be construed.

2. In its rules on international responsibility and warfare on land and at sea, international customary law provides the bulk of the rules governing the laws of international economic torts and economic warfare.

3. 117 Recueil des Cours 1, 12, 14   Hague Academy of International Law. (1966–I). Reprinted by permission of the

3. By the treaties and parallel national practices to which, in an evolution extending over nearly a millennium, International Economic Law has given rise, it has made two major contributions to international law at large. By way of generalization of rules originally limited to foreign merchants, it has laid the foundations for the rules of general international customary law on the freedom of the seas in times of peace and war, and for the rule on the minimum standard for the treatment of foreign nationals.

The growth of the rules on the exhaustion of local remedies, denial of justice, the outlawry of piracy *jure gentium,* and the transformation of the right of shipwreck into the law of salvage are further illustrations of the contributions made by International Economic Law to general international customary law.

GEORG SCHWARZENBERGER, EQUALITY AND DISCRIMINATION IN INTERNATIONAL ECONOMIC LAW[4]

* * * In the absence of bilateral and multilateral treaty obligations to the contrary, international law does not ordain economic equality between States nor between their subjects. Economic sovereignty reigns supreme. It is for each subject of international law to decide for itself whether and, if so, in which form, it desires to grant equal treatment to other States and their subjects or give privileged treatment to some and discriminate against others.

———

Sometimes it is claimed that the principle of "non-discrimination", often termed the "Most–Favored–Nation" obligation, is a norm of customary international law, a question to which we will return in Chapter 10. In addition, in the international discourse of today there is often argument over whether there exists in international law some general obligation to assist developing countries in their efforts to make economic progress. Some of these ideas have been incorporated into treaty-based law (such as Part IV of GATT, or resolutions of the United Nations Conference on Trade and Development), so it may no longer be necessary to base such arguments solely on customary law. Again these are subjects to which later chapters, particularly Chapter 25, return.

(C) ECONOMIC TREATIES

No attempt will be made here to canvass or catalogue the myriad of bilateral economic treaties. Perhaps most important of these are "BITs" (bilateral investment treaties), "FCN" (Friendship–Commerce–Naviga-

---

4. 25 Yearbook of World Affairs 163,   of Stevens & Sons, Ltd., London.
163 (1971). Reprinted with the permission

tion) treaties, "Economic Cooperation Agreements,"[5] the various treaties for the avoidance of multiple taxation, a long line of "commercial treaties" dealing with tariffs and customs matters (often superseded by modern multilateral agreements), and particular commercial treaties dealing with a specific product group (e.g., textiles or meat).[6] Many bilateral treaties deal with taxation, and other more specialized subjects of economic regulation.

The brief materials that follow should help to lend perspective to materials in the rest of this book that focus on modern multilateral agreements as a source of international regulatory obligation.

ERIC V. YOUNGQUIST, UNITED STATES COMMERCIAL TREATIES: THEIR ROLE IN FOREIGN ECONOMIC POLICY[7]

FUNCTIONS OF THE FCN TREATY

As its title suggests, the traditional friendship, commerce and navigation treaty is designed to establish an agreed framework within which mutually beneficial economic relations between two countries can take place, creating a basic accord governing day-to-day intercourse between them. It is bilateral, rather than multilateral in nature. Such a treaty is "one of the most familiar instruments known to diplomatic tradition" and probably the simplest type of general agreement with meaningful provisions available in United States treaty practice. It sets forth the terms upon which trade and shipping are conducted, and governs the rights of individuals and firms from one state living, doing business, or owning property within the jurisdiction of the other state. * * *

* * *

The commercial treaty occupied a central foreign policy role during the formative years of the Republic. It served both as a symbol of peaceful relations and a protector of vital commercial interests. In a world of exclusively bilateral relations, it was virtually the sole instrument for important peacetime agreements between nations. The history of this country's foreign economic policy is written in the negotiations on commercial treaties.

* * *

5. See, e.g., U.S.-China Accord on Industrial and Technological Cooperation, signed and entered into force, January 12, 1984.

6. See, e.g., U.S. Dept. of State, Treaties in Force (A list of Treaties and Other International Agreements of the United States in Force).

7. Reprinted from Studies in Law and Economic Development, Vol. II, study no. 1, at 72, 73–76, George Washington University International Law Society (May, 1967). Reprinted by Permission of the George Washington University International Law Society. "Studies in Law and Economic Development" continues as the *Journal of International Law and Economics*.

THE MODERN FCN TREATY PROGRAM—1945 TO PRESENT

After World War II, as after the First World War, the United States decided to revise the FCN treaty and employ it in a program aimed at modernizing its commercial treaty relations with other countries.

* * *

These postwar FCN treaties retained many of the traditional provisions of the older treaties. They differed from their predecessors primarily in that they placed greater emphasis on the right of establishment and promotion of private foreign investment, as opposed to trade and shipping, which were the areas of greatest concern in negotiation of earlier FCN treaties. This change in emphasis was a direct reflection of the increased foreign investment role of American business firms after World War II as well as the fact that, after 1934, the trade promotion aspects of commercial treaties had largely been taken over by the reciprocal trade agreements program, and that the General Agreement on Tariffs and Trade (GATT) provided the principal forum for negotiating tariff adjustment and furthering trade promotion objectives after World War II. * * *

KENNETH J. VANDEVELDE, U.S. BILATERAL INVESTMENT TREATIES: THE SECOND WAVE[8]

* * * By 1967, however, there appeared to be no other countries willing to conclude a U.S. FCN treaty. Accordingly, the FCN program expired in the mid–1960s.

At the very time the U.S. FCN program was drawing to a close, several European States were enjoying considerable success negotiating bilateral investment protection agreements which differed from the U.S. FCNs in that they were devoted exclusively to investment protection. After repeated calls from Congress and the U.S. business community for a U.S. investment treaty program similar to the European programs, the State Department decided in 1977 to launch the U.S. BIT program.

The BIT program, as it was conceived in the mid–1970s, had a number of purposes. One of the most important, at least in the minds of the early proponents of these treaties, was to counter the claim made during the 1970s by many developing countries that customary international law no longer required that expropriation be accompanied by prompt, adequate, and effective compensation, if indeed it ever had. This claim was embodied most visibly in the U.N. General Assembly's adoption in 1974 of the Charter of Economic Rights and Duties of States (CERDS), which had provided that compensation for expropriation was to be measured by the law of the expropriating State. That is, the

8. 14   Mich.J.Intl.L.   621,   624–626   Michigan Journal of International Law. (1993). Reprinted with permission of the

CERDS seemed not only to challenge the standard of prompt, adequate, and effective compensation, but to assume that there was no international minimum standard at all. The United States hoped to create a network of bilateral treaties embracing the prompt, adequate, and effective standard that would counter assertions that State practice no longer supported that standard.

A second purpose was to protect existing stocks of investment owned by U.S. nationals and companies in the territory of other States. U.S. BIT negotiators, at least at the inception of the program, did not consider the promotion of future investment to be a goal of the BITs. The promotion of investment in particular countries would have been inconsistent with the U.S. policy of letting the market direct investment flows and could have raised opposition to these treaties on the part of labor groups concerned about the loss of jobs. Even had the promotion of foreign investment been a goal of the program, U.S. negotiators saw no evidence that a BIT actually would result in increased investment in a particular country. Rather, investment decisions were based on numerous factors—such as political stability, the availability of low wage labor or natural resources, the development of the infrastructure, the size of the domestic market, and the legal climate—very few of which were addressed by a BIT.

A third purpose of the BITs was to depoliticize investment disputes. Traditionally, the remedies available to an investor whose investment was expropriated or otherwise injured by actions of the host State depended upon the involvement of the investor's government in the dispute. This resulted in the U.S. government's routine involvement in disputes between individual investors and foreign States, which inevitably complicated the conduct of foreign policy. The BITs were intended to establish legal remedies for investment disputes that would not necessitate the involvement of the investor's own government.

Note

As of November 2000, the United States was a party to 32 BITs.[9] A number of other BITs had been negotiated and signed, but not yet ratified. Worldwide, more than 1800 BITs had been negotiated at the end of the 1990's.[10]

SECTION 5.4   THE BRETTON WOODS SYSTEM AND WORLD ECONOMIC RELATIONS

At the core of contemporary international regulation of economic relations is a group of institutions and multilateral international agreements which can be termed the "Bretton Woods System." There are

9. List of U.S. Bilateral Investment Treaties, Office of Investment Affairs (IFD/OIA), Bureau of Economic and Business Afairs, U.S. Dept. of State, November 1, 2000, http://www.state.gov/www/issues/economic/bilateral.htm (visited April 17, 2001).

10. UNCTAD, Bilateral Investment Treaties 1959–1999, UNCTAD/ITE/IIAIZ.

numerous other institutions and agreements besides those that are generally considered part of the Bretton Woods System, and the next section of this book will take up some of those other institutions. However, to understand international regulation of economic relations, it is essential initially to study the Bretton Woods System, comprising the International Monetary Fund (IMF), the International Bank for Reconstruction and Development (IBRD—the "World Bank") and the General Agreement on Tariffs and Trade (GATT). These institutions and agreements were developed during a series of conferences beginning near the end of World War II, extending to the end of the 1940's. In 1944, the Bretton Woods conference itself was held at Bretton Woods, New Hampshire, in the United States. This conference developed the institutions and agreements on the financial side of economic relations, namely the IMF and IBRD. The General Agreement, however, was developed in a series of conferences beginning in the Fall of 1946, and extending to mid–1948.[1] In this section our focus is on the IMF; in the next chapter we study GATT and its successor—the World Trade Organization (WTO).

GERALD M. MEIER, THE BRETTON WOODS AGREEMENT—25 YEARS AFTER[2]

I. The Bretton Woods System as a Code of International Economic Conduct

The term "Bretton Woods system" incorporates the GATT as well as the IMF and World Bank, because the Bretton Woods Conference looked forward to the creation of an ancillary institution that would reduce obstacles to international trade and give effect to the principle of multilateral nondiscriminatory trade. Although the initial plans for the Havana Charter and the creation of an International Trade Organization were not carried out, the GATT emerged as a multilateral agreement embodying commercial policy provisions essentially similar to the Havana Charter chapter on commercial policy. While the IMF was intended to repair the disintegration that had befallen the international monetary system prior to the War, and the World Bank was designed to stimulate and support foreign investment, which had declined to insignificant amounts, the GATT was intended to reverse the protectionist and discriminatory trade practices that had multiplied during the pre-war depression years. The Fund and GATT were to collaborate on exchange policies and trade policies. In combination, the Fund, the Bank, and GATT were designed to help the advanced industrial countries achieve

1. See generally The International Monetary Fund, 1945–1965 (J. Keith Horsefield ed., 3 vols. 1969); IMF, The International Monetary Fund 1966–1971 (1984); Edward S. Mason & Robert E. Asher, The World Bank Since Bretton Woods (1973); Roberto Lavalle, Le Banque Mondiale et ses Filiales (1972); Richard N. Gardner, Sterling–Dollar Diplomacy (new expanded ed. with rev. intro. 1980).

2. 39 Stanford L.Rev. 235, 237, 245–246 (1971). Reprinted by permission of the Board of Trustees of the Leland Stanford Junior University.

the multiple objectives of full employment, freer and expanding trade, and stable exchange rates. * * *

* * *

A. *The Uneasy Triangle*

The overriding international economic policy question for most nations has been whether they can attain simultaneously the multiple objectives of high levels of employment (as stated in article I of the Fund Agreement), trade liberalization (as proposed by GATT), and balance-of-payments equilibrium with stable exchange rates (as proposed by the IMF). To the extent that these objectives conflict, some policy tradeoffs must occur.

In their efforts to achieve full employment, countries have often resorted to import restrictions. Even though international trade theory would label the advocacy of trade restrictions in order to promote full employment as a "non-argument" or as a "third, fourth, or "best" policy measure, governmental policies have often in reality had this neomer-cantilistic aspect. The pursuit of full employment also can entail balance-of-payments disequilibrium or departure from the condition of a fixed exchange rate. As a country undertakes expansionary domestic measures to achieve full employment, it is probable that its imports will increase and/or its exports fall so much that a deficit arises in the country's international payments balance. Some tradeoff must then occur between full employment and balance-of-payments equilibrium with stable exchange rates, or between full employment and trade liberalization. Finally, if a balance-of-payments deficit arises, the country will likely attempt to remedy the situation either by undertaking measures that restrict employment and contract income, in order to reduce imports and stimulate exports, or by imposing trade restrictions.

When confronted by these policy conflicts, most governments have allowed the objective of full employment to dominate national economic policy making even at the cost of a retreat from trade liberalization or pressure on their balance of payments. The central challenge to the operation of the Bretton Woods system has therefore been how to allow nations to pursue their domestic economic objectives without having to forgo the gains from trade or suffer balance-of-payments disequilibrium.

(A) THE INTERNATIONAL MONETARY FUND[3]

In a later chapter we will take a more detailed look at the operations of the International Monetary Fund (known as the IMF or simply the Fund). In this subsection, however, a few of the basic constitutional and structural aspects of the IMF will be taken up, so that these can be

3. For information about the IMF, the reader is directed to the numerous works by Sir Joseph Gold, former General Counsel to the Fund. See, e.g., Gold, The IMF and International Law (1996), Gold, Legal and Institutional Aspects of the International Monetary System: Selected Essays (2 vols. 1984); Gold, Developments in the International Monetary System, the International Monetary Fund, and International Monetary Law Since 1971, 174 Recueil des Cours 107 (1982–I).

compared and contrasted with other institutions (such as GATT and the WTO), and so that we will have an overall view with which to approach some of the problems concerning the "constitutional" questions of international economic law. For example, it is important to know in this connection, what are the necessary steps (both internationally and nationally) that must be taken in order to amend the IMF Articles of Agreement. In addition, it is important to know who has the definitive authority to interpret the IMF articles, how decisions are made, what is the nature of the voting and what procedures exist for dispute resolution and sanctions.

The United States has participated in the IMF (and other Bretton–Woods institutions, such as the World Bank), under the authority of the Bretton–Woods Agreements Act of 1945, as amended.[4] Several salient provisions of that act are as follows:

BRETTON WOODS AGREEMENTS ACT[5]

Sec. 4(b)(4). Whenever, under the Articles of Agreement of the Fund or the Articles of Agreement of the Bank, the approval, consent or agreement of the United States is required before an act may be done by the respective institutions, the decision as to whether such approval, consent, or agreement, shall be given or refused shall (to the extent such decision is not prohibited by section 5 of this Act) be made by the Council [a group consisting of the Secretaries of State, Treasury and Commerce, the Chairman of the Board of Governors of the Federal Reserve System, the President of the Export–Import Bank and a representative of the President], under the general direction of the President. No governor, executive director, or alternate representing the United States shall vote in favor of any waiver of condition under article V, section 4, or in favor of any declaration of the United States dollar as a scarce currency under article VII, section 3, of the Articles of Agreement of the Fund, without prior approval of the Council.

Sec. 5. Unless Congress by law authorizes such action, neither the President nor any person or agency shall on behalf of the United States (a) request or consent to any change in the quota of the United States under article III, section 2(a), of the Articles of Agreement of the Fund; (b) propose a par value for the United States dollar under paragraph 2, paragraph 4, or paragraph 10 of schedule C of the Articles of Agreement of the Fund; (c) propose any change in the par value of the United States dollar under paragraph 6 of schedule C of the Articles of Agreement of the Fund, or approve any general change in par values under paragraph 11 of schedule C; (d) subscribe to additional shares of stock under article II, section 3, of the Articles of Agreement of the Bank; (e) accept any amendment under article XXVIII of the Articles of Agreement of the Fund or article VIII of the Bank; (f) make any loan to the Fund or the Bank or (g) approve either the disposition of more than 25 million ounces of Fund gold for the benefit of the Trust Fund established by the

---

4. 22 U.S.C.A. secs. 286–86gg.

5. As amended, secs. 4(b)(4), 5, 26; 22 U.S.C.A. secs. 286b(b)(4), 286c, 286e–6.

Fund on May 6, 1976, or the establishment of any additional trust fund whereby resources of the International Monetary Fund would be used for the special benefit of a single member, or of a particular segment of the membership, of the Fund. Unless Congress by law authorizes such action, no governor or alternate appointed to represent the United States shall vote for an increase of capital stock of the Bank under article II, section 2, of the Articles of Agreement of the Bank, if such increase involves an increased subscription on the part of the United States. Neither the President nor any person or agency shall, on behalf of the United States, consent to any borrowing (other than a borrowing from a foreign government or other official public source) by the Fund of funds denominated in United States dollars, unless the Secretary of the Treasury transmits a notice of such proposed borrowing to both Houses of the Congress at least 60 days prior to the date on which such borrowing is scheduled to occur.

Sec. 26. The United States Governor of the Fund is directed to vote against the establishment of a Council authorized under Article XII, Section 1 of the Fund Articles of Agreement as amended, if under any circumstances the United States' vote in the Council would be less than its vote in the Fund.

———

Congress has attempted to keep control of U.S. participation in the IMF in other ways as well. For example, the U.S. representative is to work against any extension of assistance to a country whose government harbors terrorists, 22 U.S.C.A. sec. 286e–11, and to seek to assure that no IMF decision will undermine the U.S. policy regarding comparable treatment of public and private creditors. 22 U.S.C.A sec. 286e–8. In 1983, Congress adopted numerous directives to the Executive Branch as to what policies it should espouse and when it should consult with senior Members of Congress in respect of the IMF. See Pub.L.No. 98–181, title 8, 97 Stat. 1267. One addition requires the U.S. representative to work to have the IMF, as a condition of extending financial assistance, obtain the beneficiary's agreement to eliminate unfair trade and investment practices that the U.S. Trade Representative determines to be deleterious to the international trading system. 22 U.S.C.A. sec. 286gg(b).

(B) STRUCTURE OF THE FUND AND VOTING

IMF SURVEY, SUPPLEMENT ON THE FUND
September 2000

Organization

The IMF's Articles of Agreement provide for a Board of Governors, an Executive Board, a Managing Director, and a staff of international civil servants.

The Board of Governors, the highest decision-making body of the IMF, consists of one governor and one alternate for each member country. The governor, appointed by the member country, is usually the minister of finance or the central bank governor. The Board of Governors has delegated to the Executive Board all except certain reserved powers. It normally meets once a year.

The Executive Board (the Board) is responsible for conducting the business of the IMF. It is composed of 24 directors, who are appointed or elected by member countries or groups of countries. The Managing Director serves as its chairman. Meeting several times a week, the Board deals with a wide variety of policy, operational, and administrative matters, including surveillance of members' exchange rate policies, provision of IMF financial assistance to member countries, and discussion of systemic issues in the global economy.

Selected by the Executive Board, the IMF's Managing Director serves as the head of the organization's staff. Under the Board's direction, the Managing Director is responsible for conducting the ordinary business of the IMF. The Managing Director serves a five-year term and may be reelected to successive terms.

QUOTAS

Subscription: A member's IMF quota is its subscription in the organization. A member must pay its subscription in full: up to 25 percent in reserve assets specified by the IMF (SDRs or "usable" currencies) and the rest in its own currency.

Voting power: Each IMF member has 250 basic votes plus 1 additional vote for each SDR 100,000 of quota. Thus, the quota defines a member's voting power in IMF decisions.

THE INTERNATIONAL MONETARY FUND: ITS EVOLUTION, ORGANIZATION AND ACTIVITIES[6]

VOTING

Most decisions taken by the Board of Governors or the Executive Board are adopted by a simple majority of the votes cast. However, for more important decisions, a larger majority is required. Broadly, a 70 percent majority of the total voting power is needed to resolve such operational issues as rates of charges on the use of the Fund's resources and the rate of interest on holdings of SDRs. An 85 percent majority (often referred to as a "high" majority) is required to decide matters concerned with, for example, the structure of the Fund, changes in quotas, the allocation of SDRs, and the disposition of the Fund"s gold. The United States alone, or the members of the European Community or the group of developing countries when voting together, can veto proposals subject to a high majority. In practice, formal votes are rarely taken

6. International Monetary Fund Pamphlet Series No. 37, at 18–19 (David D.   Driscoll ed., 4th ed. 1984).

by the Executive Board. In most cases, decisions in the Board are arrived at by consensus; however, these decisions usually take cognizance of the distribution of voting power among members.

VOTING IN THE IMF

(March 19, 2001)[7]

	Votes	Percent of IMF Total
United States	371,743	17.16
Japan	133,378	6.16
Germany	130,332	6.02
France	107,635	4.97
United Kingdom	107,635	4.97
Saudi Arabia	70,105	3.24
China	63,942	2.95
Russia	59,704	2.76

Questions

What power does the United States have in the process of amending the Articles of the Fund? See Article XXVIII. What about the EU? Under Article XVI, 4, decisions regarding allocations and cancellations of special drawing rights require approval by 85% of the Fund's voting power. What powers do the United States and the EU have in these decisions? What international and national procedures are required to amend the Charter of the IMF?

(C) INTERPRETATION OF THE ARTICLES OF THE FUND

JOSEPH GOLD, THE RULE OF LAW IN THE INTERNATIONAL MONETARY FUND
43–46 (1980)[8]

QUESTIONS OF INTERPRETATION

Article XXIX is an obvious provision under which specific complaints or disputes can be considered. The original provision was modified by the First Amendment of the Articles, but no substantial change was made in it by the Second Amendment. The heart of the provision is the following sentence:

> Any question of interpretation of the provisions of this Agreement arising between any member and the Fund or between any members of the Fund shall be submitted to the Executive Board for its decision.

The provision was unusual when adopted because it created jurisdiction for the Fund to settle within the organization itself questions of interpretation of the Articles that arose between any member and the Fund

---

7. IMF Executive Directors and Voting Power, March 19, 2001, *http://www.imf. org/external/np/sec/memdir/eds.htm* (visited 2 April 2001).

8. See also Joseph Gold, Interpretation: The IMF and International Law 115–16 (1996).

or between members. The provision required members seeking a resolution of these questions to submit them to the Fund and to no other authority, required the Fund to decide the questions when submitted to it, and provided that the decisions of the Fund on the questions were to be final. The sentence quoted above referred to questions and not to complaints or disputes in order to broaden the category of issues to which the provision related, but there was no doubt that a question of interpretation that was the subject of, or arose from, a complaint or dispute fell within the scope of the provision. None of these aspects of the original provision has been modified.

* * *

An explanation of the disuse of the formal procedure for interpretation is that in these matters, as well as in others, the Fund has preferred informal procedures. Only ten questions of interpretation have been settled by recourse to the formal procedure. The last of these interpretations was adopted on July 24, 1959. Nine of the interpretations were adopted at the request of individual members or at the instance of the Fund on the assumption that questions had arisen between a member and the Fund, although this assumption was not based on anything like a dispute between a member and the organization. There was tacit agreement, concurred in by the Fund and members, that clarifications by way of interpretation would be helpful for various reasons. The remaining interpretation was the result of a dispute between the Fund and a member.

A multitude of other questions of interpretation have been settled by decisions of the Executive Board without resort to the formal procedure. These decisions are reached by the same legal techniques as are formal decisions on questions of interpretation and are treated with the same respect by members and the Fund. Few of the decisions reached by the informal procedure have been prompted by anything resembling complaints or disputes.

Question

Why do you think that there is a preference for informal resolution of interpretative questions?

(D) SANCTIONS AND THE FUND

Joseph Gold has pointed out that the International Monetary Fund has made very little use of sanctions.[9] "The Articles authorize the Fund to take certain actions of which some are clearly sanctions and others have been regarded as comparable to sanctions if only because there is a tacit view that they involve an adverse judgment on the member against which (*sic*) the action is taken." Such sanctions or sanction-like measures include a declaration of ineligibility to use the Fund's resources when a member is "using the resources of the Fund in a manner

9. Joseph Gold, Some Characteristics of Operation—The Avoidance of Sanctions, from Horsefield, supra note 28, vol. II, at 578.

contrary to the purposes of the Fund," or when it "fails to fulfill any of its obligations." Members can even be required to withdraw from the Fund when, after a reasonable period of time, a member persists in its failure to fulfill any of its obligations or if a difference between the member and the Fund persists regarding unauthorized change of par value. The relatively sparse use of sanctions by the Fund has at least something to do, says Gold, with the fact that "there has been a high degree of observance by members, but not complete impeccability, and sanctions could have been applied more frequently than they have been."

Note

Next to the core Bretton Woods system institutions described above, there are of course numerous other international economic organizations. These include the Organization for Economic Cooperation and Development (OECD) and the United Nations Conference on Trade and Development (UNCTAD) that are of particular importance in international trade relations, but also organizations such as the International Finance Corporation (IFC), the International Development Association (IDA), the International Center for Settlement of Investment Disputes (ICSID), the International Labour Organization (ILO) etc.[10]

10. See generally Union of International Associations (ed.), Yearbook of International Organizations (published annually); Marcel A.G. van Meerheaghe, International Economic Institutions (1992); Bernard Co- las, Global economic co-operation : a guide to agreements and organizations (2nd ed. 2000); Michel Bélanger, Institutions économiques internationales: la mondialisation économique et ses limites (6th ed. 1997).

Chapter 6

THE LEGAL STRUCTURE OF
THE WTO/GATT SYSTEM

SECTION 6.1 INTRODUCTION: THE
NEW WORLD TRADING SYSTEM[1]

The end of the eight-year Uruguay Round of trade negotiations in 1994 brought a profound change in the legal structure of the institutions for international trade. Since 1947, the General Agreement on Tariffs and Trade (the General Agreement or GATT) was the principal international multilateral treaty for trade, although technically it was only in force "provisionally." In theory, the General Agreement did not establish an "organization," although in practice GATT operated like one. The Uruguay Round resulted in the creation of a new and better defined international organization and treaty structure—a World Trade Organization (WTO)—to carry forward GATT's work. Some have suggested that this is the most significant result of the Uruguay Round, and that it

1. See generally John H. Jackson, World Trade and the Law of GATT (1969); John H. Jackson, The World Trading System (2nd ed. 1997); John H. Jackson, Restructuring the GATT System (1990); William J. Davey, The WTO/GATT World Trading System: An Overview, *in* Pierre Pescatore, William J. Davey & Andreas F. Lowenfeld, Handbook of GATT Dispute Settlement (1994); Dominique Carreau et al., Droit International Economique (3d ed. 1990); John H. Jackson, The Jurisprudence of GATT and the WTO (2000); Kenneth W. Dam, The GATT: Law and International Economic Organization (1970); Thiébaut Flory, L'Organization Mondial du Commerce: Droit International et Substantiel (1999); Robert E. Hudec, Enforcing International Trade Law (1993); Robert E. Hudec, The GATT Legal System and World Trade Diplomacy (1975); Robert E. Hudec, Essays on the Nature of International and Trade Law (1999); Pierre Lortie, Economic Integration and the Law of GATT (1975); Edmond McGovern, International Trade Regulation (3rd ed. 1999); The GATT Uruguay Round: A Negotiating History: 1986–1992 (Terence P. Stewart ed., 1993); Pieter Verloren van Themaat, The Changing Structure of International Economic Law (1981); Executive Branch GATT Studies, Nos. 1–13, Senate Comm. on Finance, Subcomm. on International Trade, 93d Cong., 1st Sess. (Compilation of 1973 Studies prepared by the Executive Branch: Comm. Print, March 1974). GATT published an annual report entitled "GATT Activities In 19___." It also published a compilation of Basic Instruments and Selected Documents (BISD), which includes the major actions taken by the GATT contracting parties. See also GATT, Analytical Index (6th ed. 1994), a provision-by-provision analysis of the General Agreement that cites relevant GATT actions interpreting and applying each of them, and GATT, Status of Legal Instruments (looseleaf). The WTO publishes an annual report, volumes of "Dispute Settlement Reports" and a looseleaf WTO Status of Legal Instruments.

is part of a series of circumstances (including economic integration in Europe and North America) that may be the most profound change in international economic institutions since the Bretton Woods Conference of 1944.

The institutional reforms of the Uruguay Round include not only the WTO, but also substantial revisions of the dispute settlement procedures, which will be taken up in the next chapter. In this chapter, we will explore the history and characteristics of GATT, as predecessor (and still the existing treaty source for substantive norms) to the WTO. We will then examine the WTO itself, and follow this with explorations of certain institutional questions, such as membership and decision making, provisions for future trade negotiation rounds and the domestic law effect of the GATT, WTO and related treaties. Before doing this, however, a brief overview of the treaty structure may assist readers to better understand the material that follows. (The reader should examine the structure of these treaties in the Documents Supplement, as he or she reads the brief description that follows.)

The General Agreement is a treaty that deals almost entirely with trade in products. The Uruguay Round for the first time has produced a comparable treaty for trade in services (broadly defined) and a new treaty dealing with intellectual property. These three treaties form the core and bulk of the substantive international rules that will be administered by the WTO. What do these treaties provide?

GATT 1947 & 1994: The General Agreement on Tariffs and Trade, completed in late 1947 and amended and embellished with a variety of treaty instruments (about 200), provides an important "code" of rules applying to government actions which regulate international trade. The basic purpose of the General Agreement is to constrain governments from imposing or continuing a variety of measures that restrain or distort international trade. Such measures include tariffs, quotas, internal taxes and regulations which discriminate against imports, subsidy and dumping practices, state trading, as well as customs procedures and a plethora of other "non-tariff measures" that discourage trade. The basic objective of the rules is to "liberalize trade" so that the market can work to achieve the policy goals outlined in Chapter 1. An additional and very important rule is the "MFN" or Most Favored Nation Clause of Article I, which provides that government import or export regulations should not discriminate between other countries' products. Likewise Article III establishes the "national treatment" obligation of non-discrimination against imports. Article II establishes that the tariff limits expressed in each contracting party's "schedule of concessions" shall not be exceeded. The thrust of the General Agreement is to channel all "border protection" against imports into tariffs, and provide for agreements for tariff reductions, which are "bound" in the schedules and reinforced by Article II rules and the rest of the agreement.

The General Agreement also has a number of exceptions, such as those for national security, health and morals, safeguards or escape clauses (for temporary restraint of imports), free trade agreements, and the like.

Annex 1A to the WTO Agreement incorporates a document labeled GATT 1994 which is essentially GATT 1947 as amended and changed through the Uruguay Round, along with all the ancillary agreements pertaining to trade in goods.

GATS: The General Agreement on Trade in Services resulted from negotiations in the Uruguay Round on one of the "new subjects." The word "services" embraces more than a hundred different service sectors, such as banking, tourism, communications, medical, legal, insurance, brokerage, transport, etc. Many of these sectors are difficult and complex to regulate. The policy makers of the 1980's felt that global economic trends were making services an ever larger portion of international and national markets, thus necessitating some type of multilateral rule structure comparable to that for goods, in order to inhibit a growing tendency of governments to limit competition with restrictions and protectionist measures. The trade negotiators naturally tended to use analogies to GATT rules to try to regulate services, although sometimes the analogies did not work too well. Nevertheless, the GATS agreement has counterpart provisions to MFN and national treatment. It also has a system of "schedules of concessions." The GATS, however, also includes rules on competition and monopoly policy (antitrust). It contains exceptions clauses similar to GATT's on safeguards, health and morals, and national security. It also includes clauses on "transparency," calling for openness and publication of information affecting traders.

TRIPS: The Agreement on Trade–Related Aspects of Intellectual Property Rights is designed to provide rules requiring governments to ensure a certain minimum level of protection for patents, copyrights, industrial designs, trademarks, business secrets and similar matters. It incorporates provisions of some of the major intellectual property treaties (such as the Berne Convention concerning copyrights and the Paris Convention on patents). One of the major goals of proponents of this agreement was to add a measure of "enforceability" through a GATT-type dispute settlement system to intellectual property norms. Rules included in this agreement also require governments to provide civil and administrative procedures and remedies for rights-holders to pursue. This agreement also has clauses concerning MFN treatment, national treatment and transparency, as well as exceptions for national security.

Added to these three major substantive agreements, are the WTO Charter itself, an understanding on dispute settlement provisions, a "Trade Policy Review Mechanism," and an annex with two so-called "plurilateral agreements" (there were originally four in 1995, but two of them—the dairy and meat agreements—are no longer in effect). A chart showing the relationship follows:

WTO CHARTER

Annex 1: Multilateral Agreements
            Annex 1A: GATT 1994 (including agreements on trade in goods, understandings and the Marrakesh Protocol)
            Annex 1B: GATS
            Annex 1C: TRIPS
Annex 2: Dispute Settlement Rules
Annex 3: Trade Policy Review Mechanism
Annex 4: Plurilateral Agreements (optional)
            Annex 4A: Civil Aircraft
            Annex 4B: Government Procurement

By adhering to the WTO Charter, countries become subject to all of the annexed agreements, except the plurilateral agreements, adherence to which is optional. There are also, as part of the April 1994 Final Act that established the WTO structure, an assortment of appended Ministerial Decisions, Declarations, Understandings and Recommendations.

SECTION 6.2 GATT AND ITS TROUBLED HISTORY[1]

(A) GATT'S ORIGINS AND "BIRTH DEFECTS"[2]

National leaders never intended for the GATT to become the central international trade organization. The original idea was to create a broader international organization to be named the "International Trade Organization" (ITO), but history was not kind to that idea.

The initiatives towards the development of a GATT and an ITO began during World War II and came principally from the United States. Two strands of American economic policy converged to encourage these initiatives. The first strand was the general "Reciprocal Trade Agreements" program of the United States, originating with the 1934 Act that enabled the President to negotiate mutual reductions of tariffs. Weaknesses of the bilateral approach became apparent, however, and a multilateral approach seemed to offer some solutions for those weaknesses.

A second strand of American policy recognized the role of international economic affairs in causing World War II and sought to prevent a reoccurrence of such an event. It was recognized by American policy makers that organizations to regulate national practices affecting inter-

---

1. See John H. Jackson, World Trade and the Law of GATT (1969); Richard N. Gardner, Sterling–Dollar Diplomacy (new expanded ed. with rev. introd. 1980).

2. See Jackson, supra note 1, ch. 2; Gardner, supra note 2; William A. Brown, Jr., The United States and the Restoration of World Trade (1950); Clair Wilcox, A Charter for World Trade (1949); William Diebold, The End of the I.T.O. (Essays in International Finance No. 16, Princeton University, 1952).

national monetary flows, as well as trade, would be needed, and in 1944 a monetary conference was held at Bretton Woods.

In 1945 Congress again extended the Reciprocal Trade Agreements Act.[3] Late in that year, the United States Department of State invited a number of other nations to enter into multinational negotiations for the reduction of tariffs. At about the same time the United Nations was beginning its work, and the U.N. Economic and Social Council (ECOSOC) was established. At the first ECOSOC meeting in February 1946, the United States introduced a resolution, which was adopted, calling for the convening of a "United Nations Conference on Trade and Employment" with the purpose of drafting a charter for an international trade organization.[4]

The first preparatory committee for this effort convened in the Fall of 1946 in London, to consider a "Suggested Charter for an International Trade Organization" drafted by the United States government.[5] Following this meeting, a drafting subcommittee met at Lake Success, New York, early in 1947,[6] and then the full preparatory conference convened again in Geneva from April to October, 1947.[7] At this conference, the multilateral tariff negotiations were conducted, in addition to the continuing work on a draft charter for the ITO that was to be concluded at the Havana conference during the early part of 1948.

The General Agreement on Tariffs and Trade (GATT) was drafted at the Geneva conference, simultaneously with the tariff negotiations and the work on the ITO charter. The basic idea for the General Agreement was that it would be an agreement to embody the results of the tariff negotiations, but that it would also include some of the general protective clauses that would prevent evasion of the tariff commitments. It was not contemplated that GATT would be an organization; indeed, when early drafts of the General Agreement included terminology that suggested an organization, these were intensely criticized in hearings before U.S. congressional committees on the grounds that the President had no authority to accept international organization membership for the United States without congressional approval.[8] It was understood that an ITO charter would be submitted to Congress (or to the Senate) for approval. The tariff agreements (including the General Agreement) were being negotiated under the authority of the Reciprocal Trade

3. An Act to Extend the Authority of the President Under section 350 of the Tariff Act of 1930, 79th Cong. 1st Sess., 59 Stat. 410 (1945).

4. U.S. State Dept. Press Release, Dec. 16, 1945, reproduced in 13 Dept. State Bull. 970 (1945); 1 U.N. ECOSOC Res. 13, U.N. Doc. E/22 (1946); see Jackson, supra note 1, sec. 2.2.

5. See London Report, First Session of the Preparatory Committee (1946); U.N. Doc. EPCT/CII/1–66 (1946).

6. See New York Report, U.N. Doc. EPCT/34 (1947); U.N. Doc. EPCT/C.6/W.58 (1947).

7. See U.N. Docs. EPCT/A/SR/1–43; EPCT/B/SR/1–33 (1947); U.N. Doc. EPCT/TAC/SR. 1–28 (1947).

8. See Hearings on the Trade Agreements Act and the Proposed ITO Before the House Ways and Means Comm., 80th Cong. 1st Sess. (1947); Hearings on Operation of the Trade Agreements Act and Proposed ITO Before the Senate Finance Comm., 80th Cong. 1st Sess. (1947).

Agreements Act extension of 1945. However, the General Agreement was intended to be a subsidiary agreement under the ITO charter, and to depend upon the ITO charter and the ITO secretariat for servicing and enforcement. Indeed, most of its general clauses were drawn from comparable clauses drafted for the ITO, and it was understood that most of these clauses would be changed to conform to the corresponding version of the ITO charter that emerged from the later Havana conference.[9]

The United States tariff agreements authority was going to expire in the middle of 1948, and it was obvious that an ITO charter would not be in effect by then. Partly for these reasons, the United States and other countries desired to have the General Agreement accepted and implemented as soon as possible. Because some countries would require parliamentary action in order to accept many of GATT's general clauses, the General Agreement itself was not applied. Instead, a "Protocol of Provisional Application" (PPA) was signed in late 1947, by the twenty-two original members of GATT, and this protocol became effective on January 1, 1948.[10] It is only through this protocol that the General Agreement is applied. Originally it was thought that after the ITO charter came into force, the Protocol of Provisional Application would fall by the wayside, and the General Agreement would be applied definitively.

The Havana conference in early 1948 completed the draft charter of the ITO, but since the United States was the strongest economy in the post-war world, and since the initiative for an agreement came from the United States, other countries waited to see if the United States would accept the ITO. The ITO was several times submitted to Congress and extensive hearings were held upon it, but by the late 1940's the enthusiasm of international cooperation that prevailed immediately after World War II had faded, and the composition of Congress had shifted to a stance less liberal on trade matters and less internationally oriented. Recognizing the inevitable, in December 1950, the Executive Branch announced that it would not re-submit the ITO charter to Congress for approval, so for all practical purposes the ITO charter was dead.[11]

The death of the ITO meant that GATT was, by default, the central organization for coordinating national policies on international trade. By now somewhat enlarged by additional members, the GATT countries recognized that the General Agreement was ill-suited to perform the role that had been thrust upon it. Consequently it was decided to overhaul it and establish a small organization to operate it, to be known as the Organization for Trade Cooperation (OTC). The ninth session of the Contracting Parties of GATT, (October 1954 to May 1955), was the

---

9. See Jackson, supra note 1, sec. 2.4.

10. Protocol of Provisional Application to the General Agreement on Tariffs and Trade, Oct. 30, 1947, 61 Stat. pts. 5, 6, TIAS No. 1700, 55 UNTS 308; see also Jackson, supra note 1, sec. 3.2.

11. See Diebold, supra note 2; Jackson, supra note 1, sec. 2.5.

"review session" at which a number of amendments to GATT were prepared, and a draft charter for the OTC completed.[12]

The OTC charter met the same fate as the earlier ITO Charter. Congress would not accept it.[13] A number of the amendments to the General Agreement, however, were ultimately brought into force, accepted for the United States under the authority of the current Trade Agreements Act. Subsequently, it was amended only once, with the 1964 amendments to add Part IV relating to developing countries.[14]

One legacy of this troubled history has been a long festering quarrel in the United States over the "legality" of GATT, a subject that we take up below in Section 6.7.

GATT's troubled history explains why the nation participants in GATT were not called "members," but instead were called "contracting parties." This terminology tends to down play the notion of "organization."

When the Uruguay Round commenced, it was possible to list a number of serious problems facing GATT, most of which could be traced to "birth defects" dating from this troubled history of its origins:

1) GATT application was controversial, flawed and still "provisional," although the GATT rules did apply as binding international treaty obligations. Grandfather rights still existed, even though they were originally intended to be temporary. A number of other institutional problems stemmed from this basic treaty structure, including the difficulty of the amendment process, its uncertain relationship to domestic laws, the lack of a unified dispute settlement procedure, questions of membership, and the ill-defined powers of the contracting parties.

2) The amending provisions of the General Agreement were such that it was considered nearly impossible to amend it. The delay required by the treaty acceptance process, the difficulty of obtaining the required number of acceptances, the shift in bargaining power involved under the amending procedure in the context of a large membership and the fact that even when an amendment is effective it will not apply to countries which do not accept it, are all reasons why the amending procedure had fallen into disuse. This caused a certain rigidity and inability to develop rules to accommodate the many new developments in international trade and other economic interdependence subjects. One result was the development of an elaborate system of "side agreements or codes," which created additional problems.

3) A key problem was the relationship to GATT of these many side agreements, which in most cases were stand-alone treaties, but which were intimately linked to the GATT treaty structure itself. It was

12. See GATT, 3d Supp. BISD (1955); Agreement on the Organization for Trade Cooperation, GATT Doc. Final Act, 9th Session; see also Jackson, supra note 1, § 2.5.

13. See Jackson, supra note 1, at 51.

14. Id., sec. 3.4. and Appendix C, at 888–897, list of GATT Protocols and Agreements. See GATT, Status of Legal Instruments.

unclear in some circumstances what this relationship was and whether an obligation contained in a side agreement would prevail over one contained in the General Agreement or vice versa. In any event, since the side agreements tended to have a series of separate procedures for various matters including dispute settlement, there was a certain inefficiency in the potential "forum shopping." Side agreements bound only governments that accepted them, and the opportunity for countries to pick and choose led to "GATT a la carte."

4) The relationship of the GATT treaty system to domestic law in a variety of GATT member countries was very murky. This might have existed in any event, regardless of the basic treaty structure, since national legal systems differ so widely. Nevertheless, it seemed that some more attention could be given to the possibility of certain international treaty obligations with respect to how the trade and economic rules should be implemented domestically. More attention has been given to this question in recent years, sometimes under the rubric "transparency." It should be noted that the General Agreement itself has several clauses (e.g., Article X) that are related to transparency, dealing with publication and administration of trade regulations.

5) There were a number of troublesome problems with respect to membership, or "contracting party status," in the GATT system. There were various ways by which a nation could become a "member" of GATT or one of the side agreements. In some cases, membership could be obtained by a territory that did not have full independent international sovereignty. In certain cases, former colonies could be sponsored for membership and enter GATT with very little substantive commitment, reducing the "terrain of reciprocity," and leading to criticisms of unfairness. The General Agreement had an "opt out" clause (Article XXXV) by which individual GATT contracting parties could opt out of a GATT relationship with other parties, at one time only (when one of them originally enters GATT). Furthermore, there were a number of instances where there was an effective "opt out" at a later time, with murky legal results. Article XXI with an exception for "national security" purposes is related to this issue.

6) The powers of the Contracting Parties defined in the General Agreement were very ambiguous. Indeed, they were so broad that they could be the subject of abuse (although they have not been so abused). There were a number of unsettled and disquieting issues, such as the power of the contracting parties to interpret the General Agreement and the relationship of actions of the contracting parties to some of the side agreements. Furthermore, the decision making process left much to be desired. The so-called "consensus approach," which had evolved to ameliorate some of the problems of a one-nation one-vote structure, had slowed the decision making process and made it hard to confront difficult issues. The GATT Council had been created out of whole cloth by resolution of the Contracting Parties, and had been delegated almost all of their powers, but had no treaty status.

7) The dispute settlement processes of GATT were one of the more intriguing institutional developments of the institution. The treaty language was very sparse indeed, but many decades of practice had resulted in a considerable amount of exegesis. A Tokyo Round "understanding" elaborated and formalized many of the dispute settlement procedures that had developed in the early decades of GATT practice.

8) Finally, there was a long festering problem with respect to the relationship of GATT to the other Bretton Woods institutions, particularly the International Monetary Fund and the World Bank.

(B) THE GATT LEGAL STRUCTURE

The General Agreement, including the remarkably detailed commitments on tariffs that comprise the "Tariff Schedules," fills many volumes of treaty text. The "General Articles" of General Agreement comprise the basic trade policy commitments. These articles, now numbering thirty-eight and covering seventy pages of text (see Documents Supplement), contain a number of detailed rules and obligations designed generally to prevent nations from pursuing "beggar-thy-neighbor" trade policies which would be self-defeating if emulated by other nations. GATT is not a single agreement, but is a series of over two hundred agreements, protocols, procès-verbaux, etc.[15] Some of these protocols are amendments to the text of the general articles, while many are corrections or revisions (in the light of renegotiations) of the tariff schedules.

As noted above, the beginning point for understanding the GATT obligations is Article II, relating to the tariff schedules, in which each country commits to limit its tariffs on particular items to the level it negotiated. Many of the remaining GATT obligations are designed in large part to reinforce the basic tariff obligations. In addition, there are two broad non-discrimination obligations: (i) Article I contains the "Most Favored Nation" clause, which effectively prohibits discrimination amongst other parties in respect of imports or exports, and (ii) Article III contains the national treatment obligation, which specifies that imports shall be treated no worse than domestically produced goods under internal taxation or regulatory measures.

In addition to *obligations*, however, the General Agreement contains a large number of exceptions. It has been said that the agreement is "riddled with exceptions," and that "a lawyer could drive a four-horse team through any obligation that anybody had." The exceptions include those for escape clause actions against injurious and increasing imports; for balance of payments problems; for customs unions and free trade areas; for health and conservation measures; and for national security.

The General Agreement, central as it was to international trade regulation from 1948 to 1994, was never itself applied definitively. Rather, it was applied by the "Protocol of Provisional Application"

15. See Jackson, supra note 1, ch. 3.

(PPA), signed October 30, 1947, the key paragraphs of which which reads as follows:[16]

PROTOCOL OF PROVISIONAL APPLICATION OF THE GENERAL AGREEMENT ON TARIFFS AND TRADE

1.   [Australia, Belgium, Canada, France, Luxembourg, the Netherlands, the United Kingdom and the United States] undertake, provided that this protocol shall have been signed on behalf of all the foregoing Governments not later than 15 November 1947, to apply provisionally on and after 1 January 1948:

    (a) Parts I and III of the General Agreement on Tariffs and Trade, and

    (b) Part II of that Agreement to the fullest extent not inconsistent with existing legislation.

2.   The foregoing Governments shall make effective such provisional application of the General Agreement, in respect of any of their territories other than their metropolitan territories, on or after 1 January 1948, upon the expiration of thirty days from the day on which notice of such application is received by the Secretary–General of the United Nations.

* * *

5.   Any Government applying this Protocol shall be free to withdraw such application, and such withdrawal shall take effect upon the expiration of sixty days from the day on which written notice of such withdrawal is received by the Secretary–General of the United Nations.

———

Each time a country later became a party to GATT, it did so under a protocol with essentially the same terms (but different dates) or through a procedure by which it is deemed to come within such a protocol.[17] While GATT Article XXXI allowed a country to withdraw from GATT after six months' notice, the PPA shortened that notice period to sixty days.

The most important clause of the PPA, however, was the "existing legislation clause" of paragraph 1(b), the clause giving rise to what are known as "grandfather rights." Those grandfather rights were a source of difficulties, acrimony and dispute throughout the existence of GATT. Early practice in GATT established that in order for a grandfather right

16. Protocol of Provisional Application of the General Agreement on Tariffs and Trade, Oct. 30, 1947, 61 Stat. pts. 5, 6, TIAS No. 1700, 55 UNTS 308; see also Jackson, supra note 1, sec. 3.2.

17. See Jackson, supra note 1, secs. 3.2, 4.4.

to be invocable by a party, the existing legislation must be "mandatory." This follows from the history of GATT that the principal reason for the PPA was to provide an opportunity for countries to accept the General Agreement provisionally without having to submit it to their parliamentary approval procedures. Thus, if the executive had the authority to conform governmental measures to GATT obligations, it was argued, there should be no "existing legislation exception."

Although grandfather rights have had a troubled history in GATT, in later years they became less and less important, partly because many of them have withered away. One of the features of the WTO Charter is that it definitively put to rest the open-ended concept of grandfather rights. However, one GATT grandfather right was perpetuated in the WTO Charter's definition of GATT 1994 (the U.S. Jones Act).

SECTION 6.3   THE WORLD TRADE ORGANIZATION

(A) ORIGINS OF THE NEW CHARTER

Although there was substantial realization that GATT was handicapped in many ways because of the circumstances surrounding its origins, there was no indication during the 1980's and during the preparations for the Uruguay Round negotiations that there would be a proposal for a new organization during the round. There seemed to be a fear that such a proposal would attract too much opposition, especially in the U.S. Congress, which had twice before struck down such proposals in the trade area. The agenda and negotiating structure that resulted from the ministerial meeting launching the new round at Punta del Este, Uruguay, in September 1986, did not include any indication that a new charter would be considered. It did include a negotiating topic on, and a group charged with considering, the "Future of the GATT System" (the acronym "FOGS" was considered appropriate). The FOGS group, however, focused on GATT's relationship to the monetary part of the Bretton Woods system and on designing the new Trade Policy Review Mechanism (TPRM). It did not attempt more ambitious restructuring of the international trade institutions. A separate negotiating group was assigned the task of revising the dispute settlement procedures.

Only later did the ideas for a new organization begin to emerge. The Government of Canada first put forth a formal proposal (in May of 1990) for a WTO—World Trade Organization. Later that year, the European Union indicated it favored a similar organization, but preferred the name MTO—Multilateral Trade Organization. At the December 1990 Brussels Ministerial Meeting (which resulted in an impasse), the draft documents only mentioned the possibility of future exploration of a new organization.

After regrouping from the Brussels impasse, the then GATT Director–General, Arthur Dunkel, spurred the negotiators to produce in December 1991 a complete rough draft of the negotiation results, pasting together tentative texts of the entire package (with many holes and text in square brackets indicating unresolved matters). In this draft, for the first time, the world saw a draft charter for a new organization—an MTO. During 1992 and 1993 the negotiators worked on this draft in the face of various objections, particularly from the United States, to revise it and make it more acceptable. Finally, in the final hours of the December 1993 negotiations, there was agreement (including the United States) to a charter proposal, but the name was changed back to WTO, as it now stands. This proposal was then finalized in Morocco in April 1994, and submitted to governments for ratification.

It is important to realize that the WTO is not the ITO (the 1948 International Trade Organization.) The ITO Charter included five sizeable chapters filled with substantive rules concerning international economic behavior, plus a chapter with an elaborate set of institutional clauses. The WTO Charter by comparison, is a "mini-charter," relatively spare regarding institutional measures and containing no substantive rules, although large texts of such matter are included in Annexes. This overall structure of the WTO is itself significant. It suggests a spirit of flexibility, which allows for texts to be added or subtracted over time and for the evolution of institutions necessary for implementation of the rules.

(B) THE STRUCTURE OF THE WTO

The WTO Charter is confined to institutional measures, but the charter explicitly outlines four important annexes that technically contain thousands of pages of substantive rules. Indeed it is reported that the total "package" of the text of the Uruguay Round results weighs 385 pounds and consists of over 22,000 pages, including annexes and schedules.

The annex structure is important; the different annexes have different purposes and different legal impacts:

Annex 1 contains the "Multilateral Agreements," which comprise the bulk of the Uruguay Round results and which are all "mandatory," in the sense that these texts impose binding obligations on all members of the WTO. This reinforces the single package idea of the negotiators, departing from the Tokyo Round approach of "pick and choose" side texts, or "GATT a la carte." As outlined above, the Annex 1 texts include the following:

Annex 1A consists of GATT 1994, which includes the revised General Agreement with new understandings, side agreements on 12 topics ranging from agriculture to preshipment inspection, and the vast "schedules of tariff concessions" that make up the large bulk of pages in the official treaty text. The schedule for each of the major trading countries, the United States, Japan, and the European Union, constitutes a volume of printed tariff listings. There are a number of "side agreements," some originating from the Tokyo Round results (as revised in the Uruguay Round). These are as follows:

Agriculture (see Section 9.2 infra)

Application of Sanitary and Phytosanitary Measures (Section 14.2)

Textiles and Clothing (Section 9.2)

Technical Barriers to Trade (Standards) (Section 14.3)

Trade–Related Investment Measures (TRIMs) (Section 12.3)

Implementation of Article VI of GATT 1994 (Dumping) (Chapters 16–17)

Implementation of Article VII of GATT 1994 (Valuation) (Section 8.3(C))

Preshipment Inspection

Rules of Origin (Section 8.3(D))

Import Licensing Procedures (Section 9.1)

Subsidies and Countervailing Measures (Chapters 17–18)

Safeguards (Chapter 15)

Annex 1B consists of the General Agreement on Trade in Services (GATS), which also incorporates a series of schedules of concessions (Chapter 19).

Annex 1C consists of the Agreement on Trade–Related Aspects of Intellectual Property (TRIPS) (Chapter 20).

Annex 2 has the dispute settlement rules, which are obligatory on all members, and which form (for the first time) a unitary dispute settlement mechanism covering all the agreements listed in Annex 1, Annex 2 and Annex 4 (i.e., all but the TPRM procedures) (Chapter 7).

Annex 3 establishes the Trade Policy Review Mechanism (TPRM), by which the WTO will review the overall trade policies of each member on a periodic and regular basis, and report on those policies. The approach is not supposed to be "legalistic," and questions of consistency with WTO and Annex obligations are not the focus; rather the focus is the general impact of the trade policies, both on the country being examined and on its trading partners.

Annex 4 contains the four agreements that are "optional," termed "plurilateral agreements." This is a slight departure from the single package ideal, but the agreements included tend to be either targeted to a few industrial countries, or to be more "hortatory" in nature without real legal impact. The four agreements deal with government procurement (see Section 12.5 infra), trade in civil aircraft, bovine meat and dairy products. The latter two have been terminated. Clearly this annex, which may be added to, leaves open some important flexibility for the WTO to evolve and redirect its attention and institutional support for important new subjects that may emerge during the next few decades.

(C) LEGAL PERSONALITY AND ORGANIZATIONAL ATTRIBUTES

Unlike the General Agreement, the WTO Charter clearly establishes an international organization, endows it with legal personality, and supports it with the traditional treaty organizational clauses regarding "privileges and immunities," secretariat, director general, budgetary measures, and explicit authority to develop relations with other intergovernment organizations and, important to some interests, non-government organizations. The charter prohibits staff of the Secretariat from seeking or accepting instructions from any government "or any other authority external to the WTO."

(D) CONTINUITY WITH THE GATT

There is strong indication in various parts of the WTO Charter to promote a sense of legal and practice continuity with GATT. Except as otherwise provided, the WTO and the Multilateral Trade Agreements shall "be guided by the decisions, procedures and customary practices followed by [GATT 1947]." Art. XVI:1. The secretariat of the GATT 1947 became the WTO secretariat.

(E) IMPACT ON NATIONAL LAWS

An interesting new clause is included in the WTO Charter, which reads:

Each Member shall ensure the conformity of its laws, regulations and administrative procedures with its obligations as provided in the annexed Agreements.

Art. XVI:4.

(F) GOVERNING STRUCTURE

The governing structure of the WTO follows some of the GATT 1947 model, but departs from it substantially. At the top there is a "Ministerial Conference," which meets not less often than every two years. Next there is not one, but four "Councils." The "General Council" has overall supervisory authority, including responsibility for carrying out many of the functions of the Ministerial Conference between Ministerial Conference sessions. Presumably, the "General Council" will meet at least as often as the GATT Council, which met monthly (with some exceptions). In addition, however, there is a Council for each of the Annex 1 agreements, thus:

Council for Trade in Goods

Council for Trade in Services, and

Council for Trade–Related Aspects of Intellectual Property Rights

A "Dispute Settlement Body" (DSB) is established to supervise and implement the dispute settlement rules in Annex 2. The General Council is authorized to perform the DSB tasks. Likewise there is a TPRM Body for the Trade Policy Review Mechanism.

(G) APPRAISING THE NEW CHARTER

JOHN H. JACKSON, TESTIMONY BEFORE
THE SENATE FINANCE COMMITTEE,
March 23, 1994

First, the WTO essentially will continue the GATT institutional ideas and many of its practices, in a form better understood by the public, media, government officials and lawyers. To some small extent, a number of the GATT "birth defects" are overcome in the WTO. The WTO Charter (XVI:1) expressly states the intention to be guided by GATT practices, decisions, and procedures to the extent feasible.

Second, the WTO structure offers some important advantages for assisting the effective implementation of the Uruguay Round. For example, a "new GATT 1994" is created and thus countries effectively withdraw from the old GATT and become members of the new GATT. This procedure avoids the constraints of the amending clause of the old GATT that might make it quite difficult to bring the Uruguay Round into legal force.

Third, the WTO ties together the various texts developed in the Uruguay Round and reinforces the "single package" idea of the negotiators, namely, that countries accepting the Uruguay Round must accept the entire package (with a few exceptions).

Fourth, another important aspect of the WTO structure is that it facilitates the extension of the institutional structure (GATT-like) to the new subjects negotiated in the Uruguay Round, particularly services and intellectual property. Without some kind of legal mechanism such as the WTO, this would have been quite difficult to do since the GATT itself only applies to goods. The new GATT structure separates the institutional concepts from the substantive rules. The GATT 1994 will remain a substantive agreement (with many of the amendments and improvements developed throughout its history, including in the Uruguay Round.) The WTO has a broader context.

Fifth, similarly the WTO will be able to apply a unified dispute settlement mechanism, and the Trade Policy Review Mechanism to all of the subjects of the Uruguay Round, for all nations who become members.

Sixth, the WTO Charter offers considerably better opportunities for the future evolution and development of the institutional structure for international trade cooperation. Even though the WTO Charter is minimalist, the fact that there is provision for explicit legal status, and the traditional organizational privileges and immunities to improve the efficiency of an organization helps in this regard. With the WTO focusing on the institutional side, it also offers more flexibility for future inclusion of new negotiated rules or measures which can assist nations to face the constantly emerging problems of world economics. For example, already mentioned for such attention are environmental policies and competition policies.

There is some confusion about the effect of a WTO and its actions on U.S. law. It is almost certain to be the case (as Congress has provided in recent trade agreements) that the WTO and the Uruguay Round treaties will not be self-executing in U.S. law. Thus they do not automatically become part of U.S. law. Nor do the results of panel dispute settlement procedures automatically become part of U.S. law. Instead the U.S. must implement the international obligations or the result of a panel report, often through legislation adopted by the Congress. In a case where the U.S. feels it is so important to deviate from the international norms that it is willing to do so knowing that it may be acting inconsistently with its international obligations, the U.S. government still has that power under its constitutional system. This can be an important constraint if matters go seriously wrong. It should not be lightly used of course. In addition, it should also be noted that governments as members of the WTO have the right to withdraw from the WTO with six months notice (XV:1). Again, this is a drastic action that would not likely be taken, but it does provide some checks and balances to the overall system.

SECTION 6.4 DECISION MAKING IN GATT AND THE WTO

Since GATT was not viewed as an organization, it is not surprising that the General Agreement had little in it about decision making. Article XXV called for one-nation one-vote and decision by a majority of votes cast, unless otherwise provided. The language reads:

> 1. Representatives of the contracting parties shall meet from time to time for the purpose of giving effect to those provisions of this Agreement which involve joint action and, generally, with a view to facilitating the operation and furthering the objectives of this Agreement. Wherever reference is made in this Agreement to the contracting parties acting jointly they are designated as the CONTRACTING PARTIES.

This language is remarkably broad. Although cautiously utilized (at least in the early years), it was the basis for much GATT activity. For the United States, for instance, this language posed a danger. First, the United States could have been outvoted in a GATT with over 120 members, over two-thirds of which are developing countries, and over half of which are formally associated in one status or another with the European Union. Second, a nation's vote is cast by the Executive Branch of its government, and for the United States (and possibly other countries as well) an Executive decision to vote for a measure could result in its acceptance of a binding international obligation, without participation of its Legislative Branch. In practice, however, this was probably not a realistic danger, since the preparatory work, the failure of the ITO and OTC, the criticism of Congress, and the worry over voting strength, led the Contracting Parties to be cautious in voting additional obligations. Moreover, a short withdrawal notice period and the relative ease of breaching obligations have also been sources of caution. Most efforts in GATT got accomplished through a process of negotiation and compromise, with varying degrees of formality and a tacit understanding that agreement was necessary among countries with important economic influence.

One important question of the scope of authority under Article XXV was whether the Contracting Parties had the power to make definitive interpretations of the General Agreement, binding on all members. For example, the Contracting Parties, in a decision of 9 August, 1949, ruled:[1]

> The reduction of the rate of duty on a product, provided for in a schedule to the General Agreement, below the rate set forth therein, does not require unanimous consent of the Contracting Parties.

From time to time, various working groups or panels of GATT have reported their interpretations of the General Agreement, and these reports have been "adopted" by the Contracting Parties. In addition, once in a while the chairman of the Contracting Parties has made an "interpretative ruling," and no objection has been raised in the Contracting Parties' meeting.[2]

The General Agreement also had measures specifying the procedure and votes for amending the agreement and for waivers.

The WTO Charter substantially changes all of this and contains an elaborate matrix of decision making procedures, with important constraints around them. Basically there are five different techniques for making decisions or formulating new or amended rules of trade policy in the WTO Charter: decisions on various matters, "interpretations," waivers, amendments to the agreements, and, finally, negotiation of new agreements. The following chart summarizes the provisions. Examination of the WTO Charter provisions in the Documents Supplement will reveal even more complexity!

WTO DECISION MAKING

ORDINARY DECISIONS: ARTICLE IX:1

The WTO Charter specifies that the GATT practice of decision making by consensus is to be continued for the WTO Ministerial Conference (MC) and General Council (GC), but when consensus cannot be achieved, decisions will be made on the basis of the majority of votes cast, with each member having one vote, unless otherwise provided.

INTERPRETATIONS: ARTICLE IX:2

The MC and GC have exclusive authority to adopt interpretations of the WTO Charter and the Multilateral Trade Agreements. Interpretations of the Annex 1 agreements are to be based on a recommendation of the Council for that agreement and require an affirmative

---

1. GATT, II BISD 11 (1952); see also John H. Jackson, World Trade and the Law of GATT 21 (1969).

2. See GATT, II BISD 12 (1952) (Ruling by the Chairman on 24 August 1948).

vote from three-quarters of the overall WTO membership. Interpretations are not to be used to undermine Article X's amendment procedures.

WAIVERS: ARTICLE IX:3

The MC may waive an obligation under the WTO Charter and the Annex 1 Multilateral Trade Agreements. If consensus cannot be reached, the grant of a waiver requires an affirmative vote of three-quarters of the overall WTO membership. In the case of Annex 1 agreements, the waiver request is to be submitted to the relevant Council (e.g., Goods, Services or TRIPS), which will submit a report to the MC. Article IX:4 provides that any waiver granted shall specify the exceptional circumstances justifying it and a termination date. Waivers are subject to annual MC review.

AMENDMENTS: ARTICLE X

Amendments to the WTO Charter and the Annex 1 Multilateral Trade Agreements may be proposed to the MC by members or Councils. If consensus cannot be reached, the approval of an amendment for submission to the members requires a two-thirds vote of the overall WTO membership. Generally, amendments come into force on acceptance by two-thirds of the members. If it has been determined that the amendment will not affect member rights and obligations, it comes into force for all members at that time. Otherwise, amendments come into force only for those members accepting them, unless by a three-quarters vote of the overall WTO membership, it is decided that if a member does not accept the amendment it shall be free to withdraw or remain a member with permission of the MC. (In the case of GATS, amendments to certain provisions come into force on a two-thirds vote. For the other provisions, they come into effect for those approving them, but are subject to the same three-quarters vote procedure.)

Amendments to certain rules take effect only upon acceptance by all members: WTO decision making and amendment rules (Arts. IX, X); GATT Arts. I (MFN) & II (Tariff Schedules); GATS Art. II:1 (MFN); TRIPS Art. 4 (MFN).

Amendments to Annexes 2 (Dispute Settlement) & 3 (TPRM) can be made by MC action alone (without member acceptance), but for Annex 2, approval must be by consensus. Art. X:8

NEGOTIATING OTHER AGREEMENTS: ARTICLE III:2

The WTO is to provide a forum for negotiations on agreements contained in its annexes. It may also provide a forum for other negotiations on trade relations and a framework for the implementation of the results of such negotiations, by decision of the MC.

ANNEX 4: PLURILATERAL AGREEMENTS

Decision making and amendments under these agreements is governed by the rules contained in each agreement. (Arts. IX:5, X:10)

The MC may add trade agreements to Annex 4 by consensus; it may delete agreements from Annex 4 on the request of the members party to the agreement. Art. X:9.

In addition, it is important to understand the potential of the dispute settlement procedures, and the panel and Appellate Body reports that result (the subject of the next chapter), on the change or evolution of the trade rules.

In GATT there was some worry about waivers being used as a sort of "easy track" substitute for amendments. Some GATT documents discussed this problem,[3] but the practice of GATT was rather relaxed on this point. The WTO Charter stiffens considerably the rules regarding waivers and makes explicit the power of the organization to terminate waivers (an issue of some contention in GATT.) See Article IX:3.

Likewise in GATT there was concern about the amending rules (contained in Article XXX). The unanimity required for certain amendments had never been achieved, and the requirement otherwise of two-thirds (but not binding on hold-outs) was increasingly difficult to fulfill as the number of GATT contracting parties increased. This difficulty was a major factor in the Tokyo Round negotiations, leading the participants to utilize "side" codes or agreements on a number of GATT subjects as a way to avoid the need for amendments. But these codes only bound governments which accepted them, and in the Uruguay Round it was decided that a "single package" approach should be followed, so that all governments that became members of the WTO would be obligated to accept almost all of the agreements and rules. The whole package itself is being accepted as a totally new treaty, thus avoiding the GATT amending procedure (and probably resulting in technical withdrawals from the old GATT). The amending rules of this new package are somewhat similar to the GATT rules, so it is possible that the inconveniences of the GATT rules will continue to be a problem. However, the WTO rules do have some areas of greater flexibility for changing trade rules.

SECTION 6.5   TRADE NEGOTIATING ROUNDS

(A) OVERVIEW

One of the more important roles that GATT has played during the last four decades has been its sponsorship of a series of major multinational trade negotiations. So far there have been eight such trade negotiating "rounds." The rounds are summarized by the following chart:[1]

---

3. GATT Doc. L/403, 7th Sept. 1955.

1. For the first five rounds, see Gerard Curzon, Multilateral Commercial Diplomacy 81 (1965). For the Kennedy Round, see John W. Evans, The Kennedy Round in American Trade Policy 281 (1971). For the

Tokyo Round, see GATT, The Tokyo Round of Trade Negotiations: Report by the Director–General of GATT 118 (1979) and GATT, The Tokyo Round of Trade Negotiations: Supplementary Report by the Director–General of GATT 6 (1980) (collec-

	Countries Participating	Trade Affected
1. Geneva, Switzerland 1947	23	$10 Billion
2. Annecy, France 1948	33	Unavailable
3. Torquay, England 1950	34	Unavailable
4. Geneva 1956	22	$2.5 Billion
5. "Dillon Round," Geneva 1960–61	45	$4.9 Billion
6. "Kennedy Round," Geneva 1964–67	48	$40 Billion
7. "Tokyo Round," Geneva 1973–1979	99	$155 Billion
8. "Uruguay Round," Geneva 1986–94	120+	$3.7 Trillion

The first five of these rounds focused on negotiations for the reduction of tariffs. As it turned out, the sixth round also focused on tariffs, although one of the expressed goals for the round was to deal significantly with non-tariff barriers. The seventh round was predominantly concerned with non-tariff measures, although considerable attention was still given to tariff reductions. (The negotiation procedures and problems concerning tariffs will be discussed in Chapter 8.) Finally, the Uruguay Round continued detailed work on many non-tariff measures, but greatly expanded the scope of the trading system by adding services and intellectual property subjects, and, as previously indicated, created significant new institution. Preliminary estimates of the trade affected by the Uruguay Round include $2.7 trillion for goods, plus approximately $1 trillion for services.

(B) TOKYO ROUND (1973–1979)

JOHN H. JACKSON, RESTRUCTURING THE GATT SYSTEM 26–29 (1990)[2]

In [the Tokyo MTN] round non-tariff in addition to tariff measures were addressed extensively for the first time. Except for the original drafting of the GATT itself, the MTN results may well be the most far-reaching and substantively important product of the seven major trade rounds. The MTN results included, in addition to tariff reduction protocols, nine special agreements, and four "understandings," dealing with subjects as follows:

Agreements on:

1) Technical Barriers to Trade

2) Government Procurement

3) Interpretation and Application of Articles VI, XVI & XXIII (Subsidies)

tively, the GATT Tokyo Round Reports). For the Uruguay Round generally, see The GATT Uruguay Round: A Negotiating History: 1986–1992 (Terence P. Stewart ed., 1993).

2. Reprinted by permission of The Royal Institute of International Affairs. *Restruc-*

turing the GATT System was published by Pinter for the Royal Institute of International Affairs, London. It was published in North America for the RIIA by the Council on Foreign Relations Press, New York.

4) Arrangement Regarding Bovine Meat

5) International Dairy Arrangement

6) Implementation of Article VII (Custom Valuation)

7) Import Licensing Procedures

8) Trade in Civil Aircraft

9) Implementation of Article VI (Anti–Dumping duties)

Understandings on:

1) Differential and More Favorable Treatment, Reciprocity and Fuller Participation of Developing Countries

2) Declaration on Trade Measures Taken for Balance-of-Payments Purposes

3) Safeguard Action for Development Purposes

4) Understanding Regarding Notification, Consultation, Dispute Settlement and Surveillance

The overall impact of these results was to substantially broaden the scope of coverage of the GATT system.

The legal status of these various agreements and understandings, however, was not always clear. The nine agreements are drafted as "stand-alone" treaties, each with signatory clauses, and in most cases with institutional measures which include a committee of signatories with certain powers, and a dispute settlement mechanism (part of the "Balkanization" mentioned earlier.) Of these agreements, seven have sufficiently precise obligations to be called "codes." The others tend to confine their terms to the development of consultation mechanisms, statements of objectives, and only a few weak provisions which actually provide binding obligations. In one case, an agreement has been sufficiently troubled that the United States and some other signatories have formally withdrawn from it.

The "understandings," have a much more ambiguous status. These instruments mostly express goals or very general obligations, or (in the case of dispute settlement) describe procedures which arguably were already followed. These are not signed as independent agreements. The CONTRACTING PARTIES in November 1979, adopted these understandings. The implication of some of the provisions in these understandings is such as to suggest a "waiver" from other GATT obligations, while other provisions elaborate procedures in the manner in which a "decision" under GATT Article XXV might do. The understanding regarding dispute settlement, has been extremely important, since the GATT treaty provisions on this subject are so slim. This understanding (which, however, has a number of ambiguities) has provided a reasonably definitive account of the practice which had developed over the decades of GATT activity.

As "stand-alone" treaties, the "codes" obligate only those nations which sign and ratify them. A number of questions can then be raised about the legal relationship of these codes to the GATT itself. First, in theory, GATT parties which do not sign the agreements are not bound by them, and no provision of a "code" can alter their GATT rights. Since the GATT obligations include the most-favored-nation clause, however, if a code provides treatment for the trade of any other code signatory which is more favorable than that provided in GATT, such treatment is arguably required to benefit a GATT member which has not signed the code. The GATT CONTRACTING PARTIES in November 1979 adopted a decision which takes this position. However, some codes may not fall within the terms of the GATT MFN clause, for example, Government Procurement.

Some of the "codes" have titles which relate them to the GATT, such as the "Agreement on Implementation of Article VI," and another on "Interpretation and Application of" several GATT Articles. Again, non-signatories can argue that they are in no way bound by such codes. However, if these codes can be deemed to be "practice" of the GATT contracting parties, they could themselves be evidence of evolving interpretation of the GATT language itself. This could be especially true if further practice in GATT develops, without protest from non-signatories of the codes, which follows a code interpretation. In these ways GATT parties who have not signed a code may find that they effectively become obligated to code terms which "interpret" the GATT.

(C) URUGUAY ROUND (1986–1994)

Much of the preceding parts of this chapter present the results of the Uruguay Round. It is an extraordinarily broad and detailed product that resulted in an overhaul of the entire GATT system, embracing over 50 separate texts brought into one single package through the WTO charter. The following is one illustrative comment about that round:

STATEMENT OF GATT DIRECTOR–GENERAL PETER SUTHERLAND [3]

In every sense, the Uruguay Round is a global negotiation with a global result. For the first time, a negotiation under the auspices of GATT has covered virtually every sector of world trade. For the first time too, participation has been global. Indeed, perhaps the most significant feature about this negotiation has been the large number of developing countries taking part, and taking part actively. Their contribution to the Round has been a vital one, reflecting the importance of the multilateral system in creating and maintaining opportunities for sustainable development.

Important new areas of the world economy have been brought under multilateral disciplines. The General Agreement on Trade in Services provides for a new set of multilateral rules for the conduct of services trade. It simultaneously creates a framework for a continuing process of

---

3. GATT, News of the Uruguay Round,   NUR 081, Dec. 21, 1993, at 2.

liberalization. These rules take account of the particular features of trade in services and are based on fundamental principles of non-discrimination and national treatment. The outlook for job creation in this fast growing and dynamic sector, which accounts for over 60 percent of world production, is now better than ever.

* * *

The results on market access for goods represent a major milestone in the history of the GATT. Tariffs are expected to have been reduced by around 40 percent. Of equally far reaching importance is the substantial rise in security in the world trading system by virtue of the large increase in tariff bindings, not only but especially by developing countries, many of whom have undertaken wide-ranging economic reforms in recent years intended to achieve fuller integration with world markets. And if we factor in comprehensive tariffication of the measures affecting trade in agriculture, over 95 percent of world merchandise products will now be secured by tariff bindings, representing an enormous advance in predictability and stability of trading operations.

(D) FUTURE NEGOTIATIONS

At the end of the Uruguay Round there was considerable speculation about the prospects for another, ninth, round. Many observers expressed the view that the era of "rounds" was over, that the world could no longer wait for ten or more years between rounds to solve pressing and fast changing problems of international economic relations, and that rounds were so cumbersome and hard to manage that they should give way to other techniques of negotiation and rule making for the international trading system.

On the other hand, some of the advantages of rounds continued to be pointed out. For example, a round often provides more "trading material," in the sense that different nations have different objectives and may be more willing to yield in certain areas, if there are other relatively unrelated matters which attract them to an overall package. In addition, world leaders are more likely to become directly and personally involved in a "large package" negotiation than one that merely involves small bits of rather technical material.

In the late 1990's important agreements on telecommunications and financial services were successfully negotiated in the context of the services agreement. But the attempt to launch a ninth round of multilateral trade negotiations at the WTO Ministerial Meeting in Seattle in December 1999 failed after a week in which street protests caught global media attention. The events in Seattle have been described in terms of an "inside problem," and an "outside problem." The "inside problem" was what was really going on in the negotiations and the disagreement among Members over a wide array of old and new issues (agriculture, the position of developing countries, the question which new issues to deal with and whether to launch a full new round or deal with different issues one at a time etc.). The "outside problems" were the demonstrations, the tensions involved with that and the organization of NGOs and public participation. These relate to issues of "transparency" and "participation" in dispute settlement, negotiations and decision-making mechanisms.

It is hard to tell what may happen in the future. One thing is clear, there is much left to do, and a number of new subjects are competing for attention of the world trading system. Some of the Uruguay Round texts already contemplated further negotiation on certain matters (see the text on services and the text on agriculture.) Furthermore, relevant Ministerial Meetings have issued some indications of future agenda for the WTO system. High on the list of items for consideration are environment and trade problems, development, competition policy and trade problems, and perhaps some type of consideration of selected labor standards (although this was very controversial).

A complete inventory of potential agenda items for a possible new Round could be very long. In addition to the issues mentioned above, some of the other rules of the GATT system need further attention. These include subsidies, anti-dumping, product standards, the "process-product" problem of non-tariff measures, rules of origin, rules regarding customs unions and free trade areas, further evolution of some of the institutional provisions of the WTO, etc. It has been suggested that many of these issues should be considered at the technical level and possibly in a series of overlapping, but not necessarily simultaneous, "mini-rounds," such as a round on "environment," a round on "services," etc. See chapter 27 for further developments.

SECTION 6.6   ACCESSION AND MEMBERSHIP

(A) INTRODUCTION AND GATT HISTORY

In this section we will discuss the process by which a country can become a Member of the WTO. After a brief overview of the procedures that existed under the original GATT, subsection B will discuss the procedures for accession to the WTO and how they differ from those under the old GATT. In section C we will look at the possibilities that exist to "opt-out" of WTO commitments with other Members at the time of accession. Finally section D will look more specifically at the accession of the People's Republic of China to the WTO. We will also look at the problems under U.S. law related to the granting of Permanent Normal Trade Relations to China.

Following the fiction that GATT was not an organization, its participating nations or customs territories were called "Contracting Parties," and not "members." The WTO Charter changed this. The new charter designates participants as "Members." A bit of the GATT history on accession is relevant, however, because it clearly influences the interpretations and practices under the WTO Charter. Indeed, the process of negotiating accession remains largely the same.

There were basically two ways by which a country could become a contracting party to the General Agreement on Tariffs and Trade (other than as an original signatory to the Protocol of Provisional Application). Article XXXIII specified the "normal" procedure for membership. This article required a decision of two-thirds majority of the existing contracting parties, and accession to GATT on terms "to be agreed between such government and the CONTRACTING PARTIES." The article, however, only hints at the most important prerequisite to becoming a member through this procedure—the "ticket of admission" required from the acceding country by way of trade and tariff commitments negotiated at the time of entry.

Suppose, for example, an industrialized country wished to join GATT. The existing members of GATT, through previous tariff and trade negotiating rounds, had each committed themselves not only to the general provisions of the Agreement, but in most cases to extensive and detailed commitments contained in a schedule for each country. For a new country to enter GATT without agreeing to comparable tariffs would allow it to obtain a "free ride" in receiving the previously negotiated concessions of the existing members. Consequently, the existing members appropriately desired a negotiation with the applicant country, which must result in the applicant agreeing to a series of tariff concessions that the existing members feel are reciprocally balanced to those commitments that they have already made in GATT. Often this negotiation has been held in the context of a general trade or tariff round, For example, Japan negotiated for entry during the 1955 Geneva Round.

A first step for membership may be no more than to obtain "observer status" for the applicant. Following this, there may be a declaration by the Contracting Parties of special commercial relationships, often providing that existing GATT parties will extend GATT treatment, including MFN, to the new participant, if the new participant reciprocates. Sometimes such a declaration is called a declaration of "provisional accession" and it results in "de facto" application of the General Agreement. Finally, a protocol for accession itself will be negotiated and after the necessary decision by the Contracting Parties, will be open for signature (although as soon as the applicant country signs, the protocol becomes effective under its terms, since the Contracting Parties' vote is acceptance for GATT). The process suggests that the Contracting Parties acting jointly have legal personality under international law, enabling them to enter into an international agreement directly with the country.

A second way by which countries could become GATT parties was through "sponsorship" under Article XXVI:5(c). This paragraph applied primarily to countries that had become independent after having been ruled by a GATT Contracting Party that had applied the General Agreement to the territory in question. The first country to accede under these provisions was Indonesia in 1950, and over the years, many other nations became contracting parties by this route. It was generally agreed that the sponsored new member would apply the General Agreement as its parent sponsor was applying it on the date of sponsorship, including the "grandfather" clauses of the Protocol of Provisional Application or similar accession protocol.

Most significantly, a sponsored country did not need to negotiate a "ticket of admission." If the parent country had negotiated a separate schedule on behalf of the territory that had become a country, the commitments in that tariff schedule would become the schedule of the newly independent country in GATT. In practice, the separate schedules for colonial territories were very brief, often containing only a few tariff commitments. In some cases, there were no such tariff schedules at all. Thus, this meant that some parties had no schedule, i.e. no tariff commitments in GATT.[1] As noted earlier, this was raised fairness problems in the eyes of some.

(B) MEMBERSHIP AND ACCESSION TO THE WTO

Articles XI and XII of the WTO Charter state the requirements for membership of and accession to the WTO. It is generally assumed that countries that accede to the WTO as new Members will also have to comply with the requirements that Article XI sets out for the original Members. It is interesting to note, however, that the Charter does not specifically require this.

Article XI

ORIGINAL MEMBERSHIP

1. The contracting parties to GATT 1947 as of the date of entry into force of this Agreement, and the European Communities, which accept this Agreement and the Multilateral Trade Agreements and for which Schedules of Concessions and Commitments are annexed to GATT 1994 and for which Specific Commitments are annexed to GATS shall become original Members of the WTO.

2. The least-developed countries recognized as such by the United Nations will only be required to undertake commitments and concessions to the extent consistent with their individual development, financial and trade needs or their administrative and institutional capabilities.

Article XII

ACCESSION

1. Any State or separate customs territory possessing full autonomy in the conduct of its external commercial relations and of the other matters provided for in this Agreement and the Multilateral Trade Agreements may accede to this Agreement, on terms to be agreed between it and the WTO. Such accession shall apply to this Agreement and the Multilateral Trade Agreements annexed thereto.

---

1. See generally John H. Jackson, World Trade and the Law of GATT, secs. 4.5, 10.1 (1969).

2. Decisions on accession shall be taken by the Ministerial Conference. This Ministerial Conference shall approve the agreement on the terms of accession by a two-thirds majority of the Members of the WTO.

3. Accession to a Plurilateral Trade Agreement shall be governed by the provisions of that Agreement.

It can be seen that some of the GATT concepts have been carried over, such as the "ticket of admission," and "independent customs territory" status. There is, however, no provision in the WTO Charter comparable to GATT Article XXVI providing for easy accession by sponsorship of a former colonial mother country. All WTO Members, both original Members and those seeking accession, are expected to have tariff and service schedules, even if they contain relatively few meaningful commitments. The phrase in Article XII "on terms to be agreed" is obviously crucial and GATT procedures and practice have clearly influenced the direction taken in the WTO.

Often the initial approach of a potential applicant for WTO membership is a request to become an observer. When a country or separate customs territory decides that it wants to become a Member of the WTO it submits a communication to the Director General of the WTO indicating its desire to accede to the WTO under Article XII. This communication is then circulated to all Members and the General Council can decide to establish a Working Party. The Applicant is then required to submit a Memorandum describing in detail its foreign trade regime, its rules, regulations, and economic policies related to international trade in goods, services, and intellectual property rights, as well as certain economic statistics. The Secretariat can provide technical assistance. The Memorandum is sent to the Secretariat and circulated to all Members who are invited to submit questions. The Working Party will then start discussions with the Applicant about the Memorandum, the questions submitted by Members, and the changes that may be needed in its trade regime. When these consultations have sufficiently advanced, members may initiate bilateral accession negotiations on market access for goods and services and on the other terms to be agreed. When the Working Party and the bilateral negotiations have been concluded, a Schedule of Concessions and Commitments to GATT 1994 and a Schedule of Specific Commitments to the GATS will be prepared. These will then be reviewed multilaterally and annexed to the Protocol of Accession, of which they become an integral part. The Protocol of Accession contains the terms of accession for the Member agreed by the Applicant and the Members of the Working Party. The Working Party must approve a report that includes the draft Protocol. In the WTO this approval has generally been by "consensus." This Protocol of Accession is submitted to the General Council or Ministerial Conference together with a summary of the Working Party's discussions and a draft Decision. A two-thirds majority in the General Council is required for adoption of the Protocol. The Protocol of Accession will enter into force thirty days after the Applicant has signed or, if parliamentary approval is required, after it has deposited the Instrument of Ratification.

(C) NON–APPLICATION

When GATT was negotiated, the original text required a unanimous decision to accept a new Contracting Party. After the 1948 Havana Conference, however, this provision was changed to a two-thirds majority. Nevertheless, it was felt that no country should be forced to accept a trade agreement with another country without its own decision to do so. For that reason a "non-application" or "opt-out" provision was added to the Agreement. Thus, Article XXXV of GATT was designed to allow, on a one-time availability basis, an option to either a newly acceding state or any existing Contracting Party, to table a notification that as between the acceding state and that existing Contracting Party, the Agreement would not apply, even after the accession. Often political considerations enter into the decision to opt out of a trading relationship, as suggested by the past invocation of the option by India and Pakistan against South Africa. The most extensive set of "opt out" invocations were those exercised by a number of countries against Japan at the time Japan entered GATT in the middle of the 1950's. Subsequently, most of those countries withdrew their Article XXXV invocation, often after individual bilateral negotiations with the government of Japan resulting from special commitments. This "opt-out" or "non-application" provision has been used under the GATT approximately eighty-six times (most of these invocations have subsequently been withdrawn).[2]

Article XIII of the WTO Charter is an updated version of Article XXXV of GATT. It states:

Article XIII

NON–APPLICATION OF MULTILATERAL TRADE AGREEMENTS BETWEEN PARTICULAR MEMBERS

1. This Agreement and the Multilateral Trade Agreements in Annexes 1 and 2 shall not apply as between any Member and any other Member if either of the Members, at the time either becomes a Member, does not consent to such application.

2. Paragraph 1 may be invoked between original Members of the WTO which were contracting parties to GATT 1947 only where Article XXXV of that Agreement had been invoked earlier and was effective as between those contracting parties at the time of entry into force for them of this Agreement.

3. Paragraph 1 shall apply between a Member and another Member which has acceded under Article XII only if the Member not consenting to the application has so notified the Ministerial Conference before the approval of the agreement on the terms of accession by the Ministerial Conference.

2. See Analytical Index: Guide to GATT Law and Practice, Geneva 1995, p. 1034.

4. The Ministerial Conference may review the operation of this Article in particular cases at the request of any Member and make appropriate recommendations.

5. Non-application of a Plurilateral Trade Agreement between parties to that Agreement shall be governed by the provisions of that Agreement.

Article XIII of the WTO is largely a continuation of GATT Article XXXV. In contrast to GATT 1947 Article XXXV, however, Article XIII of the WTO Charter no longer contains a provision stating that the Agreement shall not apply between two Members if they have not entered into tariff negotiations. Article XIII also differs from the old system in that it explicitly requires notification to the Ministerial Conference. The United States has invoked WTO Article XIII four times, including a "carried over" case from GATT Article XXXV.

(D) CHINA'S ACCESSION TO THE WTO

The potential accession and integration of China to the WTO is one of the most important challenges and opportunities for the WTO and its Members. China's accession differs in scope and in political implications from the normal process of accession, but nevertheless provides a clear example of how accession works in practice.

China was one of the original 1948 GATT Contracting Parties, but the government representing China at GATT, the "Nationalist Chinese" or Taiwan, withdrew China from the GATT in 1950. Over time the PRC government assumed China's seat in many international organizations, including the United Nations and the International Monetary Fund. In more recent years, the PRC joined the Multifiber Arrangement associated with the GATT, and became an observer at GATT. Some argue that the withdrawal of China from GATT was attempted by a government that was not in control, and therefore was not effective. However, several counterarguments have been made, such as China's decade-long absence from GATT. It was nevertheless agreed that for the PRC's "re-entry" into the GATT the accession procedures would be used. When the Uruguay Round terminated the GATT and created the WTO, it was clear that the WTO accession procedures would apply.

Nicholas Lardy has indicated a number of reasons why WTO accession is of great importance to China, the United States, and the world trading system in general.[3] He observes that China has become a major player in international investment and trade but that it needs to be further integrated into the global economic system. China's leaders, he says, have staked their legitimacy on their ability to create economic growth. Continued economic growth has thus become a sine qua non to stay in power. Especially after the Asian crisis, many Chinese leaders have seen globalization of production as the only viable alternative, and,

---

3. See for a more complete overview of his views: Nicholas R. Lardy, Issues in China's WTO Accession, Congressional Testimony, U.S.-China Security Review Commission, May 9, 2001.

indeed, one that China could benefit from. Chinese leadership has also started to realize that further integration into the world economy requires development of a market economy. WTO Membership will oblige China to comply with the rules of the world trade system. Reform-minded Chinese leaders can use the WTO obligations as a lever to complete transition to a market-oriented economy.

China's accession, says Lardy, is also of great importance to the United States and the world trading system in general. For many years, China has been the single largest country outside the trading system. China's WTO Membership will also greatly increase the possibilities for foreign direct investment in the Chinese market (telecommunications, distribution, financial services) and will increase market access and leads to the availability of lower cost imports for consumers in the United States. Further economic integration may also make China a "more constructive participant" in new trade negotiation rounds. The increased ability to achieve economic reform and liberalization will allow China to meet the needs and expectations of its population, will create greater stability, and will be beneficial to the rest of the world too. Better economic conditions may, in the long term, also lead to a more pluralistic political system, and will likely "lead to stronger trade and investment ties between China and Taiwan that may contribute to a gradual reduction of tensions between the two."

A substantial barrier to overcome for China's WTO accession in the United States was parts of the 1974 Trade Act relating to trade relations with communist countries (so called Non–Market Economies or NMEs).[4] Under these statutes, the United States cannot grant MFN treatment (or as it has been termed in U.S. law since 1998 "normal trade relations") to products of an NME that denies its citizens the right to emigrate, or imposes sanctions on emigration.[5] Section 402 of the Trade Act of 1974, the so-called Jackson–Vanik Amendment, allows the President to waive these requirements, subject to annual review.[6] Although the United States and the PRC entered into a bilateral trade agreement in 1979, the PRC was subject to this annual review process. In light of China's WTO accession, several arguments were made that it was important for the United States to allow Permanent Normal Trade Relations (PNTR) with China. The most important was that it would ensure compliance with the WTO requirement of "unconditional most favored nation treatment," and would ensure that the United States reap the full benefits of China's WTO accession.[7] In September 2000 the U.S. Congress passed a bill giving the President the right to decide, after accession of the PRC to the WTO, that trade relations with China will no

---

4. See generally, Sylvia A. Rhodes, John H. Jackson, United States Law and China's WTO Accession Process, Journal of International Economic Law 2(3) (1999), 497–510.

5. Trade Act of 1974 secs. 401ff., 19 U.S.C.A. secs. 2431ff. (West 1980 and Supp. 1999).

6. Trade Act of 1974 secs. 402.

7. See for an overview of arguments John H. Jackson, Letter to U.S. Representatives Jim Kolbe, Cal Dooley, Robert Matsui and David Dreier, March 21, 2000, Inside US Trade vol. 18, No. 14, April 7, 2000.

longer be subject to annual review and will be granted MFN treatment on a permanent basis.

Note

In June 2001, China reached agreement with the United States, and, shortly thereafter, with the European Union as well, on bilateral concessions relating to China's WTO accession. In June 2001 President Bush informed Congress of his intent to extend normal trade relations to China under the Jackson–Vanik Amendment. At the time of this writing (August 2001) it was expected that the full terms of China's accession could be agreed upon by the end of 2001. The U.S. President will likely grant Permanent Normal Trade Relations to China around the time of its actual accession.

SECTION 6.7   EFFECT OF THE WTO/GATT AGREEMENTS ON DOMESTIC LAW

(A) THE GENERAL AGREEMENT IN U.S. LAW

A final issue to consider is that there are vast differences among nations about how they approach the issue of "direct application" of treaties in their domestic law. Here we treat the question from a U.S. perspective. This material relates to matters taken up in Chapter 3, but here we focus particularly on the General Agreement on Tariffs and Trade and the WTO Charter.

The General Agreement was an executive agreement entered into by the President of the United States. Because Congress never explicitly approved it, questions have been raised from time to time as to whether the President had the authority to enter into it and as to its status in domestic U.S. law, i.e. is it a self-executing agreement and did it apply to the states?[1] When the WTO entered into force on January 1, 1995, some of these questions became moot. The GATT text is now part of Annex 1 to the WTO and no longer has a separate legal status. This history, however, still has context significance and illustrates some of the issues of treaty application in US law.

As to the question of GATT's self-executing nature, one of the authors has argued that although the General Agreement itself was to be self-executing, application under the Protocol of Provisional Application is not self-executing. Nevertheless, under statutory authority giving the President the power to "proclaim" trade agreements,[2] if the President had the authority to enter into the General Agreement, he had the authority to make it part of United States domestic law, which he did for all except Part IV, which was added in the 1960's.

As to the more basic question of whether the President exceeded his powers under his trade agreements authority when he entered into the General Agreement, consider the following:

1. In Section 3.4 supra, we dealt generally with the problems in U.S. law of international agreements, both in respect of how they are properly accepted by the United States as binding agreements and their application as domestic law.

2. See discussion in Section 3.4(C) supra.

JOHN H. JACKSON, THE GENERAL AGREEMENT
ON TARIFFS AND TRADE IN UNITED
STATES DOMESTIC LAW [3]

From examining the text of the [trade agreements authority], one can see that it places no *explicit* hurdle against multilateral trade agreements. Furthermore, it was stressed in testimony before the congressional committee that the 1947 GATT negotiations would in reality be "bilateral," as before, with the results of the many bilateral negotiations simply drawn together in one instrument, for the sake of convenience. Even an opposing Congressman commented that merely because the result was one instrument signed by all, did not in itself mean that the President had exceeded his statutory authority. Thus, one can conclude that GATT does not go beyond the statutory authority merely because of its multilateral nature.

A more serious statutory assault on GATT is the argument that specific provisions of GATT exceed the authority delegated to the President by the Trade Agreements Act. Careful analysis is required to evaluate this argument, but to discuss each clause of GATT here would be tedious and lengthy. Appendix A outlines the sources, if the reader wishes to pursue the matter as to any specific article of GATT. Without reference to specific GATT provisions, however, the arguments for the statutory validity of our adherence to GATT can be summarized as follows: (1) the language of the Statute can be read to permit United States entry into GATT, since it authorizes "trade agreements" either without explicit limitation or with limitations that can be interpreted not to preclude an agreement such as GATT; (2) the legislative history shows that provisions such as those in GATT were contemplated by Congress; (3) prior trade agreements known to Congress had provisions like those of GATT, thus further evidencing congressional intent; (4) later actions of Congress can be taken as recognizing or accepting GATT; and (5) several court cases, while not directly litigating the validity of GATT, have resulted in decisions and opinions that necessarily imply its validity.

———

In the early years of GATT, congressional antagonism led Congress on at least one occasion to specify in a statute that "no trade agreement * * * shall be applied in a manner inconsistent with the requirements of this section."[4] In extensions of the trade agreements authority in 1953, 1954, 1955 and 1958, Congress inserted a clause which read, "the enactment of this Act shall not be construed to determine or indicate the approval or disapproval by the Congress of the Executive Agreements

3. 66 Mich.L.Rev. 249, 294 (1967). This and other excerpts from this publication in this chapter are reprinted by permission of the Michigan Law Review Association.

4. 65 Stat. 75 (1951).

known as the General Agreement on Tariffs and Trade."[5] In the Trade Act of 1974, Congress for the first time explicitly provided authority to appropriate funds to meet the U.S. obligation to contribute to the GATT budget. (Prior to that action the President had used other funding sources under his control, such as his contingency funds, but always reported to Congress on his action.) The 1974 statutory clause (Section 121(d)) reads (still somewhat begrudgingly!): "This authorization does not imply approval or disapproval by the Congress of *all* articles of the General Agreement on Tariffs and Trade" (emphasis supplied).

It would seem that an issue like this, after such a long history of recognition by the U.S. government of the validity and binding nature of GATT, would be laid to rest. Yet in a 1983 report by the House Commerce Committee concerning a proposal for a "domestic content" requirement on automobiles sold in the United States, the Committee stated: "GATT is an executive agreement, never ratified by the Senate under the Constitution."[6] A footnote to the statement reads as follows:

> The American Law Division of the Congressional Research Service (CRS) in a June 6, 1983 memorandum commented on the legal nature of GATT and said:
>
> Some ambiguity surrounds the precise legal nature of the General Agreement on Tariffs and Trade (GATT). GATT came into force for the United States on January 1, 1948, pursuant to a Protocol of Provisional Application to which the United States agreed to (sic) by way of an executive agreement. Some courts apparently refuse to give full legal effect to GATT since Congress never ratified it. See, e.g., Sneaker Circus, Inc. v. Carter, 457 F.Supp. 771, (E.D.N.Y.1978), aff'd 614 F.2d 1290 (2d Cir.1979).
>
> The Conference Report (H.Rept. No. 93–1644, December 19, 1974, p. 27) concerning the Trade Act of 1974 notes a provision was added to section 121 of the Act stating that the authorization of appropriations for payment by the United States of its share of expenses to GATT "does not imply approval or disapproval by the Congress of all articles of the GATT."

The footnote is somewhat misleading. The Second Circuit did not find it necessary to address this issue in *Sneaker Circus*. In the lower court, Judge Costantino had stated, "Plaintiff's claim that the President's action violated the General Agreement on Tariff and Trade * * * is likewise without merit, since Congress has never ratified GATT," 457 F.Supp. at 795, citing United States v. Yoshida Intl., Inc., 526 F.2d 560, 575 n. 22 (C.C.P.A.1975). (The *Yoshida* court did *not* hold that the General Agreement was not a binding international agreement.) Judge Costantino's statement seems to be directly inconsistent with the Supreme Court's holding in the *Belmont* case, discussed in Section 3.4

---

5. 72 Stat. 673 (1958); 69 Stat. 162 (1955); 68 Stat. 360 (1954); 67 Stat. 472 (1953).

6. H.Rep. No. 98–287, 98th Cong., 1st Sess., part I, at 22 (1983).

supra. He went on to note, however, that "even if GATT were applicable," its provisions were complied with. Id.

In any event, having made the above quoted statement, the Committee did not claim that the General Agreement was an invalid agreement, but rather went on to argue that the proposal was consistent with it. The fact that the Committee felt it necessary to argue that the proposal was GATT consistent is itself very interesting to the question of appraising GATT's effectiveness.

The authors are aware of no U.S. state or federal court which held the General Agreement not to be a binding international agreement for the United States, and many cases have applied GATT rules.[7] The situation as to the agreements resulting from the GATT-sponsored Tokyo Round negotiation was entirely different, as discussed below, and of course the WTO and Uruguay Round texts have a different status now.

A more complicated issue was the extent to which GATT rules could be used to defend or attack an administrative agency's interpretation of U.S. law. Of course, if there is a direct conflict between a U.S. statute and the General Agreement, the U.S. statute controls. But what if there is no direct conflict? What was the relevance of the GATT rules in interpreting the U.S. statute? Consider the following excerpt from Suramerica de Aleaciones Laminadas, C.A. v. United States, 966 F.2d 660, 667–668 (Fed.Cir.1992):

> [E]ven if we were convinced that Commerce's interpretation [of the U.S. statutory requirements for filing an antidumping investigation] conflicts with the GATT, which we are not, the GATT is not controlling. While we acknowledge Congress's interest in complying with U.S. responsibilities under the GATT, we are bound not by what we think Congress should or perhaps wanted to do, but by what Congress in fact did. The GATT does not trump domestic legislation; if the statutory provisions at issue here are inconsistent with the GATT, it is a matter for Congress to decide and remedy.

Questions

Do you agree? Is the court's approach consistent with the Restatement (Third) of the Foreign Relations Law of the United States (1987), § 114, which states, "Where fairly possible, a United States statute is to be construed so as not to conflict with international law or with an international agreement of the United States?" Other courts discussing this issue include Mississippi Poultry Assn., Inc. v. Madigan, 992 F.2d 1359 (5th Cir.1993)(en banc review pending); Footwear Distributors & Retailers of America v. United States, 852 F.Supp. 1078 (CIT 1994).

7. See e.g., Baldwin–Lima–Hamilton Corp. v. Superior Court, 208 Cal.App.2d 803, 25 Cal.Rptr. 798 (1962); Bethlehem Steel Corp. v. Board of Commrs., 276 Cal. App.2d 221, 80 Cal.Rptr. 800 (1969) (Section 3.6 supra); Hawaii v. Ho, 41 Hawai'i 565 (1957) (Section 12.4 infra).

(B) THE GENERAL AGREEMENT AND STATE LAWS

There is, however, a perplexing question of international law effect the relation of GATT and WTO obligations to state laws in the United States. This stems from the language of GATT Article XXIV, paragraph 12, which reads:

> 12. Each contracting party shall take such reasonable measures as may be available to it to ensure observance of the provisions of this Agreement by the regional and local governments and authorities within its territory.

The following 1967 extract may help to focus the issues presented by this paragraph.

JOHN H. JACKSON, THE GENERAL AGREEMENT ON TARIFFS AND TRADE IN UNITED STATES DOMESTIC LAW [8]

Simple and straightforward as it appears, this language contains an ambiguity that has an important impact on the domestic law application of GATT. The opposing interpretations can be expressed as follows:

(A) The language does not change the binding application of GATT to political subdivisions, but it recognizes that in a federal system certain matters are legally within the power of subdivisions and beyond the control of the central government. In such a case, the central government is not in breach of its international obligations when a subdivision violates GATT, as long as the central government does everything *within its power* to ensure local observance of GATT.

(B) On the contrary, this language indicates that GATT was not intended to apply as a matter of law against local subdivisions at all, and even when the central government has legal power to require local observance of GATT, it is not obligated under GATT to do so, but merely to take "reasonable measures."

If the second interpretation is correct, then GATT cannot be invoked as a matter of law in any state proceeding involving state law. This precise issue has risen in several cases, including a very recent California case. The unanimous conclusion of the courts thus far has been that GATT does apply to and override state or territorial law. However, the State Department took the contrary position in a letter to the Hawaii Territorial Supreme Court in the earliest of these cases. This letter, signed by the then State Department Legal Advisor, Herman Phleger, referring to Article XXIV:12, stated:

> This provision * * * has always been interpreted as preventing the General Agreement from overriding legislation of political subdivisions of contracting parties inconsistent with the provisions of the Agreement; by placing upon contracting parties the obligation to take reasonable measures to obtain observance of the Agreement by

8. Supra note 3, at 302–304.

such subdivisions, the parties indicated that as a matter of law the General Agreement did not override such laws. * * * In light of the provisions of paragraph 12 of Article XXIV * * * the reliance by the Supreme Court of the Territory on Article VI, clause 2 of the United States Constitution to invalidate the legislation would appear to have been based on a misconception of the General Agreement and of its effect on the legislation of the parties to it * * * it is suggested that you might desire to request a rehearing of the case on the basis that the particular constitutional grounds relied on are not appropriate in view of paragraph 12 of Article XXIV.

This letter is consistent with the testimony of a State Department official in hearings before a Senate Committee in 1949, one-and-one-half years after GATT was signed. * * *

The actual drafting history of GATT, however, leaves one with a somewhat different impression. The language of article XXIV:12 was drawn directly from an identical provision that was in the draft ITO Charter at the time the GATT draft was formulated.

What, then, can be concluded from the preparatory history of article XXIV:12? The fragments of that history that were recorded suggest that this clause was intended to apply only to the situation in which the central government did not have the constitutional power to control the subsidiary governments. Australia and other countries made reference to this situation. The United States delegate did likewise, adding his tentative judgment that the United States did not find itself in this circumstance. Thus, it can be argued that the interpretation which was presented at the outset of this section is the correct one, despite the opposing view expressed in the 1949 Senate Finance Committee hearings.

In the Uruguay Round, this situation was addressed by the adoption of an understanding on Article XXIV:12. It provides:

ARTICLE XXIV:12

13.   Each Member is fully responsible under the GATT 1994 for the observance of all provisions of the GATT 1994, and shall take such reasonable measures as may be available to it to ensure such observance by regional and local governments and authorities within its territory.

14.   The provisions of Articles XXII and XXIII of the GATT 1994 as elaborated and applied by the Understanding on Rules and Procedures Governing the Settlement of Disputes may be invoked in respect of measures affecting its observance taken by regional or local governments or authorities within the territory of a Member. When the Dispute Settlement Body has ruled that a provision of the GATT 1994 has not been observed, the responsible Member shall

take such reasonable measures as may be available to it to ensure its observance. The provisions relating to compensation and suspension of concessions or other obligations apply in cases where it has not been possible to secure such observance.

15. Each Member undertakes to accord sympathetic consideration to and afford adequate opportunity for consultation regarding any representations made by another Member concerning measures affecting the operation of the GATT 1994 taken within the territory of the former.

Does this clarify the issues raised above?

(C) IMPLEMENTATION OF THE URUGUAY ROUND

The Uruguay Round Agreements are not self-executing and thus have no direct "statute-like" effect in U.S. law, although the agreements can and should have an indirect effect on U.S. courts and officials when they interpret provisions of U.S. law.

DAVID W. LEEBRON, IMPLEMENTATION OF THE URUGUAY ROUND RESULTS IN THE UNITED STATES 212–214[9]

In short, the Uruguay Round Agreements themselves are unlikely to be directly applied in any proceeding other than a proceeding brought by the United States for the purpose of enforcing obligations under the agreements. To the extent that the agreements are fully implemented by the statutory language, this is not a matter of concern, but many aspects of the agreement were not explicitly implemented by the legislation. The agreements, including authoritative interpretations by the WTO or decisions of dispute settlement panels, might still be applied either by a court to resolve ambiguities in the language of a statute or by administrative agencies in promulgating rules and regulations. But such applications could not lead to an interpretive result that was contrary to any clearly expressed intent of Congress.

These restrictive aspects of United States implementation are consistent with United States practice since the Tokyo Round. What is newer is the attempt to circumscribe the effect of the statute itself. Generally speaking, statutes later in time take precedence over both earlier statutes and treaties. Although every effort will be made to construe statutes in order to avoid conflicts, implementation of the language and purpose of the later statute will prevail when two statutes cannot be reconciled. A critical question is how broadly a statute should be interpreted when it arguably conflicts with previous legislation. This was a matter of considerable concern in the implementation of the Uruguay Round Agreements, particularly regarding environmental pro-

9. Reprinted from John H. Jackson & Alan O. Sykes (eds.), Implementing the Uruguay Round (1997).

tection and product standards. Congress included provisions intended to limit the potential effects of not only the Uruguay Round Agreements, but also the implementing legislation itself. Section 102(a)(2) of the URAA provides:

Construction.—Nothing In This Act Shall Be Construed

(A) To amend or modify any law of the United States, including any law relating to—

    (i) the protection of human, animal, or plant life or health,

    (ii) the protection of the environment, or

    (iii) worker safety, or

(B) To limit any authority conferred under any law of the United States, including Section 301 of the Trade Act of 1974, Unless specifically provided for in this Act.

The effect of this provision is to greatly limit the extent to which the Act may be interpreted as altering laws (which for this purpose include administrative regulations). * * * If any statutes of the United States not specified in the implementing legislation need to be amended to conform to the Uruguay Round Agreements (whether as a result of dispute settlement or a voluntary determination by the United States), the normal legislative process would have to be followed.

Note on U.S. Participation in the WTO

As already noted in Section 3.6 supra, the 1994 Uruguay Round Agreements Act provides that U.S. federal law prevails over a Uruguay Round agreement in event of a conflict, section 102(a), and that Uruguay Round agreements prevail over state law, but only in actions brought by the U.S. government. Section 102(b)(2). In addition, under the Act no person (except the United States) has a cause of action or defense under any Uruguay Round agreement by virtue of congressional approval thereof, nor may any person challenge a federal, state or local law or action or inaction on the grounds that it is inconsistent with a Uruguay Round agreement, nor may a private party rely on the results of an action brought by the federal government. Section 102(c). The Statement of Administrative Action that accompanied the bill also stresses that the agreements are not self-executing.

In addition, the Act provides for much closer congressional oversight of U.S. WTO/GATT participation than in the past. It establishes a number of reporting and congressional consultation requirements (i.e., with the Ways and Means and Finance Committees), particularly in respect of WTO decision making and dispute settlement. Sections 122, 123, 127. In particular, the Act provides that the United States shall work for continuation in the WTO of the GATT practice of decision making by consensus, section 122(a), and for increased transparency in the WTO in general. Section 126. It also provides for five-year reviews of U.S. participation. Section 125.

Chapter 7

DISPUTE SETTLEMENT

SECTION 7.1   INTRODUCTION

(A) INTRODUCTION

The question of dispute settlement in international affairs was raised earlier in Chapter 5, where the topic was discussed in general terms. In this chapter, we look more closely at the dispute settlement procedures of the WTO system. We begin this chapter with a discussion of whether a legalistic-adjudicative/rules-oriented approach or a pragmatic-negotiation/power-oriented approach is the best way to resolve trade disputes in the WTO system. After a detailed examination of how the WTO's Dispute Settlement Understanding operates in practice, we then consider a number of key issues that have arisen, such as: What sort of claims may be brought? How are those claims evaluated? What remedies are available? How are conflicting norms resolved? What rights do non-governments have?

(B) GOALS AND METHODS

A fundamental question that arises in constructing and evaluating dispute settlement systems at the international level is whether the systems should be primarily designed to adjudicate disputes or to mediate them. If mediation is the goal, then a dispute settlement system must emphasize methods designed to encourage the contending parties to negotiate a solution to their dispute. If adjudication is the goal, then a system must be able to apply the relevant rules consistently and ensure that the decisions produced by the system are implemented. In tracing the history of GATT dispute settlement in Section 7.2, we will see that the GATT system became more and more adjudicative over the years. Not everyone is convinced that this evolution has been desirable. The following articles argue that an adjudicative, rule-based system is superior to a negotiation, power-based system. In reading them, consider whether you agree.

WILLIAM J. DAVEY, DISPUTE SETTLEMENT IN GATT[1]

What are the goals of GATT dispute settlement, and would they be better achieved by emphasizing adjudication or negotiation?

1. GOALS OF GATT DISPUTE SETTLEMENT

The GATT dispute settlement system was intended to resolve two types of disputes that may arise among GATT members: first, claims by one party that another has violated the provisions of the General Agreement. * * *

In the case of an alleged rule violation, the principal goal of a dispute settlement system is to stop the violation. Even if the dispute settlement system cannot compel compliance with the rule, and even if compliance without compulsion is unlikely, a lesser goal—such as achieving compliance with a watered-down version of the rule—or a goal that ignores the rule altogether would undermine the rule, and by implication all other GATT rules. GATT rules would become meaningless. So as long as there are agreed-upon rules, their enforcement must be the principal goal of the dispute settlement system. This conclusion suggests that in determining whether the GATT dispute settlement system should be more or less adjudicative in nature, the issue is whether a more adjudicative system would promote greater compliance with GATT rules.

* * *

2. ADJUDICATION OR NEGOTIATION

One result of emphasizing adjudication in the GATT dispute settlement system would likely be an increase in the number of cases considered by panels. While an emphasis on adjudication is not inconsistent with negotiated resolution of trade disputes, participants believing that attempts at a negotiated solution had failed would naturally request a dispute settlement panel. The existence of this possibility means that parties would probably abandon attempts at negotiated solutions more quickly than under a system where negotiation was the only alternative. Critics of the adjudication model argue that such increased use would poison the atmosphere within the GATT system to the eventual detriment of all parties, and that it could lead to the collapse of GATT, particularly if so-called "wrong" cases are brought. Proponents argue that it would increase overall compliance with GATT rules to the general benefit of all. These contentions are explored below.

a. *Poisoning the Atmosphere*

Critics of the adjudication model claim that it will promote conflict and contentiousness in an organization that must promote negotiated

1. 11 Fordham Intl.L.J. 51, 67–78 Fordham International Law Journal. (1987). Reprinted with permission of the solutions to achieve its goals. The need to promote negotiated solutions is said to exist because even if a panel report vindicated the complaining party, there is no guarantee that the other party will correct its violation. Thus, obtaining the other party's compliance with the violated GATT rule will necessarily be the subject of negotiations as to the exact form and timing of compliance. Since such diplomatic contracts will almost always be required, the legalistic approach is viewed as counterproductive because it poisons the atmosphere in which those contacts take place. Moreover, economic relations between the contending parties may deteriorate generally as positions in the dispute harden and bad feelings spill over into other areas.

It is difficult to analyze this criticism. Whether or not the atmosphere between two parties had been poisoned cannot objectively be determined by examining tangible evidence. If the atmosphere has been tainted, it is because one or both of the parties has deemed it so. One can evaluate, however, some of the reasons that are given as causes of a poisoned atmosphere.

First, it is suggested that the publicity associated with use of the dispute settlement system will make it more difficult to resolve the dispute. Publicity may embarrass the respondent by publicly labeling it a wrongdoer, thereby causing it to become intransigent. To the extent that positions taken by the parties become public, it becomes more difficult for them to modify these positions without appearing to back down. This situation impedes settlement of the dispute because neither side wants to appear to lose. These arguments seem rather weak because trade disputes are not secret. Even if they are handled through negotiations, one side will argue publicly that the other side has done something wrong. In addition, general positions on the issues will usually become known, at least to those who have an interest in the dispute.

Second, it is suggested that the filing of a complaint is a contentious act in itself, which will worsen relations. The weight of this argument would seem to depend on how frequently the dispute settlement system is used. If it is used only infrequently and only a few parties ever lose, initiation of a complaint would be something of a slap in the face. The ignominy of a loss would also loom larger. But to the extent that there are many cases, and the major trading nations are both winners and losers, this argument loses whatever force it had. So long as the dispute settlement system is viewed as a mechanism for resolving the myriad disputes, both major and minor, that arise between ninety-odd countries on a reasonably regular basis, there should be no poisoning of the atmosphere. As use grows, the system will be viewed as a normal part of the relationships between countries.

Third, it can be argued that a complaint will lead the respondent in that case to bring an action against the original complainant on other grounds. If this occurs, it will increase the number of disputes the system must handle, but that in itself is not undesirable. Indeed, if more complaints lead to a higher level of compliance with GATT rules, it would be beneficial. It could be argued, however, that more cases will result in more unresolved disputes, which could adversely affect GATT's prestige. For example, an increase in the number of disputes between two parties could make resolution of any one dispute more difficult if its resolution is tied to resolution of all others. While this may occur, it would occur in a system emphasizing negotiation as well. In any event, the tying together of different issues is not necessarily a negative result. Disputes that cannot be solved individually may be disposed of as part of a global solution. By indicating which party is in the right on the individual disputes, the dispute settlement system can play an important role in pushing the ultimate global settlement toward compliance with GATT rules. If the disputes are left entirely to negotiations, it is less clear that there would be any factor pushing the solution toward that suggested by the GATT rules.

All in all, the argument that an adjudicative system will poison the atmosphere of GATT is not compelling. Moreover, it is arguable that such a system will improve the atmosphere of GATT. Emphasis on negotiation is likely to lead some countries to use their relative political and economic strength to take advantage of weaker countries, a situation fundamentally incompatible with a system that stresses rules. Rules tend to treat everyone in the same fashion. Negotiated settlements tend to favor the party with the best negotiating position, which often will be the more economically powerful party. This is probably why smaller countries often support a legalistic system, as they perceive that they will be treated more fairly under such a system. As such, it can be argued that an adjudicative approach would improve the atmosphere of GATT by stressing fairness.

b. Wrong Cases

A second objection made to be a legalistic system is that it will result in what Professor Hudec has called "wrong" cases being brought into the system. A wrong case is a dispute the resolution of which undermines the GATT trading system. Several kinds of wrong cases have been suggested.

First, there is the case where a country has violated the rules of the General Agreement, but has done so unavoidably. Typically such violation would occur because of domestic pressures that the government cannot ignore. It is argued that condemning that government for violating the General Agreement in such circumstances is both unfair and inappropriate. It is considered unfair because the government is perceived to have no choice but to do what it did. It is considered inappropriate because the domestic political pressures will prevent the government from correcting the situation.

This sort of wrong case is not likely to damage GATT. The argument that it will seems to be based on a criminal law analogy. This analogy holds that an adverse decision by a dispute settlement panel is wrong and unfair because such decision is tantamount to convicting the respondent of a criminal act that it did not intend and could not prevent. This analogy is, however, inappropriate. Even assuming that the respondent really could not prevent the violation and did not intend it, a violation occurred. Since the General Agreement contains a negotiated balance of obligations, it is difficult to see why one country that has upset that balance should be able to do so without any offsetting penalty. While it might be inappropriate to punish a government that was helpless to prevent the violation, it does seem appropriate to put pressure on the government to correct the violation and, perhaps, to award relief to those countries adversely affected by the violation. Surely there is nothing unfair about such an outcome. Moreover, such action is appropriate since it will likely promote compliance with GATT rules. In particular, it may help respondent's government counteract domestic pressures if that government can honestly argue that condemnation by GATT is likely and retaliation by trading partners is possible. To the extent that such an argument is successful, compliance with the General Agreement will be improved. In short, in some cases noncompliance may be inevitable, but there would be more compliance if GATT condemned rule violations than if GATT ignored them.

The second example of a wrong case is one that is initiated in respect of an issue on which the GATT community has either not yet reached a consensus or on which past consensus has broken down. In such a case it is unthinkable that both parties will accept the panel's decision, whatever it may be. Examples of such cases would include those challenging agricultural trade practices, such as those of the EC, the 1962 Uruguayan complaint against numerous developed country import restrictions, and the U.S. complaint against EC tax systems in the DISC case.

Cases such as these undeniably put strains on the GATT system. The panel reports may generate considerable controversy, especially if they uphold the complainant's position. Moreover, the strains endure in time, as these cases are likely to remain unresolved for years. The critical point to remember, however, is that GATT has survived these wrong cases. Indeed, the United States and the EC have resolved a number of agricultural disputes through GATT, and the Uruguayan complaint, while not achieving what Uruguay sought, did lead to some reduced import restrictions. Thus, the "wrong" cases that GATT has faced so far might better be viewed as difficult cases that sorely tested the system, but that did not damage it.

What about the future possibility of wrong cases such as these? An adjudicative model of dispute settlement allows parties to push for interpretations of rules that are not commonly agreed upon. The risk exists in any system, but in a legalistic system it is more serious because the system guarantees that the party pressing the claim can obtain a decision, whereas in a system based on negotiated solutions the claim is never seriously considered. But does guaranteeing consideration of such claims undermine GATT. To begin with, it is quite possible that the panel will reject the controversial interpretation, particularly if it is novel. Even if the claim is accepted, several points are worth noting. First, the fact that it is accepted suggests that there is some basis for it. Second, if all of the contracting parties—or at least two-thirds of them—agreed that compliance with the panel decision should not be required, they could grant a waiver of the obligation at issue. Third, so long as there is the possibility that the GATT Council must approve a panel report, an outlandish complaint leading to an unacceptable result seems remote. Nonetheless, it must be conceded that a profusion of wrong cases such as those mentioned above might weaken GATT.

c. Compliance With GATT Rules

The principal argument in favor of a relatively more legalistic system is that it would better promote compliance with GATT rules than would a negotiation/consensus system.

An adjudicative system would promote compliance with GATT rules in two ways. First, it would discourage infractions of GATT rules. To the extent that countries know that they will be called to account if they violate the rules, they will be less likely to do so because the perceived cost of a violation will rise. In a more legalistic system the cost may include counteraction that negates any benefits from violating the rules. Further costs involve being labeled as a rule violator, a status that in and of itself imposes some cost, particularly in future negotiations over trade issues. Thus, to the extent that an adverse dispute panel decision is anticipated, countries will hesitate to violate the rules. Indeed, domestic political pressures may be directed elsewhere when the government can make a case against noncompliance with GATT. By contrast, in a negotiation/consensus system, the only cost may be unpleasant diplomatic exchanges, a negligible cost compared to the domestic political and economic benefits obtained by violating the rules.

Second, to the extent that an adjudicative approach produces more panel decisions, compliance with GATT rules will improve simply because panel decisions tend to be implemented, if not immediately, then over time. In general there has been an excellent, though admittedly at times slow, record of compliance with dispute settlement decisions that have been adopted by the Council. So long as most decisions are respected, adherence to the rules under a legalistic system will be better than in a negotiation/consensus system.

Furthermore, even if one party initially refuses to comply with a dispute settlement decision, that decision will affect the relative negotiating positions of the two contending parties. At the very least, the loser will suffer embarrassment. Moreover, that nation will have to justify its noncompliance with the panel decision. Such noncompliance, having been sanctioned, must be dealt with in other areas which are the subject of negotiations. In these other areas, as well as in negotiations directly on the subject matter of the dispute, the winner will gain leverage from having its positions vindicated by the panel report.

Thus, all other things being equal, it is likely that compliance with panel decisions will be increased and adherence to GATT rules better served by a more legalistic system. With an increase in the number of decisions, the obligations of GATT members will become clearer and better defined. Thus, the increased compliance with GATT rules will be compliance with more precisely defined rules.

JOHN H. JACKSON, THE WORLD TRADING SYSTEM 109–111 (2d ed. 1997)[2]

POWER-ORIENTED DIPLOMACY CONTRASTED WITH RULE-ORIENTED DIPLOMACY

One way to explore the questions raised above is to compare two techniques of modern diplomacy: a "rule-oriented" technique and a "power-oriented" technique. This perhaps puts the issue in too simple a dichotomy (because in practice the observable international institutions and legal systems involve some mixture of both), but it is nevertheless a useful way to examine the policy issues involved. This dichotomy can be explained as follows:

In broad perspective one can roughly divide the various techniques for the peaceful settlement of international disputes into two types: settlement by negotiation and agreement with reference (explicitly or implicitly) to relative power status of the parties; or settlement by negotiation or decision with reference to norms or rules to which both parties have previously agreed.

For example, countries A and B have a trade dispute regarding B's treatment of imports from A to B of widgets. The first technique mentioned would involve a negotiation between A and B by which the most powerful of the two would have the advantage. Foreign aid, military maneuvers, or import restrictions on other key goods by way of retaliation would figure in the negotiation. A small country would hesitate to challenge a large one on whom its trade depends. Implicit or explicit threats (e.g., to impose quantitative restrictions on some other product) would be a major part of the technique employed. Domestic political influences would probably play a greater part in the approach of the respective negotiators in this system, particularly on the negotiator for the more powerful party.

On the other hand, the second suggested technique—reference to agreed rules—would see the negotiators arguing about the application of the rule (e.g., was B obligated under a treaty to allow free entry of A's goods in question?). During the process of negotiating a settlement it would be necessary for the parties to understand that an unsettled dispute would ultimately be resolved by impartial third-party judgments based on the rules so that the negotiators would be negotiating with reference to the respective predictions as to the outcome of those judgments and not with reference to potential retaliation or actions exercising power of one or more of the parties to the dispute.

In both techniques negotiation and private settlement of disputes is the dominant mechanism for resolving differences; but the key is the perception of the participants as to what are the "bargaining chips." Insofar as agreed rules for governing the economic relations between the parties exist, a system which predicates negotiation on the implementation of those rules would seem for a number of reasons to be preferred. The mere existence of the rules, however, is not enough. When the issue is the application or interpretation of those rules (rather than the formulation of new rules), it is necessary for the parties to believe that if their negotiations reach an impasse the settlement mechanisms which take over for the parties will be designed to apply fairly or to interpret the rules. If no such system exists, then the parties are left basically to rely upon their respective "power positions," tempered (it is hoped) by the good will and good faith of the more powerful party (cognizant of its long-range interests).

All diplomacy, and indeed all government, involves a mixture of these techniques. To a large degree, the history of civilization may be described as a gradual evolution from a power-oriented approach, in the state of nature, towards a rule-oriented approach. However, never is the extreme in either case reached. In modern Western democracies, as we know them, power continues to play a major role, particularly political power of voter acceptance, but also to a lesser degree economic power such as that of labor unions or large corporations. However, these governments have passed far along the scale toward a rule-oriented approach, and generally have an elaborate legal system involving court procedures and a monopoly of force, through a police and a military, to ensure the rules will be followed. The U.S. government has indeed proceeded far in this direction, as the resignation of a recent president demonstrates. When one looks at the history of England over the last thousand years, I think that the evolutionary hypothesis from power to rule can be supported. And more recently, when one looks at the evolution of the EC, one is struck by the evolution toward a system that is remarkably elaborate in its rule structure, effectuated through a court of justice, albeit without a monopoly of force.

In international affairs, a strong argument can be made that to a certain extent this same evolution must occur, even though currently it has not progressed very far. The initiatives of the World War II and immediate postwar periods toward developing international institutions is part of this evolution, but as is true in most evolutions there have been setbacks, and mistakes have been made. Likewise when one focuses on international economic policy, we find that the dichotomy between power-oriented diplomacy and rule-oriented diplomacy can be seen. We have tried to develop rules, in the context of the International Monetary Fund and the GATT. The success has been varied.

Nevertheless, a particularly strong argument exists for pursuing gradually and consistently the progress of international economic affairs toward a rule-oriented approach. Apart from the advantages which accrue generally to international affairs through a rule-oriented approach—less reliance on raw power, and the temptation to exercise it or flex one's muscles, which can get out of hand; a fairer break for the smaller countries, or at least a perception of greater fairness; the development of agreed procedures to achieve the necessary compromises—in economic affairs there are additional reasons.

Economic affairs tend (at least in peace time) to affect more citizens directly than may political and military affairs. Particularly as the world becomes more economically interdependent, more and more private citizens find their jobs, their businesses, and their quality of life affected if not controlled by forces from outside their country's boundaries. Thus they are more affected by the economic policy pursued by their own country on their behalf. In addition, the relationships become increasingly complex—to the point of being incomprehensible to even the brilliant human mind. As a result, citizens assert themselves, at least within a democracy, and require their representatives and government officials to respond to their needs and their perceived complaints. The result of this is increasing citizen participation, and more parliamentary or congressional participation in the processes of international economic policy, thus restricting the degree of power and discretion which the executive possesses.

This makes international negotiations and bargaining increasingly difficult. However, if citizens are going to make their demands heard and influential, a "power-oriented" negotiating process (often requiring secrecy, and executive discretion so as to be able to formulate and implement the necessary compromises) becomes more difficult, if not impossible. Consequently, the only appropriate way to turn seems to be toward a rule-oriented system, whereby the various citizens, parliaments, executives and international organizations will all have their inputs, arriving tortuously to a rule—which, however, when established will enable business and other decentralized decision makers to rely upon the stability and predictability of governmental activity in relation to the rule.

Notes and Questions

(1) The WTO Dispute Settlement Understanding (see Documents Supplement) states in Article 3(2), "The dispute settlement system of the WTO is a central element in providing security and predictability to the multilateral trading system." While there had been some controversy in GATT over whether the purpose of dispute settlement was to provide a negotiating forum or a more judicial-like setting, at least some drafters favored the latter approach. One stated at preparatory meetings that the agreement "should deal with these subjects in precise detail so that the obligations of member governments would be clear and unambiguous. Most of these subjects readily

lend themselves to such treatment. Provisions on such subjects, once agreed upon, would be self-executing * * *."[3]

(2) There are significant advantages to a rule-based system. Former GATT Director–General Arthur Dunkel once noted:[4]

International economic policy commitments, in the form of agreed rules, have far-reaching domestic effect. * * * They are the element which secures the ultimate co-ordination and mutual compatibility of the purely domestic economic policies. They form the basis from which the government can arbitrate and secure an equitable and efficient balance between the diverse domestic interest: producers v. consumers, export industries v. import-competing industries.

In the same vein, they also allow planning by private parties.

(3) Does Professor Davey dismiss too easily the problems of using adjudicative methods to solve disputes among sovereign states? For example, for the adjudicative approach to work, nations must generally follow the decisions. What if they do not? In particular, what if the most powerful nation does not? Professor Hudec, a leading scholar on GATT dispute settlement, has expressed concern that the Uruguay Round reforms, which adopt and even go beyond those suggested by Professor Davey for making the system more adjudicative, may be the "worst of all worlds." He writes:

[The reforms] will assert the authority of GATT law more forcefully, but if the major GATT countries are not ready to change their behavior, these stronger demands will only produce more visible and dramatic legal failures. And if that were to happen, the credibility of GATT legal obligations would almost certainly plunge.[5]

Professor Hudec conditions his fears by noting that a successful Uruguay Round, with substantive agreements that do not paper over disputes as happened in the Tokyo Round, would reduce the likelihood of a dispute settlement failure. He further notes that a failure to strengthen significantly the dispute settlement system in the Uruguay Round might undermine its past successes. These successes have raised expectations that if not met would have "an extremely discouraging impact for a long time to come."[6]

One of the main reasons for Professor Hudec's concern is his view of U.S. behavior in GATT dispute settlement cases in the late 1980's and 1990's. During this period, the U.S. exercised its power to delay and, in some cases, block the adoption of panel reports by the GATT Council (or Code committee) and failed to implement promptly certain adopted panel reports. If the U.S. attitude persists, what effect would that have on the WTO dispute settlement system? Is that possibility reason enough to raise doubts about the desirability of the adjudicative approach? As you read the next section, consider whether there is evidence to date that the WTO reforms

3. Statement of U.S. delegate Harry Hawkins, UN Doc. EPCT/C.II/PV.2, 8 (1946), quoted in John H. Jackson, World Trade and the Law of GATT, 12 n.1 (1969).

4. GATT/1312 (Mar. 5, 1982).

5. Robert E. Hudec, Enforcing International Trade Law: The Evolution of the Modern GATT Legal System 364 (1993).

6. Id. at 365. For Professor Hudec's evaluation of the new system after three years, see Robert E. Hudec, The New WTO Dispute Settlement Procedure: An Overview of the First Three Years, 8 Minn. J. Global Trade 1 (1999).

went too far in adopting an adjudicative approach. As we will see in Section 7.3(B) infra, implementation of DSB recommendations has sometimes been slow, but in general has occurred as of mid–2001. Whether that record will be maintained remains to be seen.

(4) The problems of non-compliance would be exacerbated to the extent that a dispute settlement system produces results that state parties believe impose obligations beyond those to which they agreed. Given this consideration, should those charged with dispute settlement be more conservative in interpreting international obligations that national courts may be in interpreting national statutes? In particular, should international dispute settlement bodies be hesitant to adopt expansive interpretations of vague rules, even if such interpretations are consistent with broadly worded objectives of an agreement? In the international arena, is it rather the province of negotiators to refine obligations? After all, international agreements are consensual arrangements entered into by sovereigns. We will explore this and related issues in Section 7.4(B) infra.

(5) Should individuals have the right to invoke the WTO dispute settlement system? Would it lead to stricter enforcement of international rules because affected individuals could be counted upon to try to enforce their rights where governments might not for a variety of political or other reasons? Would such a possibility cause governments to hesitate to enter into broad commitments?[7] To date, there seems to have been little interest among most WTO members in allowing private party involvement in dispute settlement proceedings, even as observers. We will explore this and related issues in Section 7.4(F) infra. We will see in Section 10.3 infra that private parties are involved in certain of the dispute settlement mechanisms of the U.S.-Canada and North American Free Trade Agreements. For example, private parties have the right to appeal administrative decisions in anti-dumping and countervailing duty matters to binational panels, where they brief and argue their positions. In addition, private parties may demand third-party arbitration of investment disputes with NAFTA governments (see Chapter 24 infra), and they have limited rights to cause the initiation of enforcement reviews under the NAFTA environmental side agreement.[8]

SECTION 7.2   DISPUTE SETTLEMENT IN THE GATT SYSTEM

There are 19 clauses in the General Agreement which obligate GATT parties to consult in specific instances.[1] These provisions cover such varied subjects as customs valuation and invocation of the Escape Clause. Likewise, there are sprinkled throughout the General Agreement at least seven different provisions for compensatory withdrawal or suspension of concessions.

7. See Jackson, supra note 3, at 187; John H. Jackson, Jean–Victor Louis & Mitsuo Matsushita, Implementing the Tokyo Round 204 (1984); see generally Ernst–Ulrich Petersmann, Constitutional Functions and Constitutional Problems of International Economic Law (1991). See Section 27.3 infra.

8. See North American Agreement on Environmental Cooperation, arts. 14(1), 15(4).

1. This paragraph is based on John H. Jackson, World Trade and the Law of GATT, sec. 8.2, at 164 (1969).

While Article XXIII is GATT's the principal dispute settlement provision, it contains very little procedural detail. Consequently, the GATT parties had to improvise and develop procedures through practice over the years. Initially, the Contracting Parties considered disputes at their regular meetings. In some cases, working parties were used. A working party is understood in the GATT context to mean a body whose members are "nations," so that each nation may send a representative of its own choice. In the 1950's, largely as a result of the influence of then GATT Director–General Eric Wyndham–White, it became the practice to use panels to consider disputes. A panel is composed of individuals acting in their individual capacities, and not as national representatives. Interestingly, this shift early on in GATT's history shows a desire in GATT to emphasize adjudication by independent decision makers as opposed to negotiated settlements of differences by national representatives. The panel members, usually three in number, were in fact often chosen from available national representatives to GATT. Their reports were then (usually) adopted by consensus in the GATT Council.

The procedures used in the GATT system were codified in a 1979 Tokyo Round understanding.[2] There were also two further declarations on dispute settlement in the mid 1980's[3] and then a series of improvements agreed upon at the Uruguay Round midterm review session in 1989.[4] These procedures were largely carried over in the WTO procedures.

The GATT system experienced some problems with delays and failures to adopt reports because of blocking tactics by losing parties that prevented a consensus in the GATT Council. We will see how the WTO system addresses those problems in the next section. Generally, however, the GATT dispute settlement system can be viewed as relatively successful. Many disputes were settled without resort to the panel procedures. Indeed, only about 40% of the disputes resulted in a panel report adopted by the Council.[5] As to the results of the system, Professor Hudec concluded in his comprehensive study that of the 139 complaints through 1989 that he found to have been valid, conceded as valid, settled or withdrawn despite their probable validity, the complaining party received full satisfaction in 60% of the cases and partial satisfaction in another 29%.[6] This success rate—almost 90%—is extremely high. Few, if any, international dispute settlement systems can claim such success rates over a similarly long time period.

SECTION 7.3 THE WTO DISPUTE SETTLEMENT UNDERSTANDING

The WTO Agreement provides that one of the principal functions of the WTO is the administration of the Understanding on Rules and

2. Understanding Regarding Notification, Consultation, Dispute Settlement and Surveillance, 26th Supp. BISD 210 (1980).

3. 1982 Ministerial Declaration on Dispute Settlement Procedures, 29th Supp. BISD 13 (1983); 1984 Action on Dispute Settlement Procedures, 31st Supp. BISD 9 (1985).

4. 1989 Improvements to the GATT Dispute Settlement Rules and Procedures, 36th Supp. BISD 61 (1990).

5. Robert E. Hudec, Enforcing International Trade Law 375–83 (1993).

6. Id. at 285–87.

Procedures Governing the Settlement of Disputes, which is Annex 2 to the WTO Agreement and which is set out in the Documents Supplement. Indeed, the Dispute Settlement Understanding (DSU) states that the dispute settlement system "is a central element in providing security and predictability to the multilateral trading system" (art. 3.2). The DSU sets forth a comprehensive statement of dispute settlement rules and, while it builds on the past GATT practices, it makes several fundamental changes in the operation of the system. The DSU is administered by the Dispute Settlement Body (DSB), which is the WTO General Council acting in a specialized role under a separate chair. The DSU regulates dispute settlement under all covered WTO agreements, although under some agreements special rules and procedures will be applicable.[1]

The general philosophy of WTO dispute settlement is set out in Article 3 of the DSU. Among the principles that are enshrined in that article are the following:

First, it is recognized that the system serves to preserve the rights and obligations of Members and to clarify the existing provisions of the WTO agreements in accordance with the customary rules of interpretation of public international law. In this regard, it is also noted that the prompt settlement of disputes is essential to the functioning of the WTO and the maintenance of a proper balance between the rights and obligations of WTO Members.

Second, it is agreed that the results of the dispute settlement process cannot add to or diminish the rights and obligations provided in the WTO agreements. In this regard, the DSU explicitly notes the right of Members to seek authoritative interpretation of provisions pursuant to Article IX of the WTO Agreement, which itself provides that it is the exclusive means for interpreting the WTO Agreement.

Third, several provisions highlight that the aim of dispute settlement is to secure a positive solution to a dispute and that a solution that is acceptable to the parties and consistent with the WTO agreements is clearly to be preferred.

Fourth, although the DSU provides for the eventuality of noncompliance, it is explicitly stated in DSU Article 3.7 that "the first

---

1. Appendix 2 to the Dispute Settlement Understanding lists the special or additional dispute settlement rules and procedures. There are special rules, in particular, under the Antidumping and Subsidies Agreements. The DSU explicitly provides that the DSB Chair may decide what rules and procedures to follow when there is a dispute. DSU, art. 1.2. This unification of dispute settlement procedures eliminated forum shopping, which was a problem after the Tokyo Round because many Tokyo Round agreements had their own dispute settlement procedures, under the control of each agreement's supervisory body. See John H. Jackson, GATT Machinery and the Tokyo Round Agreements, *in* William Cline (ed.), Trade Policy in the 1980s, at 159, 185–87 (1983).

objective of the dispute settlement mechanism is usually to secure the withdrawal of the measures concerned if these are found to be inconsistent with the provisions of any of the covered agreements". Retaliatory action is described as the last resort.

(A) THE DSU PROCEDURES[2]

The key stages in a WTO dispute settlement proceeding are outlined and explained below. There are four major phases of WTO dispute settlement: First, the parties must attempt to resolve their differences through consultations. Second, if that fails, the complaining party may demand that a panel of independent experts be established to rule on the dispute. Third, and new under the DSU, is the possibility of an appeal by any party to the dispute to the Appellate Body. Finally, if the complaining party succeeds, the DSB is charged with monitoring the implementation of its recommendations. If the recommendations are not implemented, the possibility of negotiated compensation or authorization to withdraw concessions arises. The following materials describe the issues relevant at each of these stages, with particular emphasis on how the DSU deals with them, and, in particular, on the innovations it introduced compared to the GATT system.

(1) Consultations

The requirement that disputing parties consult with a view toward satisfactorily adjusting the matter is contained in Article XXIII itself. The hope is that the parties will resolve their dispute without having to invoke the formal dispute settlement procedures. The rules regarding consultations are set out in article 4 of the DSU. The manner in which the consultations are conducted is up to the parties. The DSU has no rules on consultations beyond that they are to be entered into in good faith and are to be held with 30 days of a request. During the consultations, both parties try to learn more about the facts and the legal arguments of the other party. Despite the fact that the structure of consultations is undefined and there are no rules for conducting them, a significant number of cases end at the consultations stage (either through settlements or abandonment of a case). If consultations fail to settle a dispute within 60 days after the request therefor, the complaining party may request the establishment of a panel. Art. 4.7. In fact, consultations often go on for more than 60 days.

(2) Panel Process

Under the DSU, the right of party to have a panel established is clearly set out in article 6.1. If consultations fail to resolve a dispute within the 60–day time frame specified in article 4, a complainant may insist on the establishment of a panel and, at the meeting following that

---

2. This section is based in part on William J. Davey, The WTO Dispute Settlement System, *in* Gary P. Sampson & W. Bradnee Chambers (eds.), Trade, Environment and the Millennium 119–142 (United Nations University Press 1999) (2d ed. 2001); see also David Palmeter & Petros C. Mavroidis, Dispute Settlement in the World Trade Organization: Practice and Procedure (1999).

at which the request first appears on the DSB's agenda, the DSB is required to establish a panel unless there is a consensus in the DSB not to establish a panel. Since the complaining party may prevent the formation of this "reverse" consensus, there is effectively a right to have a panel established. This is in contrast to the GATT system. Although persistent complainants virtually always succeeded in getting the GATT Council to establish a panel, their success sometimes came only after long periods of delay.

(a) Setting up the panel

Once a panel is established, it is necessary to select the three individuals who will serve as panelists. DSU article 8 provides for the Secretariat to propose potential panel members to the parties, who are not to object except for compelling reasons. In practice, parties are relatively free to reject proposed panelists, but if the parties do not agree on panel members within 20 days of establishment, any party may request the WTO Director–General to appoint the panel on his or her own authority. Art. 8.7. In recent years, the Director–General has appointed some members of almost one-half of the panels composed.

Article 8.1 of the DSU provides that panels shall be composed of

> "well-qualified governmental and/or non-governmental individuals, including persons who have served on or presented a case to a panel, served as a representative of a Member or of a contracting party to GATT 1947 or as a representative to the Council or Committee of any covered agreement or its predecessor agreement, or in the Secretariat, taught or published on international trade law or policy, or served as a senior trade policy official of a Member."

These criteria could be roughly summarized as establishing three categories of panelists: government officials (current or former), former Secretariat officials and trade academics or lawyers. It is specifically provided that panelists shall not be nationals of parties or third parties, absent agreement of the parties. It is also specified that in a case involving a developing country, one panelist must be from a developing country (if requested). Of the individuals actually chosen for panel service, it appears that the vast majority (over 80%) are current or former government officials.

The DSU provides that panelists serve in their individual capacities and that Members shall not give them instructions or seek to influence them. In addition, the DSB has adopted rules of conduct applicable to participants in the WTO dispute settlement system. The rules require that panelists "be independent and impartial, shall avoid direct or indirect conflicts of interest and shall respect the confidentiality of proceedings." To ensure compliance with the rules, such persons are to disclose "the existence or development of any interest, relationship or matter that person could reasonable be expected to know and that it likely to affect, or give rise to justifiable doubts as to, that person's independence or impartiality." Disputing parties have the right to raise an alleged material violation of the rules, which if upheld, would lead to the replacement of the challenged individual.[3]

(b) The task of panels

The DSU provides in article 7.1 for standard terms of reference (absent agreement to the contrary). The standard terms direct a panel "To examine, in the light of the relevant provisions in (name of the covered agreement/s cited by the parties to the dispute), the matter referred to the DSB by (name of party) in document DS/ . . . and to make such findings as will assist the DSB in making the recommendations or in giving the rulings provided for in that/those agreement/s." The Appellate Body has emphasized in its rulings that panels may not stray beyond their terms of reference. In practice, the document mentioned above will be the panel request made pursuant to article 6.2, which requires that the request "specify the measures at issue and provide a brief summary of the legal basis of the complaint sufficient to present the problem clearly." There are often lengthy arguments over whether second requirement has been met.[4]

More generally, DSU Article 11 provides that a panel shall make an objective assessment of the matter before it, including an objective assessment of the facts of the case and the applicability of and conformity with the relevant WTO agreements. In the *Hormones* case (see Section 14.2 infra), the Appellate Body elaborated on this requirement as follows (para. 133):

> [W]hen may a panel be regarded as having failed to discharge its duty under Article 11 of the DSU to make an objective assessment of the facts before it? Clearly, not every error in the appreciation of the evidence (although it may give rise to a question of law) may be characterized as a failure to make an objective assessment of the facts. In the present appeal, the European Communities repeatedly claims that the Panel disregarded or distorted or misrepresented the evidence submitted by the European Communities and even the opinions expressed by the Panel's own expert advisors. The duty to make an objective assessment of the facts is, among other things, an obligation to consider the evidence presented to a panel and to make factual findings on the basis of that evidence. The deliberate disregard of, or refusal to consider, the evidence submitted to a panel is incompatible with a panel's duty to make an objective assessment of the facts. The wilful distortion or misrepresentation of the evidence put before a panel is similarly inconsistent with an objective assessment of the facts. "Disregard" and "distortion" and "misrepresentation" of the evidence, in their ordinary signification in judicial and

3. WT/DSB/RC/1. See generally Gabrielle Marceau, Rules on Ethics for the New World Trade Organization Dispute Settlement Mechanism, *Journal of World Trade*, vol. 32, no. 3, June 1998, page 57.

4. See William J. Davey, WTO Dispute Settlement: Segregating the Useful Political Aspects and Avoiding "Over-legalization", *in* Marco Bronckers & Reinhard Quick (eds.), New Directions in International Economic Law: Essays in Honor of Professor John H. Jackson 291–307 (2000).

quasi-judicial processes, imply not simply an error of judgment in the appreciation of evidence but rather an egregious error that calls into question the good faith of a panel. A claim that a panel disregarded or distorted the evidence submitted to it is, in effect, a claim that the panel, to a greater or lesser degree, denied the party submitting the evidence fundamental fairness, or what in many jurisdictions is known as due process of law or natural justice.

EC Measures Concerning Meat and Meat Products (Hormones), WT/DS26 & 48/AB/R, adopted by the DSB on February 13, 1998. While the Appellate Body found some instances where it concluded that the panel's representations of its experts' view were not accurate, it found that the EC failed to establish a violation of article 11.

(c) Panel procedures

A panel normally meets with the parties shortly after its selection to set its working procedures and time schedule. The DSU's standard proposed timetable for panels makes provision for two meetings between the panel and the parties to discuss the substantive issues in the case. Each meeting is preceded by the filing of written submissions. The DSU permits other WTO members to intervene as third parties and present arguments to the panel. Otherwise, the panel proceedings are not open to the public. It was firmly established by the Appellate Body in the *Bananas* case, however, that a party is free to choose the members of its delegation to hearings.[5] Thus, parties may be assisted, and often are, by private counsel.

Among the most fundamental issues that arises in assessing a complaint is the assignment of the burden of proof. Generally speaking, the decisions of the Appellate Body have held that the burden of proof rests upon the party who asserts the affirmative of a particular claim or defense. If that party adduces sufficient evidence to raise a presumption that what is claimed is true, then the burden shifts to the other party to rebut the presumption.[6] The Appellate Body has also spoken in terms of the need for a claimant to establish a *prima facie* case.

In GATT dispute settlement, it was often the case that factual issues were not that important. The basic issue was typically whether a particular governmental measure violated GATT rules. To date, comparatively more WTO disputes have involved disputed factual issues. In order to establish facts, panels normally ask oral and written questions to which the parties are expected to respond. The parties often bring government experts versed in the relevant field to panel meetings. Some parties have submitted affidavit evidence to establish facts. By and large, the fact-finding procedures of panels are relatively less sophisticated that

5. European Communities—Regime for the Importation, Sale and Distribution of Bananas, WT/DS27/AB/R, paras. 4–12, Appellate Body Report adopted by the DSB on September 25, 1997.

6. United States—Measures Affecting Imports of Woven Wool Shirts and Blouses, WT/DS33/AB/R, pp. 12–17, Appellate Body Report adopted by the DSB on May 23, 1997.

those of national courts, although it can be expected that more sophisticated fact-finding techniques will develop as the need for fact-finding becomes more acute.

One area in which panels have already become more sophisticated is in the use of experts in scientific matters. In this regard, the DSU provides that if a panel deems it appropriate, it may consult either individuals experts or form an expert review group to advise it on technical and scientific issues. Panels have consulted multiple experts on an individual basis in the three cases arising under the SPS Agreement (see Section 14.2), in one case involving health issues and in one case involving environmental issues. In each case, the panel asked the parties to suggest possible experts and sought information from the relevant international scientific agency. The parties were also invited to comment on the questions that the panel proposed to ask the experts. Following receipt of the experts' answers, the parties had the opportunity to comment in writing on the answers and an "experts' meeting" was held at which the panel and the parties could question the experts.

One basic issue faced by panels is what sort of standard of review should be applied in reviewing challenged measures. Of course, in some cases that issue is not particularly significant. The only issue is whether the measure violates a WTO rule. But in an increasing number of cases, the assessment of a measure's consistency with WTO rules involves an assessment of the justification for a measure, for example, of whether a measure is "necessary" within the terms of an exception contained GATT Article XX or whether a measure is "based on" or rationally related to a risk assessment in the case of an SPS (health) measure. In such a case, to what extent should a panel or the Appellate Body defer to the challenged government's assessment of necessity or rationality? The DSU gives no guidance on this issue beyond directing panels to make an objective assessment of the matter before them. This is obviously a key issue and we consider it in detail below in Section 7.4(B).

After hearings and deliberations, the panel prepares a report detailing its conclusions. Traditionally, the panel has submitted its description of the dispute and of the parties' arguments to the parties for comment. Under the DSU, panels are required to submit an interim report containing their legal analysis for comment as well. Art. 15. Appendix 3 of the DSU specifies time limits for implementations of the various stages in the panel process. Those time limits suggest that the panel report should normally be issued within six to eight months of the establishment of the panel. In practice, cases typically take more time than that.

(d) Consideration and adoption of panel reports

Under GATT dispute settlement practice prior to conclusion of the Uruguay Round, after a panel issued its report, it was considered for adoption by the GATT Council. Traditionally, decisions in the Council were made by consensus, which meant that any party—including the losing party—could prevent the Council from adopting a panel report. If unadopted, a report would represent only the view of the individual panel members. While parties did not often permanently block adoption of reports, some reports were never adopted (even when the underlying dispute was resolved) and others were adopted only after months of delay. Many commentators felt that this was a major failing in what was otherwise a fairly successful GATT dispute settlement system. Indeed, it is difficult to explain to someone new to the subject why the losing party by itself should be able to prevent adoption of a panel report.

The DSU fundamentally changed this procedure. It eliminates the possibility of blockage by providing in Article 16 that a panel report shall be adopted unless there is an appeal (see below) or a "reverse consensus," i.e., a consensus *not* to adopt the report. This switch from requiring a consensus for adoption to requiring a consensus to block adoption is a very significant change. It appears that it was adopted in hopes that it would satisfy U.S. complaints about weaknesses in the GATT system and thereby result in the United States using the system in the future instead of taking unilateral action as it had done sometimes in the past. Basically, other GATT parties were willing to make the change as a way to rein in U.S. unilateralism in trade matters. Indeed, article 23.1 of the DSU requires WTO members to use the WTO dispute settlement system exclusively if they "seek the redress of a violation of obligations or other nullification or impairment of benefits under the covered agreements." We will consider the effect of this provision on U.S. law and practice in Section 7.4(G), where we examine the results of an EC challenge in WTO dispute settlement to so-called Section 301 of the 1974 Trade Act, as amended, which is the statute typically invoked by the United States when it applies unilateral trade measures.

(3) The Appellate Body

The change in the consensus rule described above was paired with the introduction of a right to appeal a panel decision. The DSU creates a standing Appellate Body with seven members, appointed for four-year terms and representative of WTO membership.[7] Only one reappointment is permitted. The Appellate Body is authorized to draw up its own working procedures, in consultation with the Chairman of the DSB and the Director–General. These procedures regulate the operation of the Appellate Body and process by which appeals are made and considered. They are available at the WTO website.

7. The first seven members of the Appellate Body were James Bacchus (US), Christopher Beeby (New Zealand), Claus–Dieter Ehlermann (Germany), Florentino Feliciano (the Philippines), Said El Naggar (Egypt), Julio Lacarte Muro (Uruguay) and Mitsuo Matsushita (Japan). Ehlermann, Feliciano and Lacarte–Muro were deemed to have initial two-year terms and were later reappointed to four-year terms expiring in December 2001. They were replaced by Luiz Olavo Baptista (Brazil), John S. Lockhart (Australia) and Giorgio Sacerdoti (Italy). Bacchus and Beeby were re-appointed in 1999 to terms expiring in December 2003. However, Beeby later died and was replaced by Yasuhei Taniguchi (Japan). El Naggar and Matsushita were replaced by Georges Abi–Saab (Egypt) and A.V. Ganesan (India).

The Appellate Body hears appeals of panel reports in divisions of three, although its rules provide for the division hearing a case to exchange views with the other four Appellate Body members before the division finalizes its report. The members of the division that hears a particular appeal are selected by a secret procedure that is based on randomness, unpredictability and the opportunity for all members to serve without regard to national origin. The Appellate Body is required to issue its report within 60 (at most 90) days from the date of the appeal, and its report is to be adopted automatically by the DSB within 30 days, absent consensus to the contrary (as explained above). The appealed panel report is also adopted at that time, as modified by the Appellate Body report.

The Appellate Body's review is limited to issues of law and legal interpretation developed by the panel. However, the Appellate Body has taken a broad view of its power to review panel decisions. It has the express power to reverse, modify or affirm panel decisions, but the DSU does not include a possibility of remanding a case to a panel. Partly as a consequence, the Appellate Body has adopted the practice, where possible in light of a panel's factual findings, of completing the analysis of particular issues in order to resolve cases where it has significantly modified a panel's reasoning. This avoids requiring a party to start the whole proceeding over as a result of those modifications.

There had been 58 WTO dispute settlement cases where reports had been adopted by the DSB as of September 1, 2001 (including compliance cases). In 40 of those cases, there was an Appellate Body report. In seven cases, panels were upheld; in one case, the panel was reversed. In the remaining 32 cases, the Appellate Body modified, sometimes extensively, the panel's findings. In all but one of those 32 cases, however, the basic finding of a violation reached by the panel was upheld, albeit sometimes to a different degree and/or on the basis of quite different reasoning. Eighteen panel reports had been adopted without an appeal. Thus, slightly more than two-thirds of the cases had been appealed.

It is probably much too early to judge an institution that has been in operation for only five and one-half years. Yet a number of points may be made. First, although the Appellate Body has never articulated a standard of review that it will apply on appeals of panel reports, it has engaged in fairly intensive review of such reports. In doing so, it has in general left its stamp clearly on most areas of WTO law that have been appealed. Indeed, in respect of GATT Articles III and XX, and the SPS, Safeguards and Subsidies Agreements, the Appellate Body jurisprudence is particularly rich and far-reaching. While strict notions of "stare decisis" do not apply in the WTO, it is clear that prior cases do play an important role in dispute settlement, especially those considered to be well-reasoned and persuasive. Indeed, the Appellate Body noted early on that adopted GATT panel reports created "legitimate expectations" that similar matters would be handled similarly,[8] and both panels and the

---

8. Japan—Taxes on Alcoholic Beverages, WT/DS8, 10 & 11/AB/R, pp. 12–14, Appellate Body Report adopted by the DSB on November 1, 1996.

Appellate Body frequently support their decisions by extensive citation and quotation of prior decisions. Thus, it is appropriate to speak of the Appellate Body's effect on "WTO law".

Generally speaking, the Appellate Body tends to rely heavily on close textual interpretation of the WTO provisions at issue, stressing that a treaty interpreter must look to the ordinary meaning of the relevant terms, in their context and in light of the object and purpose of the relevant agreement (a requirement of Article 31 of the Vienna Convention of the Law of Treaties) and must not interpret provisions so as to render them devoid of meaning. The Appellate Body has expressed the need to respect due process and procedural rights of Members in the dispute settlement process, but by and large it has recognized considerable discretion on the part of panels, which has led it in the end to reject most procedural/due process challenges. On the whole, it is difficult to characterize the Appellate Body as being more or less deferential to Member discretion than panels. While it has significantly cut back on the scope of panel rulings in some cases, it has significantly expanded the scope of liability in others.

(4) Implementation and Suspension of Concessions

If it is found that a complaint is justified, the panel/Appellate Body report typically recommends that the offending member cease its violation of WTO rules, normally by withdrawing the offending measure. After it adopts a report, the DSB monitors whether or not its recommendations are implemented. The DSU requires a losing respondent to indicate what actions it plans to take to implement the panel's recommendations. If immediate implementation is impracticable, then implementation is required within a reasonable period of time. Art. 21.3. The reasonable period of time is normally set by agreement of the contending parties, or, absent agreement, by arbitration. Normally, the period is not to exceed 15 months; a range of 8–10 months is average.

If the recommendations are not implemented, the prevailing party is entitled to seek compensation from the non-complying member or request DSB authority to suspend concessions previously made to that member (sometimes referred to as "retaliation"). Art. 22.1. In this regard, the DSU modifies past GATT practice. Article XXIII permitted GATT contracting parties to authorize the prevailing party to retaliate if the losing party failed to end its violation of GATT rules. Such authorization was granted only once, however, and that was in 1955 to allow the Netherlands to suspend concessions made to the United States in a case involving GATT-inconsistent U.S. quotas on Dutch agricultural products. The Netherlands apparently never utilized the authorization. Attempts to obtain authorizations in the 1980's failed because of the consensus rule, with the target country opposing the authorization. Now, under the DSU, suspension of concessions is to be authorized automatically in the absence of implementation or compensation, absent a consensus in the DSB to the contrary. Art. 22.6. There are specific arbitration procedures for determining the level of such a suspension if no agreement can be reached.

The DSU provides: "Prompt compliance with recommendations or rulings of the DSB is essential in order to ensure the effective resolution of disputes to the benefit of all Members" (art. 21.1). The DSB will normally recommend the withdrawal of any measure found to be inconsistent with a member's obligations, and the DSU explicitly provides that withdrawal of a nonconforming measure is preferred to compensation or suspension of concessions. Art. 22.1. Compensation and suspensions of concessions are viewed as "temporary measures," to be used when a report is not implemented in a reasonable time. The preference for withdrawal is also found in the WTO Agreement itself, where article XVI:4 provides that "[e]ach Member shall ensure the conformity of its laws, regulations and administrative procedures with its obligations as provided in the annexed Agreements." Thus, there would appear to be an international law obligation to implement recommendations to withdraw inconsistent measures.

The application of the foregoing procedures on implementation and retaliation has been controversial. We will discuss why and other related issues in respect of remedies in Section 7.4(C) infra.

Notes and Questions

(1) In 1987, Professor Davey summarized the principal complaints about the GATT dispute system as follows: (i) disuse, (ii) delays in the establishment of panels, (iii) delays in appointing panel members, (iv) delays in the completion of panel reports; (v) uncertain quality and neutrality of panelists and panel reports, (vi) blocked panel reports and (vii) non implementation of panel reports.[9] These problems were epitomized by the so-called *DISC* case, involving an EC challenge to a U.S. tax law and a counter-challenge by the U.S. against the tax rules of several European countries. Over a year elapsed between the start of consultations and the decision to establish a panel, and roughly two and one-half years passed before the members were selected. While the panel reports were issued promptly, their quality and content were severely criticized and they lingered on the Council's agenda for several years before action was finally taken.[10] The problem of disuse (only 38 complaints made in the 1960's and 1970's combined) disappeared in the 1980's (115 complaints).[11] As to the other problems, how does the DSU deal with each of them? Does more need to be done?

(2) The Uruguay Round changes have not received universal acclaim. Perhaps the most serious concern raised is the one raised at the end of Section 7.1—if a major economic power (such as the United States, the EU

---

9. William J. Davey, Dispute Settlement in GATT, 11 Fordham J.Intl.L. 51, 81–89 (1987). See also U.S. Int'l Trade Comm'n, Pub. No. 1793, Review of the Effectiveness of Trade Dispute Settlement Under the GATT and the Tokyo Round Agreements (1985).

10. See John H. Jackson, The Jurisprudence of International Trade: The *DISC* Case in GATT, 72 Am.J.Intl.L. 747 (1978).

11. Robert E. Hudec, Enforcing International Trade Law 590–608 (1993).

or Japan) refuses to comply with adverse panel or Appellate Body decisions, will the WTO dispute settlement system collapse? In addition, more specific concerns have been raised.[12] Will the existence of the Appellate Body reduce the prestige of panel service and the quality of panel reports? Who will serve on the seven-person Appellate Body? Will they view their role more as mediators or as judges? If the former, what will be the effect on the dispute settlement system? Will the right of appeal increase delays? Will the opportunity of the parties to comment on the legal reasoning of the panel in its draft report cause panels to be too solicitous of the parties' positions? Will the reforms dilute the positive role that the Secretariat's legal staff played in improving the quality of panel reports? Given the experience of the six and one-half years since 1995, how would you evaluate these concerns?

(3) As noted above, one of the complaints about the GATT dispute settlement system arose from the effect of the consensus rule—the ability of the losing party to block adoption of the panel report. While this practice can certainly be criticized, it is worth remembering that the consensus rule provided GATT panel reports with political legitimacy—the organization adopted the panel reports without objection. Automatic adoption removes this political cover. Will that in itself reduce the legitimacy, and therefore the effectiveness, of the dispute settlement system? Will the existence of the Appellate Body provide an adequate substitute for adoption by consensus? There were other proposals to deal with the blockage problem. The principal one was the "consensus minus two" solution, which would not allow the parties to the dispute to block adoption of the panel report. Would that change have been better than automatic adoption? How could the system prevent the blocking of adoption by proxies (i.e., parties not directly involved in the dispute but willing to "represent" the losing party and block consensus, perhaps because of interests similar to the losing party or simply as a favor)?

(4) Note the provisions that govern a dispute arising under GATT Articles VI, XIX or XXVIII, and note that in each of these cases reaction by the aggrieved nation (with countervailing duties to a subsidy, with compensatory import restraints to an escape clause action and with compensatory withdrawal of tariff bindings to a prior withdrawal) requires no international permission, i.e. it can be effected unilaterally, if necessary. Compare these provisions with the DSU. If your country took an action which could be interpreted as either an escape clause action or a violation of a GATT binding (nullification and impairment), would you prefer a construction of the action as a violation, or as the exercise of a right under Article XIX? Which would most likely result in counter-response from the other side? Is there an anomaly in a situation which "rewards" violations compared to exercise of rights?

(5) Could monopoly or cartel practices give rise to an Article XXIII complaint? One GATT report suggested that such practices should not be the basis of such a complaint, because it was "dangerous" to use Article

---

12. See William J. Davey, The GATT Dispute Settlement System: Proposals for Reform in the Uruguay Round, in Work- shop on the Multilateral Trade Negotiations of GATT (1992).

XXIII in these circumstances.[13] Why? Are there any definable boundaries to the use of the dispute settlement procedures?

(6) The DSU provides for other alternatives than formal dispute settlement if parties cannot resolve their disputes. Article 5 includes provisions on good offices, conciliation and mediation, and provides specifically that the Director–General may offer to provide such services in an effort to assist members in resolving disputes. These informal methods may be used in addition to or in lieu of the panel process. As of mid–2001, these alternative procedures had not been used, although in July 2001 the Director–General urged WTO members to consider using them.

(B) THE OPERATION OF THE WTO DISPUTE SETTLEMENT SYSTEM: 1995–2001

The WTO dispute settlement system has been quite active since the founding of the WTO on January 1, 1995. As of September 1, 2001, there had been 237 consultation requests. The annual number of consultation requests peaked at 50 in 1997 and more recently has been running at an annual rate of around 30 or so. It appears that roughly one-half of the cases are settled (sometimes after commencement of panel proceedings) or abandoned (in the sense that one year after the consultation request, no panel has been requested).

The panel system and the Appellate Body have seen their work load increase significantly in recent years, in part because of compliance cases, which are expedited proceedings to determine if DSB recommendation have been implemented. The activity of this part of the system can be seen in the following table of panel/Appellate Body reports adopted on a year-to-year basis demonstrates:

Year	Reports adopted	Compliance reports adopted	Total
1995	–	–	–
1996	2	–	2
1997	5	–	5
1998	11	–	11
1999	9	1	12
2000	14	4	20
2001 (to Sept. 1)	11	1	12
Total	52	6	58

In addition, there have been four arbitrations concerning the level of retaliation to be authorized. As of September 1, 2001, there were 12 active cases at the panel or Appellate Body stage, plus 6 cases in the panel composition stage.

The DSU provides that panel reports should be circulated within nine months of the establishment of the panel. To date, panels have

---

13. GATT, 9th Supp. BISD 172 (1961); see John H. Jackson, World Trade and the Law of GATT 181 (1969).

often missed this deadline—sometimes because of the complexity of the cases or the need to consult experts, sometimes simply because of translation delays. Nonetheless, given the circumstances, the reports have generally appeared reasonably close to the DSU requirements. In the case of the Appellate Body, it has seldom missed its 90 day deadline for circulating its reports. Thus, the system has largely eliminated delays that characterized some periods of GATT dispute settlement.

WTO dispute settlement proceedings have produced a huge corpus of what might be called WTO law. While the 40 reports of the Appellate Body have probably received the most attention, it is important to remember that 58 panel reports have also been adopted by the DSB and in many of the 40 cases that were appealed, the panel reports rule on issues that were not appealed. Compared to GATT cases, WTO cases have tended to involve more issues and often involve claims under more than one agreement. Thus, there is a very rich body of material interpreting WTO obligations.

The WTO system has had a reasonably good overall implementation record. As of September 1, 2001, panel and/or Appellate Body reports had been adopted in 52 cases (not including compliance proceedings). In 8 cases, no implementation was required; in 7 cases the period for implementation had not expired. Of the remaining 37 cases, implementation had occurred in 30, or approximately 75% of the cases. In some of these cases implementation was not completely accepted by the complaining party, but no further proceedings were initiated. In addition, implementation was not always timely; nonetheless it ultimately occurred in these cases. Of the seven remaining cases, four were in compliance proceedings to determine whether implementation had taken place. In the other three cases, where non-compliance had been found or admitted, retaliatory measures had been authorized. The three cases were *EC Bananas*,[14] where a settlement had been provisionally announced and the retaliatory measures withdrawn in mid–2001 (see Section 7.4(C) infra for a description of the implementation issues raised by this case); *EC Hormones*,[15] where retaliatory measures were in place (see Section 14.2 infra); and *Brazil Aircraft Subsidies*,[16] where retaliatory measures had been authorized but not implemented. These cases were the exceptions to an otherwise strong record in compliance. The existence of these cases (and cases where complainants have not obtained timely or complete satisfaction) has raised the question, however, of whether the remedies available under WTO rules need to be improved. It can be argued that the current structure of compliance proceedings encourages foot-dragging and that the ultimate WTO remedy for compli-

14. European Communities—Regime for the Importation, Sale and Distribution of Bananas, WT/DS27.

15. European Communities—Measures Affecting Livestock and Meat (Hormones), WT/DS26 & 48.

16. Brazil—Export Financing Programme for Aircraft, WT/DS46.

ance—"retaliation" through trade sanctions—may not always be effective. We explore this further below in Section 7.4(D) infra.

SECTION 7.4   CRITICAL ISSUES IN WTO DISPUTE SETTLEMENT

In this section, we will consider a number of critical issues that have arisen in respect of WTO dispute settlement. We have had to be quite selective in choosing these issues, as the subject of WTO dispute settlement could probably now support a course by itself. The seven issues we will examine are (i) the concept of nullification or impairment in GATT Article XXIII, both in violation and non-violation cases, (ii) the appropriate standard of review to be applied by panels to government measures, (iii) implementation procedures, (iv) the problem of providing for effective remedies, (v) resolving conflicts of norms within the WTO system and between the WTO and other international legal systems, (vi) transparency and participation by non-members; (vii) the problem of unilateralism and the DSU, and (viii) the special problems of developing countries.

Some of these issues were considered in a review of the operation of the DSU that was undertaken in 1998–1999, pursuant to a ministerial decision in the Uruguay Round. Although many proposals and comments were made in the review process, it appeared that in the main WTO members were generally satisfied with the operation of the dispute settlement system. In any event, no agreement was reached on implementing changes and the review ended with the system described above remaining in effect and unchanged.

(A) GATT ARTICLE XXIII AND THE CONCEPT OF NULLIFICATION AND IMPAIRMENT

As in the case of the GATT dispute settlement system, the wording and structure of GATT Article XXIII play an important role in the WTO system. The other WTO agreements either expressly incorporate Article XXIII as the standard for dispute settlement or contain a provision very similar to it. In addition, DSU Article 3.1 provides: "Members affirm their adherence to the principles for the management of disputes heretofore applied under Article XXII and XXIII of GATT 1947."

A careful look at Article XXIII reveals a number of troublesome and peculiar characteristics. In fact (as one of the authors has written elsewhere), the draftsmen of the General Agreement had at least three objectives in mind for Article XXIII, and it is not likely that those objectives are consistent one with another.[1] The first objective was that Articles XXII (a general provision on consultations) and XXIII were to be the framework of a dispute settlement procedure, stressing the general obligation to consult on any matter relating to GATT. The second objective was that Article XXIII would play an important role in obtain-

---

1. John H. Jackson, World Trade and the Law of GATT 167–69 (1969).

ing compliance with the GATT obligations. The customary international law analogy of *retorsion* was used. A third goal for these provisions of GATT was to establish a means for ensuring continued "reciprocity and balance of concessions" in the face of changing circumstances. This third goal is more in the nature of an "escape clause" or "changed circumstances" provision.

The structure of Article XXIII is complex. In order to prevail under the terms of Article XXIII, a complainant must show that either

(i) benefits accruing to it under the General Agreement are being nullified or impaired; or

(ii) the attainment of an objective of the General Agreement is being impeded.

GATT disputes have virtually always turned on whether benefits have been nullified or impaired, with the result that the meaning of the second quoted phrase is unclear.

In addition, the complainant must show that such nullification or impairment (or impedance of objective) is a result of:

(i) a breach of obligation by the respondent contracting party;

(ii) the application of any measure by the respondent contracting party, whether it conflicts with the General Agreement or not; or

(iii) the existence of any other situation.

Under the language of Article XXIII, as traditionally interpreted, a violation of the General Agreement was by itself neither sufficient nor necessary to entitle a party to relief. Over time, however, more emphasis in the dispute settlement process has been placed on whether a violation of the General Agreement has been shown.

For example, in 1962, Uruguay brought an Article XXIII complaint against a broad range of trade restrictions it alleged were maintained by 15 industrialized GATT parties. In deciding how it would handle the complaint, the panel noted the following:[2]

> In cases where there is a clear infringement of the provisions of the General Agreement, or in other words, where measures are applied in conflict with the provisions of GATT and are not permitted under the terms of the relevant protocol under which the GATT is applied by the contracting party, the action would, *prima facie*, constitute a case of nullification or impairment and would *ipso facto* require consideration of whether the circumstances are serious enough to justify the authorization of suspension of concessions.

The *prima facie* concept was also applied in situations involving quotas or domestic subsidies on products subject to agreed upon tariff limitations (i.e., tariffs bound under Article II, see Section 8.2 infra).[3]

---

2. Uruguayan Recourse to Article XXIII, 11th Supp. BISD 95, 100 (Panel report adopted Nov. 16, 1962).

3. See generally Jackson, supra note 1, at 182.

In this section, we examine how the concept of nullification or impairment is treated in the DSU and in WTO cases. Since the rules and the cases differentiate between cases based on Article XXIII:1(a)—claims that a party failed to "carry out its obligations" (violation cases) and (ii) those based on Article XXIII:1(b)—claims involving no alleged violation (nonviolation cases), we will consider first dispute settlement rules particularly relevant to violation cases and then those applied to nonviolation cases.

(1) *Nullification or Impairment in Violation Cases*

By far the most common claim raised in GATT and WTO dispute settlement is that one party has violated its GATT/WTO obligations. The evolution of the nullification or impairment concept in violation cases (see below for discussion of non-violation cases) is quite interesting. As noted above, Article XXIII, by its terms, in a violation case, requires both a violation ("failure * * * to carry out its obligations") and that a "benefit accruing to [the complaining party] directly or indirectly under the Agreement is being nullified or impaired."[4] In early violation cases, the panel turned to the issue of nullification or impairment after finding a GATT violation. For example, in *Italian Discrimination Against Imported Agricultural Machinery*, see Section 12.2 infra, the panel noted that it "considered whether [the violation] had caused injury to the United Kingdom's commercial interests, and whether such an injury represented an impairment of benefits."[5] But in the Uruguayan case, as noted above, the concept of *prima facie* nullification or impairment was introduced.

UNITED STATES—TAXES ON PETROLEUM AND CERTAIN IMPORTED SUBSTANCES

34th Supp. BISD 136 (1988).
Panel Report adopted June 17, 1987.

[Certain U.S. legislation, known as the Superfund Act, deals with the cleanup of hazardous waste sites. The Act imposed a tax of 8.2 cents per barrel on domestic crude oil received at a U.S. refinery and a tax of 11.7 cents per barrel for petroleum products entered into the U.S. for consumption, use or warehousing. It was effectively conceded by the U.S. that the tax violated the national treatment requirement of GATT Article III:2. Instead, the main U.S. contention was that] the tax differential was so small that its trade effects were minimal or nil and that the tax differential—whether it conformed to Article III:2, first sentence, or not—did not nullify or impair benefits accruing to Canada, the EEC and Mexico under the General Agreement. Canada, the EEC and Mexico considered this defence to be neither legally valid nor factually correct. * * *

4. In lieu of nullification or impairment, relief under Article XXIII would also be available if it were established that "the attainment of an objective of the Agreement is being impeded." No adopted panel reports have turned on this issue.

5. 7th Supp. BISD 60, 65 (Panel report adopted Oct. 23, 1958).

5.1.3 Under Article XXIII of the General Agreement contracting parties may bring complaints, inter alia, if they consider that benefits accruing to them under that Agreement are nullified or impaired. According to established GATT practice, described in the Annex to the 1979 Understanding on dispute settlement, "where there is an infringement of the obligations assumed under the General Agreement, the action is considered prima facie to constitute a case of nullification or impairment" (BISD 26S/216). The question raised by the case before the Panel is whether the presumption that a measure inconsistent with the General Agreement causes a nullification or impairment of benefits accruing under that Agreement is an absolute or a rebuttable presumption and, if rebuttable, whether a demonstration that a measure inconsistent with Article III:2, first sentence, has no or insignificant effects on trade is a sufficient rebuttal.

* * *

5.1.6 The Panel examined how the CONTRACTING PARTIES have reacted in previous cases to claims that a measure inconsistent with the General Agreement had no adverse impact and therefore did not nullify or impair benefits accruing under the General Agreement to the contracting party that had brought the complaint. The Panel noted such claims had been made in a number of cases but that there was no case in the history of the GATT in which a contracting party had successfully rebutted the presumption that a measure infringing obligations causes nullification and impairment. * * *

5.1.7 The Panel concluded from its review of the above and other cases that, while the CONTRACTING PARTIES had not explicitly decided whether the presumption that illegal measures cause nullification or impairment could be rebutted, the presumption had in practice operated as an irrefutable presumption.

5.1.8 The Panel then examined whether—even assuming that the presumption could be regarded as rebuttable in the present case—a demonstration that the trade effects of the tax differential were insignificant would constitute a proof that the benefits accruing to Canada, the EEC and Mexico under Article III:2, first sentence, had not been nullified or impaired.

5.1.9 An acceptance of the argument that measures which have only an insignificant effect on the volume of exports do not nullify or impair benefits accruing under Article III:2, first sentence, implies that the basic rationale of this provision—the benefit it generates for the contracting parties—is to protect expectations on export volumes. That, however, is not the case. Article III:2, first sentence, obliges contracting parties to establish certain competitive conditions for imported products in relation to domestic products. Unlike some other provisions in the General Agreement, it does not refer to trade effects. The majority of the members of the Working Party on the "Brazilian Internal Taxes" therefore correctly concluded that the provisions of Article III:2, first sentence, "were equally applicable, whether imports from other contracting parties were substantial, small or non-existent" (BISD Vol. II/185). The Working Party also concluded that "a contracting party was bound by the provisions of Article III whether or not the contracting party in question had undertaken tariff commitments in respect of the goods concerned" (BISD Vol. II/182), in other words, the benefits under Article III accrue independent of whether there is a negotiated expectation of market access or not. Moreover, it is conceivable that a tax consistent with the national treatment principle (for instance, a high but non-discriminatory excise tax) has a more severe impact on the exports of other contracting parties than a tax that violates that principle (for instance a very low but discriminatory tax). The case before the Panel illustrates this point: the United States could bring the tax on petroleum in conformity with Article III:2, first sentence, by raising the tax on domestic products, by lowering the tax on imported products or by fixing a new common tax rate for both imported and domestic products. Each of these solutions would have different trade results, and it is therefore logically not possible to determine the difference in trade impact between the present tax and one consistent with Article III:2, first sentence, and hence to determine the trade impact resulting from the non-observance of that provision. For these reasons, Article III:2, first sentence, cannot be interpreted to protect expectations on export volumes; it protects expectations on the competitive relationship between imported and domestic products. A change in the competitive relationship contrary to that provision must consequently be regarded ipso facto as a nullification or impairment of benefits accruing under the General Agreement. A demonstration that a measure inconsistent with Article III:2, first sentence, has no or insignificant effects would therefore in the view of the Panel not be a sufficient demonstration that the benefits accruing under that provision had not been nullified or impaired even if such a rebuttal were in principle permitted.

* * *

Notes and Questions

(1) The DSU provides in article 3.8:

> In cases where there is an infringement of the obligations assumed under a covered agreement, the action is considered *prima facie* to constitute a case of nullification or impairment. This means that there is normally a presumption that a breach of the rules has an adverse impact on other Members parties to that covered agreement, and in such cases, it shall be up to the Member against whom the complaint has been brought to rebut the charge.

Both sentences appeared in the 1979 Understanding, but not together. In the panel's view, in the 1979 Understanding, the second sentence followed a sentence discussing when consideration should be given to authorizing retaliatory action. As such, the panel did not consider it to be directly on point as to whether it was appropriate to find nullification or impairment for purposes of a recommendation to bring an offending measure into compliance with GATT obligations. Does the new position of this sentence in the

DSU affect the panel's reasoning? In WTO practice to date, panel reports usually contain a sentence in the concluding section that cites article 3.8 and notes that in light of the violation found, benefits accruing to the complaining member have been nullified or impaired.

(2) Do you agree with the analysis in the *Superfund* case? As a policy matter, if a violation in fact has no trade impact, why should the offending party have to correct it?

(3) Suppose a party prevails in a dispute settlement proceeding without showing any trade effects of a violation. If the other party fails to implement the DSB's recommendation to withdraw the nonconforming measure, and no agreement on compensation can be reached between the parties, is the prevailing party entitled to suspend concessions? In what amount? See DSU, art. 22.4 ("The level of the suspension of concessions or other obligations * * * shall be equivalent to the level of nullification or impairment.")

(4) In light of the *Superfund* decision, would you think that a law violates GATT rules if it authorizes, but does not require, the administrative authorities of a country to violate the General Agreement? A GATT panel once stated that:

> that panels had consistently ruled that legislation which mandated action inconsistent with the General Agreement could be challenged as such, whereas legislation which merely gave the discretion to the executive authority of a contracting party to act inconsistently with the General Agreement could not be challenged as such; only the actual application of such legislation inconsistent with the General Agreement could be subject to challenge.

United States—Measures Affecting the Importation, Internal Sale and Use of Tobacco, 41st Supp. BISD 131, para. 118, adopted on October 4, 1994. While a number of WTO panels have followed this approach, the Appellate Body has yet to consider it. A more nuanced approach was taken in the *Section 301* case, which is excerpted in Section 7.4(G) infra. Is Article XVI:4 of the WTO Agreement relevant to this issue?

(5) The evolution of the need to establish nullification or impairment in GATT dispute settlement is a fascinating study in international rule making. In GATT, a system of case-by-case decision making gradually elaborated the sparse language of Article XXIII into a complex set of rules, which in time were ratified by inclusion in the DSU (and in its predecessor decisions on dispute settlement). This is a "bottom up" approach that is quite different than the "top down" procedure that normally might be expected in the international context.

(2) Nullification or Impairment in Nonviolation Cases

As we have already noted, the vast majority of GATT dispute settlement panel decisions have involved alleged violations of the General Agreement, but from the very early years of GATT, there have been occasional cases claiming nullification or impairment of benefits arising out of actions that are not claimed to be GATT violations, including the following controversial case.

JAPAN—MEASURES AFFECTING CONSUMER PHOTOGRAPHIC FILM AND PAPER

WT/DS44/R

Panel Report adopted by the DSB on April 22, 1998

[The United States claimed that through the application of three broad categories of liberalization "countermeasures" the Japanese Government for more than 30 years had inhibited the distribution and sale of imported consumer photographic film and paper in Japan. These three categories of measures included: (1) distribution measures, which allegedly encouraged and facilitated the creation of a market structure for photographic film and paper in which imports were excluded from traditional distribution channels; (2) restrictions on large retail stores, which allegedly restricted the growth of an alternative distribution channel for imported film; and (3) promotion measures, which allegedly disadvantaged imports by restricting the use of sales promotion techniques. The United States alleged that the above measures, individually and collectively, nullified or impaired benefits accruing to the United States within the meaning of GATT Article XXIII:1(b). In addition, it alleged that the distribution measures were inconsistent with GATT Article III:4, and that certain unpublished enforcement actions and unpublished administrative guidance were inconsistent with GATT Article X:1. The following excerpt examines the rationale for nonviolation claims and lays out the basic elements of such a claim. The panel ultimately rejected the US claim and the US did not appeal.]

10.35   The underlying purpose of Article XXIII:1(b) was cogently explained by the panel on *EEC—Oilseeds*:

"The idea underlying [the provisions of Article XXIII:1(b)] is that the improved competitive opportunities that can legitimately be expected from a tariff concession can be frustrated not only by measures proscribed by the General Agreement but also by measures consistent with that Agreement. In order to encourage contracting parties to make tariff concessions they must therefore be given a right of redress when a reciprocal concession is impaired by another contracting party as a result of the application of any measure, whether or not it conflicts with the General Agreement".

. . .

"The Panel considered that the main value of a tariff concession is that it provides an assurance of better market access through improved price competition. Contracting parties negotiate tariff concessions primarily to obtain that advantage. They must therefore be assumed to base their tariff negotiations on the expectation that the price effect of the tariff concessions will not be systematically offset. If no right of redress were given to them in such a case they would be reluctant to make tariff concessions and the General Agreement would no longer be useful as a legal framework for incorporating the results of trade negotiations".[6]

Clearly, the safeguarding of the process and the results of negotiating reciprocal tariff concessions under Article II is fundamental to the balance of rights and obligations to which all WTO Members subscribe.

10.36 Although the non-violation remedy is an important and accepted tool of WTO/GATT dispute settlement and has been "on the books" for almost 50 years, we note that there have only been eight cases in which panels or working parties have substantively considered Article XXIII:1(b) claims. This suggests that both the GATT contracting parties and WTO Members have approached this remedy with caution and, indeed, have treated it as an exceptional instrument of dispute settlement. We note in this regard that both the European Communities and the United States in the *EEC—Oilseeds* case, and the two parties in this case, have confirmed that the non-violation nullification or impairment remedy should be approached with caution and treated as an exceptional concept. The reason for this caution is straightforward. Members negotiate the rules that they agree to follow and only exceptionally would expect to be challenged for actions not in contravention of those rules.

* * *

10.38 In GATT jurisprudence, most of the cases of non-violation nullification or impairment have dealt with situations where a GATT-consistent domestic subsidy for the producer of a product has been introduced or modified following the grant of a tariff concession on that product. The instant case presents a different sort of non-violation claim. At the outset, however, we wish to make clear that we do not *a priori* consider it inappropriate to apply the Article XXIII:1(b) remedy to other governmental actions, such as those designed to strengthen the competitiveness of certain distribution or industrial sectors through non-financial assistance. Whether assistance is financial or non-financial, direct or indirect, does not determine whether its effect may offset the expected result of tariff negotiations. Thus, a Member's industrial policy, pursuing the goal of increasing efficiency in a sector, could in some circumstances upset the competitive relationship in the market place between domestic and imported products in a way that could give rise to a cause of action under Article XXIII:1(b). In the context of a Member's distribution system, for example, it is conceivable that measures that do not infringe GATT rules could be implemented in a manner that effectively results in a disproportionate impact on market conditions for imported products. In this regard, however, we must also bear in mind that tariff concessions have never been viewed as creating a guarantee of trade volumes, but rather, as explained below, as creating expectations as to competitive relationships.

* * *

6. [original note 1202] *EEC—Oilseeds*, adopted on 25 January 1990, BISD 37S/86, 128–129, paras. 144, 148.

10.41   We now return to our more detailed examination of the scope of Article XXIII:1(b). Article XXIII:1(b) provides in relevant part:

> "If any Member should consider that any *benefit* accruing to it directly or indirectly under this Agreement is being *nullified or impaired* . . . as the result of . . . (b) the *application* by another Member of any *measure*, whether or not it conflicts with the provisions of this Agreement . . ." (emphasis added).

The text of Article XXIII:1(b) establishes three elements that a complaining party must demonstrate in order to make out a cognizable claim under Article XXIII:1(b): (1) application of a measure by a WTO Member; (2) a benefit accruing under the relevant agreement; and (3) nullification or impairment of the benefit as the result of the application of the measure. We shall proceed with our analysis by considering in turn each of these three elements.

(a) APPLICATION OF A MEASURE

* * *

10.43   The ordinary meaning of *measure* as it is used in Article XXIII:1(b) certainly encompasses a law or regulation enacted by a government. But in our view, it is broader than that and includes other governmental actions short of legally enforceable enactments. * * *

10.44   In Japan, it is accepted that the government sometimes acts through what is referred to as administrative guidance. In such a case, the company receiving guidance from the Government of Japan may not be legally bound to act in accordance with it, but compliance may be expected in light of the power of the government and a system of government incentives and disincentives arising from the wide array of government activities and involvement in the Japanese economy. As noted by the parties, administrative guidance in Japan takes various forms. Japan, for example, refers to what it calls "regulatory administrative guidance", which it concedes effectively substitutes for formal government action. It also refers to promotional administrative guidance, where companies are urged to do things that are in their interest to do in any event. In Japan's view, this sort of guidance should not be assimilated to a measure in the sense of Article XXIII:1(b). * * *

10.45   Our review of GATT jurisprudence, particularly the panel report on *Japan-Semi-conductors*, teaches that where administrative guidance creates incentives or disincentives largely dependent upon governmental action for private parties to act in a particular manner, it may be considered a governmental measure. In that case, the panel found that although a measure was not mandatory, it could be considered a *restriction* subject to Article XI:1 because

> "sufficient incentives or disincentives existed for non-mandatory measures to take effect . . . [and] the operation of the measures . . . was essentially dependent on Government action or intervention [because in such a case] the measures would be operating in a manner equivalent to mandatory requirements such that the differ-

ence between the measures and mandatory requirements was only one of form and not of substance . . .".[7]

* * *

10.49 * * * In our view, a government policy or action need not necessarily have a substantially binding or compulsory nature for it to entail a likelihood of compliance by private actors in a way so as to nullify or impair legitimately expected benefits within the purview of Article XXIII:1(b). Indeed, it is clear that non-binding actions, which include sufficient incentives or disincentives for private parties to act in a particular manner, can potentially have adverse effects on competitive conditions of market access. For example, a number of non-violation cases have involved subsidies, receipt of which requires only voluntary compliance with eligibility criteria. Moreover, we also consider it conceivable, in cases where there is a high degree of cooperation and collaboration between government and business, e.g., where there is substantial reliance on administrative guidance and other more informal forms of government-business cooperation, that even non-binding, hortatory wording in a government statement of policy could have a similar effect on private actors to a legally binding measure or what Japan refers to as regulatory administrative guidance. Consequently, we believe we should be open to a broad definition of the term *measure* for purposes of Article XXIII:1(b), which considers whether or not a non-binding government action has an effect similar to a binding one.

10.49 We reach this conclusion in considering the purpose of Article XXIII:1(b), which is to protect the balance of concessions under GATT by providing a means to redress government actions not otherwise regulated by GATT rules that nonetheless nullify or impair a Member's legitimate expectations of benefits from tariff negotiations. To achieve this purpose, in our view, it is important that the kinds of government actions considered to be measures covered by Article XXIII:1(b) should not be defined in an unduly restrictive manner. Otherwise, there is the risk of cases, in which governments have been involved one way or another in the nullification or impairment of benefits, that will not be redressable under Article XXIII:1(b), thereby preventing the achievement of its purpose. We would stress, however, that giving a broad definition to *measure* does not expand the scope of the Article XXIII:1(b) remedy because it remains incumbent on the complaining Member to clearly demonstrate how the measure at issue results in or causes nullification or impairment of benefits, and as explained below, in the final analysis the responding Member's government is only responsible for what it has itself caused.

* * *

(ii) Governmental versus private actions

10.52 As the WTO Agreement is an international agreement, in respect of which only national governments and separate customs terri-

---

7. [original note 1211] *Japan—Semiconductors*, BISD 35S/116, 155.

tories are directly subject to obligations, it follows by implication that the term *measure* in Article XXIII:1(b) and Article26.1 of the DSU, as elsewhere in the WTO Agreement, refers only to policies or actions of governments, not those of private parties. But while this "truth" may not be open to question, there have been a number of trade disputes in relation to which panels have been faced with making sometimes difficult judgments as to the extent to which what appear on their face to be private actions may nonetheless be attributable to a government because of some governmental connection to or endorsement of those actions.

* * *

10.56   These past GATT cases demonstrate that the fact that an action is taken by private parties does not rule out the possibility that it may be deemed to be governmental if there is sufficient government involvement with it. It is difficult to establish bright-line rules in this regard, however. Thus, that possibility will need to be examined on a case-by-case basis.

* * *

(b) Benefit Accruing under the GATT

10.61   The second required element which must be considered to establish a case of non-violation nullification or impairment under Article XXIII:1(b) is the existence of a benefit accruing to a WTO Member under the relevant agreement (in this case, GATT 1994). In all but one of the past GATT cases dealing with Article XXIII:1(b) claims, the claimed benefit has been that of legitimate expectations of improved market-access opportunities arising out of relevant tariff concessions. This same set of GATT precedents suggests that for expectations to be legitimate, they must take into account all measures of the party making the concession that could have been reasonably anticipated at the time of the concession. * * *

10.62   In the particular case before us, the question of legitimate expectations of benefits accruing to the United States is complicated by the fact that the United States is claiming to have had expectations of improved market access benefits in respect of four different products (each under a different tariff line), granted during three successive rounds of multilateral trade negotiations. This claim raises two general issues. First, may the benefits legitimately expected by a Member derive from successive rounds of tariff negotiations? [The panel answered this question in the affirmative, based in part on the WTO Agreement's definition of GATT 1994 and in part on past GATT cases.] Second, what factors should be considered to determine if a Member should have reasonably anticipated measures that it claims nullified or impaired benefits?

* * *

10.72   The text of Article XXIII:1(b) simply refers to "a benefit accruing, directly or indirectly, under this Agreement" and does not further define or explain what benefits are referred to. Past GATT panel reports have considered that such benefits include those that a Member reasonably expects to obtain from a tariff negotiation.

10.76 [After reviewing those materials, the panel continued:] As suggested by the 1961 report, in order for expectations of a benefit to be legitimate, the challenged measures must not have been reasonably anticipated at the time the tariff concession was negotiated. If the measures were anticipated, a Member could not have had a legitimate expectation of improved market access to the extent of the impairment caused by these measures.

10.77 Thus, under Article XXIII:1(b), the United States may only claim impairment of benefits related to improved market access conditions flowing from relevant tariff concessions by Japan to the extent that the United States could not have reasonably anticipated that such benefits would be offset by the subsequent application of a measure by the Government of Japan. * * *

* * *

10.79 We consider that the issue of reasonable anticipation should be approached in respect of specific "measures" in light of the following guidelines. First, in the case of measures shown by the United States to have been introduced subsequent to the conclusion of the tariff negotiations at issue, it is our view that the United States has raised a presumption that it should not be held to have anticipated these measures and it is then for Japan to rebut that presumption. Such a rebuttal might be made, for example, by establishing that the measure at issue is so clearly contemplated in an earlier measure that the United States should be held to have anticipated it. However, there must be a clear connection shown. In our view, it is not sufficient to claim that a *specific* measure should have been anticipated because it is consistent with or a continuation of a past *general* government policy. As in the *EEC— Oilseeds* case, we do not believe that it would be appropriate to charge the United States with having reasonably anticipated all GATT-consistent measures, such as "measures" to improve what Japan describes as the inefficient Japanese distribution sector. Indeed, if a Member were held to anticipate all GATT-consistent measures, a non-violation claim would not be possible. Nor do we consider that as a general rule the United States should have reasonably anticipated Japanese measures that are similar to measures in other Members' markets. In each such instance, the issue of reasonable anticipation needs to be addressed on a case-by-case basis.

Second, in the case of measures shown by Japan to have been introduced prior to the conclusion of the tariff negotiations at issue, it is our view that Japan has raised a presumption that the United States should be held to have anticipated those measures and it is for the United States to rebut that presumption. In this connection, it is our view that the United States is charged with knowledge of Japanese government measures as of the date of their publication. We realize that knowledge of a measure's existence is not equivalent to understanding the impact of the measure on a specific product market. For example, a vague measure could be given substance through enforcement policies that are initially unexpected or later changed significantly. However, where the United States claims that it did not know of a measure's relevance to market access conditions in respect of film or paper, we would expect the United States to clearly demonstrate why initially it could not have reasonably anticipated the effect of an existing measure on the film or paper market and when it did realize the effect. Such a showing will need to be tied to the relevant points in time (i.e., the conclusions of the Kennedy, Tokyo and Uruguay Rounds) in order to assess the extent of the United States' legitimate expectations of benefits from these three Rounds. A simple statement that a Member's measures were so opaque and informal that their impact could not be assessed is not sufficient. While it is true that in most past non-violation cases, one could easily discern a clear link between a product-specific action and the effect on the tariff concession that it allegedly impaired, one can also discern a link between general measures affecting the internal sale and distribution of products, such as rules on advertising and premiums, and tariff concessions on products in general.

* * *

(c) NULLIFICATION OR IMPAIRMENT OF BENEFIT: CAUSALITY

10. 82   The third required element of a non-violation claim under Article XXIII:1(b) is that the benefit accruing to the WTO Member (e.g., improved market access from tariff concessions) is *nullified or impaired as the result of* the application of a measure by another WTO Member. In other words, it must be demonstrated that the competitive position of the imported products subject to and benefitting from a relevant market access (tariff) concession is being *upset by* ("nullified or impaired ... as the result of") the application of a measure not reasonably anticipated. The equation of "nullification or impairment" with "upsetting the competitive relationship" established between domestic and imported products as a result of tariff concessions has been consistently used by GATT panels examining non-violation complaints. For example, the *EEC—Oilseeds* panel, in describing its findings, stated that it had "found ... that the subsidies concerned had impaired the tariff concession because they *upset the competitive relationship between domestic and imported oilseeds*, not because of any effect on trade flows".[8] The same language was used in the *Australian Subsidy* and *Germany— Sardines* cases. Thus, in this case, it is up to the United States to prove that the governmental measures that it cites have upset the competitive relationship between domestic and imported photographic film and paper in Japan to the detriment of imports. In other words, the United States

---

8.   [original note 1241] Follow-up on the Panel Report, *EEC—Oilseeds*, BISD 39S/91, 114–115, para. 77 (emphasis added).

must show a clear correlation between the measures and the adverse effect on the relevant competitive relationships.

10.83 We consider that this third element—causality—may be one of the more factually complex areas of our examination. In this connection, we note that in the three prior non-violation cases in which panels found that the complaining parties had failed to provide a detailed justification to support their claims, the issue turned primarily on the lack of evidence of causality. Four issues related to causation merit general discussion. First, the question of the degree of causation that must be shown—"but for" or less. Second, the relevance of the origin-neutral nature of a measure to causation of nullification or impairment. Third, the relevance of intent to causality. And fourth, the extent to which measures may be considered collectively in an analysis of causation.

10.84 As to the first issue, * * * [i]n our view, Japan should be responsible for what is caused by measures attributable to the Japanese Government as opposed, for example, to what is caused by restrictive business conduct attributable to private economic actors. At this stage of the proceeding, the issue is whether such a measure has caused nullification or impairment, i.e., whether it has made more than a *de minimis* contribution to nullification or impairment.

10.85 In respect of the second issue, * * * [i] n our view, even in the absence of *de jure* discrimination (measures which on their face discriminate as to origin), it may be possible for the United States to show *de facto* discrimination (measures which have a disparate impact on imports). However, in such circumstances, the complaining party is called upon to make a detailed showing of any claimed disproportionate impact on imports resulting from the origin-neutral measure. * * *

* * *

10.87 The third issue is the relevance of intent to causality. * * * Article XXIII:1(b) does not require a proof of intent of nullification or impairment of benefits by a government adopting a measure. What matters for purposes of establishing causality is the impact of a measure, i.e. whether it upsets competitive relationships. Nonetheless, intent may not be irrelevant. In our view, if a measure that appears on its face to be origin-neutral in its effect on domestic and imported products is nevertheless shown to have been intended to restrict imports, we may be more inclined to find a causal relationship in specific cases, bearing in mind that intent is not determinative where it in fact exists. * * *

10.88 Finally, as for the US position that the Panel should examine the impact of the measures *in combination* as well as individually (a position contested by Japan), we do not reject the possibility of such an impact. * * *

* * *

DISTRIBUTION "MEASURES"

10.90   The US case against distribution "measures" may best be understood in the context of the general theme advanced by the United States to the effect that there exists in Japan a unique relationship between government and industry. The US argument is that for Japan to develop and implement its industrial policy, the government relies heavily on different types of quasi-governmental entities, including, *inter alia*, fair trade councils, advisory committees, study groups, research institutes, and chambers of commerce. The US position is that the participation of these entities in the "concerted adjustment" process increases the "peer pressure" on these entities to comply with the industrial policies adopted by the government.

* * *

10.92   The United States argues that when the liberalization of international trading conditions became imminent, MITI and Japanese industry recognized the superiority of foreign firms which could create serious competition for Japanese manufacturers and their products. MITI and Japanese manufacturers, it is argued, consequently devised a plan to streamline Japan's distribution system in order to bring it under the control of domestic producers. The basic US position is that MITI sought to strengthen vertical distribution channels that would handle the products of a particular domestic manufacturer exclusively.

10.93   As noted above, the United States claims that Japan's application of the following eight distribution "measures" encouraged and facilitated the creation of a market structure for photographic film and paper in Japan in which imports are excluded from traditional distribution channels, thereby nullifying or impairing benefits accruing to the United States under Article XXIII:1(b):

(1) 1967 Cabinet Decision;

(2) 1967 JFTC Notification 17 on premiums to businesses;

(3) 1968 Sixth Interim Report on Distribution Modernization Outlook and Issues;

(4) 1969 Seventh Interim Report on Systemization of Distribution Activities;

(5) 1969 Survey Report regarding Transaction Terms;

(6) 1970 Guidelines for Rationalizing Terms of Trade for Photographic Film;

(7) 1971 Basic Plan for the Systemization of Distribution; and

(8) 1975 Manual for Systemization of Distribution by Industry: Camera and Film.

* * *

10.204   The essence of the US claim in respect of distribution "countermeasures" is that Japan created vertical integration and single-brand distribution in the Japanese film and paper market. In the US view, this was done through standardization of transaction terms, systemization and limitations on premiums to businesses. As we have found above, the United States has not been able to show that the various "measures" it cites have upset competitive relationships between domestic and US film and paper in Japan, principally because single-brand distribution appears to have occurred before and independently of those "measures", but also because the United States has not demonstrated that these "measures" are directed at promoting vertical integration or single-brand distribution. In answering the timing problem, the United States has provided no convincing evidence or arguments that the cited "measures" in fact had the effect of reinforcing single-brand distribution. Equally, the United States has not explained why the vertically integrated, single-brand distribution structure of the film sector in Japan—a state of affairs that the evidence suggests is similar to that occurring elsewhere in the world (including in the United States)— would have broken down in the absence of continuing government intervention.

10.205 In respect of a number of distribution "measures", the United States argues that they have continued in effect even though they may be dated or have been formally revoked. In our view, the United States has not shown that the 1967 Cabinet Decision, the Sixth and Seventh Interim Reports, the 1969 Survey Report, the 1970 Guidelines, the 1971 Basic Plan and the 1975 Manual are today upsetting competitive relationships between domestic and US film and paper in Japan.

10.206 We note that the Sixth and Seventh Interim Reports, the 1969 Survey Report, the 1971 Basic Plan and the 1975 Manual refer to "foreign capital" and the need to prepare for its imminent appearance in Japan. In each case, however, the focus of these "measures" is not on foreign capital, but on general reform of the Japanese distribution sector for reasons unrelated to foreign capital (e.g. labour shortages). We do not suggest that proof of intent to nullify or impair benefits is required under Article XXIII:1(b). We merely note that in our review of these "measures", we were not convinced that foreign capital was a major factor in their adoption or implementation.

10.207 To the extent that the alleged "measures" exist and should not have been reasonably anticipated by the United States, legitimate expectations in relation to these "measures" only exist for black and white film and paper. We note in this connection that today the black and white film market in Japan is insignificant as compared to colour film. The parties agree that it is on the order of three per cent. Moreover, proof of causation with regard to black and white film is undermined by an apparent increase, according to Japan, in market share from around 6.6 per cent in 1965 to a peak of around 41.4 per cent in 1985, despite the alleged impact of the "measures" in the 1965–1975 timeframe. The United States has submitted alternative statistics concerning the market shares in the photographic materials market that do not separately break out black and white film from colour film.

Notes and Questions

(1) The only successful nonviolation claim since the early 1950's arose out of EU duty-free tariff bindings on oilseeds made in 1962. In a case brought by the United States, the U.S. claimed that subsequent to making this binding, the EU adopted agricultural support programs that created an incentive to produce oilseeds in the EU that impaired benefits it could reasonably expect to accrue to it under the tariff concessions for oilseeds. The essential EU defense was that it is not legitimate to expect the absence of production subsidies even after the grant of a tariff concession because GATT Articles III:8(b) and XVI:1 explicitly recognize the right of parties to grant production subsidies. The panel rejected that argument. It also noted:

148. * * * At issue in the case before it are product-specific subsidies that protect producers completely from the movement of prices for imports and thereby prevent tariff concessions from having any impact on the competitive relationship between domestic and imported oilseeds. The Panel considered that the main value of a tariff concession is that it provides an assurance of better market access through improved price competition. Contracting parties negotiate tariff concessions primarily to obtain that advantage. They must therefore be assumed to base their tariff negotiations on the expectation that the price effect of the tariff concessions will not be systematically offset. * * *

150. * * * The Panel noted that the CONTRACTING PARTIES have consistently interpreted the basic provisions of the General Agreement on restrictive trade measures as provisions establishing conditions of competition. * * * [I]n the tariff negotiations in the framework of GATT, contracting parties seek tariff concessions in the hope of expanding their exports, but the commitments they exchange in such negotiations are commitments on conditions of competition for trade, not on volumes of trade.

151. * * * The approach of the CONTRACTING PARTIES reflects the fact that governments can often not predict with precision what the impact of their interventions on import volumes will be. * * * The provisions of Article XXIII:1(b) could therefore in practice hardly be applied if a contracting party claiming nullification or impairment had to demonstrate not only that an adverse change in competition has taken place but also that the change has resulted in a decline in imports.

EEC—Payments and Subsidies Paid to Processors and Producers of Oilseeds and Related Animal–Feed Proteins, 37th Supp. BISD 86, adopted on January 25, 1990.

(2) There were two cases from the early 1950's that accepted the legitimacy of non-violation complaints. In one case, Chile complained when Australia changed its policy on subsidizing fertilizer so as to remove the subsidy on the type of fertilizer that Chile had been exporting to Australia, while maintaining it on the type of fertilizer produced domestically. The Australian Subsidy on Ammonium Sulphate, II BISD 188 (1952) (Working party report adopted April 3, 1950). Chile claimed that this action nullified

or impaired the tariff concession on fertilizer that it had obtained from Australia, and the working party agreed (II BISD at 193):

> It was agreed that such impairment would exist if the action of the Australian Government which resulted in upsetting the competitive relationship between [the two fertilizers] could not reasonably have been anticipated by the Chilean Government, taking into consideration all pertinent circumstances and the provisions of the General Agreement, at the time it negotiated the duty-free binding on [the fertilizer that it produced].

In another case, which is discussed in Section 10.2(B) infra, Norway successfully brought a complaint protesting a German change in tariff rates on products that had formerly been treated the same, with the result that relatively higher tariffs were imposed on the Norwegian product compared to competing products from other countries. Treatment by Germany of Imports of Sardines, 1st Supp. BISD 53 (1953) (Panel report adopted Oct. 31, 1952).

(3) Despite the long history of nonviolation claims, they remain controversial. In the Chile–Australia case, the Australian representative made the following statement in response to the panel decision:

> In view of * * * the fact that the working party has also found that the Australian subsidy on ammonium sulphate [fertilizer] is completely in accordance with the provisions of the Agreement including the provisions specifically relating to subsidies, Australia cannot consider it a sound argument that what a country might now say was its reasonable expectation three years ago in respect of a particular tariff concession should be the determining factor in establishing the existence of impairment in terms of Article XXIII. If it were accepted by the CONTRACTING PARTIES, then this interpretation of Article XXIII would require a complete re-examination of the principles on which Australia (and, we had supposed, all other countries) had hitherto granted tariff concessions. The history and practice of tariff negotiations show clearly that if a country seeking a tariff concession on a product desires to assure itself of a certain treatment for that product in a field apart from rates of duty *and to an extent going further than is provided for in the various articles of the General Agreement,* the objective sought must be a matter for negotiation in addition to the actual negotiation respecting the rates of duty to be applied.

> If this were not so, and if an expectation (no matter how reasonable) which has never been expressed, discussed or attached to a tariff agreement as a condition is interpreted in the light of the arguments adduced in the report of the working party, then tariff concessions and the binding of a rate of duty would be extremely hazardous commitments and would only be entered into after an exhaustive survey of the whole field of substitute or competitive products and detailed analyses of probable future needs of a particular economy.

Do you agree? Are cases like this, which do not involve alleged violations of rules, appropriate for consideration in a dispute settlement system? Or do they present differences over policy issues that ought to resolved through negotiation of applicable rules? What problems may arise if policy disputes are adjudicated in a dispute settlement system?

(4) How does the DSU deal with nonviolation complaints under Article XXIII:1(b)? Examine DSU, art. 26.1. Are there any differences in the procedures to be followed or the remedies available under Article 26.1 cases compared to regular cases? The Agreement on Trade–Related Aspects of Intellectual Property Rights provides that complaints based on Article XXIII:1(b) and (c) will not be permitted for five years and during that time the governing body shall consider whether such complaints are to be allowed. TRIPS Agreement, art. 64. (The TRIPS Council has not taken any decision on the subject.) The General Agreement on Trade in Services allows for certain of such complaints. See GATS, art. XXIII:3.

(5) There have been no GATT or WTO decisions that have recognized nullification or impairment resulting from a complaint based on Article XXIII:1(c). How does the DSU treat such complaints? See DSU, art. 26.2.

(6) Is "nullification or impairment" a useful concept on which to base dispute settlement? Why not always require a breach of obligations? Isn't the nullification or impairment concept more compatible with negotiated dispute settlement as opposed to adjudication? It does allow consideration of problems that the rules fail to cover. But with only one adopted panel report recognizing such a situation since 1952, one can argue that it does not fill a pressing need. Moreover, nullification or impairment seems to be based on the idea that there is a reciprocal balance of concessions that should be maintained. Yet after almost 50 years of negotiations on an ever-broadening range of issues in the WTO, that idea of broad-based reciprocity may not be meaningful. One could argue that what is more important is that the agreed-upon rules are obeyed, and that if they are not, then offsetting compensation is afforded to balance the effect of the rule violations.

(B) STANDARDS OF REVIEW[9]

One of the more difficult problems faced in recent years by the WTO dispute settlement system is the choice of appropriate standards of review. The issue arises when the panel must review a national statute or administrative action where the issue is whether a specified standard contained in the WTO rules has been met. To take concrete examples, how much deference should a panel give to the decision of a national antidumping authority that the facts presented demonstrate material injury to domestic industry? How much deference should be given to a national health authority's decision to adopt a national safety standard that is stricter than an existing internationally accepted standard, where the national authority argues that its standard is appropriate given the state of (or lack of) scientific knowledge? In each of these cases, the basic question is whether the panel may (or should) reassess the facts presented to the national decisionmaker to determine if the panel agrees that they meet the WTO rule. Similar issues arise in national court review of administrative agency action. See Section 3.5 supra.

9. Generally on this subject see, Steven P. Croley & John H. Jackson, WTO Dispute Procedures, Standard of Review, and Deference to National Governments, 90 Am. J.Intl.L. 193 (1996), revised version in John H. Jackson, The Jurisprudence of GATT and the WTO, ch. 11 (2000).

(1) WTO Rules on Standard of Review

This problem had already arisen frequently in antidumping cases considered by panels established under the 1979 Antidumping Code. In large part as a result of concerns raised by the United States, the WTO Antidumping Agreement provides in article 17.6 that

> (i) in its assessment of the facts of the matter, the panel shall determine whether the [national antidumping] authorities establishment of the facts was proper and whether their evaluation of those facts was unbiased and objective. If the establishment of the facts was proper and the evaluation was unbiased and objective, even though the panel might have reached a different conclusion, the evaluation shall not be overturned;

> (ii) the panel shall interpret the relevant provisions of the [Antidumping] Agreement in accordance with customary rules of interpretation of public international law. Where the panel finds that a relevant provision of the Agreement admits of more than one permissible interpretation, the panel shall find the authorities' measure to be in conformity with the Agreement if it rests upon one of those permissible interpretations.

Do you think that this provision effectively prevents panels from second-guessing factual determinations of national authorities? If so, do you think it is appropriate? What does the second clause mean? What are the customary rules? See Section 5.2(C) supra (Vienna Convention on the Law of Treaties). How often would you expect panels to decide that the agreement could be interpreted in several different ways? It is worth noting that in the national context, respecting administrative discretion on the interpretation of a rule does not necessarily lead to inconsistent application of a rule, so long as the agency acts on a consistent basis. But on the international level, allowing different interpretations of a WTO agreement by national authorities means that there is no consistency because there is no longer one international rule. What other standards might be used to control panel discretion?

On the general issue of the standard of review in WTO cases, the Appellate Body had the following to say in the *Hormones* case (discussed in Section 14.2 infra):

> 114.   The first point that must be made in this connection, is that the *SPS Agreement* itself is silent on the matter of an appropriate standard of review for panels deciding upon SPS measures of a Member. Nor are there provisions in the DSU or any of the covered agreements (other than [Article 17.6(i) of] the *Anti-Dumping Agreement*) prescribing a particular standard of review. * * * Textually, Article 17.6(i) is specific to the *Anti-Dumping Agreement*.

> 115.   The standard of review appropriately applicable in proceedings under the *SPS Agreement*, of course, must reflect the balance established in that Agreement between the jurisdictional competences conceded by the Members to the WTO and the jurisdictional

competences retained by the Members for themselves. To adopt a standard of review not clearly rooted in the text of the *SPS Agreement* itself, may well amount to changing that finely drawn balance; and neither a panel nor the Appellate Body is authorized to do that.

116. We do not mean, however, to suggest that there is at present no standard of review applicable to the determination and assessment of the facts in proceedings under the *SPS Agreement* or under other covered agreements. In our view, Article 11 of the DSU bears directly on this matter and, in effect, articulates with great succinctness but with sufficient clarity the appropriate standard of review for panels in respect of both the ascertainment of facts and the legal characterization of such facts under the relevant agreements. Article 11 reads thus:

> * * * [A] panel should make an <u>objective assessment of the matter before it,</u> including <u>an objective assessment of the facts</u> of the case and the <u>applicability of and conformity with the relevant covered agreements,</u> * * * (underlining by Appellate Body)

117. So far as fact-finding by panels is concerned, their activities are always constrained by the mandate of Article 11 of the DSU: the applicable standard is neither *de novo* review as such, nor "total deference", but rather the "objective assessment of the facts". Many panels have in the past refused to undertake *de novo* review, wisely, since under current practice and systems, they are in any case poorly suited to engage in such a review. On the other hand, "total deference to the findings of the national authorities", it has been well said, "could not ensure an 'objective assessment' as foreseen by Article 11 of the DSU".[10]

118. In so far as legal questions are concerned—that is, consistency or inconsistency of a Member's measure with the provisions of the applicable agreement—a standard not found in the text of the *SPS Agreement* itself cannot absolve a panel (or the Appellate Body) from the duty to apply the customary rules of interpretation of public international law. It may be noted that the European Communities refrained from suggesting that Article 17.6 of the *Anti-Dumping Agreement* in its entirety was applicable to the present case. Nevertheless, it is appropriate to stress that here again Article 11 of the DSU is directly on point, requiring a panel to "make an objective assessment of the matter before it, including an objective assessment of the facts of the case and the applicability of and conformity with the relevant covered agreements . . .".

119. We consider, therefore, that the issue of failure to apply an appropriate standard of review, raised by the European Communities, resolves itself into the issue of whether or not the Panel, in

---

10. [original note 82] Panel Report, *United States—Underwear,* adopted 25 February 1997, WT/DS24/R, para. 7.10.

making the above and other findings referred to and appealed by the European Communities, had made an "objective assessment of the matter before it, including *an objective assessment of the facts ...*". This particular issue is addressed (in substantial detail) below. Here, however, we uphold the findings of the Panel appealed by the European Communities upon the ground of failure to apply either a "deferential reasonableness standard" or the standard of review set out in Article 17.6(i) of the *Anti-Dumping Agreement*.

European Communities—Measures Affecting Livestock and Meat (Hormones), WT/DS26 & 48/AB/R, adopted by the DSB on February 13, 1998.

Notes and Questions

(1) To say that article 11 provides the appropriate standard of review is only a starting point. The next question is how does one perform an objective assessment of the facts. So far, the Appellate Body has seemed to suggest that in matters involving health, governments should be afforded considerable discretion in their decisions on what protections are needed. For example, in the *Hormones* case, the Appellate Body noted (para. 194):

> [R]esponsible and representative governments tend to base their legislative and administrative measures on "mainstream" scientific opinion. In other cases, equally responsible and representative governments may act in good faith on the basis of what, at a given time, may be a divergent opinion coming from qualified and respected sources. By itself, this does not necessarily signal the absence of a reasonable relationship between the SPS measure and the risk assessment, especially where the risk involved is life-threatening in character and is perceived to constitute a clear and imminent threat to public health and safety.

In another part of the *Hormones* report, the Appellate Body stated: "We cannot lightly assume that sovereign states intended to impose upon themselves the more onerous, rather than the less burdensome obligation by mandating conformity or compliance with such standards, guidelines and recommendations. To sustain such an assumption and to warrant such a far-reaching interpretation, treaty language far more specific and compelling than that found in Article 3 of the SPS Agreement would be necessary." In a footnote it then referred to the principle of *in dubio mitius,* which it explained as follows: " 'The principle * * * applies in interpreting treaties, in deference to the sovereignty of states. If the meaning of a term is ambiguous, that meaning is to be preferred which is less onerous to the party assuming an obligation * * * ' " (para. 165 & n. 154, quoting R. Jennings & A. Watts (eds.), Oppenheim's International Law (9th ed. 1992)).

Similarly in the *Asbestos* case (see Section 13.1 infra), the Appellate Body accorded considerable to France's decision on the level of protection needed to halt the spread of asbestos-related health risks:

> 174. In our view, France could not reasonably be expected to employ *any* alternative measure if that measure would involve a continuation of the very risk that the Decree seeks to "halt". Such an alternative measure would, in effect, prevent France from achieving its chosen level of health protection. * * *

178. * * * In justifying a measure under Article XX(b) of the GATT 1994, a Member may also rely, in good faith, on scientific sources which, at that time, may represent a divergent, but qualified and respected, opinion. A Member is not obliged, in setting health policy, automatically to follow what, at a given time, may constitute a majority scientific opinion. * * *

European Communities—Measures Affecting Asbestos and Asbestos–Containing Products, WT/DS135/AB/R, adopted by the DSB on April 5, 2001.[11]

In contrast, in trade-remedy cases, the Appellate Body has not been as deferential. For example, in United States—Safeguard Measures on Imports of Fresh, Chilled or Frozen Lamb Meat from New Zealand and Australia, WT/DS177 & 178/AB/R, adopted by the DSB on May 16, 2001, the Appellate Body described the requirements of article 11 in a safeguards case (see Chapter 15 infra) as follows:

103. * * * [A]n "objective assessment" of a claim under Article 4.2(a) of the *Agreement on Safeguards* has, in principle, two elements. First, a panel must review whether competent authorities have evaluated *all relevant factors*, and, second, a panel must review whether the authorities have provided a *reasoned and adequate explanation* of how the facts support their determination. Thus, the panel's objective assessment involves a *formal* aspect and a *substantive* aspect. The formal aspect is whether the competent authorities have evaluated "all relevant factors". The substantive aspect is whether the competent authorities have given a reasoned and adequate explanation for their determination.

104. This dual character of a panel's review is mandated by the nature of the specific obligations that Article 4.2 of the *Agreement on Safeguards* imposes on competent authorities. Under Article4.2(a), competent authorities must, as a formal matter, evaluate "all relevant factors". However, that evaluation is not simply a matter of form, and the list of relevant factors to be evaluated is not a mere "check list". Under Article 4.2(a), competent authorities must conduct a substantive evaluation of "the *'bearing'*, or the *'influence'* or *'effect'*"[12] or *"impact"* that the relevant factors have on the "situation of [the] domestic industry". (emphasis added) By conducting such a substantive evaluation of the relevant factors, competent authorities are able to make a proper overall determination, *inter alia*, as to whether the domestic industry is seriously injured or is threatened with such injury as defined in the Agreement.

105. It follows that the precise nature of the examination to be conducted by a panel, in reviewing a claim under Article 4.2 of the

11. Other examples are cited in John H. Jackson, Dispute Settlement and the WTO: Emerging Problems, 1 J.Intl.Econ.L. 329, 342 n.29 (1998), including the following statement in United States—Standards for Conventional and Reformulated Gasoline, WT/DS2/AB/R, p. 30: "WTO Members have a large measure of autonomy to determine their own policies on the environment (including its relationship with trade), their environmental objectives and the environmental legislation they enact and implement.".

12. [original note 62] Appellate Body Report, *United States—Wheat Gluten Safeguard*, footnote 19, para. 71.

Agreement on Safeguards, stems, in part, from the panel's obligation to make an "objective assessment of the matter" under Article 11 of the DSU and, in part, from the obligations imposed by Article 4.2, to the extent that those obligations are part of the claim. Thus, as with any claim under the provisions of a covered agreement, panels are required to examine, in accordance with Article 11 of the DSU, whether the Member has complied with the obligations imposed by the particular provisions identified in the claim. By examining whether the explanation given by the competent authorities in their published report is reasoned and adequate, panels can determine whether those authorities have acted consistently with the obligations imposed by Article 4.2 of the *Agreement on Safeguards*.

106.   We wish to emphasize that, although panels are not entitled to conduct a *de novo* review of the evidence, nor to *substitute* their own conclusions for those of the competent authorities, this does *not* mean that panels must simply *accept* the conclusions of the competent authorities. To the contrary, in our view, in examining a claim under Article 4.2(a), a panel can assess whether the competent authorities' explanation for its determination is reasoned and adequate *only* if the panel critically examines that explanation, in depth, and in the light of the facts before the panel. Panels must, therefore, review whether the competent authorities' explanation fully addresses the nature, and, especially, the complexities, of the data, and responds to other plausible interpretations of that data. A panel must find, in particular, that an explanation is not reasoned, or is not adequate, if some *alternative explanation* of the facts is plausible, and if the competent authorities' explanation does not seem adequate in the light of that alternative explanation. Thus, in making an "objective assessment" of a claim under Article 4.2(a), panels must be open to the possibility that the explanation given by the competent authorities is not reasoned or adequate.

How does the text we have underlined compare to the approach followed in *Hormones* and *Asbestos*? Are there reasons to have a stricter standard of review in trade-remedy cases, as opposed to health-related cases?

(2) The Canada–United States Free Trade Agreement and the North American Free Trade Agreement each established a mechanism for panel review of administrative decisions in antidumping and countervailing duty cases. A decision by a panel may be brought before an extraordinary challenge committee on the grounds, inter alia, that the panel applied an inappropriate standard of review. To date, the challenge committees have hesitated to second-guess the panel decisions, even where they have indicated that the panel had probably misapplied the applicable standard of review. One such case is excerpted in Section 11.3(C)(2) infra.

(2) Techniques of Judicial Restraint

WILLIAM J. DAVEY, HAS THE WTO DISPUTE SETTLEMENT SYSTEM EXCEEDED ITS AUTHORITY?[13]

To date, I do not believe that the results of WTO dispute settlement evidence to any substantial degree over-reaching by the Appellate Body or panels so as to impose new obligations on Members or to limit inappropriately the discretion of Member government policy-making. * * *

* * * However, I have also noted a few examples (and there are more) where language in a specific case is capable of broad interpretation in the future. Thus, to the extent that it is believed that the WTO system has been too intrusive or might be in the future, it is appropriate to consider whether the WTO dispute settlement system should make greater use of what I term "issue-avoidance" techniques.[14] Over time, courts have developed a variety of such techniques to dispose of cases or issues within cases where a decision seems unnecessary, inappropriate or perhaps simply too controversial. Among the techniques used are

— limitations on the parties who may bring an action (e.g., "standing" or legal interest requirements);

— restrictions limiting the time at which an action may be brought (e.g., categorizing actions as too late (mootness) or too early (ripeness or failure to exhaust other remedies));

— Categorization of actions as inappropriate for judicial consideration (e.g., political questions, *non liquet*); and

— exercise of judicial economy so as avoid considering issues (e.g., strict interpretation of terms of reference; resolution of only necessary issues).

Readers familiar with WTO/GATT dispute settlement case-law will recognize that panels and the Appellate Body have considered all of these issues: (i) standing—*Bananas*; (ii) mootness—*Indonesia Autos*; (iii) ripeness—*Section 301*; (iv) exhaustion—*US Salmon* (GATT Antidumping Code); (v) political-judicial balance—*India QR*; (vi) non-liquet—*Coconuts, EEC Wheat Flour Export Subsidies* (Tokyo Round Subsidies Code); (vii) terms of reference—*Bananas, India Patents I, Korea Dairy*; and (viii) judicial economy—*Wool Shirts, Salmon*. In this section, I will consider the US and international law rules in respect of these techniques and then consider whether the right balance has been struck by the WTO dispute settlement system in using them in the mentioned and other similar cases.

13. 4 Journal of International Economic Law 79, 96–110 (2001) *and in* T. Cottier, P. Mavroidis & P. Blatter (eds.), The Role of the Judge: Lessons for the WTO (forthcoming Univ. Mich. Press 2002). Reprinted with permission.

14. [original note 24] See also Jeffrey L. Dunoff, The Death of the Trade Regime, European Journal of International Law, vol. 10, no. 4, at 733, 757–760.

A. Standing or Legal Interest

The issue considered under the heading of "standing" is whether the complaining party is entitled to have the court decide the merits of the dispute. Or, put another way, whether the complainant has a legal interest that a court will protect.

* * *

In WTO dispute settlement, the issue of standing or legal interest was presented in the *Bananas* case. The EC argued that the panel should reject the US claims made in respect of GATT 1994 because the US did not export bananas and thus had no legal interest in claims related to trade in bananas as goods. The panel noted that there is no explicit requirement in the DSU that a complaining party must have a legal interest in order to bring a case. It also noted that GATT rules were concerned with competitive opportunities and that the US did produce bananas. Moreover, the US market was affected indirectly by the EC import regime for bananas. In the panel's view, a potential trading interest and a Member's interest in a determination of rights and obligations under the various WTO agreements were each sufficient.

On appeal, the Appellate Body noted that the case-law of the International Court of Justice did not indicate that there was a general international law rule that a party must have a legal interest to bring a case. In turning to the wording of GATT Article XXIII, the Appellate Body stressed that it provided that "If any *Member should consider* that any benefit accruing to it is being nullified or impaired ...", the Member is permitted to initiate consultations and thereafter dispute settlement proceedings. It also noted the language of DSU Article 3.7, which requires Members to exercise judgment in deciding whether to bring cases. For the Appellate Body, these provisions suggest that it is largely up to the WTO Member concerned to decide for itself whether it wishes to start an action and whether it will be fruitful.

In addition, the Appellate Body noted that the US did in fact have a potential export interest in bananas as a producer and that the internal market of the United States could be affected by the EC regime. It noted its agreement with the panel that

> "with increased interdependence of the global economy ... Members have a greater stake in enforcing WTO rules than in the past since any deviation from the negotiated balance of rights and obligations is more likely than ever to affect them, directly or indirectly."

Finally, it noted that the GATT claims were closely related to the GATS claims and that there was no question that the US had a right to bring the GATS claims.

From the foregoing, it would appear that a standing or legal interest requirement does not exist under the DSU. However, the Appellate Body concluded its discussion of standing in *Bananas III* by stating that while the above mentioned factors taken together were enough to give the US the right to bring claims under GATT in that case, that did not mean that "one or more of the factors we noted in this case would necessarily be dispositive in another case". There have been no other cases to date, so the meaning of the Appellate Body's remark remains uncertain.

It is instructive to consider whether the factors cited as supporting the doctrine of standing in the US are relevant for WTO dispute settlement. The requirements under US law of redressable injury caused by the respondent arise from the US constitutional limitation of federal court jurisdiction to "cases" and "controversies". These requirements are not relevant to WTO dispute settlement since the DSU does not require injury to be shown (nullification or impairment is presumed if a rule violation is established) and redress in the form of a recommendation to bring a measure into conformity with WTO rules is always available. The other three factors, based on prudential concerns, do not seem relevant to WTO dispute settlement either. The rights asserted in WTO dispute settlement are by their nature the rights of a Member. Thus, the rules against third-party standing and generalized grievances seem inappropriate and the requirement that a plaintiff must be within the zone of interests protected by a statute in always met. Moreover, to the extent that the WTO Agreement represents a balance struck by all Members, the general concern about intermeddling does not seem applicable to the WTO. Thus, in my view, there does not seem to be a need to have a standing requirement in WTO dispute settlement proceedings.

B.   Mootness

* * *

C.   Ripeness (Mandatory vs. Discretionary Measures)

The doctrine of ripeness is concerned with ensuring that cases presented to a court are ready for review in the sense that they are not too speculative. It is designed both to avoid cases about injury that may never occur and to ensure that a proper record exists on which a decision can be based. There is an obvious overlap with standing requirements, insofar as they require a plaintiff to show injury, but ripeness focuses on whether there has been injury as opposed to who has been injured.

* * *

In the WTO and GATT before it, much has been made of the ripeness issue. As a general rule, it has been said that under GATT dispute settlement precedents, if a measure is mandatory, i.e., if certain circumstances occur, the government does not have discretion as to whether or not to apply the measure, then it is challengeable in GATT dispute settlement proceedings even if it has not been applied and even if it has not yet come into effect. However, a discretionary measure is not challengeable.[15] The principal case involving this issue in the WTO is the *Section 301* case [excerpted in Section 7.4(G) infra]. The US and the EC devoted the lion's share of their arguments to exploring this distinction.

---

15. [original note 46] See, e.g., Panel Report on United States—Measures Affecting the Importation, Internal Sale and Use of Tobacco, adopted October 4, 1994, BISD 41S/131, 174–175 at para. 118 (and cited cases).

The panel concluded that the issue had to be decided on a case by case basis by examining the WTO provisions at issue. In that case, it found essentially that a discretionary statute could be challenged under certain WTO rules because of the nature of the obligations contained in those rules. [It is not clear how much of a precedent this case is, as the panel itself stressed the special factors applicable to claims under article 23 of the DSU and, in fact, subsequent panel reports have tended to follow the GATT distinction.]

* * *

In the end, the clearest justification for allowing a WTO challenge to discretionary legislation is that such legislation may have an impact on trade, even if it has not (yet) been applied. Indeed, panels in the past have refused to consider that the long-time and consistent non-enforcement of mandatory legislation renders it immune from challenge. Given the focus of WTO rules on competitive opportunities, this would argue for not strictly applying the discretionary/mandatory legislation rule. I tend to think, however, that panels and the Appellate Body should exercise some restraint in this area. I can imagine laws that do affect trade even though they are not applied; while others would likely not. It would probably be prudent to avoid rulings in the latter cases. Indeed, one can imagine cases where a Member believes that it is politically necessary for it to have certain measures on the statute books that may be of questionable WTO-consistency, but not politically necessary for that Member to take action under such measures.

D.   Exhaustion of Available Remedies/Abstention

The requirement that a plaintiff exhaust available remedies (i.e., more appropriate remedies available in another forum) is a device to provide for orderly consideration of issues. It is designed in part to ensure the use of the more appropriate tribunal to decide cases.

* * *

A requirement to exhaust national remedies would too often be tantamount to denying effective enforcement of WTO obligations for too long a period of time and would not seem to be an appropriate mechanism for avoiding difficult issues.

E.   Political–Judicial Balance

In the United States, the US Supreme Court has developed the so-called political question doctrine, which it invokes to avoid decisions in certain cases that have political ramifications. Of course, any court decision may have such ramifications, but the political question doctrine is designed to avoid decision by the Court that would bring it into conflict with politics. As expressed in *Baker v. Carr*:

> "Prominent on the surface of any case held to involve a political question is found a textually demonstrable commitment of the issue to a coordinate political department; or a lack of judicially discoverable and manageable standards for resolving it; or the impossibility

of deciding without an initial policy determination of a kind clearly for nonjudicial discretion; or the impossibility of a court's undertaking independent resolution without expressing lack of respect due coordinate branches of government; or an unusual need for unquestioning adherence to a political decision already made; or the potentiality of embarrassment from multifarious departments on one question."[16]

While commentators have viewed these criteria of limited use, the Court has often quoted this language. In practical terms, the Court has declined to rule, inter alia, on whether a state has a republican form of government as required by Article IV(4) of the US Constitution, on matters related to congressional governance, on the process for ratifying constitutional amendments and on some matters related to foreign policy. Its decisions are not that consistent, however, and counter-examples in the above categories may be found.

The ICJ has generally not accepted arguments that it should decline to rule on an issue because it is a political question. Rather, it has noted that many disputes have political ramifications, but that is not an excuse not to examine the legal issues presented.

As noted in Part I of this paper, in the GATT/WTO context, a political-question type issue has arisen in respect of whether certain matters arising under the balance-of-payments exceptions in GATT Articles XII and XVIII:B and under the regional trade rules of Article XXIV should be subject to review by panels and the Appellate Body. Generally, I conclude above that in considering the issue of balance within the WTO system, it is important that panels and the Appellate Body do not create rules that cause them to reject cases on *a priori* grounds. To do so risks upsetting the balance of rights and obligations among Members. The fundamental purpose of the dispute settlement system is to provide security and predictability to the multilateral trading system. It cannot do that if certain obligations are viewed as too political to be reviewed in dispute settlement. It may well be that panels and the Appellate Body should defer to a Member's decision in a specific case (e.g., where the issue of whether a measure meets the terms of an exception is a close one), but that does not mean that the dispute settlement system should not consider the claims in the first instance.

I would take this position even in cases where the respondent invokes GATT Article XXI–the national security exception. Of course, given the wording of Article XXI ("any action which *it considers* necessary"), I would expect panels and the Appellate Body to afford considerable discretion to the Member invoking that exception. Nonetheless, the possibility of dispute settlement review to prevent abusive invocations is appropriate.

16. [original note 51] 369 U.S. 186, 217 (1962).

F. *Non liquet*

A *non liquet* occurs when a judicial body decides not to rule on a case because the law is not clear or, put another way, there is a gap in the law. As so formulated, it is not an issue-avoidance technique found in US constitutional law, although it is not all that dissimilar to certain techniques discussed herein. The authorization to the ICJ to use general principles of international law as a source of law has been viewed as an attempt to prevent the use of *non liquet* by the ICJ.

The prime example of *non liquet* in GATT dispute settlement was the unadopted panel report in *EEC Wheat Flour Export Subsidies*, where in a somewhat confusing panel report, the panel, inter alia, noted an absence of legal certainty as to the meaning of the Tokyo Round Subsidies Code. That panel report is generally viewed as unsatisfactory. In WTO jurisprudence, the *Coconuts* case has been viewed as a *non liquet*.[17] In that case, the complainant was essentially denied WTO relief, but in circumstances where it could have pursued a claim under the Tokyo Round Anti-dumping Agreement.

Generally speaking, I think that *non liquet* is and should be a disfavored judicial technique. The WTO dispute settlement system is typically asked if a measure violates one or more of the covered agreements. Normally, the Appellate Body and panels should be able to answer that question using standard treaty interpretation methods. If a complainant is unable to establish a violation of an agreement, it will simply lose for that reason. Thus, I think that *non liquet* is not a technique that WTO dispute settlement should embrace.

G. Terms of Reference

* * *

H. Judicial Economy

GATT and WTO panels have traditionally ruled only on those claims of a party that must be addressed in order to resolve the matter at issue. Thus, if an aspect of a measure has been found to violate one GATT provision, panels have typically not considered whether it violates another provision as well. This practice, referred to as judicial economy, has been approved by the Appellate Body, although it has not always been followed.

There are essentially two pressures that have caused panels not to exercise as much judicial economy as they could. First, the advent of intensive appellate review has caused some panels to consider additional issues so as to provide alternative bases for findings that will increase the chance that their basic decision will be upheld or so as to enable the Appellate Body to have more of a record of factual determinations in the

---

17. [original note 56] See Pierre Pesca-tore, untitled article in Antonio Perez van Kappel & Wolfgang Heusel, Free World Trade and the European Union: The Reconciliation of Interests and the Review of the Understanding on Dispute Settlement in the Framework of the World Trade Organization 9, 21–22 (Academy of European Law, Trier).

event it decides to "complete the analysis" in respect of an issue not dealt with by the panel.

Second, the Appellate Body has stated that panels should not exercise judicial economy to the extent that only a partial resolution of the matter results. In its words:

> "A panel has to address those claims on which a finding is necessary in order to enable the DSB to make sufficiently precise recommendations and rulings so as allow for prompt compliance by a Member with those recommendations and rulings 'in order to ensure effective resolution of dispute to the benefit of all Members' (quoting DSU Article 21.1).

> In this case, for the Panel to make findings concerning violation of Article 5.1 with respect to other Canadian [i.e. other than ocean-caught wild Pacific] salmon, without also making findings under Articles 5.5 and 5.6, would not enable the DSB to make sufficiently precise recommendations and rulings so as to allow for compliance by Australia with its obligations under the *SPS Agreement*, in order to ensure the effective resolution of this dispute with Canada. An SPS measure, which is brought into consistency with Article 5.1, may still be inconsistent with either Article 5.5 or Article 5.6, or with both."[18]

It is unclear how this guidance should be interpreted. It could be read to reject the very notion of judicial economy since more information about what would comply with an agreement would always be useful for implementation purposes.

As a general matter, I think that judicial economy is an appropriate technique for panels to use to avoid controversial issues. If a measure can be found to be inconsistent with WTO rules without addressing a difficult issue in the case, panels should not hesitate to avoid the difficult issue. Perhaps the issue will arise again, but perhaps it will not.

It should be noted that it is evident from the discussion of the exercise of judicial economy—in the argument sections of panel reports, in the interim review process and in the Appellate Body—that parties are often frustrated by the exercise of judicial economy. This is understandable, as a party may have devoted considerable time and effort to make a whole range of arguments and feel quite frustrated if many of them are not even considered. In my view, however, if the panel accepts one of a party's theories as to why a measure is WTO-inconsistent, that should be sufficient, particularly where the additional arguments may be difficult or controversial. For me, if anything, panels should probably be more willing to exercise judicial economy than they seem to be nowadays.

18. [original note 62] Appellate Body Report, *Salmon*, paras. 223–224.

I.   Scope of Appellate Review and Appellate Judicial Economy

The Appellate Body has never articulated a standard of review to apply to its consideration of appeals. While DSU Article 17.12 provides that the AB shall "address each of the issues raised", it would seem that the AB has the flexibility of exercising judicial economy as well. It can simply say that having addressed certain issues, the remaining issues do not need to be considered separately. That statement, in itself, "addresses" the remaining issues.

To date, the Appellate Body does not seem to have exercised much judicial economy, except when it has declared that appealed issues are factual in nature and therefore beyond its purview. * * * For me, the Appellate Body could appropriately deal with more issues on the basis of judicial economy.

CONCLUSION

In general, I do not believe that the Appellate Body and panels have over-reached in the various reports adopted through September 25, 2000, in the WTO dispute settlement system, except perhaps in the few, relatively minor, matters mentioned at the end of Part I. In respect of issue-avoidance techniques, I think that over time the WTO system could profitably make more use of such techniques in respect of the timing of consideration of issues (mootness and ripeness) and the exercise of judicial economy. This is particularly true in the case of the Appellate Body in respect of mootness and judicial economy. The one caveat has been noted in connection with the discussion of judicial economy—it is necessary to have clear standards as to when these techniques will be used, so as to avoid having some Members believe that they have been unfairly treated differently than other Members.

Notes and Questions

(1) Does Professor Davey reach the right balance on which of these avoidance techniques should be used?

(2) In reading its decisions in some of the more controversial cases to date in Chapters 13 and 14 (such as the *Asbestos, Gasoline, Shrimp* and *Hormones* cases), consider whether the Appellate Body has generally acted in a way so as to afford considerable discretion to WTO members and in tune with prevailing political sentiments in at least the major powers in the WTO.

(3) Standard of Review and Its Impact on Potential Imbalances in Political and Judicial Power

Because of the reverse consensus rule, the results of the dispute settlement system are adopted automatically. In comparison, because of the tradition of consensus decisionmaking in other WTO bodies, it may often be very difficult, if not impossible, for the General Council to change an interpretation of a WTO agreement by a panel or the Appellate Body. For example, as discussed in Section 7.3(F) infra, the Appellate Body has ruled that it has the power to accept amicus submissions from non-WTO members, and in the *Asbestos* case (discussed in Sections 12.4 and 13.1 infra) it circulated procedures as to how it would decide whether to accept such submissions in that case (WT/DS135/9, Nov. 8, 2000). Its decision was harshly criticized in a special meeting of the General Council.

DECISION BY THE APPELLATE BODY CONCERNING *AMICUS CURIAE* BRIEFS

Statement by Uruguay at the General Council
on 22 November 2000, WT/GC/38 (Dec. 12, 2000)

The dispute settlement system of this Organization has been described as the "jewel" of the achievements of the Uruguay Round. We must not allow this jewel to lose its brilliance or its value. If the Members cease to have confidence in this dispute settlement system—which is unique at the international level—they will lose a fundamental tool for the defence of their interests and will find themselves worse off than before.

* * *

The WTO is an agreement of a contractual nature that is qualitatively different from other international agreements in the sense that the obligations that flow from this contract include the strict fulfilment of the decisions of the Dispute Settlement Body to the extent of diminishing the decision-making capacity of the Members. Insofar as the Members are mainly States, the political effect of this situation is of no little consequence. It is for this reason that any decision by the bodies that make up the system cannot be taken lightly, but must be firmly based on the provisions of the Agreements that were duly signed and ratified by the respective governments and parliaments.

It is in this context that we view with very great concern the appearance and mass circulation outside the Organization of document WT/DS135/9 in which the Appellate Body has established an additional procedure for the submission of written briefs from persons or institutions that are neither parties nor third parties in a particular dispute that is at the appeal stage. Our concern is based on the fact that notwithstanding the positive intention that inspired this document its form, its substance and the way it has been handled affect the rights and obligations of the Members of the Organization and, moreover, alter the relationship between the bodies within the system.

* * *

Although this document is presented to us as an explanatory note under Rule 16(1) of the [Appellate Body] Working Procedures, its practical effect is that the Appellate Body is adopting decisions on relations with NGOs, and such decisions * * * statutorily belong to the General Council [pursuant to WTO Agreement, art. V:2]. Consequently, this is not a matter of clarifying procedures, but of upsetting the balance of the functions of each body involved.

In view of this practical outcome, we do not agree that it is a matter of procedure, but rather, in our opinion, a matter of substance which affects the working procedures and which should at least be subject to consultation with the Chairman of the DSB and the Director–General, in accordance with [DSU] Article 17.9.

* * *

As for the substance, we believe that the practical effect has been to grant individuals and institutions outside the [WTO] a right that the Members themselves do not possess. In fact, this procedure allows such institutions to present their points of view and possibly even influence a purely legal and interpretative decision of the rules in a specific case, while that right is reserved solely to the parties and third parties to a dispute, even being refused to the other Members of the [WTO]. We consider this to be highly inappropriate because it alters an Agreement negotiated and adopted multilaterally and, in particular, because this subject was discussed during the negotiations of the Uruguay Round, but was not incorporated into the DSU.

Furthermore, the procedure limits the rights of the parties and third parties. The last paragraph of Section 1 of the factual background note states that the decision gives the parties and the third parties a full and adequate opportunity to comment on and respond to the submissions. However, the fact is that this is not possible within the short and mandatory time-limits which the Appellate Body has to meet in its work.

* * *

In conclusion, Mr. Chairman, the preceding analysis, although extensive, has been necessary to justify the following positive conclusions:

(a) The decision of the Division of the Appellate Body in this case, despite its praise-worthy intentions, * * * has had the practical effect of altering the agreements, which it is not in its terms of reference to do.

(b) The Appellate Body must restrict itself to establishing whether a Panel has correctly applied or interpreted the rules in a specific case. However, insofar it knows that its decisions will set precedents, when it identifies difficulties that arise from the wider interpretation of the Agreements it should inform the General Council so that the latter may take the decisions incumbent upon it. Thus, we believe that in the *US–Shrimp* case, * * * when the Appellate Body decided to reject the Panel's interpretation of its powers under Article 13 of the DSU, it should have informed the General Council of this situation so as to obtain an interpretation that could be applied in other cases.

(c) The General Council has begun today its consideration of the *amicus curiae* briefs sent to the Panels and the Appellate Body. This is a matter of interpretation having systemic effects that is the responsibility of the General Council. Consequently, we request that this matter be placed on the regular agenda of the General Council and that the

Chairman take the appropriate measures in the case so that this Council can adopt an interpretation of general application.

(d) Panels and the Appellate Body should refrain from acting in this matter until the General Council has given its interpretation.

Notes and Questions

(1) What is your reaction? Do you agree with Uruguay?

(2) Reportedly, only the United States defended the Appellate Body's decision.

(3) While the Appellate Body ultimately decided not to accept any such submissions, the controversy underscored the relative weakness in practice of the General Council's decision-making powers compared to the automatic procedure by which the results of dispute settlement cases are adopted. Does this argue that panels and the Appellate Body should exercise judicial restraint to a greater degree than national courts, where decisions on statutory interpretation are much more easily changed by the legislature?

(C) IMPLEMENTATION AND RETALIATION PROCEDURES

The operation of the DSU's provisions on determining implementation and authorizing retaliation has been quite controversial because of certain ambiguities in the provisions of articles 21 and 22 of the DSU. The relevant provisions are:

> Article 21.5, which provides that "[w]here there is a disagreement as to the existence or consistency with a covered agreement of measures taken to comply with [DSB recommendations] such dispute shall be decided through recourse to these dispute settlement procedures, including wherever possible resort to the original panel;" and

> Article 22.2, which provides that "[i]f the Member concerned fails to bring the measure found to be inconsistent with a covered agreement into compliance therewith * * * within the reasonable period of time" and "[i]f no satisfactory compensation has been agreed to within 20 days after the date of the expiry of the reasonable period of time", the prevailing party "may request authorization from the DSB to suspend * * * concessions * * * ." Pursuant to article 22.6, "[w]hen the situation described in paragraph 2 occurs, the DSB, upon request, shall grant authorization to suspend concessions or other obligations within 30 days of the expiry of the reasonable period of time unless the DSB decides by consensus to reject the request."

In the *EC Bananas* case, the EC argued that since there was a dispute over whether its implementing measure was consistent with WTO rules, there had to be a determination under article 21.5, before suspension of concession could be authorized. The US argued that article 22 did not impose such a condition and that, as a practical matter, it would lose the right to have suspension of concessions approved by reverse consensus if its request were not acted upon within 30 days of the expiration of the reasonable period of time. In that regard, it noted that a panel would never be able to complete work within such a time frame.

Ultimately, after a week-long DSB meeting and much controversy, the US request was ruled to be in order. The EC then requested an arbitration under article 22.6 to determine the level of suspension, which is required by article 22.4 to be "equivalent to the level of nullification or impairment". The arbitrators were the members of the original panel, who were contemporaneously conducting an article 21.5 proceeding brought a few weeks earlier by Ecuador (one of the original complainants with the US). They simultaneously ruled in both matters that the EC implementing measures were not WTO-consistent and in the arbitration set the level of suspension at $191 million (as opposed to the US request of $520 million). The rulings were issued within the article 21.5 timeframe of 90 days, but not within the 30 day timeframe specified for the arbitration. At the end of that 30 day period, the US unilaterally imposed sanctions in an amount of $520 million (which it later reduced to $191 million). The EC initiated a panel proceeding, which reached the obvious conclusion that the unilateral US action violated various rules, including article 23 of the DSU. United States—Import Measures on Certain Products from the European Communities, WT/DS165R & AB/R, adopted by the DSB on January 10, 2001.

In subsequent cases, parties have generally agreed that both the 21.5 and arbitration procedures will be commenced promptly after the end of the expiry of the reasonable period of time, but that the arbitration will be suspended until the 21.5 panel rules (and in some cases until any appeal has been concluded). A proposal to clarify articles 21 and 22 so as to establish a sequence of procedures such as those now typically agreed to garnered substantial support immediately prior to the Seattle ministerial conference in 1999, but has never been adopted. Since providing for such a sequence required an overall lengthening of the time for completing a typical case and since there was a desire not to lengthen the overall process, a number of adjustments were made in the consultation and panel stages to reduce the time devoted thereto. Some developing countries have opposed shortening these timeframes, while other members (including the EC and the US) have withheld support from the proposal in an attempt to have other DSU reforms included.

Notes and Questions

(1) As of September 1, 2001, there had been 11 article 21.5 proceedings. Does this suggest that some WTO members are taking questionable implementation measures as a way to postpone full compliance?

(2) Can a 21.5 panel consider whether the implementing measure violates WTO rules that were not at issue in the original dispute? What would be the consequences of a negative answer? See page 782 infra.

(3) As of September 1, 2001, there had been 5 completed article 22 arbitrations—two in *EC Bananas*, two in *EC Hormones* and one in *Brazil Aircraft Subsidies*—and two were pending, waiting completion of article 21.5 proceedings. Interestingly, in *EC Bananas*, which involved claims relating to

the goods and services agreements, Ecuador was authorized to suspend obligations under the TRIPS Agreement because it successfully argued under article 22.3 that, for the most part, it would not be practicable or effective for it to suspend obligations owed to the EC under GATT or GATS. European Communities—Regime for the Importation, Sale and Distribution of Bananas—Recourse to Arbitration by the European Communities under Article 22.6 of the DSU, Decision by the Arbitrators, WT/DS27/ARB/ECU (March 24, 2000).

(D) EFFECTIVE REMEDIES

(1) Current Rules

In line with DSU article 19.1, the normal practice of panels is to propose that the DSB recommend that the WTO member whose measure has been found in violation of an agreement bring that measure into conformity with that agreement. The following case raises issues as to whether broader relief would be appropriate.

NORWAY—PROCUREMENT OF TOLL COLLECTION EQUIPMENT FOR THE CITY OF TRONDHEIM

40th Supp. BISD 319
Panel Report adopted May 13, 1992 by the Committee
on Government Procurement

[This case arose under the Government Procurement Code, which is described in Section 11.4 supra. The panel concluded that Norway had violated the Code because the City of Trondheim had not instituted an open bidding procedure in respect of its procurement of certain highway toll collection equipment. The following part of the decision deals with the appropriate remedy for this violation.]

4.17   The panel then turned its attention to the recommendations that the United States had requested it to make. In regard to the United States' request that the Panel recommend that Norway take the necessary measures to bring its practices into compliance with the Agreement with regard to the Trondheim procurement, the Panel noted that all the acts of non-compliance alleged by the United States were acts that had taken place in the past. The only way mentioned during the Panel's proceedings that Norway could bring the Trondheim procurement into line with its obligations under the Agreement would be by annulling the contract and recommencing the procurement process. The Panel did not consider it appropriate to make such a recommendation. Recommendations of this nature had not been within customary practice in dispute settlement under the GATT system and the drafters of the Agreement on Government Procurement had not made specific provision that such recommendation be within the task assigned to panels under standard terms of reference. Moreover, the Panel considered that in the case under examination such a recommendation might be disproportionate, involving waste of resources and possible damage to the interests of third parties.

4.18   The United States had further requested the Panel to recommend that Norway negotiate a mutually satisfactory solution with the United States that took into account the lost opportunities in the procurement of United States' companies, including Amtech. Finally, the United States had requested the Panel to recommend that, in the event that the proposed negotiation did not yield a mutually satisfactory result, the Committee be prepared to authorize the United States to withdraw benefits under the Agreement from Norway with respect to opportunities to bid of equal value to the Trondheim contract. * * *

4.19   In examining these requests, the Panel first noted that, as instructed in its terms of reference, it had given Norway and the United States full opportunity to develop a mutually satisfactory solution. The Panel also noted that nothing prevented the two governments from negotiating at any time a mutually satisfactory solution that took into account the lost opportunities of United States' suppliers, provided such solution was consistent with their obligations under this and other GATT agreements. The issue was whether the Panel should recommend this and further recommend that the Committee be prepared to authorize the withdrawal of benefits under the Agreement from Norway if such a solution were not negotiated.

* * *

4.21   [Beyond noting that the US was somewhat inconsistent in its requests to the Panel], the Panel observed that, under the GATT, it was customary for panels to make findings regarding conformity with the General Agreement and to recommend that any measures found inconsistent with the General Agreement be terminated or brought into conformity from the time that the recommendation was adopted. The provision of compensation had been resorted to only if the immediate withdrawal of the measure was impracticable and as a temporary measure pending the withdrawal of the measures which were inconsistent with the General Agreement. Questions relating to compensation or withdrawal of benefits had been dealt with in a stage of the dispute settlement procedure subsequent to the adoption of panel reports.

4.22   * * * [T]he Panel noted the argument of the United States that, because benefits accruing under the Agreement were primarily in respect of events (the opportunity to bid), rather than in respect of trade flows, and because government procurement by its very nature left considerable latitude for entities to act inconsistently with obligations under the Agreement in respect of those events even without rules or procedures inconsistent with those required by the Agreement, standard panel recommendations requiring an offending Party to bring its rules and practices into conformity would, in many cases, not by themselves constitute a sufficient remedy and would not provide a sufficient deterrent effect.

4.23   In considering this argument, the Panel was of the view that situations of the type described by the United States were not unique to government procurement. Considerable trade damage could be caused in other areas by an administrative decision without there necessarily being any GATT inconsistent legislation, for example in the areas of discretionary licensing, technical regulations, sanitary and phytosanitary measures, and subsidies. Moreover, there had been cases where a temporary measure contested before the GATT had been lifted before a Panel had been able to report.

4.24   The Panel also believed that, in cases concerning a particular past action, a panel finding of non-compliance would be of significance for the successful party: where the interpretation of the Agreement was in dispute, panel findings, once adopted by the Committee, would constitute guidance for future implementation of the Agreement by Parties.

4.25   Moreover, the Panel was not aware of any basis in the Agreement on Government Procurement for panels to adopt, with regard to the issues under consideration, a practice different from that customary under the General Agreement, at least in the absence of special terms of reference from the Committee.

4.26   In the light of the above, the Panel did not consider that it would be appropriate for it to [make the recommendation requested by the United States].

Notes and Questions

(1) Did the United States receive adequate redress in the *Trondheim* case? If the DSU had been in effect, would the U.S. have had a better argument for broader relief?

(2) Suppose that a panel concludes that a country has inappropriately applied antidumping duties to imports from a complainant. Would it be appropriate to recommend that the duties be refunded? This occurred in New Zealand—Imports of Electrical Transformers from Finland, 32nd Supp. BISD 55 (1986) (Panel report adopted July 18, 1985), but the United States blocked adoption of a panel report to the Antidumping Committee that recommended that the U.S. reimburse such duties in a case involving certain Swedish steel exports to the U.S. The U.S. has argued that the proposed recommendation was "of an extraordinary retroactive and specific nature." GATT Activities 1992, at 40.

(3) Under the DSU, one 21.5 panel recommended that a government, which had granted an WTO-inconsistent export subsidy, could "withdraw the subsidy" as required by article 4.7 of the Subsidies Agreement only by obtaining full repayment. The result was quite controversial and heavily criticized at the DSB meeting at which the panel report was adopted. (There was no appeal because of a prior agreement that neither side would appeal the panel report.) Australia—Subsidies Provided to Producers and Exporters of Automotive Leather, WT/DS126/RW, adopted by the DSB on February 11, 2000.

(2) The Efficacy of Retaliation as a Solution to Trade Disputes

As explained in Section 7.3 supra, suspension of concessions was only authorized once in GATT's history and that occasion was in the

1950's. As also noted there, under the DSU, suspension of concessions has been authorized in three cases (*Bananas, Hormones* and *Brazil Aircraft Subsidies*), but as of September 1, 2001, was in effect only in one (*Hormones*). Do you think that such actions are an appropriate means of resolving trade disputes?

Professor Davey argued in 1987 that[19]

there are good reasons why GATT should authorize retaliation more regularly. First, the novelty of retaliation will decrease with use and it will eventually be accepted as the normal consequence of an inability to resolve a dispute. This will lessen the poisonous effects that retaliation entails. Second, retaliation would improve the efficiency of the GATT dispute settlement system by encouraging speedy conflict resolution. Third, retaliation is fair because it reestablishes the balance of concessions between the two parties, a balance that is thrown into disequilibrium when one party has violated GATT's rules. Fourth, and most important, retaliation will often occur anyway if disputes are not resolved. Given that this is the case, it would be desirable for GATT to exercise greater control over retaliation when it occurs. Indeed, it is possible that retaliation will become more common, in the future, because of its proven effectiveness in recent U.S.-EC trade disputes. With GATT supervision some control can be exercised, particularly as to the amount of retaliation, which reduces the likelihood that a massive trade war would erupt.

Notes and Questions

(1) Is there a significant risk of starting a trade war if one side suspends concessions? Or does that risk already exist, such that attempting to control the use of such suspensions in the WTO framework is an improvement on the prior GATT system? As noted earlier, there is a hope on the part of many countries that the U.S. will be less likely to act unilaterally under these new rules.

(2) It should be noted that Article XXIII suspensions are *not* limited by the text of that article to compensatory amounts (as compared to punitive amounts) and are not limited to actions by a nation which has been harmed. Theoretically, a "sanction" could authorize suspensions of major concessions by many, if not all, WTO members and could even be the basis for an effective expulsion. The DSU, however, limits suspensions to those that have "invoked the dispute settlement procedures" (art. 22.2) and provides that the level of suspension "shall be equivalent to the level of the nullification or impairment." Art. 22.4.

(3) There is some question whether retaliation works that well in practice. In Section 21.1 infra, we will consider an historical study of the use of sanctions to achieve economic and political goals that questions whether sanctions are all that effective. As noted in Section 7.3(B), overall the record

---

19. Dispute Settlement in GATT, 11 Fordham Intl.L.J. 51, 101–102 (1987). Re-   printed by permission.

of compliance by WTO Members with DSB recommendations has been relatively good. However, there are examples of "foot-dragging" in implementation. In the two cases where retaliation was authorized and implemented—the *Bananas* and *Hormones* cases—it did not lead quickly to compliance, although the *Bananas* case was settled two years after retaliation was authorized. In the third case where retaliation was authorized—the *Brazil Aircraft Subsidies* case, Canada has not taken advantage of the authorization, apparently in part because of some concerns about its efficacy. Consequently, the question becomes whether improvements are needed in respect of the WTO remedies available for noncompliance.

WILLIAM J. DAVEY

WTO DISPUTE SETTLEMENT (2001)

In considering remedies in the WTO system, it is important to recall that the existing remedies are prospective—whether in the form of compensation or retaliation. In addition, it is important to consider their two principal aims–to restore the balance of concessions that was upset when one member violated its obligations (a temporary aim since compliance is the preferred result); and to give that member an incentive to comply. The current problem with achieving the first aim—rebalancing—is that if retaliation is authorized, rebalancing takes place at a lower level of trade liberalization than had been agreed to. It would be desirable if a remedy could be devised that would not lead to less liberalization overall. One could consider monetary payments or requiring the payment of compensation through a reduction in other tariffs or trade restrictions maintained by the non-complying Member.[20]

In respect of the second aim—incentive to comply—there are two issues—timing and level of compensation or retaliation. At present, because remedies are prospective, there is an incentive initially to delay the time at which point they might be implemented, such as by seeking a long reasonable period of time for compliance and then forcing the victor to go through an article 21.5 panel (and Appellate Body) proceeding. Moreover, if the threat of retaliation does not work, it is possible that the actual existence of retaliation will become viewed as the status quo and a long-term solution, even though the WTO rules in theory require compliance. This fear that retaliation will lose effect over time explains in part the US desire to implement the so-called carousel provision, by which the products targeted by retaliatory action would change on a regular basis once retaliation is authorized. A preferable solution may be to create incentives for early compliance, such as by providing that any retaliation will be calculated from a date prior to the date set for implementation or by providing for increasing retaliation over time.

---

20. See Joost Pauwelyn, Enforcement and Countermeasures in the WTO, 94 Am. J.Intl.L. 335 (2000).

These issues will require careful thought. While retaliation seems to work when threatened by a large country against a smaller one, and has worked as between two large countries, it may not be an effective remedy for a small country (even if it can target sensitive large country sectors such as copyright holders). Moreover, the *Bananas* and *Hormones* cases show that it is not always effective between the large players. Its inefficacy and the unfavorable position in which it leaves developing countries may soon combine to create a serious credibility problem for the system that must be confronted.

In considering how to improve WTO remedies, it will be necessary to consider whether there are other forms of remedies beyond compensation and retaliation that might be more effective. One possibility would be the payment of fines or damages. One obvious problem would be the disparity in fine-paying ability among WTO members. Any such system would have to be designed to avoid the possibility that rich members could effectively buy their way out of obligations in a way not available to the poor members. One alternative would be to tie the amount of fines to the size of the member's economy, or otherwise provide for a sliding scale that would minimize "discrimination" against poor members. To avoid the perception that the payment of fines is simply an alternative to compliance, the fines could be assessed annually (or on some other periodic basis) and could be increased over time. Such a system could serve as a method of rebalancing if the fines are paid to the member owed compliance and could promote prompter compliance if the fines are increased over time. While a system of fines has not been discussed in detail in the past, the exploration by the US administration in 2001 of the possibility of using fines for environmental and labor rules violations (instead of trade sanctions) could lead to a more serious consideration of such an alternative.[21]

A different sort of alternative would be to suspend certain WTO rights for the period of time that a member is not in compliance with its obligations. There are a wide variety of rights or benefits that might be suspended: voting rights, participation rights in meetings, technical cooperation, dispute settlement rights.[22] Given the lack of voting in the WTO, suspension of voting rights would not seem to be an alternative. The limitation of participation rights might be difficult to define—it would not be in the interest of the WTO or its members to exclude one member from trade liberalization negotiations. Suspension of technical cooperation could also be self-defeating since it is usually concerned with implementation issues, and in any event, it would be applicable only to developing countries. The most promising area in which to consider suspension of rights would be in respect of dispute settlement. If a member refuses to comply with the results of dispute settlement when it

---

21. USTR, Concept Paper, Using Monetary Assessments to Enforce Panel Decisions under Bilateral Free–Trade Agreements, reproduced in Inside US Trade under the heading Internal USTR Paper on Monetary Fines (April 2001).

22. See generally Henry G. Schermers & Niels M. Blokker, International Institutional Law, secs. 1445–1561 (3d rev. ed. 1999).

loses, simple notions of fairness would argue that it should not be able to invoke the system against others. It would be necessary to define the rights to be suspended: at a minimum, five rights are easily identified– the right to request consultations, the right to request a panel, the right to request authority to suspend concessions, the right to participate as a third party and the right to participate in DSB meetings. It would be possible to create a scheme that would phase-in a loss of the foregoing rights over time.

Notes and Questions

(1) Which of the foregoing ideas seems to be most plausible–in terms of likely effectiveness and acceptance by WTO members?

(2) What others remedies might be considered?

(E) CONFLICTS OF NORMS[23]

Given the wide scope of the WTO agreements, it seems inevitable that there may be overlapping or even conflicting obligations in some cases. While the agreements themselves provide some means for resolving potential conflicts, others potential conflicts are not dealt with at all.

The WTO Agreement provides in Article XVI:3 that in the event of a conflict between it and any of the other WTO agreements, the WTO Agreement prevails. In the event of a conflict between GATT 1994 and any of the other Annex 1A agreements (i.e., the other agreements on trade in goods), the provisions of the other agreement prevail. WTO Agreement, Annex 1A, general interpretative note. There are no provisions, however, that deal generally with conflicts between the various agreements on trade in goods, although there are specific provisions in certain cases. For example, the Agriculture Agreement provides that GATT 1994 and the other Annex 1A agreements are subject to it (art. 21.1). There are also no general provisions dealing with conflicts involving the agreements on services (GATS) or intellectual property (TRIPS Agreement).

Under the general rules of public international law on conflicts, a treaty interpreter should attempt to interpret the relevant agreements so that there is no conflict, i.e., so that the agreements are compatible. However, as regards treaties having incompatible provisions, the relation of treaties between the same parties and with overlapping provisions is primarily a matter of interpretation, aided by presumptions. First, it is to be presumed that a later treaty prevails over an earlier treaty concerning the same subject matter. Second, a treaty may provide expressly that it is to prevail over subsequent incompatible treaties. These principles are not very pertinent for resolving the relationship between GATT, GATS and the TRIPS Agreement or between the various Annex 1A agreements. All agreements within the WTO framework

---

23. This section draws extensively upon William J. Davey & Werner Zdouc, The Triangle of TRIPS, GATT and GATS, in Thomas Cottier & Petros C. Mavroidis (eds.), Intellectual Property: Trade, Competition and Sustainable Development (forthcoming).

have been concluded as a single treaty and at the same time—including GATT 1994—which renders the later-in-time rule inapposite. To some extent, the principle of effective treaty interpretation may be useful in avoiding incompatibilities between obligations provided for in the various WTO agreements.

WTO panels and the Appellate Body have considered conflict problems in the context of the relationships among the Annex 1A agreements and the relationship of GATT and GATS. They have also had to define the notion of conflict for purposes of applying the General Interpretative Note to Annex 1A, which provides that in the even of a conflict between GATT 1994 and the other agreements on trade in goods, the other agreements prevail. In *EC—Bananas,* the panel concluded that the national treatment and MFN clauses of GATT 1994 and provisions of the TRIMs Agreement and the Agreement on Import Licensing Procedures (Licensing Agreement) could simultaneously apply to the same measure, i.e., the EC regime on the importation, sale and distribution of bananas. In dicta, the panel developed a broad notion of "conflict" between obligations contained in GATT 1994 and those provided for in the other Annex 1A agreements. It presumed such a conflict to exist— and thus the rule of the other Annex 1A agreement to prevail over the general rule of GATT 1994—not only in a situation where one agreement explicitly mandates what another agreement explicitly prohibits, but also in a situation where one agreement explicitly permits what another explicitly forbids. The panel acknowledged that in the latter case a Member could comply with both rules by renouncing to resort to the right conferred by the permissive rule in order not to violate the prohibitive rule. However, it deemed such a result to be contrary to the principle of effective treaty interpretation because no meaning would be given to the permissive rule which would become entirely redundant. The panel gave the example of quantitative restrictions permitted by the safeguard provisions of the Agreement on Textiles and Clothing (ATC) which on their face are incompatible with the general prohibition of quantitative restrictions in Article XI of GATT, but follow a somewhat similar rationale as safeguard measures justifiable under Article XIX of GATT.

In the *Indonesia–Autos* case, this reasoning was taken somewhat out of context by Indonesia which used it to buttress the argument that GATT Article III and the provisions of the Subsidies Agreement could not apply simultaneously to the same measure, especially in light of the exemption of production subsidies in Article III:8(b) from the coverage of the national treatment clause. The panel in *Indonesia–Autos* adopted a narrower notion of what constitutes a conflict than had the *Bananas* panel, essentially concluding that a conflict in the meaning of the Note to Annex 1A exists only in cases where one rule explicitly prohibits what another rule explicitly requires a Member to do. It is unclear, however, whether—as a result of this narrower notion of conflict—that panel would have answered differently the hypothetical posed by the *Bananas* panel, i.e., the relation between a prohibitive and a permissive rule.

Given the *Indonesia–Autos* panel's reliance in general on the principle of effective treaty interpretation, it is probably more appropriate to assume that this panel would have reached a conclusion similar to that of the *Bananas* panel. However, it would probably have reached that conclusion without labeling the relationship between a prohibitive and a permissive rule a situation of conflict, but it would likely have reasoned that effective treaty interpretation required it to give meaning to the conditional derogation under the safeguards clause of the ATC from the general prohibition of quotas under GATT.

The relationship of GATT and GATS has been explored in the two cases—*Canada—Periodicals* and *EC—Bananas.* The panel and the Appellate Body in *Canada—Periodicals* held that the creation of GATS did not carve out part of the pre-existing coverage of GATT 1947 or 1994. Therefore, the fact that Canada had not committed itself to grant market access or national treatment in a certain service sector (e.g., advertising services) did not exempt a measure directly affecting this service sector (e.g., an excise tax on products) from the potential coverage of the GATT national treatment clause.[24] In *EC—Bananas,* the Appellate Body distinguished between three different situations: (1) measures that only affect trade in goods, (2) measures that only affect trade in services, and (3) measures that affect trade in goods as well as trade in services such as measures involving a service relating to a particular good or a service supplied in conjunction with a particular good. It noted that while a measure falling in category (3) could be scrutinized under both GATT and GATS, the specific aspects of the measure examined under each agreement could be different. Under GATT, the focus would be on how the measure affects the goods involved, whereas under GATS the focus would be on how the same measure affects the supply of the service or the service supplier involved.[25]

Notes and Questions

(1) Are you satisfied that the foregoing WTO cases dealing with conflicts adequately address the issues? The GATT-GATS relationship is further explored in Chapter 19.

(2) How should a conflict between an obligation in a WTO agreement and a non-WTO-related agreement be analyzed? Consider the principles outlined above and article 31 of the Vienna Convention on the Law of Treaties (Chapter 5.2 supra). See Section 13.4 infra.

(F) TRANSPARENCY AND PARTICIPATION OF NON–MEMBERS

One of the more controversial issues faced by the WTO dispute settlement system is how to deal with complaints by non-governmental

24. *Canada—Certain Measures Concerning Periodicals*, WT/DS31/AB/R, pp. 17–20, adopted by the DSB on 30 July 1997.

25. European Communities—Regime for the Importation, Sale and Distribution of Bananas, WT/DS27/AB/R, paras. 217–222, adopted by the DSB on September 25, 1997.

organizations (NGOs) and others that the system lacks transparency and does not permit sufficient access for non-Members.

(1) Transparency

Currently, panel and Appellate Body proceedings are closed to the public. Only the parties and, to a limited extent, third parties may attend the proceedings. The parties and third parties may make public their own submissions to a panel or the Appellate Body, but they are not required to do so. For parties who do not make their submissions public, the DSU requires them, on request, to provide a non-confidential summary that could be made public (art. 18.2). In practice, such summaries are often very brief and prepared only after considerable delay. The arguments of the parties and third parties are described in great detail in (or even attached to) panel reports and are summarized relatively concisely in Appellate Body reports. Since panel and Appellate Body reports (and all other WTO documents relating to specific disputes) are issued as unrestricted documents and placed on the WTO website on the same day as their distribution to WTO members, the parties' arguments become known in due course.

The United States has proposed that dispute settlement proceedings be open to the public and that submissions be made public when filed with the WTO. Should the WTO dispute settlement system adopt such or similar transparency rules? What are the advantages and disadvantages of more transparency? In that regard, what is the practice of other national and international tribunals—are their proceedings public? When are party submissions made public?

(2) Participation of Non-members

Even more controversial than transparency, is the proposal by the United States that non-parties should be permitted to make amicus ("friend-of-the-court") submissions to panels and the Appellate Body. When the US proposals were discussed in the review of the DSU conducted in 1998–1999, there was considerable opposition to them. Many developing country Members view the WTO system as exclusively intergovernmental in nature and hesitate to open it in any way to non-governments. In their view, if an NGO wants to make an argument to a panel, it should convince one of the parties to make it, and if no party makes the argument, those members would view that as evidence that the argument is not meritorious. Moreover, they view such openness as favoring the positions espoused by western, developed country NGOs, which they view as likely not to be in their interest. Others argue that the credibility of the system would be much enhanced if it were more open and that openness would have no significant disadvantages.

While the DSU review was ongoing, the Appellate Body ruled that panels have the right to accept non-requested submissions from non-parties (such as NGOs).[26] It reversed a panel report that had concluded

---

26. United States—Import Prohibition of Certain Shrimp and Shrimp Products, WT/DS58/AB/R, paras. 99–110, adopted on 6 November 1998.

that while panels had the right to "seek" information under DSU article 13.1, they did not have the power to accept information that had not been sought. The Appellate Body criticized the panel for reading article 13 "in too literal a manner" (para. 107). The Appellate Body also ruled, however, that the panel's decision in that case to call the submissions to the attention of the parties and ask if the parties wished to adopt all or part of them was an appropriate exercise of its discretion.

Notwithstanding considerable criticism of the foregoing decision, the Appellate Body later ruled that it also had the power to accept amicus submissions, even though its working procedures and the DSU provisions applicable to it contained no provision like article 13.[27] Later, in the *Asbestos* case, the Appellate Body announced specific procedures for considering whether to accept amicus submissions in that case. That decision was harshly criticized in a special General Council meeting called to discuss the issue. The reader should review the statement by Venezuela on this issue, which we excerpted in Section 7.4(B)(3) supra.

Notes and Questions

(1) Should the WTO dispute settlement system permit amicus submission? What are the advantages and disadvantages of doing so? In that regard, what is the practice of other national and international tribunals?

(2) One concern is that panels will be deluged with amicus submissions. Do you think that is likely? How might the problem be minimized?

(3) There is a concern that parties will not know on which, if any, amicus arguments or facts a panel or the Appellate Body intends to rely, and therefore will not be in a position to respond appropriately. What procedures could be devised to address this concern?

(4) Given popular fears of globalization and the WTO's connection therewith, could increased transparency and participation rights in dispute settlement play an important role in increasing the credibility of the WTO in a way that may be essential to ensure the future effectiveness of the WTO itself, as well as the dispute settlement system?

(5) Should there be disclosure rules for NGOs wishing to submit amicus briefs so that their sources of financial support and ties to interested parties are known?

(6) See generally Gabrielle Marceau and Matthew Stilwell, Practical Suggestions for *amicus curiae* Briefs before WTO Adjudicating Bodies, 4 Journal of International Economic Law 155–187 (2001).

(G) UNILATERALISM AND THE DSU

Section 301 of the U.S. Trade Act of 1974 has engendered tremendous controversy through the years. Broadly speaking, it authorizes the

---

27. United States–Imposition of Countervailing Duties on Certain Hot–Rolled Lead and Bismuth Carbon Steel Products Originating in the United Kingdom, WT/ DS138/AB/R, paras. 139–142, Appellate Body Report adopted by the DSB on June 7, 2000.

United States Trade Representative to take retaliatory action against foreign trade practices that the United States deems "unfair." Prior to the entry into force of the Uruguay Round Agreements, when GATT dispute resolution proceedings could be "blocked" by any party, the United States regularly invoked Section 301 to threaten and in some cases carry out retaliatory measures against a wide range of foreign practices. In some cases, the United States took the position that the practice in question was a violation of GATT, and that unilateral action was its only recourse given the weakness of GATT dispute resolution. In other cases, the United States attacked practices that were not covered by GATT, such as a lack of protection for U.S. intellectual property rights.

The wisdom of Section 301 was hotly debated. Critics labeled it a form of "aggressive unilateralism," with the United States seen as unjustifiably taking the law into its own hands. Objections were made to the fact that the United States could unilaterally decide whether its rights were violated under GATT (although in practice it would respect the decisions of GATT panels if the other disputant consented to a panel), and to the fact that the United States at times retaliated against practices that were indisputably legal under international law.

Defenders of Section 301 argued that if it was used wisely, it was a reasonable self-help measure in the face of ineffective GATT dispute resolution as well as the broad gaps in the coverage of GATT commitments.[28] Further, Section 301 provides to the Executive Branch authority over trade policy that ordinarily resides with the Congress, and thus puts the U.S. President on a par with other world leaders whose constitutional systems already afford them much latitude in the formulation of trade policy.

Regardless of who had the better of the argument, many believe that the existence of Section 301 (and perhaps parallel legislation in Europe) was the catalyst for the movement to the new WTO dispute resolution system. Now that disputants can no longer block the process from going forward, the United States can no longer claim a need for self help when violations arise. And because WTO commitments are much broader than those of the GATT (including services and intellectual property, for

---

28. For a flavor of some of the debate, see Aggressive Unilateralism (Jagdish Bhagwati & Hugh Patrick eds. 1989); Thomas Bayard & Kimberly Elliott, Reciprocity and Retaliation in U.S. Trade Policy (1994); Jagdish Bhagwati, Protectionism (1988); Daniel Partan, Retaliation in United States and European Community Trade Law, 8 B.U.Intl.L.J. 333, 337–38 (1990); Powell, Why Trade Retaliation Closes Markets and Impoverishes People, CATO Policy Analysis No. 143, Nov. 1990; Alan O. Sykes, Constructive Unilateral Threats in International Commercial Relations: The Limited Case for Section 301, 23 L. & Pol.Intl.Bus. 263 (1992); . Discussions of the efficacy of retaliation from the game theoretic perspective, at varying levels of technical complexity, include the Sykes paper, cited above; the McMillan paper in the Aggressive Unilateralism volume; Dixit, How Should the United States Respond to Other Countries' Trade Policies?, in U.S. Trade Policies in a Changing World Economy (R. Stern ed., 1987); Baldwin, Optimal Tariff Retaliation Rules, in The Political Economy of International Trade (R. Jones & A. Krueger eds., 1990); and Eaton & Engers, Sanctions, 100 J.Pol.Econ. 899 (1992).

example), it is much harder to argue that gaps in international law require unilateral measures. Accordingly, although Section 301 remains on the books, it now bears little connection to "unilateralism" as a practical matter. Rather, it provides a vehicle whereby private industry can petition the government to take cases to the WTO, and it provides the Executive Branch with the statutory authority to implement WTO-authorized retaliatory sanctions. Because it *could* be used in a manner inconsistent with WTO obligations, however, some U.S. trading partners remain uneasy about its potential to cause mischief. In the hope of eliminating it once and for all, the European Community brought a challenge to it before the WTO.

UNITED STATES—SECTIONS 301–310
OF THE TRADE ACT OF 1974

WT/DS152/R
Panel Report adopted by the DSB on January 27, 2000

7.2   The EC claims that by adopting, maintaining on its statute book and applying Sections 301–310 of the 1974 Trade Act after the entry into force of the Uruguay Round Agreements, the US has breached the historical deal that was struck in Marrakech between the US and the other Uruguay Round participants. According to the EC, this deal consists of a trade-off between, on the one hand, the practical certainty of adoption by the Dispute Settlement Body ("DSB") of panel and Appellate Body reports and of authorization for Members to suspend concessions—in the EC's view, an explicit US request—and, on the other hand, the complete and definitive abandoning by the US of its long-standing policy of unilateral action. The EC submits that the second leg of this deal, which is, in its view, the core of the present Panel procedure, has been enshrined in the following WTO provisions: Articles 3, 21, 22 and, most importantly, 23 of the DSU and Article XVI:4 of the WTO Agreement.

* * *

7.4   The EC submits that Sections 301–310, on their face, mandate unilateral action by the US authorities in breach of Article 23 of the DSU and consequently of Articles I, II, III, VIII and XI of the GATT 1994. * * *

7.5   In addition, the EC argues that Sections 301–310—even if they could be interpreted to permit the USTR to avoid WTO-inconsistent determinations and actions—cannot be regarded as a sound legal basis for the implementation of the US obligations under the WTO. For the EC, the lack of this "sound legal basis" produces a situation of threat and legal uncertainty against other WTO Members and their economic operators that fundamentally undermines the "security and predictability" of the multilateral trading system.

* * *

7.9 The US responds that the EC has brought a political case that is in search of a legal argument. It submits that * * * Sections 301–310 permit the US to comply with DSU rules and procedures in every case. * * *

* * *

7.29 The EC claims that Section 304 mandates the USTR to make a "unilateral" determination on whether another WTO Member has violated US rights under the WTO. The EC submits that this determination by the USTR has to be made within 18 months after the initiation of an investigation under Section 302, a date that normally coincides with the request for consultations under the DSU. According to the EC, DSU procedures can, however, be assumed to take 19 [or more] months. The EC submits that, as a result of the 18 months deadline, the determination under Section 304 is required even if the DSB has not yet adopted a report with findings on the matter, contrary to Article 23.2(a) of the DSU.

7.30 The US responds that nothing in Section 304 compels the USTR to make a specific determination that US rights have been denied in the absence of panel or Appellate Body findings, adopted by the DSB. In its second submission, the US goes even further and submits that since Section 304 determinations have to be made on the basis of WTO dispute settlement proceedings pursuant to Section 304 (a)(1), a determination that US rights have been denied before the adoption of DSB findings is *precluded*. According to the US, Section 304 only requires the USTR to "determine *whether*"–not to determine *that*–US rights have been denied. In the US view, the USTR has the discretion to determine that no violation has occurred, that no violation has been confirmed by the DSB, that a violation will be confirmed on the date the DSB adopts panel or Appellate Body findings or that the ongoing investigation must terminate. The US also argues that the relevant period for DSU procedures to be completed–from the request for consultations to the adoption of reports by the DSB–is not 19 [or more] months, as claimed by the EC, but 16 months and 20 days.

7.31 As regards the statutory language of Section 304, we consider it sufficient to make the following findings based upon examination of the text itself, the evidence and arguments submitted to us in this respect as well as interpretation, where applicable, of the relevant provisions of the WTO.

    (a) First, as a matter of fact, we find that under the statutory language of Section 304 (a)(2), the USTR is mandated, i.e. obligated in law, to make a determination on whether US rights are being denied within 18 months after the request for consultations. This is a mandatory feature of Section 304 in which the Legislature left no discretion to the Executive Branch.

    (b) Second, as a matter of law, since most of the time-limits in the DSU are either minimum time-limits without ceilings or maximum time-limits that are, nonetheless, indicative only, DSU proceedings–from the request for consultations to the adoption of findings by the DSB–may take longer than 18 months and have in practice often led to time-frames beyond 18 months. As a result, the USTR could be obligated in certain cases brought by the US–and indeed in certain cases has already been so obligated–to make a unilateral determination as to whether US rights are being denied before the completion of multilateral DSU proceedings.

(c) Third, as a matter of fact, we find that even though the USTR is obligated to make a determination within the 18 months time-frame, under the broad discretion allowed under Section 304 there are no circumstances which would compel him or her to make a determination to the effect that US rights under the WTO Agreement have been denied–hereafter referred to as a "determination of inconsistency"–before the exhaustion of DSU proceedings.

Section 304 (a) requires the USTR to determine *whether* US rights are being denied within 18 months. It does not require the USTR to determine *that* US rights are being denied at the 18 months deadline. The criteria referred to in Section 304 (a) on which the USTR has to base its determination–"the investigation initiated under section 302 ... and the consultations (and the proceedings, if applicable) under section 303"–allow the USTR to exercise wide discretion in all cases concerning the actual content of the determination he or she has to make.

As will be seen below, however, this discretion does not necessarily absolve Section 304 from a breach of the DSU.

(d) Fourth, as a matter of fact, we find that even though the USTR is not *obligated*, under any circumstance, to make a Section 304 determination of inconsistency prior to exhaustion of DSU proceedings, it is not *precluded* by the statutory language of Section 304 itself from making such a determination. We find that the broad discretion given to the USTR allows him or her to do exactly what the statutory language suggests: to determine *whether* US rights have been denied, i.e. to determine that they have *not* been denied but also to determine that they *have* been denied.

7.32   In conclusion, the statutory language of Section 304 *mandates* the USTR in certain cases to make a unilateral determination on whether US rights have been denied even *before* the adoption by the DSB of its findings on the matter. However, the statutory language of Section 304 neither *mandates* the USTR to make a determination of inconsistency nor *precludes* him or her from making such a determination.

7.33   Critically, the statutory language of Section 304 reserves to the USTR when exercising his or her mandatory duty after 18 months, the right to make a unilateral determination of inconsistency even prior to exhaustion of DSU proceedings.

* * *

7.35 Article 23 of the DSU deals, as its title indicates, with the "Strengthening of the Multilateral System". Its overall design is to prevent WTO Members from unilaterally resolving their disputes in respect of WTO rights and obligations. It does so by obligating Members to follow the multilateral rules and procedures of the DSU.

* * *

7.38 [After describing Article 23.1 and 23.2, the panel stated:] we conclude as follows:

    (a) It is for the WTO through the DSU process—not for an individual WTO Member—to determine that a WTO inconsistency has occurred (Article 23.2(a)).

    (b) It is for the WTO or both of the disputing parties, through the procedures set forth in Article 21—not for an individual WTO Member—to determine the reasonable period of time for the Member concerned to implement DSB recommendations and rulings (Article 23.2(b)).

    (c) It is for the WTO through the procedures set forth in Article 22—not for an individual WTO Member—to determine, in the event of disagreement, the level of suspension of concessions or other obligations that can be imposed as a result of a WTO inconsistency, as well as to grant authorization for the actual implementation of these suspensions.

* * *

7.41 As a general proposition, GATT *acquis*, confirmed in Article XVI:4 of the WTO Agreement and recent WTO panel reports, make abundantly clear that legislation as such, independently from its application in specific cases, may breach GATT/WTO obligations:

    (a) In GATT jurisprudence, to give one example, legislation providing for tax discrimination against imported products was found to be GATT inconsistent even before it had actually been applied to specific products and thus before any given product had actually been discriminated against.

    (b) Article XVI:4 of the WTO Agreement explicitly confirms that legislation as such falls within the scope of possible WTO violations. It provides as follows:

> "Each Member shall ensure the conformity of its *laws, regulations and administrative procedures* with its obligations as provided in the annexed Agreements" (emphasis added).

The three types of measures explicitly made subject to the obligations imposed in the WTO agreements—"laws, regulations and administrative procedures"—are measures that are applicable generally; not measures taken necessarily in a specific case or dispute. Article XVI:4, though not expanding the material obligations under WTO agreements, expands the type of measures made subject to these obligations.

(c) Recent WTO panel reports confirm, too, that legislation as such, independently from its application in a specific case, can be inconsistent with WTO rules.

7.42   Legislation may thus breach WTO obligations. This must be true, too, in respect of Article 23 of the DSU. * * *

* * *

7.46   * * * A violation of the explicit provisions of Article 23 can, therefore, be of two different kinds. It can be caused

(a) by an *ad hoc*, specific action in a given dispute, or

(b) by measures of general applicability, e.g. legislation or regulations, providing for a certain process to be followed which does not, say, include recourse to the DSU dispute settlement system or abide by the rules and procedures of the DSU.

* * *

7.51   The parties focused much of their arguments on the kind of legislation which could be found to be inconsistent with WTO obligations. The US submitted forcefully that only legislation *mandating* a WTO inconsistency or *precluding* WTO consistency, can, as such, violate WTO provisions. This was at the very heart of the US defence. On this US reading it followed that since Section 304 never mandates a specific determination of inconsistency prior to exhaustion of DSU proceeding nor, in the US view, precludes the US from acting consistently with its WTO obligations in all circumstances, the legislation, in and of itself could not be in violation of Article 23.2(a) of the DSU.

7.52   The EC submitted with equal force that also certain types of legislation under which a WTO inconsistent conduct is not *mandated* but is *allowed*, could violate WTO obligations. The EC considered that Section 304 is of such a nature.

7.53   Despite the centrality of this issue in the submissions of both parties, we believe that resolving the dispute as to which type of legislation, *in abstract*, is capable of violating WTO obligations is not germane to the resolution of the type of claims before us. In our view the appropriate method in cases such as this is to examine with care the nature of the WTO obligation at issue and to evaluate the Measure in question in the light of such examination. The question is then whether, on the correct interpretation of the specific WTO obligation at issue, only mandatory or also discretionary national laws are prohibited. We do not accept the legal logic that there has to be one fast and hard rule covering all domestic legislation. After all, is it so implausible that the framers of the WTO Agreement, in their wisdom, would have crafted some obligations which would render illegal even discretionary legislation and crafted other obligations prohibiting only mandatory legislation? Whether or not Section 304 violates Article 23 depends, thus, first and foremost on the precise obligations contained in Article 23.

* * *

7.59 The text of Article 23.1 is simple enough: Members are obligated generally to (a) have recourse to and (b) abide by DSU rules and procedures. These rules and procedures include most specifically in Article 23.2(a) a prohibition on making a unilateral determination of inconsistency prior to exhaustion of DSU proceedings. As a plain textual matter, therefore, could it not be said that statutory language of a Member specifically authorizing a determination of inconsistency prior to exhaustion of DSU procedures violates the ordinary meaning of Members' obligations under Article 23?

7.60 Put differently, cannot the raw text of Articles 23.2(a) and 23.1 be read as constituting a mutual promise among WTO members giving each other a guarantee enshrined in an international legal obligation, that certain specific conduct will not take place? Does not the text of Article 23.1 in particular suggest that this promise has been breached and the guarantee compromised when a Member puts in place legislation which explicitly allows it to do that which it promised not to do?

7.61 On this reading, the very discretion granted under Section 304, which under the US argument absolves the legislation, is what, in our eyes, creates the presumptive violation. The statutory language which gives the USTR this discretion on its face precludes the US from abiding by its obligations under the WTO. In each and every case when a determination is made whilst DSU proceedings are not yet exhausted, Members locked in a dispute with the US will be subject to a mandatory determination by the USTR under a statute which explicitly puts them in that very danger which Article 23 was intended to remove.

7.62 It could be said that this is a danger which can never be entirely removed. After all, even those Members which do not have any internal "trade legislation" can any day of the week decide to violate their WTO obligations including the obligations under Article 23.

7.63 In our view, when a WTO Member has *not* enacted specific legislation providing for procedures to enforce WTO rights, normally only the first type of violation of Article 23 can occur, i.e. a breach of the promise not to make determinations of inconsistency before the adoption of DSB findings in *specific* disputes. Certain WTO Members, however, including the US and the EC, *have* enacted legislation for seeking redress of WTO inconsistencies. There can be very good reasons related to norms of transparency, democracy and the rule of law which explain why Members may wish to have such legislation. However, when a

Member adopts any legislation it has to be mindful that it does not violate its WTO obligations. Trade legislation, important or positive as it may be, which statutorily reserves the right for the Member concerned to do something which it has promised *not* to do under Article 23.2(a), goes, in our view, against the ordinary meaning of Article 23.2(a) read together with Article 23.1.

7.64   It is notoriously difficult, or at least delicate, to construe the requirement of the Vienna Convention that a treaty shall be interpreted in good faith in third party dispute resolution, not least because of the possible imputation of bad faith to one of the parties. We prefer, thus, to consider which interpretation suggests "better faith" and to deal only briefly with this element of interpretation. Applying the good faith requirement to Article 23 may not lead to a conclusive result but impels us in the direction suggested by our examination of the ordinary meaning of the raw text.

7.65   Imagine two farmers with adjacent land and a history of many disputes concerning real and alleged mutual trespassing. In the past, self help through force and threats of force has been used in their altercations. Naturally, exploitation of the lands close to the boundaries suffers since it is viewed as dangerous terrain. They now sign an agreement under which they undertake that henceforth in any case of alleged trespassing they will abjure self help and always and exclusively make recourse to the police and the courts of law. They specifically undertake never to use force when dealing with alleged trespass. After the entry into force of their agreement one of the farmers erects a large sign on the contested boundary: "No Trespassing. Trespassers may be shot on sight".

7.66   One could, of course, argue that since the sign does not say that trespassers *will* be shot, the obligations undertaken have not been violated. But would that be the "better faith" interpretation of what was promised? Did they not after all promise *always and exclusively* to make recourse to the police and the courts of law?

7.67   Likewise, is it a good faith interpretation to construe the obligations in Article 23 to allow a Member that promised its WTO partners–under Articles 23.1 and 23.2(a)–that it will generally, including in its legislation, have recourse to and abide by the rules and procedures of the DSU which specifically contain an undertaking not to make a determination of inconsistency prior to exhaustion of DSU proceedings, to put in place legislation the language of which explicitly, *urbi et orbi*, reserves to its Executive Branch the right to make a determination of inconsistency–that which it promised it would not do? This Panel thinks otherwise.

7.68   The good faith requirement in the Vienna Convention suggests, thus, that a promise to have recourse to and abide by the rules and procedures of the DSU, also in one's legislation, includes the undertaking to refrain from adopting national laws which threaten prohibited conduct.

* * *

7.71 What are the objects and purposes of the DSU, and the WTO more generally, that are relevant to a construction of Article 23? The most relevant in our view are those which relate to the creation of market conditions conducive to individual economic activity in national and global markets and to the provision of a secure and predictable multilateral trading system.

7.72 Under the doctrine of direct effect, which has been found to exist most notably in the legal order of the EC but also in certain free trade area agreements, obligations addressed to States are construed as creating legally enforceable rights and obligations for individuals. Neither the GATT nor the WTO has so far been interpreted by GATT/WTO institutions as a legal order producing direct effect. Following this approach, the GATT/WTO did *not* create a new legal order the subjects of which comprise both contracting parties or Members and their nationals.

7.73 However, it would be entirely wrong to consider that the position of individuals is of no relevance to the GATT/WTO legal matrix. Many of the benefits to Members which are meant to flow as a result of the acceptance of various disciplines under the GATT/WTO depend on the activity of individual economic operators in the national and global market places. The purpose of many of these disciplines, indeed one of the primary objects of the GATT/WTO as a whole, is to produce certain market conditions which would allow this individual activity to flourish.

* * *

7.75 Providing security and predictability to the multilateral trading system is another central object and purpose of the system which could be instrumental to achieving the broad objectives of the Preamble. Of all WTO disciplines, the DSU is one of the most important instruments to protect the security and predictability of the multilateral trading system and through it that of the market-place and its different operators. DSU provisions must, thus, be interpreted in the light of this object and purpose and in a manner which would most effectively enhance it. * * *

* * *

7.77 Trade is conducted most often and increasingly by private operators. It is through improved conditions for these private operators that Members benefit from WTO disciplines. The denial of benefits to a Member which flows from a breach is often indirect and results from the impact of the breach on the market place and the activities of individuals within it. Sections 301–310 themselves recognize this nexus. One of the principal triggers for US action to vindicate US rights under covered agreements is the impact alleged breaches have had on, and the complaint emanating from, individual economic operators.

* * *

7.83   It is commonplace that domestic law in force imposing discriminatory taxation on imported products would, in and of itself, violate Article III irrespective of proof of actual discrimination in a specific case. Furthermore, a domestic law which exposed imported products to future discrimination was recognized by some GATT panels to constitute, by itself, a violation of Article III, even before the law came into force. Finally, and most tellingly, even where there was no certainty but only a risk under the domestic law that the tax would be discriminatory, certain GATT panels found that the law violated the obligation in Article III. A similar approach was followed in respect of Article II of GATT 1994 by the WTO panel on *Argentina–Textiles and Apparel (US)* when it found that the very change in system from *ad valorem* to specific duties was a breach of Argentina's *ad valorem* tariff binding even though such change only brought about the potential of the tariff binding being exceeded depending on the price of the imported product.

7.84   The rationale in all types of cases has always been the negative effect on economic operators created by such domestic laws. An individual would simply shift his or her trading patterns–buy domestic products, for example, instead of imports–so as to avoid the would-be taxes announced in the legislation or even the mere risk of discriminatory taxation. Such risk or threat, when real, was found to affect the relative competitive opportunities between imported and domestic products because it could, in and of itself, bring about a shift in consumption from imported to domestic products: This shift would be caused by, for example, an increase in the cost of imported products and a negative impact on economic planning and investment to the detriment of those products. * * *

* * *

7.87   To be sure, in the cases referred to above, whether the risk materialised or not depended on certain market factors such as fluctuating reference prices on which the taxation of the imported product was based by virtue of the domestic legislation. In this case, whether the risk materializes depends on a decision of a government agency. From the perspective of the individual economic operator, however, this makes little difference. Indeed, it may be more difficult to predict the outcome of discretionary government action than to predict market conditions, thereby exacerbating the negative economic impact of the type of domestic law under examination here.

7.88   When a Member imposes unilateral measures in violation of Article 23 in a specific dispute, serious damage is created both to other Members and the market-place. However, in our view, the creation of damage is not confined to actual conduct in specific cases. A law reserving the right for unilateral measures to be taken contrary to DSU

328 DISPUTE SETTLEMENT Ch. 7

rules and procedures, may–as is the case here–constitute an ongoing threat and produce a "chilling effect" causing serious damage in a variety of ways.

* * *

7.91 In conclusion, the risk of discrimination was found in GATT jurisprudence to constitute a violation of Article III of GATT—because of the "chilling effect" it has on economic operators. The risk of a unilateral determination of inconsistency as found in the statutory language of Section 304 itself has an equally apparent "chilling effect" on both Members and the market-place even if it is not quite certain that such a determination would be made. The point is that neither other Members nor, in particular, individuals can be reasonably certain that it will not be made. Whereas States which are part of the international legal system may expect their treaty partners to assume good faith fulfillment of treaty obligations on their behalf, the same assumption cannot be made as regards individuals.

* * *

7.96 Consequently, the statutory language of Section 304—by mandating a determination *before* the adoption of DSB findings and statutorily reserving the right for this determination to be one of inconsistency–must be considered presumptively to be inconsistent with the obligations in Article 23.2(a). The discretion given to the USTR to make a determination of inconsistency creates a real risk or threat for both Members and individual economic operators that determinations prohibited under Article 23.2(a) will be imposed. The USTR's discretion effectively to make such determinations removes the guarantee which Article 23 is intended to give not only to Members but indirectly also to individuals and the market place. In this sense, the USTR's discretion under Section 304 does not—as the US argued—ensure the consistency of Section 304. On the contrary, it is the core element of the *prima facie* inconsistency of the statutory language of Section 304.

* * *

7.98 In the previous analysis we have deliberately referred to the "statutory language" of Section 304 and likewise we have deliberately concluded that the statutory language creates a *prima facie* violation. We did not conclude that a violation has been confirmed. This is so because of the special nature of the Measure in question. The Measure in question includes statutory language as well as other institutional and administrative elements. To evaluate its overall WTO conformity we have to assess all of these elements together.

* * *

7.101 One can imagine different ways to remove the *prima facie* violation. If, for example, the statutory language itself were modified so that the USTR were not under an obligation to make a determination within the 18 months time-frame, but could, for example, await the making of any determination until such time as DSU procedures were completed the guarantee that Article 23 was intended to create would remain intact and the *prima facie* inconsistency would not exist. Likewise, if, by a change in the statutory language, the USTR's discretion to make a determination of inconsistency prior to exhaustion of DSU proceedings were curtailed, once again the *prima facie* inconsistency would no longer exist.

7.102   Changing the statute is not the only way to remove the *prima facie* inconsistency. If the possibility of the USTR making a determination of inconsistency prior to exhaustion of DSU proceedings were lawfully curtailed in a different manner, the same legal effect would be achieved. The obligation on Members to bring their laws into conformity with WTO obligations is a fundamental feature of the system and, despite the fact that it affects the internal legal system of a State, has to be applied rigorously. At the same time, enforcement of this obligation must be done in the least intrusive way possible. The Member concerned must be allowed the maximum autonomy in ensuring such conformity and, if there is more than one lawful way to achieve this, should have the freedom to choose that way which suits it best.

7.103   Critically, the offending discretionary element has to be *lawfully* curtailed since, as found in WTO case law, conformity with WTO obligations cannot be obtained by an administrative promise to disregard its own binding internal legislation, i.e. by an administrative undertaking to act illegally.

7.104   For the following reasons we find that the *prima facie* violation has in fact in this case been lawfully removed and no longer exists.

* * *

7.108   The language of Section 304 allows the existence of multilateral dispute resolution proceedings to be taken into account. It also allows for determinations of inconsistency to be postponed until after the exhaustion of DSU proceedings. This language surely permits the Administration to limit the discretion of the USTR so that no determination of inconsistency would be made before the exhaustion of DSU proceedings. The wide discretion granted as to the content of the determination to be made should be interpreted as including the power of the US Administration to adopt an administrative decision limiting the USTR's discretion in a manner consistent with US international obligations.

7.109   For reasons we explain below, we find that this is precisely the situation in the present case. Briefly, the US Administration has carved out WTO covered situations from the general application of the Trade Act. It did this in a most authoritative way, *inter alia*, through a Statement of Administrative Action ("SAA") submitted by the President to, and approved by, Congress. Under the SAA so approved "... it is the expectation of the Congress that future administrations would observe and apply the [undertakings given in the SAA]''. One of these undertakings was to "base any section 301 determination that there has been a violation or denial of US rights ... on the panel or Appellate Body findings adopted by the DSB." This limitation of discretion would effectively preclude a determination of inconsistency prior to exhaustion of DSU proceedings. The exercise of discretion under the statutory scheme is in the hands of the Administration and it is the Administration which has given this undertaking. We recognize of course that an undertaking given by one Administration can be repealed by that Administration or by another Administration. But this is no different from the possibility that statutory language under examination by a panel be amended subsequently by the same or another Legislator. The critical question is whether the curtailment of discretion is lawful and effective. This Panel finds that it is.

* * *

7.112   In the SAA the US Administration indicated its interpretation of Sections 301–310 as well as the manner in which it intends to use its discretion under Sections 301–310, as follows (emphases added):

"Although it will enhance the effectiveness of section 301, the DSU does not require any significant change in section 301 *for investigations that involve an alleged violation of a Uruguay Round agreement or the impairment of U.S. benefits under such an agreement.* In such cases, *the Trade Representative will*:

— invoke DSU dispute settlement procedures, as required under current law;

— base any section 301 determination that there has been a violation or denial of U.S. rights under the relevant agreement on the panel or Appellate Body findings adopted by the DSB;

— following adoption of a favourable panel or Appellate Body report, allow the defending party a reasonable period of time to implement the report's recommendations; and

— if the matter cannot be resolved during that period, seek authority from the DSB to retaliate" (emphasis added).

This official statement in the SAA–in particular, the commitment undertaken in the second bullet point–approved by the US Congress in the expectation that it will be followed by future US Administrations, is a major element in our conclusion that the discretion created by the statutory language permitting a determination of inconsistency prior to exhaustion of DSU proceeding has effectively been curtailed. As we already noted, we find that this decision of the US Administration on the manner in which it plans to exercise its discretion, namely to curtail it in such a way so as never to adopt a determination of inconsistency prior to the adoption of DSB findings, was lawfully made under the statutory language of Section 304.

* * *

7.115   The international legal relevance of the US commitments in the SAA were confirmed and amplified also in the context of the very proceedings before this Panel. In response to our very insistent questions, the US explicitly, officially, repeatedly and unconditionally confirmed the commitment expressed in the SAA namely that the USTR would "... base any section 301 determination that there has been a violation or denial of U.S. rights under the relevant agreement on the panel or Appellate Body findings adopted by the DSB".

* * *

7.126   The aggregate effect of the SAA and the US statements made to us is to provide the guarantees, both direct to other Members and indirect to the market place, that Article 23 is intended to secure. Through the SAA and the US statements, as we have construed them, it is now clear that under Section 304, taking account of the different elements that compose it, the USTR is precluded from making a determination of inconsistency contrary to Article 23.2(a). As a matter of international law, the effect of the US undertakings is to anticipate, or discharge, any would-be State responsibility that could have arisen had the national law under consideration in this case consisted of nothing more than the statutory language. It of course follows that should the US repudiate or remove in any way these undertakings, the US would incur State responsibility since its law would be rendered inconsistent with the obligations under Article 23.

[The panel then went on to make similar findings with respect to the allegation that Section 306 of the Trade Act of 1974 is inconsistent with Article 23.2(a) of the DSU, as well as the allegation that Sections 305 and 306 of the Act are inconsistent with Article 23.2(c) of the DSU.]

Notes and Questions

(1)   The decision was not appealed, as both sides claimed victory. Did the panel successfully defuse what might have become a "wrong case"? Was it appropriate to give so much weight to statements by the US administration and USTR lawyers?

(2)   The panel explicitly notes that WTO rules do not have "direct effect" as that term is used in the EU (see Section 4.2(B) supra). It then discusses at length the impact of WTO rules on individuals (paras. 7.72–7.88). Is that appropriate in this case?

(3)   The United States relied heavily in its defense on the "mandatory" vs. "discretionary" distinction, borrowed from old GATT cases—legislation did not on its face [as opposed to as applied] violate GATT obligations as long as the authorities charged with administering the legislation retained discretion to apply it consistently with the GATT. Is the panel persuasive in its rejection of that distinction when it notes, among other things, that uncertainty about government action can be greater than uncertainty about market fluctuations (para. 7.87)? What if domestic law embodies a general obligation on officials to act in accordance with international law?

(4) The panel noted that the question whether "discretionary" legislation violates the WTO perhaps need not be answered the same way for all WTO provisions. (para. 7.53) What conclusion do you draw about DSU article 23 on the basis of its text alone?

(5) Section 301 predated the Uruguay Round, and the challenged provisions may retain some vitality with respect to disputes involving matters not covered by WTO law and actions involving non-members. Is the panel's reference to the hypothetical sign, "Trespassers May Be Shot on Sight," a convincing analogy under these circumstances (para. 7.65)? Would it be a more accurate analogy to imagine that after the agreement between the two farmers, one of them keeps their gun to guard against third parties?

(6) Is there any argument for the view that no violation should be deemed to exist under a law or regulation until it is *applied* in a way that violates WTO law? Suppose that a panel finds a law to be inconsistent with WTO obligations on its face, but it has not been so applied. The losing disputant refuses to alter the law. What remedy?

A Short Note on the History and Procedures of Section 301

In 1962, partly because of the dissatisfaction of Congress with the way in which the Executive Branch had responded to citizen complaints against foreign government actions affecting international trade, Congress granted certain explicit powers to the President, authorizing retaliation with trade measures against certain foreign government actions.[29] Although this was by no means the first statute of this type,[30] it was a fairly unique statute. This statute was replaced and considerably expanded by title III of the Trade Act of 1974, and particularly Section 301 thereof, which granted similar powers to the President. The Act also provided explicit procedures under which U.S. citizens could petition the U.S. government for action against harmful foreign government activities. This part of the 1974 Act, from which the "Section 301 Procedure" derives its name, was amended in 1979, 1984 and 1988.[31] See Documents Supplement.

The 1988 amendments were extensive, transferring decision making authority from the President to USTR, and introducing a number of other wrinkles that we note briefly below. They also created two other statutory provisions, popularly known as "Special 301" and "Super 301." The Special 301 provisions address intellectual property issues, while the Super 301 provisions were designed to force the Executive Branch to self initiate Section 301 proceedings against certain "priority" nations that engaged in egregious practices.

The United States Trade Representative (USTR) may initiate Section 301 investigations upon citizen petition or upon its own initiative.

---

29. Trade Expansion Act of 1962, sec. 252, Pub.L. No. 87–794, 75 Stat. 879.

30. See, e.g., An Act to authorize the President of the United States to lay, regulate and revoke embargoes, 1 Stat. 372 (1794).

31. See Trade Act of 1974, secs. 301–06 (codified at 19 U.S.C.A. secs. 2411–16), as amended, Pub.L. No. 96–39, tit. IX, 93 Stat. 295 (1979); Pub.L. No. 98–573, secs. 304, 306, 98 Stat. 3002 (1984); Pub.L. No. 100–418, secs. 1301–02.

Most cases result from petitions. After a petition is filed, USTR decides within 45 days whether or not to "initiate" the investigation. Reasonably tight time limits apply for the completion of investigations, although USTR may extend the time by a number of months in "complicated" cases.

These investigations are quite informal. The petitioner and other interested parties (including the foreign government respondent) are afforded an opportunity to present their views, including a public hearing if requested. "Briefs" will typically be filed during the course of the process, but any hearing will be conducted by mid-level USTR staff, and there are no formal rules of procedure. The statute contains no provisions for judicial review, and to date such review has not occurred.

The 1988 amendments to Section 301 divided the statute into two sections—Section 301(a) governing unfair practices that require "mandatory" action, and Section 301(b) governing cases that require only "discretionary" action. Focusing for the moment on Section 301(a), this provision applies to any foreign government practice that "violates, or is inconsistent with ... or otherwise denies benefits to the United States" under a trade agreement, or "is in violation of, or inconsistent with" other international legal rights of the United States and "burdens or restricts United States Commerce."[32] The terms "inconsistent" and "otherwise denies benefits" are not defined, but seemingly include practices that frustrate the reasonable expectations of the United States even if the practices do not technically violate the letter of any trade agreement. After initiating an investigation pursuant to Section 301(a), USTR must request informal consultations with the country in question. If these consultations do not yield a satisfactory solution, USTR may then invoke formal dispute resolution under the procedures set forth in the agreement at issue. No later than eighteen months after the initiation of the case, whether or not the international dispute resolution process has concluded, USTR must make a determination whether the practice in question violates the legal rights of the United States. If that determination is affirmative, USTR must simultaneously determine what action to take in response to the practice. No retaliatory action is necessary if the international dispute resolution process finds against the United States, if the foreign government agrees to conform its practice to the U.S. view of its international obligations, or if the foreign government provides the United States with satisfactory compensation for the violation in the form of trade concessions on other goods or services.[33] Otherwise, retaliation is "mandatory,"[34] though "subject to the specific direction, if any, of the President." Absent an agreement on modification of the challenged practice or compensation, the statute provides a range of retaliatory options, including duties or other restrictions upon exports

32. See 19 U.S.C.A. secs. 2411(a)(1), 2411(d)(4)(A) (1988).

33. 9 U.S.C.A. sec. 2411(c)(1)(C).

34. More on the "mandatory" retaliation provisions may be found in Sykes, Mandatory Retaliation for Breach of Trade Agreements: Some Thoughts on the Strategic Design of Section 301, 8 Bos. Univ.Intl.L.J. 301 (1990).

of goods or services from the country under investigation.[35] These sanctions must "be devised so as to affect goods or services of the foreign country in an amount that is equivalent in value to the burden being imposed by that country on U.S. commerce."[36]

Foreign government practices that do not violate Section 301(a) may nevertheless violate Section 301(b) if they are "unreasonable" or "discriminatory," and also "burden or restrict United States commerce." An "unreasonable" act is defined constructively as one that is "unfair and inequitable." The statute provides a non-exhaustive list of examples of unreasonable acts, including denial of "market opportunities" or "opportunities for the establishment of an enterprise," failure to protect intellectual property rights, export targeting, toleration of anticompetitive practices by private firms, and denial of worker rights.[37] The statute offers no comprehensive definition of "discriminatory" acts. It does indicate, however, that such acts include a denial of most-favored-nation or national treatment in "appropriate" cases involving goods, services, or investment.[38]

A few other features of the statutory scheme warrant a mention. The 1984 amendments introduced a requirement that the Executive Branch produce a "National Trade Estimates" (NTE) report, to identify important barriers to U.S. exports. Such barriers were deemed to include a denial of protection for U.S. intellectual property.[39] In 1988, a new "Special 301" section was added to require USTR to use the NTE report as a basis for identifying "priority foreign countries" which deny "adequate and effective" intellectual property rights and which are not making progress to eliminate the problem.[40] Having done so, it must then self-initiate an investigation of those countries unless it determines that to do so would be detrimental to U.S. economic interests.[41] These investigations proceed as "discretionary" action cases.

One can certainly wonder whether, after the Uruguay Round Agreement on Trade Related Aspects of Intellectual Property, there is any remaining need for Special 301. In that regard, note the transitional provisions in Article of that Agreement relating to developing countries, and also that a country may behave "unreasonably" in denying intellectual property protection to U.S. firms, even if it is in compliance with the Uruguay Round TRIPS Agreement. See Section 301(d)(3) of the Trade Act of 1974.

The Omnibus Trade and Competitiveness Act of 1988 also created "Super 301," which expired in 1990, but was temporarily renewed for a time thereafter. Behind the enactment of "Super 301" lay Congressional concern "that certain foreign countries, most notably Japan, engage in broad and consistent patterns of unfair practices that serve to keep their home markets free of significant competition from U.S. and other foreign

35. 19 U.S.C.A. sec. 2411(c).
36. Id. sec. 2411(a)(3).
37. Id. sec. 2411(d)(3)(B).
38. Id. sec. 2411(d)(4)(B).

39. See 19 U.S.C.A. sec. 2241.
40. See 19 U.S.C.A. sec. 2242.
41. See 19 U.S.C.A. sec. 2412(b)(2).

firms.''[42] With the inventory of foreign practices in the National Trade Estimates Report as a base, the "Super 301" process requires the identification of "priority practices, including major barriers and trade distorting practices, the elimination of which are likely to have the most significant potential to increase United States exports." It also requires the identification of "priority foreign countries," taking into account the number and pervasiveness of priority practices in that country, the level of U.S. exports of goods and services "that would be reasonably expected from full implementation of existing trade agreements to which that foreign country is a party," and the volume of U.S. exports lost because of the priority practices. Within twenty-one days after the "Super 301" report is sent to the Congress, the USTR must initiate Section 301 investigations of each priority practice by each priority country.

Implementation of the "Super 301" provision began with USTR's identification, on May 26, 1989, of six priority practices by three priority countries. Three of the identified practices were Japanese: exclusionary government procurement practices in the supercomputer sector which barred foreign suppliers, a ban on procurement by the government of foreign-made satellites, and technical barriers affecting the import of forest products into Japan. Two of the identified practices were by India: one relating to investment restrictions, and the other to impediments to insurance sales. The last was an import licensing scheme administered by Brazil. A Section 301 investigation of each was initiated in June of 1989.

Each country reacted angrily. The Government of Japan stated repeatedly, for example, that it would not negotiate under the threat of retaliation. But over the next year, Japan and the United States entered agreements settling each of the cases, with Japan agreeing at least on paper to meet many of the U.S. demands.[43] Brazil settled its case by agreeing to remove a number of quantitative restrictions. The disputes with India were resolved by a agreement to negotiate over services and investment policy during the Uruguay Round.

(H) DEVELOPING COUNTRIES IN THE DISPUTE SETTLE-MENT SYSTEM

One difficult problem facing the WTO system is how to integrate developing countries into the system. This problem is discussed generally in Chapter 25 infra, but it is a particular problem in respect of dispute settlement. In 1962, Uruguay brought a series of complaints in GATT against 15 developed countries, alleging that dozens of practices by those countries had restricted Uruguayan export opportunities and thereby nullified and impaired its benefits under the General Agreement. The complaint was viewed more as an attempt to call attention to the problems of developing countries than as an attempt to obtain specific

42. See Senate Finance Committee Report on Omnibus Trade Act of 1987, S. Rep. No. 71, 100th Cong., 1st Sess., p. 77 (1987).

43. See Grier, The Use of Section 301 to open Japanese markets to Foreign Firms, 17 N.C.J.Intl.L. & Com.Reg. 1 (1992).

relief for Uruguay. Nonetheless, the whole process demonstrated that small countries have basic problems in trying to invoke the dispute settlement system, particularly when they need to collect extensive information to support complicated legal arguments. While smaller countries are undoubted better off by having WTO rules limiting the freedom of developed countries to impose trade restrictions than they would be in the absence of such rules, they clearly are not as able to use the dispute settlement system as developed countries to enforce WTO rules. This disparity is particularly evident when the question of suspending concessions is considered. Such an action by a large, powerful country against the trade of a small, developing country could be devastating, but retaliation by a small country against a large one may go virtually unnoticed in the large country and may even be counterproductive to the interests of the smaller country.

In 1965 and 1966 a GATT Committee on Legal and Institutional Framework created an Ad Hoc Group on Legal Amendments to consider proposals to amend Article XXIII. Such proposals included the provision of financial compensation to a developing country damaged by actions violating GATT, the automatic release of a developing country from GATT obligations toward an offending developed GATT member and a provision for collective GATT action against an offending party.[44] A procedure for developing country complaints was adopted as a GATT decision in 1966,[45] providing for time limits and heavy reliance on mediation by the Director–General of GATT, but the proposals mentioned above were not adopted. The special procedures were invoked only infrequently; they were, however, carried over into the DSU.

What special rules, if any, do you think that should apply to dispute settlement matters involving developing countries? What would your position be on the desirability of the above-mentioned proposals? The DSU contains a number of provisions calling for special treatment of developing and least developed countries. How significant of an impact would you expect these rules to have?

In 2001, the Advisory Centre on WTO Law was established as an intergovernmental organization to provide legal services and training to developing countries in respect of WTO matters. What else should be done to address the problems of developing countries in this area?

SECTION 7.5   DISPUTE SETTLEMENT IN FREE TRADE AREAS

We have already examined dispute settlement in one free trade area–the European Union. The EU is, of course, much more than a free trade area and its dispute settlement mechanism–the Court of Justice–is more a regular court of law than an international dispute settlement

---

44. GATT, 14th Supp. BISD 139 (1969).

45. Procedures under Art. XXIII, Decision of 5th April, 1966, GATT, 14th Supp.

BISD 18 (1966); see also, Robert E. Hudec, The GATT Legal System and World Trade Diplomacy, chs. 18 22 (1975).

system. But the EU system suggests that as countries integrate their economies through free trade areas, there is a need for effective dispute settlement to enforce the terms of the free trade agreement. We will examine the dispute settlement provisions of the Canada–U.S. FTA and the North American Free Trade Agreement in Section 11.3 infra.

Chapter 8

BORDER MEASURES I: TARIFFS AND CUSTOMS RULES

SECTION 8.1 INTRODUCTION

(A) REGULATORY PRINCIPLES AND IMPORT RESTRAINTS: THE CORE OF THE SYSTEM

So far, we have examined the international economic system and its institutions in a general way, focusing on fundamental and institutional legal questions. Our objective has been to give the reader an understanding of the three levels of the international economic system (private transactions, national regulation and regional or international regulation), how these levels fit together and what the principal legal notions are that motivate or constrain policy and activity in this system.

Now, we turn to a series of functional subjects. The first seven chapters were horizontal in structure, presenting the international economic system in layers (private transactions at the bottom, national regulation next, and international regulation on top), while the next chapters are structured vertically, that is to say, a functional subject is explored through all three levels of analysis, or at least through the top two—national and international—since the focus will be upon WTO rules and U.S. law.

The next 11 chapters deal with the most fundamental aspects of regulation of international economic relations. Any person involved with international trade policy, whether in government or in private life, will find that discourse generally assumes a knowledge of these topics. These subjects are essentially legal in the sense that they embody rules and principles similar to those found in legal systems, and there is a *comparatively* high degree of consensus and compliance with the rules.

The starting point—Chapter 8—is an examination of tariffs—the basic import restraint—and national customs laws related to tariffs. Chapter 9 considers quotas and other non-tariff barriers. Chapter 10 deals with the most-favored-nation (MFN) obligation, while Chapter 11 examines the far reaching exception from MFN treatment for free trade areas and customs unions. Then, in Chapter 12, we examine the national treatment obligation. The MFN and national treatment obligations are probably the two most fundamental principles of international trade regulation. Chapter 13 analyzes certain exceptions to those fundamental principles, looking in particular at the question of how environmental and health concerns are treated. Chapter 14 then considers the special problems of product standards, which are the subject of two WTO agreements. Chapter 15 looks at the problem of safeguards, which are measures taken to protect domestic industry from injurious foreign competition. The so-called Escape Clause permits safeguards in certain situations, thereby providing some flexibility in the rules. Chapters 16 to 18 introduce the problems raised when foreign exporters or countries use unfair export methods to the detriment of importing country producers. In particular, we examine two such methods—dumping and subsidies—and how they are controlled by international and national rules.

(B) INTRODUCTION TO CHAPTERS 8 AND 9

We began in Chapter 1 with an overview of the economic theories that underlie international economic policies. We have seen how the view that free trade is desirable and reduces the likelihood of armed conflict played a central role in the establishment of GATT. Throughout the rest of the book, the reader will see how the factors introduced in Chapter 1 have affected the creation of the international rules and national practices under them. In particular, we will see how the WTO rules enshrine the basic principles of free international trade, but at the same time allow exceptions to them, particularly in cases where imports are viewed as unfairly traded or as injurious to local industry, and we will see played out time and again the struggle between advocates of a broader national interest—free trade—and those defending the interests of a particular industry.

At the time that General Agreement on Tariffs and Trade was drafted in 1947, four techniques were considered to be the primary governmental methods of import restraint:[1] the tariff, the quota, subsidies and state trading enterprises. The basic and most prominent of these is the tariff, which is a tax imposed at the border on imported goods. Generally there are three types of tariffs: ad valorem, specific and mixed. An ad valorem tariff is a tax set as a percentage of the value of the imported goods. Thus, if a product valued at $100 were subject to a 10% ad valorem tariff, $10.00 would be due upon importation. A specific tariff is a flat charge per unit or quantity of goods, such as $1.00 per ton. A mixed tariff combines these two concepts, such as 5 cents per pound plus 10% of value. There are also "tariff quotas," which provide a different tariff rate depending upon the amount already imported into a country. For instance, a tariff quota might provide that the first 1,000,-000 tons of an imported product would be subject to a tariff of 10%, with all additional imports subject to a 20% tariff.

1. See generally John H. Jackson, World Trade and the Law of GATT 305–08, 625–38 (1969).

In order to apply tariffs, a nation needs a complex set of regulations, including a detailed list of goods indicating the tariff for each product, as the accompanying excerpt from the U.S. tariff schedule demonstrates.[2]

HARMONIZED TARIFF SCHEDULE of the United States
(1994)—Supplement 1

Annotated for Statistical Reporting Purposes

Heading/ Subheading	Stat. Suffix	Article Description	Units of Quantity	Rates of Duty 1 General	Rates of Duty 1 Special	2
8512		Electrical lighting or signaling equipment (excluding articles of heading 8539), windshield wipers, defrosters and demisters, of a kind used for cycles or motor vehicles; parts thereof:				
8512.10		Lighting or visual signaling equipment of a kind used on bicycles:				
8512.10.20	00	Lighting equipment.........	X	7.6%	Free (A, E, IL, J, MX) 3% (CA)	45%
8512.10.40	00	Visual signaling equipment ..	X	2.7%	Free (A, E, IL, J, MX) 1% (CA)	35%
8512.20		Other lighting or visual signaling equipment:				
8512.20.20		Lighting equipment.........	....	Free		25%
	40	For the vehicles of subheading 8701.20 or heading 8702, 8703, 8704, 8705 or 8711	X			
	80	Other	X			
8512.20.40		Visual signaling equipment ..	....	2.7%	Free (A, B, E, IL, J, MX) 1% (CA) [1]	35%
	40	For the vehicles of subheading 8701.20 or heading 8702, 8703, 8704, 8705 or 8711	X			
	80	Other	X			
8512.30.00		Sound signaling equipment	....	2.7%	Free (A, B, E, IL, J, MX) 1% (CA) [1,2]	35%
	20	Horns	X			
	40	Other	X			
8512.40		Windshield wipers, defrosters and demisters:				
8512.40.20	00	Defrosters and demisters	X	3.9%	Free (A, E, IL, J, MX) 1.5% (CA) [2]	35%
8512.40.40	00	Windshield wipers	X	3.1%	Free (A, B, E, IL, J, MX) 1.2% (CA)[2]	25%
8512.90		Parts:				
8512.90.20	00	Of signaling equipment	X	2.7%	Free (A, B, E, IL, J, MX) 1% (CA) [1]	35%
8512.90.40	00	Of lighting equipment: Of a kind used on bicycles	X	7.6%	Free (A, E, IL, J, MX) 3% (CA)	45%
8512.90.60	00	Other	X	Free		25%
8512.90.70	00	Of defrosters and demisters	X	3.9%	Free (A, E, IL, J, MX) 1.5% (CA) [2]	35%
8512.90.90	00	Other	X	3.1%	Free (A, B, E, IL, J, MX) 1.2% (CA) [2]	25%
8513		Portable electric lamps designed to function by their own source of energy (for example, dry batteries, storage batteries, magnetos), other than lighting equipment of heading 8512; parts thereof:				
8513.10		Lamps:				
8513.10.20	00	Flashlights	No	25%	Free (A, E, IL, J, MX) 10% (CA)	35%

2. The Harmonized Tariff Schedule of the United States is published annually by the United States International Trade Commission.

Heading/ Subheading	Stat. Suffix	Article Description	Units of Quantity	Rates of Duty		
				General	1 Special	2
8513.10.40	00	Other	No	6.9%	Free (A, E, IL, J, MX) 2.7% (CA)	40%
8513.90 8513.90.20	00	Parts: Of flashlights	X	25%	Free (A, E, IL, J, MX) 10% (CA)	35%
8513.90.40	00	Other	X	6.9%	Free (A, E, IL, J, MX) 2.7% (CA)	40%

1 See subheading 9905.85.56.
2 See subheading 9905.00.00.

Note the detail of the classification and the fine gradations in tariff rates between what might be viewed as similar goods (e.g., signaling devices for vehicles or miscellaneous auto parts). The above excerpt applied immediately before implementation of the Uruguay Round tariff reductions. Over time, tariff negotiations tend to lead to reduced and more standardized tariff rates. For example, as of 2001, after implementation of the Uruguay Round reductions, the items under heading 8512 were all subject to a column 1 duty of 2.5%, except for lighting equipment and parts (0%) and visual signaling equipment for bikes (2.7%). The rates under heading 8513 had been reduced by half.

The schedule has three columns, each with different tariff rates. The tariff rate applied depends upon the origin or source of the goods. Column 1 of the U.S. tariff indicates the general or "normal trade relations" rate, formerly known as the "MFN" rate. It is the rate applied to imports from countries receiving most-favored-nation treatment from the United States (see Chapter 10). Column 2 shows the "statutory rate," which is the rate imposed by the Smoot–Hawley Tariff Act of 1930,[3] as amended from time to time. The column 2 rate is applied to products from countries which do not receive normal (MFN) or special treatment.[4] Finally, there is a third column—the Special column. The rates in that column apply mainly to imports from countries who are beneficiaries of a U.S. tariff preference. Generally, when a preferential arrangement is fully implemented, goods benefiting from it are admitted duty free. The beneficiaries of U.S. preferences include Canada, Israel and Mexico, each of which has entered into a free trade agreement with the United States; most African, Caribbean and Andean countries (see Section 25.3(B) infra); and those countries which qualify for the U.S. Generalized System of Preferences (GSP) scheme, also discussed in Section 25.3(B) below.[5]

3. Ch. 497, 46 Stat. 590 (1930), codified in 19 U.S.C.A. secs. 1202–1677k.

4. Only a few countries fell into this category as of June 2001: Afghanistan, Cuba, Laos, Montenegro, North Korea, Serbia and Vietnam. U.S. Harmonized Tariff Schedule, General Note 3(a).

5. The letters in the Special column in the excerpted tariff schedule refer to the following preferences: A = GSP beneficiaries; CA = Canada; E = Caribbean Basin Economic Recovery Act beneficiaries; IL = Israel; J = Andean Trade Preferences Act beneficiaries; MX=Mexico. In the 2001 Schedule, D = African Growth and Opportunity Act beneficiaries and R = U.S.-Caribbean Basin Trade Partnership Act beneficiaries. As of 2001, there were four classes of industrial products that receive special treatment: civil aircraft under the GATT agreement on civil aircraft (indicated by C); certain Canadian automotive products and motor vehicles under the Automotive Products Trade Act (B); certain pharmaceuticals (K); and certain intermediate chemicals for dyes (L).

Conceivably, a country could have many more columns in its tariff schedule. If it did not grant MFN treatment to other nations, it could have a tariff schedule with as many columns as there are nations with whom it trades. Obviously, this would be a very complex system to administer, and the origin of goods could be very critical in terms of the rate actually applied. Thus, questions of how to ascertain the true origin of goods (and prevent fraud) would loom large.

As discussed in Chapter 1, the amount of a tariff is a cost of business to the importer that must be recovered when the good is sold in the importing country. Since domestically produced goods are not subject to the tariff, the domestic producer often may charge a higher price for its goods than it could in the absence of a tariff. In this sense tariffs protect domestic industries from foreign competition.

While tariffs are the most common import restraint, the quota or quantitative restriction is the most prominent of the plethora of nontariff barriers (NTBs) through which countries can restrain imports. A quota specifies the quantity of a particular good that a country will allow to be imported during a specified time period. The quota may be global, in the sense that it expresses the total amount that can be imported from all sources; or it may be divided into country quotas that specify import limits on goods from specific countries (e.g., 1000 widgets each year from Japan, 500 from Taiwan, etc.). Quotas will be analyzed in more detail in Chapter 9 infra.

A subsidy can be used as a protective device if it is granted for the domestic production of goods, so that such goods can be priced lower in the domestic market than the comparable imported goods. Consequently, in contrast to tariffs and quotas, which result in higher prices, subsidies lead to lower prices, thereby favoring the consumer (at the expense of the taxpayer, of course). If sufficiently subsidized, domestic goods might be sold at a price so low as to drive all imports out of the domestic market, and therefore no imports would occur. WTO rules on subsidies are explained in Chapter 18.

State trading enterprises can also be used to restrict imports. They operate as follows: The government decrees that a particular corporation (usually government-owned) shall be the only entity allowed to import a certain type of commodity (such as tobacco or steel). The state trading corporation will then purchase goods abroad and resell them on the domestic market in competition with domestically produced goods. The degree of protection that this device affords will depend upon the mark-up which the state trading corporation imposes on the goods. If it purchases a product for $100 and resells it on the domestic market for $200, it has imposed a 100% mark-up. This can operate similarly to a 100% tariff, and reduces the demand for imported goods in competition with domestic goods. A state trading corporation can also use its purchases and sales to have the effect of a quota. For example, it may simply refuse to purchase more than a specified amount of foreign goods for domestic resale, thereby limiting the quantity of imports to that amount. GATT rules on state trading are examined in Chapter 9.

The GATT approach to these four basic protective devices differs considerably. Basically, GATT prefers the tariff, as do international economists generally. Tariffs, it is argued, are more visible, capture for the government much of the "monopoly profit" which they create, do not need licensing to administer, do not require government funds (in contrast to a subsidy), and give only a limited amount of protection, so that if a foreign-based industry is efficient enough, it will still be able to export to the tariff-imposing country. GATT therefore permits tariffs and if a country has not agreed to a limit on its tariff for a particular product, it is permitted under GATT rules to impose any tariff it wishes. Another advantage of tariffs is that tariff reduction is relatively easy to negotiate and the GATT structure provides for multilateral, international negotiations on the level of individual tariffs. In Section 8.2 we consider the basic GATT obligations in respect of tariffs. In Section 8.3 we look at tariffs from the national perspective, which essentially involves consideration of the basic issues of customs law.

In comparison, quotas are thought to entail the risk of government corruption in the licensing process. They also tend to conceal from the public the degree and cost of the protection being afforded domestic producers. Moreover, unless quota rights are sold, which is rarely the case, the extra profits that they yield go to the foreign seller, instead of the government, as would be the case with a tariff. On the other hand, quotas facilitate economic planning since the precise amount of imports can be predicted, which is not the case with tariffs. Nonetheless, as discussed in Chapter 9, GATT rules prohibit the use of quotas (with certain specified exceptions). WTO/GATT rules also limit the use of subsidies or state trading for restraining imports.

Beyond the basic four protective devices discussed above, there is a large number of other nontariff barriers (NTBs) and we will have occasion to examine them throughout the book, particularly in Chapter 9.

SECTION 8.2   GATT TARIFF COMMITMENTS: THE BINDINGS

When it was negotiated in 1947, the basic purpose of the General Agreement on Tariffs and Trade was to cut tariffs significantly and to protect those cuts from indirect evasion through discriminatory internal taxes or other measures. After the failure of the International Trade Organization ratification process (described in Chapter 6), GATT assumed a broader role in regulating international trade than originally intended. Nonetheless, the negotiation and enforcement of tariff commitments has remained central to GATT. In this section, we trace the history of tariff negotiations in GATT and examine the basic GATT rules applicable to tariff commitments: the bindings made under Article II and the various tariff renegotiation provisions.

(A) GATT TARIFF NEGOTIATIONS

The various rounds of GATT negotiations have been previously described generally in Chapter 6; here we focus on tariff negotiations. In all trade negotiation rounds, a first important step has been the establishment of a tariff negotiations committee, consisting of a representative from each of the countries which are participating in the negotiations. Often countries that were not GATT Contracting Parties participated in GATT tariff negotiations, usually in anticipation of joining GATT. If such a country did not become a GATT party, it typically agreed to observe certain GATT-based rules so as to guarantee its tariff concessions.[1]

(1) The Early Years (1947–1961)

The first five tariff negotiating rounds were conducted under procedures following generally those established by the first round and can be summarized as follows: the first step was for each country to submit a "request list" on which it detailed for every other participant the concessions (specified product by product) which it desired the other country to make. Thus, if the United States felt that it had a potential for shipping aircraft to the United Kingdom, it would ask the United Kingdom for a tariff commitment on aircraft which would likely permit more U.S. sales of aircraft to the United Kingdom.

Next, each country would analyze the requests submitted to it and prepare an "offer list," which would indicate what tariff concessions it was willing to make in exchange for obtaining favorable treatment on its requests. Each of the request and offer lists would be furnished to every country participating in the negotiation.

A third step was a series of bilateral conferences between negotiating countries to begin to develop the bargain between them. The objective was to obtain concessions roughly equivalent in value to those that a country gave up. In general, offers on particular products would be extended to the country which was the "principal supplier" of that product to the offering country. Thus, if country X imported bicycles from countries A, B and C, with A supplying 60%, B supplying 30%, and C supplying 10%; then X would make its tariff offer to A, which supplied most of the bicycles and would stand to benefit most from a concession. Nevertheless, once A and X had come to a tentative agreement, then X would begin negotiating with B with respect to the same concession, trying to obtain from B some reciprocal concessions for the advantage B would automatically obtain under the MFN clause by the concession X was willing to extend to A.

Gradually, toward the end of this process, more and more concessions would fall into place and third party benefits would be reciprocated as the circle of bilateral negotiations was extended. Finally, all countries would finalize their offer lists. At this point, each country would have to evaluate the total concessions of all the other participants in the negotia-

---

1. See Protocol of Bulgaria, GATT, 26th   Supp. BISD 189 (1980).

tions, to see whether it felt that as a whole they were equivalent in value to the concessions which it was giving. If it felt this was not the case, it would then notify the other participants that it was withdrawing some of its offers to remove the imbalance. Needless to say, a withdrawal could create a ripple effect of counter withdrawals, which could extend through the entire negotiation and destroy the results obtained so far. This stage of the negotiation has been accompanied with a considerable amount of bluff, tension, late night sessions and a certain amount of mediation by the secretariat.

By the time of the "Dillon Round" (1960–61), the item-by-item approach to tariff negotiations proved extraordinarily cumbersome. The technical problem of dealing with thousands of specific products was formidable enough. The process was further complicated, however, because the European Community, one of the main participants, had to negotiate internally in order to establish a common position among its six member states before it could negotiate on an item in GATT. Thus, it became almost impossible to make progress in the negotiations.

(2) *The Kennedy Round (1963–1967)*[2]

The difficulties in negotiating tariff cuts in the Dillon Round led the GATT Contracting Parties to conclude that it would be necessary for future tariff negotiating rounds to establish new procedures, and, in particular, it was decided to utilize a "linear technique" for negotiating tariff reductions. The precise negotiating rules implementing such a technique for the Kennedy Round were agreed upon in May 1964.[3] Basically, the rules called for offers of a 50% cut in tariffs as a "working hypothesis," except for most agricultural products. Countries then tabled "exceptions lists," specifying the products that they wished exempted from these general tariff cuts. The negotiations then focused principally upon the exceptions lists.

Several developed countries (Australia, Canada, South Africa and New Zealand) and all of the developing countries were exempted from making offers based on the linear technique. The four developed countries asked for an exemption because they depended heavily upon agriculture and raw material exports. Since these products were generally not included in the linear offers, if these countries were required to offer 50% tariff cuts on industrial products, they felt that they could not hope to achieve reciprocal concessions from other developed countries. As for the developing countries, they argued that under Part IV of GATT (added in 1964) they were not expected to offer reciprocal concessions in GATT trade negotiations and should therefore not be required to make

---

2. See generally John W. Evans, The Kennedy Round in American Trade Policy (1971); John H. Jackson, World Trade and the Law of GATT, sec. 10.5 (1969); Kenneth W. Dam, The GATT: Law and International Economic Organization 68–77 (1970).

3. GATT, 12th Supp. BISD 47, para. A4 (1964); GATT, 13th Supp. BISD 109–10 para. A (1965). See Dam, supra note 2, at 69–70; Evans, supra note 2, at 184–202; Jackson, supra note 2, at 223–27.

the linear offer,[4] although they desired industrialized country 50% offers to include products of special interest to them.

Just before U.S. negotiating authority ran out on June 30, 1967, the Kennedy Round participants completed their agreements. The tariff reductions were substantial. The main industrialized countries—the EU, Japan, Sweden, Switzerland, the United Kingdom and the United States—made concessions on imports valued at $32 billion. Duty reductions affected 70% of these countries' dutiable imports, and the majority of these reductions were of 50% or more.

(3) The Tokyo Round Tariff Negotiations[5]

The Tokyo Round was supposed to focus on nontariff barriers, and in fact it did. However, the tariff negotiations, especially in the early years of the negotiation, remained very significant. Some have observed that this may have been due to the momentum of bureaucratic habits. Others suggested that during periods when the overall negotiation was largely stalled, the continuation of detailed and often mathematical talks about tariffs provided the continuity or "glue" which held the negotiation together, by providing a joint sense of purpose and movement, and a focus for lower level officials to continue their activities, thus maintaining the governmental structure necessary to accomplish the intense work that would come when the overall negotiation began to move forward.

In the case of the United States, the Trade Act of 1974 contained the tariff negotiating authority for the Tokyo Round. Initial proposals for the Act would have given the Executive unlimited tariff negotiating authority. Partly because of the "Watergate" climate and a weak (and perhaps disinterested) Executive, the tariff authority that finally emerged in the Trade Act allowed a 60% cut in any tariff existing on January 1, 1975, with provision for abolition of tariffs which on that date were not more than 5% ad valorem. Arguably this was extensive: One can compare it with the 50% tariff authority of the 1962 Act. On the other hand, by 1975 industrialized country tariff levels were generally between 8% and 9%, so that a 60% cut meant about a 5 percentage point reduction in tariff levels, while in previous negotiations a 50% cut could give an average reduction of 6 percentage points or more. Furthermore, given the swings in exchange rates in the early 1970's (as much as 20% in the dollar's relation to other currencies), exchange rate swings could have many times the influence of the authorized tariff rate changes under the 1974 Trade Act.

One of the serious controversies to be addressed in the Tokyo Round tariff negotiations was the so-called "disparities issue," which first arose in the Kennedy Round.[6] In the 1960's the European Union had imple-

---

4. GATT, Art. XXXVI:8; GATT, Annex I, Ad Art. XXXVI:8.

5. See generally GATT, The Tokyo Round of Trade Negotiations: Report by the Director–General of GATT (1979); GATT, The Tokyo Round of Trade Negotiations:

Supplementary Report by the Director–General of GATT (1980); Gilbert R. Winham, International Trade and the Tokyo Round Negotiation (1986).

6. See A.H.M. Albregts & A.J.W. van de Gevel, Negotiating Techniques and Issues mented a common external tariff, which tended to be the average of the tariffs of its member states. As a result, it was a more uniform tariff without the "peaks and valleys" often found in a traditional national tariff schedule, such as the U.S. schedule. The EU argued that a 50% reduction in peak tariffs would not have an equivalent trade effect to a 50% reduction in its flatter tariff. For example, halving a 40% tariff would result in a 20% tariff, which would still offer considerable protection against imports. On the other hand, if a 20% tariff were cut in half, the resulting 10% tariff might not suffice to inhibit greatly increased imports.

This issue was resolved in the Tokyo Round by an agreement to use an algebraic formula for the initial tariff reduction offers. A variant of the following formula was used: $Z = (A \text{ times } X)$ divided by $(A + X)$; with X representing the initial rate of import duty applied, A a coefficient to be agreed upon, and Z the resulting reduced rate of duty.[7] Under this formula, if A were set at 16, then a 10% duty would be reduced to 6.15% (a cut of 38.5%), while a 20% duty would be reduced to 8.88% (a cut of 55.6%). In fact, there were considerable variations in the way this formula was applied, but it generally led to significant tariff cuts. The EU, Austria, Canada, Finland, Japan, Norway, Sweden, Switzerland and the United States agreed to reduce their weighted average tariffs on industrial products from 7.0% to 4.7% (10.4% to 6.4% based on simple tariff averages). In addition, the use of the tariff-cutting formula reduced the differences in their tariff levels by 25%, measured by standard deviation of national averages.[8]

(4) The Uruguay Round Tariff Negotiations (1986–1994)[9]

Like the Tokyo Round, the Uruguay Round was intended to focus on nontariff issues, but as in all GATT negotiating rounds, there were significant negotiations on tariffs. As in the Tokyo Round, the U.S. President was authorized to make 50% cuts in U.S. tariffs, with the proviso that tariffs of under 5% could be reduced to zero.[10]

Initially, the Uruguay Round had a tariff negotiating subgroup, as well as a number of other subgroups dealing with market access issues relating to specific products, such as tropical products and agriculture. The 1988 midterm review session in Montreal (which was completed in

in the Kennedy Round, *in* Economic Relations After the Kennedy Round 20, 23–31 (Frans A.M. Alting von Geusau ed., 1969); Thomas B. Curtis & John R. Vastine, Jr., The Kennedy Round and the Future of American Trade 82–91 (1971); Dam, supra note 2, at 73–76; Evans, supra note 2, at 186–200.

7. See GATT, The Tokyo Round of Multilateral Trade Negotiations: Report by the Director–General of GATT 46–48 (1979).

8. GATT, The Tokyo Round of Multilateral Trade Negotiations, Supplementary Report by the Director–General of GATT 3–7 (1980).

9. See generally John Croome, Reshaping the World Trading System: A History of the Uruguay Round (2d ed. 1999)(written for the WTO); The GATT Uruguay Round: A Negotiating History (1986–1992) (Terence P. Stewart ed., 1993).

10. Omnibus Trade and Competitiveness Act of 1988, sec. 1102(a), 19 U.S.C.A. sec. 2902(a).

Geneva in April 1989) reached an agreement to cut tariffs on tropical products, an issue of particular interest to developing countries.

The Uruguay Round negotiations were later reorganized and one negotiating group was given a broad range of market access issues including tariffs. There were considerable difficulties in agreeing on an approach to tariff reduction—with the United States pushing for negotiations on an item-by-item basis, and many other countries arguing for a formula approach of the type used in the Tokyo Round. Ultimately, both were used. In the end, the GATT Secretariat reported on April 12, 1994, that implementation of the Uruguay Round tariff commitments would result in an overall decrease of 38% in average developed country tariffs (from 6.3% to 3.9%). In addition, there would be an increase in the number of industrial products receiving duty-free treatment in developed countries from 20% to 43%.

The round also resulted in a significant increase in the number of tariff lines "bound" under Article II. In the case of developed countries, the increase was from 78% to 99%; in the case of developing countries, it was from 22% to 72%; and in the case of countries in transition, it was from 73% to 98%.

(5) Tariff Negotiations in the WTO

As of mid–2001, there had been no general tariff negotiations under the auspices of the WTO, although such negotiations are expected whenever a new round of trade negotiations is launched. In 1996, however, there were negotiations in respect of tariffs on information technology products, and at the Singapore Ministerial Meeting at the end of 1996, a significant number of WTO Members agreed to eliminate tariffs on such products.

(6) Problems of Tariff Negotiations

There are two particular problems that stand out in tariff negotiations.[11] First, the MFN obligation, providing for a generalization of each nation's concessions to all other GATT members, tends to restrain willingness to make offers and concessions, particularly if some participants are dragging their feet. A foot dragger, whose offered concessions are relatively meager, stands to gain from the free ride effect of MFN if the other countries go ahead despite the foot dragging. The formula cuts described above are intended to reduce this problem, but to the extent that the full participation of smaller countries is often not crucial to the deals struck by the major trading nations, these smaller countries may evade the full effect of the formula through invocation of comparatively extensive exceptions or, in nonformula negotiations, through limited offers.

How would you expect the extent of free riding to be affected, if at all, by the choice of negotiating method for tariff cutting, for example, between item-by-item cuts or formula reductions? Are there other nego-

---

11. See Jackson, supra note 2, at 240–248.

tiation techniques that would reduce the likelihood of free riding? Despite the obvious interest of these questions, we have found no studies reaching firm conclusions on these issues.

A second difficulty arises from the reciprocity principle. While economists may believe that unilateral tariff cuts benefit a country's economy in the long run (see Chapter 1), tariff negotiations under GATT's auspices have typically been carried out with the objective in each participant's mind of gaining tariff concessions from others to match those that it makes itself. However, it is extremely difficult to measure the trade effects of tariff changes because the necessary information (e.g., price elasticities of the relevant products) is often nonexistent or unreliable and because many other unpredictable, nontariff related events (such as exchange rate shifts) may have much more important price effects than tariff cuts. The only easily available measure of tariff cuts is to multiply the tariff reduction times a recent year's import value figure. Thus, if a tariff is reduced from 20% to 10% and the total imports of the product were valued at $1 million in a recent year, the value of the reduction for purposes of comparing it to other reductions is 10% of $1 million or $100,000. Obviously, this measure is extremely imprecise.

Despite these problems, the notion of reciprocity has had enormous political impact. The idea of achieving equivalent concessions in tariff reductions appeals to laymen and politicians as "fair" and has helped to achieve the great reductions of tariffs that have occurred in the last 50 years. Perhaps reciprocity can be termed a "useful myth," but it would be nice if some new principles with comparable political appeal could be discovered. Perhaps a concept of "sector harmonization" will serve some of these functions. Such an approach was followed in the Tokyo Round agreement on civil aircraft, which provided for duty-free treatment for civil aircraft and engines and their parts.[12] In the Uruguay Round, a number of major trading nations agreed to eliminate tariffs on many pharmaceutical and chemical products, and as noted above, in 1996, a significant number of WTO Members agreed to eliminate tariffs on information technology products.

(B) THE OBLIGATION TO LIMIT TARIFFS

The central obligation of the General Agreement on Tariffs and Trade is that in Article II, which requires nations to limit their tariffs on particular goods to a specified maximum.[13] The current GATT tariff commitments or "bindings," as they are often called, are the result of eight major rounds of negotiation. They are contained in country-by-country schedules which are appended to the General Agreement and incorporated into it by reference in Article II. Each contracting party's schedule is, of course, different. A nation's GATT tariff schedule may differ from its national tariff schedule, in that the GATT schedule

---

12. Agreement on Trade in Civil Aircraft, GATT, 26th Supp. BISD 162 (1980).

13. See Jackson, supra note 2, at 201–211. See also Richard E. Caves & Ronald W. Jones, World Trade and Payments 281–86 (1973); Gerard Curzon, Multilateral Commercial Diplomacy 70–123 (1965); Dam, supra note 2, at 17, 18, 25–55.

specifies the maximum tariff which can be applied for each product listed. The national tariff schedule, on the other hand, sets the actual rate applied by that country for each product. For products which are not on its GATT schedule, a country may charge any tariff it pleases. For products which are listed on the GATT schedule, it may charge a tariff below the GATT maximum, if it so desires. If it charges a tariff in excess of the GATT maximum, however, it is violating its GATT obligations, unless a GATT exception applies, such as Article VI (antidumping and countervailing duties) or Article XIX (the Escape Clause).

There are a number of significant legal problems raised by the Article II obligation.[14] The GATT obligations relating to a tariff commitment can be divided into two groups. The first group consists of those obligations which relate specifically to a tariff binding and are triggered by the existence of that tariff binding on the GATT schedule. A second group of obligations consists of the more general GATT obligations (a sort of "code of good conduct for trade policy"), which relate not only to the treatment of goods that are listed on a schedule, but to all goods. These latter obligations (such as obligations on the use of quotas or national treatment obligations relating to internal taxation and regulations) have as *one* of their purposes the prevention of evasion of the GATT tariff binding. Since the objective of obtaining a binding is to gain market access and since nontariff barriers inhibit such access, any NTB is, to a certain extent, an evasion of the GATT tariff bindings. Thus, all GATT rules limiting NTBs serve to protect the Article II bindings.

The group of obligations in the General Agreement which relate more directly to the tariff bindings and are generally limited to goods that are listed on the GATT tariff schedule, include the following:

(1) The tariff maximum or ceiling, as expressed in the schedule (see Article II:1 which obligates treatment "no less favorable" than that specified in the schedule).

(2) Other provisions of Article II designed to protect the value of the concession from encroachment by other governmental measures, such as "other charges," new methods of valuing goods, reclassification of goods (see Article II:3 & 5) and currency revaluations (Article II:6). See Section 8.3 infra.

(3) Limits on the protection against imports of a particular product which can be afforded by the use of an import monopoly (Article II:4). See Chapter 9 infra.

(4) A GATT interpretation that new subsidies granted on products covered in a nation's schedule, after the schedule has been negotiated, shall be considered a "prima facie nullification" for purposes of complaints under Article XXIII. See Section 7.4(A)(2) supra.

---

14. For a discussion of these and other   at 211–217.
legal problems, see J. Jackson, supra note 2,

It should be emphasized that the GATT obligation refers to goods "which are the products of territories of other contracting parties." Thus if A and B are GATT parties and C is not, a company in A cannot buy products from C, ship them to B, and demand the GATT schedule treatment so long as the goods retain their C origin. See Section 8.3(D) infra.

Notes and Questions

(1) There have been a number of WTO disputes concerning the interpretation of tariff and other schedules. In EUROPEAN COMMUNITIES–CUSTOMS CLASSIFICATION OF CERTAIN COMPUTER EQUIPMENT, WT/DS62, 67 & 68/AB/R, adopted by the DSB on June 22, 1998, the Appellate Body noted:

> 84. * * * Tariff concessions provided for in a Member's Schedule—the interpretation of which is at issue here—are reciprocal and result from a mutually-advantageous negotiation between importing and exporting Members. A Schedule is made an integral part of the GATT 1994 by Article II:7 of the GATT 1994. Therefore, the concessions provided for in that Schedule are part of the terms of the treaty. As such, the only rules which may be applied in interpreting the meaning of a concession are the general rules of treaty interpretation set out in the *Vienna Convention*.

In applying the rules of the Vienna Convention, the Appellate Body noted that it would be relevant in tariff classification cases to examine the Harmonised System and its Explanatory Notes, as well as decisions taken by the Harmonised System Committee of the World Customs Organization (see Section 8.3(B)(1) infra). The Appellate Body rejected the panel's position that the legitimate expectations of the exporting party were of particular relevance, at least insofar as violation cases were concerned. In its view:

> 109. * * * Tariff negotiations are a process of reciprocal demands and concessions, of "give and take". It is only normal that importing Members define their offers (and their ensuing obligations) in terms which suit their needs. On the other hand, exporting Members have to ensure that their corresponding rights are described in such a manner in the Schedules of importing Members that their export interests, as agreed in the negotiations, are guaranteed. There was a special arrangement made for this in the Uruguay Round. For this purpose, a process of verification of tariff schedules took place from 15 February through 25 March 1994, which allowed Uruguay Round participants to check and control, through consultations with their negotiating partners, the scope and definition of tariff concessions. Indeed, the fact that Members' Schedules are an integral part of the GATT 1994 indicates that, while each Schedule represents the tariff commitments made by *one* Member, they represent a common agreement among *all* Members.

> 110. * * * We consider that any clarification of the scope of tariff concessions that may be required during the negotiations is a task for *all* interested parties.

See also Canada—Measures Affecting the Importation of Milk and the Exportation of Dairy Products, WT/DS103 & 113/AB/R, paras. 125–143, adopted by the DSB on October 27, 1999.

(2) What happens when a new product is developed? Can a GATT tariff binding ever cover a product that did not exist when the binding was made? What if the new product is very similar, at least in some respects, to a product that it is subject to a tariff binding? To take an actual case,[15] if Greece had bound a specific tariff rate on records (e.g., x drachmas per record), could it apply a higher rate to long-playing records on the grounds that such records did not exist at the time it made the binding, that long-playing records contained up to five times the volume of recordings of conventional records and that they were lighter and made of different material than conventional records? Would it matter that other countries distinguished between long-playing and conventional records? If the Greek binding had been set as an *ad valorem* duty, would this problem have arisen?

The GATT Contracting Parties did not definitively resolve this dispute. In the course of their consideration of it, they requested an advisory opinion from the Customs Co-operation Council, the body responsible for the Brussels Tariff Nomenclature (BTN), which at the time was the basis on which many countries classified goods for tariff purposes. See Section 8.3(B) infra. Although the Council declined to give such an opinion, it noted the BTN principle that "[g]oods not falling within any heading of the Nomenclature shall be classified under the heading appropriate to the goods to which they are most akin," but also noted that this principle did not apply if a tariff classification contained a residual heading, i.e., "other articles not elsewhere specified." Despite the lack of a resolution of the dispute, one of the co-authors of this book has concluded that "it seems that several principles are accepted by most contracting parties: (1) new products must be deemed within bound Schedule items where the description clearly covers them; (2) reference will be made to the national law of the party whose Schedule is under dispute to determine the principles of classification; but the national law is not determinative."[16]

(3) The two foregoing notes involved disputes over the scope of a GATT tariff binding. An analogous problem arises when a WTO member claims that under the MFN clause one of its products should receive the same favorable tariff treatment as a similar product from another country. See the *SPF Dimension Lumber* and *Spanish Coffee* cases, excerpted in Section 10.2 infra.

(4) What arguments might an adversely affected WTO member make in response to an unanticipated classification change, even if a technical violation of the tariff concession does not occur. See the *German Sardines* case, excerpted in Section 10.2 infra.

(5) Article II:2(c) provides that Article II tariff bindings do not prevent a party from imposing a fee or other charge "commensurate with the cost of services provided." Article VIII provides that import fees "shall be limited in amount to the approximate cost of services rendered" and shall not repre-

15. Greek Increase In Bound Duty, Report by the Group of Experts, GATT Doc. L/580 (Nov. 9, 1956).

16. Jackson, supra note 2, at 214.

sent indirect protection or taxation. These provisions would clearly permit a party to impose a reasonable fee for a necessary health or safety-related inspection of imported goods. Would they permit a country to impose a fee designed to recover the entire cost of its customs service? The United States claimed that they did, and in 1986 it attempted to do so by imposing a customs user fee of 0.22% (reduced to 0.17% in subsequent years). Under the U.S. system, an import valued at $1 million would have to pay a $1700 fee, while one valued at $1000 would be charged $1.70. Are these fees commensurate with the cost of services rendered? A GATT panel concluded they were not because there was no demonstrable relation between the fee and the cost of processing *specific* transactions. The panel felt that the phrase "cost of services rendered" meant the "approximate cost of customs processing for the individual entry in question." U.S. Customs User Fee, GATT, 35th Supp. BISD 245, 290 (Panel report adopted Feb. 2, 1988). The panel also ruled that certain costs of the U.S. Customs Service could not be recovered because they were not services rendered in connection with dutiable imports. The United States revised its fee structure so that the 0.17% fee was subject to a $21 minimum and $400 maximum (slightly more for manual entries).[17] Given the panel's decision as described above, does this new fee comply with Articles II and VIII? Based on the wording of these two articles, do you think that the panel correctly concluded that the articles applied to a general fee like the U.S. user fee (as opposed to finding that they applied only to fees for special services not generally provided, such as health inspections)?

(6) Article II:1(b) provides that duties shall not exceed those set forth in a party's Schedule, "subject to the terms, conditions and qualifications set forth in that Schedule." Does the quoted language allow a party to make a duty rate subject to terms that would otherwise violate the General Agreement? For example, could a quota scheme that would normally violate Articles XI and XIII be saved by being expressed as a condition to a tariff rate under Article II? See U.S. Restrictions on Imports of Sugar, GATT, 36th Supp. BISD 331 (Panel report adopted June 22, 1990)(no). Accord, European Communities—Regime for the Importation, Sale and Distribution of Bananas, WT/DS27/R, paras. 7.112–7.118, adopted by the DSB on September 25, 1997.

(C) RENEGOTIATION OF TARIFF BINDINGS

Although the tariff binding is an obligation to limit the tariff on a particular product to the maximum listed in the tariff binding, the General Agreement contains a number of provisions that give considerable flexibility to this commitment.[18] These provisions are basically of two types: provisions that enable tariff bindings to be suspended temporarily and provisions that enable a particular tariff binding to be changed permanently. The first type is more appropriately the subject of discussion of GATT exceptions such as the Escape Clause (Chapter 15),

17. Customs and Trade Act of 1990, sec. 111, 104 Stat. 635.

18. See generally Anwarul Hoda, Tariff Negotiations and Renegotiations Under the GATT and the WTO: Procedures and Practices (2001); Jackson, supra note 2, at 229–238.

retaliation-sanction type provisions of Article XXIII (Chapter 7), and provisions for waivers (Chapter 6). The second type of provision, however, deals with the procedures for negotiating and renegotiating the permanent schedule of obligations themselves. Although the great bulk of tariff reductions are negotiated during one or another of the so-called rounds described in Section (A), GATT is in fact the locus of more or less continuous tariff negotiations. For example, a particular binding accepted by a nation during the Uruguay Round may later prove (due to changing circumstances or changing political context in the obligated nation) to be impractical or too onerous for the nation to follow. There are provisions in the General Agreement whereby that nation is entitled to reopen the matter and substitute other commitments in place of the one which it now desires to remove. In fact, a full survey of all the various types of changes which can be accomplished, as well as the techniques for obtaining new bindings, would include the following:

NEW NEGOTIATIONS

1) Bindings resulting from a negotiating "round" (Article XXVIII bis).

2) Negotiations for the accession of new members (WTO Article XIII) (described in Chapter 6).

3) Various other negotiations not specifically authorized by the General Agreement. Nations may, of course, negotiate with any other nation on an ad hoc basis for the reduction of tariff maximums below GATT scheduled rates. These negotiations need not be conducted in the context of GATT, but if any member of the negotiation is a WTO member, it is obligated under the MFN clause of GATT Article I to generalize the treatment promised. While these ad hoc bindings may or may not be included in the GATT schedules, they nevertheless will affect the trade of all WTO members.

RENEGOTIATIONS, MODIFICATIONS, RECTIFICATIONS

1) Reopening every three years (Article XXVIII:1).

2) Special circumstance renegotiations (Article XXVIII:4).

3) Reserved renegotiations (Article XXVIII:5).

4) Compensatory renegotiations due to formation of a customs union or free trade area (Article XXIV:6).

5) Renegotiations by developing countries (Article XVIII:7).

6) Withdrawal of concessions initially negotiated with a country that fails to become or ceases to be a GATT party (Article XXVII).

7) Rectifications (corrections of mistakes and other minor changes).

This is not the place to discuss each of these articles in detail, but a brief summary of several of the renegotiation provisions may assist the reader in understanding the GATT system.

Originally, the General Agreement was negotiated with the idea that tariff concessions would extend for only a three-year period, after which they would be renewed or modified. Article XXVIII embodied this principle by authorizing, after a three-year period, any nation to withdraw any concession or binding. If a binding were withdrawn, however, then the countries with whom the original binding had been negotiated or other countries which were major beneficiaries of the obligated tariff treatment, were entitled either to make reciprocal compensatory withdrawals of their own or to obtain from the withdrawing party substitute concessions of equivalent value. Article XXVIII details some of the procedures by which these renegotiations would occur. Subsequently, it was amended so that it specified that this "reopener" would occur every three years from January 1, 1958. At the time of the reopener, some WTO members have followed the practice of reserving rights to reopen beyond the technical time limit period provided in Article XXVIII.

Another important renegotiation provision is that which pertains to the formation of a customs union or free trade area.[19] Under Article XXIV, groups of nations can, under certain circumstances, join together into a customs union or free trade area and depart from the most-favored-nation obligation to the extent necessary to give duty-free treatment to other members of the customs union or free trade area. We discuss Article XXIV in Chapter 11 infra. In the case of a customs union, a common external tariff is substituted for the individual national tariffs of the members, and when this is done it is very likely that some of the tariffs of the common external tariff will be higher than some individual GATT tariff bindings made by members of the union. When this occurs, Article XXIV, paragraph 6, provides that "the procedure set forth in Article XXVIII shall apply." Unfortunately, the Article XXVIII description of procedures is quite skeletal and a number of difficult problems arise when these procedures are applied to the customs union case. Two important rounds of GATT negotiations have occurred in connection with these types of rights, both in the context of the development of the European Union.

The EC Treaty provided for a staged development of a common external tariff (CXT) and the elimination of separate national tariffs. Since the CXT tended to be an average of EU member state tariffs, whenever the lowest EU member state tariff on a product was bound in GATT and was raised above the binding to the EU average, renegotiation rights arose in non-EU countries. Most of the renegotiations concerned with the development of the EU occurred simultaneously with and as part of the Kennedy Round. One of the features of these renegotiations was the withdrawal by the EU of most GATT bindings on agricultural goods, particularly grains, since it was developing a common agricultural policy (CAP), with provision for high and variable tariffs, which would be inconsistent with those bindings. Since the United States was by then a major exporter of agricultural goods, particularly

19. See generally Jackson, supra note 2, at 575–623.

grains, to the EU it was seriously concerned with the loss of its trading rights and the imbalance in such rights that would allegedly ensue between the United States and the EU. Two particular disputes arose out of those renegotiation procedures: one called the "Chicken War," and the other called the "Standstill on Grain Rights."

The Chicken War[20] occurred when, after a dramatic increase in the export of U.S. frozen poultry and poultry parts to EU countries, the EU took action under its CAP to limit imports of these goods, thereby contravening a GATT binding. The matter was treated by the United States as a withdrawal of a concession on the part of several European countries, and the United States asserted its renegotiation rights under Article XXVIII. Since the EU was unprepared to grant the United States satisfactory substitute concessions, the United States indicated that it would withdraw concessions equivalent in value to the trade it lost because of the EU policy. The negotiations broke down, however, on the question of what was the value of the trade loss. Article XXVIII is not very satisfactory in the case of a breakdown of negotiations, since unilateral responses by each negotiating party could draw counter-responses and escalate the conflict. Recognizing the need for some kind of arbitral procedure to prevent such escalation, the Director–General of GATT, Eric Wyndham–White, was induced to suggest the appointment of a special panel composed of representatives from nondisputants, which would be charged with determining the precise issue of the amount of the trading rights which the United States had lost. This panel received briefs and oral arguments from both sides, the United States arguing that its trading rights had a value considerably more than that which the EU was willing to recognize. The panel came to a determination of that value somewhat in between,[21] and the United States and the EU agreed to abide by that determination. The United States then proceeded to withdraw its own concessions on brandy, trucks, starch and dextrin.[22] Since withdrawals under Article XXVIII are designed to be on an MFN basis, the United States had to choose products which were mostly supplied by EU countries, so that its withdrawal would hopefully only affect the export trade of those countries. Nevertheless, one country which was hurt by the "fall-out effect" of these withdrawals was Spain, and subsequently a lawsuit was brought in U.S. courts arguing that the President did not have authority to make the withdrawals in the manner in which he did.[23] The withdrawals did not result in a change in EU policies.

---

20. Dam, supra note 2, at 87–88; Evans, supra note 2, at 173–180; L. Thomas Galloway, Star Industries Inc. v. United States: Sequel to the Chicken War, 6 Intl.Lawyer 48, 49–52 (1972); Herman Walker, Dispute Settlement: The Chicken War, 58 Am. J.Intl.L. 671 (1964).

21. GATT Doc. L/2088 (1963); reprinted in 3 Intl. Legal Materials 116 (1964).

22. Presidential Proclamation No. 3564, 28 Fed.Reg. 13247 (1963).

23. United States v. Star Industries, Inc., 462 F.2d 557 (C.C.P.A.1972), cert. denied, 409 U.S. 1076, 93 S.Ct. 678, 34 L.Ed.2d 663 (1972), sustained the President's authority.

The grains rights problem was also very difficult. Again, the problem was that the CAP called for the withdrawal of EU member state concessions on the importation of grains, which had mostly been with the United States. Because no satisfactory resolution of the matter could be obtained during the Kennedy Round, the EU and the United States agreed to extend the grains rights to the United States until such time at some future negotiation when the United States would be able to "cash in" its rights.[24]

Another important round of customs unions renegotiation occurred when the EU was enlarged by the admission to membership of the United Kingdom, Denmark and Ireland. The treaty of enlargement became effective January 1, 1973, with the extension of the common external tariff to the new members' markets. Once again a series of GATT bindings that had been in effect for those new members was withdrawn. An elaborate negotiation took place, which was called the "Twenty-four-Six" negotiation (GATT Article XXIV:6).

Initially the EU argued that the tariff reductions that the three acceding countries were implementing far outweighed the tariff increases involved in their joining the EU and that no other adjustments were necessary. The U.S. position was that it should be compensated for the loss of the lower tariff rates in the three acceding countries. In particular, the United States was unwilling to accept reduced industrial tariffs as an offset to loss of market access in the agricultural area. In 1974, the dispute was settled after the EU agreed, inter alia, to increase U.S. market access for tobacco, oranges and grapefruits, kraft paper, photographic film, non-agricultural tractors, excavating machinery, diesel and marine engines and outboard motors, engine additives, measuring instruments, pumps, plywood and other items.[25]

The accessions of Greece to the EU in 1981 and of Austria, Finland and Sweden in 1995 occurred without causing any major problems in EU–U.S. trade relations. The accession of Spain and Portugal in 1986 again raised the issue of how the United States was to be compensated for its loss of agricultural markets. The dispute was resolved in the Uruguay Round.[26]

SECTION 8.3   CUSTOMS LAW

(A) INTRODUCTION

Customs law is a very detailed and specialized subject. It is important for the general study of trade policy, however, to understand certain

---

24. See Agreements between United States and EEC of March 7, 1962, relating to grains and to wheat. 13 UST 958 & 960, TIAS Nos. 5034 and 5035. See also Agreement between the EEC and the United States entered into June 30, 1969, suspending agreements of March 7, 1962, relating to quality wheat and other grains. 20 UST 2864, TIAS No. 6761, 723 UNTS 411.

25. See Trade Agreement between the United States and the European Community, 10 Weekly Comp.Pres.Doc. 366 (1974).

26. Office of the U.S. Trade Representative, 1994 National Trade Estimate Report on Foreign Trade Barriers 73–74.

of its basic principles because customs rules can be manipulated to have a significant impact on international trade flows. The rules we will examine concern the three determinations that customs officials must make in order to administer tariffs and quotas. First, they must classify the goods, identifying them under one of the categories in the tariff schedule. (Are they handkerchiefs or scarves? Shoes or sandals?) Second, the goods must be valued so that the ad valorem tariff rate can be applied. Third, the origin of the goods must be determined so that it is possible to apply the appropriate tariff rate within the specific category. Only after those steps are completed, can customs officials specify the exact amount of tariff due on imported goods.

After a brief description of the few GATT rules that are applicable to tariff administration and an overview of U.S. customs procedures, we will examine the three issues mentioned above: classification, valuation and origin. In each case, we will first discuss the applicable international rules and then look at national (mainly U.S.) practice.

A number of GATT articles (particularly Articles VII through X) impose some international standards on the customs procedures followed by GATT parties. For example, Article X requires that customs laws and regulations be published promptly and that a tribunal be available to hear appeals from decisions by customs officials. As we saw in the preceding section (the *U.S. Customs User Fee* case), Article VIII limits the fees, formalities and penalties that can be imposed on imported products. Article IX limits the use of origin marking requirements, in particular by requiring MFN treatment, while Article VII deals with valuation of goods, a subject also dealt with in Tokyo and Uruguay Round agreements and to which we return below.

The administration of tariffs varies from country to country. Since our focus is on U.S. rules, we start with an overview of U.S. customs law.[1] When foreign goods reach the United States, they must be either formally entered into the United States at a port of entry or held in a bonded facility pending later entry or re-export.[2] Entry may be accomplished by the consignee (importer), its authorized regular employee or its agent.[3] After entry has been filed, the port director of customs will

---

1. The basic laws affecting customs are codified in 19 U.S.C.A., and the rules and regulations of the Customs Service are collected in 19 C.F.R. There are a number of useful secondary sources on customs law, including in particular Ruth F. Sturm, Customs Law and Administration (3d ed. loose-leaf); Bureau of National Affairs, International Trade Reporter (consisting of two basic volumes on trade laws, weekly reports and a selection of recent decisions in the area that are issued periodically as bound volumes entitled "International Trade Reporter Decisions" or "ITRD"); David Serko, Import Practice: Customs and International Trade Law (2d ed. 1991). For EC customs law, see Dominik Lasok, The Customs Law of the European Economic Community (3d ed. 1998); Stefano Inama & Edwin A. Vermulst, Customs and Trade Laws of the European Community (1998).

2. Merchandise may also be imported by mail. See 19 CFR pt. 145 (2001).

3. Entry may also be made by the exporter or his agent in the United States. The primary requirements are that the surety for any required bond be incorporated in the United States and that the party or agent be authorized to accept service of process in the state of the port of entry. For regulations pertaining to the entry of merchandise, see 19 CFR pts. 141–43 (2001).

designate representative quantities for examination by customs officials, make an estimate of duties for deposit and release the bulk under bond.[4] The examination is necessary to determine the classification, value and origin of the goods for duty assessment and to ensure that country of origin or other special marking requirements have been met, that no prohibited articles are present, that the shipment has been correctly invoiced and that no quantitative discrepancies exist. It is also at this time that a number of health and safety regulations are applied.[5] Likewise in some cases there are quotas on the amount of goods which can be imported and customs officials, usually in conjunction with a licensing system, administer these quotas.

The final determination of the rate and amount of duty is termed "liquidation." The importer is notified of any variance from the estimate deposited; any increase must be paid, and any excess is automatically refunded (except for de minimis amounts). If the importer wishes to contest the liquidation, it must file a protest with the appropriate customs office to secure an administrative review. If the protest is denied and all assessed duties have been paid, the denial may be appealed to the Court of International Trade (CIT), which has exclusive jurisdiction over all such actions and which is headquartered in New York City. In the CIT, there is a trial de novo of the issues,[6] but Customs is presumed to have acted correctly. Neither the Government nor importers are bound by prior decisions.[7] Appeals from the CIT go to the Court of Appeals for the Federal Circuit.[8]

(B) CLASSIFICATION

The problem of classifying goods for customs purposes is a difficult one. So long as tariffs vary by product, it is necessary to have a system of categorizing every conceivable tradable good. At the same time, this system must be simple enough that it can be applied consistently by hundreds of customs inspectors to thousands of transactions daily. In this section, we examine first the international system that has been designed for the classification of goods and then turn to a number of classification issues that have arisen under U.S. law.

(1) International Rules: The Harmonized System

The desirability of a uniform, internationally accepted classification system has long been recognized.[9] It would ease international trade flows

---

4. Some classes of goods not intended for sale (e.g., goods imported for repair, professional equipment and samples) may be imported free under bond for their exportation within one year. 19 CFR secs. 10.31–.40 (2001).

5. 19 CFR secs. 12, 161, 133 (2001).

6. 28 U.S.C.A. sec. 2640(a).

7. United States v. Stone & Downer Co., 274 U.S. 225, 47 S.Ct. 616, 71 L.Ed. 1013

(1927); United States v. Ralph Boone, 188 F.2d 808, 38 C.C.P.A. 89 (1951).

8. For a discussion of these courts and a brief selection of their jurisprudence, see Section 3.5 supra.

9. For a more thorough discussion of the history of efforts to develop a uniform classification system, see Howard L. Friedenberg, The Development of a Uniform International Tariff Nomenclature: From 1853 to 1967 with Emphasis on the Brus-

and tariff negotiations and make international trade statistics more reliable and useful. Following World War II a European Customs Union Study Group was established in Brussels and it developed a classification system variously known as the Brussels Tariff Nomenclature (BTN) and the Customs Cooperation Council Nomenclature. As part of its efforts, the Customs Cooperation Council (CCC) was established,[10] with one of its major purposes being to assume responsibility for supervising the application and interpretation of the Nomenclature. Over time, all major GATT members made the Nomenclature the basis of their customs tariffs, with the exception of the United States and Canada, and by 1967, three-quarters of the free-world's exports and imports were classified according to the Nomenclature for tariff purposes.[11]

The United States joined the CCC in 1970, but it did not adopt the Nomenclature, partly on the grounds that it had become outmoded and that a better and more modern classification system was needed. Subsequently, the CCC developed, with U.S. participation, the Harmonized Commodity Description and Coding System (the Harmonized System), which entered into force on January 1, 1988.[12] The United States adopted the Harmonized System, effective January 1, 1989.

There is another international classification system, which is utilized by the United Nations for reporting of trade statistics and which is entitled "Standard International Trade Classification" (SITC).[13] The Harmonized System is based in part on the SITC.

Notes and Questions

(1) The Harmonized System Committee meets regularly, under the auspices of the CCC, also known now as the World Customs Organization (WCO), to consider specific classification problems and review the operation of the Harmonized System and update it and the explanatory notes as necessary, acting by consensus. The U.S. implementing legislation authorizes the President, upon recommendation of the U.S. International Trade Commission, to proclaim modifications to the U.S. tariff schedule to reflect changes in the Harmonized System. The changes are to be substantially rate neutral and must be reported to Congress prior to taking effect.[14]

(2) GATT contains no specific rules on customs classification, except that Article II:5 provides for negotiations "with a view to a compensatory adjustment" when a tariff classification ruling prevents implementation of a negotiated concession. As noted in Section 8.2, GATT tariff schedules are interpreted under normal treaty interpretation rules.

sels Tariff Nomenclature (U.S. Tariff Commn., TC Pub.No. 237, 1968).

10. 22 UST 320, TIAS No. 7063, 157 UNTS 129.

11. Customs Cooperation Council, The Activities of the Council (July, 1967 to June, 1969) 28 (1970).

12. International Convention on the Harmonized Commodity Description and Coding System, done at Brussels on June

14, 1983, and the Protocol thereto, done at Brussels on June 24, 1986. 1035 UNTS 3; KAV 2260.

13. Department of Economic and Social Affairs, Statistical Office of the United Nations, Series M, No. 34, Standard International Trade Classification, Revised (1961); Revision 2 (1975); Revision 3 (1986).

14. 19 U.S.C.A. sec. 3006.

(3) Classification issues have arisen in two other important contexts in GATT. One early GATT case recognized that a legitimate tariff reclassification could nullify or impair the reasonable anticipation of a party, giving rise to a claim for compensation under Article XXIII. In addition, there have been GATT cases involving claims that a classification system denied MFN treatment to the complaining country's products by classifying them differently than essentially the same products from other countries. These cases are analyzed in Section 10.2 infra.

(2) Classification Under U.S. Law

The currently effective Harmonized Tariff Schedule of the United States (HTS or HTSUS), which is based upon the CCC's Harmonized System, came into effect on January 1, 1989.[15] According to the U.S. International Trade Commission, "the most noteworthy observation [about the implementation of the HTS] is the overall absence of complaints from the private sector."[16] It noted that the administrative agencies involved in customs administration welcomed the HTS because it provided better statistical data on trade that was more comparable to the data of U.S. trading partners and because it simplified the classification process (see Note 9 below).

The HTS contains some 8,500 8–digit legal tariff lines. The classification rules used to determine under which subdivision a product falls are complex. We will not attempt to cover these rules in a comprehensive fashion, but the following materials should give the reader a flavor of the issues involved in classification disputes. We excerpt first the general U.S. interpretative rules, which are those of the Harmonized System, and then examine a typical appellate court decision on classification.

HARMONIZED TARIFF SCHEDULE OF THE UNITED STATES (2001)(Rev. 1)

GENERAL RULES OF INTERPRETATION

Classification of goods in the tariff schedule shall be governed by the following principles:

1.   The table of contents, alphabetical index, and titles of sections, chapters and sub-chapters are provided for ease of reference only; for legal purposes, classification shall be determined according to the terms of the headings and any relative section or chapter notes and, provided such headings or notes do not otherwise require, according to the following provisions:

2.   (a) Any reference in a heading to an article shall be taken to include a reference to that article incomplete or unfinished, provided that, as entered, the incomplete or unfinished article has the essential character of the complete or finished

---

15. 19 U.S.C.A. sec. 1202.

16. U.S. Intl. Trade Commn., Investigation No. 332–274, at v (USITC Pub. 2296, June 1990).

article. It shall also include a reference to that article complete or finished (or failing to be classified as complete or finished by virtue of this rule), entered unassembled or disassembled.

(b) Any reference in a heading to a material or substance shall be taken to include a reference to mixtures or combinations of that material or substance with other materials or substances. Any reference to goods of a given material or substance shall be taken to include a reference to goods consisting wholly or partly of such material or substance. The classification of goods consisting of more than one material or substance shall be according to the principles of rule 3.

3. When, by application of rule 2(b) or for any other reason, goods are, prima facie, classifiable under two or more headings, classification shall be effected as follows:

(a) The heading which provides the most specific description shall be preferred to headings providing a more general description. However, when two or more headings each refer to part only of the materials or substances contained in mixed or composite goods or to part only of the items in a set put up for retail sale, those headings are to be regarded as equally specific in relation to those goods, even if one of them gives a more complete or precise description of the goods.

(b) Mixtures, composite goods consisting of different materials or made up of different components, and goods put up in sets for retail sale, which cannot be classified by reference to 3(a), shall be classified as if they consisted of the material or component which gives them their essential character, insofar as this criterion is applicable.

(c) When goods cannot be classified by reference to 3(a) or 3(b), they shall be classified under the heading which occurs last in numerical order among those which equally merit consideration.

4. Goods which cannot be classified in accordance with the above rules shall be classified under the heading appropriate to the goods to which they are most akin.

* * *

6. For legal purposes, the classification of goods in the subheadings of a heading shall be determined according to the terms of those subheadings and any related subheading notes, and, mutatis mutandis, to the above rules, on the understanding that only subheadings at the same level are comparable. For the purposes of this rule, the relative section, chapter and subchapter notes also apply, unless the context otherwise requires.

ADDITIONAL U.S. RULES OF INTERPRETATION

1. In the absence of special language or context which otherwise requires—

   (a) a tariff classification controlled by use (other than actual use) is to be determined in accordance with the use in the United States at, or immediately prior to, the date of importation, of goods of that class or kind to which the imported goods belong, and the controlling use is the principal use;

   (b) a tariff classification controlled by the actual use to which the imported goods are put in the United States is satisfied only if such use is intended at the time of importation, the goods are so used and proof thereof is furnished within 3 years after the date the goods are entered;

   (c) a provision for parts of an article covers products solely or principally used as a part of such articles but a provision for "parts" or "parts and accessories" shall not prevail over a specific provision for such part or accessory; * * *

LYNTEQ, INC. v. UNITED STATES

United States Court of Appeals, Federal Circuit, 1992.
976 F.2d 693.

LOURIE, CIRCUIT JUDGE:

[This case involves an appeal by the United States of a CIT decision overruling the Customs Service's classification of a product known as "Cromophyl–L," which is incorporated into poultry feed in order to enhance the yellow color of chicken skin and egg yolks. The color enhancing properties of Cromophyl–L are derived from marigold meal, which is a rich source of xanthophyll pigment, but compared to marigold meal, Cromophyl–L is more stable, easier to incorporate into poultry feed and more readily absorbed by poultry.

The applicable provisions of the HTSUS are as follows:

Heading 3203.00—Coloring matter of vegetable or animal origin (including dyeing extracts but excluding animal black), whether or not chemically defined; preparations as specified in note 3 to this chapter based on coloring matter of vegetable or animal origin:

Subheading 3203.00.10—Annato, archil, cochineal, cudbear, litmus, logwood and marigold meal . . . . Duty Free

Subheading 3203.00.50—Other 3.1%

Note 3 provides: "[Heading 3203] appl[ies] also to preparations based on coloring matter * * * of a kind used for coloring any material or used as ingredients in the manufacture of coloring preparations."]

* * * The ultimate issue as to whether particular merchandise has been classified under an appropriate tariff provision necessarily depends

on the meaning of the terms of that provision, which is a question of law subject to de novo review. Thus, we need not afford deference to the trial court's decision regarding the proper scope of subheading 3203.00.10. Customs' classification of imported merchandise is presumed to be correct, 28 U.S.C. sec. 2639(a)(1) (1988), and the burden of proof is upon the party challenging the classification.

I. PREPARATIONS

Neither party disputes that Cromophyl–L is properly classified under heading 3203.00. * * * We must thus decide which of the two subdivisions of heading 3203.00 is applicable to Cromophyl–L. Resolution of that issue necessarily entails deciding whether subheading 3203.00.10 encompasses not only the enumerated coloring matter, but preparations based on that coloring matter as well.

The trial court determined that subheadings 3203.00.10 and 3203.00.50 encompass "not only coloring matter of animal or vegetable origin, but also preparations based thereon of a kind used for coloring any material or used as ingredients in the manufacture of coloring preparations." The trial court, however, failed to articulate any reasoning supporting that conclusion other than that it was based on the court's reading of the language of heading 3203.00 in conjunction with Note 3 to Chapter 32. We conclude that the trial court's broad interpretation of the scope of subheading 3203.00.10 was erroneous.

"In determining the scope of a statute, we look first to its language. If the statutory language is unambiguous, in the absence of a 'clearly expressed legislative intent to the contrary, that language must ordinarily be regarded as conclusive.' " United States v. Turkette, 452 U.S. 576, 580 (1981) (quoting Consumer Prod. Safety Comm'n v. GTE Sylvania, Inc., 447 U.S. 102, 108 (1980)). The language of subheading 3203.00.10 is clear and unambiguous. That eo nomine[17] subheading, by its very terms, covers only coloring matter which comes within the common meaning of the items that are specifically enumerated therein: annato, archil, cochineal, cudbear, litmus, logwood, and marigold meal. See Rule 6, General Rules of Interpretation of the Harmonized System [excerpted above].

An eo nomine provision which does not specifically provide for preparations does not encompass preparations within its ambit. Cf. United States v. Bruckmann, 582 F.2d 622, 625 (CCPA 1978) ("It is fairly well-settled law that an eo nomine provision which does not specifically provide for parts does not include parts."). Indeed, if Congress had intended to include Cromophyl–L or other preparations under subheading 3203.00.10, Congress could easily have done so, for example, by simply drafting the subheading so as to cover "Annato, archil, cochineal, cudbear, litmus, logwood, marigold meal and preparations based thereon." Congress did not do so and we decline to act where Congress has not.

---

17. "Eo nomine" means "by or under that name." Webster's Third New Interna- tional Dictionary (Unabridged) (1981).

Accordingly, all products coming within the scope of heading 3203.00, including preparations, that are not specifically enumerated in subheading 3203.00.10 are covered by the residual subheading 3203.00.50, and are thus not entitled to duty-free treatment. * * * In order for the imported merchandise to be properly classified under subheading 3203.00.10, it must come within the meaning of the term "marigold meal." As the trial court correctly determined, it does not.

II. MARIGOLD MEAL

Tariff terms contained in the statutory language "are to be construed in accordance with their common and popular meaning, in the absence of contrary legislative intent." E.M. Chemicals v. United States, 920 F.2d 910, 913 (Fed.Cir.1990). "To assist it in ascertaining the common meaning of a tariff term, the court may rely upon its own understanding of the terms used, and it may consult lexicographic and scientific authorities, dictionaries, and other reliable information sources." Brookside Veneers, Ltd. v. United States, 847 F.2d 786, 789 (Fed.Cir.1988). The term "marigold meal" is not defined by the HTSUS, and thus we must consult other acceptable and reliable sources of information.

"Marigold" refers to "a plant of the genus Tagetes." Webster's Third New International Dictionary 1381 (1986). "Meal" is defined, inter alia, as: "1. the ground seeds of a cereal grass or pulse esp. when coarsely ground and unbolted and usu. excluding flour of wheat ..."; and "2. the product resembling seed meal in particle size, texture, or other quality...." Id. at 1398. Thus, the tariff term "marigold meal" fairly refers to the product produced by the coarse grinding of the marigold plant.

In the absence of contrary legislative intent, an eo nomine designation without terms of limitation includes all forms of the article. The record, however, is replete with evidence that Cromophyl–L is not a form of marigold meal and thus that it is beyond the scope of the common meaning of that tariff term. For example, at least 94% or more of the xanthophyll present in marigold meal exists in the form of xanthophyll esters, not xanthophyll free alcohol. In contrast, Cromophyl–L, derived from marigold meal through saponification, is an aqueous extract of xanthophyll in which 98+% of the xanthophyll is present in its free alcohol form. The inherent characteristics of Cromophyl–L (e.g. stability, aqueous form, coloring efficiency) that distinguish it from other by-products of the marigold plant make it the preferred color-enhancing food additive in the poultry industry. Thus, we find no error in the trial court's determination that the imported merchandise "possesses qualities altogether different from those present in the raw material from which it is derived, that it can no longer be deemed to be marigold meal for classification purposes." However, for reasons stated above, we reach a different conclusion as to the proper classification of the imported merchandise. Because we find that Cromophyl–L does not come within the meaning of the term "marigold meal," we must conclude that it is properly classified under subheading 3203.00.50, dutiable at 3.1% ad valorem, and not under subheading 3203.00.10.

Notes and Questions

(1) In one of its rare classification opinion, the U.S. Supreme Court recently held that ruling letters issued by the Customs Service are not entitled to so-called *Chevron* deference when challenged in court. United States v. Mead, 533 U.S. 218, 121 S.Ct. 2164, 150 L.Ed.2d 292 (2001).

(2) The *Lynteq* case lays out some of the basic principles of classification. In particular, the court's approach to interpreting the words of the schedule by relying on common meanings is typical. Note also that tariff classification schemes often have a general heading, followed by a number of specific headings and concluded by an "other" category. Indeed, this pattern sometimes repeats itself within the "other" category so that a product may be classified under a general heading as "Other, other, other." Normally the specific headings are designed to give either favorable or unfavorable treatment to specific products.

(3) An interesting EU case, E.I. DU PONT DE NEMOURS INC. v. COMMISSIONERS OF CUSTOMS & EXCISE, Case 234/81, [1982] ECR 3515, involved the classification of the Du Pont product Corian, which resembles marble in appearance, but consists by weight of about two-thirds aluminum hydroxide obtained from bauxite ore and one-third polymethyl methacrylate, an artificial plastic material. Should Corian be classified as artificial stone (heading 68.11) or a methacrylic polymer (heading 39.02)? Consider General Rule 2(b), excerpted above. The EC Court of Justice ruled that since Corian contained a material specified in heading 39.02, it was prima facie classifiable there under General Rule 2(b). (This rule could not be applied to classify Corian as an ore or as aluminum hydroxide, because the relevant notes excluded ores submitted to a chemical process and included aluminum hydroxide only as a separate element or chemically defined compound, which was not true in the case of Corian). As to the possibility of the artificial stone heading, the Court ruled:

> There is no universally accepted interpretation of [the] concept [of artificial stone] in either trade or scientific circles, although the prevailing view is that "artificial stone contains natural stone."

> * * * According to [the Explanatory] Notes, "artificial stone is an imitation of natural stone usually obtained by agglomerating pieces of natural stone, crushed or powdered natural stone * * * with lime or cement or other binders (e.g., artificial plastic material)."

> It was submitted by Du Pont * * * that the word "usually" * * * implies that there may be exceptions * * *. That argument cannot be accepted, however, for the position of the word "usually", which precedes the words "by agglomerating" and not the words "powdered natural stone", indicates in fact that an exception might be made at most to allow for the possibility of using a manufacturing process other than the agglomeration of binders with powdered natural stone, but not for the case where no natural stone is used.

The Court concluded that even if Corian were prima facie classifiable as artificial stone, Rule 3 would dictate the choice of heading 39.02 over heading 68.11. Do you see why? The Court relied on Rule 3(a), not 3(c).

(4) How would you classify a stereo component system including the following five components, with their respective values indicated separately in deutsche marks:

compact disc player (DM 164)

amplifier (DM 173.50)

tuner (DM 124)

double cassette recorder (DM 179)

record player (DM 55)?

Assume your choices are:

(1) 8519 9910—other sound-producing apparatus with laser optical reading systems (based on CD player);

(2) 8527—radio reception apparatus (based on tuner);

(3) 8519 3900—record player, or

(4) 8520 3190—double cassette player.

What result under Rule 3? The German Federal Supreme Finance Court concluded that Rules 3a and 3b were not helpful, leaving Rule 3c as determinative. In re Import of a Compact Disc Player, [1993] 1 CMLR 780 (Case VII K 2/91, Bundes-finanzhof, June 2, 1992). Note that the system had originally been classified as a CD player, which meant that it was subject to antidumping duties.

(5) One of the more controversial trade issues between the United States and Japan in 1992–1993 was whether minivans should be classified as trucks or cars. As noted in Section 8.2, as a result of the Chicken War, the U.S. raised its MFN tariff on trucks, and it remains at 25%, while the MFN tariff on cars is 2.5%. Although the increased tariff was designed to "punish" Germany, its effect in recent years has been to limit Japanese exports of trucks to the United States. Under the HTSUS, the choice for classifying minivans is between heading 8703 (Motor cars and other motor vehicles principally designed for the transport of persons)("cars") and heading 8704 (motor vehicles for the transport of goods)("trucks"). The U.S. has long classified as minivans as cars,[18] but after Treasury Department officials overruled a Customs Service decision to reclassify them as trucks, that decision was criticized by then presidential candidate Bill Clinton. Assuming there are no helpful notes, under which heading do you think minivans should be classified? Why? What information would be relevant to your decision? Would it matter if minivans were more closely related to trucks than cars as to some (or most) basic engineering factors? That minivans were subject to lower environmental and safety standards than regular passenger cars? That the auto industry reports minivan sales under the general heading of "light truck" sales? See Marubeni America Corp. v.

18. It appears that the punitive tariff on trucks, which dates from 1963, was not intended to apply to the Volkswagen "box-on-wheels" station wagon, which arguably is a predecessor of today's minivans. See N.Y.Times, Jan. 7, 1964, at 39, col 4.

United States, 821 F.Supp. 1521 (CIT 1993) (two-door sports utility vehicles should be classified as cars; key issue is whether they are for the purpose of transporting passengers or goods; rejects other factors such as those listed above). If the U.S. reclassifies minivans as trucks, what claims might Japan bring in the WTO? Who would likely prevail?

(6) Assume your client wants to import educational construction kits into the United States. The kits are designed for teenage children and consist of instructions and materials by which a small (and not very durable) electronic speedometer can be constructed, suitable for attaching to a bicycle or automobile. Assuming that only the asterisked tariff classifications are relevant, what duty will be imposed on the kits?

Tariff Heading	Article Description	Duty
8712.00	Bicycles and other cycles * * *	
8714.00	Parts * * * of vehicles of headings 8711 to 8713	
8714.99	Other	
*8714.99.80	Other	10%
9029	Revolution counters, * * *, speedometers	
9029.20	Speedometers and tachometers * * *	
*9029.20.20	Bicycle speedometers	6%
*9029.20.40	Other speedometers * * *	Free
9029.90	Parts and accessories	
*9029.90.40	Of bicycle speedometers	6%
*9029.90.80	Other	Free
9503	Other toys; reduced-sized ("scale") models * * *	
*9503.20.00	Reduced-size ("scale") model assembly kits, whether or not working models	Free
9503.30.00	Other construction sets and constructional toys	Free

The former U.S. tariff schedules contained a note to the effect that toys were articles chiefly used for the amusement of children or adults. Would this note be helpful in classifying the kits? In terms of strategy, the best rate is "other speedometers" while the worst is "bicycle speedometers." What is the danger of arguing for the "other speedometers" rate?

(7) Should "bicycle-type" speedometers, suitable for use on bicycles, but in fact used primarily on exercisers, be classified in the speedometers heading under the subheading "Bicycle speedometers and parts thereof" or "Other"? See Additional U.S. Rules excerpted above; Stewart–Warner Corp. v. United States, 748 F.2d 663 (Fed.Cir.1984)(based on chief use, should be "other").

(8) Which General Rule would you rely upon to classify a box containing several major elements of a tape recorder and the necessary parts to assemble it? What if some of the elements were imported separately?

(9) The Harmonized System approach to classification differs from the old U.S. system in a number of ways. Probably the most important changes are that (i) the old U.S. system often focused on use, while the HS attempts to classify goods according to their essential character; and (ii) the change in the case of textiles from classification on the basis of the fiber of chief value to the fiber of chief weight. In each case, the aim is to reduce uncertainty by reducing disputes over actual use or value. (The concept of use, of course, has not been eliminated. See Notes 6 and 7 above.)

(10) Classification is important only as long as tariff rates vary by product. Why are they likely to do so?

(C) VALUATION

Most tariffs are ad valorem, which means that the value of the goods subject to them must be ascertained in order to calculate the amount of tariff due. In this section, we describe the detailed valuation rules agreed upon in the Tokyo Round's Customs Valuation Code, which were largely left unchanged in the Uruguay Round, and then examine how U.S. courts have applied those rules.

(1) The GATT Customs Valuation Code

Prior to the Tokyo Round (1979), customs valuation was a controversial issue. Although GATT Article VII regulated valuation to some degree, it was not adequate. Indeed, an examination of the interpretative notes to Article VII demonstrates the wide disparities in practices that were permitted by Article VII. The U.S. system for valuation of goods for customs purposes, which benefited from the grandfather provisions of the Protocol of Provisional Application, was so complex and cumbersome that it was deemed to be a non-tariff barrier by many trading nations.[19] For its part, the United States objected to the imprecise and unpredictable valuation practices of many other countries. This dissatisfaction led to the negotiation in the Tokyo Round of a GATT Customs Valuation Code.[20] The background and the results of the negotiations are described in the Senate Report on the Trade Agreements Act of 1979.

SENATE REPORT 96–249

96th Cong., 1st Sess. 108–10 (1979)

The basis and complexity of customs valuation systems used throughout the world vary considerably. Some systems, such as the Brussels Definition of Value (BDV) used by the European Communities (EC) and most of the countries in the world, employ a "notional" standard for valuation purposes. Under this system, the customs value of an imported product is the price at which that product *would be* sold if the actual transaction in question were a perfectly competitive transaction. Adjustments to the actual value to reach the ideal value are made, and such adjustments are often criticized as arbitrary and almost always increase the value and, therefore, the tariff liability. Other customs valuation systems, such as the U.S. system, use a "positive" standard, where customs value is usually the price at which goods are sold in the actual transaction. In certain circumstances, such systems also provide for alternative definitions of value for use in those cases where the price cannot be used. Still other systems assess customs duties primarily on

---

19. The former U.S. valuation system is described and contrasted with those of other countries in U.S. Tariff Commn., Customs Valuation (TC Pub.No. 180, 1966).

20. Agreement on Implementation of Article VII & Protocol, GATT, 26th Supp. BISD 116 (1980).

the basis of national or official values which are arbitrary and are used to increase duties collected and/or to protect domestic industries, or primarily on the basis of the domestic selling price of the goods in the country of exportation. Other aspects of customs valuation systems making for complexity and controversy include: The existence in some systems of numerous alternative definitions of value; complex laws and administrative regulations making it difficult to easily predict the amount of duty that will be owed; the absence of requirements and procedures for review of valuation decisions; and the absence of published administrative regulations and decisions.

Against this background, negotiations in the [Tokyo Round] on an international set of rules for customs valuation took place with the active participation of the major industrialized countries and many of the developing countries.

* * *

SUMMARY OF THE AGREEMENT

Methods of Customs Valuation.—The Customs Valuation Agreement establishes five alternative methods of customs valuation. Each is summarized briefly below in the order in which it would be applied.

1. *The transaction value of the imported goods,* i.e., the price actually paid or payable for the goods with adjustments for certain specified costs, charges, and expenses which are incurred but not reflected in the price actually paid or payable for the goods (including selling commissions, container costs, packing costs, certain royalties and licenses fees, and assists) (article 1 of the agreement).

2. If the transaction value of the imports cannot be determined or used, then the *transaction value of identical goods* sold for export to the same country, and exported at or about the same time as the imported goods (article 2 of the agreement).

3. If the transaction value of identical goods cannot be determined, then the *transaction value of similar goods* sold for export to the same country and exported at or about the same time as the imported goods (article 3 of the agreement).

4. If customs value cannot be determined by looking to transaction value, then the *deductive* value or *computed* value, as the importer chooses. The *deductive* value for the imported goods is determined by the price at which the imported goods, or identical or similar imported goods, are sold in the greatest aggregate quantity to unrelated persons in the country of importation in the same condition as imported (or after further processing), with deductions for commissions or profit, general expenses, transport and insurance costs, customs duties and certain other costs, charges and expenses incurred as a result of reselling the goods. (Article 5 of the agreement.)

5. The *computed value* of the imported goods, determined by summing the cost of producing the article in the country of exportation, an amount for general expense and profit, and the cost or value of all other expenses necessary to reflect the valuation option (i.e., f.o.b. or c.i.f.) chosen by the signatory. (Article 6 of the Agreement.)

In those rare instances where a value cannot be determined under any of the valuation methods described above, the agreement provides that "the value shall be determined using reasonable means consistent with the principles and general provisions of this code...." The customs values determined under this residual method "should be based to the greatest possible extent on previously determined customs values." Several valuation methods are specifically precluded from being used as a basis for determining customs value, including methods such as the American selling price (ASP) and foreign value methods currently used in the United States.

Circumstances Under Which the Transaction Value Will Not Be Used. The most significant circumstance under the agreement which would result in the transaction value not being used is when the transaction in question is between related parties. If the buyer and seller are related, the transaction value may not be used unless an examination of the circumstances surrounding the sale demonstrates that such relationship did not influence the price, or the importer demonstrates that the transaction value closely approximates one of several other enumerated values, subject to other criteria of the agreement.

Notes and Questions

(1) The Valuation Code was not significantly changed in the Uruguay Round. See Documents Supplement for the WTO Customs Valuation Agreement.

(2) Despite the special provisions designed to ease adherence to the Valuation Code by developing countries, many did not join. The principal reasons given were problems in respect of training customs personnel, determining proper procedures to apply the agreement, loss of revenue, providing guidance to importers and preparation of the necessary laws and regulations.[21] While all WTO members are required to accept the WTO Customs Valuation Agreement, many developing countries have continued to postpone implementation. WTO, 2001 Annual Report, at 51.

(3) The Committee on Customs Valuation established by the Code reported in 1983 that experience in the first year "indicated that, in line with the Agreement's objectives, the vast majority of customs entries were being valued on the basis of transaction value."[22] The Committee has studied

21. Report of the Committee on Customs Valuation, GATT, 30th Supp. BISD 56, 61 (1984).

22. Id., at 59. A study by the U.S. Customs Service found that over 94% of entries in the ports examined were made on the basis of transaction value. U.S. General Accounting Office, New U.S. Valuation System for Imported Products is Better and Easier to Administer (Report No. B–201765, 1982).

a couple of areas where interpretative difficulties have arisen under the Code, including the proper valuation of computer software and the treatment of interest charges in cases of deferred payment.[23]

(4) For more information on the Code, see Saul L. Sherman & Hinrich Glashoff, Customs Valuation: Commentary on the GATT Customs Valuation Code (1988).

(2) U.S. Valuation Rules

The Customs Valuation Code was implemented into U.S. law by title II of the Trade Agreements Act of 1979 (See Documents Supplement, Tariff Act of 1930, sec. 402; 19 U.S.C.A. sec. 1401a).[24] It is generally perceived in the United States that valuation disputes have declined with implementation of the Code.[25]

GENERRA SPORTSWEAR CO. v. UNITED STATES

United States Court of Appeals, Federal Circuit, 1990.
905 F.2d 377.

MAYER, CIRCUIT JUDGE:

Generra Sportswear Company of Seattle, Washington, contracted to purchase 595 women's 100% cotton knit blouses from Bagutta Garment Ltd. of Hong Kong at a price of $6.00 each. Bagutta agreed to obtain Type A Transfer quota for category 338/339 at $0.95 per unit.[26] Bagutta obtained quota for the shipment from LCL Manufacturer Co., Ltd. of Hong Kong at $1.28 per unit,[27] the cost of quota having gone up since Bagutta received Generra's purchase order.

The issue on this appeal, whether the quota charges were properly included in transaction value, is a matter of statutory construction. * * *

[B]ecause section 1401a(b) does not precisely address whether or not quota payments may be included in transaction value, we determine whether the appraisal was based on a permissible construction of the statute. Customs' interpretation will be accepted if it is "sufficiently reasonable." Unless it is clear that Congress' intent was to the contrary,

---

23. Reports of the Committee on Customs Valuation, GATT, 31st Supp. BISD 273, 274 (1985). As a result of a committee decision on software, the EU determined not to include the value of the software in determining the value of goods containing software. Council Regulation 1055/85, [1985] Eur.Comm.O.J. No. L 112/50.

24. Pub.L. No. 96–39, 93 Stat. 144 (codified at 19 U.S.C.A. sec. 1401a). See Edward J. Hayward & Julie Long, Comparative Views of U.S. Customs Valuation Issues in light of the U.S. Customs Modernization Act, 5 Minn. J. Global Trade 311 (1996).

25. Munford P. Hall, II, Value's Greatest Hits (and Misses): A Complete History of Judicial Decisions Concerning Value Under the Trade Agreements Act of 1979—Volume I, 25 L. & Poly.Intl.Bus. 51, 67 (1993).

26. [original note 2] As a means of complying with voluntary restraint agreements with the United States, Hong Kong requires that an export license be obtained for each shipment for export. * * *

27. [original note 3] An exporter can obtain an export license by purchasing quota from another party. * * *

courts normally defer to the agency's construction of the statutory scheme it administers.

We think Customs' construction of section 1401a(b), that transaction value may include quota charges, is permissible. It is reasonable to conclude that these charges were part of the "price actually paid or payable," defined in subsection 1401a(b)(4)(A) as "the total payment . . . made, or to be made, for imported merchandise by the buyer to, or for the benefit of, the seller." The total payment from Generra to Bagutta was $6.95 per unit. The term "total payment" is all-inclusive. If Congress had intended to exclude quota payments from transaction value, it could have included them among the explicit exclusions enumerated in section 1401a(b)(3).

It is not important that the buyer itself did not pay the seller for the quota charges; the payment was made on behalf of Generra by its Hong Kong buying agent. Further, Generra admits that the "question whether or not the seller benefitted from the quota payment is a non-issue in this case." When the payment is made to the seller, it is not necessary to get into whether the seller benefitted; the statute is written in the alternative: "to, or for the benefit of, the seller." 19 U.S.C. sec. 1401a(b)(4)(A).

The thrust of Generra's argument, and the essence of the trial court's reasoning, is that the quota payment was not "for imported merchandise." * * *

Accepting the stipulated fact that $0.95 of the total payment to Bagutta was for quota charges, it was reasonable for Customs to conclude that the entire payment was "for imported merchandise" within the meaning of subsection 1401a(b)(4)(A). A permissible construction of the term "for imported merchandise" does not restrict which components of the total payment may be included in transaction value. Congress did not intend for the Customs Service to engage in extensive fact-finding to determine whether separate charges, all resulting in payments to the seller in connection with the purchase of imported merchandise, are for the merchandise or for something else. As we said in Moss Mfg. Co. v. United States, 896 F.2d 535, 539 (Fed.Cir.1990), the "straightforward approach [of section 1401a(b)] is no doubt intended to enhance the efficiency of Customs' appraisal procedure; it would be frustrated were we to parse the statutory language in the manner, and require Customs to engage in the formidable fact-finding task, envisioned by [appellant]."

As long as the quota payment was made to the seller in exchange for merchandise sold for export to the United States, the payment properly may be included in transaction value, even if the payment represents something other than the per se value of the goods. The focus of transaction value is the actual transaction between the buyer and the seller; if quota payments were transferred by the buyer to the seller, they are part of transaction value. That transaction value may encompass items other than the pure cost of the imported merchandise is reflected in section 1401a(b)(3), governing exclusions from transaction value. If excludable costs or charges are not identified separately from the price actually paid or payable, they are included in transaction value.

It was not necessary for the Customs Service to find that the quota charge was imposed as a condition of sale before considering it part of the "price actually paid or payable" under subsection 1401a(b)(4)(A). Nothing in the statute requires that. On the other hand, that a foreign seller must obtain quota before he can export goods to the United States reasonably indicates that quota payments are part of the "price actually paid or payable for the merchandise when sold for exportation to the United States." 19 U.S.C. sec. 1401a(b)(1).

That was the case here. Bagutta applied for an export license from the Hong Kong Department of Trade before shipping the blouses to Generra; the license form required Bagutta to name the quota holder, the quota reference and the quantity being shipped in quota units. The export license accompanied the goods out of Hong Kong as proof that Bagutta had quota for the shipment. Indeed, if quota were not a prerequisite to exportation, one wonders why Bagutta paid more than the contract price for quota, taking a loss, or even agreed to obtain quota in the first place.

Notes and Questions

(1) The EC Court of Justice reached the opposite result in a similar case under the EC regulation implementing the GATT Code, Ospig Textilgesellschaft KG W. Alhers v. Hauptzollamt Bremen–Ost, Case 7/83, [1984] ECR 609, as had the Court of Customs and Patent Appeals under prior U.S. law. United States v. Getz Bros. & Co., 55 C.C.P.A. 11 (1967). Do you agree with the Court's result? Should it matter that the identical product sold for the same price may be valued differently, depending on the cost of the quota rights? That the seller of the product may not benefit from the quota charge payment? Is the court right to ask only who paid how much to whom? To stress the need for simplicity?

(2) Suppose a Hong Kong business contracts with a U.S. client to supply a made-to-measure suit that it will purchase in Hong Kong and deliver to the client in the United States. On entry of the suit into the United States, should it be valued at the price paid by the Hong Kong business or the price its client will pay to the Hong Kong business? Review the wording of Section 402(b)(1) of the Tariff Act of 1930, 19 U.S.C.A. sec. 1401a(b)(1). When is this merchandise "sold for exportation to the United States?" See E.C. McAfee Co. v. United States, 842 F.2d 314 (Fed.Cir.1988)(value is price paid by middleman). Accord, Nissho Iwai American Co. v. United States, 982 F.2d 505 (Fed.Cir.1992)(Japanese subway cars). How could you argue that this result is not consistent with *Generra Sportswear*?

(3) Suppose the importer has paid the supplier $100 for the product at the time of importation, but later receives a $10 rebate. What effect does the rebate have on the value of the product for customs purposes? Consider Section 402(b)(4)(B) of the Tariff Act of 1930, 19 U.S.C.A. sec. 1401a(b)(4)(B).

(4) Notice that the value of any "assist" is added to the transaction value (see the definition in Section 402(h), 19 U.S.C.A. sec. 1401a(h)), as is any royalty or license fee related to the imported goods that the buyer is required to pay "as a condition of the sale of the imported merchandise." Tariff Act of 1930, sec. 402(b)(1)(C)-(D), 19 U.S.C.A. sec. 1401a(b)(1)(C)-(D).

(5) Your client wishes to ascertain the likely duty to be assessed on a product, made by its European parent, that it plans to import into the United States for resale. The normal duty rate for the product is 10% and the stated CIF invoice price is $1000. Shipping costs are $50, insurance $10 and packing $5. In addition, your client pays certain royalties to its parent on each resale. Your client has not been doing well financially and the parent has allowed it to defer inter-company payments indefinitely and such amounts are now between 30 and 90 days past due. Discuss the problems that might arise in determining the applicable duty amount.

(6) The United States has always utilized an FOB method of valuation for customs purposes, whereas most of its trading partners use CIF.[28] This, of course, means that a 10% tariff applied by the United States produces less revenue and is less of a trade barrier than a 10% tariff applied by a country using CIF valuation—the difference being equal basically to 10% of the shipping and insurance costs, a fact negotiators must keep in mind when discussing reciprocal tariff concessions.

It has been argued that it would be unconstitutional for the United States to use CIF prices for customs valuation.[29] The constitutional provisions at issue are Article I, section 8, clause 1, and section 9, clause 6, which read, respectively:

> The Congress shall have power to lay and collect taxes, duties, imposts, and excises, * * * but all duties, imposts, and excises shall be uniform throughout the United States.

> No preference shall be given by any regulation of commerce or revenue to the ports of one state over those of another * * *.

It can be argued that CIF valuation would mean that identical goods, sold for the same price (excluding freight and insurance) would be taxed in different amounts on entry into the United States, thereby violating the uniformity clause. Similarly, CIF valuation would give a preference to U.S. ports closer to the port of dispatch. (Of course, if the cost of bringing goods to the United States is properly considered as part of their value, then FOB valuation leads to nonuniformity and gives a preference to distant ports.) What do you think of this constitutional argument? At the time this issue was discussed during the Tokyo Round, the chairman of the Senate Finance Committee was from Louisiana. Which system favors New Orleans?

28. An FOB price is the price at the point of shipment for the goods only, while a CIF price is the price for the goods plus an amount covering transportation and insurance to a specified destination. See Section 2.2(B)(2) supra. The relevant U.S. statute is Tariff Act of 1930, sec. 402(b)(4)(A), 19 U.S.C.A. sec. 1401a(b)(4)(A) (dutiable value excludes "any costs, charges, or expenses incurred for transportation, insurance, and related services incident to the international shipment of the merchandise" to the United States).

29. This issue is discussed in U.S. Tariff Commission, Customs Valuation, Report to Senate Comm. on Finance, 93d Cong., 1st Sess. 83–86 (Comm.Print 1973).

(7) The U.S. valuation law prior to 1979 was a pastiche of provisions, some perpetuated from prior laws by special interest lobbying with Congress. No less than nine different standards were applied, depending on the product or circumstance. The most controversial standard was the American Selling Price (ASP) rule, which derived from the Tariff Act of 1922,[30] and which provided that where the statutory tariff did not equalize the difference between foreign and domestic costs of production, the President could change the valuation basis of the article to the ASP. The ASP was defined as the usual wholesale price, including preparation for shipping, at which an article manufactured in the United States was freely offered for sale. Prior to the Tokyo Round, the rule was applied to benzenoid chemicals, certain rubber-soled footwear, certain canned clams, and low-value wool-knit gloves. Although in 1969 less than one percent of United States imports were subject to the ASP rule,[31] the effect where applied was considerable. According to a Tariff Commission study of ASP imports in 1964, a 20% duty on some chemicals and footwear was the equivalent of up to 58% at normal customs value.[32]

The ASP method of customs valuation was not consistent with Article VII of GATT. Because ASP was law prior to GATT, however, it benefited from the "grandfather" clause of the Protocol of Provisional Application.[33] During the Kennedy Round of trade negotiations, an agreement was reached whereby the United States would eliminate ASP in exchange for certain European and Japanese concessions (mainly tariff reductions on chemicals and a French agreement to change their method of taxing automobiles so that United States auto exports would be more competitive in the French market). This agreement required approval by the U.S. Congress, which was never given. After several extensions of the deadline for acceptance of the agreement and in the face of congressional inaction, European parties to the agreement indicated in 1972 that they were not prepared to accept a further extension, and the agreement lapsed. The ASP system was eliminated when the United States implemented the Customs Valuation Code as described above. Its only importance today is that it is remembered by U.S. trading partners as a particularly objectionable nontariff barrier, one which the President agreed to eliminate in the Kennedy Round, but was unable to do so because of congressional inaction.

(D) RULES OF ORIGIN

Once goods have been classified and valued, it is necessary to determine their origin so that the proper tariff rate may be applied. Origin determinations would be unnecessary if tariffs were applied on a uniform, most-favored-nation basis, but increasingly nations have entered into preferential trading arrangements, such as free trade areas, customs unions and various programs favoring developing countries. The result has been that origin problems have become more significant in

30. Act of Sept. 21, 1922, ch. 356, sec. 315, 42 Stat. 941.

31. U.S. Tariff Commn., Customs Valuation: Report to the Senate Comm. on Finance, 93d Cong., 1st Sess. 71 (Comm.Print 1973).

32. U.S. Tariff Commission, Trade Barriers, pt. II, vol. 6, at 193 n. 1 (TC Pub.No. 665, 1974).

33. See Section 6.2(B) supra.

recent years. Moreover, origin determinations have become increasingly necessary to the administration of other non-tariff trade laws: origin-marking requirements, quota administration and application of anti-dumping and countervailing duties. The problems of determining origin have been compounded by recent trends toward global sourcing and multinational manufacturing, where different stages in manufacturing are performed in different countries, in part to take advantage of lower costs, but also in some cases with an eye toward establishing favorable origin. Here we will consider briefly the international rules on origin and then consider how origin rules are typically applied.

(1) The International Rules on Origin

The General Agreement does not treat origin rules per se, although origin marking rules are dealt with in Article IX, which most fundamentally requires MFN treatment. Art. IX:1. The other provisions of Article IX are aimed at minimizing the use of origin marking requirements to hinder trade. For example, countries are to allow origin to be marked at the time of importation (if practicable) and in a way that is not too costly or damaging to the imported product. In addition, there have been various reports and recommendations on origin in GATT.[34] Prior to the Uruguay Round, the principal international agreement dealing with origin issues was the Kyoto Convention, which establishes only very general rules relating to origin.[35]

The Uruguay Round negotiations resulted in a WTO Agreement on Rules of Origin. The agreement calls for the harmonization of non-preferential origin rules through a work program to be undertaken by the WTO Committee on Rules of Origin and the World Customs Organization (WCO). Article 2 of the agreement contains a number of general rules that are applicable to non-preferential origin rules until such time as the harmonization work program is completed. For example, such rules are to be clearly defined; they are not to be used as instruments to pursue trade objectives; they are not by themselves to create restrictive, distorting or disruptive effects on international trade; the rules applicable to imports and exports are not to be more stringent that those applicable for determining domestic origin; they are to be based on positive standards (specification of what is required to achieve origin, not what is insufficient); and certain procedural rights are to be respected. After the harmonization program is completed, Article 3 of the agreement provides that origin rules are to apply equally for all purposes (i.e., for MFN purposes, antidumping and countervailing duty purposes, safeguard purposes, origin marking purposes and any discriminatory quotas or tariffs, as well as for government procurement and trade statistics purposes) and that generally the "last substantial transformation" stan-

34. John H. Jackson, World Trade and the Law of GATT, sec. 17.8 (1969); see also the GATT reports published in: GATT, 1st Supp. BISD 100 (1953); GATT, 2d Supp. BISD 53 (1954); GATT, 5th Supp. BISD 33, 102 (1957).

35. International Convention on the Simplification and Harmonization of Customs Procedures, done at Kyoto May 18, 1973, entered into force Sept. 25, 1974, for the United States, Jan. 28 1984 (subject to reservations). KAV 2259.

dard shall be used to determine origin. That standard may be implemented through the use of such criteria as change in tariff heading, value added or completion of specific processes. The agreement is mainly concerned with non-preferential origin rules, but an annex contains a declaration on preferential rules, which requires, inter alia, that such rules be clearly defined and based on positive standards. The text of the agreement is in the Documents Supplement. As of mid–2001, negotiations on non-preferential origin rules were continuing.

(2) The Application of Origin Rules

The application of origin rules is a complex subject. At the outset, it should be clear that a product made in country A and transshipped via country B to country X is unlikely to be considered to have originated in B when it arrives in X. The difficult question arises when work is performed on a product in two (or more) countries. To take the prior example, how much must be done in B to give the product B origin? If B is the beneficiary of a preferential tariff, should the origin rule be different?

SUPERIOR WIRE v. UNITED STATES

United States Court of International Trade, 1987.
669 F.Supp. 472, affd., 867 F.2d 1409 (Fed.Cir.1989).

RESTANI, JUDGE:

[Superior began importing wire rod from Spain into Canada in 1984 following the imposition of preliminary antidumping and countervailing duties on wire rod imported from Spain into the United States. In a newly-established wire drawing facility in Canada, Superior drew the wire rod into wire before shipping the wire to its wire mesh operation in Michigan. It claimed Canada as the country of origin instead of Spain. Superior's practice continued after the United States entered into a Voluntary Restraint Agreement (VRA) with Spain covering wire and wire rod. In 1987, the Customs Service refused entry to Superior's imports of drawn wire from Canada on the grounds that they were of Spanish origin and lacked the proper certificates that would permit entry under the Spanish VRA.[36]

The process by which rod is drawn into wire is as follows: The rod is uncoiled, cleaned and coated with a lubricant/rust preventative. The rod is then typically drawn through two dies. "The final result is a substantially stronger product, which is also cleaner, smoother, 'less springy,' less ductile, and cross-sectionally more uniform. Seventy percent of the wire imported by [Superior] is intended for use in making wire mesh for concrete sewer pipe reinforcement. * * * The sizes of rod imported produce a range of sizes of wire, but the physical properties of the rod limit the range of sizes of wire which may be effectively or economically produced from a particular size of rod. * * * [T]he chemical content of

---

36. This description of the facts is taken from the CIT and Federal Circuit decisions.

the rod and the cooling processes used in its manufacture determine the properties that the wire will have after drawing. * * * [T]he value added in terms of cost of the drawing process is about fifteen percent."]

The court now turns to the fundamental question of whether under generally applicable precedent a substantial transformation of the wire rod from Spain occurs when it becomes wire, so as to make the wire a product of Canada, and thus not subject to VRA restrictions. The basic test cited by the parties was set forth in a drawback case, Anheuser–Busch Brewing Ass'n v. United States, 207 U.S. 556, 562 (1908), which held that a product would be considered the manufacture or product of the United States if it was transformed into a new and different article "having a distinctive name, character or use." The test has been applied in various situations. * * *

Although all recent cases cite the Anheuser–Busch test, they apply it differently, and modify it somewhat. A name change, for example, is not always considered determinative. Therefore, although it is clear that a name change from "wire rod" to "wire" occurred here, this fact is not necessarily determinative. It may support, however, a finding of substantial transformation, as it did in Ferrostaal [Metals Corp. v. United States, 664 F.Supp. 535 (CIT 1987) (galvanizing of steel sheet effected substantial transformation)]. Likewise the change in tariff classification which occurred here is not dispositive, although it also may be supportive.

In recent years the courts have concentrated on change in use or character, finding various subsidiary tests appropriate depending on the situation at hand. An inquiry that is sometimes treated as a type of cross-check or additional factor to be considered in substantial transformation cases is whether significant value is added or costs are incurred by the process at issue. See United States v. Murray, 621 F.2d 1163 (1st Cir.1980) (blending of glues added no significant value). In National Juice [Prod. Assn. v. United States, 628 F.Supp. 978 (CIT 1986), which involved dilution of concentrated juice], values of between one and eight percent were not found to be significant. In Uniroyal v. United States, 542 F.Supp. 1026 (CIT 1982) (addition of outer sole did not substantially transform shoe upper under marking laws), no percentage was specified, but the cost of the alleged transformation was deemed insignificant. In *Ferrostaal*, on the other hand, a value, attributable to the transformation of at least thirty-six to nearly fifty percent of the value of the heat treated steel, reinforced the court's conclusion that galvanizing and annealing steel constituted a substantial transformation.

A value added test has appeal in many situations because it brings a common sense approach to a fundamental test that may not be easily applied to some products. The fifteen percent added value figure for the wire standing alone does not pull in either direction, but related concepts, including the amount of labor required to accomplish the change and the capital investment required relative to that required to produce the entire article, are also relevant to a determination of whether the change involves minor processing. Minimal processing is part of the factual background of cases such as *Murray, National Juice* and *Uniroyal,* all of which involve findings of no substantial transformation. The differences in capital investment and labor needed in the production of wire rod versus wire are enormous. Comparing only the production of wire from wire rod, versus the production of wire rod from billet, it becomes apparent that the processing performed in Canada is a minor finishing step which may be accomplished easily anywhere with a minimal amount of effort and investment. By itself such analysis may not provide the entire answer as to whether a substantial transformation has taken place, but it should comprise part of the analysis in a case involving the type of products and processes at issue here.

Turning to past precedent, the court observes that cases dealing with substantial transformations are very product specific and are often distinguishable on that basis, rather than by their statutory underpinnings. It is difficult to generalize from cases involving combinations of articles to those that involve processing of a single material. In addition, it is frequently difficult to take concepts applicable to products such as textiles and apply them to combinations of liquids or fabrication of steel articles. To determine whether the goods at hand are substantially transformed for purposes of VRA enforcement, the court should examine cases involving processing of metal objects without combination or assembly operations. Torrington Co. v. United States, 764 F.2d 1563 (1985) is one such case. As indicated, it involved the manufacture of needles in a beneficiary developing country [i.e., a country benefiting from the U.S. Generalized System of Preferences (GSP) for developing countries, which provides duty-free treatment to qualifying imports]. In the first stage of production of needles, a wire is straightened, cut, beveled, and drawn to form a needle blank. The blank is only useful in the needle-making process. In the next stage, an eye is struck into the needle, a groove is made for thread, and the needle is finished by various processes, including hardening, sharpening, and polishing. The *Torrington* court found that in order for plaintiff to prevail under the GSP statute, two substantial transformations were necessary; the court found both the first and second stages to be substantial transformations.

The second stage of processing discussed in the *Torrington* case involved a transformation from producers' to consumers' goods. * * * Although some of the processes involved here are the same as those involved in the second phase of *Torrington*, there is no clear change from producers' to consumers' goods. Wire rod is primarily intended for wire production, which, in turn, is primarily intended to be used for making wire mesh for concrete pipe reinforcement.

The processes involved in the first stage of *Torrington* are closer to the ones involved here. In fact, the *Torrington* court cited in support of its holding a Treasury Decision involving use of dies to draw plate steel into a cup-shaped rear engine housing. Two factors distinguish this aspect of *Torrington* from the case at hand. First, once the needle blanks were drawn they were fit for only one purpose; the raw material was then destined for one end use. This type of transformation does not occur when wire rod is drawn into wire. The composition of the wire rod determines what uses the wire may have. Although the steel and wire industries may have different names for the products, wire rod and wire may be viewed as different stages of the same product. The difference in stages may be important for tariff purposes but it is not determinative here. In contrast, the *Torrington* court stated, "the initial wire is a raw material and possesses nothing in its character which indicated either the swages [blanks] or the final product." Here, the wire rod dictates the final form of the finished wire. Second, the court cannot escape the statutory basis of the *Torrington* opinion. Apart from direct references to the purpose of the GSP already mentioned, the court also noted, " * * * Torrington Portuguesa could do no more than it already does in the production of needles. In these circumstances we think Congress intended the GSP statute to apply."

The engine housing decision cited by *Torrington* also differs from the case at hand. Like the wire to needle blank change, the product was transformed from basic steel into a part with a unique destiny. In addition, the decision noted the involvement of a series of dies. Essentially only two die passes are involved here. The wire emerges stronger and rounder after the passes, but the wire loses a few other advantages, such as greater ductility, in the process. It looks much the same. Its strength characteristic, which is important to its end use, is altered, but the parameters of the strength increase was metallurgically predetermined in the creation of the steel billet and very specifically through the fabrication of the wire rod. Under these circumstances the court does not find a significant change in use or character to have occurred.

The court should also mention here the *Ferrostaal* case. The hot-dipped galvanizing processes involved there, which involved substantial chemical changes, were different from the cold drawing processes involved here. Although, applying broader analytical concepts, the changes in use and character were not greatly different from those involved here, the value added was significant. It appears that a larger capital investment, as well as possibly significant labor, was required to accomplish the transformation in *Ferrostaal*. Taken together these differences are sufficient to distinguish *Ferrostaal* from the case at hand.

Here only the change in name test is clearly met, and such a change has rarely been dispositive. No transformation from producers' to consumers' goods took place; no change from a product suitable for many uses to one with more limited uses took place; no complicated or expensive processing occurred, and only relatively small value was added. Overall, the court views the transformation from wire rod to wire to be minor rather than substantial. Accordingly, the country of origin of the wire must be considered Spain rather than Canada.

Notes and Questions

(1) The *Superior Wire* decision mentions many of the tests used for origin purposes. Although the court focused on the substantial transforma-

tion test, it also considered the impact of (i) a change in four-digit tariff heading, a test used in U.S. and EU free trade area agreements (subject to many exceptions) and (ii) the value added in the claimed country of origin, a standard which is also used extensively in preferential agreements, sometimes as a fall-back provision applicable when there has been no change in tariff heading. There are also special origin rules for certain products that specify in detail the processes that must have been performed on the product in a country in order to obtain origin. For example, the U.S. has special origin rules generally applicable to textile products; the EC for semiconductors.[37] Given the *Anheuser-Busch* test—transformation into a new article having a distinctive name, character or use—was it appropriate for the court to consider the value added in Canada? How relevant is that to determining whether the three *Anheuser-Busch* criteria have been met?

(2) The purpose of the U.S. GSP scheme is to promote trade, while the purpose of a steel VRA is to limit trade. Should these different purposes influence origin decisions? Do you think that the district court in *Superior Wire* was in fact influenced by these purposes? Are you convinced by the court's distinction of *Torrington* in *Superior Wire*? In affirming the *Superior Wire* decision, the Federal Circuit noted that "[o]ur decision, should, therefore, not be understood to entirely rule out consideration of the context in which a country of origin determination must be made." 867 F.2d at 1415 n.2. For a fascinating description of the evolution of CIT and Federal Circuit thinking on this issue, see N. David Palmeter, Rules of Origin in the United States, *in* Rules of Origin in International Trade: A Comparative Study 27, 37–42 (Edwin Vermulst, Jacques Bourgeois & Paul Waer eds., 1994).

(3) Origin rules impact trade and investment decisions. Obviously, they are used to determine origin for applying the appropriate duty rate and other customs rules. As such, in order to gain favorable origin treatment, particularly where value-added rules apply, an exporter may choose to purchase components of its products from suppliers whose goods will help meet the value-added requirement. For example, in order to meet the 62.5% value-added requirement for automobiles under NAFTA, auto assemblers in NAFTA have an incentive to buy NAFTA origin parts so they will more easily meet NAFTA's preferential origin requirements when they export their autos to the other NAFTA members. Similarly, auto part makers may choose to locate their plants where their customers will most benefit from origin rules. When there is some doubt as to whether origin rules can be satisfied, the rules promote investment in the largest market in the free trade area. Do you see why? NAFTA origin rules are explored in Section 11.3(C) infra.

Nonpreferential origin rules may also influence the location and scope of plants built to supply particular markets, especially when the aim is to create origin so as to avoid duties (whether regular, antidumping or counter-

---

37. 19 CFR sec. 12.130 (2001) (certain combining, cutting, trimming, joining and finishing operations not sufficient to confer origin). See Mast Industries, Inc. v. Regan, 596 F.Supp. 1567 (CIT 1984); Note, The 1984 "Country of Origin" Regulations for Textile Imports: Illegal Administrative Action Under Domestic and International Law, 14 Ga.J.Intl. & Comp.L. 573 (1984); Edwin Vermulst & Paul Waer, European Community Rules of Origin as Commercial Policy Instruments?, 24 J.World Trade, June 1990, at 55.

vailing), quotas or other restrictive trade measures. See generally Rules of Origin in International Trade: A Comparative Study (Edwin Vermulst, Jacques Bourgeois & Paul Waer eds., 1994).

(4) Under the U.S. origin rules for GSP treatment, which affords duty-free entry to certain products of developing countries, the product (1) must be transported directly to the United States from the country of origin and (2) the sum of (a) the cost or value of the materials produced in the beneficiary country plus (b) the direct costs of processing operations performed in such country must not be less than 35% of the value of the product when imported into the United States.[38] Under certain circumstances groups of countries may count as one under these rules, e.g., the Andean nations, the ASEAN nations and members of the Caribbean Common Market.[39]

As evidenced by the discussion of the *Torrington* case in *Superior Wire*, the phrase "materials produced in the beneficiary country" includes products manufactured there out of inputs from third countries. One of the difficult determinations that must be made under the GSP and other similar value-added origin tests is whether an input from a third country has been substantially transformed into an intermediate product, which then counts as a beneficiary country product for the value-added test when it is incorporated into the exported product. In *Torrington*, the court found that wire had been transformed into an intermediate product—needle blanks or swages—and permitted the value of the swages to count toward meeting the 35% test for value added in Portugal even though they were made of imported, non-Portuguese wire. Despite the *Torrington* result, courts often find that an intermediate product has not been produced if all of the processing takes place within a single plant. See, e.g., F.F. Zuniga v. United States, 996 F.2d 1203 (Fed.Cir.1993); Azteca Milling Co. v. United States, 890 F.2d 1150 (Fed.Cir.1989).

Similar problems arose under the U.S.-Canada Free Trade Agreement (FTA). In one controversial case, a Japanese automobile maker (Honda) exported automobile engines to Canada after assembly and some manufacture in the U.S.[40] The engines were installed in automobiles in Canada, and Honda then exported the autos to the U.S. The engines contained a substantial component of U.S. materials and labor and were treated as originating in the U.S. by Canadian authorities on their export to Canada. Nonetheless,

---

38. HTS, Headnote 4(c); 19 CFR sec. 10.171–.178 (2001). The EU preferential rules generally focus on whether the four-digit tariff classification number of the product changes, although there are many special exceptions. See Ian S. Forrester, EEC Customs Law: Rules of Origin and Preferential Duty Treatment, 5 Eur.L.Rev. 167, 257 (1980). See generally Thomas P. Cutler, The United States Generalized System of Preferences: The Problem of Substantial Transformation, 5 N.Car.J.Intl.L. & Com.Reg. 393 (1980); UNCTAD, Rules of Origin in the General Scheme of Preferences in Favour of the Developing Countries (U.N. Doc. TD/B/AC.5/3/Rev. 1, 1969).

39. HTS, Headnote 4(a). In the case of the beneficiaries of the Caribbean Basin Economic Recovery Act, if part of the value of a product consists of materials produced in the United States, an amount not to exceed 15% of the products value that is attributed to the United States may be counted toward the 35% requirement. 19 CFR sec. 10.195 (2001).

40. See David Palmeter, The Honda Decision: Rules of Origin Turned Upside Down, CCH Free Trade Law Reports, The Free Trade Observer, No. 32A (June 1992); Frédéric P. Cantin & Andreas F. Lowenfeld, Rules of Origin, The Canada–U.S. FTA, and the *Honda* Case, 87 Am.J.Intl.L. 375 (1993).

U.S. Customs treated them as non-U.S. parts for FTA origin rule purposes when the completed cars were exported from Canada to the United States. For reasons that are too technical to explore here, the U.S. authorities took a different and much stricter view of how to interpret the FTA origin rules than had the Canadians. As a consequence, the automobiles failed (barely) to meet the 50% value-added test specified in the FTA and were subject to the MFN duty on automobiles, rather than being admitted duty free under the FTA. The U.S. and Canada agreed to settle their dispute over the Honda case by using the special origin rules for automobiles in the North American Free Trade Agreement. NAFTA, art. 403. Under those rules, the value on importation of all non-NAFTA origin components will be subtracted from the net cost to see if the 62.5% value-added threshold for automobiles is met. Thus, imported components will not count towards the value-added requirement, even if they have been manufactured into intermediate products. NAFTA, art. 403(1). For goods not subject to the special rules for autos, imported products manufactured into intermediate products would count toward NAFTA origin, just as the needle blanks did in the *Torrington* case. NAFTA, art. 402(4). Why not apply the NAFTA auto origin rule generally and never count imported components to determine if a value-added threshold has been met? See Section 11.3(C) infra.

(5) Assume that a New Zealand owned, but Soviet registered fishing boat catches fish known as New Zealand Hoki in New Zealand's exclusive economic zone or EEZ (i.e., within 200 miles of New Zealand) but outside New Zealand's traditional territorial waters (i.e., beyond 12 miles of New Zealand). Assume further that the fish are beheaded, de-tailed, eviscerated and frozen on the boat and then landed and stored in New Zealand. Then assume that the fish are sent to South Korea for skinning, boning, trimming, glazing and packaging. Should the fish package be marked as a product of the Soviet Union, New Zealand or South Korea? In a case involving these facts, the U.S. Customs Service initially claimed that under the U.S. origin marking statute, 19 U.S.C.A. sec. 1304(a), the fish were a product of the Soviet Union since they were caught on the high seas by a Soviet boat. The exporter claimed they were a product of New Zealand since they were caught in New Zealand territory. The court rejected the latter argument on the grounds that the EEZ could not be considered New Zealand territory under international law, even though New Zealand had preferential rights to resources in its EEZ. The court would have concluded that the fish were a Soviet product except that it found that the fish were substantially transformed in South Korea where they arrived as "headed and gutted" Hoki and left as "individually quick frozen fillets." Koru North America v. United States, 701 F.Supp. 229 (CIT 1988). As a fish consumer, would you find it helpful to read that these fish were a product of South Korea?

(6) The goal of customs law is to establish simple rules that can be consistently applied. In light of the foregoing materials, how close would you say that U.S. origin rules come in meeting this standard? How precise and predictable is the substantial transformation test? What about a change of tariff heading test? Does it take adequate account of the concerns underlying origin rules? Recall that under that test the wire in *Superior Wire* would have had Canadian origin. Would a value added test be sufficiently precise? Or do the problems in Note 4 above suggest that it also is an inadequate

solution? In addition to the problems discussed there, there are difficulties in deciding what non-material and non-labor costs should be counted in determining the value added in each jurisdiction. For NAFTA purposes, origin marking is now based on change of tariff heading rules. See Bestfoods v. United States, 110 F.Supp.2d 965 (CIT 2000)(and prior history); Donna L. Bade, Beyond Marking: Country of Origin Rules and the Decision in CPC International, 31 John Marshall L. Rev. 179 (1997).

(E) OTHER CUSTOMS ISSUES

There are two additional areas of U.S. Customs Law that may be of particular interest: special rules to assist exports and enforcement issues.

(1) Export Promotion: Foreign Trade Zones and Drawback

The aim of customs law is to tax goods that enter the United States for consumption. To the extent goods are not going to be used in the United States, no duty is applied. The simplest example of this principle is embodied in the rules on transit; goods passing through the United States on the way to another destination are not subject to duties.[41] In fact, such goods may even be stored and/or processed in the United States in special bonded customs warehouses.[42]

More complex are rules designed to promote U.S. exports. For example, under the foreign trade zone rules goods may enter a designated foreign trade zone in the United States without payment of duty, be processed and then exported.[43] If the resultant product is "exported" to the United States, duty is assessed on the new product, although arrangements may be made so that duties are assessed on the basis of the amount of the imported goods used in the product sold in the United States.

Similarly, since the aim of the customs law is to tax imported goods consumed in the United States, if imported goods are incorporated in a product that is exported from the United States, there are rules that permit 99% of the duties paid on the incorporated product to be recovered.[44] These so-called drawback rules are also designed to promote the United States as a place for manufacture of export goods. The rules for drawback are procedurally complex and any company hoping to avail itself of the rules should make sure it has complied in all respects in advance of exportation. Special rules on "substitution" are designed to allow drawback on a pro rata basis in the situation where domestic-origin and foreign-origin components are used in producing merchandise.

---

41. See generally 19 U.S.C.A. secs. 1551–65; 19 CFR secs. 18.1–18.45 (2001). Of course, care is taken to exclude the possibility that the goods will be consumed or used in the United States without payment of duty. For example, goods in transit must generally be entered with the customs authorities, transported by bonded carrier and checked out of the United States. See 19 CFR secs. 18.20–18.22 (2001).

42. See generally 19 CFR secs. 19.1–19.96 (2001).

43. See generally 19 U.S.C.A. secs. 81a–81u; 19 CFR secs. 146.0–146.49 (2001).

44. See generally 19 U.S.C.A. sec. 1313; 19 CFR secs. 191.0–191.195 (2001).

Under these rules, if a foreign-origin component was used in a domestically sold item and a like domestic-origin component was used in an exported item, drawback would still be allowed.

Finally, another rule that is designed to promote U.S. manufacturing provides that the value for duty purposes of imported goods assembled abroad of U.S. components is reduced by the value of the U.S. components.[45] This provision provides some incentive for U.S. manufacturers to keep at least part of their production processes in the United States.

(2) Customs Law Enforcement

Section 592 of the Tariff Act of 1930 provides that no person shall enter merchandise into the United States by means of a document or statement that is material and false or by means of an omission that is material.[46] Penalties for this civil violation range from the value of the merchandise in the case of fraud to the lesser of that amount or twice the duties of which the United States is or may be deprived in the case of negligence.[47]

Prior to 1978, the penalty provisions of the U.S. law, which provided for forfeiture in all cases of violation, were claimed to be in violation of GATT Article VIII, paragraph 3, which prohibits substantial penalties for minor breaches.[48]

45. 19 CFR secs. 10.11–10.26 (2001).

46. 19 U.S.C.A. sec. 1592(a)(1). Clerical errors or factual mistakes are not considered violations unless they are part of a pattern of negligence. 19 U.S.C.A. sec. 1592(a)(2).

47. 19 U.S.C.A. sec. 1592(c). If the violation did not affect the assessment of duties, the penalty for negligence may be 20% of the value. The penalties for gross negligence are twice those for negligence (i.e. four times the duties/40% of the value).

48. See American Bar Assn., Section of Intl.Law, Report to the House of Delegates 2–3 (1975) to accompany resolution on section 502 adopted at the August 1975 meeting.

Chapter 9

BORDER MEASURES II: QUOTAS AND NON–TARIFF BARRIERS

Tariffs are the preferred trade barrier under the GATT rules, as we saw in Chapter 8, while quotas and other non-tariff barriers (NTBs) are disfavored. The economic effects of quotas have already been described in the Appendix to Chapter 1. In Section 9.1, we will see that GATT rules generally ban the use of quotas on imports and exports. That ban has not always been easy to implement, however, so we will have occasion to examine certain formal and "informal" exceptions whereby the use of quotas and similar measures was permitted or tolerated. In particular, we will look in Section 9.2 at the history and current use of quotas and similar measures in the areas of textiles and clothing, and in agriculture. In Section 9.3, we will examine GATT rules on state trading, a mechanism that may be used by governments to duplicate the effect of tariffs and quotas. Finally, in Section 9.4, we will consider more generally the WTO's approach to NTBs, with special reference to its rules on transparency.

SECTION 9.1   ARTICLE XI

Article XI is commonly described as GATT's quota prohibition, but it is far broader than that. It provides as follows:

1.   No prohibitions or restrictions *other than duties, taxes or other charges*, whether made effective through quotas, import or export licenses or other measures shall be instituted or maintained by any contracting party on the importation of any product of the territory of any other contracting party or on the exportation or sale for export of any product destined for the territory of any other contracting party. (Emphasis added.)

The broad sweep of this provision underscores the basic philosophy of the General Agreement in respect of import restraints. Such restraints are to be in the form of tariffs, and maximum tariff levels are to be negotiated by the contracting parties. Article XI bans other forms of import restraints, and once imported goods are admitted to a country,

Article III generally prohibits the application to them of discriminatory internal taxes or other regulatory measures.

Probably the most difficult interpretative issue presented by Article XI is defining its scope. By its wording, it applies to all import restrictions "other than duties, taxes or other charges." Obviously, Article XI prohibits straightforward quotas on imports. But to what extent does it cover other measures that adversely affect imports? For example, does it apply to minimum import price requirements or to investment-related performance requirements? How "mandatory" must a government policy be in order to fall within the prohibition?

JAPAN—TRADE IN SEMI–CONDUCTORS
GATT Panel Report Adopted May 4, 1988.
35th Supp. BISD 116 (1989).

[In the mid–1980's, there was considerable friction between the United States and Japan over trade in semi-conductors, which resulted in the initiation of antidumping investigations and a Section 301 investigation of Japanese exports of semi-conductors. Following protracted negotiations, the U.S. and Japan formally concluded an Arrangement concerning Trade in Semi–Conductor Products (the "Arrangement") on September 2, 1986. Under the Arrangement, the U.S. unfair trade investigations were suspended in return for Japanese commitments to expand foreign access to the Japanese semi-conductor market and to prevent dumping.]

99. [After concluding the Arrangement,] the Japanese Government:

— requested Japanese producers and exporters of semi-conductors covered by the Arrangement not to export semi-conductors at prices below company-specific costs [i.e., not to dump, see Chapter 16 infra];

— collected data on company and product-specific costs from producers; introduced a statutory requirement, reinforced by penal servitude not exceeding six months or a fine not exceeding Y 200,000, for exporters of semi-conductors to report data on export prices;

— systematically monitored company and product-specific cost and export price data on semi-conductors which were sold for export to certain contracting parties other than the United States;

— instituted quarterly supply and demand forecasts and communicated to manufacturers its concern about the need to accommodate their production levels to the forecasts as compiled by MITI [Ministry of International Trade and Investment].

[Initially the cost and export price data were examined in connection with the decision on whether to issue an export license under Japan's COCOM regulations. Later, the examination of the data and the COCOM screening process were administratively separated. (COCOM was the international arrangement under which high tech exports to the former Soviet bloc were controlled by the U.S. and its Cold War allies.)]

* * *

102.   The Panel understood the main contentions of the parties to the dispute on the consistency of the measures set out in paragraph 99 with Article XI:1 of the General Agreement to be the following. The EEC considered that such measures constituted restrictions on the sale for export of semi-conductors at prices below company-specific costs through measures other than duties, taxes or charges within the meaning of Article XI:1. Japan contended that there were no governmental measures limiting the right of Japanese producers and exporters to export semi-conductors at any price they wished. The Government's measures to avoid sales at dumping prices were not legally binding and therefore did not fall under Article XI:1. Exports were limited by private enterprises in their own self-interest and such private action was outside the purview of Article XI:1.

103.   As for the export approval system, the EEC [asked the Panel to examine] the delays in the issuing of export licenses resulting from the monitoring of costs and export prices. The EEC considered that these delays constituted restrictions on exportation made effective through export licenses within the meaning of Article XI:1. Japan maintained that the delays in the granting of export licenses resulting from the monitoring of costs and export prices had occurred for purely administrative reasons and did not constitute restrictions within the meaning of Article XI:1, since no export license had ever been denied for reasons related to export pricing.

104.   The Panel examined the parties' contentions in the light of Article XI:1 * * *. The Panel noted that [the wording of Article XI:1] was comprehensive: it applied to all measures instituted or maintained by a contracting party prohibiting or restricting the importation, exportation or sale for export of products other than measures that take the form of duties, taxes or other charges.

105.   The Panel noted that the CONTRACTING PARTIES had decided in a previous case that the import regulation allowing the import of a product in principle, but not below a minimum price level, constituted a restriction on importation within the meaning of Article XI:1. The Panel considered that the principle applied in that case to restrictions on imports of goods below certain prices was equally applicable to restrictions on exports below certain prices.

106.   The Panel then examined the contention of the Japanese Government that the measures complained of were not restrictions within the meaning of Article XI:1 because they were not legally binding or mandatory. In this respect the Panel noted that Article XI:1, unlike other provisions of the General Agreement, did not refer to laws or regulations but more broadly to measures. This wording indicated clearly

that any measure instituted or maintained by a contracting party which restricted the exportation or sale for export of products was covered by this provision, irrespective of the legal status of the measure.

107. Having reached this finding on the basis of the wording and purpose of the provision, the Panel looked for precedents that might be of further assistance to it on this point. It noted that the CONTRACTING PARTIES had addressed a case relating to the interpretation of Article XI:2(c) in the report of the Panel on "Japan—Restrictions on Imports of Certain Agricultural Products." [BISD 35S/163 (1989)] Under Article XI:2(c) import restrictions might be imposed if they were necessary to the enforcement of "governmental measures" restricting domestic supplies. The complaining party argued in the earlier panel proceedings that some of the measures which Japan had described as governmental measures were in fact "only an appeal for private measures to be taken voluntarily by private parties" and could therefore not justify the import restrictions. Japan replied that "to the extent that governmental measures were effective, it was irrelevant whether or not the measures were mandatory and statutory," that the governmental measures "were effectively enforced by detailed directives and instructions to local governments and/or farmers' organizations" and that "such centralized and mutually collaborative structure of policy implementation was the crux of government enforcement in Japan." The Panel which examined that case had noted that "the practice of 'administrative guidance' played an important role" in the enforcement of the Japanese supply restrictions, that this practice was "a traditional tool of Japanese government policy based on consensus and peer pressure" and that administrative guidance in the special circumstances prevailing in Japan could therefore be regarded as a governmental measure enforcing supply restrictions. The Panel recognized the differences between Article XI:1 and Article XI:2(c) and the fact that the previous case was not the same in all respects as the case before it, but noted that the earlier case supported its finding that it was not necessarily the legal status of the measure which was decisive in determining whether or not it fell under Article XI:1.

108. The Panel recognized that not all non-mandatory requests could be regarded as measures within the meaning of Article XI:1. Government-industry relations varied from country to country, from industry to industry, and from case to case and were influenced by many factors. There was thus a wide spectrum of government involvement ranging from, for instance, direct government orders to occasional government consultations with advisory committees. The task of the Panel was to determine whether the measures taken in this case would be such as to constitute a contravention of Article XI.

109. In order to determine this, the Panel considered that it needed to be satisfied on two essential criteria. First, there were reasonable grounds to believe that sufficient incentives or disincentives existed for non-mandatory measures to take effect. Second, the operation of the measures to restrict export of semi-conductors at prices below company-

specific costs was essentially dependent on Government action or intervention. The Panel considered each of these two criteria in turn. The Panel considered that if these two criteria were met, the measures would be operating in a manner equivalent to mandatory requirements such that the difference between the measures and mandatory requirements was only one of form and not of substance, and that there could be therefore no doubt that they fell within the range of measures covered by Article XI:1.

[The Panel concluded, *inter alia*, that at least by April 1987, producers and exporters in Japan knew that the Japanese Government had made an undertaking to the United States to stop dumping, and that a failure by the Government to fulfil the commitment would have adverse consequences for Japan. They also knew that the Government had the fullest information available to identify any producers or exporters selling at prices below costs.]

111.   The Panel considered that, in the above circumstances, the Japanese Government's measures did not need to be legally binding to take effect, as there were reasonable grounds to believe that there were sufficient incentives or disincentives for Japanese producers and exporters to conform. * * *

[The Panel then considered the second criterion—whether the measures were essentially dependent on the Government. In its analysis, the Panel cited Government descriptions of its role, the extensive monitoring scheme and collection of information on costs and export prices, and the government forecasts of supply and demand.]

116.   * * * [Finally,] the Panel noted that Japan had stated in the proceedings of the Panel that "although monitoring by MITI was limited in scope, it was still meaningful because MITI represented a neutral and objective figure overseeing the entire industry while taking into account costs and prices among competing companies in Japan. Monitoring also helped to stamp out suspicion among companies that others were cheating or resorting to dumping." Japan had further stated that "if the semiconductor manufacturers were to pursue their own profits and ignore MITI's concern, the whole dumping prevention mechanism would collapse," and that "the administration presents (firms) with objective facts and considerations and others that are usually not obtainable by one firm alone." The Panel considered that these statements concerning the way in which the Government exercised its authority were a further confirmation of the fact that the Government's involvement was essential to the prevention of sales below company-specific costs.

117.   All these factors led the Panel to conclude that an administrative structure had been created by the Government of Japan which operated to exert maximum possible pressure on the private sector to cease exporting at prices below company-specific costs. This was exercised through such measures as repeated direct requests by MITI, combined with the statutory requirement for exporters to submit information on export prices, the systematic monitoring of company and

product-specific costs and export prices and the institution of the supply and demand forecasts mechanism and its utilization in a manner to directly influence the behavior of private companies. These measures operated furthermore to facilitate strong peer pressure to comply with requests by MITI and at the same time to foster a climate of uncertainty as to the circumstances under which their exports could take place. The Panel considered that the complex of measures exhibited the rationale as well as the essential elements of a formal system of export control. The only distinction in this case was the absence of formal legally binding obligations in respect of exportation or sale for export of semi-conductors. However, the Panel concluded that this amounted to a difference in form rather than substance because the measures were operated in a manner equivalent to mandatory requirements. The Panel concluded that the complex of measures constituted a coherent system restricting the sale for export of monitored semi-conductors at prices below company-specific costs to markets other that the United States, inconsistent with Article XI:1.

118.   The Panel then reverted to the issue raised by the EEC concerning the delays of up to three months in the issuing of export licenses that had resulted from the monitoring of costs and export prices of semi-conductors destined for contracting parties other than the United States. It examined whether the measures taken by Japan constituted restrictions on exportation or sale for export within the meaning of Article XI:1. It noted that the CONTRACTING PARTIES had found in a previous case that automatic licensing did not constitute a restriction within the meaning of Article XI:1 and that an import license issued on the fifth working day following the day on which the license application was lodged could be deemed to have been automatically granted. The Panel recognized that the above applied to import licenses but it considered that the standard applicable to import licenses should, by analogy, be applied also to export licenses because it saw no reason that would justify the application of a different standard. The Panel therefore found that export licensing practices by Japan, leading to delays of up to three months in the issuing of licenses for semi-conductors destined for contracting parties other than the United States, had been non-automatic and constituted restrictions on the exportation of such products inconsistent with Article XI:1.

[The Panel also concluded that the violation could not be excused by Article VI relating to dumping, since that article only authorized action by importing countries.]

Notes and Questions

(1) The *Japanese Semi-conductor* case is important because of its analysis of how GATT rules apply to voluntary export restraints. We examine such restraints in Chapter 15, which deals with the Escape Clause (Article XIX) and safeguard measures generally.

(2) In a 1999 case, *India—Quantitative Restrictions on Imports of Agricultural, Textile and Industrial Products*, WT/DS90/R, adopted by the DSB

on September 22, 1999, a panel found that certain Indian measures—discretionary (non-automatic) import licensing systems; canalization of certain imports through government agencies; and a system allowing imports of certain products only by actual users, which precluded imports of consumer goods by wholesalers or retailers—violated Article XI:1. India had notified the measures as quantitative restrictions, but claimed that they were permitted for balance-of-payments reasons. This defense was rejected, as explained in Chapter 22.

(3) Related to the question of what sort of measure is a governmental measure is the question of how to deal with actions taken by state trading companies. Consider the Interpretative Note Ad Articles XI–XIV & XVIII, which provides that the terms "import restrictions" and "export restrictions" in those articles include restrictions made effective through state-trading operations. We discuss the problems associated with state trading companies in Section 9.3.

(4) Article XI speaks of "prohibitions or restrictions * * * *on the importation* of any product." Does this phrase include measures that are applied after importation if those measures deter or effectively prevent the import of products by making it difficult or impossible to sell them? In this regard, is there any significance to the difference in wording in Article XI between the phrase dealing with "importation" and that dealing with "exportation or sale for export".

In 1984, a GATT panel analyzed Canadian practices whereby foreign companies were permitted to invest in manufacturing plants in Canada only if they undertook that those plants would purchase inputs and other goods of Canadian origin in preference to imported goods. In response to a U.S. argument that this practice violated Article XI, the panel responded:[1]

> The Panel shares the view of Canada that the General Agreement distinguishes between measures affecting the "importation" of products, which are regulated in Article XI:1, and those affecting "imported products," which are dealt with in Article III. If Article XI:1 were interpreted broadly to cover also internal requirements, Article III would be partly superfluous. Moreover, the exceptions to Article XI:1, in particular those contained in Article XI:2, would also apply to internal requirements restricting imports, which would be contrary to the basic aim of Article III. The Panel did not find, either in the drafting history of the General Agreement or in previous cases examined by the CONTRACTING PARTIES, any evidence justifying such an interpretation of Article XI.

The Uruguay Round on Trade–Related Investment Measures (TRIMs) provides that it violates Article XI:1 for a government to (i) restrict imports by an enterprise, either generally or by reference to its exports, or (ii) restrict exports, either in terms of specific products, in terms of volume or value of products, or in terms of a proportion of its local production. TRIMS Agreement, Annex, Illustrative List, para. 2. See Documents Supplement. We will consider in Chapter 12 how Article III deals with restrictions on imported products and with trade-related investment measures. In that regard, consid-

---

1. Canada—Administration of the Foreign Investment Review Act, GATT, 30th   Supp. BISD 140, para. 5.14 (Panel report adopted Feb. 7, 1984).

er whether the division in the TRIMs Agreement between the measures that are deemed to violate Article III:4 and those that violate Article XI:1 supports the panel's distinction. The TRIMs Agreement is examined in Chapter 24.

(5) The Interpretative Note Ad Article III provides that an internal tax or regulation that is applied to imported and domestic products and is collected or enforced in the case of the imported product at the border is nevertheless to be regarded as an internal tax or regulation subject to Article III. Does this note support the distinction made by the panel in the preceding note or does it mean only that Article III applies, without implying anything about the application of Article XI? In practice, GATT and WTO panels have tended to examine non-state trading measures applying to both imported and domestic products under Article III and not Article XI, but the issue is often not discussed, so the precise relationship of the two articles remains somewhat unclear.

(6) Assuming that an exception to Article XI:1 applies, must quotas be utilized consistently with the MFN obligation of Article I? Is it consistent with MFN treatment to allocate quota shares among WTO members? See Article XIII.

(7) When quotas are imposed, a licensing system is often used to determine who has the right to import under the quota. One of the Tokyo Round agreements was the Agreement on Import Licensing Procedures.[2] The basic provision of the Agreement—Article 1(3)—calls for the rules for import licensing procedures to be "neutral in application and administered in a fair and equitable manner." Article 1 of the Agreement requires the relevant rules and changes to them and the products to which they apply to be published promptly. It calls for forms and procedures to be kept "simple," and bans refusals of applications for minor documentation errors. It also provides that importations shall not be refused for minor deviations in value, weight or quantity from the licensed amount. Additional provisions in Article 3 require that all persons meeting the importing country's legal requirements be eligible to apply for licenses. In allocating licenses, consideration is to be given to an applicant's past performance and to ensuring a reasonable distribution of licenses to new importers, particularly those importing products from the least developed countries or developing countries. The provisions of the Agreement are essentially designed to prevent licensing procedures from constituting trade barriers in themselves. The Agreement was modified in the Uruguay Round, but the above-mentioned basic provisions were carried forward.

(8) GATT rules and the Import Licensing Agreement do not mandate how quotas are to be allocated among individual suppliers (as opposed to countries). Under the general U.S. rules on quota procedures, the United States in theory allocates quotas on a first-come, first-served basis, which involves some risk for an exporter since the goods may arrive at U.S. customs just as the quota has been filled. See 19 CFR sec. 132 (2001). In fact, the U.S. often relies on special arrangements with exporting countries, rather than these general rules. As we saw in the *Generra* and *Superior Wire* cases in the preceding chapter, entry to the United States was contingent on

---

2. GATT, 26th Supp. BISD 154 (1980).

presentation of a document issued by the exporting country. One interesting development in U.S. law with respect to quotas was the authorization in the 1988 Trade Act of the use of auctions to distribute quotas. One of the principal criticisms of quotas has been that they allow the foreign supplier to capture monopoly profits in the form of higher, scarcity-induced prices in the importing countries (compared to tariffs, which would have a similar effect, but benefit the government through higher tax collections). The sales of quota rights by auction would allow the government to capture these monopoly profits. Would the auction of quota rights be permissible under GATT rules? Consider Articles II and VIII.

(9) In the EC Treaty, Article 28 [formerly 30] provides: "Quantitative restrictions on imports and all measures having equivalent effect shall * * * be prohibited between Member States." Is this broader, narrower or the same as GATT Article XI:1? The EC Court of Justice initially gave Article 28 a much broader reading than the GATT panel gave Article XI:1 in the *Canadian Foreign Investment* case quoted above. In PROCUREUR DU ROI v. DASSONVILLE, Case 8/74, [1974] ECR 837, the Court stated:

> All trading rules enacted by the Member States which are capable of hindering, directly or indirectly, actually or potentially, intra-Community trade are to be considered as measures having an effect equivalent to quantitative restrictions.

This broad reading of Article 28 has led the Court of Justice to uphold challenges to many Member States measures. See George A. Bermann et al., European Community Law ch. 13 (2d ed. 2002). Is Article XI:1 capable of supporting a similarly broad reading? Should it be given one? In recent years, the Court of Justice has cut back on its expansive reading of Article 28. Keck & Mithouard, Cases C–267 & 268/91, 1993 ECR–I 6097. We will consider the EC approach to discrimination against imports in more detail in Section 14.4.

A Note on Export Controls

International trade policy and rules tend to focus on market access issues, with the goal of reducing import restrictions. However, exports are mentioned in GATT in at least 13 clauses and are related to obligations in several others.[3] The most significant obligations in GATT relating to treatment of exports are the most-favored-nation treatment obligation of Article I, and the ban on prohibitions and quantitative restrictions of Article XI, which applies to exports as well as imports. Problems stemming from export promotion activities, such as subsidies, will be treated in Chapter 18. Of course, GATT clauses that apply generally to customs procedures, in many cases apply to those procedures affecting exports as well as imports.[4] The basic problem with GATT obligations relating to exports, however, stems

---

3. See generally Michael Rom, Export Controls in GATT, 18 J.World Trade L. 125 (1984). GATT Art. I (MFN), para. 1; Art. VI (antidumping), paras. 1, 5, 6(b), 7(a); Art. VIII (fees and formalities), paras. 1, 4; Art. IX (marks of origin), para. 2; Art. X (publication), para. 1; Art. XI (quantitative restrictions), paras. 1, 2; Art. XIII (nondiscriminatory administration of quantitative restrictions), paras. 1, 5; Art. XVI (subsidies), Section B; Art. XX (general exceptions), paras. (i), (j); see John H. Jackson, World Trade and the Law of GATT 497–506 (1969).

4. See, e.g., GATT Arts. VIII and IX: (9).

from two facts: 1) There is no GATT obligation against the use of export taxes or fees; and 2) the exception to the GATT obligations restraining use of export restrictions are quite broad.

While Article XI prohibits export restrictions, it provides an exception for restrictions "temporarily applied to prevent or relieve critical shortages of foodstuffs or other products essential to the exporting contracting party."[5] Article XX provides two broad and vague exceptions for restrictions on exports "necessary to ensure essential quantities of such materials to a domestic processing industry during periods when the domestic price of such materials is held below the world price as part of a government stabilization plan,"[6] and restrictions "essential to the acquisition or distribution of products in general or local short supply," provided that an equitable share principle is followed.[7] With these exceptions, a WTO member has considerable discretion to apply export restrictions. In the cases where it feels restrained by GATT rules from using quantitative restrictions, it can, of course, utilize export taxes or fees.

There have been relatively few complaints in GATT/WTO about export restrictions.[8] In 1949, Czechoslovakia brought a complaint against the United States in respect of controls that the US had imposed on exports to Czechoslovakia, arguing that the US controls discriminated against Czechoslovakia. The US controls were part of the national security measures imposed by the US on trade with the Soviet Bloc during the Cold War. The Contracting Parties, however, formally decided that the United States had not "failed to carry out its obligations under the Agreement through its administration of the issue of export licenses." The principal recent case on export controls was the *Japanese Semiconductor* case, excerpted above.

In the 1970's, many countries became concerned about export restrictions, particularly on oil as a result of the Arab oil embargo on the US and the Netherlands, but also on other commodities as a result of the US export restrictions on soybeans imposed in 1973 to relieve domestic shortages. These concerns resulted in negotiations on the subject of access to supplies of raw materials and finished goods in the Tokyo Round. These negotiations were difficult because they raised questions concerning national sovereignty over natural resources. The only result was an understanding that the GATT export provisions should be reassessed in the near future.[9] Except for negotiations on safeguards, export controls were not a significant issue in the Uruguay Round. It is worth noting, however, that in recent years, there has been increased concern over regulating exports of waste or domestically-banned products.[10]

---

5. GATT Art. XI, para. 2(a).

6. GATT Art. XX, para. (i).

7. GATT Art. XX, para. (j).

8. See Frieder Roessler, GATT and Access to Supplies, 9 J.World Trade L. 25, 30 (1975).

9. See GATT, The Tokyo Round of Multilateral Trade Negotiations: Report by the Director–General of GATT 152 (1979).

10. Joy Clairmont, Imports and Exports of Hazardous Waste: Implementation of OECD Council Decision C(92)39 Concerning the Transfrontier Movements of Recoverable Wastes, 3 Environmental Lawyer 545 (Feb. 1997).

The potential for future disputes over export controls should not be underemphasized, however. They figured prominently in the relationships between nations prior to World War II and arguably were one of the causes, or at least a trigger, of the outbreak of that war in the Pacific.[11]

In the case of the United States, the Constitution prohibits export taxes, but the US imposes other export restrictions. Under the Export Administration Act, the President is given the power to "prohibit or curtail the export of any goods subject to the jurisdiction of the United States or exported by any person subject to the jurisdiction of the United States" for reasons of national security, foreign policy or short supplies.[12] The Department of Commerce has primary responsibility for the administration of the EAA, and its Bureau of Export Administration has issued extensive regulations based on the Act.[13] The State Department is in charge of arms exports. The US cooperates with its NATO and other allies to control exports of so-called dual-use goods–those goods that are not munitions, but that may be used for both military and non-military purposes. It is important to bear in mind that other U.S. regulations may restrict export transactions with certain countries, such as those subject to general economic sanctions implemented by the President under the International Emergency Economic Powers Act. We discuss sanctions for political and national security purposes in Chapter 21 infra.

SECTION 9.2   EXCEPTIONS TO ARTICLE XI

The General Agreement contains two important exceptions to the quota ban in Article XI:1. First, Article XI:2 permits the use of (a) export restrictions to relieve critical shortages, (b) import and export restrictions necessary to apply certain commodity standards and (c) import restrictions to enforce certain government agricultural programs. Second, Articles XII and XVIII permit the use of quotas in the event of balance-of-payments problems. In addition, in practice many GATT parties have historically used quotas or similar measures to restrict imports of clothing and textile products and of agricultural products (other than under Article XI:2). As described below, one of the most important achievements of the Uruguay Round was to make those products effectively subject to the disciplines of Article XI:1. In this section, we look briefly at the use of quotas and similar measures to restrict imports of agricultural and clothing and textiles products. The balance-of-payments exception is analyzed in Chapter 22.

11. James H. Herzog, Closing the Open Door: American–Japanese Diplomatic Negotiations 1936–1941, at 92–101, 163–86, Naval Inst. Press (1973); Herbert Feis, The Road to Pearl Harbor: The Coming of the War Between the United States and Japan 107–09, 205–08, 267–70 (1950).

12. See 50 U.S.C.A.App. secs. 2404(a), 2405(a), 2406(a). In the case of national security controls, the authorization to con-trol extends to technology, as well as goods. 50 U.S.C.A.App. sec. 2404(a). In the case of foreign policy controls, it extends to technology or other information. 50 U.S.C.A.App. sec. 2405(a).

13. 15 CFR pts. 730–74 (2001). See William A. Root & John R. Liebman, United States Export Controls (4th ed. 2000).

(A) AGRICULTURAL PRODUCTS[1]

Historically, GATT rules were not rigorously applied to agricultural trade, on either the import or export side. As for agricultural imports, the United States obtained a waiver from the Article XI quota ban for certain of its agricultural programs in 1955.[2] Although few other formal waivers were granted in respect of agricultural products, other countries sometimes acted as if they viewed the U.S. waiver as generally applicable. This lack of discipline was also exemplified by the agricultural trade policies of the European Community. In constructing its Common Agricultural Policy (CAP), the EC unbound most of its tariffs on agricultural products, which meant that it was free to charge any import duty it wished on those products. In fact, the EC often implemented the CAP by using variable levies, which were flexible import charges set (and adjusted regularly) so as to make imported agricultural products more expensive than the comparable EC product. They effectively kept imports out of the European market. Developing countries often claimed authority to impose quotas on agricultural products pursuant to the balance-of-payments exception. While GATT panel decisions in the late 1970's and 1980's strictly enforced the agricultural exceptions in Article XI:2, the import restrictions applied by the U.S., the EC and developing countries were not challenged (and may not have been challengeable) under Article XI. One of the main issues in the Uruguay Round was how to reestablish GATT disciplines on agricultural trade.

In the Uruguay Round Agreement on Agriculture, WTO members agreed to convert their nontariff import restrictions on agricultural products to tariffs and not to use such restrictions in the future except pursuant to the Agreement's special safeguard provisions and certain exceptions.[3] The initial tariffs have been set to approximate the current level of protection, but are to be reduced by 36% over a six-year period (24% over 10 years for developing countries). Current market access is to be maintained and certain minimum market access is to be provided if current access is less than three percent of domestic production (rising to five percent over the implementation period).[4] As a result of the tariffication commitment, the exceptions for agricultural programs in Article XI:2 are of little importance today.

Agricultural trade flows are often affected by national subsidies paid to farmers. These subsidies may result in a significant expansion in production of agricultural products, which causes pressures to restrict competing imports and to subsidize exports to get rid of surpluses. In the Uruguay Round Agreement on Agriculture, developed WTO members agreed to cut certain specified domestic subsidies by 20% over the

---

1. See generally Davey, The Rules for Agricultural Trade in GATT, in M. Honma, A. Shimizu & H. Funatsu (eds.), GATT and Trade Liberalization in Agriculture (1993).

2. Decision of March 5, 1955, 3rd Supp. BISD 32.

3. WTO Agreement on Agriculture, art. 4(2).

4. GATT Focus, December 1993, at 6.

specified implementation period.[5] One aim of the agreement is to promote the use of subsidies that do not promote production or distort trade flows, such as those aim at only income support for farmers.[6]

Article XVI:3 of the General Agreement was designed to limit export subsidies on primary products. It did not ban them, but provided that they should not be used to obtain a "more than equitable share of world export trade" in a product, a concept that was refined in the Tokyo Round Subsidies Code.[7] In practice, however, the use of export subsidies on primary products was not effectively controlled by the "equitable share" language. While one early, pre-Subsidies Code GATT decision suggested that this standard could be used to control effectively the use of export subsidies,[8] a later decision by a panel appointed under the Subsidies Code essentially concluded that the language was too imprecise to be applied to world wheat trade.[9] The panel was criticized by some for having abdicated its responsibility, and its report was never adopted by the Subsidies Code governing committee, the body responsible for dispute settlement under the Subsidies Code. Indeed, one result of the decision was that dispute settlement under the Subsidies Code broke down completely during the 1980's as one or more signatories blocked the adoption of all subsequent panel reports issued under the Code's dispute settlement provisions during that time period.

The Uruguay Round Agreement on Agriculture takes a different approach to controlling agricultural export subsidies. It requires that they be reduced over the implementation period, compared to a 1986–1990 base period, by 36% in terms of value and by 21% in respect of the volume of exports benefiting from them.[10] (The WTO Subsidies Agreement now bans the use of export subsidies, but it is explicitly made subject to the Agreement on Agriculture.)

It remains to see how much the Uruguay Round Agreement on Agriculture increases agricultural trade. The commitments described above are generally limited in scope and time. It is obviously unknown at this point whether and to what extent these commitments will be extended in the future. Many countries are very concerned with the security of their food supplies, and it will very difficult to convince them to take measures that will result in their basic foodstuffs (e.g., rice in the case of Japan and Korea) being significantly supplied by imports as

5. GATT Focus, December 1993, at 7.

6. See WTO Agreement on Agriculture, annex 2.

7. Agreement on Interpretation and Application of Articles VI, XVI and XXIII of the General Agreement on Tariffs and Trade (the Subsidies Code), art. 10; 26th Supp. BISD 56, 69.

8. French Assistance to Exports of Wheat and Wheat Flour, 7th Supp. BISD 46; see also European Communities—Refunds on Exports of Sugar, 26th Supp. BISD 290; European Communities—Re-

funds on Exports of Sugar—Complaint by Brazil, 27th Supp. BISD 69.

9. European Economic Community—Subsidies on Exports of Wheat Flour, GATT Doc. SCM/42. See 31st Supp. BISD 259. The text of the report can be found in 18 BNA U.S. Export Weekly 899–916 (1983).

10. WTO Agreement on Agriculture, art. 9(2)(b)(iv). For developing countries, the respective percentages are 24% and 14%.

opposed to domestic production. For many countries this is a matter of national security.[11]

The Agreement on Agriculture provided for further negotiations on agricultural trade, which started in 2000. It is too early to tell how successful they will be. On one side are those that want to eliminate export subsidies and improve market access. On the other, are those that want recognition that agricultural subsidies serve multiple purposes (e.g., environmental, rural preservation and development) and therefore should not be subject to strict controls.

(B) CLOTHING AND TEXTILE PRODUCTS

GATT SECRETARIAT STUDY, TEXTILES AND CLOTHING IN THE WORLD ECONOMY
6–8, 74–76, 82–83 (1984)

The most common feature of trade policies in the textiles (and later clothing) area over the past century is the above-average level of government intervention. With the exception of the United Kingdom and Japan, tariff protection of the textile industry has been commonplace from the nineteenth century to the present. Stimulated by the Great Depression and competition from Japan, the interwar period witnessed a dramatic increase in protection of the mature textile industries against competition from Japan, other newcomers and one another. The first known voluntary export restraint (VER) in textiles, involving Japan's textile exports to the United States, was adopted in 1936.

Most of the developed countries, particularly in Western Europe, began the postwar period with very restrictive trade régimes. As the 1950s progressed, many of these policies were liberalized under the auspices of the GATT and the Organization for European Economic Cooperation (OEEC). Trade policies affecting textiles, and in particular discriminatory policies against Japan, some developing countries, and some East European countries not only remained mainly untouched by this liberalization, but tended to increase in restrictiveness.

During the early postwar years, a number of developing countries either continued to apply import-substitution policies for textiles, or introduced such programmes for the first time. * * *

Japan's accession to the GATT in 1955, the move to external convertibility of West European currencies in 1958 (which removed the balance-of-payments justification for existing quantitative restraints) and the emergence of important developing country exporters combined to create pressure for alternative approaches to controlling "low wage imports" into the industrial countries. * * *

---

11. See generally McGeorge, Accommodating Food Security Concerns in a World of Comparative Advantage: A Challenge for GATT's International Trade System, 71 Nebraska L. Rev. 368 (1992).

Although cotton textiles and clothing were not the only products caught up in this process, they were clearly the main concern, as is evidenced by the fact that they have been the only products to be formally exempted from the regular GATT rules and given a régime of their own. Initially this took the form of the Short–Term Arrangement Regarding International Trade in Textiles (the STA), which was in force from October 1961 until September 1962. In October 1962 the Long–Term Arrangement Regarding International Trade in Cotton Textiles (the LTA) came into force, lasting (with extensions) until 1973.

These agreements were significant events in GATT's history. An important part of world trade was formally exempted from GATT rules, in particular the non-discrimination rule and the general prohibition of quantitative restrictions. The new rules operated principally to affect exports from Japan and the developing countries.

Notes and Questions

(1) The LTA was replaced by the Multifibre Arrangement (MFA) in 1974. The MFA was modified from time to time, but remained in effect until the WTO Agreement came into force in 1995. Over time, the MFA came to cover a much broader range of textiles than cotton textiles. It permitted the use of safeguard mechanisms in certain defined circumstances, but provided for the growth over time in the quotas imposed on textile and clothing imports. Developing countries were particularly dissatisfied with this treatment of clothing and textile products and the issue of bringing GATT disciplines back into this sector was a major one in the Uruguay Round.

(2) The WTO Agreement on Textiles and Clothing (ATC) provides for the gradual reintegration of textile and clothing products into the General Agreement, so that they will in the future be subject to normal GATT rules.[12] As a first step, the ATC requires that

> [o]n the entry into force of the WTO Agreement, each Member shall integrate into GATT 1994 products which accounted for not less than 16 per cent of the total volume of the Member's 1990 imports of the products in the Annex, in terms of [Harmonized System] lines or categories. The products to be integrated shall encompass products from each of the following four groups: tops and yarns, fabrics, made-up textile products, and clothing.[13]

An additional 17 per cent are to be reintegrated at the beginning of the fourth year; 18 per cent at the beginning of the eighth year and the rest (49 per cent) at the beginning of the eleventh year.[14] In addition, remaining MFA quotas are to be expanded faster than had been agreed upon under the MFA.[15] The agreement allows the use of special transitional safeguard measures, but once textile and clothing products have been reintegrated into GATT, the Escape Clause of Article XIX, as interpreted by the Safeguards

---

12. See generally 1 Terence P. Stewart (ed.), The GATT Uruguay Round: A Negotiating History (1986–1992), at 255–361 (1993).

13. ATC, art. 2(6).

14. ATC, art. 2(8).

15. ATC, art. 2(13)-(14).

Agreement, would be the applicable safeguard provision.[16] See Chapter 15 supra.

(3) Developing countries have been quite dissatisfied with the implementation of the ATC by the US, the EC and Canada. To date, one-third of tariff lines, as defined above, have been reintegrated, but in fact there were few restrictions imposed on products falling under those lines. Thus, developing countries feel that the benefits they were promised have yet to materialize. See generally Chapter 25 infra.

(4) In mid–2001, there were proposals that a special trading regime should be established for steel products. Would that be a good idea?[17]

SECTION 9.3   STATE TRADING

(A) THE INTERFACE PROBLEM[1]

A basic structural assumption of the General Agreement is an international, free market system for trading. Many GATT rules make sense only in the context of such a market system. They restrict the types of regulations which governments can impose on international traders, but do not purport to regulate the traders themselves. If the government is the trader or controls the trader, the rules may be ineffective since decisions ostensibly made independently by the trader may in fact reflect actions of the government.

This problem can be seen in a number of different contexts. For example, how can the GATT Article XI rule against use of quantitative restrictions—one of the basic principles of the General Agreement—be applied effectively where a government agency or a government-controlled company determines import and export levels through its purchasing and sales decisions? Even more basic, how can negotiations over tariff levels—one of the essential subjects of GATT negotiations—be meaningful if import levels are determined not by tariffs and prices, but rather by economic plans or decisions of government-controlled import monopolies? The following hypothetical situation illustrates this problem.

Let us assume that country M, a market economy country, and country S, a state trading country, are both members of the WTO. The General Agreement limits the use of quantitative restrictions on the importation of goods in Article XI, and provides for negotiation leading to tariff bindings under Article II that restrict the level of tariffs that a country can impose on its imports from other GATT members. Suppose countries M and S have negotiated between themselves and M has promised to bind its tariff on bicycles and widgets at no more than 10%. Suppose S has agreed to bind its tariffs on automobiles and gadgets at no more than 8% and 12%, respectively. In the case of M, private traders

---

16. ATC, art. 6.

17. The problems of the steel industry were treated in Chapter 26.4 of the 1995 edition of this casebook.

1. See generally Interface One (Don Wallace et al. eds., 1980).

will send goods to M, with the confidence that they will be able to import them without incurring more than a 10% tariff charge. They can price their goods accordingly and proceed to import goods. If the tariff has been higher previously, the lower price allowed by the lower tariff should result in an increase in imports.

In the case of S, however, importing is accomplished only through a state trading monopoly, which is regulated by the government and pursues its import plans according to the economic plan of the country (and other foreign policy considerations). If the state trading monopoly can decide, as a matter of enterprise decision, to import no more than a given quantity of automobiles or gadgets, or to import those only from country A or B, rather than M, the fact that S's tariff on M's automobiles and gadgets has been lowered would not necessarily result in an increase of imports. If the import monopoly has complete discretion in determining the sales price of the imports, it may offset the effect of a tariff reduction by raising prices. Consequently, M may not receive reciprocal benefits for its trade concessions to S. S can sell more goods to M, through M's private traders; but M cannot sell more goods to S, if S's state trading agency has simply decided not to purchase more goods or to maintain prior retail prices.

In an oversimplified form, this hypothetical situation illustrates the major problem of establishing trade relations between nonmarket economies on the one hand, and the industrialized free market economies on the other. The same problem arises, of course, to a lesser degree in relations between market economies wherever state trading monopolies exist. This problem is not the only one. Other GATT rules can be applied to nonmarket economies only with great difficulty. For example, the dumping rules require comparing export prices of a product to its normal value in the home market. But in a nonmarket economy there is no freely determined price in that economy to which the export price can be compared. Similarly, how can the rules against subsidies be applied when government control so permeates an economy that either everything or nothing can be considered a subsidy?

In the next section, we review Articles XVII and II:4—the GATT provisions dealing with state trading and nonmarket economies. You should consider whether these provisions adequately address the problems raised in the foregoing paragraphs. In particular, consider whether they are sufficient to deal with the problems that would be presented by the accession to the WTO of countries still in transition to market economy status.

(B) GATT REGULATION OF STATE TRADING[2]

(1) State Trading Enterprises Defined

The principal GATT provision regulating state trading is Article

---

2. See generally Thomas Cottier & Petros C. Mavroidis, eds., State Trading in the Twenty–First Century (1998); John H. Jackson, World Trade and the Law of GATT, ch. 14 (1969); M.M. Kostecki, East–West Trade and the GATT System (1978); Edmond M. Ianni, The International Treatment of State Trading, 16 J. World Trade

XVII, which applies to state trading enterprises.[3] Exactly what enterprises are covered by Article XVII? By its terms, Article XVII applies to "State enterprises" and enterprises to which a party has granted "exclusive or special privileges." These terms have been further refined through various GATT actions. For example, the 1994 Understanding on Article XVII adopts the following "working definition" of state trading enterprises:

> Governmental and non-governmental enterprises, including marketing boards, which have been granted exclusive or special rights or privileges, including statutory or constitutional powers, in the exercise of which they influence through their purchases or sales the level or direction of imports or exports.

In addition, a 1960 report, which was adopted by the GATT contracting parties, discussed the meaning of "enterprise" as follows:[4]

> 21. [T]he Panel did not use the word "enterprise" to mean any instrumentality of government. There would be nothing gained in extending the scope of the notification provisions of Article XVII to cover governmental measures that are covered by other articles of the General Agreement. * * *

More recently, the WTO has adopted an illustrative list:

ILLUSTRATIVE LIST OF RELATIONSHIPS BETWEEN GOVERNMENTS AND STATE TRADING ENTERPRISES AND THE KINDS OF ACTIVITIES ENGAGED IN BY THESE ENTERPRISES

(Adopted by the WTO Goods Council on October 15, 1999).

I. INTRODUCTORY COMMENTS

1. Pursuant to paragraph 5 of the Understanding on the Interpretation of Article XVII of the General Agreement on Tariffs and Trade 1994 ("the Understanding"), this Illustrative List shows the kinds of relationships which exist between governments and state trading enterprises and the kinds of activities which such enterprises engage in, which may be relevant for the purposes of Article XVII. It is based on the Article XVII notifications made since 1980.

2. The List does not represent a definition of what constitutes a state trading enterprise or an attempt to further refine or interpret the definition of "state trading enterprise" as provided in Article XVII of GATT 1994 and its Interpretative Notes or the working definition contained in the Understanding. Rather, the List is based on a catalogue

L. 480 (1982); Eliza R. Patterson, Improving GATT Rules for Non–Market Economies, 20 J. World Trade L. 185 (1986).
3. William J. Davey, Article XVII GATT: An Overview, in Cottier & Mavroidis, supra note 2, at 17.

4. Notifications of State–Trading Enterprises, Final Report adopted on May 24, 1960, 9th Supp. BISD 179, 183–84 (1961).

of those relationships and entities which have been previously included in notifications and, as such, reflects examples of relationships with governments and activities which various individual Members considered relevant in their notification of state trading enterprises. While this List reflects the past practice of individual Members rather than consensus standards, Members could find the List useful in guiding their notification decisions.

* * *

II. USER'S GUIDE TO THE ILLUSTRATIVE LIST

5. It is recalled that three fundamental elements are identified in the working definition of "state trading enterprise" contained in paragraph 1 of the Understanding:

(i) a governmental or non-governmental entity, including marketing boards;

(ii) the granting to the enterprise of exclusive or special rights or privileges; and

(iii) a resulting influence, through the enterprise's purchases or sales, on the level or direction of imports or exports.

6. Thus, a notifiable state trading enterprise has a relationship to the government through the latter's granting of a right or privilege and conducts an activity which influences the level or direction of imports or exports. It is suggested that, by looking at the type of relationship the entity has with the government as a result of the latter's granting of an exclusive or special right or privilege, at the type of activity the enterprise engages in and through which it influences the level or direction of imports or exports, and finally by examining the interaction between the two, the Member may be better able to determine whether the enterprise should be notified. The lists in Sections III and IV which follow are included for this purpose. It should be noted that the activities of a state trading enterprise may not be limited to those derived from the rights/privileges granted to it and may include other activities.

* * *

III. RELATIONSHIPS WITH GOVERNMENT

8. The following types of relationships between enterprises and governments should be considered as possible indications of the existence of a state trading enterprise. As mentioned in the section on "Introductory Comments", no one relationship described necessarily identifies an enterprise as falling within the agreed WTO definitions of "state trading enterprise".

The enterprise[5] which is granted exclusive or special rights or privileges in the exercise of which it influences through its purchases or sales the level or direction of imports or exports is:

---

5. [original note] Not included are entities, or government Ministries, that have only regulatory authority in areas relevant to international trade.

   (a) a branch of government or a government-owned (or partially owned) enterprise; *or*

   (b) entirely separate from government (i.e. neither a branch of government nor fully or partially owned by the government), whether established to carry out government-mandated policies or programmes subject to legislated controls, or whether established for commercial purposes; this includes entities which are established and maintained under legislation and financed and controlled by the producers of the product over which they have marketing authority.

In addition, the enterprise purchases or sells a given product or group of products, either directly or indirectly through third parties under contract or transfer of right; *and* one or more of the following applies:

   (i) the enterprise is specially authorized or mandated by the government to do one or more of the following:

      — control and/or conduct import or export operations;

      — distribute imports;

      — control domestic production, processing, or distribution.

   (ii) all or part of the enterprise's activities are supported by government in one or more of the following ways, and the support afforded is specific or more favourable to the enterprise and not generally available to other entities, or is not warranted by purely commercial considerations:

      — budget allocations;

      — interest rate/tax concessions;

      — guarantees (e.g. for loans or against business failure);

      — revenue from the collection of tariffs;

      — preferential access to foreign exchange;

      — any off-budget support or assistance.

IV. ACTIVITIES ENGAGED IN BY STATE TRADING ENTERPRISES

9. The following activities are of the kind which might be engaged in by a state trading enterprise. An enterprise might engage in one or more of these activities, which can be directly related to importation, exportation, or the trade regime, or which can be related to trade in an indirect way. As mentioned in the section on "Introductory Comments", no one activity or combination of activities necessarily identifies an enterprise as falling within the agreed WTO definitions of "state trading enterprise".

   (a) Controls or conducts imports or exports;

(b) Administers multilaterally or bilaterally agreed quotas, tariff quotas or other restraint arrangements, or other import or export regulations;

(c) Issues licences/permits for importation or exportation;

(d) Determines domestic sales prices of imports.

(e) Enforces the statutory requirements of an agricultural marketing scheme and/or stabilization arrangement;

The following activities were included in some notifications:

(i) Authorizes or manages domestic production and/or processing of domestic production;

(ii) Determines the purchase price and/or sales price of domestic production;

(iii) Manages domestic distribution of domestic production and/or imports;

(iv) Undertakes purchases and sales of domestic production based on pre-determined floor and ceiling prices (intervention purchases/sales);

(v) Issues credit guarantees for producers, processors, exporters, or importers;

(vi) Engages in export-and support-related activities such as storage, shipping, processing, packaging, and insurance;

(vii) Controls or conducts marketing or distribution of processed products through subsidiaries or joint ventures in import markets;

(viii) Exercises quality control functions for imports or domestic production, including for export;

(ix) Engages in promotional activities for exports and/or domestic consumption;

(x) Procures and maintains emergency stocks of certain strategic and/or agricultural goods;

(xi) Negotiates or administers long-term bilateral contracts (including government-to-government) for exports and/or imports;

(xii) Undertakes purchases or sales necessary to fulfil contractual obligations entered into by the government.

Notes and Questions

Often, it is clear whether an enterprise falls within Article XVII's definition. But there are difficult issues raised by some cases. For example, does the existence of some right to control some (perhaps peripheral) aspect of importation or exportation result in state-trading-enterprise status? Is every government agency with some control over imports or exports covered? How would you answer those questions in light of the foregoing materials?

(2) Article XVII

Article XVII imposes both notification and substantive obligations in respect of state trading enterprises. First, Article XVII:4(a), as interpreted by GATT practice and the 1994 Understanding on Article XVII, requires notification of state trading enterprises. These notifications are designed to provide transparency in trade matters—one of GATT's basic goals. When the existence of such enterprises and their activities are revealed, other members are able to consider whether and how they are affected by them so that they may take appropriate measures.

More significantly, Article XVII regulates the activities of state trading enterprises, although its rules have not generally been considered to be very stringent. Under Article XVII:1(a), WTO members undertake that if they maintain a state trading enterprise, that enterprise shall act in a manner consistent with GATT's general principles of nondiscriminatory treatment. This requirement is explained in Article XVII:1(b) to mean that such enterprises will make purchases and sales solely on the basis of commercial considerations.

Professor Jackson has concluded from these provisions that a modified or relaxed form of the most-favored-nation obligation seems to be the general thrust of Article XVII:[6]

> The preparatory work reflects that the words "general principles of nondiscriminatory treatment" were inserted in Article XVII, paragraph 1(a), at Geneva (1947) in order to allay the doubt that " 'commercial principles' [in Article XVII, paragraph 1(b)] meant that exactly the same price would have to exist in different markets." Thus it appears that what is meant by "nondiscriminatory treatment" is a Most–Favored–Nation principle tempered by "commercial considerations," such as those listed in Article XVII, paragraph 1(b). The obligation in this paragraph also requires that adequate opportunity be granted to the other contracting parties' enterprises to compete "in accordance with customary business practice," which the draftsmen understood was "intended to cover business practices customary in the respective line of trade."

It can be argued that the preparatory work for the drafting of the General Agreement seems to limit the scope of Article XVII:1's nondiscriminatory treatment obligation to an MFN obligation and indicates that it was not intended to require also a national treatment standard. Thus, under that reading of Article XVII, the enterprise would be entitled to discriminate between domestic and foreign products in its purchases or its sales, as long as it does so on an MFN basis.[7] To date, GATT dispute settlement panels have not explicitly endorsed the limitation of Article XVII to MFN treatment, but one panel indicated that it "saw great force in [the] argument that only the most-favoured-nation

---

6. Jackson, supra note 2, at 346.

7. The General Agreement on Trade in Services (see Chapter 19 supra) requires WTO members to ensure that any monopoly service provider does not act in a manner inconsistent with their obligations under GATS Article II (MFN) and their specific commitments. GATS, art. VIII:1.

and not the national treatment obligations fall within the general principles referred to in Article XVII:1(a)."[8]

However, other GATT panels have applied Article III to the activities of state trading enterprises. In a case involving a Canadian provincial requirement that required imported beer to be transported to retail sales outlets by the provincial liquor authority, the panel found that Article III:4 had been violated because (i) domestically produced beer could be delivered by the brewer or other private haulers to retail outlets without provincial involvement and (ii) Canada could not show that the treatment of imported beer in this regard was not less favorable than the treatment of domestically produced beer.[9]

An important interpretative note to the General Agreement explicitly provides that the term "quantitative restrictions," which restrictions are prohibited or governed by Articles XI through XIV and Article XVIII of GATT, includes restrictions "made effective through state trading operations."[10] Thus, import restrictions that would violate Article XI if imposed by a government cannot be made effective through the use of import monopolies.[11]

(3) Article II:4

GATT Article II, paragraph 4, relating to import monopolies, adds another obligation in respect of import monopolies, which normally would be state trading enterprises (although the converse is not necessarily true). Article II:4 provides that if a product is subject to a GATT tariff binding in the schedule of a country, the country may not evade that binding through the use of an import monopoly to provide protection in excess of that provided for in the schedule. A note to this provision provides that it will be applied in light of the provisions of Article 31 of the Havana Charter. The provision has been interpreted by several GATT panels, including two dealing with complaints about Canadian provincial liquor authorities, which have import monopolies. These complaints alleged, inter alia, that the Canadian authorities marked up the cost prices of imported alcoholic beverages more than they did the comparable prices of domestic beverages. The panel concluded in the first such case that[12]

---

8. Canada—Administration of the Foreign Investment Review Act, 30th Supp. BISD 140, 163 (Panel report adopted Feb. 7, 1984).

9. Canada—Import, Distribution and Sale of Certain Alcoholic Drinks by Provincial Marketing Agencies, 39th Supp. BISD 27, 77–80 (Panel report adopted Feb. 18, 1992). See also Canada—Import, Distribution and Sale of Alcoholic Drinks by Canadian Provincial Marketing Agencies, 35th Supp. BISD 37, 90 (Panel report adopted Mar. 22, 1988).

10. GATT Annex I, Note ad Articles XI, XII, XIII, XIV and XVIII; see Jackson, supra note 2, at 348.

11. Japan—Restrictions on Imports of Certain Agricultural Products, 35th Supp. BISD 163, 229 (Panel report adopted Mar. 22, 1988).

12. Canada—Import, Distribution and Sale of Alcoholic Drinks by Canadian Provincial Marketing Agencies, 35th Supp. BISD 37, 88 (Panel report adopted Mar. 22, 1988). See also Canada—Import, Distribution and Sale of Certain Alcoholic Drinks by Provincial Marketing Agencies, 39th Supp.

[M]ark-ups which were higher on imported than on like domestic alcoholic beverages (differential mark-ups) could only be justified under Article II:4, to the extent that they represented additional costs necessarily associated with marketing of the imported products, * * * [and] that the burden would be on Canada if it wished to claim that additional costs were necessarily associated with marketing of the imported products.

The panel rejected the Canadian argument that the differential mark-ups could be justified on the grounds that they represented a policy of revenue maximization, which charged higher mark-ups on imports in order to exploit the lower price elasticities for premium imported products. As so interpreted, Article II:4 represents a significant constraint on the pricing policies of import monopolies that deal with bound products. Article 31.5 of the Havana Charter also restricted the ability of import monopolies to restrict the volume of imports. It provided that such monopolies shall "import and offer for sale such quantities of the product as will be sufficient to satisfy full domestic demand for the imported product [subject to any rationing rules then in effect]." Article II:4 only applies to import monopolies, not to state trading enterprises generally.

Notes and Questions

(1) In light of the foregoing description of the GATT rules on state trading, how effectively would you say that they deal with the interface problems outlined at the beginning of this section?

(2) Do you think that Article XVII imposes a national treatment obligation as one of the commercial considerations that state trading enterprises are supposed to follow? Should it?

(3) As noted earlier, the Uruguay Round negotiations produced an Understanding on Article XVII, which is reproduced in the Documents Supplement. To what extent did the understanding strengthen GATT regulation of state trading enterprises? What additional changes in GATT rules would you propose?

SECTION 9.4   NON–TARIFF BARRIERS

The discovery of new protective devices appears to be an endless process. As soon as the international system establishes restraints or regulations on a particular protective device, government officials and human ingenuity seem able to turn up some other measures to accomplish at least part of their protective purposes. Consequently, any international economic regulatory system must be designed so as to cope with the constant change in protectionist techniques.

While there are hundreds of distinct nontariff barriers, many of them can be cataloged under one of a dozen or so general headings:

BISD 27 (Panel report adopted Feb. 22, 1992).

customs valuation, import licensing rules, subsidies, investment performance requirements, rules restricting government procurement to domestic producers, compatibility standards, quality standards, health and safety regulations, labeling laws, inspection and testing requirements, and lack of intellectual property protection.[1]

The WTO agreements have two methods of attacking nontariff barriers. First, the general WTO requirements on transparency ensure that information about measures that may constitute such barriers should be available to traders. Second, there are agreements on specific nontariffs barriers, as well as general GATT rules that may restrict their use in specific situations.

(A) TRANSPARENCY

One of the most useful underlying principles of the WTO Agreement is that international trade regulations should be transparent. A major hindrance to international trade is the difficulty of finding out the rules that are applicable in faraway markets. The WTO's rules on transparency are designed to address this issue. There are three kinds of transparency provisions.

First, GATT Article X requires the publication of laws, regulations, judicial decisions and administrative rulings pertaining to a wide range of trade issues. It also requires mechanisms to review customs' decisions. A similar publication requirement is found in GATS Article III.

Second, most WTO agreements require notification to the WTO of various and sundry laws and regulations. In addition, they often require WTO members to establish enquiry points where further information can be obtained about such laws and regulations. The WTO maintains these notifications in a central registry.

Third, there are regular procedures for reviews of WTO members' trade policies and regulations. The most far-reaching review is thorough the Trade Policy Review Mechanism, pursuant to which the trade policies of members are reviewed by the Secretariat and other members on a regular basis. The major four trading countries are reviewed every two years; the next sixteen, every four years: and the rest, every six years or so. The procedure provides for memoranda on a country's trade policies and trade regime to be prepared by both the country and the

---

1. Numerous attempts have been made to catalog NTBs. A GATT effort in the 1960's produced an inventory of over 800 NTBs. More recently, the USTR has been publishing an annual list of NTBs used by U.S. trading partners in its "National Trade Estimate Reports on Foreign Trade Barriers." The Industrial Structure Council of Japan also publishes an annual "Report on Unfair Trade Policies by Major Trading Partners," while the EC publishes an annual report on "U.S. Trade Barriers and Unfair Practices." In addition, the GATT Secretariat discusses NTBs in its reports under the Trade Policy Review Mechanism. Often more difficult than cataloging such barriers is measuring their effects. Attempts have been made to compute a "tariff equivalent effect" of NTBs, but this has proved to be very difficult to do. Alan V. Deardorff & Robert M. Stern, Methods of Measurement of Nontariff Barriers (prepared for the United Nations Conference on Trade and Development, UNCTAD document UNCTAD/ST/MD/28, 2 January 1985).

secretariat. These are then discussed in a meeting of the Trade Policy Review Body, which is the General Council performing the trade policy review function under a separate chair.

In addition to the TPR process, a number of WTO agreements require discussion of members' laws in specific areas. For example, the TRIPS Council undertakes a review of members' intellectual property laws. These reviews typically allow other members to make inquiries about one member's laws and receive clarifications. As such, they are an important, albeit indirect, means of promoting compliance with WTO obligations. The discussions in these reviews also generally serve a valuable education and clarification function, as they allow the membership to express its views on the meaning of many WTO obligations.

(B) AGREEMENTS AND RULES ON NON–TARIFF BARRIERS

A number of NTBs were dealt with in Tokyo and Uruguay Round agreements, including the Customs Valuation Agreement (discussed in Section 8.3(C)); the Import Licensing Agreement (discussed in Section 9.1); the Agreement on Pre–Shipment Inspection; the Agreement on Rules of Origin (discussed in Section 8.3(D)); the Agreement on Technical Barriers to Trade, known as the TBT Agreement (discussed in Section 14.3)); the Agreement on Sanitary and Phytosanitary Measures, known as the SPS Agreement, discussed in Section 14.2; the Agreement on Trade–Related Investment Measures, known as the TRIMs Agreement, discussed in Sections 9.1 & 12.4(B), as well as in Chapter 24; and the Agreement on Government Procurement (discussed in Section 12.5). We will deal with the varied forms of NTBs throughout this book because many NTBs are arguably governed by GATT rules on most-favored-nation treatment, national treatment or subsidies. However, as noted above, the ingenuity of man is such that new varieties of trade barriers crop up constantly. Although their effect on trade is clear, many of these barriers are not easy to fit within the traditional categories of import restraints. They involve subtle concepts such as the effect of government "targeting" policies, or societal differences such as language or quality preference. A major question facing international trade negotiators, as well as theorists, is which NTBs are really trade barriers that should be regulated by international rules and which are actions that affect trade but are really legitimate government policies that are not intended to discriminate against foreign products or are simply societal preferences that give one country certain advantages over another so that trade is possible in the first place.

Review Problems for Chapters 8 and 9

Assume that Atlonia and Bugslavia are members of the WTO, while Xonia is not. Atlonia's schedule contains the following binding:

Handkerchiefs, cotton ... 10%

This concession was negotiated at the most recent round of negotiations, partly pursuant to a request of a country named "Categorica" which at the time was the second largest exporter of handkerchiefs to

Atlonia. The largest exporter to Atlonia at that time was "Dominata." Today, the largest two exporters of handkerchiefs to Atlonia are "Exportonia" (first), and "Factonia" (second.) All these countries are members of the WTO.

Bugslavia ships products to Atlonia, and the following cases arise. In each case indicate whether the Atlonia practice is consistent with GATT or not. (Refer to the GATT agreement in the Documents Supplement.)

(1) A tariff is imposed on the imports of cotton handkerchiefs produced in Bugslavia at the rate of:

(a) 12%.

(b) 8%.

(c) Specific rate of one drachma, and the handkerchiefs are valued at 8 drachmas each.

(d) Same, except value is 12 drachmas each.

(2) Imports are of handkerchiefs made of 50% cotton and 50% synthetic fiber; tariff imposed is 20%.

(3) Besides the tariff, a customs administration fee of 1 drachma per handkerchief is imposed, and mandatory import entry invoice forms are sold for 1 drachma each.

(4) All textile imports are valued by the highest price found for like goods in any market of the world.

(5) Textile imports are valued by applying Atlonia production cost factors, using standard Atlonia collective bargaining labor wage rates.

(6) All imports are valued for customs purposes as if their value included the standard Atlonia 10% domestic sales tax applied to all goods, domestic or foreign.

(7) After the binding was negotiated, Atlonia granted to its domestic textile industry an accelerated income tax depreciation rate for new capital expenses by that industry.

(8) Atlonia maintains a state trading monopoly for textile imports and imported handkerchiefs are sold at a 40% mark-up, after they have cleared customs and paid duty.

(9) Atlonia abolishes its state trading monopoly, but establishes an import quota for handkerchiefs at 1 million units per year. (Past imports have never exceeded 700,000 units per year.)

(10) A Bugslavia firm buys handkerchiefs from Xonia and ships them to Atlonia for resale. A tariff of 20% is imposed.

(11) On compact disc players, Atlonia has made no GATT binding. Atlonia now charges a tariff of 10% on imports of this product, but is developing a domestic industry to produce such players. It wishes to exclude imports of these products and consults you, its lawyer, about ways to accomplish this. Advise on the relative merits of the following proposals:

(a) Impose a ban on imports of the product.

(b) Subsidize with direct government grant equal to 50% of the cost of producing each item.

(c) Raise the tariff from 10% to 100%.

(d) Raise the tariff to 1000%.

(e) Raise the tariff to 50% ad valorem, but provide that imported CD players shall be valued for customs purposes equal to the average price charged in the domestic market for domestically produced CD players.

(f) Impose a requirement that imported CD players be stored in a warehouse for one year after importation, before resale.

(12) Suppose Atlonia had bound its tariff on CD players at 50%. Would that cause you to change your advice on the alternatives listed in (11)?

(13) Suppose its GATT binding of 50% were on "CD players," and Atlonia now decided to change its domestic tariff schedule to appear as follows:

CD Players:

Portable   100%

All other   50%

Could Atlonia do this without being in contravention of GATT rules?

(14) Some other techniques for Atlonia to consider (discussed in later chapters):

(a) Leave the tariff at 10%, but impose an internal excise sales tax of 50% which is waived on domestically produced goods.

(b) Require the exchange rate to be used in purchases of CD players to allow one-half the amount of Atlonia currency per unit of foreign currency.

(c) Require importers to deposit with an Atlonia bank an amount equal to the value of CD player imports, such amount to be refundable after six months (but with no interest).

(d) Allow imports of CD players only from countries which import a like amount of such product from Atlonia.

(e) Allow imports of CD players only from countries which themselves have a zero tariff on imports of CD players.

(15) If Atlonia decides to withdraw its tariff binding on handkerchiefs, what procedures in the WTO does it face? Which WTO members will have "negotiating" rights?

(16) If, at a new negotiation, Atlonia is prepared to reduce its tariff on silk handkerchiefs from 20% to 10%, and has recently been importing one million units of this product from Bugslavia, two million from Categorica, and three million from Dominata, all at a wholesale customs entry valuation of the equivalent of $1.00 per unit (before tariff), what value of concessions is Atlonia entitled to ask from each of these countries? How should one measure the value of a concession?

Chapter 10

NONDISCRIMINATION AND THE MOST–FAVORED– NATION CLAUSE

SECTION 10.1 INTRODUCTION[1]

(A) THE POLICIES UNDERLYING THE MFN PRINCIPLE

"The unconditional most-favored-nation (MFN) provision is the cornerstone of the international trade rules embodied in the General Agreement on Tariffs and Trade (GATT).

"The basic rationale for MFN is that if every country observes the principle, all countries will benefit in the long run through the resulting more efficient use of resources. Furthermore, if the principle is observed, there is less likelihood of trade disputes."[2]

1. For references on MFN in addition to those excerpted in this chapter, see generally John H. Jackson, World Trade and the Law of GATT ch. 11 (1969); Thomas Cottier & Petros C. Mavroidis (eds.), Regulatory Barriers and the Principle of Non–Discrimination in World Trade Law (2000); John H. Jackson, The World Trading System ch. 6 (2d ed. 1997); John H. Jackson, Equality and Discrimination in International Economic Law (XI): The General Agreement on Tariffs and Trade, Brit.Yb.World Aff. 1983, at 224 (1983); Warren Schwartz & Alan O. Sykes, Toward a Positive Theory of the Most Favored Nation Obligation and its Exceptions in the WTO/GATT System, 16 Int'l Rev. L. & Econ. 27 (1996); Warren Schwartz & Alan O. Sykes, Most Favored Nation Obligations in International Trade, New Palgrave Dictionary of Economics and the Law, Vol. 2 660 (Peter Newman ed. 1998); League of Nations Economic Comm., Equality of Treatment in the Present State of International Commercial Relations: The Most–Favoured–Nation Clause, L.N.Doc.C. 379, M. 250. 1936 II.B.; Gardner Patterson, Discrimination in International Trade: The Policy Issues, 1945–1965 (1966); Richard C. Snyder, The Most–Favored–Nation Clause: An Analysis with Particular Reference to Recent Treaty Practice and Tariffs (1948); Hector Gros Espiell, The Most–Favoured–Nation Clause, 5 J. World Trade L. 29 (1971); Theodore C. Sorensen, Most Favored and Less Favorite Nations, 52 Foreign Affairs 273 (1974). In the context of the Tokyo Round, see Gary C. Hufbauer, J. Sheldon Erb & H.P. Starr, The GATT Codes and the Unconditional Most–Favored–Nation Principle, 12 Law & Poly.Intl. Bus. 59 (1980); Report of the International Law Commission on it Thirtieth Session, Draft Articles on Most–Favoured–Nation Clauses and Commentary, in Yearbook of the International Law Commission 1978, at 8–73 (Vol. 2, pt. 2, 1979) (U.N.Doc. A/CN.4/ SER.A/1978/Add. 1 (Part 2)).

2. Executive Branch GATT Studies, No. 9, The Most–Favored–Nation Provision, at 133, Subcomm. on International Trade, Senate Comm. on Finance, 93d Cong., 2d Sess. (Compilation of 1973 studies prepared by the Executive Branch: Comm.Print 1974).

The importance of the most-favored-nation principle has been further underscored by GATT economists who have noted five significant benefits flowing from the principle.[3]

First, "[f]rom the economic viewpoint, [the MFN principle] ensures that each country will satisfy its total import needs from the most efficient sources of supply, allowing the operation of comparative advantage." If a country's tariff rates on a product vary and a higher rate is applied to the nearest or most efficient producer, then that producer may not be able to compete in the country's market, raising prices and costs in that market and reducing efficiency worldwide.

Second, "[f]rom the trade policy viewpoint, the MFN commitment protects the value of bilateral concessions and 'spreads security around' by making them the basis for a multilateral system." Because MFN treatment generalizes market-opening measures, it is a positive force for multilateral trade liberalization. It can be expected that more liberalization will be achieved with MFN than without. This is of great importance because without MFN, discrimination leads inevitably to more discrimination and all suffer, even if discrimination sometimes appears to be in the short-run interest of the discriminating country.

Third, "[f]rom the international-political viewpoint, the commitment to the MFN clause mobilizes the power of the large countries behind the main interest and aspiration of the small ones which is to be treated equally. It represents the only way to realize the ideal of sovereign equality of nations; in more practical terms, it guarantees the access of newcomers into international markets." This result may significantly reduce international tensions because those nations denied special trade advantages will resent it, and the more special advantages that are created, the more disputes that can be expected.

Fourth, "[f]rom the domestic-political viewpoint, the MFN commitment makes for more straightforward and transparent policies and for greater simplicity of administration of protection." For example, with general MFN treatment, special origin rules would be unnecessary.

Fifth, "[u]ltimately, the unconditional MFN commitment is of a constitutional significance. It serves as the safe constraint on the delegated discretionary powers of the executive branch in trade matters." If a government has a strong commitment to an MFN policy, special interests will be less likely to try to obtain and even less likely to get special discriminatory trade measures. Thus, trade generally will be freer of government interference.

MFN has sometimes been described as the "central" policy of GATT and the post World War II trading system. Certainly it is one of the central policies, and the fact that it is Article I of General Agreement reinforces that position. Indeed, the "existing legislation" exception of the GATT 1947's Protocol of Provisional Application did not apply to

---

3. GATT Focus, Sept.–Oct. 1984, at 3.

Part I of the General Agreement, which includes Article I (as well as the tariff concessions article, Article II, discussed in the previous chapter).

The MFN principle of non-discrimination (one of GATT's two major non-discrimination principles, the other being the national treatment principle, taken up in Chapter 12), has been the center of considerable discussion and controversy in recent years. In this introductory section, after a description of the history of MFN, we consider whether there is any MFN obligation in customary international law, apart from treaty obligation. In Section 10.2, we look at the operation of the GATT MFN clause, examining the GATT and WTO decisions that have interpreted its scope and the major GATT-authorized exceptions to MFN treatment. MFN obligations exist in a number of treaties besides the General Agreement, and we consider how different wordings of MFN clauses can effect the application of the principle in other contexts.

We conclude this chapter with an examination of U.S. legislative approaches to the MFN principle, where we will find examples of support for the principle, but also derogations from it. In this connection, we consider the results of the Tokyo and Uruguay Rounds and the related U.S. implementing legislation.

Despite its centrality in the WTO/GATT system, some question the future of the MFN rule as a fundamental principle of international trade agreements. They note that the MFN principle is now being eroded rapidly by the extensive use of exceptions to it and by various bilateral arrangements between nations which depart from the spirit if not the letter of the MFN obligations. In Chapter 11, we examine the most significant MFN exception—that for customs unions and free trade areas. In Chapter 25, we will explore the Generalized System of Preferences, which is designed to aid developing countries, but which is a departure from MFN.

Apart from exceptions to the MFN clause, there are some policy problems with the MFN principle itself.

JOHN H. JACKSON, THE WORLD TRADING SYSTEM 160–62 (2d ed. 1997)[4]

A second set of counterarguments stresses the risk of a unilateral unconditional MFN approach. These are the "foot-dragger" and "free-rider" arguments. To negotiate a general rule applicable to all nations in a system that stresses unanimity and consensus often means that a hold-out nation can prevent agreement or cause its provisions to be reduced to the least common denominator. This can greatly inhibit needed improvement in substantive or procedural rules.

On the other hand, for like-minded nations to go ahead with reforms and agreements without the "foot dragger," but to grant (as uncondi-

---

4. © 1997 by The Massachusetts Institute of Technology. Reprinted by permis-   sion of The MIT Press.

tional MFN requires) all the benefits of the new approach to the non-agreeing parties, gives the latter unreciprocated benefits without any of the obligations. This furnishes an incentive to nations to stay out of the agreement. This is what led the United States to require nations to accept the Subsidies Code obligations as a condition to receiving beneficial U.S. treatment in countervailing duty cases (as specified in the Tokyo Round code).

* * *

CONDITIONAL AND UNCONDITIONAL MFN; CODE CONDITIONALITY

Under conditional MFN, when country A grants a privilege to country C while owing MFN to country B, then country A must grant the equivalent privilege to B—but only after B has given A some reciprocal privilege to "pay for it."

Under unconditional MFN, in the case above A must grant the equivalent privilege to country B without receiving anything in return from B. The United States pursued a "conditional MFN" policy prior to World War I, although many other major nations had by that time moved to an unconditional approach. The United States changed to an unconditional policy in 1923.

Several arguments are often voiced in preference of the unconditional approach over the conditional. In the first place, it is very difficult to negotiate for reciprocal concessions from a third-party beneficiary of benefits. When A grants to C a privilege, and B knows that MFN obligations require that privilege to go to B also, albeit after "payment," there is not a very strong incentive for B to be forthcoming in a bargaining process with A. Such negotiations can generate more rancor and trouble than they are worth. Second, unconditional MFN can help spread trade liberalization faster, given that any concession by a particular country is generalized to apply very broadly. The GATT MFN clause is clearly unconditional.

A different type of MFN concept has arisen in connection with various "codes," or side agreements on trade matters, negotiated in the Tokyo Round. In some of these codes, certain code members have taken the position that the benefits of code treatment would only be granted to nations that became members of the code (or at least reciprocated with code treatment). Thus, if A, B, and C belonged to a code which calls for an "injury" test requirement before countervailing duties can be applied to imports, A could argue that it need not give such "test" to the imports from X, which was not a code member. Sometimes this has been called "conditional MFN," but in fact it is not the same as the traditional "conditional MFN" concept, since it does not require a particular negotiation of reciprocal benefits. Instead, the code itself defines the nature of the reciprocity that is owed in order to receive the advantage of this type of MFN. The advantage of "code conditionality" is that it creates an incentive for other nations to join a code and submit to its discipline. If a general MFN obligation (e.g., in GATT) required all code

nations to grant the favorable code treatment to nations that did not
become code members, there would be substantially less incentive for
such nations to join. They can take a "free-rider" approach, and claim
the benefits without having to incur the discipline of code membership.

———

Two of the Tokyo Round agreements, and the U.S. statute implementing three of the Tokyo Round agreements, seemed to limit the
benefits of those agreements to the countries which assumed the obligations of the particular agreement, a sort of "agreement" or "code"
conditional MFN. See Section 10.3 infra. In considering the materials
below, the reader should keep in mind the difference between traditional
conditional MFN and code conditional MFN. Under the WTO Agreement, there are now only two plurilateral agreements with limited
membership–the revised Government Procurement Agreement and the
Tokyo Round Civil Aircraft Agreement.

(B) THE HISTORY OF MFN

THE MOST–FAVORED–NATION PROVISION, EXECUTIVE BRANCH GATT STUDIES, NO. 9, 133–35 (1973)[5]

HISTORY

The concept embodied in the MFN clause has been traced to the
12th century, although the phrase "most-favored-nation" did not appear
until the end of the 17th century. The emergence of the MFN provision
is largely attributable to the growth of world commerce in the 15th and
16th centuries. At that time England and Holland were competing with
Spain and Portugal, and the French and the Scandinavians were challenging the Hanseatic League and the Italian Republics. Each country,
seeking maximum advantage for its trade, found itself compelled to
grant concessions in return. The role of the MFN provision was to link
commercial treaties through time and between states. At first, the MFN
provision applied to concessions granted only to specified states, but
gradually the clause became generalized to apply to concessions granted
to all countries.

The trend toward wide use of the MFN clause necessarily coincided
with the decline of mercantilism. The mercantilist view that in any
commercial exchange one nation wins and the other loses does not mix
with the concept of reciprocal arrangements implicit in the MFN principle.

The unconditional form of the MFN clause—guaranteed equal treatment without requiring directly reciprocal compensation—was used ex-

5. Subcomm. on Intl. Trade, Senate (Compilation of 1973 studies prepared by Comm. on Finance, 93d Cong., 2d Sess. the Executive Branch: Comm. Print 1974).

clusively until the late 18th century. In fact, conditional MFN—equal treatment conditional upon adequate compensation—was inaugurated in 1778 by the United States. During the first half of the 19th century, the conditional form was common in treaties in Europe and elsewhere. The wave of liberalism that swept Europe in the second half of the 19th century brought a return to use of the unconditional MFN clause in keeping with the free trade sentiment of the time. While European countries ultimately returned to the unconditional form, the United States was consistent until 1923 in its adherence to the conditional form. It should be noted, however, that in practice only a limited amount of United States trade was affected by reciprocal treaties involving conditional MFN. The United States consistently applied a single-schedule tariff to imports from all countries. Reciprocal treaties granting reductions from the general tariff rates were few in number at any given time.

The United States began granting conditional MFN with its first treaty after independence, the United States–France treaty of 1778. Article II provided that, "The Most Christian King and the United States engage mutually not to grant any particular favor to other nations in respect of commerce and navigation, which shall not immediately become common to the other party, who shall enjoy the same favor, Freely, If The Compensation Was Freely Made, Or On Allowing The Same Compensation, If The Concession Was Conditional" (caps added). Similar provisions in treaties with Prussia (1785) and Sweden (1793) served to establish the "American interpretation" that special favors must be specifically bought.

The position of the United States as a newcomer to world commerce largely accounts for its novel interpretation of the MFN clause. With the colonial ties to the British Empire broken, the United States had difficulty establishing an equal footing for trade with other nations. France and Spain, as well as Britain, attempted to exclude the Americans from trading with their overseas possessions. At the same time, these countries sought to penetrate the American market. Given European reluctance to grant initial reciprocity, the United States policy was to establish high duties and grant access to the American market only in return for access to markets controlled by Europe. Under the circumstances then prevailing the conditional MFN clause enabled the United States to maximize its bargaining leverage by offering no gratuitous access privileges.

The American principle of conditional MFN had a growing effect on commercial policy abroad, reaching its peak roughly between 1830 and 1860. The year 1810 marked the first conditional MFN clause in a treaty between European states (Great Britain and Portugal). In 1824 the clause was introduced to South America, where it remained dominant for the next 25 years. Of all European states, England was the most consistent in adhering to the unconditional MFN form through the first half of the 19th century, although the conditional clause was not uncommon in its treaties during that period.

Beginning with the Cobden treaty between France and England in 1860, the unconditional form of the MFN clause again prevailed in European commercial treaties. The benefits of the Cobden treaty were conditionally extended to other countries by France and unconditionally extended to others by England. It soon became apparent to England that under this arrangement the balance of advantages was in favor of France. To compensate for this, England launched a successful drive to conclude unconditional MFN treaties with other countries. The unconditional MFN clause was used exclusively in Europe after that time, in spite of a return to protectionism on the Continent after 1875.

While the United States and Europe were consistent in following their respective interpretations of the MFN clause during the latter 19th century, practice in other parts of the trading world varied. In South and Central America, for example, both forms of the clause were used with no clear-cut pattern, although the conditional form was used consistently in treaties between American states. Japan also used both forms.

The divergent interpretations of the MFN principle during the late 19th century were largely a manifestation of the economic relationship between the United States and Europe. World War I altered this relationship dramatically. Following the war, the United States no longer stood to Europe as an underdeveloped nation, dependent upon Europe for industrial goods and capital, content to export to Europe its raw materials. American products were now much in demand in Europe and American capital financed European factories. Therefore, in the 1920's United States policy changed, reflecting its broader and more important export interests. By offering complete and continuous nondiscriminatory treatment the United States sought to obtain the same treatment from other countries, thus reducing discrimination against United States exports.

JOHN H. JACKSON, WORLD TRADE AND
THE LAW OF GATT 250–251 (1969)[6]

One of Wilson's fourteen points in 1918 urged "the establishment of an equality of trade conditions among all the nations consenting to the Peace," which was explained to mean "whatever tariff any nation might deem necessary for its own economic service, be that tariff high or low, it should apply equally to all foreign nations." The League of Nations Covenant likewise mentioned the goal of "equitable treatment for the commerce of all members" and the 1919 peace treaties contained MFN clauses. The League occupied itself with various economic and financial matters, but one prominent topic was MFN, on which the League prepared a series of reports and studies.

In 1936, the League published a study that included legal language for a recommended MFN clause, as well as a discussion of various

---

problems, ambiguities, and policy questions of scope. At the same time, as chronicled elsewhere, international trade in the interwar period was breaking down and a variety of trade barriers were spreading from nation to nation. In 1930, the United States enacted the infamous Smoot–Hawley tariff and one reaction that has been attributed to this act was the introduction of a preferential trade system for the British Commonwealth. In 1934, the United States accepted Cordell Hull's reciprocal trade agreement program but, although MFN clauses were universally included in the trade agreements negotiated pursuant to that act, the treaties with Commonwealth nations excepted the Commonwealth preferences from MFN operation.

One of the prime post-World War II objectives of the United States was the dismantling of trade preferences, especially the Commonwealth system. The details of the clash between United States and British policy and public opinion in this respect are set forth in Richard Gardner's book *Sterling-Dollar Diplomacy*. The United States' preoccupation with Commonwealth preferences was so intense that an administrative spokesman told Congress in 1947 that eliminating these preferences was almost a *sine qua non* of success at the Geneva Conference. Failure to achieve this result has been blamed as one of the causes for the failure of the United States to accept the Havana Charter, thus causing the ITO to fail to materialize.

(C) THE NONDISCRIMINATION OBLIGATION IN CUSTOMARY INTERNATIONAL LAW

From time to time it is argued that countries are obligated under customary international law to extend nondiscriminatory treatment to other nations. Prior to World War I, there was no such obligation. As summarized by Professor Georg Schwarzenberger, customary law of the time recognized that:[7] "Freedom of commerce is a purely optional pattern of international economic law. As distinct from freedom of trade, it is compatible with monopoly of trade, preferential treatment and equality of treatment for foreign commerce. * * * The most important [optional standards for equality of commerce] are the standards of most-favoured-nation, national, identical and equitable treatment."

In the 1950's, some East European scholars argued that the United Nations principle of state equality applied to international commercial relations, thereby prohibiting the discrimination to which these countries were then subject.[8] These scholars stressed the noncommercial aspects of nondiscrimination, such as the promotion of friendly relations between states. Western scholars generally rejected that view, express-

---

7. Georg Schwarzenberger, Equality and Discrimination in International Economic Law (I), 25 Yearbook of World Affairs 163, 164–65 (1971). Reprinted by permission of Stevens and Sons Ltd., London.

8. This debate is ably described in John N. Hazard, Editorial Comment: Commercial Discrimination and International Law, 52 Am.J.Intl.L. 495 (1958).

ing, inter alia, the difficulty of applying traditional international commercial considerations to state trading countries at all.[9]

In 1978, the United Nations International Law Commission concluded its work on 30 draft articles on most-favored-nation clauses and recommended to the U.N. General Assembly that U.N. member states should conclude a convention based on those articles.[10] The articles specifically provide that MFN treatment is treaty-based.[11]

SECTION 10.2   THE MOST FAVORED NATION OBLIGATION IN GATT

(A) INTRODUCTION

In this section we explore the MFN obligations in the General Agreement on Tariffs and Trade. We first consider the scope and meaning of GATT Article I, and then we examine the exceptions to the MFN obligation. The problems at the end illustrate the complexity and variety of legal questions which can arise in connection with MFN obligations.

The GATT MFN article is a fundamental and central obligation of international trade policy, but it is not without interpretive problems, as its drafters realized.[1] The most difficult issues concern the scope of the clause's coverage. In the first instance, the clause applies to customs duties and any other import or export charges, the methods of levying them, all rules and formalities in connection with importation or exportation, and internal taxation and sales regulations. Second, the clause requires that any advantage granted in respect of these matters in respect of one product must be granted to the like product from other parties.

Three definitional issues are obvious. First, what are rules and formalities in connection with importation and exportation? What are import or export charges? Second, what is an advantage? Third, what is a like product? We explore these issues in the following materials and in the problems at the end of this section.

In discussing the scope of the MFN requirement of Article I, it must be kept in mind that many other provisions of the General Agreement have nondiscrimination requirements similar to Article I. Thus, the fact that an action taken by a contracting party does not fall within the scope of Article I, does not mean that discrimination will be permitted. For example, as we discuss below, there are nondiscrimination requirements

9. See generally Martin Domke & John N. Hazard, State Trading and the Most–Favored–Nation Clause, 52 Am.J.Intl.L. 55 (1958).

10. See Report of the International Law Commission, supra note 1, at 16. For a description of an earlier UN project relevant to this issue, see Piet Hein Houben, Principles of International Law Concerning Friendly Relations and Co-operation Among States, 61 Am.J.Intl.L. 703, 722–23 (1967).

11. Report of the International Law Commission, supra note 1, at 25 (Art. 8).

1. See generally John H. Jackson, World Trade and the Law of GATT (1969), ch. 11, note particularly sec. 11.2 discussing the drafter's views.

in Articles XIII (quota administration) and XX (general exceptions). Other MFN or nondiscrimination clauses include: Article IV(b) (cinema films); Article III:7 (international mixing requirements); Article V:2, 5 & 6 (transit of goods); Article IX:1 (marks of origin); Article XVII:1 (state trading); and Article XVIII:20 (measures to assist economic development).[2] There are, however, provisions of the General Agreement that authorize general nonobservance of Article I, such as the customs union and free trade area exception of Article XXIV, and GATT practices that do likewise, such as the authorization of discrimination in tariff matters in favor of developing countries.

(B) THE SCOPE OF THE MFN OBLIGATION

The general scope of the MFN obligation was discussed by the Appellate Body in EUROPEAN COMMUNITIES—REGIME FOR THE IMPORTATION, SALE AND DISTRIBUTION OF BANANAS, WT/DS27/AB/R, adopted by the DSB on September 25, 1997. In that case the EC argued that there were two separate EC import regimes for bananas, the preferential regime for traditional ACP bananas and the *erga omnes* regime for all other imports of bananas. According to the EC, the non-discrimination obligations of Articles I:1, X:3(a) and XIII of the GATT 1994 and Article 1.3 of the Licensing Agreement, applied only within each of these separate regimes. In response, the Appellate Body stated:

190.   The issue here is not whether the European Communities is correct in stating that two separate import regimes exist for bananas, but whether the existence of two, or more, separate EC import regimes is of any relevance for the application of the non-discrimination provisions of the GATT 1994 and the other Annex 1A agreements. The essence of the non-discrimination obligations is that like products should be treated equally, irrespective of their origin. As no participant disputes that all bananas are like products, the non-discrimination provisions apply to all imports of bananas, irrespective of whether and how a Member categorizes or subdivides these imports for administrative or other reasons. If, by choosing a different legal basis for imposing import restrictions, or by applying different tariff rates, a Member could avoid the application of the non-discrimination provisions to the imports of like products from different Members, the object and purpose of the non-discrimination provisions would be defeated. It would be very easy for a Member to circumvent the non-discrimination provisions of the GATT 1994 and the other Annex 1A agreements, if these provisions apply only within regulatory regimes established by that Member.

191.   Non-discrimination obligations apply to all imports of like products, except when these obligations are specifically waived or are otherwise not applicable as a result of the operation of specific provisions of the GATT 1994, such as Article XXIV. In the present case, the non-discrimination obligations of the GATT 1994, specifi-

2.   See id. at 255.

cally Articles I:1 and XIII, apply fully to all imported bananas irrespective of their origin, except to the extent that these obligations are waived. * * *

The difficult cases involving Article I:1 issues have tended to be of two types: First, there have been cases where the key issue is the likeness of the products at issue for tariff purposes. Second, there have been cases where the grant of favorable tariff treatment to products imported by specific importers is alleged to result in de facto discrimination against the like products from some other WTO members. In this section, we will examine examples of both types of cases.

(1) The Concept of Like Product for Tariff Purposes

JAPAN—TARIFF ON IMPORT OF SPRUCE–PINE–FIR (SPF) DIMENSION LUMBER

GATT Panel Report adopted July 19, 1989
36th Supp. BISD 167 (1990)

[Canada complained that Japan's tariffs on certain lumber cut to specified dimensions ("dimension lumber") violated the most-favored-nation clause of Article I. Lumber of some species of coniferous trees was tariff-free; lumber of other species was dutiable at 8%.]

5.4 According to Canada, Article I:1 required Japan to accord also to SPF dimension lumber the advantage of the zero tariff granted by Japan * * * to planed and sanded lumber of "other" coniferous trees * * *.

5.5 The Panel noted that the tariff classification * * * had been established autonomously by Japan, with negotiation.

* * *

5.7 In view of analysing the factual situation submitted to it under its terms of reference, the Panel had first to consider the legal framework in which the Canadian complaint had been raised. In substance, Canada complains of the fact that Japan had arranged its tariff classification in such a way that a considerable part of Canadian exports of SPF dimension lumber to Japan was submitted to a customs duty of 8 per cent, whereas other comparable types of dimension lumber enjoy the advantage of a zero-tariff duty. The Panel considered it impossible to appreciate fully the Canadian complaint if it had not in a preliminary way clarified the bearing of some principles of the GATT-system in relation to tariff structure and tariff classification.

5.8 The Panel noted in this respect that the General Agreement left wide discretion to the contracting parties in relation to the structure of national tariffs and the classification of goods in the framework of such structure [citing the *Spanish Coffee* case, which follows this case]. The adoption of the Harmonized System, to which both Canada and Japan have adhered, had brought about a large measure of harmonization in the field of customs classification of goods, but this system did not entail any obligation as to the ultimate detail in the respective tariff classifications. Indeed, the nomenclature has been on purpose structured in such a way that it leaves room for further specifications.

5.9   The Panel was of the opinion that, under these conditions, a tariff classification going beyond the Harmonized System's structure is a legitimate means of adapting the tariff scheme to each contracting party's trade policy interests, comprising both its protection needs and its requirements for the purposes of tariff and trade negotiations. It must however be borne in mind that such differentiations may lend themselves to abuse, insofar as they may serve to circumscribe tariff advantages in such a way that they are conducive to discrimination among like products originating in different contracting parties. A contracting party prejudiced by such action may request therefore that its own exports be treated as "like products" in spite of the fact that they might find themselves excluded by the differentiations retained in the importing country's tariff.

5.10   Tariff differentiations being basically a legitimate means of trade policy, a contracting party which claims to be prejudiced by such practice bears the burden of establishing that such tariff arrangement has been diverted from its normal purpose so as to become a means of discrimination in international trade. Such complaints have to be examined in considering simultaneously the internal protection interest involved in a given tariff specification, as well as its actual or potential influence on the pattern of imports from different extraneous sources. The Canadian complaint and the defense of Japan will have to be viewed in the light of these requirements.

5.11   "Dimension lumber" as understood by Canada is defined by its presentation in a standard form of measurements, quality-grading and finishing. It appears from the information provided by Canada that this type of lumber is largely used in platform-house construction in Canada as well as in the United States and that it has found also widespread use in Japan, is testified by the existence of a Japanese technical standard known under the name of "JAS 600".

5.12   Japan objected to this claim on different grounds. Japan explained that dimension lumber was only one particular type of lumber among many other possible presentations and that house-building is only one of the many possible uses of this particular kind of lumber. From the legal point of view, Japan contended that the concept of "dimension lumber" is not used either in any internationally accepted tariff classification, or in the Japanese tariff classification. In accordance with the Harmonized System, [the Japanese tariff heading at issue] embraces all types of coniferous wood "sawn or chipped lengthwise ... exceeding 6mm". Apart from the thickness and the grade of finishing, customs treatment of lumber according to the Japanese Tariff was determined exclusively on the basis of a distinction established between certain biological genera or species. Dimension lumber was therefore not identified as a particular category in the framework of the Japanese tariff classification.

5.13   The Panel considered that the tariffs referred to by the General Agreement are, quite evidently, those of the individual contracting parties. This was inherent in the system of the Agreement and appeared also in the current practice of tariff negotiations, the subject matter of which were the national tariffs of the individual contracting parties. It followed that, if a claim of likeness was raised by a contracting party in relation to the tariff treatment of its goods on importation by some other contracting party, such a claim should be based on the classification of the latter, i.e. the importing country's tariff.

5.14   The Panel noted in this respect that "dimension lumber" as defined by Canada was a concept extraneous to the Japanese Tariff. It was a standard applied by the Canadian industry which appeared to have some equivalent in the United States and in Japan itself, but it could not be considered for that reason alone as a category for tariff classification purposes, nor did it belong to any internationally accepted customs classification. The Panel concluded therefore that reliance by Canada on the concept of dimension lumber was not an appropriate basis for establishing "likeness" of products under Article I:1 of the General Agreement.

5.15   At the same time, the Panel felt unable to examine the Canadian complaint in a broader context, as Canada had declared expressly that the issue before the Panel should not be confused by broadening the scope of the Panel's examination beyond "dimension lumber" to planed lumber generally. Canada's complaint was limited to the specific product known in North America, and also in Japan, as dimension lumber. Canada did not contend that different lumber species per se should be considered like products, regardless of the product-form they might take. Thus there appeared to be no basis for examining the issue raised by Canada in the general context of the Japanese tariff classification.

SPAIN—TARIFF TREATMENT
OF UNROASTED COFFEE

GATT Panel Report adopted June 11, 1981
28th Supp. BISD 102 (1982)

[Prior to 1979, Spain had classified all unroasted, non-decaffeinated coffee under one tariff heading. In 1979, Spain subdivided its classification for such coffee into five parts, to three of which a 7% duty was applied and to two of which no duty was applied. Brazil, which was the principal supplier of the type of coffee subjected to duty, complained in GATT and a panel was established to consider the dispute. The Spanish tariff was not bound under GATT Article II.]

4.6   The Panel examined all arguments that had been advanced during the proceedings for the justification of a different tariff treatment for various groups and types of unroasted coffee. It noted that these arguments mainly related to organoleptic differences resulting from geographical factors, cultivation methods, the processing of the beans, and the genetic factor. The Panel did not consider that such differences were sufficient reason to allow for a different tariff treatment. It pointed out that it was not unusual in the case of agricultural products that the taste and aroma of the end-product would differ because of one or several of the above-mentioned factors.

4.7 The Panel furthermore found relevant to its examination of the matter that unroasted coffee was mainly, if not exclusively, sold in the form of blends, combining various types of coffee, and that coffee in its end-use, was universally regarded as a well-defined and single product intended for drinking.

4.8 The Panel noted that no other contracting party applied its tariff régime in respect of unroasted, non-decaffeinated coffee in such a way that different types of coffee were subject to different tariff rates.

4.9 In the light of the foregoing, the Panel *concluded* that unroasted, non-decaffeinated coffee beans * * * should be considered as "like products" within the meaning of Article I:1.

4.10 The Panel further noted that Brazil exported to Spain mainly "unwashed Arabica" and also Robusta coffee which were both presently charged with higher duties than that applied to "mild" coffee. Since these were considered to be "like products", the Panel *concluded* that the tariff régime as presently applied by Spain was discriminatory vis-à-vis unroasted coffee originating in Brazil.

Notes and Questions

(1) The concept of like products is a crucial one for the MFN clause of Article I:1. The same or similar language appears in other GATT provisions as well. For example, as we will see in Chapter 12, the obligation to provide national treatment under Article III is limited in part to like products. Under the provisions of Article VI, contracting parties are permitted to impose antidumping or countervailing duties on dumped or subsidized imports that materially injure domestic producers of the like product. The Escape Clause of Article XIX allows parties to restrict imports when the imports seriously injure a domestic industry producing like or directly competitive products.

It is agreed that the term "like product" should not necessarily be interpreted the same way in each of these provisions, and we will consider cases in several chapters dealing with these definitions. But how should the definition of the term should vary from clause to clause? Since both Articles I and III are basic antidiscrimination provisions at the heart of the General Agreement, it can be argued that the term should be construed broadly in those articles, so as to strike down discriminatory measures wherever possible. On the other hand, it can be argued that the term should be interpreted most narrowly in the case of Article VI, since that article establishes an exception to general GATT rules. However, the Article VI exception exists because it is felt by many that dumped and subsidized imports are unfair, suggesting a broader interpretation perhaps. We will revisit the definition of like product in later chapters when we discuss the foregoing provisions.

(2) Would you characterize the *SPF* interpretation of the term like product as narrow or broad? What about the interpretation given in the *Spanish Coffee* case? Are they consistent? If not, which do you think was the preferable interpretation? In that connection, are you persuaded, as the *Spanish Coffee* panel seemed to be, that coffee is coffee? Does the market recognize any differences in types of coffee?

(3) The MFN clause has been characterized as an antidiscrimination provision. Do you think that the discrimination challenged in *SPF* and *Spanish Coffee* was the type of discrimination that the clause was designed to combat? Or should countries be free to classify products as finely as they wish for tariff purposes? How does the GATT principle, discussed in Section 8.1, that import protection should be afforded principally by tariffs relate to this issue?

Historically, one impact of MFN on tariff negotiations is to encourage the use of narrower and narrower classifications of goods, as negotiating countries try to limit the benefit of a tariff binding to the nation with whom it is negotiating, preventing "free-rider" benefits to third parties. Thus if A and B both export brandy to the United States, and the United States wishes to reciprocate concessions made by A but not B, then the fact (if true) that most of A's brandy is high priced and most of B's brandy is low priced, will suggest to the United States that its "concession" to A should be only on high priced brandy and not on all brandy. The classic example of this technique was the product description contained in the Swiss–German Treaty of 1904, reducing German tariffs on the importation of "large dapple mountain cattle or brown cattle reared at a spot at least 300 metres above sea level and having at least one month's grazing each year at a spot at least 800 metres above sea level."[3]

What limits are there (or should there be) on such attempts to distinguish what on the surface appear to be identical products (i.e. brandy or cows)? Must there be some structural difference in the products? Is it enough that identical products were produced under different conditions? Sold at different prices?

What other arguments, not based on Article I, might be raised under Article XXIII to challenge a discriminatory tariff classification? Consider the following GATT panel report.

TREATMENT BY GERMANY OF IMPORTS OF SARDINES

GATT Panel Report Adopted October 31, 1952
1st Supp. BISD 53 (1953)

[In 1951, the Federal Republic of Germany began imposing an import duty of 14 per cent on preparations of clupea pilchardus as

---

3. See Gerard Curzon, Multilateral Commercial Diplomacy: The General Agreement on Tariffs and Trade and Its Impact on National Commercial Policies and Techniques 60 & n. 1 (1965).

compared with a duty of 20 per cent for clupea harengus and 25 per cent for clupea sprattus. The products were also treated differently in respect of internal taxes and quantitative restrictions. Although the parties disputed whether these three products were "like products" for the purposes of Articles I and XIII, the panel did not decide that issue. It simply noted that the history of the negotiations suggested that the parties had not considered them to be like products. The panel did consider, however, whether in the absence of a violation of Articles I and XIII, Norway's anticipated benefits under the General Agreement had been nullified or impaired.]

16. The Panel * * * agreed that such impairment would exist if the action of the German Government, which resulted in upsetting the competitive relationship between preparations of clupea pilchardus and preparations of the other varieties of the clupeoid family could not reasonably have been anticipated by the Norwegian Government at the time it negotiated for tariff reductions on preparations of clupea sprattus and clupea harengus. The Panel concluded that the Government of Norway had reason to assume, during these negotiations that preparations of the type of clupeae in which they were interested would not be less favourably treated than other preparations of the same family and that this situation would not be modified by unilateral action of the German Government. In reaching this conclusion, the Panel was influenced in particular by the following circumstances:

(a) the products of the various varieties of clupeae are closely related and are considered by many interested parties as directly competitive;

(b) that both parties agreed that the question of the equality of treatment was discussed in the course of the Torquay negotiations; and

(c) although no conclusive evidence was produced as to the scope and tenor of the assurances or statements which may have been given or made in the course of these discussions, it is reasonable to assume that the Norwegian delegation in assessing the value of the concessions offered by Germany regarding preparations of clupeae and in offering counter concessions, had taken into account the advantages resulting from the continuation of the system of equality which had prevailed ever since 1925.

17. As the measures taken by the German Government have nullified the validity of the assumptions which governed the attitude of the Norwegian delegation and substantially reduced the value of the concessions obtained by Norway, the Panel found that the Norwegian Government is justified in claiming that it had suffered an impairment of a benefit accruing to it under the General Agreement.

18.   In the light of the considerations set out above, the Panel suggests to the CONTRACTING PARTIES that it would be appropriate for the CONTRACTING PARTIES to make a recommendation to Germany and Norway in accordance with the first sentence of paragraph 2 of Article XXIII. This recommendation should aim at restoring, as far as practicable, the competitive relationship which existed at the time when the Norwegian Government negotiated at Torquay and which that Government could reasonably expect to be continued.

Notes and Questions

(1)   Do think that there was adequate evidence to show that Norway met the requirements for establishing a "non-violation" claim under the Article XXIII? Non-violation claims are discussed generally in Section 7.3(A) supra.

(2)   The GATT MFN clause applies only "to any product," and thus does not apply to services or consular rights and business establishment. An important policy question faced in the Uruguay Round was whether and to what extent a GATT Article I-type MFN obligation should be included in an agreement on trade in services. See Chapter 19 infra. The same issue arose in respect of the TRIPS Agreement. See Chapter 20 infra.

(2) The Breadth of the MFN Obligation

CANADA—CERTAIN MEASURES AFFECTING THE AUTOMOTIVE INDUSTRY

WT/DS139 & 142/AB/R, adopted by the DSB on June 19, 2000

7.   The Canadian measure at issue in this appeal is duty-free treatment provided to imports of automobiles, buses and specified commercial vehicles ("motor vehicles") by certain manufacturers under the Customs Tariff, the Motor Vehicles Tariff Order, 1998 (the "MVTO 1998") and the Special Remission Orders (the "SROs"). The conditions under which eligibility for the import duty exemption is determined are set out in the MVTO 1998, the SROs and certain Letters of Undertaking (the "Letters").

8.   The MVTO 1998 has its origins in the Agreement Concerning Automotive Products Between the Government of Canada and the Government of the United States of America (the "Auto Pact"), which was implemented domestically in Canada [in 1965].

9.   Under the MVTO 1998, the import duty exemption is available to manufacturers of motor vehicles on imports "from any country entitled to the Most–Favoured–Nation Tariff", if the manufacturer meets the following three conditions: (1) it must have produced in Canada, during the designated "base year", motor vehicles of the class imported; (2) the ratio of the net sales value of the vehicles *produced in Canada* to the net sales value of all vehicles of that class *sold* for consumption *in Canada* in the period of importation must be "equal to or higher than" the ratio in the "base year", and the ratio shall not in any case be lower than 75:100 (the "ratio requirements"); and (3) the

amount of Canadian value added in the manufacturer's local production of motor vehicles must be "equal to or greater than" the amount of Canadian value added in the local production of motor vehicles of that class during the "base year" (the "CVA requirements").

10. The Panel found that, as a matter of fact, the average ratio requirements applicable to the MVTO 1998 beneficiaries are "as a general rule" 95:100 for automobiles, and "at least" 75:100 for buses and specified commercial vehicles.

11. The MVTO 1998 states that the CVA used by a particular manufacturer shall be calculated based on the "aggregate" of certain listed costs of production, which are, broadly speaking:

— the cost of parts produced in Canada and of materials of Canadian origin that are incorporated in the motor vehicles;

— transportation costs;

— labour costs incurred in Canada;

— manufacturing overhead expenses incurred in Canada;

— general and administrative expenses incurred in Canada that are attributable to the production of motor vehicles;

— depreciation in respect of machinery and permanent plant equipment located in Canada that is attributable to the production of motor vehicles; and

— a capital cost allowance for land and buildings in Canada that are used in the production of motor vehicles.

12. Through the SROs, Canada has also designated certain other companies, in addition to those qualifying under the MVTO 1998, as eligible to import motor vehicles duty-free. Canada promulgated the SROs under the authority of the Financial Administration Act for certain companies that had not met the original conditions of the MVTO 1965. The SROs entitle motor vehicles imported by these companies to receive the import duty exemption as long as they meet certain designated conditions. Specifically, the SROs provide for the remission of duties on imports of motor vehicles where conditions relating to certain specified production-to-sales ratio requirements and CVA requirements are fulfilled.

13. With respect to the actual ratio and CVA requirements under the SROs, each SRO sets out specific ratio and CVA requirements to be met by the company receiving the SRO. For ratio requirements, the SROs issued before 1977 set the production-to-sales ratios at 75:100. Since then, almost all SROs have set ratios at 100:100. For CVA, requirements under the SROs range from 40 to 60 per cent, as follows.

14. In accordance with its obligations under the CUSFTA [Canada–United States Free Trade Agreement], since 1989, Canada has not designated any additional manufacturers to be eligible for the import duty exemption under the MVTO 1998, nor has Canada promulgated any new SROs. Also, the MVTO 1998 specifically excludes vehicles imported

by a manufacturer which did not qualify before 1 January 1988. Thus, the list of manufacturers eligible for the import duty exemption is closed.

* * *

69.   On appeal, the issue before us is whether the import duty exemption accorded by this measure is consistent with Canada's obligations under Article I:1 of the GATT 1994. We are confronted with the daunting task of interpreting certain aspects of the "most-favoured-nation" ("MFN") principle that has long been a cornerstone of the GATT and is one of the pillars of the WTO trading system.

70.   In examining the measure in issue, we note that the import duty exemption is afforded by Canada to imports of some, but not all, motor vehicles. We observe, first of all, that the Canadian Customs Tariff provides that a motor vehicle normally enters Canada at an MFN tariff rate of 6.1 per cent. This is also the bound *ad valorem* rate in Canada's WTO Schedule of Concessions. The MVTO 1998 and the SROs modify this rate by providing the import duty exemption for motor vehicles imported by certain manufacturers meeting certain ratio requirements and CVA requirements. The MVTO 1998 accords the import duty exemption in the form of a "reduced rate of customs duty", established in the amended Canadian Customs Tariff as "free". The SROs accord the import duty exemption in the form of a full duty "remission".

71.   Although the measure on its face imposes no formal restriction on the *origin* of the imported motor vehicle, the Panel found that, in practice, major automotive firms in Canada import only their own make of motor vehicle and those of related companies. Thus, according to the Panel,

> General Motors in Canada imports only GM motor vehicles and those of its affiliates; Ford in Canada imports only Ford motor vehicles and those of its affiliates; the same is true of Chrysler and of Volvo. These four companies all have qualified as beneficiaries of the import duty exemption. In contrast, other motor vehicle companies in Canada, such as Toyota, Nissan, Honda, Mazda, Subaru, Hyundai, Volkswagen and BMW, all of which also import motor vehicles only from related companies, do not benefit from the import duty exemption.

72.   Therefore, the Panel considered that, in practice, a motor vehicle imported into Canada is granted the "advantage" of the import duty exemption only if it originates in one of a small number of countries in which an exporter of motor vehicles is affiliated with a manufacturer/importer in Canada that has been designated as eligible to import motor vehicles duty-free under the MVTO 1998 or under an SRO.

73.   Since 1989, no manufacturer not already benefiting from the import duty exemption on motor vehicles has been able to qualify under the MVTO 1998 or under an SRO. The list of manufacturers eligible for the import duty exemption was closed by Canada in 1989 in fulfilment of Canada's obligations under the CUSFTA.

74.   Thus, in sum, while the Canadian Customs Tariff normally allows a motor vehicle to enter Canada at the MFN duty rate of 6.1 per cent, the same motor vehicle has the "advantage" of entering Canada duty-free when imported by a designated manufacturer under the MVTO 1998 or under the SROs.

75.   In determining whether this measure is consistent with Article I:1 of the GATT 1994, we begin our analysis, as always, by examining the words of the treaty. Article I:1 states, in pertinent part:

> With respect to customs duties and charges of any kind imposed on or in connection with importation or exportation . . . *any* advantage, favour, privilege or immunity granted by any Member to *any* product originating in or destined for any other country shall be accorded *immediately and unconditionally* to the *like product* originating in or destined for the territories of *all other Members*. (emphasis added)

76.   The applicability of certain elements of Article I:1 is not in dispute in this case. First, the parties do not dispute that the import duty exemption is an "advantage, favour, privilege or immunity granted by any Member to any product". Second, it is not disputed that some, but not all, motor vehicles imported from certain Members are accorded the import duty exemption, while some, but not all, like motor vehicles imported from certain other Members are not. Third, the Panel's interpretation that the term "unconditionally" refers to advantages conditioned on the "situation or conduct" of exporting countries has not been appealed.

77.   One main issue remains in dispute: has the import duty exemption, accorded by the measure to motor vehicles originating in some countries, in which affiliates of certain designated manufacturers under the measure are present, also been accorded to like motor vehicles from all other Members, in accordance with Article I:1 of the GATT 1994?

78.   In approaching this question, we observe first that the words of Article I:1 do not restrict its scope only to cases in which the failure to accord an "advantage" to like products of all other Members appears *on the face* of the measure, or can be demonstrated on the basis of the words of the measure. Neither the words *"de jure"* nor *"de facto"* appear in Article I:1. Nevertheless, we observe that Article I:1 does not cover only "in law", or *de jure*, discrimination. As several GATT panel reports confirmed, Article I:1 covers also "in fact", or *de facto*, discrimination.[4] Like the Panel, we cannot accept Canada's argument that

---

4.   [original note 70] We note, though, that the measures examined in those reports differed from the measure in this case. Two of those reports dealt with "like" product issues: *Spain–Tariff Treatment of Unroasted Coffee; Japan–Tariff on Imports of Spruce, Pine, Fir (SPF) Dimension Lumber*. In this case, as we have noted, there is no dispute that the motor vehicles subject to the import duty exemption are "like" products. Furthermore, two other reports dealt with measures which, on their face, discriminated on a strict "origin" basis, so that, at any given time, either *every* product, or *no* product, of a particular origin was accorded an advantage. See panel report, *Belgian Family Allowances*, G/32, adopted 7 November 1952, BISD 1S/59;

Article I:1 does not apply to measures which, on their face, are "origin-neutral".

79.   We note next that Article I:1 requires that *"any advantage, favour, privilege or immunity granted by any Member to any product originating in or destined for any other country shall be accorded immediately and unconditionally to the like product originating in or destined for the territories of all other Members."* (emphasis added) The words of Article I:1 refer not to *some* advantages granted "with respect to" the subjects that fall within the defined scope of the Article, but to *"any advantage"*; not to *some* products, but to *"any product"*; and not to like products from *some* other Members, but to like products originating in or destined for *"all other"* Members.

80.   We note also the Panel's conclusion that, in practice, a motor vehicle imported into Canada is granted the "advantage" of the import duty exemption only if it originates in one of a small number of countries in which an exporter of motor vehicles is affiliated with a manufacturer/importer in Canada that has been designated as eligible to import motor vehicles duty-free under the MVTO 1998 or under an SRO.

81.   Thus, from both the text of the measure and the Panel's conclusions about the practical operation of the measure, it is apparent to us that "[w]ith respect to customs duties...imposed on or in connection with importation...," Canada has granted an "advantage" to some products from some Members that Canada has not "accorded immediately and unconditionally" to "like" products "originating in or destined for the territories of *all other Members.*" (emphasis added) And this, we conclude, is not consistent with Canada's obligations under Article I:1 of the GATT 1994.

82.   The context of Article I:1 within the GATT 1994 supports this conclusion. Apart from Article I:1, several "MFN-type" clauses dealing with varied matters are contained in the GATT 1994. The very existence of these other clauses demonstrates the pervasive character of the MFN principle of non-discrimination.

83.   The drafters also wrote various exceptions to the MFN principle into the GATT 1947 which remain in the GATT 1994. Canada invoked one such exception before the Panel, relating to customs unions and free trade areas under Article XXIV. This justification was rejected by the Panel, and the Panel's findings on Article XXIV were not appealed by Canada. Canada has invoked no other provision of the GATT 1994, or of any other covered agreement, that would justify the inconsistency of the import duty exemption with Article I:1 of the GATT 1994.

84.   The object and purpose of Article I:1 supports our interpretation. That object and purpose is to prohibit discrimination among like products originating in or destined for different countries. The prohibi-

panel report, *European Economic Community–Imports of Beef from Canada*, L/5099, adopted 10 March 1981, BISD 28S/92. In this case, motor vehicles imported into Canada are not disadvantaged in that same sense.

tion of discrimination in Article I:1 also serves as an incentive for concessions, negotiated reciprocally, to be extended to all other Members on an MFN basis.

85.   The measure maintained by Canada accords the import duty exemption to certain motor vehicles entering Canada from certain countries. These privileged motor vehicles are imported by a limited number of designated manufacturers who are required to meet certain performance conditions. In practice, this measure does not accord the same import duty exemption immediately and unconditionally to like motor vehicles of *all* other Members, as required under Article I:1 of the GATT 1994. The advantage of the import duty exemption is accorded to some motor vehicles originating in certain countries without being accorded to like motor vehicles from *all* other Members. Accordingly, we find that this measure is not consistent with Canada's obligations under Article I:1 of the GATT 1994.

86.   We, therefore, uphold the Panel's conclusion that Canada acts inconsistently with Article I:1 of the GATT 1994 by according the advantage of the import duty exemption to motor vehicles originating in certain countries, pursuant to the MVTO 1998 and the SROs, which advantage is not accorded immediately and unconditionally to like products originating in the territories of all other WTO Members.

Notes and Questions

(1) INDONESIA—CERTAIN MEASURES AFFECTING THE AUTO-MOTIVE INDUSTRY, WT/DS54, 55, 59 & 64/R, adopted by the DSB on July 23, 1998 (not appealed), involved a challenge by Japan, the EC and the U.S. to certain exemptions from Indonesian customs duties and internal taxes, which were alleged to be conditional and available *de facto* only to imports of motor vehicles from Korea but not to imports of like products from other WTO Members. The Indonesian measure at issue benefited imports by PT PTN, a private Indonesian company, of certain cars ("National Cars") made for it by Kia, a Korean company. The panel rejected Indonesia's argument that a private-sector choice, not government direction, was the reason why there were imports from Korea and that such a private choice was not within the scope of Article I. In the view of the panel:

> 14.143   * * * The GATT case law is clear to the effect that any such advantage (here tax and customs duty benefits) cannot be made conditional on any criteria that is not related to the imported product itself. [The panel cited *Belgian Family Allowances*, 1st Supp. BISD 59 (Panel report adopted November 7, 1952), involving a Belgian charge levied on purchases by public authorities that was applicable depending on whether products originated in a country that had a system of family allowances meeting certain criteria].

* * *

> 14.145   Indeed, it appears that the design and structure of the [challenged Indonesian measure] is such as to allow situations where another Member's like product to a National Car imported by PT PTN

from Korea will be subject to much higher duties and sales taxes than those imposed on such National Cars. * * * The distinction as to whether one product is subject to 0% duty and the other one is subject to 200% duty * * * depends on whether or not PT TPN had made a "deal" with that exporting company to produce that National Car, and is covered by the authorization of June 1996 with specifications that correspond to those of the Kia car produced only in Korea. In the GATT/WTO, the right of Members cannot be made dependent upon, conditional on or even affected by, any private contractual obligations in place. The existence of these conditions is inconsistent with the provisions of Article I:1 which provides that tax and customs duty benefits accorded to products of one Member (here on Korean products) be accorded to imported like products from other Members "immediately and unconditionally".

The finding of a violation by the panel in *Indonesia–Autos* does not seem to depend on a showing of *de facto* discrimination, but rather only on the fact that some autos from Korea received more favorable tariff treatment than like autos from the complainants. The panel in *Canada–Autos* rejected this broad interpretation of Article I. In its view, the use of the word "unconditionally" in Article I:1 did not mean that the availability of a tariff rate could not be made subject to conditions, but rather that such conditions could not result in *de facto* discrimination. WT/DS139 & 142/R, paras. 10.18–10.30. The Appellate Body report does not explicitly address this issue. In your view, which panel report correctly interprets Article I:1? Could Article XVII have been invoked in these cases?

(2) How narrowly should like products be defined in a case like *Canada–Autos*? In United States—Denial of Most–Favored–Nation Treatment as to Non-rubber Footwear From Brazil, 39th Supp. BISD 128 (1993), adopted June 19, 1992, Brazil complained that the procedures under which U.S. countervailing duties were revoked (i.e., terminated) violated the most-favored-nation clause of Article I. It claimed that the U.S. applied different rules to goods imported under the U.S. Generalized System of Preferences (GSP) than were applied to Brazilian imports. In its examination, the panel noted that the GSP products to which the allegedly more favorable procedures had actually been applied (industrial fasteners, industrial lime, automotive glass) were not like the product to which the less favorable procedures had been applied in the case of Brazil (non-rubber footwear). However, the panel noted that Brazil not only claimed that the application of these two procedures in concrete cases was inconsistent with Article I:1 of the General Agreement but also that the U.S. rules themselves were inconsistent with that provision. As such, it noted that the products to which one rule accords advantages were therefore in principle the same products to which the other rule denies the advantages. Was the panel's application of "like product" consistent with those of the prior cases in this section?

(3) Because Article I's MFN obligation applies to internal taxes and sales regulations subject to Article III's national treatment obligation, the scope of the MFN obligation depends in part on the scope of Article III.

(C) GATT AND THE MFN EXCEPTIONS

The most significant GATT exceptions to MFN are found in two Articles related in one way or another to the issue of preferential trade arrangements. These are Article I:2 dealing with tariff preferences in force when the General Agreement was drafted and Article XXIV which allows for the formation of customs unions and free trade areas.

Article I:2 has become less significant over the years as the number of colonies declined drastically and the related colonial preferences largely disappeared. In practical terms, however, these preferences have effectively been replaced and vastly expanded under the so-called Generalized System of Preferences (GSP). This system was instituted under a 10 year GATT waiver obtained in 1971 by various industrial countries for the benefit of developing countries. Since the Tokyo Round, the GSP preferences have been maintained under the authority of the so-called Enabling Clause, which was adopted by the Contracting Parties at the conclusion of the Tokyo Round. See Decision of the Contracting Parties of Nov. 28, 1979, on Differential and More Favourable Treatment, Reciprocity and Fuller Participation of Developing Countries, 26th Supp. BISD 203 (1980). There is considerable controversy over the adequacy and desirability of developing country preferences. We will explore these issues in detail in Chapter 25.

Traditionally there has been an exception to MFN obligations for border traffic and limited regional arrangements, and so when GATT was drafted it was natural to include such an exception in GATT Article XXIV. It was generally thought that a customs union or free trade area, whereby associated countries eliminated barriers on each other's trade, would be a further step towards general trade liberalization and therefore should be permitted, at least as long as the preferential arrangement did not harm the trade of nonmembers. As we will see in Chapter 11, the economic desirability of such arrangements is now questioned by some. We will also examine in Chapter 11 the detailed conditions that customs unions and free trade areas must meet under Article XXIV.

There are also a few, less important exceptions to the General Agreement's preference for nondiscriminatory treatment. For example, Article VI allows imposition of countervailing and antidumping duties on subsidized exports or imports sold at less than domestic prices, resulting in injury to domestic industries. Article XIV permits discrimination in certain cases in the application of quotas justified on balance of payments grounds. Article XIX permits a country affected by another country's invocation of the Escape Clause to suspend concessions it had made to that country. Under Article XXI, deviations from MFN are permitted for national security reasons. Paragraph 2 of Article XXIII allows a country to be authorized to suspend concessions made to another contracting party that has nullified or impaired its benefits under the General Agreement.

(D) NON–GATT MFN CLAUSES—NOTECASES

The following three notecases are examples of national courts applying MFN clauses.

(1) MARJORIE M. WHITEMAN, 14 DIGEST OF INTERNATIONAL LAW 755 (1970): In an early French case (1913), the French Court of Cassation had to decide whether certain procedural requirements for bringing suit as provided in a French–Swiss Convention on jurisdiction and execution of judgments applied also to German nationals as a result of a most-favored-nation clause in a Franco–German Commercial Treaty. The Franco–German Treaty guaranteed most-favored-nation treatment in their commercial relations including the "admission and treatment of subjects of the two nations." The decision of the Court was based in part on the following propositions: that "these provisions pertain exclusively to the commercial relations between France and Germany, considered from the viewpoint of the rights under international law, but they do not concern, either expressly or implicitly, the rights under civil law, particularly, the rules governing jurisdiction and procedure that are applicable to any disputes that develop in commercial relations between the subjects of the two States;" and that "the most-favored-nation clause may be invoked only if the subject of the treaty stipulating it is the same as that of the particularly favorable treaty the benefit of which is claimed." (Translation.) *Braunkohlen Briket Verkaufsverein Gesellschaft c. Goffart, ès qualités,* Arrêt de la Cour de Cassation du 22 décembre 1913. The decision may be found in *Case Concerning Rights of Nationals of the United States of America in Morocco* (France v. United States of America), II *Pleadings, Oral Arguments, Documents,* I.C.J. (1952) 84–85.

(2) C. TENNANT, SONS & CO. v. DILL, 158 F.Supp. 63 (S.D.N.Y. 1957) concerned the imposition in 1957 by the United States of a quota on importation of Paraguayan tung oil. At the time the quota was imposed, plaintiff had a shipment of tung oil en route to the United States and a second followed shortly thereafter. Plaintiff was unable to import all of its tung oil because the first shipment exceeded the available monthly quota. In an action to force the Collector of Customs to admit the tung oil to the United States, plaintiff relied on GATT Article XIII(3)(b) (the "en route clause") and the most-favored-nation clause of the United States–Paraguay International Trade Agreement. The court analyzed plaintiff's argument as follows:

> Paraguay was not a signatory to GATT (see table following 19 U.S.C.A. sec. 1351). Nevertheless, the plaintiff contends that by reason of the "most-favored-nation" clause contained in Article I of the Paraguayan Trade Agreement, Paraguay is a beneficiary of the en route clause in GATT and that, therefore, the quota restriction here at issue does not apply to plaintiff's en route tung oil. This contention, in my opinion, lacks merit. Article I, subdivision 1, of the Trade Agreement with Paraguay in effect requires the signatories to grant each other unconditional and unrestricted "most-favored-nation" treatment in all matters concerning:

1. Customs duties and subsidiary charges of every kind;

2. The method of levying such duties and charges;

3. The rules, formalities and charges imposed in connection with clearing goods through customs;

4. All laws or regulations affecting the sale, taxation, distribution or use of imported goods within the country.

Subdivision 2 of Article I in substance requires that each of the signatories be accorded treatment equal to that accorded any third country with respect to "duties, taxes or charges" or "any rules or formalities."

The subjects covered by subdivisions 1 and 2 of Article I are described with clarity and particularity. The phrase "import restriction" and the word "quota" nowhere appear. Furthermore, these subdivisions do not, in my opinion, contain language from which their applicability to import restrictions involving the fixing of quotas can be implied.

It is interesting to note that Article I of the Trade Agreement with Paraguay is considerably more explicit and restrictive than are certain other parts of the Trade Agreement. For example, Article III, subdivision 1 of the Agreement employs the language "no prohibition or restriction of any kind" and in Article XII, subdivision 1 the all-inclusive terms "concession" and "customs treatment" are used.

It seems clear, therefore, that the "most-favored-nation" clause contained in the Trade Agreement with Paraguay is not sufficiently broad to entitle Paraguay, and, hence, the plaintiff, to the benefits of the en route provision of GATT.

(3) In MENTULA v. STATE LAND BOARD, 244 Or. 229, 417 P.2d 581 (1966), the Oregon Supreme Court considered a petition of the Consul General of Finland to have proceeds of the estate of a decedent paid to him, to transmit to the sole heir residing in Finland and presumed living. The United States–Finnish Treaty of Friendship and Commerce authorized a Consul General to collect and receive property from estates if he could show that he would remit to the heir. The Treaty also had an MFN clause as to "all the rights, privileges, exemptions and immunities which are enjoyed by officers of the same grade of the most-favored-nation * * *" and on the basis of this the petitioner claimed the estate proceeds *without* the necessity of proving remittance to the heir. The court said (at 233):

Despite centuries of use in many forms of treaties there is a dearth of authority on the meaning and purpose of the most-favored-nation clause. It is held that "This clause means that each signatory grants to the other the broadest rights and privileges which it accords to any other nation in the treaties it has made or will make." Kolovrat v. Oregon, 1961, 366 U.S. 187, 193, 81 S.Ct. 922, 6 L.Ed.2d 218; Ljubich v. Western Cooperage Co., 1919, 93 Or. 633, 637, 184 P. 551. This tells us that we may look to treaties executed both before and after the treaty with Finland was proclaimed. It does not aid in deciding whether or not the grant of additional general authority to a Consular officer by the most favored nation clause includes the specific authority asserted here. No one would dispute that the most favored nation clause does enhance the authority of a Consul to perform his more normal commercial functions, but does the general grant of most favored nation treatment expand the Consul General's specific grant of authority to collect and receipt for his absent countryman in addition to the restricted authority stated in Article XXIX of this particular treaty? We think it does.

(E) PROBLEMS

A, B and C are nations which are members of the WTO. X, Y and Z are nations which do not belong to the WTO, but A and X have a bilateral agreement in which each extends MFN to the other as to tariff duties.

(1) A charges a 10% tariff on bicycles from B. C, X and Y also export bicycles to A; what rate are they entitled to?

(2) X charges a 5% tariff on clock radios from Y. What rate are such products from A, B and Z entitled to when imported into X?

(3) A's GATT binding for toy clocks is 10%. Its custom bureau currently charges 5% tariff on toy clocks from Y. What rate should be applied by A to toy clocks from B, C and X?

(4) A's GATT binding for FM radios is 5%, but A's customs bureau is charging a 10% tariff pursuant to a statute just passed by its Parliament. What recourse do importers of FM radios from B, X or Y have against A? What procedures can be followed?

(5) A charges a tariff of 5% on motorcycle imports, and in addition imposes a quota on motorcycles from B, while prohibiting motorcycle imports from C, X and Y altogether. What rights have B, C, X and Y?

(6) A charges a 5% tariff on imports of autos which weigh less than 2000 pounds; a 20% tariff on other autos. B and X produce only autos weighing less than 2000 pounds; C and Y produce only autos heavier than that. What are the rights of C and Y?

(7) A charges a 5% tariff on imports of autos which operate on less than 20 miles per gallon; a 20% tariff on the rest. B and X autos use less than 20 miles per gallon; C and Y autos more. What are the rights of C and Y?

(8) A charges a 5% tariff on imports of autos without shatter-proof glass; but 20% for autos equipped with shatter-proof glass. A has a large domestic industry which produces shatter-proof glass, and so does B. B sells such glass to its own auto makers and to those of X, both of whom export autos to A. Do B and X have a valid complaint?

(9) A charges a 5% tariff on automobiles from countries with average auto industry wage rates over $4.00 per hour; 20% for autos from other countries. B and X auto wage rates are under $4.00 per hour, C and Y rates are over that amount. Do B and X have a valid complaint?

(10) A charges a 5% tariff on textile imports from countries with a per capita gross national product less than $1000 per year; a 20% tariff on the rest. C and Z are textile exporting countries with per capita annual GNP less than $1000. Do B, X and Y have any recourse?

(11) B imports hand-crafted baskets from Y in bulk lots of 1000, repackages them individually, and exports them to A. A's GATT binding on baskets is 10% but it charges a 30% tariff on these basket imports. Can B complain?

(12) A normally charges 5%, its GATT binding, on imports of cooking pans. Under a national countervailing duty law, its officials have determined that B's grants of low interest "development loans" to the cooking pan industry, for encouraging exports, are "subsidies" and consequently A imposes a countervailing duty of another 10% on pots and pans produced in B. C, X and Y have similar programs of government export encouraging loans and their cooking pan industries, as well as their basket weaving industries, benefit. However, A does not impose countervailing duties on either cooking pans or baskets from C, X or Y. Does B have a valid complaint?

(13) B's countervailing duty law exempts all imports from countries which have per capita annual GNP of less than $1000. Does A or Y have a valid complaint?

(14) Suppose B's countervailing duty law exemption were not explicit, but merely a "practice" of its officials?

(15) C, a developing country, exports bauxite (for aluminum production). It imposes: a) a ban on bauxite exports to A; b) a 50% export tax on exports of bauxite to X and Y, but not Z or B. What rights do A, X and Y have?

SECTION 10.3   MOST FAVORED NATION OBLIGATION IN THE UNITED STATES

(A) THE TRADE ACT OF 1974

United States law specifies MFN treatment for most imports. Section 126(a) of the Trade Act of 1974 requires (unless otherwise provided by law) "any duty or other import restriction or duty-free treatment proclaimed in carrying out any trade agreement under this [Act] shall apply to products of all foreign countries, whether imported directly or indirectly."[1] For tariff purposes, the following countries did not receive

---

1. 19 U.S.C.A. sec. 2136. By its terms, section 126(a) only applied to duties or restrictions proclaimed in implementing the Tokyo Round agreements, which includes

such treatment as of June 2001: Afghanistan, Cuba, Laos, Montenegro, North Korea, Serbia and Vietnam. U.S. Harmonized Tariff Schedule (2001), General Note 3(a).

Today, the major exceptions to the above rule are (i) the Generalized System of Preferences for developing countries, created by title V of the 1974 Act and described in Chapter 25 infra; (ii) similar, but more extensive, preferences for African, Caribbean and Andean countries under specific legislation described in Chapter 25 infra; and (iii) the U.S. Free Trade Agreements with Israel and with Canada and Mexico (NAFTA), described in Section 11.3 infra. Formerly, another major exception to the MFN requirement was for Communist countries, but as explained below in recent years, most such countries have received MFN treatment, either by statute or through a special waiver procedure under title IV of the 1974 Act.

Several other provisions of the 1974 Act permit departures from MFN treatment, most notably the balance-of-payments (BOP) authority (Section 122(a)(2)) and the revised retaliatory authority (originally Sections 301–302, now Sections 301–310)).

(B) U.S. IMPLEMENTATION OF THE TOKYO AND URUGUAY ROUND AGREEMENTS AND MFN

As has been discussed previously, the Tokyo Round resulted in a whole series of side agreements on various trade issues. Generally, these agreements had procedural and governance provisions that gave a voice only to signatories. In that sense, even if the tangible benefits of the agreements accrued to all GATT members because of GATT's MFN requirements, nonsignatory members of GATT were treated differently. Much more significantly, two of the side agreements—the Subsidies Code and the Government Procurement Code—only obligated the parties thereto to apply the provisions of the Code to other parties.[2]

In implementing the Subsidies Code and the Government Procurement Code, as well as the Standards Code,[3] the U.S. Trade Agreements Act of 1979 provided that the benefits of each of the three codes were to be available only to other parties of the code in question, and, in the case of the Subsidies Code, only to parties who had assumed obligations to the United States which were substantially equivalent to U.S. obligations

most of those now in force, but its effect has been extended to apply to the results of the Uruguay Round. Omnibus Trade and Competitiveness Act of 1988, sec. 1105(a)(codified at 19 U.S.C.A. sec. 2904). This policy predates the 1974 Act. For example, Section 251 of the 1962 Trade Expansion Act required that trade agreements concessions negotiated with one country be automatically extended to all others— whether or not an international commitment such as the GATT would entitle others to such concessions—so long as the re-

cipient did not discriminate against U.S. trade. Pub.L.No. 87–794, 76 Stat. 872 (1962).

2. Agreement on Interpretation and Implementation of Article VI, XVI and XXIII, art. 1, GATT, 26th Supp. BISD 56, 57 (1980); Agreement on Government Procurement, art. II(1), GATT, 26th Supp. BISD 33, 35 (1980).

3. Agreement on Technical Barriers to Trade, GATT, 26th Supp. BISD 8 (1980).

under the Code, which excluded some developing country parties to the Code.[4]

Notes and Questions

(1) An interesting question is whether the GATT MFN obligations could have been interpreted to require the United States to apply the rules of the Subsidies Code to nonsignatories who were GATT members and to signatories that the United States believed had not fully implemented the Code. Nonapplication by the United States would have meant that a Code party would not have been entitled to an injury determination before countervailing duties were imposed on its exports to the U.S. Not requiring such a determination would have made it far more likely that duties would be imposed. In the early 1980's, the United States refused to apply the Code to India on the grounds that even though India was a Code signatory, it had not undertaken the same obligations that the U.S. had undertaken in the Code. India claimed that the United States had violated its basic obligations under Article I of GATT and invoked the GATT dispute settlement procedures. India later dropped its complaint when the United States announced that it would apply the Code to India.[5] Would India have won if its dispute with the United States had been considered by a GATT panel? The issue in the Indian case was complicated by the fact that the old U.S. countervailing duty law benefited from the existing legislation exception of the Protocol of Provisional Application.

(2) Under the WTO, parties that join the WTO must adhere to all of the various annexed agreements, with the exception of those dealing with government procurement and civil aircraft. As a result, the MFN problems presented by the Tokyo Round side agreements, all of which had limited memberships, should not arise in implementation of the Uruguay Round results.

(3) For the most part, the U.S. still limits the benefits of the Government Procurement Agreement to other parties to that agreement.[6] Does that practice violate Article I of GATT? Consider GATT Articles III:8 and XVII:1 in framing an answer. Could an MFN clause in a typical FCN agreement be invoked to claim MFN treatment in government procurement matters? For example, the U.S.-German Friendship, Commerce and Navigation Treaty of October 29, 1954, 7 U.S.T. 1839, TIAS 3593, provides in Article XVII:2 that

> [e]ach party shall accord to the nationals, companies and commerce of the other Party fair and equitable treatment, as compared with that accorded to the nationals, companies and commerce of any third country, with respect to: (a) the governmental purchase of supplies; (b) the awarding of concessions and other government contracts * * *.

4. Trade Agreements Act of 1979, secs. 101, 301, 422, 19 U.S.C.A. secs. 1671(a), 2511, 2552.

5. 46 Fed.Reg. 48391 (1981). An Indian representative at GATT stated to the Committee on Subsidies that Indian legislation did not contain provisions in conflict with the Subsidies Code and that it would comply with the Code if it took countervailing action. GATT, 28th Supp. BISD 28 (1982). See also GATT, 29th Supp. BISD 113 (1983) (report of settlement).

6. Trade Agreements Act of 1979, sec. 301, 19 U.S.C.A. sec. 2511(b).

Could the United States discriminate against Germany in the area of government procurement? Would the "fair and equitable" language allow such discrimination so long as Germany had not made concessions on government procurement similar to those made by the favored country? In 1993, Germany took the position, over EU protests, that this clause prohibited Germany from discriminating against U.S. companies in certain procurement matters, even though there was an EC directive requiring such discrimination.[7]

(C) THE UNITED STATES AND COMMUNIST COUNTRIES

During the Cold War, the United States restricted its trade with Communist countries. In the case of exports, those countries were the main target of U.S. export controls based on national security concerns and a frequent target of controls based on general foreign policy reasons. In the case of imports, the United States generally did not provide MFN treatment to imports from Communist countries, did not allow them to benefit from the U.S. GSP program, and enacted a number of statutes (e.g., the antidumping laws and section 406 of the 1974 Trade Act) that provided means to restrict Communist country imports on the basis of more easily met standards than applicable to imports in general. This disparate treatment is becoming less significant as the United States normalizes its relations with ex-Communist countries. Accordingly, in this section we will describe only briefly the history and current status of U.S. controls on imports from Communist countries.

The United States extended most-favored-nation treatment to the Soviet Union in 1937.[8] However, in 1951 Congress directed that MFN treatment be withdrawn from all countries controlled or dominated by the World Communist movement.[9] In 1972, the United States entered into a trade agreement with the Soviet Union, which provided that Soviet exports to the United States were to receive MFN treatment.[10] The President proposed approval of the MFN agreement as part of the general trade bill introduced in 1973, which eventually was adopted as the Trade Act of 1974. The provisions dealing with MFN and Communist countries were the most controversial in the proposed legislation. The controversy centered on the extent to which the United States should use the prospect of granting MFN treatment to the Soviet Union as a lever to extract Soviet policy changes in other areas, and, in particular, the expansion of emigration opportunities for Soviet citizens.

As enacted, title IV of the Trade Act of 1974 (i) required that the President continue to deny MFN treatment to those countries not then receiving it,[11] (ii) established a procedure by which MFN treatment could

---

7. 10 BNA Intl. Trade Rptr. 974 (1993).

8. Presidential Proclamation, 50 Stat. 1619 (1937).

9. Pub.L.No. 49, Ch. 139, sec. 5, 65 Stat. 73 (1951).

10. U.S.-U.S.S.R. Agreement Regarding Trade, with annexes and exchange of let-ters; signed at Washington, 18 Oct. 1972. For reasons made clear in the text of this section, this agreement failed to enter into force.

11. Trade Act of 1974, sec. 401; 19 U.S.C.A. sec. 2431.

be granted to such countries in the future,[12] and (iii) established a special procedure for limiting imports from Communist countries if the imports caused market disruption.[13] The Trade Act constituted a congressional rejection of granting MFN treatment to the Soviet Union and the 1972 trade agreement never came into effect.

The 1974 Trade Act tied the President's power to enter into commercial agreements with a Communist country and to grant MFN treatment to such country to the emigration rules of that country. The Act also provided, however, that the President could waive the free-emigration rule in certain circumstances. To prevent presidential misuse of the waiver power, the Act provided an elaborate process through which Congress had an annual right to review individual waivers granted by the President.

For the next twenty years, the result of these waiver procedures and other trade measures taken for foreign policy reasons was an ever changing U.S. policy toward these countries. While most ex-Communist countries now receive MFN treatment, some are still subject to the annual waiver procedure. In the case of China, the annual process has been particularly controversial, although MFN status has continued in effect since first extended in 1979. Indeed, the term "most-favored-nation treatment" has been changed to "normal trade relations", to prevent critics from claiming that China was getting particularly favorable treatment as a *most* favored nation.[14] In 2000, Congress approved permanent normal trade relations status for China, conditional on its accession to the WTO.[15]

Notes and Questions

(1) Why is MFN treatment important? Without MFN treatment, what chance do a country's exports have in the U.S. market?

(2) If you were advising a business client about the long term stability of trade relations between the United States and any of the countries subject to the annual waiver process, what would you advise?

(3) The general wisdom of linking trade policy to other policies, such as human rights, worker rights or arms sales, is discussed in Chapter 21.

---

12. Trade Act of 1974, secs. 402–405; 19 U.S.C.A. secs. 2432–35.

13. Trade Act of 1974, sec. 406; 19 U.S.C.A. sec. 2436.

14. Pub. L. 105–201, sec. 5003(b)(2), July 22, 1998, 112 Stat. 685, 789, substitut- ed "normal trade relations" for "most-favored-nation treatment" wherever appearing in Section 402 of the 1974 Trade Act.

15. Pub. L. 106–286, October 10, 2000, 114 Stat. 880.

Chapter 11

FREE TRADE AREAS AND CUSTOMS UNIONS

SECTION 11.1 INTRODUCTION

(A) THE GROWTH OF REGIONALISM

In Chapter 10, we introduced the most favored nation concept and its important exceptions. The most important of all has proven to be the Article XXIV exception for customs unions and free trade areas, so important that we treat it in a separate chapter.

Arrangements that reduce or eliminate trade barriers between two or more political units while maintaining barriers against imports from outside regions date back to the 19th century.[1] Customs unions, as they were generally called, were established by means of treaties or agreements between and among the various states of the German, Austrian and British empires. In the first half of the 20th century, before the establishment of GATT, there were customs unions between European, African and South American states. Since the formation of GATT, regional economic groups have continued to flourish.

Western Europe has the European Union (EU), formerly known as the European Economic Community (EEC), the European Free Trade Area (EFTA) and the European Economic Area (EEA). See Section 4.2 supra. The United States has free trade agreements with Canada and Mexico (NAFTA) as well as Israel. Many Latin American countries have expressed interest in expanding the NAFTA to create a hemispheric free trade arrangement to be called the Free Trade Agreement of the Americas. Other regional initiatives abound.

(B) THE CONSEQUENCES OF REGIONALISM

The trend toward regional integration has uncertain consequences for the world trading system. Economists divide the consequences of preferential trading arrangements into two categories—"trade creation" and "trade diversion."[2] Trade creation refers to the expansion of trade

---

1. See J. Viner, The Customs Union Issue (1950).

2. See J. Meade, The Theory of Customs Unions (1955); T. Scitovsky, Economic The-

with efficient suppliers inside the customs union or free trade area. Trade diversion refers to a shift in trade from efficient suppliers outside the regional arrangement, to inefficient suppliers inside it, driven by the desire to take advantage of trade preferences.

For example, suppose that prior to NAFTA, the United States imports significant quantities of winter vegetables from Mexico because Mexico produces them efficiently and transport costs are low. After NAFTA, tariffs on these goods fall, and imports rise. The usual argument for gains from trade should apply, and both countries will benefit from this liberalization of trade—trade creation. By contrast, suppose that prior to NAFTA, the United States imports large quantities of textile products from India. And suppose that after NAFTA, investors establish textile factories in Mexico to produce for the U.S. market solely because Mexico enjoys preferential access to the United States and is able to outcompete India for that reason. From the global perspective, specialization on the basis of comparative advantage has now been distorted—trade diversion. The consequences are particularly severe from India's perspective, as its exports contract due to the diversion of textile trade to Mexico. Even the United States may be worse off because of the diversion of trade. U.S. consumers gain to be sure, but the U.S. government has lost tariff revenue on imports from India, and it is possible that the loss in tariff revenue may exceed the gains to consumers. Some further considerations are developed in the following excerpts.

PAUL R. KRUGMAN, IS BILATERALISM BAD?[3]

As a general source of concern, however, the risk of trade diversion seems a weak point. It shows that under certain circumstances a customs union could be a mistake—but this is true of many economic policies, and policy concern based on the possibility of wide spread stupidity by governments may be realistic though not very interesting. Also, while a customs union with a *given* external tariff may be harmful to the members, a customs union that adjusts its tariff optimally is always beneficial; while optimal adjustment may be unlikely in practice, again this seems to reduce the concern over bilateralism to a fear that governments will make mistakes.

The point that a customs union is always potentially beneficial to its members has been made formally by Kemp and Wan. It may be useful to state the point informally. Suppose that two countries that happen to

ory and Western European Integration (1958); Lipsey, The Theory of Customs Unions: A General Survey, in R. Caves and H. Johnson (eds.), A.E.A. Readings in International Economics, Vol. XI (1968); B. Balassa, The Theory of Economic Integration (1961); J. Vanek, General Equilibrium of International Discrimination: The Case of Customs Unions, Harvard Economic Studies, Vol. CXXIII (1965); M. Krauss (ed.), The Economics of Integration (1973). J.

Pelkmans (ed.), Market Integration in the European Community (1984); A. El–Algraa & A. Jones, Theory of Customs Unions (1981).

3. From International Trade and Trade Policy 9 (E. Helpman & A Razia, eds., 1991). Copyright © 1991 by the Massachusetts Institute of Technology. Reprinted with permission of the MIT Press.

have the same tariff rate form a customs union. If they did not alter their external tariff rate, the increased trade within the union would represent a mixture of trade creation and trade diversion. Since the trade diversion would be harmful while the trade creation would be beneficial, the overall welfare effect would be ambiguous. (There may also be a terms of trade effect, to which we return below). The Kemp–Wan point, however, is that by adjusting the external tariff, the members of a customs union can always ensure a gain. Specifically, by reducing the tariff to the point at which external trade remains at its preunion level, the countries can ensure that there is no trade diversion. Also, since at this reduced tariff rate the offer to the rest of the world would be unchanged, the terms of trade of the customs union would also remain the same. So the welfare effect of a customs union that lowers its external tariff enough to prevent trade diversion is unambiguously positive. Now, in general, the customs union may choose to have a different tariff level than this; but if it does so, it is because this other tariff level yields still higher welfare. Thus a customs union is always potentially beneficial.

So far as good. But the last point—that a customs union may choose a tariff rate that is different from the one that leaves external trade at its preunion level—raises a potential negative possibility. The reason is that almost surely the optimal tariff rate for the customs union will be higher than this constant-trade level because the customs union will want to take advantage of its size to improve its terms of trade. Indeed, we may expect as a general presumption that a customs union, being a larger unit with more market power than any of its constituent members, will have an optimal external tariff that is higher than the preunion tariff rates of the member nations. Thus while our proof of potential gains relies on the hypothetical case of a customs union that does not lead to any trade diversion, in fact a customs union ordinarily will choose policies that do lead to trade diversion.

But this means that the formation of a customs union, while necessarily beneficial to the members, will certainly be harmful to the rest of the world and may reduce the welfare of the world as a whole (if such a measure can be defined).

Now let us return to the concern over bilateral and regional trading arrangements. One way to rationalize the concern of the trade negotiation professionals is the following: They fear that there may be a Prisoner's Dilemma at work in the formation of trading blocs. Imagine a world consisting of four countries, A, B, C, and D. Let A and B form a customs union; then other things equal they will be better off. However, they will have an incentive to improve their terms of trade by maintaining an external tariff that induces trade diversion—indeed, probably an external tariff that is higher than either of them would have on their own—and which therefore leaves C and D worse off. Similarly, C and D will be better off, other things equal, if they form a customs union, but their optimal external tariff will similarly induce trade diversion in the effort to achieve improved terms of trade. What could happen is that the resulting tariff war will induce enough trade diversion to leave everyone worse off than if they had not formed the customs unions.

ROBERT Z. LAWRENCE, EMERGING REGIONAL ARRANGEMENTS: BUILDING BLOCKS OR STUMBLING BLOCKS?[4]

The major regional initiatives currently under way are more likely to represent the building blocks of an integrated world economy than stumbling blocks which prevent its emergence. To be sure, there are risks that these initiatives could go astray. But the forces initiating these developments are the very opposite of protectionism. They represent positive, integrative responses to the pressures exerted by globalization. If accompanied by parallel progress at the GATT, regionalization could be a potent mechanism for freeing world trade and investment and harmonizing national institutional practices.

Growth. One key benefit to the rest of the world comes from the impact of regional arrangements in stimulating growth and thus demand for extra-regional exports. These growth effects stem from several sources. One is the income effect of the gains from trade. Secondly, such increased income induces increased investment. For example, Richard Baldwin estimates that the removal of trade and other internal barriers to trade and investment within Europe as a part of the Single Market will stimulate sufficient increases in investment to produce "dynamic" growth effects that will be greater than the "static" efficiency gains: up to a 10 per cent increase in total output, as compared to the 4.5 per cent figure (for static gains alone) estimated in the official Cecchini report prepared for the Commission.

External barriers. Open regional blocs can actually promote and facilitate external liberalization, that is, trade with parties outside blocs. On the political front, regions might be more willing to agree to liberalization than individual countries. The postwar experience with the EC is heartening. Increased European integration after the Treaty of Rome was quite compatible with the lowering of Europe's external barriers. Gary Hufbauer, for example, has argued that the Kennedy Round of trade negotiations would not have occurred in the absence of the EC. "France and Italy, in particular, would have strongly resisted making any trade concessions in the 1960s, and Germany would not have made trade concessions in isolation from its continental partners." With the noteworthy exception of agriculture, therefore (an exception for which the EC was not solely to blame), increased regional integration among the original six members of the EC was associated with extensive participation in multilateral tariff reductions. Indeed the formation of the EEC was an important impulse for the Kennedy Round.

---

4. From Finance and the International   Reprinted with permission.
Economy 23 (Richard O'Brien, ed., 1991).

The European experience also demonstrates that excluded countries have stronger incentives to liberalize in a system with emerging regional arrangements. Instead of the fragmentation process some fear, an expansionary dynamic is likely. The prospects (indeed, the actuality) that major trading partners could move into arrangements from which they are excluded could well drive countries to join regional liberalization schemes.

Motivation. * * * The motive for completing the internal market [in Europe] is not to secure the European market for European producers by providing them preferential access, but instead to facilitate the free movement of goods, services, labour and capital throughout the Community. The EC Single Market initiative reflects the recognition that as the European economies became increasingly integrated, it was necessary to move beyond simply removing border barriers to achieve a much deeper degree of integration. To be sure, there is the hope that a larger market will improve European efficiency, but enhanced competition is precisely the mechanism by which the gains from trade are achieved.

Moreover deeper integration within Europe will facilitate trade with the rest of the world. A common set of standards, for example, makes it easier for all who wish to sell in Europe—not just insiders. A tough set of rules which inhibits governments from subsidizing domestic firms aids all their competitors, not only those located in the European Community. Once the larger European economies are committed to allow the free flow of resources within Europe, they will no longer be able to ensure each has a national champion in every industry, located within its territories. This undermining of the nationalist sentiments which drives much of the protectionism in the larger European countries will benefit outsiders. In addition, some of the mechanisms developed by the EC to deal with national diversity could serve as a model for further integration between the EC and its trading partners.

————

Despite theoretical uncertainty about the consequences of preferential arrangements, empirical economists typically argue that existing regional arrangements tend to have positive economic effects for their members and no more than minimal adverse effects on the rest of the world. With particular regard to NAFTA, surveys of some of the empirical work may be found in North American Free Trade: Assessing the Impact (N. Lustig, B. Bosworth & R. Lawrence eds., Brookings, 1992) and G. Hufbauer & J. Schott, North American Free Trade: Issues and Recommendations (Inst. for Intl. Econ. 1992).

Finally, although the normative theory and consequences of regional arrangements have received considerable attention, less attention has been devoted to positive questions such as what determines when regional arrangements are formed, what determines who joins, what determines whether the arrangement is a customs union or a free trade area, and why is it the case in practice (if indeed it is) that most regional arrangements seem to have favorable economic consequences. For an early effort to address some of these issues, see Johnson, An Economic Theory of Protectionism, Tariff Bargaining, and the Formation of Customs Unions, 73 J.Pol.Econ. 256 (1965).

Notes and Questions

(1) Krugman's concern is that regional arrangements may try to take advantage of their enhanced "monopoly power" in trade to raise their external tariffs to the "optimal" level—recall the discussion of the optimal tariff in Chapter 1. Putting aside the question whether governments in practice are motivated by the pursuit of the optimal tariff, look at Article XXIV to see whether governments can in fact do so under GATT. Suppose first that the arrangement is a customs union—what constraints are apparent in the text? What if it is a free trade area?

(2) In response to Lawrence's optimism, is there a danger that regional arrangements will create new interest groups as a result of trade diversion whose economic survival depends upon the maintenance of trade preferences? And if so, to what extent will those interest groups impede multilateral liberalization over the long haul?

SECTION 11.2   THE ARTICLE XXIV EXCEPTION

(A) HISTORY OF ARTICLE XXIV

JOHN H. JACKSON, WORLD TRADE AND THE LAW OF GATT 576–77 (1969) [1]

* * * The GATT draftsmen * * * termed the regional exception a "standard clause in all commercial treaties." By custom as well as explicit provision, certain regional arrangements had long been considered as an exception to the Most–Favored–Nation clause in commercial treaties. But regional arrangements had posed a difficult dilemma for commercial treaty draftsmen because of the danger of diluting the Most–Favored–Nation clause. * * *

* * * One of the major purposes that the United States sought to accomplish through GATT and the ITO was the dismantlement of trading preferences, especially the Commonwealth preferences. Yet even the United States recognized the legitimacy of an exception for customs unions. The original United States draft included clauses excepting such

---

1. Copyright 1969, by The Bobbs–Merrill Company Inc. Reprinted by Permission. All rights reserved. See also John H. Jackson, The World Trading System 141 (1989); John H. Jackson, Regional Trade Blocs and GATT, 16 The World Economy 121 (1993); Uster, The MFN Customs Union Exception, 15 J. World Trade L. 377 (1981); J. Allen, The European Common Market and the GATT (1960); P. Lortie, Economic Integration and the Law of GATT (1975); V. Curzon, The Essentials of Economic Integration: Lessons of EFTA Experience (1974); Dam, Regional Economic Arrangements and the GATT: The Legacy of a Misconception, 30 U.Chi.L.Rev. 615 (1963).

arrangements from Most–Favored–Nation and other obligations. But the problem was how to define such exception without opening the door to the introduction of all preferential systems under the guise of a customs union. The United States draft solution to this danger was to define a customs union to be the arrangement where "all tariffs and other restrictive regulations of commerce as between the ... members of the union are substantially eliminated" and where a uniform external tariff and regulation system exists for the union. In addition, the United States draft required that the common external tariff and regulation "shall not on the whole be higher or more stringent than the average level of the duties and regulations of commerce applicable in the constituent territories prior to the formation of such union." The United States representative explained this as follows: "Customs unions are desirable, provided that they [do] not cause any disadvantage to outside countries, in comparison with their trade before the customs union [was] effected."

Delegates from other nations at the 1946–1947 preparatory conferences urged, however, that a period of transition to form a customs union be allowed. The United States agreed that an "interim period" was reasonable, but "only after it had been definitely agreed to establish such a customs union." Ultimately, the Geneva draft ITO and the original GATT contained clauses incorporating these suggestions.

———

Although both customs unions and free trade areas in principle require the elimination of substantially all trade impediments between their members, in practice matters have worked out differently. A large number of regional associations have claimed the GATT Article XXIV exception, although arguably only a very few could really qualify. Yet even in questionable cases the preference system has been tolerated, and legal arguments have been ignored or resulted in a standoff without resolution. We consider below the extent to which the new WTO dispute settlement system has changed this situation.

(B) THE REQUIREMENTS OF ARTICLE XXIV

The Article XXIV MFN exception for trade groupings applies to three types of associations:

>(1) A free trade area (defined in Article XXIV, paragraph 8(b), as an association of nations that eliminates barriers to imports from members on "substantially all" trade among them).

>(2) A customs union (defined in Article XXIV, paragraph 8(a), as an association of nations that eliminates barriers to imports from members on "substantially all" trade among them and that further puts in place a common level of external tariffs for imports from nonmembers).

>(3) An interim agreement leading to one of the above within a "reasonable period of time."

Among the issues that arise in its application and implementation are:[2]

(i) What is a "reasonable time" for an interim agreement to become a customs union or free trade area under paragraph 5?

(ii) What is "substantially all" trade under paragraph 8 and what "other restrictive regulations of commerce" must be eliminated?

(iii) What does it take for imports to qualify as originating from a member state, i.e., what are the rules of origin and does Article XXIV place any constraints upon them?

(iv) With respect to a customs union, how does one ensure under paragraph 5 that tariffs and other barriers to trade with the customs union are "not on the whole * * * higher or more restrictive than the general incidence of the duties and regulations of commerce applicable in the constituent territories prior to the formation of such union," as required by Article XXIV(5)(a)?

Under the old GATT system, these questions were never given clear answers. The compatibility of a free trade area or customs union agreement with the provisions of Article XXIV would be examined by a working party, which reported its findings and discussion to the Contracting Parties. These reports would discuss the relevant issues, but would not reach firm conclusions. Although numerous customs union and free-trade area agreements were considered by GATT, few were approved by any formal action by the Contracting Parties.[3] For example, despite extensive discussions, the GATT Contracting Parties never took a position on the EEC or its three enlargements, a fact highlighted in 1983 when the compatibility with Article XXIV of Greece's accession was the subject of an inconclusive working party report.[4] Indeed, in November 1992, it was stated at a GATT Council meeting that "over fifty previous working parties on individual customs unions or free-trade areas had been unable to reach unanimous conclusions as to the GATT consistency of those agreements. On the other hand, no such agreements had been disapproved explicitly."[5]

The new WTO Understanding on the Interpretation of Article XXIV of the General Agreement on Tariffs and Trade 1994 provides greater guidance on some issues. For example, Paragraph 3 provides that "[t]he 'reasonable length of time' (allowed for an interim agreement to produce a completed customs union or free trade area)* * * should exceed 10 years only in exceptional cases." It remains to be seen how frequently exceptional cases will be found. The Understanding also provides in Paragraph 10 that if an interim agreement does "not include a plan and schedule, contrary to paragraph 5(c) of Article XXIV, the working party in its report shall recommend such a plan and schedule."

2. See generally Jackson, supra note 1, ch. 24, especially secs. 24.6, 24.7, 24.8.

3. See generally WTO, Regionalism and the World Trading System (1995).

4. GATT, 30th Supp. BISD 168–90 (1984).

5. GATT, Analytical Index 760 (6th ed. 1994).

More fundamentally, a controversial issue in the GATT was whether the compatibility of an arrangement with Article XXIV could be raised in dispute settlement proceedings, particularly in cases where the working party examination had been completed and no action had been taken by the Contracting Parties. This question was discussed at some length in connection with a U.S. challenge to the EU's trading arrangements with a number of Mediterranean countries in the early 1980's. Although the panel established to consider the case found that U.S. benefits under the General Agreement had been nullified or impaired, the report was never adopted.[6] The Uruguay Round Understanding on Article XXIV seeks to resolve this issue:

> 12. The provisions of Articles XXII and XXIII of GATT 1994 * * * may be invoked with respect to any matters arising from the application of those provisions of Article XXIV relating to customs unions, free-trade areas or interim agreements leading to the formation of a customs union or free-trade area.

The most prominent WTO dispute to date concerning what might be characterized as a regional trading arrangement was the *Bananas* case,[7] involving preferential treatment by the European Union of banana imports from certain countries. Because the preferences were ostensibly authorized by a waiver granted in relation to the Lomé Convention, however, the legal issues there involved the interpretation of the Convention and the waiver. The EU did not claim that Article XXIV was applicable. Article XXIV issues did arise to a great extent, however, in a lesser known case involving a dispute between India and Turkey over Turkey's textile imports policy following its entry into a customs union agreement with the European Union.

TURKEY—RESTRICTIONS ON IMPORTS OF TEXTILE AND CLOTHING PRODUCTS
WT/DS34/AB/R
Appellate Body Report adopted by the DSB on November 19, 1999

2. On 6 March 1995, the Turkey–EC Association Council adopted Decision 1/95, which sets out the rules for implementing the final phase of the customs union between Turkey and the European Communities. Article 12(2) of this Decision states:

> In conformity with the requirements of Article XXIV of the GATT Turkey will apply as from the entry into force of this Decision, substantially the same commercial policy as the Community in the textile sector including the agreements or arrangements on trade in textile and clothing.

In order to apply what it considered to be "substantially the same commercial policy" as the European Communities on trade in textiles

---

6. See GATT, GATT Activities 1983, at 42–43; GATT, GATT Activities 1984, at 36–38.

7. European Communities–Regime for the Importation, Sale and Distribution of Bananas, WT/DS27.

and clothing, Turkey introduced, as of 1 January 1996, quantitative restrictions on imports from India on 19 categories of textile and clothing products.

3.   The Panel considered claims by India that the quantitative restrictions introduced by Turkey were inconsistent with Articles XI and XIII of the GATT 1994, and Article 2.4 of the Agreement on Textiles and Clothing (the "*ATC*"). In the Panel Report, circulated on 31 May 1999, the Panel reached the conclusion that the quantitative restrictions were inconsistent with the provisions of Articles XI and XIII of the GATT 1994 and consequently with those of Article 2.4 of the *ATC*, and rejected Turkey's defence that the introduction of any such otherwise GATT/ WTO incompatible import restrictions is permitted by Article XXIV of the GATT 1994.

* * *

41.   * * * The issue raised by Turkey in this appeal is whether these quantitative restrictions are nevertheless justified by Article XXIV of the GATT 1994.

42.   In examining Turkey's defence that Article XXIV of the GATT 1994 allowed Turkey to adopt the quantitative restrictions at issue in this appeal, the Panel looked, first, at Article XXIV:5(a) and, then, at Article XXIV:8(a) of the GATT 1994. The Panel examined the ordinary meaning of the terms of these provisions, in their context and in the light of the object and purpose of the *WTO Agreement*. The Panel reached the following conclusions:

> With regard to the specific relationship between, in the case before us, Article XXIV and Articles XI and XIII (and Article 2.4 of the ATC), we consider that the wording of Article XXIV does not authorize a departure from the obligations contained in Articles XI and XIII of GATT and Article 2.4 of the ATC.

* * *

> [Paragraphs 5 and 8 of Article XXIV] do not . . . address any specific measures that may or may not be adopted on the formation of a customs union and importantly they do not authorize violations of Articles XI and XIII, and Article 2.4 of the ATC. . . . We draw the conclusion that even on the occasion of the formation of a customs union, Members cannot impose otherwise incompatible quantitative restrictions.

Consequently, the Panel rejected Turkey's defence that Article XXIV justifies the introduction of the quantitative restrictions at issue. Turkey appeals the Panel's interpretation of Article XXIV.

43.   We note that, in its findings, the Panel referred to the chapeau of paragraph 5 of Article XXIV only in a passing and perfunctory way. The chapeau of paragraph 5 is not central to the Panel's analysis, which focuses instead primarily on paragraph 5(a) and paragraph 8(a). However, we believe that the chapeau of paragraph 5 of Article XXIV is the key

provision for resolving the issue before us in this appeal. In relevant part, it reads:

> Accordingly, the provisions of this Agreement *shall not prevent*, as between the territories of contracting parties, *the formation of a customs union* ...; *Provided* that: ... (emphasis added)

44. To determine the meaning and significance of the chapeau of paragraph 5, we must look at the text of the chapeau, and its context, which, for our purposes here, we consider to be paragraph 4 of Article XXIV.

45. First, in examining the text of the chapeau to establish its ordinary meaning, we note that the chapeau states that the provisions of the GATT 1994 *"shall not prevent"* the formation of a customs union. We read this to mean that the provisions of the GATT 1994 *shall not make impossible* the formation of a customs union. Thus, the chapeau makes it clear that Article XXIV may, under certain conditions, justify the adoption of a measure which is inconsistent with certain other GATT provisions, and may be invoked as a possible "defence" to a finding of inconsistency.[8]

46. Second, in examining the text of the chapeau, we observe also that it states that the provisions of the GATT 1994 shall not prevent *"the formation of a customs union"*. This wording indicates that Article XXIV can justify the adoption of a measure which is inconsistent with certain other GATT provisions only if the measure is introduced upon the formation of a customs union, and only to the extent that the formation of the customs union would be prevented if the introduction of the measure were not allowed.

47. It follows necessarily that the text of the chapeau of paragraph 5 of Article XXIV cannot be interpreted without reference to the definition of a "customs union". This definition is found in paragraph 8(a) of Article XXIV, which states, in relevant part:

> A customs union shall be understood to mean the substitution of a single customs territory for two or more customs territories, so that

> (i) duties and other restrictive regulations of commerce (except, where necessary, those permitted under Articles XI, XII, XIII, XIV, XV and XX) eliminated with respect to *substantially all the trade* between the constituent territories of the union or at least with respect to substantially all the trade in products originating in such territories, and,

---

8. [original note 13] * * * The chapeau of paragraph 5 refers only to the provisions of the GATT 1994. It does not refer to the provisions of the *ATC*. However, Article 2.4 of the *ATC* provides that "[n]o new restrictions ... shall be introduced *except under* the provisions of this Agreement or *relevant GATT 1994 provisions.*" (emphasis added) In this way, Article XXIV of the GATT 1994 is incorporated in the *ATC* and may be invoked as a defence to a claim of inconsistency with Article 2.4 of the *ATC*, provided that the conditions set forth in Article XXIV for the availability of this defence are met.

(ii) ... *substantially the same* duties and other regulations of commerce are applied by each of the members of the union to the trade of territories not included in the union. (emphasis added)

48. Sub-paragraph 8(a)(i) of Article XXIV establishes the standard for the *internal trade* between constituent members in order to satisfy the definition of a "customs union". It requires the constituent members of a customs union to eliminate "duties and other restrictive regulations of commerce" with respect to "substantially all the trade" between them. Neither the GATT Contracting Parties nor the WTO Members have ever reached an agreement on the interpretation of the term "substantially" in this provision. It is clear, though, that "substantially all the trade" is not the same as *all* the trade, and also that "substantially all the trade" is something considerably more than merely *some* of the trade. We note also that the terms of sub-paragraph 8(a)(i) provide that members of a customs union may maintain, where necessary, in their internal trade, certain restrictive regulations of commerce that are otherwise permitted under Articles XI through XV and under Article XX of the GATT 1994. Thus, we agree with the Panel that the terms of sub-paragraph 8(a)(i) offer "some flexibility" to the constituent members of a customs union when liberalizing their internal trade in accordance with this sub-paragraph. Yet we caution that the degree of "flexibility" that sub-paragraph 8(a)(i) allows is limited by the requirement that "duties and other restrictive regulations of commerce" be "eliminated with respect to substantially all" internal trade.

49. Sub-paragraph 8(a)(ii) establishes the standard for the trade of constituent members *with third countries* in order to satisfy the definition of a "customs union". It requires the constituent members of a customs union to apply "substantially the same" duties and other regulations of commerce to external trade with third countries. The constituent members of a customs union are thus required to apply a common external trade regime, relating to both duties and other regulations of commerce. However, sub-paragraph 8(a)(ii) does *not* require each constituent member of a customs union to apply *the same* duties and other regulations of commerce as other constituent members with respect to trade with third countries; instead, it requires that *substantially the same* duties and other regulations of commerce shall be applied. We agree with the Panel that:

> [t]he ordinary meaning of the term "substantially" in the context of sub-paragraph 8(a) appears to provide for both qualitative and quantitative components. The expression "substantially the same duties and other regulations of commerce are applied by each of the Members of the [customs] union" would appear to encompass both quantitative and qualitative elements, the quantitative aspect more emphasized in relation to duties.

50. We also believe that the Panel was correct in its statement that the terms of sub-paragraph 8(a)(ii), and, in particular, the phrase "substantially the same" offer a certain degree of "flexibility" to the constit-

uent members of a customs union in "the creation of a common commercial policy." Here too we would caution that this "flexibility" is limited. It must not be forgotten that the word "substantially" qualifies the words "the same". Therefore, in our view, something closely approximating "sameness" is required by Article XXIV:8(a)(ii). * * *

51. Third, in examining the text of the chapeau of Article XXIV:5, we note that the chapeau states that the provisions of the GATT 1994 shall not prevent the formation of a customs union *"Provided that"*. The phrase *"provided that"* is an essential element of the text of the chapeau. In this respect, for purposes of a "customs union", the relevant proviso is set out immediately following the chapeau, in Article XXIV:5(a). It reads in relevant part:

> with respect to a customs union ..., the duties and other regulations of commerce imposed at the institution of any such union ...
> in respect of trade with contracting parties not parties to such union ... shall not on the whole be higher or more restrictive than the general incidence of the duties and regulations of commerce applicable in the constituent territories prior to the formation of such union ...;

52. Given this proviso, Article XXIV can, in our view, only be invoked as a defence to a finding that a measure is inconsistent with certain GATT provisions to the extent that the measure is introduced upon the formation of a customs union which meets the requirement in sub-paragraph 5(a) of Article XXIV relating to the "duties and other regulations of commerce" applied by the constituent members of the customs union to trade with third countries.

53. With respect to "duties", Article XXIV:5(a) requires that the duties applied by the constituent members of the customs union *after* the formation of the customs union "shall *not* on the whole be *higher* ... than the *general incidence*" of the duties that were applied by each of the constituent members before the formation of the customs union. Paragraph 2 of the *Understanding on Article XXIV* requires that the evaluation under Article XXIV:5(a) of the *general incidence of the duties* applied before and after the formation of a customs union "shall ... be based upon an overall assessment of weighted average tariff rates and of customs duties collected." Before the agreement on this Understanding, there were different views among the GATT Contracting Parties as to whether one should consider, when applying the test of Article XXIV:5(a), the *bound* rates of duty or the *applied* rates of duty. This issue has been resolved by paragraph 2 of the *Understanding on Article XXIV*, which clearly states that the *applied* rate of duty must be used.

54. With respect to "other regulations of commerce", Article XXIV:5(a) requires that those applied by the constituent members *after* the formation of the customs union "shall *not* on the whole be ... *more restrictive* than the *general incidence*" of the regulations of commerce that were applied by each of the constituent members *before* the formation of the customs union. Paragraph 2 of the *Understanding on Article*

XXIV explicitly recognizes that the quantification and aggregation of regulations of commerce other than duties may be difficult, and, therefore, states that "for the purpose of the overall assessment of the incidence of other regulations of commerce for which quantification and aggregation are difficult, the examination of individual measures, regulations, products covered and trade flows affected may be required."

55.   We agree with the Panel that the terms of Article XXIV:5(a), as elaborated and clarified by paragraph 2 of the *Understanding on Article XXIV*, provide:

> . . . that the effects of the resulting trade measures and policies of the new regional agreement shall not be more trade restrictive, overall, than were the constituent countries' previous trade policies.

and we also agree that this is:

> an "economic" test for assessing whether a specific customs union is compatible with Article XXIV.

56.   The text of the chapeau of paragraph 5 must also be interpreted in its context. In our view, paragraph 4 of Article XXIV constitutes an important element of the context of the chapeau of paragraph 5. The chapeau of paragraph 5 of Article XXIV begins with the word "accordingly", which can only be read to refer to paragraph 4 of Article XXIV, which immediately precedes the chapeau. Paragraph 4 states:

> The contracting parties recognize the desirability of increasing freedom of trade by the development, through voluntary agreements, of closer integration between the economies of the countries parties to such agreements. They also recognize that the purpose of a customs union or of a free-trade area should be to facilitate trade between the constituent territories and not to raise barriers to the trade of other contracting parties with such territories.

57.   According to paragraph 4, the purpose of a customs union is "to facilitate trade" between the constituent members and "not to raise barriers to the trade" with third countries. This objective demands that a balance be struck by the constituent members of a customs union. A customs union should facilitate trade within the customs union, but it should *not* do so in a way that raises barriers to trade with third countries. We note that the *Understanding on Article XXIV* explicitly reaffirms this purpose of a customs union, and states that in the formation or enlargement of a customs union, the constituent members should "to the greatest possible extent avoid creating adverse affects on the trade of other Members". Paragraph 4 contains purposive, and not operative, language. It does not set forth a separate obligation itself but, rather, sets forth the overriding and pervasive purpose for Article XXIV which is manifested in operative language in the specific obligations that are found elsewhere in Article XXIV. Thus, the purpose set forth in paragraph 4 informs the other relevant paragraphs of Article XXIV, including the chapeau of paragraph 5. For this reason, the chapeau of paragraph 5, and the conditions set forth therein for establishing the

availability of a defence under Article XXIV, must be interpreted in the light of the purpose of customs unions set forth in paragraph 4. The chapeau cannot be interpreted correctly without constant reference to this purpose.

58.   Accordingly, on the basis of this analysis of the text and the context of the chapeau of paragraph 5 of Article XXIV, we are of the view that Article XXIV may justify a measure which is inconsistent with certain other GATT provisions. However, in a case involving the formation of a customs union, this "defence" is available only when two conditions are fulfilled. First, the party claiming the benefit of this defence must demonstrate that the measure at issue is introduced upon the formation of a customs union that fully meets the requirements of sub-paragraphs 8(a) and 5(a) of Article XXIV. And, second, that party must demonstrate that the formation of that customs union would be prevented if it were not allowed to introduce the measure at issue. Again, *both* these conditions must be met to have the benefit of the defence under Article XXIV.

59.   We would expect a panel, when examining such a measure, to require a party to establish that both of these conditions have been fulfilled. It may not always be possible to determine whether the second of the two conditions has been fulfilled without initially determining whether the first condition has been fulfilled. In other words, it may not always be possible to determine whether not applying a measure would prevent the formation of a customs union without first determining whether there *is* a customs union. In this case, the Panel simply assumed, for the sake of argument, that the first of these two conditions was met and focused its attention on the second condition.

60.   More specifically, with respect to the first condition, the Panel, in this case, did not address the question of whether the regional trade arrangement between Turkey and the European Communities is, in fact, a "customs union" which meets the requirements of paragraphs 8(a) and 5(a) of Article XXIV. The Panel maintained that "it is arguable" that panels do not have jurisdiction to assess the overall compatibility of a customs union with the requirements of Article XXIV. We are not called upon in this appeal to address this issue, but we note in this respect our ruling in *India–Quantitative Restrictions on Imports of Agricultural, Textile and Industrial Products* [affirming] the jurisdiction of panels to review the justification of balance-of-payments restrictions under Article XVIII:B of the GATT 1994. The Panel also considered that, on the basis of the principle of judicial economy, it was not necessary to assess the compatibility of the regional trade arrangement between Turkey and the European Communities with Article XXIV in order to address the claims of India. Based on this reasoning, the Panel assumed *arguendo* that the arrangement between Turkey and the European Communities is compatible with the requirements of Article XXIV:8(a) and 5(a) and limited its examination to the question of whether Turkey was permitted to introduce the quantitative restrictions at issue. The assumption by the Panel that the agreement between Turkey and the European Communities is a

"customs union" within the meaning of Article XXIV was not appealed. Therefore, the issue of whether this arrangement meets the requirements of paragraphs 8(a) and 5(a) of Article XXIV is not before us.

61. With respect to the second condition that must be met to have the benefit of the defence under Article XXIV, Turkey asserts that had it not introduced the quantitative restrictions on textile and clothing products from India that are at issue, the European Communities would have "exclud[ed] these products from free trade within the Turkey/EC customs union". According to Turkey, the European Communities would have done so in order to prevent trade diversion. Turkey's exports of these products accounted for 40 per cent of Turkey's total exports to the European Communities. Turkey expresses strong doubts about whether the requirement of Article XXIV:8(a)(i) that duties and other restrictive regulations of commerce be eliminated with respect to "substantially all trade" between Turkey and the European Communities could be met if 40 per cent of Turkey's total exports to the European Communities were excluded. In this way, Turkey argues that, unless it is allowed to introduce quantitative restrictions on textile and clothing products from India, it would be prevented from meeting the requirements of Article XXIV:8(a)(i) and, thus, would be prevented from forming a customs union with the European Communities.

62. We agree with the Panel that had Turkey not adopted the same quantitative restrictions that are applied by the European Communities, this would not have prevented Turkey and the European Communities from meeting the requirements of sub-paragraph 8(a)(i) of Article XXIV, and consequently from forming a customs union. We recall our conclusion that the terms of sub-paragraph 8(a)(i) offer some–though limited–flexibility to the constituent members of a customs union when liberalizing their internal trade. As the Panel observed, there are other alternatives available to Turkey and the European Communities to prevent any possible diversion of trade, while at the same time meeting the requirements of sub-paragraph 8(a)(i). For example, Turkey could adopt rules of origin for textile and clothing products that would allow the European Communities to distinguish between those textile and clothing products originating in Turkey, which would enjoy free access to the European Communities under the terms of the customs union, *and* those textile and clothing products originating in third countries, including India. In fact, we note that Turkey and the European Communities themselves appear to have recognized that rules of origin could be applied to deal with any possible trade diversion. Article 12(3) of Decision 1/95 of the EC–Turkey Association Council, which sets out the rules for implementing the final phase of the customs union between Turkey and the European Communities, specifically provides for the possibility of applying a system of certificates of origin. A system of certificates of origin would have been a reasonable alternative until the quantitative restrictions applied by the European Communities are required to be terminated under the provisions of the *ATC*. Yet no use was made of this

possibility to avoid trade diversion. Turkey preferred instead to introduce the quantitative restrictions at issue.

63.   For this reason, we conclude that Turkey was not, in fact, required to apply the quantitative restrictions at issue in this appeal in order to form a customs union with the European Communities. Therefore, Turkey has not fulfilled the second of the two necessary conditions that must be fulfilled to be entitled to the benefit of the defence under Article XXIV. Turkey has not demonstrated that the formation of a customs union between Turkey and the European Communities would be prevented if it were not allowed to adopt these quantitative restrictions. Thus, the defence afforded by Article XXIV under certain conditions is not available to Turkey in this case, and Article XXIV does not justify the adoption by Turkey of these quantitative restrictions.

64.   For the reasons set out in this report, the Appellate Body concludes that the Panel erred in its legal reasoning by focusing on sub-paragraphs 8(a) and 5(a) and by failing to recognize the crucial role of the chapeau of paragraph 5 in the interpretation of Article XXIV of the GATT 1994, but upholds the Panel's conclusion that Article XXIV does not allow Turkey to adopt, upon the formation of a customs union with the European Communities, quantitative restrictions on imports of 19 categories of textile and clothing products which were found to be inconsistent with Articles XI and XIII of the GATT 1994 and Article 2.4 of the *ATC*.

65.   We wish to point out that we make no finding on the issue of whether quantitative restrictions found to be inconsistent with Article XI and Article XIII of the GATT 1994 will *ever* be justified by Article XXIV. We find only that the quantitative restrictions at issue in the appeal in this case were not so justified. Likewise, we make no finding either on many other issues that may arise under Article XXIV. The resolution of those other issues must await another day. We do not believe it necessary to find more than we have found here to fulfill our responsibilities under the DSU in deciding this case.

66.   The Appellate Body recommends that the DSB request that Turkey bring its measures which the Panel found to be inconsistent with Articles XI and XIII of the GATT 1994 and Article 2.4 of the *ATC* into conformity with its obligations under these agreements.

Notes and Questions

(1) Does the Appellate Body's decision place significant roadblocks in the way of creating free trade areas and customs unions? Consider the extent to which the exception of Article XXIV has been limited by the Appellate Body's interpretation of the chapeau of paragraph 5 (see para. 46).

(2) Note the Appellate Body's view that Article XXIV is a defense and that the respondent must establish that it fully meets the requirements of Article XXIV:8 (paras. 58–60). How will panels decide if those requirements are met? If there are doubts, does the respondent lose? If so, does this case suggest that Article XXIV will likely be interpreted strictly in the future,

despite the longstanding tolerance by GATT/WTO members of a very loose interpretation? Is it appropriate for the dispute settlement system to implement that change, as opposed to the political organs of the WTO? Recall the discussion in Section 7.4(B) supra.

(3) Does the Appellate Body offer much guidance regarding the phrase "substantially all" trade? The European Union once urged 80% of all trade as a benchmark[9]—would that standard pass muster? Is there a principled way to give content to the "substantially all" requirement? Can that be done without a convincing theory of why it is there in the first place? Why should the GATT Contracting Parties have viewed small departures from the MFN obligation as unacceptable, yet have been willing to allow quite massive departures as long as they satisfy the "substantially all" criterion?

(4) The *Wheat Gluten* case in Section 15.3 examines the rules of the Safeguards Agreement that are applicable to the use of safeguards by a member of a free trade area.

(5) An interesting further issue arises for nations that use tariffs as an important source of government revenue—what if the elimination of trade barriers in the pursuit of a customs union or free trade area might impair the ability of the government to raise needed revenues? Should there be an exception to the requirement that duties be eliminated on "substantially all" trade for "non-protective revenue duties?" See European Economic Community—Agreement of Association With Malta, Working Party Report adopted on May 29, 1972. GATT, 19th Supp. BISD 94–95 (1973).

(6) Customs unions and free trade areas with developing countries raise still further issues regarding the ability of developing nations to invoke GATT exceptions for infant industry protection, and so on, when to do so might mean that they have failed to eliminate barriers on "substantially all" trade. There is an additional question whether preferential arrangements with developing nations are to be classified as arrangements subject to Article XXIV, or mere preferences for developing country exports permitted by other GATT provisions or decisions. See European Economic Community—Association Agreements With African and Malagasy States and Overseas Countries and Territories, Working Party Report adopted on April 4, 1966. GATT, 14th Supp. BISD 100–06 (1966). For the conclusions of the Contracting Parties adopted on the same date, see id., at 22.

(7) Departures from the most-favored-nation principle, including customs unions and free trade areas, necessitate rules of origin to determine whether or not imported merchandise is entitled to preferential treatment. Often, the origin of a good is obvious, as when it is produced entirely within the borders of a single exporting nation. But when a finished good has been through several stages of processing in different countries, the matter is more complex. The greater the degree to which processing must occur within the customs union or free trade area before a good will be deemed to have originated there, the greater the extent to which the preferential arrangement may cause trade diversion. Thus, countries that are not a party to the regional arrangement will prefer less restrictive rules of origin to minimize the impact of preferences on their exports. Countries within the regional

9.   GATT, 6th Supp. BISD 70, 99 (1958).

arrangement, by contrast, may prefer restrictive rules of origin so that the benefits of the trade preferences do not extend much beyond the borders of regional agreement.

The rules in use within various regional arrangements vary considerably, and have been a source of some concern within GATT through the years. See European Free Trade Association—Examination of the Stockholm Convention, Working Party Report adopted on June 4, 1960, GATT, 9th Supp. BISD 71–73 (1961); European Communities—Agreements With Portugal, Working Party Report adopted on October 19, 1973, GATT, 20th Supp. BISD 177–81 (1974). The WTO Agreement on Rules of Origin aims at harmonization of such rules over time, but is in the main focused on nonpreferential rules of origin. See Section 8.3(D) supra.

(8) The GATS analog to Article XXIV is GATS Article V. How does it differ from Article XXIV?

SECTION 11.3   U.S. PARTICIPATION IN REGIONAL ARRANGEMENTS

(A) HISTORY PRIOR TO NAFTA

The United States remained outside the global trend toward customs unions and free trade areas until 1985, when it entered into a free trade agreement with Israel.[1] Under that agreement all duties would be eliminated in four stages by January 1, 1995.[2] The agreement also covers nontariff barriers. For example, Israel committed to eliminate export subsidy programs on industrial products and processed agricultural products within six years. In a number of other respects, such as import licensing and government procurement, the agreement establishes more stringent rules than did the Tokyo Round agreements.[3]

The U.S.–Israel agreement was no doubt motivated more by political and military concerns than economic concerns. It provides a way for the United States to encourage economic growth and investment in Israel without the need for direct, on-budget subsidization. But while negotiations with Israel were proceeding, the United States was also exploring the possibility of a free trade arrangement with its largest trading partner—Canada. The 1974 Trade Act stated that it was the sense of Congress that the United States should enter into a free trade agreement with Canada, and the President was authorized to initiate negotia-

1. Negotiation of the agreement was authorized in 1984. Trade and Tariff Act of 1984, title IV; 19 U.S.C.A. sec. 2112. Under the trade agreement negotiating authority of the 1974 Trade Act, as modified in the 1984 Act for application to a U.S.–Israel trade agreement, congressional approval of legislation implementing the agreement was required. Such legislation was handled under the "fast-track" procedures and was approved in June 1985. Pub.L. No. 99–47, 99 Stat. 82. See House Rep. No. 99–64, 99th Cong., 1st Sess. (1985).

2. Agreement on the Establishment of a Free Trade Area Between the Government of the United States of America and the Government of Israel, signed April 22, 1985.

3. Id., arts. 12, 15. The minimum limit for contracts subject to the government procurement provisions is $50,000, about one-third of that of the Tokyo Round Agreement on Government Procurement.

tions with Canada.[4] The result was the Canada–United States Free Trade Agreement (CUSFTA), which was signed on January 2, 1988 and came into effect on January 1, 1989.

The CUSFTA was a sweeping accord, reducing or eliminating most duties between the two nations over a period of years. It contained additional provisions relating to rules of origin, technical barriers to trade, agricultural market access and subsidization, safeguards measures, government procurement, trade in services, investment and temporary migration for business persons. Its coverage was substantially broader than that of GATT prior to the end of the Uruguay Round, particularly as to its provisions on services, investment, agriculture and rules of origin. With respect to services and investment in particular, the cornerstone of the CUSFTA commitments was national treatment—in general, the United States and Canada were to afford the same treatment to each other as to their own citizens, with some exceptions.

Some of the most important innovations of the CUSFTA were found in Part VI, which contained the institutional provisions. A Canada–United States Trade Commission was established, with its principal functions relating to dispute settlement. In the event of disputes arising under the agreement (with certain exceptions, i.e. those involving financial services, safeguards and antidumping and countervailing duties), the Commission would undertake to resolve the disputes through consultations and negotiations. If that proved unsuccessful, a dispute settlement panel would be appointed from a list of potential panelists to consider the dispute and issue a ruling promptly. If the Commission was unable to agree on the settlement of the dispute after the panel's ruling, the aggrieved party was authorized to suspend concessions under the CUSFTA to offset its claimed disadvantage. The procedure was modeled somewhat on the GATT system and the grounds for invoking the process included the GATT-based concept of nullification or impairment of benefits (art. 2011). But the system sought to avoid the problems of the GATT system that became evident prior to the Uruguay Round, such as delays, inexperienced panelists and blockage by one party, through imposition of strict deadlines (the process should be completed in 8 or 9 months), the use of a roster from which panelists would be selected and the authorization of compensatory action if no final agreement was reached on the implementation of the panel's decision. In addition to the process described above, the CUSFTA provided for the possibility of binding arbitration (in safeguard disputes). This binding arbitration procedure was similar to the general dispute settlement process except that only the prevailing party was authorized to take compensatory action in the event no settlement was reached.

---

4. Trade Act of 1974, sec. 612, 19 U.S.C.A. sec. 2486(a). In 1979, Congress ordered the President to study the desirability of entering into trade agreements with countries in the northern portion of the Western hemisphere. Trade Agreements Act of 1979, sec. 1104, 19 U.S.C.A. sec. 2486(b). See U.S.Intl.Trade Commn., Background Study of the Economies and International Trade Patterns of the Countries of North America, Central America and the Caribbean (Inv. No. 332–119, 1981).

Chapter 19 established special dispute settlement procedures for antidumping and countervailing duty issues. Under its provisions, so-called binational panels considered claims that amendments to existing antidumping and countervailing duty laws were inconsistent with the relevant GATT Codes and heard appeals from administrative decisions under such laws when requested by an affected party from the other country. Thus, the panels replaced judicial review in such cases. This provision was considered absolutely essential by the Canadians, who felt that the procedure would discourage U.S. administrative authorities from deciding cases on essentially political grounds.

(B) THE NORTH AMERICAN FREE TRADE AGREEMENT (NAFTA)

In 1990, President Bush informed Congress of his intention to enter into negotiations with Mexico toward a free trade agreement, pursuant to negotiating authority contained in the Omnibus Trade and Competitiveness Act of 1988.[5] Since the agreement was intended to include Canada, it would be known as the North American Free Trade Agreement (NAFTA). The NAFTA negotiations were concluded in 1992 and the agreement was signed on December 17, 1992. Political opposition in the United States subsequently led to the negotiation of three "side agreements" covering environmental issues, labor issues and import surges. After a heated political battle, the agreement was approved in Congress and came into effect in 1994.

NAFTA is similar to the CUSFTA, although it goes beyond it in a number of respects. Effectively, the CUSFTA is merged into NAFTA, although formally NAFTA replaces the CUSFTA and the bilateral obligations of the CUSFTA are "suspended."[6]

Part One (Chapters One and Two) of NAFTA lays out objectives and general definitions. Part Two deals with trade in goods. Chapter Three establishes a general requirement of national treatment and provides for the phased elimination of tariffs over a ten year period, with most tariffs eliminated within five years and subject to a fifteen year period in a few cases. Quotas and licensing requirements are also to be eliminated. Chapter Four contains the rules of origin, which generally confer NAFTA origin on a product if (i) it is wholly obtained or produced entirely within the territory of NAFTA, (ii) each of the non-originating components of the product changes tariff heading or (iii) a minimum value added test is met (e.g., 50% of net cost consists NAFTA regional value). Among the many special cases under the origin rules are those that effectively subject automobiles to a 62.5% value added requirement and require most apparel to be sewn from NAFTA origin yarn or fibers. These two rules are somewhat controversial and are more difficult to meet than the analogous rules under the U.S.-Canada FTA. Part Two

---

5. See Pub. L. 100–418, secs. 1102–03, 102 Stat. 1107 (1988), 19 U.S.C. secs. 2902–03.

6. See North American Free Trade Agreement Implementation Act, sec. 107, Pub. L. 103–182, 107 Stat. 2057 (1993).

also contains special provisions for customs procedures (Chapter Five), energy (Chapter Six), agriculture (Chapter Seven) and emergency safeguards (Chapter Eight).

Part Three (Chapter Nine) contains rules governing the use of technical barriers to trade. This provision, along with similar rules in respect of sanitary and phytosanitary measures in Chapter Seven, has been controversial because of a fear by some U.S. environmental and consumer groups that the rules would force the United States to relax health, safety and other standards. Article 906(2) provides, however, that harmonization efforts will be undertaken "[w]ithout reducing the level of safety or of protection of human, animal or plant life or health, the environment or consumers."

Part Four (Chapter Ten) deals with procurement by specified government agencies of specified goods and services. The threshold for coverage is $50,000 ($6.5 million for construction services). Unlike the CUSFTA, which mainly incorporated the provisions of the GATT Government Procurement Code, NAFTA has detailed rules on procurement practices.

Part Five contains provisions on investment (Chapter Eleven), Services (Chapter Twelve), telecommunications (Chapter Thirteen), financial services (Chapter Fourteen), competition policy (Chapter Fifteen) and temporary entry of business persons (Chapter Sixteen). Among the more interesting differences relative to the CUSFTA are in the investment chapter and govern disputes between one of the parties and an investor of another party. They allow a U.S. investor, for example, to seek arbitration of an investment dispute with Mexico. The disputes covered are those arising out of a violation of NAFTA's rules on investment and certain rules in Chapter Fifteen on monopolies and state enterprises. Thus, a U.S. investor could seek arbitration if it claimed that it did not receive the required compensation on expropriation of its investment, or if the expropriation was not for a public purpose, or if one of the other rules (e.g., national/MFN treatment) of Chapter Eleven were not followed. We consider arbitral decisions under this provision in Chapter 24 infra.

Part Six (Chapter Seventeen) establishes detailed rules with respect to intellectual property, a subject not treated in the CUSFTA to any significant degree. Essentially, the provisions are aimed at ensuring that Mexico provides the sort of protection that the U.S. and Canada provide to intellectual property. Consequently, this chapter contains specific rules on what kinds of intellectual property are to be protected and what protections are to be afforded. In addition, it requires the parties to provide effective domestic law remedies for violations of intellectual property rights, and specifies in some detail procedural and remedial rules.

Part Seven contains institutional provisions that are similar to those of the CUSFTA, adjusted to take account of the existence of three parties. Chapter Nineteen carries over the system of binational panel review of antidumping and countervailing duty decisions reached by administrative agencies. NAFTA provides for a number of changes to the current process. Perhaps the most interesting are the inclusion of a requirement that "[t]he roster * * * include judges or former judges to the fullest extent practicable" (Annex 1901.2), the specification that a panel's failure to apply the appropriate standard of review is grounds for an extraordinary challenge committee to overrule the panel's decision (Article 1904(13)(a)(iii)), and a provision for safeguarding the panel review system (Article 1905), pursuant to which one of the three parties may claim that another party has thwarted the operation of the panel review system and, if the claim is upheld by a special committee, suspend the operation of the binational review process or take certain other action. The first two provisions seem to be designed to make panels less likely to reverse the rulings of administrative agencies, something that they have done relatively often, most often to the displeasure of U.S. industry. Their impact is uncertain since it may be difficult to find judges willing to serve and a recent extraordinary challenge committee has already effectively implemented the second change, but still declined to reverse the panel, despite its disagreement with the panel's intensive review. The third provision was apparently included because of concerns about Mexico's judicial system.

Chapter Twenty provides for the establishment of the Free Trade Commission and the secretariat, and contains NAFTA's general dispute resolution procedures, which are similar to those under Article 18 of the CUSFTA. The parties are generally free to invoke their rights under either GATT dispute settlement procedures or NAFTA procedures, except that a defending party may insist on using the NAFTA procedures in cases involving health or environmental measures that raise factual issues concerning the environment, health, safety or conservation or in cases subject to Article 104, which provides that certain environmental agreements prevail over NAFTA. In addition, Annex 2004 places some limits on nullification or impairment claims in the absence of a technical violation.

As noted, three side agreements were negotiated prior to the approval of NAFTA by the U.S. Congress. The agreement on import surges relates to safeguards measures. The other two agreements address environmental and labor matters. Both of these agreements are structured similarly, in that they create a bureaucracy with the capacity to investigate matters of concern under the side agreement and to promote cooperative activity toward improvement in labor and environmental standards. They also obligate each party to NAFTA to enforce its own laws respecting labor and the environment, and to provide private parties with an opportunity to enforce their rights under national laws. Further, if another party believes that a government is not enforcing its domestic law, a procedure is established through which a complaint may be filed. Should an accord not be reached after such a complaint, a dispute resolution process may be pursued with the possibility of monetary penalties against the recalcitrant government. It is noteworthy that neither side agreement obligates parties to follow any particular labor or environmental standards or to change existing national laws; rather, parties simply covenant to enforce whatever standards have already been enacted or will be enacted in the future in the ordinary course.[7] Consequently, one might question whether the side agreements will prove to be of much consequence in practice.[8]

In 2001, the General Accounting Office compiled a study of the environmental and labor side agreements and summarized experience to date as follows:[9]

> [In the case of the environmental side agreement,] to date, 31 submissions have been filed with the Secretariat. Of these submissions, 8 were against the United States, 13 were against Mexico, and 10 were against Canada. These submissions have raised a wide range of concerns, from narrow questions of a government's failure to effectively enforce environmental laws in a particular instance, to broader concerns about enforcement in general. The submission process can lead to the publication of a "factual record," a report that outlines the history of the issue, a Party's obligations under the law in question, and the facts relevant to assertions made in the submission. Of the submissions made to date, only two have resulted in completed factual records, and neither of those completed factual records has involved the United States.

> [In the case of the labor side agreement,] to date, 23 submissions have been filed, with 7 against the United States, 14 against Mexico, and 2 against Canada. Although these submissions have covered a broad range of issues, a majority of them have raised concerns about freedom of association. Thus far, no submission has reached the dispute settlement phase.

(C) SELECTED ISSUES

With time, a substantial body of "case law" will develop pursuant to the NAFTA dispute resolution provisions, and indeed many decisions have already been rendered.[10] The bulk of these cases pertain to topics that are the subject of subsequent chapters of this book, and we will occasionally note them in passing. In particular, we examine dispute settlement cases in respect of U.S. measures taken against Canadian subsidies on softwood lumber (Chapter 18) and a Mexican challenge to

7. Texts of the side agreements are in the Documents Supplement. The labor agreement text may be found in BNA, 1993 Daily Rep. Executives 177 d92 (September 15, 1993), and the environment agreement may be found in BNA, 1993 Daily Rep. Executives 175 d70 (September 13, 1993). A summary of both agreements, prepared by USTR, may be found in BNA, 1993 Daily Rep. Executives 156 d54 (August 16, 1993).

8. See Taylor, NAFTA's Green Accords: Sound and Fury Signifying Little, CATO

Policy Analysis No. 198 (November 17, 1993).

9. US General Accounting Office, North American Free Trade Agreement: U.S. Experience With Environment, Labor, and Investment Dispute Settlement Cases, Report No. GAO–01–933 (July 20, 2001).

10. See generally Ralph Folsom, Michael Gordon & John Spanogle, Handbook of NAFTA Dispute Settlement Vols. I & II (2000).

U.S. limitations on its provision of trucking services in the U.S. market (Chapter 19). In addition, we consider how arbitral tribunals have applied NAFTA Chapter 11 on investment in Chapter 24.

We conclude this chapter with brief attention to the dispute resolution system of NAFTA, as well as its predecessor under the CUSFTA, and the interface of this transnational dispute resolution process with the national legal system of the United States. We also touch briefly on the important topic of rules of origin.

(1) Constitutional Concerns

Article 19 of the NAFTA, like Article 19 of the CUSFTA, provides that appeals from administrative determinations in antidumping and countervailing duty cases may be taken to a "binational panel." Appellate review by the panel replaces ordinary judicial review—in the United States, the Court of International Trade would otherwise have jurisdiction. The decisions of a binational panel are reviewable on limited grounds by an "extraordinary challenge committee,"[11] but are never appealable to a U.S. court. As such, the operation of these binational panels is quite different than WTO dispute settlement. The panels are substituting for national courts, they are applying national law and their decisions are virtually self executing.

Both the binational panel and the extraordinary challenge committee consist of individuals appointed by the involved nations. A panel consists of five members, two appointed by each disputant nation, and the fifth by agreement of the disputant nations or, failing such agreement, by one of them chosen by lot. The extraordinary challenge committee is similarly constructed, except that it consists of only three individuals. NAFTA requires that panel members be judges or former judges "to the extent practicable." Members of an extraordinary challenge committee must be judges or former judges.

In the United States, the institution of binational panel review raises some constitutional questions. First, the "transfer" of appellate jurisdiction from the Court of International Trade and the Court of Appeals for the Federal Circuit—both Article III courts—to a binational panel, has led some commentators to argue that the panel mechanism impermissibly deprives litigants of judicial review by an Article III court. Second, the "Appointments Clause" vests the power to appoint "officers of the United States" with the President, subject to Senate confirmation, except for "inferior officers" who may be appointed by Department heads. As noted, members of binational panels are appointed by both parties to the dispute. If such panelists are "officers of the United States," as some commentators have argued on the grounds that they provide appellate review under U.S. law, then the fact that some are appointed by a foreign government could be of concern. Likewise, the fact that the U.S. panelists are appointed by USTR may be of concern

---

11. See NAFTA, Article 1904(13) and Annex 1904.13.

unless they may be viewed as "inferior officers."[12] Thus far, however, the NAFTA panel mechanism has survived constitutional challenge, although the merits of the issues are not yet resolved.[13]

(2) Extraordinary Challenges and the Standard of Review

The binational panel review process was included in the CUSFTA at the insistence of Canada, which felt that agency decisions in the United States were politicized and that existing appellate review was too deferential to provide foreign respondents with much protection against agency politics. But similar concerns arise with binational panel review—will the panels undertake to follow the law carefully in accordance with their obligations, or will political factors intrude, perhaps causing panel decisions to turn on which country has the panel majority?

The primary check on panels that go astray is the extraordinary challenge process, itself potentially imperfect because the members of the extraordinary challenge committee are appointed in much the same way as those of the binational panel. The extraordinary challenge committee may review the actions of panels for misconduct or conflict of interest on the part of a panelist, for failure to follow appropriate procedures, or for exceeding their authority as by failing to apply the correct standard of review.[14] NAFTA attempts to reduce the degree to which the extraordinary challenge committee may be influenced by politics by *requiring* that all committee members have judicial experience. Whether these provisions will suffice to ensure a reality and a perception of fairness and unbiasedness remains to be seen.

---

12. Much was written on these issues after the entry into force of the CUSFTA. The NAFTA panel review mechanism differs from the of the CUSFTA in some respects that might have constitutional significance, such as in the capacity of a party to suspend it and revert to ordinary judicial review under certain exceptional conditions. Nevertheless, the constitutional concerns about the CUSFTA panels might also be raised, in slightly modified form, about the NAFTA panels.

Among the numerous papers on this set of issues, all written with particular reference to the CUSFTA, are Christenson & Gambrel, Constitutionality of Binational Panel Review in Canada–U.S. Free Trade Agreement, 23 Intl.Law. 401 (1989); Davey, The Appointments Clause and International Dispute Settlement Mechanisms: A False Conflict, 49 Wash. & Lee L.Rev. 1315 (1992); Morrison, Appointments Clause Problems in the Dispute Resolution Provisions of the United States–Canada Free Trade Agreement, 49 Wash. & Lee L.Rev. 1299 (1992); Note, The Binational Panel Mechanism for Reviewing United States–Canadian Antidumping and Countervailing Duty Determinations: A Constitutional Dilemma?, 29 Va.J.Intl.L. 681 (1989); Note, Chapter 19 of the Canada–United States Free Trade Agreement: An Unconstitutional Preclusion of Article III Review, 5 Conn. J.Intl.L. 317 (1989); Note, The Constitutionality of Chapter 19 of the United States–Canada Free Trade Agreement: Article III and the Minimum Scope of Judicial Review, 89 Colum.L.Rev. 897 (1989).

13. Challenges to the constitutionality of binational review under the CUSFTA were mounted prior to NAFTA, but dismissed on jurisdictional grounds. See, e.g., National Council for Industrial Defense v. United States, 827 F.Supp. 794 (D.D.C. 1993). A similar case after NAFTA dismissed on standing grounds was American Coalition for Competitive Trade v. Clinton, 128 F.3d 761 (D.C.Cir.1997).

14. NAFTA, art. 1904(13).

IN RE LIVE SWINE FROM CANADA

Panel No. ECC–93–1904–01USA.

1993 FTAPD LEXIS 1 (1993).

This memorandum opinion and order arises from the extraordinary challenge proceeding conducted pursuant to Article 1904.13 and Annex 1904.13 of the United States–Canada Free–Trade Agreement ("FTA") in the matter of Live Swine From Canada. The proceeding followed a Request For An Extraordinary Challenge Committee ("Request") filed by the Office of the United States Trade Representative ("USTR"). * * *

An Extraordinary Challenge Committee ("ECC") does not serve as an ordinary appellate court. Article 1904.13 provides that a Party may avail itself of the extraordinary challenge procedure only if it satisfies each prong of a three-part threshold test.[15] If the USTR fails to meet its burden, we must affirm the Panel's decision. The ECC should be perceived as a safety valve in those extraordinary circumstances where a challenge is warranted to maintain the integrity of the binational panel process. * * * The exceptional nature of an extraordinary challenge was accentuated by the drafters of the FTA by limiting extraordinary challenges to the United States and Canadian governments, and not to other Participants in the Panel's proceedings. * * *

III. ALLEGATION OF ERROR BY THE USTR

The USTR on behalf of the Government of the United States argues that the Panel Majority in Decision II manifestly exceeded its jurisdiction by failing to apply the appropriate standard of judicial review, and in particular by reversing Commerce's specificity determination and "supplanting it" with "the appropriate test" announced by the Panel Majority in its opinion. The USTR asserts that such error materially affected the Panel's decision and thereby threatened the integrity of the binational panel review process. Based on the oral and written record, the Committee is not persuaded that the USTR has sustained its burden of proving that the Panel manifestly exceeded its jurisdiction by failing to apply the correct standard of judicial review.

The North American Free Trade Agreement ("NAFTA") makes explicit what was implicit in the FTA, that if a panel fails to apply the appropriate standard of review, it manifestly exceeds "its powers, authority or jurisdiction," the first prong of our three-part test, FTA Article 1904.13(a)(iii). The equivalent provision in the NAFTA reads:

15. Article 1904.13 reads:

Where, within a reasonable time after the panel decision is issued, a Party alleges that:

  a) i) a member of the panel was guilty of gross misconduct, bias, or a serious conflict of interest, or otherwise materially violated the rules of conduct,

    ii) the panel seriously departed from a fundamental rule of procedure, or

    iii) the panel manifestly exceeded its powers, authority or jurisdiction set forth in this Article, and

  b) any of the actions set out in subparagraph (a) has materially affected the panel's decision and threatens the integrity of the binational panel review process,

that Party may avail itself of the extraordinary challenge procedure set out in Annex 1904.13.

"the panel manifestly exceeded its powers, authority or jurisdiction set out in this Article, for example, by failing to apply the appropriate standard of review . . ."

During oral argument, Counsel for the Canadian government argued that it was required that a Panel "expressly refuse" to apply a standard of review prescribed in applicable domestic law in order to conclude that the Panel "manifestly exceeded its . . . jurisdiction." Expressed rejection is not required. The appropriate test is whether the Panel accurately articulated the scope of review and * * * whether it "has been conscientiously applied." Although we cannot say here, based upon the record before us, that the Panel did not conscientiously apply the appropriate standard of review, that is not to say that in another case if a panel simply cites the correct standard of review and the record does not reflect the conscientious application of it, that panel would not be manifestly exceeding its jurisdiction.

The Panel correctly cited the standard of review it had to follow under U.S. law. The Panel appropriately looked first to section 516A(b)(1)(B) of the Tariff Act of 1930, as amended, (19 U.S.C. § 1516a(b)(1)(B) (1992)) for its scope of review. Section 516A(b)(1)(B) provides that the Panel "shall hold unlawful any determination by Commerce found * * * to be unsupported by substantial evidence on the record, or otherwise not in accordance with law." In addition, both Parties and the Panel correctly recognized that the "Special Rule," 19 U.S.C. § 1677(5)(B) (1992), applied to the underlying dispute. This provision requires that Commerce determine whether a "bounty, grant or subsidy" was provided to a "specific enterprise or industry . . . ," but is silent as to how Commerce should do so (emphasis added). 19 U.S.C. § 1677(5)(B) (1992). Because this statutory provision is silent, the Panel properly recognized that it was required to give deference to Commerce's statutory interpretation. The Panel appropriately cited Chevron, U.S.A. v. Natural Res. Def. Council, 467 U.S. 837 (1984) through its progeny in support of this proposition. The Panel stated: "In the absence of clearly discernible legislative intent, panels must limit their inquiry to whether Commerce's statutory interpretations are 'sufficiently reasonable.' In this regard, '[t]he agency's interpretation need not be the only reasonable construction or the one the court would adopt had the question initially arisen in a judicial proceeding.' Id . . ." The Panel also recognized that "under [its standard of review], binational panels may not engage in de novo review or simply impose their constructions of the statute upon the agency."

Not only did the Panel accurately articulate its standard of review * * * [it]concluded after a brief discussion of the specificity test that Commerce's determination was not in accordance with law, nor based on substantial evidence. Although we need not and will not reach a decision on the merits of these conclusions, the Committee felt the Panel may have erred. Nonetheless, on balance, the Committee was not persuaded that the Panel failed to apply the properly articulated standard of review. Because the Committee was not persuaded that the Panel manifestly exceeded the appropriate standard of review, the Committee need not address the second and third prongs of our test as set forth in FTA Article 1904.13(b).

Question

What does the extraordinary challenge committee do here to verify that the proper standard of review was "conscientiously applied?" What should it do?

(3) Rules of Origin

DONALD HARRISON & KENNETH WEIGEL, CUSTOMS PROVISIONS AND RULES OF ORIGIN UNDER NAFTA[16]

Chapter 4 contains the basic NAFTA Rules of Origin. These origin rules—or, more strictly speaking, standards of preference—raised some of the more controversial and difficult issues in the NAFTA negotiations. The governments involved, as well as many of the important economic and political interests in the three countries, were very concerned that the reduced duties available under the NAFTA only benefit products that involve significant manufacturing and other economic activity in the three countries. For example, the governments and other interests did not want Mexico, with its lower wage rates and other costs, to be used as an "export platform" for entry into the United States of goods that consisted largely of third-country materials. Controversies involved in the United States Customs Service's administration of the CFTA's [Canadian Free Trade Agreement's] origin rules also increased interest in the NAFTA origin rules.

* * *

A.   Originating Goods—Article 401

Article 401 of the NAFTA provides the basic tests for determining whether a good will be considered to originate in the territory of a Party to the NAFTA. The basic standard, which is similar to that in the CFTA, involves a change in tariff classification approach. Specifically, article 401 provides that a good will qualify as an originating good when each of the nonoriginating materials used to produce the good undergoes an applicable change in tariff classification, as set forth in Annex 401, as a result of production occurring entirely in the territory of one or more of the Parties. As noted above, Annex 401 is a 168–page annex providing specific rules for each chapter of the HTS. Additionally, in many cases the good must also satisfy a minimum regional value content requirement. Article 401 also permits a good to qualify where nonoriginating materials provided for as "parts" under the HTS do not undergo a

---

16.   27 Intl.Law. 647, 653–59 (1993). Copyright © 1993 American Bar Associa-   tion. Reprinted with permission.

change in tariff classification because of two types of circumstances, with the further proviso of a minimum regional value content.

B. REGIONAL VALUE CONTENT—ARTICLE 402

1. Basic Definitions

Article 402 explains the calculation of the regional value content of a good where the specific origin rules in Annex 401 require such a calculation. Article 402 generally provides that this regional value content (RVC) may be calculated on the basis of either the transaction-value method or the net-cost method.

Under the transaction-value method, the NAFTA expresses the RVC as a percentage equal to the transaction value of the goods (adjusted to an F.O.B. basis) (TV), less the value of nonoriginating materials (VNM) used by the producer in the production of the good, divided by the TV, multiplied by 100, that is: RVC = (TV − VNM)/TV times 100.

Under the net-cost method, the NAFTA calculates the RVC as a percentage equal to the net cost of the good (NC), less the value of nonoriginating materials (VNM) used by the producer in the production of the good, divided by the NC, multiplied by 100, that is: RVC = (NC − VNM)/NC times 100.

The NAFTA defines the net cost in turn, as the "total cost" less the following specific costs: "sales promotion, marketing and after-sales service costs, royalties, shipping and packing costs, and non-allowable interest costs that are included in the total cost." Article 402 further provides that in calculating the net cost, the producer may use several allocation methods, provided the chosen method is consistent with Uniform Regulations to be established under article 511. The producer may, for example, reasonably allocate each cost that forms part of the total cost incurred with respect to the good so that the aggregate of these costs does not include any of the items excluded from the net cost definition.

* * *

3. Transaction–Value Method versus Net–Cost Method

One basic difference between the two RVC methods in the NAFTA is that the transaction-value method includes some costs that are excluded in the net-cost method. Thus, the net-cost method excludes such costs as "sales promotion, marketing and after-sales service costs," and does not include profit. The NAFTA bases transaction-value method on "the price actually paid or payable for a good or material," and may thus include all costs plus profit. To compensate for this difference the transaction-value method requires a higher percentage of RVC. Additionally, article 402 provides for certain circumstances where the exporter or producer of the good must calculate the RVC using the net-cost method. Finally, the exporter/producer of a good may also calculate using the net-cost method where it initially used the transaction-value method. But this method is determined to be "unacceptable" during a verification.

4.   The Value of Nonoriginating Materials

As noted, both the transaction-value method and the net-cost method require the calculation of the value of nonoriginating materials. NAFTA bases this value generally on the transaction value of such materials determined in accordance with article 1 of the Customs Valuation Code, that is, the price actually paid or payable for the material. Also included in this value are the costs to transport the material to the location of the producer, such as freight, insurance, and packing. Additionally, the value includes duties taxes and customs brokerage fees, as well as the cost of waste and spoilage, less the value of renewable scrap or by-product.

In most cases, the decision of whether materials used by a producer are originating or nonoriginating is made on an all-or-nothing basis. That is, if the material qualifies as originating under the NAFTA origin rules, then no portion of its value is treated as nonoriginating, even if the material is comprised in part of nonoriginating submaterials. This result may be referred to as the "roll-up" of the value of the nonoriginating submaterials. Similarly, if the material does not qualify as originating—for example, because it does not satisfy the change in tariff classification requirement or the minimum RVC requirement—the full value is treated as nonoriginating, including any originating submaterials and regional value added. This result may be referred to as the "roll-down" of the originating material and regional value added. * * *

5.   Intermediate Materials

The term "intermediate material" refers to material that a producer creates and then uses in the production of another good. Both the CFTA and the NAFTA implicitly or explicitly recognize that such seller-produced materials can qualify as originating materials. In an effort to deal with a concern about roll-up, however, the NAFTA provides that where the intermediate material is subject to an RVC requirement, the producer may not designate as an intermediate material any other self-produced material also subject to an RVC requirement that was used to produce that intermediate material. This restriction deals with so-called "cascading roll-up," which was also the subject of CFTA concern.

C.   Automotive Goods—Article 403

Consistent with the enormous importance of automotive manufacturing and trade in and among the three countries involved, article 403 includes separate origin rules for automotive goods. One significant aspect of these rules concerns the provision for tracing the value of nonoriginating materials. As noted above, most materials are subject to an all-or-nothing approach based on whether the material does or does not qualify as "originating" under the NAFTA rules. For most motor vehicles, however, article 403 requires the tracing of the actual value of most if not all nonoriginating materials, even if those materials are imported by a supplier that uses them to produce a qualifying originating material. Specifically, for most motor vehicles, including passenger automobiles and light trucks, the value of nonoriginating materials includes the delivered value of all nonoriginating materials that are (1) imported from outside the territory of the three NAFTA Parties, (2) classified under certain tariff provisions listed in Annex 403.1, and (3) used in the production of either the good or any material used in the production of the good. This provision means that producers of these goods will have to develop procedures to calculate the value of these nonoriginating materials, even if a supplier or subsupplier imports the materials.

* * *

D.   ACCUMULATION—ARTICLE 404

Article 404 provides that in determining whether a good qualifies as originating, the exporter/producer of the good can "accumulate" production of the good by other producers, provided that on this accumulated basis all nonoriginating materials undergo the required tariff classification change and the good satisfies any applicable RVC requirement. This article would apparently permit, for example, a good that producer A processed initially in Mexico and that Producer B imported and further processed in the United States to qualify as an originating good on the basis of the overall production by producers A and B when the good is exported to Canada.

Notes and Questions

(1) Plainly, it will not be possible for the Customs Service to verify the accuracy of all claims of origination made under this system, and it will be forced to rely on periodic audits or "verifications" to police compliance. Even so, it should be clear from the excerpt why the costs of adherence to rules of origin, both for the government and for private parties, are a non-trivial matter under a preferential trading arrangement. Likewise, even when goods are eligible for preferential treatment, the costs of establishing eligibility may at times exceed the gains.

(2) Suppose a company is caught in an audit claiming NAFTA origin for goods that do not qualify—what should the penalty be?

Chapter 12

THE NATIONAL TREATMENT CLAUSE

SECTION 12.1   INTRODUCTION

The national treatment obligation of the General Agreement on Tariffs and Trade, like the MFN obligation, is a rule of nondiscrimination.[1] In the case of MFN, the obligation prohibits discrimination as between the same goods from different exporting countries. The national treatment clause, in contrast, imposes the principle of nondiscrimination as between domestically produced goods and the same imported goods. It is a central feature of international trade rules and policy,[2] and exists within the WTO/GATT system to prevent government practices that evade tariff and other market access obligations.

Article III is the central national treatment obligation of the General Agreement. Paragraph 1 establishes the general principle that internal taxes and regulations "should not be applied * * * so as to afford protection to domestic production." In some cases, this principle is specifically incorporated into the obligations established in the other provisions of Article III. Paragraph 2 of Article III requires national treatment in respect of internal taxation (such as sales, excise or value added taxes), while paragraph 4 requires it in respect of regulations affecting the sale and use of goods generally. The other paragraphs of Article III deal with particular situations, including paragraph 8, which carves out important exceptions for government procurement and subsidization.

Article III is closely related to a number of other GATT provisions, particularly Articles I, II, XI, XVII and XX, and it is helpful at this point

---

1. Many trade treaties negotiated prior to the General Agreement on Tariffs and Trade included a clause which imposed a "national treatment" obligation upon the parties. See John H. Jackson, World Trade and the Law of GATT 277 & nn. 7 & 8 (1969).

2. In addition to the references in the text of this chapter, the reader may find the following references useful in further re-

search on the national treatment obligation: Jackson, supra note 1, ch. 12; U.S. Tariff Commn., Trade Barriers, pts. 1–4, Report to the Committee on Finance of the United States Senate and its Subcomm. on International Trade (USTC Pub. No. 665 1974); Kenneth W. Dam, The GATT: Law and International Economic Organization ch. 7 (1970).

to preview those interactions. For example, the subject matter of Article III, paragraphs 2 and 4 (internal taxation and sales regulations), is incorporated into Article I. Thus, in respect of those matters, both GATT nondiscrimination principles are applicable.

Article III acts to reinforce the tariff bindings made pursuant to Article II by limiting the circumstances in which it is permissible for a nation to provide treatment for domestic goods in its national legislation and programs which is more favorable than that for imported goods. Such treatment will tend to disfavor the importation and purchase of imported goods, and consequently it is a form of protection, which can be even more severe than tariffs. A GATT binding to limit a tariff on a particular commodity would be valueless if there were not some limitations on the types of internal taxation or regulation which a country could impose to afford protection against such imports. To cite one easy example: Suppose tariffs on widgets were bound at 10%, but a country imposed an internal excise or sales tax on all widgets, in an amount of 5% for domestic goods and 10% for imported goods. The effect would be similar to adding 5% to the tariff. Such a practice is proscribed by Article III. This result underlines the philosophy of the General Agreement: protection should be transparent and in the form of tariffs.

The interaction of Articles III and XI was explored in Section 9.1. As noted there, it has been said that Article XI applies to measures that affect the actual importation of products, while Article III deals with measures affecting imported products. This line may sometimes be hard to draw. A note to Article III provides that measures applied to domestic products, which are applied to imported products at the time of importation, may be analyzed under Article III.

There is also a complex relationship between Article III and XVII, which was examined in Section 9.3. Article XVII deals with state trading enterprises and imposes certain obligations on them. It has sometimes been claimed to impose a sort of national treatment obligation, although as noted above some interpretative material suggests the contrary.

The interrelationship of Article III and Article XX, GATT's general exceptions clause, sometimes presents extremely difficult problems. Article XX, which itself contains language that imposes a kind of loose national treatment obligation, allows government actions that violate GATT obligations but that are justifiable on health, safety and similar grounds. There are broad policy issues raised by the interaction of the trade liberalization function of Article III and the exceptions established by Article XX. A nation may have a wide variety of domestic programs and legislation designed to promote health, welfare and various economic goals. It may regulate the sale of goods, so as to assure their reasonable safety when used by the public. It may regulate the production of goods in order to prevent pollution of the atmosphere or of water. It may design a tax structure to assist depressed areas of the country or to redistribute wealth from the rich to the poor. Few would advocate a system of international economic rules that would prevent nations from exercising their sovereignty to promote domestic policy goals in these various ways. But to the extent that these policies tend to disfavor imports, there may be a conflict between the liberal trade goals of international economic policy and national policy goals embodied in a wide variety of local and national laws and regulations.

The more the international economic system imposes rules to limit such hidden protectionism, however, the less freedom there is for national or local governmental units to pursue even their legitimate domestic policies. These same issues arise in any federal system—such as that of the United States or the EU—where there are different levels of government with overlapping responsibilities and powers over some subject matters. The question is which level of government should appropriately have the authority to make certain types of decisions. If too much decision-making is centralized at the federal level, then local governments cannot use initiative and cannot respond to constituents, even though they may be closer to the particular problems of those constituents. Some central control may be necessary, however, as there seems to be a natural tendency for local government units to establish policies which favor their constituents at the expense of constituents located in other government units, to the general detriment of the federal system. We have already examined some aspects of this issue in Sections 3.6 (U.S. federal-state relations) and 4.2 (the subsidiarity issue in the EU).

We will consider the Article XX exceptions in some detail in Chapter 13. In Chapter 14, we will examine the problems of technical barriers to trade, including the U.S. and EU approaches to these problems at the domestic level, in addition to the applicable WTO rules at the international level. One interesting question will be whether differing degrees of integration (economic, political, social) within an entity necessitate different approaches to these problems. In this regard, recall the discussion of the economic integration of Europe in Section 4.2(D) supra.

In the next sections of this chapter, we first take up the national treatment obligation generally, with excerpts from two of the most important GATT panel reports on Article III. We then consider in Section 12.3 the prohibition on discriminatory internal taxes found in Article III:2. In analyzing this provision, close attention is given to the text and interpretative notes of Article III. A key issue is distinguishing like products, directly competitive or substitutable products, and other products. In Section 12.4, we turn to an examination of Article III:4, which requires that imported products be given no less favorable treatment than like domestic products in respect of certain internal regulations. The concept of like product is crucial here too, but different considerations apply. Finally, we take a quick look at the exceptions contained in Article III:8, and specifically the one for government procurement. We will revisit the issue of national treatment in Chapter 19 on trade in services since one of the major questions that arose in negotiating the General Agreement on Trade in Services was the extent to which a national treatment obligation should apply to banking, insurance and other services.

SECTION 12.2   THE NATIONAL TREATMENT OBLIGATION: THE BASIC RULE

Numerous GATT and WTO panel and Appellate Body decisions have addressed the interpretation of Article III. Historically, the following two decisions are probably the most important, with the first decision giving a broad reading to paragraph 4 in the early days of GATT dispute settlement and the second one building on it 20 years later in 1979. In reading these cases, the student should focus on the scope of Article III. Exactly how far does it go in preventing discriminatory treatment of imports? Might it require comparatively favorable treatment of imports?

ITALIAN DISCRIMINATION AGAINST IMPORTED AGRICULTURAL MACHINERY

GATT Panel Report adopted October 23, 1958
7th Supp. BISD 60 (1959)

[The United Kingdom challenged an Italian law (no. 949) pursuant to which the Italian Government had established a fund, used to grant special credit terms for the purchase of Italian agricultural machinery. The loans were granted at 3 per cent; purchasers of foreign agricultural machinery on credit would receive less favorable terms. During the period 1952–1957 the purchasers of about half of the Italian tractors sold in Italy (i.e., about one-third of all tractors sold in the country) benefited from these credit facilities. In 1949, before the entry into force of Law No. 949, Italian import duties on various types of tractors and other agricultural machinery had been bound under GATT Article II.]

5.   The United Kingdom delegation noted that Article III:4 of the General Agreement provided that products imported into the territory of any contracting party "shall be accorded treatment no less favourable than that accorded to like products of national origin in respect of all laws, regulations and requirements affecting their internal sale, offering for sale, purchase, transportation * * *" etc. As the credit facilities provided under the Italian Law were not available to the purchasers of imported tractors and other agricultural machinery these products did not enjoy the equality of treatment which should be accorded to them. The fact that these credit facilities were reserved exclusively to the purchasers of Italian tractors and other agricultural machinery represented a discrimination and the operation of the Law involved an inconsistency with the provisions of Article III of the General Agreement which provides that laws, regulations and requirements affecting internal sale should not be applied to imported products so as to afford protection to domestic producers. The United Kingdom would not challenge the consistency with the General Agreement of subsidies which the Italian Government might wish to grant to domestic producers of tractors and other agricultural machinery in accordance with the terms of paragraph 8(b) of Article III. However, in the case of the Italian Law the

assistance by the State was not given to producers but to the purchasers of agricultural machinery; a case which is not covered by the provisions of paragraph 8(b). Even in the case of subsidies granted to producers the rights of the United Kingdom under Article XXIII of the General Agreement would be safeguarded as was recognized by the CONTRACT-ING PARTIES in paragraph 13 of the Report on Other Barriers to Trade which they approved during the course of the Review Session.[1]

6. The Italian delegation considered that the General Agreement was a trade agreement and its scope was limited to measures governing trade; thus the text of paragraph 4 of Article III applied only to such laws, regulations and requirements which were concerned with the actual conditions for sale, transportation, etc., of the commodity in question and should not be interpreted in an extensive way. In particular, the Italian delegation stated that the commitment undertaken by the CONTRACTING PARTIES under that paragraph was limited to qualitative and quantitative regulations to which goods were subjected, with respect to their sale or purchase on the domestic market.

7. It was clear in their view that the Law No. 949 which concerned the development of the Italian economy and the improvement in the employment of labour was not related to the questions of sale, purchase or transportation of imported and domestically produced products which were the only matters dealt with in Article III.

8. Moreover the Italian delegation considered that the text of Article III:4 could not be construed in such a way as to prevent the Italian Government from taking the necessary measures to assist the economic development of the country and to improve the conditions of employment in Italy.

9. Finally, the Italian delegation, noting that the United Kingdom delegation recognized that the Italian Government would be entitled to grant subsidies exclusively to domestic producers, stressed it would not be logical to exclude this possibility in the case of credit facilities which had a far less pronounced effect on the terms of competition.

10. In the view of the Italian delegation it would be inappropriate for the CONTRACTING PARTIES to construe the provisions of Article III in a broad way since this would limit the rights of contracting parties in the formulation of their domestic economic policies in a way which was not contemplated when they accepted the terms of the General Agreement.

11. The Panel agreed that the question of the consistency of the effects of the Italian Law with the provisions of the General Agreement raised a problem of interpretation. It had the impression that the contention of the Italian Government might have been influenced in part by the slight difference of wording which existed between the French

1. [original note] Third Supplement, Basic Instruments and Selected Documents, page 224. [This refers to the possibility of a bringing a non-violation case on the grounds that a tariff concession had been nullified by domestic subsidies. See Section 7.4(A) supra.]

and the English texts of paragraph 4 of Article III. The French text which had been submitted to the Italian Parliament for approval provided that the imported products "ne seront pas soumis à un traitement moins favorable" whereas the English text read "the imported product shall be accorded treatment no less favourable". It was clear from the English text that any favourable treatment granted to domestic products would have to be granted to like imported products and the fact that the particular law in question did not specifically prescribe conditions of sale or purchase appeared irrelevant in the light of the English text. It was considered, moreover, that the intention of the drafters of the Agreement was clearly to treat the imported products in the same way as the like domestic products once they had been cleared through customs. Otherwise indirect protection could be given.

12.   In addition, the text of paragraph 4 referred both in English and French to laws and regulations and requirements *affecting* internal sale, purchase, etc., and not to laws, regulations and requirements governing the conditions of sale or purchase. The selection of the word "affecting" would imply, in the opinion of the Panel, that the drafters of the Article intended to cover in paragraph 4 not only the laws and regulations which directly governed the conditions of sale or purchase but also any laws or regulations which might adversely modify the conditions of competition between the domestic and imported products on the internal market.

13.   The Italian delegation alleged that the provisions of paragraph 8(b) which exempted the granting of subsidies to producers from the operation of this Article showed that the intention of the drafters of the Agreement was to limit the scope of Article III to laws and regulations directly related to the conditions of sale, purchase, etc. On the other hand, the Panel considered that if the Italian contention were correct and if the scope of Article III was limited in this way (which would, of course, not include any measure of subsidization) it would have been unnecessary to include the provisions contained in paragraph 8(b) since they would be excluded *ipso facto* from the scope of Article III. The fact that the drafters of Article III thought it necessary to include this exemption for production subsidies would indicate that the intent of the drafters was to provide equal conditions of competition once goods had been cleared through customs.

14.   Moreover, the Panel agreed with the contention of the United Kingdom delegation that in any case the provisions of paragraph 8(b) would not be applicable to this particular case since the credit facilities provided under the Law were granted to the purchasers of agricultural machinery and could not be considered as subsidies accorded to the producers of agricultural machinery.

15.   The Panel also noted that if the Italian contention were correct, and if the scope of Article III were limited in the way the Italian delegation suggested to a specific type of laws and regulations, the value of the bindings under Article II of the Agreement and of the general

rules of non-discrimination as between imported and domestic products could be easily evaded.

16.   The Panel recognized and the United Kingdom delegation agreed with this view that it was not the intention of the General Agreement to limit the right of a contracting party to adopt measures which appeared to it necessary to foster its economic development or to protect a domestic industry, provided that such measures were permitted by the terms of the General Agreement. The GATT offered a number of possibilities to achieve these purposes through tariff measures or otherwise. The Panel did not appreciate why the extension of the credit facilities in question to the purchasers of imported tractors as well as domestically produced tractors would detract from the attainment of the objectives of the Law, which aimed at stimulating the purchase of tractors mainly by small farmers and co-operatives in the interests of economic development. If, on the other hand, the objective of the Law, although not specifically stated in the text thereof, were to protect the Italian agricultural machinery industry, the Panel considered that such protection should be given in ways permissible under the General Agreement rather than by the extension of credit exclusively for purchases of domestically produced agricultural machinery.

* * *

25.   In the light of the considerations set out above the Panel suggests to the CONTRACTING PARTIES that it would be appropriate for them to make a recommendation to the Italian Government in accordance with paragraph 2 of Article XXIII. The Panel considers that the recommendation should draw the attention of the Italian Government to the adverse effects on United Kingdom exports of agricultural machinery, particularly tractors, of those provisions of Law 949 limiting the prescribed credit facilities to purchasers of Italian produced machinery and suggest to the Italian Government that it consider the desirability of eliminating within a reasonable time the adverse effects of the Law on the import trade of agricultural machinery by modifying the operation of that Law or by other appropriate means.

UNITED STATES—SECTION 337 OF THE TARIFF ACT OF 1930

GATT Panel Report adopted November 7, 1989
36th Supp. BISD 345 (1990)

[This case arose out of a complaint by the European Community that Section 337 of the U.S. Tariff Act of 1930 violated Article III.]

2.2   Under Section 337 of the United States Tariff Act of 1930 unfair methods of competition and unfair acts in the importation of articles into the United States, or in their sale, are unlawful if these unfair acts or methods of competition have the effect or tendency to (i) destroy or to substantially injure an industry efficiently and economically operated in the United States, (ii) prevent the establishment of such an industry, or (iii) restrain or monopolise trade and commerce in the United States. The unfair acts and methods of competition in question include the importation or sale of goods that infringe valid United States patents. * * * Since it was revised in the Trade Act of 1974, the majority of investigations under the Section 337 have concerned alleged infringements of patents. * * *

2.3   Remedies available under Section 337, in the event of a violation of the Section, consist of orders excluding the articles concerned from importation into the United States (exclusion orders) and/or cease and desist orders directing parties violating Section 337 to stop the act or method of competition found to be unfair. The exclusion order may be a general order covering all imports that, in a patent-based case, infringe the United States patent in question, or may be limited to goods produced by a respondent in the case.

2.4   Investigations under Section 337 are carried out by the United States International Trade Commission (USITC). The USITC is an independent administrative agency of the United States Government. The USITC is not created as a court under Article III of the United States Constitution, but is authorised and directed by Congress to conduct proceedings under Section 337 which are similar to court proceedings. Section 337 proceedings are subject to the Administrative Procedure Act, which governs similar "quasi-judicial proceedings" conducted by numerous agencies of the United States Federal Government.

* * *

V.   FINDINGS

[Although Section 337 applies to more than patent disputes, the Panel noted that the complaint in this case and the submissions of the parties concentrated on the application of Section 337 to patent-based cases, and the Panel's findings and conclusions are limited to such cases.]

5.4   The central and undisputed facts before the Panel are that, in patent infringement cases, proceedings before the USITC under Section 337 are only applicable to imported products alleged to infringe a United States patent; and that these proceedings are different, in a number of respects, from those applying before a federal district court when a product of United States origin is challenged on grounds of patent infringement. The [European] Community maintained that the differences between the two proceedings are such that the treatment accorded to imported products is less favorable than that accorded to like products of United States origin, inconsistently with Article III:4 of the General Agreement, and that this less favorable treatment cannot be justified under Article XX(d) of the General Agreement. The United States maintained that Section 337 is justifiable under Article XX(d) and, in any event, is not inconsistent with Article III:4 since it does not accord imported products less favorable treatment than that accorded to like products of United States origin.

* * *

(iii) Relation of Article III to Article XX(d)

5.8 The parties to the dispute agreed that Article III:4 applies to substantive patent law, since such law affects the "internal sale, offering for sale, purchase, transportation or use" of imported and domestic products. They also agreed that the consistency of the substantive provisions of United States patent law with the General Agreement is not at issue. Further, the parties agreed that Section 337, when applied in cases of alleged patent infringement, is a means to secure compliance with United States patent law in respect of imported products. They disagreed, however, on the question of whether a measure to secure compliance with patent laws—in contrast to the substantive patent law itself—is covered by Article III:4. * * *

5.9 The Panel noted that Article XX is entitled "General Exceptions" and that the central phase in the introductory clause reads: "nothing in this Agreement shall be construed to prevent the adoption or enforcement ... of measures ... ". Article XX(d) thus provides for a limited and conditional exception from obligations under other provisions. The Panel therefore concluded that Article XX(d) applies only to measures inconsistent with another provision of the General Agreement, and that, consequently, the application of Section 337 has to be examined first in the light of Article III:4. If any inconsistencies with Article III:4 were found, the Panel would then examine whether they could be justified under Article XX(d).

(iv) Article III:4

(a) Meaning of "Laws, Regulations and Requirements" in Article III:4

5.10 The Panel then examined Section 337 in the light of Article III:4. The Panel first addressed the issue of whether only substantive laws, regulations and requirements or also procedural laws, regulations and requirements can be regarded as "affecting" the internal sale of imported products. * * * The Panel noted that the text of Article III:4 makes no distinction between substantive and procedural laws, regulations or requirements and it was not aware of anything in the drafting history that suggests that such a distinction should be made. A previous Panel had found that "the selection of the word 'affecting' would imply ... that the drafters of the Article intended to cover in paragraph 4 not only the laws and regulations which directly governed the conditions of sale or purchase but also any laws or regulations which might adversely modify the conditions of competition between the domestic and imported products on the internal market," [citing para. 12 of the *Italian Agricultural Machinery* case, excerpted earlier in this section]. In the Panel's view enforcement procedures cannot be separated from the substantive provisions they serve to enforce. If the procedural provisions of internal law were not covered by Article III:4, contracting parties could escape the national treatment standard by enforcing substantive law, itself meeting the national treatment standard, through procedures less favorable to imported products than to like products of national origin. The interpretation suggested by the United States would therefore defeat the purpose of Article III, which is to ensure that internal measures "not be applied to imported or domestic products so as to afford protection to domestic production" (Article III:1). The fact that Section 337 is used as a means for the enforcement of United States patent law at the *border* does not provide an escape from the applicability of Article III:4; the interpretative note to Article III states that any law, regulation or requirement affecting the internal sale of products that is enforced in the case of the imported product at the time or point of importation is nevertheless subject to the provisions of Article III. Nor could the applicability of Article III:4 be denied on the ground that most of the procedures in the case before the Panel are applied to persons rather than products, since the factor determining whether persons might be susceptible to Section 337 proceedings or federal district court procedures is the source of the challenged products, that is whether they are of United States origin or imported. For these reasons, the Panel found that the procedures under Section 337 come within the concept of "laws, regulations and requirements" affecting the internal sale of imported products, as set out in Article III of the General Agreement.

(b) The "No Less Favorable" Treatment Standard of Article III:4

5.11 The Panel noted that, as far as the issues before it are concerned, the "no less favorable" treatment requirement set out in Article III:4, is unqualified. These words are to be found throughout the General Agreement and later agreements negotiated in the GATT framework as an expression of the underlying principle of equality of treatment of imported products as compared to the treatment given either to other foreign products, under the most favored nation standard, or to domestic products, under the national treatment standard of Article III. The words "treatment no less favorable" in paragraph 4 call for effective equality of opportunities for imported products in respect of the application of laws, regulations and requirements affecting the internal sale, offering for sale, purchase, transportation, distribution or use of products. This clearly sets a minimum permissible standard as a basis. On the one hand, contracting parties may apply to imported products different formal legal requirements if doing so would accord imported products more favorable treatment. On the other hand, it also has to be recognised that there may be cases where application of formally identical legal provisions would in practice accord less favorable treatment to imported products and a contracting party might thus have to apply different legal provisions to imported products to ensure that the treatment accorded them is in fact no less favorable. For these reasons, the mere fact that imported products are subject under section 337 to legal provisions that are different from those applying to products of national origin is in itself not conclusive in establishing inconsistency with Article III:4. In such cases, it has to be assessed whether or not such differences in the legal provisions applicable do or do not accord to imported products less favorable treatment. Given that the underlying objective is to guarantee equality of treatment, it is incumbent on the contracting party applying differential treatment to show that, in spite of such differences, the no less favorable treatment standard of Article III is met.

5.12   The Panel noted the differing views of the parties on how an assessment should be made as to whether the differences between Section 337 and federal district court procedures do or do not accord imported products less favorable treatment than that accorded to products of United States origin. In brief, the United States believed that this determination could only be made on the basis of an examination of the *actual results* of past Section 337 cases. It would follow from this reasoning that any unfavorable elements of treatment of imported products could be offset by more favorable elements of treatment, provided that the results, as shown in past cases, have not been less favorable. The Community's interpretation of Article III:4 would require that Section 337 not be *capable* of according imported products less favorable treatment; elements of less and more favorable treatment could thus only be offset against each other to the extent that they always would arise in the same cases and necessarily would have an offsetting influence on each other.

5.13   The Panel examined these arguments carefully. It noted that a previous Panel had found that the purpose of the first sentence of Article III:2, dealing with internal taxes and other internal charges, is to protect "expectations on the competitive relationship between imported and domestic products".[2] Article III:4, which is the parallel provision of Article III dealing with the "non-charge" elements of internal legislation, has to be construed as serving the same purpose. Article III:4 would not serve this purpose if the United States interpretation were adopted, since a law, regulation or requirement could then only be challenged in GATT after the event as a means of rectifying less favorable treatment of imported products rather than as a means of forestalling it. In any event, the Panel doubted the feasibility of an approach that would require it to be demonstrated that differences between procedures under Section 337 and those in federal district courts had actually caused, in a given case or cases, less favorable treatment. The Panel therefore considered that, in order to establish whether the "no less favorable" treatment standard of Article III:4 is met, it had to assess whether or not Section 337 in itself may lead to the application to imported products of treatment less favorable than that accorded to products of United States origin. It noted that this approach is in accordance with previous practice of the CONTRACTING PARTIES in applying Article III, which has been to base their decisions on the distinctions made by the laws,

---

2. [original note] Report of Panel on United States—Taxes on Petroleum and Certain Imported Substances (L/6175, para-graph 5.1.9), adopted by the Council on June 17, 1987.

regulations or requirements themselves and on their potential impact rather than on the actual consequences for specific imported products.

5.14   The Panel further found that the "no less favorable" treatment requirement of Article III:4 has to be understood as applicable to each individual case of imported products. The Panel rejected any notion of balancing more favorable treatment of some imported products against less favorable treatment of other imported products. If this notion were accepted, it would entitle a contracting party to derogate from the no less favorable treatment obligation in one case, or indeed in respect of one contracting party, on the ground that it accords more favorable treatment in some other case, or to another contracting party. Such an interpretation would lead to great uncertainty about the conditions of competition between imported and domestic products and thus defeat the purposes of Article III.

(c) Appraisal of Section 337 in Terms of Article III:4

5.15   The United States contended that Section 337 accords imported products more favorable treatment than that accorded to domestic products in district court proceedings because of [several factors.] The Panel examined whether these elements of claimed more favorable treatment could within the meaning of Article III:4 offset any elements of less favorable treatment of imported products alleged by the Community.

5.16   As has already been stated above, an element of more favorable treatment would only be relevant if it would always accompany and offset an element of differential treatment causing less favorable treatment. * * *

5.17   The Panel noted that some of the procedural advantages that, according to the United States, are given to respondents could operate in all cases. The Panel also recognised that the substantive economic requirements put procedural burdens not only on the respondent but also on the complainant, which has the burden of proof on these matters, and that these procedural burdens could operate in all cases. The Panel took these factors into account to the extent that they might be capable of exerting an offsetting influence in each individual case of less favorable treatment resulting from an element cited by the Community.

5.18   In cases concerning imported products over which both federal district courts and the USITC have jurisdiction, the complainant has the choice of which forum to use, or possibly to initiate a complaint in both fora; no equivalent choice of forum is available to a plaintiff in a case concerning products of United States origin. This option was referred to on numerous occasions by the Community and by third contracting parties making submissions. The Panel found that, given the differences between the proceedings of the USITC and of federal courts, to provide the complainant with the choice of forum where imported products are concerned and to provide no corresponding choice where domestically-produced products are concerned is in itself less favorable treatment of imported products and is therefore inconsistent with Article

III:4. It is also a reason why in practice Section 337 is more likely to be employed in those cases where the specific elements that might accord less favorable treatment to imported products are significant. The complainant will tend to avoid recourse to Section 337 in cases where elements of more favorable treatment of the respondent than that accorded in federal district court litigation might play a role, for example where public interest or policy considerations might be expected to intervene.

5.19　The Panel considered the specific differences between Section 337 proceedings and those in federal district courts referred to by the Community to assess whether they accord less favorable treatment to imported products than that accorded to products of United States origin in patent-based cases: * * *

(d) Summary of Findings Under Article III:4

5.20　The Panel *found* that Section 337, inconsistently with Article III:4 of the General Agreement, accords to imported products alleged to infringe United States patents treatment less favorable than that accorded under federal district court procedures to like products of United States origin as a result of the following factors:

(i) the availability to complainants of a choice of forum in which to challenge imported products, whereas no corresponding choice is available to challenge products of United States origin.

(ii) the potential disadvantage to producers or importers of challenged products of foreign origin resulting from the tight and fixed time-limits in proceedings under Section 337, when no comparable time-limits apply to producers of challenged products of United States origin;

(iii) the non-availability of opportunities in Section 337 proceedings to raise counterclaims, as is possible in proceedings in federal district court;

(iv) the possibility that general exclusion orders may result from proceedings brought before the USITC under Section 337, given that no comparable remedy is available against infringing products of United States origin.

(v) the automatic enforcement of exclusion orders by the United States Customs Service, when injunctive relief obtainable in federal court in respect of infringing products of United States origin requires for its enforcement individual proceedings brought by the successful plaintiff;

(vi) the possibility that producers or importers of challenged products of foreign origin may have to defend their products both before the USITC and in federal district court, whereas no corresponding exposure exists with respect to products of United States origin.

5.21 The Panel considered whether all these differences of treatment could be traced back to one common cause, this being the structure of the USITC which is fundamentally not a court of law but an administrative agency, and whether this structural difference could be said to entail in itself treatment incompatible with the requirements of Article III. The Panel however reached no conclusion in this respect, as this question had not been raised in such general terms by the Community.

Notes and Questions

(1) Relying principally on these two cases (and the *Superfund* case cited in the *Section 337* footnote), the Appellate Body summarized the purpose of Article III as follows:

> The broad and fundamental purpose of Article III is to avoid protectionism in the application of internal tax and regulatory measures. More specifically, the purpose of Article III "is to ensure that internal measures 'not be applied to imported or domestic products so as to afford protection to domestic production' ".[3] Toward this end, Article III obliges Members of the WTO to provide equality of competitive conditions for imported products in relation to domestic products.[4] "[T]he intention of the drafters of the Agreement was clearly to treat the imported products in the same way as the like domestic products once they had been cleared through customs. Otherwise indirect protection could be given".[5] Moreover, it is irrelevant that "the trade effects" of the tax differential between imported and domestic products, as reflected in the volumes of imports, are insignificant or even non-existent; Article III protects expectations not of any particular trade volume but rather of the equal competitive relationship between imported and domestic products.[6] Members of the WTO are free to pursue their own domestic goals through internal taxation or regulation so long as they do not do so in a way that violates Article III or any of the other commitments they have made in the *WTO Agreement*.

Japan—Taxes on Alcoholic Beverages, WT/DS8, 10 & 11/AB/R, at 16, adopted by the DSB on November 1, 1996.

(2) The *Section 337* case is unusual in that it effectively overruled a prior panel decision. In United States—Imports of Certain Automotive Spring Assemblies, GATT, 30th Supp. BISD 107 (Panel report adopted May 26, 1983), the use of Section 337 had been upheld in a specific case, but when the GATT Council adopted the panel report it did so in light of an understanding that adoption of the report "shall not foreclose future examination of the use of Section 337 to deal with patent infringement cases from the point of view of consistency with Articles III and XX of the General Agreement." GATT Doc. C/M/168, item 7. We examine Section 337 and the U.S. implementation of the panel's findings in Chapter 20 infra.

3. quoting *Section 337*, para. 5.10.
4. quoting *Superfund*, para. 5.1.9.
5. quoting *Italian Agricultural Machinery*, para. 11.
6. quoting *Superfund*, para. 5.1.9.

(3) The broad scope of Article III:4 is underscored by these panel decisions. The concluding lines of paragraphs 11 and 12 of the *Italian Agricultural Machinery* case are particularly noteworthy, as they stress the role of Article III in (i) limiting protective measures to border measures (mainly tariffs) and (ii) preventing evasion of tariff bindings. How does the *Section 337* decision build on these conclusions of the *Italian Agricultural Machinery* case? See, in particular, para. 5.11. What does it mean to say

> that the words "treatment no less favorable" in paragraph 4 call for *effective equality of opportunities* for imported products in respect of the application of laws, regulations and requirements affecting the internal sale, offering for sale, purchase, transportation, distribution or use of products (emphasis added)?

Suppose that the market for cigarettes in a country had been closed to imports and dominated by a domestic monopoly. If the market is opened to imports, but at the same time advertising of cigarettes is banned, could the exporting countries claim that in order to provide effective equality of opportunities, they must be allowed some freedom to advertise their products? See Thailand—Restrictions on Importation of and Internal Taxes on Cigarettes, GATT, 37th Supp. BISD 200, 224 (1991) (Panel report adopted Nov. 7, 1990) (panel suggested that even if an advertising restriction were found to violate Article III, the restriction might be justified as necessary under Article XX(b)).

(4) The *Italian Agricultural Machinery* panel's rejection of Italy's paragraph 8(b) defense is typical. If interpreted broadly, any discrimination against imports could be characterized as a government subsidy to domestic producers and therefore exempt under paragraph 8(b). This would obviously completely eviscerate the substantive provisions of Article III. See also United States—Measures Affecting Alcoholic and Malt Beverages, 39th Supp. BISD 206 (Panel report adopted June 19, 1992)(rejected U.S. attempt to justify lower taxes on domestic products and tax credits available only in respect of domestic products by reference to Article 8(b)). Yet, does it make much sense to distinguish a subsidy to sellers from a subsidy to purchasers? How are they different in their economic impact?

(5) How does the *Section 337* panel deal with the problem of measuring the effect of a violation? Did it focus on the actual impact of Section 337 or the potential impact? Over time, it has become accepted in GATT that a mandatory law that might result in a GATT violation violates the General Agreement on its face and no negative impact need be shown. The explanation for this expansive interpretation is in part given in para. 5.13, where it is noted that Article III is aimed at protecting expectations on competitive relationships between imports and domestic products. We previously discussed aspects of this issue in Section 7.4(A) on dispute settlement.

(6) Note that the panel did not rule out the possibility that a party could treat imported and domestic products differently without violating Article III (para. 5.11). Who would have the burden of proving the different treatment afforded no less favorable treatment? How easy do you think it would be to meet this burden? Note also that the panel rejected the notion of balancing more favorable and less favorable aspects of a law. (para. 5.14) This is consistent with the interpretation that has been given to Article I, as

we saw in Section 9.2(B)(2). We examine the question of what constitutes less favorable treatment in Section 12.4 infra.

(7) What does national treatment mean in a federal system? Suppose that Michigan favors its own citizens over those of neighboring U.S. states. If a national treatment obligation applies to Michigan, does Michigan owe Canadians the treatment it gives its own citizens or only the most favorable treatment that it gives noncitizens?

SECTION 12.3   DISCRIMINATORY TAXES: ARTICLE III:2

In this section, we look at the problem of discriminatory taxation. While most product-based taxes are applied uniformly across a broad range of products (such as general sales taxes or value added taxes), certain excise or registration taxes may vary greatly depending on product definitions. In particular, various national systems for taxing alcoholic beverages have often been alleged to provide protection to domestic products, whether intentionally or otherwise. As we will see, Article III:2 can be used to attack these systems in two ways: First, it can be claimed that the products involved are all like products and that only one tax rate can be applied. Second, even if the beverages are not like products, Article III:2, second sentence, can be invoked to claim that the tax system is being used to protect some domestic products, in contravention of Article III:1 and 2. In reading the following Appellate Body report, consider the following questions: How does the Appellate Body's analysis of the like product issue compare to the *SPF* and *Spanish Coffee* cases in Section 10.2? If different, are the differences justified? How does the second sentence of Article III:2 affect, if at all, the like-product issue? Does it justify (or obviate the need for) a broad definition of like product? What differences are there in the way that the two sentences of Article III:2 operate?

JAPAN—TAXES ON ALCOHOLIC BEVERAGES
WT/DS8, 10 & 11/AB/R
Appellate Body Report adopted by the DSB on November 1, 1996

[Canada, the EC and the United States challenged the Japanese law on liquor taxation on the grounds that it violated Article GATT III:2 by taxing a Japanese product—shochu—less heavily than certain like or competitive imported products (including vodka, gin, whisky, brandy, rum and liqueurs). The Panel concluded that (i) shochu and vodka were like products and Japan, by taxing the latter in excess of the former, violated Article III:2, first sentence and (ii) shochu and the other products were "directly competitive or substitutable products" and Japan, by not taxing them similarly, violated Article III:2, second sentence. A 1987 GATT case had found the prior Japanese liquor tax system to violate Article III.

At issue in the WTO case was the proper interpretation of Article III:2, the second sentence of which specifically refers to Article III:1 and is the subject of an interpretative note. These provisions should be reviewed before studying the Appellate Body's report.]

The terms of Article III must be given their ordinary meaning—in their context and in the light of the overall object and purpose of the WTO Agreement. Thus, the words actually used in the Article provide the basis for an interpretation that must give meaning and effect to all its terms. The proper interpretation of the Article is, first of all, a textual interpretation. Consequently, the Panel is correct in seeing a distinction between Article III:1, which "contains general principles", and Article III:2, which "provides for specific obligations regarding internal taxes and internal charges". Article III:1 articulates a general principle that internal measures should not be applied so as to afford protection to domestic production. This general principle informs the rest of Article III. The purpose of Article III:1 is to establish this general principle as a guide to understanding and interpreting the specific obligations contained in Article III:2 and in the other paragraphs of Article III, while respecting, and not diminishing in any way, the meaning of the words actually used in the texts of those other paragraphs. In short, Article III:1 constitutes part of the context of Article III:2, in the same way that it constitutes part of the context of each of the other paragraphs in Article III. Any other reading of Article III would have the effect of rendering the words of Article III:1 meaningless, thereby violating the fundamental principle of effectiveness in treaty interpretation. Consistent with this principle of effectiveness, and with the textual differences in the two sentences, we believe that Article III:1 informs the first sentence and the second sentence of Article III:2 in different ways.

Article III:2, First Sentence

Article III:1 informs Article III:2, first sentence, by establishing that if imported products are taxed in excess of like domestic products, then that tax measure is inconsistent with Article III. Article III:2, first sentence does not refer specifically to Article III:1. There is no specific invocation in this first sentence of the general principle in Article III:1 that admonishes Members of the WTO not to apply measures "so as to afford protection". This omission must have some meaning. We believe the meaning is simply that the presence of a protective application need not be established separately from the specific requirements that are included in the first sentence in order to show that a tax measure is inconsistent with the general principle set out in the first sentence. However, this does not mean that the general principle of Article III:1 does not apply to this sentence. To the contrary, we believe the first sentence of Article III:2 is, in effect, an application of this general principle. The ordinary meaning of the words of Article III:2, first sentence leads inevitably to this conclusion. Read in their context and in the light of the overall object and purpose of the WTO Agreement, the words of the first sentence require an examination of the conformity of an internal tax measure with Article III by determining, first, whether the taxed imported and domestic products are "like" and, second, whether the taxes applied to the imported products are "in excess of" those applied to the like domestic products. If the imported and domestic products are "like products", and if the taxes applied to the imported products are "in excess of" those applied to the like domestic products, then the measure is inconsistent with Article III:2, first sentence.

This approach to an examination of Article III:2, first sentence, is consistent with past practice under the GATT 1947. Moreover, it is consistent with the object and purpose of Article III:2, which the panel in the predecessor to this case dealing with an earlier version of the Liquor Tax Law, rightly stated as "promoting non-discriminatory competition among imported and like domestic products [which] could not be achieved if Article III:2 were construed in a manner allowing discriminatory and protective internal taxation of imported products in excess of like domestic products".

(a) "Like Products"

Because the second sentence of Article III:2 provides for a separate and distinctive consideration of the protective aspect of a measure in examining its application to a broader category of products that are not "like products" as contemplated by the first sentence, we agree with the Panel that the first sentence of Article III:2 must be construed narrowly so as not to condemn measures that its strict terms are not meant to condemn. Consequently, we agree with the Panel also that the definition of "like products" in Article III:2, first sentence, should be construed narrowly.

How narrowly is a matter that should be determined separately for each tax measure in each case. We agree with the practice under the GATT 1947 of determining whether imported and domestic products are "like" on a case-by-case basis. The Report of the Working Party on *Border Tax Adjustments*, adopted by the CONTRACTING PARTIES in 1970, set out the basic approach for interpreting "like or similar products" generally in the various provisions of the GATT 1947:

> ... the interpretation of the term should be examined on a case-by-case basis. This would allow a fair assessment in each case of the different elements that constitute a "similar" product. Some criteria were suggested for determining, on a case-by-case basis, whether a product is "similar": the product's end-uses in a given market; consumers' tastes and habits, which change from country to country; the product's properties, nature and quality.[1]

This approach was followed in almost all adopted panel reports after *Border Tax Adjustments*. This approach should be helpful in identifying on a case-by-case basis the range of "like products" that fall within the narrow limits of Article III:2, first sentence in the GATT 1994. Yet this approach will be most helpful if decision makers keep ever in mind how narrow the range of "like products" in Article III:2, first sentence is

---

1. [original note 45] Report of the Working Party on *Border Tax Adjustments*, BISD   18S/97, para. 18.

meant to be as opposed to the range of "like" products contemplated in some other provisions of the GATT 1994 and other Multilateral Trade Agreements of the *WTO Agreement*. In applying the criteria cited in *Border Tax Adjustments* to the facts of any particular case, and in considering other criteria that may also be relevant in certain cases, panels can only apply their best judgement in determining whether in fact products are "like". This will always involve an unavoidable element of individual, discretionary judgement. * * *

No one approach to exercising judgement will be appropriate for all cases. The criteria in *Border Tax Adjustments* should be examined, but there can be no one precise and absolute definition of what is "like". The concept of "likeness" is a relative one that evokes the image of an accordion. The accordion of "likeness" stretches and squeezes in different places as different provisions of the *WTO Agreement* are applied. The width of the accordion in any one of those places must be determined by the particular provision in which the term "like" is encountered as well as by the context and the circumstances that prevail in any given case to which that provision may apply. We believe that, in Article III:2, first sentence of the GATT 1994, the accordion of "likeness" is meant to be narrowly squeezed.

The Panel determined in this case that shochu and vodka are "like products" for the purposes of Article III:2, first sentence. We note that the determination of whether vodka is a "like product" to shochu under Article III:2, first sentence, or a "directly competitive or substitutable product" to shochu under Article III:2, second sentence, does not materially affect the outcome of this case.

* * *

(b) *"In Excess Of"*

The only remaining issue under Article III:2, first sentence, is whether the taxes on imported products are "in excess of" those on like domestic products. If so, then the Member that has imposed the tax is not in compliance with Article III. Even the smallest amount of "excess" is too much. "The prohibition of discriminatory taxes in Article III:2, first sentence, is not conditional on a 'trade effects test' nor is it qualified by a *de minimis* standard."[2] * * *

ARTICLE III:2, SECOND SENTENCE

Article III:1 informs Article III:2, second sentence, through specific reference. Article III:2, second sentence, contains a general prohibition against "internal taxes or other internal charges" applied to "imported or domestic products in a manner contrary to the principles set forth in paragraph 1". As mentioned before, Article III:1 states that internal taxes and other internal charges "should not be applied to imported or

---

2. [original note 51] *United States— Measures Affecting Alcoholic and Malt Bev-* *erages*, BISD 39S/206, para 5.6. * * *

domestic products so as to afford protection to domestic production". Again, *Ad* Article III:2 states as follows:

> A tax conforming to the requirements of the first sentence of paragraph 2 would be considered to be inconsistent with the provisions of the second sentence only in cases where competition was involved between, on the one hand, the taxed product and, on the other hand, a directly competitive or substitutable product which was not similarly taxed.

Article III:2, second sentence, and the accompanying *Ad* Article have equivalent legal status in that both are treaty language which was negotiated and agreed at the same time. The *Ad* Article does not replace or modify the language contained in Article III:2, second sentence, but, in fact, clarifies its meaning. Accordingly, the language of the second sentence and the *Ad* Article must be read together in order to give them their proper meaning.

Unlike that of Article III:2, first sentence, the language of Article III:2, second sentence, specifically invokes Article III:1. The significance of this distinction lies in the fact that whereas Article III:1 acts implicitly in addressing the two issues that must be considered in applying the first sentence, it acts explicitly as an entirely separate issue that must be addressed along with two other issues that are raised in applying the second sentence. Giving full meaning to the text and to its context, three separate issues must be addressed to determine whether an internal tax measure is inconsistent with Article III:2, second sentence. These three issues are whether:

(1) the imported products and the domestic products *are "directly competitive or substitutable products" which are in competition with each other*;

(2) the directly competitive or substitutable imported and domestic products *are "not similarly taxed"*; and

(3) the dissimilar taxation of the directly competitive or substitutable imported domestic products *is "applied ... so as to afford protection to domestic production"*.

Again, these are three separate issues. Each must be established separately by the complainant for a panel to find that a tax measure imposed by a Member of the WTO is inconsistent with Article III:2, second sentence.

(a) "Directly Competitive or Substitutable Products"

If imported and domestic products are not "like products" for the narrow purposes of Article III:2, first sentence, then they are not subject to the strictures of that sentence and there is no inconsistency with the requirements of that sentence. However, depending on their nature, and depending on the competitive conditions in the relevant market, those same products may well be among the broader category of "directly competitive or substitutable products" that fall within the domain of

Article III:2, second sentence. How much broader that category of "directly competitive or substitutable products" may be in any given case is a matter for the panel to determine based on all the relevant facts in that case. As with "like products" under the first sentence, the determination of the appropriate range of "directly competitive or substitutable products" under the second sentence must be made on a case-by-case basis.

In this case, the Panel emphasized the need to look not only at such matters as physical characteristics, common end-uses, and tariff classifications, but also at the "market place". This seems appropriate. The GATT 1994 is a commercial agreement, and the WTO is concerned, after all, with markets. It does not seem inappropriate to look at competition in the relevant markets as one among a number of means of identifying the broader category of products that might be described as "directly competitive or substitutable".

Nor does it seem inappropriate to examine elasticity of substitution as one means of examining those relevant markets. The Panel did not say that cross-price elasticity of demand is *"the* decisive criterion" for determining whether products are "directly competitive or substitutable". The Panel stated the following:

> In the Panel's view, the decisive criterion in order to determine whether two products are directly competitive or substitutable is whether they have common end-uses, *inter alia*, as shown by elasticity of substitution.

We agree. And, we find the Panel's legal analysis of whether the products are "directly competitive or substitutable products" in paragraphs 6.28–6.32 of the Panel Report to be correct.

* * *

(b) *"Not Similarly Taxed"*

To give due meaning to the distinctions in the wording of Article III:2, first sentence, and Article III:2, second sentence, the phrase "not similarly taxed" in the *Ad* Article to the second sentence must not be construed so as to mean the same thing as the phrase "in excess of" in the first sentence. On its face, the phrase "in excess of" in the first sentence means *any* amount of tax on imported products "in excess of" the tax on domestic "like products". The phrase "not similarly taxed" in the *Ad* Article to the second sentence must therefore mean something else. It requires a different standard, just as "directly competitive or substitutable products" requires a different standard as compared to "like products" for these same interpretive purposes.

* * *

* * * Thus, in any given case, there may be some amount of taxation on imported products that may well be "in excess of" the tax on domestic "like products" but may not be so much as to compel a conclusion that "directly competitive or substitutable" imported and domestic products are "not similarly taxed" for the purposes of the *Ad* Article to Article III:2, second sentence. * * * We agree with the Panel that this amount of differential taxation must be more than *de minimis* to be deemed "not similarly taxed" in any given case. And, like the Panel, we believe that whether any particular differential amount of taxation is *de minimis* or is not *de minimis* must, here too, be determined on a case-by-case basis. Thus, to be "not similarly taxed", the tax burden on imported products must be heavier than on "directly competitive or substitutable" domestic products, and that burden must be more than *de minimis* in any given case.

In this case, the Panel applied the correct legal reasoning in determining whether "directly competitive or substitutable" imported and domestic products were "not similarly taxed". However, the Panel erred in blurring the distinction between that issue and the entirely separate issue of whether the tax measure in question was applied "so as to afford protection". Again, these are separate issues that must be addressed individually. * * *

(c) "So As To Afford Protection"

This third inquiry under Article III:2, second sentence, must determine whether "directly competitive or substitutable products" are "not similarly taxed" in a way that affords protection. This is not an issue of intent. It is not necessary for a panel to sort through the many reasons legislators and regulators often have for what they do and weigh the relative significance of those reasons to establish legislative or regulatory intent. If the measure is applied to imported or domestic products so as to afford protection to domestic production, then it does not matter that there may not have been any desire to engage in protectionism in the minds of the legislators or the regulators who imposed the measure. It is irrelevant that protectionism was not an intended objective if the particular tax measure in question is nevertheless, to echo Article III:1, "*applied* to imported or domestic products so as to afford protection to domestic production". This is an issue of how the measure in question is *applied*.

* * *

Although it is true that the aim of a measure may not be easily ascertained, nevertheless its protective application can most often be discerned from the design, the architecture, and the revealing structure of a measure. The very magnitude of the dissimilar taxation in a particular case may be evidence of such a protective application, as the Panel rightly concluded in this case. Most often, there will be other factors to be considered as well. In conducting this inquiry, panels should give full consideration to all the relevant facts and all the relevant circumstances in any given case.

* * *

[As noted earlier], having stated the correct legal approach to apply with respect to Article III:2, second sentence, the Panel then equated dissimilar taxation above a *de minimis* level with the separate and distinct requirement of demonstrating that the tax measure "affords protection to domestic production". * * * [I]n every case, a careful, objective analysis, must be done of each and all relevant facts and all the relevant circumstances in order to determine the existence of protective taxation. Although the Panel blurred its legal reasoning in this respect, nevertheless we conclude that it reasoned correctly that in this case, the Liquor Tax Law is not in compliance with Article III:2. As the Panel did, we note that:

> ... the combination of customs duties and internal taxation in Japan has the following impact: on the one hand, it makes it difficult for foreign-produced shochu to penetrate the Japanese market and, on the other, it does not guarantee equality of competitive conditions between shochu and the rest of white and brown spirits. Thus, through a combination of high import duties and differentiated internal taxes, Japan manages to "isolate" domestically produced shochu from foreign competition, be it foreign produced shochu or any other of the mentioned white and brown spirits.

Our interpretation of Article III is faithful to the "customary rules of interpretation of public international law". WTO rules are reliable, comprehensible and enforceable. WTO rules are not so rigid or so inflexible as not to leave room for reasoned judgements in confronting the endless and ever-changing ebb and flow of real facts in real cases in the real world. They will serve the multilateral trading system best if they are interpreted with that in mind. In that way, we will achieve the "security and predictability" sought for the multilateral trading system by the Members of the WTO through the establishment of the dispute settlement system.

Notes and Questions

(1) The Appellate Body report is particularly interesting for the interpretative method that it lays out. For those familiar with the arguments in the case, however, the report was unusual in the way it dealt with those arguments. While the views of the Appellate Body on meaning of "like product" are clear, it does not specifically discuss the alternative meaning put forward by both Japan and the United States (and opposed by the EC and Canada). While there were subtle differences in their approach, Japan and the U.S. had essentially argued that in determining the likeness of products it is necessary to consider the aims and effect of the measure at issue to determine whether the tax or regulatory distinction made by the measure is "so as to afford protection," in the words of Article III:1. If there were no such aim or effect, then the products would not be like and would not be subject to Article III:2, first sentence. The policy justification for such an interpretation would be to avoid a mechanical application of the like products test of Article III that could lead to a finding that a non-protectionist measure designed to achieve legitimate policy goals denied national

treatment in violation of Article III. The so-called aims and effect test had been used in one adopted GATT panel report,[3] along with more traditional factors, in defining product likeness and had been used as the sole basis for determining likeness in one unadopted report.[4]

The panel in the instant case declined to follow the aims and effect test on the grounds that it lacked a textual basis in Article III. After all, even if Article III:1 provides context for interpretation of Article III:2, how can it justify changing an examination of the likeness of products into an examination of the purpose or effect of legislation? Moreover, application of such a test could have the effect of converting an Article XX defense that a respondent would normally have the burden of establishing (e.g., the safety exception of Article XX(b)) into an element of the complainant's case (e.g., the products are like because there is a protectionist aim and effect to the measure and not a safety rationale), thereby making it more difficult to establish an Article III violation.

In your view, should the aims and effect test have been accepted by the Appellate Body? If Article III:1 is the context for all of Article III, why shouldn't it be necessary to establish a violation of any part of Article III to show that a measure is applied so as to afford protection? How does the Appellate Body deal with the relationship between Article III:1 and the two sentences of Article III:2? To the extent that the policy justification for that test is to avoid invalidating legitimate regulations, do you see how a narrow view of the scope of the phrase "like products" in Article III:2 largely accomplishes that goal? Different considerations may apply in the case of Article III:4, which we consider in the next section.

(2) There have been two other WTO alcohol tax cases–one involving Korea and the other Chile. Those cases follow the outlines established in the Japan case, but they also examine in more detail the definitions of "competitive or substitutable products" and "not similarly taxed". Korea–Taxes on Alcoholic Beverages, WT/DS75 & 84/R & AB/R, adopted by the DSB on February 17, 1999; Chile–Taxes on Alcoholic Beverages, WT/DS87 & 110/R & AB/R, adopted by the DSB on January 12, 2000.

(3) What are the key factors in determining the third element of a violation of Article III:2, second sentence? In other words, how does one establish that a measure is applied so as to afford protection? Do you think that the existence of domestic production should suffice to establish the lack of protection (or discrimination)? If so, how much domestic production should be necessary?

(4) More generally, what are the stakes in applying Article III:2? Is it simply a matter of protecting expectations generated during tariff negotiations? If so, does that imply that changes in domestic policies are the real problem? Why does the national treatment article not then "grandfather" certain pre-existing discriminatory policies? Should "like product" be defined primarily with reference to what the negotiators understood or would have reasonably understood to be its scope? Might tariff classification

---

3. Panel Report on United States–Measures Affecting Alcoholic and Malt Beverages, BISD 39/206, 294–295 (adopted on June 19, 1992).

4. Panel Report on United States–Taxes on Automobiles, GATT Doc. DS31/R (Sept. 29, 1994)(not adopted).

headings not be quite helpful on this point? Is discrimination among reasonably close substitutes problematic for reasons other than a possible frustration of expectations? Are MacIntosh computers "like" IBM computers? Are minivans "like" passenger sedans?

(5) In the drafting history of Article III:2, the following example is given of the type of protection that the Article III:2, second sentence, is designed to prevent. Suppose that a country produces apples and imports oranges, which it cannot produce. An internal tax on oranges, but not on fruits grown domestically (such as apples), could operate to protect the domestic apple industry. The drafting history suggests that the orange exporting country could rely on Article III:2, second sentence, in attacking the tax on oranges in GATT. The tariff on oranges, as a practical matter, would have to be bound in order to make this argument attractive. Why?

(6) Article 90 of the EC Treaty provides:

> No Member State shall impose, directly or indirectly, on the products of other Member States any internal taxation of any kind in excess of that imposed directly or indirectly on similar domestic products. Furthermore, no Member State shall impose on the products of other Member States any internal taxation of such a nature as to afford indirect protection to other products.

In applying it, the EC Court of Justice has concluded that significantly different tax rates on wine versus beer and grain-based spirits versus wine- or fruit-based spirits violate Article 90. The court has not always made it clear whether it relied on the first sentence or second sentence of Article 90. See Commission v. France (Alcohol excise tax), Case 168/78, [1980] ECR 347; Commission v. United Kingdom (Wine and beer taxes), Case 170/78, [1983] ECR 2265. Would you expect such a result to be reached in GATT under Article III under the reasoning of the *Japanese Alcoholic Beverages* case?

(7) Suppose a country applies a tax on the purchase of new cars. Suppose further that the tax due increases progressively as the car's horsepower increases, up to a maximum of 1100 francs, but that there is a special 5000 franc tax on high horsepower cars, all of which are imported. These facts gave rise to an EC Court of Justice ruling that the French tax system violated Article 90 of the EC Treaty, which is set out in Note 6 above.

In HUMBLOT v. DIRECTEUR DES SERVICES FISCAUX, Case 112/84, [1985] ECR 1367, the court ruled:

> [13] Such a system of domestic taxation is, however, compatible with Article [90] only in so far as it is free from any discriminatory or protective effect.

> [14] That is not true of a system like the one at issue in the main proceedings. Under that system there are two distinct taxes: a differential tax which increases progressively and is charged on cars not exceeding a given power rating for tax purposes and a fixed tax on cars exceeding that rating which is almost five times as high as the highest rate of the differential tax. Although the system embodies no formal distinction based on the origin of products it manifestly exhibits discriminatory or protective fea-

tures contrary to Article [90], since the power rating determining liability has been fixed at a level such that only imported cars, in particular from other Member States, are subject to the special tax whereas all cars of domestic manufacture are liable to the distinctly more advantageous differential tax.

[15] In the absence of considerations relating to the amount of the special tax, consumers seeking comparable cars as regards such matters as size, comfort, actual power, maintenance costs, durability, fuel consumption and price would naturally choose from among cars above and below the critical power rating laid down by French law. However, liability to the special tax entails a much larger increase in taxation than passing from one category of car to another in a system of progressive taxation embodying balanced differentials like the system on which the differential tax is based. The resultant additional taxation is liable to cancel out the advantages which certain cars imported from other Member States might have in consumers' eyes over comparable cars of domestic manufacture, particularly since the special tax continues to be payable for several years. In that respect the special tax reduces the amount of competition to which cars of domestic manufacture are subject and hence is contrary to the principle of neutrality with which domestic taxation must comply.

The U.S. claimed in 1956 that the French tax violated Article III, but no GATT panel examined it. In 1994, a GATT panel examined an EU challenge to several U.S. auto measures: a "gas guzzler" tax,[5] a luxury tax[6] and the Corporate Average Fuel Efficiency (CAFE) rules.[7] The EU claimed that although EU-origin cars hold only four percent of the U.S. market, 88% of the revenue collected from these levies is from EU cars. The panel upheld the luxury and gas guzzler taxes, but found certain averaging formulae in the CAFE rules violated Article III:4 by treating domestic and foreign cars differently, in a manner not acceptable under Article XX(g). GATT Doc. DS31/R (Sept. 29, 1994). The report was never adopted.

(8) Assume that the United States adopts legislation that imposes (i) a tax on certain chemicals sold or imported into the United States and (ii) a tax on certain imported substances containing chemicals subject to the first tax. The tax on imported substances is set so that a substance would bear the same tax as it would if it had been made in the U.S. from chemicals subject to the first tax. The taxes are used to fund the so-called Superfund, which is used to cleanup hazardous waste sites in the United States. Is the tax on imported substances permissible under Article III?

An affirmative answer was given by a GATT panel in UNITED STATES—TAXES ON PETROLEUM AND CERTAIN IMPORTED SUB-

---

5. 26 U.S.C.A. sec. 4064 (taxes range from $1000 for cars with fuel efficiency rating of less than 22.5 miles per gallon to $7700 for cars below 12.5 MPG).

6. 26 U.S.C.A. sec. 4001 (to be phased out in 2002).

7. 49 U.S.C.A. secs. 32901–32919 (civil penalties payable based on the extent to which an automaker's product line fails to achieve average fuel economy standards specified by Secretary of Transportation).

STANCES, GATT, 34th Supp. BISD 136 (1988)(Panel report adopted June 17, 1987), which was also excerpted in Section 7.4(A)(dispute settlement):

5.2.3 The Panel noted that the United States justified the tax on certain imported substances as a border tax adjustment corresponding in its effect to the internal tax on certain chemicals from which these substances were derived. The Panel further noted that the EEC considered the tax on certain chemicals not to be eligible for border tax adjustment because it was designed to tax polluting activities that occurred in the United States and to finance environmental programs benefiting only United States producers. Consistent with the Polluter–Pays Principle, the United States should have taxed only products of domestic origin because only their production gave rise to environmental problems in the United States. * * *

5.2.4 The report of the Working Party on Border Tax Adjustments, adopted by the CONTRACTING PARTIES in 1970, concluded the following on the rules of the General Agreement relating to tax adjustments applied to goods entering into international trade:

"There was convergence of views to the effect that taxes directly levied on products were eligible for tax adjustment. Examples of such taxes comprised specific excise duties, sales taxes and cascade taxes and the tax on value added ... Furthermore, the Working Party concluded that there was convergence of views to the effect that certain taxes that were not directly levied on products were not eligible for tax adjustment. Examples of such taxes comprised social security charges whether on employers or employees and payroll taxes" (BISD 18S/100–101).

As these conclusions of the CONTRACTING PARTIES clearly indicate, the tax adjustment rules of the General Agreement distinguish between taxes on products and taxes not directly levied on products; they do not distinguish between taxes with different policy purposes. Whether a sales tax is levied on a product for general revenue purposes or to encourage the rational use of environmental resources, is therefore not relevant for the determination of the eligibility of a tax for border tax adjustment. For these reasons the Panel concluded that the tax on certain chemicals, being a tax directly imposed on products, was eligible for border tax adjustment independent of the purpose it served. The Panel therefore did not examine whether the tax on chemicals served environmental purposes and, if so, whether a border tax adjustment would be consistent with these purposes.

Note the distinction made by the GATT Working Party between taxes imposed on products and taxes imposed on income. As is brought out in the review problems which follow, it is generally accepted that Article III applies to the former, and not the latter. But what if an income tax benefit (e.g., deduction or credit) is tied to the purchase of a domestic product?

Review Problems

Consider whether each situation described below is consistent or inconsistent with GATT Article III:

(1) Suppose the United States imposed a tax on automobiles which cannot operate more efficiently than 15 miles per gallon of gasoline, but rebates 50% of that tax to any domestic automobile company for use solely in research on auto energy conservation. See United States–Measures Affecting Alcoholic and Malt Beverages, GATT, 39th Supp. BISD 206 (1993)(Panel report adopted June 19, 1992)(excise tax credits available only to domestic brewers violate Article III).

(2) A special accelerated depreciation income tax deduction is granted to domestic manufacturing companies, but not to foreign manufacturers, even when they derive locally taxable income from sales of imported goods.

(3) Suppose U.S. purchasers of automobiles are granted a gasoline tax rebate of $300 for the year in which they purchased a new *domestically produced* automobile.

(4) Suppose U.S. law imposes a 10% excise tax on the sale of domestically produced or imported cars, but provides that such excise tax shall be one percentage point less than 10% for each 5% improvement in the officially rated gas mileage of each particular current year's make and model, over the model's rating for 1990. That is, if a car was rated at 20 miles-per-gallon in 1990, and 22 miles-per-gallon in 1992, then the 10% improvement would result in an 8% excise tax on the 1993 model, rather than a 10% tax. Suppose further, that it can be established that the best selling *imported* cars in 1990 had miles-per-gallon ratings of 30% to 50% over most American domestically made models (and that therefore much improvement would be more difficult for the imported makes). Would such a law be consistent with U.S. WTO obligations?

SECTION 12.4 DISCRIMINATORY REGULATIONS: ARTICLE III:4

Article III:4 requires that imported products receive no less favorable treatment than domestic like products in respect of laws, regulations and requirements affecting their internal sale, offering for sale, purchase, transportation, distribution or use. We have already examined two older Article III:4 cases—*Italian Agricultural Machinery* and *Section 337*—and seen that it has been interpreted broadly. In this section, we focus on the actual terms of Article III:4. First, we examine how the concept of "like product" should be interpreted. Does the phrase have the same meaning that it does in Article III:2? What considerations argue for a different scope? Second, what is treatment "no less favorable"? We saw that the *Section 337* panel concluded that identical treatment may not be required, but when is non-identical treatment less favorable? For both of the foregoing issues–like product and less favorable treatment—what role should Article III:1, which is not mentioned in Article III:4, play in their interpretation? Third, while the definition of "laws" and "regulations" may be relatively clear, what are "requirements" for purposes of Article III:4?

(A) LIKE PRODUCTS

EUROPEAN COMMUNITIES—MEASURES AFFECTING ASBESTOS AND ASBESTOS-CONTAINING PRODUCTS

WT/DS135/AB/R
Appellate Body Report adopted by the DSB on April 5, 2001

[This case involved a Canadian challenge of a French regulation that prohibits the manufacture, processing, sale, import, marketing and transfer of all varieties of asbestos fibres, regardless of whether these substances have been incorporated into materials, products or devices, subject to a limited exception in cases where no substitute product exists. Canada claimed that the regulation is inconsistent with GATT Articles III and XI and Article 2 of the TBT Agreement, and that under GATT Article XXIII:1(b), it nullified or impaired advantages accruing to Canada directly or indirectly under WTO Agreement (a non-violation claim). The panel ruled that in general the TBT Agreement did not apply to the regulation (a finding reversed by the Appellate Body), that like products were involved such that Article III:4 was violated (also reversed), but that the regulation fell within the exception of GATT Article XX(b) and did not nullify or impair advantages accruing to Canada. We discuss the first issue in Section 14.3, the second issue in this section and the third issue in Section 13.1.

The panel found that chrysotile asbestos fibres are "like" polyvinyl alcohol, cellulose and glass fibres ("PCG fibres") and that cement-based products containing chrysotile asbestos fibres are "like" cement-based products containing one of the PCG fibres. The Panel also concluded that all these cement-based products are "like".]

88. [After noting that the term "like products" appears in a number of different provisions in several WTO agreements, the Appellate Body noted:] [T]he term must be interpreted in light of the context, and of the object and purpose, of the provision at issue, and of the object and purpose of the covered agreement in which the provision appears. * * *

89. It follows that, while the meaning attributed to the term "like products" in other provisions of the GATT 1994, or in other covered agreements, may be relevant context in interpreting Article III:4 of the GATT 1994, the interpretation of "like products" in Article III:4 need not be identical, in all respects, to those other meanings.

90. Bearing these considerations in mind, we turn now to the ordinary meaning of the word "like" in the term "like products" in Article III:4. According to one dictionary, "like" means:

Having the same characteristics or qualities as some other . . . thing; of approximately identical shape, size, etc., with something else;

similar.[1]

91.   This meaning suggests that "like" products are products that share a number of identical or similar characteristics or qualities. The reference to "similar" as a synonym of "like" also echoes the language of the French version of Article III:4, *"produits similaires"*, and the Spanish version, *"productos similares"*, which, together with the English version, are equally authentic.

92.   However, as we have previously observed, "dictionary meanings leave many interpretive questions open." In particular, this definition does not resolve three issues of interpretation. First, this dictionary definition of "like" does not indicate *which characteristics or qualities are important* in assessing the "likeness" of products under Article III:4. For instance, most products will have many qualities and characteristics, ranging from physical properties such as composition, size, shape, texture, and possibly taste and smell, to the end-uses and applications of the product. Second, this dictionary definition provides no guidance in determining the *degree or extent to which products must share qualities or characteristics* in order to be "like products" under Article III:4. Products may share only very few characteristics or qualities, or they may share many. Thus, in the abstract, the term "like" can encompass a spectrum of differing degrees of "likeness" or "similarity". Third, this dictionary definition of "like" does not indicate *from whose perspective* "likeness" should be judged. For instance, ultimate consumers may have a view about the "likeness" of two products that is very different from that of the inventors or producers of those products.

93.   To begin to resolve these issues, we turn to the relevant context of Article III:4 of the GATT 1994. In that respect, we observe that Article III:2 of the GATT 1994, which deals with the internal tax treatment of imported and domestic products, prevents Members, through its first sentence, from imposing internal taxes on imported products "in excess of those applied ... to *like* domestic products." (emphasis added) In previous Reports, we have held that the scope of "like" products in this sentence is to be construed "narrowly". This reading of "like" in Article III:2 might be taken to suggest a similarly narrow reading of "like" in Article III:4, since both provisions form part of the same Article. However, both of these paragraphs of Article III constitute specific expressions of the overarching, "general principle", set forth in Article III:1 of the GATT 1994. As we have previously said, the "general principle" set forth in Article III:1 "informs" the rest of Article III and acts "as a guide to understanding and interpreting the specific obligations contained" in the other paragraphs of Article III, including paragraph 4. Thus, in our view, Article III:1 has particular contextual significance in interpreting Article III:4, as it sets forth the "general principle" pursued by that provision. Accordingly, in interpreting the term "like products" in Article III:4, we must turn, first, to the

1.   [original note 61] *The New Shorter Oxford English Dictionary*, Lesley Brown   (ed.) (Clarendon Press, 1993), Vol. I, p. 1588.

"general principle" in Article III:1, rather than to the term "like products" in Article III:2.

94.   In addition, we observe that, although the obligations in Articles III:2 and III:4 both apply to "like products", the text of Article III:2 differs in one important respect from the text of Article III:4. Article III:2 contains *two separate* sentences, each imposing *distinct* obligations: the first lays down obligations in respect of "like products", while the second lays down obligations in respect of "directly competitive or substitutable" products. By contrast, Article III:4 applies only to "like products" and does not include a provision equivalent to the second sentence of Article III:2. * * *

95.   For us, this textual difference between paragraphs 2 and 4 of Article III has considerable implications for the meaning of the term "like products" in these two provisions. In *Japan–Alcoholic Beverages*, we concluded, in construing Article III:2, that the two separate obligations in the two sentences of Article III:2 must be interpreted in a harmonious manner that gives meaning to *both* sentences in that provision. We observed there that the interpretation of one of the sentences necessarily affects the interpretation of the other. Thus, the scope of the term "like products" in the first sentence of Article III:2 affects, and is affected by, the scope of the phrase "directly competitive or substitutable" products in the second sentence of that provision. * * *

96.   In construing Article III:4, the same interpretive considerations do not arise, because the "general principle" articulated in Article III:1 is expressed in Article III:4, not through two distinct obligations, as in the two sentences in Article III:2, but instead through a single obligation that applies solely to "like products". Therefore, the harmony that we have attributed to the two sentences of Article III:2 need not and, indeed, cannot be replicated in interpreting Article III:4. Thus, we conclude that, given the textual difference between Articles III:2 and III:4, the "accordion" of "likeness" stretches in a different way in Article III:4.

[After recalling its statement of the purpose of Article III in *Japan Alcoholic Beverages*, quoted in Note 1 to Section 12.2 supra, the Appellate Body continued:]

98.   As we have said, although this "general principle" is not explicitly invoked in Article III:4, nevertheless, it "informs" that provision. Therefore, the term "like product" in Article III:4 must be interpreted to give proper scope and meaning to this principle. In short, there must be consonance between the objective pursued by Article III, as enunciated in the "general principle" articulated in Article III:1, and the interpretation of the specific expression of this principle in the text of Article III:4. This interpretation must, therefore, reflect that, in endeavouring to ensure "equality of competitive conditions", the "general principle" in Article III seeks to prevent Members from applying internal taxes and regulations in a manner which affects the competitive

relationship, in the marketplace, *between the domestic and imported products involved*, "so as to afford protection to domestic production."

99.   As products that are in a competitive relationship in the marketplace could be affected through treatment of *imports* "less favourable" than the treatment accorded to *domestic* products, it follows that the word "like" in Article III:4 is to be interpreted to apply to products that are in such a competitive relationship. Thus, a determination of "likeness" under Article III:4 is, fundamentally, a determination about the nature and extent of a competitive relationship between and among products. In saying this, we are mindful that there is a spectrum of degrees of "competitiveness" or "substitutability" of products in the marketplace, and that it is difficult, if not impossible, in the abstract, to indicate precisely where on this spectrum the word "like" in Article III:4 of the GATT 1994 falls. We are not saying that *all* products which are in *some* competitive relationship are "like products" under Article III:4. In ruling on the measure at issue, we also do not attempt to define the precise scope of the word "like" in Article III:4. Nor do we wish to decide if the scope of "like products" in Article III:4 is co-extensive with the combined scope of "like" and "directly competitive or substitutable" products in Article III:2. However, we recognize that the relationship between these two provisions is important, because there is no sharp distinction between fiscal regulation, covered by Article III:2, and non-fiscal regulation, covered by Article III:4. Both forms of regulation can often be used to achieve the same ends. It would be incongruous if, due to a significant difference in the product scope of these two provisions, Members were prevented from using one form of regulation—for instance, fiscal—to protect domestic production of certain products, but were able to use another form of regulation—for instance, non-fiscal—to achieve those ends. This would frustrate a consistent application of the "general principle" in Article III:1. For these reasons, we conclude that the scope of "like" in Article III:4 is broader than the scope of "like" in Article III:2, first sentence. Nonetheless, we note, once more, that Article III:2 extends not only to "like products", but also to products which are "directly competitive or substitutable", and that Article III:4 extends only to "like products". In view of this different language, and although we need not rule, and do not rule, on the precise product scope of Article III:4, we do conclude that the product scope of Article III:4, although broader than the *first* sentence of Article III:2, is certainly *not* broader than the *combined* product scope of the *two* sentences of Article III:2 of the GATT 1994.

100.   We recognize that, by interpreting the term "like products" in Article III:4 in this way, we give that provision a relatively broad product scope—although no broader than the product scope of Article III:2. In so doing, we observe that there is a second element that must be established before a measure can be held to be inconsistent with Article III:4. Thus, even if two products are "like", that does not mean that a measure is inconsistent with Article III:4. A complaining Member must still establish that the measure accords to the group of "like" *imported*

products "less favourable treatment" than it accords to the group of "like" *domestic* products. The term "less favourable treatment" expresses the general principle, in Article III:1, that internal regulations "should not be applied ... so as to afford protection to domestic production". If there is "less favourable treatment" of the group of "like" imported products, there is, conversely, "protection" of the group of "like" domestic products. However, a Member may draw distinctions between products which have been found to be "like", without, for this reason alone, according to the group of "like" *imported* products "less favourable treatment" than that accorded to the group of "like" *domestic* products. In this case, we do not examine further the interpretation of the term "treatment no less favourable" in Article III:4, as the Panel's findings on this issue have not been appealed or, indeed, argued before us.

101. We turn to consideration of how a treaty interpreter should proceed in determining whether products are "like" under Article III:4. As in Article III:2, in this determination, "[n]o one approach ... will be appropriate for all cases." Rather, an assessment utilizing "an unavoidable element of individual, discretionary judgement" has to be made on a case-by-case basis. The Report of the Working Party on *Border Tax Adjustments* outlined an approach for analyzing "likeness" that has been followed and developed since by several panels and the Appellate Body. This approach has, in the main, consisted of employing four general criteria in analyzing "likeness": (i) the properties, nature and quality of the products; (ii) the end-uses of the products; (iii) consumers' tastes and habits—more comprehensively termed consumers' perceptions and behaviour—in respect of the products; and (iv) the tariff classification of the products. We note that these four criteria comprise four categories of "characteristics" that the products involved might share: (i) the physical properties of the products; (ii) the extent to which the products are capable of serving the same or similar end-uses; (iii) the extent to which consumers perceive and treat the products as alternative means of performing particular functions in order to satisfy a particular want or demand; and (iv) the international classification of the products for tariff purposes.

102. These general criteria, or groupings of potentially shared characteristics, provide a framework for analyzing the "likeness" of particular products on a case-by-case basis. These criteria are, it is well to bear in mind, simply tools to assist in the task of sorting and examining the relevant evidence. They are neither a treaty-mandated nor a closed list of criteria that will determine the legal characterization of products. More important, the adoption of a particular framework to aid in the examination of evidence does not dissolve the duty or the need to examine, in each case, *all* of the pertinent evidence. In addition, although each criterion addresses, in principle, a different aspect of the products involved, which should be examined separately, the different criteria are interrelated. For instance, the physical properties of a product shape and limit the end-uses to which the products can be

devoted. Consumer perceptions may similarly influence—modify or even render obsolete—traditional uses of the products. Tariff classification clearly reflects the physical properties of a product.

103.   The kind of evidence to be examined in assessing the "likeness" of products will, necessarily, depend upon the particular products and the legal provision at issue. When all the relevant evidence has been examined, panels must determine whether that evidence, as a whole, indicates that the products in question are "like" in terms of the legal provision at issue. We have noted that, under Article III:4 of the GATT 1994, the term "like products" is concerned with competitive relationships between and among products. Accordingly, whether the *Border Tax Adjustments* framework is adopted or not, it is important under Article III:4 to take account of evidence which indicates whether, and to what extent, the products involved are—or could be—in a competitive relationship in the marketplace.

[The Appellate Body then examined the Panel's findings that the products at issue were like, considering what the Panel had said with respect to each of the four *Border Taxes* criteria. With respect to the "properties, nature and quality of the products", it noted that the Panel found that it was not decisive that the products "do not have the same structure or chemical composition", nor that asbestos is "unique". Instead, the Panel focused on "market access" and whether the products have the "same applications" and can "replace" each other for some industrial uses. In its examination of this criterion, the Panel declined to consider health risks of the products.

In respect of "end-use", the Appellate Body noted that the Panel stated that it had already found, under the first criterion, that the products have "certain identical or at least similar end-uses" and that it did not, therefore, consider it necessary to elaborate further on this criterion. The Panel declined to "take a position" on "consumers' tastes and habits", the third criterion, "[b]ecause this criterion would not provide clear results". Finally, the Panel did not regard as "decisive" the different "tariff classification" of the fibres.

The Appellate Body then considered in detail the Panel's evaluation of likeness under the four criteria. In this regard, it stated:]

111.   We believe that physical properties deserve a separate examination that should not be confused with the examination of end-uses. Although not decisive, the extent to which products share common physical properties may be a useful indicator of "likeness". Furthermore, the physical properties of a product may also influence how the product can be used, consumer attitudes about the product, and tariff classification. It is, therefore, important for a panel to examine fully the physical character of a product. We are also concerned that it will be difficult for a panel to draw the appropriate conclusions from the evidence examined under each criterion if a panel's approach does not clearly address each criterion separately, but rather entwines different, and distinct, elements of the analysis along the way.

112.   In addition, we do not share the Panel's conviction that when two products can be used for the same end-use, their *"properties* are then *equivalent*, if not identical." (emphasis added) Products with quite different physical properties may, in some situations, be capable of performing similar or identical end-uses. Although the *end-uses* are then *"equivalent"*, the physical properties of the products are not thereby altered; they remain different. Thus, the physical "uniqueness" of asbestos that the Panel noted does not change depending on the particular use that is made of asbestos.

* * *

114.   [As to the appropriateness of considering the health risks of the products, the Appellate Body stated that this] carcinogenicity, or toxicity, constitutes, as we see it, a defining aspect of the physical properties of chrysotile asbestos fibres. The evidence indicates that PCG fibres, in contrast, do not share these properties, at least to the same extent. We do not see how this highly significant physical difference *cannot* be a consideration in examining the physical properties of a product as part of a determination of "likeness" under Article III:4 of the GATT 1994.

115.   We do not agree with the Panel that considering evidence relating to the health risks associated with a product, under Article III:4, nullifies the effect of Article XX(b) of the GATT 1994. Article XX(b) allows a Member to "adopt and enforce" a measure, *inter alia*, necessary to protect human life or health, even though that measure is inconsistent with another provision of the GATT 1994. Article III:4 and Article XX(b) are distinct and independent provisions of the GATT 1994 each to be interpreted on its own. The scope and meaning of Article III:4 should not be broadened or restricted beyond what is required by the normal customary international law rules of treaty interpretation, simply because Article XX(b) exists and may be available to justify measures inconsistent with Article III:4. The fact that an interpretation of Article III:4, under those rules, implies a less frequent recourse to Article XX(b) does not deprive the exception in Article XX(b) of *effet utile*. Article XX(b) would only be deprived of *effet utile* if that provision could *not* serve to allow a Member to "adopt and enforce" measures "necessary to protect human . . . life or health". Evaluating evidence relating to the health risks arising from the physical properties of a product does not prevent a measure which is inconsistent with Article III:4 from being justified under Article XX(b). We note, in this regard, that, different inquiries occur under these two very different Articles. Under Article III:4, evidence relating to health risks may be relevant in assessing the *competitive relationship in the marketplace* between allegedly "like" products. The same, or similar, evidence serves a different purpose under Article XX(b), namely, that of assessing whether a *Member* has a sufficient basis for "adopting or enforcing" a WTO-inconsistent measure on the grounds of human health.

116. We, therefore, find that the Panel erred in excluding the health risks associated with chrysotile asbestos fibres from its examination of the physical properties of that product.

117. Before examining the Panel's findings under the second and third criteria, we note that these two criteria involve certain of the key elements relating to the competitive relationship between products: first, the extent to which products are capable of performing the same, or similar, functions (end-uses), and, second, the extent to which consumers are willing to use the products to perform these functions (consumers' tastes and habits). Evidence of this type is of particular importance under Article III of the GATT 1994, precisely because that provision is concerned with competitive relationships in the marketplace. If there is—or could be—*no* competitive relationship between products, a Member cannot intervene, through internal taxation or regulation, to protect domestic production. Thus, evidence about the extent to which products can serve the same end-uses, and the extent to which consumers are—or would be—willing to choose one product instead of another to perform those end-uses, is highly relevant evidence in assessing the "likeness" of those products under Article III:4 of the GATT 1994.

118. We consider this to be especially so in cases where the evidence relating to properties establishes that the products at issue are physically quite different. In such cases, in order to overcome this indication that products are *not* "like", a higher burden is placed on complaining Members to establish that, despite the pronounced physical differences, there is a competitive relationship between the products such that *all* of the evidence, taken together, demonstrates that the products are "like" under Article III:4 of the GATT 1994. In this case, where it is clear that the fibres have very different properties, in particular, because chrysotile is a known carcinogen, a very heavy burden is placed on Canada to show, under the second and third criteria, that the chrysotile asbestos and PCG fibres are in such a competitive relationship.

119. [The Appellate Body then concluded] that the Panel did not adequately examine the evidence relating to end-uses.

120. The Panel declined to examine or make any findings relating to the third criterion, consumers' tastes and habits, "[b]ecause this criterion would not provide clear results". There will be few situations where the evidence on the "likeness" of products will lend itself to "clear results". In many cases, the evidence will give conflicting indications, possibly within each of the four criteria. For instance, there may be some evidence of similar physical properties and some evidence of differing physical properties. Or the physical properties may differ completely, yet there may be strong evidence of similar end-uses and a high degree of substitutability of the products from the perspective of the consumer. A panel cannot decline to inquire into relevant evidence simply because it suspects that evidence may not be "clear" or, for that matter, because the parties agree [according to Canada] that certain

evidence is not relevant. In any event, we have difficulty seeing how the Panel could conclude that an examination of consumers' tastes and habits "would not provide clear results", given that the Panel did not examine *any* evidence relating to this criterion.

121. Furthermore, in a case such as this, where the fibres are physically very different, a panel *cannot* conclude that they are "like products" if it *does not examine* evidence relating to consumers' tastes and habits. In such a situation, if there is *no* inquiry into this aspect of the nature and extent of the competitive relationship between the products, there is no basis for overcoming the inference, drawn from the different physical properties of the products, that the products are not "like".

122. In this case especially, we are also persuaded that evidence relating to consumers' tastes and habits would establish that the health risks associated with chrysotile asbestos fibres influence consumers' behaviour with respect to the different fibres at issue. We observe that, as regards *chrysotile asbestos and PCG fibres*, the consumer of the fibres is a *manufacturer* who incorporates the fibres into another product, such as cement-based products or brake linings. We do not wish to speculate on what the evidence regarding these consumers would have indicated; rather, we wish to highlight that consumers' tastes and habits regarding *fibres*, even in the case of commercial parties, such as manufacturers, are very likely to be shaped by the health risks associated with a product which is known to be highly carcinogenic.[2] A manufacturer cannot, for instance, ignore the preferences of the ultimate consumer of its products. If the risks posed by a particular product are sufficiently great, the ultimate consumer may simply cease to buy that product. This would, undoubtedly, affect a manufacturer's decisions in the marketplace. Moreover, in the case of products posing risks to human health, we think it likely that manufacturers' decisions will be influenced by other factors, such as the potential civil liability that might flow from marketing products posing a health risk to the ultimate consumer, or the additional costs associated with safety procedures required to use such products in the manufacturing process.

* * *

124. We observe also that the Panel did not regard as decisive the different tariff classifications of the chrysotile asbestos, PVA, cellulose and glass fibres, each of which is classified under a different tariff heading. In the absence of a full analysis, by the Panel, of the other three criteria addressed, we cannot determine what importance should be attached to the different tariff classifications of the fibres.

2. [original note 103] We recognize that consumers' reactions to products posing a risk to human health vary considerably depending on the product, and on the consumer. Some dangerous products, such as tobacco, are widely used, despite the known health risks. The influence known dangers have on consumers' tastes and habits is, therefore, unlikely to be uniform or entirely predictable.

125. In sum, in our view, the Panel reached the conclusion that *chrysotile asbestos and PCG fibres* are "like products" under Article III:4 of the GATT 1994 on the following basis: the Panel disregarded the quite different "properties, nature and quality" of chrysotile asbestos and PCG fibres, as well as the different tariff classification of these fibres; it considered no evidence on consumers' tastes and habits; and it found that, for a "small number" of the many applications of these fibres, they are substitutable, but it did not consider the many other end-uses for the fibres that are different. Thus, the only evidence supporting the Panel's finding of "likeness" is the "small number" of shared end-uses of the fibres.

[Accordingly, the Appellate Body reversed the panel's conclusion that chrysotile and PCG fibres are "like products". It reached the same result in respect of the Panel's finding that cement products containing asbestos and those containing PCG fibres are like. It then made its own examination of likeness:]

134. We address first the "likeness" of *chrysotile asbestos fibres* and *PCG fibres*. As regards the physical properties of these fibres, we recall that the Panel stated that:

> * * * The parties agree that none of the substitute fibres mentioned by Canada in connection with Article III:4 has the same structure, either in terms of its form, its diameter, its length or its potential to release particles that possess certain characteristics. Moreover, they do not have the same chemical composition, which means that, in purely physical terms, none of them has the same nature or quality.
>
> . . .

135. We also see it as important to take into account that, since 1977, chrysotile asbestos fibres have been recognized internationally as a known carcinogen because of the particular combination of their molecular structure, chemical composition, and fibrillation capacity. * * * In contrast, the Panel found that the PCG fibres "are not classified by the WHO at the same level of risk as chrysotile." The experts also confirmed, as the Panel reported, that current scientific evidence indicates that PCG fibres do "not present the same risk to health as chrysotile" asbestos fibres.

136. It follows that the evidence relating to properties indicates that, physically, chrysotile asbestos and PCG fibres are very different. As we said earlier, in such cases, in order to overcome this indication that products are *not* "like", a high burden is imposed on a complaining Member to establish that, despite the pronounced physical differences, there is a competitive relationship between the products such that, *all* of the evidence, taken together, demonstrates that the products are "like" under Article III:4 of the GATT 1994.

137. The Panel observed that the end-uses of chrysotile asbestos and PCG fibres are the same "for a small number" of applications. The Panel simply adverted to these overlapping end-uses and offered no elaboration on their nature and character. We note that Canada argued

before the Panel that there are some 3,000 commercial applications for asbestos fibres. Canada and the European Communities indicated that the most important end-uses for asbestos fibres include, in no particular order, incorporation into: cement-based products; insulation; and various forms of friction lining. Canada noted that 90 percent, by quantity, of French imports of chrysotile asbestos were used in the production of cement-based products. This evidence suggests that chrysotile asbestos and PCG fibres share a small number of similar end-uses and, that, as Canada asserted, for chrysotile asbestos, these overlapping end-uses represent an important proportion of the end-uses made of chrysotile asbestos, measured in terms of quantity.

138. There is, however, no evidence on the record regarding the nature and extent of the many end-uses for chrysotile asbestos and PCG fibres which are *not* overlapping. Thus, we do not know what proportion of all end-uses for chrysotile asbestos and PCG fibres overlap. Where products have a wide range of end-uses, only some of which overlap, we do not believe that it is sufficient to rely solely on evidence regarding the overlapping end-uses, without also examining evidence of the nature and importance of these end-uses in relation to all of the other possible end-uses for the products. In the absence of such evidence, we cannot determine the significance of the fact that chrysotile asbestos and PCG fibres share a small number of similar end-uses.

139. As we have already stated, Canada took the view, both before the Panel and before us, that consumers' tastes and habits have no relevance to the inquiry into the "likeness" of the fibres. We have already addressed, and dismissed, the arguments advanced by Canada in support of this contention. We have also stated that, in a case such as this one, where the physical properties of the fibres are very different, an examination of the evidence relating to consumers' tastes and habits is an indispensable—although not, on its own, sufficient—aspect of any determination that products are "like" under Article III:4 of the GATT 1994. If there is no evidence on this aspect of the nature and extent of the competitive relationship between the fibres, there is no basis for overcoming the inference, drawn from the different physical properties, that the products are not "like". However, in keeping with its argument that this criterion is irrelevant, Canada presented *no* evidence on consumers' tastes and habits regarding chrysotile asbestos and PCG fibres.

140. Finally, we note that chrysotile asbestos fibres and the various PCG fibres all have different tariff classifications. While this element is not, on its own, decisive, it does tend to indicate that chrysotile and PCG fibres are not "like products" under Article III:4 of the GATT 1994.

141. Taken together, in our view, all of this evidence is certainly far from sufficient to satisfy Canada's burden of proving that chrysotile asbestos fibres are "like" PCG fibres under Article III:4 of the GATT 1994. Indeed, this evidence rather tends to suggest that these products

are not "like products" for the purposes of Article III:4 of the GATT 1994.

* * *

149.   One Member of the Division hearing this appeal wishes to make a concurring statement. * * *

151.   In paragraph 113 of the Report, we state that "[w]e are very much of the view that evidence relating to the health risks associated with a product may be pertinent in an examination of 'likeness' under Article III:4 of the GATT 1994." We also point out, in paragraph 114, that "[p]anels must examine fully the physical properties of products. In particular, ... those physical properties of products that are likely to influence the competitive relationship between products in the market place. In the cases of chrysotile asbestos fibres, their molecular structure, chemical composition, and fibrillation capacity are important because the microscopic particles and filaments of chrysotile asbestos fibres are carcinogenic in humans, following inhalation." This carcinogenicity we describe as "a defining aspect of the physical properties of chrysotile asbestos fibres", which property is not shared by the PCG fibres, "at least to the same extent." We express our inability to "see how this highly significant physical difference *cannot* be a consideration in examining the physical properties of a product as part of a determination of 'likeness' under Article III:4 of the GATT 1994." (emphasis in the original) We observe also that the Panel, after noting that the carcinogenicity of chrysotile asbestos fibres has been acknowledged by international bodies and confirmed by the experts the Panel consulted, ruled that it "[has] sufficient evidence that *there is in fact a serious carcinogenic risk associated with the inhalation of chrysotile fibres.*" (emphasis added) In fact, the scientific evidence of record for this finding of carcinogenicity of chrysotile asbestos fibres is so clear, voluminous, and is confirmed, a number of times, by a variety of international organizations, as to be practically overwhelming.

152.   In the present appeal, considering the nature and quantum of the scientific evidence showing that the physical properties and qualities of chrysotile asbestos fibres include or result in carcinogenicity, my submission is that there is ample basis for a definitive characterization, on completion of the legal analysis, of such fibres as *not* "like" PCG fibres. PCG fibres, it may be recalled, have not been shown by Canada to have the same lethal properties as chrysotile asbestos fibres. That definitive characterization, it is further submitted, may and should be made even in the absence of evidence concerning the other two *Border Tax Adjustments* criteria (categories of "potentially shared characteristics") of end-uses and consumers' tastes and habits. It is difficult for me to imagine what evidence relating to economic competitive relationships as reflected in end-uses and consumers' tastes and habits could outweigh and set at naught the undisputed deadly nature of chrysotile asbestos fibres, compared with PCG fibres, when inhaled by humans, and thereby

compel a characterization of "likeness" of chrysotile asbestos and PCG fibres.

153.   The suggestion I make is not that *any* kind or degree of health risk, associated with a particular product, would *a priori* negate a finding of the "likeness" of that product with another product, under Article III:4 of the GATT 1994. The suggestion is a very narrow one, limited only to the circumstances of this case, and confined to chrysotile asbestos fibres as compared with PCG fibres. To hold that these fibres are not "like" one another in view of the undisputed carcinogenic nature of chrysotile asbestos fibres appears to me to be but a small and modest step forward from mere reversal of the Panel's ruling that chrysotile asbestos and PCG fibres are "like", especially since our holding in completing the analysis is that Canada failed to satisfy a complainant's burden of proving that PCG fibres are "like" chrysotile asbestos fibres under Article III:4. That small step, however, the other Members of the Division feel unable to take because of their conception of the "fundamental", perhaps decisive, role of economic competitive relationships in the determination of the "likeness" of products under Article III:4.

154.   My second point is that the necessity or appropriateness of adopting a "fundamentally" economic interpretation of the "likeness" of products under Article III:4 of the GATT 1994 does not appear to me to be free from substantial doubt. Moreover, in future concrete contexts, the line between a "fundamentally" and "exclusively" economic view of "like products" under Article III:4 may well prove very difficult, as a practical matter, to identify. It seems to me the better part of valour to reserve one's opinion on such an important, indeed, philosophical matter, which may have unforeseeable implications, and to leave that matter for another appeal and another day, or perhaps other appeals and other days. I so reserve my opinion on this matter.

Notes and Questions

(1) The concurring statement is the first in the history of the Appellate Body. Is it really a dissent? What about the substantive point? Does the majority put too much emphasis on the view of the market?

(2) In light of the Appellate Body decisions in the *Japan–Alcoholic Beverages* and the *Asbestos* cases, it would seem that a panel would always be well advised to consider the *Border Tax Adjustments* criteria carefully in any analysis of product likeness. It also seems clear that a panel should examine any other relevant factors. What other factors are relevant in determining likeness? To what extent are those other factors secondary in importance to a market analysis?

(3) It has often been assumed in GATT/WTO discussions that determining the likeness of products cannot be based on an analysis of the way in which the products were made. Otherwise, countries would be tempted to discriminate against products from countries following policies or in a state of development below their own. Thus, it has been argued that it would be inappropriate to distinguish between products on the grounds of whether

they are produced in an environmentally friendly way or by workers benefiting from certain labor rights or wage levels. For example, in BELGIAN FAMILY ALLOWANCES, 1st Supp. BISD 59–62 (1953)(Panel report adopted Nov. 7, 1952), a GATT panel was faced with a Belgian law that levied a charge on foreign goods purchased by public authorities when those goods originated in a country whose system of family allowances did not meet specific requirements. The panel noted that some countries had been exempted from the charge and concluded that if the General Agreement were definitively in force "it is clear that that exemption would have to be granted unconditionally to all other contracting parties (including [the complaining countries of] Denmark and Norway). The consistency or otherwise of the system of family allowances in force in the territory of a given contracting party with the requirements of the Belgian law would be irrelevant in this respect."

Under the Appellate Body's *Asbestos* decision, would it be appropriate to consider such distinctions in making a likeness determination? Would it be necessary to show that the market recognized the distinctions? How significant would that market differentiation have to be? Given that products come with histories and origins and distinctions can be made on those bases, why couldn't those distinctions offer a basis for calling some products unlike other products? In this connection, does GATT ever allow discrimination on the basis of how a product is produced? See Article XX(e) (prison labor).

(4) In *Asbestos*, the Appellate Body suggests that the breadth of the definition of like products for purposes of Article III:4 includes products that would be considered to be directly competitive or substitutable for purposes of Article III:2 (para. 99). To establish a violation of Article III:2 in respect of such products, it would be necessary to show that the taxation at issue was dissimilar and applied so as to afford protection. For purposes of establishing a violation of Article III:4, less favorable treatment need be shown, but not protection. Does this suggest that Article III:4 in practice restricts government discretion much more than Article III:2?

(5) Given the broader coverage of Article III:4 would it make sense to consider whether the "aims and effect" test mentioned in the preceding section should be used for purposes of defining likeness in Article III:4?

(6) Would you say that the emphasis on markets and the competitiveness of products is likely to lead to fewer or more findings of product likeness?

(B) LESS FAVORABLE TREATMENT

In most Article III:4 cases, the question of whether a measure affords less favorable treatment has not been a major issue. However, it worth remembering that not all different treatment is necessarily less favorable. Thus, there are occasions when it is necessary to decide precisely what this aspect of Article III:4 means.

KOREA—MEASURES AFFECTING IMPORTS OF
FRESH, CHILLED AND FROZEN BEEF

WT/DS161 & 169/AB/R

Appellate Body Report adopted by the DSB on January 10, 2001

[Australia and the United States challenged a number of aspects of Korean treatment of imported beef, including the so-called dual retail system, which required that imported and domestic beef be sold in different stores (or, in the case of large stores, in different sections). The Panel found that the dual retail system accords treatment less favorable to imported beef than to like Korean beef, and is, thus, inconsistent with Article III:4 of the GATT 1994. This finding was based on the Panel's view that any measure based exclusively on criteria relating to the origin of a product is inconsistent with Article III:4 and on the Panel's assessment of how the dual retail system modifies the conditions of competition between imported and like domestic beef in the Korean market. Korea argued on appeal that the system does not accord treatment less favorable to imported beef than to like domestic beef and therefore does not violate Article III:4.

[The Appellate Body began by recalling its description of the purpose of Article III, as set out earlier in this chapter in *Japan–Alcoholic Beverages*, and the analysis of the *Section 337* panel in section 5.11 of its report, also set above. It then continued:]

137. A formal difference in treatment between imported and like domestic products is thus neither necessary, nor sufficient, to show a violation of Article III:4. Whether or not imported products are treated "less favourably" than like domestic products should be assessed instead by examining whether a measure modifies the *conditions of competition* in the relevant market to the detriment of imported products.

138. We conclude that the Panel erred in its general interpretation that "[a]ny regulatory distinction that is based exclusively on criteria relating to the nationality or the origin of the products is incompatible with Article III."

139. The Panel went on, however, to examine the conditions of competition between imported and like domestic beef in the Korean market. The Panel gave several reasons why it believed that the dual retail system alters the conditions of competition in the Korean market in favour of domestic beef. First, it found that the dual retail system would "limit the possibility for consumers to compare imported and domestic products", and thereby "reduce opportunities for imported products to compete directly with domestic products". Second, the Panel found that, under the dual retail system, "the only way an imported product can get on the shelves is if the retailer agrees to substitute it, not only for one but for all existing like domestic products." This disadvantage would be more serious when the market share of imports (as is the case with imported beef) is small. Third, the Panel found that

the dual retail system, by excluding imported beef from "the vast majority of sales outlets", limits the potential market opportunities for imported beef. This would apply particularly to products "consumed on a daily basis", like beef, where consumers may not be willing to "shop around". Fourth, the Panel found that the dual retail system imposes more costs on the imported product, since the domestic product will tend to continue to be sold from existing retail stores, whereas imported beef will require new stores to be established. Fifth, the Panel found that the dual retail system "encourages the perception that imported and domestic beef are different, when they are in fact like products belonging to the same market", which gives a competitive advantage to domestic beef, "based on criteria not related to the products themselves". Sixth, the Panel found that the dual retail system "facilitates the maintenance of a price differential" to the advantage of domestic beef.

* * *

141.   It will be seen below that we share the ultimate conclusion of the Panel in respect of the consistency of the dual retail system for beef with Article III:4 of the GATT 1994. Portions, however, of the Panel's analysis *en route* to that conclusion appear to us problematic. For instance, while limitation of the ability to compare visually two products, local and imported, at the point of sale may have resulted from the dual retail system, such limitation does not, in our view, necessarily reduce the opportunity for the imported product to compete "directly" or on "an equal footing" with the domestic product. Again, even if we were to accept that the dual retail system "encourages" the perception of consumers that imported and domestic beef are "different", we do not think it has been demonstrated that such encouragement necessarily implies a competitive advantage for domestic beef. Circumstances like limitation of "side-by-side" comparison and "encouragement" of consumer perceptions of "differences" may be simply incidental effects of the dual retail system without decisive implications for the issue of consistency with Article III:4.

142.   We believe that a more direct, and perhaps simpler, approach to the dual retail system of Korea may be usefully followed in the present case. In the following paragraphs, we seek to focus on what appears to us to be the fundamental thrust and effect of the measure itself.

143.   Korean law in effect requires the existence of two distinct retail distribution systems so far as beef is concerned: one system for the retail sale of domestic beef and another system for the retail sale of imported beef. A small retailer (that is, a non-supermarket or non-department store) which is a "Specialized Imported Beef Store" may sell any meat *except domestic beef*; any other small retailer may sell any meat *except imported beef*. A large retailer (that is, a supermarket or department store) may sell both imported and domestic beef, as long as the imported beef and domestic beef are sold in separate sales areas. A

retailer selling imported beef is required to display a sign reading "Specialized Imported Beef Store".

144.   Thus, the Korean measure formally separates the selling of imported beef and domestic beef. However, that formal separation, *in and of itself*, does not necessarily compel the conclusion that the treatment thus accorded to imported beef is less favourable than the treatment accorded to domestic beef.[3] To determine whether the treatment given to imported beef is less favourable than that given to domestic beef, we must, as earlier indicated, inquire into whether or not the Korean dual retail system for beef modifies the *conditions of competition* in the Korean beef market to the disadvantage of the imported product.

145.   When beef was first imported into Korea in 1988, the new product simply entered into the pre-existing distribution system that had been handling domestic beef. The beef retail system was a unitary one, and the conditions of competition affecting the sale of beef were the same for both the domestic and the imported product. In 1990, Korea promulgated its dual retail system for beef. Accordingly, the existing small retailers had to choose between, on the one hand, continuing to sell domestic beef and renouncing the sale of imported beef or, on the other hand, ceasing to sell domestic beef in order to be allowed to sell the imported product. Apparently, the vast majority of the small meat retailers chose the first option. The result was the virtual exclusion of imported beef from the retail distribution channels through which domestic beef (and until then, imported beef, too) was distributed to Korean households and other consumers throughout the country. Accordingly, a new and separate retail system had to be established and gradually built from the ground up for bringing the imported product to the same households and other consumers if the imported product was to compete at all with the domestic product. Put in slightly different terms, the putting into legal effect of the dual retail system for beef meant, in direct practical effect, so far as imported beef was concerned, the sudden cutting off of access to the normal, that is, the previously existing, distribution outlets through which the domestic product continued to flow to consumers in the urban centers and countryside that make up the Korean national territory. The central consequence of the dual retail system can only be reasonably construed, in our view, as the imposition of a drastic reduction of commercial opportunity to reach, and hence to generate sales to, the same consumers served by the traditional retail channels for domestic beef. In 1998, when this case began, eight years after the dual retail system was first prescribed, the consequent reduction of commercial opportunity was reflected in the much smaller number of specialized imported beef shops (approximately 5,000 shops) as compared with the number of retailers (approximately 45,000 shops) selling domestic beef.

3.   [original note 85] Apart from the display sign requirement, dealt with in para. 151.   [See Note (4).]

146. We are aware that the dramatic reduction in number of retail outlets for imported beef followed from the decisions of individual retailers who could choose freely to sell the domestic product or the imported product. The legal necessity of making a choice was, however, imposed by the measure itself. The restricted nature of that choice should be noted. The choice given to the meat retailers was *not* an option between remaining with the pre-existing unified distribution set-up or going to a dual retail system. The choice was limited to selling domestic beef only or imported beef only. Thus, the reduction of access to normal retail channels is, in legal contemplation, the effect of that measure. In these circumstances, the intervention of some element of private choice does not relieve Korea of responsibility under the GATT 1994 for the resulting establishment of competitive conditions less favourable for the imported product than for the domestic product.

147. We also note that the reduction of competitive opportunity through the restriction of access to consumers results from the imposition of the dual retail system for beef, notwithstanding [what Korea describes as] "perfect regulatory symmetry" of that system, and is not a function of the limited volume of foreign beef actually imported into Korea. The fact that the WTO-consistent quota for beef has, save for two years, been fully utilized does not detract from the lack of equality of competitive conditions entailed by the dual retail system.

148. We believe, and so hold, that the treatment accorded to imported beef, as a consequence of the dual retail system established for beef by Korean law and regulation, is less favourable than the treatment given to like domestic beef and is, accordingly, not consistent with the requirements of Article III:4 of the GATT 1994.

149. It may finally be useful to indicate, however broadly, what we are *not* saying in reaching our above conclusion. We are *not* holding that a dual or parallel distribution system that is *not* imposed directly or indirectly by law or governmental regulation, but is rather solely the result of private entrepreneurs acting on their own calculations of comparative costs and benefits of differentiated distribution systems, is unlawful under Article III:4 of the GATT 1994. What is addressed by Article III:4 is merely the *governmental* intervention that affects the conditions under which like goods, domestic and imported, compete in the market within a Member's territory.

Notes and Questions

(1) Korea invoked the exception in Article XX(d) to justify the dual retail system and we examine that issue in the next chapter.

(2) In contrast to its analysis in the *Asbestos* case, the Appellate Body does not emphasize (or even mention) the role of Article III:1 in interpreting the second element of Article III:4. Should it have done so? Does an examination of whether conditions of competition have been modified to the detriment of imports necessarily address whether a measure has been applied so as to afford protection to domestic production?

(3) More generally, could the no-less-favorable-treatment be interpreted with reference to Article III:1 in order to achieve the goal sought by the proponents of the "aims and effect" test for like products that we have previously examined in this chapter? That is, could (or should) the requirement of no less favourable treatment be read to include an element of protection, such that the lack of protection could be used as a defense to a claim of less favorable treatment?

(4) As part of the dual retail system, Korea required that stores selling imported beef display a sign declaring "Specialized Imported Beef Store". The Panel found that the requirement was ancillary to the dual retail system and as that violated Article III:4, so did the sign requirement. The Appellate Body did not review that finding, noting that "[w]hen considered independently from a dual retail system, a sign requirement might or might not be characterized legally as consistent with Article III:4." (para. 151) Suppose Korea abolished the dual retail system, but kept the sign requirement. How would you analyse a challenge to that requirement under Article III:4?

Consider the following cases. HAWAII v. HO, 41 Hawaii 565 (1957) involved a law making it unlawful for any person to sell imported eggs unless a placard bearing the words "WE SELL FOREIGN EGGS" was displayed in a conspicuous place. The court concluded that such a requirement violated Article III:4 since a similar requirement was not imposed on domestic eggs. As to Article XX, the Court found it inapplicable because deceptive practices could better be prevented by a straightforward origin-marking requirement. Moreover, "[w]e think that the additional requirement of a placard of origin only in the case of foreign eggs constitutes a disguised restriction on international trade." Do you agree?

An April, 1967 order of the United States Federal Trade Commission changed its labeling rules concerning fur products, by requiring an animal formerly designated as "Mink, Japanese" to be henceforth designated as "Japanese Weasel." See 16 C.F.R. sec. 301.0 (2001). A Wall Street Journal article of May 8, 1967, entitled "FTC Labels a 'Mink' from Japan a Weasel—and the Fur Flies," notes that all mink whether Asian or American are members of the weasel family, and implies that the desire of the FTC to require Japanese mink to be labeled weasel may stem from a desire to protect U.S. mink ranchers from competition of the Japanese fur. Did the FTC action violate Article III:4?

In dealing with a similar issue, the EC Court of Justice once held that an origin-marking requirement applicable to domestic and imported products violates Article 28 of the EC Treaty, which prohibits quantitative restrictions and measures having equivalent effect. In Commission v. United Kingdom (Marks of origin), Case 207/83, [1985] ECR 1201, it wrote:

> [I]t has to be recognized that the purpose of indications of origin or origin-marking is to enable consumers to distinguish between domestic and imported products and that this enables them to assert any prejudices which they may have against foreign products. * * * [The EC Treaty] seeks to unite national markets in a single market having the characteristics of a domestic market. Within such a market, the origin-marking requirement * * * makes the marketing in a Member State of goods produced in other Member States * * * more difficult.

For all of the foregoing situations, how does GATT Article IX impact your analysis?[4]

(5) The Agreement on Trade–Related Investment Measures (TRIMs Agreement) contains a list of examples of measures that violate Article III:4. The list includes measures which require "the purchase or use by an enterprise of products of domestic origin * * *, whether specified in terms of particular products, in terms of volume or value of products, or in terms of a proportion of volume or value of its local production; or that an enterprise's purchases or use of imported products be limited to an amount related to the volume of value of local products that it exports." Do you see why these measures satisfy the terms of Article III:4, and, in particular, the no less favorable treatment requirement?

(C) LAWS, REGULATIONS AND REQUIREMENTS

Article III:4 applies to laws, regulations and requirements affecting the internal sale, etc. of imported goods. We saw at the outset of this chapter that the term "affecting" has been interpreted broadly. This has also been true of the term "requirements". For example, a measure that conditions a governmental benefit on certain action is viewed as a requirement, although in fact there is not obligation to take action. For example, the TRIMs Agreement's illustrative list of investment measures related to trade in goods (TRIMs) that are inconsistent with Article III:4 includes measures "compliance with which is necessary to obtain an advantage".

In the *Japan-Film* case, the panel assumed for purposes of its analysis of the Article III claims that the phrase "laws, regulations and requirements" should be given a broad reading, basically equivalent to the term "measures" in Article XXIII:1(b). Japan—Measures Affecting Photographic Film and Paper, WT/DS44/R, para. 10.376 (adopted by the DSB on April 22, 1998). The *Film* panel's broad reading of the term "measures" for purposes of Article XXIII had been based in part on the Article XI cases, such as *Japan—Semiconductors* discussed in Section 9.1 supra, that had concluded that so-called administrative guidance fell within the definition of "other measures" for purposes of Article XI.

SECTION 12.5   GOVERNMENT PURCHASES

Because of the explicit exception in paragraph 8(a), government purchases are not limited by Article III's national treatment obligation, and because of the language of Article I, it is generally considered that the MFN obligation also does not apply to government purchases,[1] although Article XVII contains a modest constraint on purchases of state enterprises. Consequently, prior to the Tokyo Round, governments were generally free in their procurement policies to discriminate in favor of domestic goods, or in favor of the goods of one country over another, and they often did.

---

4. John H. Jackson, World Trade and the Law of GATT 461 (1969).

1. See John H. Jackson, World Trade and the Law of GATT 291 (1969).

The existence of statutes or policies favoring domestic suppliers was a source of considerable aggravation, particularly to those industries (e.g., aircraft and electric turbines) whose products are often purchased by governments. Moreover, in some countries it seemed that the government owned or operated sector of the economy represented an increasing percentage of the whole economy, with the result that an increasing amount of economic activity was escaping the discipline of the international trade rules. This was a significant part of the motivation which led major nations to undertake, in the Tokyo Round, to negotiate a code on government purchases.[2] Prior to the Tokyo Round, government procurement policies had been the subject of considerable work in the OECD. This work was made available to the Tokyo Round negotiators and the result of the negotiations was a side agreement on government procurement, which entered into force in 1981. It was amended in 1987.

(A) THE 1994 AGREEMENT ON GOVERNMENT PROCUREMENT

Concurrently with the Uruguay Round, a new Agreement on Government Procurement (GPA) was negotiated, and it entered into force on January 1, 1996.[3] The GPA is attached to the WTO Agreement as a plurilateral agreement in Annex 4. As such, it is not part of the "single undertaking" to which all WTO members must subscribe, and its membership is limited mainly to more industrialized WTO members. As of 2001, the parties to the GPA were Canada, the EC and its member states, Hong Kong China, Iceland, Israel, Japan, Korea, Liechtenstein, Netherlands on behalf of Aruba, Norway, Singapore, Switzerland and the United States. Bulgaria, Estonia, Jordan, Kyrgyz Republic, Latvia and Panama were negotiating accession.

With respect to government procurement covered by the GPA, the GPA requires that a party give no less favorable treatment to products, services and suppliers of another GPA party than it gives (i) to its own domestic products, services and suppliers and (ii) to the products, services and suppliers of any other GPA party (Article III:1). In other words, the GPA imposes national treatment and MFN obligations in respect of government procurement. In addition, Article III:2 bans discrimination against locally-established suppliers on the basis of their foreign ownership or affiliation or on the basis of the foreign source of their goods or services (provided the source is a GPA party).

The coverage of the GPA extends to central government entities, sub-central government entities and other entities (such as utilities) that are listed in annexes 1 to 3 of a party's schedule. It covers procurement above certain thresholds by those entities of goods, services (to the

---

2. See generally Report of the Director–General of GATT, The Tokyo Round of Multilateral Trade Negotiations 76–77 (1979); Senate Report No. 96–249, 96th Cong., 1st Sess. 128 (1979).

3. Bernard M. Hoekman & Petros C. Mavroidis, eds., Law and Policy in Public Purchasing: The WTO Agreement on Government Procurement (1997); Arie Reich, International Public Procurement Law: The Evolution of International Regimes on Public Purchasing (1999).

extent specified in annex 4) and construction services (to the extent specified in annex 5). There is variation in the thresholds, which are expressed in terms of IMF special drawing rights (1 SDR was equivalent to $1.29 on August 31, 2001). For the US, federal entities are covered for goods and services procurement in excess of SDR 130,000 and in excess of SDR 5 million for construction services. Sub-federal entities have a higher threshold for goods and services (SDR 355,000), as do other entities (SDR 400,000). In the case of the EC, the thresholds are generally the same, except that sub-federal entities are subject to a SDR 200,000 threshold. There are, however, various exceptions found in the annexes and in the general notes to each party's schedule. For example, the U.S. notes provide that its obligations are subject to continuation of set asides for minority and small businesses. More generally, the GPA has exceptions similar to those found in GATT Articles XX and XXI.

In addition to the non-discrimination requirements, the GPA contains transparency requirements designed to ensure that the rules governing procurement are published and requires parties to report statistics annually on procurement covered by the agreement (Article XIX). In addition, it contains detailed rules on procurement procedures, aimed at ensuring that foreign supplies and suppliers are given an equal opportunity to compete for covered procurement contracts. For example, in cases of limited tenders, where bids are accepted only from qualified suppliers, the agreement has rules on how suppliers are qualified. The GPA also requires parties to establish so-called challenge procedures under which interested suppliers have a right of recourse to an impartial and independent review body before which they may argue that the requirements of the GPA were not met in a specific case (Article XX).

The GPA contains a couple of specific substantive provisions that ban certain policies. First, the use of offsets (e.g., domestic content or counter-trade requirements) is prohibited (Article XVI). Second, Article VI aims at ensuring that technical specifications are not used to discriminate against foreign products or services.

Finally, it should be noted that the GPA contains a number of special provisions for developing countries, designed to encourage their accession.

Notes and Questions

(1) The basic federal Buy–American provision is the Buy American Act of 1933.[4] Subject to exceptions, such as resulted from implementing the GPA, the law essentially requires federal agencies to buy domestically produced goods unless the price is unreasonable or such purchase is otherwise not in the public interest. Under the Federal Acquisition Regulations, domestic suppliers are generally favored if their offer price is not more than six percent above that offered by foreign suppliers.[5] The preference is 50

---

4. 41 U.S.C.A. secs. 10a–10d.

5. 48 CFR sec. 25.105 (2001)(12 percent, if the domestic offer is from a small business concern).

percent in the case of the Defense Department.[6] The U.S. law implementing the 1979 and 1994 Agreements is Sections 301–308 of the Trade Agreements Acts of 1979, as amended (Documents Supplement).

(2) There were three dispute panel reports issued under the Tokyo Round Code. In the first case, it was determined that VAT and applicable taxes and duties should be included in determining whether a contract met the Code's minimum threshold.[7] In a 1992 report, a panel concluded that the U.S. had violated the Code by excluding an EU supplier from bidding on a sonar mapping system for Antarctica.[8] The U.S., which never permitted the adoption of the panel report, claimed that the contract was not subject to the Code because it involved the provision of services, as well as goods. Also in 1992, in response to a U.S. complaint, a panel concluded that Norway had violated the Code in connection with procurement of toll collection equipment for the City of Trondheim.[9] The basic issue in the case was whether the contract fell within the Code's research and development/prototype exception. The panel concluded that it did not, essentially because it resulted in the procurement by Trondheim of a complete toll collection system. As we saw in Chapter 7 on dispute settlement, this case highlights the problem of effective remedies: To what relief is an aggrieved foreign bidder entitled? The GPA requires that challenge procedures must provide for the possibility of obtaining rapid interim relief (e.g., suspension of the procurement process), but it does not require that such relief must necessarily be given (e.g., the tribunal may take into account "overriding adverse consequences for the interests concerned, including the public interest") (Article XX(7). What are the advantages and disadvantages of requiring interim relief?

(3) As permitted by the Dispute Settlement Understanding, the GPA provides that the DSU will apply to GPA disputes, subject to certain specific rules (Article XXII). For purposes of such disputes, the DSB consists of only GPA parties. As of 2001, dispute settlement panels had been established in two cases brought under the GPA. One involved a challenge by the EC and Japan to the Massachusetts law that was the subject of the *Crosby* case, excerpted in Section 3.6 supra. After the panel had been composed but before any submissions had been made to it, the proceeding was suspended and later abandoned when the law was struck down by the U.S. federal courts. The second case involved a U.S. challenge to Korean procurement in connection with the new Seoul airport at Inchon. The case turned on whether the Korean schedule included the entity responsible for the airport and the panel concluded that it did not. It also rejected a non-violation claim brought by the U.S. in the alternative. The U.S. did not appeal the decision. Korea—Measures Affecting Government Procurement, WT/DS163/R (adopted by the DSB on June 19, 2000).

---

6. 48 CFR sec. 252.225–7001 (2001).

7. See GATT, 29th Supp. BISD 41 (1983); GATT, 30th Supp. BISD 36 (1984); GATT, 31st Supp. BISD 247 (1985); GATT, 34th Supp. BISD 177, 179 (1988); Eur. Comm. O.J. C 25/2 (Jan. 30, 1988)(EU lowered threshold applicable to it by 13% to reflect VAT applied in EU).

8. GATT Doc. GPR.DS1/R (Apr. 23, 1992).

9. Norway–Procurement of Toll Collection Equipment for the City of Trondheim, GATT Doc. GPR.DS2/R (April 28, 1992)(Panel report adopted May 13, 1992, by the Committee on Government Procurement). The U.S. later decided that Norway had adequately implemented the decision. 57 Fed. Reg. 46232 (1992).

(4) The WTO has estimated that government procurement represents 10–15% of GDP. According to statistics collected under the Tokyo Round Code for the period 1990–1994, it applied to roughly $30 billion in annually procurement. The GPA was expected to increase that number by a factor of ten. GPA parties are required to report statistics annually that indicate the extent of the coverage of the GPA, but the parties have not done so on a systematic basis.

(5) A multilateral working group on transparency in government procurement practices was established at the 1996 Singapore Ministerial with the aim of developing elements for inclusion in a future agreement on the subject.

(6) Government procurement was treated in both the U.S.-Canada Free Trade Agreement and the North American Free Trade Agreement. In the FTA, the provisions of the GATT Agreement were incorporated by reference, with the threshold being lowered to US$25,000. FTA, arts. 1303–1304. In addition, there were some expanded procedural and reporting obligations agreed to. Id., arts. 1305–1306. Since Mexico was not a signatory to the GATT Agreement (and did not subsequently become a party to the GPA), NAFTA contains detailed provisions on government procurement. NAFTA, ch. 10. Its provisions expand the number of covered entities and the type of contract covered (e.g., $50,000 for contracts for goods, services or any combination; $6.5 million for construction services), subject in each case to various specific exceptions.

(B) SUB–FEDERAL GOVERNMENT PROCUREMENT PREFERENCES

The desire to favor local suppliers is found at all levels of government. In the United States, as we saw in Section 3.6 supra, many states and localities give some form of preferential treatment to local, state or national bidders.[10] It was estimated in 1990 that all but a very few states had some form of domestic preference policy. The form of preference varies widely. They have been categorized as comprehensive, product-specific, flexible, absolute, buy-state or buy-local.[11] A comprehensive law is one that applies to all government procurement; a product-specific law is one that applies only to a specified product or group of products. In the United States, the steel industry has managed to have a number of states adopt Buy–American statutes for steel.[12] A flexible law gives procurement officials discretion to take into account such factors as quality and price differences. Many of the state statutes are buy-national statutes, which means that there is no discrimination against other states. But some statutes give preferences to state or local producers.

Prior to the GPA, U.S. state and local preferences in government procurement were not subject to U.S. international obligations. That remains largely true, although some procurement by most states is now

10. See generally Robert Fraser Miller, Buy–American Statutes: An Assessment of Validity Under Present Law and a Recommendation for Preemption, 23 Rutgers L.J. 137 (1991).

11. See id. at 140–41.

12. We have already seen one such example in the *Trojan Technologies* case, discussed in Section 3.6 supra.

covered by the GPA. While state and local restrictions can be attacked as interfering with the federal government's exclusive foreign affairs powers, such as we saw in the *Bethlehem* case in Section 3.6 supra, other cases have rejected that claim, as we saw in the *Trojan Technologies* case in the same section. Moreover, the Supreme Court has permitted states to discriminate against interstate commerce in procurement matters under the market participant doctrine, which was also discussed in Chapter 3.

Chapter 13

ARTICLE XX: THE GENERAL EXCEPTIONS

In this chapter, we will examine the general exceptions to GATT rules that are contained in Article XX.[1] In particular, we will examine the exceptions for health (Article XX(b)), enforcement (Article XX(d)) and conservation measures (Article XX (g)). There are, of course, other provisions containing exceptions to GATT rules, but we will focus on Article XX and these three exceptions because they are frequently invoked and have been the subject of an extraordinarily detailed Appellate Body jurisdiction developed during the first seven years of the WTO's existence.

The general exceptions clause of Article XX is of particular importance to one of the most controversial subjects that the WTO has had to confront in recent years—the relationship between trade rules and environmental measures. Insofar as the charge is made that the WTO's rules inappropriately find fault with environmental measures, the extent to which the exceptions to those rules permit the maintenance of the challenged environmental measures is critical. Indeed, the trade-environment conflict first burst on the scene in a case involving US rules banning imports of tuna not taken with dolphin-friendly methods. While the results of the two cases dealing with that issue were never adopted by the GATT Council, the cases received widespread attention and caused many to view GATT in a very unfavorable light. In this chapter, we will treat extensively a case similar to the so-called *Tuna-Dolphin* case, involving US rules banning imports of shrimp not taken with turtle-friendly methods. The difference in approach between the two sets of cases has led some to argue that the trade-environment conflict may not be so deep after all. (We deal with the general relationship between trade and the environment in Chapter 21 infra.)

At the outset of our examination of Article XX, it is useful to consider its structure. It consists of two parts: an introductory clause (often referred to as the chapeau) and a list of types of measures that fall within its scope. That list includes measures:

1. See generally John H. Jackson, World Trade and the Law of GATT, ch. 28 (1969).

(a) necessary to protect public morals;

(b) necessary to protect human, animal or plant life or health;

(c) relating to the importation or exportation of gold or silver;

(d) necessary to secure compliance with laws or regulations which are not inconsistent with GATT rules themselves;

(e) relating to the products of prison labor;

(f) imposed for the protection of national treasures;

(g) relating to the conservation of exhaustible natural resources;

(h) undertaken pursuant to obligations of certain international commodity agreements;

(i) involving restrictions on exports necessary to ensure domestic supplies when the domestic price is held below the world price by the government for price stabilization reasons; and

(j) essential to the acquisition or distribution of products in short supply.

As noted above, there is detailed jurisprudence on clauses (b), (d) and (g), but not in respect of the others. It is worth noting that while the scope of these other clauses is for the most part fairly well defined, the reach of clause (a), which permits measures necessary to protect public morals, has never been the subject of interpretation in dispute settlement proceedings and its breadth is potentially far-reaching. Could it, for example, justify measures taken to protest an exporter's human rights policies? The issue of linking trade to non-trade policies is considered generally in Chapter 21 infra.

The Appellate Body has stressed that a proper analysis of an Article XX defense must in all cases begin with a consideration of whether the measure at issue is a type covered by Article XX.[2] For example, is it a measure necessary to protect human health (clause (b)) or one that is related to conservation of exhaustible natural resources (clause (g))? If the measure falls under one of the enumerated clauses, such that it can be "provisionally justified," then it is necessary to see if the measure complies with the requirements of the chapeau, which provides that the exceptions of Article XX are only available if the measure at issue is "not applied in a manner which would constitute a means of arbitrary or unjustifiable discrimination between countries where the same conditions prevail, or a disguised restriction on international trade." Consequently, in this chapter we will first examine WTO cases that consider whether a measure falls within the list of measures covered by Article XX and then consider how the requirements of the chapeau have been interpreted.

---

2. United States—Import Prohibition of Certain Shrimp and Shrimp Products, WT/DS58/AB/R, paras. 118–121, Appellate Body Report adopted by the DSB on November 6, 1998; United States–Standards for Reformulated and Conventional Gasoline, WT/DS2 & 4/AB/R, p. 22, Appellate Body Report adopted by the DSB on May 20, 1996.

SECTION 13.1   ARTICLE XX(b)—
HEALTH MEASURES

Article XX(b) covers measures "necessary to protect human, animal or plant life or health". Two WTO agreements are related to Article XX(b). First, the Agreement on Sanitary and Phytosanitary Measures (the SPS Agreement) applies in general to measures taken to protect human, animal and plant life or health from certain specified risks. The SPS Agreement explicitly provides that measures conforming to its provisions "shall be presumed to be in accordance with * * * GATT 1994 * * *, in particular the provisions of Article XX(b)" (SPS art. 2(4)). Second, the Agreement on Technical Barriers to Trade (the TBT Agreement) applies to technical regulations and standards, which often have a safety or health basis, although the overlap with Article XX(b) is more limited than in the case of the SPS Agreement. The TBT Agreement does not specify how it relates to Article XX, which has lead to some interpretative uncertainties. These two agreements are analyzed in Chapter 14.

Our consideration of Article XX(b) starts with the Appellate Body's decision in the *Asbestos* case. Although the Appellate Body ruled that the products at issue were not like (see Section 12.4(A) supra), which meant that the EC had not violated any WTO rules, the Appellate Body examined the panel's conclusion that even though the measure violated Article III, it could be justified under Article XX(b).

EUROPEAN COMMUNITIES—MEASURES AFFECTING ASBESTOS AND ASBESTOS–CONTAINING PRODUCTS

WT/DS135/AB/R

Appellate Body Report adopted by the DSB on April 5, 2001

[The underlying facts of this case are set out in Section 12.4(A) supra.]

155.   Under Article XX(b) of the GATT 1994, the Panel examined, first, whether the use of chrysotile-cement products poses a risk to human health and, second, whether the measure at issue is "necessary to protect human ... life or health". * * *

* * *

157.   On the issue of whether the use of chrysotile-cement products poses a risk to human health sufficient to enable the measure to fall within the scope of application of the phrase "to protect human ... life or health" in Article XX(b), the Panel stated that it "considers that the evidence before it *tends to show* that handling chrysotile-cement products constitutes a risk to health rather than the opposite." (emphasis added) On the basis of this assessment of the evidence, the Panel concluded that:

"the EC has made a prima facie case for the existence of a health risk in connection with the use of chrysotile, in particular as regards lung cancer and mesothelioma in the occupational sectors downstream of production and processing and for the public in general in relation to chrysotile-cement products. This prima facie case has not been rebutted by Canada. Moreover, the Panel considers that the comments by the experts confirm the health risk associated with exposure to chrysotile in its various uses. *The Panel therefore considers that the EC have shown that the policy of prohibiting chrysotile asbestos implemented by the Decree falls within the range of policies designed to protect human life or health. . . .*" (emphasis added)

Thus, the Panel found that the measure falls within the category of measures embraced by Article XX(b) of the GATT 1994.

* * *

162. * * * [W]e have examined the seven factors on which Canada relies in asserting that the Panel erred in concluding that there exists a human health risk associated with the manipulation of chrysotile-cement products. We see Canada's appeal on this point as, in reality, a challenge to the Panel's assessment of the credibility and weight to be ascribed to the scientific evidence before it. Canada contests the conclusions that the Panel drew both from the evidence of the scientific experts and from scientific reports before it. As we have noted, we will interfere with the Panel's appreciation of the evidence only when we are "satisfied that the panel has *exceeded the bounds of its discretion*, as the trier of facts, in its appreciation of the evidence." (emphasis added) In this case, nothing suggests that the Panel exceeded the bounds of its lawful discretion. To the contrary, all four of the scientific experts consulted by the Panel concurred that chrysotile asbestos fibres, and chrysotile-cement products, constitute a risk to human health, and the Panel's conclusions on this point are faithful to the views expressed by the four scientists. In addition, the Panel noted that the carcinogenic nature of chrysotile asbestos fibres has been acknowledged since 1977 by international bodies, such as the International Agency for Research on Cancer and the World Health Organization. In these circumstances, we find that the Panel remained well within the bounds of its discretion in finding that chrysotile-cement products pose a risk to human life or health.

* * *

164. On the issue of whether the measure at issue is "necessary" to protect public health within the meaning of Article XX(b), the Panel stated:

In the light of France's public health objectives as presented by the European Communities, the Panel concludes that the EC has made a prima facie case for the non-existence of a reasonably available alternative to the banning of chrysotile and chrysotile-cement products and recourse to substitute products. Canada has not rebutted the presumption established by the EC. We also consider that the EC's position is confirmed by the comments of the experts consulted in the course of this proceeding.

165. Canada argues that the Panel erred in applying the "necessity" test under Article XX(b) of the GATT 1994 "by stating that there is a high enough risk associated with the manipulation of chrysotile-cement products that it could in principle justify strict measures such as the Decree." Canada advances four arguments in support of this part of its appeal. First, Canada argues that the Panel erred in finding, on the basis of the scientific evidence before it, that chrysotile-cement products pose a risk to human health. Second, Canada contends that the Panel had an obligation to "quantify" itself the risk associated with chrysotile-cement products and that it could not simply "rely" on the "hypotheses" of the French authorities. Third, Canada asserts that the Panel erred by postulating that the level of protection of health inherent in the Decree is a halt to the spread of asbestos-related health risks. According to Canada, this "premise is false because it does not take into account the risk associated with the use of substitute products without a framework for controlled use." Fourth, and finally, Canada claims that the Panel erred in finding that "controlled use" is not a reasonably available alternative to the Decree.

166. With respect to Canada's first argument, we note simply that we have already dismissed Canada's contention that the evidence before the Panel did not support the Panel's findings. We are satisfied that the Panel had a more than sufficient basis to conclude that chrysotile-cement products do pose a significant risk to human life or health.

167. As for Canada's second argument, relating to "quantification" of the risk, we consider that, as with the *SPS Agreement*, there is no requirement under Article XX(b) of the GATT 1994 to *quantify*, as such, the risk to human life or health. A risk may be evaluated either in quantitative or qualitative terms. In this case, contrary to what is suggested by Canada, the Panel assessed the nature and the character of the risk posed by chrysotile-cement products. The Panel found, on the basis of the scientific evidence, that "no minimum threshold of level of exposure or duration of exposure has been identified with regard to the risk of pathologies associated with chrysotile, except for asbestosis." The pathologies which the Panel identified as being associated with chrysotile are of a very serious nature, namely lung cancer and mesothelioma, which is also a form of cancer. Therefore, we do not agree with Canada that the Panel merely relied on the French authorities' "hypotheses" of the risk.

168. As to Canada's third argument, relating to the level of protection, we note that it is undisputed that WTO Members have the right to determine the level of protection of health that they consider appropriate in a given situation. France has determined, and the Panel accepted, that the chosen level of health protection by France is a "halt" to the spread of *asbestos*-related health risks. By prohibiting all forms of

amphibole asbestos, and by severely restricting the use of chrysotile asbestos, the measure at issue is clearly designed and apt to achieve that level of health protection. Our conclusion is not altered by the fact that PCG fibres might pose a risk to health. The scientific evidence before the Panel indicated that the risk posed by the PCG fibres is, in any case, *less* than the risk posed by chrysotile asbestos fibres , although that evidence did *not* indicate that the risk posed by PCG fibres is non-existent. Accordingly, it seems to us perfectly legitimate for a Member to seek to halt the spread of a highly risky product while allowing the use of a less risky product in its place. In short, we do not agree with Canada's third argument.

169. In its fourth argument, Canada asserts that the Panel erred in finding that "controlled use" is not a reasonably available alternative to the Decree. This last argument is based on Canada's assertion that, in *United States—Gasoline* [see Section 13.3], both we and the panel held that an alternative measure "can only be ruled out if it is shown to be impossible to implement." We understand Canada to mean by this that an alternative measure is only excluded as a "reasonably available" alternative if implementation of that measure is "impossible". We certainly agree with Canada that an alternative measure which is impossible to implement is not "reasonably available". But we do not agree with Canada's reading of either the panel report or our report in *United States—Gasoline*. In *United States—Gasoline*, the panel held, in essence, that an alternative measure did not *cease* to be "reasonably" available simply because the alternative measure involved *administrative difficulties* for a Member. The panel's findings on this point were not appealed, and, thus, we did not address this issue in that case.

170. Looking at this issue now, we believe that, in determining whether a suggested alternative measure is "reasonably available", several factors must be taken into account, besides the difficulty of implementation. In *Thailand—Restrictions on Importation of and Internal Taxes on Cigarettes*, the panel made the following observations on the applicable standard for evaluating whether a measure is "necessary" under Article XX(b):

> The import restrictions imposed by Thailand could be considered to be "necessary" in terms of Article XX(b) only if there were no alternative measure consistent with the General Agreement, or less inconsistent with it, which Thailand could *reasonably be expected to employ to achieve its health policy objectives*.[3] (emphasis added)

171. In our Report in *Korea—Beef* [see Section 13.2], we addressed the issue of "necessity" under Article XX(d) of the GATT 1994. In that appeal, we found that the panel was correct in following the standard set forth by the panel in *United States—Section 337 of the Tariff Act of 1930*:

3. [original note 163] Adopted 20 February 1990, BISD 37S/200, para. 75.

It was clear to the Panel that a contracting party cannot justify a measure inconsistent with another GATT provision as "necessary" in terms of Article XX(d) if an alternative measure which it could reasonably be expected to employ and which is not inconsistent with other GATT provisions is available to it. By the same token, in cases where a measure consistent with other GATT provisions is not reasonably available, a contracting party is bound to use, among the measures reasonably available to it, that which entails the least degree of inconsistency with other GATT provisions.[4]

172. We indicated in *Korea–Beef* that one aspect of the "weighing and balancing process . . . comprehended in the determination of whether a WTO-consistent alternative measure" is reasonably available is the extent to which the alternative measure "contributes to the realization of the end pursued". In addition, we observed, in that case, that "[t]he more vital or important [the] common interests or values" pursued, the easier it would be to accept as "necessary" measures designed to achieve those ends. In this case, the objective pursued by the measure is the preservation of human life and health through the elimination, or reduction, of the well-known, and life-threatening, health risks posed by asbestos fibres. The value pursued is both vital and important in the highest degree. The remaining question, then, is whether there is an alternative measure that would achieve the same end and that is less restrictive of trade than a prohibition.

173. Canada asserts that "controlled use" represents a "reasonably available" measure that would serve the same end. The issue is, thus, whether France could reasonably be expected to employ "controlled use" practices to achieve its chosen level of health protection—a halt in the spread of asbestos-related health risks.

174. In our view, France could not reasonably be expected to employ *any* alternative measure if that measure would involve a continuation of the very risk that the Decree seeks to "halt". Such an alternative measure would, in effect, prevent France from achieving its chosen level of health protection. On the basis of the scientific evidence before it, the Panel found that, in general, the efficacy of "controlled use" remains to be demonstrated. Moreover, even in cases where "controlled use" practices are applied "with greater certainty", the scientific evidence suggests that the level of exposure can, in some circumstances, still be high enough for there to be a "significant residual risk of developing asbestos-related diseases." The Panel found too that the efficacy of "controlled use" is particularly doubtful for the building industry and for DIY [do-it-yourself] enthusiasts, which are the most important users of cement-based products containing chrysotile asbestos. Given these factual findings by the Panel, we believe that "controlled use" would not allow France to achieve its chosen level of health protection by halting the spread of asbestos-related health risks. "Con-

4. [original note 165] Adopted 7 November 1989, BISD 36S/345, para. 5.26; we expressly affirmed this standard in our Report in *Korea–Beef*, para. 166.

trolled use" would, thus, not be an alternative measure that would achieve the end sought by France.

175. For these reasons, we uphold the Panel's finding * * * that the European Communities has demonstrated a *prima facie* case that there was no "reasonably available alternative" to the prohibition inherent in the Decree. As a result, we also uphold the Panel's conclusion * * * that the Decree is "necessary to protect human ... life or health" within the meaning of Article XX(b) of the GATT 1994.

Notes and Questions

(1) Part of Canada's appeal of the panel's findings on Article XX(b) was cast as a failure by the panel to make an "objective assessment" of the evidence it had presented, as required by DSU article 11. In responding to that argument, the Appellate Body stated:

> 178. * * * [I]n the context of the SPS Agreement, we have said previously, in *European Communities—Hormones*, that "responsible and representative governments may act in good faith on the basis of what, at a given time, may be a divergent opinion coming from qualified and respected sources." (emphasis added) In justifying a measure under Article XX(b) of the GATT 1994, a Member may also rely, in good faith, on scientific sources which, at that time, may represent a divergent, but qualified and respected, opinion. A Member is not obliged, in setting health policy, automatically to follow what, at a given time, may constitute a majority scientific opinion. Therefore, a panel need not, necessarily, reach a decision under Article XX(b) of the GATT 1994 on the basis of the "preponderant" weight of the evidence.

The *Hormones* case is discussed in Chapter 14 infra. In light of this statement and the Appellate Body's foregoing analysis of Article XX(b), how would you characterize the extent of a WTO member's discretion in imposing health-related product measures? To what extent did the seriousness of the health threat play a role in the *Asbestos* decision? For example, would a decision by a member to "halt" a less significant, non-life threatening health risk be afforded the same deference in a determination of necessity? What factors should be taken into account in deciding this issue?

(2) The *Thai Cigarettes* case referred to by the Appellate Body in paragraph 170 above involved an attempt by Thailand to invoke Article XX(b) to defend discriminatory taxes it imposed on foreign cigarettes in violation of Article III:2. The panel in that case concluded that such measures were not necessary in that Thailand could accomplish its claimed health goal through nondiscriminatory taxes that were consistent with GATT rules.

SECTION 13.2   ARTICLE XX(d)— ENFORCEMENT MEASURES

Article XX(d) provides an exception to GATT rules for measures "necessary to secure compliance with laws or regulations which are not inconsistent with the provisions of this Agreement, including those relating to customs enforcement, the enforcement of monopolies operated under paragraph 4 of Article II and Article XVII, the protection of patents, trade marks and copyrights, and the prevention of deceptive practices." The following case examines the criteria for establishing this exception.

KOREA—MEASURES AFFECTING IMPORTS OF FRESH, CHILLED AND FROZEN BEEF

WT/DS161 & 169/AB/R
Appellate Body Report adopted by the DSB on January 10, 2001

[The Panel was established to consider a complaint by Australia and the United States with respect to Korean measures that affected the importation of certain beef products. We have already considered in Section 12.4(B) the finding of the Appellate Body that Korea's separate retail distribution channels for imported and domestic beef products (the so-called "dual retail system") violated GATT Article III. Here we examine Korea's invocation of Article XX(d).]

157.   For a measure, otherwise inconsistent with GATT 1994, to be justified provisionally under paragraph (d) of Article XX, two elements must be shown. First, the measure must be one designed to "secure compliance" with laws or regulations that are not themselves inconsistent with some provision of the GATT 1994. Second, the measure must be "necessary" to secure such compliance. A Member who invokes Article XX(d) as a justification has the burden of demonstrating that these two requirements are met.

158.   The Panel examined these two aspects one after the other. The Panel found, "despite ... troublesome aspects, ... that the dual retail system was put in place, at least in part, in order to secure compliance with the Korean legislation against deceptive practices to the extent that it serves to prevent acts inconsistent with the *Unfair Competition Act*." It recognized that the system was established at a time when acts of misrepresentation of origin were widespread in the beef sector. It also acknowledged that the dual retail system "does appear to reduce the opportunities and thus the temptations for butchers to misrepresent [less expensive] foreign beef for [more expensive] domestic beef". The parties did not appeal these findings of the Panel.

159.   We turn, therefore, to the question of whether the dual retail system is "necessary" to secure compliance with the *Unfair Competition Act*. Once again, we look first to the ordinary meaning of the word "necessary", in its context and in the light of the object and purpose of Article XX, in accordance with Article 31(1) of the *Vienna Convention*.

160.   The word "necessary" normally denotes something "that cannot be dispensed with or done without, requisite, essential, needful". We note, however, that a standard law dictionary cautions that:

[t]his word must be considered in the connection in which it is used, as it is a word susceptible of various meanings. It may import

absolute physical necessity or inevitability, or it may import that which is only convenient, useful, appropriate, suitable, proper, or conducive to the end sought. It is an adjective expressing degrees, and may express mere convenience or that which is indispensable or an absolute physical necessity.[5]

161.   We believe that, as used in the context of Article XX(d), the reach of the word "necessary" is not limited to that which is "indispensable" or "of absolute necessity" or "inevitable". Measures which are indispensable or of absolute necessity or inevitable to secure compliance certainly fulfil the requirements of Article XX(d). But other measures, too, may fall within the ambit of this exception. As used in Article XX(d), the term "necessary" refers, in our view, to a range of degrees of necessity. At one end of this continuum lies "necessary" understood as "indispensable"; at the other end, is "necessary" taken to mean as "making a contribution to." We consider that a "necessary" measure is, in this continuum, located significantly closer to the pole of "indispensable" than to the opposite pole of simply "making a contribution to".

162.   In appraising the "necessity" of a measure in these terms, it is useful to bear in mind the context in which "necessary" is found in Article XX(d). The measure at stake has to be "necessary to ensure compliance with laws and regulations ..., *including* those relating to customs enforcement, the enforcement of [lawful] monopolies ..., the protection of patents, trade marks and copyrights, and the prevention of deceptive practices". (emphasis added) Clearly, Article XX(d) is susceptible of application in respect of a wide variety of "laws and regulations" to be enforced. It seems to us that a treaty interpreter assessing a measure claimed to be necessary to secure compliance of a WTO-consistent law or regulation may, in appropriate cases, take into account the relative importance of the common interests or values that the law or regulation to be enforced is intended to protect. The more vital or important those common interests or values are, the easier it would be to accept as "necessary" a measure designed as an enforcement instrument.

163.   There are other aspects of the enforcement measure to be considered in evaluating that measure as "necessary". One is the extent to which the measure contributes to the realization of the end pursued, the securing of compliance with the law or regulation at issue. The greater the contribution, the more easily a measure might be considered to be "necessary". Another aspect is the extent to which the compliance measure produces restrictive effects on international commerce, that is, in respect of a measure inconsistent with Article III:4, restrictive effects *on imported goods*. A measure with a relatively slight impact upon imported products might more easily be considered as "necessary" than a measure with intense or broader restrictive effects.

164.   In sum, determination of whether a measure, which is not "indispensable", may nevertheless be "necessary" within the contempla-

---

5.   [original note 103] *Black's Law Dic-   tionary*, (West Publishing, 1995), p. 1029.

tion of Article XX(d), involves in every case a process of weighing and balancing a series of factors which prominently include the contribution made by the compliance measure to the enforcement of the law or regulation at issue, the importance of the common interests or values protected by that law or regulation, and the accompanying impact of the law or regulation on imports or exports.

165. The panel in *United States—Section 337* described the applicable standard for evaluating whether a measure is "necessary" under Article XX(d) in the following terms [quoted in *Asbestos*, Section 13.1 supra].

166. The standard described by the panel in *United States—Section 337* encapsulates the general considerations we have adverted to above. In our view, the weighing and balancing process we have outlined is comprehended in the determination of whether a WTO-consistent alternative measure which the Member concerned could "reasonably be expected to employ" is available, or whether a less WTO-inconsistent measure is "reasonably available".

167. The Panel followed the standard identified by the panel in *United States—Section 337*. It started scrutinizing whether the dual retail system is "necessary" under paragraph (d) of Article XX by stating:

> Korea has to convince the Panel that, contrary to what was alleged by Australia and the United States, no alternative measure consistent with the WTO Agreement is reasonably available at present in order to deal with misrepresentation in the retail market as to the origin of beef.

168. The Panel first considered a range of possible alternative measures, by examining measures taken by Korea with respect to situations involving, or which could involve, deceptive practices similar to those which in 1989–1990 had affected the retail sale of foreign beef. The Panel found that Korea does not require a dual retail system in *related product areas*, but relies instead on traditional enforcement procedures. There is no requirement, for example, for a dual retail system separating domestic Hanwoo beef from domestic dairy cattle beef. Nor is there a requirement for a dual retail system for any other meat or food product, such as pork or seafood. Finally, there is no requirement for a system of separate restaurants, depending on whether they serve domestic or imported beef, even though approximately 45 per cent of the beef imported into Korea is sold in restaurants. Yet, in all of these cases, the Panel found that there were numerous cases of fraudulent misrepresentation. For the Panel, these examples indicated that misrepresentation of origin could, in principle, be dealt with "on the basis of basic methods ... such as normal policing under the Korean *Unfair Competition Act*."

169. Examining enforcement measures applicable to the same illegal behavior relating to like, or at least similar, products does not necessarily imply the introduction of a "consistency" requirement into the "necessary" concept of Article XX(d). Examining such enforcement

measures may provide useful input in the course of determining whether an alternative measure which could "reasonably be expected" to be utilized, is available or not.

170. For Korea, alternative measures must not only be reasonably available, but must also *guarantee* the level of enforcement sought which, in the case of the dual retail system, is the *elimination* of fraud in the beef retail market. With respect to investigations, Korea argues that this tool can only reveal fraud *ex post*, whereas the dual retail system can combat fraudulent practices *ex ante*. Korea contends that *ex post* investigations do not *guarantee* the level of enforcement that Korea has chosen, and therefore should not be considered. With respect to policing, Korea believes that this option is not "reasonably available", because Korea lacks the resources to police thousands of shops on a round-the-clock basis.

171. We share the Panel's conclusion. We are not persuaded that Korea could not achieve its desired level of enforcement of the *Unfair Competition Act* with respect to the origin of beef sold by retailers by using conventional WTO-consistent enforcement measures, if Korea would devote more resources to its enforcement efforts on the beef sector. It might also be added that Korea's argument about the lack of resources to police thousands of shops on a round-the-clock basis is, in the end, not sufficiently persuasive. Violations of laws and regulations like the Korean *Unfair Competition Act* can be expected to be routinely investigated and detected through selective, but well-targeted, controls of potential wrongdoers. The control of records will assist in selecting the shops to which the police could pay particular attention.

172. There is still another aspect that should be noted relating to both the method actually chosen by Korea—its dual retail system for beef—and alternative traditional enforcement measures. Securing through conventional, WTO-consistent measures a higher level of enforcement of the *Unfair Competition Act* with respect to the retail sale of beef, could well entail higher enforcement costs for the national budget. It is pertinent to observe that, through its dual retail system, Korea has in effect shifted all, or the great bulk, of these potential costs of enforcement (translated into a drastic reduction of competitive access to consumers) to imported goods and retailers of imported goods, instead of evenly distributing such costs between the domestic and imported products. In contrast, the more conventional, WTO-consistent measures of enforcement do not involve such onerous shifting of enforcement costs which ordinarily are borne by the Member's public purse.

Notes and Questions

(1) Do you see any differences between the Appellate Body's view of the "necessity" requirement under Article XX(d) as compared to it view of the requirement under Article XX(b), which we examined in the *EC Asbestos* case in Section 13.1 supra. For example, in light of paragraph 163, should there have been a consideration of the impact of the French regulation on imported goods? Or is that irrelevant in the case of a health measure?

(2) How does the fact that there are "numerous cases" of origin fraud in other contexts suggest that the enforcement mechanisms used in those contexts are adequate (para. 168)? Despite its protest to the contrary (para. 169), does the Appellate Body effectively endorse a consistency test? What problems do you see in relying on such a test?

(3) Is the Appellate Body's rejection of Korea's argument that it wished to guarantee a specific, high level of enforcement consistent with its acceptance of the French desire to halt exposure to asbestos? How does a panel or the Appellate Body judge how "vital or important * * * common interests or values are" (para. 162)? How much should be left to the discretion of the government concerned?

SECTION 13.3 ARTICLE XX(g)— CONSERVATION MEASURES

Article XX(g) contains an exception to general GATT rules for measures "relating to the conservation of exhaustible natural resources if such measures are made effective in conjunction with restrictions on domestic production or consumption." This clause has been interpreted in two landmark Appellate Body decisions, including the following decision, which was the first issued by the Appellate Body.

UNITED STATES—STANDARDS FOR REFORMULATED AND CONVENTIONAL GASOLINE

WT/DS2/AB/R, pp. 13–20
Appellate Body Report adopted by the DSB on May 20, 1996

[This case involved a dispute between the United States and Venezuela, later joined by Brazil. The dispute related to the implementation by the US Environmental Protection Agency (EPA) through its so-called Gasoline Rule of provisions of the US Clean Air Act of 1990 (CAA), which were designed to ensure (i) that pollutants in major population centres were reduced and (ii) that pollution from gasoline combustion did not exceed 1990 levels. To achieve the first goal, the Rule provided that only so-called reformulated gasoline was permitted to be sold in certain large metropolitan (and some other) areas that had experienced significant summertime ozone pollution in the past. Conventional gasoline could only be sold outside of these areas. To achieve the second goal, the Gasoline Rule relied on the use of 1990 baselines as described below.

The CAA required reformulated gasoline to meet certain specifications. In addition, it imposed "non-degradation" rules, which required that certain quality aspects of reformulated gasoline not fall below 1990 baseline levels for gasoline generally. In order to prevent the dumping of pollutants extracted from reformulated gasoline into conventional gasoline, the CAA required that conventional gasoline remain as clean as 1990 baseline levels. Consequently, in respect of both reformulated and conventional gasoline, the 1990 baselines were an integral element of the Gasoline Rule, and it contained detailed baseline establishment rules.

Baselines could be either individual (established on the basis of the records of the individual) or statutory (established by the EPA and intended to reflect average 1990 US gasoline quality). Any domestic refiner which was in operation for at least six months in 1990 was required to establish an individual baseline representing the quality of gasoline produced by that refiner in 1990. In contrast, the Gasoline Rule did not provide for individual baselines for foreign refiners. Although the EPA at one time proposed allowing limited use by importers of such baselines, Congress enacted legislation specifically denying the funding necessary to implement the proposal.

The Panel Report concluded that the above described rules violated Article III:4, essentially because imported gasoline was required to meet the statutory baseline (with effectively no option to benefit from an individual baseline) while domestic gasoline needed only to meet the applicable individual baseline. In fact, the vast majority of domestic gasoline did not meet the statutory baseline. It should be noted that after January 1, 1998, all reformulated gasoline had to meet the same specified standard, so the Gasoline Rule in respect of individual baselines for reformulated gasoline was essentially a transitional provision for the benefit of US refiners.

The US did not appeal the Panel's finding that Article III:4 had been violated, nor did it appeal the Panel's finding that the Gasoline Rule could not be justified as a health measure under Article XX(b). It did, however, appeal the Panel's rejection of its Article XX(g) defense. While the Panel found that clean air was an exhaustible natural resource for purposes of Article XX(g), it concluded that the less favourable baseline establishment methods at issue were not "primarily aimed" at the conservation of exhaustible natural resources and thus fell outside the justifying scope of Article XX(g).]

The Panel, addressing the task of interpreting the words "relating to", quoted with approval the following passage from the panel report in the 1987 *Herring and Salmon* case:[6]

> as the preamble of Article XX indicates, the purpose of including Article XX:(g) in the General Agreement was not to widen the scope for measures serving trade policy purposes but merely to ensure that the commitments under the General Agreement do not hinder the pursuit of policies aimed at the conservation of exhaustive natural resources. The Panel concluded for these reasons that, while a trade measure did not have to be necessary or essential to the conservation of an exhaustible natural resource, it had to be *primarily aimed* at the conservation of an exhaustible natural resource to be considered as "relating to" conservation within the meaning of Article XX:(g). (emphasis added by the Panel)

6. *[original note 30] Canada—Measures Affecting Exports of Unprocessed Herring and Salmon,* BISD 35S/98, para. 4.6; adopted on 22 March 1988.

The Panel Report then went on to apply the 1987 *Herring and Salmon* reasoning and conclusion to the baseline establishment rules of the Gasoline Rule in the following manner:

> The Panel then considered whether the precise aspects of the Gasoline Rule that it had found to violate Article III—the less favourable baseline establishment methods that adversely affected the conditions of competition for imported gasoline—were primarily aimed at the conservation of natural resources. The Panel saw no direct connection between less favourable treatment of imported gasoline that was chemically identical to domestic gasoline, and the US objective of improving air quality in the United States. Indeed, in the view of the Panel, being consistent with the obligation to provide no less favourable treatment would not prevent the attainment of the desired level of conservation of natural resources under the Gasoline Rule. Accordingly, it could not be said that the baseline establishment methods that afforded less favourable treatment to imported gasoline were primarily aimed at the conservation of natural resources. In the Panel's view, the above-noted lack of connection was underscored by the fact that affording treatment of imported gasoline consistent with its Article III:4 obligations would not in any way hinder the United States in its pursuit of its conservation policies under the Gasoline Rule. Indeed, the United States remained free to regulate in order to obtain whatever air quality it wished. The Panel therefore concluded that the less favourable baseline establishment methods at issue in this case were not primarily aimed at the conservation of natural resources.

It is not easy to follow the reasoning in the above paragraph of the Panel Report. In our view, there is a certain amount of opaqueness in that reasoning. The Panel starts with positing that there was "*no direct connection*" between the baseline establishment rules which it characterized as "less favourable treatment" of imported gasoline that was chemically identical to the domestic gasoline and "the US objective of improving air quality in the United States." Shortly thereafter, the Panel went on to conclude that "*accordingly, it could not be said that* the baseline establishment rules that afforded less favourable treatment to imported gasoline *were primarily aimed at* the conservation of natural resources" (emphasis added). The Panel did not try to clarify whether the phrase "direct connection" was being used as a synonym for "primarily aimed at" or whether a new and additional element (on top of "primarily aimed at") was being demanded.

One problem with the reasoning in that paragraph is that the Panel asked itself whether the "less favourable treatment" of imported gasoline was "primarily aimed at" the conservation of natural resources, rather than whether the "measure", i.e. the baseline establishment rules, were "primarily aimed at" conservation of clean air. In our view, the Panel here was in error in referring to its legal conclusion on Article III:4 instead of the measure in issue. The result of this analysis is to turn Article XX on its head. Obviously, there had to be a finding that the measure provided "less favourable treatment" under Article III:4 before the Panel examined the "General Exceptions" contained in Article XX. That, however, is a conclusion of law. The chapeau of Article XX makes it clear that it is the "measures" which are to be examined under Article XX(g), and not the legal finding of "less favourable treatment."

* * *

A principal difficulty, in the view of the Appellate Body, with the Panel Report's application of Article XX(g) to the baseline establishment rules is that the Panel there overlooked a fundamental rule of treaty interpretation [i.e., Article 31 of the Vienna Convention on the Law of Treaties].

* * *

Applying the basic principle of interpretation that the words of a treaty, like the *General Agreement*, are to be given their ordinary meaning, in their context and in the light of the treaty's object and purpose, the Appellate Body observes that the Panel Report failed to take adequate account of the words actually used by Article XX in its several paragraphs. In enumerating the various categories of governmental acts, laws or regulations which WTO Members may carry out or promulgate in pursuit of differing legitimate state policies or interests outside the realm of trade liberalization, Article XX uses different terms in respect of different categories:

"necessary"—in paragraphs (a), (b) and (d);

"relating to"—in paragraphs (c), (e) and (g);

"for the protection of"—in paragraph (f);

"in pursuance of"—in paragraph (h);

"involving"—in paragraph (i); and

"essential"—in paragraph (j).

It does not seem reasonable to suppose that the WTO Members intended to require, in respect of each and every category, the same kind or degree of connection or relationship between the measure under appraisal and the state interest or policy sought to be promoted or realized.

At the same time, Article XX(g) and its phrase, "relating to the conservation of exhaustible natural resources," need to be read in context and in such a manner as to give effect to the purposes and objects of the *General Agreement*. The context of Article XX(g) includes the provisions of the rest of the *General Agreement*, including in particular Articles I, III and XI; conversely, the context of Articles I and III and XI includes Article XX. Accordingly, the phrase "relating to the conservation of exhaustible natural resources" may not be read so expansively as seriously to subvert the purpose and object of Article III:4. Nor may Article III:4 be given so broad a reach as effectively to emasculate Article XX(g) and the policies and interests it embodies. The relationship between the affirmative commitments set out in, *e.g.*, Articles I, III and XI, and the policies and interests embodied in the "General Exceptions" listed in Article XX, can be given meaning within the framework of the *General Agreement* and its object and purpose by a treaty interpreter only on a case-to-case basis, by careful scrutiny of the factual and legal context in a given dispute, without disregarding the words actually used by the WTO Members themselves to express their intent and purpose.

The 1987 *Herring and Salmon* report, and the Panel Report itself, gave some recognition to the foregoing considerations of principle. As earlier noted, the Panel Report quoted the following excerpt from the *Herring and Salmon* report:

> as the preamble of Article XX indicates, the purpose of including Article XX(g) in the General Agreement was not to widen the scope for measures serving trade policy purposes but merely *to ensure that the commitments under the General Agreement do not hinder the pursuit of policies* aimed at the conservation of exhaustible natural resources. (emphasis added)

All the participants and the third participants in this appeal accept the propriety and applicability of the view of the *Herring and Salmon* report and the Panel Report that a measure must be "primarily aimed at" the conservation of exhaustible natural resources in order to fall within the scope of Article XX(g). Accordingly, we see no need to examine this point further, save, perhaps, to note that the phrase "primarily aimed at" is not itself treaty language and was not designed as a simple litmus test for inclusion or exclusion from Article XX(g).

Against this background, we turn to the specific question of whether the baseline establishment rules are appropriately regarded as "primarily aimed at" the conservation of natural resources for the purposes of Article XX(g). We consider that this question must be answered in the affirmative.

The baseline establishment rules, taken as a whole (that is, the provisions relating to establishment of baselines for domestic refiners, along with the provisions relating to baselines for blenders and importers of gasoline), need to be related to the "non-degradation" requirements set out elsewhere in the Gasoline Rule. Those provisions can scarcely be understood if scrutinized strictly by themselves, totally divorced from other sections of the Gasoline Rule which certainly constitute part of the context of these provisions. The baseline establishment rules whether individual or statutory, were designed to permit scrutiny and monitoring of the level of compliance of refiners, importers and blenders with the "non-degradation" requirements. Without baselines of some kind, such scrutiny would not be possible and the Gasoline Rule's objective of stabilizing and preventing further deterioration of the level of air pollution prevailing in 1990, would be substantially frustrated. The relationship between the baseline establishment rules and the "non-degradation" requirements of the Gasoline Rule is not negated by the inconsistency, found by the Panel, of the baseline establishment rules with the terms of Article III:4. We consider that, given that substantial relationship, the baseline establishment rules cannot be regarded as merely incidentally or inadvertently aimed at the conservation of clean air in the United States for the purposes of Article XX(g).

[The Appellate Body then considered the third clause of Article XX(g), i.e., whether the baseline establishment rules were "made effective in conjunction with restrictions on domestic production or consumption", an issue that the Panel had not considered. In that connection, the Appellate Body noted that it viewed that clause] as a requirement that the measures concerned impose restrictions, not just in respect of imported gasoline but also with respect to domestic gasoline. The clause is a requirement of *even-handedness* in the imposition of restrictions, in the name of conservation, upon the production or consumption of exhaustible natural resources.

There is, of course, no textual basis for requiring identical treatment of domestic and imported products. Indeed, where there is identity of treatment—constituting real, not merely formal, equality of treatment—it is difficult to see how inconsistency with Article III:4 would have arisen in the first place. On the other hand, if *no* restrictions on domestically-produced like products are imposed at all, and all limitations are placed upon imported products *alone*, the measure cannot be accepted as primarily or even substantially designed for implementing conservationist goals. The measure would simply be naked discrimination for protecting locally-produced goods.

In the present appeal, the baseline establishment rules affect both domestic gasoline and imported gasoline, providing for—generally speaking—individual baselines for domestic refiners and blenders and statutory baselines for importers. Thus, restrictions on the consumption or depletion of clean air by regulating the domestic production of "dirty" gasoline are established jointly with corresponding restrictions with respect to imported gasoline. That imported gasoline has been determined to have been accorded "less favourable treatment" than the domestic gasoline in terms of Article III:4, is not material for purposes of analysis under Article XX(g). * * *

We do not believe, finally, that the clause * * * was intended to establish an empirical "effects test" for the availability of the Article XX(g) exception. * * *

[The Appellate Body then considered whether the requirements of the chapeau to Article XX had been met and concluded that they had not been. Its reasoning on that issue is considered in the notes following the principal case in Section 13.4, where we examine the meaning of the chapeau to Article XX.]

Notes and Questions

(1) Although the United States ultimately lost its appeal, it expressed great satisfaction with the Appellate Body's analysis of Article XX(g). Past GATT panels had focused, as had the *Gasoline* panel, on whether the GATT-

inconsistent aspect of a measure was "primarily aimed at" conservation. The Appellate Body's decision that it was necessary to look at the broader measure—the baseline establishment rules generally—and examine whether they were aimed at conservation significantly expanded the scope of Article XX(g). Do you agree with the Appellate Body's approach?

(2) The Appellate Body had the occasion to consider again the scope of Article XX(g) in the *Shrimp* case, which we examine in detail in the next section of this chapter dealing with the chapeau to Article XX. In respect of Article XX(g), one of the issues in the *Shrimp* case was a claim that the phrase "exhaustible natural resources" referred only to minerals and not to living things. Not surprisingly, the Appellate Body rejected that argument; there was ample GATT and WTO authority finding other fish and clean air to be exhaustible natural resources. Significantly, however, the Appellate Body scarcely mentioned the prior cases, but rather undertook a wide-ranging analysis of the words at issue in light of contemporary understanding:

128. Textually, Article XX(g) is *not* limited to the conservation of "mineral" or "non-living" natural resources. * * * "[E]xhaustible" natural resources and "renewable" natural resources are [not] mutually exclusive. One lesson that modern biological sciences teach us is that living species, though in principle, capable of reproduction and, in that sense, "renewable", are in certain circumstances indeed susceptible of depletion, exhaustion and extinction, frequently because of human activities. Living resources are just as "finite" as petroleum, iron ore and other non-living resources.

129. The words of Article XX(g), "exhaustible natural resources", were actually crafted more than 50 years ago. They must be read by a treaty interpreter in the light of contemporary concerns of the community of nations about the protection and conservation of the environment. While Article XX was not modified in the Uruguay Round, the preamble attached to the *WTO Agreement* shows that the signatories to that Agreement were, in 1994, fully aware of the importance and legitimacy of environmental protection as a goal of national and international policy. The preamble of the *WTO Agreement*—which informs not only the GATT 1994, but also the other covered agreements—explicitly acknowledges "the objective of *sustainable development*": * * *

130. From the perspective embodied in the preamble of the *WTO Agreement*, we note that the generic term "natural resources" in Article XX(g) is not "static" in its content or reference but is rather "by definition, evolutionary".[7] It is, therefore, pertinent to note that modern international conventions and declarations make frequent references to

---

7. [original note 109] See *Namibia (Legal Consequences) Advisory Opinion* (1971) I.C.J. Rep., p. 31. The International Court of Justice stated that where concepts embodied in a treaty are "by definition, evolutionary", their "interpretation cannot remain unaffected by the subsequent development of law .... Moreover, an international instrument has to be interpreted and applied within the framework of the entire legal system prevailing at the time of the interpretation." See also *Aegean Sea Continental Shelf Case*, (1978) I.C.J. Rep., p. 3; Jennings and Watts (eds.), *Oppenheim's International Law*, 9th ed., Vol. I (Longman's, 1992), p. 1282 and E. Jimenez de Arechaga, "International Law in the Past Third of a Century", (1978–I) 159 *Recueil des Cours* 1, p. 49.

natural resources as embracing both living and non-living resources. [The Appellate Body then referred to, inter alia, the 1982 United Nations Convention on the Law of the Sea; the Convention on Biological Diversity; Agenda 21; the Resolution on Assistance to Developing Countries, adopted in conjunction with the Convention on the Conservation of Migratory Species of Wild Animals; and the Convention on International Trade in Endangered Species of Wild Fauna and Flora ("CITES")].

United States—Restrictions on Importation of Certain Shrimp and Shrimp Products, WT/DS58/AB/R, Appellate Body Report adopted by the DSB on November 6, 1998. Exactly how does the Preamble to the WTO Agreement make the term "natural resources" "by definition, evolutionary"? Of what importance is the establishment of a new organization under a new agreement as of January 1, 1995? Does the Appellate Body's reasoning on the evolutionary nature of generic terms apply to all parts of the WTO Agreement? If not, to which parts does it apply? Does this interpretation suggest that there is a "constitutional", as opposed to a mere contractual, aspect to the WTO Agreement? Is it consistent with the notion of looking to the "ordinary meaning" of the terms of a treaty?

(3) The Appellate Body also considered in *Shrimp,* whether the US statute was "related to" conservation. It expressed itself as follows:

141. In its general design and structure, therefore, Section 609 is not a simple, blanket prohibition of the importation of shrimp imposed without regard to the consequences (or lack thereof) of the mode of harvesting employed upon the incidental capture and mortality of sea turtles. Focusing on the design of the measure here at stake, it appears to us that Section 609, *cum* implementing guidelines, is not disproportionately wide in its scope and reach in relation to the policy objective of protection and conservation of sea turtle species. The means are, in principle, reasonably related to the ends. The means and ends relationship between Section 609 and the legitimate policy of conserving an exhaustible, and, in fact, endangered species, is observably a close and real one, a relationship that is every bit as substantial as that which we found in *United States—Gasoline* between the EPA baseline establishment rules and the conservation of clean air in the United States.

142. In our view, therefore, Section 609 is a measure "relating to" the conservation of an exhaustible natural resource within the meaning of Article XX(g) of the GATT 1994.

Does the Appellate Body simply apply its approach in *Gasoline* here? Or do the phrases "not disproportionately wide in its scope" and "means * * * reasonably related to the ends" suggest additional tests for determining whether a measure is one "relating" to conservation? Should there be such tests? Note that the phrase "primarily aimed at" is not used.

(4) There were inconsistent, but unadopted panel reports that addressed the question of whether Article XX(g) could be invoked to justify measures effectively applicable beyond the territory of a Member. Compare United States—Restrictions on Imports of Tuna (Mexico), DS21/R (September 3, 1991), BISD 39S/155 (not adopted) with United States—Restrictions

on Imports of Tuna (EC), DS29/R (May 20, 1994) (not adopted). In the *Shrimp* case, the Appellate Body wrote the following on that issue:

133. The sea turtle species here at stake, i.e., covered by Section 609, are all known to occur in waters over which the United States exercises jurisdiction. Of course, it is not claimed that *all* populations of these species migrate to, or traverse, at one time or another, waters subject to United States jurisdiction. Neither the appellant nor any of the appellees claims any rights of exclusive ownership over the sea turtles, at least not while they are swimming freely in their natural habitat—the oceans. We do not pass upon the question of whether there is an implied jurisdictional limitation in Article XX(g), and if so, the nature or extent of that limitation. We note only that in the specific circumstances of the case before us, there is a sufficient nexus between the migratory and endangered marine populations involved and the United States for purposes of Article XX(g).

Should there be "an implied jurisdictional limitation" in Article XX(g)?

SECTION 13.4   THE CHAPEAU TO ARTICLE XX

The introductory clause to Article XX, which is commonly referred to as the chapeau, conditions the availability of the Article XX exception for measures listed in the specific clauses as follows:

Subject to the requirement that such measures are not applied in a manner which would constitute a means of arbitrary or unjustifiable discrimination between countries where the same conditions prevail, or a disguised restriction on international trade, nothing in this Agreement shall be construed to prevent the adoption or enforcement by any Member of measures: [(a)-(j)].

The most detailed consideration of the meaning of the chapeau is found in the following case:

UNITED STATES—IMPORT PROHIBITION OF CERTAIN SHRIMP AND SHRIMP PRODUCTS
WT/DS58/AB/R
Appellate Body Report adopted by the DSB on November 6, 1998

[This case involved a prohibition imposed by the United States on the importation of certain shrimp and shrimp products. The roots of the case go back to 1987, when the US issued regulations, pursuant to the 1973 Endangered Species Act, that in their final form required all US shrimp trawlers to use turtle excluder devices ("TEDs") in areas where there is a likelihood that shrimp trawling will interact with sea turtles, subject to certain limited exceptions. The regulations became fully effective in 1990.

In 1989, Section 609 of Public Law 101–162 was enacted (16 USC sec. 1537). Among other things, Section 609(b) imposed, not later than 1 May 1991, an import ban on shrimp harvested with commercial fishing technology which may adversely affect sea turtles. It also provided that the import ban would not apply to harvesting nations that are certified as (i) having a fishing environment (e.g., lack of sea turtles or use of artisinal harvesting methods) which does not pose a threat of the incidental taking of sea turtles in the course of shrimp harvesting or (ii) providing documentary evidence of a regulatory program governing the incidental taking of sea turtles in the course of shrimp trawling comparable to the US program *and* having an average rate of incidental taking of sea turtles comparable to that of US vessels.

The State Department's 1991 Guidelines limited the geographical scope of the import ban imposed by Section 609 to countries in the wider Caribbean/western Atlantic region, and granted these countries a three-year phase-in period. In December 1995, the US Court of International Trade (CIT) found that this geographical limitation violated Section 609 and directed the State Department to extend the ban worldwide not later than May 1, 1996. On April 19, 1996, the State Department issued its 1996 Guidelines, extending Section 609 to all foreign countries effective May 1, 1996.

The 1996 Guidelines provided that all shrimp imported into the US must be accompanied by a form attesting that the shrimp was harvested either in the waters of a certified nation or under conditions that do not adversely affect sea turtles. In late 1996, the CIT ruled that the 1996 Guidelines were in violation of Section 609 in allowing the import of shrimp from non-certified countries (except where taken manually by methods not harming sea turtles). In 1998, the US Court of Appeals vacated the CIT ruling. In practice, however, import of TED-caught shrimp from non-certified countries was not possible while the dispute was pending.

The panel report concluded that the measures at issue violated Article XI and that they were not covered by Article XX. The US had not contested that the measures violated GATT rules but rather claimed they were permitted by Article XX(g), and it appealed the panel's rejection of that defense. The Appellate Body concluded that the measure fell within the scope of Article XX(g), as explained in Notes 2 and 3 to the preceding section.

Then, before turning to a detailed analysis of whether the measures satisfied the terms of the chapeau, the Appellate Body underlined that the Uruguay Round negotiators had effectively qualified the original objectives of GATT 1947 by adding a clause to the preamble to the WTO Agreement on the objective of sustainable development and the protection and preservation of the environment. It went on to note "that this language demonstrates a recognition by WTO negotiators that optimal use of the world's resources should be made in accordance with the objective of sustainable development. As this preambular language reflects the intentions of negotiators of the *WTO Agreement*, we believe it must add color, texture and shading to our interpretation of the agreements annexed to the *WTO Agreement*, in this case, the GATT 1994" (para. 153). It then recalled other more recent developments that in its view helped to elucidate the objectives of WTO members with respect to the relationship between trade and the environment, highlighting in particular the establishment of a permanent Committee on Trade and Environment (the "CTE").]

150.   We commence the second tier of our analysis with an examination of the ordinary meaning of the words of the chapeau. The precise language of the chapeau requires that a measure not be applied in a manner which would constitute a means of "arbitrary or unjustifiable discrimination between countries where the same conditions prevail" or a "disguised restriction on international trade." * * * In order for a measure to be applied in a manner which would constitute "arbitrary or unjustifiable discrimination between countries where the same conditions prevail", three elements must exist. First, the application of the measure must result in *discrimination*. As we stated in *United States— Gasoline*, the nature and quality of this discrimination is different from the discrimination in the treatment of products which was already found to be inconsistent with one of the substantive obligations of the GATT 1994, such as Articles I, III or XI. Second, the discrimination must be *arbitrary* or *unjustifiable* in character. We will examine this element of *arbitrariness* or *unjustifiability* in detail below. Third, this discrimination must occur *between countries where the same conditions prevail*. In *United States—Gasoline*, we accepted the assumption of the participants in that appeal that such discrimination could occur not only between different exporting Members, but also between exporting Members and the importing Member concerned. Thus, the standards embodied in the language of the chapeau are not only different from the requirements of Article XX(g); they are also different from the standard used in determining that Section 609 is violative of the substantive rules of Article XI:1 of the GATT 1994.

* * *

156.   Turning then to the chapeau of Article XX, we consider that it embodies the recognition on the part of WTO Members of the need to maintain a balance of rights and obligations between the right of a Member to invoke one or another of the exceptions of Article XX, specified in paragraphs (a) to (j), on the one hand, and the substantive rights of the other Members under the GATT 1994, on the other hand. Exercise by one Member of its right to invoke an exception, such as Article XX(g), if abused or misused, will, to that extent, erode or render naught the substantive treaty rights in, for example, Article XI:1, of other Members. Similarly, because the GATT 1994 itself makes available the exceptions of Article XX, in recognition of the legitimate nature of the policies and interests there embodied, the right to invoke one of those exceptions is not to be rendered illusory. The same concept may be expressed from a slightly different angle of vision, thus, a balance must be struck between the *right* of a Member to invoke an exception under Article XX and the *duty* of that same Member to respect the treaty rights

of the other Members. To permit one Member to abuse or misuse its right to invoke an exception would be effectively to allow that Member to degrade its own treaty obligations as well as to devalue the treaty rights of other Members. If the abuse or misuse is sufficiently grave or extensive, the Member, in effect, reduces its treaty obligation to a merely facultative one and dissolves its juridical character, and, in so doing, negates altogether the treaty rights of other Members. The chapeau was installed at the head of the list of "General Exceptions" in Article XX to prevent such far-reaching consequences.

157. In our view, the language of the chapeau makes clear that each of the exceptions in paragraphs (a) to (j) of Article XX is a *limited and conditional* exception from the substantive obligations contained in the other provisions of the GATT 1994, that is to say, the ultimate availability of the exception is subject to the compliance by the invoking Member with the requirements of the chapeau. This interpretation of the chapeau is confirmed by its negotiating history * * * [which] confirms that the paragraphs of Article XX set forth *limited and conditional* exceptions from the obligations of the substantive provisions of the GATT. Any measure, to qualify finally for exception, must also satisfy the requirements of the chapeau. This is a fundamental part of the balance of rights and obligations struck by the original framers of the GATT 1947.

158. The chapeau of Article XX is, in fact, but one expression of the principle of good faith. This principle, at once a general principle of law and a general principle of international law, controls the exercise of rights by states. One application of this general principle, the application widely known as the doctrine of *abus de droit*, prohibits the abusive exercise of a state's rights and enjoins that whenever the assertion of a right "impinges on the field covered by [a] treaty obligation, it must be exercised bona fide, that is to say, reasonably." An abusive exercise by a Member of its own treaty right thus results in a breach of the treaty rights of the other Members and, as well, a violation of the treaty obligation of the Member so acting. Having said this, our task here is to interpret the language of the chapeau, seeking additional interpretative guidance, as appropriate, from the general principles of international law.

159. The task of interpreting and applying the chapeau is, hence, essentially the delicate one of locating and marking out a line of equilibrium between the right of a Member to invoke an exception under Article XX and the rights of the other Members under varying substantive provisions (e.g., Article XI) of the GATT 1994, so that neither of the competing rights will cancel out the other and thereby distort and nullify or impair the balance of rights and obligations constructed by the Members themselves in that Agreement. The location of the line of equilibrium, as expressed in the chapeau, is not fixed and unchanging; the line moves as the kind and the shape of the measures at stake vary and as the facts making up specific cases differ.

160. With these general considerations in mind, we address now the issue of whether the *application* of the United States measure, although the measure itself falls within the terms of Article XX(g), nevertheless constitutes "a means of arbitrary or unjustifiable discrimination between countries where the same conditions prevail" or "a disguised restriction on international trade". We address, in other words, whether the application of this measure constitutes an abuse or misuse of the provisional justification made available by Article XX(g). We note, preliminarily, that the application of a measure may be characterized as amounting to an abuse or misuse of an exception of Article XX not only when the detailed operating provisions of the measure prescribe the arbitrary or unjustifiable activity, but also where a measure, otherwise fair and just on its face, is actually applied in an arbitrary or unjustifiable manner. The standards of the chapeau, in our view, project both substantive and procedural requirements.

161. We scrutinize first whether Section 609 has been applied in a manner constituting "unjustifiable discrimination between countries where the same conditions prevail". Perhaps the most conspicuous flaw in this measure's application relates to its intended and actual coercive effect on the specific policy decisions made by foreign governments, Members of the WTO. Section 609, in its application, is, in effect, an economic embargo which requires *all other exporting Members*, if they wish to exercise their GATT rights, to adopt *essentially the same* policy (together with an approved enforcement program) as that applied to, and enforced on, United States domestic shrimp trawlers. As enacted by the Congress of the United States, the *statutory* provisions of Section 609(b)(2)(A) and (B) do not, in themselves, *require* that other WTO Members adopt *essentially the same* policies and enforcement practices as the United States. Viewed alone, the statute appears to permit a degree of discretion or flexibility in how the standards for determining comparability might be applied, in practice, to other countries. However, any flexibility that may have been intended by Congress when it enacted the statutory provision has been effectively eliminated in the implementation of that policy through the 1996 Guidelines promulgated by the Department of State and through the practice of the administrators in making certification determinations.

162. According to the 1996 Guidelines, certification "shall be made" under Section 609(b)(2)(A) and (B) if an exporting country's program includes a requirement that all commercial shrimp trawl vessels operating in waters in which there is a likelihood of intercepting sea turtles use, at all times, TEDs comparable in effectiveness to those used in the United States. Under these Guidelines, any exceptions to the requirement of the use of TEDs must be comparable to those of the United States program. Furthermore, the harvesting country must have in place a "credible enforcement effort". The language in the 1996 Guidelines is mandatory: certification "shall be made" if these conditions are fulfilled. However, we understand that these rules are also applied in an *exclusive* manner. That is, the 1996 Guidelines specify the

only way that a harvesting country's regulatory program can be deemed "comparable" to the United States' program, and, therefore, they define the *only* way that a harvesting nation can be certified under Section 609(b)(2)(A) and (B). Although the 1996 Guidelines state that, in making a comparability determination, the Department of State "shall also take into account other measures the harvesting nation undertakes to protect sea turtles", in practice, the competent government officials only look to see whether there is a regulatory program requiring the use of TEDs or one that comes within one of the extremely limited exceptions available to United States shrimp trawl vessels.

163. The actual *application* of the measure, through the implementation of the 1996 Guidelines and the regulatory practice of administrators, *requires* other WTO Members to adopt a regulatory program that is not merely *comparable*, but rather *essentially the same*, as that applied to the United States shrimp trawl vessels. Thus, the effect of the application of Section 609 is to establish a rigid and unbending standard by which United States officials determine whether or not countries will be certified, thus granting or refusing other countries the right to export shrimp to the United States. Other specific policies and measures that an exporting country may have adopted for the protection and conservation of sea turtles are not taken into account, in practice, by the administrators making the comparability determination.

164. We understand that the United States also applies a uniform standard throughout its territory, regardless of the particular conditions existing in certain parts of the country. * * * It may be quite acceptable for a government, in adopting and implementing a domestic policy, to adopt a single standard applicable to all its citizens throughout that country. However, it is not acceptable, in international trade relations, for one WTO Member to use an economic embargo to *require* other Members to adopt essentially the same comprehensive regulatory program, to achieve a certain policy goal, as that in force within that Member's territory, *without* taking into consideration different conditions which may occur in the territories of those other Members.

165. Furthermore, when this dispute was before the Panel and before us, the United States did not permit imports of shrimp harvested by commercial shrimp trawl vessels using TEDs comparable in effectiveness to those required in the United States if those shrimp originated in waters of countries not certified under Section 609. In other words, *shrimp caught using methods identical to those employed in the United States* have been excluded from the United States market solely because they have been caught in waters of *countries that have not been certified by the United States*. The resulting situation is difficult to reconcile with the declared policy objective of protecting and conserving sea turtles. This suggests to us that this measure, in its application, is more concerned with effectively influencing WTO Members to adopt essentially the same comprehensive regulatory regime as that applied by the United States to its domestic shrimp trawlers, even though many of those Members may be differently situated. We believe that discrimina-

tion results not only when countries in which the same conditions prevail are differently treated, but also when the application of the measure at issue does not allow for any inquiry into the appropriateness of the regulatory program for the conditions prevailing in those exporting countries.

166. Another aspect of the application of Section 609 that bears heavily in any appraisal of justifiable or unjustifiable discrimination is the failure of the United States to engage the appellees, as well as other Members exporting shrimp to the United States, in serious, across-the-board negotiations with the objective of concluding bilateral or multilateral agreements for the protection and conservation of sea turtles, before enforcing the import prohibition against the shrimp exports of those other Members. The relevant factual finding of the Panel reads:

> . . . However, *we have no evidence that the United States actually undertook negotiations on an agreement on sea turtle conservation techniques which would have included the complainants before the imposition of the import ban as a result of the CIT judgement.* From the replies of the parties to our question on this subject, in particular that of the United States, we understand that the United States did not propose the negotiation of an agreement to any of the complainants until after the conclusion of negotiations on the Inter–American Convention for the Protection and Conservation of Sea Turtles, in September 1996, i.e. well after the deadline for the imposition of the import ban of 1 May 1996. Even then, it seems that the efforts made merely consisted of an exchange of documents. We therefore conclude that, in spite of the possibility offered by its legislation, the United States did not enter into negotiations before it imposed the import ban. As we consider that the measures sought by the United States were of the type that would normally require international cooperation, we do not find it necessary to examine whether parties entered into negotiations in good faith and whether the United States, absent any result, would have been entitled to adopt unilateral measures. (emphasis added)

167. *A propos* this failure to have prior consistent recourse to diplomacy as an instrument of environmental protection policy, which produces discriminatory impacts on countries exporting shrimp to the United States with which no international agreements are reached or even seriously attempted, a number of points must be made. First, the Congress of the United States expressly recognized the importance of securing international agreements for the protection and conservation of the sea turtle species in enacting this law. Section 609(a) *directs* the Secretary of State to:

> (1) *initiate negotiations as soon as possible for the development of bilateral or multilateral agreements with other nations* for the protection and conservation of such species of sea turtles;

> (2) *initiate negotiations as soon as possible* with all foreign governments which are engaged in, or which have persons or companies

engaged in, commercial fishing operations which, as determined by the Secretary of Commerce, may affect adversely such species of sea turtles, *for the purpose of entering into bilateral and multilateral treaties with such countries to protect such species of sea turtles*;
* * *

Apart from the negotiation of the Inter–American Convention for the Protection and Conservation of Sea Turtles (the "Inter–American Convention") which concluded in 1996, the record before the Panel does not indicate any serious, substantial efforts to carry out these express directions of Congress.

168. Second, the protection and conservation of highly migratory species of sea turtles, that is, the very policy objective of the measure, demands concerted and cooperative efforts on the part of the many countries whose waters are traversed in the course of recurrent sea turtle migrations. The need for, and the appropriateness of, such efforts have been recognized in the WTO itself as well as in a significant number of other international instruments and declarations. As stated earlier, the Decision on Trade and Environment, which provided for the establishment of the CTE and set out its terms of reference, refers to both the Rio Declaration on Environment and Development and Agenda 21. Of particular relevance is Principle 12 of the Rio Declaration on Environment and Development, which states, in part:

> Unilateral actions to deal with environmental challenges outside the jurisdiction of the importing country should be avoided. *Environmental measures addressing transboundary or global environmental problems should, as far as possible, be based on international consensus.* (emphasis added)

[The Appellate Body then quoted analogous language calling for multilateral cooperation from Agenda 21 (para, 2.22(i)); the Convention on Biological Diversity (art. 5); and the Convention on the Conservation of Migratory Species of Wild Animals.] Furthermore, we note that WTO Members in the Report of the CTE, forming part of the Report of the General Council to Ministers on the occasion of the Singapore Ministerial Conference, endorsed and supported:

> ... *multilateral solutions based on international cooperation and consensus as the best and most effective way for governments to tackle environmental problems of a transboundary or global nature.* WTO Agreements and multilateral environmental agreements (MEAs) are representative of efforts of the international community to pursue *shared goals*, and in the development of a mutually supportive relationship between them, *due respect must be afforded to both.* (emphasis added)

169. Third, the United States did negotiate and conclude one regional international agreement for the protection and conservation of sea turtles: The Inter–American Convention. This Convention was opened for signature on 1 December 1996 and has been signed by five countries, in addition to the United States, and four of these countries

are currently certified under Section 609. This Convention has not yet been ratified by any of its signatories. The Inter–American Convention provides that each party shall take "appropriate and necessary measures" for the protection, conservation and recovery of sea turtle populations and their habitats within such party's land territory and in maritime areas with respect to which it exercises sovereign rights or jurisdiction. Such measures include, notably,

> [t]he reduction, to the greatest extent practicable, of the incidental capture, retention, harm or mortality of sea turtles in the course of fishing activities, through the appropriate regulation of such activities, as well as the development, improvement and use of appropriate gear, devices or techniques, including the use of turtle excluder devices (TEDs) pursuant to the provisions of Annex III [of the Convention].

Article XV of the Inter–American Convention also provides, in part:

Article XV

Trade Measures

1. *In implementing this Convention, the Parties shall act in accordance with the provisions of the Agreement establishing the World Trade Organization* (WTO), as adopted at Marrakesh in 1994, including its annexes.

2. In particular, and *with respect to the subject-matter of this Convention, the Parties shall act in accordance with the provisions of* the Agreement on Technical Barriers to Trade contained in Annex 1 of the WTO Agreement, as well as *Article XI of the General Agreement on Tariffs and Trade of 1994.* ... (emphasis added)

170.   The juxtaposition of (a) the *consensual* undertakings to put in place regulations providing for, *inter alia*, use of TEDs *jointly determined* to be suitable for a particular party's maritime areas, with (b) the reaffirmation of the parties' obligations under the *WTO Agreement*, including the *Agreement on Technical Barriers to Trade* and Article XI of the GATT 1994, suggests that the parties to the Inter–American Convention together marked out the equilibrium line to which we referred earlier. The Inter–American Convention demonstrates the conviction of its signatories, including the United States, that consensual and multilateral procedures are available and feasible for the establishment of programs for the conservation of sea turtles. Moreover, the Inter–American Convention emphasizes the continuing validity and significance of Article XI of the GATT 1994, and of the obligations of the *WTO Agreement* generally, in maintaining the balance of rights and obligations under the *WTO Agreement* among the signatories of that Convention.

171.   The Inter–American Convention thus provides convincing demonstration that an alternative course of action was reasonably open to the United States for securing the legitimate policy goal of its

measure, a course of action other than the unilateral and non-consensual procedures of the import prohibition under Section 609. It is relevant to observe that an import prohibition is, ordinarily, the heaviest "weapon" in a Member's armory of trade measures. The record does not, however, show that serious efforts were made by the United States to negotiate similar agreements with any other country or group of countries before (and, as far as the record shows, after) Section 609 was enforced on a world-wide basis on May 1, 1996. Finally, the record also does not show that the appellant, the United States, attempted to have recourse to such international mechanisms as exist to achieve cooperative efforts to protect and conserve sea turtles[8] before imposing the import ban.

172. Clearly, the United States negotiated seriously with some, but not with other Members (including the appellees), that export shrimp to the United States. The effect is plainly discriminatory and, in our view, unjustifiable. The unjustifiable nature of this discrimination emerges clearly when we consider the cumulative effects of the failure of the United States to pursue negotiations for establishing consensual means of protection and conservation of the living marine resources here involved, notwithstanding the explicit statutory direction in Section 609 itself to initiate negotiations as soon as possible for the development of bilateral and multilateral agreements. The principal consequence of this failure may be seen in the resulting unilateralism evident in the application of Section 609. As we have emphasized earlier, the policies relating to the necessity for use of particular kinds of TEDs in various maritime areas, and the operating details of these policies, are all shaped by the Department of State, without the participation of the exporting Members. The system and processes of certification are established and administered by the United States agencies alone. The decision-making involved in the grant, denial or withdrawal of certification to the exporting Members, is, accordingly, also unilateral. The unilateral character of the application of Section 609 heightens the disruptive and discriminatory influence of the import prohibition and underscores its unjustifiability.

173. The application of Section 609, through the implementing guidelines together with administrative practice, also resulted in other differential treatment among various countries desiring certification. Under the 1991 and 1993 Guidelines, to be certifiable, fourteen countries in the wider Caribbean/western Atlantic region had to commit themselves to require the use of TEDs on all commercial shrimp trawling vessels by 1 May 1994. These fourteen countries had a "phase-in" period of three years during which their respective shrimp trawling sectors could adjust to the requirement of the use of TEDs. With respect to all other countries exporting shrimp to the United States (including the

---

8. [original note 174] While the United States is a party to CITES, it did not make any attempt to raise the issue of sea turtle mortality due to shrimp trawling in the CITES Standing Committee as a subject requiring concerted action by states. In this context, we note that the United States, for example, has not signed the Convention on the Conservation of Migratory Species of Wild Animals or UNCLOS, and has not ratified the Convention on Biological Diversity.

appellees, India, Malaysia, Pakistan and Thailand), on December 29, 1995, the United States Court of International Trade directed the Department of State to apply the import ban on a world-wide basis not later than May 1, 1996. On April 19, 1996, the 1996 Guidelines were issued by the Department of State bringing shrimp harvested in *all* foreign countries within the scope of Section 609, effective May 1, 1996. Thus, all countries that were not among the fourteen in the wider Caribbean/western Atlantic region had only four months to implement the requirement of compulsory use of TEDs. We acknowledge that the greatly differing periods for putting into operation the requirement for use of TEDs resulted from decisions of the Court of International Trade. Even so, this does not relieve the United States of the legal consequences of the discriminatory impact of the decisions of that Court. The United States, like all other Members of the WTO and of the general community of states, bears responsibility for acts of all its departments of government, including its judiciary.

174.   The length of the "phase-in" period is not inconsequential for exporting countries desiring certification. That period relates directly to the onerousness of the burdens of complying with the requisites of certification and the practical feasibility of locating and developing alternative export markets for shrimp. The shorter that period, the heavier the burdens of compliance, particularly where an applicant has a large number of trawler vessels, and the greater the difficulties of re-orienting the harvesting country's shrimp exports. The shorter that period, in net effect, the heavier the influence of the import ban. The United States sought to explain the marked difference between "phase-in" periods granted to the fourteen wider Caribbean/western Atlantic countries and those allowed the rest of the shrimp exporting countries. The United States asserted that the longer time-period was justified by the then undeveloped character of TED technology, while the shorter period was later made possible by the improvements in that technology. This explanation is less than persuasive, for it does not address the administrative and financial costs and the difficulties of governments in putting together and enacting the necessary regulatory programs and "credible enforcement effort", and in implementing the compulsory use of TEDs on hundreds, if not thousands, of shrimp trawl vessels.

175.   Differing treatment of different countries desiring certification is also observable in the differences in the levels of effort made by the United States in transferring the required TED technology to specific countries. Far greater efforts to transfer that technology success-fully were made to certain exporting countries—basically the fourteen wider Caribbean/western Atlantic countries cited earlier—than to other exporting countries, including the appellees. The level of these efforts is probably related to the length of the "phase-in" periods granted—the longer the "phase-in" period, the higher the possible level of efforts at technology transfer. Because compliance with the requirements of certification realistically assumes successful TED technology transfer, low or merely nominal efforts at achieving that transfer will, in all probability,

result in fewer countries being able to satisfy the certification requirements under Section 609, within the very limited "phase-in" periods allowed them.

176.   When the foregoing differences in the means of application of Section 609 to various shrimp exporting countries are considered in their cumulative effect, we find, and so hold, that those differences in treatment constitute "unjustifiable discrimination" between exporting countries desiring certification in order to gain access to the United States shrimp market within the meaning of the chapeau of Article XX.

* * *

185.   In reaching these conclusions, we wish to underscore what we have *not* decided in this appeal. We have *not* decided that the protection and preservation of the environment is of no significance to the Members of the WTO. Clearly, it is. We have *not* decided that the sovereign nations that are Members of the WTO cannot adopt effective measures to protect endangered species, such as sea turtles. Clearly, they can and should. And we have *not* decided that sovereign states should not act together bilaterally, plurilaterally or multilaterally, either within the WTO or in other international fora, to protect endangered species or to otherwise protect the environment. Clearly, they should and do.

186.   What we *have* decided in this appeal is simply this: although the measure of the United States in dispute in this appeal serves an environmental objective that is recognized as legitimate under paragraph (g) of Article XX of the GATT 1994, this measure has been applied by the United States in a manner which constitutes arbitrary and unjustifiable discrimination between Members of the WTO, contrary to the requirements of the chapeau of Article XX. For all of the specific reasons outlined in this Report, this measure does not qualify for the exemption that Article XX of the GATT 1994 affords to measures which serve certain recognized, legitimate environmental purposes but which, at the same time, are not applied in a manner that constitutes a means of arbitrary or unjustifiable discrimination between countries where the same conditions prevail or a disguised restriction on international trade. As we emphasized in *United States—Gasoline*, WTO Members are free to adopt their own policies aimed at protecting the environment as long as, in so doing, they fulfill their obligations and respect the rights of other Members under the *WTO Agreement*.

Notes and Questions

(1) The Appellate Body also found that Section 609 had been applied in a manner constituting "arbitrary discrimination". First, it noted that there was little or no flexibility in how officials made the certification determinations and that this rigidity and inflexibility constituted "arbitrary discrimination" within the meaning of the chapeau. Second, it found that the certification process was not transparent or predictable. It highlighted that there was no formal opportunity for an applicant country to be heard, or to respond to any arguments that might be made against it, in the course of the

certification process before a decision to grant or to deny certification is made. Countries whose applications are denied also do not receive notice of such denial (other than by omission from the list of approved applications) or of the reasons for the denial. No procedure for review of, or appeal from, a denial of an application is provided. "It appears to us that, effectively, exporting Members applying for certification whose applications are rejected are denied basic fairness and due process, and are discriminated against, *vis-à-vis* those Members which are granted certification" (para. 181). The Appellate Body also noted that these procedural defects were "contrary to the spirit, if not the letter, of Article X:3 of the GATT 1994" (para. 183). The potential scope (and, indeed, the precise source) of this due process requirement remains somewhat unclear, but it could obviously have major ramifications over time.

(2) The panel in *Shrimp* had been particularly concerned with the unilateral nature of the U.S. measure and the fact that it was designed to force other countries to change conservation policy across the board (as opposed simply to meet U.S. production standards in respect of products exported to the United States). In the panel's view, this broader purpose was simply not permitted by the chapeau. In commenting on this view, the Appellate Body stated:

> 121. * * * The Panel, in effect, constructed an *a priori* test that purports to define a category of measures which, *ratione materiae*, fall outside the justifying protection of Article XX's chapeau. In the present case, the Panel found that the United States measure at stake fell within that class of excluded measures because Section 609 conditions access to the domestic shrimp market of the United States on the adoption by exporting countries of certain conservation policies prescribed by the United States. It appears to us, however, that conditioning access to a Member's domestic market on whether exporting Members comply with, or adopt, a policy or policies unilaterally prescribed by the importing Member may, to some degree, be a common aspect of measures falling within the scope of one or another of the exceptions (a) to (j) of Article XX. Paragraphs (a) to (j) comprise measures that are recognized as *exceptions to substantive obligations* established in the GATT 1994, because the domestic policies embodied in such measures have been recognized as important and legitimate in character. It is not necessary to assume that requiring from exporting countries compliance with, or adoption of, certain policies (although covered in principle by one or another of the exceptions) prescribed by the importing country, renders a measure *a priori* incapable of justification under Article XX. Such an interpretation renders most, if not all, of the specific exceptions of Article XX inutile, a result abhorrent to the principles of interpretation we are bound to apply.

(3) In the *Gasoline* case (see Section 13.3 supra), the Appellate Body concluded that the U.S. measures at issue did not meet the terms of the chapeau for the following reasons (p. 27):

> We have above located two omissions on the part of the United States: to explore adequately means, including in particular cooperation with the governments of Venezuela and Brazil, of mitigating the administra-

tive problems relied on as justification by the United States for rejecting individual baselines for foreign refiners; and to count the costs for foreign refiners that would result from the imposition of statutory baselines [in contrast to its view that application of the statutory baseline to domestic producers in 1995 would have been physically and financially impossible]. In our view, these two omissions go well beyond what was necessary for the Panel to determine that a violation of Article III:4 had occurred in the first place. The resulting discrimination must have been foreseen, and was not merely inadvertent or unavoidable. In the light of the foregoing, our conclusion is that the baseline establishment rules in the Gasoline Rule, in their application, constitute "unjustifiable discrimination" and a "disguised restriction on international trade."

There was no explanation of why these two shortcomings constituted a disguised restriction on international trade in addition to being discriminatory. The lack of consultations or negotiations with foreign governments was a major factor in the *Shrimp* case. Where else in this chapter has a failure to consider the excessive costs imposed on imports (as opposed to domestic products) been a factor in determining the applicability of Article XX?

(4) Precisely why did the Appellate Body find that the US actions in *Shrimp* constituted unjustifiable or arbitrary discrimination? In respect of each of these reasons, what would the US have to do to bring its measure into conformity with its WTO obligations? Consider how the Appellate Body dealt with these issues:

UNITED STATES—IMPORT PROHIBITION OF CERTAIN SHRIMP AND SHRIMP PRODUCTS

(Recourse to Article 21.5 by Malaysia)
WT/DS58/AB/RW
Appellate Body Report adopted by the DSB on November 21, 2001

[Malaysia brought an Article 21.5 action claiming that the United States had failed to bring Section 609 into conformity with its WTO obligations within the agreed-upon reasonable period of time for implementation. Thus, the compliance panel focused on the actions taken by the United States subsequent to the original *Shrimp* decision. The panel described the US implementing measures as (i) the adoption of the 1999 Guidelines and (ii) US efforts to negotiate an agreement on the conservation of sea turtles with the Governments of the Indian Ocean region and to provide technical assistance on the use of TEDs.

According to the 1999 Guidelines,[1] Section 609 does not apply to shrimp or products of shrimp harvested under specified conditions in which harvesting does not adversely affect sea turtles. These conditions include shrimp harvested in aquaculture; shrimp harvested by trawlers using TEDs comparable in effectiveness to those required in the United States; shrimp harvested exclusively by artisanal means; and shrimp

---

1. 64 Fed. Reg. 36949 (1999).

harvested in any other manner that the State Department determines does not pose a threat of the incidental taking of sea turtles.

Under the 1999 Guidelines, importation of shrimp into the US must be accompanied by a declaration attesting that the shrimp at issue were harvested (i) under the conditions defined above or (ii) in waters subject to the jurisdiction of a nation currently certified pursuant to Section 609.

The 1999 Guidelines provide for certification on the basis that the particular fishing environment of the harvesting nation does not pose a threat of incidental taking of sea turtles (e.g., the relevant species of sea turtles are not found in its waters; shrimp are harvested exclusively by means that do not pose a threat to sea turtles, e.g., artisanal means; shrimp trawling takes place exclusively in waters in which sea turtles do not occur). The Guidelines also provide for certification on the basis that a government has adopted and credibly enforced a TEDs program. Moreover, they also allow for the possibility that a country may be certified on the basis of having a regulatory programme not involving the use of TEDs if it demonstrates that it has implemented and is enforcing a comparably effective regulatory program to protect sea turtles in the course of shrimp trawl fishing without the use of TEDs. In making the latter determination, the State Department is required to take fully into account any demonstrated differences between the shrimp fishing conditions in the United States and in the country in question. In either case, there is also a requirement that the rate of incidental taking of sea turtles must be comparable to the US rate.

The Revised Guidelines also revise the procedures under which the certification process operates. They also indicate that they may be revised in the future to take into consideration additional information on the interaction between sea turtles and shrimp fisheries, changes in the US program and in light of the results of pending litigation in US courts.

The Article 21.5 panel found that the US had made adequate efforts to negotiate an agreement with South East Asia nations. It also concluded that the US had satisfactorily dealt with the other aspects of the unjustifiable discrimination found by the Appellate Body, which it noted were agreed by the parties to be: (i) the insufficient flexibility of the 1996 Guidelines, in particular the absence of consideration of the different conditions that may exist in the exporting nations; (ii) the prohibition of importation of shrimp caught in uncertified countries, even when that shrimp had been caught using TEDs; (iii) the length of the "phase-in" period; and (iv) the differences in the level of efforts made by the United States to transfer successfully TED technology to exporting countries. Similarly, it found that the US had corrected the problems of arbitrary discrimination found by the Appellate Body through the adoption of new procedures.

On appeal Malaysia's arguments concerned (i) the nature and extent of the duty of the United States to pursue international cooperation in protecting and conserving endangered sea turtles and (ii) the flexibility of the Revised Guidelines.]

The Nature and the Extent of the Duty of the United States to Pursue International Cooperation in the Protection and Conservation of Sea Turtles

119. * * * In *United States—Shrimp*, we stated that the measure at issue there resulted in "unjustifiable discrimination", in part because, as applied, the United States treated WTO Members differently. The United States had adopted a cooperative approach with WTO Members from the Caribbean/Western Atlantic region, with whom it had concluded a multilateral agreement on the protection and conservation of sea turtles, namely the Inter–American Convention. Yet the United States had not, we found, pursued the negotiation of such a multilateral agreement with other exporting Members, including Malaysia and the other complaining WTO Members in that case.

* * *

122. We concluded in *United States—Shrimp* that, to avoid "arbitrary or unjustifiable discrimination", the United States had to provide all exporting countries "similar opportunities to negotiate" an international agreement. Given the specific mandate contained in Section 609, and given the decided preference for multilateral approaches voiced by WTO Members and others in the international community in various international agreements for the protection and conservation of endangered sea turtles that were cited in our previous Report, the United States, in our view, would be expected to make good faith efforts to reach international agreements that are comparable from one forum of negotiation to the other. The negotiations need not be identical. Indeed, no two negotiations can ever be identical, or lead to identical results. Yet the negotiations must be *comparable* in the sense that comparable efforts are made, comparable resources are invested, and comparable energies are devoted to securing an international agreement. So long as such comparable efforts are made, it is more likely that "arbitrary or unjustifiable discrimination" will be avoided between countries where an importing Member concludes an agreement with one group of countries, but fails to do so with another group of countries.

123. Under the chapeau of Article XX, an importing Member may not treat its trading partners in a manner that would constitute "arbitrary or unjustifiable discrimination". With respect to this measure, the United States could conceivably respect this obligation, and the conclusion of an international agreement might nevertheless not be possible despite the serious, good faith efforts of the United States. Requiring that a multilateral agreement be *concluded* by the United States in order to avoid "arbitrary or unjustifiable discrimination" in applying its measure would mean that any country party to the negotiations with the United States, whether a WTO Member or not, would have, in effect, a veto over whether the United States could fulfill its WTO obligations. Such a requirement would not be reasonable. For a variety of reasons, it may be possible to conclude an agreement with one group of countries but not another. The conclusion of a multilateral agreement requires the

cooperation and commitment of many countries. In our view, the United States cannot be held to have engaged in "arbitrary or unjustifiable discrimination" under Article XX solely because one international negotiation resulted in an agreement while another did not.

124. As we stated in *United States—Shrimp*, "the protection and conservation of highly migratory species of sea turtles … demands concerted and cooperative efforts on the part of the many countries whose waters are traversed in the course of recurrent sea turtle migrations". Further, the "need for, and the appropriateness of, such efforts have been recognized in the WTO itself as well as in a significant number of other international instruments and declarations". For example, Principle 12 of the Rio Declaration on Environment and Development states, in part, that "[e]nvironmental measures addressing transboundary or global environmental problems should, as far as possible, be based on international consensus". Clearly, and "as far as possible", a multilateral approach is strongly preferred. Yet it is one thing to *prefer* a multilateral approach in the application of a measure that is provisionally justified under one of the subparagraphs of Article XX of the GATT 1994; it is another to require the *conclusion* of a multilateral agreement as a condition of avoiding "arbitrary or unjustifiable discrimination" under the chapeau of Article XX. We see, in this case, no such requirement.

* * *

130. * * * The Panel compared the efforts of the United States to negotiate the Inter–American Convention with one group of exporting WTO Members with the efforts made by the United States to negotiate a similar agreement with another group of exporting WTO Members. The Panel rightly used the Inter–American Convention as a factual reference in this exercise of comparison. It was all the more relevant to do so given that the Inter–American Convention was the only international agreement that the Panel could have used in such a comparison. As we read the Panel Report, it is clear to us that the Panel attached a relative value to the Inter–American Convention in making this comparison, but did not view the Inter–American Convention in any way as an absolute standard. Thus, we disagree with Malaysia's submission that the Panel raised the Inter–American Convention to the rank of a "legal standard". The mere use by the Panel of the Inter–American Convention *as a basis for a comparison* did not transform the Inter–American Convention into a "legal standard". Furthermore, although the Panel could have chosen a more appropriate word than "benchmark" to express its views, Malaysia is mistaken in equating the mere use of the word "benchmark", as it was used by the Panel, with the establishment of a legal standard.

131. The Panel noted that while "factual circumstances may influence the duration of the process or the end result, … any effort alleged to be a 'serious good faith effort' must be assessed against the efforts made in relation to the conclusion of the Inter–American Convention." Such a comparison is a central element of the exercise to determine

whether there is "unjustifiable discrimination". The Panel then analyzed the negotiation process in the Indian Ocean and South–East Asia region to determine whether the efforts made by the United States in those negotiations were serious, good faith efforts comparable to those made in relation with the Inter–American Convention. In conducting this analysis, the Panel referred to the following elements:

— A document communicated on 14 October 1998 by the United States Department of State to a number of countries of the Indian Ocean and the South–East Asia region. This document contained possible elements of a regional convention on sea turtles in this region.

— The contribution of the United States to a symposium held in Sabah on 15–17 July 1999. The Sabah Symposium led to the adoption of a Declaration calling for the negotiation and implementation of a regional agreement throughout the Indian Ocean and South–East Asia region.

— The Perth Conference in October 1999, where participating governments, including the United States, committed themselves to developing an international agreement on sea turtles for the Indian Ocean and South–East Asia region.

— The contribution of the United States to the Kuantan round of negotiations, 11–14 July 2000. This first round of negotiations towards the conclusion of a regional agreement resulted in the adoption of the Memorandum of Understanding on the Conservation and Management of Marine Turtles and their Habitats of the Indian Ocean and South–East Asia (the "South–East Asian MOU"). The Final Act of the Kuantan meeting provided that before the South–East Asian MOU can be finalized, a Conservation and Management Plan must be negotiated and annexed to the South–East Asian MOU. At the time of the Panel proceedings, the Conservation and Management Plan was still being drafted.

132.   On this basis and, in particular, on the basis of the "contribution of the United States to the steps that led to the Kuantan meeting and its contribution to the Kuantan meeting itself", the Panel concluded that the United States had made serious, good faith efforts that met the "standard set by the Inter–American Convention." In the view of the Panel, whether or not the South–East Asian MOU is a legally binding document does not affect this comparative assessment because differences in "factual circumstances have to be kept in mind". Furthermore, the Panel did not consider as decisive the fact that the final agreement in the Indian Ocean and South–East Asia region, unlike the Inter–American Convention, had not been concluded at the time of the Panel proceedings. According to the Panel, "at least until the Conservation and Management Plan to be attached to the MOU is completed, the United States efforts should be judged on the basis of its active participation and its financial support to the negotiations, as well as on the basis of its

previous efforts since 1998, having regard to the likelihood of a conclusion of the negotiations in the course of 2001."

133. We note that the Panel stated that "any effort alleged to be a 'serious good faith effort' must be assessed against the efforts made in relation to the conclusion of the Inter–American Convention." In our view, in assessing the serious, good faith efforts made by the United States, the Panel did not err in using the Inter–American Convention as an *example*. In our view, also, the Panel was correct in proceeding then to an analysis broadly in line with this principle and, ultimately, was correct as well in concluding that the efforts made by the United States in the Indian Ocean and South–East Asia region constitute serious, good faith efforts comparable to those that led to the conclusion of the Inter–American Convention. We find no fault with this analysis.

134. In sum, Malaysia is incorrect in its contention that avoiding "arbitrary and unjustifiable discrimination" under the chapeau of Article XX requires the *conclusion* of an international agreement on the protection and conservation of sea turtles. Therefore, we uphold the Panel's finding that, in view of the serious, good faith efforts made by the United States to negotiate an international agreement, "Section 609 is now applied in a manner that no longer constitutes a means of unjustifiable or arbitrary discrimination, as identified by the Appellate Body in its Report".

The Flexibility of the Revised Guidelines

* * *

135. Malaysia disagrees with the Panel that a measure can meet the requirements of the chapeau of Article XX if it is flexible enough, both in design and application, to permit certification of an exporting country with a sea turtle protection and conservation programme "comparable" to that of the United States. According to Malaysia, even if the measure at issue allows certification of countries having regulatory programs "comparable" to that of the United States, and even if the measure is applied in such a manner, it results in "arbitrary or unjustifiable discrimination" because it conditions access to the United States market on compliance with policies and standards "unilaterally" prescribed by the United States. * * *

* * *

140. In *United States—Shrimp*, we concluded that the measure at issue there did not meet the requirements of the chapeau of Article XX relating to "arbitrary or unjustifiable discrimination" because, through the application of the measure, the exporting members were faced with "a single, rigid and unbending requirement" to adopt *essentially the same* policies and enforcement practices as those applied to, and enforced on, domestic shrimp trawlers in the United States. In contrast, in this dispute, the Panel found that this new measure is more flexible than the original measure and has been applied more flexibly than was the original measure. In the light of the evidence brought by the United

States, the Panel satisfied itself that this new measure, in design and application, does *not* condition access to the United States market on the adoption by an exporting Member of a regulatory programme aimed at the protection and the conservation of sea turtles that is *essentially the same* as that of the United States.

141. As the Panel's analysis suggests, an approach based on whether a measure requires "essentially the same" regulatory programme of an exporting Member as that adopted by the importing Member applying the measure is a useful tool in identifying measures that result in "arbitrary or unjustifiable discrimination" and, thus, do *not* meet the requirements of the chapeau of Article XX. However, this approach is not sufficient for purposes of judging whether a measure *does* meet the requirements of the chapeau of Article XX. * * *

* * *

143. Given that the original measure in that dispute required "essentially the same" practices and procedures as those required in the United States, we found it necessary in that appeal to rule only that Article XX did not allow such inflexibility. Given the Panel's findings with respect to the flexibility of the new measure in this dispute, we find it necessary in this appeal to add to what we ruled in our original Report. The question raised by Malaysia in this appeal is whether the Panel erred in inferring from our previous Report, and thereby finding, that the chapeau of Article XX permits a measure which requires only "comparable effectiveness".

144. In our view, there is an important difference between conditioning market access on the adoption of essentially the same programme, and conditioning market access on the adoption of a programme *comparable in effectiveness*. Authorizing an importing Member to condition market access on exporting Members putting in place regulatory programmes *comparable in effectiveness* to that of the importing Member gives sufficient latitude to the exporting Member with respect to the programme it may adopt to achieve the level of effectiveness required. It allows the exporting Member to adopt a regulatory programme that is suitable to the specific conditions prevailing in its territory. As we see it, the Panel correctly reasoned and concluded that conditioning market access on the adoption of a programme *comparable in effectiveness*, allows for sufficient flexibility in the application of the measure so as to avoid "arbitrary or unjustifiable discrimination". We, therefore, agree with the conclusion of the Panel on "comparable effectiveness".

* * *

146. We note that the Revised Guidelines contain provisions that permit the United States authorities to take into account the specific conditions of Malaysian shrimp production, and of the Malaysian sea turtle conservation programme, should Malaysia decide to apply for certification. The Revised Guidelines explicitly state that "[if] the gov-

ernment of a harvesting nation demonstrates that it has implemented and is enforcing a comparably effective regulatory program to protect sea turtles in the course of shrimp trawl fishing without the use of TEDs, that nation will also be eligible for certification." Likewise, the Revised Guidelines provide that the "Department of State will take fully into account any demonstrated differences between the shrimp fishing conditions in the United States and those in other nations as well as information available from other sources."

147.   Further, the Revised Guidelines provide that the import prohibitions that can be imposed under Section 609 do not apply to shrimp or products of shrimp "harvested in any other manner or under any other circumstances that the Department of State may determine, following consultations with the [United States National Marine Fisheries Services], does not pose a threat of the incidental taking of sea turtles." * * * Additionally, Section II.B(c)(iii) states that "[i]n making certification determinations, the Department shall also take fully into account other measures the harvesting nation undertakes to protect sea turtles, including national programmes to protect nesting beaches and other habitat, prohibitions on the direct take of sea turtles, national enforcement and compliance programmes, and participation in any international agreement for the protection and conservation of sea turtles." * * *

148.   These provisions of the Revised Guidelines, on their face, permit a degree of flexibility that, in our view, will enable the United States to consider the particular conditions prevailing in Malaysia if, and when, Malaysia applies for certification. As Malaysia has not applied for certification, any consideration of whether Malaysia would be certified would be speculation.

149.   We need only say here that, in our view, a measure should be designed in such a manner that there is sufficient flexibility to take into account the specific conditions prevailing in *any* exporting Member, including, of course, Malaysia. Yet this is not the same as saying that there must be specific provisions in the measure aimed at addressing specifically the particular conditions prevailing in *every individual* exporting Member. Article XX of the GATT 1994 does not require a Member to anticipate and provide explicitly for the specific conditions prevailing and evolving in *every individual* Member.

150.   We are, therefore, not persuaded by Malaysia's argument that the measure at issue is not flexible enough because the Revised Guidelines do not explicitly address the specific conditions prevailing in Malaysia.

151.   Malaysia argues, finally, that the Panel should have scrutinized the decision of the CIT in the *Turtle Island* case and assessed, in the light of that decision, the likelihood and consequences of the Revised Guidelines being modified in the future. According to Malaysia, the Panel should have come to the conclusion that the Revised Guidelines are not flexible enough because the CIT ruled that the part of the Revised Guidelines allowing TED-caught shrimp from non-certified har-

vesting countries to be imported into the United States is contrary to Section 609. As we have already ruled, we are of the view that, when examining the United States measures, the Panel took into account the status of municipal law at the time, and reached the correct conclusion. The CIT decision in the *Turtle Island* case has not modified the legal effect or the application of the Revised Guidelines; hence, we are not persuaded by this argument of Malaysia.

153.   For all these reasons, we uphold the finding of the Panel, in paragraph 6.1 of the Panel Report, that "Section 609 of Public Law 101–162, as implemented by the Revised Guidelines of 8 July 1999 and as applied so far by the [United States] authorities, is justified under Article XX of the GATT 1994 as long as the conditions stated in the findings of this Report, in particular the ongoing serious, good faith efforts to reach a multilateral agreement, remain satisfied".

Notes and Questions

(1) In respect of the condition in paragraph 153, the Appellate Body noted that the United States had negotiated and concluded a Memorandum of Understanding with certain countries in the Indian Ocean and South–East Asia region, the South–East Asian MOU, which took effect on September 1, 2001.

(2) On the key issue of negotiations, do you agree with the Appellate Body? Does it let the US off too easily? What of the fact that the negotiations took place while the US measure remained in effect? The panel in fact noted (in para. 5.73) "that, in that context, negotiators may have found themselves constrained to accept conditions that they may not have accepted had Section 609 not been applied. Even if Section 609 as currently applied takes more into account the existence of different conservation programs, it can still influence the outcome of negotiations. This is why the Panel feels it is important to take the reality of international relations into account and considers that the standard of review of the efforts of the United States on the international plane should be expressed as follows: whether the United States made serious good faith efforts to negotiate an international agreement, taking into account the situations of the other negotiating countries."

(3) As the description of the factual background of the initial Appellate Body Report in this case makes clear, there has been considerable controversy in the US over the meaning of Section 609. Environmental, animal rights and sea turtle advocacy groups have succeeded in forcing the US government to apply Section 609 more broadly than it wished. As of this writing, those groups have successfully challenged in the Court of International Trade the State Department's decision to permit imports of shrimp taken with TEDs, but from uncertified countries. The CIT did not, however, enjoin enforcement of the 1999 Guidelines. Turtle Island Restoration Network v. Mallett, 110 F.Supp.2d 1005 (CIT 2000). If the government loses on appeal, what impact would that have on the question of whether the US has adequately implemented the original *Shrimp* decision? In that regard, re-read para. 165 in the original Appellate Body Report. Note how the possibility of such an event was handled in the compliance proceeding.

(4) In light of the *Shrimp* decisions, how would you characterize the extent of WTO Members to take unilateral action for the protection of the environment? What are the limits on that discretion? What is the relevance of the product-process distinction (noted in connection with like-product analysis in Chapter 12) in an analysis under the chapeau of Article XX?

(5) The stress on negotiations should remind one that are many multilateral agreements dealing with environmental issues. How should a conflict between a WTO requirement and a requirement of a multilateral environmental agreement (MEA) be resolved? By whom? Suppose the MEA authorizes, but does not require, an action that is inconsistent with WTO requirements? To what extent can Article XX be used to excuse compliance with WTO requirements in such a situation? Interestingly, the preamble to the Cartegena Protocol to the Convention on Biological Diversity provides that the Protocol shall not be interpreted as implying a change in the rights and obligations of a party under any existing international agreements, but that this statement is not intended to subordinate the protocol to other international agreements. The negotiations on environmental issues, including the relationship between MEAs and the WTO, that were agreed upon at the Doha Ministerial are described in more detail in Section 27.1 infra.

Chapter 14

TECHNICAL REGULATIONS AND PRODUCT STANDARDS: THE SPS AND TBT AGREEMENTS

In this chapter, we examine the problems that arise from the application of technical regulations and standards, including measures taken for health reasons. We first consider why these issues are important in international trade. We then examine the two WTO agreements specifically addressing these problems—the Agreement on Sanitary and Phytosanitary Measures (the SPS Agreement), which applies in general to measures taken to protect human, animal and plant life or health from certain specified risks; and the Agreement on Technical Barriers to Trade (the TBT Agreement), which applies to the use of technical regulations and standards. The SPS Agreement has been the subject of several important dispute settlement proceedings, which are discussed below. Somewhat surprisingly, there have been no cases interpreting the substance of the TBT Agreement, or its Tokyo Round predecessor. In the last section of the chapter, we consider how the EC, the US and the free trade agreements to which the US is a party address these problems, which by their nature arise in all federal systems. A key issue in all cases is the extent to which it is appropriate for international (or federal) rules to limit national (or local) discretion in these matters, especially if there is strong popular and political support for the national (or local) measures. Indeed, some question whether trade agreements are the appropriate place to regulate such issues at all.

SECTION 14.1 INTRODUCTION

We begin in this section with an overview of the problems associated with technical regulations and product standards. In the following materials, consider the extent to which the SPS and TBT Agreements address the various types of problems noted by Professor Sykes:

ALAN O. SYKES, PRODUCT STANDARDS FOR INTERNATIONALLY INTEGRATED GOODS MARKETS 1–9 (1995)[1]

As tariffs have diminished pursuant to the GATT and other international agreements, the significance of non-tariff impediments to international trade has increased relatively and in some instances absolutely. Diverse standards and regulations governing the sale of products in national markets are a potential source of these non-tariff impediments, and in modern parlance may become "technical barriers to trade."

It is ironic that product standards and regulations should create trade barriers, as many of them evolved for the purpose of promoting trade. Familiar weights and measures developed to facilitate the description of goods in commerce and to obviate problems of fraud. Voltage standards allow electrical products to operate satisfactorily in different geographic areas. Standardized television broadcast formats enable programs of varying origin to be viewed on receivers of varying manufacture, a similar function being performed by standard operating systems for microcomputers. Regulations governing the wholesomeness of foodstuffs serve in part to reassure consumers of their safety and thereby to expand the market of willing buyers. Innumerable other examples might be offered.

Yet, it is not difficult to appreciate how these same measures can diverge across national markets and become trade impediments. Standards and regulations may be deliberately crafted to impose a cost disadvantage on foreign competitors. They may also differ across jurisdictions as a result of divergent tastes, because of variations in technology, income or resource endowments, or even by chance. It is thus common for goods that conform to all pertinent standards and regulatory requirements in their country of origin to fail to conform elsewhere. And, even when conformity to foreign standards and regulations is not difficult, the burden of *demonstrating* conformity to the satisfaction of consumers or regulators abroad can still be considerable. "Technical barriers" thus arise both from the divergence of standards and regulations across nations, and from the burden of establishing conformity with them whether or not they are divergent.

It is useful to begin with some terminology. I define a product "standard" as a specification or set of specifications that relates to some characteristic of a product or its manufacture. It may relate to its size, its dimensions, its weight, its design, its function, its ingredients, or any number of other product attributes. It may or may not be formally promulgated by a private or public standard-setting entity. The distinguishing feature of a "standard" is that compliance is *voluntary*. Thus, products that do not conform to a standard are legally permitted to be

1. © 1995 The Brookings Institution. Reprinted with the permission of The Brookings Institution. See also Alan O. Sykes, Regulatory Protectionism and the Law of International Trade, 66 U.Chi. L.Rev. 1 (199).

sold and any penalty for non-conformity is a market one. A "regulation" differs from a standard only in this key respect—it too may relate to any aspect of product characteristics or manufacture, but compliance with a regulation is legally *mandatory*. It is not uncommon for standards to be converted into regulations by government fiat.

* * *

* * * [T]he trading community needs more information about technical barriers. Their importance sector by sector is generally unknown, as is their impact on economic welfare. Additional, systematic research into their incidence and magnitude would be immensely beneficial. And, because information about the problem is so scant, my remaining conclusions must be viewed as quite tentative.

In brief, I conclude that many problems of potential technological *incompatibility* are handled adequately by existing institutions. Decentralized market forces suffice to avoid unproductive incompatibilities (not all are undesirable) in a considerable percentage of cases. Other problems are averted through the work of international standardizing bodies such as the International Organization for Standardization (ISO), which facilitate cooperative activity among national standardizers and do much to avoid unproductive incompatibilities that might otherwise arise by accident.

Nevertheless, some notable compatibility problems have arisen that market forces and international standardizing bodies have not averted, the bulk of which fall into two categories. The first involves incompatibilities that predate extensive international trade or modern international standardization efforts, such as those due to differences between the imperial and metric systems. The second involves incompatibilities associated with new, proprietary technologies, where the selection of a standard necessarily favors one producer group over another and national or sub-national interest groups may block the consensus needed for the adoption of an international (or even national) standard. Historical controversies over television broadcast format standards are illustrative here.

Little can be done at the global level about most problems that fall into the first category. At bottom, the question is whether the nations that adhere to a minority standard would benefit on balance from switching given all of the costs involved, a question that is not always easy to answer (consider the debate in the United States over metric conversion). If the answer is yes, government action will be necessary to make the change for a variety of reasons. But these are primarily matters of national rather than international policy, and I do not dwell on them at length.

As for the second group of incompatibility problems, it is not easy to imagine any reform of international institutions that would eliminate them, and that would also be politically feasible. Outside of the European Community, nations have shown no willingness to cede sovereignty to a central authority with the power to compel them to follow a particular technological standard. Treaty covenants to utilize international standards such as those in the GATT system are also unlikely to be effective, either because the adoption of an international standard is blocked by a lack of consensus or because nations will opt out (as GATT allows). Consequently, when divergence of producer interests threatens to create inefficient incompatibilities in global markets, the best hope for solution may lie in explicit or implicit side payments among producers, as through joint ventures or mergers.

Turning to matters of product *quality*, I find it helpful to distinguish between technical barriers that result from a divergence of national goals and preferences regarding quality, and barriers that result from a divergence in the means selected to achieve similar goals and preferences. I recognize that this line is not always easy to draw, but it can be operationalized easily in many cases and is quite a useful analytical construct.

Legal constraints upon national sovereigns such as those in the GATT system—an approach that I term "policed decentralization"—can respond fairly well in principle to the barriers that result from divergent means to the same end. The most important legal constraint here is the "least restrictive means principle." Related or corollary principles include nondiscrimination requirements, generality requirements, an obligation to employ existing international standards and to afford mutual recognition where adequate to meet domestic objectives, an obligation to justify a refusal of mutual recognition, and others. Adherence to these principles can readily avert technical barriers that result from chance differences in national standards and regulations, and to a lesser extent can police problems of capture by exposing them and subjecting nations that use quality measures for protectionist purposes to reputational penalties or retaliation. In the end, however, the effectiveness of the GATT system or any other legal system for policing these technical barriers also depends upon diligence in enforcement and compliance efforts. On this score, the GATT is apparently less successful to date (though systematic information is again lacking). Recent improvements in GATT dispute resolution as a result of the Uruguay Round have the potential to considerably strengthen the effectiveness of the system, as does the extension of GATT obligations to matters not previously covered (such as process and production standards). * * *

When technical barriers result from genuine differences in national goals and objectives regarding quality, general legal obligations such as those in the GATT system can accomplish much less. Indeed, it is precisely here that "technical barriers" may be economically efficient, and it becomes difficult to know whether anything ought be done about them at all. The reduction of technical barriers in this category will likely come primarily from international cooperation to achieve complete or partial harmonization. * * *

SECTION 14.2   THE SPS AGREEMENT

One of the major goals of the Uruguay Round negotiations was to bring agricultural trade back within GATT disciplines. As noted earlier (Section 9.2), for most of GATT's existence its disciplines were not very effective in the agricultural sector because of waivers, lack of tariff bindings and the widespread use of some questionable non-tariff barriers. Among the non-tariff barriers that concerned negotiators were measures ostensibly taken for sanitary or phytosanitary (SPS) purposes. The attention given this subject ultimately resulted in a separate WTO agreement—the Agreement on Sanitary and Phytosanitary Measures, better known as the SPS Agreement.

The basic obligations of the SPS Agreement are set out in article 2. In essence, while article (2)1 recognizes the right of WTO members to take SPS measures necessary to protect life or health, article 2(2) requires them to apply such measures only to the extent necessary to protect life or health, to base them on scientific principles and not to maintain them without sufficient scientific evidence (subject to a precautionary principle exception). In addition, article 2(3) requires that SPS measures not arbitrarily or unjustifiably discriminate between WTO members where identical or similar conditions prevail and not be applied in a manner that would constitute a disguised restriction on international trade.

Article 3(1) of the SPS Agreement requires WTO members to base their SPS measures on international standards where they exist and if they do so, they are presumed to be in compliance with the agreement (article 3(2)). However, article 3(3) allows them to introduce SPS measures that result in a higher level of SPS protection than would be achieved by measures based on international standards, so long as they are scientifically justified, i.e., based on a risk assessment conducted pursuant to article 5 of the agreement. As a result, it can be said that the SPS Agreement promotes international harmonization, but does not require it.

The SPS Agreement has been the subject of three disputes that have resulted in panel and Appellate Body decisions—dealing with measures to protect human, animal and plant health. The following is the best known and most controversial of the three cases. It focuses in particular on the risk assessment and other requirements of article 5 of the SPS Agreement.

EC MEASURES CONCERNING MEAT AND MEAT PRODUCTS (HORMONES)
WT/DS26 & 48AB/R
Appellate Body Report adopted by the DSB on February 13, 1998

2.   The Panel dealt with a complaint against the European Communities relating to an EC prohibition of imports of meat and meat products derived from cattle to which either the natural hormones:

oestradiol–17β, progesterone or testosterone, or the synthetic hormones: trenbolone acetate, zeranol or melengestrol acetate ("MGA"), had been administered for growth promotion purposes.

* * *

179.   Article 5.1 of the *SPS Agreement* provides:

> Members shall ensure that their sanitary or phytosanitary measures are <u>based on an assessment, as appropriate to the circumstances, of the risks to human</u>, animal or plant <u>life or health</u>, taking into account risk assessment techniques developed by the relevant international organizations. (underlining added)

180.   At the outset, two preliminary considerations need to be brought out. The first is that the Panel considered that Article 5.1 may be viewed as a specific application of the basic obligations contained in Article 2.2 of the *SPS Agreement*, which reads as follows:

> Members shall ensure that any sanitary or phytosanitary measure is applied only <u>to the extent necessary to protect</u> human, animal or plant life or health, is <u>based on scientific principles</u> and is not maintained without <u>sufficient scientific evidence</u>, except as provided for in paragraph 7 of Article 5. (underlining added)

We agree with this general consideration and would also stress that Articles 2.2 and 5.1 should constantly be read together. Article 2.2 informs Article 5.1: the elements that define the basic obligation set out in Article 2.2 impart meaning to Article 5.1.

181.   The second preliminary consideration relates to the Panel's effort to distinguish between "risk assessment" and "risk management". The Panel observed that an assessment of risk is, at least with respect to risks to human life and health, a "scientific" examination of data and factual studies; it is not, in the view of the Panel, a "policy" exercise involving social value judgments made by political bodies. The Panel describes the latter as "non-scientific" and as pertaining to "risk management" rather than to "risk assessment". We must stress, in this connection, that Article 5 and Annex A of the *SPS Agreement* speak of "risk assessment" only and that the term "risk management" is not to be found either in Article 5 or in any other provision of the *SPS Agreement*. Thus, the Panel's distinction, which it apparently employs to achieve or support what appears to be a restrictive notion of risk assessment, has no textual basis. The fundamental rule of treaty interpretation requires a treaty interpreter to read and interpret the words actually used by the agreement under examination, and not words which the interpreter may feel should have been used.

182.   Paragraph 4 of Annex A of the *SPS Agreement* sets out the treaty definition of risk assessment: This definition, to the extent pertinent to the present appeal, speaks of:

> . . . the evaluation of the <u>potential for adverse effects on human</u> or animal <u>health</u> arising from the presence of additives, contaminants,

toxins or disease-causing organisms in food, beverages or feedstuffs.
(underlining added)

183. Interpreting the above definition, the Panel elaborates risk
assessment as a two-step process that "should (i) *identify* the *adverse
effects* on human health (if any) arising from the presence of the
hormones at issue when used as growth promoters *in meat* . . ., and (ii) if
any such adverse effects exist, *evaluate* the *potential* or probability of
occurrence of such effects".

184. The European Communities appeals from the above interpretation as involving an erroneous notion of risk and risk assessment.
Although the utility of a two-step analysis may be debated, it does not
appear to us to be substantially wrong. What needs to be pointed out at
this stage is that the Panel's use of "probability" as an alternative term
for "potential" creates a significant concern. The ordinary meaning of
"potential" relates to "possibility" and is different from the ordinary
meaning of "probability". "Probability" implies a higher degree or a
threshold of potentiality or possibility. It thus appears that here the
Panel introduces a quantitative dimension to the notion of risk.

185. In its discussion on a statement made by Dr. Lucier at the
joint meeting with the experts in February 1997, the Panel states the
risk referred to by this expert is an estimate which ". . . only represents
a statistical range of 0 to 1 in a million, not a scientifically identified
risk". The European Communities protests vigorously that, by doing so,
the Panel is in effect requiring a Member carrying out a risk assessment
to quantify the potential for adverse effects on human health.

186. It is not clear in what sense the Panel uses the term "scientifically identified risk". The Panel also frequently uses the term "identifiable risk", and does not define this term either. The Panel might
arguably have used the terms "scientifically identified risk" and "identifiable risk" simply to refer to an ascertainable risk: if a risk is not
ascertainable, how does a Member ever know or demonstrate that it
exists? In one part of its Reports, the Panel opposes a requirement of an
"identifiable risk" to the uncertainty that theoretically always remains
since science can *never* provide *absolute* certainty that a given substance
will not *ever* have adverse health effects. We agree with the Panel that
this theoretical uncertainty is not the kind of risk which, under Article
5.1, is to be assessed. In another part of its Reports, however, the Panel
appeared to be using the term "scientifically identified risk" to prescribe
implicitly that a certain *magnitude* or threshold level of risk be demonstrated in a risk assessment if an SPS measure based thereon is to be
regarded as consistent with Article 5.1. To the extent that the Panel
purported to require a risk assessment to establish a minimum magnitude of risk, we must note that imposition of such a quantitative
requirement finds no basis in the *SPS Agreement*. A panel is authorized
only to determine whether a given SPS measure is "based on" a risk
assessment. As will be elaborated below, this means that a panel has to

determine whether an SPS measure is sufficiently supported or reasonably warranted by the risk assessment.

187.   Article 5.2 of the *SPS Agreement* provides an indication of the factors that should be taken into account in the assessment of risk. Article 5.2 states that:

> In the assessment of risks, Members shall take into account available scientific evidence; relevant processes and production methods; relevant inspection, sampling and testing methods; prevalence of specific diseases or pests; existence of pest- or disease-free areas; relevant ecological and environmental conditions; and quarantine or other treatment.

The listing in Article 5.2 begins with "available scientific evidence"; this, however, is only the beginning. We note in this connection that the Panel states that, for purposes of the EC measures in dispute, a risk assessment required by Article 5.1 is "a *scientific* process aimed at establishing the *scientific* basis for the sanitary measure a Member intends to take". To the extent that the Panel intended to refer to a process characterized by systematic, disciplined and objective enquiry and analysis, that is, a mode of studying and sorting out facts and opinions, the Panel's statement is unexceptionable. However, to the extent that the Panel purports to exclude from the scope of a risk assessment in the sense of Article 5.1, all matters not susceptible of quantitative analysis by the empirical or experimental laboratory methods commonly associated with the physical sciences, we believe that the Panel is in error. Some of the kinds of factors listed in Article 5.2 such as "relevant processes and production methods" and "relevant inspection, sampling and testing methods" are not necessarily or wholly susceptible of investigation according to laboratory methods of, for example, biochemistry or pharmacology. Furthermore, there is nothing to indicate that the listing of factors that may be taken into account in a risk assessment of Article 5.2 was intended to be a closed list. It is essential to bear in mind that the risk that is to be evaluated in a risk assessment under Article 5.1 is not only risk ascertainable in a science laboratory operating under strictly controlled conditions, but also risk in human societies as they actually exist, in other words, the actual potential for adverse effects on human health in the real world where people live and work and die.

188.   Although it expressly recognizes that Article 5.1 does *not* contain any specific procedural requirements for a Member to base its sanitary measures on a risk assessment, the Panel nevertheless proceeds to declare that "there is a minimum procedural requirement contained in Article 5.1". That requirement is that "the Member imposing a sanitary measure needs to submit evidence that at least it actually *took into account* a risk assessment when it enacted or maintained its sanitary measure in order for that measure to be considered as *based on* a risk assessment". The Panel goes on to state that the European Communities did not provide any evidence that the studies it referred to

or the scientific conclusions reached therein *"have actually been taken into account by the competent EC institutions* either when it *enacted* those measures (in 1981 and 1988) or *at any later point in time"*. (emphasis added) Thereupon, the Panel holds that such studies could not be considered as part of a risk assessment on which the European Communities based its measures in dispute. Concluding that the European Communities had not met its burden of proving that it had satisfied the "minimum procedural requirement" it had found in Article 5.1, the Panel holds the EC measures as inconsistent with the requirements of Article 5.1.

189. We are bound to note that, as the Panel itself acknowledges, no textual basis exists in Article 5 of the *SPS Agreement* for such a "minimum procedural requirement". The term "based on", when applied as a "minimum procedural requirement" by the Panel, may be seen to refer to a human action, such as particular human individuals "taking into account" a document described as a risk assessment. Thus, "take into account" is apparently used by the Panel to refer to some subjectivity which, at some time, may be present in particular individuals but that, in the end, may be totally rejected by those individuals. We believe that "based on" is appropriately taken to refer to a certain *objective relationship* between two elements, that is to say, to an *objective situation* that persists and is observable between an SPS measure and a risk assessment. Such a reference is certainly embraced in the ordinary meaning of the words "based on" and, when considered in context and in the light of the object and purpose of Article 5.1 of the *SPS Agreement*, may be seen to be more appropriate than "taking into account". We do not share the Panel's interpretative construction and believe it is unnecessary and an error of law as well.

190. Article 5.1 does not insist that a Member that adopts a sanitary measure shall have carried out its own risk assessment. It only requires that the SPS measures be "based on an assessment, as appropriate for the circumstances . . . ". The SPS measure might well find its objective justification in a risk assessment carried out by another Member, or an international organization. The "minimum procedural requirement" constructed by the Panel, could well lead to the elimination or disregard of available scientific evidence that rationally supports the SPS measure being examined. This risk of exclusion of available scientific evidence may be particularly significant for the bulk of SPS measures which were put in place before the effective date of the *WTO Agreement* and that have been simply maintained thereafter.

191. In the course of demanding evidence that EC authorities actually "took into account" certain scientific studies, the Panel refers to the preambles of the EC Directives here involved. The Panel notes that such preambles did not mention any of the scientific studies referred to by the European Communities in the panel proceedings. Preambles of legislative or quasi-legislative acts and administrative regulations commonly fulfil requirements of the internal legal orders of WTO Members. Such preambles are certainly not required by the *SPS Agreement*; they

are not normally used to demonstrate that a Member has complied with its obligations under international agreements. The absence of any mention of scientific studies in the preliminary sections of the EC Directives does not, therefore, prove anything so far as the present case is concerned.

192. Having posited a "minimum procedural requirement" of Article 5.1, the Panel turns to the "substantive requirements" of Article 5.1 to determine whether the EC measures at issue are "based on" a risk assessment. In the Panel's view, those "substantive requirements" involve two kinds of operations: first, identifying the scientific conclusions reached in the risk assessment and the scientific conclusions implicit in the SPS measures; and secondly, examining those scientific conclusions to determine whether or not one set of conclusions matches, i.e. conforms with, the second set of conclusions. Applying the "substantive requirements" it finds in Article 5.1, the Panel holds that the scientific conclusions implicit in the EC measures do not conform with any of the scientific conclusions reached in the scientific studies the European Communities had submitted as evidence.

193. We consider that, in principle, the Panel's approach of examining the scientific conclusions implicit in the SPS measure under consideration and the scientific conclusion yielded by a risk assessment is a useful approach. The relationship between those two sets of conclusions is certainly relevant; they cannot, however, be assigned relevance to the exclusion of everything else. We believe that Article 5.1, when contextually read as it should be, in conjunction with and as informed by Article 2.2 of the *SPS Agreement*, requires that the results of the risk assessment must sufficiently warrant—that is to say, reasonably support—the SPS measure at stake. The requirement that an SPS measure be "based on" a risk assessment is a substantive requirement that there be a rational relationship between the measure and the risk assessment.

194. We do not believe that a risk assessment has to come to a monolithic conclusion that coincides with the scientific conclusion or view implicit in the SPS measure. The risk assessment could set out both the prevailing view representing the "mainstream" of scientific opinion, as well as the opinions of scientists taking a divergent view. Article 5.1 does not require that the risk assessment must necessarily embody only the view of a majority of the relevant scientific community. In some cases, the very existence of divergent views presented by qualified scientists who have investigated the particular issue at hand may indicate a state of scientific uncertainty. Sometimes the divergence may indicate a roughly equal balance of scientific opinion, which may itself be a form of scientific uncertainty. In most cases, responsible and representative governments tend to base their legislative and administrative measures on "mainstream" scientific opinion. In other cases, equally responsible and representative governments may act in good faith on the basis of what, at a given time, may be a divergent opinion coming from qualified and respected sources. By itself, this does not necessarily signal the absence of a reasonable relationship between the SPS measure and

the risk assessment, especially where the risk involved is life-threatening in character and is perceived to constitute a clear and imminent threat to public health and safety. Determination of the presence or absence of that relationship can only be done on a case-to-case basis, after account is taken of all considerations rationally bearing upon the issue of potential adverse health effects.

195. We turn now to the application by the Panel of the substantive requirements of Article 5.1 to the EC measures at stake in the present case. The Panel lists the following scientific material to which the European Communities referred in respect of the hormones here involved [list omitted].

196. Several of the above scientific reports appeared to the Panel to meet the minimum requirements of a risk assessment, in particular, the Lamming Report [commissioned by the EC] and the 1988 and 1989 JECFA Reports [prepared for Codex Alimentarius–a FAO–WHO body]. The Panel assumes accordingly that the European Communities had demonstrated the existence of a risk assessment carried out in accordance with Article 5 of the *SPS Agreement*. At the same time, the Panel finds that the conclusion of these scientific reports is that the use of the hormones at issue (except MGA) for growth promotion purposes is "safe". The Panel states:

> ... none of the scientific evidence referred to by the European Communities which specifically addresses the safety of some or all of the hormones in dispute when used for growth promotion, indicates that an identifiable risk arises for human health from such use of these hormones if good practice is followed. All of the scientific studies outlined above came to the conclusion that the use of the hormones at issue (all but MGA, for which no evidence was submitted) for growth promotion purposes is safe; most of these studies adding that this conclusion assumes that good practice is followed.

197. Prescinding from the difficulty raised by the Panel's use of the term "identifiable risk", we agree that the scientific reports listed above do not rationally support the EC import prohibition.

198. With regard to the scientific opinion expressed by Dr. Lucier at the joint meeting with the experts, and as set out in paragraph 819 of the Annex to the US and Canada Panel Reports[2], we should note that this opinion by Dr. Lucier does not purport to be the result of scientific studies carried out by him or under his supervision focusing specifically on residues of hormones in meat from cattle fattened with such hor-

---

2. This paragraph reads in relevant part: "For every million women alive in the United States, Canada, Europe today, about a 110,000 of those women will get breast cancer. This is obviously a tremendous public health issue. Of those 110,000 women [who] get breast cancer, maybe several thousand of them are related to the total intake of exogenous oestrogens from every source, including eggs, meat, phyto-oestrogens, fungal oestrogens, the whole body burden of exogenous oestrogens. And by my estimates one of those 110,000 would come from eating meat containing oestrogens as a growth promoter, if used as prescribed." [Note that Dr. Lucifer was explaining here his earlier expressed view that the risk was between zero and one in a million–see para. 185.]

mones. Accordingly, it appears that the single divergent opinion expressed by Dr. Lucier is not reasonably sufficient to overturn the contrary conclusions reached in the scientific studies referred to by the European Communities that related specifically to residues of the hormones in meat from cattle to which hormones had been administered for growth promotion.

199. The European Communities laid particular emphasis on the 1987 IARC [International Agency for Research on Cancer] Monographs and the articles and opinions of individual scientists referred to above. The Panel notes, however, that the scientific evidence set out in these Monographs and these articles and opinions relates to the carcinogenic potential of entire *categories* of hormones, or of the hormones at issue *in general*. The Monographs and the articles and opinions are, in other words, in the nature of general studies of or statements on the carcinogenic potential of the named hormones. The Monographs and the articles and opinions of individual scientists have not evaluated the carcinogenic potential of those hormones when used specifically *for growth promotion purposes*. Moreover, they do not evaluate the specific potential for carcinogenic effects arising from the presence *in "food"*, more specifically, "meat or meat products" of residues of the hormones in dispute. The Panel also notes that, according to the scientific experts advising the Panel, the data and studies set out in these 1987 Monographs have been taken into account in the 1988 and 1989 JECFA Reports and that the conclusions reached by the 1987 IARC Monographs are complementary to, rather than contradictory of, the conclusions of the JECFA Reports. The Panel concludes that these Monographs and these articles and opinions are insufficient to support the EC measures at issue in this case.

200. We believe that the above findings of the Panel are justified. The 1987 IARC Monographs and the articles and opinions of individual scientists submitted by the European Communities constitute general studies which do indeed show the existence of a general risk of cancer; but they do not focus on and do not address the particular kind of risk here at stake—the carcinogenic or genotoxic potential of the residues of those hormones found in meat derived from cattle to which the hormones had been administered for growth promotion purposes—as is required by paragraph 4 of Annex A of the *SPS Agreement*. Those general studies, are in other words, relevant but do not appear to be sufficiently specific to the case at hand.

201. With regard to risk assessment concerning MGA, the European Communities referred to the 1987 IARC Monographs. These Monographs deal with, *inter alia*, the category of progestins of which the hormone progesterone is a member. The European Communities argues that because MGA is an anabolic agent which mimics the action of progesterone, the scientific studies and experiments relied on by the 1987 IARC Monographs were highly relevant. However, the Monographs and the articles and opinions of the individual scientists did not include any study that demonstrated how closely related MGA is chemically and

pharmacologically to other progestins and what effects MGA residues would actually have on human beings when such residues are ingested along with meat from cattle to which MGA has been administered for growth promotion purposes. It must be recalled in this connection that none of the other scientific material submitted by the European Communities referred to MGA, and that no international standard, guideline or recommendation has been developed by Codex relating specifically to MGA. The United States and Canada declined to submit any assessment of MGA upon the ground that the material they were aware of was proprietary and confidential in nature. In other words, there was an almost complete absence of evidence on MGA in the panel proceedings. We therefore uphold the Panel's finding that there was no risk assessment with regard to MGA.

202.   The evidence referred to above by the European Communities related to the biochemical risk arising from the ingestion by human beings of residues of the five hormones here involved in treated meat, where such hormones had been administered to the cattle in accordance with good veterinary practice. The European Communities also referred to distinguishable but closely related risks—risks arising from failure to observe the requirements of good veterinary practice, in combination with multiple problems relating to detection and control of such abusive failure, in the administration of hormones to cattle for growth promotion.

203.   The Panel considers this type of risk and examines the arguments made by the European Communities but finds no assessment of such kind of risk. Ultimately, the Panel rejects those arguments principally on *a priori* grounds. First, to the Panel, the provisions of Article 5.2 relating to "relevant inspection, sampling and testing methods":

> ... do not seem to cover the general problem of control (such as the problem of ensuring the observance of good practice) which can exist for any substance. The risks related to the general problem of control do not seem to be specific to the substance at issue but to the economic or social incidence related to a substance or its particular use (such as economic incentives for abuse). These non-scientific factors should, therefore not be taken into account in a risk assessment but in *risk management*. (underlining added)

Moreover, the Panel finds that, assuming these factors could be taken into account in a risk assessment, the European Communities has not provided convincing evidence that the control or prevention of abuse of the hormones here involved is more difficult than the control of other veterinary drugs, the use of which is allowed in the European Communities. Further, the European Communities has not provided evidence that control would be more difficult under a regime where the use of the hormones in dispute is allowed under specific conditions than under the current EC regime of total prohibition both domestically and in respect of imported meat. The Panel concludes by saying that banning the use of a substance does not necessarily offer better protection of human health than other means of regulating its use.

204. The European Communities appeals from these findings of the Panel principally on two grounds: firstly, that the Panel has misinterpreted Article 5.2 of the *SPS Agreement*; secondly, that the Panel has disregarded and distorted the evidence submitted by the European Communities.

205. In respect of the first ground, we agree with the European Communities that the Panel has indeed misconceived the scope of application of Article 5.2. It should be recalled that Article 5.2 states that in the assessment of risks, Members shall take into account, in addition to "available scientific evidence", "relevant processes and production methods; [and] relevant inspection, sampling and testing methods". We note also that Article 8 requires Members to "observe the provisions of Annex C in the operation of control, inspection and approval procedures ... ". The footnote in Annex C states that "control, inspection and approval procedures include, *inter alia*, procedures for sampling, testing and certification". We consider that this language is amply sufficient to authorize the taking into account of risks arising from failure to comply with the requirements of good veterinary practice in the administration of hormones for growth promotion purposes, as well as risks arising from difficulties of control, inspection and enforcement of the requirements of good veterinary practice.

206. Most, if not all, of the scientific studies referred to by the European Communities, in respect of the five hormones involved here, concluded that their use for growth promotion purposes is "safe", if the hormones are administered in accordance with the requirements of good veterinary practice. Where the condition of observance of good veterinary practice (which is much the same condition attached to the standards, guidelines and recommendations of Codex with respect to the use of the five hormones for growth promotion) is *not* followed, the logical inference is that the use of such hormones for growth promotion purposes may or may not be "safe". The *SPS Agreement* requires assessment of the potential for adverse effects on human health arising from the presence of contaminants and toxins in food. We consider that the object and purpose of the *SPS Agreement* justify the examination and evaluation of all such risks for human health whatever their precise and immediate origin may be. We do not mean to suggest that risks arising from potential abuse in the administration of controlled substances and from control problems need to be, or should be, evaluated by risk assessors in each and every case. When and if risks of these types do in fact arise, risk assessors may examine and evaluate them. Clearly, the necessity or propriety of examination and evaluation of such risks would have to be addressed on a case-by-case basis. What, in our view, is a fundamental legal error is to exclude, on an *a priori* basis, any such risks from the scope of application of Articles 5.1 and 5.2. We disagree with the Panel's suggestion that exclusion of risks resulting from the combination of potential abuse and difficulties of control is justified by

distinguishing between "risk assessment" and "risk management". As earlier noted, the concept of "risk management" is not mentioned in any provision of the *SPS Agreement* and, as such, cannot be used to sustain a more restrictive interpretation of "risk assessment" than is justified by the actual terms of Article 5.2, Article 8 and Annex C of the *SPS Agreement*.

207.   The question that arises, therefore, is whether the European Communities did, in fact, submit a risk assessment demonstrating and evaluating the existence and level of risk arising in the present case from abusive use of hormones and the difficulties of control of the administration of hormones for growth promotion purposes, within the United States and Canada as exporting countries, and at the frontiers of the European Communities as an importing country. Here, we must agree with the finding of the Panel that the European Communities in fact restricted itself to pointing out the condition of administration of hormones "in accordance with good practice" "without further providing an assessment of the potential adverse effects related to non compliance with such practice". The record of the panel proceedings shows that the risk arising from abusive use of hormones for growth promotion combined with control problems for the hormones at issue, may have been examined on two occasions in a scientific manner. The first occasion may have occurred at the proceedings before the Committee of Inquiry into the Problem of Quality in the Meat Sector established by the European Parliament, the results of which constituted the basis of the Pimenta Report of 1989. However, none of the original studies and evidence put before the Committee of Inquiry was submitted to the Panel. The second occasion could have been the 1995 EC Scientific Conference on Growth Promotion in Meat Production. One of the three workshops of this Conference examined specifically the problems of "detection and control". However, only one of the studies presented to the workshop discussed systematically some of the problems arising from the combination of potential abuse and problems of control of hormones and other substances. The study presented a theoretical framework for the systematic analysis of such problems, but did not itself investigate and evaluate the actual problems that have arisen at the borders of the European Communities or within the United States, Canada and other countries exporting meat and meat products to the European Communities. At best, this study may represent the beginning of an assessment of such risks.

208.   In the absence of any other relevant documentation, we find that the European Communities did not actually proceed to an assessment, within the meaning of Articles 5.1 and 5.2, of the risks arising from the failure of observance of good veterinary practice combined with problems of control of the use of hormones for growth promotion purposes. The absence of such a risk assessment, when considered in conjunction with the conclusion actually reached by most, if not all, of the scientific studies relating to the other aspects of risk noted earlier, leads us to the conclusion that no risk assessment that reasonably

supports or warrants the import prohibition embodied in the EC Directives was furnished to the Panel. We affirm, therefore, the ultimate conclusion of the Panel that the EC import prohibition is not based on a risk assessment within the meaning of Articles 5.1 and 5.2 of the *SPS Agreement* and is, therefore, inconsistent with the requirements of Article 5.1.

Notes and Questions

(1) The Appellate Body dealt with many other issues on this appeal. In particular, it ruled that the burden of proof to show a violation of Article 5 was on the complainants. It upheld a number of important procedural rulings made by the panel, in particular in respect of the selection and use of experts under DSU article 13. It also established a standard for determining whether a panel had failed to meet its obligation under DSU article 11 to make an objective assessment of the matter before it (see Section 7.3 infra). In that respect, it engaged in a searching and often critical examination of how the panel had evaluated certain evidence.

(2) The EC measures at issue were adopted and came into effect before 1995, the effective date of the WTO Agreement. Why were they subject to the risk assessment requirements of the SPS Agreement at all?

(3) Article 5(7) of the SPS Agreement contains a version of what is known as the precautionary principle. To be specific, it provides:

> In cases where scientific evidence is insufficient, a [WTO] Member may provisionally adopt [SPS] measures on the basis of available pertinent information, including that from the relevant international organizations as well as from [SPS] measures applied by other Members. In such circumstances, Members shall seek to obtain the additional information necessary for a more objective assessment of risk and review the [SPS] measure accordingly within a reasonable period of time.

In response to a question from the panel, the EC declined to invoke this provision. On appeal, however, it argued that there was the precautionary principle had become a general customary rule of international law or at least a general principle of law on which it could rely to justify its measures. In response, the US suggested that the precautionary principle was more an "approach" than a "principle". Canada took the view that the principle had not yet been incorporated into the corpus of public international law, even though it might in the future crystallize as a general principle of law. The Appellate Body addressed the argument as follows:

> 123.   The status of the precautionary principle in international law continues to be the subject of debate among academics, law practitioners, regulators and judges. The precautionary principle is regarded by some as having crystallized into a general principle of customary international *environmental* law. Whether it has been widely accepted by Members as a principle of *general* or *customary international law* appears less than clear. We consider, however, that it is unnecessary, and probably imprudent, for the Appellate Body in this appeal to take a position on this important, but abstract, question. We note that the Panel itself did not make any definitive finding with regard to the status

of the precautionary principle in international law and that the precautionary principle, at least outside the field of international environmental law, still awaits authoritative formulation.

124. It appears to us important, nevertheless, to note some aspects of the relationship of the precautionary principle to the *SPS Agreement*. First, the principle has not been written into the *SPS Agreement* as a ground for justifying SPS measures that are otherwise inconsistent with the obligations of Members set out in particular provisions of that Agreement. Secondly, the precautionary principle indeed finds reflection in Article 5.7 of the *SPS Agreement*. We agree, at the same time, with the European Communities, that there is no need to assume that Article 5.7 exhausts the relevance of a precautionary principle. It is reflected also in the sixth paragraph of the preamble and in Article 3.3. These explicitly recognize the right of Members to establish their own appropriate level of sanitary protection, which level may be higher (i.e., more cautious) than that implied in existing international standards, guidelines and recommendations. Thirdly, a panel charged with determining, for instance, whether "sufficient scientific evidence" exists to warrant the maintenance by a Member of a particular SPS measure may, of course, and should, bear in mind that responsible, representative governments commonly act from perspectives of prudence and precaution where risks of irreversible, e.g. life-terminating, damage to human health are concerned. Lastly, however, the precautionary principle does not, by itself, and without a clear textual directive to that effect, relieve a panel from the duty of applying the normal (i.e. customary international law) principles of treaty interpretation in reading the provisions of the *SPS Agreement*.

125. We accordingly agree with the finding of the Panel that the precautionary principle does not override the provisions of Articles 5.1 and 5.2 of the *SPS Agreement*.

Japan invoked the SPS Agreement's precautionary principle in the so-called *Apples* case, but was found not to have shown that it had taken any action to comply with the second sentence of article 5(7). Japan—Measures Affecting Agricultural Products, WT/DS76/AB/R, paras. 86–94 (Appellate Body Report adopted by the DSB on March 19, 1999).

(4) The panel in *EC Hormones* found that the EC also violated article 5(5) of the SPS Agreement, which provides as follows:

> With the objective of achieving consistency in the application of the concept of appropriate level of [SPS] protection against risks to human life or health, or to animal and plant life or health, each Member shall avoid arbitrary or unjustifiable distinctions in the levels it considers to be appropriate in different situations, if such distinctions result in discrimination or a disguised restriction on international trade.

In particular, the panel concluded that the EC had made an arbitrary or unjustifiable distinction in banning the use of hormones for growth promotion purposes in meat production, but not regulating their natural occurrence in meat and other foods (and that such distinction had resulted in discrimination or a disguised restriction on trade). On appeal, the Appellate

Body reversed the panel's finding of an arbitrary or unjustifiable distinction, noting:

> 221. We do not share the Panel's conclusions that the above differences in levels of protection in respect of added hormones in treated meat and in respect of naturally-occurring hormones in food, are merely arbitrary and unjustifiable. To the contrary, we consider there is a fundamental distinction between added hormones (natural or synthetic) and naturally-occurring hormones in meat and other foods. In respect of the latter, the European Communities simply takes no regulatory action; to require it to prohibit totally the production and consumption of such foods or to limit the residues of naturally-occurring hormones in food, entails such a comprehensive and massive governmental intervention in nature and in the ordinary lives of people as to reduce the comparison itself to an absurdity. The other considerations cited by the Panel, whether taken separately or grouped together, do not justify the Panel's finding of arbitrariness in the difference in the level of protection between added hormones for growth promotion and naturally-occurring hormones in meat and other foods.

Do you agree? Are Dr. Lucifer's comments, in footnote 2 supra, on the cancer-causing impact of "exogenous oestregens" relevant? How does one decide what situations are comparable? How many health measures could be justified if they were compared to toleration of smoking?

(5) Consider the obligations in article 2(3) of the SPS Agreement. How do those obligations relate to the obligations in article 5(5)? Could there be a violation of article 5(5) without there being a violation of article 2(3)? In particular, what does the "distinctions" requirement of article 5(5) add?

(6) A violation of article 5(5) was found in the *Australia Salmon* case. Australia—Measures Affecting the Importation of Salmon, WT/DS18 (Appellate Body Report and Panel Report as modified adopted by the DSB on November 6, 1998; Compliance Panel Report adopted by the DSB on March 20, 2000). In respect of that case, Professor Davey has written:

> In the *Salmon* case, the panel looked at three warning signals (the arbitrariness and unjustifiability of the distinctions in the level of protection provided by different, but comparable, Australian SPS measures; the substantial size of those distinctions; the inconsistency of the Australian measure with SPS Articles 5.1 and 2.2) and three additional factors (the substantial difference in the SPS measures applied by Australia in comparable situations; the change in the conclusions between the draft risk assessment and the final risk assessment; and the absence of measures controlling internal fish movements within Australia) that it cumulated to find discrimination or a disguised restriction. Panel Report, paras. 8.146–8.160. The panel's analysis was upheld by the Appellate Body, although it found that the first additional factor was equivalent to the first warning signal. Appellate Body Report, paras. 159–178. The compliance panel, in examining the new Australian measure implemented in response to the panel/Appellate Body reports, found that there was no longer an unjustifiable or arbitrary distinction between comparable situations. It also noted the absence of two of the three warning signals and of all of the additional factors noted in the

original case. Accordingly, no violation of Article 5.5 was found. Compliance Panel Report, paras. 7.86–7.108.

The use of "warning signals" and "additional factors" to determine whether Article 5.5 has been violated is not very satisfactory. Perhaps it is only a matter of language, but there is a suggestion by using those two categories that there is a missing third category–"factors establishing a violation". In other words, the warning signals cause you to be suspicious that there might be a violation (but by definition cannot establish it) and the additional factors support your finding that there is a violation, but do not themselves establish the violation. In the future, more precise standards for the application of Article 5.5 need to be established with respect to this third factor. In doing so, it needs to be considered what, if anything, Article 5.5 adds to what is already covered by Article 2.3.

William J. Davey, Has the WTO Dispute Settlement System Exceeded Its Authority?: A Consideration of Deference Shown by the System to Member Government Decisions and Its Use of Issue–Avoidance Techniques, *in* 4 Journal of International Economic Law 79, 91–92 (2001) *and in* T. Cottier & P. Mavroidis (eds.), The Role of the Judge: Lessons for the WTO (forthcoming 2002).

(7) The SPS Agreement establishes a committee to administer the agreement. It consists of all WTO members and meets regularly to discuss issues that have arisen under the SPS Agreement. Since members are obligated to notify new and proposed SPS measures, the committee often has occasion to discuss such measures. In 2000, the committee issued "Guidelines to Further the Practical Implementation of Article 5.5" (G/SPS/15, July 18, 2000).

SECTION 14.3   THE TBT AGREEMENT

Like the SPS Agreement, the WTO Agreement on Technical Barriers to Trade (the TBT Agreement) is much more than an exception to GATT rules. Unlike the SPS Agreement, the TBT Agreement has not been interpreted to any significant degree in WTO (or GATT) dispute settlement proceeding, despite having been in existence since the Tokyo Round, where it was known as the Standards Code. The TBT Agreement appears in the Documents Supplement. For the purposes of the following notes and questions, the student should, at a minimum, read Article 2 and Annex 1.1–1.2 carefully and skim the preamble and Articles 3–6. As you study the TBT Agreement, consider whether and to what extent it goes beyond the provisions of GATT Articles III and XI.

Notes and Questions

(1) The TBT agreement deals with technical regulations and standards. Annex 1.1 defines a "technical regulation" as follows:

Document which lays down product characteristics or their related processes and production methods, including the applicable administrative provisions, with which compliance is mandatory. It may also include or deal exclusively with terminology, symbols, packaging, marking or labeling requirements as they apply to a product, process or production method.

A "standard" is defined in Annex 1.2 as a "[d]ocument approved by a recognized body, that provides for repeated use, rules, guidelines or characteristics for products or related processes and production methods, with which compliance is not necessary."

In the *Asbestos* case (excerpted in Sections 12.4(A) and 13.1 supra), the panel had ruled that a prohibition on the marketing of a product would not fall within the definition of technical regulation as set out above. The Appellate Body reversed, noting (para. 75):

> Viewing the measure as an integrated whole [including both the basic prohibition and exceptions], we see that it lays down "characteristics" for all products that might contain asbestos, and we see also that it lays down the "applicable administrative provisions" for certain products containing chrysotile asbestos fibres which are excluded from the prohibitions in the measure. Accordingly, we find that the measure is a "document" which "lays down product characteristics ... including the applicable administrative provisions, with which compliance is mandatory."

(2) How do the provisions of article 2 of the TBT Agreement compare to GATT Article III? Note in article 2.1, there is a MFN and national treatment obligation. As in the case of Article III, the obligation is based on according most favorable treatment to "like products." This means that the controversy we noted in respect of Article III over whether identical products produced by different processes or under different conditions must be treated as like products will arise under the TBT Agreement. See notes to Section 12.4(A) supra. Suppose a violation of article 2.1 is found because a technical regulation fails to accord no less favorable treatment to the imported like product at issue. Could the exceptions of GATT Article XX be invoked?

(3) Labeling rules are subject to the TBT Agreement. Would it be possible to impose a labeling rule that differentiated products on the basis of the process or production method by which they were made? Would it matter whether difference was revealed in the product itself?

(4) The heart of the TBT Agreement's obligations on trade barriers is contained in articles 2.2–2.5. Consider, in particular, the language of article 2.2:

> Members shall ensure that technical regulations are not prepared, adopted or applied with a view to or with the effect of creating unnecessary obstacles to international trade. For this purpose, technical regulations shall not be more trade-restrictive than necessary to fulfil a legitimate objective, taking account of the risks non-fulfillment would create. Such legitimate objectives are, *inter alia*, national security requirements; the prevention of deceptive practices; protection of human health or safety, animal or plant life or health, or the environment. In assessing such risks, relevant elements of consideration are, *inter alia*, available scientific and technical information, related processing technology or intended end-uses of products.

The key question presented is how to interpret the word "necessary." How much freedom do parties have to choose their own level of protection for human health? To what extent is the jurisprudence under GATT Article XX(b) and (d) relevant?

(5) Suppose a country wishes to implement a technical regulation on a product in respect of which there is an international standard. Under article 2.4, what freedom does it have to impose restrictions that are stricter than the international standard? Who decides whether the international standard is inadequate or ineffective? Consider article 2.5. How would this issue be handled under the SPS Agreement? Consider SPS article 3(3).

(6) Why do you think that the TBT Agreement establishes a preference for performance characteristics rather than design or descriptive characteristics? See article 2.8.

(7) To what extent does the TBT Agreement apply to local governments and nongovernment organizations? See article 3. What is the extent of the U.S. obligation under article 3.1? Compare GATT Article XXIV:12, as interpreted by the Understanding on the Interpretation of Article XXIV. See Section 6.7(B) supra.

(8) To what extent does the TBT Agreement effectively restrict the ability of a country to insist on proof that imported products comply with its national standards? To what extent must it accept proof of tests conducted outside the country? See articles 5 and 6.

(9) One of the main goals of the TBT Agreement is transparency, to ensure that those who will be affected by new regulations and standards are informed in time to participate in the drafting process. Do you think that it achieves this goal?

(10) The U.S. implemented the Tokyo and Uruguay Round agreements in the Trade Agreements Act of 1979, secs. 401–453, as amended.

SECTION 14.4 ALTERNATIVE APPROACHES TO CONTROLLING DISGUISED DISCRIMINATION

The SPS and TBT Agreements try to discourage the use of measures that will adversely affect international trade flows. One can debate whether they strike a proper balance between the interests of free trade and national sovereignty. In considering whether they are too solicitous of countries wanting to impose their own idiosyncratic standards or too intrusive, it is useful to consider the rules applied by the EU and the United States to control discrimination against products from other Member States or States. We look first at an EC case; then at a U.S. one. The U.S. case involves an analysis of the so-called Dormant Commerce Clause, which we examined in Section 3.6 supra. The EC Treaty provisions at issue in the EC case are Article 28, which bans quantitative restrictions and measures having equivalent effect and which was excerpted in Chapter 9 supra, and Article 30, which lists a number of exceptions to Article 28 of the type contained in GATT Article XX. The notes explore the approaches taken in the U.S. free trade agreements, which can be usefully compared to those taken by in the WTO and the EC.

REWE-ZENTRAL AG v. BUNDESMONOPOLVERWAL-TUNG FÜR BRANNTWEIN (CASSIS DE DIJON)

Court of Justice of the European Community, 1979.
Case 120/78, [1979] ECR 649.

[2]   It appears from the order making the reference that the plaintiff in the main action intends to import a consignment of "Cassis de Dijon" originating in France for the purpose of marketing it in the Federal Republic of Germany.

The plaintiff applied to the Bundesmonopolverwaltung (Federal Monopoly Administration for Spirits) for authorization to import the product in question and the monopoly administration informed it that because of its insufficient alcoholic strength the said product does not have the characteristics required in order to be marketed within the Federal Republic of Germany.

* * *

Those provisions lay down that the marketing of fruit liqueurs, such as "Cassis de Dijon", is conditional upon a minimum alcohol content of 25%, whereas the alcohol content of the product in question, which is freely marketed as such in France, is between 15 and 20%.

* * *

[8]   In the absence of common [EC] rules relating to the production and marketing of alcohol * * * it is for the Member States to regulate all matters relating to the production and marketing of alcohol and alcoholic beverages on their own territory.

Obstacles to movement within the Community resulting from disparities between the national laws relating to the marketing of the products in question must be accepted in so far as those provisions may be recognized as being necessary in order to satisfy mandatory requirements relating in particular to the effectiveness of fiscal supervision, the protection of public health, the fairness of commercial transactions and the defense of the consumer.

[9]   The Government of the Federal Republic of Germany, intervening in the proceedings, put forward various arguments which, in its view, justify the application of provisions relating to the minimum alcohol content of alcoholic beverages, adducing considerations relating on the one hand to the protection of public health and on the other to the protection of the consumer against unfair commercial practices.

[10]   As regards the protection of public health the German Government states that the purpose of the fixing of minimum alcohol contents by

national legislation is to avoid the proliferation of alcoholic beverages on the national market, in particular alcoholic beverages with a low alcohol content, since, in its view, such products may more easily induce a tolerance towards alcohol than more highly alcoholic beverages.

[11]   Such considerations are not decisive since the consumer can obtain on the market an extremely wide range of weakly or moderately alcoholic products and furthermore a large proportion of alcoholic beverages with a high alcohol content freely sold on the German market is generally consumed in a diluted form.

[12]   The German Government also claims that the fixing of a lower limit for the alcohol content of certain liqueurs is designed to protect the consumer against unfair practices on the part of producers and distributors of alcoholic beverages.

This argument is based on the consideration that the lowering of the alcohol content secures a competitive advantage in relation to beverages with a higher alcohol content, since alcohol constitutes by far the most expensive constituent of beverages by reason of the high rate of tax to which it is subject.

Furthermore, according to the German Government, to allow alcoholic products into free circulation wherever, as regards their alcohol content, they comply with the rules laid down in the country of production would have the effect of imposing as a common standard within the Community the lowest alcohol content permitted in any of the Member States, and even of rendering any requirements in this field inoperative since a lower limit of this nature is foreign to the rules of several Member States.

[13]   As the Commission rightly observed, the fixing of limits in relation to the alcohol content of beverages may lead to the standardization of products placed on the market and of their designations, in the interests of a greater transparency of commercial transactions and offers for sale to the public.

However, this line of argument cannot be taken so far as to regard the mandatory fixing of minimum alcohol contents as being an essential guarantee of the fairness of commercial transactions, since it is a simple matter to ensure that suitable information is conveyed to the purchaser by requiring the display of an indication of origin and of the alcohol content on the packaging of products.

[14]   It is clear from the foregoing that the requirements relating to the minimum alcohol content of alcoholic beverages do not serve a purpose which is in the general interest and such as to take precedence over the requirements of the free movement of goods, which constitutes one of the fundamental rules of the Community.

In practice, the principle effect of requirements of this nature is to promote alcoholic beverages having a high alcohol content by excluding from the national market products of other Member States which do not answer that description.

It therefore appears that the unilateral requirement imposed by the rules of a Member State of a minimum alcohol content for the purposes of the sale of alcoholic beverages constitutes an obstacle to trade which is incompatible with the provisions of Article [28] of the Treaty.

There is therefore no valid reason why, provided that they have been lawfully produced and marketed in one of the Member States, alcoholic beverages should not be introduced into any other Member State; the sale of such products may not be subject to a legal prohibition on the marketing of beverages with an alcohol content lower than the limit set by the national rules.

[15] Consequently, * * * the concept of "measures having an effect equivalent to quantitative restrictions on imports" contained in Article [28] of the Treaty is to be understood to mean that the fixing of a minimum alcohol content for alcoholic beverages intended for human consumption by the legislation of a Member State also falls within the prohibition laid down in that provision where the importation of alcoholic beverages lawfully produced and marketed in another Member State is concerned.

Notes and Questions

(1) After the *Cassis de Dijon* judgment appeared, the EC Commission issued a Communication, in which it indicated that the main lesson to be drawn from the decision was: "Any product lawfully produced and marketed in one Member State must, in principle, be admitted to the market of any other Member State." Eur. Comm. O.J. C 256/2 (Oct. 3, 1980). This has been referred to as the mutual trust or mutual recognition principle. The Commission and others have relied on the *Cassis de Dijon* decision to attack successfully many similar restrictions. Among the best known cases are Commission v. Germany (German beer), Case 178/84, [1987] ECR 1227 (German beer purity law cannot be used to block sale of beer lawfully produced in other EC member states); 3 Glocken GmbH v. USL Centro–Sud, Case 407/85, [1988] ECR 4233 (Italian rules on pasta composition cannot be used to block imports of pasta from other EC member states). The recent decision in the *Keck* case, described in Chapter 9, does not affect this line of cases, which deal with product standards, not business practices.

It is noteworthy that in its list of factors that might justify product standards (see para. 8), the EC Court included factors not found in Article 30,[3] such as fairness of commercial transactions and consumer protection. The Court has since added environmental considerations to this list.

---

3. Article 30 provides: "The provisions of Articles 28 and 29 shall not preclude prohibitions or restrictions on imports, exports or goods in transit justified on grounds of public morality, public policy or public security; the protection of health and life of humans, animals or plants; the protection of national treasures possessing artistic, historic or archaeological value or the protection of industrial and commercial property. Such prohibitions or restrictions shall not, however, constitute a means of

(2) Subsequent to the *Cassis de Dijon* decision, the EC Treaty was amended by the Single European Act, effective in 1987, which added Article 95(4), which provides:

> If, after the adoption of a harmonization measure by the Council * * *, a Member State deems it necessary to apply national provisions on grounds of major needs referred to in Article 30, or relating to protection of the environment or the working environment, it shall notify the Commission of these provisions.

> The Commission shall confirm the provisions involved after having verified that they are not a means of arbitrary discrimination or a disguised restriction on trade between Member States.

New article 176 provided: "The protective measures adopted in common pursuant to Article 175 [relating to the environment] shall not prevent any Member State from maintaining or introducing more stringent protective measures compatible with this Treaty." This article was revised slightly by the Maastricht Treaty in 1993, which added similar language to the Treaty's provisions on consumer protection. How do these provisions affect the decision in *Cassis de Dijon*, if at all?

(3) If an EC member state wanted to implement a ban on beef from cattle fed hormones, how would the issue be treated under the *Cassis de Dijon* analysis? Assume that the EC has taken no action one way or the other on the use of hormones and that the some other member states permit their use. Who would have the burden of proof under the *Cassis de Dijon* case?

(4) What differences exist between the EC and WTO regimes that may make the mutual trust or recognition principle unsuitable or unacceptable for use in the WTO? Are these differences immutable, or would you expect them to change over time?

(5) In the U.S.-Canada Free Trade Agreement (the CUSFTA), the problem of product standards was dealt with generally in Chapter 6 and in Article 708 in respect of agricultural, food, beverages and certain related goods. Chapter 6 did not apply to state or provincial governments. Art. 601(2). The basic obligation of Chapter 6 is in Article 603, which provides:

> Neither party shall maintain or introduce standards-related measures or procedures for product approval that would create unnecessary obstacles to trade between the territories of the Parties. Unnecessary obstacles to trade shall not be deemed to be created if: a) the demonstrable purpose of such measure or procedure is to achieve a legitimate domestic objective; and b) the measure or procedure does not operate to exclude goods of the other Party that meet that legitimate domestic objective.

According to Article 609, "legitimate domestic objective means an objective whose purpose is to protect health, safety, essential security, the environment, or consumer interests." If these had been the applicable rules in the EC, would the *Cassis de Dijon* case have come out differently? How would the hormones dispute be resolved? Would you characterize the CUSFTA approach as more EC-like or more WTO-like?

arbitrary discrimination or a disguised re-   striction on trade between Member States."

(6) CUSFTA Article 708.2(a), which is in the chapter on agriculture, provides that the parties shall prevent the introduction of a standard that constitutes an arbitrary, unjustifiable or disguised restriction on trade. After adopting new standards for milk, Puerto Rico barred the import of ultra-high temperature (UHT) milk from Quebec as of December 31, 1991, principally affecting the Quebec company Lactel, which had supplied UHT milk to the Puerto Rican market from 1977 to 1991. The new standards were those applied in the continental U.S. A panel under Chapter 18 of the CUSFTA concluded that the Puerto Rican measure was a restriction, but that it was not disguised or arbitrary. As to the issue of justifiability, the panel concluded that it was not unjustifiable for the U.S. to insist on a study to demonstrate that the standards applied in Quebec were equivalent to the Puerto Rican standards, although it felt that the U.S. conduct in delaying resolution of the equivalency issue was less than exemplary. Indeed, although the panel concluded that Article 708 had not been violated, it concluded that because of U.S. footdragging Canada's reasonable expectations under the FTA had been nullified and impaired by the UHT milk ban. In re Puerto Rico Regulations on the Import, Distribution and Sale of U.H.T. Milk from Quebec, Case No. USA–93–1807–01 (Panel Report of June 3, 1993).

(7) In the North American Free Trade Agreement (NAFTA), because of concerns expressed by environmental groups, the issue of product standards was dealt with in more detail than in the CUSFTA. See Documents Supplement, NAFTA arts. 904–908, especially art. 904(4)(similar to CUSFTA Article 603 quoted above). NAFTA Article 904(2) states that "Notwithstanding any other provision of this Chapter, each Party may, in pursuing its legitimate objectives * * * establish the levels of protection that it considers appropriate in accordance with Article 907(2)." Article 907(2) provides that a Party "*should* avoid arbitrary or unjustifiable distinctions between similar goods or services in the level of protection it considers appropriate, where the distinctions: (a) result in arbitrary or unjustifiable discrimination against goods or services providers of another Party; (b) constitute a disguised restriction on trade between the Parties; or (c) discriminate between similar goods or services for the same use under the same conditions that pose the same level of risk and provide similar benefits." (Emphasis added.) Is NAFTA more or less protective of idiosyncratic standards than the CUSFTA? Than the TBT Agreement? How would the hormones disputes be resolved under these NAFTA provisions? NAFTA contains specific rules for SPS measures in Chapter 7B. How would the hormones dispute be resolved under those provisions? See, in particular, Article 712.

(8) In Article 906(2), NAFTA effectively calls for the harmonization of standards "[w]ithout reducing the level of safety or of protection of human, animal or plant life or health, the environment or consumers." See also NAFTA, arts. 713–714 (use of international standards and pursuit of equivalence, without reducing protection levels). How does this compare to the *Cassis de Dijon* approach? It is noteworthy that the EC Commission so heartily embraced the mutual recognition doctrine in *Cassis* because it had found it so difficult to harmonize standards otherwise.

MINNESOTA v. CLOVER LEAF CREAMERY CO.

Supreme Court of the United States, 1981.
449 U.S. 456, 101 S.Ct. 715, 66 L.Ed.2d 659.

JUSTICE BRENNAN:

In 1977, the Minnesota Legislature enacted a statute banning the retail sale of milk in plastic nonreturnable, nonrefillable containers, but permitting such sale in other nonreturnable, nonrefillable containers, such as paperboard milk cartons. Respondents contend that the statute violates the Equal Protection and Commerce Clauses of the Constitution.

I

The purpose of the Minnesota statute is set out as section 1:

"The legislature finds that the use of nonreturnable, nonrefillable containers for the packaging of milk and other milk products presents a solid waste management problem for the state, promotes energy waste, and depletes natural resources. The legislature therefore * * * determines that the use of nonreturnable, nonrefillable containers for packaging milk and other milk products should be discouraged and that the use of returnable and reusable packaging for these products is preferred and should be encouraged."

[A lower state court concluded that the Act would not achieve the legislature's policy goals and found that the actual purpose (as opposed to the above-quoted stated purpose) "was to promote the economic interests of certain segments of the local dairy and pulpwood industries at the expense of the economic interests of other segments of the diary industry and the plastics industry." It consequently enjoined enforcement of the Act under the Due Process Clauses of the Minnesota and U.S. Constitutions and under the U.S. Constitution's Equal Protection and Commerce Clauses.]

The State appealed to the Supreme Court of Minnesota, which affirmed the District Court on the federal equal protection and due process grounds, without reaching the Commerce Clause or state-law issues. Unlike the District Court, the State Supreme Court found that the purpose of the Act was "to promote the state interests of encouraging the reuse and recycling of materials and reducing the amount and type of material entering the solid waste stream," and acknowledged the legitimacy of this purpose. Nevertheless, relying on the District Court's findings of fact, the full record, and an independent review of documentary sources, the State Supreme Court held that "the evidence conclusively demonstrates that the discrimination against plastic nonrefillables is not rationally related to the Act's objectives."

[In Part II, the Court concluded that the Minnesota statute did not violate the Equal Protection Clause because it bore a rational relation to Minnesota's objectives. The Court stressed in Part II that it was not appropriate under the federal Equal Protection Clause for a state court to substitute its judgment on policy issues for that of the state legislature. Although the state supreme court had not considered the Commerce Clause issue, the Supreme Court did.]

III

The District Court also held that the Minnesota statute is unconstitutional under the Commerce Clause because it imposes an unreasonable burden on interstate commerce. We cannot agree.

When legislating in areas of legitimate local concern, such as environmental protection and resource conservation, States are nonetheless limited by the Commerce Clause. If a state law purporting to promote environmental purposes is in reality "simple economic protectionism," we have applied a "virtually per se rule of invalidity." Philadelphia v. New Jersey, 437 U.S. 617, 624 (1978).[4] Even if a statute regulates "evenhandedly," and imposes only "incidental" burdens on interstate commerce, the courts must nevertheless strike it down if "the burden imposed on such commerce is clearly excessive in relation to the putative local benefits." Pike v. Bruce Church, Inc., 397 U.S. 137, 142 (1970). Moreover, "the extent of the burden that will be tolerated will of course depend on the nature of the local interest involved, and on whether it could be promoted as well with a lesser impact on interstate activities." Ibid.

Minnesota's statute does not effect "simple protectionism," but "regulates evenhandedly" by prohibiting all milk retailers from selling their products in plastic, nonreturnable milk containers, without regard to whether the milk, the containers, or the sellers are from outside the State. This statute is therefore unlike statutes discriminating against interstate commerce, which we have consistently struck down.

Since the statute does not discriminate between interstate and intrastate commerce, the controlling question is whether the incidental burden imposed on interstate commerce by the Minnesota Act is "clearly excessive in relation to the putative local benefits." Pike v. Bruce Church, Inc., supra, at 142. We conclude that it is not.

The burden imposed on interstate commerce by the statute is relatively minor. Milk products may continue to move freely across the Minnesota border, and since most dairies package their products in more than one type of containers, the inconvenience of having to conform to different packaging requirements in Minnesota and the surrounding States should be slight. Within Minnesota, business will presumably shift from manufacturers of plastic nonreturnable containers to producers of paperboard cartons, refillable bottles, and plastic pouches, but

4. [original note 15] A court may find that a state law constitutes "economic protectionism" on proof either of discriminatory effect, or of discriminatory purpose. Respondents advance a "discriminatory purpose" argument, relying on a finding by the District Court that the Act's "actual basis was to promote the economic inter-ests of certain segments of the local dairy and pulpwood industries at the expense of the economic interests of other segments of the dairy industry and the plastics industry." We have already considered and rejected this argument in the equal protection context, and do so in this context as well.

there is no reason to suspect that the gainers will be Minnesota firms, or the losers out-of-state firms. Indeed, two of the three dairies, the sole milk retailer, and the sole milk container producer challenging the statute in this litigation are Minnesota firms.

Pulpwood producers are the only Minnesota industry likely to benefit significantly from the Act at the expense of out-of-state firms. Respondents point out that plastic resin, the raw material used for making plastic nonreturnable milk jugs, is produced entirely by non-Minnesota firms, while pulpwood, used for making paperboard, is a major Minnesota product. Nevertheless, it is clear that respondents exaggerate the degree of burden on out-of-state interests, both because plastics will continue to be used in the production of plastic pouches, plastic returnable bottles, and paperboard itself, and because out-of-state pulpwood producers will presumably absorb some of the business generated by the Act.

Even granting that the out-of-state plastics industry is burdened relatively more heavily than the Minnesota pulpwood industry, we find that this burden is not "clearly excessive" in light of the substantial state interest in promoting conservation of energy and other natural resources and easing solid waste disposal problems, which we have already reviewed in the context of equal protection analysis. We find these local benefits ample to support Minnesota's decision under the Commerce Clause. Moreover, we find that no approach with "a lesser impact on interstate activities," Pike v. Bruce Church, Inc., supra, at 142, is available. Respondents have suggested several alternative statutory schemes, but these alternatives are either more burdensome on commerce than the Act (as, for example, banning all nonreturnables) or less likely to be effective (as, for example, providing incentives for recycling).

In Exxon Corp. v. Governor of Maryland, 437 U.S. 117 (1978), we upheld a Maryland statute barring producers and refiners of petroleum products-all of which were out-of-state businesses-from retailing gasoline in the State. We stressed that the Commerce Clause "protects the interstate market, not particular interstate firms, from prohibitive or burdensome regulations." Id., at 127–128. A nondiscriminatory regulation serving substantial state purposes is not invalid simply because it causes some business to shift from a predominantly out-of-state industry to a predominantly in-state industry. Only if the burden on interstate commerce clearly outweighs the State's legitimate purposes does such a regulation violate the Commerce Clause.

Notes and Questions

1. How would you compare the US approach–as set out in *Clover Leaf Creamery*—to the NAFTA, CUSFTA, EC and WTO approaches to the product standards problem?

2. As all of the foregoing highlights, as economic integration goes forward, more harmonization or acceptance of differences seems inevitable. At any given time, of course, it is impossible to predict how fast the process will occur.

Chapter 15

ESCAPE CLAUSES, SAFEGUARDS AND ADJUSTMENT POLICIES

SECTION 15.1 INTRODUCTION

(A) SCOPE OF THE CHAPTER

Traditionally, international trade rules have distinguished between the ways in which an importing nation can respond to "fair" trade practices on the one hand, and "unfair" trade practices on the other hand. "Safeguards" measures are available under certain conditions to respond to fairly traded imports, while more extensive counter-measures are permitted to respond to imports that are "dumped," subsidized, or otherwise considered to be in violation of international rules of conduct. We discuss safeguard measures in response to fair trade in this chapter, with discussion of unfair trade practices to follow.

Prior to the Uruguay Round, safeguards measures were governed solely by Article XIX of GATT—often referred to as GATT's escape clause. It specifies standards that are supposed to be met before safeguards measures can be imposed. Safeguards measures were to be used only when, "as a result of unforeseen developments and of the effect of obligations incurred" under the GATT, "increased imports" caused or threatened "serious injury" to a domestic industry.

Over time, GATT members began to ignore aspects of these standards in their safeguards policies, and also turned to other techniques for protecting domestic industries such as "voluntary" export restraints and orderly marketing agreements in place of formal actions under Article XIX. Such trade came to be known as "gray area" measures. Although they technically violated the legal requirements of GATT, they nevertheless embodied government-to-government accords and nations had little incentive to complain about them. A rough consensus arose prior to the Uruguay Round, however, that their proliferation was undermining GATT commitments. The result was a strong initiative to bring them under GATT discipline, and the new Uruguay Round Agreement on Safeguards requires that virtually all gray area measures be eliminated. If the new Agreement is respected, therefore, we may anticipate that formal reliance upon Article XIX could become more important in the years to come. The Safeguards Agreement also adds substantial clarification and tightening to the rules of safeguards, and has already spawned an interesting set of WTO cases. In addition to our study of the WTO law of safeguards, we will examine the safeguards policies of the United States and the U.S. law that governs them.

We are also concerned briefly in this chapter with measures that do not interfere directly in trade, but that nevertheless serve to aid firms or workers harmed by import competition. Subsidies to firms to adapt their product mix to changing competitive conditions, for example, or aid to workers for retraining, may serve as a substitute for or supplement to traditional safeguards measures. These types of programs are often termed "adjustment assistance," and will be the subject of the last section of the chapter.

(B) THE POLICIES OF SAFEGUARDS

What is the logic of affording protection to domestic industries "seriously injured" by import competition? A variety of economic and non-economic arguments for safeguards have been advanced through the years.

(1) Compensation and Adjustment Costs

One theory of safeguards actions is that they might serve to "compensate" those who suffer from trade liberalization. Even granting that increased imports may promote productive efficiency and give the consumer more choice at less expense, the argument runs, the domestic producers of import-competing products may find that they can no longer compete successfully. Businesses may be forced to change their product lines or to go out of business entirely, workers may become unemployed, and communities that were heavily dependent on such businesses may find their tax bases eroded and their local economies in shambles. The injured businesses and workers can argue that they have been made to bear an undue proportion of the costs for society's general gains and that society through government action should help them "adjust" to their new situation. They may urge an analogy here between compensation for trade-related injury and the governmental obligation to compensate property owners when property is taken for governmental purposes.

(2) Restoring Competitiveness

"The argument for safeguards measures to restore 'competitiveness' is straightforward. Safeguards actions provide ailing firms with an increase in profits, enabling them to invest in new technology and modern equipment, which will later allow them to compete successfully in the international marketplace. The purported source of net gains to the international community (and to the importing nation) lies with the eventual emergence of efficient competitors. The premise is that the protected industry will in time lower its costs of production to the point that protection is no longer necessary to its survival, and that the eventual savings in production costs (or perhaps the elimination of distortions attributable to monopoly power that would otherwise exist) will more than offset the short-term inefficiencies that arise during the period of protection."[1]

(3) *The Safety Valve Hypothesis*

"Policymakers need safety valves to pursue a long-term strategy of free trade. * * * [P]olitical pressures for protecting special interests can overwhelm the consensus favoring free trade. The dangers are greatest during periods of general economic distress, which can produce legislated quotas (as in the case of the textile bill passed recently) or voluntary restraint agreements or more formal agreements negotiated by the executive branch but motivated by congressional pressure (as in the case of quotas on automobiles, steel and textiles). Safety valves that relieve protectionist pressure, diverting it from the purely political arena, can therefore be extremely useful. They can facilitate trade liberalization and better enable lawmakers to withstand demands for protectionist policies."[2]

(4) *The Public Choice/Contractarian Perspective*

"Note that the revocation of a particular [trade] concession benefits import-competing firms in the revoking country but hurts exporters abroad. Those exporters will complain to their political officials about the loss of access to their overseas market, and likely withdraw some political support from the officials who were responsible for obtaining the original concession. Indeed, depending upon the form of government, a loss of export earnings may directly reduce the welfare of officials in power. A [politically sophisticated trade] agreement will nevertheless permit "escape" in states of the world in which the attendant political gains to officials in the importing country "outweigh" the costs to the officials in the exporting country. Suppose, for example, that in some state of the world, the concession by one country is highly disadvantageous to its officials, and the costs to officials in the other country if the concession is revoked would be modest. The parties may then benefit from an agreement to allow the first country to escape its concession in that state of the world. The quid pro quo from the perspective of officials in the other country is an agreement to let them escape their concessions in the same or some other state of the world in which they would gain considerably and the costs to officials in their trading partner would be modest."[3]

---

1. Alan Sykes, Protectionism as a "Safeguard": A Positive Analysis of the GATT "Escape Clause" With Normative Speculations, 58 U.Chi.L.Rev. 255, 263–64 (1991). Reprinted with permission.

2. Robert Lawrence & Robert Litan, Saving Free Trade 23–24 (1986).

3. Alan Sykes, Protectionism as a "Safeguard," supra note 1, at 281–82.

How convincing are these various arguments? The literature on the wisdom of safeguards policy is extensive—in addition to the sources quoted above, see Paul R. Krugman, Competitiveness: A Dangerous Obsession, Foreign Affairs, Mar./Apr. 1994 and the three papers by Sykes, Lawrence and Trebilcock in Reforming Trade Remedy Laws (Michael Trebilcock and Robert York eds., 1990).

SECTION 15.2   SAFEGUARD ACTIONS UNDER U.S. LAW

In the United States, the procedures for obtaining escape clause relief have varied significantly over time, often reflecting general congressional attitudes towards the desirability of free trade. Currently under U.S. law, an escape clause proceeding begins with a petition to the International Trade Commission (ITC) by representatives of the allegedly injured domestic industry (such as a trade association, individual firm, union or group of workers), or with a request to the ITC by the President, the U.S. Trade Representative, the Senate Finance Committee, or the House Ways and Means Committee, or upon initiation by the ITC itself. The ITC, formerly known as the Tariff Commission, consists of six Commissioners, not more than three of whom belong to the same political party. A petition for relief must give information justifying relief, including extensive data on imports, domestic production and injury, as well as an explanation of how the industry is making an effort to compete with the imports and how it will adjust if relief is granted. The ITC then determines whether the prerequisites of U.S. law are fulfilled. Its investigation and report must be completed within six months. If it makes an affirmative determination (including a tie vote), those Commissioners voting in the affirmative recommend a remedy and pass the matter on to the President, who must usually act within 60 days. The President has fairly broad discretion to reject the ITC recommendation, or to alter the recommended remedy, and not infrequently the President has done so.

Interested parties typically submit written materials and present testimony at ITC hearings. Decisions of the ITC are generally reviewable in the Court of International Trade or (in some cases) the Court of Appeals for the Federal Circuit. In escape clause cases, however, in large part because of the involvement of the President, judicial review is extremely limited—essentially to questions of procedural regularity. See Maple Leaf Fish Co. v. United States, 762 F.2d 86 (Fed.Cir.1985).

We will consider the legal issues raised by escape clause proceedings in the following order. First, in this section, we examine: (1) The requirement of increased imports; (2) the task of defining the domestic industry that competes with them; (3) the requirement of serious injury; (4) the requirement of causation; (5) the remedy phase before the President and the duration of relief.

(A) INCREASED IMPORTS

The first prerequisite for escape clause relief is the existence of increased imports. An increase in imports can be said to occur in one of two ways: (1) The absolute volume of imports may increase or (2) the import share of the domestic market may increase, even though the total volume of imports declines. An issue on which neither the WTO nor the U.S. statute provides much guidance concerns the time period over which the existence of an increase is measured. What if imports have increased in absolute terms over a one-or two-year period, but are below their absolute and relative peaks, which occurred several years earlier?

STAINLESS STEEL AND ALLOY TOOL STEEL

U.S. Intl. Trade Commn. (1976).[1]

VIEWS OF COMMISSIONERS MOORE AND BEDELL

* * *

We consider the increased imports requirement satisfied because imports increased between 1964 and 1975. We have used this time frame to avoid a determination based solely on a time period in which abnormal economic conditions existed. For example, the time period 1968–74 was not only one of unusual market conditions, but one in which unique governmental actions distorted stainless steel and alloy tool steel import levels. During this period the domestic industry was adversely affected by the Voluntary Restraint Agreement (VRA) and its subsequent changes, a world-wide nickel strike, two recessions, and domestic price controls.

Since 1964, total imports of stainless steel and alloy tool steel have tripled, imports of stainless sheets and strip have more than doubled, and other stainless steel and alloy tool steel articles have increased threefold to tenfold.

The act also states that the Commission should examine whether imports increased relative to domestic production. Imports increased from 116,000 tons in 1973 to 151,000 tons in 1974. During January–September 1975, imports increased to 120,000 tons, compared with 95,000 tons entered during the corresponding period in 1974. The ratio of imports to U.S. production has more than doubled, rising from 9.9 percent in 1973 to 23.1 percent during the most recent period, January–September 1975. Facts developed during the Commission's investigation indicate that imports will continue their upward trend.

* * *

VIEWS OF VICE CHAIRMAN MINCHEW

* * *

---

1. Inv. No. TA–201–5, Pub. No. 756, 1　ITRD 5404 (1976)

It is my view that, in the absence of extraordinary circumstances, the Commission should look at the increase in imports resulting from only the most recent trade concessions, so that the injury considered would be a new and continuing injury from increased imports as opposed to an "old" injury. The Senate Finance Committee Report at page 120 states:

> The increase in imports referred to would generally be such increases as have occurred since the effectiveness of the most recent trade-agreement concessions proclaimed by the President, i.e., as of now, the effectiveness of the Kennedy Round concessions beginning in 1968.

In certain circumstances in the past I have been willing to look at a shorter time frame to determine the trend of increasing imports, as I feel is my prerogative under the statute, but to look back beyond the last trade-agreement concessions would require extraordinary circumstances. In the present case, despite some out-of-the-ordinary occurrences since 1968, I do not feel that these occurrences warrant my looking beyond the 1968 trade-agreement concessions for purposes of determining increased import trends.

* * *

Views of Commissioner Ablondi

* * *

Increased Imports

Inseparably connected to the issue of "increased" imports is the selection of a time period over which imports are to be measured. In my judgment the relevant measuring period in the instant case is confined to the period since 1968.

Section 201(b)(1) of the act requires the Commission to determine "whether an article *is being imported* into the United States in such increased quantities as to be a substantial cause of serious injury, or the threat thereof, to the domestic industry * * *" (Emphasis added). By using the present tense, Congress clearly intended that the Commission consider only imports which have occurred during a period relative to the alleged injury. The act requires that imports be related to the injury claimed, and that the injury be current, or "new" injury. The relevant period of importation, then, must necessarily be close to the time of the injury (that is, to the present time) rather than during earlier periods of importation having little or no impact on present industry conditions.

* * *

It has been argued that the period since 1968 is unrepresentative and that the Commission should therefore consider imports which occurred prior to that time. I disagree. The factors cited by advocates of a longer measuring period are insufficient to warrant a departure from the measuring period outlined by Congress.

Many of the factors which are asserted to be the cause of unusual market conditions during the period 1968–74 have been encountered in each investigation conducted by this Commission under section 201. The effects of recessions, dollar devaluations, and price controls were national in scope and not confined to the specialty steel industry. Furthermore, market factors which related specifically to specialty steel during the period 1968–74 did not so distort market conditions as to necessitate the adoption of an alternate measuring period. The nickel strike of 1969 was clearly a temporary condition which served merely to delay imports until the following year. The two affirmative determinations of this Commission under the Antidumping Act each affected only one product from one exporting country. Finally, although the Voluntary Restraint Agreement (VRA) did affect import levels, its impact was limited by several factors, including the voluntary nature of the agreement—which in many instances caused imports to vary both above and below quota levels—and the fact that a substantial number of specialty steel exporters were not parties to the agreement. Clearly, the aforementioned factors are neither unique to the subject industry nor so pervasive as to substantially distort market conditions. Accordingly, there is no basis on which to adopt a measuring period extending before 1968.

In selecting the appropriate measuring period, it has been the established practice of this Commission under section 301 of the Trade Expansion Act as well as under section 201 of the 1974 Trade Act to analyze imports over a period of time of sufficient length to establish trends and thereby put aberrant or temporary conditions into proper perspective. Generally, the period of time selected by the Commission has been 5 years or so. On the basis of such a period, it can be seen that since 1970 total imports of stainless steel and alloy tool steel have declined absolutely and relative to domestic production. In 1974 total imports were over 7,000 tons less than in 1970. During 1970–74, annual U.S. production of stainless and alloy tool steel increased steadily from 700,000 tons to more than 1,325,000 tons. In the same period, the ratio of imports to domestic production was nearly halved, dropping from 24.4 percent to 12.3 percent.

During the recessionary period of 1974 and the first part of 1975, imports did increase relative to domestic production. However, a substantial part of the increase can be attributed to importers' lead times, which at the end of the third quarter of 1974 were roughly twice as long as domestic lead times. Such a differential meant that deliveries on orders placed with foreign producers during the boom period of 1974 continued through the fourth quarter of 1974 and the first and second quarters of 1975—a period during which domestic production fell almost 50 percent below 1974 levels. Clearly, these increases were inconsistent with the general downward trend evidenced during the period 1970–74 and, as such, are not sufficient to satisfy the requirement of "increased" imports.

Notes and Questions

(1) Suppose that imports have declined in absolute terms, but increased in relative terms. Can it fairly be said that "increased imports" are causing injury, or would it be more accurate to say that something else is injuring both the suppliers of imports and their domestic competitors? We will consider related matters at length in the materials on causation.

(2) The five year rule of thumb mentioned in Commissioner Ablondi's opinion has become conventional in more recent cases, at least as far as the Commission's data gathering efforts are concerned—staff reports usually contain data on imports and other industry variables for the most recent five year period for which data can be assembled. Still, it is not uncommon for respondents to urge that an apparent increase in imports over the past five years is misleading for some reason, or for petitioners to urge that an apparently flat five year trend is the product of some abnormally high import level in the base year. Can anything of a principled nature be said about the proper base period to utilize in these cases? We will see in the next section that the WTO Appellate Body seems to emphasize recent trends as most relevant.

(B) INDUSTRY DEFINITION

The petitioners before the ITC typically specify the imports to be investigated, and that choice alone allows an assessment of whether imports have increased absolutely. But before the market share of imports can be measured, and before the "serious injury" analysis can be undertaken, it is necessary to identify the domestic "industry" that competes with the imports under investigation.

GATT Article XIX requires that the increased imports injure producers of "like or directly competitive products," language that carries over into U.S. law. The concept of like products is found in other GATT provisions (e.g., Arts. III, VI), but the addition of the words "directly competitive" suggests that a more expansive definition is intended here. Indeed, it could be argued that if an industry is seriously injured by imports, that is evidence that it produces "directly competitive products."[2]

In addition to determining what products are competitive with the imports, the ITC must at times address the question of whether to include products that are partially manufactured abroad. On this matter both the statute and the WTO Safeguards Agreement provide little guidance.

WOOD SHAKES AND SHINGLES
U.S. Intl. Trade Commn. (1986)[3]

VIEWS OF CHAIRWOMAN STERN, COMMISSIONER ECKES, COMMISSIONER LODWICK AND COMMISSIONER ROHR

* * *

2. See J. Jackson, World Trade and the Law of GATT 561 n. 16 (1969).

3. Inv. No. TA 201–56, Pub. No. 1826.

Section 201(b)(1) defines the term "industry" in terms of the producers of articles "like or directly competitive" with the imported articles at issue. The statute does not define the terms "like" or "directly competitive." However, the legislative history of the Trade Act of 1974 discusses them as follows: "The words 'like' and 'directly competitive' as used previously and in this bill, are not to be regarded as synonymous or explanatory of each other ... 'like' articles are those which are substantially identical in inherent or intrinsic characteristic (i.e., materials from which made, appearance, quality, texture, and etc.), and 'directly competitive' articles are those which, although not substantially identical in their inherent or intrinsic characteristics, are substantially equivalent for commercial purposes, that is, are adapted to the same uses and are essentially interchangeable therefore."

* * *

In addition, section 601(5) of the Trade Act of 1974 specifies that the term "directly competitive with" a domestic article may include an imported article at an earlier or later stage of processing if the importation of the article has an economic effect on producers of the domestic article comparable to the effect of the importation of an article at the same stage of processing as the domestic article.

The imported articles at issue in this investigation are wood shakes and shingles. The respondents in this investigation, producers and importers of wood shakes and shingles from Canada, argued that the Commission should conclude that there are four domestic industries. They argued that the imports are properly disaggregated into shakes of western red cedar, shingles of western red cedar, remanufactured shingles of western red cedar, and shingles of northern white cedar, and that a separate industry produces each of these articles.

It is clear that there are both similarities and differences between the various shakes and shingles at issue in this investigation. Western red cedar shakes and shingles are manufactured from the same raw material, frequently in the same facility, and may be manufactured by the same persons, although using somewhat different equipment. Similarly, northern white cedar shingles are manufactured in the same manner, using the same type of equipment, as western red cedar shingles, and can be used for the same purposes, but are manufactured from a different species of tree and are generally produced and marketed in different geographical areas of the United States. Furthermore, the choice of whether to use shakes or shingles in a particular building application appears to be dictated by factors other than the inherent characteristics of the articles, such as consumer preferences and geography.

In determining which producers constitute the domestic industry, the Commission generally considers the productive facilities, manufacturing processes, and the markets for the products at issue in the investigation. In this investigation, approximately 50 percent of the domestic mills produce both shakes and shingles. In addition, both shakes and shingles are marketed for the most part through wholesale distributors and sold to the construction industry.

The various articles at issue here are, to a greater or lesser extent, interchangeable. The choice between western red cedar and northern white cedar shingles, for instance, appears to be largely a function of geographical region (northern white cedar is most popular in the northeast and the Atlantic seaboard, while western red cedar is most popular in the west and southwest), and the particular appearance desired (northern white cedar ages to a silvery grey, while western red cedar ages to a deep reddish brown). In addition, shakes have a more rustic appearance than do shingles. However, both shakes and shingles are used for fundamentally the same purpose, the outside covering of buildings, particularly in residential applications. In this investigation, we conclude that it is appropriate to find a single domestic industry, devoted to the production of wood shakes and shingles.

Respondents suggested that if the Commission were to determine that there is a single industry producing wood shakes and shingles, it should expand the industry definition to include other roofing and siding products, such as asphalt shingles, clay title, and aluminum siding, which they argue are directly competitive with wood shakes and shingles. While it is true that these products have some common ultimate uses as the outside covering of a structure, they are not necessarily equivalent for commercial purposes. The analysis of "like or directly competitive" under section 201 focuses on the question of whether products are essentially interchangeable in the sense of being substantially equivalent for commercial purposes. A contractor or homeowner is not likely to consider products of such fundamentally different appearance as asphalt shingles or clay tiles as the commercial equivalent of wood shakes and shingles. Moreover, roofing products such as asphalt shingles or clay tiles are not suitable for use as siding. In addition, the productive facilities and manufacturing processes for these other roofing and siding products are significantly different from those of wood shakes and shingles. Moreover pricing of these other products appears to be more responsive to forces other than those significant to the pricing of wood shakes and shingles. For instance, the price of asphalt shingles appears to be primarily responsive to the price of oil, a primary input in the manufacture of asphalt shingles.

CERTAIN CAMERAS
U.S. Intl. Trade Commn. (1990)[4]

ADDITIONAL VIEWS OF ACTING CHAIRMAN ANNE E. BRUNSDALE

I present these additional views to elaborate on what I consider the most complex issue in this case—that is, how the Commission should consider the activities and products of U.S. firms that have assembly operations or parts manufacturing facilities abroad. In my view, this is a

4. Inv. No. TA 201–62, Pub. No. 2315.

serious question, less for its bearing on this particular case, than for its likely importance in future cases.

* * *

In this case, the Commission had to decide how to assess Kodak's domestic operations related to the production of 35mm and 110 cameras that were assembled or partially manufactured in Mexico and Brazil. Further, the Commission had to determine whether those Kodak cameras that are considered to be imports for customs purposes should also be considered imports for the purpose of this investigation. The main argument for using final assembly to determine the country of origin is that final assembly is the stage that transforms parts into the relevant "like or directly competitive article." If all parts are made in the U.S. but assembled abroad, then, it is argued, the U.S. is simply a parts manufacturer and not a manufacturer of the like or directly competitive product. Since the court held in United Shoe Workers of America, AFL–CIO v. Bedell, 506 F.2d (D.D.C.1974), a case involving the trade adjustment assistance laws, that parts are not to be considered as like or directly competitive with the finished article, it purportedly follows that final assembly is the critical factor.

I believe that such an argument is simplistic and that a distinction should be made between a mere manufacturer of component parts (as in United Shoe) and a manufacturer of the like product, such as Kodak, that has assembly operations abroad. * * * While it may make sense for final assembly to be the decisive factor in the determination of an import for customs purposes, it makes little sense for the Commission to adopt this standard without careful consideration of the consequences. Taken to their extreme, the problems with placing such importance on final assembly become obvious. A domestic screwdriver plant set up only to assemble imported parts would be able to seek relief from products that, except for assembly, are made in the United States. Using a customs standard, we would ignore the fact that the domestic content was substantially higher in the product assembled abroad. Therefore, granting relief to the so-called domestic industry would actually decrease productive activity in the United States. Perversely, the foreign country that supplied parts to the screwdriver plant would be the main beneficiary of such an action. This scenario demonstrates that a simplistic or arbitrary definition of imports or domestic production may prove to be detrimental to U.S. competitiveness in the long run. Therefore, the Commission should look further.

* * *

Since domestic productive activity is the most important focus of the law, I favor an approach that considers the domestic industry to be all such domestic activity that adds value to the like product. I see no basis for giving greater weight to one kind of value-added activity over another. In addition, I would prefer not to exclude certain domestic productive activity because it contributed an insufficient percentage of domestic value-added to the ensuing final product. After all, there may be more domestic employment and investment generated from a product with a relatively low percentage of domestic value-added than from a product with a relatively high percentage of domestic value-added.

The difficulty with a strict value-added approach is that it cannot be used unless the data are presented in such a way as to allow consideration of all domestic value-added activities. In many cases, it would be impossible to allocate profits and employment in any reliable way. Without such data, Commissioners cannot carry out their statutory obligation to determine the impact of imports on the condition of the domestic industry in a rigorous way. When the data are not available to make a determination based strictly on domestic value-added, I would try to make distinctions for particular products. I would determine whether a good was domestic or imported, initially looking at its share of domestic content, both absolutely and in comparison to the industry average.

In this case, petitioner Keystone contends that the domestic industry should be defined to exclude the operations related to Kodak cameras that have value added in Mexico and Brazil. Kodak, on the other hand, suggests that all of its U.S. camera production activity should be included with the domestic industry, even if the camera is partially manufactured and/or assembled abroad. While I agree with Kodak in principle, the available data do not permit me to evaluate the domestic industry in the manner it suggested. A strict value-added approach in this case would not have allowed Commissioners to address the question of injury to the domestic industry producing conventional cameras. Therefore, I used an alternative approach whereby each product is considered domestic or imported based on its share of domestic content. * * * Both Keystone and Kodak cameras that are assembled in the United States should be considered as domestic products based on their share of domestic content. Kodak 110 cameras assembled in Mexico should also be considered as domestic products. * * * I do not believe that the percentage of domestic content in Kodak's 35mm cameras partially manufactured in Brazil and Mexico is sufficient to consider them as domestic products.

* * *

Kodak undertakes R & D activity and the manufacturing of camera parts and sub-assemblies in the U.S. and has generated the bulk of employment in the camera industry, particularly if one considers the total wage bill. Kodak stated that some camera models would not be competitive unless a certain portion of their production was done abroad. By assembling those cameras abroad, Kodak has found a way to be competitive in the long run while maintaining significant domestic activity—the very purpose behind this import relief law. Excluding its activities from the domestic industry would undermine the very purpose of this law.

Notes and Questions

(1) Reflect on the possible stakes in the industry definition battle. Petitioners will typically propose a definition of industry that gives them as much protection as possible against competing imports, without broadening the industry so much that they cannot meet the statutory requirements of increased imports, serious injury and causation. Respondents may pursue a strategy of dividing the proposed industry into several, hoping that at least some of their exports will remain free of restraint even if others do not, or of proposing a broader industry that would cause the petitioners to be aggregated with other domestic firms that are doing well. We see elements of both approaches in the *Shakes and Shingles* case. Can you isolate the Commission's basis for treating white cedar shingles as part of the same industry as red cedar products? If builders in the principal markets for red cedar products often choose between red cedar shakes and tile for the roofs of high-end homes, but virtually never consider white cedar shingles as an option, does it make sense to say that white cedar products are part of the industry but tile products are not?

(2) The statutory definition, "like or directly competitive," on its face emphasizes the degree of substitutability between products from the perspective of purchasers. If data are available, this "demand side" substitutability can be analyzed in part by efforts to estimate the "cross-price elasticity" of demand between two products—the degree to which the demand for one product changes with the price of the other. A large, positive cross-price elasticity (an increase in the price of one product increases greatly the demand for the other) suggests that the products are close substitutes for consumers.

(3) As the materials above make clear, the ITC also looks closely at the "supply side," to see whether the products are made by the same firms or in the same facilities. What is the logic of this attention to the "supply side?"

(4) With reference to the *Cameras* case, consider an industry with two domestic firms. One is doing well because it imports semifinished products from abroad and completes their manufacture in the United States, perhaps allowing much of the work that is intensive in relatively unskilled labor to be done overseas. The other firm is doing poorly because it tries to do all of its manufacturing domestically. If the two firms are aggregated, the analysis of serious injury becomes a close call; if only the second is included in the domestic "industry," the criteria for relief are easily met. Which is the proper way to proceed?

(C) SERIOUS INJURY

Escape clause relief is only permissible under WTO and U.S. law if the increased imports cause or threaten to cause serious injury to the domestic industry. (Later in the book we will see that for relief in dumping and subsidies cases, the domestic industry must be "materially" injured—a test thought to be easier to meet than "serious" injury.) With rare exception, the petitioners allege that serious injury exists already and do not rely solely on threat.

Under U.S. law, the ITC must consider, with respect to serious injury, the following:[5]

the significant idling of productive facilities in the domestic industry, the inability of a significant number of firms to carry out domestic production operations at a reasonable level of profit, and significant unemployment or underemployment within the domestic industry.

In evaluating the threat of serious injury, the ITC is to consider:[6]

a decline in sales or market share, a higher and growing inventory * * * and a downward trend in production, profits, wages, productivity or employment (or increasing underemployment); the extent to which firms in the domestic industry are unable to generate adequate capital to finance the modernization of their domestic plants and equipment, or are unable to maintain existing levels of expenditures for research and development; and the extent to which the United States market is the focal point for the diversion of exports of the article concerned by reason of [third country import restraints].

The law goes on to provide that the presence or absence of any factor is not necessarily to be determinative.

The following two cases highlight some of the difficulties in finding concrete standards for analyzing the seriousness of injury. Both involved the U.S. footwear industry, a beneficiary of earlier import restraints that had been lifted at the time these cases were filed. The first investigation was instituted as a result of an industry petition; the second investigation, only about a year later, was instituted at the request of the Senate Finance Committee.

NONRUBBER FOOTWEAR
U.S. Intl. Trade Commn. (1984)[7]

VIEWS OF COMMISSIONERS STERN, LIEBELER AND ROHR

* * *

In this investigation, the Commission has made a negative finding because it has concluded that the domestic nonrubber footwear industry is not currently experiencing "serious injury." Section 201 does not specifically define the term "serious injury." The legislative history makes clear, however, that mere injury is not sufficient to meet the statutory standard:

It is not intended that the escape clause criteria go from one extreme of excessive rigidity to complete laxity. An industry must be seriously injured or threatened with serious injury before an affirmative determination should be made.

---

5. Trade Act of 1974 sec. 202(c)(1)(A).

6. Id., sec. 202(c)(1)(B).

7. Inv. No. TA–201–50, Pub. No. 1545, 6 ITRD 1992 (1984).

We believe that Congress intended that we not make an affirmative finding unless the injury suffered by an industry is indeed severe.

In order to guide the Commission, the statute does list specific economic factors the Commission should consider in reaching its determination as to whether an industry is seriously injured, as follows:

> the significant idling of productive facilities in the industry, the inability of a significant number of firms to operate at a reasonable level of profit, and significant unemployment or underemployment within the industry.

The statute also provides that the Commission may take into consideration any other economic factors it considers relevant. In this investigation, we have found the indicators of the performance of the domestic industry to be mixed; some are characteristic of an industry suffering injury while others are characteristic of a healthy industry. We are mindful of the admonition from Congress in the Trade Act of 1974:

> The Committee did not intend that an industry would automatically satisfy the criteria for import relief by showing that all, or some of the enumerated factors, were present at the time of its petition to the [ITC]. That is a judgment to be made by the [ITC] on the basis of all factors it considers relevant.

We have analyzed and weighed all of the factors we have considered relevant to this industry, including those enumerated. Our analysis of all the indicators of this industry's performance leads us to conclude that it is not currently experiencing serious injury.

Production

The first factor that we have considered is the "significant idling of productive facilities." The data presented to the Commission indicate that total domestic production of nonrubber footwear declined during 1979–83. The major portion of this decline occurred between 1981–82. Between 1982 and 1983, in contrast, the decline in domestic production was small, indicating that production has stabilized.

The Commission received conflicting data on the closings of plants and firms in the industry during the period of investigation. Department of Commerce data indicate that there have been both plant and firm closings during the period of investigation. These data reflect also that the number of such closings was at or below the average annual number of closings in this industry for the last 20 years. Further, the petitioners' data indicate that the closings that occurred during the period of import relief during 1977–81 had a substantially greater effect on capacity than have closings since that time. The Commission also cannot ignore that this industry has historically been characterized by low barriers to entry and exit.

* * *

In analyzing the performance of the productive facilities in the industry, we conclude that, at this time, although there has been some idling of productive facilities, the evidence does not establish the serious injury required in the statute, especially when viewed in the context of the industry's total performance. The data reveal an industry that is smaller and more concentrated than in prior years. But a smaller and more concentrated industry is not necessarily a seriously injured industry.

Profitability

The second indicator we have analyzed is the profitability of the industry. In its analysis, the Commission considered only the profit data of operations producing domestic footwear.

Overall, profits on domestic nonrubber footwear operations increased during the 1979–83 period. The ratio of net operating profit to net sales increased from 6.8 percent in 1979 to 10.0 percent in 1981, then fell to 8.2 percent in 1982 before rising again in 1983 to 8.8 percent. Compared with other domestic industries and total U.S. production of durable goods, these ratios are impressive. In 1982, total U.S. manufacturing showed a ratio of operating income to net sales of 6.3 percent. For the first three quarters of 1983, that ratio was 6.6 percent.

We have also looked at the performance of the industry using the traditional indicators used by financial analysts. These indicators suggest that a reasonably healthy industry currently exists. As a ratio to total assets, profits reached a five-year high in 1983. Profits as a percentage of net worth, a measure of the returns in this industry, were also sharply above 1979 levels, and in three years, 1980, 1981, and 1983, were over 30 percent.

* * *

[Although some smaller firms have been unprofitable, the] larger companies producing 1 to 2 million pairs annually, accounting for 17 percent of production in 1982 performed considerably better than the smaller firms. The ratios of operating profit to net sales for these firms were 6.3 percent in 1979, 12.6 percent in 1980, and 9.4 percent in 1983. The profitability ratios for firms producing 2 to 4 million pairs annually, which accounted for 15 percent of production in 1982, were 7.0 percent in 1979, 8.5 percent in 1981, and 7.2 percent in 1983. The largest firms, those producing over 4 million pairs annually and accounting for 53 percent of production, showed ratios of net operating profit to net sales of 7.9 percent in 1979, 11.2 percent in 1981, 11.9 percent in 1982, and 11.2 percent in 1983. The financial indicators of the performance of these groups of producers also remained stable or showed improvement.

Thus, the profit data of these three latter categories of firms, representing about 85 percent of domestic production, establish that this industry is not suffering serious injury financially and is, in fact, healthy. Our analysis of all of the segments of the industry indicates to us that only a small number of firms are experiencing injury. We cannot base a finding of serious injury on the ill-health of a very small portion of domestic production.

Employment

A third factor which we have considered is whether there is significant unemployment or underemployment in the industry. It is clear that there are fewer shoeworkers employed in the industry now than in 1981, at the end of the last period of import relief for this industry. In assessing these levels of employment, we recognize that viewed solely in an historical context there is a significant employment problem in the footwear industry. We cannot, however, view employment solely in its historical context. We must also consider employment in the context of the current industry.

Bureau of Labor Statistics estimates show that after a sharp increase in the number of unemployed workers between 1981 and 1982, there was a significant drop in the number of unemployed workers in the industry between 1982 and 1983. At the same time, the Commission's survey indicates that for those firms currently producing footwear, total employment increased slightly between 1982 and 1983 and increased by 7 percent over the period of investigation.

Further, in interpreting employment data, we must also consider the level of compensation paid to workers in the industry. The average hourly compensation paid to production and related workers increased by 31 percent from $4.79 to $6.27 over the 1979–83 period. The Commission does not infer from these wage increases that workers in this industry are overpaid. Wages in this industry have historically been below those in other industries which this Commission has recently examined. Nevertheless, wage trends in this industry do not support a finding of serious injury.

Thus, the employment picture in this industry is mixed. Were we to look solely at the historic employment patterns, we might indeed find that there was significant unemployment and underutilization of capacity in this industry. Our investigation, however, must include other indicia of injury and we do not find, on the basis of the totality of the information before the Commission, including production, profitability, and employment, that the domestic industry is currently experiencing serious injury.

Threat of Serious Injury

* * *

The legislative history states that a threat exists "when serious injury, although not yet existing, is clearly imminent if import trends continued unabated." The Commission traditionally has interpreted the standard to require that threat be real rather than speculative, and that serious injury be highly probable in the foreseeable future. We have considered each of the economic factors enumerated in the statute and have concluded that the data fail to indicate a threat of serious injury at this time. In doing so, we have focused in particular upon the data for 1982 and 1983.

In terms of revenues, net sales of domestically produced footwear have remained essentially stable during the past three years. Although production has declined over the period of investigation, it now appears to have stabilized. According to official statistics, there was only a very slight decline in production between 1982–83. Profits in the industry, although varying by the size of the firm, have been stable or increasing for most firms in the industry during the past two years. As noted above, the unemployment rate in the industry declined during 1983 and the absolute number of employees increased slightly. Further, hourly wages throughout the industry have increased over the period of investigation. Further, the ratio of inventories to shipments, which indicates the potential threat of inventory overhang, remained relatively constant.

NONRUBBER FOOTWEAR

U.S. Intl. Trade Commn. (1985)[8]

VIEWS OF CHAIRWOMAN STERN

* * *

One year ago, I joined my colleagues in concluding that the U.S. footwear industry had been successful and would continue to be successful in meeting competition from abroad. Notwithstanding, I now find the increased imports threaten this industry with serious injury. Why is a different conclusion now warranted? What has changed since 1984 that now justifies a five year period of import relief? How could the Commission which found neither serious injury nor causation one year later find both? Is the present finding the correction of some unacknowledged error? Were increasing imports threatening this industry with serious injury in 1984? Readers will find that I have not recanted. Rather, my present findings stem from changes in the factual situation.

In 1984, imports were penetrating the U.S. market rapidly. Imports had increased an average of 25 percent a year since 1981. In the first quarter of 1984 this pace continued. But the data then indicated that the composition of these imports was such that direct competition with domestic production was limited. The vast majority of the increase in imports between 1979 and 1983 was imports of low-cost footwear, and attributable to a new, strong demand for athletic shoes. Many domestic producers were not seriously affected by this increase in imports—in fact almost half of the imports were imported by the domestic producers themselves. Moreover, the industry's economic indicators, while neither uniformly positive or negative, did not reflect a seriously injured industry.

* * *

---

8. Inv. No. TA–201–55, ITC Pub. No. 1717.

In 1985, the Commission has a more complete, and more recent, picture. Now there are distinct, declining trends in production, capacity, shipments, and employment, which could not be foreseen in the last investigation.

* * *

Production. Data from the Department of Commerce in our previous investigation indicated that domestic nonrubber footwear production had declined from 372 million pairs in 1981 to 342 million pairs in 1982. However, in 1983, domestic production appeared to stabilize at 341 million pairs.

Updated information now shows that the overall pattern is one of constant decline in production since 1981. Production fell from 372 million pairs in 1981 to 359 million pairs in 1982. In 1983, production fell to 344 million pairs. The decline continued into 1984, when production reached only 298 million pairs.

Rather than an industry that appeared to be experiencing stability, the picture is now one of a 17 percent decline since 1982, with most of that reduction occurring in 1984. Moreover, production was 20 percent less during the last half of 1984 than in the first part of the year. * * *

Similarly, in the last investigation, capacity appeared to be stabilizing. Although there had been a decline between 1981 and 1982 coincident with the lifting of the [Orderly Marketing Arrangements] with Taiwan and the Republic of Korea, in 1983 capacity stood approximately at its 1982 level.

Now that 1984 figures have been added to previous data, it is clear that capacity has not stabilized. Rather, capacity has fallen 9 percent since 1982. Despite this decline in capacity, domestic producers have been unable to increase their capacity utilization rates. Utilization of domestic capacity has remained at 70 percent since 1983.

This decline in domestic capacity has clearly been the result of a striking increase in the number of firms that have recently closed. While only 3 plants closed in 1980, 11 in 1981 and 1982, and 14 in 1983; in 1984, an alarming 84 plants closed. * * *

Financial Health of the Industry. In 1984, the Commission saw an industry that experienced several years of high and stable profits, as well as an overall healthy balance sheet. Operating income rose from 9.1 percent of net sales in 1980 to 10.1 percent of net sales in 1981. Once import relief was removed in 1982, the industry's profit level fell slightly to 8.0 percent of net sales. However, in 1983, operating profits rose to 8.7 percent of net sales. These profit levels compared favorably with other U.S. manufacturing industries. Financial ratios were also quite healthy.

In 1984, operating income on domestic footwear operations fell to 5.8 percent of net sales. In contrast, average operating profits for all manufacturing increased to 6.8 percent. Moreover, while data in the previous investigation showed the producers of the majority of domestic production were experiencing strong profits, our most recent data show otherwise. * * *

The overall decline in the industry's profitability is apparently attributable to a particularly severe drop in operating profits during the last half of 1984. While the profits were a reasonable 6.4 percent during the first half of 1984, near the level of those for all manufacturing, during the latter half of the year, they fell to 5.3 percent.

* * *

Employment. Whereas the employment picture was mixed in last year's investigation, this year's questionnaire data shows that overall employment in this industry has in fact fallen 8 percent since 1983. The number of workers in this industry has fallen gradually since 1981. The drop to only 87,000 workers in 1984, however, is much sharper than in earlier periods.

The new information presented in this investigation thus shows that by the end of 1984 and continuing into 1985, this industry is clearly becoming less able to meet the increasing intensity of global competition than the industry the Commission examined in its last investigation.

Notes and Questions

(1) Look carefully at the two cases—how much had things really changed in a year?

(2) The current statutory provision that no single factor is "dispositive" stems at least in part from the first *Footwear* case, where the profitability data was thought by some to have "trumped" the data on declining production and employment. Is there any principled way to attach relative weight to the various factors that the statute mentions and the ITC considers? For example, might it be argued that if the purpose of the escape clause is to address dislocation, unemployment or underemployment ought be the center of attention, while a loss of profits (especially when firms are owned by diversified shareholders) is of little interest? Or are profits important because shareholders are at least as likely to contribute to national political campaigns as workers? If profits are high and unemployment is high as well, does that argue for adjustment assistance as a remedy? What about "idling of productive facilities" and low rates of capacity utilization generally—should such factors receive any weight if profits are healthy and employment is stable?

(D) CAUSATION

In addition to finding "serious injury," the ITC must also find that the serious injury has been caused by the increased imports. As noted, the U.S. statutory provisions on the causation issue have changed over time. In the 1951 law, the imports in question had to "cause" or threaten serious injury. The 1955 amendment provided that it was enough that such imports "contributed substantially" to causing or threatening serious injury, while the 1962 Trade Expansion Act provided that imports had to be "the major factor" in causing, or threatening to cause, serious injury. At present, Section 201 requires that the increased imports be a "substantial cause" of serious injury, with substantial cause defined as an "important" cause that is "not less than" any other cause. Interestingly, GATT Article XIX and the Safeguards Agreement require simply that increased imports "cause or threaten to cause" serious injury.

You should also reflect on the following conundrum, present under both the WTO and U.S. law formulations of the causation inquiry. To illustrate it, suppose that consumers in the United States lose interest in domestically produced video games, and shift their purchases to games produced abroad simply because they find them more entertaining. As a result, imports of video games increase dramatically, contemporaneously with a decline in the fortunes of U.S. manufacturers. Here, although increased imports arise at a time of industrial decline domestically, both phenomena are "caused" by something else in the ordinary sense of that word—namely, a change in consumer tastes. Yet, the law treats "increased imports" as a causal variable. To an economist, this formulation makes little sense because the quantity of imports, as in our example, is always an "effect," with the forces of supply and demand (tastes, income, technology, input prices, and so forth) being "causal." How is someone charged with administering the law to make sense of increased imports as a "cause" in light of this observation?

CERTAIN MOTOR VEHICLES

U.S. Intl. Trade Commn. (1980)[9]

VIEWS OF CHAIRMAN ALBERGER

* * *

I have found the decline in demand for new automobiles and light trucks owing to the general recessionary conditions in the United States economy to be a far greater cause of the domestic industries' plight than the increase in imports.

* * *

One noticeable factor in this case is the apparent lack of correlation between the growth in import volume and the state of health of domestic producers. Our investigation reveals that the period 1976–78 was characterized by strong domestic sales and record profits. Yet it was during this period that the largest increase in total imports occurred. Imports actually declined in 1979, when the recession began in earnest. Even Japanese imports grew most dramatically in the prior period, and remained about steady in 1979. While Japanese imports have increased by a more alarming rate in the first 6 months of 1980 (by about 200,000 units over the comparable period of 1979), imports from other sources have declined. This juxtaposition of events becomes even more curious

9. Inv. No. TA–201–44, Pub. No. 1110, 2 ITRD 5241 (1980).

when we consider the testimony of petitioners that the injury began in early 1979 and has deepened over the past 18 months. Given the relatively slight import growth in that period, and considering how healthy the monthly sales figures were before 1979, one obviously begins to look for other explanations of the current injury.

One figure that stands out in stark contrast to the rather marginal import increases for 1979–80 is the very large decline in overall consumption of both passenger autos and light trucks. Consumption of passenger autos fell by almost 1 million units in 1979, a decline of 7.8 percent. Moreover, consumption in January–June 1980 was 1.1 million units or 18.5 percent below the figure for January–June 1979.

* * *

At the most fundamental level, then, it is useful to allocate the decline in domestic producers' shipments in 1979 and 1980 into two basic components: that portion accounted for by the reduced overall consumption of autos and light trucks because of general economic conditions, and that portion attributable to the increasing market share of import vehicles. The relative magnitude of these two causes can be assessed by comparing the actual decline in domestic shipments to the decline that might have occurred if imports had not increased their market share in 1979–80, i.e., if imports and domestic vehicles had shared equally in the overall decline in sales. The difference between these two figures represents the maximum potential loss in sales due to increased imports. This amount can then be compared to the volume of loss attributable *solely* to reduced demand.

* * *

[Such analysis suggests] that declining demand accounted for over 80 percent of the net decline in U.S. producers' domestic shipments of both automobiles and trucks from 1978 to 1979, as compared with less than 20 percent of the decline in U.S. producers' domestic shipments being attributable to imports' increasing share of U.S. consumption. Between January–June 1979 and January–June 1980, about two-thirds of the decline in U.S. producers' domestic shipments was attributable to declining demand and only a third was due to the increased share of the U.S. market accounted for by imports. Thus, even if the import share had been held constant during these critical 18 months, and even if all of those sales which went into the increased import share had instead gone to U.S. producers, domestic firms' sales still would have fallen by over 80 percent of their actual decline in 1979 and by over 60 percent of their actual decline in January–June 1980.

Petitioners would perhaps dispute the conclusions I draw [because they] fail to allow for the theory that an import increase in the earlier period of 1976–78 could be accountable for injury which did not become manifest until 1979. However, even if average imports, consumption and domestic shipments for 1976–78 are compared to the 1979 figures, the decline in demand is still greater than the import factor.

* * *

It has been argued in this case that the downturn in demand is itself a result of several factors, and that each should be assessed individually to determine whether any single factor is greater than increasing imports. To consider demand in the aggregate, the argument goes, is to cumulate artificially what are clearly separate causal elements in a manner inconsistent with the purposes or legislative history of Section 201. Among the separate and identifiable causes mentioned in this case are inflation, unemployment, rising interest rates, and higher energy costs. Undoubtedly, all of these factors played a part in bringing about the present recession in new vehicle sales. Supporters of the petition contend that none of these factors *alone* played as great a role in bringing about the injury as increasing imports. In fact, the UAW brief contends that increasing imports brought on much of the recession, and so the recession should be viewed as an effect rather than a cause.

All of these contentions seek to isolate and weigh separately the various components of a general economic downturn. In reality, most of the factors mentioned above have worked in unison to bring about what is commonly termed a "recession." * * * Recessions are often characterized by rising prices, high interest rates and unemployment. But to say they are comprised of a multitude of causes is not to say that reduced demand in a recession cannot be cited as a single cause for purposes of section 201. In fact, I have cited this very factor in several past cases, particularly where we were considering highly cyclical industries which fluctuate with the general economy. The reason for such a policy is readily apparent; if decline in demand for the product is a consequence of a general economic downturn, then the inevitable recovery from the recession will restore health to the industry. This is precisely what happened to the automobile industry after the downturn in 1974–75. Cyclical downturns in the economy are to be expected, and must not force a reliance on unnecessary import remedies. The problem which auto producers confront is one which confronts many sectors of the economy (the building industry, for example), and it cannot be solved by import relief.

* * *

VIEWS OF VICE CHAIRMAN CALHOUN

* * *

I have found two factors which seem to be more important causes of the industry's problems than are increased imports.

First, the demand for the type of automobile desired by a significant portion of the buying public is shifting from a product line roughly described as larger, less fuel-efficient automobiles to smaller, more fuel-efficient automobiles. * * *

Second, there has been an overall decline in demand for automobiles that is largely associated with the general decline in the economy.

A. Shift in Demand

With regard to the shift in consumer preference from one type of automobile to another, petitioners argued that if such a shift exists it is nothing more than a shift from the purchase of domestic cars to the purchase of imported cars with a resulting increase in imported automobiles. The reason for the increase in imports, they argued, is unimportant to our determination under section 201. Moreover, their view continued, section 201 is specifically designed to provide a remedy in precisely those circumstances in which domestic sales are displaced by sales of imports. While I do not refute this view of the policy underlying section 201 I must take exception, both in concept and in fact, with the view that in this case the shift in consumer preference merely explains why imports might have increased and is not cognizable as an independent source of injury to the domestic industry.

* * *

For me the decisive precedent for the integrity of demand shift as a concept distinct from a shift to imports in a circumstance of increasing and competitive imports is *Wrapper Tobacco,* Investigation No. TA–201–3, USITC Pub. No. 746 (1975). *Wrapper Tobacco* has a particular precedential appeal because the behavior of imports in the marketplace was especially strong. First, imports had more than tripled their market penetration over a four-year period while domestic production and total consumption were in decline. Second, the prices of the bulk of the imported articles tended to be below the price of the domestic articles, but certain high-grade imports were priced considerably higher than the domestic product. Third, while some of the imports were considered to be of higher quality than the domestic article, most of the imports were used to produce product lines that competed with those using the domestic product.

In the face of this extremely competitive position of imports, the Commission in *Wrapper Tobacco* made a unanimous negative determination. Four Commissioners relied upon the change in consumer tastes from larger cigars to smaller cigars and other tobacco products as the primary reason for the decline in demand they viewed as a cause of injury more important than increasing imports. Thus, the majority of the Commission had no difficulty in concept or in fact in differentiating between a shift from the domestic article and a shift to imports.

* * *

Moreover, where in both concept and in fact a shift in demand is distinguishable from a shift to imports, not to make it a factor in the consideration of causality transforms section 201 from an import relief provision to an industrial relief provision. Under such a view, whenever an industry is in decline because of internal structural changes or exogenous occurrences in the society independent of imports, an industry need only show that imports are increasing concomitant with its difficulty and it could receive relief. While one could make very good arguments supporting the need for an industrial policy which would provide assistance to worthy industries suffering generalized difficulty unassociated with imports, section 201 cannot be so construed. It is plainly and simply an import relief provision and, therefore, our fundamental task on the face of it and from the legislative history is to determine that *imports* are an important cause of the injury and to determine that no other cause is more important than imports. Thus, any other factors that may have contributed to injury must be measured against the contribution made by imports.

Having established the validity of the concept of a product line shift as a factor to be assessed in this case, establishing the fact of the shift and assessing what weight it ought to be given is not difficult.

* * *

Between 1975 and 1979, large domestic car sales grew at an annual rate of 2.4 percent while sales of imports grew at an annual rate of 6.4 percent. Eclipsing both of these were sales of small domestic cars which grew 9.6 percent during this period. Comparing the first half of 1980 to the first half of 1979, in 1980 sales of large domestic cars declined 48.5 percent, and sales of imports and domestic small cars each grew 1.8 percent. The failure of small domestic cars to keep pace with their earlier rate of sales growth and with the growth rate of imports for the first half of 1980 might be viewed as proof that consumption has, in fact, shifted to imports *qua* imports. But precisely the opposite is the case.

The significant growth in demand for domestic small cars caught up with production during the first half of 1980, exceeding the ability of the domestic producers to supply the market. During the first six months of 1980, several producers were at or above their full capacity for small cars. Others were either experiencing serious recall problems on their major small car models or were suffering from major adverse publicity on their products' quality and safety. Both of these factors had a considerable impact on sales.

* * *

VIEWS OF COMMISSIONER STERN

* * *

Although there is serious injury present in the passenger car industry, I have determined that increased imports do not constitute a substantial cause of the existing serious injury.

* * *

There is scant legislative direction on which alternative causes should be weighed against increased imports.

The Senate Finance Committee Report does direct the Commission to examine the injury attributable to increased imports or of other causes, "such as change in technology or in consumer tastes, domestic competition from substitute products, plant obsolescence, or poor management." By not shackling the Commission to an approach so finely detailed as to be unworkable in all potential cases, the statute gives the Commission maximum flexibility and discretion. Within these broad boundaries lies the responsibility for the Commission's determination to be "clear, well documented, and ... decisive."

* * *

I have attempted to concentrate on those phenomena that are relatively independent. To the extent that an increase in imports seemed to be merely incidental to a far more fundamental phenomenon, I have decided to analyze that fundamental phenomenon as a separate cause. Under the rubric "imports as an independent cause," I shall treat those sales which imports have captured in head-on competition with domestic autos due to attributes such as price, design, and quality that attract customers.

A full understanding of the industry's problems necessitates an examination of a complex web of events. The injury sustained by the automobile industry can best be explained by analyzing four fundamental phenomena:

(1) A general decline in demand due to rapidly increasing costs of car ownership and operation (added to normal—if not precisely predictable—recessionary effects on consumer income and confidence);

(2) A seemingly permanent shift in consumer tastes to relatively smaller, more fuel-efficient autos;

(3) A substantially negative accounting impact on profits resulting from huge investments to transform the industry; and

(4) Success of imports in head-to-head competition.

The decline in demand and shift in demand are more important causes of injury to the auto industry than increasing imports, *per se.* I have not been able to evaluate fully the relative significance of the massive capital costs of transforming the industry; however, I believe that their impact on domestic industry performance is at least of the same magnitude as that of imports. It is doubtful that in the absence of the first three causes the remaining injury attributable to imports would be serious.

HEAVYWEIGHT MOTORCYCLES

U.S. Intl. Trade Commn. (1983)[10]

VIEWS OF CHAIRMAN ECKES

* * *

Finally, imports of finished heavyweight motorcycles pose a "substantial cause" of threat of serious injury. Under section 201(b)(4), a "substantial cause" is "a cause which is important and not less than any other cause." In my view, there is no cause more important than imports threatening injury to the domestic motorcycle industry.

In reaching this conclusion I have considered the significance of the present recession in my analysis. Without a doubt the unusual length and severity of the present recession has created unique problems for the domestic motorcycle industry. Without a doubt the rise in joblessness, particularly among blue-collar workers, who constitute the prime market for heavyweight motorcycles, has had a severe impact on the domestic industry. Nonetheless, if the Commission were to analyze the causation question in this way, it would be impossible in many cases for a cyclical industry experiencing serious injury to obtain relief under section 201 during a recession. In my opinion Congress could not have intended for the Commission to interpret the law this way.

There are other reasons for doubting the domestic recession is a substantial cause of injury or threat to the U.S. industry. During the current recession, imports from Japan have increased their market share from domestic producers, gaining nearly six percentage points. Imports have taken market share from the domestic facilities of Honda and Kawasaki as well as Harley–Davidson.

Moreover, while the current recession has undoubtedly depressed demand for heavyweight motorcycles, economic conditions are beginning to improve in this country. Automobile sales are moving up, and so are housing starts and other important leading indicators. As demand responds to this improvement, the domestic industry will be pre-empted from participating in any growth because of the presence of a one-year supply of motorcycles poised and ready to capture market share. Consequently, not the recession, but the inventory of motorcycles coupled with anticipated future imports constitute the greatest threat of injury in the months ahead.

UNWROUGHT COPPER

U.S. Intl. Trade Commn. (1984)[11]

VIEWS OF COMMISSIONERS ECKES, LODWICK AND ROHR

* * *

---

10. Inv. No. TA–201–47, Pub. No. 1342, 4 ITRD 2469 (1983).

11. Inv. No. TA–201–52, Pub. No. 1549, 6 ITRD 1708 (1984).

During the period of investigation world copper prices fell from 85 cents per pound to 63 cents per pound while average U.S. production costs have decreased from 88 cents to 82 cents. In our view market pressures resulting from this relatively low world price have had a significant negative impact on the domestic copper industry's ability to compete with foreign copper producers. The world price, however, cannot be viewed as an isolated cause of injury existing independent of the overall world supply and demand picture as well as factors of comparative advantage. Indeed,

> (s)uch a line of reasoning would result in the entire U.S. market being taken over by imports. * * * It must be clearly understood that imports are the vehicle by which the effects of low world prices are transmitted to the U.S. industry. Increased imports in particular are the cause of those negative effects previously detailed.

* * *

Of all the conditions of production affecting the domestic copper industry, declining ore grades have been characterized as an irreparable cause of injury. While we recognize that ore grades are a natural bounty subject to depletion we disagree that the rising costs associated with depletion are irreparable. The domestic industry has already demonstrated that through improved technology domestic producers have improved their production efficiencies and reduced the cost per pound of production.

* * *

We reject the notion that the Commission must determine whether the domestic industry has a comparative advantage in a product before making an affirmative recommendation. Such a requirement would thwart the purpose of section 201. It would also ignore the reality that costs and conditions of production change and that section 201 is intended to enable an industry to use a period of shelter in order to adjust to shifts in these costs and conditions.

EXTRUDED RUBBER THREAD
U.S. Intl. Trade Commn. (1992)[12]

VIEWS OF CHAIRMAN NEWQUIST AND COMMISSIONERS ROHR AND NUZUM

* * *

The cost advantage arguments raised by respondents help explain why increasing imports are an important cause of serious injury to the domestic industry. Imports may enjoy a cost advantage which, particularly in the case of products that are relatively fungible, enables them to displace sales of competing domestically produced product. This advantage often is one of lower labor or raw material costs. These types of

---

12. Inv. No. TA–201–63, Pub. No. 2563.

underlying factors, however, cannot constitute "alternative causes" under the Act. Rather, Congress directed the Commission to consider whether alternative causes in the U.S. market or among U.S. producers, such as changes in technology or in consumer tastes, domestic competition from substitute products, plant obsolescence, or poor management were a more important cause of injury than increased imports. Thus, it is the entry of these imports in increased quantities, irrespective of any competitive attributes of those imports derived from their home market, that the Commission must consider.

CERTAIN CAMERAS

U.S. Intl. Trade Commn. (1990)[13]

VIEWS OF THE COMMISSION

* * *

We find other causes are more important than the increased imports. In reaching this decision, we have focused on the causes of serious injury or threat thereof to [petitioner] Keystone, which is the only firm alleging that increased imports are a substantial cause of serious injury or threat.

In our view, several decisions of Keystone's prior management are more important than increased imports in explaining the serious injury or threat of serious injury. The brief investment by a wholly owned subsidiary of Keystone in the videocassette business was a disaster with long-term financial consequences for the camera company. Keystone's management also seemed unable to adapt to changes in the camera market. In particular, Keystone was not able to gain a strong foothold in the market for 35mm cameras where demand has been growing rapidly. Keystone's management failed to pursue a consistent and effective plan to develop brand name recognition or to develop a distinctive market niche. In a market where brand names command significant price premiums and where new models, features, and concepts rapidly capture market share, Keystone followed no consistent approach to expand its sales and profits. Instead, it sporadically invested in advertising and developed primarily cheaper versions of existing models. In this particular industry, such an approach has not proven to be effective or profitable. Perhaps most telling is Keystone's adjustment plan, which suggests a number of revised management strategies.

* * *

Whether we view the videocassette venture and the camera-related business decisions of Keystone as two independent causes or, alternatively, as a single cause, namely "poor management," we conclude that other causes are more important than increased imports. Accordingly, we render a negative determination.

13. Inv. No. TA–201–62, Pub. No. 2315.

WOOD SHAKES AND SHINGLES

U.S. Intl. Trade Commn. (1986)[14]

VIEWS OF VICE CHAIRMAN SUSAN W. LIEBELER
AND COMMISSIONER ANNE E. BRUNSDALE

* * *

Section 201 requires that increased imports be a substantial cause of serious injury or threat of serious injury to the domestic industry. * * * The ordinary meaning of the term cause is "anything producing an effect or result." Thus, to begin with, it is important to distinguish causes from effects. The fact that the quantity of imports has increased and that the domestic industry is injured does not necessarily mean that imports are a cause of injury, much less a substantial cause of injury. The coincidence of increases in imports and injury to the domestic industry may be due entirely to changes in other factors. For example, an increase in the domestic industry's costs could cause a reduction in domestic production and an increase in domestic price that could attract increased imports. Injury to the domestic industry would be caused by these higher costs, not by the increase in imports; that is, the increase in imports would be an effect rather than a cause of the injury. Under these conditions, were the Commission to find a positive association between the imports and the injury, it would be making a decision based on a spurious correlation—i.e., a correlation suggesting a causal relationship that does not in fact exist. * * *

Our approach to analyzing causation is guided by the principle that it is imperative to be able to distinguish between cause and effect. In addition, it is important to select a method of analysis that not only incorporates the specific variables cited by Congress as relevant to escape clause cases, but does so in a manner that is coherent and internally consistent. We sought a framework that makes it possible to distinguish situations where "increased imports" are a substantial cause of serious injury from situations where the increase in imports is an effect of changes in other factors operating in the domestic market.

Economic analysis is very useful when examining cause and effect. The framework we adopt is a traditional demand and supply analysis that explains how the price and quantity of a product are determined in a market. This framework has three general components: (1) the domestic demand for the product, (2) the domestic supply of U.S. producers, and (3) the import supply of foreign producers. Each component incorporates the influence of (or depends on) a different collection of specific variables. Indeed, this framework is particularly useful because it enables us to consider the influence of any particular variable deemed relevant to the study of a market.

For example, such things as consumer tastes, construction activity, and prices of substitute products (like asphalt shingles, clay tile, alumi-

---

14. Inv. No. TA 201–56, Pub. No. 1826.

num siding, and slate) each influence the domestic demand for shakes and shingles. Consumer tastes and construction activity affect the market for shakes and shingles only in so far as they affect demand; they do not directly affect either domestic supply or import supply, although both the quantity of domestic shipments and the quantity of imports will in general change in response to the change in demand.

Domestic supply depends on a different collection of variables, including production technology and the supply conditions in the United States of production input like labor and red cedar logs. Similarly, import supply depends on yet another collection of variables, comprised of foreign demand and input supply conditions that are found abroad.

* * *

By defining "substantial cause" as a cause "which is important and not less than any other cause," the statute requires the Commission to compare and weigh causes. We believe that it is important to examine causes at a comparable level of aggregation and generality and to do so in a consistent manner from case to case so that all participants in escape clause investigations are fully aware of what is involved. We are mindful of the concern of Congress that escape clause cases "provide a fair and reasonable test for any industry which is being injured by imports...." We believe such a test is possible with a causation analysis framed in terms of the three basic components (domestic demand, domestic supply, and import supply), since they are at a comparable level of aggregation and generality.

* * *

The evidence before us suggests that domestic supply did not shift adversely (e.g., domestic technology and input prices did not change significantly). Therefore, we confine our attention to changes in domestic demand and in import supply. * * * To find out how domestic demand and import supply have changed, we examined the data for domestic consumption, quantity of imports, and domestic price. Consumption was about 20 percent lower in 1984 and 1985 than it was in 1978 and approximately equal to the level in 1980. The quantity of imports increased by 20 percent between 1978 and 1984 and 17 percent between 1980 and 1984. An index for deflated composite U.S. prices for western red cedar shakes and shingles shows that the real price dropped about 50 percent between 1978 and 1985 and about 30 percent since 1980. It is clear from these results that an increase in imports cannot be the only cause of injury to domestic producers of shakes and shingles. If domestic supply and demand had not changed, an increase in import supply would have caused an increase in domestic consumption as well as a decrease in price. Since consumption has either fallen or remained constant (depending on the base period used for comparison), domestic demand must have decreased. Therefore, even if the level of imports had remained constant, the domestic shakes and shingles industry would nevertheless be injured by the lower prices necessary to keep cedar shakes and shingles competitive with other products.

At the same time, the evidence on the change in domestic prices and domestic production, together with the increase in imports from Canada, shows that the fall in domestic demand for cedar shakes and shingles is not the only adverse change affecting this industry. The increased quantity of imports at lower prices could only have occurred with an increase in Canadian supply to the U.S. market.

The statute requires that we determine which of these two factors, decreased demand or increased import supply, is more important in causing injury to the domestic shake and shingle industry. The answer to this question turns on the sensitivity or responsiveness of domestic demand and import supply to changes in the domestic price. As explained below, we find that domestic demand is highly sensitive to price while import supply is relatively insensitive to price. Under these conditions, an increase in import supply does not and cannot exert a significant depressing effect on the domestic price. Rather, the primary effect is to increase the quantity of imports and also to increase domestic consumption. Because the effect on the price was minor, the effect on domestic producers was also minor. Hence the increase in import supply cannot be a cause of serious injury to the domestic industry. In contrast, when domestic demand falls and supply is relatively insensitive to changes in price, the result is a sharp decline in market price. As a consequence, there is also a substantial adverse effect on the domestic industry. Therefore, the contraction in domestic demand is a greater cause of injury to the domestic industry than the increase in imports.

Notes and Questions

(1) In one of the few GATT disputes under Article XIX to proceed through the dispute resolution process, the United States had imposed restrictions on imports of hat parts. (The case is popularly known as the Hatters' Fur Case, Sales No. GATT/1951–3 (Nov. 1951.)) In the course of defending its position, the United States contended that a change in fashion had led consumers to prefer imports over domestically-produced products. Although the substantial cause test was not then in effect or at issue in the working party's deliberations, for whom does that theory cut under the current statute?

(2) Commissioner Alberger's approach in the *Automobiles* case was sometimes known as "shift-share analysis," comparing the effects of a decline in consumption (holding the import market share constant) to the increase in import market share (at either the old or the new level of consumption). How would you attack this method if you were a petitioner today? How would you attack this method as a respondent?

(3) After the 1988 amendments, the ITC may not "aggregate the causes of declining demand associated with a recession or economic downturn ... into a single cause." What does this mean—could the ITC conclude in an appropriate case that a recession is attributable to a single cause, or is the statute an irrebuttable presumption to the contrary? How about the follow-

ing disaggregation of causes—a recession is 99% the result of a tight monetary policy, and 1% the result of unknown factors? Is the approach urged by Liebeler and Brunsdale in the *Shakes and Shingles* case permissible under this standard?

(4) If imports have a "cost advantage," petitioner's case may be strengthened. If the domestic industry has "poor management," by contrast, the respondent's case is strengthened. How is poor management to be distinguished from a cost disadvantage? More generally, when imports are outcompeting domestic products in the market, how does one determine whether the cause is the competitive advantage of imports or the competitive disadvantage of domestic producers?

(5) The *Cameras* case suggests that poor management will stand in the way of relief; *Unwrought Copper* suggests that poor ore quality in domestic mines will not. Is not the former problem far more likely to be remediable than the latter? Has the ITC got it backwards, or is its position defensible?

(6) To an economist, the view that import supply, domestic supply and domestic demand represent distinct collections of causal variables comes quite naturally. To defend the proposition that each is a "single cause" in the legal sense, however, is it sufficient to suggest that they are at comparable "levels of aggregation and generality" (the argument of Liebeler and Brunsdale)?

(7) In addition to identifying the possible alternative causes of injury and deciding which ones "count" in the analysis, the ITC must proceed to weigh them against "increased imports." How is this accomplished as a practical matter? Suppose, for example, that as between "increased imports" and "poor management," there is a stronger contemporaneous correlation between rising imports and industrial decline than between demonstrably poor management decisions and industrial decline. How persuasive is this fact for petitioners?

(8) One advantage of the Liebeler–Brunsdale framework in the *Shakes and Shingles* case is that it does permit more systematic analysis of the relative importance of possible causes. Did you understand how the hypothesized slopes of the supply and demand relationships (their "elasticity") was being used?

(9) It is possible to go beyond the qualitative approach of Liebeler and Brunsdale in the *Shakes and Shingles* case to produce statistical models of supply and demand, and to use the models to analyze counterfactual scenarios in which one or another "causal" variable is manipulated. An interesting effort in this regard was made by respondents in the *Unwrought Copper* case (to no avail at the ITC as it turned out). That study, which concluded that a recession and rising labor costs were a more important cause of decline in the U.S. industry than imports, is discussed in Pindyck & Rotemberg, Are Imports to Blame? Attribution of Injury Under the 1974 Trade Act, 30 J. L. & Econ. 101 (1987). In light of what you have seen about alternative causes at the ITC, is it surprising that the study had little impact? In any case, the approach discussed in that paper provides another response to the question of how the quantity of imports nay be viewed as a causal variable. In effect, it asks how much better off the domestic industry would have been had there been a quota in place freezing imports at their base period level.

(10) Suppose petitioners argue that the declining price of imports during the period of investigation is the substantial cause of their injury. Respondents contend, correctly, that the price decline is entirely attributable to a general appreciation of the dollar relative to foreign currencies, making imports cheaper in dollar terms. Who wins?

LAMB MEAT

U.S. Intl. Trade Commn. (1999)[15]

Views of the Commission

[W]e find that increased imports of lamb meat are a "substantial cause" of the threat of serious injury to the domestic lamb meat industry under section 202(b)(1)(B). * * *

Imports reached record levels in 1996, and increased another 19.2 percent in 1997. Imports will exceed even those record levels based on annualized data from interim 1998. Australian and New Zealand firms submitting questionnaire responses to the Commission themselves project that their exports to the United States will increase further in 1999. These firms' 1999 projections were 21 percent above projections for full year 1998. * * * As of the time of the Commission's vote on injury, the Australian Government had projected a 6 percent increase in exports to the United States. * * *

Increases in import volume are likely to have further negative effects on the domestic industry's prices, shipment volumes, and financial condition in the imminent future. With regard to prices, given the inability of domestic growers and feeders to reduce production in the short run, the increase in imports has caused prices to fall in the short run. The unit value of domestic, Australian, and New Zealand lamb meat dropped in interim 1998 as compared to interim 1997; over the same period imports (on an annualized basis) increased by the greatest amount of any year during the period of investigation. Moreover, U.S., Australian, and New Zealand lamb meat prices were in most cases lower for the products surveyed in the second half of 1997 and the first 3 quarters of 1998 than in comparable quarters in 1996 and the first half of 1997. Any further increases in the volume of imports would be expected to put further downward pressure on prices in the U.S. market.

With regard to market share, the share of the domestic market held by imports, as measured both in quantity and value, more than doubled during the period of investigation, from 11.2 percent in 1993 (as measured in quantity) to 23.3 percent in January–September 1998, and from 11.9 percent in 1993 (as measured in share of value) to 30.7 percent in January–September 1998. Most of this increase occurred in 1997 and 1998. The 1997 increase in imports of 9.7 million pounds was mirrored by a decline in U.S. lamb shipments of 8.4 million pounds, suggesting that imports captured market share directly from U.S. producers.

15. Inv. No. TA–201–68, Pub. No. 3176, April 1999.

With regard to the domestic industry's financial condition, we found above that financial performance of the various segments worsened due to declining sales and falling prices, a result of the increase in imports. In addition, the increased imports directly captured market share from the domestic producers. Thus, the increase in imports is likely to have a negative impact on the industry's shipments, prices, and financial performance.

As required by the statute, we considered whether any other causes might be a more important cause of the threat of serious injury than increased imports. First, we examined whether termination of payments under the National Wool Act of 1954 ("Wool Act") might be a more important cause. Congress enacted legislation ending the Wool Act in 1993, and the support payments were phased out largely in 1994 and 1995, before the increase in imports that began in 1996. Petitioners claim that the loss of the payments had been largely absorbed by the growers and feeders before the increase in imports. Respondents assert that the industry cannot be expected to absorb so quickly the effects of the loss of such a longstanding payment program.

We have no doubt that the loss of Wool Act payments hurt lamb growers and feeders and caused some to withdraw from the industry. We also believe that it is unrealistic to conclude that the effects of the termination of Wool Act payments had completely disappeared as of 1997. However, the industry had experienced some recovery since full termination in 1996, and the effects of termination of Wool Act payments can be expected to recede further with each passing month. In addition, the termination of the Wool Act could only have had an indirect effect on the financial condition of the packers and breakers, who never received payments under the Wool Act. We find that in the imminent future, the recent loss of Wool Act payments is a less important cause of the threat of serious injury than imports of lamb meat.

We also considered whether competition from other meat products, such as beef, pork, and poultry, might be a more important cause of the threat of serious injury. Although such products appear to compete with lamb to a certain extent, we find no evidence that such competition is a more important cause of future imminent serious injury than imports of lamb meat. As noted above, per capita consumption of lamb meat has been relatively steady since 1995. We also considered whether increased input costs, alleged overfeeding of lambs, and increased concentration in the packer segment might individually be more important causes of the threat of serious injury than the increased imports. We find that they are not. Expenses for growers rose at a modest rate and then fell in January–September 1998. Expenses for feeders increased at a faster pace but not at a dramatic pace. Similarly, costs of inputs for packers and breakers rose moderately in line with production. Thus, there has been no significant increase in input costs that explains the sharp decline in industry profits, and no increase is predicted in the imminent future.

Respondents allege that some U.S. feeders in 1997 held lambs unduly long in feed lots in order to maximize revenue while prices were high, and that these lambs went to slaughter on the heavy side and sold at lower prices, which pulled down other domestic prices. Petitioners disagree, pointing out that the percentage of domestic lamb carcasses with higher fat content as measured by the USDA grading system was lower in 1997 than in 1993 and 1994. Even if we accept respondents' arguments, these "fat" lambs would have accounted for no more than a small share of total domestic lamb production. In any event, respondents do not allege that overfeeding is currently taking place or represents a future threat.

We also considered whether concentration in the packer segment of the industry might be a more important cause of the threat of serious injury. USDA data indicate that nine domestic packing plants accounted for 85 percent of the sheep and lambs slaughtered in 1997. However, petitioners claim that packer concentration has actually decreased over the past 5 years. An undue level of concentration among packers would have suggested that they would have been sheltered from the effects of low-priced imports and would have been able to pass through lower prices more readily to feeders and growers. However, packers, like other segments of the lamb meat industry, experienced deteriorating profits in the latter part of the period of investigation and operated at a loss in January–September 1998. Thus, we conclude that concentration in the packer segment of the industry is a less important cause of the threat of serious injury than increased imports.

Finally, we considered whether the failure to develop and implement an effective marketing program for lamb meat was a more important cause of the threat of serious injury, particularly in light of the repeal of the longstanding Wool Act payment program. While an effective marketing program to bolster domestic demand could have had an important impact on the industry, in view of the foregoing discussion, we do not find that failure to implement such a program is a more important cause of the threat of serious injury than increased imports. * * *

Notes and Questions

The Lamb investigation resulted in restrictions on lamb imports that were challenged before the WTO. An excerpt from that challenge discussing the ITC's analysis of causation follows in the next section. Before reading what the WTO Appellate Body has to say, ask yourself whether you are convinced by the ITC's reasoning. Does the ITC do enough to rule out other possible causes of threatened injury, or is its discussion too conclusory? What more should it do, if anything?

(E) SAFEGUARDS REMEDIES: THE PRESIDENTIAL PHASE

Under Section 203 of the 1974 Trade Act, the remedies open to the President include a range of options. He can increase duties, impose quotas or tariff rate quotas, or enter into "agreements" with exporting nations (subject to new WTO discipline after the Uruguay Round). The

President also has broad discretion to impose as large a trade restriction as he considers necessary to achieve the purposes of Section 201. Indeed, the existence of the President's power to take effective remedial action where appropriate has not been an issue. Rather, the questions have concerned his willingness to use his power.

One of the significant legislative issues in the drafting of the 1974 Act was how much discretion to give to the President to depart from findings or recommendations of the ITC. Some urged that the ITC determination and remedy be final; while others urged that for foreign policy reasons as well as broader economic policy reasons, the President should have the final say in all of these cases. In the Act as passed, there was a large but not complete measure of discretion for the President,[16] which can be contrasted with the U.S. laws regarding dumping and subsidies, where there is almost no discretion in the executive. The 1974 Act tried to achieve a balance between those who wanted more and those who wanted no presidential discretion, and sections 202 and 203 reflected this. The 1988 amendments struck the balance slightly differently, and Section 203 now states that that the President "shall take all appropriate and feasible action within his power which the President determines will facilitate efforts by the domestic industry to make positive adjustment to import competition and provide greater economic and social benefits than costs." Later clauses give the President the right to consider, for example, the impact of relief upon consumers and competition, the burden on the economy of any compensation that may be required to trading partners under GATT, and national security.

Thus, the President considers a substantially broader set of interests than the ITC, and it is not surprising that the President has with some regularity elected not to grant the relief recommended by the ITC. In the original Section 203, a legislative veto was included to allow the Congress by concurrent resolution to force the President to follow the ITC recommendation. After the U.S. Supreme Court's decision in *Chadha*, discussed in Section 3.2(B)(2) supra, the validity of this congressional veto provision was in doubt. In the 1984 Trade and Tariff Act, Congress amended Section 203 to eliminate this veto, and provided that Congress may override the President and cause the recommendation of the ITC to come into effect by adopting a joint resolution to that effect. This change eliminates the problems raised by *Chadha* since the President may veto any such resolution. Neither the concurrent resolution procedure before 1984 nor the joint resolution procedure in effect since has ever been successfully invoked, however, so that the President's decisions have in practice proven final.

Notes and Questions

(1) The role of the attorney in the Presidential phase of the escape clause investigation resembles that of the typical Washington lobbyist, striving to build a political coalition for or against import relief. The

---

16. The courts have not attempted to control this discretion. See, e.g., Maple Leaf Fish Co. v. United States, 762 F.2d 86 (Fed. Cir.1985).

potential members of the coalition on the petitioners' side are to a great degree obvious—the beneficiaries of protection, typically the petitioning industry itself. How does one proceed on the respondents' side, given that foreign exporters have no vote in U.S. elections? In reflecting on this issue, it is perhaps instructive to recall what happened after the ITC determinations in the *Automobiles* case and the *Unwrought Copper* case, supra. In the *Automobiles* case, the President eventually secured a voluntary restraint arrangement with Japan (which lasted, at least on paper, until 1994) despite the negative vote by the ITC. In the *Unwrought Copper* case, by contrast, the President declined to grant relief despite a unanimous affirmative vote. Of what significance is the fact that the burden of auto restraints fell upon individual American consumers, while the burden of restrictions on refined copper imports would have also fallen on industrial consumers such as the wire and brass industries?

(2) The lobbyists for respondents' interests are retained and paid in many cases by foreign companies or governments. Such "foreign agents" (to use the language of the federal statute that requires them to register their activities with the Justice Department) are regularly the target of criticism and derision by domestic interests, even to the point of suggesting that they are unpatriotic. Should lawyers have any qualms about such representation? Suppose, for example, that respondents' domestic representatives purchase a number of tickets to a $1,000 a plate fundraiser for the Chairman of the Ways and Means Committee. Undue influence, or government as usual?

(3) GATT Article XIX provides that relief may be afforded "for such time as may be necessary to remedy" the injury to the domestic industry. Thus, it was contemplated that relief would be temporary, but firm requirements to that end were lacking. An importing nation could always claim that injury or threat was ongoing and required a lengthy period of protection. The Uruguay Round Agreement on Safeguards responds in Article 7 with several more specific restrictions. The general rule is that safeguards measures should not last more than four years "unless extended" on the basis of an additional investigation to establish that serious injury or threat continues, and that "the industry is adjusting." Even with an extension, the total period of protection is not to exceed eight years. Further, in the case of any measure that lasts over two years, no *new* safeguards measures are permitted after the expiration of the previous measures for a period of time equal to the length of time that protection was in place. Finally, there is a requirement that restrictions to last over one year be "progressively liberalized" at "regular intervals," and that measures lasting over three years be reviewed at their midpoint to assess whether withdrawal or accelerated liberalization is appropriate. U.S. law was already roughly in accord with these requirements and has now been amended to comply fully. It provides that protection shall ordinarily be phased down during the period of relief. It also provides in Section 203 for a four year period of relief, which can be extended to a total of eight years if the ITC makes a determination that an extension is needed to prevent injury and that a positive adjustment is occurring. The result is that the ITC must undertake a scaled down version of the original investigation after a few years, known as a "203 review" (a review of the President's action taken under Section 203). Respondents have the opportunity to appear and to argue anew that protection is not necessary

or that its costs exceed its benefits. Similar opportunities for "203 reviews" existed under prior law.

SECTION 15.3   WTO DEVELOPMENTS

A number of WTO cases have now been brought concerning safeguard measures imposed since the Uruguay Round, including two involving U.S. actions under Section 201. In reading through the excerpts that follow, you may want to reflect on the general question of whether the reasoning of the U.S. ITC in the cases in Section 15.2 could survive WTO challenges today. We examine two cases in detail. In the first case, which involved an Argentine safeguard on footwear, the Appellate Body lays out its views on the basic prerequisites for safeguards relief (increased imports, serious injury and causation). The second case, involving the U.S. *Lamb Meat* decision excerpted above, deals with the relationship of GATT Article XIX and the Safeguards Agreement to the question of industry definition. Most critically for the United States, it also examines in detail the U.S. approach to causation.

ARGENTINA—SAFEGUARD MEASURES ON IMPORTS OF FOOTWEAR

WT/DS121/AB/R
Appellate Body Report adopted by the DSB on January 12, 2000

1.   Argentina and the European Communities appeal certain issues of law and legal interpretation in the Panel Report, *Argentina—Safeguard Measures on Imports of Footwear* (the "Panel Report"). The Panel was established to consider a complaint by the European Communities with respect to the application by Argentina of certain safeguard measures on imports of footwear.

* * *

5.   The Panel concluded that "the definitive safeguard measure on footwear based on Argentina's investigation and determination is inconsistent with Articles 2 and 4 of the Agreement on Safeguards" and, therefore, "that there is nullification or impairment of the benefits accruing to the European Communities under the Agreement on Safeguards within the meaning of Article 3.8 of the DSU." * * *

* * *

123.   Articles 2.1 and 4.2 of the *Agreement on Safeguards* provide as follows:

ARTICLE 2

Conditions

1.   A Member may apply a safeguard measure to a product only if Member has determined, pursuant to the provisions set out below, that such product is being imported into its territory in such

increased quantities, absolute or relative to domestic production, and under such conditions as to cause or threaten to cause serious injury to the domestic industry that produces like or directly competitive products.

ARTICLE 4

Determination of Serious Injury or Threat Thereof

2. (a) In the investigation to determine whether increased imports have caused or are threatening to cause serious injury to a domestic industry under the terms of this Agreement, the competent authorities shall evaluate all relevant factors of an objective and quantifiable nature having a bearing on the situation of that industry, in particular, the rate and amount of the increase in imports of the product concerned in absolute and relative terms, the share of the domestic market taken by increased imports, changes in the level of sales, production, productivity, capacity utilization, profits and losses, and employment.

(b) The determination referred to in subparagraph (a) shall not be made unless this investigation demonstrates, on the basis of objective evidence, the existence of the causal link between increased imports of the product concerned and serious injury or threat thereof. When factors other than increased imports are causing injury to the domestic industry at the same time, such injury shall not be attributed to increased imports.

(c) The competent authorities shall publish promptly, in accordance with the provisions of Article 3, a detailed analysis of the case under investigation as well as a demonstration of the relevance of the factors examined.

124. We recall the Panel's ultimate conclusions on Articles 2.1 and 4.2:

> For the foregoing reasons, we conclude that Argentina's investigation did not demonstrate that there were increased imports within the meaning of Articles 2.1 and 4.2(a); that the investigation did not evaluate all relevant factors of an objective and quantifiable nature having a bearing on the situation of the domestic industry within the meaning of Article 4.2(a); that the investigation did not demonstrate on the basis of objective evidence the existence of a causal link between increased imports and serious injury within the meaning of Article 2.1 and 4.2(b); that the investigation did not adequately take into account factors other than increased imports within the meaning of Article 4.2(b); and that the published report concerning the investigation did not set forth a complete analysis of the case under investigation as well as a demonstration of the relevance of the factors examined within the meaning of Article 4.2(c).

> Therefore, we find that Argentina's investigation and determinations of increased imports, serious injury and causation are inconsis-

tent with Articles 2 and 4 of the Safeguards Agreement. As such, we find that Argentina's investigation provides *no* legal basis for the application of the definitive safeguard measure at issue, or any safeguard measure.

Increased Imports

125. With respect to the requirement relating to "increased imports", the Panel stated as follows:

> The Agreement on Safeguards requires an increase in imports as a basic prerequisite for the application of a safeguard measure. The relevant provisions are in Articles 2.1 and 4.2(a).

> * * *

> Thus, to determine whether imports have increased in "such quantities" for purposes of applying a safeguard measure, these two provisions require an analysis of the rate and amount of the increase in imports, in absolute terms and as a percentage of domestic production.

126. In its evaluation of whether the investigation by the Argentine authorities demonstrated the required increase in imports under Articles 2.1 and 4.2(a), the Panel stated the following:

> ... *the Agreement requires not just an increase (i.e., any increase) in imports, but an increase in "such ... quantities" as to cause or threaten to cause serious injury*. The Agreement provides no numerical guidance as to how this is to be judged, nor in our view could it do so. But this does not mean that this requirement is meaningless. To the contrary, we believe that it means that the increase in imports must be judged in its full context, in particular with regard to its "rate and amount" as required by Article 4.2(a). Thus, considering the changes in import levels over the entire period of investigation, as discussed above, seems unavoidable when making a determination of whether there has been an increase in imports "in such quantities" in the sense of Article 2.1. (emphasis added).

127. [Eds. note: Argentina had examined imports over a five-year period of investigation from 1991 through 1995.] The Panel concluded that Argentina did not adequately consider the "intervening trends in imports, in particular the steady and significant declines in imports beginning in 1994, as well as the sensitivity of the analysis to the particular end points of the investigation period used." For these reasons, the Panel concluded that "Argentina's investigation did not demonstrate that there were increased imports within the meaning of Articles 2.1 and 4.2(a)". The Panel, though, rejected an argument made by the European Communities "that only a 'sharply increasing' trend in imports at the end of the investigation period can satisfy this requirement."

128. Argentina maintains that, in its interpretation and application of the requirement of "increased imports" in Articles 2.1 and 4.2 of the

Agreement on Safeguards, the Panel "impose[d] a variety of methodological hurdles which must be overcome before a finding of 'increased imports' can be justified." In particular, Argentina argues that the Panel misinterpreted the word "rate" in Article 4.2(a) to include "direction", and found that there could only be "increased imports" if: (i) a change in the base year from 1991 to 1992 would still result in an increase; (ii) the analysis of end points and interim periods is mutually reinforcing; and (iii) it is found that the decrease in imports in 1994 and 1995 was temporary. Argentina also asserts that the Panel "collapsed" the "increased imports" requirement "with the other qualitative requirements of Article" and wrongly treated it as a *"qualitative,* rather than a separate *quantitative* requirement." The ordinary meaning of "increased imports", in Argentina's view, is that imports have become greater, and Argentina argues that there is no factual or contextual support for any additional requirements in the *Agreement on Safeguards.*

129. We agree with the Panel that Articles 2.1 and 4.2(a) of the *Agreement on Safeguards* require a demonstration not merely of *any* increase in imports, but, instead, of imports "in such increased quantities ... and under such conditions as to cause or threaten to cause serious injury." In addition, we agree with the Panel that the specific provisions of Article 4.2(a) require that "the rate *and amount* of the increase in imports ... in absolute and relative terms" (emphasis added) must be evaluated. Thus, we do not dispute the Panel's view and ultimate conclusion that the competent authorities are required to consider the *trends* in imports over the period of investigation (rather than just comparing the end points) under Article 4.2(a). As a result, we agree with the Panel's conclusion that "Argentina did not adequately consider the intervening trends in imports, in particular the steady and significant declines in imports beginning in 1994, as well as the sensitivity of the analysis to the particular end points of the investigation period used."

130. All the same, while we do not find that the Panel erred in its application of the requirement in Article 2.1 of the *Agreement in Safeguards* that the *"product is being imported* ... in such increased quantities", we do find the Panel's interpretation of that requirement somewhat lacking. We note that the Panel characterized this condition in Article 2.1 on several occasions in the Panel Report simply as "increased imports". However, the actual requirement, and we emphasize that this requirement is found in both Article 2.1 of the *Agreement on Safeguards* and Article XIX:1(a) of the GATT 1994, is that "such product *is being imported* ... in such increased quantities", "and under such conditions as to cause or threaten to cause serious injury to the domestic industry". (emphasis added) Although we agree with the Panel that the "increased quantities" of imports cannot be just *any* increase, we do not agree with the Panel that it is reasonable to examine the trend in imports over a five-year historical period. In our view, the use of the present tense of the verb phrase "is being imported" in both Article 2.1 of the *Agreement on Safeguards* and Article XIX:1(a) of the GATT 1994

indicates that it is necessary for the competent authorities to examine recent imports, and not simply trends in imports during the past five years—or, for that matter, during any other period of several years. In our view, the phrase "is being imported" implies that the increase in imports must have been sudden and recent.

131. * * * We also believe that the phrase "in *such* increased quantities" in Article 2.1 of the *Agreement on Safeguards* and Article XIX:1(a) of the GATT 1994 is meaningful to this determination. In our view, the determination of whether the requirement of imports "in such increased quantities" is met is not a merely mathematical or technical determination. In other words, it is not enough for an investigation to show simply that imports of the product this year were more than last year—or five years ago. Again, and it bears repeating, not just *any* increased quantities of imports will suffice. There must be "*such* increased quantities" as to cause or threaten to cause serious injury to the domestic industry in order to fulfil this requirement for applying a safeguard measure. And this language in both Article 2.1 of the *Agreement on Safeguards* and Article XIX:1(a) of the GATT 1994, we believe, requires that the increase in imports must have been recent enough, sudden enough, sharp enough, and significant enough, both quantitatively and qualitatively, to cause or threaten to cause "serious injury".

Serious Injury

132. With respect to the requirement relating to "serious injury", Article 4.2(a) of the *Agreement on Safeguards* provides, in relevant part:

> In the investigation to determine whether increased imports have caused or are threatening to cause serious injury to a domestic industry under the terms of this Agreement, the competent authorities *shall evaluate all relevant factors* of an objective and quantifiable nature *having a bearing on the situation of that industry, in particular,* . . . the share of the domestic market taken by increased imports, changes in the level of sales, production, productivity, capacity utilization, profits and losses, and employment.

133. The Panel stated that the requirements of Article 4.2(a) obliged it to:

> . . . consider, first, whether all injury factors listed in the Agreement were considered by Argentina, as the text of Article 4.2(a) of the Agreement ("all relevant factors . . . including . . . changes in the level of sales, production, productivity, capacity utilisation, profits and losses, and employment") is unambiguous that at a minimum each of the factors listed, in addition to all other factors that are "relevant", must be considered.

The Panel also concluded that, pursuant to the provisions of Article 4.2(c) and, by reference, Article 3 of the *Agreement on Safeguards*, it was required to examine whether Argentina's findings and conclusions on "serious injury" were supported by the evidence before the Argentine authorities.

134. The Panel read Article 4.2(a) literally to mean that all the listed factors: "changes in the level of sales, production, productivity, capacity utilisation, profits and losses, and employment"—must be evaluated in every investigation. In addition, the Panel stated that all other relevant factors having a bearing on the situation of the industry must also be evaluated. As the Panel found that Argentina had not evaluated two of the listed factors, capacity utilization and productivity, the Panel concluded that Argentina's investigation was not consistent with the requirements of Article 4.2(a).

135. Argentina submits that the Panel erred in its analysis of Argentina's determination of "serious injury". According to Argentina, Article 4.2(c) of the *Agreement on Safeguards* requires only a demonstration of the relevance of the factors examined, rather than an examination of all the listed factors as relevant. In response to the Panel's finding that Argentina had not properly evaluated the factors of capacity utilization and productivity, Argentina replies by maintaining that the factor of productivity is explicitly mentioned in Act 338 and that data sufficient to calculate capacity utilization was available to the Argentine authorities. Furthermore, Argentina argues that neither capacity utilization nor productivity was a principal or a significant issue in the investigation. Argentina also takes issue with the Panel's view that the available data for 1996 should have been examined by Argentina in its investigation of "serious injury". Here, Argentina responds that the record clearly shows that the data for 1996 was incomplete, and Argentina submits that it was appropriate and reasonable to use a single review period for which all the data was available as a basis for its determination of "serious injury". In addition, Argentina argues that the Panel erred in several aspects of its examination of the evidence considered by the Argentine authorities.

136. We agree with the Panel's interpretation that Article 4.2(a) of the *Agreement on Safeguards* requires a demonstration that the competent authorities evaluated, at a minimum, each of the factors listed in Article 4.2(a) as well as all other factors that are relevant to the situation of the industry concerned. Furthermore, we do not dispute the Panel's finding that Argentina did not evaluate all of the listed factors, in particular, capacity utilization and productivity. We consider the other points that Argentina has raised in this appeal, relating to the availability of data for 1996 and to the Panel's evaluation of the evidence considered by the Argentine authorities, to relate to matters of fact which are not within our mandate, under Article 17.6 of the DSU, to examine on appeal.

137. For these reasons, we uphold the Panel's conclusion that Argentina did not evaluate "all relevant factors of an objective and quantifiable nature having a bearing on the situation of that industry" as required by Article 4.2(a) of the *Agreement on Safeguards*.

138. However, although it was not necessary for the Panel to go beyond where it did in this case, as the Panel found that Argentina had

not evaluated all of the required listed factors, we do not believe that an evaluation of the listed factors in Article 4.2(a) is all that is required to justify a determination of "serious injury" under the *Agreement on Safeguards*. We note, in this respect, that there is a definition of "serious injury" in Article 4.1(a) of the *Agreement on Safeguards*, which reads as follows:

> "serious injury" shall be understood to mean a *significant overall impairment* in the position of a domestic industry. (emphasis added)

And we note that, in its legal analysis of "serious injury" under Article 4.2(a), the Panel made no use whatsoever of this definition.

139.   In our view, it is only when the *overall position* of the domestic industry is evaluated, in light of all the relevant factors having a bearing on a situation of that industry, that it can be determined whether there is "a significant overall impairment" in the position of that industry. Although Article 4.2(a) technically requires that certain listed factors must be evaluated, and that all other relevant factors must be evaluated, that provision does not specify what such an evaluation must demonstrate. Obviously, any such evaluation will be different for different industries in different cases, depending on the facts of the particular case and the situation of the industry concerned. An evaluation of each listed factor will not necessarily have to show that each such factor is "declining". In one case, for example, there may be significant declines in sales, employment and productivity that will show "significant overall impairment" in the position of the industry, and therefore will justify a finding of serious injury. In another case, a certain factor may not be declining, but the overall picture may nevertheless demonstrate "significant overall impairment" of the industry. Thus, in addition to a technical examination of whether the competent authorities in a particular case have evaluated all the listed factors and any other relevant factors, we believe that it is essential for a panel to take the definition of "serious injury" in Article 4.1(a) of the *Agreement on Safeguards* into account in its review of any determination of "serious injury".

Causation

140.   With respect to the requirement of causation, Article 4.2(b) of the *Agreement on Safeguards* provides that a determination of serious injury:

> . . . shall not be made unless this investigation demonstrates, on the basis of objective evidence, the existence of the causal link between increased imports of the product concerned and serious injury or threat thereof. When factors other than increased imports are causing injury to the domestic industry at the same time, such injury shall not be attributed to increased imports.

141.   The Panel interpreted the requirements of Article 4.2(b) as follows:

... we will consider whether Argentina's causation analysis meets these requirements on the basis of (i) whether an upward trend in imports coincides with downward trends in the injury factors, and if not, whether a reasoned explanation is provided as to why nevertheless the data show causation; (ii) whether the conditions of competition in the Argentine footwear market between imported and domestic footwear as analysed demonstrate, on the basis of objective evidence, a causal link of the imports to any injury; and (iii) whether other relevant factors have been analysed and whether it is established that injury caused by factors other than imports has not been attributed to imports.

142.   On causation, the Panel stated:

> ... the *trends*—in both the injury factors and the imports—matter as much as their absolute levels. In the particular context of a causation analysis, we also believe that this provision means that it is the *relationship* between the movements in imports (volume and market share) and the movements in injury factors that must be central to a causation analysis and determination.
>
> In practical terms, we believe therefore that this provision means that if causation is present, an increase in imports normally should coincide with a decline in the relevant injury factors. While such a coincidence by itself cannot *prove* causation (because, *inter alia*, Article 3 requires an explanation—i.e., "findings and reasoned conclusions"), its absence would create serious doubts as to the existence of a causal link, and would require a *very* compelling analysis of why causation still is present.

143.   Argentina argues on appeal that the Panel erred in establishing and applying three "standards" in its analysis of causation. First, Argentina maintains that the Panel required that an upward trend in imports must *coincide* with a *downward* trend in the injury factors. On this point, Argentina maintains that Article 4.2(c) of the *Agreement on Safeguards* refers to "changes" and not to "downward trends", so that there is no requirement that there be a "downward trend" in each year of the period of investigation. Moreover, Argentina maintains that the Panel's requirement of "coincidence" in time is not implied by the term "cause". Second, Argentina asserts that the Panel used the phrase "under such conditions" to develop a requirement that the "conditions of competition" between imported and domestic footwear in the Argentine market demonstrate a causal link between the increased imports and injury. Argentina asserts that there is no basis in the *Agreement on Safeguards* for this requirement. Third, Argentina maintains that the Panel required the Argentine authorities to establish that other relevant factors had been analyzed, and that injury caused by factors other than imports is not evidence of serious injury caused by imports. In Argentina's opinion, this requirement goes far beyond what is actually required in Article 4.2(b) of the *Agreement on Safeguards*.

144. We note that Article 4.2(a) requires the competent authorities to evaluate "the rate and amount of the increase in imports", "the share of the domestic market taken by increased imports", as well as the "changes" in the level of factors such as sales, production, productivity, capacity utilization, and others. We see no reason to disagree with the Panel's interpretation that the words "rate and amount" and "changes" in Article 4.2(a) mean that "the *trends*—in both the injury factors and the imports—matter as much as their absolute levels." We also agree with the Panel that, in an analysis of causation, "it is the *relationship* between the *movements* in imports (volume and market share) and the *movements* in injury factors that must be central to a causation analysis and determination." (emphasis added) Furthermore, with respect to a "coincidence" between an increase in imports and a decline in the relevant injury factors, we note that the Panel simply said that this should "normally" occur if causation is present. The Panel qualified this statement, however, in the following sentence:

> While such a coincidence by itself cannot *prove* causation (because, *inter alia*, Article 3 requires an explanation—i.e., "findings and reasoned conclusions"), its absence would create serious doubts as to the existence of a causal link, and would require a *very* compelling analysis of why causation still is present.

145. We are somewhat surprised that the Panel, having determined that there were no "increased imports", and having determined that there was no "serious injury", for some reason went on to make an assessment of causation. It would be difficult, indeed, to demonstrate a "causal link" between "increased imports" that did not occur and "serious injury" that did not exist. Nevertheless, we see no error in the Panel's interpretation of the causation requirements, or in its interpretation of Article 4.2(b) of the *Agreement on Safeguards*. Rather, we believe that Argentina has mischaracterized the Panel's interpretation and reasoning. Furthermore, we agree with the Panel's conclusions that "the conditions of competition between the imports and the domestic product were not analysed or adequately explained (in particular price); and that 'other factors' identified by the CNCE in the investigation were not sufficiently evaluated, in particular, the tequila effect."

146. For all these reasons, we uphold the Panel's conclusion that "Argentina's findings and conclusions regarding causation were not adequately explained and supported by the evidence."

Notes and Questions

(1) With regard to "increased imports," how can one determine whether an increase has been "recent enough, sudden enough, sharp enough, and significant enough, both quantitatively and qualitatively, to cause or threaten to cause 'serious injury' "? (para. 134) Does the Appellate Body in paragraph 130 impliedly accept the European argument that "only a 'sharply increasing' trend in imports at the end of the investigation period can satisfy the [increased imports] requirement?" Is it wise to focus so heavily on the immediate past, or will trends over a larger window of time be more

informative as to the competitive position of a domestic industry in relation to imports?

(2) In its analysis of "serious injury," has the Appellate Body done more than merely create hoops for national authorities to jump through in their discussion of the issue—could Argentina have avoided the problems it encountered simply by reciting that it had duly "considered" all the factors listed in the Safeguards Agreement or raised during the investigation? What greater degree of discipline over national authorities is practicable?

(3) Is it fair to characterize the Appellate Body's discussion of causation as suggesting that the contemporaneous correlation (or absence of correlation) between increased imports and indicators of industrial decline must be the centerpiece of the analysis?

UNITED STATES—SAFEGUARD MEASURES ON IMPORTS OF FRESH, CHILLED OR FROZEN LAMB MEAT FROM NEW ZEALAND AND AUSTRALIA

WT/DS177 & 178/AB/R
Appellate Body Report adopted by the DSB on May 16, 2001

2. On 7 October 1998, the United States International Trade Commission (the "USITC") initiated a safeguard investigation into imports of lamb meat. By Proclamation of the President of the United States, dated 7 July 1999, the United States imposed a definitive safeguard measure, in the form of a tariff-rate quota, on imports of fresh, chilled and frozen lamb meat, effective as of 22 July 1999. * * *

* * *

4. * * * [T]he Panel concluded:

(a) that the United States has acted inconsistently with Article XIX:1(a) of GATT 1994 by failing to demonstrate as a matter of fact the existence of "unforeseen developments";

(b) that the United States has acted inconsistently with Article 4.1(c) of the Agreement on Safeguards because the USITC, in the lamb meat investigation, defined the domestic industry as including input producers (i.e., growers and feeders of live lamb) as producers of the like product at issue (i.e. lamb meat);

* * *

(f) that the United States has acted inconsistently with Article 4.2(b) of the Agreement on Safeguards because the USITC's determination in the lamb meat investigation in respect of causation did not demonstrate the required causal link between increased imports and threat of serious injury, in that the determination did not establish that increased imports were by themselves a necessary and sufficient cause of threat of serious injury, and in that the determination did not ensure that threat of serious injury caused by "other factors" was not attributed to increased imports;

(g) that by virtue of the above violations of Article 4 of the Agreement on Safeguards, the United States also has acted inconsistently with Article 2.1 of the Agreement on Safeguards.

* * *

Unforeseen Developments

65.   Before the Panel, Australia and New Zealand claimed that the United States failed to comply with the requirements of Article XIX:1(a) of the GATT 1994 regarding "unforeseen developments". The Panel found:

> Article XIX:1 read in the context of SG Article 3.1 requires the competent national authority, in its determination, to reach a conclusion demonstrating the existence of "unforeseen developments" in the sense of GATT Article XIX:1.

* * *

68.   We begin by noting that the claim made by both Australia and New Zealand before the Panel was that the United States acted inconsistently with its obligation in Article XIX:1(a) of the GATT 1994 relating to "unforeseen developments". Article XIX:1(a) of the GATT 1994 reads:

> If, as a result of unforeseen developments and of the effect of the obligations incurred by a Member under this Agreement, including tariff concessions, any product is being imported into the territory of that Member in such increased quantities and under such conditions as to cause or threaten serious injury to domestic producers in that territory of like or directly competitive products, the Member shall be free, in respect of such product, and to the extent and for such time as may be necessary to prevent or remedy such injury, to suspend the obligation in whole or in part or to withdraw or modify the concession.

69.   In our Reports in *Argentina—Footwear Safeguard* and *Korea—Dairy Safeguard*, we examined the relationship between Article XIX of the GATT 1994 and the *Agreement on Safeguards* and, in particular, whether, with the entry into force of the *Agreement on Safeguards*, Article XIX continues to impose obligations on WTO Members when they apply safeguard measures. We observed in those two appeals that "the provisions of Article XIX of the GATT 1994 *and* the provisions of the *Agreement on Safeguards* are *all* provisions of one treaty, the *WTO Agreement*", and we said that these two texts must be read "harmoniously" and as "an inseparable package of rights and disciplines". We derived support for this interpretation from Articles 1 and 11.1(a) of the *Agreement on Safeguards*. We observed, in both the Reports, that:

> Article 1 states that the purpose of the *Agreement on Safeguards* is to establish "rules for the application of safeguard measures which shall be understood to mean *those measures provided for in* Article XIX of GATT 1994." (emphasis added) The ordinary meaning of the

language in Article 11.1(a)—"unless such action conforms with the provisions of that Article applied in accordance with this Agreement"—is that any safeguard action *must conform* with the provisions of Article XIX of the GATT 1994 *as well as* with the provisions of the *Agreement on Safeguards*. Thus, any safeguard measure imposed after the entry into force of the *WTO Agreement* must comply with the provisions of *both* the *Agreement on Safeguards* and Article XIX of the GATT 1994.

70. We reiterate: Articles 1 and 11.1(a) of the *Agreement on Safeguards* express the full and continuing applicability of Article XIX of the GATT 1994, which no longer stands in isolation, but has been clarified and reinforced by the *Agreement on Safeguards*.

71. Based on this interpretation of the relationship between Article XIX of the GATT 1994 and the *Agreement on Safeguards*, we found in both these previous Reports:

> The first clause in Article XIX:1(a)—"as a result of unforeseen developments and of the obligations incurred by a Member under the Agreement, including tariff concessions ..."—is a dependent clause which, in our view, is linked grammatically to the verb phrase "is being imported" in the second clause of that paragraph. Although we do not view the first clause in Article XIX:1(a) as establishing independent *conditions* for the application of a safeguard measure, additional to the *conditions* set forth in the second clause of that paragraph, we do believe that the first clause describes certain *circumstances* which must be demonstrated as a matter of fact in order for a safeguard measure to be applied consistently with the provisions of Article XIX of the GATT 1994. In this sense, we believe that there is *a logical connection* between the circumstances described in the first clause—"as a result of unforeseen developments and of the effect of the obligations incurred by a Member under this Agreement, including tariff concessions ..."—and the conditions set forth in the second clause of Article XIX:1(a) for the imposition of a safeguard measure.

72. Although we stated in these two Reports that, under Article XIX:1(a) of the GATT 1994, unforeseen developments "must be demonstrated as a matter of fact", we did not have occasion, in those two appeals, to examine when, where or how that demonstration should occur. In conducting such an examination now, we note that the text of Article XIX provides no express guidance on this issue. However, as the existence of unforeseen developments is a prerequisite that must be demonstrated, as we have stated, "in order for a safeguard measure to be applied" consistently with Article XIX of the GATT 1994, it follows that this demonstration must be made *before* the safeguard measure is applied. Otherwise, the legal basis for the measure is flawed. We find instructive guidance for where and when the "demonstration" should occur in the "logical connection" that we observed previously between the two clauses of Article XIX:1(a). The first clause, as we noted,

contains, in part, the "circumstance" of "unforeseen developments". The second clause, as we said, relates to the three "conditions" for the application of safeguard measures, which are also reiterated in Article 2.1 of the *Agreement on Safeguards*. Clearly, the fulfilment of these conditions must be the central element of the report of the competent authorities, which must be published under Article 3.1 of the *Agreement on Safeguards*. In our view, the logical connection between the "conditions" identified in the second clause of Article XIX:1(a) and the "circumstances" outlined in the first clause of that provision dictates that the demonstration of the existence of these circumstances must also feature in the same report of the competent authorities. Any other approach would sever the "logical connection" between these two clauses, and would also leave vague and uncertain how compliance with the first clause of Article XIX:1(a) would be fulfilled.

73.   In this case, we see no indication in the USITC Report that the USITC addressed the issue of "unforeseen developments" at all. It is true that the USITC Report identifies two changes in the type of lamb meat products imported into the United States. These were: the proportion of imported fresh and chilled lamb meat increased in relation to the proportion of imported frozen lamb meat; and, the cut size of imported lamb meat increased. The USITC Report mentions the first of these changes in examining the "like products" at issue, and mentions both changes under the heading "causation" while describing the substitutability of domestic and imported lamb meat in the domestic marketplace. However, we observe that the USITC Report does not discuss or offer any explanation as to why these changes could be regarded as "unforeseen developments" within the meaning of Article XIX:1(a) of the GATT 1994. It follows that the USITC Report does not *demonstrate* that the safeguard measure at issue has been applied, *inter alia*, ". . . as a result of unforeseen developments . . .".

74.   The USITC's failure to address the existence of unforeseen developments, in the USITC Report of April 1999, is not surprising, as the USITC is not obliged by any United States legislation, regulation, or other domestic rule, to examine the existence of unforeseen developments in its investigation into the situation of a domestic industry. Although the United States has subsequently modified its position on this issue,[1] we recall that, as a third participant in both *Korea—Dairy Safeguard* and *Argentina—Footwear Safeguard*, the United States argued that the omission of unforeseen developments from the *Agreement on Safeguards* meant that it was no longer necessary to demonstrate the existence of unforeseen developments. Our Reports in *Korea—Dairy Safeguard* and *Argentina—Footwear Safeguard*, in which we found that unforeseen developments must be demonstrated as a matter of fact, were circulated on 14 December 1999, that is to say, more than seven months *after* the report of the USITC on the domestic lamb meat industry was

---

1.   [original note 40] At the oral hearing, the United States indicated that it is no longer of the view that it is unnecessary to   demonstrate the existence of unforeseen developments.

published in April 1999. Our two Reports were, therefore, not known to the USITC when it rendered its report in the present case.

75.   Accordingly, although we do not agree with every aspect of the Panel's reasoning, we uphold the Panel's conclusion, in paragraphs 7.45 and 8.1(a) of the Panel Report, "that the United States has failed to demonstrate as a matter of fact the existence of unforeseen developments as required by Article XIX:1(a) of GATT 1994". * * *

76.   We emphasize that neither Australia nor New Zealand has claimed that the United States acted inconsistently with Article 3.1 of the *Agreement on Safeguards* with respect to unforeseen developments. We do not, therefore, rule on whether the USITC, and, hence, the United States, acted inconsistently with Article 3.1 of the *Agreement on Safeguards* because the USITC failed to "set[] forth ... findings and reasoned conclusions" on this issue. Nonetheless, we observe that Article 3.1 requires competent authorities to set forth findings and reasoned conclusions on "all pertinent issues of fact and law" in their published report. As Article XIX:1(a) of the GATT 1994 requires that "unforeseen developments" must be demonstrated, as a matter of fact, for a safeguard measure to be applied, the existence of "unforeseen developments" is, in our view, a "pertinent issue[] of fact and law", under Article 3.1, for the application of a safeguard measure, and it follows that the published report of the competent authorities, under that Article, must contain a "finding" or "reasoned conclusion" on "unforeseen developments".

Domestic Industry

77.   The USITC defined the domestic industry in this case to include growers and feeders of live lambs, as well as packers and breakers of lamb meat. The USITC did so because it considered that there was a "continuous line of production from the raw to the processed product", and that there was a "substantial coincidence of economic interests" between and among the growers and feeders of live lambs, and the packers and breakers of lamb meat.

* * *

81.   The United States ... argues that the USITC's determination of "domestic industry" is correct, in particular, in its reliance on the criteria of a "continuous line of production" and a "coincidence of economic interests" to assess which producers make up the domestic industry. The United States argues that the *Agreement on Safeguards* allows Members some discretion when defining the term "producers" in the light of the facts and circumstances of each case. Moreover, the United States argues that the Panel's own criteria for determining the scope of the domestic industry are devoid of a textual basis. In this respect, the United States asserts that the Panel incorrectly stated that the USITC had found growers and feeders to be producers of a product separate and distinct from lamb meat. The United States maintains that

the USITC's approach in this case is appropriate in order to capture in full the affected domestic industry.

82.   As a preliminary matter, we note that the USITC clearly stated in its report that the issue of whether the producers of an input product could be included in the domestic industry producing the processed product is not addressed in the United States safeguard statute. In response to questioning at the oral hearing, the United States confirmed that the two-pronged test applied by the USITC in deciding this issue is not mandated either by the United States safeguard statute or by any provision of the United States Code of Federal Regulations that applies to safeguard investigations and determinations. The United States also confirmed, at the oral hearing, that the USITC has adopted this test for defining a "domestic industry" in safeguard actions as a matter of practice in the evolution of its own case law; for safeguard actions, the test has not been enacted into law or promulgated as a regulation.

83.   We begin our analysis with the definition of the term "domestic industry" in Article 4.1(c) of the *Agreement on Safeguards*, which reads:

> (c) in determining injury or threat thereof, a "domestic industry" shall be understood to mean the *producers* as a whole *of the like or directly competitive products* operating within the territory of a Member, or those whose collective output *of the like or directly competitive products* constitutes a major proportion of the total domestic production of *those products*. (emphasis added)

84.   The definition of "domestic industry" in this provision refers to two elements. First, the industry consists of "producers". As the Panel indicated, "producers" are those who grow or manufacture an article; "producers" are those who bring a thing into existence. This meaning of "producers" is, however, qualified by the second element in the definition of "domestic industry". This element identifies the particular products that must be produced by the domestic "producers" in order to qualify for inclusion in the "domestic industry". According to the clear and express wording of the text of Article 4.1(c), the term "domestic industry" extends solely to the "producers ... *of the like or directly competitive* products". (emphasis added) The definition, therefore, focuses exclusively on the producers of a very specific group of products. Producers of products that are *not* "like or directly competitive products" do not, according to the text of the treaty, form part of the domestic industry.

* * *

87.   Accordingly, the first step in determining the scope of the domestic industry is the identification of the products which are "like or directly competitive" with the imported product. Only when those products have been identified is it possible then to identify the "producers" of those products.

88. There is no dispute that in this case the "like product" is "lamb meat", which is the imported product with which the safeguard investigation was concerned. The USITC considered that the "domestic industry" producing the "like product", lamb meat, includes the growers and feeders of live lambs. The term "directly competitive products" is not, however, at issue in this dispute as the USITC did not find that there were any such products in this case.[2]

89. The United States argues, nevertheless, that it is permissible, on the facts and circumstances of this case, to include in the "domestic industry" the growers and feeders of live lambs because, as the USITC has found: (1) there is a "continuous line of production" from the raw product, live lambs, to the end-product, lamb meat; and (2) there is a "substantial coincidence of economic interests" between the producers of the raw product and the producers of the end-product.

90. This interpretation may well have a basis in the USITC case law, but there is no basis for this interpretation in the *Agreement on Safeguards*. The text of Article 4.1(c) defines the "domestic industry" exclusively by reference to the "producers ... of the like or directly competitive product". There is no reference in that definition to the two criteria relied upon by the United States. In our view, under Article 4.1(c), input products can only be included in defining the "domestic industry" if they are "like or directly competitive" with the end-products. If an input product and an end-product are not "like" or "directly competitive", then it is irrelevant, under the *Agreement on Safeguards*, that there is a continuous line of production between an input product and an end-product, that the input product represents a high proportion of the value of the end-product, that there is no use for the input product other than as an input for the particular end-product, or that there is a substantial coincidence of economic interests between the producers of these products. In the absence of a "like or directly competitive" relationship, we see no justification, in Article 4.1(c) or any other provision of the *Agreement on Safeguards*, for giving credence to any of these criteria in defining a "domestic industry".

91. In this respect, we are not persuaded that the words "as a whole" in Article 4.1(c), appearing in the phrase "producers as a whole", offer support to the United States' position. These words do not alter the requirement that the "domestic industry" extends only to producers of "like or directly competitive products". The words "as a whole" apply to "producers" and, when read together with the terms "collective output" and "major proportion" which follow, clearly address the *number* and the *representative nature* of producers making up the domestic industry. The words "as a whole" do not imply that producers of *other* products,

---

2. [original note 50] We note that two Commissioners (Askey and Crawford) did not join in the findings of the USITC on this point. These two Commissioners both found that *live lambs*, produced by growers and feeders, are directly competitive with lamb *meat* and that, accordingly, the "do- mestic industry" includes the producers of these competing products. The United States has not argued, before the Panel or before us, that *live lambs* are directly com- petitive with lamb *meat*, and that issue as we stated earlier, does not form part of this appeal.

which are *not* like or directly competitive with the imported product, can be included in the definition of domestic industry. Like the Panel, we see the words "as a whole" as no more than "a *quantitative* benchmark for the proportion of producers ... which a safeguards investigation has to cover." (emphasis added)

* * *

Causation

162.   In assessing the claims made by Australia and New Zealand relating to causation, the Panel began with a "[g]eneral interpretative analysis" of the relevant provisions of the *Agreement on Safeguards*, before turning to the application of that interpretation to the facts of this dispute. The Panel took note of the terms of Articles 4.2(a) and 4.2(b) of that Agreement and, after examining the ordinary meaning of the word "cause", stated:

> It is not enough that increased imports cause just some injury which may then be intensified to a "serious" level by factors other than increased imports. In our view, therefore, the ordinary meaning of these phrases describing the Safeguards Agreement's causation standard indicates that increased imports must not only be *neces-sary*, but also *sufficient* to cause or threaten a degree of injury that is *"serious"* enough to constitute a significant overall impairment in the situation of the domestic industry. (underlining added)

163.   The Panel added that:

> ... the second sentence of SG Article 4.2(b) also makes clear ... that increased imports need *not* be the *sole* or exclusive causal factor present in a situation of serious injury or threat thereof, as the requirement not to attribute injury caused by other factors by implication recognises that *multiple* factors may be present in a situation of serious injury or threat thereof.

* * *

> ... where a number of factors, one of which is increased imports, are sufficient *collectively* to cause a significant overall impairment of the position of the domestic industry, but increased imports *alone* are not causing injury that achieves the threshold of "seriousness" set up by SG Article 4.2(a) and 4.2(b), the conditions for imposing a safeguard measure are not satisfied. While we believe that a Member remains free to determine any appropriate method of assessing causation, any method that it selects would need to ensure that the injury caused by increased imports, considered alone, is "serious injury", i.e., causing a significant overall impairment in the situation of the domestic industry. Moreover, we cannot see how a causation standard that does not examine whether increased imports are both a *necessary* and *sufficient* cause for serious injury or threat thereof would ensure that injury caused by factors other than

increased imports is not attributed to those imports. (underlining added)

164. The United States appeals the Panel's finding that the USITC's causation analysis was inconsistent with the *Agreement on Safeguards*. According to the United States, there is no basis in Article 4.2(b) of that Agreement to support the Panel's interpretation that increased imports must be a "necessary and sufficient cause" of, or must, "considered alone", cause, serious injury or a threat thereof. The United States asserts that the Panel's approach is indistinguishable from the approach of the panel in *United States—Wheat Gluten Safeguard*, which we reversed on appeal. The United States concludes that, for the reasons we gave in that appeal, we must also reverse the Panel's findings on causation in this dispute.

165. We agree with the United States that the Panel's interpretation of the causation requirements in Articles 4.2(a) and 4.2(b) of the *Agreement on Safeguards* is very similar to the interpretation of the same provisions by the panel in *United States—Wheat Gluten Safeguard*. Both panels reasoned that increased imports, considered on their own, must be capable of causing, or threatening to cause, injury which is "serious". Both panels stated that increased imports must be "sufficient" to cause serious injury. Moreover, both panels accepted that the situation of the domestic industry may be aggravated by other factors which are also contributing to the injury and, therefore, that increased imports need not be the sole cause of injury, but may be one of several causes. Furthermore, we note that, in this case, the Panel relied on the interpretation of the causation requirements given by the panel in *United States—Wheat Gluten Safeguard* and stated that its interpretation of causation "is *consistent* as well with the findings of the Panel in *US—Wheat Gluten* ... (emphasis added) As the United States points out, we did indeed reverse those findings on appeal in our own Report in *United States—Wheat Gluten Safeguard*.

166. In that appeal, in examining the causation requirements in the *Agreement on Safeguards*, we observed that the first sentence of Article 4.2(b) of the *Agreement on Safeguards* provides that a determination "shall not be made unless [the] investigation demonstrates ... the existence of *the causal link* between increased imports ... and serious injury or threat thereof." (emphasis added) In interpreting this phrase, we said:

> ... the term "the causal link" denotes, in our view, a relationship of cause and effect such that increased imports contribute to "bringing about", "producing" or "inducing" the serious injury. Although that contribution must be sufficiently clear as to establish the existence of "the causal link" required, the language in the first sentence of Article 4.2(b) does *not* suggest that increased imports be *the sole* cause of the serious injury, or that *"other* factors" causing injury must be excluded from the determination of serious injury. To the contrary, the language of Article 4.2(b), as a whole, suggests that

"the causal link" between increased imports and serious injury may exist, *even though other factors are also contributing, "at the same time", to the situation of the domestic industry.*

167. We also noted in that appeal the crucial significance of the second sentence of Article 4.2(b), which states that competent authorities "shall not . . . attribute" to increased imports injury caused by other factors, and we found that:

> Clearly, the process of attributing "injury", envisaged by this sentence, can only be made following a separation of the "injury" that must then be properly "attributed". What is important in this process is separating or distinguishing the *effects* caused by the different factors in bringing about the "injury".

168. We emphasized there that the non-attribution language in the second sentence of Article 4.2(b) means that the effects of increased imports, as separated and distinguished from the effects of other factors, must be examined to determine whether the effects of those imports establish a "genuine and substantial relationship of cause and effect" between the increased imports and serious injury.

169. We also addressed, in that appeal, the language in Articles 2.1 and 4.2(a) of the *Agreement on Safeguards*, which we found to support our reading of the non-attribution language in the second sentence of Article 4.2(b). By way of conclusion, we:

> . . . reverse[d] the Panel's interpretation of Article 4.2(b) of the *Agreement on Safeguards* that increased imports "alone", "in and of themselves", or *"per se"*, must be capable of causing injury that is "serious".

170. In view of the close similarity between the respective interpretations of the causation requirements in the *Agreement on Safeguards* given by this Panel and by the panel in *United States—Wheat Gluten Safeguard*, we are of the view that, for the reasons we gave in *United States—Wheat Gluten Safeguard*, the Panel in this dispute erred in its interpretation of the causation requirements in the *Agreement on Safeguards*. As we held in *United States—Wheat Gluten Safeguard*, the *Agreement on Safeguards* does not require that increased imports be "sufficient" to cause, or threaten to cause, serious injury. Nor does that Agreement require that increased imports "alone" be capable of causing, or threatening to cause, serious injury.

171. Accordingly, we reverse the Panel's interpretation of the causation requirements in the *Agreement on Safeguards*.

172. Having reversed the Panel's "[g]eneral interpretative analysis" of "causation", we go on to consider whether the Panel was correct nonetheless in concluding that the United States acted inconsistently with the causation requirements in Article 4.2 of the *Agreement on Safeguards*. Our own examination of this issue is based *exclusively* on the facts presented in the USITC Report, which form part of the Panel record and are uncontested. Furthermore, notwithstanding the findings

we have made previously in this appeal, we must *assume* in our examination: first, that the definition of the domestic industry given by the USITC is correct, *and*, second, that the USITC correctly found that the domestic industry is threatened with serious injury. On this basis, we must examine whether the USITC properly established, in accordance with the *Agreement on Safeguards*, the existence of the required "causal link" between increased imports and threatened serious injury.

173.   At the outset, we note that this appeal does *not* involve any claim relating to the causation standard set forth in the United States statute. The Panel issued a preliminary ruling that the United States statute *as such* does not fall within the Panel's terms of reference, and this ruling has not been appealed. Therefore, like the Panel, our task on this issue is confined to examining the *application* of the United States' statutory causation standard by the USITC in its determination in the lamb meat investigation for its consistency with the *Agreement on Safeguards*.

174.   The claims by Australia and New Zealand relating to causation focus principally on the requirement, in Article 4.2(b) of the *Agreement on Safeguards*, that injury caused by factors other than increased imports should not be "attributed" to those imports. In the view of Australia and New Zealand, it is uncontested that the USITC acknowledged that other factors were having injurious effects on the domestic industry. However, Australia and New Zealand argue that the USITC failed to explain what the injurious effects of the other factors were, and, therefore, that the United States failed to demonstrate compliance with the "non-attribution" requirement in the second sentence of Article 4.2(b) of the *Agreement on Safeguards*.

175.   Accordingly, we must consider whether the USITC properly ensured that injury caused, or threatened, by factors other than increased imports was not attributed to increased imports, as required by Article 4.2(b). In so considering, we recall that, as we have already elaborated at some length in this Report, when examining a claim under Article 4.2 of the *Agreement on Safeguards*, panels must review whether the competent authorities have acted consistently with the obligations in Article 4.2 by examining whether those authorities have given a reasoned and adequate explanation as to how the facts support their determination.

176.   Article 4.2(b) of the *Agreement on Safeguards* provides:

(b) The determination referred to in [Article 4.2(a)] shall not be made unless this investigation demonstrates, on the basis of objective evidence, the existence of the causal link between increased imports of the product concerned and serious injury or threat thereof. *When factors other than increased imports are causing injury to the domestic industry at the same time, such injury shall not be attributed to increased imports.* (emphasis added)

177.   In our Report in *United States—Wheat Gluten Safeguard*, we said:

Article 4.2(b) presupposes, therefore, as a first step in the competent authorities' examination of causation, that the injurious effects caused to the domestic industry by increased imports are *distinguished from* the injurious effects caused by other factors. The competent authorities can then, as a second step in their examination, attribute to increased imports, on the one hand, and, by implication, to other relevant factors, on the other hand, "injury" caused by all of these different factors, including increased imports. Through this two stage process, the competent authorities comply with Article 4.2(b) by ensuring that any injury to the domestic industry that was *actually* caused by factors other than increased imports is not "attributed" to increased imports and is, therefore, not treated as if it were injury caused by increased imports, when it is not. In this way, the competent authorities determine, as a final step, whether "the causal link" exists between increased imports and serious injury, and whether this causal link involves a genuine and substantial relationship of cause and effect between these two elements, as required by the *Agreement on Safeguards*.

178. We emphasize that these three steps simply describe a logical process for complying with the obligations relating to causation set forth in Article 4.2(b). These steps are not legal "tests" mandated by the text of the *Agreement on Safeguards*, nor is it imperative that each step be the subject of a separate finding or a reasoned conclusion by the competent authorities. Indeed, these steps leave unanswered many methodological questions relating to the non-attribution requirement found in the second sentence of Article 4.2(b).

179. The primary objective of the process we described in *United States—Wheat Gluten Safeguard* is, of course, to determine whether there is "a genuine and substantial relationship of cause and effect" between increased imports and serious injury or threat thereof. As part of that determination, Article 4.2(b) states expressly that injury caused to the domestic industry by factors other than increased imports "shall not be attributed to increased imports." In a situation where *several factors* are causing injury "at the same time", a final determination about the injurious effects caused by *increased imports* can only be made if the injurious effects caused by all the different causal factors are distinguished and separated. Otherwise, any conclusion based exclusively on an assessment of only one of the causal factors—increased imports—rests on an uncertain foundation, because it *assumes* that the other causal factors are *not* causing the injury which has been ascribed to increased imports. The non-attribution language in Article 4.2(b) precludes such an assumption and, instead, requires that the competent authorities assess appropriately the injurious effects of the other factors, so that those effects may be disentangled from the injurious effects of the increased imports. In this way, the final determination rests, properly, on the genuine and substantial relationship of cause and effect between increased imports and serious injury.

180. As we said in our Report in *United States—Wheat Gluten Safeguard*, the non-attribution language in Article 4.2(b) indicates that, logically, the final identification of the injurious effects caused by increased imports must follow a prior separation of the injurious effects of the different causal factors. If the effects of the different factors are not separated and distinguished from the effects of increased imports, there can be no proper assessment of the injury caused by that single and decisive factor. As we also indicated, the final determination about the existence of "the causal link" between increased imports and serious injury can only be made *after* the effects of increased imports have been properly assessed, and this assessment, in turn, follows the separation of the effects caused by all the different causal factors.

181. We emphasize that the method and approach WTO Members choose to carry out the process of separating the effects of increased imports and the effects of the other causal factors is not specified by the *Agreement on Safeguards*. What the Agreement requires is simply that the obligations in Article 4.2 must be respected when a safeguard measure is applied.

182. In this case, the USITC Report states that the "worsen[ing]" financial situation of the domestic industry, as defined by the USITC, had occurred as "a result of the increase in imports." The USITC identified six factors other than increased imports which were alleged to be contributing to the situation of the domestic industry at the same time. Applying the statutory standard established in United States law, the USITC considered whether, individually, each of these six factors was a "more important cause" of the threat of serious injury than the increased imports. The USITC concluded that each of these factors was not a more important cause than the increased imports. The USITC then concluded, echoing the United States statutory standard, that "the increased imports are an important cause, and a cause no less important than any other cause, of the threat of serious injury".

183. According to Australia and New Zealand, the USITC's determination on this issue is inconsistent with Article 4.2(b) of the *Agreement on Safeguards* because the methodology used by the USITC did not ensure that injury caused by the six other factors was not attributed to increased imports. Our examination, therefore, focuses on the issue of non-attribution. As we have just stated, in a situation such as this, where there are several causal factors, the process of ensuring that injury caused by other causal factors is not attributed to increased imports must include a separation of the effects of the different causal factors.

184. By examining the *relative* causal importance of the different causal factors, the USITC clearly engaged in some kind of process to separate out, and identify, the effects of the different factors, including increased imports. Although an examination of the *relative* causal importance of the different causal factors may satisfy the requirements of United States law, such an examination does not, for that reason, satisfy

the requirements of the *Agreement on Safeguards*. On the record before us in this case, a review of whether the United States complied with the non-attribution language in the second sentence of Article 4.2(b) can only be made in the light of the explanation given by the USITC for its conclusions on the relative causal importance of the increased imports, as distinguished from the injurious effects of the other causal factors.

185. In that respect, we see nothing in the USITC Report to indicate how the USITC complied with the obligation found in the second sentence of Article 4.2(b) and, therefore, we see no basis for either the Panel or us to assess the adequacy of the USITC process with respect to the "non-attribution" requirement of Article 4.2(b) of the *Agreement on Safeguards*. The USITC Report, on its face, does not explain the process by which the USITC separated the injurious effects of the different causal factors, nor does the USITC Report explain how the USITC ensured that the injurious effects of the other causal factors were not included in the assessment of the injury ascribed to increased imports. The USITC concluded only that each of four of the six "other factors" was, relatively, a less important cause of injury than increased imports. As Australia and New Zealand argue, and as the Panel expressly found, in doing so, the USITC acknowledged implicitly that these factors were actually causing injury to the domestic industry at the same time. But, to be certain that the injury caused by these other factors, whatever its magnitude, was not attributed to increased imports, the USITC should also have assessed, to some extent, the injurious effects of these other factors. It did not do so. The USITC did not explain, in any way, what injurious effects these other factors had on the domestic industry. For instance, of the six "other factors" examined, the USITC focused most on the cessation of the payments under the National Wool Act of 1954 (the "Wool Act") subsidy. The USITC recognized that the Wool Act subsidies represented an important contribution to the profits of the growers and feeders of live lambs. Yet the USITC's analysis of the injurious effects of this "factor" is confined largely to the statement that "the loss of Wool Act payments *hurt* lamb growers and feeders and caused some to withdraw from the industry." (emphasis added) This explanation provides no insight into the nature and extent of the "hurt" caused to the domestic industry by this factor. The USITC stated also that "the effects of termination of the Wool Act payments can be expected to recede further with each passing month." The USITC, thereby, acknowledged that the Wool Act will have on-going effects, but it did not elaborate on what these effects are likely to be nor how quickly they will disappear. In varying degree, the same is true as well for the remaining "other factors" examined. Thus, although the USITC acknowledged that these other factors were having *some* injurious effects, it did not explain what these effects were, nor how those injurious effects were separated from the threat of serious injury caused by increased imports.

186. In the absence of any meaningful explanation of the nature and extent of the injurious effects of these six "other" factors, it is

impossible to determine whether the USITC properly separated the injurious effects of these other factors from the injurious effects of the increased imports. It is, therefore, also impossible to determine whether injury caused by these other factors has been attributed to increased imports. In short, without knowing anything about the nature and extent of the injury caused by the six other factors, we cannot satisfy ourselves that the injury deemed by the USITC to have been caused by increased imports does not include injury which, in reality, was caused by these factors.

187. In this respect, we also recall that, on this issue, the Panel concluded:

> ... that the USITC's application of the "substantial cause" test in the lamb meat investigation as reflected in the USITC report did not ensure that threat of serious injury caused by other factors has not been attributed to increased imports.

188. For the foregoing reasons, we find that the USITC, in its Report, did not adequately explain how it ensured that injury caused to the domestic industry by factors other than increased imports was not attributed to increased imports. In the absence of such an explanation, we uphold, albeit for different reasons, the Panel's conclusions that the United States acted inconsistently with Article 4.2(b) of the *Agreement on Safeguards*, and, hence, with Article 2.1 of that Agreement.

Notes and Questions

(1) The "unforeseen developments" language in GATT Article XIX was largely ignored by GATT members for many decades, which explains why U.S. law makes no reference to it in its instructions to the ITC. The Appellate Body has now clearly resurrected the requirement (sound?), but the question remains how nations must meet it. The developments in question must be unforeseen—by whom? at what point in time? Suppose that the last tariff concession on a particular product was during the Kennedy Round. Can anything that happens today be said to have been "foreseen" by negotiators that long ago? Is that the test? What do you see as the purpose of the "unforeseen developments" requirement in GATT Article XIX?

(2) Could the United States properly include growers in the industry by making the move embraced by two ITC Commissioners, namely, holding that lamb meat and live lambs are "directly competitive?" Does it make sense to exclude producers at prior stages of processing from the "industry" that is injured or threatened with injury by imports? If they are to be included in some cases, why limit those cases to the agricultural sector (as had largely been ITC practice)?

(3) How is the ITC to proceed to ensure that injury caused by other factors is not "attributed" to imports? Is anything short of a multiple regression study acceptable? What if the data for such a study are unavailable? How is the econometrician hired to perform such a study to deal with the puzzle of how to treat changes in the quantity of imports as a causal variable?

(4) In the *Wheat Gluten* case, mentioned by the Appellate Body in the course of its *Lamb* opinion, the EU claimed that the ITC had neglected to analyze a "relevant factor" under Article 4.2(a) of the Safeguards Agreement, namely, whether the depressed price of wheat gluten in the United States might be due to unusually high protein content in domestic wheat gluten that reduced demand for it (rather than primarily to increased imports, as the ITC had found). The Panel Report in the case held that it was unnecessary for the ITC to consider that issue because it was not "clearly raised" by the parties to the ITC proceeding. The Appellate Body disagreed, holding that the obligation to consider all "relevant factors" extended to matters not clearly raised by interested parties to the safeguards investigation. Sound? Is that not an invitation to strategic behavior by respondents, who will raise arguments in a WTO proceeding that they suppressed before national authorities?

(5) When a nation suspends concessions as a "safeguard", what is the law regarding compensation to affected countries? Article XIX of GATT, paragraphs 2 and 3, contemplate negotiations over compensation, followed by a withdrawal of equivalent concessions by the nations affected by safeguards if the parties cannot agree on compensation. But in the period leading up to the Uruguay Round, there was a feeling that the compensation requirement of Article XIX discouraged the use of formal safeguards measures and encouraged resort to less-disciplined voluntary restraint and orderly marketing agreements. The final Uruguay Round Agreement weakens the commitment to compensation in an important way. In Article 8.1, it provides that countries proposing to apply a safeguards measure "shall endeavour to maintain a substantially equivalent level of concessions," and must negotiate over the provision of trade compensation. Article 8.2 then provides for the withdrawal of substantially equivalent concessions in the event that agreement fails. But in Article 8.3, however, this right of withdrawal is restricted—it is not to be exercised during the first three years of safeguards measures *if* those measures are a response to an *absolute* increase in imports and otherwise conform with the Agreement.

(6) Another issue in the *Wheat Gluten* case concerned the obligation under Article 12.1 of the Safeguards Agreement to notify the Committee on Safeguards "immediately" about the initiation of a safeguards proceeding, about a finding of serious injury caused by imports, and about a decision to apply a safeguards measure. The Appellate Body found that delays of a few weeks in providing notice on the first two matters violated U.S. obligations. The United States was also found to have violated its obligation to afford an opportunity for prior consultations regarding the goal of maintaining the balance of concessions (see Article 12.3 and Article 8.1) because it failed to provide adequate notice of the safeguards measures that it eventually undertook in advance of putting them in place. What should be the remedy for such misconduct, if a nation otherwise complies with all its obligations under Article XIX and the Safeguards Agreement?

(7) Is it permissible under WTO law for a nation to apply an escape clause remedy on a basis other than MFN? For many years, this issue of "selectivity" was among the most controversial aspects of safeguards policy. The next excerpt from the *Wheat Gluten* case addresses one important

dimension of the matter—safeguard preferences for members of customs unions and free trade areas.

UNITED STATES—DEFINITIVE SAFEGUARD MEASURES ON IMPORTS OF WHEAT GLUTEN FROM THE EUROPEAN COMMUNITIES

WT/DS166/AB/R

Appellate Body Report adopted by the DSB on January 19, 2001

1.　The United States and the European Communities appeal certain issues of law and legal interpretations in the Panel Report, *United States–Definitive Safeguard Measures on Imports of Wheat Gluten from the European Communities* (the "Panel Report"). The Panel was established to consider a complaint by the European Communities with respect to a definitive safeguard measure imposed by the United States on certain imports of wheat gluten.

2.　On 1 October 1997, the United States International Trade Commission (the "USITC") initiated a safeguard investigation into certain imports of wheat gluten. By Proclamation of the President of the United States, dated 30 May 1998, the United States imposed a definitive safeguard measure, in the form of a quantitative restriction on imports of wheat gluten, effective as of 1 June 1998. Products from Canada, a partner with the United States in the North American Free–Trade Agreement ("NAFTA"), and certain other countries were excluded from the application of the safeguard measure. * * *

* * *

93.　Before the Panel, the European Communities claimed that the United States' treatment of imports of wheat gluten from Canada, its partner in the North American Free Trade Agreement ("NAFTA"), was inconsistent with Articles 2.1 and 4.2 of the *Agreement on Safeguards*. On this issue, the Panel concluded that:

> . . . in this case, the United States has acted inconsistently with Articles 2.1 and 4.2 SA by excluding imports from Canada from the application of the safeguard measure (following a separate and subsequent inquiry concerning whether imports from Canada accounted for a "substantial share" of total imports and whether they "contributed importantly" to the "serious injury" caused by total imports) after including imports *from all sources* in its investigation of "increased imports" of wheat gluten into its territory and the consequent effects of such imports on its domestic wheat gluten industry. (emphasis in original)

94.　On appeal, the United States challenges the Panel's interpretation of Articles 2.1 and 4.2 of the *Agreement on Safeguards,* and argues that the Panel failed to take sufficient account of the fact that, in this case, following its determination that imports from all sources were causing serious injury, the USITC conducted a "separate and subsequent examination", as part of the same investigation, concerning Canadian

imports alone. In that examination, the USITC found that, although
"imports from Canada account for a substantial share of total imports",
those imports were "not contributing importantly to the serious injury
caused by imports". On the basis of this examination, the USITC
recommended that imports from Canada be excluded from any safeguard
measure adopted. The United States considers that, for these reasons, it
was justified in excluding imports of wheat gluten from Canada from the
scope of application of the safeguard measure. The United States adds
that the Panel erred in failing to assess the legal relevance of footnote 1
to the *Agreement on Safeguards* and Article XXIV of the GATT 1994 to
this issue.

95.   In considering the appeal of the United States on this point, we
turn first to Article 2.1 of the *Agreement on Safeguards*, which provides
that a safeguard measure may only be applied when "such increased
quantities" of a *"product* [are] *being imported* into its territory . . .
under such conditions as to cause or threaten to cause serious injury to
the domestic industry". As we have said, this provision, as elaborated in
Article 4 of the *Agreement on Safeguards*, sets forth the *conditions* for
imposing a safeguard measure. Article 2.2 of the *Agreement on Safeguards*, which provides that a safeguard measure "shall be applied to a
product being imported irrespective of its source", sets forth the rules on
the *application* of a safeguard measure.

96.   The same phrase—"product. . .being imported"—appears in
both these paragraphs of Article 2. In view of the identity of the language
in the two provisions, and in the absence of any contrary indication in
the context, we believe that it is appropriate to ascribe the *same* meaning
to this phrase in both Articles 2.1 and 2.2. To include imports from all
sources in the determination that increased imports are causing serious
injury, and then to exclude imports from one source from the application
of the measure, would be to give the phrase "product being imported" a
different meaning in Articles 2.1 and 2.2 of the *Agreement on Safeguards*. In Article 2.1, the phrase would embrace imports from *all*
sources whereas, in Article 2.2, it would exclude imports from certain
sources. This would be incongruous and unwarranted. In the usual
course, therefore, the imports included in the determinations made
under Articles 2.1 and 4.2 should correspond to the imports included in
the application of the measure, under Article 2.2.

97.   In the present case, the United States asserts that the exclusion of imports from Canada from the scope of the safeguard measure
was justified because, following its investigation based on imports from
all sources, the USITC conducted an additional inquiry specifically
focused on imports from Canada. The United States claims, in effect,
that the scope of its initial investigation, *together with its subsequent and
additional inquiry* into imports from Canada, did correspond with the
scope of application of its safeguard measure.

98.   In our view, however, although the USITC examined the importance of imports from Canada separately, it did not make any explicit

determination relating to increased imports, *excluding imports from Canada*. In other words, although the safeguard measure was applied to imports from all sources, *excluding* Canada, the USITC did not establish explicitly that imports from these *same* sources, excluding Canada, satisfied the conditions for the application of a safeguard measure, as set out in Article 2.1 and elaborated in Article 4.2 of the *Agreement on Safeguards*. Thus, we find that the separate examination of imports from Canada carried out by the USITC in this case was not a sufficient basis for the safeguard measure ultimately applied by the United States.

99. Lastly, we note that the United States has argued that the Panel erred in failing to address Article XXIV of the GATT 1994, and in failing to set out a "basic rationale" for finding that footnote 1 to the *Agreement on Safeguards* did not affect its reasoning on this issue. In this case, the Panel determined that this dispute does not raise the issue of whether, as a general principle, a member of a free-trade area can exclude imports from other members of that free-trade area from the application of a safeguard measure. The Panel also found that it could rule on the claim of the European Communities without having recourse to Article XXIV or footnote 1 to the *Agreement on Safeguards*. We see no error in this approach, and make no findings on these arguments.

100. We, therefore, uphold the Panel's finding, in paragraph 8.182 of the Panel Report, that the United States acted inconsistently with its obligations under Articles 2.1 and 4.2 of the *Agreement on Safeguards*.

Notes and Questions

(1) The Agreement on Safeguards provides in Article 5 that the "allocation of shares" in any quota system may be worked out "by agreement" with nations having a "substantial interest" in the matter. When agreement is not "practicable," shares are to be allocated based on the shares of trading partners in trade with the importing nation "during a previous representative period," with due account taken of any "special factors" that may have been affecting trade during that period. Likewise, an importing nation may depart even from these principles in allocating shares after prior consultation with the Committee on Safeguards, and a showing that departure is justified because imports from certain nations have "increased in disproportionate percentage," and that departure from the principles above is "justified" and "equitable." In short, the Agreement leaves some room for quantitative measures that are more restrictive of imports from nations that have recently increased their market shares.

(2) As a policy matter, when if ever should the WTO permit "selective" safeguards?

SECTION 15.4   ADJUSTMENT ASSISTANCE

The Department of Labor administers a program of trade-related adjustment assistance for workers[1], while the Department of Commerce,

---

1. See generally M. Trebilcock, M. Chandler & R. Howse, Trade and Transi-

Economic Development Administration administers a program of technical assistance for firms and industries. The Labor Department program is by far the larger of the two.

U.S. COMMISSION ON INTERNATIONAL TRADE AND INVESTMENT POLICY (THE WILLIAMS COMMISSION), REPORT 47–49 (1971)

CHOOSING AMONG OPTIONS

Adjustment assistance and [import restrictions] differ importantly in their impact on the economy. While adjustment assistance is focused on the particular firms or workers injured by increased imports, the impact of tariff relief or "voluntary" export restraints cannot be confined to those firms actually suffering injury. All producers of the protected product, whether or not they have been injured, benefit from lessened competition.

As opposed to adjustment assistance, both escape-clause relief and orderly marketing agreements would also impose in differing degrees the various costs that are associated with increased protection against imports. * * *

Adjustment assistance, unlike import restriction, would impose direct monetary costs on the taxpayer. But by creating more flexible industries and more highly skilled workers—thus benefiting the entire economy—successful programs of adjustment assistance should offset part or all of their tax cost.

Use of adjustment assistance also avoids the adverse effects on costs of U.S.–produced goods in both domestic and foreign markets, the restriction on access for those goods to markets abroad, and the strains on U.S. foreign relations that may arise when the escape clause is used or when pressure is applied in an effort to obtain "voluntary" export restraints. Hence the Commission feels that in general the government should encourage adjustment rather than impose restrictions—except in those circumstances, outlined below, where protection may be more appropriate.

Under some circumstances, adjustment assistance will be difficult to apply. An industry may require only a brief period of protection, say five years, but no other aid from government programs to improve its competitive position. Or the industry may be so large that a program of adjustment assistance might need an extraordinarily high budgetary appropriation. As a general principle, therefore, in instances where an entire industry—not simply certain of its firms—is seriously injured,

tions: A Comparative Analysis of Adjustment Policies (1990); Richardson, Worker Adjustment to U.S. International Trade: Programs and Prospects, in W. Cline (ed.), Trade Policy in the 1980s, at 393 (1983) (with bibliography); Bratt, Issues in Worker Certification and Questions of Future Direction in the Trade Adjustment Assistance Program, 14 Law & Pol.Intl.Bus. 819, 823 (1982).

temporary import restrictions, coupled with maximum possible adjustment assistance, would be appropriate.

FORMER EMPLOYEES OF SHAW PIPE, INC. v. UNITED STATES SECRETARY OF LABOR

988 F.Supp. 588 (CIT 1997)

CARMAN, CHIEF JUDGE: Shaw Pipe, Incorporated ("Shaw Pipe") closed its pipe coating operations in Highspire, Pennsylvania on August 12, 1994, resulting in a group of approximately thirty-five workers losing their jobs. On January 3, 1995, three former employees filed a petition with the Department of Labor on the behalf of all the separated employees seeking certification to receive trade adjustment assistance benefits. Plaintiffs characterize Shaw Pipe's Highspire, Pennsylvania facility as having produced "small diameter steel pipe coated with polyethylene coating" and "large diameter steel pipe coated with concrete coating." Plaintiffs' petition for certification to receive trade adjustment assistance benefits was denied and plaintiffs' appealed the Secretary's determination to this Court.

On January 9, 1997, this Court found the Department of Labor's determination that plaintiffs were not eligible for certification to receive trade adjustment assistance benefits was not supported by substantial evidence on the record and was not otherwise in accordance with law, and remanded the matter to Labor for further consideration. *See FEO Shaw Pipe, 957 F. Supp. at 244.* In compliance with this Court's order, Labor filed a Supplemental Administrative Record providing further support for its determination with the Court on May 5, 1997.

* * *

In reviewing determinations of the Department of Labor denying certification of eligibility to receive trade adjustment assistance benefits, this Court will sustain the Department's determination when it is supported by substantial evidence on the record and is otherwise in accordance with law. * * *

In reviewing Labor's determination, this Court will give deference "to the agency's chosen [investigative] technique, only remanding a case if that technique is so marred that the Secretary's finding is arbitrary or of such a nature that it could not be based on" substantial evidence.

In order for the Secretary of Labor to certify a group of workers to receive trade adjustment assistance benefits as provided for under Section 222 of the Trade Act of 1974, it must be determined:

(1) that a significant number or proportion of the workers in such workers' firm or an appropriate subdivision of the firm have become totally or partially separated, or are threatened to become totally or partially separated,

(2) that sales or production, or both, of such firm or subdivision have decreased absolutely, and

(3) that increases of imports of articles like or directly competitive with articles produced by such workers' firm or an appropriate subdivision thereof contributed importantly to such total or partial separation, or threat thereof, and to such decline in sales or production.

19 U.S.C. sec. 2272(a)(1994). Case law clearly establishes that plaintiffs must satisfy all three of these statutory requirements in order to receive trade adjustment assistance benefits.

The conditions established by 19 U.S.C. sec. 2272(a)(1) and (a)(2) are not at issue in this matter. Rather, at issue in this matter is whether there is substantial evidence on the record to support the Secretary's determination that plaintiffs are ineligible to receive trade adjustment assistance benefits because they fail to satisfy the two requirements within 19 U.S.C. sec. 2272(a)(3). In order to satisfy the first requirement of 19 U.S.C. sec. 2272(a)(3), it must be determined that plaintiffs' were employed at a firm which "produce[s]" an article. As noted above, the statutory language has been interpreted to require the firm at which applicants were employed to "create or manufacture a tangible commodity, or transform it into a new and different article." The second condition of 19 U.S.C. sec. 2272(a)(3) which must be met in order to be eligible for certification to receive trade adjustment assistance benefits requires that "imports of articles like or directly competitive with articles produced by [plaintiffs'] firm ... contributed importantly to [plaintiffs'] total or partial separation." * * *

In responding to plaintiffs' Motion for Judgment Upon the Agency Record, defendant first argues the Supplemental Administrative Record contains substantial evidence supporting the Secretary's determination that employees of Shaw Pipe's Highspire, Pennsylvania pipe coating operation were not eligible for certification to receive trade adjustment benefits because the Highspire facility did not "create or manufacture a tangible commodity, or transform it into a new and different article." One basis for the determination is the observation in the Department's Notice of Negative Determination of Reconsideration On Remand that "the pipe used for pipeline transmission could be used without the protective coating, but it is not likely." Additionally, in arguing Shaw Pipe's application of protective coatings did not transform the pipe, defendant asserts "just because pipe is coated for protection from the elements does not change its fundamental purpose, character, or use."

The Court remains unpersuaded by defendant's assertions that the record compiled in this matter contains substantial evidence supporting the Secretary's determination that Shaw Pipe's Highspire pipe coating operation did not "create or manufacture a tangible commodity or transform it into a new and different article." The Department's determination that coated and uncoated pipes are "not likely" to be used interchangeably in pipeline construction suggests to the Court that coated and uncoated pipe have different properties or characteristics which make one type of pipe preferable to the other in certain applications.

As noted in Pemberton v. Marshall, 639 F.2d 798, 800 (D.C.Cir. 1981), an important consideration in evaluating whether an item is transformed into a new and different article is whether a "new [product] is entered into the stream of commerce." The Court believes the Department's statement that coated and uncoated pipe are "not likely" to be used interchangeably in pipeline construction suggests the two types of pipe are different products and thus suggests plaintiffs did cause a new product to be entered into the stream of commerce. These observations contradict Labor's determination that Shaw Pipe's Highspire operation did not "create or manufacture a tangible commodity, or transform it into a new and different article."

These considerations would also seem to raise questions about the accuracy of defendant's statement that the "fundamental purpose, character, [and] use" of coated and uncoated pipe are identical. While the utilization of both coated and uncoated pipe in pipeline construction suggests the two types of pipe have a similar fundamental purpose, the Department's determination that coated and uncoated pipe are "not likely" to be used interchangeably suggests differences in their character and use which appear to contradict defendant's argument.

Additionally, the Court is not persuaded by defendant's application of the relevant case law interpreting the statutory requirements placed on recipients of trade adjustment assistance benefits. Defendant focuses particular attention on the decisions in Pemberton, 639 F.2d at 802 (sustaining determination that shipyard employees who repaired engines, removed barnacles and painted and repaired hulls provided a service, and thus were ineligible to receive trade adjustment assistance benefits), and Woodrum v. Donovan, 564 F. Supp. 826, 828 (1983), aff'd, 737 F.2d 1575 (Fed.Cir.1984) (sustaining determination that employees responsible for inspecting new cars prior to sale, including "setting the timing, front end alignments, checking the oil, inspecting the rods, tightening the wheels, and other tasks" provided a service and thus were not eligible for certification to receive trade adjustment assistance benefits).

The Court observes the products involved in the Pemberton and Woodrum decisions (i.e., completely manufactured boats and automobiles) are products which are significantly more complicated than steel pipe. Because steel pipe is a simple product, minor changes could reasonably be found to result in a transformation of the pipe into a new and different article. The suggestion in the Supplemental Administrative Record that coated and uncoated pipe are different products with different characteristics and uses would appear to confirm this observation. In contrast, the Pemberton and Woodrum decisions emphasize that minor alterations to or repairs made on more complex and intricate products are unlikely to result in the alteration or transformation of the underlying product.

Based on these considerations, the Court finds the Secretary's determination that plaintiffs are not eligible for certification to receive trade adjustment assistance benefits because Shaw Pipe's Highspire operation did not "create or manufacture a tangible commodity, or transform it into a new and different article" is not supported by substantial evidence on the record and is not otherwise in accordance with law.

As noted above, case law clearly establishes that in order to be eligible for certification to receive trade adjustment assistance benefits, applicants must satisfy all the statutory requirements upon which certification is conditioned. In order for applicants for certification to receive trade adjustment assistance benefits to satisfy the requirements of 19 U.S.C. sec. 2272(a)(3), it must be determined not only that the applicants' former firm "create[s] or manufacture[s] a tangible commodity, or transform[s] it into a new and different article", but also that imports of a like or competitive product contributed importantly to the applicants losing their jobs. * * *

* * *

Defendant's second argument asserts plaintiffs are not eligible for certification to receive trade adjustment assistance benefits because "evidence contained in the administrative record and the supplemental administrative record demonstrates that increases in imports of articles like or directly competitive with the pipe produced by plaintiffs did not contribute importantly to their separation." Defendant's argument is supported by Labor's determination in the Supplemental Administrative Record that "remand findings also show that the subject firm closed the Highspire, Pennsylvania plant because the contract with the primary customer was not renewed. The customer [steel company] awarded the contract to another domestic company."

Plaintiffs' only response to the Department's determination that plaintiffs lost their job when the pipe coating contract was awarded to a different domestic company is the assertion that "the [Department's] finding . . . is not within reason of the record in this case." Other than making this assertion, however, plaintiffs' brief makes no effort to challenge or rebut the Department's finding that plaintiffs lost their jobs when Shaw Pipe's pipe coating contract was not renewed and was awarded to a domestic competitor.

* * *

Because the administrative record contains substantial evidence plaintiffs did not lose their jobs as the result of increases in imports of like or competitive articles "that contributed importantly to [plaintiffs'] total or partial separation," this Court determines plaintiffs have failed to satisfy the requirements of 19 U.S.C. sec. 2272(a) (1994) for eligibility for certification to receive trade adjustment assistance benefits.

Notes and Questions

(1) What is the logic of conditioning adjustment assistance in part on whether the petitioning workers are producers of an "article?"

(2) If the plant closed because its principal customer switched to another domestic supplier, is that enough to establish that imports did not "contribute importantly" to the closing? Suppose the new supplier won the account after it reduced its prices in response to increased import competition that freed up capacity to serve other customers? Or suppose that the petitioners' firm was unable to secure replacement business because of import competition?

(3) Is there any principled justification for providing more safety net benefits to workers displaced by changes in trade patterns than by changes in, say, technology or consumer tastes?

(4) What role should the availability of adjustment assistance play in the decision to afford an industry import relief under the escape clause? If sufficient adjustment assistance is available, should import restraints ever be imposed? If so, when?

Chapter 16

THE REGULATION OF DUMPING

SECTION 16.1 INTRODUCTION

(A) RESPONSES TO UNFAIR ACTS IN INTERNATIONAL TRADE

The eight preceding chapters have dealt primarily with the substantive obligations of international trade rules and the exceptions to those rules. In particular, Chapter 15 explored exceptions designed to allow an economy to implement an orderly adjustment to increased imports. In this chapter, the focus shifts. There are a number of practices of governments or private firms which are designed to influence international trade flows, other than through the use of restraints on imports. In particular, both governments and private firms may wish to promote exports by the use of discriminatory pricing or by subsidies. For decades, certain of these practices have been considered "unfair." First in bilateral, and then in multilateral trade treaties, nations have agreed that unilateral responses to some of these practices should be permitted under international trade rules. The purpose of this chapter and the three following ones is to examine several different types of governmental responses that are designed to counteract foreign trade policy actions which affect trade differently from the free market mechanism. The distinction between escape clause actions and the types of actions considered in these chapters is that escape clause actions are taken for purposes of adjustment to imports, which come about through the natural application of liberal trade policies; whereas the responses considered in Chapters 16–18 are designed to counteract foreign measures which are considered in some sense "unfair" or "market distorting."

The distinction made in international trade law between "fair" and "unfair" trade, such as is reflected in the differences between titles II and III of the Trade Act of 1974, is not airtight. In practice, there tends to be a blurring of the differences between fair and unfair trade. Arguments about "unfairness" are sometimes made in escape clause proceedings, where fairness is not technically relevant, and the difficulty of defining "unfair" leads to suspicions that some proceedings alleging unfairness are really disguised attempts to obtain escape clause type relief.

One of the rationales behind the unfair trade rules we will examine is similar to that behind the antitrust and unfair competition laws that exist to a greater or lesser degree in every country. Just as it is believed that certain domestic activities, such as monopolization, price fixing or market sharing are undesirable, it is thought that certain international trade practices are undesirable and should be regulated. The basic idea behind such rules is sometimes expressed as a desire to create a level playing field where the producers of the world all have an equal chance to compete.

We will see that while there is a considerable degree of agreement in the international trading system on the general sort of practices that are unfair, there is some controversy over how to define those practices precisely. Moreover, in the case of one practice—subsidization by governments—there is considerable disagreement over what responses should be permitted. Indeed, it is in the general area of export promotion by governments that the international consensus breaks down. It is agreed that cash bounties paid to exporters to encourage greater exports are unacceptable. But it is not really agreed how to evaluate, and to what extent retaliatory responses should be allowed to offset, many other government policies that directly or indirectly assist exporters. Such policies may range from operating subsidies, to provision of cheap raw materials, to government policies promoting education and research and development, to government encouragement of the commercialization of certain products, to a full-scale governmental industrial policy.

Moreover, even to the extent that the accepted international rules embodied in the WTO agreements reflect the views of the international trading community as to what is unfair, economists have challenged the underlying premises of certain of those rules and have argued that they do not make sense economically (just as they have raised similar questions about aspects of national antitrust laws).

The problems we will consider in this chapter and the following chapters can be seen in the following four situations:

(1) Tractor producers in Bavonia export to Avaly and sell their tractors in the Avaly market for less than they sell the same product in the home market of Bavonia. Competing Avaly tractor manufacturers complain that this import competition is unfair and that the tractors are being "dumped" in Avaly.

(2) Caldonia manufacturers produce watches, and the Caldonia government grants to each producer a subsidy of the equivalent of $20 for each watch. Because of the subsidy, Caldonia watchmakers are able to sell their products in the Avaly market for up to $20 less than Avaly-made watches and the Avaly watch producers cannot compete in Caldonia. The Avaly watchmakers cry "foul."

(3) Duglavsky producers of electronic calculators produce and use a special integrated circuit which is patented in Avaly, but refuse to obtain a patent license or to pay royalties to the Avaly patent holder. Nevertheless, they attempt to export some of these

calculators to Avaly where they compete with Avaly-made calculators, whose producers pay royalties to the patent holder. The patent holder, as well as the Avaly producers, seeks to prevent those imports.

(4) Xonia normally imports shoes from Avaly, but decides to ban Avaly shoes so as to protect its home shoe industry. Avaly's shoe exporters are disturbed and seek to have Avaly ban imports of silk cloth from Xonia (which are normally substantial).

These cases involve a variety of problems. For example, it has already been noted that some actions affect a country's *exports* in a way which makes other nations feel aggrieved, while other actions affect a country's *imports* in a way which aggrieves others. In some cases the action is by private firms or manufacturers, (e.g., dumping), in others it is by governments (e.g., subsidies). In some cases an action may breach an international obligation, but in other cases there may be no such breach (or there may be no existing international norm on the subject), yet a trading partner will still feel aggrieved and seek a response.

We will consider each of these problems. First, in Chapters 16 and 17, we will consider the policy issues, international rules and U.S. laws applicable to the "dumping" of foreign goods. In Chapter 18, we will examine the same questions in respect of subsidies. Additionally, in Chapter 20 where our focus will be on international rules in respect of intellectual property, we will also consider Section 337 of the Tariff Act of 1930, which has been invoked to protect U.S. industry from patent infringement and similar actions. More generally, recall that in Chapter 7, we considered Section 301 of the Trade Act of 1974, a statute giving the U.S. President broad authority to take retaliatory measures against what he determines to be unfair trade practices.

Before turning to these detailed discussions, however, there are two general issues affecting all of them that should be considered at the outset. One is sometimes referred to as the problem of interface: How should the world trading system handle problems arising from the fact that different nations have different philosophies of organizing and directing economic activities? The second is the question of how rules on international trade practices should be applied—in a legalistic manner with frequent recourse to courts to establish precise rules of conduct or more flexibly with a view toward government or industry negotiated settlements of disputes?

(B) THE INTERFACE THEORY OF ECONOMIC RELATIONS

Many of the "unfair" trading practices that we will examine have been considered unfair because they interfere with or distort free market economy principles. The WTO, of course, is largely based upon such principles. It is not surprising, therefore, that it is often difficult to apply its trading rules to nonmarket economies. In addition, even between the relatively similar western industrial market economies, there are wide differences regarding the degree of government involvement in the economy, by regulation or ownership of various industrial or other economic segments. As world economic interdependence has increased, it has become more difficult to manage relationships between various economies. This problem can be analogized to the difficulties involved in trying to get two computers of different makes to work together. To do so, one needs an "interface" mechanism to mediate between the two computers. Likewise in international economic relations, and particularly trade, some interface mechanism may be necessary to allow different economic systems to trade together harmoniously.

These problems can be easily seen in the chapters on dumping and subsidies. We will see that part of the definition of dumping is selling for export at below home-market prices or costs. But for nonmarket economies, are there meaningful costs and prices? In the case of subsidies, it may be easy to identify cash payments to an exporter, but there are a myriad of government policies that affect the competitiveness of a business. If the goal is really to achieve a "level playing field," does that imply that the world's governments must adopt uniform policies? If not, how will it be humanly possible to analyze (or in these days, to program a computer to analyze) the effect of different policies? Besides, isn't trade to some degree based on differences between countries?

In some cases, the problem involves questions of preventing or inhibiting what are deemed unfair practices, such as dumping or export subsidies. As the subject of unfair practices develops, however, it becomes clear that it reaches deeply into matters of domestic concern to governments, and the question of unfairness becomes more controversial. In many cases of subsidies, for example, the government providing such subsidies feels that they are an essential and praiseworthy tool of government, sometimes useful to correct disparities of income, or to help disadvantaged groups or regions. With respect to dumping, for example, it is argued that such a practice, a form of "price discrimination," actually has beneficial effects on world and national prosperity, encouraging competition. The rules for responding to some unfair trade practices allow use of import restrictions, such as added duties, which can be anticompetitive and can reduce world welfare. In some cases, exporting nations feel bitterness towards these import restrictions on their trade, and argue that the rules on unfair trade are being manipulated by special interests for effectively protectionist reasons.

An example of the interface problem and the difficulties of defining unfairness can be seen in the following problem, which focuses on so-called variable cost analysis. It may arise in the context of two economies that differ only slightly in respect of their acceptance of basic free market economic principles. As the problem demonstrates, even given such similarities, there may be differences in the way the respective economies operate over the course of the business cycle that may create situations that are considered unfair by some, even though these differences may not have resulted from any conscious unfair policies or practices.

Take an industrial sector (such as steel) in two economies (such as the United States and Japan) with the following characteristics:

Society A

Worker tenure (no layoffs of workers)

Capitalization with a high debt-equity ratio (e.g., 90% debt)

Society B

No worker tenure (wages for workers are therefore variable costs)

Capitalization with low debt-equity ratio (e.g., less than 50%) (dividends can be skipped)

In times of slack demand, economists note that it is rational for a firm to continue to produce as long as it can sell its product at or above its short-term variable costs. This is true because it must in any event pay its fixed costs. Of course, this is true only for limited periods; presumably over the regular course of the business cycle, the firm must not incur losses in the long term.

An analysis of the short-term variable costs of firms in Societies A and B can be done as follows:

Costs of a Firm (per unit of production)	Society A	Society B
Plant Upkeep	20 fixed	20 fixed
Debt Service	90 fixed	50 fixed
Dividends (cost of capital)	10 variable	50 variable
Worker Costs	240 fixed	240 variable
Cost of Materials	240 variable	240 variable
Total Costs (per unit of production)	600	600
Fixed	350	70
Variable	250	530

As noted above, it will be rational for producers in Society A to continue production so long as they can obtain a price of 250, while producers in Society B need to receive a price of 530. Thus, in a period of falling prices and demand, the producers in Society A can be expected to garner, through exports to Society B, an increasing share of the Society B market. Suppose this happens, and the firms in Society B close. Are Society A's exports to Society B unfair?

There are no easy answers to the questions raised above. Indeed, they are in fact probably more complicated than the foregoing would indicate because whatever general rules exist, it is argued that special considerations should apply to developing countries. We will discuss these issues in more detail at the end of the book, where we look at the special problems posed by trade rules and policies that must take account of developing countries (Chapter 25).

(C) THE PROBLEM OF LEGALIZATION

As we proceed through the next few chapters, the reader will note that application of the major statutes on unfair trade practices, such as dumping and subsidization, is characterized, particularly in the United States, by complex rules and proceedings and by extensive involvement of lawyers and courts. While our examination of other legal systems will not be extensive, it is fair to say that proceedings in those systems are more informal, and therefore less costly. It can be argued that the added expense of the U.S. approach is worth its cost, a matter we will discuss in more detail in Chapter 26 infra. More frequent judicial review leads to more detailed rules and allows parties to tailor their conduct to avoid violations. Of course, at the same time it may lead to the creation of unintended loopholes that allow certain conduct because it is considered to be technically outside the rules, even though an unbiased observer would probably conclude that the rules were meant to apply to such conduct, and vice versa.

The lack of precisely defined rules leaves considerable discretion in the hands of those officials who apply the rules. They may as a result be in a position to use the rules only when appropriate to effectuate the real purpose of the rules. Their exercise of discretion will be difficult to review, however, and this, of course, presents serious problems of potential abuse, problems which may be magnified since those seeking protection from the officials are constituents of sorts of the officials, while those who will be adversely affected are foreigners.

The reader should consider, as we proceed through these chapters, whether the U.S. system has struck the proper balance between flexibility and reasonable cost, on the one hand, and predictability and "over legalization," on the other hand.

SECTION 16.2   ANTIDUMPING LAWS: THE UNDERLYING POLICY ISSUES[1]

(A) INTRODUCTION

Dumping is broadly defined as exporting at prices below those charged on the domestic market (or, if none, on a third-country market) or at prices insufficient to cover the cost of the goods sold. For example, if a U.S. industry sells its product in the U.S. market for $10/unit and sells the same product on the same terms for export to the EU at an equivalent price of $9/unit, it would be dumping the product in the EU market. Under the rules discussed below, if the dumping caused material injury to the EU industry (or threatened it), the EU would be permitted

---

1. There are numerous books and articles on dumping, and space constraints preclude listing more than a few. A particularly useful book that compares U.S., EC, Canadian and Australian antidumping laws and contains an extensive bibliography, as well as comments by many experts, is John H. Jackson & Edwin A. Vermulst, eds., Antidumping Law and Practice: A Comparative Study (1989). See also Bernard M. Hoekman, Free Trade and Deep Integration: Antidumping and Antitrust in Regional Agreements (1998); USITC, The Economic Effects of Antidumping and Countervailing Duty Orders and Suspensions Agreements (1995); Richard Boltuck & Robert E. Litan, eds., Down in the Dumps (1991); Jacob Viner, Dumping: A Problem in International Trade (1923).

to impose antidumping duties of $1/unit to offset the dumping. In addition, if it cost an EU company $20/unit to produce its product and it sold the product in the U.S. and EU at $18/unit, it would be engaged in dumping in the U.S. in the amount of $2/unit. The former case involves what is sometimes referred to as international price discrimination; the latter as below-cost sales.

Whether dumping should be controlled through the use of offsetting, antidumping (AD) duties is a matter of some controversy within the world of international trade specialists, so we begin with an examination of the underlying policy issues raised by AD laws. Then, after a look at the international rules on dumping, we undertake a detailed analysis of U.S. AD rules.

Part of the reason for the controversy over the use of AD duties stems from the fact that in recent years several major trading countries have used them extensively, which has raised concerns that they may have become a disguised form of protectionism. At the same time, a number of developing countries have started to make use of such laws, which has further heightened those concerns. WTO statistics indicate that in the 1980s, the average number of AD investigations initiated per year was around 140 cases and four countries—the U.S., the EC, Canada and Australia were by far the major users of antidumping measures. From 1990 to 1994, the annual rate of initiations almost doubled to 250 cases per year, an average rate that continued from 1995 to 1999. The increase in the use of AD measures in the last decade is largely explained by the fact that, in addition to the U.S., the EC, Canada and Australia, a much broader range of WTO members is now making frequent use of antidumping measures—principally Argentina, Brazil, India, Mexico and South Africa. The traditional big four users of antidumping measures imposed almost 75% of the AD measures reported as outstanding at the end of 1995, but only about 50% of those outstanding at the end of 2000. Now India and South Africa have joined the U.S. and the EC as the four major imposers of antidumping measures, and overall at least 24 WTO members had antidumping measures in place at the end of 2000.

(B) THE POLICY DEBATE OVER ANTIDUMPING LAWS

As noted above, dumping can be broadly defined as selling for export at prices below (i) those prevailing in the home market (international price discrimination) or (ii) those necessary to cover production costs (below cost sales). In each case, some international trade scholars question the desirability of using AD duties to offset such behavior. Nevertheless, the laws have strong supporters. Consider the following two excerpts.

WILLIAM J. DAVEY, ANTIDUMPING LAWS: A TIME FOR RESTRICTION[2]

PRICE DISCRIMINATION

Price discrimination is possible when a seller is able to identify separate markets for its product and charge a higher price in the market that attaches a greater utility to the product. [T]he seller must possess sufficient market power to have some autonomy in its pricing decisions, and there must be some barrier between the markets so that the lower-priced goods are not resold in the higher-priced market by an arbitrageur. Internationally, price discrimination * * * may occur when demand in the export market is more elastic than in the domestic market, i.e. more responsive to lower prices, and where arbitrage is prevented by barriers such as tariffs, transport costs or any one of a variety of nontariff barriers.

The prerequisites for price discrimination—the existence of market power in the hands of the seller and the concomitant absence of perfect competition—indicate that a less than optimum competitive situation exists in the relevant market. It is not clear, however, that price discrimination makes this suboptimal competitive situation any less desirable, or in economists' terms, less efficient, than it would be in the absence of price discrimination. There are, of course, income or distribution effects resulting from price discrimination. It generally makes consumers in the higher-priced market worse off and the producer better off. But it does not follow that the economy itself is worse off overall. Indeed, it seems logical that the price discriminator will probably increase its output in order to supply the lower-priced market, a result that economists would usually view as desirable because it offsets the undesirable supply-restricting behavior that would otherwise occur.

Even if one is not prepared to conclude that price discrimination may be beneficial, it seems clear that price discrimination cannot be condemned *per se*. The issue is arguably more complex, however, when two national markets are involved because, even if price discrimination is not detrimental to the world as a whole, it could be beneficial to one national economy and detrimental to the other. * * *

Two effects of international price discrimination are typically noted for the exporting country. First, there may be a price effect. Whether the price will rise or fall in the exporting country is not clear. * * *

* * *

[I]f dumping does harm the exporting economy because of an adverse effect on price levels in that economy, the most appropriate remedy would be the removal of the market imperfections that made the higher prices possible. While antidumping duties imposed by the importing country to counteract dumping might have a minor beneficial effect on prices in the exporting country, they certainly could not be expected to correct the basic market imbalances that led to those higher prices.

The second effect that dumping may have on the exporting country is to harm users of the dumped product located in that country. This harm can occur only when the dumped product is an intermediate product, i.e. a component of a final product. In such cases, if users of the dumped product compete with users in the exporting country, those users will have a cost advantage because of their access to the lower-priced, dumped product and they may be able to sell final products incorporating the dumped component more cheaply, thereby gaining an advantage over competing producers in the exporting country. The significance of this advantage would depend on the importance of the dumped component in the cost of the final product and the extent of competition between producers in the two countries. * * *

In conclusion, it is not clear on the basis of economic analysis that dumping harms the exporting country on balance, although it is probably the case that the benefit to the dumper outweighs possible losses to consumers. Much more telling is the fact that exporting countries have generally not thought it worthwhile to control dumping, which strongly suggests that dumping does not have any significant adverse effect on the exporting country. Thus, economic justification for antidumping laws must be found elsewhere.

Since the economic effect on the exporting country cannot justify antidumping laws, the key question becomes whether the effect on the importing country provides a rationale for them. There is considerable controversy over what this effect is. It is generally agreed that consumers in the importing country will benefit from the lower prices resulting from dumping (at least in the short run) and that producers (the "domestic producers") in the importing countries who compete with the dumpers will be injured because they will lose market share to the dumpers. * * *

To determine if the benefits to consumers in the importing country outweigh the harm to the domestic producers, it is first necessary to consider the extent of such benefits, and, in particular, whether the benefits are only temporary. Consumers might not benefit from dumping if the lower, dumping prices prevail for only a short time and result in higher prices later. Defenders of antidumping laws usually rely very heavily on the argument that the consumer benefit is transitory, often virtually conceding that in the short run consumer benefits probably outweigh producer injury. The contention that the consumer benefits are temporary therefore requires very careful consideration. Two reasons are advanced to support it—(1) the dumper may be engaged in predatory conduct with the aim of driving domestic producers out of the market so that it can ultimately raise its prices to monopolistic levels or (2) the dumping may be the result of a temporary market condition, perhaps a recession in the dumper's home market, and will end when the dumper's home market sales improve. In the latter case, domestic producers could incur substantial adjustment costs when they idle capacity as they lose market share to the dumper and then incur significant readjustment costs when they reactivate their plants when the dumper leaves the market. * * *

How likely is predatory dumping? Many economists think predatory behavior is rare and unlikely to occur. This is because to be sure of success, the predatory dumper would have to know in advance (i) the price levels necessary to drive the domestic producers out of business and (ii) whether it could thereafter raise its prices sufficiently high to offset the losses associated with its predatory prices, without drawing other competitors (back) into the market. It seems impossible that this information could be firmly known in advance. Indeed, uncertainty about such factors is particularly great in this day and age because the internationalization of the world economy means that it is likely in almost every industry that low cost producers in newly industrialized or developing countries will enter a market if there are significant profits to be made. Consequently, although the identity of the competitors (or the location of their plants) may change, competition is likely to remain healthy.

* * *

* * * The mere existence of multinationals producing many products and the continuing industrialization of less developed world, all would seem to virtually guarantee a continuing supply of competitors and low-priced products, so long as protectionist trade barriers are not erected. The small possibility of predatory conduct does not justify antidumping laws, especially since the antitrust laws can effectively penalize predatory behavior in the event that it occurs.

The second question to consider is: Will producer adjustment costs resulting from temporary dumping outweigh the benefit to consumers of lower prices? If the dumper does not leave the domestic market, the domestic producers will have to adjust only once. Thereafter, they will engage in different, but presumably more efficient activity. This analysis is the same as that which generally supports free international trade, and this shifting of activities is what is supposed to happen in a free market economy. However, if the dumper leaves the domestic market and domestic producers reenter it, they will incur readjustment costs that they may try to recover through increased prices. Two issues are presented: Is the dumper likely to abandon the domestic market? If so, will domestic producers then raise their prices so high as to offset the benefit consumers gained from lower, dumped prices?

It is difficult to see, absent capacity limitations, why the dumper would leave the domestic market since it will have invested time and money to open and develop that market. Indeed, this argument is inconsistent with the predatory view of dumping where the dumper is assumed to enter the domestic market permanently. Recent experience with exporters to the United States, whether dumpers or not, suggest that they will go to considerable efforts (including cutting their profit margins) in order to maintain their newly won U.S. market shares. This is not to say that a dumper's export prices will not rise over time. For example, if the impetus for dumping came from a recession in its home market, it is possible that the dumper will raise its export prices when the recession is over, but, absent capacity limitations, as long as it wishes to retain its market share, its prices presumably will remain below those prevailing prior to its entry into the domestic market. More importantly, as long as the dumper remains in the domestic market, the domestic industry will not incur readjustment costs.

Suppose, however, that the dumper does abandon the domestic market, in whole or in part, either because of capacity limitations or because it raises prices to the extent that it loses market share to domestic industry. Will domestic industry then raise its prices so much that there will be no long-term benefit to consumers from dumping? No precise answer can be given. To the extent the dumper remains a force in the market, it seems likely that its mere presence as an additional competitive force will limit any price increases. Moreover, even if the dumper does abandon the market, domestic producers may not raise prices so much as to offset the initial benefits of dumping. Evidence that this is the likely result can be found in the economic literature on the effect of price wars or cutthroat competition among domestic oligopolists. Typically, after such a war, prices are raised. Studies by economists indicate, however, that consumers benefit overall from such price wars, because the temporary lower prices are not more than offset by price increases occurring at the end of the price war. A similar result in the dumping context—lower prices prevailing while the dumper is in the market, domestic industry then raising its prices when the dumper leaves, but not enough to offset the beneficial effect of the period of lower prices—would mean that consumers benefit from dumping.

Thus, the best view seems to be that consumers benefit from international price discrimination or dumping and that the benefit is a long-term one. Any "harm" to domestic industry is properly viewed as that naturally occurring from international trade or shifts in a domestic economy between sectors or individual domestic producers. Overall, the economy is better off. It may be appropriate to assist domestic industry to adjust, but as is discussed later, antidumping duties are, in any event, an ineffective and inefficient method of assisting domestic industry. In short, economic analysis does not support the application of antidumping duties to counteract price discrimination so as to protect the market into which goods are dumped.

BELOW-COST SALES

In recent years, it has become accepted internationally that anti-dumping laws apply when an exporter exports goods at prices that do not cover the cost of their production. At first view, it may strike one as unfair to sell goods at a price below what it costs to produce them. On reflection, however, it is more useful to consider the appropriateness of such activity in light of its duration and motivation. Since a company would fail if it priced its products below cost in the long run, below-cost sales are likely to be temporary. The motives for such sales vary. They could be made by a predatory competitor in order to destroy its competition. As noted above, such a motivation is probably rare, and where found, such behavior can be punished under the antitrust laws.

It is more likely that below-cost sales occur because (1) the seller wishes to gain market share or (2) the seller believes it is more profitable (in the sense of avoiding even greater losses) to sell goods at a loss in the short run than it is to not sell any goods at all. A desire to gain market share may be motivated by the existence of unused capacity or by a belief that producers not having a certain minimum market share will not be able to survive. Whatever the reason, the displacement of one competitor by another is not cause for concern, assuming the behavior of the winner is not predatory.

Sales at a loss that are motivated by a desire to avoid greater losses may occur when a producer faces unavoidable, fixed costs and the marginal revenue of an additional sale exceeds the marginal cost of that sale (even though the additional revenue does not cover the total cost of the product sold). Because economists believe that the appropriate price for a rational producer to charge is the price at which marginal revenue from the sale of a product is equal to its marginal cost, they view short-term below-cost sales under such circumstances to be rational, and such sales are not generally viewed as predatory under the antitrust laws. In the short run, therefore, it sometimes will make sense for a producer to sell goods at a price below their total cost. In the long run, all costs are variable and prices have to cover the producer's costs or the producer goes bankrupt. But in the short-run, below-cost sales are rational if marginal costs do not exceed marginal revenues and should not be controlled.

As in the case of price discrimination, one can ask if the temporary nature of sales below cost means that dumping of this sort in general is harmful because the benefits to consumers are short-lived and the domestic producers will suffer as they lose market share to the dumpers. As discussed above, there is no reason to protect one set of competitors in preference to another set so long as competition in the market is not affected. Moreover, as also noted above, consumer benefits are likely to be long lived. There is no reason to assume the dumper will leave the market when the economy recovers, even if its prices rise. In addition, even if domestic producers do later expand their output and thereby incur readjustment costs, it is unlikely that those costs will offset the benefits to consumers of the temporarily lower prices.

One objection to this analysis is that failure to prevent below-cost sales will allow a recession-bound economy to export the recession (or at least part of the adjustment burden) to its trading partners. To some degree this may be true, but to the extent that we have free international trade, it would seem to be inevitable that economies will be interdependent. Under such circumstances, it seems fairest to let the strongest companies survive (wherever located) and to assist the others to adjust. To argue otherwise requires one to support the position that domestic producers have a government-protected entitlement to a certain market position. While the government may wish to provide such a guarantee for some industries, for defense or other strategic purposes, such as the perceived importance of an industry in the future world economy, the general proposition is completely inconsistent with a free and open economy. Moreover, the desire or need to protect a few key industries does not justify a general antidumping law; it justifies special government programs, such as subsidies, for those industries. * * *

In short, there is no economic rationale to penalize most short-run, below-cost sales. The fact that countries generally did not even try to do so until the last decade is further evidence that such rules are unnecessary and unjustified.

EC COMMISSION, ELEVENTH ANNUAL REPORT ON THE COMMUNITY'S ANTI-DUMPING AND ANTI-SUBSIDY ACTIVITIES PARAS. 2.2–2.3 (1993)

Rationale

The reasons why the GATT considers injurious dumping as unfair are:

— dumping requires that the exporting market be segregated and that the importing market be open. These substantially different degrees of market access makes international trade fundamentally different to trade within an integrated market;

— operating from a segregated market can confer on exporters an advantage which is not due to higher efficiency and cannot be matched by his competitors in the importing country;

— this provides the dumper with the opportunity to maximize profits or minimize losses and can be highly injurious for the importing country's industry.

Dumping in integrated and international markets

Domestic trade within an integrated market economy is governed by the freedom of movement of goods, services, capital and people which create a level playing field and give maximum impact to the role of market forces which compel firms to price in relation to efficiency. Under such conditions, there is only room for very limited and short term price discrimination between different parts of the market, by the operator (or a group of operators) because this would lead to immediate arbitrage or retaliation by competitors.

An integrated market is also a very hostile environment for those who attempt to gain by sustained selling below cost. There is little incentive to carry out such a strategy, on any other than a short term basis, given that competitors are free to retaliate with equally low prices. It would simply force all prices down with no offsetting gain in terms of increased market share. With these "inbuilt" constraints on unfair pricing, competition rules can be restricted to maintaining the level playing field, through action, for example, against cartels or abuse of dominant position.

The international environment is very different to the situation prevailing in integrated markets. The rules applying to international trade have so far not been able to ensure equal access to all or, at least, the most important markets, nor do they cover international competition. Even between the main players in world trade there are still significant differences in tariff rates. Non-tariff barriers are numerous, ranging from outright quotas and so-called "voluntary restraint agreements" to a multitude of measures impeding market access by foreign competitors such as elaborate customs procedures, discriminatory standards and other technical barriers, discriminatory patent regulations, non-enforced or biased anti-trust legislation, exclusive import groupings, close-bidding practices, etc. As a consequence large scale price discrimination between different national markets is possible and can become a strategy for companies operating in foreign trade from a "closed" market.

The effects of dumping

a) Position of the dumper and the exporting country

Provided its home market is shielded against arbitrage or retaliation, and a consequent price drop (which would neutralize the discrimination), dumping can have clear advantages for the individual exporter. A profitable home market provides a platform which may be used to operate in export markets at prices much lower than could have been possible without market segregation. The low export prices generate further sales which in turn lower the costs of production, an advantage which benefits both export and home sales. Under such conditions, dumping becomes an economic behaviour of great efficiency, the benefits of which do not necessarily reflect a genuine competitive advantage to the dumper.

Dumping can also be beneficial to dumpers, even in situations where home market sales are made at a loss. As long as the latter cover fixed costs, export sales can be priced as low as variable cost, a strategy which permits production and employment to be maintained in a recession or enables the aggressor to obtain considerable advantages when going for economies of scale, etc. * * *

The benefits of dumping for the exporting country's economy are that domestic industries develop capacities which far exceed the size of the national market. This allows high economic growth and high production levels, even in periods of domestic or world-wide recession. Furthermore, it facilitates strategic targeting of key industrial sectors in important markets. This can result in a high trade surplus and possibly dominant positions in the industrial sectors concerned. The advantages derived from dumping can thus outweigh disadvantages stemming from protection of the home market, in particular relatively high consumer prices.

b) Effects for the importing country

A domestic industry facing dumped imports is in a difficult position. The normal reaction to the low prices of a competitor would be to sell on the latter's home market at equally low prices, but this is not always possible because of access barriers. Instead, it has to reduce its domestic prices to the level of the dumped import prices or lose market share. Its position becomes the more difficult as the dumper may be able to sustain losses on its export business for long periods because of its "guaranteed" home market profits. The resulting cost increases and losses may affect also the industry's position in third markets. As a result, its overall productivity and investment strength is weakened. In addition, dumping creates uncertainty for investment. Even correct investment planning may be frustrated by less efficient competition with the result that resources in the importing country are wasted.

Users and consumers are likely to enjoy short term benefits from dumped imports through low prices, but the position may be less favourable in the longer term. Where domestic producers are forced to lower production or to cease it altogether, competition is reduced, a situation which, in the long run, is unlikely to serve consumer interests.

The impact of dumping on the importing country as a whole is the reverse of the impact on the exporting country. There may be an immediate advantage through the cheap imports, but account has to be taken of the total costs of dumping to the domestic economy, i.e. lost capacities, lost investments, the loss of technology especially in promising or strategic sectors, a shrinking industrial base, and the social costs of unemployment and the contraction or elimination of whole industries.

Different Dumping Strategies

In a number of instances, dumping is not or not sufficiently harmful to justify defensive action. Short term dumping, e.g. for the purpose of ensuring market entry, as a general rule may only involve limited damage to domestic producers and therefore constitutes insufficient reason to warrant protection. Even where long-term dumping takes place, anti-dumping action is justified only if and when it leads or threatens to lead to significant injury, e.g. in terms of market shares or through price under-cutting or price depression. The GATT and Council Regulation (EEC) No. 2423/88 consequently stipulate that anti-dumping action is dependent upon the finding of material injury caused by the dumping to the domestic industry of the importing country.

There are three types of dumping which are particularly damaging:

— state trade dumping from economies whose main aim may not be cost efficiency but to earn hard currency at any price. In these cases the margins by which the prices of the Community producers are under-cut may be unusually high. Because the exporters in question often do not follow normal business behaviour, this type of dumping in unpredictable in view of its occurrence, volume, price and duration;

— "cyclical" dumping occurs in industries subject to periodic excess supply and capacity in which there is an incentive to export during the period of shrinking domestic demand to dump the excess produc-tion at prices below full cost, thus exporting unemployment. Cyclical dumping can be expected in industries with high investment and consequently high fixed costs, like the steel or chemical industry, and has the effect of exacerbating the difficulties facing an industrial sector in the importing country which is already affected by economic recession;

— strategic dumping aimed at achieving, through an aggressive export strategy, a strong position on important export markets. The long-term character of such dumping usually stems from the fact that the dumper operates from a home market base where foreign competition is weak or non-existent. This strategy has as its main aim the expansion of production to benefit from scale and learning economies for products such as in the electronics sector.

Notes and Questions

(1) AD laws also have strong supporters in the U.S. Congress, and it seems unlikely that they will disappear in the near future. While AD laws tend to be replaced by rules on competition (antitrust laws) in respect of trade between members of advanced free trade areas (integrated markets), such as the EU, the European Economic Area, and the Australia–New Zealand pact, they continue to be used often in looser free trade areas, such as NAFTA.

(2) Among the reasons why AD laws seem likely to persist are first, on the part of Congress, members find it convenient to deflect complaints about import competition by referring constituents to the AD procedures, and second, many people, particularly in import sensitive industries, feel strongly that dumping is unfair. One may speculate, however, that congressional support may ebb in the future, if the spread of AD laws leads to increased complaints by U.S. exporters about the need to protect U.S. industry by *toughening* the international rules on dumping to reduce the use of AD laws against them. On the other hand, to the extent that the international rules contain extensive procedural requirements, it may be difficult for developing countries to use them effectively.

(3) The fundamental complaint about dumping is that it is an unfair business practice, one "condemned" in GATT Article VI when it causes injury. But how unfair is dumping? One way to evaluate whether and to what extent dumping is unfair is to consider how domestic legal systems treat dumping-like behavior. We have seen that dumping consists of price discrimination and below-cost sales. The question then becomes: What rules limit price discrimination and below-cost sales by domestic firms in the domestic market? In the case of the United States, domestic price discrimi-

nation is regulated by the Robinson–Patman Act.[3] How does that law compare with the U.S. AD statute? As a general rule, it would seem that U.S. AD laws are applied in a much more restrictive manner than the Robinson–Patman Act. There are, for example, a number of defenses to price discrimination under Robinson–Patman, but virtually none to dumping. Court decisions interpreting the Robinson–Patman Act state that ultimately its purpose is to protect competition, not individual competitors,[4] while the AD laws seem designed to protect domestic competitors whatever the effect on overall domestic competition.[5] These differences in the rules applied to price discrimination domestically and internationally, which allow more price discrimination domestically, suggest that price discrimination is perhaps not so unfair. In the case of below-cost sales, there is acceptance of that practice in the United States, so long as it is not predatory.[6] Indeed, in a recession where all steel producing companies are losing money, U.S. steelmakers do not sue each other for making below-cost sales, but they do bring AD actions against imports. In light of this, would you say that the existence of AD laws is consistent with the WTO's general philosophy of requiring national treatment? Should the scope of AD laws be limited to the scope of domestic rules against price discrimination and below-cost sales? What might justify differential treatment of imports?

(4) A second aspect of the unfairness argument is that AD laws are appropriate in times of recession because without them the country with the most open markets will suffer most because it will become a dumping ground for producers in other countries who have protected markets. (The EC Commission's defense of AD laws is based on the existence of such a protected market, although imposition of AD duties is not conditional on showing that the exporter's home market is protected.) AD laws in such circumstances can ensure that the burdens of recession are equitably shared. One can argue, however, that the safeguard procedures described in Chapter 15 offer a better method for dealing with this problem. The relief afforded by U.S. AD rules is based on the amount (margin) of dumping and is not adjusted to reflect the extent of injury suffered by domestic industry. Since there is no necessary relationship between the margin of dumping and that injury, are AD laws well suited as an adjustment mechanism? Would your answer differ if available safeguard procedures were more expensive than AD procedures and rarely invoked successfully?

(5) On the unfairness issue more generally, one study concluded, after examining all 174 final affirmative injury findings of the International Trade Commission in antidumping and countervailing duty cases between 1980 and 1988, that

---

3. 15 U.S.C.A. sec. 13. See Stephen F. Ross, Principles of Antitrust Law ch. 7 (1993).

4. Brooke Group Ltd. v. Brown & Williamson Tobacco Corp., 509 U.S. 209, 113 S.Ct. 2578, 125 L.Ed.2d 168 (1993).

5. See Ronald A. Cass, Price Discrimination and Predation Analysis in Antitrust and International Trade: A Comment, 61 U.

Cincinnati L.Rev. 877 (1993); Report of the Ad Hoc Committee on Antitrust and Antidumping of the American Bar Association Section on Antitrust Law, 46 Antitrust L.J. 653, 691–693 (1974).

6. See Brooke Group Ltd. v. Brown & Williamson Tobacco Corp., 509 U.S. 209, 113 S.Ct. 2578, 125 L.Ed.2d 168 (1993).

in 84% of the countervailing duty cases, 59% of the antidumping cases, and 67% of the joint antidumping/countervailing duty cases, the dumping (or subsidy) margin and the market share of unfair imports were too small (less than 5%) to expect that unfair imports have a significant impact on competing domestic industries.[7]

In the words of the authors, "Despite the importance of the fairness issue, there is surprisingly little information about the extent to which [dumped and subsidized] imports actually harm domestic producers."[8]

(6) As noted above, to some extent AD laws seem inconsistent with the philosophy of antitrust laws because they focus on the protection of individual competitors rather than overall competition. This concern is underscored by studies that show that the most frequent users of AD actions are concentrated industries,[9] and by concerns raised when AD cases are "settled" by agreements to raise prices or cease exporting. Do you think that AD laws should be modified to include a consideration of consumer and/or competitive interests? How could this be done? The EC AD rules call for consideration of "Community interest" in deciding whether to impose AD duties, but the provision has seldom been invoked to reduce AD duty levels.

(7) To what extent do the inefficiencies cited by the EC Commission report have negative effects in the dumper's home market, as opposed to the importing country's market? Should the importing country care about inefficiencies in the dumper's home market?

(8) Some argue that the WTO system should expand the scope of AD laws to cover "social" or "exchange rate" dumping. "Social" dumping occurs when import prices are low because of comparatively lower wages and less strict environmental rules and factory safety rules in the exporting countries. "Exchange rate" dumping occurs when import prices decline because of shifts in exchange rates. Would such an expansion be appropriate in your view? If there were to be such an expansion, what sort of definitional issues would have to be addressed? We explore the issue of linkages between international trade and worker rights generally in Chapter 21.

SECTION 16.3   THE INTERNATIONAL RULES ON DUMPING

(A) THE EVOLUTION OF THE INTERNATIONAL OBLIGATIONS

During the latter part of the nineteenth century, several European countries, primarily Great Britain and the Netherlands, complained about the dumping of sugar, and in 1902 an agreement was signed to counteract it. Ten European nations adhered to this pact during its eighteen-year life, but there was little success in concluding agreements to cover other products.

---

7. Morris E. Morkre & Kenneth Kelly, Perspectives on the Effects of Unfair Imports on Domestic Industries, 61 U. Cincinnati L. Rev. 919, 944 (1993).

8. Id. at 920, citing as a "notable exception" one study of four industries: brass sheet, unfinished mirrors, candles and oil country tubular goods.

9. Davey, supra note 2, at 8–33 to 8–36.

Beginning with Canada in 1904, nations started unilaterally to legislate against dumping in order to protect domestic industries from a perceived threat of predatory behavior from abroad. In the case of Canada, one apparent concern was U.S. steel exports. By the time the League of Nations in the 1920's, and the World Economic Conference in 1933, had considered the problem, the national laws were of as much concern as the dumping practices themselves. Nations feared that their trading partners would use the laws as protectionist devices, rather than as simple regulatory measures to deal with patently unfair practices. When the preliminary ITO–GATT work began, the United States offered a proposal for standards modeled upon its own 1921 Antidumping Act. The need for such standards seems to have been generally recognized, and the result was GATT Article VI, which deals with both antidumping and countervailing duties.[1]

Article VI is relatively brief and says little about many of procedural and substantive issues that arise in AD cases. Consequently, there were efforts in GATT to reach agreement on more specific standards for these cases. These efforts culminated in 1967 with the signing of an Agreement on Interpretation of Article VI (the 1967 Antidumping Code) by the United States and 17 other nations.[2] In addition to specifying minimal procedural standards for AD cases, the Code also required that dumping be the "principal" cause of the material injury to domestic industry.

Unfortunately, the U.S. President had received no authorization from Congress to negotiate and enter into such an agreement.[3] As a consequence, even though it is arguable that the Code was consistent with the wording of the then effective U.S. statute,[4] certain congressional leaders were incensed at the President's action, and took action that, according to then Senate Finance Committee Chairman Russell B. Long, meant that "Congress has forbidden the Executive Branch and the Tariff Commission to interpret the Antidumping Act more narrowly in the future than in the past by virtue of the negotiation of the [1967] Antidumping Code."[5] This dispute is now of only historical interest since the United States implemented the Tokyo Round substitute for the Code, but it highlights the uncertainty that surrounds the negotiation of agreements by the United States if those agreements need congressional approval, as well as the rancor that occasionally develops between the President and Congress over trade matters. In addition, the whole affair

1. See generally John J. Jackson, World Trade and the Law of GATT 403–424 (1969), for a discussion of the development and meaning of both Article VI and the 1967 Antidumping Code.

2. GATT, 15th Supp. BISD 74 (1968).

3. The Senate Finance Committee Report on the Trade Expansion Act of 1962, which provided authorization for Kennedy Round negotiations, explicitly stated that the then current antidumping statute was "not intended to be affected." S.Rep. No. 2059, 87th Cong., 2d Sess. 19 (1962).

4. See generally John J. Barcelo, III, Antidumping Laws as Barriers to Trade: The United States and the International Antidumping Code, 57 Cornell L.Rev. 491 (1972).

5. Russell B. Long, United States Law and the International Anti-dumping Code, 3 Intl. Lawyer 464, 486 (1969).

had an adverse impact on the U.S. image as a responsible participant in trade negotiations, an impact that did not quickly dissipate.

There were extensive negotiations during the Tokyo Round concerning a code on subsidies, which we will discuss in Chapter 18. When those negotiations were completed, it was agreed that provisions in the 1967 Antidumping Code should be conformed to their analogues in the Subsidies Code.[6] In addition, the requirement that dumping be the principal cause of injury was omitted. The result was a new Agreement on Implementation of Article VI, which effectively replaced the 1967 Antidumping Code.[7] The U.S. Congress had authorized these negotiations and the 1979 Code was implemented by the United States through the 1979 Trade Agreements Act.

In the Uruguay Round, it was not initially expected that the 1979 Code would be a major subject of negotiations. But as the negotiations unfolded, it turned out that many contracting parties were dissatisfied with GATT regulation of AD procedures and substance. On the one hand, the U.S. and the EU were concerned about gaining GATT acceptance of the use of certain devices to prevent the circumvention of AD duties. They were also interested in regulating more closely the procedures used in AD actions in light of the increased use by Mexico and other developing countries of AD laws. On the other hand, many of the countries commonly targeted by AD actions, including countries in East Asia and Scandinavia, pressed for changes in the substantive rules applied in AD cases so as to make them less susceptible to use for protectionist purposes. The ensuing negotiations were among the more hotly contested in the Round. The result of the negotiations was a bit of a compromise: The procedural rules were tightened, while there was some, rather minimal, tightening of the substantive rules. No agreement was reached, however, on anticircumvention measures. Implementation of the Uruguay Round Antidumping Agreement was quite controversial in the U.S. Supporters of AD laws tried to limit the effect of the liberalizing aspects of the Agreement and proposed other changes in U.S. law designed to "toughen" it. By and large, the changes were at a level of detail that is beyond the coverage of this Chapter.

AD rules continue to be controversial in the WTO. Japan and a number of other newly industrialized and developing countries would like the next round of WTO negotiations to include serious negotiations on AD rules. The United States has been generally opposed to including AD rules in such negotiations.

(B) THE WTO RULES ON DUMPING

We will not discuss the provisions of Article VI and the WTO Antidumping Agreement in any detail. By and large, they have been implemented by the United States, and we will discuss U.S. law in the

---

6. GATT, The Tokyo Round of Multilateral Trade Negotiations, Report by the Director–General of GATT 181 (1979).

7. GATT, 26th Supp. BISD 171 (1980).

following section. Here, we will highlight in a series of notes and questions, some of the general issues relating to AD actions that have arisen in GATT and in the WTO, generally and in dispute settlement proceedings.

Notes and Questions

(1) One key fact about Article VI and GATT regulation of dumping is that the General Agreement does not forbid dumping; it only authorizes, as an exception to other GATT obligations, the imposition of AD duties to offset dumping if the dumping causes material injury to a domestic industry. The lack of a prohibition is not surprising. After all, companies, not governments, dump. Nonetheless, governments could have agreed to make dumping unlawful under national law or to make a dumper liable for any damages caused, but they have not done so. As a consequence, it is generally believed that a dumping company is not liable for dumping (beyond the potential assessment of AD duties) under national law. Do you think that the fact that dumping is not considered to be illegal (and therefore not punishable by law), increases the likelihood of its occurrence?

In light of the foregoing and your analysis of Article VI and the WTO AD Agreement, would it be consistent under those rules for a country to create a private right of action for damages resulting from dumping, such that a domestic industry could sue for lost profits if it could establish injury caused by dumping in a domestic legal proceeding? Would it be necessary that an identical or analogous right of action existed in respect of injury from price discrimination or below-cost sales by other domestic entities? Is the *Section 337* case discussed in Section 12.2 relevant?

In the United States, the Antidumping Act of 1916 (15 U.S.C.A. sec. 72) makes certain intentional dumping unlawful and provides for the recovery of treble damages in private actions. On challenge by the EC and Japan, the Appellate Body upheld panel findings that the Act violated GATT Article VI and provisions of the AD Agreement. The Appellate Body laid particular stress on article 1 of the AD Agreement, which provides that "An antidumping measure shall be applied only under the circumstances provided for in Article VI of GATT 1994 and pursuant to an investigation initiated and conducted in accordance with the provisions of this Agreement," and article 18.1, which provides that "No specific action against dumping of exports * * * can be taken except in accordance with the provisions of GATT 1994, as interpreted by this Agreement." United States—Antidumping Act of 1916, WT/DS136 & 162/AB/R, adopted by the DSB on September 26, 2000.

(2) Would it be permissible under GATT Article VI and the AD Agreement to pay the amount of money collected as AD duties to the companies that had been injured by the dumping? Such payments have recently been authorized in the United States pursuant to the so-called Byrd Amendment (the Continued Dumping and Subsidy Offset Act of 2000, 19 U.S.C.A. sec. 1675c), which is currently being challenged in a WTO panel proceeding by 11 WTO members. WT/DS217 & 234. How will the case be decided?

(3) If a European manufacturer makes widgets from scratch and sells them at a loss in the United States, it is dumping. What if the European manufacturer buys widget components at below-cost prices from unrelated

companies, assembles them into widgets and sells them in the United States at a small profit? Is it dumping? Is there any real difference in the two cases? The second situation is called downstream dumping, and it is generally agreed it is not covered by existing law, although there have been proposals to change the law to cover it explicitly, one of which was adopted in the House (but not in the final) version of the 1984 Trade and Tariff Act.[8] Would such a provision be consistent with GATT Article VI? With the WTO AD Agreement?

(4) Article VI does not contain any rules on the procedures to be followed to decide whether to impose AD duties, although the WTO Anti-dumping Agreement does. Assume that a country suspects that companies in another country are dumping. Can it impose duties immediately and then proceed to investigate? Article 5 of the Agreement specifies in detail the information that the authorities must have before an investigation may be initiated. So far, panels have strictly enforced these requirements. Guatemala—Definitive Anti-dumping Measure regarding Grey Portland Cement from Mexico, WT/DS156/R, adopted by the DSB on November 17, 2000. If a country fails to follow all of the rules in initiating an AD action, but properly finds that dumping and material injury have occurred, do the shortcomings in the initiation procedure mean that it cannot impose duties, but rather must recommence the investigation. In other words, is or should there be a notion of harmless error? If not, how can respect of the initiation rules be ensured?

(5) AD laws typically allow AD duties to be imposed on a preliminary or provisional basis after an AD proceeding has been initiated, but before the investigation has been completed. Such duties are refunded if no dumping is ultimately found. What limits does the WTO AD Agreement place on the use of such provisional AD measures? For example, is a country permitted to impose provisional duties, subject to refund, within a few days of the filing of a complaint? Is there some minimal preliminary investigation that is required? See art. 7.3. As long as any provisional duties are refunded if no dumping is found, why restrict their use? In this connection, what effect on imports of a product would you expect to result from the initiation of an AD investigation? From the imposition of provisional AD duties on the product?

(6) An examination of the WTO AD Agreement reveals a number of specific procedural requirements that must be satisfied before imposing AD duties. Article 5's requirements for initiating investigations have been noted above. Article 6 requires certain rights to be afforded to those accused of dumping, such as notice, a right to a full opportunity for the defense of their interests, and notice of the essential facts on which definitive action is to be taken, in sufficient time to respond. Article 12.2 requires public notice of a determination to impose AD duties and a report setting forth in sufficient detail the findings and conclusions reached on all issues of fact and law considered material by the investigative authorities. Article 13 requires the maintenance of judicial, arbitral or administrative tribunals or procedures to review administrative actions relating to final determinations. To what extent do you think that the burdens of meeting those requirements may impede the use of AD laws by developing countries? See Guatemala—

8. See House Conference Rep. No. 98– 1156, 98th Cong., 2d Sess. 171–72 (1984).

Definitive Anti-dumping Measure regarding Grey Portland Cement from Mexico, WT/DS156/R, adopted by the DSB on November 17, 2000 (numerous procedural defects found).

(7) Is there an MFN requirement applicable to the application of AD duties? If so, exactly what does that mean? Suppose that companies in two exporting countries are dumping by an identical amount. Must identical AD duties be imposed? What if there is a difference in the injury caused (for example, although each is dumping in the same amount, the prices of one exporter are higher)? In 1960, a GATT committee report, adopted by the contracting parties, stated:[9] "In equity, and having regard to the most-favored-nation principle, the Group considered that where there was dumping to the same degree from more than one source and where that dumping caused or threatened material injury to the same extent, the importing country ought normally to be expected to levy antidumping duties equally on all the dumped imports." Given the foregoing, how would you assess the amount of discretion that a country has in differentiating among exporters in respect of AD duties? In the WTO AD Agreement, Article 5.8 provides that no AD duties should be imposed if certain *de minimis* standards are met, i.e., the dumping margin is less than 2% or the dumped imports from a particular country are less than 3% of the total imports (unless countries individually accounting for less than 3%, collectively account for more than 7% of the imports).

(8) So far in this chapter, we have defined dumping to include below-cost sales, but is it clear that Article VI permits the imposition of AD duties in respect of below-cost sales in the absence of international price discrimination? If Article VI does not explicitly permit such a practice, how could you fashion an argument based on language in Article VI to support it? It is now taken for granted that Article VI applies to below-cost sales, although objections were raised in GATT when the U.S. law was applied in this manner in the 1970's.[10] Those countries imposing duties in such cases argue that below-cost domestic sales are not made in the ordinary course and thus can be excluded from consideration in calculating normal value. If so many sales are excluded on that basis such that no domestic price may be calculated, Article VI(1)(b) allows normal value to be based on cost of production. When normal value is set by calculating the cost of production, below-cost sales will obviously be found to have been dumped. Article 2.2.1 of the WTO AD Agreement specifies the circumstances under which below-cost sales constitute dumping.

(9) The WTO AD Agreement contains a special standard of review applicable in WTO dispute settlement proceedings for evaluating administrative actions imposing AD duties and AD statutes in general. See Section 7.4(B) supra.

(10) There have been more ten AD cases considered in WTO dispute settlement and many more are pending. For the most part, they involve technical matters beyond the level of our treatment of AD issues, although we will refer to a number of them in the remainder of the chapter.

---

9. GATT, 9th Supp. BISD 194, 198 (1961).

10. See, e.g., GATT, 22nd Supp. BISD 24 (1976); GATT. 24th Supp. BISD 19–20 (1978).

(C) DUMPING AND U.S. FREE TRADE AGREEMENTS

The Canada–U.S. Free Trade Agreement (FTA) established special dispute settlement procedures for AD and countervailing duty (CVD) issues. Similar procedures now apply under the North American Free Trade Agreement (NAFTA). Under Chapter 19 (of both agreements), so-called binational panels are provided for to hear appeals from administrative decisions under U.S., Canadian and Mexican AD or CVD laws when requested by an affected party from one of the other countries.[11] These procedures are described in more detail in Section 11.3 supra. The panels effectively replace judicial review in such cases.

In the negotiations on the FTA, the Canadian government had hoped to exempt Canadian goods from U.S. AD and CVD laws. As we noted earlier, in some free trade areas, AD laws have been eliminated for trade within the area. The U.S. refused to agree to such an exemption. In its place, Canada accepted the binational review procedure as a means of placing some limits on the use of these laws by U.S. authorities. The Canadian government had been particularly upset in 1986 when the U.S. Commerce Department had reversed its 1983 decision that certain government timber programs in Canada did not involve countervailable subsidies. (This controversy is described in more detail in Chapter 18.) FTA Article 1906 provided that the binational panel procedures would be used for five years (extendable to seven years) "pending the development of a substitute system of rules in both countries for antidumping and countervailing duties as applied to their bilateral trade." No such system was agreed upon, and NAFTA does not provide for further negotiations on the subject. It appears that the binational panel system may be in place for a long time. Should such a system be generalized under the auspices of the WTO?

SECTION 16.4   UNITED STATES ANTIDUMPING LAW[1]

Prior to the Tokyo Round U.S. antidumping (AD) law was not entirely consistent with GATT Article VI, principally because it required domestic producers to show only injury, not material injury. It also granted a great deal of discretion to the administrators of the law—the Treasury Department and the International Trade Commission—who exercised that discretion in a way that seldom resulted in the imposition of AD duties, which caused many in Congress to believe that the

---

11. Binational panels may also be established to consider claims that amendments to existing AD and CVD laws are inconsistent with the relevant WTO rules.

1. The basic U.S. antidumping statute was enacted by the Trade Agreements Act of 1979, which added a new title VII to the Tariff Act of 1930 (see Documents Supplement). Those sections of title VII that are particularly relevant to AD actions are Sections 731–39 (AD investigations), Sections 751–52 (reviews) and Sections 771–83 (definitions and procedures). Those sections are codified, as amended, at 19 U.S.C.A. secs. 1673–73h; 1675–75a, 1677–77n. The basic statute governing appeals from administrative decisions in AD cases is Section 516A of the Tariff Act, 19 U.S.C.A. sec. 1516a.

Executive Branch did not take the enforcement of the AD laws seriously enough.

The implementation of the Tokyo Round agreements was the occasion for a substantial restructuring of U.S. AD law. It can be argued that the changes in substance were not all that great—after all, the Tokyo Round agreement was a somewhat watered-down version of the 1967 Code that the Treasury Department had contended was consistent with U.S. law. The changes in procedure, however, were fundamental in nature. Since 1980 the administration of the U.S. AD law has been split between the International Trade Administration of the U.S. Department of Commerce (typically referred to as the "ITA" or "Commerce"), which determines whether dumping has occurred, and the International Trade Commission (typically referred to as the "ITC" or the "Commission"), which determines whether U.S. industry has demonstrated sufficient injury.[2]

In this section, we will first focus on the procedural aspects of U.S. law and then examine the substantive issues of AD law. As a consequence of the changes in procedure in 1979, AD proceedings in the United States have become very formalized and are played out according to a complex set of rules, largely designed to minimize administrative discretion. The notes following our description of U.S. procedures will contrast a number of U.S. practices with those of the EU and Canada.

(A) PROCEDURAL ASPECTS OF U.S. ANTIDUMPING LAW

JOHN H. JACKSON & WILLIAM J. DAVEY, REFORM OF THE ADMINISTRATIVE PROCEDURES USED IN U.S. ANTIDUMPING AND COUNTERVAILING DUTY CASES[3]

* * * There are three distinct stages in U.S. AD and CVD [countervailing duty] cases: First, the initial investigation, which determines whether or not an AD/CVD order will be issued. Second, the annual review procedure, in which the actual amount of AD/CV duties to be collected is established. Third, the revocation procedures, by which cases are finally terminated. In addition, there is judicial review of all final determinations in these three stages.

1. Initial Investigations

An AD or CVD proceeding is typically commenced by the filing of a petition in respect of a specific product on behalf of the U.S. domestic

---

2. The AD rules of the ITA are found at 19 C.F.R. pt. 351 (2001). Those of the ITC are at 19 C.F.R. pt. 207 (2001). As to basic source material, actions taken by the ITA are published in the Federal Register and the available on the ITA website. Notices of determinations by the ITC are also published in the Federal Register and the decisions are available on the ITC website.

3. This report to the Administrative Conference of the United States was published in Administrative Conference of the United States: Recommendations and Reports 909 (1991) and reprinted in a slightly revised version in 6 The Admin.L.J.Am.U. 399 (1992).

industry producing that product. Thereafter, the statute establishes strict deadlines for completion by the ITA [International Trade Administration, Commerce Department] and the ITC [International Trade Commission] of the various phases of the initial investigation. Once an investigation is opened, the ITA is responsible for determining the extent of dumping or subsidization, while the ITC determines whether U.S. industry has suffered material injury. The order of their determinations is as follows: First, the ITC makes a preliminary injury determination; then the ITA makes both its preliminary and final dumping/subsidy determination; and finally the ITC makes its final injury determination. The time limits established by Congress for these determinations is as follows:

Action	Days After Petition Filed	
	AD	CVD
ITA decision to initiate investigation	20	20
ITC preliminary injury determination	45	45
ITA preliminary dumping/subsidy determination	160	85
ITA final dumping/subsidy determination	235	160
ITC final injury determination	280	205

[These deadlines are subject to modification in certain cases, which means that AD cases usually take longer than 280 days to complete.]

The decision by the ITA on whether to initiate an investigation is largely pro forma. At this stage, the ITA determines whether the petition properly alleges the basis for an action, contains information reasonably available to the petitioner in support thereof and is filed by an appropriate party.[4] The ITA does not permit arguments against initiation to be made by respondents.

If the ITA initiates an investigation, the ITC determines whether there is a reasonable indication that U.S. industry has been materially injured by the allegedly dumped or subsidized imports. To make that determination, the ITC collects information from the U.S. industry and others through questionnaires and uses other information available to it about the industry. * * *

If the ITC preliminary determination is affirmative, the ITA continues its preliminary investigation (which goes forward in any event during the ITC's preliminary investigation). The ITA sends question-

---

4. [original note 41] 19 C.F.R. sec. [351.203]. Petitions may be filed by a manufacturer, producer or wholesaler in the United States of a like product; a certified union or recognized union or group of workers representative of an industry in the United States engaged in the manufacture, production or wholesale of a like product; a trade or business association a majority of whose members manufacture, produce or wholesale a like product in the United States; and an association, a majority of whose members is composed of the foregoing. There is a special rule for processed agricultural products. Tariff Act of 1930, sec. 771(9)(C)-(G); 19 U.S.C. sec. 1677(9)(C)-(G).

naires to the exporters, importers and other parties known to be involved in the case, including the relevant foreign government in a CVD case. The questionnaires aim to establish the information needed to determine whether dumping or subsidization has occurred, i.e. information on domestic and export prices, information concerning adjustments needed to make those prices "comparable," information about costs if there are allegations of below-cost sales, information about government programs and information about receipt of government benefits by individual companies. On the basis of the questionnaire responses, or, in the absence of adequate information from a respondent, the best information available to it (which may be information supplied by the petitioner), the ITA determines on a preliminary basis whether the foreign goods are being sold in the United States at less than fair value or have been subsidized. It does so by calculating the preliminary subsidy margin or dumping margin, i.e. the difference between the [export] price and the [normal] value of the goods in question. In the case of an affirmative determination, the Customs Service is directed to "suspend liquidation" of all subsequent imports of the product in question and to collect a deposit or bond thereon equal to the preliminary margin. Suspension of liquidation means that the final amount of duty owed on the imported goods is held open for later determination. A preliminary negative decision does not end the case, however, as the ITA is required to proceed to a final determination.

Between its preliminary and final determinations, the ITA verifies the questionnaire responses, typically by sending ITA personnel to conduct an on-site examination of the books and records of the respondent. In addition, both the respondent and the petitioner typically file comments in respect of the preliminary determination. In its final determination, the ITA responds to these comments and revises its preliminary determination in light of those comments that it accepts and whatever additional relevant information has come to its attention.

* * *

If the ITA makes an affirmative preliminary dumping or subsidy determination, the ITC commences a further investigation into the injury issue. * * * In the final ITC investigation, * * * a hearing is typically scheduled, at which the parties can present witnesses and legal arguments. * * *

Assuming that the ITC makes an affirmative injury finding, an AD or CVD order is issued. The dumping or subsidy margin established in the ITA's final determination is used as the basis for establishing the precise amount of AD/CV duties owed on imports of the merchandise made between the preliminary AD/CVD determination and the final ITC injury determination. If the amount fixed in the final ITA determination exceeds that of the preliminary ITA determination, the shortfall is disregarded; if the final amount is less than that established in the preliminary determination, the excess is refunded, without interest. With respect to imports of the merchandise made after the issuance of an AD or CVD order, a duty equal to the final dumping or subsidy margin is collected provisionally as an estimated AD or CV duty. This provisional amount must normally be deposited with the U.S. government in cash. The final amount of duty owing on these imports is determined in the annual review procedure discussed below.

It is possible under the AD and CVD statutes for the foreign exporters or government to "settle" a case by agreeing to cease dumping, to cease subsidization or to revise their prices so as to eliminate the injury to U.S. industry. Such settlements, known as price undertakings in the GATT Codes and suspension agreements in U.S. law, are common in the EC and to a lesser extent in Australia and Canada, but not in the United States. As of December 31, 1990, there were five AD suspension agreements and 12 CVD suspension agreements in effect in the United States.

The principal reason that suspension agreements are not often used in the United States is that Congress has attached many conditions to their use. Under U.S. law, in order for a suspension agreement to be entered into, (i) exporters of substantially all investigated products must agree to stop exporting to the United States or agree to eliminate completely the dumping margin by raising their prices or (ii) they must agree to revise their prices so as to eliminate completely the injurious effect of exports to the United States. Use of the latter type of agreement is subject to a number of additional conditions and may be entered into only in "extraordinary circumstances." Moreover, the legislative history of the U.S. law indicates considerable congressional opposition to use of suspension agreements. This antipathy towards price undertakings seems to have originated in congressional dissatisfaction with the administration of the U.S. AD and CVD laws by the Treasury Department. Congress apparently believed that the Treasury Department imposed duties too infrequently and tended to resolve cases on terms that were too favorable to exporters.

Finally, one important procedural aspect of U.S. AD/CVD proceedings must be highlighted. Much of the information collected by the ITA and ITC is viewed by the suppliers as highly sensitive commercial information, such as detailed data on costs, prices and customers. While such information is treated as confidential by the agencies and is not available to the public or parties generally, it is available to attorneys for the parties under protective orders. This practice allows attorneys for the parties to participate much more effectively in the proceedings than would be the case if there was no access to such confidential information.

2. Administrative Reviews

As explained above, the dumping or subsidy margin determined by the ITA in its final determination in an investigation is used to set the amount that must be deposited on importation of products subject to an AD or CVD order. The ITA, at the request of an interested party, will conduct a review each year to establish the exact extent of dumping or subsidization, and the importer either receives a refund if the amount deposited was too high (plus interest) or pays an additional sum (plus interest) if it was too low. Commerce Department officials told us that such a request is received in approximately 50–60% of the cases. In those cases where no review is requested, the amount deposited as the estimated duty is collected as the definitive amount due. In the other cases, reviews are held.

* * * Essentially the same sort of information is collected in a review as in the initial investigation. * * * There [were] no strict statutory time limits for completion of reviews [until 1994,] and historically, the ITA has had a considerable backlog of reviews waiting to be processed, although it has made progress in reducing that backlog in the recent past.

3.   Revocation

AD and CVD orders remain in effect until they are revoked. Even if an annual review finds no dumping or subsidization, which means that no amount is required to be deposited on future importations, the AD/CVD order remains in effect and it is possible that a subsequent review could result in the assessment of AD or CV duties.

* * *

[First], there is a statutory provision for review of the injury determination by the ITC. If the ITC concludes that revocation would not result in material injury to U.S. industry, the ITA will revoke an AD or CVD order. Such reviews by the ITC are only rarely conducted and only a handful have succeeded.

[Second], an AD or CVD order may be revoked [by the ITA] on the basis of changed circumstances. * * * [See 19 C.F.R. secs. 351.222 (2001).]

* * *

[R]evocation is relatively rare unless there is no opposition from U.S. industry. In the three years 1988–1990, there were a total of 15 AD order revocations (197 AD orders remained outstanding at the end of 1990, compared to 163 at the end of 1988) and 13 CVD order revocations (72 CVD orders remained outstanding at the end of 1990, compared to 77 at the end of 1988). This means that the unsettling effect on international trade inherent in a U.S. AD or CVD order typically continues for a considerable period of time.

[As required by the WTO AD Agreement, the United States added a sunset review provision, to implement article 11.3 of the WTO AD Agreement, which provides for the revocation of AD orders after five years unless there is a determination that "the expiry of the duty would be likely to lead to continuation or recurrence of dumping and injury." Existing orders were deemed to have been imposed on January 1, 1995.

During 2000, more than 100 AD orders were revoked following sunset reviews.]

4.　Judicial Review

U.S. law provides for appeals from final determinations of the ITA or ITC to the Court of International Trade (CIT). * * * Decisions by the ITA not to initiate an investigation and negative preliminary decisions by the ITC are reviewed to see if they are "arbitrary, capricious, or an abuse of discretion, or otherwise not in accordance with law." Final determinations by the ITA and the ITC are reviewed to see if they are "unsupported by substantial evidence on the record, or otherwise not in accordance with law." From the CIT, cases are appealable to the Court of Appeals for the Federal Circuit, and to the Supreme Court on writ of certiorari. Decisions involving Canadian products may instead be "appealed" to binational panels under the United States–Canada Free Trade Agreement.

Prior to 1979, the law relating to judicial review in AD/CVD cases was different and there was relatively little judicial review of such cases. Now, judicial review is much more common, and it appears that most AD and CVD final determinations are appealed to the CIT. * * *

* * *

[T]he process of judicial review in the CIT often takes years. This is true despite a perception, at least on the part of the agencies, that CIT review does not cause them to change their results significantly.

Notes and Questions

(1) Although AD proceedings are administrative proceedings, the typical pattern of U.S. administrative proceedings—the use of administrative law judges and reliance on adversarial hearings—is not used in AD cases. Contested issues are resolved by the ITA staff; hearings are not used to any significant degree in the fact-finding process. Although this makes the U.S. system more informal than one might normally expect in the U.S., the U.S. system seems in general to be more formal than those of other countries. Generally, the EU, Canadian and Australian systems seem to afford more discretion to administrators and operate more informally. Judicial review is also more readily available and seems more intrusive in the United States than the other three jurisdictions. All of this means that AD proceedings in the U.S. are relatively expensive, so much so that their expense is sometimes cited as a trade barrier in itself. We discuss the cost of trade law remedies generally in Chapter 26.

Judicial review in the United States can be particularly time-consuming because the CIT often remands a decision to the ITA or the ITC for further proceedings. Appeals to the Federal Circuit are generally not permitted as long as remands are ordered. The result is that some very important issues to the administration of the AD/CVD laws go unresolved for many years when judges of the CIT (or the CIT and the ITA) disagree. For example, the first Federal Circuit opinion dealing with the key issue of CVD law—the definition of countervailable subsidy—was not rendered until 1991.

(2) Article 5.4 of the WTO AD Agreement specifies that the investigating authorities must determine the degree of support within domestic industry for opening an investigation. The minimum level of acceptable support is set at those who account for 25% of total production. The 1994 Act implements this requirement. Section 732(c)(4).

(3) As noted in the foregoing excerpt, confidential information submitted by the parties to U.S. authorities in AD/CVD cases is usually available under court protective order to attorneys for the opposing parties. This allows counsel to monitor the decisions of the authorities much more effectively. In contrast, under EU rules confidential information is generally not subject to review by the parties or their attorneys, although summaries of the information must be provided. As a result, attorneys are less able to argue their clients' cases effectively. Canadian agencies also make confidential information available to attorneys under rules similar to those used in the U.S. It appears that there have been relatively few (and largely inadvertent) violations of U.S. protective orders. Given that the information requested by the U.S. authorities often concerns very sensitive commercial information on customers, prices and costs, one might wonder why parties are willing to supply it if there is any risk at all of disclosure. The answer is that if the information requested is not submitted, the authorities are permitted to use the best information available, which may be the allegations of the opposing parties and which is likely to be very unfavorable.

(4) The results of dumping cases in the EU are much different than in the United States. The amount of the duty imposed in the EU is not necessarily the amount of the dumping margin. The EU authorities have the discretion to impose a lesser duty if it would be sufficient to eliminate the injury to EU industry, a practice endorsed but not required by the WTO AD Agreement, article 9.1. This practice is referred to in the EU as using "injury margins" or the "lesser duty rule" and a significant proportion of EU AD duties are reduced on the basis of such analysis. Moreover, the EU is required to take into account the "Community interest" in imposing duties, although this provision is not typically applied to reduce duties as the EU authorities seem to equate Community interest with complainant (and not consumer) interests in most cases. Likewise in Canada, the Canadian International Trade Tribunal may consider whether an AD duty would be in the public interest and may recommend to the relevant Minister that duties should not be imposed or should be reduced. It appears that such recommendations have been made only rarely.

Should the U.S adopt some form of lesser duty rule? What would the advantages and disadvantages of such a rule be? In particular, consider such issues as (i) is it appropriate to grant protection to an industry in excess of its injury, (ii) could the discretion of administrative agencies in setting the lesser duty be effectively monitored by courts, (iii) which U.S. agency would set the duty rate, and (iv) how would the U.S. annual review process be affected? The 1994 Act gives users a hearing, but their views need not be considered. Section 777(h).

(5) If duties are ultimately imposed in the EU, they are imposed on a prospective basis. There is no annual review to determine the precise amount of the dumping margins. While there is the possibility of obtaining a

refund if no dumping in fact occurred in a given transaction, refunds are not common because of procedural and substantive impediments in the applicable EU rules. After one year has passed, it is possible to ask the EU authorities to review and, if appropriate, revise the duty rate.

In Canada, if dumping and injury are found, Revenue Canada usually sets the normal value for the product in question by establishing a so-called benchmark price. Future imports at less than the benchmark price are subject to a duty in the amount of the shortfall. Thus, as in the EU system, there is a prospective duty, but like the U.S. system, if the exporter stops dumping, there is usually no duty due.

Which of those systems would you say is superior? On what basis? Do you think that any one system is significantly more protectionist or expensive to administer than the others?

One problem with imposing a prospective duty as the EU does is that a dumper might choose to absorb the duty itself in order to maintain the same market price. To avoid this problem, the EU added a new provision to its AD regulation in 1988, which is designed to prevent the absorption of AD duties by the exporter or related parties. If the EU finds that they have absorbed the AD duty, an additional AD duty may be imposed. Is this consistent with the WTO AD Agreement?

(6) Generally speaking, the prospect of a fixed prospective duty such as imposed in the EU is disturbing for exporters. Even if one stops dumping, the duty may continue to be payable. To avoid this kind of duty, companies subject to EU investigations typically have made so-called price undertakings, pursuant to which they settle the case by agreeing to respect certain price levels in their exports to the EU and to report their prices to the EU regularly. From 1980 to 1989, of those cases in which dumping and injury were found, 183 cases (66%) were concluded by undertakings, while in 96 cases (34%) duties were imposed. In the first nine months of 2000, undertakings were less common in the EU, but were involved in more than one-third of the cases where AD duties were imposed. Undertakings are also common in Canada.

Are the provisions of the U.S. statute that discourage the use of undertakings (called suspension agreements in U.S. law) consistent with the letter of the WTO AD Agreement? With its spirit? Should the U.S. make more extensive use of undertakings? What are the risks of using them? For example, do you see the potential for antitrust problems? For enforcement problems?

(B) THE SUBSTANTIVE RULES: DETERMINATIONS OF DUMPING

The U.S. antidumping statute provides that if imports occur at "less than fair value" and are causing or threatening material injury, then an antidumping duty will be assessed equal to the amount by which the "normal value" exceeds the "export price."[5] The U.S. statute does not

---

5. The relevant statutory sections are 731 (imposition of AD duties), 772 (definition of export price) and 773 (definition of normal value). 19 U.S.C.A. secs. 1673, 1677a, 1677b.

actually define "less than fair value," although it is generally assumed that if normal value (as defined in the statute) exceeds the export price (also defined) then imports are occurring at "less than fair value."

The process of establishing the export price and the normal value is very complex. Typically, invoice prices are the starting point. Various adjustments are then made because export sales may be made on quite different terms than sales on the home market, thereby making inappropriate a simple comparison of invoice prices. To take an example, exports may be sold on a CIF basis for cash and with a limited warranty, while domestic sales may be made on an FOB basis on 60 days credit and with full warranty. The adjustment process tries to compensate for such differences. It essentially attempts to arrive at comparable "ex factory" prices for the exports and for the similar products sold in the home market.

Much work is involved in this effort to establish comparable values. Often, accountants and economic consultants work with the lawyers in these cases, and since comparisons with foreign markets are involved, not only are language skills essential, but analysts must have knowledge of different accounting standards. The adjustment process can be very confusing, but the key is to focus on whether a proposed adjustment expands the difference (called the dumping margin) between the export price and the normal value or decreases it. Generally speaking, the petitioners (domestic industry) will want to minimize the export price and maximize the normal value, while the respondents (exporters) will want to do the opposite.

The following case and notes focus only on some of the more basic issues raised in AD cases. We cannot in this book do more than introduce these intricate and complex matters.

(1) Calculating the Dumping Margin

We start by examining a recent, relatively straightforward AD case involving hot-rolled steel products from India. While AD cases may be much more complex, involving many exporters and a multitude of product models, this case provides a useful introduction to the basic issues in an AD proceeding. It discusses the basic U.S. rules on calculating the export price and normal value—the two items that are compared to determine if dumping has occurred. It also contains a couple of examples of the kind of adjustments necessary to make the export price and normal value comparable. Following the Commerce Department's determination are notes and questions that focus on the key aspects of each of the subdivisions of this case. It may be helpful to refer to the corresponding note after reading each section of Commerce's determination.

CERTAIN HOT–ROLLED CARBON STEEL FLAT PRODUCTS FROM INDIA[6]

We preliminarily determine that certain hot-rolled carbon steel flat products (HRS) from India are being sold, or are likely to be sold, in the United States at less than fair value (LTFV), as provided in section 733 of the Act. The estimated margins of sales at LTFV are shown in the Suspension of Liquidation section of this notice.

Case History

This investigation was initiated on December 4, 2000. * * * On December 28, 2000, the United States International Trade Commission (ITC) preliminarily determined that there is a reasonable indication that imports of the products subject to this investigation from Argentina, China, India, Indonesia, Kazakhstan, the Netherlands, Romania, South Africa, Taiwan, Thailand, and Ukraine, are materially injuring an industry in the United States producing the domestic like product.

The Department issued antidumping questionnaires to the two mandatory respondents in India on January 11, 2001. [Section A of the questionnaire requests general information concerning a company's corporate structure and business practices, the merchandise under investigation that it sells, and the manner in which it sells that merchandise in all of its markets. Section B requests a complete listing of all home market sales, or, if the home market is not viable, of sales in the most appropriate third-country market (this section is not applicable to respondents in non-market economy (NME) cases). Section C requests a complete listing of U.S. sales. Section D requests information on the cost of production (COP) of the foreign like product and the constructed value (CV) of the merchandise under investigation. Section E requests information on further manufacturing.] We received responses to our questionnaire from both mandatory respondents, Ispat Industries Ltd. (Ispat) and Essar Steel Ltd. (Essar). We issued supplemental questionnaires, pertaining to sections A, B, C, and D of the antidumping questionnaire, to Ispat and Essar in March 2001. Ispat and Essar responded to these supplemental questionnaires in April 2001.

* * *

Period of Investigation

The period of investigation (POI) for this investigation is October 1, 1999, through September 30, 2000. This period corresponds to the four most recent fiscal quarters prior to the month of the filing of the petition (i.e., November 2000).

Scope of Investigation

6. U.S. Department of Commerce, International Trade Administration, Notice of Preliminary Determination of Sales at Less Than Fair Value and Postponement of Final Determination, 66 Fed.Reg. 22157 (May 3, 2001).

For purposes of these investigations, the products covered are certain hot-rolled carbon steel flat products * * * .

Selection of Respondents

Section 777A(c)(1) of the Act directs the Department to calculate individual dumping margins for each known exporter and producer of the subject merchandise. Where it is not practicable to examine all known producers/exporters of subject merchandise, section 777A(c)(2) of the Act permits the Department to investigate either (1) a sample of exporters, producers, or types of products that is statistically valid based on the information available at the time of selection, or (2) exporters and producers accounting for the largest volume of the subject merchandise that can reasonably be examined. Using company-specific export data for the POI, which we obtained from the American Embassy in New Delhi, India, we found that four Indian exporters shipped HRS to the United States during the POI. Due to limited resources we determined that we could investigate only the two largest producers/exporters, accounting for more than 60 percent of total exports to the United States. Therefore, we designated Ispat and Essar as mandatory respondents and sent them the antidumping questionnaire.

Product Comparisons

In accordance with section 771(16) of the Act, all products produced by the respondents covered by the description in the Scope of Investigation section, above, and sold in India during the POI are considered to be foreign like products for purposes of determining appropriate product comparisons to U.S. sales. Where there were no sales of identical merchandise in the home market to compare to U.S. sales, we compared U.S. sales to the next most similar foreign like product on the basis of the characteristics listed above.

Fair Value Comparisons

To determine whether sales of HRS from India were made in the United States at LTFV, we compared the export price (EP) to the normal value (NV), as described in the Export Price and Normal Value sections of this notice. In accordance with section 777A(d)(1)(A)(i) of the Act, we calculated weighted-average EPs. We compared these to weighted-average home market prices.

* * *

Export Price

For the price to the United States, we used EP, in accordance with section 772(a) of the Act, because Ispat and Essar sold the merchandise directly to unaffiliated U.S. customers or sold the merchandise to unaffiliated trading companies, with knowledge that these companies in turn sold the merchandise to U.S. customers, and constructed export price was not otherwise warranted. For both Ispat and Essar, we calculated EP using the packed prices charged to the first unaffiliated customer in the United States (the starting price).

We deducted from the starting price, where applicable, amounts for discounts and rebates, and movement expenses in accordance with section 772(c)(2)(A) of the Act. In this case, movement expenses include foreign inland freight, international freight, foreign and U.S. brokerage and handling charges, insurance, U.S. duties and U.S. inland freight.

Duty Drawback

In the instant investigation, Ispat and Essar have claimed a duty drawback adjustment for the Government of India's Duty Entitlement Passbook Scheme ("DEPB"). Under the DEPB program, exporters are granted a credit which is equivalent to 14 percent of the FOB value of exports. The exporters then use this credit to offset the customs duty payment on imported inputs used to manufacture exported products.

* * *

The Department has repeatedly rejected the claim for duty drawback under the DEPB, based on the fact that the applicants received a drawback for the full amount of dutiable imports although there is no direct linkage between the material actually imported and the refunded amount. The record evidence in this investigation demonstrates that neither Essar nor Ispat was able to "link" the import duties paid on the input, and then rebated upon exportation. Rather the evidence on the record demonstrates that the DEPB program is a refund of duties calculated on an aggregated basis rather than on an input-specific basis. * * *

Normal Value

A.   Selection of Comparison Market

Section 773(a)(1) of the Act directs that NV be based on the price at which the foreign like product is sold in the home market, provided that the merchandise is sold in sufficient quantities (or has sufficient aggregate value, if quantity is inappropriate) and that there is no particular market situation in the home market that prevents a proper comparison with the EP transaction. The statute contemplates that quantities (or value) will normally be considered insufficient if they are less than five percent of the aggregate quantity (or value) of sales of the subject merchandise to the United States.

For this investigation, we found that Ispat and Essar each had a viable home market for HRS. Thus, the home market is the appropriate comparison market in this investigation, and we used the respondents' submitted home market sales data for purposes of calculating NV.

In deriving NV, we made adjustments as detailed in the Calculation of NV Based on Home Market Prices and Calculation of NV Based on CV, sections below.

B.   Affiliated–Party Transactions and Arm's-Length Test

* * * Ispat reported that it made home market sales to other affiliated companies. We applied the arm's-length test to sales from Ispat to these affiliated companies by comparing them to sales of identical merchandise from Ispat to unaffiliated home market customers. If these affiliated party sales satisfied the arm's-length test, we used them in our analysis. Sales to affiliated customers in the home market which were not made at arm's-length prices were excluded from our analysis because we considered them to be outside the ordinary course of trade.

* * *

C.   Cost of Production [COP] Analysis

Concurrent with the filing of the original petition, the petitioners alleged that sales of HRS in the home market of India were made at prices below the fully absorbed COP, and accordingly, requested that the Department conduct a country-wide sales-below-COP investigation. Based upon the comparison of the adjusted prices from the petition for the foreign like product to its COP, and in accordance with section 773(b)(2)(A)(i) of the Act, we found reasonable grounds to believe or suspect that sales of HRS manufactured in India were made at prices below the COP. As a result, the Department has conducted an investigation to determine whether Ispat and Essar made sales in the home market at prices below their respective COPs during the POI within the meaning of section 773(b) of the Act. We conducted the COP analysis described below.

1.   Calculation of COP. In accordance with section 773(b)(3) of the Act, we calculated a weighted-average COP for each respondent based on the sum of the cost of materials and fabrication for the foreign like product, plus amounts for the home market general and administrative (G & A) expenses and interest expenses. We relied on the COP data submitted by Ispat and Essar in their cost questionnaire responses, except, as noted below, in specific instances where Ispat's submitted costs were not appropriately quantified or valued.

a.   Changes to Ispat's Cost of Production. Based on the information on the record, it appears that Ispat reached commercial levels of production prior to the POI. Therefore, we disallowed the start-up adjustment claimed by Ispat. We adjusted the reported costs to include depreciation expenses and certain raw material costs that were omitted. We recalculated Ispat's G & A expense ratio using its company-wide G & A costs from its fiscal year 2000 audited financial statements. We adjusted Ispat's financial expense ratio to include the net exchange rate difference and loss on cancellation of forward contract per its audited financial statements.

2.   Test of Home Market Sales Prices. On a model-specific basis, we compared the revised COP to the home market prices, less any applicable discounts and rebates, movement charges, selling expenses, commissions, and packing. We then compared the adjusted weighted-average COP to the home market sales of the foreign like product, as required under section 773(b) of the Act, in order to determine whether these sales had been made at prices below the COP within an extended period of time (i.e., a period of one year) in substantial quantities and whether

such prices were sufficient to permit the recovery of all costs within a reasonable period of time.

3.   Results of the COP Test. Pursuant to section 773(b)(2)(C) of the Act, where less than 20 percent of a respondent's sales of a given product were at prices less than the COP, we did not disregard any below-cost sales of that product because we determined that the below-cost sales were not made in "substantial quantities." Where 20 percent or more of a respondent's sales of a given product during the POI were at prices less than the COP, we determined such sales to have been made in "substantial quantities" within an extended period of time in accordance with section 773(b)(2)(B) or the Act. In such cases, because we compared prices to POI average costs, we also determined that such sales were not made at prices that would permit recovery of all costs within a reasonable period of time, in accordance with section 773(b)(2)(D) of the Act. Therefore, we disregarded the below-cost sales.

We found that, for certain models of HRS, more than 20 percent of the home market sales by Ispat and Essar were made within an extended period of time at prices less than the COP. Further, the prices did not provide for the recovery of costs within a reasonable period of time. We therefore disregarded these below-cost sales and used the remaining sales as the basis for determining NV, in accordance with section 773(b)(1) of the Act.

D.   Calculation of NV Based on Home Market Prices

We based home market prices on the packed prices to unaffiliated purchasers in India. We adjusted, where applicable, the starting price for discounts and rebates. We made adjustments for any differences in packing, in accordance with section 773(a)(6)(A) and 773(a)(6)(B)(i) of the Act, and we deducted movement expenses and domestic brokerage and handling, pursuant to section 773(a)(6)(B)(ii) of the Act. In addition, where applicable, we made adjustments for differences in circumstances of sale (COS) pursuant to section 773(a)(6)(C)(iii) of the Act * * * . We also made COS adjustments, where applicable, by deducting direct selling expenses incurred for home market sales (credit expense and warranty) and adding U.S. direct selling expenses. We also made adjustments, pursuant to 19 CFR 351.410(e), for indirect selling expenses incurred on comparison-market or U.S. sales where commissions were granted on sales in one market but not in the other (the commission offset). No other adjustments to NV were claimed or allowed.

E.   Calculation of NV Based on CV [Constructed Value]

Section 773(a)(4) of the Act provides that, where NV cannot be based on comparison-market sales, NV may be based on CV. Accordingly, for those models of HRS for which we could not determine the NV based on comparison-market sales, either because there were no sales of a comparable product or all sales of the comparison products failed the COP test, we based NV on CV.

F.   Level of Trade (LOT)

In accordance with section 773(a)(1)(B) of the Act, to the extent practicable, we determine NV based on sales in the comparison market at the same LOT as the U.S. transaction (in this case EP transactions). The NV LOT is that of the starting-price sales in the comparison market or, when NV is based on CV, that of the sales from which we derive selling, general, and administrative (SG & A) expenses and profit. For EP sales, the U.S. LOT is also the level of the starting-price sale, which is usually from exporter to importer.

To determine whether NV sales are at a different LOT than EP transactions, we examine stages in the marketing process and selling functions along the chain of distribution between the producer and the unaffiliated customer. If the comparison market sales are at a different LOT and the difference affects price comparability, as manifested in a pattern of consistent price differences between the sales on which NV is based and comparison market sales at the LOT of the export transaction, we make a LOT adjustment under section 773(a)(7)(A) of the Act.

In implementing these principles in this investigation, we obtained information from the respondents about the marketing stages involved in the reported U.S. and home market sales, including a description of the selling activities performed by the respondents for each channel of distribution. In identifying LOTs for EP and home market sales, we considered the selling functions reflected in the starting price before any adjustments. In this investigation, neither Ispat nor Essar requested a LOT adjustment [and we made none in light of the facts.]

Currency Conversions

We made currency conversions into U.S. dollars in accordance with section 773A of the Act based on exchange rates in effect on the dates of the U.S. sales, as obtained from the Federal Reserve Bank (the Department's preferred source for exchange rates).

Verification

In accordance with section 782(i) of the Act, we intend to verify all information relied upon in making our final determination.

All Others Rate

Recognizing the impracticality of examining all producers and exporters in all cases, section 735(c)(5)(A) of the Act provides for the use of an "all others" rate, which is applied to non-investigated firms. See SAA at 873. This section states that the all others rate shall generally be an amount equal to the weighted average of the weighted-average dumping margins established for exporters and producers individually investigated, excluding any zero and de minimis margins, and any margins based entirely upon the facts available. Therefore, we have preliminarily assigned to all other exporters of Indian HRS, an "all others" margin that is the weighted average of the margins calculated for Ispat and Essar.

Suspension of Liquidation

In accordance with section 733(d) of the Act, we are directing the U.S. Customs Service (Customs Service) to suspend liquidation of all entries of HRS from India that are entered, or withdrawn from warehouse, for consumption on or after the date of publication of this notice in the Federal Register. We will instruct the Customs Service to require a cash deposit or the posting of a bond equal to the weighted-average amount by which NV exceeds EP, as indicated in the chart below. We will adjust the deposit requirements to account for any export subsidies found in the companion countervailing duty investigation. These suspension-of-liquidation instructions will remain in effect until further notice. The weighted-average dumping margins are as follows:

Manufacturer/exporter	Margin (percent)
Ispat Industries Ltd	39.36
Essar Steel Ltd	34.55
All Others	34.75

Notes and Questions

The following notes and questions relate for the most part to issues considered in the *India HRS* case.

(1) The foregoing decision is a preliminary determination. During the next phase of the investigation, Commerce receives comments from the parties on its preliminary determination and verifies the information submitted by respondents by sending Commerce officials to examine their books and records. It is not unusual for there to be significant changes in the dumping calculation as a result of the comments and verification.

(2) As the foregoing decision makes clear, respondents were required on short notice to submit detailed information on their domestic and export sales and their production costs. While it is not made clear in the parts of the decision that are excerpted, Commerce requires the information to be supplied in specific formats so that it can be easily processed. The information supplied by exporters is made available to petitioners' attorneys under protective orders forbidding disclosure to the petitioners. This enables the attorneys to comment meaningfully on the Commerce decision. One might legitimately ask why would a foreign company supply such detailed and sensitive information? As noted earlier, the answer is that a failure to provide the information would result in a decision by Commerce to use the "information available," which might well be the allegations of the petitioners and which might lead to the imposition of very high duties. See Section 782(d). Annex II to the WTO AD Agreement sets standards for the use of best information available. Certain U.S. practices regarding information available were found to violate WTO rules in United States—Anti–Dumping Measures on Certain Hot–Rolled Steel Products from Japan, WT/DS184/AB/R, adopted by the DSB on August 24, 2001.

(3) *Product Comparisons.* There are subtle distinctions drawn between the goods considered in establishing the export price, the normal value and injury. The basic function of Commerce is to determine whether "a class or kind of foreign merchandise" is being sold in the United States at less than

its fair value. To do so, it calculates the normal value of the "foreign like product," a phrase defined in Section 771(16). The ITC determines whether there has been injury to U.S. "industry," a term defined in Section 771(4) to mean the U.S. producers of a "domestic like product," which is itself defined in Section 771(10). By narrowly defining the class of goods investigated, the likelihood of dumping and injury findings may be increased, but the opportunities for circumvention of a dumping order may be greater. We discuss the problems of circumvention below.

(4) *Fair Value Comparisons.* The traditional method of calculating a dumping margin is somewhat unusual and raises serious fairness questions in the minds of some. Take the following example: In the home market, seven sales are shown to occur, one each at a price of 20, 21, 22, 23, 24, 25, 26. Seven imports into the United States are also made, at the same time, one at each of those prices. Obviously the average in both cases is 23. But this does not mean that there is no dumping. The normal value has typically been calculated as an average, i.e. 23. But *each* shipment to the U.S. has been compared (after a dumping order issues) to that average, so three of the imports (those made at 20, 21 and 22) would be below the average and could be assessed a duty equal to the difference (3, 2 and 1, respectively). Furthermore, if it could be shown that the cost of production in the home market was 22, the sales at 20 and 21 may be omitted in calculating the home market average, which would make the home market average equal to 24, and would result in even more shipments being assessed AD duties.

Some countries urged in the Uruguay Round that the GATT Antidumping Code be amended to require that the export and home market prices be established by the use of average prices over the same time period. In the example given above, this would mean that no dumping would be found, as the average price would be the same in both markets, i.e., 23. Ultimately, a compromise was reached that provided that in AD investigations average-to-average comparisons should be the normal calculation method, unless the authorities find "a pattern of export prices which differ significantly among different purchasers, regions or time periods," which cannot be taken into account appropriately by an average-to-average comparison. WTO AD Agreement, art. 2.4.2. It is uncertain how widely applicable this exception will prove to be in practice. As of 2001, both the U.S. and the EU had been found to apply averaging techniques in violation of this new rule. European Communities—Anti–Dumping Duties on Imports of Cotton–Type Bed–Linen from India, WT/DS141/AB/R, adopted by the DSB on March 12, 2001; United States—Anti–Dumping Measures on Stainless Steel Plate in Coils and Stainless Steel Sheet and Strip from Korea, WT/DS179/R, adopted by the DSB on February 1, 2001. In the U.S., the 1994 Act implements this rule, but permits the use of monthly normal values in the administrative review process in which AD duties are actually determined and collected. Section 777A(d). Note that average-to-average comparisons were used in investigation phase of the *India HRS* case.

Should there be a dumping margin so small that no duties should be imposed? Prior to the Uruguay Round, the U.S. used a 0.5% cutoff, but in the Uruguay Round it was agreed that a margin of less than 2% should be deemed de minimis. WTO AD Agreement, art. 5.8. Sections 733(b)(3), 735(a)(4). If an AD order is issued because of non de minimis margins, would the de minimis rule apply in the annual reviews to set the actual amount of duties collected?

(5) *Export Price.* The calculation of export price is relatively straightforward when sales are made to unrelated parties prior to importation into the U.S., as was the case in *India HRS*. The main adjustment that is made to the invoice price is to eliminate transportation and related "movement" expenses so as to arrive at an ex-factory price. Can you explain why it would have been appropriate, if the appropriate direct connection had been established, to allow a duty-drawback adjustment to the export price in *India HRS*?

When the goods have not been sold to an unrelated party before importation into the U.S., U.S. law provides for the use of a constructed export price. A typical example of such a situation would be a foreign manufacturer that sells goods to a U.S. distribution subsidiary, which imports the products into the United States and then resells them to unrelated parties. If the constructed export price is used to establish the export price, then any U.S. distribution costs (and any additional U.S. manufacturing costs) are factored out of the price charged to the first unrelated party. The rules also provide for an adjustment to normal value to the extent that it includes indirect selling expenses that are comparable to indirect selling expenses that are deducted from the constructed export price because they were incurred in the U.S. This adjustment, known as the constructed export price offset, cannot exceed the amount of indirect selling expenses deducted from the constructed export price. 19 C.F.R. sec. 351.412(f) (2001). What explains the special rules applicable in the constructed export price situation?

(6) *Normal Value.* The calculation of normal value is more complex. In the first instance, Commerce determines whether there are sufficient sales in the home market, defined as at least 5% of sales to the U.S., to serve as a basis for normal value. See Section 773(a). If there are not adequate sales in the home market, then Commerce has a choice of establishing normal value through the use of export prices to third countries or constructed value, which is discussed below. Although the regulations indicate a preference for using third-country sales, constructed value is often used. 19 C.F.R. sec. 351.404(f) (2001). What might explain the preference for using third-country exports instead of constructed value for setting normal value?

(7) *Cost of Production.* As explained in *India HRS*, Commerce may exclude below-cost sales from consideration in calculating normal value in certain circumstances. If the volume of the remaining above-cost sales is inadequate, constructed value is used to set foreign market value. Section 773(b)(1) provides that "sales made at less than the cost of production * * * within an extended period of time in substantial quantities, and * * * not at prices which would permit recovery of all costs within a reasonable period of time" may be disregarded in determining normal value. A number of questions are presented. What is an extended period of time? What are substantial quantities? What is a reasonable period of time? How does Commerce answer these questions in the *India HRS* case? Do you agree with its answers? See WTO AD Agreement, art. 2.2.1 (including the footnotes!).

As noted in the first section of this chapter, economists would expect a profit-maximizing firm to produce at a loss, at least in the short run, if it was recovering its marginal, as opposed to average, costs. Does the Commerce rule reflect that expectation? How should end-of-season sales be treated under Section 773(b)? How should sales of perishable products be treated? What about sales of airplanes that had incurred such massive development costs that those costs will be recovered only after several years of sales?

(8) *Price-to-Price Comparisons*. In order to make the export price and the normal value comparable, certain non-movement adjustments must also be made. The basic rules are laid out in Sections 772(c)-(f) and 773(a)(6)-(7), and, in particular, in specific Commerce regulations on adjustments for quantities,[7] different physical characteristics,[8] and different circumstances of sale.[9] Adjustments for quantity differences are relatively unusual. Adjustments for physical differences are usually based on cost differences. The most common and controversial adjustments are for differences in the circumstances of sale. The regulation provides:[10]

> (b) *In general*. * * * [T]he Secretary will make circumstances of sale adjustments under Section 773(a)(6)(C)(iii) of the Act only for direct selling expenses and assumed expenses.

> (c) *Direct selling expenses*. "*Direct selling expenses*" are expenses, such as commissions, credit expenses, guarantees, and warranties, that result from, and bear a direct relationship to, the particular sale in questions.

> (d) *Assumed expenses*. Assumed expenses are selling expenses that are assumed by the seller on behalf of the buyer, such as advertising expenses.

The way in which Commerce treats advertising and technical services is elaborated in the following excerpt from its Antidumping Manual, ch. 8, pp. 26–30 (1998):

Advertising and Sales Promotion

Most advertising expenses are aimed at the customer of the producer or exporter and as such they are not adjusted for as COS adjustments because they are considered indirect in nature. Advertising and sales promotion expenses can, however, be "assumed" by the producer or exporter on behalf of its customer. If this is the case, a COS adjustment is warranted. The most common types of assumed advertising expenses are consumer advertising costs paid for totally by the producer and cooperative (co-op) consumer advertising which is paid for jointly by the producer and first unrelated purchaser and aimed at customers of the first purchaser.

When considering claims for COS adjustments for assumed media advertising costs, we examine specific examples of the advertisements and the media in which the ads are placed. The advertising must be directed toward the specific product under investigation. The following examples

---

7. 19 CFR sec. 351.409 (2001).

8. 19 CFR sec. 351.411 (2001).

9. 19 CFR sec. 351.410 (2001).

10. Id.

are illustrative of different advertising scenarios that you may encounter and what [Commerce's] position would be on allowing an adjustment: 1) we disallow COS claims for advertising in trade journals when the sales under consideration are directly to an end-user because there is no further sale of the merchandise by the end user; 2) trade journal advertising expenses would be adjusted for as a COS if the sales under consideration were to distributors and the advertisements in the trade journal were aimed at retailers; 3) we make a COS adjustment for consumer advertising expenses when they involve sales made to distributors and/or retailers and the final sales of the merchandise are to consumers. These types of advertisements are usually placed in general circulation magazines, in newspapers, on television, or other broadcast media.

Another type of assumable expense involves sales promotional materials. These materials often take the form of free give-away merchandise supplied by the exporter to be given away to its customers' customers. In order to qualify for a COS adjustment, promotional materials must directly reference the merchandise under consideration. Examples of give-away merchandise would be athletic bags, t-shirts, and key chains. If these types of costs do not qualify as assumable, they would be considered indirect selling expenses.

* * *

Technical Services

Another area of claims for adjustments for differences in COS is technical service expenses. These claims are particularly common in cases where the merchandise under investigation or review is sold to an industrial user. Such claims are usually made for services involving the use of an industrial material in a manufacturing process or the operation of machinery. Where technical services are rendered as part of a sales agreement, all, or some portion of them, may constitute COS expenses. Many claims, however, relate to services provided for purposes of determining new uses for a product in future production. Such services are considered to constitute goodwill or sales promotion and as such the expenses are not considered directly related to the sales under consideration.

Claims for technical services rendered in assisting the customer in solving problems with products purchased are adjusted for as COS to the extent that the variable costs can be segregated from the fixed costs. The allowable variable costs are usually travel expenses and contracted services by unrelated technicians as these expenses would not have been incurred if the sales in question had not been made. Salaries of technicians employed by the exporter usually would not be allowed as a COS adjustment because they are usually fixed costs which are incurred whether or not the sales are made. Therefore, they are usually indirect selling expenses.

(9) *Constructed Value.* If constructed value is used, there have been two noteworthy problems under U.S. law. First, there has been the question of how to allocate research and development and start-up costs. For some

products, these costs may be substantial and whether or not there is dumping found may turn on how they are allocated. If these costs are spread over a short time period, the constructed value of the product (i.e. its normal value) will be much higher. See Section 773(f)(1)(C). Second, prior to the 1994 Act, the U.S. statute required a minimum of 10% to be added for "administrative costs," and 8% for "profits." Particularly as to the latter figure, questions were raised whether the U.S. requirement was consistent with U.S. international obligations under GATT and the Antidumping Code, because often in times of recession, or for certain types of products, profits are not nearly so high as 8%. The current rule is in Section 773(e)(2). See WTO AD Agreement, art. 2.2.2.

(10) *Currency Conversion.* Suppose a French exporter establishes price lists annually and adheres strictly to them. When the prices are set on January 1, the ex-factory price to French customers is 50FF/kg. For U.S. customers, it is a CIF price of $6/kg, where $1/kg represents the cost of shipping and insurance. On January 1, the FF:US$ exchange rate is 10:1. Is the U.S. price a dumping price? On February 1, the rate is 9:1. Is the U.S. price a dumping price? For six months, the rate remains at 9:1. Is there dumping? On September 1, the rate falls to 10:1, but shipping costs have increased $0.25/kg. Is the U.S. price a dumping price? Should it be? See WTO AD Agreement, art. 2.4.1; Section 773A.

(11) *Critical Circumstances.* Suppose you are a foreign exporter bent on dumping. You decide the best approach is to dump a massive amount of goods into the United States within a short time period and then stop for several months. If an investigation is opened, there will be no imports on which duties can be applied. If one is not opened for a year, you plan to do the same thing again. Are you safe from duties? Consider Section 733(e). See also WTO AD Agreement, art. 10.

(12) *Suspension of Liquidation.*[11] AD investigations are opened in respect of a specific product from a specific country. It is not unusual, however, for the same imports from several countries to be investigated simultaneously. Commerce issues a decision in respect of imports from each country investigated, although the ITC may issue one report on injury covering several countries. In its decision, Commerce calculates a specific AD duty rate for each manufacturer or exporter investigated. Subsequent exports by an entity not specifically mentioned in the Commerce decision will be required to deposit estimated duties at the "all others" rate. There are procedures by which a new exporter can obtain a specific rate.

Problems

(1) Firm E in Country X has sold 500,000 pairs of sunglasses to M, a United States importer, at a price of $5.00 per unit. Included in this price are the following: $.40 per unit for extra packaging and handling costs in preparing the sunglasses for a transoceanic voyage; a $15,000 shipment charge for the entire lot (delivery will be in five installments); $.50 per unit

11. "Liquidation" is the process of settling the duty due on an import into the United States. That process is suspended in AD cases because the duty due is not finally determined until completion of the review process described in Section 16.4(A).

to cover the export tax imposed by X. E and M have no particular commercial ties.

Firm E also sells this line of sunglasses in X, at a price of $4.75 a pair. Using only the information here provided, will the Commerce Department find the sunglasses to be sold at less than fair value if a complaint is brought by a United States manufacturer of sunglasses? If so, how much additional duty will be imposed?

(2) Assuming the information in Problem (1), will any of the following factors change your answer?

(a) E has no advertising costs in the United States, but it spends approximately $.12 per unit sold for advertising in X.

(b) Although E offers discount quantity sales to buyers in X, no buyer has ordered more than 500 pairs at one time. All sunglasses sold are produced in the same plant in X, and are stored in the same warehouse before shipment.

(c) M paid in advance for the entire lot, whereas buyers in X always choose to be billed after shipment. The cost of insuring against default and of handling the extra paperwork averages out to $.05 per pair in X.

(d) E offers to refund the purchase price to any consumer in X who is unhappy, for any reason, with the sunglasses. In the past few years, the cost of such refunds (often unreasonably requested) has averaged $.03 on each pair actually sold.

(2) *Nonmarket Economies and Antidumping Rules*

In an economy where the government exercises complete control over price and allocation decisions, it is difficult to apply AD rules. The government control means that the home market price is not a real price in the sense that term is used in market economies. Consequently, an interpretative note to Article VI notes that special difficulties in applying AD rules arise when the allegedly dumped imports come from an economy where all prices are fixed by the state and there is a state monopoly of foreign trade. In such cases, the note states that a strict comparison of prices may not be appropriate.

In practice, the U.S., the EU and others have applied AD duties on products from state-controlled economies on the basis of surrogate market prices and costs. Under a definition added by the 1988 Trade Act, nonmarket economies are defined in Section 771(18) as those that do "not operate on market principles of cost or pricing structures, so that sales of merchandise in such country do not reflect the fair value of the merchandise." The factors to be considered by the ITA in determining nonmarket economy status include (i) the convertability of the currency, (ii) the extent to which wage rates are set by free bargaining, (iii) the extent to which foreign ventures are permitted to operate in the country, (iv) the extent of government ownership of the means of production and (v) the extent of government control over resource allocation. Id. Determinations by the ITA of nonmarket economy status are not appealable.

For nonmarket economies, normal value is to be based on constructed value, where the costs are derived from a market economy country or countries considered to be appropriate by the ITA, or, if such information is inadequate, on the basis of sales prices of comparable merchandise from a market economy country. In each case, the market economy country chosen is to be at a level of development comparable to that of the nonmarket economy country. Section 773(c). For example, under the U.S. statute, the inputs of a product are determined (so many pounds of steel, so many hours of labor) and then the cost of those inputs in a comparable, market-economy country is used to arrive at a minimum appropriate price for the imports from the state-controlled economy. If the actual export price is below that price, AD duties may be applied, assuming injury has been found. An alternative method is to compare the export price of the allegedly dumped product with the price for a comparable product produced in a surrogate country. This is the typical EU approach and is a possible, but not the preferred approach, under the U.S. statute.

Notes and Questions

(1) Would you cooperate with a U.S. AD investigation by supplying price and cost information if you were a producer in a proposed surrogate country? What advantages might result for you? What disadvantages? For example, would you risk an AD proceeding if data you provided showed sales at dumping prices? For whatever reasons, it is not always possible to obtain cooperation.

(2) The U.S. statute specifies that the surrogate country is to be at about the same level of development, which the regulations indicate is normally determined by considering comparative per capita GDP. 19 C.F.R. sec. 351.408(b) (2001). Is there any real reason to believe that prices and costs in the surrogate country accurately reflect what prices and costs would have been in a nonmarket economy if it were a market economy? Given the importance of the choice of the surrogate country—it essentially determines whether dumping will be found—should there be more precise standards for selecting such a country? What standards would you propose? In respect of wages, the ITA has adopted a methodology that does not rely on comparable wages in a single surrogate country.

(3) How should the recent economic reforms in Communist countries be handled? U.S. practices takes account of these reforms in two ways. First, it is possible to establish that a specific industry is sufficiently market-oriented such that the normal rules are applied. To establish this requires a showing that (i) there is virtually no government involvement in setting prices or production quantities; (ii) the industry is characterized by private or collective ownership; and (iii) market-determined prices are paid for all significant inputs. Second, it is possible to establish that an individual firm is sufficiently independent of government control (both de jure and de facto) that it is entitled to a separate rate, as opposed to being subject to the country-wide rate. ITA, Antidumping Manual, ch. 8, pp. 90–92 (1998). For the moment, the ITA continues to treat China and Russia generally as non-market economies.

(C) ANTICIRCUMVENTION MEASURES

In the late 1980's, there was considerable concern in the U.S. and the EU that AD duties were being circumvented and that it was necessary to take action to prevent such circumvention. How might AD duties might be circumvented? First, since the duties are applicable to goods coming from a specific country, it may be possible to change the origin of the goods by shifting production to a third country. Second, since the duties apply to imports of a specific product, it may be possible to change the characteristics of that product so that it is no longer the product specified in the order imposing AD duties. Third, it may be possible to import components of the product (assuming they are not subject to AD duties themselves) and assemble the product in the country imposing the AD duties.

In June 1987, the EU amended its AD regulation to provide that AD duties could be imposed on products assembled in the EU if (i) an AD duty had previously been imposed on similar products when imported, (ii) the products were assembled in substantially increased quantities in the EU by a company related to one subject to such AD duty and (iii) the value of the parts and materials from the country subject to AD duties that were contained in the product assembled in the EU exceeded by 50% the value of all other parts and materials used in the product.[12] Following a complaint by Japan in GATT, this provision was found by a GATT dispute settlement panel to violate GATT Article III.[13] In the view of the panel, the charges imposed by the EU rules were internal taxes subject to Article III:2, not duties under Article II:1(b), because they were imposed on the assembled products, not the imported parts and components, and they were collected when the assembled products were introduced into EU commerce, not at the EU border. Do you agree? Since the EU did not impose such taxes on domestic producers of the like products, the panel concluded that the measures violated Article III:2.

The United States addressed the circumvention issue in the 1988 Trade Act, which added a series of anticircumvention provisions as Section 781 of the 1930 Tariff Act. For example, Section 781, as amended in 1994, allows the ITA to expand the scope of an AD order to cover components of a product subject to the order if those components are imported into the United States for assembly where the U.S. assembly process is minor or insignificant and the value of the components is a significant portion of the total value of the product. In making its decision, the ITA is to consider whether there was an increase in component imports into the United States after the AD order was issued and whether the exporter of the components is related to the assembler. A related provision with similar rules would cover the situation where the components are exported to a third country, assembled and then exported to the United States. These two provisions are designed to

---

12. EC Regulation 2423/88, art. 13 (10)(a), in Eur.Comm.O.J., L 209 (Aug. 2, 1988).

13. EEC—Regulation on Imports of Parts and Components, 37th Supp. BISD 132 (1990)(Panel report adopted May 16, 1990).

prevent circumvention of an AD order by importing disassembled or unfinished merchandise into the United States (or a third country) for assembly in the United States (or that third country). The Act also allows the ITA to expand the scope of an AD order to include (i) later developed, but essentially similar merchandise and (ii) merchandise that has been altered in a minor way.

The 1988 Act established a procedure by which U.S. parties can apply to have a product category created with respect to "short life cycle merchandise" if the merchandise has been subject to at least two antidumping determinations. Short life cycle merchandise is merchandise that is likely to be outmoded within four years. Such merchandise is then subject to shorter investigation deadlines. Tariff Act of 1930, Section 739.

Some of the U.S. anticircumvention provisions are somewhat similar to the EU provision, which was found to violate GATT Article III. However, because the U.S. measures would be applied as duties, at the border, at the time of entry, the reasoning of the GATT panel in the EU case would not seem to apply to the U.S. provisions. Could those provisions be attacked on other grounds? For example, could it be argued that under Article VI and the WTO AD Agreement a new injury investigation in respect of the different product must be conducted before imposing duties? The WTO AD Agreement does not deal with anticircumvention measures because no agreement could be reached on their scope.

(D) INJURY DETERMINATIONS

To impose AD duties under U.S. law, it is necessary that the International Trade Commission (ITC) find that imports of merchandise sold at less than fair value have materially injured, or threatened to materially injure, U.S. industry producing the like product or are materially retarding the establishment of such a U.S. industry. The same issue arises in CVD cases, and we will postpone general discussion of this issue until the next chapter. Here, we will introduce one related issue that arises in AD cases: In a global economy who represents the domestic industry?

This issue is raised by in an interesting case involving typewriters. In 1980, Brother Industries, a Japanese owned company, was found to be dumping portable electric typewriters into the United States, and an antidumping order remained in effect with respect to those products as of 1993. In 1991, Brother Industries (USA) Inc., a U.S. based subsidiary of that Japanese company, brought an antidumping complaint against imports of portable electric typewriters from Singapore (largely made by Smith–Corona, a U.S. owned company). The ITA determined that Brother lacked standing. 56 Fed.Reg. 49880 (1991). Although Brother assembles typewriters in Tennessee, the ITA determined that it was not a producer or manufacturer of typewriters in the United States for purposes of the antidumping law. The key factors in its decision seemed to be (i) the fact that the operation was an assembly operation, albeit a "complex" one, (ii) the low number of domestic parts used, (iii) the small amount of domestic value added and (iv) the lack of non-production activities (e.g., research, development, design, engineering) in the United States. The ITA was careful to note that the value added criteria was not determinative and in other cases it might find that a firm with a similar amount of domestic value added was a U.S. producer.

The ITA decision was reversed by the Court of International Trade in Brother Industries (USA), Inc. v. United States, 801 F.Supp. 751 (CIT 1992). The court noted:

> An antidumping proceeding shall be commenced when an "interested party" files a petition "on behalf of" the domestic industry, and meets the other requirements of the statute. 19 U.S.C.A. sec. 1673a(b)(1). An "interested party" is defined, inter alia, as a "manufacturer, producer, or wholesaler in the United States of a like product." 19 U.S.C.A. sec. 1677(9)(C).

> * * *

> * * * ITA's analysis is not supported by the statute or legislative history. * * * Here, ITA's focus on the situs of design and engineering leads to an unwarranted concern with the intrinsic nature of the product rather than the nature of production in the United States. Because ITA's determination that BIUSA [Brother] is not a manufacturer is not supported by substantial evidence and is not in accordance in law, it cannot stand. Moreover, a fair application of the ITC factors to the facts of record demonstrates that BIUSA is a United States "manufacturer" with a clear stake in the outcome of the antidumping investigation. The investment and employment levels at BIUSA, even as characterized by ITA, are not insignificant. The value-added is also significant, and at least as great as in another case where a firm has been found to be part of the domestic industry.

> Based on the record before the court, and the test selected by ITA, the fact that BIUSA performs design and engineering abroad, or that major parts are imported does not preclude a finding that it is part of the domestic industry. BIUSA's operations at Bartlett can only be described as "manufacturing." Accordingly, ITA's determination is reversed, and the case is remanded for ITA to consider whether BIUSA has filed the petition "on behalf of" the domestic industry, and if so, to proceed with an investigation under the antidumping laws.

Thereafter, the ITA reopened the investigation and concluded in its preliminary determination that Smith–Corona was dumping, with a margin of 16.02%. 58 Fed.Reg. 7537 (1993). On June 22, 1993, the ITA entered into a suspension agreement with Smith–Corona. 58 Fed.Reg. 39786 (1993).

In a related case, the ITA determined that the amount of value added in the United States by Brother was not "small" for purposes of applying the anticircumvention provisions of the antidumping law. 56 Fed.Reg. 46594, 58031 (1991). In that case, Brother, which had been subject to an antidumping order on typewriters from Japan, argued that Smith–Corona was no longer a U.S. producer and lacked standing to request an anticircumvention investigation. The ITA rejected that argument, examining the same factors cited in the prior paragraphs. The two cases highlight, however, how difficult it may become to determine the origin of products and to define "domestic industry" in a global economy. In these circumstances, do AD laws make much sense?

Chapter 17

INJURY ANALYSIS IN DUMPING
AND SUBSIDIES CASES

SECTION 17.1 INTRODUCTION

Before antidumping or countervailing duties may be imposed under WTO law, the importing nation must determine that imports of dumped or subsidized merchandise have caused material injury, or threatened material injury, to the domestic industry producing the like product, or that the imports are materially retarding the establishment of a domestic industry. See GATT Article VI, paragraph 6. This inquiry, conducted in the United States by the International Trade Commission (ITC), is known as the "injury test."

The injury test has long existed under U.S. antidumping law. U.S. countervailing duty law, by contrast, did not contain an injury requirement for many years, an omission that was "grandfathered" into GATT by the Protocol of Provisional Application. With time, an injury test was added to U.S. countervailing duty law for otherwise non-dutiable imports, and then after the Tokyo Round for all imports from Subsidies Code signatories. Under the Uruguay Round Subsidies Agreement, the United States at last extended the injury test to all countervailing duty cases involving a member of the WTO.

Through the years, the requirements of the injury test have been elaborated in both the WTO/GATT system and under U.S. law. Extensive provisions governing both substance and procedure may be found in the WTO Agreement on Implementation of Article VI (dumping) and the WTO Agreement on Subsidies and Countervailing Measures. The provisions in the two agreements relating to injury are virtually identical. The relevant portions of U.S. law, which follows the requirements of the WTO agreements fairly closely, are found in the Tariff Act of 1930, as amended. See Sections 701–705 (countervailing duties); Sections 731–35 (dumping); Section 771 (definitional section applicable to both). Because the injury analysis in dumping and countervailing duty cases is so similar, and because WTO law and U.S. law resemble each other so closely, we will treat them together in this chapter. And because few disputes on injury issues in dumping and subsidies cases have yet made their way through the WTO dispute resolution process, and those that have address fairly narrow issues,[1] our emphasis is on U.S. cases.

The injury investigation in a dumping or countervailing duty case is simpler than the injury analysis in an escape clause proceeding, particularly under U.S. law. Most importantly, there is no requirement that various "causes" of injury be compared to see which among them is most important. Rather, the proceeding simply inquires whether the unfairly traded imports cause or threaten material injury, or retard the establishment of a new industry. Concurrent causes of injury do not preclude countermeasures, save for the case where the other causes are solely responsible for whatever injury has been suffered.

Consequently, the application of the injury test requires only two or sometimes three stages of analysis. First, the relevant domestic industry must be "defined" so that the impact of imports on it can be assessed. Second, under what has sometimes been termed the "bifurcated" or "trends" version of the injury test, the domestic industry must be examined for signs of "material injury" or threat of such injury. If none are present under the bifurcated approach, analysis of causation is unnecessary. If injury or threat is present, however, the question of its cause must be reached as the third stage of analysis. An alternative approach, sometimes termed "unitary," combines these two steps—it begins by identifying the harm caused by unfair imports, and concludes with a judgment whether that harm is "material."

An examination of injury under U.S. law can occur at three different points during a dumping or countervailing duty proceeding. A "preliminary" injury investigation occurs after a case has been filed but before the Commerce Department (ITA) has made a determination whether the alleged unfair trade practice actually exists. In this preliminary investigation, the ITC decides whether there is a "reasonable indication" that the injury test can be satisfied. See Tariff Act of 1930, Sections 703, 733. If the answer is no, the investigation terminates—the idea is to "weed out" some cases early without the need for a full-blown ITA investigation or a complete injury investigation by the ITC. The "reasonable indication" standard is understood to be only a modest hurdle for petitioners.

Following an affirmative preliminary determination, the ITA investigation will proceed to conclusion. If dumping or subsidization is ulti-

---

1. In Thailand—Anti–Dumping Duties on Angles, Shapes and Sections of Iron or Non–Alloy Steel and H–Beams from Poland, WT/DS122/AB/R, adopted by the DSB on April 5, 2001, the Appellate Body held, inter alia, that the factors enumerated in article 3.4 of the Antidumping Agreement *must* be considered during the course of injury analysis by national authorities. See also European Communities—Antidumping Duties on Imports of Cotton–Type Bed Linens from India, WT/DS141/R, panel report adopted by the DSB on March 12, 2001. In Mexico—Antidumping Investigation of High Fructose Corn Syrup from the United States, WT/DS132/R, adopted by the DSB on February 24, 2000, and in the subsequent Recourse to Article 21.5 of the DSU by the United States in that proceeding, WT/DS132/WR (panel report dated June 22, 2001; appeal pending), the panel determined that the logical foundation for Mexico's finding of threatened injury was unsound.

mately determined to exist, the parties return to the ITC for the "final" injury investigation. Here, the injury test is applied more stringently and the petitioners' standard of proof is higher. An affirmative determination at this stage results in the issuance of an antidumping or countervailing duty "order," with duties to be collected by the Customs Service.

An injury analysis may also be required after a final order is issued. Prior to the Uruguay Round, exporters subject to an order could, after a time, petition for a review of the injury finding on grounds of "changed circumstances." The Uruguay Round agreements add a further requirement that antidumping and countervailing duty orders be terminated within five years of the last injury finding unless a new finding is made that they are needed to prevent the recurrence of injury.

Injury investigations under U.S. law are not governed by the Administrative Procedure Act (though some would argue that they should be), and they are typically much less formal and structured than proceedings before many other federal regulatory agencies. Nevertheless, hearings are held, and an opportunity to present briefs and witnesses is afforded to all interested parties.

The materials that follow emphasize the substantive rather than procedural aspects of injury proceedings, and are divided between the industry definition issue and the material injury/causation issues. We omit any further consideration of the "material retardation" variant of injury because reliance on that standard is quite unusual in practice, perhaps because there is no established domestic industry to petition for relief. A rare discussion of that standard may be found in BMT Commodity Corp. v. United States, 667 F.Supp. 880 (CIT 1987).

Notes and Questions

(1) Before proceeding to the details of injury analysis, it is useful to reflect on its function. Why are the ostensibly "unfair" practices of dumping and subsidization only "unfair" if injury results? Take the subsidies case in particular—might it be argued that if the purpose of WTO discipline on subsidies is to discourage governments from distorting the allocation of resources in the global marketplace, countermeasures ought be taken (indeed encouraged) whether or not producers in a particular importing nation are "injured?"

(2) Alternatively, suppose that dumping and subsidies are thought objectionable because of the adjustment costs that must be incurred by import-competing industries, costs that the injury test was conceived to detect. Which approach to injury analysis does this theory support—the bifurcated or the unitary approach?

(3) Recall that the injury test under the escape clause requires "serious injury," understood to be a greater level of injury than "material injury." Why not require "serious injury" here as well?

SECTION 17.2   INDUSTRY DEFINITION

Both WTO and U.S. law define the "industry" similarly as, in most cases, "the producers as a whole of a domestic like product" or those whose output constitutes a "major proportion" of the domestic production of the like products. See, e.g, Tariff Act of 1930, Section 771(4)(A). This last proviso is designed to permit investigations to go forward even when data from a few producers are lacking. The exception to this definition of industry, invoked on occasion, is that the industry may be limited to producers in a particular geographic area. In addition, it is permissible to exclude from the industry domestic producers that are "related" to the exporters under investigation, on the grounds that they may benefit from the unfair trade in a way that masks injury to domestic producers as a whole. Note that the "industry" here differs from that in escape clause proceedings, where the producers of "like or directly competitive products" comprise the "industry."

HIGH CAPACITY PAGERS FROM JAPAN
U.S. Intl. Trade Commn. (1983)[1]
Views of Chairman Eckes and Commissioner Haggart

* * *

Imported and domestically produced pagers are manufactured in a variety of models. The threshold issue in this investigation is whether all high capacity pagers should be considered "like products." A significant difference between pager models is the availability of a liquid crystal display which provides a combination of tone alert and a numerical readout on the display. Based upon a careful analysis of the characteristics and uses of tone-only and display pagers, we conclude that there are distinct differences in both the characteristics and uses of these respective pagers. The differences between these two types of pagers diminish the degree of substitutionality and competition between tone-only and display pagers in the subscriber market. Therefore, we conclude that tone-only and display pagers are not like products.

* * *

In addition to these differing characteristics and uses, the pricing structure of both the RCC [Radio Common Carrier] and subscriber markets indicates that tone-only and display pagers compete only to a limited extent. There are substantial price differences between these two products. RCCs generally pay a higher unit price for display pagers as compared with tone-only pagers. In addition, the subscriber pays a much higher price for the display pager and the paging service on a display pager. Because RCCs and subscribers perceive a substantial difference between the two products, they are willing to pay a premium for display pagers. Thus, the pricing structure in this market indicates that both

1. Inv. No. 731–TA–102 (Final) (Pub.   No. 1410), 5 ITRD 1721.

RCCs and their subscribers recognize that tone-only and display pagers are distinct products with different characteristics which are used to satisfy different needs.

In addition to the foregoing, the domestic industry has been able to provide the Commission with separate data on tone-only and display pagers in terms of production and profitability. This data is maintained as a matter of course by the domestic producer. The fact that separate data on the producer's profits and production are available allows the Commission to make separate assessments of the effect of imports on the production of distinct products. For the foregoing reasons, we conclude that tone-only and display pagers are distinct like products within the meaning of the statute.

Having resolved the "like product" issue, we next address the scope of the domestic industry. In the context of this investigation, the Commission must determine whether Motorola's production of Metrx and Metro–Pageboy model tone-only pagers should be considered part of the domestic industry in light of the fact that these two models are assembled in Malaysia or Korea and incorporate components sourced in the United States and abroad.

The Commission has not previously addressed the issue of what activities or specific attributes qualify a company as a domestic producer of a like product for the purposes of a final antidumping investigation. All production related activity need not occur in the United States for a firm to qualify as a domestic producer of a like product. Exclusion of firms from the domestic industry that import components or undertake some production related activities abroad would preclude relief to firms having sufficient production related activities in the United States. Our factual determination as to whether Motorola's activities with respect to its Metrx and Metro–Pageboy models are sufficient to include these particular models as part of domestic production is based on an analysis of the overall nature of Motorola's production related activities in the United States with respect to these two pager models.

Although Motorola's most obvious production related activity, the assembly and soldering of the circuit boards, occurs in Malaysia or Korea, significant production related activity occurs in the United States both before and after foreign assembly. These activities involve considerable technical experience and capital investment. The value added to Motorola's Metrx and Metro–Pageboy pagers in the United States constitutes a significant percentage of their component value and direct labor costs. Motorola has two facilities in Florida where the company employs a substantial number of workers in research and development and production activities specifically related to the Metrx and Metro–Pageboy pagers. We have concluded that the level of Motorola's production related activity which takes place in the United States with respect to the Metrx and Metro–Pageboy models is sufficient to include these two models as part of domestic production.

In summary, we conclude that tone-only and display pagers are two distinct like products. For the purposes of this investigation, we also conclude that the domestic tone-only pager industry consists of Motorola's domestic tone-only production, including production of its Metrx and Metro–Pageboy model pagers. Furthermore, we conclude that the domestic display pager industry consists of Motorola's display pager production.

* * *

VIEWS OF COMMISSIONER STERN

* * *

Generally, "like product" analysis is founded on the following points. First, "like product" covers more than virtually identical articles and may include substantially similar articles. Next, "likeness" is determined on the basis of both characteristics and uses. The definitions of "like product" and "industry" are factual determinations which involve subjective considerations based on the weight of the evidence.

The balance of factors, such as price, similarity of manufacturing processes, interchangeability in use, and customer perceptions as to competition among products is determined on a case-by-case basis. In examining prior Commission decisions regarding "like product", it emerges that certain factors receive more emphasis in specific types of investigations. In investigations involving chemicals, for example, the Commission has emphasized similarities in chemical formula and fungibility in uses.

In investigations involving "agricultural" products, the Commission has defined "like product" broadly. Thus, in *Fresh Cut Roses From The Netherlands,* 701–TA–21 (Preliminary), USITC Pub. No. 1041 [1 ITRD 5165] (1980), the Commission defined the domestic industry as producers of roses, and did not separately analyze the effect of imports on hybrid tea roses or sweetheart roses, despite a substantial difference in price and other characteristics. Similarly, in *Frozen Potato Products From Canada,* Inv. No. 701–TA–3 (Preliminary), USITC Pub. No. 1035 [1 ITRD 5161] (1980), the Commission defined the "like product" to include french fries, hash-brown potatoes, potato puffs, baked potatoes, and whole, blanched potatoes.

With respect to products manufactured to particular specifications, the Commission generally defines the domestic industry as those producers capable of satisfying the specifications of the particular type of contract. Thus, the Commission has not atomized the "like product" or "domestic industry." In this type of investigation a "like product" analysis focusing on the distinctions present in each contract or specification would result in a distorted view of the industry. An industry would consist only of the bidders on a specific contract because only those bidders could be construed as satisfying the detailed specifications. Thus, the Commission must often focus on the essential characteristics and uses of the article rather than drawing overly fine line distinctions that would render the term "industry" almost unrecognizable.

In contrast to the Commission's analysis in investigations involving agricultural products and production to specifications, the Commission has found several significant distinctions among "industrial" types of products, such as carbon steel products and pipes and tubes. In these investigations, the Commission has found that competition between separate products, and the existence of separate identifiable facilities, manpower, sales force, and/or research and development associated with the manufacture of each product warranted a finding of separate "like products." Also differences in size, shape or composition, together with varying uses and general lack of competition between products indicate the appropriateness of separate "like product" analysis. This type of analysis has resulted in finding several "like products" in an investigation, and has been applied primarily to industrial goods where differences in size or composition are significant marketplace distinctions perceived by an experienced buyer. These differences do not reflect single transaction requirements and therefore do not contradict Commission precedent in investigations of production to specifications.

There is another line of investigations which includes articles such as portable electric typewriters, televisions, and microwave ovens. Manufacturers market these products in a range of models which appeal to different customers. In some instances, the amount of competition among models is unpredictable or immeasurable. In fact, all of the models could be competing for a particular sale. In these investigations the Commission has emphasized similarity of basic uses, prices, sales force and channels of distribution. The Commission has not required fungibility or complete interchangeability as a condition for varying models to be considered "like products." Thus, in *Television Receiving Sets From Japan,* Inv. No. 751–TA–2, USITC Pub. No. 1153 [2 ITRD 5529] (1981), the Commission adopted the definition of domestic industry found in the original antidumping investigation. Throughout the Commission report distinctions between monochrome and color television receivers and distinctions in the size of the receivers were discussed. The Commission, however, did not make like product distinctions among types of television receivers on these grounds and therefore found one "domestic industry." Consideration of this pattern of prior analysis in this investigation supports my finding that there is a *single* domestic industry producing high capacity pagers.

Paging devices are essentially consumer goods which are sold in a wide range of models. Each model differs slightly from other models and is marketed to appeal to a particular segment of the pager market. This situation, for example, is similar to that in the television industry discussed above where various models differ in terms of color capabilities, size and other aspects. These differences are not sufficient to warrant separate like product analysis in an antidumping investigation.

In terms of characteristics and uses, tone-only and tone and display (display) pagers are essentially the same. Both types of pagers are produced from the same components; the same employees manufacture them in the same plants on the same machinery; and the pagers are sold or rented in the same channels of distribution. There is complete operational interchangeability and some overlap in the paging system subscribers. There is a very high degree of substitutability or interchangeability between these products in terms of their essential use.

Display pagers represent an evolving technology. Although they have an additional feature which differs from tone-only pagers, both types of pagers perform the same essential alerting function. The Commission has required more distinct differences in terms of characteristics and uses than exist here to warrant separate like product treatment of this type of good.

[There were only three Commissioners sitting in this investigation. Commissioner Stern found injury to a single domestic industry. Commissioners Eckes and Haggart found injury to the domestic tone-only pager industry, but found no injury or threat to the domestic display pager industry.]

STAINLESS STEEL FLANGES FROM INDIA AND TAIWAN

U.S. Intl. Trade Commn. (1994)[2]
Views of the Commission

* * *

The imported product subject to investigation is stainless steel flanges, both unfinished and finished, from India and Taiwan. Finished flanges are used to connect stainless pipe sections and piping system components (such as pumps, valves, tanks, gauges, etc.) at points in "process" piping systems where conditions require a connect and disconnect capability. Stainless steel flanges are manufactured in several types (blind, lap joint, slipon, socket weld, threaded, and weld neck) and sizes (most commonly ranging from one to 12 inches) for various pressure and temperature applications. Finished flanges are generally machined and drilled from forgings that are hot-forged from American Society for Testing and Materials ("ASTM") A–314 bar and that meet established specifications for annealing and tensile strength. A number of production steps are common to every type of flange from forging to finishing. There are no practical substitutes for forged stainless steel flanges.

In our preliminary determination in these investigations, we defined the like product to be stainless steel flanges, both finished and unfinished. Using the five factors of the semi-finished product analysis, we found that: the processing costs incurred in transforming the forging into a finished flange average less than the cost of producing the forging; forgings and the finished flanges are not interchangeable in use, because

2. Investigation Nos. 731–TA–639 and   640 (Final) (Pub. No. 2724).

of the necessity for further processing; when the hot bar is forged into shape it is dedicated for manufacture as a finished flange; the forging has virtually no independent use other than further processing into a finished flange; the market for the forging is limited to converters who purchase this intermediate product for the express purpose of conducting the finishing process, and thus there is no independent end-or other-use market for forgings; and finally, two of the most essential characteristics of the finished product—their metallurgy and shape which largely determine the resulting mechanical qualities—are present in both the forging and finished flange. Based on the foregoing, in particular that the forging imparts essential characteristics to the finished flange and is dedicated to use as a finished flange, and that there is no independent end-use market for forgings, the Commission determined that there was a single like product, defined as stainless steel flanges, both finished and unfinished.

* * * The additional information obtained in these final investigations is consistent with the data obtained in the preliminary investigations. The existence of common essential characteristics between the forging and the finished flange is further confirmed by the fact that a forging is dedicated to use as the exact same size finished flange. More than 97 percent of forgings are manufactured into finished flanges, confirming the absence of any significant independent uses or markets. Furthermore, the costs of processing the forging into the finished flange may vary, but average less than the cost of producing the forging. Accordingly, we reaffirm our preliminary determination that the like product is stainless steel flanges, both finished and unfinished.

* * *

If a company is a related party under section 771(4)(B), the Commission determines whether "appropriate circumstances" exist for excluding the producer in question from the domestic industry. The rationale for excluding related parties is the concern that the overall industry data may be skewed by inclusion of the related parties who are shielded from any injury that might be caused by the subject imports.

Flow Components' President acknowledged that Flow Components is the importer of record for all Taiwanese forgings that they purchase. Regarding Indian forgings, he indicated that they generally purchase forgings from a trading company which is the importer of record, such as Gulf and Northern Trading Company for Mukand products and Alkay for Akai products. He acknowledged that Flow Components has been the importer of record for purchases from a small Indian producer. Moreover, Flow Components also submitted an importer's questionnaire which reported imports of forgings from both India and Taiwan. Thus, we find that Flow Components is a related party since it has been an importer of record of subject merchandise from Taiwan and from India.

During the period of investigation, Flow Components accounted for a significant share of reported U.S. production of finished flanges. Flow Components' President stated at the conference that it shifted from domestic and other foreign producers to Indian imports of forgings for "two reasons ... availability and pricing," rather than because French and U.S. suppliers could no longer supply the product. Furthermore, there is evidence that Flow Components benefits from the LTFV imports and that inclusion of its financial data would skew the data for the domestic industry. Flow Components was on the verge of bankruptcy when it was acquired in April 1991 by a group of investors who have made changes in its operations, including the shifting of sources of its supply of forgings from the United States and France to India and Taiwan. * * * In view of all of the above, we determine that appropriate circumstances exist to exclude Flow Components as a related party.

Notes and Questions

(1) As indicated earlier, the ITC can base its findings on harm to a regional industry. The key factors are that the regional producers must sell all or almost all of their production in the region, the regional market must not be supplied to any substantial degree by U.S. producers from outside the region and all or almost all of the regional producers must be materially injured. Those requirements are discussed in a series of opinions in which the Court of International Trade found the ITC had erred in its application of the statute. Atlantic Sugar, Ltd. v. United States, 519 F.Supp. 916 (CIT 1981); 553 F.Supp. 1055 (CIT 1982); 573 F.Supp. 1142 (CIT 1983).

(2) Do you understand the logic of focusing on similarity in "characteristics and uses" to define the industry? What about "channels of distribution" and "similarity of manufacturing processes"?

(3) Because the industry is limited to "like products," the ability of "upstream" and "downstream" producers to join the "industry" is quite limited. But the *Flanges* case suggests a caveat—sometimes "finished" and "unfinished" products are combined into one "industry." How far should that be pushed? Should growers of wine grapes be entitled to complain about dumped wine imports? Should hog farmers be allowed to complain about subsidized pork imports? Should pork packers be allowed to argue that imports of subsidized hogs are not injurious to the U.S. "industry" of which they are a part? A GATT panel held in 1986 that the United States could not combine wine producers and grape growers into a single industry without violating the Tokyo Round Subsidies Code. A special statutory provision that did so was repealed by the Uruguay Round implementing legislation.

(4) In general, lower prices caused by "unfair" practices will benefit producers at downstream stages of processing (who buy their inputs at lower prices), and harm producers at upstream stages of processing (because the demand for their products as inputs downstream will diminish). What is the logic of excluding upstream and downstream producers from the injury analysis in most cases? What is the logic behind the factors used by the ITC to decide whether to combine finished and unfinished goods?

SECTION 17.3 MATERIAL INJURY OR THREAT BY REASON OF DUMPED IMPORTS

The definition of "material injury" is set out in Section 771(7) of the Tariff Act of 1930, along with the factors to be considered by the ITC in its causation analysis. These provisions should be reviewed at this time.

(A) A CONTROVERSY IN INTERPRETATION

NEW STEEL RAILS FROM CANADA

U.S. Intl. Trade Commn. (1989)[1]

On the basis of the record developed in the subject investigations, the Commission determines [by a 3–3 vote] * * * that an industry in the United States is threatened with material injury by reason of imports from Canada of new steel rails. * * *

VIEWS OF COMMISSIONERS ECKES, ROHR AND NEWQUIST

* * * We find, based on the record, that the domestic industry is currently experiencing material injury, but that the record does not support a finding that the articles subject to this investigation are a cause of material injury at the present time. However, having considered the factors set forth in the statute relevant to threat of material injury, we conclude that both the subsidized and the LTFV imports pose a real and imminent threat of material injury to the domestic industry.

* * *

Condition of the Domestic Industry

To assess the condition of the domestic industry, the Commission is directed to examine, among other factors, apparent consumption of the like product, domestic shipments and production, capacity, capacity utilization, inventories, employment, and financial performance. Examination of these factors reveals that the condition of the new steel rails industry, despite improvement in some areas, remains weak.

Data received through questionnaires indicate that from 1986 to 1987 apparent domestic consumption of new steel rails declined 8.4 percent. In 1988, domestic consumption increased, but remained below the 1986 level. During interim (January–March) 1989, apparent domestic consumption increased over interim 1988.

Both domestic production and shipments of U.S. rail mills also declined from 198 to 1987, and increased in 1988 to a level above the 1986 level. In interim 1989, production and shipments both increased further over the corresponding period in 1988.

---

1. Investigations Nos. 701–TA–297 (Fi-   nal); 731–TA–422 (Final) (Pub. No. 2217).

Capacity utilization increased from 1986 to 1987, and increased further in 1988. The rapid increase in capacity utilization reported in 1988 is attributable principally to the 1987 closure of Wheeling–Pittsburgh's plant in Monessen, PA.

Domestic rail mills generally produce rails to order and consequently maintain few or no inventories.

The number of U.S. production employees assigned to the production of new steel rails declined from 1986 to 1987, and, despite some improvement in 1988, remained below the level reported in 1986. Wages paid to production workers of new steel rails declined from 1986 to 1987. In 1988, wages showed some improvement, but still remained lower than the wages paid in 1986.

The poor condition of the industry is most evident in its financial performance. During the entire period of this investigation, U.S. producers of new steel rails sustained significant gross losses, net income losses, and operating losses. Moreover, the domestic industry suffered a negative return on assets throughout the period of investigation and negative cash flow until 1988. Capital expenditures in rail operations declined from 1986 to 1988, but recovered somewhat in the interim period; research and development expenditures followed a similar trend.

The domestic new steel rails industry, while showing improvement in some areas, overall has continued to perform negatively. Therefore, we find that the domestic industry is presently suffering material injury, but not by reason of the subject imports. We conclude, however, that the present condition of the domestic industry makes it extremely vulnerable to threatened material injury by reason of such imports.

No Material Injury by Reason of the Unfair Imports

We find that, although the domestic industry is experiencing material injury, we cannot conclude that, at the present time, the imports subject to these investigations are a cause of this injury. All imports from Canada come from two producers. One of these producers has been excluded from the countervailing duty investigation, while both are subject to the dumping investigation. Only those imports subject to investigation were considered in making our determinations in these investigations.

We note that there were substantial increases in imports, in both volume and value terms, from both producers. The same is true of their respective market shares; however, particularly in the countervailing duty investigation, the relevant market penetration was not currently significant.

The pricing information of record does not support a finding of underselling. We note that in most instances in which a Canadian producer was awarded an entire contract, it was the only responsible bidder. In most of the other instances in which Canadian product was offered in competition with domestic product, the Canadian product was initially offered at a price between the high and low domestic bids.

Finally, we note that in several instances sales of Canadian rail were made in "trial lot" sizes, purchased by railroads seeking to qualify the Canadian producer for future sales. The sales themselves were in small lots and the sale price was of little importance. Such sales do not themselves cause injury, but are a factor in our consideration of whether Canadian imports pose a threat of material injury to the domestic industry.

[In accordance with the list of factors in Section 771(F) of the Trade Act of 1930, the Commissioners proceeded to find threat of injury by reason of imports from Canada.]

Additional Views of Commissioner Eckes

In making this determination, I have employed an analytical method familiar to long-time observers of this Commission. It is the dual-requirement, or bifurcated, method for injury analysis.

When this approach is applied faithfully, an affirmative injury determination can result only if two conditions are satisfied. First, the domestic industry producing the like or directly competitive product must be materially injured. Second, less-than-fair value imports must be a cause ["by reason of"] of that material injury; in other words, the decisionmaker must find a causal nexus between unfairly traded imports and injury. And, if the evidence of record fails to satisfy both of these threshold conditions, a Commissioner, using this method, shall make a negative determination.[2]

* * *

[O]ver the last twenty-one years, twenty-two Commissioners regularly utilized bifurcated analysis and made separate findings of injury and causation. Except for Commissioner Cass, no member of the Commission since 1970, who served more than a few weeks, failed to employ this pattern of analysis. * * *

[I]t is clear from the historical record that by 1972 the Commission was routinely applying a bifurcated injury and causation analysis, and that practice has continued to recent times. Indeed, in twenty-nine of fifty-seven cases decided between May 1972 and December 1975, the bifurcated criteria were explicitly stated in the Commission's majority opinion. In the others the Commission apparently applied the two-factor test without bothering to repeat explicitly the standard. Certainly, no alternative approach was articulated. In no case did the Commission apparently adopt a unitary approach.

* * *

[T]he notion that the bifurcated approach "is not consistent with . . . Title VII" [of the Tariff Act] is erroneous. As noted earlier, both the

---

2. [original note 1] A domestic industry may also be threatened with material injury or materially retarded. At this point neither of these seems central to the debate between unitarian and traditional analyses.

Court of International Trade and the Court of Appeals for the Federal Circuit have decided that the twin-test approach is lawful.

DISSENTING VIEWS OF VICE CHAIRMAN RONALD A. CASS

I dissent from the Commission's affirmative determination in these investigations.

* * *

In these investigations, as in many others, I believe that Commissioners have reached disparate conclusions respecting the appropriate disposition of the Petition because we have very different understandings of the meaning of U.S. trade law and of this country's obligations under the General Agreement on Tariffs and Trade ("GATT"). As I will explain in detail below, I believe that our mandate under U.S. law is to determine whether dumping or subsidization of imports has caused material injury to domestic industry. At first blush, this may seem to be an uncontroversial point of view. Nevertheless, a number of cases decided by the Commission over the past few years make it quite apparent that certain of my colleagues have a radically different understanding of the task that the Commission is to perform. In my view, these Commissioners have misinterpreted the law in important respects, and are, as a consequence, contributing to an overall understanding of U.S. trade law that is contrary to Congressional intent as embodied in that law and contrary to our international obligations under the GATT. My fundamental differences with these Commissioners are outlined below.

* * *

A. Effects of Unfair Trade Practices or Effects of Imports?

First, certain of my colleagues have expressed the view that it is not the Commission's job to determine whether unfair trade practices, such as dumping or subsidization, have materially injured the domestic industry. Rather, according to these Commissioners, the Commission's task is to ascertain whether the imports that were the subject of the Commerce Department's investigation—whether or not fairly traded—caused material injury. In other words, in this view, the Commission need not make any effort to assess the effects of the unfair trade practices themselves.

Such an interpretation of our trade law is, on its face, wholly inconsistent with the GATT. The parties to the GATT have undertaken to impose antidumping duties only when it is demonstrated that "dumped imports, are through the effects of dumping, causing injury". Agreement on Implementation of Article VI of the General Agreement on Tariffs and Trade, art. 3, para. 4 (emphasis added). Similarly, in cases where subsidization is at issue, the GATT provides that countervailing duties may be imposed only where "the effect of the * * * subsidization is such as to cause or threaten material injury to an established domestic industry, or is such as to retard materially the establishment of a domestic industry". Article VI of the GATT. As other nations implementing these provisions (including Canada) have recognized, there is no doubt that these undertakings require an analysis of the effects of the unfair trade practice(s) at issue and not of imports whether or not dumped or subsidized.

An interpretation of our trade law that dispenses with any effort to assess the effects of unfair trade practices on the domestic industry is no less inconsistent with U.S. law than it is inconsistent with the GATT. The antidumping and countervailing duty laws are intended to implement and be consistent with the GATT and the GATT antidumping code. See S. Rep. No. 249, 96th Cong., 1st Sess. 57, 87 (1979); H.R. Rep. No. 317, 96th Cong., 1st Sess. 49 (1979). Of course, in any instance where GATT and Title VII of the Tariff Act of 1930 diverge, it is the U.S. law that controls our decisions. In general, however, Title VII is to be construed as being consistent with GATT, for the intention of Congress to alter such international agreements to which the United States is a party "is not to be lightly attributed to Congress". And there is no basis to suppose that Congress intended that Title VII would have the GATT-inconsistent meaning that certain of my colleagues have ascribed to it.

* * *

The difference in approaches, thus, is not between looking for effects of imports and looking for effects of unfair trade practices without regard to the role played by imports. Rather, the difference is between two approaches that look at imports. One examines the way unfairly traded imports affect the U.S. industry, in contrast to the effects that would be felt if the unfair practice did not exist. The other approach examines the effects of imports, regardless of the degree to which they are unfairly traded. On this latter view, the effect of a .05% subsidy to imported widgets is not distinguishable from that of a 50% subsidy. The critical fact for this view is the total number of widgets imported, whether the subsidy affected that number by a trivial or a massive amount. It is this view that Congress disapproved in stressing the inquiry into effects, not of imports, but of unfairly traded imports.

* * *

B. *Minimal Impact of Imports as a Predicate*
for an Injury Finding?

Those Commissioners who believe that the Commission must examine the effects of imports, rather than the effects of dumping or subsidization, also appear to believe that "even a slight contribution" to material injury from the imports subject to investigation is a sufficient basis for an affirmative determination. In other words, if the condition of the industry is such that it is deemed "materially injured" by these Commissioners, the causation requirement is considered met as long as imports subject to investigation made a "slight contribution" to that condition—even if that "contribution" was made by fairly traded imports subject to investigation. Applied literally, this standard would require an affirmative determination if the domestic industry lost any sale to the subject imports, irrespective of whether that sale was lost to imports that were fairly traded. The inconsistency between this standard and the GATT requirement that antidumping or countervailing duties be imposed only when the effects of dumping or subsidization have caused material injury to a domestic industry is so patent as to obviate the need for further discussion of that issue.

* * *

Several opinions by our reviewing courts contain dicta suggesting that this language may stand for the proposition for which it has been cited by certain of my colleagues—that is, that an affirmative determination is mandated whenever dumped or subsidized imports make a minimal contribution to adverse conditions experienced by the domestic industry. The following quote from the decision of the Court of International Trade in British Steel Corp. v. United States is representative:

> The statute's causation prerequisite to an affirmative injury determination is satisfied even if the subsidized imports contribute, even minimally, to the conditions of the domestic industry, and the Commission is precluded from weighing the causes of injury. 593 F.Supp. 405, 413 (CIT 1984).

The first point that must be emphasized about this language is that it does not quite say what it is cited as declaring. The court does not say that any harm from imports, however trivial, satisfies the causation standard of Title VII, much less that only harm from imports, subsidized or not, meets that standard. What the court does say is that this standard may be met even if the overall condition of the industry is much more affected by other factors. Neither the magnitude of the subsidized imports' contribution to the overall industry conditions nor the size of that contribution relative to other effects is dispositive under Title VII. The court's actual words, thus, merely restate the statutory directive that the Commission determine if the domestic industry is materially injured by the dumped or subsidized imports. Given that material injury is defined as "harm which is not inconsequential, immaterial or unimportant", it surely is possible that imports could cause such harm and still have only slight effect—in both absolute and relative terms—on overall industry condition. Read carefully, the court has not re-written the law to allow any contribution of imports to an industry's declining fortunes to be the basis for an affirmative decision without regard for whether the subsidized imports themselves cause (or imminently threaten) material injury.

* * *

C. Can Material Injury Be Defined in a Vacuum?

The third important respect in which my view of the law is fundamentally different from that of certain of my colleagues concerns the meaning of the term "material injury". In these investigations, as in a number of other investigations over the past several years, certain of my colleagues divide the question posed by Title VII into two independent inquiries. This bifurcated approach asks first whether the domestic industry's financial health is poor. In some investigations, this may be assessed in relation to the financial performance of other industries in the United States, although the Commission has not, to my knowledge, ever gathered, much less carefully evaluated, information on other industries with which systematically to compare the particular domestic industry before us. I can find no such evidence in the record of these investigations. In other investigations, this first inquiry refers not to the absolute state of an industry's financial health but to that health relative to some earlier period. The question, in other words, is whether the industry has suffered some adversity over the period examined in our proceeding. If the industry's health is deemed to be poor or declining, the adherents to this approach conclude that "material injury" exists. In such cases, they then attempt to ascertain whether unfairly traded imports contributed to that "injury." Where the industry is deemed to be in good health, the bifurcated approach does not address the effect of imports on the domestic industry.

By contrast, I believe that Title VII plainly contemplates a unitary approach to the analysis of causation of material injury. Such a unitary approach asks only the question that is put to us by the statute: "Has a domestic industry been materially injured by reason of dumped or subsidized imports?"

* * *

1. The Text and Structure of the Statute

First, the text and structure of our trade laws strongly suggest that Congress intended that a unitary approach be used in analyzing the question of causation of material injury in Title VII cases. The simplest and most important argument is that the text of the statute cannot be made consistent with the threshold "health" test so long as the text is read in accordance with basic precepts of the English language. The statute instructs the Commission to determine whether "an industry in the United States is materially injured, or is threatened with material injury, or the establishment of an industry in the United States is materially retarded, by reason of imports" determined by the Department of Commerce to have been sold at less than fair value or subsidized. The statute sets out clearly numerous factors that are to guide the Commission in determining what effects less than fair value ("LTFV") or subsidized imports had on the domestic industry, but it does not attempt to describe separately the factors that are relevant to "injury" and the factors that are relevant to "causation." This is significant because it suggests that Congress did not intend for the Commission to conduct independent inquiries into "injury" and "causation."

The textual argument for a unitary approach is particularly strong if one credits statutory draftsmen with basic command of the English language. The statute instructs the Commission to determine whether "an industry in the United States is materially injured, or is threatened with material injury, or the establishment of an industry in the United States is materially retarded, by reason of" imports determined by the Department of Commerce to have been sold at less than fair value or subsidized. In order to read this statutory instruction as mandating a bifurcated analysis, one would have to interpret "injury" to mean "poor health" (rather than "harm from some given action") and treat the phrase "by reason of" the relevant class of LTFV or subsidized imports as though it were introducing a concept separate from injury. The instruction, however, is a single sentence asking us to determine if there was material injury by reason of the subject imports, not two sentences asking for disjunctive determinations.

* * *

2. Legislative History

The bifurcated approach is also fundamentally at odds with the legislative history of Title VII. In 1967, when Congress was considering changes in the international obligations of the United States that might conflict with U.S. antidumping law, the Senate Finance Committee issued a report that explicitly stated:

> An industry which is prospering can be injured by dumped imports just as surely as one which is foundering although the same degree of dumping would have relatively different impacts depending upon the economic health of the industry. S. Rep. No. 1835, 90th Cong., 2d Sess. pt. 2, at 11, reprinted in 1968 U.S. Code Cong. & Admin. News 4548–49.

Subsequently, in revising the antidumping law under the Trade Agreements Act of 1979, the Senate reaffirmed its commitment to this approach. As I have stated elsewhere, these expressions of Congressional intent clearly indicate that Congress did not intend that Title VII relief be denied to an industry that is improving relative to some other period or is "healthy" (by whatever measure) compared to other domestic industries. Such an interpretation of the law is flatly inconsistent with the bifurcated approach. Plainly, if we may not deny relief to a domestic industry solely because the industry is "healthy," it is inappropriate for us to employ a standard that not only requires negative determinations where the threshold requirement of "ill health" is not met, but also, given the virtually non-existent causal requirement followed by at least some of the Commissioners who use a bifurcated analysis, makes the "health" of the industry the one critical factor in affirmative determinations.

* * *

D. Summing Up: When Is Relief Appropriate?

* * * [S]ome or all of the Commissioners who voted in the affirmative in these investigations believe that an affirmative injury determination is appropriate whenever a domestic industry is, in their view,

unhealthy in some sense, and it can be argued that imports from the country whose goods are subject to investigation, whether the particular imports were fairly traded or not, made some contribution, however minimal, to the industry's condition. Where threatened injury is in issue, rather than past injury, presumably their analytical structure remains constant while the time frame for its application changes. Accordingly, their view would be that a threatened change in the domestic industry's condition that will make the industry unhealthy, to which imports from the country whose goods are under investigation, whether fairly traded or not, threaten to contribute, in however modest amount, suffices as a basis for imposition of antidumping or countervailing duties under Title VII. Thus, for example, in this view, antidumping or countervailing duties might be seen as called for in certain sectors of the domestic economy whenever it is feared that the economy is heading into a recession. This is not a reasonable interpretation of the statutory requirement that relief be granted only when it is shown that the domestic industry is materially injured by reason of imports that have been determined to be dumped or subsidized, or is clearly threatened with imminent material injury by reason of such imports. This approach even more certainly is not a reasonable interpretation of the GATT requirement that there be evidence that the effects of dumping or subsidization, as relevant, have materially injured the domestic industry.

Notes and Questions

(1) Based on the discussion above, which approach is more likely to lead to an affirmative determination, other things being equal—the bifurcated or the unitary approach?

(2) Take a look at the Uruguay Round Agreements regarding dumping and subsidies—is there a tension between the "bifurcated" approach and WTO/GATT law? Between the interpretation of the causation requirement that Commissioner Cass criticizes (minimal impact of dumped imports) and WTO/GATT law?

(3) Commissioner Cass's opinion addresses another issue that has been controversial through the years—whether the ITC looks to the effects of the unfair imports, or the unfair trade practice. Previously, some Commissioners who answered that question in the affirmative employed a technique termed "margins analysis." They would compare the "margin" or magnitude of dumping or subsidization calculated by the ITA to the price difference between imported and domestic goods, and then decide whether the unfair trade practice was large enough to cause injury. Thus, for example, suppose that the "fair value" of imported goods is 10% higher than their actual price. The imports undersell domestic goods, however, by an average of 15%. "Margins analysis" would then conclude that dumping was not the cause of any injury on the grounds that the elimination of dumping would still leave the imports with a price advantage. Sound?

(4) A closely related issue for many years was whether the ITC should consider the magnitude of the dumping or subsidies margin in its analysis. The argument for doing so was straightforward—the greater the degree of

dumping or subsidization, the more harm it is likely to cause. But resistance was based on the language of the statute, which refers to injury "by reason of [dumped or subsidized] imports," not "by reason of" dumping or subsidization. The Uruguay Round Antidumping Agreement addressed this issue obliquely by requiring that the margin of dumping be considered (see art. 3.4); the new Subsidies Agreement does not. The Uruguay Round implementing legislation accordingly provides that, in dumping cases, the ITC "shall" evaluate the "magnitude of the margin of dumping." Is a requirement that the margin be "considered" equivalent to requiring that "dumping" be established as the cause of injury, as opposed to the "dumped imports?"

(B) INJURY ANALYSIS IN PRACTICE

CERTAIN ALL–TERRAIN VEHICLES FROM JAPAN
U.S. Int'l Trade Commission (1989)[3]

VIEWS OF THE COMMISSION

We unanimously determine that a domestic industry in the United States is not materially injured or threatened with material injury by reason of imports of all-terrain vehicles (ATVs), assembled or unassembled, from Japan that are sold at less than fair value (LTFV).

* * *

Condition of the domestic industry

In the preliminary determination, the Commission found that the indicia of the industry's condition were generally positive, based on data through the end of 1987. The data gathered in this final investigation confirm this finding.

* * *

In light of the improvement in a number of industry indicators over the period of investigation, it is questionable whether the industry is presently suffering material injury. Even assuming the domestic industry is presently suffering material injury, we base our negative determination on the lack of a causal nexus between the condition of the industry and any harm being suffered by it, and to the lack of any indication of a real and imminent threat of material injury to that industry.

No material injury by reason of LTFV imports

In considering whether the domestic industry is materially injured by reason of LTFV imports, the Commission is required to consider the volume of the imports, the effect of such imports on prices, and the impact of such imports on the domestic industry. We do not weigh causes of material injury, and the imports need not be a principal, a substantial, or a significant cause of material injury. However, we are to consider

3. Investigation No. 731–TA–388 (Final)   (Pub. No. 2163).

information that indicates that harm is caused by factors other than the LTFV imports, such as a contraction in demand, or changes in patterns of consumption or restrictive practices of and competition between the foreign and domestic producers.

* * *

After considering the record of this investigation, we find an insufficient causal link between the condition of the industry and the LTFV imports. The quantity of imports declined steadily and significantly between 1985 and 1988. The value of import shipments declined over this same period.

Import market share also steadily declined from 1985 to 1988. While the volume and market share of the imports remains substantial, the petitioner has conceded that the adverse effects of the imports were not felt until sometime in 1987, despite the fact that the volume and share of the market held by the imports were higher in 1985 and 1986. Further, we find the fact the domestic industry has gained market share over the period of investigation at the expense of the LTFV imports to be significant, particularly in light of the pronounced contraction in demand for the product. Domestic market share has steadily increased in terms of quantity and value from 1985 through 1988.

We also find no adverse price effects by the LTFV imports. As we noted in the preliminary investigation, because different models of ATVs are not fungible commodities, due to significantly different features among models, price comparisons between models are not very illuminating. We find no evidence that the LTFV imports have depressed prices, because both import and domestic prices have generally risen. The price data we obtained have generally been adjusted for rebates, discounts, holdbacks, preparation/assembly allowances and any freight absorption to ensure that increased costs for such items, not normally reflected in list prices, were properly considered in evaluating price trends. Prices have thus increased even taking into account sales incentive expenditures. * * *

We also find no evidence that the LTFV imports have prevented price increases, to any significant degree, that would otherwise have occurred. The financial data for the industry suggest that while prices have generally increased over the period of investigation, they have not risen sufficiently to offset increased costs during the latter part of the period of investigation. However, we find that the imports were not responsible to any significant degree for the failure of prices to increase still further. Rather, any difficulties in increasing prices still further is attributable to the significantly declining demand for the product. In sum, the fact that the domestic industry has been able to raise prices and increase its market share in this dramatically shrinking market is significant.

Our contacts with purchasers in the course of our investigation into alleged lost sales, and with dealers to whom Polaris alleged either stopped selling the Polaris ATV or who had declined to become a Polaris dealer, confirm the lack of a causal nexus between the imports and condition of the industry. Commission staff was able to contact and have meaningful discussions with 27 of the 34 dealers named by Polaris. Of the 27 dealers contacted, only one indicated that the imported ATVs were sold at lower prices than the domestic ATVs. One other dealer thought the Japanese were selling at lower prices but could not recall any specifics and acknowledged that even if the prices for the imported ATVs and Polaris' ATVs were the same, that purchasers would prefer the Japanese product. All the other dealers indicated other reasons for purchasing Japanese ATVs instead of the domestic product, for declining to become a Polaris dealer, or for getting out of the ATV business entirely. Those reasons included lack of demand due to the safety concerns regarding the ATVs or concerns about carrying liability insurance, quality problems with the Polaris ATVs and problems with Polaris' service and sales support, disagreements with Polaris' requirements for purchasing ATVs (such as minimum order requirements), the offering of only one engine-size by Polaris and brand-name loyalty to existing suppliers other than Polaris.

Our consideration of the impact of the imports also takes into account that at least some of the problems of the domestic industry must be attributed not to the imports, but to the domestic industry's excess and significant expansion of capacity on the erroneous assumption that domestic consumption was not going to decline as it did.

Notes and Questions

(1) The *All Terrain Vehicles* case mentions a number of factors that Commissioners have traditionally considered important to an analysis of causation—trends in the volume and market share of imports, trends in prices, evidence (or lack thereof) of price underselling, and evidence (or lack thereof) of lost sales. How useful is each factor?

(2) It has long been settled that when an investigation covers several producers from a single country, those producers may be aggregated or "cumulated" in the analysis of whether the unfair imports cause injury—a separate analysis for each producer is not required. Many cases involve allegations against producers in a number of countries, however, and the question arises whether "cumulation" is also permissible across countries. A provision to authorize such cumulation was added to U.S. law in 1984, though the ITC had cumulated on its own authority previously. See Section 771(7)(G) of the Tariff Act of 1930. The permissibility of cumulation under WTO/GATT law was resolved by the Uruguay Round. Both the dumping and subsidies agreements permit cumulation as long as the extent of the unfair practice is not "de minimis" and "a cumulative assessment of the effects of the imports is appropriate in light of the conditions of competition between imported products and the conditions of competition between the imported products and the like domestic product." See Agreement on Dumping, art. 3.3; Agreement on Subsidies, art. 15.3. The result of cumulation, of course, is that producers in a nation with a small market share, and perhaps declining exports to the United States, may be found to be a cause of material injury

because they have been aggregated with larger or more successful exporters from other nations. Is this desirable?

FRESH CUT ROSES FROM COLOMBIA AND ECUADOR

U.S. Intl. Trade Commn. 1995[4]

[W]e determine that an industry in the United States is neither materially injured nor threatened with material injury by reason of imports of fresh cut roses from Colombia and Ecuador that are sold in the United States at less than fair value (LTFV).

* * *

[W]e reaffirm our preliminary determination that there is a single like product in these investigations consisting of all fresh cut roses regardless of variety or size. Consequently, we determine that the domestic industry consists of all producers of fresh cut roses.

* * *

Because only a reasonable overlap of competition is required, we cumulatively assess the volume and price effects of all subject imports in determining whether there is material injury by reason of those imports.

IV. NO MATERIAL INJURY BY REASON OF LTFV IMPORTS

* * * For the reasons discussed below, we determine that the domestic industry producing fresh cut roses is not materially injured by reason of LTFV imports from Colombia and Ecuador.

A. *The Volume of Subject Imports*

The volume of imports from Colombia and Ecuador on a cumulated basis increased by quantity from 380.4 million stems in 1991 to 438.2 million stems in 1992 to 534.8 million stems in 1993, and was 413.2 million stems in interim 1993 compared with 467.2 million stems interim 1994. In value terms, subject imports increased from $92.6 million in 1991 to $94.4 million in 1992 to $109.2 million in 1993. In interim 1994, subject imports were valued at $101.6 million compared with $86.3 million in interim 1993. The volume of U.S. shipments of cumulated subject imports followed similar trends, increasing in absolute terms throughout the period of investigation.

Market share of cumulated subject imports increased by quantity throughout the period of investigation from 46.1 percent in 1991 to 56.0 percent in 1993; the market share of cumulated subject imports was 60.6 percent in interim 1994 compared with 57.0 percent in interim 1993. By value, the market share of cumulated subject imports increased from 39.8 percent in 1991 to 46.6 percent in 1993, and was 52.1 percent in interim 1994 compared with 47.6 percent in interim 1993. As noted above, the data for apparent U.S. consumption based on Commission questionnaire data is derived from a smaller base of domestic producers

---

4. Inv. No. 731–TA–684–85 (Final).

than data obtained from USDA. Based on apparent consumption derived from USDA data, the market share of cumulated subject imports was lower, increasing from 37.7 percent in 1991 to 41.6 percent in 1992 to 47.5 percent in 1993 by quantity.

Despite the absolute volume and market share of cumulated subject imports, and the increases in their volume and market share that occurred during the period, we do not find the volume of subject imports to be significant for several reasons. First, while absolute volume of cumulated subject imports increased by 40.6 percent from 1991 to 1993, and by 13.1 percent between interim periods, the rate of increase in their market share did not rise commensurately, increasing by 9.9 percentage points from 1991 to 1993 and by 3.6 percentage points between interim periods. This is due to the 15.6 increase in overall apparent U.S. consumption by quantity between 1991 and 1993 and the 6.3 percent increase between interim periods. This fact suggests that the subject imports were sold into important new markets and did not significantly displace domestic fresh cut roses in their existing markets.

Second, the fact that subject imports served largely to satisfy increases in demand in the mass merchandiser market further supports the conclusion that the volume of subject imports is not significant. Importers of roses from Colombia and Ecuador aggressively targeted and developed the mass merchandiser market over the period of investigation. With few exceptions, U.S. growers do not appear to have aggressively targeted this market, but rather focused primarily on their traditional retail customer base. Moreover, domestic producers reportedly would not be able to provide consistently the large quantities of roses that mass merchandisers require. Because there is substantial evidence that the mass merchandiser market is the fastest growing segment of the market, and there is no evidence that the retail florist segment is growing, we believe that the mass merchandiser market accounted for most of the growth in U.S. consumption over the period of investigation and a large proportion of subject imports served this market.

In addition, U.S. growers are unable to satisfy demand during times of peak demand, especially during the Valentine's Day season, which accounts for the largest volume of rose sales for any given period. During this period of high demand, U.S. growers in many instances can only supply partial allocations of red roses to purchasers. In addition, growers will many times force purchasers to purchase other types of flowers (e.g., non-red roses) in order to obtain the sought-after red roses. For purchasers, availability of supply is an important factor in purchasing considerations. Also, due to the limits on their ability to increase production in the short term, U.S. growers cannot sufficiently increase their rose production to meet Valentine's Day demand. Therefore, fresh cut roses have been imported to meet domestic demand both for the mass merchandiser segment of the market throughout the year, as well as other segments (e.g., retail florist segment) during periods of peak demand.

Moreover, the limited substitutability of domestic roses and subject imports, as discussed in the next section, diminishes the volume impact of the subject imports. Non-price factors have a significant impact on purchasers' decisions.

For these reasons, we find that the volumes of subject imports are not significant.

B. The Effect of Subject Imports on Domestic Prices

In evaluating the effect of LTFV imports on prices, the Commission considers whether there has been significant price underselling of imports and whether the imports depress prices to a significant degree or prevent price increases that otherwise would have occurred, to a significant degree.

A number of factors are relevant to our determination of the price effect of subject imports on domestic producers' prices including the limited degree of substitutability between the domestic and subject roses, the nature of demand for roses, and the availability of supply.

The more substitutable products are, the more likely that potential purchasers will make their relative purchasing decisions based upon price differences between the products. Conversely, where there is a high degree of product differentiation, products are less substitutable, and price is less likely to be a determining factor in purchasing decisions. Several non-price factors reduce the substitutability between domestic roses and roses from Colombia and Ecuador. As noted previously, domestic producers and producers of roses in Colombia and Ecuador grow different varieties of roses. In general, long, thick stems, large blooms, and vibrant colors are characteristics of Colombian and Ecuadorean roses that distinguish them from domestic roses. Freshness and longevity are favored characteristics of domestic roses.

We find that price plays a subordinate role to other factors such as product quality, variety, and the seasonality of demand. Most purchasers reported that domestic roses were inferior in quality to subject imports. For purchasers, product quality—which includes physical attributes such as stem length and thickness, bloom size, color, freshness, and durability (vase-life)—was more important than price. Purchasers designated bloom size and availability of particular quantities and types of roses as the two most important factors they consider when making purchases. The Commission contacted specific purchasers named in the domestic industry's lost sales allegations. Many of these purchasers confirmed that subject imports were purchased in lieu of domestic roses for non-price reasons, such as product quality and availability.

In many instances, despite the availability of lower-priced roses, sales of more expensive rose varieties increased. This further confirms that price plays a subordinate role to non-price factors such as product quality. For example, sales of the Kardinal rose, a premium quality and relatively expensive domestic rose variety, increased at a faster rate than lower-priced domestic rose varieties such as sweetheart and Cara Mia roses. The product comparisons also show that large quantities of the premium imported Madame del Bard rose (the highest rated imported rose) were sold even when they were priced higher than the domestic Kardinal rose (the highest rated domestic rose) in the same periods. In other instances, the domestic Kardinal rose oversold the Madame del Bard rose.

Because prices of roses sold on a spot basis tend to fluctuate widely, often changing several times per day, the usefulness of the pricing comparisons in these investigations is limited. In addition, certain comparisons were based on sales of significantly different quantities, which could have affected the relative prices. Due to these factors, as well as the limited substitutability of the domestic and imported products, we find that the pricing comparisons have less probative value.

Nevertheless, a consideration of the price comparisons in these investigations showed mixed underselling and overselling by the subject imports with no consistent trend across channels of distribution (e.g., sales to wholesalers versus sales to mass merchandisers) or by type of sale (e.g., spot sales versus standing order sales). For example, in most comparisons, the Madame del Bard roses from Colombia and Ecuador oversold the domestic Royalty on standing order sales to wholesalers and spot sales to mass merchandisers, but undersold the Royalty in spot sales to wholesalers. For non-red roses, on an aggregate basis, there was also mixed underselling and overselling by subject imports showing no consistent pattern. We find the low degree of substitutability and the relative importance of non-price factors discussed above diminishes the significance of any underselling.

We find little or no evidence of price depression. The pricing data we collected show that, based on quarterly f.o.b. prices, the prices for Colombian, Ecuadorean and U.S. fresh cut roses fluctuated over the period of investigation. Prices for red roses generally peaked in the first quarter of each year of the investigation, falling to lower levels during the remaining quarters and reaching their nadir in the third quarter. Prices of non-red roses also demonstrated some seasonal fluctuation, although not as dramatic. Taking into account seasonal fluctuations, prices of domestic fresh cut red roses were generally steady, decreasing only slightly during the period of investigation, despite the fact that prices for subject imports of red roses fluctuated downward. Moreover, annual unit values for red roses were relatively stable during the period of investigation. There were no consistent trends for non-red roses, which supports our conclusion that there is limited substitutability between subject imports and the domestic like product. Even if price trends are similar, however, this would not necessarily warrant a conclusion that any lower-priced Colombian and Ecuadorean fresh cut roses depressed prices of domestic fresh cut roses. Rather, we find that seasonal demand shifts are driving pricing patterns.

We also do not find that subject imports suppressed domestic fresh cut rose prices to a significant degree. Petitioners argued that they were unable to raise prices sufficiently to cover costs, but we do not find that domestic growers could have raised prices sufficiently to cover their costs even in the absence of LTFV imports from Colombia and Ecuador. Most purchasers stated that the current price of Colombian and Ecuadorean roses would have to be more than ten percent higher to cause them to shift to purchases of domestic roses. Indeed, a significant number of purchasers stated that price was not really a factor at all in their purchasing decisions, which further supports the finding of limited substitutability between subject imports and the domestic like product and minimizes the possibility of any significant adverse price effects from the subject imports. In addition, most importers stated that despite antidumping duties, their purchases of subject imports would remain unchanged. This reflects the significant influence of non-price factors in purchasing decisions and confirms our conclusion that there is limited substitutability between domestic roses and subject imports.

Given the importance of non-price factors and the lack of correlation between the prices of domestic and subject roses, we do not find that subject imports have depressed or suppressed domestic rose prices to a significant degree.

C.   The Impact of Subject Imports on the Domestic Industry

We conclude that subject imports did not have an adverse impact on the domestic industry sufficient to warrant an affirmative determination. Many U.S. producers reported that they were facing difficulties due to increased production costs and reduced volumes of rose sales, and an inability to increase rose prices. We determine, however, that any failure by the domestic industry to raise prices sufficiently, or increase their rose production to cover their costs was not due to LTFV imports to any significant degree. Although cumulated subject imports increased in volume and market share, we find that these increases, and the level of market share, have not adversely impacted the domestic industry. The growth in volume of subject imports served largely to supplement demand during peak seasons. In addition, subject imports satisfied increases in U.S. demand in the expanding mass merchandiser market, a segment of the market that domestic growers have failed to supply to any significant degree.

Further, as discussed in the previous section, purchasers tend to base their rose purchasing decisions not on price but on a variety of non-price factors, and they find subject imports and roses sold by the domestic industry are differentiated. We find that the low substitutability between imports and domestic products, as well as the inability of the domestic industry to increase production in the short term in response to any price increase, indicates that subject imports have not had an adverse impact on the domestic industry. The COMPAS (Commercial Policy Analysis System) output further supports the conclusion that domestic prices, shipment volumes, and overall revenues would not have been significantly different from their 1993 levels in the absence of unfairly traded fresh cut roses from Colombia and Ecuador. This, together with the mixed evidence of underselling and the tendency of pricing trends to track seasonal fluctuation in demand, support the conclusion that the imports had no significant impact.

Accordingly, we conclude that the domestic industry is not materially injured by reason of LTFV imports of fresh cut roses from Colombia and Ecuador.

Notes and Questions

(1) What is the ITC's response to the observation that the volume and market share of imports has risen rapidly during the period of investigation. Are you persuaded that it negates an inference of injury? What of the fact that domestic growers have difficulty meeting periods of peak demand, and imports fill the gap—does it follow that imports do not cause injury?

(2) The reference at the end of the excerpt to COMPAS (Commercial Policy Analysis System) pertains to a simulation model that is commonly used by staff economists of the ITC in dumping and countervailing duty investigations. The inputs into the simulation include baseline information on price and output, and estimates of such factors as: the elasticity of demand for domestic and imported goods; the cross-elasticity of demand (degree of substitutability) between imported and domestic goods; the elasticity of supply of domestic production, the imports under investigation, and "non-subject" imports; and the margins of dumping or subsidization. The model then estimates the impact on domestic prices and output that would result from a cessation of dumping or subsidization, or from a withdrawal of the unfair imports from the market altogether. As the *Roses* case indicates, Commissioners often pay some attention to the results of these simulations, but rarely rely on them as the primary basis for their determination. For further discussion of these more explicitly "economic" approaches to injury analysis, see Richard Boltuck, Assessing the Effects on the Domestic Industry of Price Dumping, *in* Policy Implications of Antidumping Measures 99 (P.M. Tharakan ed., 1991); Michael Knoll, An Economic Approach to the Determination of Injury Under United States Antidumping and Countervailing Duty Law, 22 N.Y.U.J.Intl.L. & Pol. 37 (1989). A survey of five "approaches" to causation analysis at the ITC may be found in Seth Kaplan, Injury and Causation in USITC Antidumping Determinations: Five Recent Approaches, *in* Policy Implications of Antidumping Measures, supra. A critical discussion of ITC practice is that of Ronald Cass & Warren Schwartz, Causality, Coherence and Transparency in the Implementation of International Trade Laws, *in* Fair Exchange: Reforming Trade Remedy Laws (Michael Trebilcock & Robert York eds., 1990). The argument that "injury" should not include a loss of monopoly profit is put forward in Diane Wood, "Unfair" Trade Injury: A Competition–Based Approach, 41 Stan.L.Rev. 1153 (1989).

(3) The two remaining excerpts in this chapter emphasize considerations that are central to the "economic" approach to injury analysis.

GERALD METALS, INC. v. UNITED STATES

United States Courts of Appeals, Federal Circuit, 1997.
132 F.3d 716.

[A] plurality of three [ITC] commissioners found material injury to the domestic industry by reason of LTFV imports of pure magnesium from Russia, Ukraine, and China; the remaining three commissioners dissented from this determination. Because the commissioners were evenly divided on the question of material injury by reason of the pure magnesium imports, the views of the plurality finding material injury constitute the determination of the Commission, pursuant to 19 U.S.C. sec. 1677(11) (1994).

* * *

Much of the record features information about imports from Russia. Specifically, the record shows, in the words of Vice Chairman Nuzum, that "a sizeable portion of the imports from Russia were fairly-traded. These imports undersold domestic product almost as frequently as did LTFV imports." Similarly the record shows, in the words of Commissioner Crawford, that "dumped Russian imports and fairly-traded Russian imports are very close, if not perfect, substitutes for each other."

All pure magnesium from Russia originates with one of two producers—Avisma Titanium–Magnesium Works (Avisma) and Solikamsk Magnesium Works (SMW). Although trading companies can import Russian pure magnesium from only these two sources, Commerce assigned zero percent dumping margins to some companies, such as Gerald Metals, while assigning margins of 100.25% to other companies. Commerce assigned to all trading companies importing pure magnesium from Ukraine margins greater than zero, ranging from 36.05% to 104.27%. Commerce assigned a margin of 108.26% to all Chinese imports.

Gerald Metals imported both fairly-traded Russian pure magnesium and LTFV Ukrainian pure magnesium. Gerald Metals reasons that because fairly-traded Russian imports are substitutes for LTFV Russian imports, domestic purchasers of magnesium products could fill their demand without resort to LTFV imports. Thus, Gerald Metals argues, the LTFV goods did not cause the injury to domestic industry. Instead, the injury was the result of market forces other than unfair trading.

The Court of International Trade found substantial evidence to support the Commission's determination. * * *

* * *

Applying an analytical framework outlined in Title 19, the Commission determines whether LTFV imports materially injure a domestic industry. Section 1677(7)(A) defines "material injury" as a "harm which is not inconsequential, immaterial, or unimportant." When determining whether imports have caused material injury to a domestic industry, the Commission evaluates:

(I) the volume of imports of the merchandise that is the subject of the investigation,

(II) the effect of imports of that merchandise on prices in the United States for domestic like products, and

(III) the impact of imports of such merchandise on domestic producers of domestic like products, but only in the context of production operations within the United States....

Additionally, the Commission "may consider such other economic factors as are relevant to the determination."

However, a showing that economic harm to domestic industry occurred when LTFV imports are also on the market is not enough to show that the imports caused a material injury. See United States Steel Group v. United States, 96 F.3d 1352, 1358 (Fed.Cir.1996) ("To claim that the temporal link between these events proves that they are causally related is ... fallacy...."). An affirmative injury determination requires both (1) present material injury and (2) a finding that the material injury is "by reason of" the subject imports. Hence, the anti-dumping statute mandates a showing of causal—not merely temporal—connection between the LTFV goods and the material injury.

Because this appeal hinges on whether the subject imports caused the injury, this court reviews the record evidence to determine whether substantial evidence supports the Commission's determination that the domestic industry was injured by reason of the subject imports. Substantial evidence is " 'such relevant evidence as a reasonable mind might accept as adequate to support a conclusion.' " * * *

The central dispute in this case is the Commission's asserted failure to incorporate the undisputed facts about fairly-traded Russian imports into its analysis of the harm caused by reason of the cumulated LTFV imports. Although the record contained surveys of purchaser comparisons of domestic product to the subject imports, there is no similar evidence of product differentiation, non-price differences, or differences in terms and conditions between the two classes of Russian imports—fairly traded and LTFV.

Indeed, only two producers were responsible for all Russian imports. The primary difference in the price and treatment of Russian pure magnesium depended on which trading company imported the product. Pricing by different trading companies, which had dumping margins of either zero percent or 100.25%, determined whether the magnesium arrived as fairly-traded or LTFV. Therefore, only one reasonable conclusion can be drawn from the record: other than differences in the trading company, the Russian imports—both fairly-traded and LTFV—were perfect substitutes for each other, if not the exact same product.

Similarly, Russian and Ukrainian pure magnesium products compete with one another. The Commission noted that the parties to the investigation did not dispute that LTFV imports from Russia and Ukraine competed with one another. Although there was some evidence of product quality differences between these imports, the Commission nonetheless concluded that its supposition was confirmed by other purchasers who stated that they did not differentiate between Russian or Ukrainian magnesium when dealing with the Commonwealth of Independent States (the association of former Soviet Union republics). Thus, the record supports the inference that Russian imports, either fairly-traded or LTFV, are substitutes for LTFV Ukrainian imports.

* * *

These aspects of the record point to a gap in the causal nexus between the LTFV Ukrainian imports and material harm to domestic industry. The Court of International Trade acknowledged this causation problem, but, without citing adequate record support, dismissed this evidence.

First, the Court of International Trade found no evidence supporting Gerald Metals' claim that fairly-traded Russian imports would have replaced all or the greater part of the subject imports. The court stated that Gerald Metals had premised this argument on the false assumption that producers would switch to different importers trading at fair value in the same way that domestic consumers switch to different trading companies when buying pure magnesium. According to the court, domestic consumers use non-price factors to select a trading partner.

A more reasonable view of the record, however, contradicts these conclusions. At the beginning of the period of investigation, the cumulated LTFV imports had a greater market share than the Russian fairly-traded imports; however, by the end of the period, the market share of the fairly-traded Russian imports was greater than that of the LTFV imports. Comparing the quantities purchased by domestic consumers during the entire period reveals that the sales of Russian LTFV product just slightly exceeded that of the fairly-traded Russian product. In fact, the quantity of all Russian pure magnesium sales—including both fairly-traded and LTFV—was three times the combined quantity of sales of LTFV imports from Ukraine and China.

The Court of International Trade apparently failed to evaluate this data in conjunction with the fact that all Russian magnesium originated from only two producers. As previously indicated, the importer, not the producer, set the price and determined whether Russian magnesium was fairly-traded or LTFV. The domestic consumption and market penetration data reveal that Russian producers sold to fairly-trading importers almost as often as to unfairly trading importers and that domestic purchasers acquired Russian imports from both types of importers in roughly similar amounts.

Indeed, this evidence demonstrates that, contrary to the Court of International Trade's analysis, domestic purchasers were not repelled from the LTFV imports as compared to fairly-traded imports because of non-price factors. This inference is underscored by the fact that the same importer, Gerald Metals, sold fairly-traded Russian product as well as

LTFV Ukrainian product to domestic purchasers. Without further explanation, this court cannot adequately review the Court of International Trade's dismissal of the prospect that fairly-traded goods would have replaced LTFV goods.

The Court of International Trade also reasoned that the Commission's injury determination did not rest upon the purported shift of all domestic purchasers of LTFV magnesium to domestic product. In fact, the domestic industry framed its material injury case not in terms of lost sales but in terms of the inability of domestic producers to raise prices without suffering lost sales volume.

After the suspension of LTFV imports of pure magnesium from Canada in 1991–92, the domestic industry apparently expected to raise prices for its pure magnesium. At this time, imports—both LTFV and fairly-traded—entered the United States due in part to liquidation of stockpiles in the former Soviet Union. These imports apparently disrupted the expectation of higher prices for domestic products. The enhanced availability on the world market of magnesium from the former Soviet Union is one of the relevant economic factors influencing both the finding of injury and causation.

Determining the accurate causation of a disrupted market expectation, however, requires careful economic evidence and analysis. The anti-dumping statute requires that the Commission consider all relevant economic factors "within the context of the business cycle and conditions of competition that are distinctive to the affected industry." Generally, a sudden increase in world supply in the face of a relatively stable demand results in lower prices. While the statute protects domestic magnesium producers from injury caused by LTFV imports, its scope of protection does not reach so far as to support artificially inflated prices when fairly-traded imports are underselling the domestic product and LTFV imports are readily convertible to fairly-traded product by merely changing importers.

The Court of International Trade erred by applying an incorrect legal test for the amount of contribution to material harm by LTFV goods necessary to satisfy the "by reason of" standard. The court stated that "even though fairly-priced imports may have been another cause of injury, the Commission has a statutory obligation not to weigh causes," and "thus ... correctly did not compare the impact of subject imports to the impact of other factors, like the fairly-traded imports." Thus, the court followed the reasoning that any contribution constitutes sufficient causation to satisfy the "by reason of" test.

To the contrary, the statute requires the injury to occur "by reason of" the LTFV imports. This language does not suggest that an importer of LTFV goods can escape countervailing duties by finding some tangential or minor cause unrelated to the LTFV goods that contributed to the harmful effects on domestic market prices. By the same token, this language does not suggest that the Government satisfies its burden of proof by showing that the LTFV goods themselves contributed only minimally or tangentially to the material harm . . .

Accordingly, this court concludes that the Court of International Trade failed to consider properly the presence of fairly-traded Russian imports in affirming the Commission's determination of material injury by reason of the LTFV goods.

Notes and Questions

(1) On remand, the ITC determined that imports of pure magnesium at less than fair value had not caused or threatened material injury, and the Court of International Trade affirmed.

(2) Even if Russian imports traded at fair value are perfectly substitutable with dumped Ukrainian imports, does it follow that dumped imports can cause no material harm? What more must be shown before that conclusion can be reached?

CERTAIN STEEL WIRE ROD FROM CANADA, GERMANY, TRINADAD & TOBAGO AND VENEZUELA

U.S. International Trade Commission 1997[5]

Dissenting Views of Commissioner Crawford

On the basis of information obtained in these investigations, I determine that the industry in the United States producing steel wire rod is materially injured by reason of imports of steel wire rod from Canada and Venezuela that the Department of Commerce has found to be subsidized. * * *

The statute calls upon us to determine whether the domestic industry is materially injured by reason of the unfairly traded imports. This case illustrates important analytical differences between my interpretation of the statute and that of my colleagues, regarding both injury and causation.

We differ regarding injury. Injury is a relative concept, not an absolute. We must in each case ask whether the industry is injured relative to what. That is, we must have a baseline, or a point of comparison, against which to measure the condition of the industry as it is factually described in the evidentiary record. The so-called "trends" analysis implicitly adopts as a baseline some unspecifed point in the past when the industry was "healthy" or "normal." Injury is then determined by comparing the industry's current condition with its past "normal" or "healthy" state, whenever it occurred, but generally within the period of investigation. If the industry is not performing as well as it was at the previous point in time selected for comparison, it is found to be injured; if it is performing as well as or better than it was at the baseline point, it is found not to be injured. In my view, this analysis is

---

5. Inv. Nos. 701–TA–368–371 (Final).

inadequate for several reasons. It lacks transparency. It arbitrarily selects a time period to define the industry's profile. It uses as a point of comparison a historical period in time largely different from the time period the Department of Commerce has reported that subsidies or dumping took place. Perhaps most important, it carries an assumption that any industry that is doing well cannot simultaneously be injured under the statute.

This case presents evidence of an industry doing well. However, in my view "doing well" is not necessarily inconsistent with being injured. * * * The measure of injury is not whether the industry is doing well, but whether it would have been doing even better had the imports not been unfairly trade. * * *

* * *

I. ANALYTICAL FRAMEWORK

* * * The statute directs that we determine whether the domestic industry is "materially injured by reason of" the unfairly traded imports. * * * To do this, as noted above, I compare the current condition of the industry to the industry conditions that would have existed without the subsidies and the dumping, that is, had subject imports all been fairly traded. I then determine whether the change in conditions constitutes material injury. Both the Court of International Trade and the United States Court of Appeals for the Federal Circuit have held that the "statutory language fits very well" with my mode of analysis, expressly holding that my mode of analysis comports with the statutory requirements for reaching a determination of material injury by reason of the subject imports. [See United States Steel Group v. United States, 96 F.3d 1352, 1361 (Fed.Cir.1996), aff'g 873 F.Supp. 673, 694–695 (CIT 1994).]

In my analysis of material injury, I evaluate the effects of the unfairly traded imports on domestic prices, domestic sales, and domestic revenues. To evaluate the effects of the unfairly traded imports on domestic prices, I compare domestic prices that existed when the imports were unfairly traded with what domestic prices would have been if the imports had been traded fairly. Similarly, to evaluate the effects of the unfairly traded imports on the quantity of domestic sales, I compare the level of domestic sales that existed when imports were unfairly traded with what domestic sales would have been if the imports had been traded fairly. The combined price and quantity effects translate into an overall domestic revenue impact. Understanding the impact on the domestic industry's prices, sales and overall revenues is critical to determining the state of the industry, because the impact on other industry indicators (e.g., employment, wages, etc.) is derived from the impact on the domestic industry's prices, sales, and revenues.

I then determine whether the price, sales and revenue effects of the unfairly traded imports, either separately or together, demonstrate that the domestic industry would have been materially better off if the imports had been traded fairly. If so, the domestic industry is materially injured by reason of the unfairly traded imports.

For the reasons discussed below, I determine that the domestic industry producing steel wire rod is materially injured by reason of subsidized imports of steel wire rod from Canada and Venezuela.

II. Conditions of Competition

To understand how an industry is affected by unfair imports, we must examine the conditions of competition in the domestic market. The conditions of competition constitute the commercial environment in which the domestic industry competes with unfair imports, and thus form the foundation for a realistic assessment of the effects of the unfairly traded imports. This environment includes demand conditions, substitutability among and between products from different sources, and supply conditions in the market.

A. Demand Conditions

An analysis of demand conditions tells us what options are available to purchasers, and how they are likely to respond to changes in market conditions, for example an increase in the general level of prices in the market. Purchasers generally seek to avoid price increases, but their ability to do so varies with conditions in the market. The willingness of purchasers to pay a higher price will depend on the importance of the product to them (e.g., how large a cost factor), whether they have options that allow them to avoid the price increase, for example by switching to alternative products, or whether they can exercise buying power to negotiate a lower price. An analysis of these demand-side factors tells us whether demand for the product is elastic or inelastic, that is, whether purchasers will reduce the quantity of their purchases if the price of the product increases. For the reasons discussed below, I find that the overall elasticity of demand for steel wire rod is relatively low.

Importance of the Product and Cost Factor. Key factors that measure the willingness of purchasers to pay higher prices are the importance of the product to purchasers and the significance of its cost. In the case of products that are incorporated into other products (e.g., a component), the importance will depend on its cost relative to the total cost of the product in which it is used. When the price of the component is a small portion of the total cost of the product in which it is used, changes in the price of the component are less likely to affect its purchase.

Record evidence shows that steel wire rod is used as a component for a host of products and that the cost component of steel wire rod in most of the end uses is moderate. This moderate cost share suggests a lower elasticity of demand for steel wire rod.

Alternative Products. Another important factor in determining whether purchasers would be willing to pay higher prices is the availability of viable alternative products. Often purchasers can avoid a price increase by switching to alternative products. If such an option exists, it can impose discipline on producer efforts to increase prices.

Steel wire rod is an intermediate product used in the production of wire and wire products. The record in these investigations indicates there are few, if any, practical substitutes for steel wire rod used in wire making. This suggests an inelastic demand for steel wire rod.

Based on the moderate cost share of steel wire in downstream products and in particular the limited availability of alternative products, I find that overall the demand for steel wire rod is inelastic. That is, purchasers will not reduce significantly the amount of steel wire rod they buy in response to a general increase in the price of steel wire rod.

B. Substitutability

Simply put, substitutability measures the similarity or dissimilarity of imported versus domestic products from the purchaser's perspective. Substitutability depends upon 1) the extent of product differentiation, measured by product attributes such as physical characteristics, suitability for intended use, design, convenience or difficulty of usage, quality, etc.; 2) differences in other non-price considerations such as reliability of delivery, technical support, and lead times; and 3) differences in terms and conditions of sale. Products are close substitutes if their product attributes, other non-price considerations and terms and conditions of sale are similar.

While price is nearly always important in purchasing decisions, non-price factors that differentiate products determine the value that purchasers receive for the price they pay. If products are close substitutes, their value to purchasers is similar, and thus purchasers will respond more readily to relative price changes. On the other hand, if products are not close substitutes, relative price changes are less important and are therefore less likely to induce purchasers to switch from one source to another.

Because demand elasticity for steel wire rod is inelastic, overall purchases will not decline significantly if the overall prices of steel wire rod increase. However, purchasers can avoid price increases from one source by seeking other sources of steel wire rod. In addition to any changes in overall demand for steel wire rod, the demand for steel wire rod from different sources will decrease or increase depending on their relative prices and their substitutability. If steel wire rod from different sources is substitutable, purchasers are more likely to shift their demand from one source when the products from that source (i.e., subject imports) experience a price increase. The magnitude of this shift in demand is determined by the degree of substitutability among the sources.

Purchasers have three potential sources of steel wire rod: domestically produced steel wire rod, subject imports, and nonsubject imports. Purchasers are more or less likely to switch from one source to another depending on the similarity, or substitutability, between and among them. I have evaluated the substitutability among steel wire rod from different sources as follows.

Based on the evidence in the record, I find that subject imports and domestic steel wire rod are good substitutes for each other. I further find that subject imports and nonsubject imports are at least moderate substitutes for each other. Thus, a shift in demand away from subject imports likely would increase demand for both nonsubject imports and domestic steel wire rod.

Purchasers noted that Canadian steel wire rod and domestic steel wire rod were equally available, had comparable delivery times, could be purchased with similar discounts, and were of the same consistent quality. A majority of purchasers reported that Venezuelan steel wire rod and domestic product had comparable delivery times, were available at similar discounts, were packaged in the same manner, and had comparable product consistency and product range. Most producers, importers and purchasers reported that German subject imports and domestic steel wire rod were used to produce the same downstream products. Most purchasers reported German subject imports to be of comparable quality, have the same product range, were offered at similar discounts and were served with comparable technical support as domestic steel wire rod. Similarly, producers, importers and purchasers generally agree that subject imports from Trinidad & Tobago and domestic steel wire rod generally can be used in the same end uses. The majority of purchasers reported that subject imports from Trinidad & Tobago were comparable as to delivery terms, discounts provided, packaging, and product quality, range and consistency. Overall a majority of purchasers reported that domestic steel wire rod and subject imports are comparable in the majority of the bases for comparison and are good substitutes for each other.

For these reasons, I find that subject imports and domestic steel wire rod are good substitutes for each other. I further find that nonsubject imports are at least moderate substitutes for domestic steel wire rod and subject imports. Therefore, all else being equal, it is likely that purchasers would have switched from purchases of subject imports to purchases of both nonsubject imports and domestic steel wire rod had the subject imports been fairly traded.

C. Supply Conditions

Supply conditions in the market are a third condition of competition. Supply conditions determine how producers would respond to an increase in demand for their product, and also affect whether producers are able to institute price increases and make them stick. Supply conditions include producers' capacity utilization, their ability to increase their capacity readily, the availability of inventories, the availability of products for export markets that can be diverted to the domestic market, production alternatives, and the level of competition in the market. For the reasons discussed below, I find that the elasticity of supply of steel wire rod is low.

Capacity Utilization and Capacity. Unused capacity can exercise discipline on prices, if there is a competitive market, as no individual producer could easily make a price increase stick. Any attempt at a price increase by any one producer would be beaten back by its competitors who have the available capacity and are willing to sell more at a lower price. In 1996, a 10.2 percent of the domestic industry's capacity to produce steel wire rod was not used and, thus only this limited amount of capacity was available to increase production. Other evidence in the record indicates that this apparent available capacity may be overstated. The domestic industry acknowledged that it did not have the capacity to serve the demand for steel wire rod in the domestic market. Several purchasers reported instances when U.S. producers could not fill orders for steel wire rod and placed the purchasers on allocation. The inability of the domestic industry to supply the domestic steel wire purchasers with adequate supply was a point emphasized by the Respondents during the investigations. Thus, the domestic industry had little, if any, actual unused capacity available to supply the demand for subject imports.

Inventories and Exports. As noted above in the Commission's opinion at Section II, the domestic industry maintained insignificant inventories throughout the period of investigation. In addition, the domestic industry's exports are insignificant, accounting for approximately 1 percent of shipments in 1996. Thus, the domestic industry did not have available inventories or exports that could have filled the demand for subject imports.

Level of Competition. The level of competition in the domestic market has a critical effect on producer responses to demand increases. A competitive market is one with a number of suppliers in which no one producer has the power to influence price significantly. There are 17 domestic producers of steel wire rod in the U.S. market, and thus there is significant competition within the domestic industry. Nonsubject imports also have been a presence in this market, accounting for 10.7 percent of consumption during 1996. Consequently, I find that there is a significant level of competition in the U.S. market for steel wire rod.

Notwithstanding the level of competition in the domestic market, I find that the elasticity of supply is low based on the domestic industry's limited ability to increase supply from existing unused capacity, inventories and exports.

III.   MATERIAL INJURY BY REASON OF SUBSIDIZED IMPORTS OF STEEL WIRE ROD FROM CANADA AND VENEZUELA

The statute requires us to consider the volume of unfairly traded imports, their effect on domestic prices, and their impact on the domestic industry. I consider each requirement in turn.

A.   *Volume of Unfairly Traded Imports*

Unfairly traded imports of steel wire rod from Canada, Venezuela, Trinidad & Tobago, and Germany increased from 943,697 short tons in 1995 to 1,312,952 short tons in 1996. The value of subject imports was $354,893,000 in 1995, and $449,927,000 in 1996. By quantity, subject imports held a market share of 12.6 percent in 1995, and 17.6 percent in

1996. Their market share by value was 13 percent in 1995, and 17.3 percent in 1996. While it is clear that the larger the volume of unfairly traded imports, the larger the effect they will have on the domestic industry, whether the volume is significant cannot be determined in a vacuum, but must be evaluated in the context of its price effects and impact. Based on the market share of unfairly traded imports and the conditions of competition in the domestic market, I find that the volume of subject imports is significant in light of its price effects and impact.

B. Effect of Unfairly Traded Imports on Domestic Prices

To determine the effect of unfairly traded imports on domestic prices, I examine whether the domestic industry could have increased its prices if the subject imports had been fairly traded. As discussed, both demand and supply conditions in the steel wire rod market are relevant. Examining demand conditions helps us understand whether purchasers would have been willing to pay higher prices for the domestic product, or buy less of it, if subject imports had been fairly traded. Examining supply conditions helps us understand whether available capacity and competition among suppliers to the market would have imposed discipline and prevented price increases for the domestic product, even if subject imports had been fairly traded.

If the unfairly traded imports had not been subsidized or dumped, their prices in the U.S. market would have increased. Thus, if subject imports had been fairly traded, they would have become more expensive relative to domestic steel wire rod and nonsubject imports. In such a case, if unfairly traded imports are good substitutes with steel wire rod from other sources, purchasers would have shifted towards the relatively less expensive products.

In these investigations, the subsidy margins and preliminary dumping margins for unfairly traded imports range from moderate to high. Thus, subject imports likely would have been priced significantly higher had they been fairly traded. Unfairly traded imports and domestic steel wire rod are good substitutes for each other. However, due to capacity limitations the domestic industry would have been able to supply only a small portion of the full demand for subject imports that likely would have shifted to domestic steel wire rod had subject imports been fairly traded. Nonsubject imports are also a presence in the market, and they are moderate substitutes with subject imports. Thus, some of the demand for subject imports likely would have shifted to nonsubject imports as well. However, it is unlikely that nonsubject imports would have captured all of the demand for unfairly traded imports because of the moderate degree of substitutability. Instead, some fairly traded subject imports would have remained in the market to serve part of the demand that the domestic industry and nonsubject imports could not supply. Overall, the shift in demand and the limited availability of supply from other sources would have allowed the domestic industry to raise its prices for steel wire rod. Overall demand would not have changed very much in response to higher prices, since demand is inelastic. Thus, had the subject imports been fairly traded, the domestic industry would have increased its prices for steel wire rod. Consequently, I find that unfairly traded imports are having a significant effect on prices for domestic steel wire rod.

C. Impact of Unfairly Traded Imports on the Domestic Industry

To assess the impact of unfairly traded imports on the domestic industry, I consider output, sales, inventories, capacity utilization, market share, employment, wages, productivity, profits, cash flow, return on investment, ability to raise capital, research and development and other relevant factors. These factors together either encompass or reflect the volume and price effects of the unfairly traded imports, and so I gauge the impact of the subsidy and dumping through those effects.

As discussed above, had subject imports been fairly traded, the domestic industry would have increased its prices significantly. However, the domestic industry would not have been able to increase its output and sales because of the low elasticity of domestic supply. Nevertheless, the domestic industry dominates the market, accounting for 71.8 percent of domestic consumption in 1996. Therefore a significant increase in the price of domestic steel wire rod would have had a significant impact on the domestic industry's revenues. Based on the increase in the domestic industry's prices, and consequently, its revenues, I conclude that the domestic industry would have been materially better off if the subject imports had been fairly traded.

IV. CONCLUSION

On the basis of the foregoing analysis, I determine that the domestic industry producing steel wire rod is materially injured by reason of subsidized imports of steel wire rod from Canada and Venezuela.

Notes and Questions

(1) Is it a matter of indifference whether the harm to the domestic industry is lower output or lower prices? Does one's view of the underlying purpose of the antidumping and countervailing duty laws have any bearing on the answer?

(2) Do you follow the various economic considerations that Commissioner Crawford brings to bear on the case? Suppose that the Commerce Department has found substantial dumping or subsidization with respect to the imports under investigation. What factors might arise that would nevertheless tend to suggest that material injury "by reason of imports" is absent?

(3) How would one adapt the "economic" approach to a case where the issue was not present injury but threatened injury? What additional information would be pertinent?

Chapter 18

SUBSIDIES AND COUNTERVAILING DUTIES

SECTION 18.1 INTRODUCTION

Disputes over government subsidies that affect trade predate the original GATT agreement, and the area remains divisive and contentious. The most difficult issues relate to the problem of distinguishing between "legitimate" government activities, on the one hand, and trade-distorting subsidies, on the other. Some progress was made during the Uruguay Round, but the problems of definition have by no means been solved. The governments of the major western trading nations continue to maintain divergent views on the role of government involvement with industry, and even more disagreement is found when the policies of developing countries are considered.

This chapter surveys the policy issues and the legal issues relating to international and national discipline of subsidies. Section 18.1 introduces the central concepts and provides a brief survey of the policy debate. Section 18.2 considers the rules on the use of subsidies found in GATT and the WTO Subsidies Agreement (also called the SCM Agreement). Section 18.3 then turns to U.S. law on subsidies and countervailing duties. In both of these sections, considerable emphasis will be placed on the difficult definitional questions raised by the subject: What is a subsidy? What subsidies are appropriate for countervailing measures? How is the amount of the subsidy calculated?

In international trade parlance, there are two types of subsidies: the "domestic" subsidy; and the "export" subsidy. The domestic subsidy is granted to an industry on all of its production of a product, regardless of whether that production is exported. It can have effects similar to those of a tariff. For example, if the domestic industry produces widgets at a cost of $1.00 each, while the foreign industry can produce and deliver widgets at a price of $.90 each, the foreign goods should compete successfully against the domestic product. But if the domestic government grants a subsidy to the widget industry of 20 cents for each widget produced, it should be able to sell the widget for 20 cents less than otherwise. Thus, it can reduce its price to a level below that of the imports, and effectively drive out the import competition. In this sense, the subsidy is protectionist, although unlike a tariff, it lowers the prices of the products concerned rather than raises them, and is thus favorable to consumers. The subsidy is also like a tariff in another sense; it can distort resource allocation by drawing resources into the production of a good or service where production would be uneconomic but for the subsidy.

An export subsidy, by contrast, is paid to an industry only on products that are exported. Thus, if the domestic industry produced widgets at a dollar each, and received a 20 cent subsidy for each widget exported, it could sell its widgets abroad for about 80 cents each. The widgets that are sold in the domestic market, however, would cost a dollar each, and presumably would be priced at or above that level. Consequently, with an export subsidy, goods tend to be sold abroad at a price below that of the goods sold in the domestic market. Like the domestic subsidy, an export subsidy can distort resource allocation by inducing production and exportation that is otherwise uneconomic.

Despite the ability of subsidies to distort the allocation of resources, it is not immediately obvious why the nations that *import* subsidized goods or services should object to them. More will be said about that issue below. Nevertheless, WTO rules allow an importing nation to respond to certain foreign subsidies by imposing "countervailing duties." These duties are set equal to the amount of the foreign subsidy, ostensibly to offset its effects on trade. The WTO system also imposes significant constraints upon the ability of governments to use both domestic and export subsidies.

Much has been written about the wisdom of WTO/GATT subsidy policies and the use of countervailing measures. The following materials provide the reader with a flavor of the literature. Very roughly, the issues divide into two categories: What is the appropriate scope of restrictions on subsidization by member nations, and when should an importing nation respond to foreign subsidies with some form of countervailing measure?

GARY C. HUFBAUER & JOANNA SHELTON ERB, SUBSIDIES IN INTERNATIONAL TRADE 5–6 (1984)[1]

THE RATIONALE FOR DISCIPLINING SUBSIDIES

Sovereign governments are free to adopt whatever macroeconomic, industrial, or social policies, including the use of subsidies, that they deem necessary to achieve their overall goals. Politicians, producers, and taxpayers may debate the relative merits of supporting one industry versus another, and whether the cost of government financial support is

---

1. © 1984, Institute for International Economics. Reproduced by permission. See also D. Wallace, F. Loftus & V. Krikorian, Interface Three: Legal Treatment of Domestic Subsidies (1984).

worth the drain on public resources. But in a representative government, the costs and benefits of public policies presumably are settled more or less to the satisfaction of the key interested parties.

An economist might, therefore, ask why the international community should concern itself with the subsidy practices of its member nations. * * *

The answer is * * * simple: unbridled and competing national subsidies can undermine world prosperity. Whatever the analytic merits of a purist free trade, turn-the-other-cheek approach, the Great Depression taught the world that protective policies can quickly and destructively spread from nation to nation. Because the concentrated interests of producers command greater political support than the diffuse interests of consumers, national governments find it much easier to emulate the vices of protection than the virtues of free trade. This lesson has prompted the international community to fashion guidelines that distinguish between acceptable and unacceptable national subsidy measures and to codify those guidelines both in bilateral treaties and in multilateral agreements. In fact, a major purpose of the General Agreement on Tariffs and Trade (GATT) is to discipline protective import policies. Robert E. Baldwin has ably summarized negotiating history since the 1930s:

> The 1930s experience with export subsidies as well as with competitive devaluation, which has the effect of a general export subsidy and import surcharge, apparently convinced the GATT founders that export subsidies exacerbate international political tensions and should be eliminated. Though consumers in the importing country gain from export subsidization by other nations, domestic-producer groups in the importing countries are forced to curtail output and incur a producer-surplus loss.... The view that domestic producers are somehow more entitled to domestic compared to foreign markets is still widely held by the general public. Thus, in the case of export subsidies, it was not necessary for the founders of GATT to implement their international political objective with regard to this distortion only gradually (as with tariffs) and export subsidies were banned outright.

WARREN F. SCHWARTZ & EUGENE W. HARPER, JR., THE REGULATION OF SUBSIDIES AFFECTING INTERNATIONAL TRADE[2]

A subsidy is treated in the GATT framework as a "distortion" of international trade, that is, as creating a disparity between the actual costs incurred in producing a particular good and those which must be borne by the firm undertaking its production. In fact, however, much

2. 70 Mich.L.Rev. 831 (1972). Reprinted   by permission.

(perhaps all) government support can be defended as being a "correction" rather than a "distortion" of the market process. The need for correction is said to derive from the existence of "externalities," that is, costs or benefits that are borne or reaped by nonparties to a transaction and are not therefore taken into account in the market process.

As a result, the issue is not that of identifying and remedying "distortions" but rather of determining if a particular measure on balance "corrects" or "distorts" the market process, that is whether it increases or decreases the efficiency with which resources are allocated. Resolution of this question turns upon theoretical and empirical judgments about how well the domestic political system performs the tasks of deciding what intervention should be undertaken and implementing the program that is adopted.

* * *

There are only a few ways in which [an international] standard could conceivably contribute to dealing with the question of subsidies. First, it could implement the notion that particular preferences, which are in fact held by the people of a country, should not be given weight by legislators in deciding whether to institute subsidies. Thus, for example, the desire to have a certain portion of the population engage in agriculture could be said to be "less important" than "efficient" agricultural production (by which is meant, of course, "efficient" in terms of all production possibilities and preferences exclusive of wanting people to engage in agriculture). However, we know of no objective basis for adopting such a standard.

The second basic notion that could be embodied in an international standard is that the domestic measure is inefficient in terms of the preferences actually held in the country. This judgment could be made on three bases.

First, it could be asserted that the structure of the domestic political process is calculated to lead to oversubsidization. There are empirical and theoretical grounds for believing that oversubsidization is likely to result under existing systems. * * *

The second respect in which it might be said that a domestic measure is inefficient is that there are better ways to accomplish its objectives. If, for example, the purpose of the measure is to increase the level of research and development in an industry rather than the output of the industry, a subsidy geared to output would be inefficient. * * *

The final respect in which the domestic process could be said to be inefficient is that implementation has been faulty. We have talked, for example, about subsidies for infant export industries. Justification for these subsidies is found in the externalities that accompany the introduction of new goods of a certain type originating in a particular country. But any effort to devise and implement a scheme of subsidies that reflects, with substantial accuracy, the externalities actually created will encounter great difficulties. The program may easily degenerate into an indiscriminate grant of subsidies, involving the risk of political corruption and adding an element of uncertainty that makes intelligent decision-making about resource allocation extremely difficult. It may be, moreover, that alternative measures, such as the government's providing information about foreign markets to domestic producers and all domestic products to foreign buyers, are better calculated to deal with the basic problem. We do not believe, however, that an international body could be empowered to make a judgment of this kind. What really must be said after all is that a domestic measure has been badly, if not corruptly, administered.

Thus we are not very sanguine that a useful international standard can be devised.

———

ALAN O. SYKES, COUNTERVAILING DUTY LAW: AN ECONOMIC CRITIQUE[3]

Subsidies arise for a variety of reasons and have a variety of consequences for the subsidizing country. Subsidies can correct market failures and enhance economic welfare in the subsidizing country, or can distort resource allocation and reduce the subsidizing country's economic welfare. They can also enhance or reduce worldwide economic welfare. Much of the existing literature on the international discipline of subsidy practices devotes considerable attention to the question whether these various categories of subsidies can be reliably distinguished. From the perspective of a country that imports the subsidized merchandise, however, these distinctions are often of no consequence. Specifically, if product and input markets in the importing country are perfectly competitive and adjust quickly to any disequilibrium, a subsidy will enhance the economic welfare of the importing country whatever the effect of the subsidy on the welfare of the subsidizing country or on the welfare of the world as a whole.

In contrast, countervailing duties will often reduce the welfare of the importing country. The principal caveat to this last proposition is that duties may improve the "terms of trade" for the importing country. A second caveat relates to the question whether countervailing duties may deter subsidization altogether and thereby confer benefits on producers in the importing country who must compete with subsidized goods in their *export* markets.

The cases in which countervailing duties might in theory generate a net benefit to the economy, however, are difficult to identify in practice. Moreover, even if the cases of potential benefit could be reliably identified, a systematic effort to impose duties in those cases might well result in a retaliatory or strategic response by trading partners that would eliminate the gains. Finally, the costs to the government of administer-

---

3. 89 Colum.L.Rev. 199 (1989). Reprint-   ed by permission.

ing the countervailing duty laws, as well as the rent-seeking expenditures of domestic producer groups seeking to avail themselves of protection, can be considerable. These costs weigh further against any type of countervailing duty policy.

It is even more clear that the *existing* U.S. countervailing duty laws cannot be explained or justified as a mechanism for the imposition of welfare-enhancing duties in competitive markets. Existing law largely ignores the factors that would be essential to ascertain the welfare consequences of duties, and the central features of existing law—the special treatment of export subsidies, the specificity test, the injury test, and so on—have little or no bearing on the welfare effects of duties in a competitive setting. Thus, a net gain to the economy under existing law can arise only by chance. In short, the economic case for applying any type of countervailing duty policy in competitive markets, let alone existing U.S. policy, appears quite weak.

* * *

JOHN H. JACKSON, THE WORLD TRADING SYSTEM 282 (2d ed. 1997)[4]

The basic problem with all of these views, however, is that they focus on too narrow a perspective—that of the importing country. When one moves to a worldwide perspective—that is, in order to explore which actions will enhance or decrease worldwide net welfare—then a stronger case can be made for providing some kind of international or national disciplines on the use of subsidies of internationally traded goods. The economists would apparently admit that in such circumstances some subsidies tend to distort international production and trading patterns, and reduce efficiency and thus reduce world welfare. This is, however, a rather peculiar argument to use within an importing nation for the application of countervailing duties. It is certainly not the basis of most of the arguments heard. Most of the arguments originate from competing producer groups, and they are most interested in their own welfare, and not in that of the world in general. On the other hand, it can be argued that if such relatively parochial or selfish motivations result in the use of measures, such as countervailing duties, that coincidentally in the long run tend to inhibit a practice (subsidization) that reduces world welfare, then why not take advantage of such parochial/selfish motivations? This argument would support the use of countervailing duties.

Notes

(1) See also the symposium beginning at 21 L. & Pol.Intl.Bus. 503 (1990); Goetz, Granet & Schwartz, The Meaning of "Subsidy" and "Injury" in the Countervailing Duty Law, 6 Intl.Rev.L. & Econ. 17 (1986); Barcelo,

Subsidies and Countervailing Duties—Analysis and a Proposal, 9 L. & Pol.Intl.Bus. 779 (1977); Schwartz, Zenith Radio Corp. v. United States: Countervailing Duties and the Regulation of International Trade, 1978 Sup. Ct. Rev. 297; Itoh & Kiyono, Welfare–Enhancing Export Subsidies, 95 J.Pol.Econ. 115 (1987).

(2) Countervailing duties are less common than antidumping duties, and were formerly mainly imposed by the United States. Indeed, according to WTO statistics, at the end of 1995, the US imposed 71 countervailing measures, almost two-thirds of the 111 measures then in place in WTO members. As of the end of 2000, that had changed significantly–the number of US measures had declined to 43 and they represented less than one-half of the 94 countervailing measures then in force. The principal new development was the increase in the use of such measures by the EC, which imposed 11 new countervailing measures in 2000 alone, which brought its total measures in force at the end of 2000 to 17. Australia, Canada and Mexico were the only other WTO members to have more than three measures in place at the end of 2000.

SECTION 18.2   INTERNATIONAL OBLIGATIONS

GATT Article XVI contains the original obligations on subsidies. It consisted originally of one paragraph (XVI:1), with a loose obligation to report all subsidies which operate to increase exports or decrease imports. The article was amended extensively during the GATT 1954–55 review session. Four paragraphs were added to Article XVI, containing two key obligations: one obligation (paragraph 3) prohibits using an export subsidy on primary products which results in obtaining more than "an equitable share of world export trade in that product;" a second obligation (paragraph 4) prohibits a subsidy on the export of non-primary products which results in an export price lower than the comparable price for like goods which are not exported (the so-called "bi-level pricing" condition).[1] These Article XVI amendments, however, were accepted only by certain industrialized nations of GATT. Developing countries objected to the differential treatment of primary and other goods.

It will be recalled that introduction of a new domestic subsidy on a product which is bound in a country's GATT schedule has been termed a "prima facie nullification or impairment" for purposes of Article XXIII complaints.[2]

Apart from obligations concerning the use of subsidies, the original GATT authorized unilateral government responses in the form of countervailing duties. Article VI of GATT governs such measures, prohibiting the use of both antidumping and countervailing duties for the same

---

1. For a complete discussion of this subject, see John H. Jackson, World Trade and the Law of GATT 372–74 (1969).

2. See discussion of the *EC Oilseeds* and the *Australia/Chile fertilizer* cases in Section 7.4(A).

situation, and imposing a "material injury" requirement as a prerequisite to the use of countervailing duties. If these conditions are met, a government is authorized to apply a countervailing duty on imported goods (in excess of regular bound duty rates), in an amount "equal to the estimated bounty or subsidy" granted directly or indirectly on the "manufacture, production or export."

In 1960, the GATT Contracting Parties adopted a report of a working party which included an "illustrative list" of practices that would be considered as "export subsidies" for purposes of GATT Article XVI, paragraph 4.[3] This list has been very important for the interpretation of GATT subsidy obligations.

In the Tokyo Round, a Subsidies Code was negotiated, and accepted by about two dozen signatories. Among other things, it tightened the restrictions on export subsidies; elaborated the procedures to be utilized by importing nations in their countervailing duty investigations; set forth criteria to be examined in the assessment of injury under the injury test; and established a Subsidies Code Committee to resolve disputes.

The Uruguay Round Subsidies Agreement is an important step forward over the Tokyo Round Code for a number of reasons. Unlike the Code, it is binding on all WTO members. It also significantly extends WTO discipline over domestic subsidies, provides some guidance on what domestic subsidies are "unfair," and encourages greater resort to WTO dispute resolution rather than unilateral countervailing measures. Its principal innovations were summarized by the GATT Secretariat as follows:[4]

> Unlike its predecessor, the [Agreement on Subsidies and Countervailing Measures] contains a definition of subsidy and introduces the concept of a "specific" subsidy—for the most part, a subsidy available only to an enterprise or industry or group of enterprises or industries within the jurisdiction of the authority granting the subsidy. Only specific subsidies would be subject to the disciplines set out in the agreement.

> The agreement established three categories of subsidies. First, it deems the following subsidies to be "prohibited": those contingent, in law or in fact, whether solely or as one of several other conditions, upon export performance; and those contingent, whether solely or as one of several other conditions, upon the use of domestic over imported goods. Prohibited subsidies are subject to new dispute settlement procedures. The main features include an expedited timetable for action by the Dispute Settlement body, and if it is found that the subsidy is indeed prohibited, it must be immediately withdrawn. If this is not done within the specified time period, the complaining member is authorized to take countermeasures.

3. GATT, 9th Supp. BISD 185 (1961); see also Jackson, supra note 1, at 385.

4. GATT Focus Newsletter, Dec. 1993, at 10–11.

The second category is "actionable" subsidies. The agreement stipulates that no member should cause, through the use of subsidies, adverse effects to the interests of other signatories, i.e. injury to domestic industry of another signatory, nullification or impairment of benefits accruing directly or indirectly to other signatories under the General Agreement (in particular the benefits of bound tariff concessions), and serious prejudice to the interests of another member. "Serious prejudice" shall be presumed to exist for certain subsidies included when the total *ad valorem* subsidization of a product exceeds 5 per cent. In such a situation, the burden of proof is on the subsidizing member to show that the subsidies in question do not cause serious prejudice to the complaining member. Members affected by actionable subsidies may refer the matter to the Dispute Settlement Body. In the event that it is determined that such adverse effects exist, the subsidizing member must withdraw the subsidy or remove the adverse effects.

The third category involves non-actionable subsidies, which could either be non-specific subsidies, or specific subsidies involving assistance to industrial research and pre-competitive development activity, assistance to disadvantaged regions, or certain type of assistance for adapting existing facilities to new environmental requirements imposed by law and/or regulations. * * * [The provisions defining non-actionable research-and environment-related subsidies expired after five years, however, and at this writing have not been renewed. Eds.]

One part of the agreement concerns the use of countervailing measures on subsidized imported goods. It sets out disciplines on the initiation of countervailing cases, investigations by national authorities and rules of evidence to ensure that all interested parties can present information and argument. Certain disciplines on the calculation of the amount of a subsidy are outlined as is the basis for the determination of injury to the domestic industry. The agreement would require that all relevant economic factors be taken into account in assessing the state of the industry and that a causal link be established between the subsidized imports and the alleged injury. Countervailing investigations shall be terminated immediately in cases where the amount of the subsidy is *de minimis* (the subsidy is less than 1 per cent *ad valorem*) or where the volume of subsidized imports, actual or potential, or the injury is negligible. Except under exceptional circumstances, investigations shall be concluded within one year after their initiation and in no case more than 18 months. All countervailing duties have to be terminated within 5 years of their imposition unless the authorities determine on the basis of a review that the expiry of the duty would be likely to lead to continuation or recurrence of subsidization and injury.

The agreement recognizes that subsidies may play an important role in economic development programmes of developing countries, and in the transformation of centrally-planned economies to market economies. Least-developed countries and developing countries that have less than $1,000 per capita GNP are thus exempted from disciplines on prohibited export subsidies, and have a time-bound exemption from other prohibited subsidies. For other developing countries, the export subsidy prohibition would take effect 8 years after the entry into force of the agreement establishing the WTO, and they have a time-bound agreement (though fewer years than for poorer developing countries) exemption from the other prohibited subsidies. Countervailing investigation of a product originating from a developing-country member would be terminated if the overall level of subsidies does not exceed 2 per cent (and from certain developing countries 3 per cent) of the value of the product, or if the volume of the subsidized imports represents less than 4 per cent of the total imports for the like product in the importing signatory. For countries in the process of transformation from a centrally-planned into a market economy, prohibited subsidies shall be phased out within a period of seven years from the date of entry into force of the agreement."

———

The new Subsidies or SCM Agreement in large part exempts agricultural subsidies, leaving them to the Agreement on Agriculture. In that Agreement, both export subsidies and domestic subsidies to agriculture are subject to a complex set of commitments for their reduction over a period of years. It treats agricultural subsidies much like bound tariffs, with country-by-country schedules indicating what is permissible, coupled with formulas for the phase down of permissible subsidies. Article 13 of the Agriculture Agreement also creates certain "safe harbor" provisions during its implementation period for measures that conform to the Agreement, exempting them from countervailing duties in some cases, and generally exempting them from the "prohibited" and "actionable" categories under the Subsidies Agreement.

The reader should review the WTO Subsidies Agreement, as well as the Agreement on Agriculture. As we proceed through this section and the next on U.S. law, it is critical to distinguish between WTO obligations restraining the use of subsidies, on the one hand, and WTO rules governing the use countervailing duties by an importing nation, on the other. Even if a subsidy is not prohibited by WTO rules, WTO law may nevertheless permit it to be offset by countervailing duties. Likewise, a subsidy against which countervailing duties are ineffectual—such as an export subsidy on goods destined for a third-country market—may nevertheless give rise to a claim of WTO violation.

A number of cases relating to subsidies have now found their way into the WTO dispute resolution system. These cases are principally concerned with defining the coverage of the obligations of the SCM Agreement. We begin here with a pair of disputes between Brazil and

Canada pertaining to subsidies to their producers of smaller commercial aircraft.

CANADA—MEASURES AFFECTING THE EXPORT OF CIVILIAN AIRCRAFT

WT/DS70/AB/R
Appellate Body Report adopted by the DSB on August 20, 1999

2.   The Panel considered claims made by Brazil relating to the activities of the Export Development Corporation (the "EDC"); the operation of Canada Account; * * * The Panel found "that Canada Account debt financing since 1 January 1995 for the export of Canadian regional aircraft" and "TPC assistance to the Canadian regional aircraft industry" constitute prohibited export subsidies inconsistent with Articles 3.1(a) and 3.2 of the *SCM Agreement*. * * *

* * *

V.   Interpretation of "Benefit" In Article 1.1(b) of the *SCM Agreement*

149.   In interpreting the term "benefit" in Article 1.1(b) of the *SCM Agreement*, the Panel found that:

> ... the ordinary meaning of "benefit" clearly encompasses some form of advantage.... In order to determine whether a financial contribution (in the sense of Article 1.1(a)(i)) confers a "benefit", *i.e.*, an advantage, it is necessary to determine whether the financial contribution places the *recipient* in a *more advantageous position than would have been the case but for the financial contribution*. In our view, the only logical basis for determining the position the recipient would have been in absent the financial contribution is the *market*. Accordingly, a financial contribution will only confer a "benefit", *i.e.*, an advantage, if it is *provided on terms that are more advantageous than those that would have been available to the recipient on the market*. (emphasis added)

150.   The Panel concluded that the notion of "cost to government" is not relevant to the interpretation and application of the term "benefit", within the meaning of Article 1.1(b) of the *SCM Agreement*. The Panel found contextual support for this reading of "benefit" in Article 14 of the *SCM Agreement*. It also found that Annex IV of that Agreement does not form part of the relevant context of "benefit" in Article 1.1(b).

151.   Canada appeals the Panel's legal interpretation of the term "benefit" in Article 1.1(b) of the *SCM Agreement*. In Canada's view, the Panel erred in its interpretation of "benefit" by focusing on the commercial benchmarks in Article 14 "to the exclusion of cost to government", and by rejecting Annex IV as relevant context. Canada maintains that Annex IV of the *SCM Agreement* supports the view that "cost to government", which is mentioned in Annex IV, is a legitimate interpre-

tation of the term "benefit". In its appellee's submission, Brazil agrees fully with the Panel's interpretation.

152. Under the heading *"Definition of a Subsidy"*, Article 1.1 of the *SCM Agreement* provides, in relevant part:

> 1.1 For the purpose of this Agreement, a subsidy shall be deemed to exist if:
>
> (a)(1) there is a financial contribution by a government or any public body within the territory of a Member (referred to in this Agreement as "government") . . .
>
> . . .
>
> and
>
> (b) *a benefit is thereby conferred.* (emphasis added)

153. In addressing this issue, we start with the ordinary meaning of "benefit". The dictionary meaning of "benefit" is "advantage", "good", "gift", "profit", or, more generally, "a favourable or helpful factor or circumstance". Each of these alternative words or phrases gives flavour to the term "benefit" and helps to convey some of the essence of that term. These definitions also confirm that the Panel correctly stated that "the ordinary meaning of 'benefit' clearly encompasses some form of advantage." Clearly, however, dictionary meanings leave many interpretive questions open.

154. A "benefit" does not exist in the abstract, but must be received and enjoyed by a beneficiary or a recipient. Logically, a "benefit" can be said to arise only if a person, natural or legal, or a group of persons, has in fact received something. The term "benefit", therefore, implies that there must be a recipient. This provides textual support for the view that the focus of the inquiry under Article 1.1(b) of the *SCM Agreement* should be on the recipient and not on the granting authority. The ordinary meaning of the word "confer", as used in Article 1.1(b), bears this out. "Confer" means, *inter alia*, "give", "grant" or "bestow". The use of the past participle "conferred" in the passive form, in conjunction with the word "thereby", naturally calls for an inquiry into *what was conferred on the recipient*. Accordingly, we believe that Canada's argument that "cost to government" is one way of conceiving of "benefit" is at odds with the ordinary meaning of Article 1.1(b), which focuses on the *recipient* and not on the *government* providing the "financial contribution".

155. We find support for this reading of "benefit" in the context of Article 1.1(b) of the *SCM Agreement*. Article 14 sets forth guidelines for calculating the amount of a subsidy in terms of "the benefit to the recipient". Although the opening words of Article 14 state that the guidelines it establishes apply "[f]or the purposes of Part V" of the *SCM Agreement*, which relates to "countervailing measures", our view is that Article 14, nonetheless, constitutes relevant context for the interpretation of "benefit" in Article 1.1(b). The guidelines set forth in Article 14 apply to the calculation of the "benefit *to the recipient* conferred *pursu-*

ant to paragraph 1 of Article 1". (emphasis added) This explicit textual reference to Article 1.1 in Article 14 indicates to us that "benefit" is used in the same sense in Article 14 as it is in Article 1.1. Therefore, the reference to "benefit *to the recipient*" in Article 14 also implies that the word "benefit", *as used in Article 1.1*, is concerned with the "benefit *to the recipient*" and not with the "cost to government", as Canada contends.

156. The structure of Article 1.1 as a whole confirms our view that Article 1.1(b) is concerned with the "benefit" to the recipient, and not with the "cost to government". The definition of "subsidy" in Article 1.1 has two discrete elements: "a financial contribution by a government or any public body" and "a benefit is thereby conferred". The first element of this definition is concerned with whether the *government* made a "financial contribution", as that term is defined in Article 1.1(a). The focus of the first element is on the action of the government in making the "financial contribution". That being so, it seems to us logical that the second element in Article 1.1 is concerned with the "benefit . . . conferred" on the *recipient* by that governmental action. Thus, subparagraphs (a) and (b) of Article 1.1 define a "subsidy" by reference, first, to the action of the granting authority and, second, to what was conferred on the recipient. Therefore, Canada's argument that "cost to *government*" is relevant to the question of whether there is a "benefit" to the *recipient* under Article 1.1(b) disregards the overall structure of Article 1.1.

157. We also believe that the word "benefit", as used in Article 1.1(b), implies some kind of comparison. This must be so, for there can be no "benefit" to the recipient unless the "financial contribution" makes the recipient "better off" than it would otherwise have been, absent that contribution. In our view, the marketplace provides an appropriate basis for comparison in determining whether a "benefit" has been "conferred", because the trade-distorting potential of a "financial contribution" can be identified by determining whether the recipient has received a "financial contribution" on terms more favourable than those available to the recipient in the market.

158. Article 14, which we have said is relevant context in interpreting Article 1.1(b), supports our view that the marketplace is an appropriate basis for comparison. The guidelines set forth in Article 14 relate to equity investments, loans, loan guarantees, the provision of goods or services by a government, and the purchase of goods by a government. A "benefit" arises under each of the guidelines if the recipient has received a "financial contribution" on terms more favourable than those available to the recipient in the market.

159. Canada has argued that the Panel erred in failing to take account of paragraph 1 of Annex IV as part of the relevant context of the term "benefit". We fail to see the relevance of this provision to the interpretation of "benefit" in Article 1.1(b) of the *SCM Agreement*. Annex IV provides a method for calculating the total *ad valorem* subsidi-

zation of a product under the "serious prejudice" provisions of Article 6 of the *SCM Agreement*, with a view to determining whether a subsidy is used in such a manner as to have "adverse effects". Annex IV, therefore, has nothing to do with whether a *"benefit"* has been conferred, nor with whether a measure constitutes a subsidy within the meaning of Article 1.1. We agree with the Panel that Annex IV is not useful context for interpreting Article 1.1(b) of the *SCM Agreement*.

160.   Canada insists that the concept of "cost to government" is relevant in the interpretation of "benefit". We note that this interpretation of "benefit" would exclude from the scope of that term those situations where a "benefit" is conferred by a private body under the direction of government. These situations cannot be *excluded* from the definition of "benefit" in Article 1.1(b), given that they are specifically *included* in the definition of "financial contribution" in Article 1.1(a)(iv). We are, therefore, not persuaded by this argument of Canada.

161.   In light of the foregoing, we find that the Panel has not erred in its interpretation of the word "benefit", as used in Article 1.1(b) of the *SCM Agreement*.

Notes and Questions

(1) Both U.S. and WTO law generally value subsidies as the benefit to the recipient rather than the cost to the government. Thus, for example, if a government borrows at 8% and lends at 10%, the recipient of the loan will still be subsidized if that recipient would otherwise have to pay 12%. In general, is the cost to the government or the benefit to the recipient the proper standard as an economic matter? How is the benefit to the recipient measured? In particular, how is *the* market interest rate determined if it is shown, as is often the case, that different banks and other financing entities offer varying rates for similar transactions? Should the market rate be an average rate? A typical rate reported in the financial press? The lowest actual rate found in the market (even if it is clearly a "loss leader" rate offered to win a new client)?

(2) An exception to this principle under WTO law may be found in item k of the Illustrative List of Export Subsidies contained in Annex I to the Subsidies Agreement. It provides that the value of an export credit subsidy is to measured against the cost of the funds to the entity that grants the subsidy. Why the distinction? Another exception arises via paragraph 1 of Annex IV, regarding serious prejudice. Again, why the difference?

CANADA—MEASURES AFFECTING THE EXPORT OF CIVILIAN AIRCRAFT—RECOURSE BY BRAZIL TO ARTICLE 21.5 OF THE DSU

WT/DS70/AB/RW

Appellate Body Report adopted by the DSB on August 4, 2000

2.   The original panel found, *inter alia*, that "Canada Account debt financing since 1 January 1995 for the export of Canadian regional aircraft" and "[Technology Partnerships Canada] assistance to the Ca-

nadian regional aircraft industry [constitute] export subsidies inconsistent with Article[s] 3.1(a) and 3.2 of the SCM Agreement" . The original panel concluded that "Canada shall withdraw [these] subsidies ... within 90 days."

* * *

4. Canada took steps to implement the recommendations and rulings of the DSB with respect to both the Canada Account and TPC. Taking the view that these measures were not consistent with Article 3.1(a) of the *SCM Agreement*, Brazil requested that the matter be referred to the original panel, pursuant to Article 21.5 of the *Understanding on Rules and Procedures Governing the Settlement of Disputes* (the "DSU"). * * *

* * *

34. Canada restructured the TPC programme by amending TPC's operating documentation, with effect from 18 November 1999. In that respect, Canada introduced, *inter alia*, the following new TPC documents: "Special Operating Agency Framework Document"; "Terms and Conditions"; "Investment Application Guide"; and, "Investment Decision Document". The new TPC "Terms and Conditions" document states that the "granting of contributions will not be contingent, either in law or in fact, upon actual or anticipated export performance" (Section 6.1). This is repeated in the TPC Investment Application Guide (Section 5). Section 5 of that Guide also states that "administering officials will not request or consider information concerning the extent to which applicant or recipient enterprises do or may export."

* * *

39. In conducting its review under Article 21.5 of the DSU, the Article 21.5 Panel declined to examine Brazil's argument that "the Canadian regional aircraft industry continues to be 'specifically targeted' for TPC assistance because of its undisputed export orientation." The Article 21.5 Panel stated that this argument "did not form part" of the reasoning of the original panel and was "not relevant to the present dispute, which concerns the issue of whether or not Canada *has implemented the DSB recommendation . . .*". (emphasis added)

40. We have already noted that these proceedings, under Article 21.5 of the DSU, concern the "consistency" of the revised TPC programme with Article 3.1(a) of the *SCM Agreement*. Therefore, we disagree with the Article 21.5 Panel that the scope of these Article 21.5 dispute settlement proceedings is limited to "the issue of whether or not Canada *has implemented the DSB recommendation*". The recommendation of the DSB was that the measure found to be a prohibited export subsidy must be withdrawn within 90 days of the adoption of the Appellate Body Report and the original panel report, as modified–that is, by 18 November 1999. That recommendation to "withdraw" the prohibited export subsidy did not, of course, cover the new measure–because

the new measure did not exist when the DSB made its recommendation. It follows then that the task of the Article 21.5 Panel in this case is, in fact, to determine whether the new measure–the revised TPC programme–is consistent with Article 3.1(a) of the *SCM Agreement*.

* * *

42.   Consequently, in these proceedings, the task of the Article 21.5 Panel was not limited solely to determining whether the revised TPC programme had been rid of those aspects of the original measure–the TPC programme, as previously constituted–that had been identified in the original proceedings, in the context of all of the facts, as not being consistent with Canada's WTO obligations. Rather, the Article 21.5 Panel was obliged to examine the revised TPC programme for its consistency with Article 3.1(a) of the *SCM Agreement*. The fact that Brazil's argument in these Article 21.5 proceedings "did not form part" of the original panel's reasoning relating to the *previous* TPC programme does not necessarily mean that this argument is "not relevant" to the Article 21.5 proceedings, which relate to the *revised* TPC programme. In our view, the Article 21.5 Panel should have examined the merits of Brazil's argument as it relates to the *revised* TPC programme. We conclude, therefore, that the Article 21.5 Panel erred by declining to examine Brazil's argument that the revised TPC programme "specifically targeted" the Canadian regional aircraft industry for assistance because of its export-orientation.

43.   With a view to resolving this dispute, and considering that the undisputed facts on the record are adequate for this purpose, we believe that we should complete the Article 21.5 Panel's analysis by examining this argument. In so doing, we observe that the essence of Brazil's argument is that the Canadian regional aircraft industry is "specifically targeted" for assistance in two different ways under the revised TPC programme.

44.   First, Brazil notes that the "Eligible Areas" for TPC assistance include "Aerospace and Defence", and that these industrial sectors are the sole such sectors to be identified expressly as eligible for TPC assistance. The other two "Eligible Areas" are "Environmental Technologies" and "Enabling Technologies", which could involve projects drawn from any industrial sector, including "Aerospace and Defence". In Brazil's view, the express identification of "Aerospace and Defence" as "Eligible Areas" puts these industrial sectors, which include the Canadian regional aircraft industry, in a privileged position and represents "specific targeting" of the Canadian regional aircraft industry. Second, Brazil maintains that the Canadian regional aircraft industry is also "specifically targeted", in practice, through the allocation of TPC funding assistance. According to Brazil, 65 per cent of TPC funding has, in the past, "gone to the [Canadian] aerospace industry".

45.   Brazil maintains that the reason for these two types of "targeting" is the high export-orientation of the industry. In support of this argument, Brazil relies on a series of statements made by Canadian

Government Ministers, Members of Parliament, other government officials, and by the TPC itself, regarding the objectives of TPC Brazil acknowledges that the statements it relies upon were made in connection with the *old* TPC programme, as *previously* constituted. Brazil argues, nevertheless, that the "specific targeting" is a fact that tends to establish that the revised TPC programme involves subsidies which are *de facto* export contingent.

46.   Canada does not contest any of the factual assertions made by Brazil in presenting its "specific targeting" argument. However, Canada emphasizes that the statements Brazil relies upon were made in relation to the *old* TPC programme, not to the *revised* programme. Canada also states that no TPC assistance has been granted or committed under the *revised* TPC programme to the Canadian regional aircraft industry. In other words, Canada asserts that there have been, thus far, no transactions involving the Canadian regional aircraft industry under this new measure. Brazil does not contest this assertion.

47.   It is worth recalling that the granting of a subsidy is not, in and of itself, prohibited under the *SCM Agreement*. Nor does granting a "subsidy", without more, constitute an inconsistency with that Agreement. The universe of subsidies is vast. Not all subsidies are inconsistent with the *SCM Agreement*. The only "prohibited" subsidies are those identified in Article 3 of the *SCM Agreement*; Article 3.1(a) of that Agreement prohibits those subsidies that are "contingent, in law or in fact, upon export performance". We have stated previously that "a subsidy is prohibited under Article 3.1(a) if it is 'conditional' upon export performance, that is, if it is 'dependent for its existence on' export performance." We have also emphasized that a "relationship of conditionality or dependence", namely that the granting of a subsidy should be "tied to" the export performance, lies at the "very heart" of the legal standard in Article 3.1(a) of the *SCM Agreement*.

48.   To demonstrate the existence of this "relationship of conditionality or dependence", we have also stated that it is *not* sufficient to show that a subsidy is granted in the knowledge, or with the anticipation, that exports will result. Such knowledge or anticipation does not, taken alone, demonstrate that the granting of the subsidy is "contingent upon" export performance. The second sentence of footnote 4 of the *SCM Agreement* stipulates, in this regard, that the "*mere fact* that a subsidy is granted to enterprises which export shall not *for that reason alone* be considered to be an export subsidy....". (emphasis added) That fact, by itself, does not, therefore, compel the conclusion that there is a "relationship of conditionality or dependence", such that the granting of a subsidy is "tied to" export performance. However, we have also said that the export-orientation of a recipient "may be taken into account as *a* relevant fact, provided it is one of several facts which are considered and is not the only fact supporting a finding" of export contingency. (underlining added)

49.   Recalling all this, at its core, we see Brazil's argument about "specific targeting" essentially as a contention that the *SCM Agreement* precludes the two types of targeting Brazil identifies simply because of the high export-orientation of the Canadian regional aircraft industry. However, in our view, the fact that an industrial sector has a high export-orientation is not, by itself, sufficient to preclude that sector from being expressly identified as an eligible or privileged recipient of subsidies. Nor does the high export-orientation of an industry limit, in principle, the amount of subsidies that may be granted to that industry. As we have said, granting subsidies, in itself, is not prohibited. Under Article 3.1(a) of the *SCM Agreement*, the subsidy must be *export contingent* to be prohibited. The two "targeting" factors *may* very well be relevant to an inquiry under Article 3.1(a) of the *SCM Agreement*, but they do not necessarily provide conclusive evidence that the granting of a subsidy is *"contingent"*, *"conditional"* or *"dependent"* upon export performance. In these proceedings, we do not see the two "targeting" factors, by themselves, as adequate proof of prohibited export *contingency*.

50.   Moreover, the evidence that Brazil relies upon in seeking to demonstrate that the Canadian regional aircraft industry is "specifically targeted" *because of* its high export-orientation relates to the TPC as *previously* constituted, and not to the *revised* TPC programme. In particular, Brazil relies upon evidence of the high proportion of TPC funding allocated to the Canadian regional aircraft industry under the *old* TPC programme and on statements made in connection with that programme by Canadian Government Ministers, Members of Parliament, officials, and by TPC itself. The burden of explaining the relevance of the evidence, in proving the claim made, naturally rests on whoever presents that evidence. Brazil has not offered any convincing explanation as to why the evidence relating to the *old* TPC programme continues to be relevant to the *revised* TPC programme. We do not believe we should simply assume that this particular evidence is relevant in respect of the revised TPC programme.

51.   For all these reasons, we find that Brazil has not sufficiently established that the Canadian regional aircraft industry is "specifically targeted" *because of* its high export-orientation.

52.   We conclude that Brazil has failed to establish that the revised TPC programme is inconsistent with Article 3.1(a) of the *SCM Agreement*. We also conclude that Brazil has failed to establish that Canada has not implemented the recommendations and rulings of the DSB. The outcome of the present proceedings does not, of course, preclude possible subsequent dispute resolution proceedings regarding the WTO-consistency of the revised TPC programme, or of specific instances of assistance actually granted under that programme.

Notes and Questions

(1) Suppose that the new TPC program continues to provide support primarily to aircraft production, and perhaps to some other export-oriented industries. Might it then become WTO illegal? On what basis?

(2) Why is WTO law particularly hostile to export subsidies?

BRAZIL—EXPORT FINANCING PROGRAMME FOR AIRCRAFT

WT/DS46/AB/R

Appellate Body Report adopted by the DSB on August 20, 1999

3. PROEX is administered by the Comitê de Crédito as Exportações (the "Committee"), an inter-agency group within the Ministry of Finance in Brazil. Day-to-day operations of PROEX are conducted by the Bank of Brazil. Under PROEX, the Government of Brazil provides interest rate equalization subsidies for sales by Brazilian exporters, including Embraer.

4. For sales of regional aircraft, PROEX interest rate equalization subsidies amount to 3.8 percentage points of the actual interest rate on any particular transaction. The lending bank charges its normal interest rate for the transaction, and receives payment from two sources: the purchaser, and the Government of Brazil. Of the total interest rate payments, the Government of Brazil pays 3.8 percentage points, and the purchaser pays the rest. In this way, PROEX reduces the financing costs of the purchaser and, thus, reduces the overall cost to the purchaser of purchasing an Embraer aircraft.

* * *

7. The Panel considered claims by Canada that PROEX is inconsistent with the prohibition on export subsidies under Article 3.1(a) of the *Agreement on Subsidies and Countervailing Measures* (the "*SCM Agreement*") ... The Panel reached the conclusion that PROEX interest rate equalization payments are subsidies within the meaning of Article 1 of the *SCM Agreement*, and are contingent upon export under Article 3.1(a) of that Agreement. In reaching this conclusion, the Panel found that the PROEX interest rate equalization payments were not "permitted" under the first paragraph of item (k) of the Illustrative List of Export Subsidies in Annex I of the *SCM Agreement* (the "Illustrative List"). The Panel also found that Brazil failed to comply with certain of the conditions of Article 27.4 of the *SCM Agreement*, and that, therefore, the prohibition in Article 3.1(a) of the *SCM Agreement* applied to Brazil. Having found that PROEX payments are inconsistent with Article 3.1(a), the Panel recommended that Brazil withdraw the subsidies within 90 days pursuant to Article 4.7 of the *SCM Agreement*.

[The Appellate Body held that Brazil, as a developing country, was not exempt from the prohibition on export subsidies because it had increased its subsidies in contravention of Article 27.4 of the SCM Agreement.]

* * *

VIII. Are PROEX Interest Rate Equalization Payments Used "To Secure a Material Advantage in the Field of Export Credit
Terms"?

165. Having determined that Brazil has not complied with the
provisions of Article 27.4, we conclude that the prohibition of Article
3.1(a) applies to Brazil in this case. We must therefore examine Brazil's
appeal of the finding of the Panel relating to Brazil's alleged "affirmative
defence" under item (k) of the Illustrative List.

* * *

168. Item (k) of the Illustrative List provides as follows:

(k) The grant by governments (or special institutions controlled by
and/or acting under the authority of governments) of export credits
at rates below those which they actually have to pay for the funds so
employed (or would have to pay if they borrowed on international
capital markets in order to obtain funds of the same maturity and
other credit terms and denominated in the same currency as the
export credit), or the payment by them of all or part of the costs
incurred by exporters or financial institutions in obtaining credits,
*in so far as they are used to secure a material advantage in the field
of export credit terms.*

Provided, however, that if a Member is a party to an international
undertaking on official export credits to which at least twelve
original Members to this Agreement are parties as of 1 January
1979 (or a successor undertaking which has been adopted by those
original Members), or if in practice a Member applies the interest
rates provisions of the relevant undertaking, an export credit practice which is in conformity with those provisions shall not be
considered an export subsidy prohibited by this Agreement. (emphasis added)

169. Before the Panel, Brazil contended that, although PROEX
payments are export subsidies, they are nevertheless "permitted" by
item (k) of the Illustrative List. The Panel noted that to rule in favour of
Brazil on this issue, it would need to find for Brazil on all of the
following three points: first, that PROEX payments are "the payment by
[governments] of all or part of the costs incurred by exporters or
financial institutions in obtaining credits"; second, that PROEX payments are not "used to secure a material advantage in the field of export
credit terms"; and, third, that a "payment" within the meaning of item
(k) which is not "used to secure a material advantage in the field of
export credit terms" is "permitted" by the *SCM Agreement* even though
it is a subsidy which is contingent upon export performance within the
meaning of Article 3.1(a) of that Agreement. The Panel also noted that
Brazil had explicitly acknowledged that the "material advantage" clause
in item (k) constitutes an "affirmative defence", and, therefore, that the
burden of establishing that "defence" was on Brazil.

170. The Panel concluded as follows:

In conclusion, we consider that an item (k) payment is "used to secure a material advantage" where the payment has resulted in the availability of export credit on terms which are more favourable than the terms that would otherwise have been available to the purchaser with respect to the transaction in question. Even if we were to assume, as argued by Brazil, that PROEX payments are the "payment by [a government] of all or part of the costs incurred by exporters or financial institutions in obtaining credits", and that such payments can be deemed to be "permitted" by item (k) where they are not "used to secure a material advantage in the field of export credit terms"—issues we need not here decide—Brazil has failed to demonstrate the PROEX payments are not "used to secure a material advantage in the field of export credit terms". Accordingly, we reject Brazil's affirmative defense based on item (k) of the Illustrative List.

* * *

177.   As always, we examine the terms of the provision at issue, in this case, the "material advantage" clause of item (k). We look first to the ordinary meaning of the language used. We agree with the Panel's statement that the ordinary meaning of the word "advantage" is "a more favorable or improved position" or a "superior position". However, we note that item (k) does not refer simply to "advantage". The word "advantage" is qualified by the adjective "material". As mentioned before, in its ultimate interpretation of the phrase "used to secure a material advantage" which the Panel finally adopted and applied to the export subsidies for regional aircraft under PROEX, the Panel read the word "material" out of item (k). This, we consider to be an error.

178.   We also note that in two of its interpretive statements, the Panel used the "marketplace" as the benchmark for comparing the subsidies on sales of regional aircraft under PROEX. However, in two other statements, the Panel made no reference to the "marketplace" as the basis for comparison. In one of those two statements, it referred, instead, more generally, to "the terms that would have been available in the absence of the payment." For the purposes of our analysis, we will assume that the Panel meant to use the "marketplace" as the benchmark for determining whether the PROEX subsidies were "used to secure a material advantage".

179.   We note that the Panel adopted an interpretation of the "material advantage" clause in item (k) of the Illustrative List that is, in effect, the same as the interpretation of the term "benefit" in Article 1.1(b) of the *SCM Agreement* adopted by the panel in *Canada–Aircraft*. If the "material advantage" clause in item (k) is to have *any* meaning, it must mean something different from "benefit" in Article 1.1(b). It will be recalled that for any payment to be a "subsidy" within the meaning of Article 1.1, that payment must consist of both a "financial contribution" and a "benefit". The first paragraph of item (k) describes a type of subsidy that is deemed to be a prohibited export subsidy. Obviously,

when a payment by a government constitutes a "financial contribution" and confers a "benefit", it is, a "subsidy" under Article 1.1. Thus, the phrase in item (k), "in so far as they are used to secure a material advantage", would have no meaning if it were simply to be equated with the term "benefit" in the definition of "subsidy". As a matter of treaty interpretation, this cannot be so. Therefore, we consider it an error to interpret the "material advantage" clause in item (k) of the Illustrative List as meaning the same as the term "benefit" in Article 1.1(b) of the *SCM Agreement*.

180. We note that there are two paragraphs in item (k), and that the "material advantage" clause appears in the first paragraph. Furthermore, the second paragraph is a proviso to the first paragraph. The second paragraph applies when a Member is "a party to an international undertaking on official export credits" which satisfies the conditions of the proviso, or when a Member "applies the interest rates provisions of the relevant undertaking". In such circumstances, an "export credit practice" which is in conformity with the provisions of "an international undertaking on official export credits" shall not be considered an export subsidy prohibited by the *SCM Agreement*. The *OECD Arrangement* is an "international undertaking on official export credits" that satisfies the requirements of the proviso in the second paragraph in item (k). However, Brazil did not invoke the proviso in the second paragraph of item (k) in its defence. Brazil argued before the Panel that it "has concluded that conformity to the OECD provisions is too expensive."

181. Thus, this case falls under the first paragraph, and not under the proviso of the second paragraph, of item (k) of the Illustrative List. Consequently, the issue here is whether the export subsidies for regional aircraft under PROEX "are used to secure" for Brazil "a material advantage in the field of export credit terms". Nevertheless, we see the second paragraph of item (k) as useful context for interpreting the "material advantage" clause in the text of the first paragraph. The *OECD Arrangement* establishes minimum interest rate guidelines for export credits supported by its participants ("officially-supported export credits"). Article 15 of the Arrangement defines the minimum interest rates applicable to officially-supported export credits as the Commercial Interest Reference Rates ("CIRRs"). Article 16 provides a methodology by which a CIRR, for the currency of each participant, may be determined for this purpose. We believe that the *OECD Arrangement* can be appropriately viewed as one example of an international undertaking providing a specific market benchmark by which to assess whether payments by governments, coming within the provisions of item (k), are "used to secure a material advantage in the field of export credit terms". Therefore, in our view, the appropriate comparison to be made in determining whether a payment is "used to secure a material advantage", within the meaning of item (k), is between the actual interest rate applicable in a particular export sales transaction after deduction of the government payment (the "*net* interest rate") and the relevant CIRR.

182. It should be noted that the commercial interest rate with respect to a loan in any given currency varies according to the length of maturity as well as the creditworthiness of the borrower. Thus, a potential borrower is not faced with a single commercial interest rate, but rather with a range of rates. Under the *OECD Arrangement*, a CIRR is the *minimum* commercial rate available in that range for a particular currency. In any given case, whether or not a government payment is used to secure a *"material* advantage", as opposed to an "advantage" that is not "material", may well depend on where the *net* interest rate applicable to the particular transaction at issue in that case stands in relation to the range of commercial rates available. The fact that a particular *net* interest rate is below the relevant CIRR is a positive indication that the government payment in that case has been "used to secure a material advantage in the field of export credit terms".

183. Brazil has conceded that it has the burden of proving an alleged "affirmative defence" under item (k). In light of our analysis, it was for Brazil to establish a *prima facie* case that the export subsidies for regional aircraft under PROEX do not result in net interest rates below the relevant CIRR. We note, however, that Brazil did not provide *any information* to the Panel on this point. We also note that Brazil declined to provide this information, even when specifically requested to do so by the Panel. Because Brazil provided *no information* on the net interest rates paid by purchasers of Embraer aircraft in actual export sales transactions, we have no basis on which to compare the net interest rates resulting from the interest rate equalization payments made under PROEX with the relevant CIRR.

184. Accordingly, we find that Brazil has failed to meet its burden of proving that export subsidies for regional aircraft under PROEX are not "used to secure a material advantage in the field of export credit terms" within the meaning of item (k) of the Illustrative List.

185. We are aware that the *OECD Arrangement* allows a government to "match", under certain conditions, officially-supported export credit terms provided by another government. In a particular case, this could result in net interest rates below the relevant CIRR. We are persuaded that "matching" in the sense of the *OECD Arrangement* is not applicable in this case. Before the Panel, Brazil argued for an interpretation of the clause "in the field of export credit terms" that would include as an "export credit term" the price at which a product is sold, and maintained that, therefore, Brazil was entitled to "offset" *all the subsidies* provided to Bombardier by the Government of Canada. The Panel rejected Brazil's argument, finding instead that "[w]e see nothing in the ordinary meaning of the phrase to suggest that 'the field of export credit terms' generally encompasses the price at which a product is sold." We note that this finding was *not* appealed by either Brazil or Canada. Even if we were to assume that the "matching" provisions of the *OECD Arrangement* apply in this case (an argument Brazil did not make), those provisions clearly do not allow a comparison to be made between the net interest rates applied as a consequence of subsidies

granted by a particular Member and the total amount of subsidies provided by another Member. We also note that under PROEX, the interest rate equalization subsidies for regional aircraft are provided at an "across-the-board" rate of 3.8 per cent for *all* export sales transactions. That rate is fixed, and does not vary depending on the total amount of subsidies provided by another Member to its regional aircraft manufacturers. Thus, we cannot accept Brazil's argument that the export subsidies for regional aircraft under PROEX should be "permitted" because they "match" the total subsidies provided to Bombardier by the Government of Canada.

186. For all these reasons, we do not agree with the Panel's interpretation of the phrase "used to secure a material advantage in the field of export credit terms" in item (k) of the Illustrative List. We do, however, agree with the Panel's conclusion that "Brazil has failed to demonstrate the PROEX payments are not 'used to secure a material advantage in the field of export credit terms'." We, therefore, uphold the Panel's rejection of the "affirmative defence" claimed by Brazil on the basis of item (k) of the Illustrative List.

187. In so doing, we do not rule on whether the export subsidies for regional aircraft under PROEX are "the payment by [governments] of all or part of the costs incurred by exporters or financial institutions in obtaining credits". Nor do we opine on whether a "payment" within the meaning of item (k) which is not "used to secure a material advantage within the field of export credit terms" is, *a contrario*, "permitted" by the *SCM Agreement*, even though it is a subsidy which is contingent upon export performance within the meaning of Article 3.1(a) of that Agreement. The Panel did not rule on these issues, and the lack of Panel findings on these issues was not appealed.

Notes and Questions

(1) What if the PROEX payments result in net interest rates of 0.5% below the pertinent CIRR benchmark. Would a violation of WTO law be proven?

(2) What was the issue left undecided regarding whether PROEX involved "the payment by [governments] of all or part of the costs incurred by exporters or financial institutions in obtaining credits?"

(3) The OECD Arrangement permits parties to match an offer by another party that is not in conformity with the Arrangement. Would such an offer fall within the terms of item (k) as quoted in paragraph 168 above? Two panels have said no, because when a party matches a derogation, it is not "in conformity with [the interest rate] provisions" of the Arrangement. Do you agree? Canada–Measures Affecting the Export of Civilian Aircraft–Recourse to Article 21.5 by Brazil, WT/DS70/RW, para. 5.114, panel report adopted by the DSB on August 4, 2000; Brazil–Export Financing Programme for Aircraft–Second Recourse to Article 21.5 by Canada, WT/DS46/RW/2, para. 5.118, panel report adopted by the DSB on August 23, 2001. The issue was not appealed in either case, but as of this writing these rulings had not been accepted by Canada (or the U.S. or EC for that matter).

UNITED STATES—TAX TREATMENT FOR "FOREIGN SALES CORPORATIONS"

WT/DS108/AB/R

Appellate Body Report adopted by the DSB on March 20, 2000

A. Overview of Relevant United States Tax Laws

6. For United States citizens and residents, the tax laws of the United States generally operate "on a worldwide basis". This means that, generally, the United States asserts the right to tax all income earned "worldwide" by its citizens and residents. A corporation organized under the laws of one of the fifty American states or the District of Columbia is a "domestic", or United States, corporation, and is "resident" in the United States for purposes of this "worldwide" taxation system. Under United States tax law, "foreign" corporations are defined as all corporations that are *not* incorporated in one of the fifty states or the District of Columbia.

7. The United States generally taxes any income earned by foreign corporations within the territory of the United States. The United States generally does not tax income that is earned by foreign corporations outside the United States. However, such "foreign-source" income of a foreign corporation generally will be subject to United States taxation when such income is "effectively connected with the conduct of a trade or business within the United States". United States tax laws and regulations provide for the tax authorities to conduct a factual inquiry to determine whether a foreign corporation's income is "effectively connected" income.

8. Many foreign corporations are related to United States corporations. Generally, a United States parent corporation is only subject to taxation on income earned by its foreign subsidiary when such income is transferred to the United States parent in the form of a dividend. The period between the earning of such income by the subsidiary and the transfer to the United States parent company of a dividend is called "deferral" under the United States tax system, because the payment of tax on that income is deferred until the income is repatriated to the United States.

9. The United States has also adopted a series of "anti-deferral" regimes that depart from the principle of deferral and that, in general, respond to specific policy concerns about potential tax avoidance by United States corporations through foreign affiliates. One of these regimes is Subpart F of the United States Internal Revenue Code (the "IRC"), which limits the availability of deferral for certain types of income earned by certain controlled foreign subsidiaries of United States corporations. Under Subpart F, certain income earned by a foreign subsidiary can be imputed to its United States parent corporation even though it has not yet been repatriated to the parent in the form of a dividend. The effect of Subpart F is that a United States parent corpora-

tion is immediately subject to United States taxation on such imputed income even while the income remains with the foreign subsidiary.

10.   These generally prevailing United States tax rules are altered for FSCs [Foreign Sales Corporations] by the FSC measure.

B.   THE FSC MEASURE

11.   FSCs are foreign corporations responsible for certain sales-related activities in connection with the sale or lease of goods produced in the United States for export outside the United States. The FSC measure essentially exempts a portion of an FSC's export-related foreign-source income from United States income tax. * * *

12.   A corporation must satisfy several conditions to qualify as an FSC. To qualify, a corporation must be a foreign corporation organized under the laws of a country that shares tax information with the United States, or under the laws of a United States possession other than Puerto Rico. The corporation must satisfy additional requirements relating to its foreign presence, to the keeping of records, and to its shareholders and directors. The corporation must also elect to be an FSC for a given fiscal year. There is no statutory requirement that an FSC be affiliated with or controlled by a United States corporation. The FSC measure is, however, such that the benefit to both FSCs and the United States corporations that supply goods for export will, as a practical matter, often be greater if the United States supplier is related to the FSC. As a result, many FSCs are controlled foreign subsidiaries of United States corporations.

13.   The foreign-source income of an FSC may be broadly divided into "foreign trade income" and all other foreign-source income. "Foreign trade income" is essentially the foreign-source income attributable to an FSC from qualifying transactions involving the export of goods from the United States. An FSC's other foreign-source income may include *inter alia* "investment income", such as interest, dividends and royalties, and active business income not deriving from qualifying export transactions. This appeal raises a number of issues with respect to the taxation of an FSC's *foreign trade income*. Foreign trade income is in turn divided into *exempt* foreign trade income and *non-exempt* foreign trade income. As explained below, the United States tax treatment of an FSC's *exempt* foreign trade income differs from the United States tax treatment of an FSC's *non-exempt* foreign trade income.

14.   An FSC's foreign trade income is its "foreign trading gross receipts" generated in qualifying transactions. Qualifying transactions involve the sale or lease of "export property" or the performance of services "related and subsidiary" to such sale or lease. "Export property" is property manufactured or produced in the United States by a person other than an FSC, sold or leased by or to an FSC for use, consumption or disposition outside the United States, and of which no more than 50 per cent of its fair market value is attributable to imports. In addition, for FSC income to be foreign trade income, certain economic

processes relating to qualifying transactions must take place outside the United States, and the FSC must be managed outside the United States.

15.   Under the FSC measure, an FSC may, at its option, choose to apply one of three transfer pricing rules in order to calculate its foreign trade income from qualifying transactions. These pricing rules serve two purposes. First, the transfer pricing rules allocate the income from transactions involving United States export property as between an FSC and its United States supplier. The part of this income attributable to the FSC is its foreign trade income (i.e. exempt and non-exempt foreign trade income). The second purpose of the transfer pricing rules is to determine how much of the income from transactions involving United States export property that is allocated to the FSC as foreign trade income is *exempt* foreign trade income, and how much of it is *non-exempt* foreign trade income. The transfer pricing rule applied to determine the amount of the FSC's foreign trade income must also be applied to determine the division of that foreign trade income into exempt and non-exempt foreign trade income.

C.   EXEMPTIONS PROVIDED BY THE FSC MEASURE

16.   The FSC measure establishes three main exemptions which affect the United States tax liability of the FSC, of its United States supplier and, possibly United States shareholders. The first exemption relates to the United States tax treatment of the foreign-source income of a foreign corporation. Under United States law generally, the foreign-source income of a foreign corporation engaged in trade or business in the United States is taxable only to the extent that it is "effectively connected with the conduct of a trade or business within the United States". This rule applies whether or not a foreign corporation is controlled by a United States corporation. To determine whether the foreign-source income of a foreign corporation is "effectively connected with the conduct of a trade or business within the United States", a factual inquiry is undertaken by the tax authorities. Under the FSC measure, however, the exempt portion of an FSC's foreign trade income is "treated as foreign source income which is not effectively connected with the conduct of a trade or business within the United States". In other words, the exempt portion of the FSC's foreign trade income is not subject to a factual inquiry to determine if it is "effectively connected with the conduct of a trade or business within the United States". Thus, under this first exemption, a portion of an FSC's foreign-source income is *legislatively determined not to be* "effectively connected" and, therefore, is not taxable in the hands of the FSC–without regard to what conclusion an administrative factual inquiry might come to in the absence of the FSC measure.

17.   The second exemption relates to the United States tax treatment of certain income earned by a foreign corporation that is controlled by a United States corporation. Under United States law generally, a United States shareholder in a controlled foreign corporation must include in his gross income each year a *pro rata* share of certain forms of

income of the foreign controlled corporation which has not yet been distributed to its United States parent. Such income is known as "Subpart F income". The United States shareholder corporation is immediately subject to United States tax on its Subpart F income, even though it has not yet received the income from its foreign affiliate. Under the FSC measure, however, the foreign trade income of an FSC is generally exempted from Subpart F. Thus, under this second exemption, the parent of an FSC is *not* required to declare its *pro rata* share of the undistributed income of an FSC that is derived from the foreign trade income of the FSC, and is *not* taxed on such income.

18.   The third exemption deals with the tax treatment of dividends received by United States corporations from foreign corporations. Under United States law generally, dividends received by a United States corporation which are derived from the foreign-source income of a foreign corporation are taxable, unless such income has already been taxed under the Subpart F rules. Under the FSC measure, however, United States corporate shareholders of an FSC generally may deduct 100 per cent of dividends received from distributions made out of the foreign trade income of an FSC. Thus, under the third exemption, the parent of an FSC is generally not taxed on dividends received that are derived from the foreign trade income of the FSC.

* * *

ARTICLE 1.1(a) OF THE *SCM AGREEMENT*

90.   We turn now to the definition of the term "subsidy" and, in particular, to Article 1.1(a)(1)(ii) [of the SCM Agreement], which provides that there is a "financial contribution" by a government, sufficient to fulfil that element in the definition of a "subsidy", where "government revenue that is *otherwise due* is foregone or not collected". (emphasis added) In our view, the *"foregoing"* of revenue *"otherwise* due" implies that less revenue has been raised by the government than would have been raised in a different situation, or, that is, "otherwise". Moreover, the word "foregone" suggests that the government has given up an entitlement to raise revenue that it could "otherwise" have raised. This cannot, however, be an entitlement in the abstract, because governments, in theory, could tax *all* revenues. There must, therefore, be some defined, normative benchmark against which a comparison can be made between the revenue actually raised and the revenue that would have been raised "otherwise". We, therefore, agree with the Panel that the term "otherwise due" implies some kind of comparison between the revenues due under the contested measure and revenues that would be due in some other situation. We also agree with the Panel that the basis of comparison must be the tax rules applied by the Member in question. To accept the argument of the United States that the comparator in determining what is "otherwise due" should be something other than the prevailing domestic standard of the Member in question would be to imply that WTO obligations somehow compel Members to choose a particular kind of tax system; this is not so. A Member, in principle, has

the sovereign authority to tax any particular categories of revenue it wishes. It is also free *not* to tax any particular categories of revenues. But, in both instances, the Member must respect its WTO obligations. What is "otherwise due", therefore, depends on the rules of taxation that each Member, by its own choice, establishes for itself.

91. The Panel found that the term "otherwise due" establishes a "but for" test, in terms of which the appropriate basis of comparison for determining whether revenues are "otherwise due" is "the situation that would prevail but for the measures in question". In the present case, this legal standard provides a sound basis for comparison because it is not difficult to establish in what way the foreign-source income of an FSC would be taxed "but for" the contested measure. However, we have certain abiding reservations about applying any legal standard, such as this "but for" test, in the place of the actual treaty language. Moreover, we would have particular misgivings about using a "but for" test if its application were limited to situations where there actually existed an alternative measure, under which the revenues in question would be taxed, absent the contested measure. It would, we believe, not be difficult to circumvent such a test by designing a tax regime under which there would be *no* general rule that applied formally to the revenues in question, absent the contested measures. We observe, therefore, that, although the Panel's "but for" test works in this case, it may not work in other cases. We note, however, that, in this dispute, the European Communities does not contest either the Panel's interpretation of the term "otherwise due" or the Panel's application of that term to the facts of this case. The United States also accepts the Panel's interpretation of that term as a general proposition.

92. The United States does, however, argue that the Panel erred because the general interpretation of the term "otherwise due" "must yield" to the standard the United States perceives in footnote 59 of the *SCM Agreement*, which the United States contends, is the "controlling legal provision" for interpretation of the term "otherwise due" with respect to a measure of the kind at issue. In the view of the United States, footnote 59 means that the FSC measure is not a "subsidy" under Article 1.1 of the *SCM Agreement*. Thus, the United States does not read footnote 59 as providing context for the general interpretation of the term "otherwise due"; rather, the United States views footnote 59 as a form of exception to that general interpretation. * * *

93. Article 1.1 sets forth the general definition of the term "subsidy" which applies "for the purpose of this Agreement". This definition, therefore, applies wherever the word "subsidy" occurs throughout the *SCM Agreement* and conditions the application of the provisions of that Agreement regarding *prohibited* subsidies in Part II, *actionable* subsidies in Part III, *non-actionable* subsidies in Part IV and countervailing measures in Part V. By contrast, footnote 59 relates to one item in the Illustrative List of Export Subsidies. Even if footnote 59 means–as the United States also argues–that a measure, such as the FSC measure, is *not* a prohibited *export* subsidy, footnote 59 does not purport to establish

an exception to the general definition of a *"subsidy"* otherwise applicable throughout the entire *SCM Agreement*. Under footnote 5 of the *SCM Agreement*, where the Illustrative List indicates that a measure is not a prohibited *export* subsidy, that measure is *not* deemed, for that reason alone, not to be a "subsidy". Rather, the measure is simply *not prohibited* under the Agreement. Other provisions of the *SCM Agreement* may, however, still apply to such a "subsidy". We note, moreover, that, under footnote 1 of the *SCM Agreement*, "the exemption of an exported *product* from duties or taxes *borne by the like product* when destined for domestic consumption . . . shall not be deemed to be a subsidy". (emphasis added) The tax measures identified in footnote 1 as not constituting a *"subsidy"* involve the exemption of exported *products* from *product-based* consumption taxes. The tax exemptions under the FSC measure relate to the taxation of *corporations* and not *products*. Footnote 1, therefore, does *not* cover measures such as the FSC measure.

94.   In light of the above, we do not accept the United States' argument that footnote 59 qualifies the general interpretation of the term "otherwise due". That being so, it is not necessary for us to examine, at this point, the United States' arguments on the interpretation of footnote 59. * * *

95.   The United States' appeal from the Panel's findings under Article 1.1 of the *SCM Agreement* is limited to its contention that the general interpretation of the term "otherwise due" is qualified by footnote 59. As we do not accept that sole ground of appeal, we uphold the Panel's finding that, under the FSC measure, the government of the United States foregoes revenue that is "otherwise due" under Article 1.1(a)(1)(ii) of the *SCM Agreement*. We note, in this respect, that the United States acknowledges that the FSC measure represents a departure from the rules of taxation that would "otherwise" apply to FSCs. We note also that the United States does not contest that, absent the FSC measure, the tax liability of the FSCs would be higher.

ARTICLE 3.1(a) OF THE *SCM AGREEMENT*

96.   The United States' appeal from the Panel's findings under Article 3.1(a) is limited to its contention that footnote 59 * * * means that the FSC measure is not an "export subsidy". Footnote 59 reads:

> The Members recognize that deferral need not amount to an export subsidy where, for example, appropriate interest charges are collected. *The Members reaffirm the principle that prices for goods in transactions between exporting enterprises and foreign buyers under their or under the same control should for tax purposes be the prices which would be charged between independent enterprises acting at arm's length.* Any Member may draw the attention of another Member to administrative or other practices which may contravene this principle and which result in a significant saving of direct taxes in export transactions. In such circumstances the Members shall normally attempt to resolve their differences using the facilities of existing bilateral tax treaties or other specific international mecha-

nisms, without prejudice to the rights and obligations of Members under GATT 1994, including the right of consultation created in the preceding sentence.

Paragraph (e) is not intended to limit a Member from taking measures to avoid the double taxation of foreign-source income earned by its enterprises or the enterprises of another Member. (emphasis added)

97. We need to examine footnote 59 sentence by sentence. The first sentence of footnote 59 is specifically related to the statement in item (e) of the Illustrative List that the "full or partial exemption remission, or deferral specifically related to exports, of direct taxes" is an export subsidy. The first sentence of footnote 59 qualifies this by stating that "deferral need not amount to an export subsidy where, for example, appropriate interest charges are collected." Since the FSC measure does not involve the *deferral* of direct taxes, we do not believe that this sentence of footnote 59 bears upon the characterization of the FSC measure as constituting, or not, an "export subsidy".

98. The second sentence of footnote 59 "reaffirms" that, in allocating export sales revenues, for tax purposes, between exporting enterprises and controlled foreign buyers, the price for the goods shall be determined according to the "arm's length" principle to which that sentence of the footnote refers. Like the Panel, we are willing to accept, for the sake of argument, the United States' position that it is "implicit" in the requirement to use the arm's length principle that Members of the WTO are not obliged to tax foreign-source income, and also that Members may tax such income less than they tax domestic-source income. We would add that, even in the absence of footnote 59, Members of the WTO are *not* obliged, by WTO rules, to tax *any* categories of income, whether foreign- or domestic-source income. The United States argues that, since there is no requirement to tax export-related foreign-source income, a government cannot be said to have "foregone" revenue if it elects not to tax that income. It seems to us that, taken to its logical conclusion, this argument by the United States would mean that there could *never* be a foregoing of revenue "otherwise due" because, in principle, under WTO law generally, *no* revenues are ever due and *no* revenue would, in this view, ever be "foregone". That cannot be the appropriate implication to draw from the requirement to use the arm's length principle.

99. Furthermore, we do not believe that the requirement to use the arm's length principle resolves the issue that arises here. That issue is *not*, as the United States suggests, whether a Member is or is not obliged to tax a particular category of foreign-source income. As we have said, a Member is not, in general, under any such obligation. Rather, the issue in dispute is whether, *having decided to tax a particular category of foreign-source income*, namely foreign-source income that is "effectively connected with a trade or business within the United States", the United States is *permitted to carve out an export contingent exemption from the category of foreign-source income that is taxed under its other*

rules of taxation. Unlike the United States, we do not believe that the second sentence of footnote 59 addresses this question. It plainly does not do so expressly; neither, as far as we can see, does it do so by necessary implication. As the United States indicates, the arm's length principle operates when a Member chooses not to tax, or to tax less, certain categories of foreign-source income. However, the operation of the arm's length principle is unaffected by the choice a Member makes as to *which* categories of foreign-source income, if any, it will not tax, or will tax less. Likewise, the operation of the arm's length principle is unaffected by the choice a Member might make to grant exemptions from the generally applicable rules of taxation of foreign-source income that it has selected for itself. In short, the requirement to use the arm's length principle does not address the issue that arises here, nor does it authorize the type of export contingent tax exemption that we have just described. Thus, this sentence of footnote 59 does not mean that the FSC subsidies are not export subsidies within the meaning of Article 3.1(a) of the *SCM Agreement.*

100. The third and fourth sentences of footnote 59 set forth rules that relate to remedies. In our view, these rules have no bearing on the substantive obligations of Members under Articles 1.1 and 3.1 of the *SCM Agreement.* So, we turn to the fifth and final sentence of footnote 59. That sentence provides:

> Paragraph (e) is not intended to limit a Member from taking measures to avoid the double taxation of foreign-source income earned by its enterprises or the enterprises of another Member.

101. On appeal, the United States maintains that the FSC measure is a measure "to avoid double taxation of foreign-source income" *under footnote 59.* As a consequence, the United States further contends that the FSC measure is excluded from the prohibition against export subsidies in Article 3.1(a) of the *SCM Agreement.* During the oral hearing, we asked the United States to identify where it had asserted before the Panel that the FSC measure is a measure "to avoid double taxation of foreign-source income" under footnote 59. That is, we asked the United States to tell us specifically where it had invoked the fifth sentence of footnote 59 as a means of justifying the FSC measure. In reply, the United States pointed to its first written submission to the Panel. In that submission, in describing the FSC measure and before setting forth its legal arguments, the United States stated that "the FSC is designed to prevent double taxation of export income earned outside the United States by exempting a portion of the FSC's income from taxation." The United States pointed also to certain general arguments it made before the Panel concerning the fifth sentence of footnote 59. However, the United States did not indicate that, in its substantive arguments to the Panel, it had justified the FSC measure as a measure "to avoid double taxation" under footnote 59. Nor do we find any indication in the Panel Record that the United States ever invoked this justification. We, therefore, conclude that the United States did not assert, far less argue, before the Panel that the FSC measure is a measure "to avoid double

taxation of foreign-source income" under footnote 59. Our conclusion is confirmed by the Panel's statement, in footnote 682 of the Panel Report, that the United States had not asserted that the fifth sentence of footnote 59 was "relevant to this dispute". It follows, therefore, that this issue was not properly litigated before the Panel and that the Panel was not asked to examine whether the FSC measure is a measure "to avoid double taxation of foreign-source income" under footnote 59.

* * *

121.   In light of all the foregoing, we uphold the Panel's conclusion, in paragraph 8.1 of the Panel Report, that the FSC tax exemptions involve subsidies contingent upon export performance that are prohibited under Article 3.1(a) of the *SCM Agreement*.

Notes and Questions

(1) A subsidy exists if tax revenue "otherwise due" is not collected, yet there is no obligation to tax anything in the first instance. Why define "subsidy" in this fashion?

(2) With reference to para. 91, when would the panel's "but for" test become problematic? What would the Appellate Body substitute for it?

(3) The FSC case has a long history. GATT disputes involving the United States, Belgium, France and the Netherlands arose in the mid–1970's, which included a challenge before a GATT panel to the U.S. tax law creating Domestic International Sales Corporations (DISC's). The panel ruled that the DISC legislation was an export subsidy. See DISC—United States Tax Legislation, GATT Doc. No. L/4422m GATT 23d Supp. BISD 98 (1977). The United States blocked adoption of the report until a compromise was reached in 1981 that resulted in a declaration that tracked closely the language of footnote 59 of the SCM Agreement. Three years later the FSC measure was enacted, which the United States insisted was consistent with the principles of the 1981 declaration. In an omitted part of the *FSC* case, the Appellate Body held that the 1981 declaration of the GATT Council had not been incorporated into GATT 1994 as an "other decision" (see definition of GATT 1994 in Annex 1A to the WTO Agreement) and did "not provide useful interpretative 'guidance' in resolving the legal issue relating to the FSC measure that is raised in this appeal" (para. 120). The U.S. FSC measure was repealed and replaced in the Extraterritorial Income Exclusion Act of 2000, which was itself the subject of an Article 21.5 challenge by the European Community on the grounds that it too was an export subsidy. The panel ruled in favor of EU, but the U.S. appealed so that the matter remains unresolved at this writing. An appellate decision is expected early in 2002.

CANADA—CERTAIN MEASURES AFFECTING THE AUTOMOTIVE INDUSTRY
WT/DS139 & 142/AB/R
Adopted by the DSB on June 19, 2000

8.   The MVTO [Motor Vehicles Tariff Order] 1998 has its origins in the Agreement Concerning Automotive Products Between the Govern-

ment of Canada and the Government of the United States of America (the "Auto Pact"), which was implemented domestically in Canada by the MVTO 1965 and the Tariff Item 950 Regulations. These legal instruments were replaced by the MVTO 1988 and later by the MVTO 1998. The MVTO 1998 is in effect today.

9. Under the MVTO 1998, [an] import duty exemption is available to manufacturers of motor vehicles on imports [of vehicles] "from any country entitled to the Most–Favoured–Nation Tariff" , if the manufacturer meets the following three conditions: (1) it must have produced in Canada, during the designated "base year", motor vehicles of the class imported; (2) the ratio of the net sales value of the vehicles *produced in Canada* to the net sales value of all vehicles of that class *sold* for consumption *in Canada* in the period of importation must be "equal to or higher than" the ratio in the "base year", and the ratio shall not in any case be lower than 75:100 (the "ratio requirements"); and (3) the amount of Canadian value added in the manufacturer's local production of motor vehicles must be "equal to or greater than" the amount of Canadian value added in the local production of motor vehicles of that class during the "base year" (the "CVA requirements").

* * *

87. Canada appeals the Panel's finding that the measure is a "subsidy" within the meaning of Article 1.1 of the *SCM Agreement*. For Canada, the measure does not, in the language of Article 1.1, forego "government revenue that is otherwise due". Canada argues that the import duty exemption at issue here cannot be equated mechanically with a tax exemption, such as the one at issue in *United States–Tax Treatment for "Foreign Sales Corporations" United States–FSC"*). For Canada, the import duty exemption should be considered a "subsidy" only if it provides an exemption from duties *in excess* of those that would have "accrued". Canada maintains, as well, that most motor vehicles benefiting from the import duty exemption could have been imported into Canada duty-free under the NAFTA.

* * *

89. * * * [W]e look first at the wording of Article 1.1 of the *SCM Agreement*, which states, *inter alia*, that a "subsidy" exists if "there is a financial contribution by a government ... and a benefit is thereby conferred". A "financial contribution" is deemed to exist, *inter alia*, where "government revenue that is *otherwise due* is foregone or not collected". (emphasis added)

* * *

91. * * * We note, once more, that Canada has established a normal MFN duty rate for imports of motor vehicles of 6.1 per cent. Absent the import duty exemption, this duty would be paid on imports of motor vehicles. Thus, through the measure in dispute, the Government of Canada has, in the words of *United States–FSC*, "given up an

entitlement to raise revenue that it could 'otherwise' have raised." More specifically, through the import duty exemption, Canada has ignored the "defined, normative benchmark" that it established for itself for import duties on motor vehicles under its normal MFN rate and, in so doing, has foregone "government revenue that is otherwise due".

92.   Canada argues that the measure is "analogous" to the situation described in footnote 1 to the *SCM Agreement*, which provides that "the exemption of an exported product from duties or taxes borne by the like product when destined for domestic consumption, or the remission of such duties or taxes in amounts not in excess of those which have accrued, shall not be deemed to be a subsidy." We do not share Canada's view. Footnote 1 to the *SCM Agreement* deals with duty and tax exemptions or remissions for *exported* products. The measure at issue applies, in contrast, to *imports* of motor vehicles which are sold for consumption in Canada. For this reason, we do not consider that footnote 1 bears upon the import duty exemption at issue in this case.

93.   In our view, it is also not relevant that motor vehicles benefiting from the import duty exemption may enter Canada duty-free if imported under the provisions of the NAFTA. Duty-free treatment under the NAFTA is not at issue in this case. The measure at issue in this case is the import duty exemption set out in the MVTO 1998 and the SROs.

94.   For these reasons, we uphold the Panel's finding that "government revenue that is otherwise due is foregone" and that the measure constitutes a "subsidy" under Article 1.1 of the *SCM Agreement*.

ARTICLE 3.1(a) OF THE SCM AGREEMENT

95.   Canada appeals the Panel's finding that the measure is a subsidy which is "contingent . . . in law . . . upon export performance" within the meaning of Article 3.1(a) of the *SCM Agreement*. * * *

* * *

97.   Article 3.1 of the *SCM Agreement* provides, in pertinent part:

Except as provided in the Agreement on Agriculture, the following subsidies, within the meaning of Article 1, shall be prohibited:

(a) subsidies contingent, in law or in fact, whether solely or as one of several other conditions, upon export performance, including those illustrated in Annex I;

* * *

99.   Although in *Canada–Aircraft* we were dealing with a subsidy that was contingent "in fact" upon export performance, we stated in that case that "the legal standard expressed by the word 'contingent' is the same for both *de jure* or *de facto* contingency." We stated, furthermore, that:

There is a difference, however, in what evidence may be employed to prove that a subsidy is export contingent. *De jure* export contingency is demonstrated on the basis of the words of the relevant legislation, regulation or other legal instrument. Proving *de facto* export contingency is a much more difficult task. There is no single legal document which will demonstrate, on its face, that a subsidy is "contingent...in fact...upon export performance". Instead, the existence of this relationship of contingency, between the subsidy and export performance, must be *inferred* from the total configuration of the facts constituting and surrounding the granting of the subsidy, none of which on its own is likely to be decisive in any given case. (emphasis in italics in the original; emphasis in underlining added)

100.   * * * In our view, a subsidy is contingent "in law" upon export performance when the existence of that condition can be demonstrated on the basis of the very words of the relevant legislation, regulation or other legal instrument constituting the measure. The simplest, and hence, perhaps, the uncommon, case is one in which the condition of exportation is set out expressly, in so many words, on the face of the law, regulation or other legal instrument. We believe, however, that a subsidy is also properly held to be *de jure* export contingent where the condition to export is clearly, though implicitly, in the instrument comprising the measure. Thus, for a subsidy to be *de jure* export contingent, the underlying legal instrument does not always have to provide *expressis verbis* that the subsidy is available only upon fulfillment of the condition of export performance. Such conditionality can also be derived by necessary implication from the words actually used in the measure.

* * *

102.   The Panel found, as a matter of fact, that:

... the ratio requirements applicable to the MVTO 1998 beneficiaries are, "as a general rule", 95:100 for automobiles, at least 75:100 for SCVs and at least 75:100 for buses. With respect, specifically, to the four automobile manufacturer beneficiaries under the MVTO 1998, Canada has stated, in response to a question from the Panel, that the amounts of the ratio requirements are confidential. Canada adds that they range from the low–80s:100 to the high–90s:100, and the average of the four amounts is approximately 95:100. * * *

* * *

104.   We agree with the Panel that "[i]n cases where the production-to-sales ratio is 100:100, the only way to import any motor vehicles duty-free is to export, and the amount of import duty exemption allowed is directly dependent upon the amount of exports achieved." Like the Panel, we fail to see how a manufacturer with a production-to-sales ratio of 100:100 could obtain access to the import duty exemption–and still maintain its required production-to-sales ratio–without exporting. A manufacturer producing motor vehicles in Canada with a sales value of 100 that does not export must sell all those motor vehicles in Canada. That manufacturer's production-to-sales ratio becomes 100:100, but without the benefit of importing duty-free one single motor vehicle. Only

if that manufacturer exports motor vehicles produced in Canada does it become entitled to import motor vehicles free of duty. The value of motor vehicles which can be imported duty-free is strictly limited to the value of motor vehicles exported. In our view, as the import duty exemption is simply not available to a manufacturer unless it exports motor vehicles, the import duty exemption is clearly conditional, or dependent upon, exportation and, therefore, is contrary to Article 3.1(a) of the SCM Agreement.

105.   Where the ratio requirements are set at less than 100:100 (for example, we know that the four MVTO automobile manufacturer beneficiaries have, on average, ratio requirements of approximately 95:100), the relationship between exports and the ability to import duty-free is less straightforward. With a ratio requirement of 95:100, a manufacturer producing motor vehicles in Canada with a sales value of 95 that does not export is nevertheless entitled to import, duty-free, additional motor vehicles with a sales value of 5. If that manufacturer doubles its Canadian production to 190, then the amount of the duty-free "allowance" also doubles, to 10; that is, the "allowance" increases in direct proportion to the increase in production. The Panel considered that, up to this amount, the import duty exemption is not contingent upon export performance. However, should a manufacturer wish to import on a duty-free basis any motor vehicles above its "allowance", that manufacturer must export motor vehicles. As in the case of a 100:100 ratio requirement, for a manufacturer with a ratio requirement less than 100:100, for any amount above this duty-free "allowance", the value of vehicles which can be imported duty-free is strictly limited, and tied to, the value of vehicles exported. The Panel found that for the amount exceeding the duty-free "allowance" there is, therefore, a clear relationship of contingency between the import duty exemption and export performance.

* * *

108.   Even where the ratio requirement for a particular manufacturer is set at less than 100:100, in our view, there is contingency "in law" upon export performance because, as a result of the operation of the MVTO 1998 and the SROs themselves, the granting of, or the entitlement to, the import duty exemption is tied to the exportation of motor vehicles by the manufacturer beneficiaries. By the very operation of the measure, the more motor vehicles that a manufacturer exports, the more motor vehicles it can import duty-free. In other words, a clear relationship of dependency or conditionality exists between the granting of the import duty exemption and the exportation of motor vehicles by manufacturer beneficiaries. We find, therefore, that, even when the ratio requirements are less than 100:100, the measure is "contingent...in law...upon export performance".

109.   For these reasons, we uphold the Panel's conclusion that the measure is a "subsidy" as that term is used in Article 1 of the *SCM Agreement* which is "contingent...in law...upon export performance" within the meaning of Article 3.1(a) of the same Agreement. Accordingly,

we also uphold the Panel's finding that Canada acts inconsistently with its obligations under Article 3.1(a) of the *SCM Agreement*.

* * *

ARTICLE 3.1(b) OF THE SCM AGREEMENT

118. The European Communities and Japan appeal the Panel's finding that they failed to demonstrate that the import duty exemption is a subsidy which is "contingent . . . upon the use of domestic over imported goods" under Article 3.1(b) of the *SCM Agreement*. They maintain that the Panel erred in concluding that the measure is not contingent "in law" upon the use of domestic over imported goods.

* * *

122. Article 3.1(b) provides as follows:

Except as provided in the Agreement on Agriculture, the following subsidies, within the meaning of Article 1, shall be prohibited:

. . .

(b) subsidies contingent, whether solely or as one of several other conditions, upon the use of domestic over imported goods.

As we have already found that the import duty exemption constitutes a "subsidy" within the meaning of Article 1 of the *SCM Agreement*, we turn to whether this subsidy is contingent "in law" upon the use of domestic over imported goods.

* * *

125. The import duty exemption at issue in this appeal is contingent on the satisfaction of three requirements: (1) manufacturing presence in Canada, (2) the ratio requirements, and (3) the CVA requirements. The Panel found that each of these requirements was a "condition" for receiving the import duty exemption. Under the measure, a manufacturer applying for the import duty exemption in a particular period is required to disclose to the Government of Canada the *aggregate* of the costs, listed in the definition of "Canadian value added" in the MVTO 1998, of producing vehicles in Canada, so as to demonstrate that the manufacturer has satisfied the CVA requirements. One of these costs–indeed, the first one listed–is Canadian parts and materials incorporated in motor vehicles in the factory of the manufacturer in Canada, that is, "domestic goods".

126. The precise issue under Article 3.1(b) is whether the *use* of domestic over imported goods is a "condition" for satisfying the CVA requirements, and, therefore, for receiving the import duty exemption.

* * *

128. * * * In its examination, however, the Panel did not conduct an analysis of how the CVA requirements under the MVTO 1998 * * * actually work. The Panel began its legal analysis by stating that "a value-added requirement is in no sense synonymous with a condition to

use domestic over imported goods." The Panel apparently reached this conclusion without any inquiry into the specific CVA requirements for specific manufacturer beneficiaries. Although the Panel did explain what *types* of costs could be used to satisfy the CVA requirements, the Panel did not, for any MVTO manufacturer * * * make any findings as to the *actual level* of CVA required. The Panel's statement that "value-added requirements" are "not synonymous" with a condition to use domestic over imported goods seems to have been based on "value-added requirements" considered *in the abstract* as opposed to the actual CVA requirements. * * *

129.   * * * The Panel simply speculated that "depending upon the factual circumstances", a manufacturer "*might well be* willing and *able* to satisfy a CVA requirement *without using any domestic goods whatsoever*". (emphasis added) The Panel did not, however, scrutinize the actual CVA requirements for MVTO and SRO manufacturers to see whether they could indeed be satisfied without using domestic goods.

130.   The Panel's reasoning implies that under no circumstances could *any* value-added requirement result in a finding of contingency "in law" upon the use of domestic over imported goods. We do not agree. We noted that the definition of "Canadian value added" in the MVTO 1998 *requires* a manufacturer to report to the Government of Canada the *aggregate* of certain listed costs of its production of motor vehicles, and that the first such cost item specified is the cost of Canadian parts and materials *used* in the production of motor vehicles in its factory in Canada. It seems to us that whether or not a particular manufacturer is able to satisfy its specific CVA requirements without using any Canadian parts and materials in its production depends very much on the *level* of the applicable CVA requirements. For example, if the level of the CVA requirements is very high, we can see that the use of domestic goods may well be a necessity and thus be, in practice, required as a *condition* for eligibility for the import duty exemption. By contrast, if the level of the CVA requirements is very low, it would be much easier to satisfy those requirements *without* actually using domestic goods; for example, where the CVA requirements are set at 40 per cent, it might be possible to satisfy that level simply with the aggregate of other elements of Canadian value added, in particular, labour costs. The multiplicity of *possibilities* for compliance with the CVA requirements, when these requirements are set at low levels, may, depending on the specific level applicable to a particular manufacturer, make the use of domestic goods only one *possible* means (means which might not, in fact, be utilized) of satisfying the CVA requirements.

* * *

132.   The Panel's failure to examine fully the legal instruments at issue here and their implications for individual manufacturers vitiates its conclusion that the CVA requirements do not make the import duty exemption contingent "in law" upon the use of domestic over imported goods. In the absence of an examination of the operation of the applica-

ble CVA requirements for individual manufacturers, the Panel simply did not have a sufficient basis for its finding on the issue of "in law" contingency. Thus, we conclude that the Panel erred in conducting its "in law" contingency analysis.

133. In *Australia–Salmon*, we stated that where we have reversed a finding of a panel, we should attempt to complete a panel's legal analysis "to the extent possible on the basis of the factual findings of the Panel and/or of undisputed facts in the Panel record". Here, as we have stated, the Panel did not identify the precise levels of the CVA requirements applicable to specific manufacturers. In addition, there are not sufficient undisputed facts in the Panel record that would enable us to examine this issue ourselves. As a result, it is impossible for us to assess whether the use of domestic over imported goods is a condition "in law" for satisfying the CVA requirements, and, therefore, is a condition for receiving the import duty exemption.

134. In light of these considerations, we are unable to complete the legal analysis necessary to determine whether the import duty exemption, through the application of the CVA requirements, is contingent "in law" upon the use of domestic over imported goods. Therefore, we make no finding and reserve our judgment on whether the import duty exemption at issue is contingent "in law" upon the use of domestic over imported goods within the meaning of Article 3.1(b) of the *SCM Agreement*.

Question

Is the Appellate Body consistent in its analysis of the ratio requirements and the value-added requirements? Why is, say, a 50:100 ratio requirement "contingent in law" on export performance while, say, a 50% value-added requirement may not be?

UNITED STATES—IMPOSITION OF COUNTERVAILING DUTIES ON CERTAIN HOT–ROLLED LEAD AND BISMUTH CARBON STEEL PRODUCTS ORIGINAT-ING IN THE UNITED KINGDOM

WT/DS138/AB/R
Appellate Body Report adopted by the DSB on June 7, 2000

2. The alleged subsidies countervailed relate principally to equity infusions granted by the British Government to a state-owned company, British Steel Corporation ("BSC"), between 1977 and 1986. In 1986, BSC and Guest, Keen and Nettlefolds ("GKN"), a privately-owned company, created United Engineering Steels Limited ("UES") as a joint venture. Both BSC and GKN provided assets to UES, in return for equal shares in the joint venture. In particular, BSC spun-off its leaded bar-producing assets to UES. Negotiations concerning the spin-off were conducted at arm's length, consistent with commercial considerations. BSC ceased producing leaded bars after the spin-off of its leaded bar-producing assets to UES. In preparation for the privatization of BSC,

British Steel plc ("BSplc") assumed, in September 1988, the property, rights and liabilities of BSC, including BSC's holding in UES. In December 1988, the British government completed the privatization through a sale of BSplc shares on the stock market. The United States Department of Commerce ("USDOC") found that the sale of BSplc shares was at arm's length, for fair market value and consistent with commercial considerations. On 20 March 1995, BSplc purchased GKN's holding in UES, whereupon UES was renamed British Steel Engineering Steels ("BSES").

3.   Countervailing duties on imports of leaded bars were originally imposed in 1993. Since then, the USDOC has undertaken a number of annual reviews of the countervailing duties applied to imports of leaded bars originating in the United Kingdom. The European Communities' claims in this case relate to the countervailing duties imposed following administrative reviews initiated in 1995, 1996 and 1997, which dealt with leaded bar imports in the calendar years 1994, 1995 and 1996, respectively. In each of these reviews, the USDOC applied its allocation methodology for untied, non-recurring subsidies to determine the amount of the benefit from the pre–1986 subsidies to BSC allocable to the relevant period of review. The USDOC also applied its "change-in-ownership" methodology to determine the extent to which the pre–1986 subsidies granted to BSC "travelled" to UES and/or BSplc/BSES. The USDOC imposed countervailing duties on the basis that a certain proportion of the subsidies granted to BSC had "passed through" to UES and BSplc/BSES. * * *

* * *

52.   The principal question before the Panel in this case was whether the countervailing duties at issue were inconsistent with the obligations of the United States under the *SCM Agreement*. The Panel concluded:

> ... the countervailing duties imposed as a result of the USDOC's 1995, 1996 and 1997 administrative reviews are not in accordance with the premise underlying Articles 19.1, 19.4 and 21.2 of the SCM Agreement, Article VI:3 of the GATT 1994, and the object and purpose of countervailing duties as expressed in footnote 36 to Article 10 ...

> Accordingly, we conclude that the countervailing duties imposed as a result of the USDOC's 1995, 1996 and 1997 administrative reviews are inconsistent with Article 10 of the SCM Agreement.

In reaching this conclusion, the Panel found:

> ... the USDOC should have examined the continued existence of "benefit" already deemed to have been conferred by the pre–1985/86 "financial contributions" to BSC, and it should have done so from the perspective of UES and BSplc/BSES respectively, and not BSC.

> ...

... fair market value was paid for all productive assets, goodwill etc. employed by UES and BSplc/BSES in the production of leaded bars imported into the United States in 1994, 1995 and 1996. In these circumstances, we fail to see how pre–1985/86 "financial contributions" bestowed on BSC could subsequently be considered to confer a "benefit" on UES and BSplc/BSES during the relevant periods of review.

The United States appeals the above findings of the Panel.

53.   Before we begin our analysis, we note that the measures at issue in this case are the duties imposed as a result of the 1995, 1996 and 1997 *administrative reviews*, not the duties imposed as a result of the original 1993 final countervailing duty determination. Nevertheless, the Panel based its reasoning in part on Articles 19.1 and 19.4 of the *SCM Agreement*, which are provisions dealing with the imposition of countervailing duties as a result of a final determination. We believe that Articles 19.1 and 19.4 provide useful context in interpreting the obligations regarding administrative reviews, but that the applicable provision covering administrative reviews is Article 21, which provides in paragraph 2:

> The authorities shall review the need for the continued imposition of the duty, where warranted, on their own initiative or, provided that a reasonable period of time has elapsed since the imposition of the definitive countervailing duty, upon request by any interested party which submits positive information substantiating the need for a review. Interested parties shall have the right to request the authorities to examine whether the continued imposition of the duty is necessary to offset subsidization, whether the injury would be likely to continue or recur if the duty were removed or varied, or both. If, as a result of the review under this paragraph, the authorities determine that the countervailing duty is no longer warranted, it shall be terminated immediately.

Pursuant to this paragraph, the authorities of a Member applying a countervailing duty must, where warranted, "review the need for the continued imposition of the duty". In carrying out such a review, the authorities must "examine whether the continued imposition of the duty is necessary to offset subsidization" and/or "whether the injury would be likely to continue or recur if the duty were removed or varied". Article 21.2 provides a review mechanism to ensure that Members comply with the rule set out in Article 21.1 of the *SCM Agreement*, which stipulates:

> A countervailing duty shall remain in force only as long as and to the extent necessary to counteract subsidization which is causing injury.

54.   Setting aside the issue of injury, which does not arise in this case, we note that in order to establish the continued need for countervailing duties, an investigating authority will have to make a finding on *subsidization*, i.e., whether or not the subsidy continues to exist. If there

is no longer a subsidy, there would no longer be any need for a countervailing duty.

55. Article 1.1 of the *SCM Agreement* defines a "subsidy" as follows:

> For the purpose of this Agreement, a subsidy shall be deemed to exist if:
>
> (a)(1) there is a financial contribution by a government or any public body within the territory of a Member . . .
>
> and
>
> (b) a benefit is thereby conferred.

The existence of a "financial contribution" is not at issue in this appeal. The principal issue in this appeal concerns the interpretation of the term "benefit" in Article 1.1 above.

56. The United States argues, on the basis of footnote 36 to Article 10 of the *SCM Agreement* and Article VI:3 of the GATT 1994, that the relevant "benefit" is a benefit to a company's *productive operations*, rather than, as the Panel held, a benefit to *legal or natural persons*. It is true, as the United States emphasizes, that footnote 36 to Article 10 of the *SCM Agreement* and Article VI:3 of the GATT 1994 both refer to subsidies bestowed or granted directly or indirectly "upon the manufacture, production or export of any merchandise". In our view, however, it does not necessarily follow from this wording that the "benefit" referred to in Article 1.1(b) of the *SCM Agreement* is a benefit to *productive operations*.

57. In our Report in *Canada–Aircraft*, we stated, with regard to the term "benefit" in Article 1.1(b):

> A "benefit" does not exist in the abstract, but must be received and enjoyed by a beneficiary or a recipient. Logically, a "benefit" can be said to arise only if a person, natural or legal, or a group of persons, has in fact received something. The term "benefit", therefore, implies that there must be a recipient. . . .

* * *

58. We, therefore, agree with the Panel's findings that benefit as used in Article 1.1(b) is concerned with the "benefit to the recipient", that such recipient must be a natural or legal person , and that in the present case:

> . . . in order to determine whether any subsidy was bestowed on the production by UES and BSplc/BSES respectively of leaded bars imported into the United States in 1994, 1995 and 1996, it is necessary to determine whether there was any "benefit" to UES and BSplc respectively (*i.e.*, the producers of the imported leaded bars at issue).

59. The United States also appeals the Panel's finding that the investigating authority must demonstrate the existence, during the relevant period of investigation or review, of a continued "benefit" from a prior "financial contribution". The United States argues that the use of the present tense of the verb "is conferred" in Article 1.1 of the *SCM Agreement* shows that an investigating authority must demonstrate the existence of "benefit" only at the time the "financial contribution" was made. The United States also relies on the context of Article 1.1, in particular Articles 14 and 27.13 of the *SCM Agreement*, in support of this interpretation.

60. Article 1.1 sets out the definition of a subsidy for the purposes of the *SCM Agreement*. However, Article 1.1 does not address the *time* at which the "financial contribution" and/or the "benefit" must be shown to exist. We therefore consider that Article 1.1 does not provide a basis for the argument made by the United States. We also find nothing in Articles 14 or 27.13 of the *SCM Agreement* that supports the United States' position.

61. We have already stated that in a case involving countervailing duties imposed as a result of an administrative review, Articles 21.1 and 21.2 of the *SCM Agreement* are relevant. As discussed above, Article 21.1 allows Members to apply countervailing duties "only as long as and to the extent necessary to counteract subsidization ...". Article 21.2 sets out a review mechanism to ensure that Members comply with this rule. In an administrative review pursuant to Article 21.2, the investigating authority may be presented with "positive information" that the "financial contribution" has been repaid or withdrawn and/or that the "benefit" no longer accrues. On the basis of its assessment of the information presented to it by interested parties, as well as of other evidence before it relating to the period of review, the investigating authority must determine whether there is a continuing need for the application of countervailing duties. The investigating authority is not free to ignore such information. If it were free to ignore this information, the review mechanism under Article 21.2 would have no purpose.

62. Therefore, we agree with the Panel that while an investigating authority may presume, in the context of an administrative review under Article 21.2, that a "benefit" continues to flow from an untied, non-recurring "financial contribution", this presumption can never be "irrebuttable". In this case, given the changes in ownership leading to the creation of UES and BSplc/BSES, the USDOC was *required* under Article 21.2 to examine, on the basis of the information before it relating to these changes, whether a "benefit" accrued to UES and BSplc/BSES. We thus agree with the Panel's finding that:

> ... the changes in ownership leading to the creation of UES and BSplc/BSES should have caused the USDOC to examine whether the production of leaded bars by UES and BSplc/BSES respectively, and not BSC, was subsidized. In particular, the USDOC should have

examined the continued existence of "benefit" already deemed to have been conferred by the pre–1985/86 "financial contributions" to BSC, and it should have done so from the perspective of UES and BSplc/BSES respectively, and not BSC.

63.   The Panel, however, also stated:

> ... when an investigation or review takes place, the investigating authority must establish the existence of a "financial contribution" and "benefit" during the relevant period of investigation or review. Only then will that investigating authority be able to conclude, to the satisfaction of Article 1.1 (and Article 21), that there **is** a "financial contribution", and that a "benefit" **is** thereby conferred.

We do not agree with the Panel's implied view that, in the context of an administrative review under Article 21.2, an investigating authority must *always* establish the existence of a "benefit" during the period of review *in the same way as* an investigating authority must establish a "benefit" in an original investigation. We believe that it is important to distinguish between the original investigation leading to the imposition of countervailing duties and the administrative review. In an original investigation, the investigating authority must establish that *all* conditions set out in the *SCM Agreement* for the imposition of countervailing duties are fulfilled. In an administrative review, however, the investigating authority must address those issues which have been raised before it by the interested parties or, in the case of an investigation conducted on its own initiative, those issues which warranted the examination.

64.   Having found that, in the particular circumstances of this case, the USDOC, in its 1995, 1996 and 1997 administrative reviews, should have examined the continued existence of a "benefit" to UES and BSplc/BSES, the Panel subsequently examined whether the "financial contributions" bestowed on BSC between 1977 and 1986 could be considered to confer a "benefit" on UES and BSplc/BSES. The Panel found that:

> ... fair market value was paid for all productive assets, goodwill etc. employed by UES and BSplc/BSES in the production of leaded bars imported into the United States in 1994, 1995 and 1996. In these circumstances, we fail to see how pre–1985/86 "financial contributions" bestowed on BSC could subsequently be considered to confer a "benefit" on UES and BSplc/BSES during the relevant periods of review.

The United States also appeals this finding.

65.   In examining this issue, we note that, according to the Panel:

> The United States has not denied that the BSC spin-off was negotiated for fair market value.

and that:

Both parties agree that the privatization of British Steel plc was "at arm's length, for fair market value and consistent with commercial considerations".

* * *

67.   Therefore, the issue before us is whether, given these factual findings, the Panel erred in finding that the "financial contributions" bestowed on BSC could not be considered to confer a "benefit" on UES and BSplc/BSES. We note that in our Report in *Canada–Aircraft*, we stated:

> ... the word "benefit", as used in Article 1.1(b), implies some kind of comparison. This must be so, for there can be no "benefit" to the recipient unless the "financial contribution" makes the recipient "better off" than it would otherwise have been, absent that contribution. In our view, the marketplace provides an appropriate basis for comparison in determining whether a "benefit" has been "conferred", because the trade-distorting potential of a "financial contribution" can be identified by determining whether the recipient has received a "financial contribution" on terms more favourable than those available to the recipient in the market.

68.   The question whether a "financial contribution" confers a "benefit" depends, therefore, on whether the recipient has received a "financial contribution" on terms more favourable than those available to the recipient in the market. In the present case, the Panel made factual findings that UES and BSplc/BSES paid fair market value for all the productive assets, goodwill, etc., they acquired from BSC and subsequently used in the production of leaded bars imported into the United States in 1994, 1995 and 1996. We, therefore, see no error in the Panel's conclusion that, in the specific circumstances of this case, the "financial contributions" bestowed on BSC between 1977 and 1986 could not be deemed to confer a "benefit" on UES and BSplc/BSES.

Notes and Questions

(1) Are you persuaded that the transfer of assets to new owners at "fair market value" cleanses them of any subsidy?

(2) Suppose a government provides a one-time grant to a company that enables it to build a new manufacturing facility. The grant is later found to be an illegal export subsidy. What is the remedy under WTO law? Such an issue arose in a dispute involving Australian subsidies to exporters of automotive leather. The panel concluded that in the circumstances of that case, repayment of the subsidy was necessary in order for the subsidy to be withdrawn as required by the SCM Agreement. Do you agree?

———

We now turn to the first and so far only case to consider the question of what constitutes "serious prejudice" within the meaning of article 5 of the SCM Agreement.

INDONESIA—CERTAIN MEASURES AFFECTING
THE AUTOMOBILE INDUSTRY

WT/DS54, 55, 59 & 64/R
Panel Report adopted by the DSB on July 23, 1998

2.15. Two sets of measures have been identified by all parties under the 1996 National Car programme:

2.16. The first set of measures—the February 1996 Programme—provides for the grant of "pioneer" or National Car company status to Indonesian car companies that meet specified criteria as to ownership of facilities, use of trademarks, and technology. Maintenance of pioneer status is dependent on the National Cars' meeting increasing local content requirements over a three year period. The benefits provided are exemption from luxury tax on sales of National Cars, and exemption from import duties on parts and components.

2.17. The second set of measures—the June 1996 Programme—provides that National Cars manufactured in a foreign country by Indonesian nationals and which fulfil the local content requirements prescribed by the Minister of Industry and Trade, shall be treated the same as National Cars manufactured in Indonesia, i.e. exempt from import duties and luxury tax. In accordance with Decree 142/96, imported National Cars are deemed to comply with the 20 per cent local content requirement for the end of the first production year if the overseas producer manufacturing the National Cars "counter-purchases" Indonesian parts and components that account for at least 25 per cent of the C & F value of the imported cars.

* * *

CLAIMS OF SERIOUS PREJUDICE UNDER PART III OF THE SCM AGREEMENT

14.153. * * * The European Communities and the United States contend that the tariff and luxury sales tax exemptions provided by Indonesia through the National Car programme are specific subsidies which have caused serious prejudice to their interests within the meaning of Article 5(c) of the Agreement on Subsidies and Countervailing Measures ("SCM Agreement"). Specifically, the complainants allege that the effect of alleged subsidies for the national car is (a) to displace or impede imports of like products of the European Communities and the United States into the Indonesian market and (b) a significant price undercutting by the subsidized national car as compared with like EC and US products in the Indonesian market. * * *

* * *

14.155. As with any analysis under the SCM Agreement, the first issue to be resolved is whether the measures in question are subsidies within the meaning of Article 1 that are specific to an enterprise or industry or group of enterprises or industries within the meaning of

Article 2. It is to be recalled that the measures in question are: import duty and luxury sales tax exemptions on CBU [completely built-up, i.e., finished] Timors [a model of compact car] imported by PT TPN [an Indonesian company] from Korea, import duty exemptions on parts and components used or to be used in the assembly of the Timor in Indonesia, and luxury sales tax exemptions on Timors assembled in Indonesia. In this case, the European Communities, the United States and Indonesia agree that these measures are specific subsidies within the meaning of those articles. * * *

14.156. Article 27 of the SCM Agreement provides significant special and differential treatment for developing country Members of the WTO, including with respect to claims of serious prejudice arising from subsidies provided by developing country Members. Thus, Article 27.9 provides that

> Regarding actionable subsidies granted or maintained by a developing country Member other than those referred to in paragraph 1 of Article 6, action may not be authorized or taken pursuant to Article 7 unless nullification or impairment of tariff concessions or other obligations under GATT 1994 is found to exist as a result of such subsidy, in such a way as to displace or impede imports of a like product into the market of the subsidizing developing country Member or unless injury to a domestic industry in the market of an importing Member occurs.

In other words, Article 27.9 provides that, *in the usual case*, developing country Members may not be subject to a claim that their actionable subsidies have caused serious prejudice to the interests of another Member. Rather, a Member may only bring a claim that benefits under GATT have been nullified or impaired by a developing country Member's subsidies or that subsidized imports into the complaining Member have caused injury to a domestic industry.

14.157 The complainants do not contest that Indonesia is a developing country Member entitled to the special and differential treatment provided by Article 27.9. Rather, they contend that Article 27.9 is not applicable in this case because the subsidies in question fall under the provisions of Article 6.1(a), i.e., that the *ad valorem* subsidization of the Timor exceeds 5 per cent. * * *

14.158 We agree that Article 27.8 allows a WTO Member to bring a serious prejudice claim with respect to subsidies provided by a developing country Member which fall within the scope of Article 6.1. Article 27.8 provides that:

> There shall be no presumption in terms of paragraph 1 of Article 6 that a subsidy granted by a developing country Member results in serious prejudice, as defined in this Agreement. Such serious prejudice, where applicable under the terms of paragraph 9, shall be demonstrated by positive evidence, in accordance with the provisions of paragraphs 3 through 8 of Article 6.

In other words, while a subsidy falling within the terms of Article 6.1 generally is presumed to cause serious prejudice to the interests of another Member, that presumption is not applicable where the subsidizing country is a developing country Member. Instead, while such a subsidy by a developing country Member may be subject to a serious prejudice challenge, a complainant does not benefit from a presumption of serious prejudice; rather, a complainant must demonstrate the existence of serious prejudice by positive evidence.

14.159   The question remains whether the subsidization challenged in this dispute satisfies the requirements of Article 6.1(a). That provision states that "[s]erious prejudice shall be deemed to exist in the case of . . . the total *ad valorem* subsidization of a product exceeding five per cent. . . ." * * *

* * *

14.161   The calculations provided by the European Communities and the United States present a variety of issues under Article 6.1(a) and Annex IV. However, we do not need in this case to calculate the precise level of *ad valorem* subsidization. Rather, we need only determine whether the *ad valorem* rate of subsidization exceeds 5 per cent. This question is not in dispute here, since Indonesia calculates that the *ad valorem* subsidization conferred by the exemption from the luxury sales tax alone is 29.54 per cent for Timors imported from Korea, 26.20 per cent for Timors assembled at the Tambun plant, and 18.68 per cent for Timors to be assembled at the Karawang plant. * * *

14.162   For the foregoing reasons, we find that the complainants are not precluded by Article 27 from seeking to demonstrate, by positive evidence, that Indonesia has caused, through the effects of the subsidies at issue in this case, serious prejudice to their interests.

* * *

LIKE PRODUCT ANALYSIS

14.164   Article 6.3 provides in relevant parts as follows:

Serious prejudice in the sense of paragraph (c) may arise in any case where one or several of the following may apply:

(a) the effect of the subsidy is to displace or impede the exports of a *like product* of another Member into the Market of the subsidizing Member;

. . .

(c) the effect of the subsidy is a significant price undercutting by the subsidized product as compared with the price of a *like product* of another Member in the same market or significant price suppression, price depression or lost sales in the same market(emphasis added).

It is clear from the text of Article 6.3 that any analysis of displacement or impedance or of price undercutting must focus on the effects of the subsidy vis à vis the like product to the subsidized product. * * *

* * *

14.175   Turning first to the argument of the European Communities that all passenger cars should be considered "like products" to the Timor, we consider that such a broad approach is not appropriate in this case. While it is true that all passenger cars "share the same basic physical characteristics and share an identical end-use", we agree with Indonesia that passenger cars are highly differentiated products. * * * Viewed from the perspective of the SCM Agreement, it is almost inconceivable that a subsidy for Timors could displace or impede imports of Rolls Royces, or that any meaningful analysis of price undercutting could be performed between these two models. In short, we do not consider that a Rolls Royce can reasonably be considered to have "characteristics closely resembling" those of the Timor.

14.176   The European Communities contend that we must consider all passenger cars to be "like" because any effort to differentiate between passenger cars with a multitude of differing characteristics would inevitably result in arbitrary divisions. We are aware that there are innumerable differences among passenger cars and that the identification of appropriate dividing lines between them may not be a simple task. However, this does not in our view justify lumping all such products together where the differences among the products are so dramatic. * * *

14.177   One reasonable way for this panel to approach the "like product" issue is to look at the manner in which the automotive industry itself has analyzed market segmentation. The United States and the European Communities have submitted information regarding the market segmentation approach taken by DRI's Global Automotive Group, a company whose clients include all major auto manufacturers, including KIA, PT TPN's national car partner. * * *

14.178   * * * DRI has in its analysis considered the physical characteristics of the cars in question when designing its segmentation. It has used as an initial filter the size of the vehicle, but it has then divided cars of a given size into upper and lower end categories, and has moved luxury cars, regardless of size, from lower segments to the E segment. We consider such an approach, which segments the market based on a combination of size and price/market position, to be a sensible one which is consistent with the criteria relevant to "like product" analysis under the SCM Agreement.

* * *

14.181   In our view, the DRI market segmentation analysis presented by the European Communities and the United States supports the view that all vehicles in the C1 Segment—including the 306, Optima and Escort—are "like products" to the Timor within the meaning of the

SCM Agreement. By contrast, the DRI analysis places the Vectra and the Neon in different market segments (D1 and C2 respectively), and this in our view weakens the complainants' view that these products should be considered to be "like" the Timor.

* * *

TREATMENT OF CARS IMPORTED UNASSEMBLED

14.194   Indonesia maintains a duty of 200 per cent on imports of passenger cars, and as a result imports of CBU passenger cars (that is, completely-built-up cars) into Indonesia are very small. In fact, almost all passenger cars imported into Indonesia, including the 306 and the Optima, are imported as CKD (completely knocked-down) kits and assembled in Indonesia. The complainants have stated that the Escort and Neon would have been imported in CKD kit form and assembled in Indonesia as well. Article 6.3 provides that serious prejudice may arise where the effect of the subsidy is "to displace or impede the imports of a like product of another Member into the market of the subsidizing Member" or is "a significant price undercutting by the subsidized product as compared with the price of a like product of another Member." Thus, in the context of a displacement or impedance claim, the question arises whether imports of CKD kits are "imports of a like product [to the Timor] of another Member" where the final passenger car assembled in Indonesia is a "like product" to the Timor. In the case of price undercutting, the related question is whether a passenger car assembled in Indonesia from an imported CKD kit is a "like product of another Member."

* * *

14.197   We do not consider that an unassembled product *ipso facto* is not a like product to that product assembled. Recalling the view of the Appellate Body that tariff classification may be a useful tool in like product analysis, we note that, under the General Rules for the Interpretation of the Harmonized System:

> Any reference in a heading to an article shall be taken to include a reference to that article incomplete or unfinished, provided that, as presented, the incomplete or unfinished article has the essential character of the complete or finished article.

We think that a comparable approach to the relation between assembled and unassembled products makes good sense in the context of this dispute. It appears that, in order to avoid paying 200 per cent duties on CBU passenger cars, EC and US car producers ship to Indonesia virtually complete CKD kits that are effectively "cars in a box." Accordingly, we believe that they can properly be considered to have characteristics closely resembling those of a completed car.

PRODUCTS NOT ORIGINATING IN A COMPLAINING MEMBER

14.198   Before turning to an analysis of adverse effects, we must first consider whether the United States may claim that it has suffered serious prejudice as a result of displacement/impedance or of price undercutting with respect to a product which does not originate in the United States solely on the basis that the producer of that product is a "US company".

* * *

14.200   In considering this issue, our starting point is that both Article XVI of GATT and the SCM Agreement are Annex 1A multilateral agreements on trade in goods. It comes as no surprise, therefore that in its discussion of serious prejudice, Article XVI:1 focuses on the effects of subsidization on trade in goods. That article provides as follows:

> If any contracting party grants or maintains any subsidy, including any form of income or price support, which operates directly or indirectly *to increase exports of any product from, or to reduce imports of any product* into, its territory, it shall notify the CON-TRACTING PARTIES in writing of the extent and nature of the subsidization, of the estimated effect of the subsidization *on the quantity of the affected product or products imported into or exported from* its territory and of the circumstances making the subsidization necessary. In any case in which it is determined that serious prejudice to the interests of any other contracting party is caused or threatened by any *such subsidization*, the contracting party granting the subsidy shall, upon request, discuss with the other contracting party or parties concerned, or with the CONTRACTING PARTIES, the possibility of limiting the subsidization. (emphasis added).

This focus on the trade effects of subsidization is carried over into Part III of the SCM Agreement. Article 5 provides that no Member should cause, through the use of any subsidy, "adverse effects to the interests of other Members." One such adverse effect is "serious prejudice to the interests of another Member," which the SCM Agreement indicates is used in the same sense as in Article XVI:1. Article 6.3 provides that serious prejudice may arise where one or several of four listed situations exist. As we have seen, the United States alleges two such situations, i.e., (i) that "the effect of the subsidy is to displace or impede the *imports of a like product of another Member* into the market of the subsidizing Member"; and (ii) that "the effect of the subsidy is a significant price undercutting by the subsidized product as compared with the price of *a like product of another Member* in the same market or significant price suppression, price depression or lost sales in the same market" (emphasis added).

14.201   In our view, the text of Article XVI and of Part III of the SCM Agreement make clear that serious prejudice may arise where a Member's trade interests have been affected by subsidization. We see nothing in Article XVI or in Part III that would suggest that the United States may claim that it has suffered adverse effects merely because it believes that the interests of US *companies* have been harmed where US *products* are not involved. The United States has cited no language in Article XVI:1 or Part III suggesting that the nationality of producers is relevant to establishing the existence of serious prejudice. Accordingly, given that serious prejudice may only arise in the case at hand where there is "displacement or impedance of imports of a like product from another Member" or price undercutting "as compared with the like product of another Member", we do not consider that the United States can convert such effects on products from the European Communities into serious prejudice to US interests merely by alleging that the products affected were produced by US companies.

14.202 In light of our view that the existence of alleged harm to US *companies* is not a basis for a claim of serious prejudice to the interests to the United States, the question remains whether one Member may bring a claim that another Member has suffered serious prejudice as a result of subsidization. In our view the answer is no. It will be recalled that Article 7 of the SCM Agreement sets forth the steps to be taken by a Member which believes that it has suffered adverse effects within the meaning of Part III. Article 7.2 provides that:

> A request for consultations under paragraph 1 shall include a statement of available evidence with regard to *(a)* the existence and nature of the subsidy in question, and *(b)* the injury caused to the domestic industry, or the nullification or impairment, or serious prejudice [footnote omitted] caused to the interests of the Member requesting consultations.

It is clear from Article 7.2 that the dispute settlement procedures set forth in Article 7 may only be invoked by a Member where that Member believes that it has itself suffered serious prejudice as a result of subsidization.

* * *

DISPLACEMENT AND IMPEDANCE

14.207 Having determined that certain EC and US passenger car models are (or, in the case of the Neon, may be) like products to the Timor, we must next examine whether the complainants have demonstrated that the effect of the subsidies provided pursuant to the National Car programme has been to displace or impede the exports of those models from the Indonesian market.

(a) Market Share Data

14.208 Before proceeding to an examination of the market share data submitted by complainants, we must consider the threshold legal issue of whether Article 6.4 of the SCM Agreement is relevant to a dispute, such as this, where the adverse effects alleged by the complainants relate to displacement or impedance of a like product into the market of the subsidizing Member under Article 6.3(a). That Article provides as follows:

> *For the purpose of paragraph 3(b),* the displacement or impeding of exports shall include any case in which, subject to the provisions of paragraph 7, it has been demonstrated that there has been a change

in relative shares of the market to the disadvantage of the non-subsidized like product (over an appropriately representative period sufficient to demonstrate clear trends in the development of the market for the product concerned, which, in normal circumstances, shall be at least one year). "Change in relative shares of the market" shall include any of the following situations: *(a)* there is an increase in the market share of the subsidized product; *(b)* the market share of the subsidized product remains constant in circumstances in which, in the absence of the subsidy, it would have declined; *(c)* the market share of the subsidized product declines, but at a slower rate than would have been the case in the absence of the subsidy. (emphasis added).

The European Communities and the United States acknowledge that Article 6.4 on its face does not apply to the displacement and impedance claims in this dispute, as their claims are based on Article 6.3(a) (effect in the market of the subsidizing Member) while Article 6.4 only applies "for the purpose of" Article 6.3(b) (effects in the market of a third country). The complainants argue, however, that there is no reason why the type of analysis set forth in Article 6.4 should not be appropriate also in the case of claims of displacement and impedance of imports from the market of the subsidizing country. Indonesia, by contrast, contends that Article 6.4 is not relevant to this dispute.

14.209   The significance of this issue in terms of the obligations on the complainants is considerable. If the type of analysis set forth in Article 6.4 is appropriate in this case, then the complainants arguably could make a *prima facie* case of displacement or impedance simply by demonstrating that the market share of a subsidized product has increased over an appropriately representative period. If, on the other hand, the type of analysis set forth in Article 6.4 is not appropriate in this case, then the complainants must demonstrate that *"the effect of the subsidy"* is to displace or impede imports into Indonesia, that is, that they have lost export sales to Indonesia that they would otherwise have made and that those export sales were lost as a result of the subsidies provided pursuant to the National Car programme.

14.210   We agree with Indonesia that Article 6.4 is not relevant in this case. The drafting of the provision is unambiguous, and the specific reference to Article 6.3(b) creates a strong inference that an Article 6.4 type of analysis is *not* appropriate in the case of Article 6.3(a) claims. The complainants have identified nothing in the context of the provision or the object and purpose of the SCM Agreement that would suggest a different conclusion.

14.211   Our conclusion does not of course mean that market share data are irrelevant to the analysis of displacement or impedance into a subsidizing Member's market. To the contrary, market share data may be highly relevant evidence for the analysis of such a claim. However, such data are no more than evidence of displacement and impedance caused by subsidization, and a demonstration that the market share of the subsidized product in the subsidizing Member has increased does not *ipso facto* satisfy the requirements of Article 6.3(a).

14.212   Having determined that the EC and US models in the C1 Segment (and arguably those in the C2 Segment) are "like" the subsidized Timor, we consider it appropriate to analyze market shares for the C Segment. A review of the data provided by Indonesia under the Annex V procedure demonstrates that the Timor quickly gained a very substantial share of the Indonesian C Segment passenger car market upon its introduction. [T]he Timor was not sold in 1995 and thus had a zero share of the C Segment market. In 1996, the year of introduction, the Timor captured a 16.9 per cent share of the Indonesian C Segment, while during the period January–May 1997 (the latest period for which we have been provided with data), that market share had climbed to 42.4 percent. Table 2 breaks this market share data down on a quarterly basis. These data indicate that Timor had no sales until the fourth quarter of 1996. In that quarter, its market share in the C Segment reached 40.9 per cent. It dropped to 38.8 per cent for the first quarter of 1997 but during the partial second quarter for which we have data (April–May) that share had climbed to 47.7 per cent.

14.213   In assessing whether this change in market share in fact amounted to a displacement or impedance of imports of EC and US origin products into Indonesia, our starting point is actual market shares for the three EC models we have found to be like products, and for the one US model which we assume *arguendo* to be a like product, to the Timor. The Neon was never introduced into the Indonesia market (allegedly because of the National Car programme), and the market share of US-origin passenger cars in the C Segment of the Indonesian passenger car market was therefore zero. Because the Escort also was never introduced into the Indonesian market, the EC market share data are based solely on sales of the 306 and the Optima. [T]he European Communities in 1995 had an Indonesian market share in the C Segment of 2.4 per cent. The EC share climbed to 5.7 per cent in 1996, but dropped to 3.7 per cent for the period for which we have data (January–May 1997). Table 2, *infra* at p. 386, breaks down these data on a quarterly basis. This analysis shows that in the first three quarters of 1996, EC market share in the C Segment ranged from 6.9 to 7.8 per cent. In the fourth quarter of 1996 (the quarter in which the Timor first entered the market), EC market share dropped to 3.7 per cent. In the first quarter of 1997, EC market share fell even further to 3.3 per cent, and remained at a relatively low 4.2 per cent in the partial second quarter for which we have data (April–May 1997).

14.214   Focusing on market shares alone, the data before us show a potentially significant correlation between the introduction of the subsidized Timor and the decline in EC market share in the C Segment of the Indonesian market. The quarterly data show that the EC market share for C Segment cars in Indonesia increased substantially during the first three quarters of 1996, but that, in the fourth quarter of 1996, coincident with the introduction of the Timor, the European models' market share dropped to 3.7 per cent, where it remained on average during the first five months of 1997. Thus, there seems to be little question that the EC market share in the C Segment dropped substantially relative to that of the subsidized Timor, and the close correlation in time between the introduction of the Timor and the drop in EC market share suggests a causal link between the two.

14.215   If Article 6.4 of the SCM Agreement applied in this dispute, this showing of a change in relative market shares to the disadvantage of the non-subsidized like product might well have been sufficient to establish the European Communities' *prima facie* case of displacement or impedance. In the absence of that article, however, it is not enough for the European Communities to demonstrate a decline in relative market share; rather, the European Communities must demonstrate that "the effect of the subsidy is to displace or impede the imports" of an EC-origin "like product" into the Indonesian market, i.e., that some imports that would have occurred did not occur as a result of the subsidies. While declining market share may be relevant to establishing such a situation, we consider that we must proceed further with the analysis and look at actual sales figures for the products in question.

14.216   In spite of their declines in market share, the absolute volume of sales of the relevant EC models did not significantly decline after the introduction of the Timor. Rather, sales of C Segment vehicles from the EC were 419 units in 1995 and 1,445 units in 1996. For 1997 we have full data from the Annex V process on the C Segment only for January–May, and this shows EC sales of 611 units, which amounts to 1,466 units on an annualized basis. We also have sales figures for the Optima (257 units) and 306 (656 units) for the period January–August 1997 from the European Communities. These figures, totalled and annualized, show sales of 1,370 units for 1997. On a quarterly basis, sales of the Optima and 306 remained relatively constant during the period from the fourth quarter of 1996 through May 1997 at between 300 and 400 units per quarter.

14.217   The explanation for the loss of market share with no decline in absolute sales volume is that the size of the Indonesian market expanded after the introduction of the Timor. What is particularly relevant here is that the increase in the size of the market was largely attributable to sales of the Timor. In particular, between the third and fourth quarters of 1996, the market for C Segment cars increased by 6,326 units, of which the Timor accounted for 4,278 units (68%). A similar pattern was evident during the first five months of 1997. Thus, relatively stable EC sales volumes in a rapidly expanding market resulted in market share declines but not in declines in absolute volumes.

14.218   We agree with the European Communities that a complainant need not demonstrate a decline in sales in order to demonstrate displacement or impedance. This is inherent in the ordinary meaning of those terms. Thus, displacement relates to a situation where sales volume has declined, while impedance relates to a situation where sales which otherwise would have occurred were impeded. The question before us is therefore whether the market share and sales data above would support a view that, but for the introduction of the subsidized Timor, sales of EC C Segment passenger cars would have been greater than they were.

14.219   In a usual case, a decline in market share in a stable or growing market, corresponding in time with the introduction of a subsidized product, might suggest that sales would have been higher but for the introduction of the subsidized product. This would be particularly the case where, in the period prior to the introduction of the subsidized product, the market share of the non-subsidized product had been rising. In this case, however, Indonesia contends that the introduction of the subsidized Timor was itself responsible for the rapid expansion of the market through the introduction of a new, highly affordable passenger car within the reach of first-time buyers. While the European Communities dismisses this argument as "purely speculative," the sales data in terms of volume of sales discussed above provide some support for this view. Thus, one possible interpretation of the data is that, if the subsidized Timor had not been introduced, the Indonesian C Segment market would have remained relatively stable or in any event would have posted during the last quarter of 1996 and the first eight months of 1997 more gradual increases, comparable to those experienced during the period between the first quarter of 1995 and the second quarter of 1996.

14.220   Assuming that, had the subsidized Timor not been introduced, the Indonesian C Segment market would have remained stable or grown at a more moderate rate during the period for which we have data, the question is whether sales of EC C Segment models in absolute terms would have been higher than those actually achieved. Here, the data are inconclusive. While the European Communities contend that its market share had been steadily increasing and that this trend would have continued but for the introduction of the subsidized Timor, actual sales consisted of only two models, the Optima and 306. As Table 2 shows, quarterly sales data for the Optima do not demonstrate any clear upward trend in the six quarters prior to the introduction of the subsidized Timor. Rather, the increase in EC sales was a result of the introduction of the 306 in the first quarter of 1996. While the European Communities state that 1996 sales of the 306 (1,086 units) were 400 units lower than planned, we have no knowledge of the basis for those sales forecasts. Sales of the 306 for partial year 1997 were at an annualized rate of between 984 units (January–August data) and 1,070 units (January to May data), down slightly from the annualized rate in the first half of 1996 of 1,214 units. Thus, if we assume that in the absence of the Timor the market would have remained stable or continued a more gradual increase through August 1997, and that the 306 would have maintained the market share it had achieved in the first half of 1996, these sales might have been expected to increase at most slightly. Such a conclusion is, in any event, highly speculative based on the facts available.

* * *

14.222 In short, the dramatic fall in EC market share in the C Segment is not in this case decisive evidence of displacement or impedance, as the data lend some credence to the Indonesian view that the introduction of the subsidized Timor actually created much of the market growth. Thus, we are required to speculate as to how the market would have performed in the absence of the introduction of the Timor, and as to the share of the market which EC models could have been expected to obtain in that hypothetical situation. It is quite possible that the Indonesian market would have remained stable or increased somewhat in late 1996 and early 1997, even without the introduction of the subsidized Timor, and that EC models would have at least maintained their market share, such that EC sales would have increased slightly. This conclusion is however highly tentative, and does not in our view satisfy the requirement, in the present case, that serious prejudice be demonstrated by positive evidence.

* * *

PRICE UNDERCUTTING

14.237 In addition to arguing that serious prejudice has been caused to their interests through displacement or impedance of their exports to Indonesia, the complainants assert that the subsidized Timor significantly undercuts the prices of EC and US like products in the Indonesian market.

14.238. In determining whether serious prejudice within the meaning of Article 5(c) arises from price undercutting, we must first consider Article 6.3(c) of the SCM Agreement. That provision states that

"serious prejudice in the sense of paragraph 5(c) may arise in any case where one or several of the following apply:

. . .

(c) the effect of the subsidy is a significant price undercutting by the subsidized product as compared with the price of a like product of another Member in the same market or significant price suppression, price depression or lost sales in the same market; . . .

Further elaboration on the application of Article 6.3(c) is provided in Article 6.5 of the SCM Agreement, which provides as follows:

For the purpose of paragraph 3(c), price undercutting shall include any case in which such price undercutting has been demonstrated through a comparison of prices of the subsidized product with prices of a non-subsidized like product supplied to the same market. The comparison shall be made at the same level of trade and at comparable times, due account being taken of any other factor affecting price comparability. However, if such a direct comparison is not possible, the existence of price undercutting may be demonstrated on the basis of export unit values.

14.239   As noted in paragraph 14.213, no U.S.-origin passenger car that is a "like product" to the subsidized Timor currently is sold in Indonesia. In the absence of any such sales in the Indonesian market, the United States by definition cannot demonstrate that the effect of the subsidies provided pursuant to the National Car programme was a significant price undercutting by the subsidized product as compared with the price of a like product of the United States in the Indonesian market. In any event, we note that the United States did not present any information regarding the price at which the Neon, the sole US-origin passenger car allegedly planned for sale in Indonesia, would have been sold in that market. Rather, the United States merely made the unsubstantiated statement that, if Chrysler had gone ahead with its plans to sell the Neon in Indonesia, the Timor would have undercut the price of the least expensive model of the Neon by more than US$5000. We do not consider that such a conclusory statement, unbacked by any supporting explanation, calculations or documentation, is sufficient to meet the United States' burden to demonstrate the existence of a significant price undercutting by positive evidence.

* * *

14.241   We now turn to the EC argument that the prices of the subsidized National Cars significantly undercut the prices of like passengers cars imported from the European Communities. In support of their price undercutting arguments, the European Communities rely on data regarding the list and market prices for passenger cars sold in Indonesia which show that the Timor has both a list and a market price which are much lower than the list and market prices for the 306 and the Optima, which we have determined to be like products (of another Member) to the Timor.

14.242   With respect to list prices, data submitted by Indonesia during the Annex V process show that the Timor had the lowest list price of any passenger car in the Indonesian market except the Mazda MR–90 as of November 1996 and March 1997. * * *

* * *

14.254.   We note that under Article 6.3(c) serious prejudice may arise only where the price undercutting is "significant." Although the term "significant" is not defined, the inclusion of this qualifier in Article 6.3(c) presumably was intended to ensure that margins of undercutting so small that they could not meaningfully affect suppliers of the imported product whose price was being undercut are not considered to give rise to serious prejudice. This clearly is not an issue here. To the contrary, it is our view that, even taking into account the possible effects of ... physical differences on price comparability, the price undercutting by the Timor of the Optima and 306 cannot reasonably be deemed to be other than significant.

14.255 Finally, we note that serious prejudice may arise under Article 6.3(c) only where the price undercutting is "the effect of the subsidy." In this case, we agree with the European Communities that Indonesia, in information that it provided in the Annex V process effectively concedes that the tariff and tax subsidies under the National Car programme are responsible for the significant level of price undercutting. * * *

14.256 For the foregoing reasons, we find that the effect of the subsidies to the Timor pursuant to the National Car programme is to cause serious prejudice to the interests of the European Communities in the sense of Article 5(c) of the SCM Agreement through a significant price undercutting as compared with the price of EC-origin like products in the Indonesian market.

Notes and Questions

(1) The decision in the *Indonesia Autos* case was not appealed. The violation of the SCM Agreement was only one of the grounds for a finding against Indonesia. The case is especially noteworthy as the first to address the "serious prejudice" idea, introduced during the Uruguay Round, which allows WTO members to challenge subsidies that displace their exports abroad even if they are not prohibited export subsidies.

(2) Was the panel faithful to the definition of "like product" in the SCM agreement? Plainly, cars were deemed "like" despite important physical differences between them. Is the panel's approach consistent with the *EC Asbestos* interpretation of GATT Article III:4 by the Appellate Body [see Section 12.4 supra]?

(3) Why limit "standing" to bring a claim to nations whose exports are curtailed, and to exclude nations whose investors' are importantly injured?

(4) Given the physical differences between the products, and any actual or perceived quality differences, how persuasive is the existence of "price undercutting" as a basis for a finding of "serious prejudice?"

A Note on Agricultural Export Subsidies

The SCM Agreement's ban on export subsidies does not apply to certain agricultural export subsidies. Such subsidies are regulated by the WTO Agreement on Agriculture, which permits export subsidies consistent with commitments (amounts) specified in individual member's schedules. Article 8. In article 9, the agreement specifies the subsidies that are subject to the scheduled commitments. Article 10(1) then provides that the "[e]xport subsidies not listed in [Article 9] shall not be applied in a manner which results in, or threatens to lead to, circumvention of export subsidy commitments; nor shall non-commercial transactions be used to circumvent such commitments. The only case examining these provisions in detail is the original and compliance proceedings in Canada—Measures Affecting the Importation of Milk and the Exportation of Dairy Products, WT/DS103 & 113. The appeal in the compliance proceeding is expected to be decided towards the end of 2001.

Problem

Under WTO rules, which of the following are export subsidies and which are domestic subsidies? Which are potentially actionable or countervailable? Does the nature of the governmental unit (federal, regional, local) affect your answer?

(1) "Tariff drawbacks," by which a firm which exports goods receives a refund of the tariffs which were imposed upon imported raw materials, or component parts, utilized in the production of the goods for export.

(2) A pro rata corporate income tax rebate for goods exported, calculated by applying the ratio of the value of goods exported over the total value of goods produced, multiplied by the corporate income tax.

(3) Export credit financing by a government agency. (a) Assume that the interest rate on the loan is at currently available market interest rates in the country of export. (b) Assume that the interest rate is lower than available market rates, but is at least as high as the government borrowing rate. (c) Assume that the interest rate is lower than available market rates and the government borrowing rate.

(4) Government grants to firms which employ previously unemployed or handicapped workers.

(5) Waivers of city real estate or corporate income tax by a municipality, for a specified period of time.

(6) Provision of a favorable lease rate on a factory built with proceeds of tax-free municipal bonds. Assume the factory exports 70% of its products.

(7) Government grants for on-the-job training for local high school students to work in a local factory that exports most of its products.

(8) Government grants to companies which train workers in certain electronic or "hi-tech" jobs.

(9) Government grants to universities to assist in developing training programs for scientists and technical workers in particular industries. Assume the industries export 50% of their products.

(10) Government research and development contracts with industries, to develop certain technologies (e.g., defense, aircraft or computer technology).

(11) Extensive fire and police protection (which reduces the insurance costs to business).

(12) Government grants to firms for use in encouraging the retirement or relocation of unneeded workers.

(13) Government grants to laid-off workers, which grants relieve firms of legal or moral obligations to make severance payments.

(14) Government grants to firms to enable the closing of unprofitable facilities.

(15) Government support to port facilities (a) to keep exporters from leaving economically depressed area or (b) for no specific purpose, although beneficial to exporters.

(16) Revision of laws for the protection of intellectual property in a way that benefits exporters of "high-tech" products.

(17) Government failure to enforce strictly its existing antipollution/antitrust laws against export industries.

SECTION 18.3   UNITED STATES COUNTERVAILING DUTY LAW

The United States has had some form of countervailing duty legislation in place since 1897. It was strengthened and elaborated in the Tariff Act of 1930, section 303, which authorized the Treasury Department to impose duties on imported merchandise to offset any "bounty or grant" bestowed upon it. This applied only to dutiable imports, but in 1974 was extended to non-dutiable imports. At the same time, an injury test was added covering non-dutiable imports, as required by Article VI of the GATT. Prior to the 1974 amendments, the absence of any injury test was protected by the "grandfather clause" in the Protocol of Provisional Application.

Neither prior law nor the 1930 Act defined the term "bounty or grant." The Treasury Department, which administered the statute until 1980, struggled with the term continually. Administrative practice failed to resolve many of the obvious issues, in part because countervailing duty actions were fairly uncommon.

Although it is difficult to compare records during the period from the first countervailing duty law in 1897 to mid–1973, it appears that there were approximately 84 countervailing duties applied under U.S. law over this 76 year span. From 1897 to 1934, there were approximately 35 duties imposed. From 1935 to 1940 there were 24, while from 1941 to 1945 there were none. The 20 year period from 1946 to 1966 saw only 13 duties imposed (3 in 1951, 2 in 1953, no more than 1 in any other year). After 1967, however, activity increased. From 1967 to 1973 there were 12 countervailing duties imposed.[1]

In 1973, the Treasury Department issued a countervailing duty order of considerable importance. The order imposed countervailing duties on tires imported from Canada and made by Michelin Tire Manufacturing Co. of Canada, Ltd.[2] The order was significant because the subsidies countervailed were domestic subsidies of the sort often granted by governmental units in the United States. Specifically, the following were held to be subsidies: Grants to Michelin by the Canadian federal and Nova Scotia governments; a special accelerated depreciation provision of the Canadian income tax law made available to Michelin;

---

1. These statistics were compiled from the reports issued in Treasury Decisions. The figures from 1897 through 1934 are difficult to compile with precision, inasmuch as the method of reporting the imposition of countervailing duties was not very systematic during those years.

2. 38 Fed.Reg. 1018 (1973); 7 Customs Bull. 24 (1973).

low-interest loans provided to Michelin by Nova Scotia; and property tax concessions provided by municipalities. These grants and concessions had been made available as part of programs to bolster the relatively weak economy of Nova Scotia. The imposition of a countervailing duty in these circumstances was apparently the first time that the U.S. statute had been applied to such subsidies.[3] Although the grants and concessions were indeed designed to help Nova Scotia's economy, a significant proportion (75%) of the tires produced needed to be exported. Since the U.S. market was the only logical export destination, is it arguable that the subsidies were in large part export subsidies because they were intended to be used to construct a plant to produce exports.

The Trade Act of 1974 made a number of additional changes in the statute. The principal changes were to require the Treasury Department to make a preliminary decision within six months of the filing date of a petition and a final decision within 12 months. The Act also required the publication of determinations by the Treasury Department and gave disappointed petitioners the right to appeal negative determinations. By so limiting the discretion of the Treasury Department as to the procedural aspects of countervailing investigations, it appeared likely that there would be a significant increase in the number of petitions filed. But Congress also realized the need for a new international agreement on subsidies and the need for the President to have some flexibility in negotiating such an agreement. The result was that the Secretary of the Treasury was given the right in Section 331(a) of the 1974 Act to waive imposition of countervailing duties if certain conditions were met. As a consequence, the 1974 Act did not lead to increased imposition of countervailing duties.

The Trade Agreements Act of 1979 implemented the Tokyo Round Subsidies Code under U.S. law. It changed the law dramatically and created procedures much like those applicable to antidumping cases. The authority to investigate allegations of subsidization was transferred from the Treasury Department to the Commerce Department, International Trade Administration (ITA). ITA was to conduct both a preliminary inquiry and a final inquiry separated by a public hearing and a process of "verification" during which the information provided by the foreign government(s) under investigation was to be audited for accuracy. Investigations were to be subjected to tight time limits, and the authority under the 1974 Act for the President to waive the imposition of countervailing duties under certain circumstances was abolished. Further, the statute directed the International Trade Commission to conduct an injury investigation in every countervailing duty case involving a signatory to the Subsidies Code, a non-signatory entitled to the same treatment by virtue of other treaty obligations, or any non-dutiable import. As with the ITA proceeding, the ITC proceeding was separated into a preliminary inquiry—to occur prior to the ITA investigation—and a final inquiry to occur after the completion of the ITA investigation. Affirma-

---

3. See generally Guido & Morrone, The Michelin Decision: A Possible New Di- rection for U.S. Countervailing Duty Law, 6 L. & Pol.Intl.Bus. 237 (1974).

tive determinations by both agencies result in the issuance of a countervailing duty "order" to be enforced by Customs. Both the ITA and ITC determinations were made appealable to the new Court of International Trade, and subsequently to the Federal Circuit. The removal of political discretion from the process had a dramatic effect in increasing the number of cases filed.

The 1979 Act also introduced some new concepts to clarify what subsidies are countervailable. Consistent with the harsh treatment of export subsidies in GATT, the Act provided that all such subsidies would be countervailable. As for domestic subsidies, the Act added the "specificity test," which provided that a countervailable "subsidy" would be found in the event that a foreign government program provided benefits to a "specific enterprise or group of enterprises." See Tariff Act of 1930 (as amended), section 771(5). The act also included a non-exhaustive list of government programs that might be deemed to constitute subsidies if specific, such as direct payments, the forgiveness of debts, or the provision of services on terms inconsistent with commercial considerations.

The implementing legislation for the Uruguay Round preserves the same basic structure of U.S. countervailing duty law. Because all WTO members are parties to the Uruguay Round accord, the injury test will apply in every countervailing duty investigation involving a WTO member. U.S. law is modified to accord with the "green light" category of non-actionable subsidies, and modified slightly to comply with the "sunset" requirement in Article 21 of the Uruguay Round Subsidies Agreement. Provisions are also added to facilitate the enforcement of U.S. rights under the Subsidies Agreement, and to authorize company specific countervailing duties.

The injury test was discussed in the preceding chapter. The materials that follow focus exclusively on the ITA portion of the countervailing duty investigation, and on the key issues that the ITA must resolve: When is a program under investigation a "subsidy" and thus countervailable? If the program is countervailable, how is the subsidy to be valued and the duty to be computed?

Because every export subsidy is countervailable under U.S. law, the only difficult issue with respect to these subsidies is one of characterization—is a program an export subsidy or not? The starting point for inquiring whether a domestic subsidy is countervailable is to ask whether it is "specific."

A NAFTA panel[4] explained its understanding of the rationale for the specificity test as follows: "Specificity analysis is required because it has long been recognized that the reach of the countervailing duty law should not extend to benefits and services, like highways, law enforcement and education, that governments routinely provide to their population at large. The statutory basis for drawing the distinction between

---

4. Pure and Alloy Magnesium From   port of August 16, 1993.
Canada, Panel No. USA–92–1904–03. Re-

such widely used and specific domestic subsidies is found in the definition of "subsidy," [which] includes domestic subsidies only if "provided to a specific enterprise or industry, or group of enterprises or industries." Legislative history of this law provides two rationales for this specificity test. First, Congress recognized that every export benefits from some general government assistance (e.g., public roads, utilities, education), and therefore, every import would arguably be subject to countervailing duties without such a test. Second, government programs which do not confer benefits selectively do not upset the free market forces that countervailing duties are meant to offset."

PPG INDUSTRIES, INC. v. UNITED STATES

United States Court of Appeals, Federal Circuit, 1991.
928 F.2d 1568.

[Eds. note. At the time of this case, Mexico was not a signatory to the Subsidies Code and was not entitled to the injury test. Thus, the case proceeded under Section 303 of the Tariff Act of 1930, now repealed. Its discussion of specificity, however, remains relevant. The current statutory language on specificity may be found in Section 771(5A) of the Tariff Act of 1930, as amended by the Uruguay Rounds Agreements Act.]

This appeal is from the decision of the United States Court of International Trade upholding the determination of the International Trade Administration (ITA or agency) that unprocessed float glass from Mexico was not subject to countervailing duties by reason of certain programs instituted by the government of Mexico, namely, the Trust Fund for the Coverage of Exchange Risks (FICORCA) and the sale of natural gas at controlled prices. * * *

The issue in this appeal broadly concerns what type of domestic subsidy received by a foreign producer from its government gives rise to a countervailing duty under 19 U.S.C. § 1303 upon importation of its goods into the United States. * * *

Under this part of the statute the question would be phrased in terms of what is a "bounty or grant." However, because of the interrelationship of section 1303 and 19 U.S.C. § 1677, the following provision of section 1677(5) is also pertinent:

> The term "subsidy" has the same meaning as the term "bounty or grant" as that term is used in section 1303 of this title, and includes, but is not limited to, the following: * * *

> (B) The following domestic subsidies, if provided or required by government action to a specific enterprise or industry, or group of enterprises or industries, whether publicly or privately owned, and whether paid or bestowed directly or indirectly on the manufacture, production, or export of any class or kind of merchandise:

>> (i) The provision of capital, loans, or loan guarantees on terms inconsistent with commercial considerations.

>> (ii) The provision of goods or services at preferential rates.

(iii) The grant of fund or forgiveness of debt to cover operating losses sustained by a specific industry.

(iv) The assumption of any costs or expenses of manufacture, production, or distribution * * *

REQUIREMENT OF SPECIFICITY

PPG first mounts a broadside attack on ITA's interpretation that a domestic subsidy must benefit a specific industry or group for such subsidy to constitute a "bounty or grant" within the meaning of § 1303. * * *

[A]s a reason to prohibit the ITA's specificity test, PPG argues that such a test yields the "absurd" result that the more widely a domestic subsidy is available and the more products that benefit from it, the less likely it would be that the subsidy would be countervailable. That is essentially the policy argument which has flared from time to time in Congress and it remains a policy choice for Congress in the first instance, not the courts. When some members of Congress in 1984 sought to make natural resource subsidies countervailable per se where an industry was a disproportionate user, the legislation failed to be enacted. Indeed, the limited scope of that proposed legislation undercuts PPG's argument that the ITA is now precluded under the statute from requiring specificity in connection with any type of domestic subsidy. * * *

Accepting that "specificity" is a requirement for countervailability of a domestic subsidy, PPG [next] argues that the requirement of specificity must be deemed met—as a matter of law—if the recipients of the subsidy are simply "identifiable." That is, if a company or companies which receive benefits can be named, they would be "identifiable" and "specific." * * *

Nothing in the statute mandates PPG's interpretation that specificity is met merely if recipients of a domestic subsidy are identifiable. Moreover, given the policy choice involved in adopting PPG's interpretation, this is a matter on which a court must defer to the agency. Thus, this argument does not require reversal. The statute does not mandate that "specific" means no more than "identifiable."

Falling back to an even narrower position, PPG asserts that the FICORCA and natural gas subsidy programs fit within the ITA's specificity standard. At this point, review of the details of these programs is appropriate.

FICORCA

FICORCA is a trust fund for the coverage of risks provided by the government of Mexico to industries on an eligibility basis.

* * *

As a result of its investigation, the ITA found:

FICORCA is a trust fund set up by the Mexican government and the Bank of Mexico operating through the country's credit institutions. All Mexican firms with registered debt in foreign currency and payable abroad to Mexican credit institutions or to foreign financial entities or suppliers may purchase, at a controlled rate, the amount in dollars necessary to pay principal on the loan. * * * We have verified documentation that the program is available to all Mexican firms with foreign indebtedness; it is not targeted to a specific industry or enterprise, groups of industries or enterprises, or to companies located in specific regions. FICORCA is also not tied in any way to exports. * * *

On that basis, the ITA determined that the FICORCA program was not countervailable. PPG attacks this conclusion because the program contains certain "eligibility requirements", which per PPG limits the group and makes it "specific."

The trial court is correct that the existence of eligibility requirements does not suffice to identify a discreet class which has been afforded the benefits of a "bounty or grant."

Although eligibility requirements may, if sufficiently narrowly tailored, de facto render the benefit one targeted to a specific industry or group of industries, the Court of International Trade and the ITA both determined that these eligibility requirements did not present such a case.

NATURAL GAS PRICING POLICY

The Mexican government holds a monopoly on the sale of basic fuels in Mexico. Operating through a state-owned facility, Petroleos Mexicanos (PEMEX), Mexico sells natural gas produced in Mexico at controlled prices. There are two categories of natural gas prices in Mexico, one for industrial use and a higher price for residential use. The prices set by the Mexican government for industrial users are well below the export price for Mexican natural gas and the world market price.

Before the ITA and the Court of International Trade, PPG asserted that preferential discounted natural gas rates were given to the float glass industry as compared to other industries, thus bringing the subsidy under section 1677(5)(B)(ii). Upon investigation, the ITA found that the evidence was to the contrary, stating:

We verified that the float glass companies paid the published price for natural gas which was available to all industries, and therefore received no benefit.

In its reply brief, PPG appears to argue for the first time that the float glass industry is part of a larger specific group, that is, "energy-intensive" industries, and that, therefore, it meets the specificity test. * * *

Neither the ITA nor the court below discussed "energy-intensive" as a category of "specific" industries, inasmuch as it appears to be an argument raised only on appeal. Nevertheless, it also appears quite clear from ITA's prior determinations that ITA does not recognize "energy-intensive" as a category of "specific" industries. In the ammonia and cement investigations, [citations omitted], the subsidized resources are reported to have accounted for eighty percent and fifty percent of cost, respectively. Here, energy is alleged to be 6.7 percent of production costs.

* * *

MICHEL, CIRCUIT JUDGE, dissenting. I respectfully dissent.

Affirming this final countervailing duty determination, as my two esteemed colleagues have voted to do, threatens to revive an old International Trade Administration ("ITA") interpretation of the statute's specificity requirement previously abrogated under settled law. Indeed, ITA itself abandoned this misinterpretation five years ago after its "general availability test" was rejected by the Court of International Trade ("CIT") in Cabot Corp. v. United States, 9 CIT 489, 620 F.Supp. 722 (1985). * * *

The mandate of Cabot is clear: ITA is required to undertake a factual investigation comparing the effects of the benefit on the foreign party named in the petition with those on other recipients of the same subsidy. Cabot, 620 F.Supp. at 732 ("The appropriate standard focuses on the de facto case by case effect of benefits.").

Despite quoting Cabot's requirement that ITA assess the "case by case effect of benefits provided to recipients," the CIT, in reviewing ITA's final determination in PPG Industries, concluded, illogically, that "[s]ince the ITA determined [that the float glass manufacturers] paid the published price for natural gas which was available to all industries, * * * ITA's determination was in substantial accordance with the statutory standard." . . . Thus, like the [majority], the [CIT] addressed only the preferential pricing allegations of PPG's ITA petition and CIT complaint, while ignoring the allegation that sales to these defendants at the published price were themselves a countervailable subsidy.

Since ITA plainly did not apply to defendants here a "specificity analysis," measuring the "case by case effect of benefits provided to recipients," to affirm its determination is wrong as a matter of law. Moreover, our affirming the CIT's erroneous holding in PPG Industries undermines subsequent CIT holdings, which uniformly and correctly applied the Cabot test.

* * *

Finally, ITA's incorrect determination, based on a statutorily incorrect test, contravenes the clear intent of Congress, which has adopted the Cabot "effect of benefits" test as reflective of its original intent. Congress amended section 1677(5)(B), originating in 1979, in the Omnibus Trade and Competitiveness Act of 1988, adding a "Special Rule":

> In applying subparagraph (A) [which includes the specificity language], the administering authority, in each investigation, shall determine whether the bounty, grant, or subsidy in law or in fact is

provided to a specific enterprise or industry, or group of enterprises or industries. Nominal general availability, under the terms of the law, regulation, program, or rule establishing a bounty, grant, or subsidy, of the benefits thereunder is not a basis for determining that the bounty, grant, or subsidy is not, or has not been, in fact provided to a specific enterprise or industry, or group thereof.

The legislative history, moreover, clearly indicates that Congress explicitly endorsed the test required in the Cabot case, H.R.Rep. No. 40, Comm. on Ways and Means, 100th Cong., 1st Sess. (H.R.Rep. No. 40), at 123–24 ("This [amendment], in effect, codifies the finding of the [CIT] decided in Cabot Corp. v. United States. * * * The test * * * is whether there is a sufficient degree of competitive advantage in international commerce being bestowed upon a discreet class of beneficiaries that would not exist but for government action." It is suggested that defeat in 1984 of an amendment to make natural energy subsidies per se countervailable proves that Congress' intent in 1979 on specificity could not cover energy subsidies even when the facts of the case warrant. The illogic of equating a per se rule of countervailability and a fact-based discretionary rule needs no elaboration. In any event, in adopting the Special Rule, Congress explicitly envisioned it being used in situations where natural energy, natural gas in particular, was the generally available benefit in question. H.R.Rep. No. 40 at 124.

Rather than upholding this incorrect determination, this court should insist that ITA apply the correct statutory test. Moreover, since the failure to assess the effects of these gas sales or look at anything more than general availability was clearly not harmless error, remand is our only proper course.

OIL COUNTRY TUBULAR GOODS FROM AUSTRIA

Intl.Trade Admin. (1985)[5]

[The ITA determined that the exporter, Voest–Alpine AG, benefited from subsidies in the form of equity infusions from the Austrian government (0.08%), grants by the Austrian government (1.60%) and subsidized export financing (0.08%), all of which are typical forms of subsidization. The ITA also examined a number of other government programs:]

D. VARIOUS CASH GRANT PROGRAMS

Petitioners alleged that the Federal government provides cash grants, equal to 100,000 Schillings per job created, to companies relocating to, or expanding plants in the special development and coal-mining areas.

The government response stated that a 100,000 Schilling Action program was established by joint resolution between Austria's federal and state governments. Funds from this program are granted (by both

---

5. Preliminary Determination, 50 Fed. Reg. 23334.

the federal and the applicable state government) as a premium in an amount no greater than 100,000 Schillings for each newly created job. To receive these cash grants, a company must meet the following requirements: (1) The recipient must have invested at least 400,000 Schillings in a newly estimated plant or 200,000 Schillings in the expansion of an old plant; (2) the character of the investment must be innovative; and (3) the recipient must make an employment guarantee of at least three years.

Under this program, Voest–Alpine AG was awarded a cash grant for the construction of its new seamless tube mill in Kindberg, Syria. Accordingly, 50 percent of any grant awarded is to be paid by the state (Syria) government and 50 percent by the federal government. The grant was approved in 1981 with payment to be made in two equal installments. The first installment was paid in May, 1983; the second installment is still outstanding. We have no information on the record that the rate of federal support does not vary from state to state and/or that the support is available in all parts of Austria. Because this program may be limited to companies located in specific regions, we preliminarily determine this grant to be countervailable.

II. PROGRAMS DETERMINED NOT TO CONFER A SUBSIDY

We preliminarily determine that subsidies are not being provided to manufacturers, producers, or exporters in Austria of oil country tubular goods under the following programs:

* * *

B. *Labor Subsidies*

Petitioners alleged that Voest–Alpine AG has received benefits from labor programs sponsored by the Austrian government.

1. *Government-Funded Labor Training.* The government response stated that under the Labor Market Promotion Act, Law No. 31/1969, companies in Austria may receive funds from the Austrian government for the establishment of in-house training programs to improve worker skills or to teach workers new vocations. In addition, under this law companies in Austria with low levels of capacity utilization may receive funds to be paid to the workers involved in training combined with reduced hours of work. Employees whose working hours are reduced receive support payments compensating them for the loss in earnings sustained. Workers receiving benefits under this program spend the difference between their reduced working hours and their normal working hours in training programs. The government's response stated that funding for these labor training programs is available to all sectors of Austrian industry and not just to the iron and steel industry or to export-related industries. Because this program is not limited to a specific enterprise or industry, or group of enterprises or industries, we preliminarily determine that the program does not constitute a subsidy.

2. *Special Assistant Act.* The Special Assistant Act of 1973, Law No. 642/1973, provides enhanced unemployment benefits for former

employees of sectors of the economy hit by the downturn which have been let go and are at least 55 years old for men or 50 years old for women. The Federal Minister of Social Affairs is empowered to determine by decree which sectors of the economy warrant application of the provisions of the law. In a decree issued on March 21, 1983, the iron and steel industry was included within the provisions of this law. The government of Austria's response stated that payments under this law are made directly to the workers who have been laid off by an employer. The employer itself is not entitled to any support or subsidies under this law and is not relieved from payment of any expenses otherwise the obligation of such employer. Because this program provides assistance to workers and does not relieve Voest–Alpine AG of any expenses or obligations, we preliminarily determine that the company does not receive a subsidy under this program.

* * *

D.   Loan Guaranty Program

Petitioners alleged that Voest–Alpine AG has received substantial loan guarantees from the Austrian government. The Austrian government's response stated that loans issued by insurance companies in Austria must meet certain strict requirements for investment security according to section 77 of the Insurance Supervisory Law of October 18, 1976. Because of these requirements, commercial loans by insurance companies must be guaranteed by the government or secured by a pledge of a real estate. The government guarantees insurance company loans to Voest–Alpine AG to enable the insurance companies to find larger-scale legally eligible investments for placement of their investment portfolios, rather than to enable Voest–Alpine AG to raise funds, which it is able to do through other sources. Accordingly, we preliminarily determine that this program does not provide subsidies to Voest–Alpine AG.

Notes and Questions

(1) To what degree can the specificity test serve to identify foreign government practices that distort the market? Might subsidies widely available to farmers create distortions even though farm subsidy programs are not legally "specific?" Might a subsidy directed to a single industry that produces a positive external benefit to the economy, such as a research and development spillover, not correct rather than create a distortion? What about targeted subsidies that help firms to comply with expensive government regulations?

(2) Does there exist any analytically sound basis for deciding when the number of recipients is small enough that the program becomes "specific?" Do the Uruguay Round Agreements Act amendments in Section 771(5A) of the Tariff Act of 1930 add any greater clarity or predictability?

UNITED STATES DEPARTMENT OF COMMERCE,
INTERNATIONAL TRADE ADMINISTRATION
IDENTIFICATION AND MEASUREMENT OF
COUNTERVAILABLE SUBSIDIES
EXCERPTS FROM 19 C.F.R.

Section 351.504—Grants

(a) *Benefit.* In the case of a grant, a benefit exists in the amount of the grant. * * *

Section 351.505—Loans

(a) *Benefit.*—(1) *In general.* In the case of a loan, a benefit exists to the extent that the amount a firm pays on the government-provided loan is less than the amount the firm would pay on a comparable commercial loan(s) that the firm could actually obtain on the market. *See* section 771(5)(E)(ii) of the Act. In making the comparison called for in the preceding sentence, the Secretary normally will rely on effective interest rates.

(2) *"Comparable commercial loan" defined.*-(i) *"Comparable" defined.* In selecting a loan that is "comparable" to the government-provided loan, the Secretary normally will place primary emphasis on similarities in the structure of the loans (*e.g.,* fixed interest rate v. variable interest rate), the maturity of the loans (*e.g.,* short-term v. long-term), and the currency in which the loans are denominated.

(ii) *"Commercial" defined.* In selecting a "commercial" loan, the Secretary normally will use a loan taken out by the firm from a commercial lending institution or a debt instrument issued by the firm in a commercial market. Also, the Secretary will treat a loan from a government-owned bank as a commercial loan, unless there is evidence that the loan from a government-owned bank is provided on non-commercial terms or at the direction of the government. However, the Secretary will not consider a loan provided under a government program, or a loan provided by a government-owned special purpose bank, to be a commercial loan for purposes of selecting a loan to compare with a government-provided loan.

(iii) *Long-term loans.* In selecting a comparable loan, if the government-provided loan is a long-term loan, the Secretary normally will use a loan the terms of which were established during, or immediately before, the year in which the terms of the government-provided loan were established.

(iv) *Short-term loans.* In making the comparison required under paragraph (a)(1) of this section, if the government-provided loan is a short-term loan, the Secretary normally will use an annual average of the interest rates on comparable commercial loans during the year in which the government-provided loan was taken out, weighted by the principal amount of each loan. However, if the Secretary finds that interest rates fluctuated significantly during the period of investigation or review, the Secretary will use the most appropriate interest rate based on the circumstances presented.

(3) *"Could actually obtain on the market" defined.*-(i) *In general.* In selecting a comparable commercial loan that the recipient "could actually obtain on the market," the Secretary normally will rely on the actual experience of the firm in question in obtaining comparable commercial loans for both short-term and long-term loans.

(ii) *Where the firm has no comparable commercial loans.* If the firm did not take out any comparable commercial loans during the period referred to in paragraph (a)(2)(iii) or (a)(2)(iv) of this section, the Secretary may use a national average interest rate for comparable commercial loans. * * *

Section 351.506—Loan guarantees

(a) *Benefit.*—(1) *In general.* In the case of a loan guarantee, a benefit exists to the extent that the total amount a firm pays for the loan with the government-provided guarantee is less than the total amount the firm would pay for a comparable commercial loan that the firm could actually obtain on the market absent the government-provided guarantee, including any difference in guarantee fees. *See* section 771(5)(E)(iii) of the Act. The Secretary will select a comparable commercial loan in accordance with section 351.505(a).

(2) *Government acting as owner.* In situations where a government, acting as the owner of a firm, provides a loan guarantee to that firm, the guarantee does not confer a benefit if the respondent provides evidence demonstrating that it is normal commercial practice in the country in question for shareholders to provide guarantees to their firms under similar circumstances and on comparable terms. * * *

Section 351.507—Equity

(a) *Benefit.*— (1) *In general.* In the case of a government-provided equity infusion, a benefit exists to the extent that the investment decision is inconsistent with the usual investment practice of private investors, including the practice regarding the provision of risk capital, in the country in which the equity infusion is made. *See* section 771(5)(E)(i) of the Act.

(2) *Private investor prices available.*—(i) *In general.* Except as provided in paragraph (a)(2)(iii) of this section, the Secretary will consider an equity infusion as being inconsistent with usual investment practice (*see* paragraph (a)(1) of this section) if the price paid by the government for newly issued shares is greater than the price paid by private investors for the same (or similar form of) newly issued shares.

(ii) *Timing of private investor prices.* In selecting a private investor price under paragraph (a)(2)(i) of this section, the Secretary will rely on sales of newly issued shares made reasonably concurrently with the newly issued shares purchased by the government.

(iii) *Significant private sector participation required.* The Secretary will not use private investor prices under paragraph (a)(2)(i) of this section if the Secretary concludes that private investor purchases of newly issued shares are not significant.

(iv) *Adjustments for "similar" form of equity.* Where the Secretary uses private investor prices for a form of shares that is similar to the newly issued shares purchased by the government (*see* paragraph (a)(2)(i) of this section), the Secretary, where appropriate, will adjust the prices to reflect the differences in the forms of shares.

(3) *Actual private investor prices unavailable.*—(i) *In general.* If actual private investor prices are not available under paragraph (a)(2) of this section, the Secretary will determine whether the firm funded by the government-provided equity was equityworthy or unequityworthy at the time of the equity infusion (*see* paragraph (a)(4) of this section). If the Secretary determines that the firm was equityworthy, the Secretary will apply paragraph (a)(5) of this section to determine whether the equity infusion was inconsistent with the usual investment practice of private investors. A determination by the Secretary that the firm was unequityworthy will constitute a determination that the equity infusion was inconsistent with usual investment practice of private investors, and the Secretary will apply paragraph (a)(6) of this section to measure the benefit attributable to the equity infusion.

(4) *Equityworthiness.*—(i) *In general.* The Secretary will consider a firm to have been equityworthy if the Secretary determines that, from the perspective of a reasonable private investor examining the firm at the time the government-provided equity infusion was made, the firm showed an ability to generate a reasonable rate of return within a reasonable period of time. The Secretary may, in appropriate circumstances, focus its equityworthiness analysis on a project rather than the company as a whole. In making the equityworthiness determination, the Secretary may examine the following factors, among others:

(A) Objective analyses of the future financial prospects of the recipient firm or the project as indicated by, *inter alia,* market studies, economic forecasts, and project or loan appraisals prepared prior to the government-provided equity infusion in question;

(B) Current and past indicators of the recipient firm's financial health calculated from the firm's statements and accounts, adjusted, if appropriate, to conform to generally accepted accounting principles;

(C) Rates of return on equity in the three years prior to the government equity infusion; and

(D) Equity investment in the firm by private investors ...

(5) *Benefit where firm is equityworthy.* If the Secretary determines that the firm or project was equityworthy (*see* paragraph (a)(4) of this section), the Secretary will examine the terms and the nature of the equity purchased to determine whether the investment was otherwise inconsistent with the usual investment practice of private investors. If

the Secretary determines that the investment was inconsistent with usual private investment practice, the Secretary will determine the amount of the benefit conferred on a case-by-case basis.

(6) *Benefit where firm is unequityworthy.* If the Secretary determines that the firm or project was unequityworthy (*see* paragraph (a)(4) of this section), a benefit to the firm exists in the amount of the equity infusion. * * *

Section 351.508—Debt forgiveness

(a) *Benefit.* In the case of an assumption or forgiveness of a firm's debt obligation, a benefit exists equal to the amount of the principal and/or interest (including accrued, unpaid interest) that the government has assumed or forgiven. In situations where the entity assuming or forgiving the debt receives shares in a firm in return for eliminating or reducing the firm's debt obligation, the Secretary will determine the existence of a benefit under section 351.507 (equity infusions). * * *

Section 351.509—Direct taxes

(a) *Benefit.*—(1) *Exemption or remission of taxes.* In the case of a program that provides for a full or partial exemption or remission of a direct tax (*e.g.,* an income tax), or a reduction in the base used to calculate a direct tax, a benefit exists to the extent that the tax paid by a firm as a result of the program is less than the tax the firm would have paid in the absence of the program.

(2) *Deferral of taxes.* In the case of a program that provides for a deferral of direct taxes, a benefit exists to the extent that appropriate interest charges are not collected. Normally, a deferral of direct taxes will be treated as a government-provided loan in the amount of the tax deferred, according to the methodology described in § 351.505. The Secretary will use a short-term interest rate as the benchmark for tax deferrals of one year or less. The Secretary will use a long-term interest rate as the benchmark for tax deferrals of more than one year. * * *

Section 351.511—Provision of goods or services

(a) *Benefit.*—(1) *In general.* In the case where goods or services are provided, a benefit exists to the extent that such goods or services are provided for less than adequate remuneration. *See* section 771(5)(E)(iv) of the Act.

(2) *"Adequate Remuneration" defined.*—(i) *In general.* The Secretary will normally seek to measure the adequacy of remuneration by comparing the government price to a market-determined price for the good or service resulting from actual transactions in the country in question. Such a price could include prices stemming from actual transactions between private parties, actual imports, or, in certain circumstances, actual sales from competitively run government auctions. In choosing such transactions or sales, the Secretary will consider product similarity; quantities sold, imported, or auctioned; and other factors affecting comparability.

(ii) *Actual market-determined price unavailable.* If there is no usea-ble market-determined price with which to make the comparison under paragraph (a)(2)(i) of this section, the Secretary will seek to measure the adequacy of remuneration by comparing the government price to a world market price where it is reasonable to conclude that such price would be available to purchasers in the country in question. Where there is more than one commercially available world market price, the Secretary will average such prices to the extent practicable, making due allowance for factors affecting comparability.

(iii) *World market price unavailable.* If there is no world market price available to purchasers in the country in question, the Secretary will normally measure the adequacy of remuneration by assessing whether the government price is consistent with market principles. * * *

Section 351.513—Worker-related subsidies

(a) *Benefit.* In the case of a program that provides assistance to workers, a benefit exists to the extent that the assistance relieves a firm of an obligation that it normally would incur. * * *

Section 351.517—Exemption or remission upon export of indirect taxes

(a) *Benefit.* In the case of the exemption or remission upon export of indirect taxes, a benefit exists to the extent that the Secretary deter-mines that the amount remitted or exempted exceeds the amount levied with respect to the production and distribution of like products when sold for domestic consumption. * * *

Section 351.518—Exemption, remission, or deferral upon export of prior-stage cumulative indirect taxes

(a) *Benefit.—* (1) *Exemption of prior-stage cumulative indirect taxes.* In the case of a program that provides for the exemption of prior-stage cumulative indirect taxes on inputs used in the production of an export-ed product, a benefit exists to the extent that the exemption extends to inputs that are not consumed in the production of the exported product, making normal allowance for waste, or if the exemption covers taxes other than indirect taxes that are imposed on the input. If the Secretary determines that the exemption of prior-stage cumulative indirect taxes confers a benefit, the Secretary normally will consider the amount of the benefit to be the prior-stage cumulative indirect taxes that otherwise would have been paid on the inputs not consumed in the production of the exported product, making normal allowance for waste, and the amount of charges other than import charges covered by the exemption.

(2) *Remission of prior-stage cumulative indirect taxes.* In the case of a program that provides for the remission of prior-stage cumulative indirect taxes on inputs used in the production of an exported product, a benefit exists to the extent that the amount remitted exceeds the amount of prior-stage cumulative indirect taxes paid on inputs that are consumed in the production of the exported product, making normal allowance for waste. If the Secretary determines that the remission of

prior-stage cumulative indirect taxes confers a benefit, the Secretary normally will consider the amount of the benefit to be the difference between the amount remitted and the amount of the prior-stage cumulative indirect taxes on inputs that are consumed in the production of the export product, making normal allowance for waste.

(3) *Deferral of prior-stage cumulative indirect taxes.* In the case of a program that provides for a deferral of prior-stage cumulative indirect taxes on an exported product, a benefit exists to the extent that the deferral extends to inputs that are not consumed in the production of the exported product, making normal allowance for waste, and the government does not charge appropriate interest on the taxes deferred. If the Secretary determines that a benefit exists, the Secretary will normally treat the deferral as a government-provided loan in the amount of the tax deferred, according to the methodology described in section 351.505. The Secretary will use a short-term interest rate as the benchmark for tax deferrals of one year or less. The Secretary will use a long-term interest rate as the benchmark for tax deferrals of more than one year. * * *

Section 351.519—Remission or drawback of import charges upon export

(a) *Benefit.*— (1) *In general.* The term "remission or drawback" includes full or partial exemptions and deferrals of import charges.

(i) *Remission or drawback of import charges.* In the case of the remission or drawback of import charges upon export, a benefit exists to the extent that the Secretary determines that the amount of the remission or drawback exceeds the amount of import charges on imported inputs that are consumed in the production of the exported product, making normal allowances for waste.

(ii) *Exemption of import charges.* In the case of an exemption of import charges upon export, a benefit exists to the extent that the exemption extends to inputs that are not consumed in the production of the exported product, making normal allowances for waste, or if the exemption covers charges other than import charges that are imposed on the input. * * *

Section 351.523—Upstream subsidies

(a) *Investigation of upstream subsidies.*—(1) *In general.* Before investigating the existence of an upstream subsidy (*see* section 771A of the Act), the Secretary must have a reasonable basis to believe or suspect that all of the following elements exist:

(i) A countervailable subsidy, other than an export subsidy, is provided with respect to an input product;

(ii) One of the following conditions exists:

(A) The supplier of the input product and the producer of the subject merchandise are affiliated;

(B) The price for the subsidized input product is lower than the price that the producer of the subject merchandise otherwise would pay another seller in an arm's-length transaction for an unsubsidized input product; or

(C) The government sets the price of the input product so as to guarantee that the benefit provided with respect to the input product is passed through to producers of the subject merchandise; and

(iii) The *ad valorem* countervailable subsidy rate on the input product, multiplied by the proportion of the total production costs of the subject merchandise accounted for by the input product, is equal to, or greater than, one percent.

(b) *Input product*. For purposes of this section, "input product" means any product used in the production of the subject merchandise.

(c) *Competitive benefit.*—(1) *In general*. In evaluating whether a competitive benefit exists under section 771A(b) of the Act, the Secretary will determine whether the price for the subsidized input product is lower than the benchmark input price. For purposes of this section, the Secretary will use as a benchmark input price the following, in order of preference:

(i) The actual price paid by, or offered to, the producer of the subject merchandise for an unsubsidized input product, including an imported input product;

(ii) An average price for an unsubsidized input product, including an imported input product, based upon publicly available data;

(iii) The actual price paid by, or offered to, the producer of the subject merchandise for a subsidized input product, including an imported input product, that is adjusted to account for the countervailable subsidy;

(iv) An average price for a subsidized input product, including an imported input product, based upon publicly available data, that is adjusted to account for the countervailable subsidy; or

(v) An unadjusted price for a subsidized input product or any other surrogate price deemed appropriate by the Secretary.

For purposes of this section, such prices must be reflective of a time period that reasonably corresponds to the time of the purchase of the input. * * *

Notes and Questions

(1) The excerpts above omit consideration of a number of other matters essential to valuing a subsidy, some of which become quite complicated. For example, the Department of Commerce must determine which products of a multiproduct firm benefit from subsidies. A further issue concerns the timing of the benefit stream. If a company receives a $50 million grant to build a factory with a useful life of 20 years, for example, how is the benefit from that grant to be allocated over the 20 year period? Subsequent sections of the proposed regulations provide formulae for doing so, as well as principles for determining when a countervailable benefit is allocated to the year of receipt or expensed over time.

(2) A much more controversial set of issues, not addressed in the regulations, involves the question whether a "subsidy" should only be found where it can be shown to have had a cross-border effect. Suppose, for purposes of illustration, that the government of Japan decides to give each Japanese automaker a billion yen on a one time basis. Suppose further that the auto companies respond by distributing the money to their shareholders as an extra dividend. By hypothesis, there is no expansion of Japanese auto production in response to the government's largesse, and thus no adverse impact of the "subsidy" on U.S. competitors. Is it nevertheless countervailable? Nothing in what you have seen above affords an obvious basis for answering in the negative, yet it has been argued through the years that a "subsidy" should only be found where the program in question can be shown to have stimulated production or exports and thus had an effect on prices abroad. Likewise, it is possible for a government to stimulate production or exports without any direct fiscal outlays, thus raising the question whether a "subsidy" can arise without any government expenditures. Such issues arose in the long running (and still unresolved) softwood lumber dispute between the United States and Canada.

CERTAIN SOFTWOOD LUMBER
PRODUCTS FROM CANADA
United States–Canada Free Trade Agreement Binational Panel Review[6]

Commerce found that different Canadian provinces sold cutting rights to timber on publicly-owned lands at "preferential rates" measured against the "benchmark" prices charged in alternative markets. As such, this provincial government action constituted a "subsidy" under 19 U.S.C. § 1677(5), requiring imposition of a countervailing duty on the various softwood lumber products generated from those logs and exported to the United States.

The provinces challenge the specific calculations which led Commerce to find preferential pricing on their part. However, the Canadian Complainants argue that even if different provincial stumpage rates were lower than prices found in alternative timber markets, this would not amount to a "subsidy" under the prevailing legislation.

That Canadian argument has two components. One component is the economic thesis that in the case of a natural resource (such as access to standing timber), while the price charged will determine the division of economic rent for that resource between its owner (here the government) and purchasers (private logging firms), such stumpage prices cannot alter the output or price of logs. For that reason, stumpage cannot affect the output or price of downstream products into which the logs are incorporated for sale in the United States. The other component of the argument is the legal contention that some such economic effect from a government's pricing policy (i.e., a "market distortion") is a necessary feature of any judgment that a "subsidy" has been conferred

---

6. Panel No. U.S.A.–92–1904–02. Report of May 6, 1993.

by a foreign government that warrants imposition of a countervailing duty upon the downstream products imported into the United States.

* * *

Commerce itself, in the introduction to its recently proposed Regulations for making CVD assessments, stated that:

Conceptually, the regulations are based upon the economic model articulated by the Department in its final determinations in Carbon Steel Wire Rod from Czechoslovakia and Carbon Steel Wire Rod from Poland and sustained by the Court in Georgetown Steel Corp. v. United States. This model, which generally defines a subsidy as a distortion of the market process for allocating an economy's resources, underlies the Department's entire methodology.

* * *

What Commerce itself has said about the model that underlies its "entire methodology"—"which generally defines a subsidy as a distortion of the market process"—cannot be legally ignored in considering whether government decisions about the pricing of access to a natural resource could influence the output and price of products generated from that resource, and thence justify imposition of a countervailing duty.

In defense of its refusal to apply "market distortion" analysis to the judgment about whether a subsidy was being offered * * *, Commerce pointed to the legislative history of the Trade Agreements Act of 1979, and in particular to the Congressional directive (at 19 U.S.C. § 1677(6)) that allowed Commerce to subtract only certain financial factors from the gross subsidy in order to arrive at a net subsidy. The specified factors do not include all offsetting costs potentially faced by subsidy recipients—such as, for example, the extra costs of operating in a remote and underdeveloped region in which the subsidy was designed to encourage development. By implication, then, Congress intended Commerce not to consider the latter amounts when calculating a net subsidy. From that premise, Commerce contended that it would be anomalous to engage in precisely this type of "net effects" analysis when determining whether a subsidy existed in the first place.

As the Canadian Complainants argue, that rationale offered by Commerce simply does not square with the broader legislative and departmental approach to cvd subsidy decisions. First, there is a clear legal distinction between § 1677(5), which governs identification of countervailable subsidies, and § 1677(6), which governs measurement of the subsidy for purposes of determining how much of a countervailing duty to impose, which distinction Commerce relies on in dismissing requests for provincial exclusions. That distinction is significant because in the case upon which Congress was focused when adopting the policy embodied in § 1677(6), there was no doubt that a government policy to grant financial benefits to firms to locate in underdeveloped regions did constitute a subsidy in the "market distortion" sense of that term. Indeed, even if a government does no more than grant sufficient benefits to a firm to offset the additional costs of locating in that region (thus leaving no net benefit at all), such a government action is designed to alter the market signal that is supposed to influence where production will be located and carried on. Thus such government action would be countervailable.

Most importantly, in this very case, Commerce in fact used the "market distortion" approach in deciding whether a subsidy had been granted in a market economy. Commerce did so with respect to British Columbia's restraints upon log exports which, according to the Department (as elaborated upon in another part of this decision), produced a drop in the aggregate market demand for British Columbia logs and thereby reduced the price that had to be paid by domestic softwood lumber producers. Though there is no explicit language in § 1677(5) covering such a governmental border measure, Commerce found that restraint of log exports was a subsidy precisely because of its alleged distorting effects on the market economy. Commerce could not, then, refuse to consider the argument that another government policy in that same market economy was not a subsidy because it did not have a market distorting effect.

* * *

No one in this case challenged the principles of classical Ricardian economic theory regarding natural resources. According to this 150–year old theory, the market for natural resources does not exhibit the normal elasticities in supply and demand whereby if prices go up (or down), purchase and production of the good will correspondingly go down (or up). Rather, because of the fact that natural resources have a basically fixed supply and strictly limited alternative uses, no such output and downstream price effects will flow from movements in resource prices, at least within what is called the "normal range." No matter how high the price charged by the owner within that range, as long as the purchaser of the right to harvest the natural resource can sell the product downstream for a higher price, the producer will harvest and sell as much of the resource as it can while making a profit on each unit sold. By the same token, no matter how low the price charged by the owner, the producer will not be able to harvest and sell more of this resource because the fixed (i.e., inelastic) supply of the latter means there is no more of the resource available for that purpose. The price set for the natural resource does play a key role in determining how the financial value—the economic rent—of the resource will be divided between owner and purchaser. It does not, however, have any market distorting impact on the output of the resource and thence on the amount and price of downstream products.

There are two important qualifications to this thesis. One concerns the situation in which the price charged for the resource is or becomes "excessive" for some reason. The resource price is excessive if, when added to the costs of harvesting and transporting the resource, it makes the total cost of production greater than the price that will be paid by downstream users. In such a case, where the producer will incur a loss on extraction and sale of each unit, reduction in price of the resource does permit an increase in levels of production. However, such a resource price effect is not market "distorting". The price has simply been moved to the normal range one would expect in a competitive market in which owners of a resource try to set their prices at a level where they can make some sales and profits, rather than leave the resource lie fallow.

A different qualification must be made at the other end of the price range. Here, rather than charge a positive price for the resource, the owners enter into a contractual arrangement whereby producers actually secure a "net benefit" from purchase and harvesting of the resource. For example, the resource may be located in a remote region where costs of extraction and transportation are themselves higher than the sale price of the same resource located in more accessible locations. If the owner (in particular, a government) has other social and political reasons for wanting to see this region developed, it may charge a nominal price for the resource, but pursuant to a contract whereby the owner makes considerably greater expenditures on extraction and transportation of the resource. This is done in order to lower the ultimate cost to producers sufficiently to make production in this location profitable. Such an in-kind net benefit will have an impact on output of the resource in question, precisely because it alters the normal market signals regarding this particular resource location. It is at this level, and only at this level, that government decisions about pricing natural resources can constitute a countervailable "subsidy" if one adopts the market distortion analysis of the legislation.

We conclude that, in this case, Commerce should have considered whether or not these provincial programs could and did have a distorting effect on the operation of normal competitive markets before concluding that these governmental policies involve the type of "preferential" pricing that constitutes a countervailable subsidy within the meaning of the Tariff Act. Accordingly, we remand this part of the stumpage decision back to Commerce for review of all the evidence regarding the natural resource market for standing timber in light of the legal principles formulated in this decision.

BRITISH STEEL CORP. v. UNITED STATES

United States Court of International Trade, 1986.
632 F.Supp. 59.

The central issue presented, having significant international trade implications for foreign governments that make "equity infusions" in state-owned enterprises in poor financial health, is: Under what circumstances are such companies "uncreditworthy" thereby making the government's investments commercially unreasonable and hence countervailable subsidies under 19 U.S.C. sec. 1677(5)(B)(i)?

* * *

Section 771(5) of the Tariff Act of 1930, as amended, 19 U.S.C. sec. 1677(5), embraces any subsidy "bestowed directly or indirectly on the manufacture, production, or export of any class or kind of merchandise" including: "[t]he provision of capital, loans or loan guarantees on terms inconsistent with commercial considerations". [Previously,] this Court construed the commercial considerations test concluding that an investment is consistent with commercial considerations if a reasonable investor could expect a reasonable rate of return on his investment within a reasonable period of time.

* * *

ITA applied the same "reasonable investor" criterion in determining [that] the British government's equity infusions in FY 1977/78—the year at issue in the present review—were "inconsistent with commercial considerations" within the meaning of the statute.

ITA reviewed BSC's financial history, commencing with its establishment in 1967. The review covered such fundamental indicia of financial condition as net income of BSC, net income before interest and taxes, cash flow from operations, coverage of interest expenses, return on equity, return on sales and current assets and liabilities.

ITA also considered such additional pertinent factors as the substantial cost of forming BSC, leading to unfavorable financial results for the first few years of the company's existence; the enormous social costs borne by BSC because of the British government's policy decisions, such as keeping high-cost plants open to preserve jobs; BSC's massive losses; the extremely bleak prospects of the company expressed by its own chairman in BSC's 1976–77 annual report; and the dismal outlook for the world steel market in general.

Based on its analysis of the foregoing factors, ITA reached the following conclusion:

> After considering the results for fiscal years 1975–76 and 1976–77 and the outlook for the world steel market in general, a reasonable investor in 1977 would not have considered British Steel with its large losses, poor return on equity, and other signs of structural problems, to be a reasonable commercial investment.

* * *

Plaintiffs argue that ITA's "reasonable investor" test is irrelevant to the commercial reasonableness of the British government's equity infusions and contrary to law. According to plaintiffs, the British government, unlike an outside investor, could not simply abandon BSC and incur no further losses if it decided to close the firm, and therefore the steps the British government took as the sole investor in the corporation were reasonably taken to minimize its prospective losses. In short, plaintiffs contend that the overall operating results and financial ratios of a loss-incurring company are irrelevant to the issue of whether the

British government's equity infusions were inconsistent with commercial considerations within the purview of the statute. [The court disagreed.]

* * *

[BSC] also urges that the Net Present Value (NPV) test be utilized in determining the commercial reasonableness of the British government's investments in BSC. [BSC] observes that under standard principles of economic analysis, the commercial reasonableness of capital expenditures by BSC on new projects must properly be judged against an evaluation of the NPV of each project. Thus, projects whose discounted cash flows show a positive NPV are commercially justified; projects whose cash flow show a negative NPV are not. According to plaintiffs, NPV analysis focuses upon whether investment in a new project is commercially worthwhile (positive), and it is irrelevant whether a capital project (or some combination of projects) returns the corporation to overall profitability. In support of NPV analysis, plaintiffs make reference to "concrete market examples" of private companies that had suffered heavy losses in successive years and nevertheless continued to make new capital investments.

Defendants, however, correctly observe that NPV analysis is largely predicated upon long-term earnings and interest-rate assumptions, which at best would be tenuous; and that BSC furnished analyses only of individual projects without any evaluation of those projects in terms of their effect upon BSC's overall operations and income-producing prospects.

While unquestionably NPV analyses were of importance to BSC's management, they were relevant to an outside investor only to the extent that the analyses showed how the investments in the individual projects would affect the overall operations and future profitability of BSC. Stated differently, from the investor's point of view, an investment would not be commercially reasonable if overall the company may still constantly lose money and never provide a reasonable return no matter how justifiable a company's decision respecting individual projects analyzed on the basis of NPV.

* * *

In sum, the court finds ITA's determination that the British government's investments in BSC in FY 1977/78 were inconsistent with commercial considerations, predicated upon its reasonable investor test, is supported by substantial evidence and otherwise in accordance with law.

Notes and Questions

(1) Take a look at section 771(6) of the Tariff Act of 1930, defining "net countervailable subsidy," and observe that the permissible deductions from an otherwise countervailable benefit are quite limited—application fees and the like. Thus, it is not permissible for a foreign government to argue that a countervailable benefit is offset by some unusual tax burden or costly regulation to which the beneficiary of the subsidy program has been subject-

ed. The desire to limit such deductions is perhaps quite understandable for administrative reasons. But does this mean that U.S. law cannot really hope to identify the *net* effect of foreign governments on the competitive positions of their industries? And, if so, what is the point of the law?

(2) In the *Softwood* excerpt concerning stumpage pricing, the panel suggests that a countervailable subsidy *would* be conferred if a firm was compensated for building a factory in an undesirable location by an amount exactly sufficient to offset the added costs—it reasoned that such a payment would have distorted the ordinary market outcome. Is that enough? Or must it also be shown that the distortion leads to increased output relative to the counterfactual world without the subsidy? That is the proposal, in essence, put forward n a paper by Goetz, Granet & Schwartz cited in the introduction to this chapter—a symposium on their proposal may be found in 21 L. & Pol.Intl.Bus. 503–770 (1990).

(3) Another issue in the softwood lumber dispute has been the suggestion by the United States that Canada's restrictions on the export of logs create a subsidy to the lumber industry by depressing the price of logs to a level below the market price that would prevail in the absence of the export restrictions. In effect, the suggestion is that a countervailable subsidy may exist even when the government has made no fiscal outlay. Is this determination consistent with the Uruguay Round Subsidies Agreement? With the U.S. implementing legislation since enacted? See United States—Measures Treating Export Restraints as Subsidies, WT/DS194/R, panel report adopted by the DSB on August 24, 2001.

(4) Is the "reasonable investor test" in *British Steel* a sensible one? Is it not the case that firms teetering on the brink of bankruptcy still have some positive value in the capital markets? What difference does it make whether the company is already wholly owned by the government? Why not let a government take account of the costs that it would incur if a company shuts down and the workers collect unemployment benefits? What if it can be shown that the government equity infusion was used for a project that was expected to have positive net present value, and that the project was indeed profitable after the fact?

(5) Do you understand how duties are calculated? Suppose that Company X produces a single product, and has one million dollars per year in total world-wide sales. Of that total, $800,000 in sales are domestic, $100,000 in sales are to the United States, and $100,000 in sales are to Europe. The company receives export subsidies of $10,000 pertaining to its U.S. sales and $20,000 pertaining to its European sales. In addition the company receives $100,000 per year in countervailable domestic subsidies. What is the appropriate countervailing duty on imports into the United States?

(6) Bear in mind that the countervailing duty rate at the conclusion of an ITA investigation is based on historical information, but will be applied prospectively. As with an anti-dumping case, therefore, the duty may not reflect the actual degree of subsidization over the period to which it applies. Consequently, the ITA periodically conducts "administrative reviews" to reassess the level of countervailable subsidies and adjust the duty accordingly. Overpayments are refunded (with interest), and the importer of record is liable to Customs for any underpayments (with interest).

(7) An issue of some remaining importance, though seemingly diminishing with time, concerns the applicability of countervailing duty laws to non-

market economies. It is now well settled that U.S. countervailing duty law is not applicable to non-market economies. See Georgetown Steel Corp. v. United States, 801 F.2d 1308 (Fed.Cir.1986). The fighting issue today is whether an economy is market-oriented or not.

(8) Note the regulations which imply that the remission or noncollection on exports of certain indirect taxes does not confer a subsidy. (19 C.F.R. secs. 351.517–519) By contrast, a remission of or exemption from direct taxes for exports is a countervailable (and WTO-illegal) export subsidy. WTO law provides for this difference in treatment, but in the view of some this situation confers an unfair advantage on U.S. trading partners. European countries, for example, rely heavily on the value added tax for revenue, an indirect tax from which exports may be exempted. The United States, by contrast, relies mainly on direct taxes for revenue from which exports may not be exempted. See Executive Branch GATT Studies No. 1, Tax Adjustments in International Trade: GATT Provisions and EEC Practices (1973). Does the difference in treatment make sense?

Chapter 19

INTERNATIONAL TRADE
IN SERVICES

SECTION 19.1   INTRODUCTION

Trade in services is of substantial and growing importance to the world and national economies. A 1991 report to the U.S. Congress estimated that such trade accounted for 25% of all world trade, for $90 billion in U.S. exports, for 60% of total U.S. output and for 90% of the growth in U.S. employment since 1980.[1] A year later, another report put U.S. services exports at $164 billion.[2] For the year 2000, the WTO reports that U.S. services exports have risen to $274 billion, and that total world trade in commercial services has reached $1.4 trillion.[3] These estimates often rest on questionable data, but there can be little doubt that trade in services is now a major component of overall world trade.

Despite its importance, trade in services was slow to come under multilateral discipline. The Treaty of Rome afforded some constraints on service sector protectionism in Europe, various friendship, commerce and navigation treaties contained limited bilateral commitments on services, and some efforts were made to discipline trade in services through the OECD.[4] The United States also pursued service sector liberalization in its free trade agreements, achieving important breakthroughs with the services provisions of the U.S.–Canada FTA and subsequently the NAFTA. But global discipline was lacking until the conclusion of the General Agreement on Trade in Services (GATS) as part of the Uruguay Round. The GATS for the first time brings world trade in services within a legal framework broadly analogous to that

---

1. See Report to the Congress on the Extension of Fast Track Procedures, March 1, 1991, at 51.

2. Office of the U.S. Trade Representative, The North American Free Trade Agreement Source Book, August 14, 1992.

3. WTO, 2001 Annual Report, Table II.4.

4. Discussion of pre-Uruguay Round agreements respecting services may be found in Geza Feketekuty, Trade in Professional Services: An Overview, in 1 U.Chi.Leg.Forum 1 (1986); John H. Jackson, International Competition in Services: A Constitutional Framework (1988); and Phedon Nicolaides, Economic Aspects of Services: Implications for a GATT Agreement, 23 J. World Trade 125 (1989).

---

governing trade in goods, and is surely among the most notable achievements of the Uruguay Round.

Why did it take so long for trade in services to be incorporated into the WTO/GATT system? One possible response is that barriers to trade in services rarely resemble the usual border measures that affect trade in goods (tariffs and quotas). Instead, domestic regulatory policies, investment restrictions and migration restrictions tend to be the principal trade impediments. As a result, agreements respecting trade in services tend to be more complex and perhaps more intrusive on entrenched domestic policies. The following materials provide some background on the distinction between goods and services and the special issues that international agreements respecting trade in services must address. We proceed in Section 19.2 to look at some services issues under NAFTA, and in Section 19.3 to consider the GATS. Section 19.4 is a discussion problem.

GEZA FEKETEKUTY, TRADE IN PROFESSIONAL SERVICES: AN OVERVIEW[5]

THE DESIRABILITY OF LIBERALIZING TRADE IN SERVICES

When goods are traded, economic principles of comparative advantage apply. Similarly, specialization and international trade in services can lead to the same economic gains as trade in goods. When imported services can be acquired more cheaply or are of higher quality than services produced at home, both economies benefit.

It is argued that gains from specialization on the basis of comparative advantage are not relevant in the service sector because services are essential to the functioning of a country and therefore must be under local control. Yet it is difficult to see a fundamental distinction between autos and insurance in this respect. Both are essential to the functioning of a country. Moreover, governments have regulatory means for assuring that broader social objectives are achieved. The argument for free service trade is not an argument for the non-observance of local regulations designed to protect the public against abuses by either local or foreign service providers. Just as an auto sold in a foreign market must meet that country's safety or environmental regulations, so must an insurance policy sold in a foreign market meet domestic regulations designed to protect the interests of policy holders.

It is also argued that service industries in many countries have not been able to develop the means to compete with foreign firms. It is suggested that if they were given enough time to invest in up-to-date equipment and management techniques, they could compete effectively. Trade in such services, therefore, should not be liberalized—at least not until local firms have become competitive.

5. 1 U.Chi.Leg.Forum 1, 3–4 (1986). Re-   printed by permission.

This is the same infant-industry argument that has been applied to trade in goods. As with goods, it is valid only up to a point. Some level of protection can give local industry more time to prepare itself for international competition; however, without some competition at the outset, and with no definite prospects for more competition in the future, local industry will not have sufficient incentive to become competitive. Moreover, by protecting its service industries, a country deprives itself of efficient, up-to-date, and moderately-priced service inputs for the production of its goods and other services. This deprivation will become increasingly detrimental to the country's ability to compete internationally as service inputs become more important to production processes.

JAGDISH BHAGWATI, ECONOMIC PERSPECTIVE ON TRADE IN PROFESSIONAL SERVICES[6]

I. THE DISTINCTION BETWEEN GOODS AND SERVICES

[T]he interest in service trade is very recent. One byproduct of this is that the relevant data are both unreliable and far too limited. The limitations on data now available are a function not only of logistical problems in data collection, but also of unresolved conceptual questions which impair our present ability to generate meaningful and adequate statistics on the matter at hand. It is still not clear, for example, how services are to be defined, or how they are different from goods.

A. *Non–Storability*

Perhaps the earliest useful attempt to define the distinction between services and goods was made by T. Hill only one decade ago. Hill focused on the non-storability of services, stressing that services must be consumed as they are produced and cannot be put into stock by producers. This key characteristic does not cover all items which we customarily report as services; "answering services," for example, do store messages nowadays. Such exceptions, however, do not detract from the usefulness of a definition of services that characterizes them as non-storable because they require simultaneous provision and use.

B. *User–Producer Interaction*

If services must be used as they are produced, there must be *interaction* between the user and the provider of the service. A producer of goods, by contrast, can generally store the finished product and transact with users at any subsequent time. This interaction, in turn, implies that we can contemplate two essential categories of services: those that necessarily require the physical proximity of the user and the

---

6. 1 U.Chi.Leg.Forum 45, 45–53 (1986). Reprinted with permission. More technical treatments of possible differences between trade in goods and trade in services include Wilfred Ethier & Henrik Horn, Services in International Trade, *in* International Trade and Trade Policy 223 (Elhanan Helpman & Assaf Razin eds., 1991); Alan Deardorff, Comparative Advantage and International Trade and Investment in Services, *in* Trade and Investment in Services: Canada/U.S. Perspectives (Robert Stern ed., 1985); and James Melvin, Trade in Producer Services: A Heckscher–Ohlin Approach, 97 J.Pol.Econ. 1180 (1989).

provider, and those that do not though such physical proximity may indeed be useful even in the second category. * * *

1. *Physical Proximity Essential.* The class of services where physical proximity between provider and user is essential is usefully thought of as consisting of three categories.

Category A: Immobile–User, Mobile–Provider. There is an important class of services which *requires* that the provider go to the user, where the reverse mobility is simply impossible. For example, when the Connecticut Turnpike was being built, an Indian or South Korean construction firm bidding for the contract could perhaps have provided the designs and skilled inputs from home base. But such a firm simply could not have supplied the labor services, except by moving Indian or South Korean labor to Connecticut where the turnpike was to be built. Services of this sort are aptly referred to as "temporary-factor-relation-requiring" services.

Category B: Mobile–User, Immobile–Provider. There is another important class of services where the user really must move to the provider rather than the provider to the user. This location-specificity of the provider arises from the fact that the service provider is a vector of characteristics, some key elements of which are simply not transferable geographically to the user's location. Complex neurosurgery for example, simply cannot be done in Gabon because, even though the Massachusetts General Hospital can fly their surgeons over there, there is no way the necessary support services and hospital care can be duplicated or even approximated.

Category C: Mobile–User, Mobile–Provider. Finally, there is a range of services where mobility is symmetrically possible. For example, haircuts and lectures are in principle transmittable between user and provider in the location of either, the only difference being the cost of providing the service in one location rather than the other.

2. *Physical Proximity Inessential: The "Long–Distance" Services.* In the second broad class of services, physical proximity between providers and users may be useful, but it is not, strictly speaking, necessary. These are basically "long-distance" services, in the sense that the transactions do not require the immediacy of geographical proximity. Traditional banking and insurance services would fall into this category, because loans and insurance policies can be secured by mail or phone. The type of legal services here discussed, however, presumable require continual contact with the client. Because an attorney serving a corporation may have to interact face-to-face with many of the corporation's employees, legal services could be provided long-distance only in an extremely inefficient and hence expensive fashion. This applies equally to a large class of other professional services such as accounting or management consulting.

II.   The Implications of This Taxonomy for Service Trade Negotiations

The above taxonomy of the service sector has significant implications for the optimal structure of international negotiations in service trade. I will focus here on the special considerations relevant to trade in temporary-factor-relocation-requiring services, which require the provider to move to the user.

First, because it requires factor relocation, trade in such services simultaneously implies *either* direct foreign investment *or* labor migration *or* both. Permitting trade in services, therefore, is tantamount to permitting such factor flows. It is thus inappropriate to think of such service trade in the customary category of trade as distinguished from the category of factor flows: the two are inextricably tied together. For this reason, it is preferable to think of service *transactions* rather than of service *trade*.

Second, the opening up of such service transactions between nations creates immediate difficulties stemming from the differences between what has traditionally been considered acceptable with regard to factor flows as against trade, differences which often reflect political sensitivities as well as economic considerations. Thus, Frank Rossi, in his excellent contribution regarding the restraints on the operations of international accounting organizations, cites as one obstacle possible restrictions on the repatriation of earnings encountered in several developing countries. Yet these are precisely the kind of restraints that apply to all direct foreign investment in these countries. Moreover, domestic enterprises in the same service sectors are subjected to the vary same restrictions arising from exchange control.

Yet analyzed as a trade issue, rather than as a transactional issue, such restraints look totally unreasonable: the trade access is not meaningful unless profits can be repatriated. * * *

The third implication of this two-sided nature of service transactions is that attention must be paid to factor-mobility restrictions. Because they are in essence factor flows, service transactions can be readily impeded simply by preventing the requisite factor flows, rather than by establishing trade tariffs or prohibitions. * * *

Restraints on factor mobility can arise simply from visa restrictions, or, as with legal services, from the restrictions imposed by regulatory bodies such as the Bar or the Bench on the foreign nationals desiring to provide such services. In the case of the United States, complications also arise from the difficulty of getting all states to adopt uniform policies, thus making the question of reciprocity as a way of opening access even more intractable than it is otherwise.

Fourth, it is important to understand why I keep emphasizing the *temporary* aspect of "factor-relocation-requiring" services. * * * ["M]igratory" (or permanent) as distinct from "transient" (or temporary) labor flows raise a different, and more difficult, set of issues which, if brought into the discussion, would compromise the possibility of making significant progress on the issue. Two critical reasons underlie this judgment.

[The first is the effects of the "brain drain" on the nations from which emigration occurs. The migrants gain from leaving, but those left behind suffer as the services provided by the migrants become more scarce and the price rises.]

* * *

The second reason for distinguishing temporary from permanent immigration is that permanent immigration is generally judged by moral-philosophical principles very different from the utilitarian calculus that underlies the economic case for free trade and free investment flows. The "right to exclude" is simply not consistent, in general, with the efficient allocation of world resources, because it prevents some labor inputs from being put to their highest valued use. Instead, a country's exclusion of immigrants is often defended on the basis of "communitarian" ideas such as those developed by philosophers such as Michael Walzer. Such communitarian arguments flatly reject efficiency as the standard against which government policy is to be judged; they are based instead on other moral judgments.

An added reason for concern is that the professional groups that fear substantial loss of earnings are exceptionally well organized, and can often adduce attractive arguments to support their protectionist goals. The American Medical Association, for example, can invoke the possibility of deleterious impact on public health to reject an open-ended services compact permitting free and permanent immigration. It is important therefore that the *temporary* nature of factor relocation, designed to permit service transactions to transpire, be made explicit in negotiations on service trade regulation. If it is not, the possibility of negotiating anything worthwhile will be lost.

U.S. NATIONAL STUDY ON TRADE IN SERVICES, A SUBMISSION BY THE UNITED STATES GOVERNMENT TO THE GENERAL AGREEMENT ON TARIFFS AND TRADE 37–39 (1982)

CONCEPTUAL ISSUES RELATED TO TRADE IN SERVICES

In examining issues surrounding services and trade in services, a number of generic issues common to many service sectors call for specific attention. Discussion of these issues may help conceptualize general principles, rules and procedures as they relate to trade in services.

Three questions regarding generic issues are considered in this section. First, how should competition between private service firms and public service monopolies be managed? This problem arises much more in services than in goods because many countries provide services through public monopolies in order to regulate service industries. Second, to what extent can trade in services and investment in services be distinguished and how important is it to be able to make that distinction clear? The answer to this question is significant as service firms may find it necessary to establish operations (i.e. invest) in the countries to which they export. In order to properly manage issues that affect service exports, countries must determine whether they should be dealt with as investment or trade problems. Third, to what extent is it necessary for countries to allow the movement of labor in order to make it possible for service companies to export? Because services are closely linked to people and the knowledge and experience they possess and because countries are sensitive to the movement of people across their borders, appropriate, balanced treatment of conflicting goals concerning immigration, employment, and trade in services is desirable.

A. Competition Between Private Firms and Government Monopolies

Many important service industries are highly regulated by national governments because the services they supply are perceived as vital to national sovereignty, well-being, and security. Indeed, many countries provide such critical services through government-owned or controlled monopolies. * * *

There are three main issues concerning competition between public and private service firms. The first concerns competition between public service monopolies and private service firms outside the national borders of the country involved. Problems arise, in particular, in transborder services between one country and another. The monopoly position at home inevitably gives public service monopolies an unequal advantage vis-à-vis private competitors from other countries in transborder services such as aviation and telecommunications. The monopolies can use their dominant position in their home market to disadvantage their foreign private competitors. Also, the allocation of rates or fees for international services are frequently established through negotiations between domestic and foreign carriers. Where this results in a negotiation between a monopoly on one side and competing foreign firms on the other side, questions can arise concerning the equity of the outcome.

Another type of issue concerns the supply of services by a public service monopoly to foreign firms. In some cases, domestic monopolies have charged foreign firms higher fees for services rendered, or have provided foreign firms a lower quality service than that provided domestic firms. These types of issues become particularly acute when the domestic monopoly also happens to be a competitor. For example, a national airline which owns the ground servicing monopoly can put competing foreign airlines at a distinct disadvantage through a variety of discriminatory practices.

A third type of issue concerns competition between public service monopolies and private foreign firms in service activities outside the scope of the domestic monopoly. There has been a growing tendency to allow public service monopolies to compete with other firms in providing services not covered by the monopoly. In such competition, the public service monopolies can use their inherent power to disadvantage foreign private competition.

In each of these areas, the issue is whether monopolies should be required to adopt an arms-length relationship between its monopoly activities and its activities as a competitor internationally, as a competitor domestically in other services, and as a supplier of services.

B. Distinguishing Trade in Services From Investment in Services

Governments have traditionally separated trade issues from investment issues, developing separate disciplines in each area. Trade rules, covering "the right to sell" abroad, have tended to be more comprehensive than investment rules. If countries are to embark on the formulation of rules for trade in services, they must know whether this can be done in a meaningful way without dealing with the more sensitive issue of investment in services.

In order to separate trade and investment issues, countries must be capable of distinguishing between the services, or the component of services, which is traded (i.e., produced abroad) and the services, or the component of a service which can only be produced locally. Thus, for example, data processing services provided by a foreign computer center through long-distance communication links is clearly trade. Data processing services provided locally by a foreign-owned computer processing facility is an investment activity.

An important issue with respect to the distinction between trade and investment concerns the distribution system. Under traditional trade concepts the question of access to the distribution system or to service/maintenance facilities is a trade issue, while ownership of the distribution system is an investment issue. Under the principles of the GATT, a product which has overcome the legitimate barriers at the border is entitled to full national treatment, i.e., there is an obligation to treat a foreign producer in the same manner as a domestic producer. Thus, a foreign producer is entitled to the same access to the domestic distribution system as a domestic producer. For example, a foreign manufacturer of autos, who has paid the tariff at the border, is entitled to have the same access to the domestic distribution system as a domestic manufacturer.

The existing GATT approach to the distribution system could be applied to trade in services. Thus, access to a local distribution system would be treated as a trade issue, while ownership of the distribution system would be treated as an investment issue. Access to the distribution system would include the right of a foreign supplier of services to negotiate a contract with local businesses to provide distribution or servicing facilities. Thus, for example, if the national treatment principle were adopted for trade in services, a foreign insurance company that was able to overcome the agreed restrictions at the border, would have a right to sign a contract with local insurance brokers or claims adjusters to sell their policies and to handle claims.

A somewhat different issue arises with respect to some service industries, such as insurance, over the matter of establishment. In a number of countries, domestic regulatory authorities require insurance companies to fully establish themselves legally before they are given a right to sell insurance to local residents. Establishment, in this case, is a requirement imposed in order to protect domestic policyholders; it is no different from any other regulatory requirement imposed by governments for the protection of local citizens, such as health, safety or environmental regulations. Under current trade rules covering trade in goods, the national treatment principle ensures that foreign producers of goods receive the same treatment under domestic regulations as domestic producers. If the national treatment principle were adopted for trade in services, a domestic regulation requiring legal establishment for insurance companies should be treated in the same way as any other domestic regulation. In other words, foreign insurance companies granted access to the local market under trade rules, would have a right to establish themselves legally under the national treatment principle.

A still different issue arises in the context of professional services, in particular professional services that require a local presence. The sale of professional services which are to be provided locally is not a trade issue as such, while the sale of professional services produced outside the importing country is clearly a trade issue. Thus, the purchase of engineering services produced outside the importing country by a foreign engineering firm would clearly be a trade issue. The establishment of a local engineering practice by a foreign engineer would not be a trade issue. Locally delivered professional services, however, could have a trade component as well as a non-trade component and trade rules would apply to the traded component. A fully accredited local engineer could, for example, establish a contractual relationship with a foreign engineering firm whereby that engineering firm would agree to provide certain engineering drawings or technical information. The drawings or information provided by the foreign engineering firm would clearly be trade. Or if the issue is put the other way, foreign suppliers of services given access to the local market under trade rules would have the right to contract with fully accredited local professionals to deliver the service. In other words, local professionals, as local businessmen, could have the right under trade rules to buy expertise, support services from a foreign firm. Issues concerning a foreign-owned professional practice or the admission of foreign professionals to a domestic practice would not be covered by international trade rules.

While it is important for trade negotiating purposes to make a distinction between trade issues and investment issues, this does not imply that investment barriers are irrelevant to trade. Indeed, in many cases, the ability to invest in elements of the distribution system or in local enterprises can substantially enhance a firm's ability to export its services. In order to exploit these trade opportunities, parallel efforts need to be pursued in other fora to reduce foreign investment barriers. The OECD Code of Liberalization of Capital Movements, one such parallel effort, has expanded investment opportunities among developed countries. Furthermore, the Code is about to be amended to include those aspects of the right of establishment most closely related to direct investment. Another effort has been the negotiation of Bilateral Investment Treaties, particularly with developing countries. These treaties cover many areas of services; though here too, efforts will need to be undertaken to improve coverage.

C. Immigration, Labor and Trade in Services

The ability of a company to conduct service business internationally depends, in many instances, on the ability of salesmen or professionals with specific skills to move across national borders. This is the case for trade in services, as it has been the case for trade in goods.

International trade depends on some movement of people. Those engaged in international sales and financing of goods frequently travel abroad to market their products, to locate sources of supply and to arrange transactions. Trade in services may depend even more heavily on the movement of people than trade in merchandise. Service professionals may have special expertise that is not available locally. For example, services industries have complained that foreign personnel that are needed to set up data processing systems, to audit financial records, to train or supervise workers and to transmit or use other special knowledge, skills, expertise or talent required for commercial activities are frequently unavailable.

These industries have expressed concern about personnel-type and professional-practice problems that exist in banking, insurance, law, engineering and construction, hotels/motels, telecommunications, data processing, accounting, advertising, franchising and health care. Among the complaints listed are work permit requirements for professional and technical personnel; minimum percentages of local nationals to be employed; hiring restrictions or quotas; citizenship or licensing requirements for foreign engineers, lawyers and other professionals.

* * *

Immigration laws that restrict the availability of many types of workers exist in many countries including the United States. * * *

The United States feels that it is unlikely that a general approach to visa or professional practice problems would be either feasible or desirable over the foreseeable future. Few, if any, countries are likely to be willing to open their borders to face international movement of people in a general way. Thus, while governments are willing to accommodate individual salesmen or professionals and while mechanisms have been developed through bilateral agreements to establish appropriate ground rules, no government has been willing to undertake generalized obligations vis-a-vis the world as a whole. This reluctance is due to a variety of political, social and cultural concerns which dominate national policy-making in this area, and which inevitably override trade concerns.

The United States does not believe that it would be useful or appropriate to negotiate immigration problems in a trade forum such as GATT nor does it believe that immigration rules should be subordinated to trade rules. Efforts to deal with disputes over the legitimacy of the rules governing the movement of labor should be dealt with under existing consular mechanisms.

Notes and Questions

(1) If an American law firm opens a branch office in Brussels, staffed in part by American citizens, is there any "trade in services," or is it an "investment" in services? What about the services provided by a Japanese manager of a Honda plant in Kentucky—are they a "Japanese export?" The Hondas produced in that plant, of course, would not be considered an export of Japan but rather part of U.S. domestic production. In the remainder of this chapter, you should be sensitive to the fuzzy distinctions between trade in services and investment in services, to the treatment for international trade accounting purposes of earnings abroad by temporary migrants, and to the legal significance of such matters in the GATS and elsewhere.

(2) Are there domestic policies at stake in services sectors that are not at stake in goods sectors? Fiduciary, solvency and prudential concerns? Professional competence concerns? How does the WTO/GATT system handle their closest analogs in goods sectors? Among other things, the Agreements on Technical Barriers and Sanitary and Phytosanitary Measures appear quite relevant.

SECTION 19.2   SERVICES UNDER NAFTA

HARRY G. BROADMAN, INTERNATIONAL TRADE AND INVESTMENT IN SERVICES: A COMPARATIVE ANALYSIS OF THE NAFTA[1]

VII.   THE SERVICES PROVISIONS OF THE NAFTA

The NAFTA's principal services provisions are contained in three core services chapters (those on cross-border trade in services, telecommunications, and financial services), two associated chapters (those on investment and temporary entry for businesspersons), and several annexes (those on land transportation, professional services, and specific reservations and exceptions to the agreement).

A.   Core Rules

The NAFTA bases its services provisions on a set of well-defined rules. First, the NAFTA extends to the services providers throughout North America the basic obligation of national treatment. Thus, each NAFTA country must treat services suppliers of the other NAFTA countries no less favorably than it treats its own services providers in like circumstances. As a corollary to the national treatment provision, within a NAFTA country, a state or province must provide services suppliers from the other NAFTA countries treatment no less favorable than the most favorable treatment that the state or province accords to

---

1. 27 Intl. Lawyer 623, 637–644 (1993)   printed with permission. copyright © American Bar Association. Re-the services suppliers of the country of which the state or province forms a part.

The NAFTA also obligates the three countries to extend MFN treatment to North American services providers. Accordingly, each NAFTA country must accord services suppliers of either of the other two countries treatment no less favorable than it accords, in like circumstances, to services providers of any country.

Additionally, under the agreement each of the NAFTA countries must accord the better of national or MFN treatment to the other NAFTA countries. This rule ensures that North American services providers will obtain the maximum liberalization of trade and investment in services offered by any of the NAFTA countries.

Another basic rule of the NAFTA's services provisions concerns the various modes for supplying services. Notwithstanding specific exceptions (described below), generally the agreement guarantees that North American services providers cannot be compelled to establish or maintain an office or other local presence, or to be a resident, in a NAFTA country as a condition for selling services in the local market. Thus, in general, the cross-border mode for supplying services is explicitly covered. Indeed, the agreement specifies that its coverage of cross-border trade in services includes the production, distribution, marketing, sale and delivery of a service (including access to and use of NAFTA countries' service) as well as the purchase, use of, or payment for a service.

Furthermore, as set out in the agreement's investment chapter, NAFTA countries must provide to services suppliers the better of national or MFN treatment for both right-of-establishment and post-establishment operations. The NAFTA thus generally covers the commercial presence mode for services supply. The agreement also covers the services supply modes of movement of consumers and temporary movement of businesspersons.

Taken together, the general prohibition on local presence as a condition for the cross-border provision of services and the agreement's general coverage of the three other modes of delivery of services means that the NAFTA will produce an open and nondiscriminatory environment for services trade and investment in the U.S., Canadian, and Mexican markets, thus creating freedom of choice for the provision of services throughout North America. In the past, Mexico has made the ability to provide various services explicitly contingent on establishment of a commercial presence in the local market.

By dint of the agreement's investment chapter, services providers establishing a commercial presence in NAFTA countries, including providers from non-NAFTA countries, will be accorded important rights and obligations, such as freedom for inward and outward transfers, prohibitions on performance requirements, internationally accepted disciplines on expropriation, and binding international arbitration for settlement of investor-state disputes.

B. Nonconforming Measures and Quantitative Restrictions

In accordance with specific terms of the agreement, each NAFTA country will be able to maintain, at various levels of government, certain existing laws and other measures pertaining to services trade and investment that do not conform with the NAFTA's enumerated rules an obligations. In particular, non-conforming existing federal measures are listed in a "reservation" annex appended to the agreement. Each NAFTA country will have up to two years after the date of entry into force of the agreement to decide which nonconforming existing state and provincial measures it wants to list in the annex. Nonconforming existing measures at the municipal or local government are not subject to the NAFTA's disciplines. Each NAFTA country may renew or amend its nonconforming measures, provided that the renewal or amendment does not make a measure more inconsistent with the agreement's rules and obligations. Importantly, once a NAFTA country liberalizes such measures they cannot thereafter be made more restrictive.

In order to provide for transparency, each NAFTA country must also publish any existing and prospective nondiscriminatory measures at the federal, state, or provincial levels that limit the number of services providers or the operations of services providers in a particular sector. Any other NAFTA country may request consultations with a view to negotiate the liberalization of such quantitative restrictions.

C. Professional Licensing and Certification

Under the agreement's provisions related to professional licensing and certification requirements and procedures, the NAFTA countries must endeavor to ensure that such requirements and procedures are based on objective and transparent criteria, are no more burdensome than is necessary to ensure the quality of the services rendered, and are not disguised restrictions on the provision of the service in question.

The agreement provides for a mechanism for the mutual recognition of licenses and certifications. While it does not require automatic recognition by one country of the credentials of services providers of another NAFTA country, the agreement does require a NAFTA country to afford the other countries the opportunity to demonstrate that their licenses and certifications should be recognized. In addition, the NAFTA countries will undertake a work program with the intention to liberalize the licensing of foreign legal consultants and the temporary licensing of civil engineer. Within two years of the implementation of the NAFTA, each country must remove any citizenship or permanent residency requirement it maintains for the licensing and certification of professional services providers from any other NAFTA country. Any failure to comply with this obligation entitles the other NAFTA countries to maintain or reinstate equivalent requirements in the same services sector.

D. Sectoral Coverage and Exceptions

The "negative list" approach governs the NAFTA's sectoral coverage for trade and investment in services. As noted earlier, if a services sector is not explicitly excluded or otherwise made subject to reservations under this approach, the sector is automatically subject to the NAFTA's rules. While general civil aviation services is the only sector explicitly carved out of the agreement, each country has take specific exceptions for various other sectors either in whole or part (apart from the reservations pertaining to citizenship of residency requirements in the professional services mentioned above).

The principal exceptions are: (1) all three countries have taken general reservations for government-provided social services, such as law enforcement and social security services; (2) all three countries have taken general reservations for the provision of basic telecommunications services; (3) Canada has taken a reservation for all "cultural industries," which applies for the entire NAFTA agreement, not just its services provisions; (4) Mexico has taken reservations for specific sectors currently reserved by the Mexican Constitution to the Mexican state or Mexican nationals (among others, various energy sectors, acquisition of land or water rights within specific proximity to the border, and participation in cooperative production enterprises); (5) the United states and Mexico have taken reservations for legal services (except foreign legal consultants) pending further work on liberalization under the work plan described earlier; and (6) all three countries have taken reservations in maritime shipping services, although in contrast to the CFTA [Canadian Free Trade Agreement], which excluded all maritime services (indeed, as note above, the CFTA services provisions excluded all transport industries), the NAFTA provides for liberalization of landside aspects of port activities.

E. Land Transportation

Although two transport services sectors, civil aviation and ocean shipping, are either effectively excepted or reserved from the NAFTA, the agreement, in a separate annex, provides for substantial liberalization in the land transport sectors of trucking, railroads, and buses. This accomplishment is significant inasmuch as over 85 percent of U.S. trade with Canada and Mexico moves by land transportation. With respect to land transport between the United States and Canada, the NAFTA locks in a bilateral 1982 national treatment agreement, ensuring that future Canadian laws, regulations, and policies do not discriminate against U.S. land transportation services providers.

Regarding land transportation between the United States and Mexico, the NAFTA provides for a gradual mutual elimination of barriers to cross-border and investment access. In particular, under the terms of the agreement, by the end of 1995 trucking of international cargo on a cross-border basis in contiguous border states of both counties and 49 percent ownership in the Mexican trucking market will be permitted. Such liberalization continues thereafter on a phased schedule that concludes with cross-border international trucking permitted throughout both countries by the end of 1999 and full ownership of international cargo companies permitted in Mexico by 2003. For buses, the NAFTA permits full cross-border carriage upon entry into force for charter and tour companies, and by the end of 1996 for scheduled route companies; however, majority ownership rights in bus companies on either side of the border will not be permitted until 2000, and full ownership will not be permitted until 2003. With respect to railroads, the agreement ensures continuation of liberalization undertaken by Mexico, permitting, among other things, U.S. railroads to market their services directly to customers, use their own locomotives, and construct and own terminals.

NAFTA also provides a framework for development of more compatible technical and safety trucking standards over a six-year period. Such standards include vehicle weights, dimensions, maintenance and repair; truck drivers' medical standards, nonmedical testing and licensing; and transportation of hazardous materials. In addition the land transportation annex provides for a review process, beginning five years after the agreement goes into effect, to consider the effectiveness of liberalization in the land transportation sector. No later than seven years after the agreement goes into effect, consultations will also address possible further liberalization.

F. Telecommunications

Because of the technical and highly regulated nature of telecommunications services, the NAFTA contains a separate chapter on access to and use of public telecommunications networks and provision of enhanced, or value-added, telecommunications services. This chapter is based on the telecommunications annex embodied in the GATS. In general the agreement: (1) obligates the three countries, upon date of entry into force, to guarantee reasonable and nondiscriminatory access to international and domestic public telecommunications networks for use in providing and operating value-added and intracorporate telecommunications services throughout North America on a cross-border basis; (2) removes existing restrictions in Mexico on U.S. and Canadian foreign investment in all value-added telecommunications services by July 1995; (3) obligates the countries to ensure that pricing of public telecommunications network services is based on economic costs; and (4) disciplines the disguised use of technical product standards as barriers to cross-border trade in telecommunications services.

G. Financial Services

The chapter on financial services establishes a comprehensive principles-based approach to disciplining measures that regulate the provision of such services in the banking, securities, insurance, and nonbanking financial service company sectors. The chapter also sets out certain country-specific liberalization commitments, including transition periods and reservations.

The chapter establishes four broad principles. First, with respect to mode of supply, financial services providers of a NAFTA country may establish a commercial presence in the other countries, and unless a country has listed a reservation, new restrictions on the cross-border sales of financial services may not be imposed; however, each country must permit its residents to purchase financial services in the territory of another NAFTA country. The NAFTA permits purchases of financial services by consumers who visit another NAFTA country. However, NAFTA countries are not required to permit financial services providers of another NAFTA country to do business or to solicit business within their territories.

Second, each country will provide both national and MFN treatment to other NAFTA financial services providers operating in its territory. Third, the NAFTA obligates each country to make transparent the procedures employed in processing applications for entry into its financial services market. Fourth, each country retains the right to take reasonable prudential measures including, under limited circumstances, the taking of such measures for balance-of payments crises.

With respect to the principal country-specific commitments, Mexico will provide access on an establishment and acquisition basis to its financial services market over a transition period. The transition period ends in 2000, and market share limits are applicable during the period. In the banking sector, at the end of the transition period, the NAFTA will not restrict the U.S. and Canadian banking presence in the Mexican market, except that the very largest Mexican banks cannot be acquired, and the form of establishment in Mexico is restricted to subsidiaries rather than branches. The agreement's rules regarding access to the Mexican securities sector are virtually the same as those in the banking sector.

In the Mexican insurance market, U.S. and Canadian providers are accorded new access through two methods over a transition period. Firms that enter through joint ventures with Mexican insurers may phase in a 100 percent equity participation over a transition period that ends in 2000, but are not subject to market share limits that terminate in 2000. U.S. and Canadian firms currently possessing ownership interests in Mexican insurers may increase their equity participation to 100 percent by 1996.

Finally, the financial services commitments of Canada and the United States to each other under the CFTA will be incorporated into the NAFTA; Canada will generally extend such commitments made to the United States to Mexico as well.

H. Dispute Settlement

The general dispute settlement mechanism in the NAFTA parallels and strengthens that of the CFTA. Analogous to the earlier accord, the NAFTA establishes a trilateral Trade Commission. The agreement incorporates provisions that, among other things, establish specific time limits for panel decision making and ensure implementation of a panel decision. Separate dispute settlement procedures also apply specifically to financial services.

* * *

Despite the breadth of NAFTA's services commitments, formal disputes relating to the services provisions have been few in number. The most visible thus far has involved the access of Mexican trucking firms to the United States market. The United States has been slow to allow access under NAFTA, alleging that safety concerns justify its hesitation. Mexico has taken the position that the safety concerns are largely baseless and that U.S. resistance is driven by protectionist interests. The matter finally proceeded to a NAFTA panel.

IN THE MATTER OF CROSS–BORDER TRUCKING SERVICES

USA–MEX–98–2008–01.
2001 FTAPD LEXIS 2 (2001).

1. The Panel in this proceeding must decide whether the United States is in breach of Articles 1202 (national treatment for cross-border services) and/or 1203 (most-favored-nation treatment for cross-border services) of NAFTA by failing to lift its moratorium on the processing of applications by Mexican-owned trucking firms for authority to operate in the U.S. border states. Similarly, the Panel must decide whether the United States breached Articles 1102 (national treatment) and/or 1103 (most-favored-nation treatment) by refusing to permit Mexican investment in companies in the United States that provide transportation of international cargo. Given the expiration on December 17, 1995 of the Annex I reservation that the United States took to allowing cross-border trucking services and investment, the maintenance of the moratorium must be justified either under the language of Articles 1202 or 1203, or by some other provision of NAFTA, such as those found in Chapter Nine (standards) or by Article 2101 (general exceptions).

* * *

66. NAFTA came into force on January 1, 1994. Under Annex I of NAFTA, the Parties are obliged to phase-out certain reservations to Articles 1102 or 1202 (national treatment) and Articles 1103 or 1203 (most-favored-nation treatment).[2]

67. With respect to cross-border trucking service, Annex I provides that a Mexican national will be permitted to obtain operating authority to provide cross-boundary trucking services in border states three years after the signing of NAFTA, i.e., December 18, 1995, and cross-border trucking services throughout the United States six years after the date of entry into force of NAFTA, i.e., January 1, 2000.

68. With respect to investment, the phase-out deadline for the reservation was three years after the signing of NAFTA, i.e., December

---

2. [original note 58] Annex I set out each Parties' reservations with respect to existing measures from the obligations imposed by Articles 1102 and 1202 and 1103 and 1203. It also set out commitments for immediate or future liberalization. The Annex I commitments oblige each party to liberalize specific sectors by dates set in the "phase-out" section of each reservation.

18, 1995, for the establishment of enterprises providing trucking services for the transport of international cargo between points within the United States; and seven years after the date of entry into force of NAFTA, i.e., January 1, 2001, for the establishment of enterprises providing bus services between points in the United States.

* * *

77. * * * [O]n December 18, 1995, [U.S. Transportation] Secretary Pena issued a press release which stated that although Mexico and the United States were working to improve Mexican truck safety, because it was not yet a completed process, the United States would accept and process applications from Mexican trucking firms, but the applications would not be finalized. Therefore, no Mexican trucks have been allowed to pass out of the pre-existing commercial zones until the United States concludes consultations with the Mexican government. Through this refusal to finalize Mexican applications, the United States essentially continued the moratorium on Mexican trucks that had been in place prior to December 18, 1995.

78. The United States explained its actions were based on the alleged lack of safety in Mexican trucks, and referred to two alleged incidents involving Mexican trucks, one in November 1995 and the other in Fall 1995, where spillages of hazardous material had occurred. In the latter alleged incident, the driver of the Mexican truck was 16 years old, carried no insurance or shipping papers and the truck involved had faulty brakes and a number of bald tires. Mexico contends that these alleged incidents are not relevant to this dispute, because Mexico could have presented information on several incidents in which U.S. truck operators caused accidents while acting in breach of U.S. law.

79. As well, in early December 1995, the GAO, the "investigative arm" of the U.S. Congress, made available to the USDOT its report on Mexican cross-border trucking. The report was officially released on February 29, 1996. The report stated that there were significant differences between United States and Mexican truck safety regulations. It reported that a Mexican truck inspection and enforcement program had been established, but was lacking the facilities and personnel to initiate it. They also reported that a large percentage of Mexican trucks operating in the commercial zones of the four U.S. border states failed to meet U.S. truck safety standards.[3]

83. The [December 18, 1995] press release [by Secretary Pena] also announced that beginning December 18, 1995, Mexican citizens would be allowed to invest in U.S. carriers engaged in international commerce.

84. Despite its assertions that Mexican citizens would be allowed to invest in U.S. carriers as of December 1995, to date the USDOT

---

3. [original note 70] Although it is undisputed that the GAO report did provide this information on the Mexican regulatory system, Mexico contends that it is not relevant to the issue to be decided. Mexico contends that its domestic regulations do not have to be harmonized with the United States domestic regulations in order to permit individual Mexican carriers to cross into the U.S. border states.

maintains a complete ban on Mexican nationals owning or controlling U.S. cargo and passenger motor carrier service providers. This ban is enforced by the application form for new operating authority, which requires that the applicant certify that the applicant is not a Mexican national, and the carriers are not owned or controlled by Mexican nationals. To gain approval of an application to acquire an existing motor carrier, the USDOT also requires that the applicant indicate whether the party acquiring rights is either domiciled in Mexico or the carrier is owned or controlled by persons of that country. These restrictions essentially ban any Mexican investment in U.S. carriers, because the applications would not be approved if they indicated Mexican ownership.

* * *

87.   As of July 20, 1999, the U.S. Department of Transportation had received 184 applications from Mexican persons to provide cross-border cargo service into the border states.

88.   The fact that differences exist in the two domestic regulatory systems is not in dispute. In their submissions, both Mexico and the United States described in detail the U.S. trucking regulatory system, and the United States compared its system to the Mexican regulatory system to illustrate the differences. Both Mexico and the United States agree that the Mexican regulatory system is not identical to that of the United States. The disagreement is therefore whether the differences in the domestic regulatory systems justify the ban of the United States of Mexican trucks entering the territory.

* * *

214.   [T]he Panel declines to examine the motivation for the U.S. decision to continue the moratorium on cross-border trucking services and investment; it confines its analysis to the consistency or inconsistency of that action with NAFTA. The Panel notes that this approach is fully consistent with the practice of the WTO Appellate Body, which in Japan—Taxes on Alcoholic Beverages, at 28, and in Chile—Taxes on Alcoholic Beverages, para. 62, has declined to inquire into the subjective motivations of government decision-makers, or examine their intent. As the Appellate Body observed in analogous circumstances, in Chile–Alcoholic Beverages, "The subjective intentions inhabiting the minds of individual legislators or regulators do not bear upon the inquiry, if only because they are not accessible to treaty interpreters."

* * *

218.   Article 102(2) provides a mandatory standard for the interpretation of the detailed provisions of NAFTA: "The Parties shall interpret and apply the provisions of this Agreement in the light of its objectives set out in paragraph 1 and in accordance with applicable rules of international law."

219. The objectives develop the principal purpose of NAFTA, as proclaimed in its Preamble, wherein the Parties undertake, inter alia, to "create an expanded and secure market for the goods and services produced in their territories." Given these clearly stated objectives and the language of the Preamble, the Panel must recognize this trade liberalization background. * * * The Panel also notes, however, that the Preamble of NAFTA reflects a recognition that the Parties intended to "preserve their flexibility to safeguard the public welfare."

220. In identifying the rules of interpretation of international law referred to in Article 102(2), the Panel need go no further than the 1969 Vienna Convention on the Law of Treaties. Both Parties agree that the Vienna Convention is appropriate for this purpose, as NAFTA Parties have agreed in the past. The guiding rule of the Vienna Convention is Article 31(1), which provides in pertinent part, "A treaty shall be interpreted in good faith in accordance with the ordinary meaning to be given to the terms of the treaty in their context and in the light of its object and purpose."

221. * * * [I]n addition to the ordinary meaning of the terms, interpretation must take into account the context, object and purpose of the treaty. The context for the purpose of the interpretation of a treaty shall comprise, in addition to the text, including its preamble and annexes, any agreement relating to the treaty. If necessary, there shall be taken into account, together with the context, any subsequent practice and any relevant rules of international law applicable in the relations between the parties.

* * *

223. Article 31, like other provisions of the Convention, must be applied in conjunction with Article 26, which provides that "Every treaty in force is binding upon the parties to it and must be performed by them in good faith," i.e., Pacta sunt servanda. The Panel must interpret the treaty provisions in dispute with the understanding that the Parties accept the binding nature of NAFTA and that its obligations shall be performed in good faith.

224. Finally, in light of the fact that both Parties have made references to their national legislation on land transportation, the Panel deems it appropriate to refer to Article 27 of the Vienna Convention, which states that "A party may not invoke the provisions of its internal law as justification for its failure to perform a treaty." This provision directs the Panel not to examine national laws but the applicable international law. Thus, neither the internal law of the United States nor the Mexican law should be utilized for the interpretation of NAFTA. To do so would be to apply an inappropriate legal framework.

* * *

228. The Panel begins its inquiry by looking at the interpretative Note ("the Note") that precedes the Parties' Schedules at pages I–1, I–2 and I–3 of Annex I. The drafters provided the interpretative Note of

Annex I to assist in the reading and understanding of the Reservations contained in Annex I. Specifically, the Note provides rules and otherwise acts as guidance for the Panel in interpreting the Annex I Schedules of Canada, Mexico and the United States, including the reservations and phase-out provisions applicable to cross-border trucking services and investment.

* * *

230.   Significantly, the Note indicates that in interpreting liberalization commitments regarding Phase–Out elements in Annex I, the elements of the reservation must be considered in the light of the relevant provisions of the Chapters against which the reservation is taken, and that the Phase–Out element of a reservation shall prevail over all other elements of the reservation.

231.   Because of its importance to this case, the reservation at issue in the Schedule of the United States Sector: Transportation, Sub–Sector: Land Transportation, Phase–Out: Cross–Border Services, Investment, pages I–U–18 to I–U–20 is quoted * * *.

"Phase-out:

Cross–Border Services

A person of Mexico will be permitted to obtain operating authority to provide:

(a) three years after the date of signature of this Agreement, cross-border truck services to or from border states (California, Arizona, New Mexico and Texas), and such persons will be permitted to enter and depart the territory of United States through different ports of entry;

(b) three years after the date of entry into force of this Agreement, cross-border scheduled bus services; and

(c) six years after the date of entry into force of this Agreement, cross-border truck services.

Investment

A person of Mexico will be permitted to establish an enterprise in the United States to provide:

(a) three years after the date of signature of this Agreement, truck services for the transportation of international cargo between points in the United States; and

(b) seven years after the date of entry into force of this Agreement, bus services between points in the United States."

* * *

235.   In light of the Note, the text of the Phase–Out elements in Annex I concerning both the liberalization of cross-border truck services and the investment in truck services is unambiguous, based on the ordinary meaning of the words. The relevant clauses establish specific

dates in Annex I for the Party to liberalize barriers to services (December 18, 1995) and investment (December 18, 1995) in land transportation cross-border trade services. The Phase–Out clauses and their context in the Annex I do not suggest that the commitment to phase-out reservations on December 18, 1995 is dependent upon any other element of the Reservation or the Note. The Panel is unaware of any agreement related to NAFTA, or any subsequent practice or legal principle, that could accommodate the perception that there is a conditional element for the execution of the liberalization commitments. Thus, it follows that the liberalization commitments were unconditional within Annex I. Any other interpretation would be contrary to what is written in NAFTA.

* * *

240.   Under these circumstances, the phase-out obligations of the United States under Annex I with regard to cross-border trucking services and investment prevail unless there is some other provision of NAFTA that could supersede these obligations. It is to those other provisions that the Panel now turns.

Services

* * *

246.   Article 1202 provides in pertinent part: "1. Each Party shall accord to service providers of another Party treatment no less favorable than it accords, in like circumstances, to its own service providers." Similarly, Article 1203 states: "Each Party shall accord to service providers of another Party treatment no less favorable than it accords, in like circumstances, to service providers of any other Party or of a non-Party."

247.   Articles 1202 and 1203 represent the obligations of national treatment (equality of treatment between foreigners and nationals) and most-favored-nation treatment (equality of treatment among foreign nationals of different states). The United States and Mexico do not question the legal force of these obligations. In its most succinct terms, the disagreement between the United States on the one hand, and Mexico and Canada on the other, is over whether the "in like circumstances" language (or some other limitation on or exception to national treatment and most-favored-nation treatment) permits the United States to deny access to all Mexican trucking firms on a blanket basis, regardless of the individual qualifications of particular members of the Mexican industry, unless and until Mexico's own domestic regulatory system meets U.S. approval. Alternatively, the issue can be stated as whether or not the United States is required to examine Mexican carriers seeking operating authority in the United States on an individual basis to determine whether each individual applicant meets (or fails to meet) the standards for carriers operating in the United States. This disagreement in turn rests on the interpretation and scope of the "in like circumstances" language, that is, whether the comparison may be applied to

"service providers" on a blanket country-by-country basis or instead must be applied to individual service provider applicants.

248. Article 1202 requires each Party to accord to service providers of another Party treatment that is no less favorable than it accords, in like circumstances, to its own service providers. Given that under U.S. law the United States treats operating authority applications received from U.S. (and Canadian)—owned and-domiciled carriers on an individual basis, the blanket refusal of the United States to review applications for operating authority from Mexican trucking service providers on an individual basis suggests inconsistency with the U.S. national treatment obligation (and from most-favored-nation treatment, given that Canadian carriers are also treated on an individual basis).

249. The Panel, in interpreting the phrase "in like circumstances" in Articles 1202 and 1203, has sought guidance in other agreements that use similar language. The Parties do not dispute that the use of the phrase "in like circumstances" was intended to have a meaning that was similar to the phrase "like services and service providers," as proposed by Canada and Mexico during NAFTA negotiations. Also, the United States contends, and Mexico does not dispute, that the phrase "in like circumstances" is not substantively different from the phrase "in like situations," as used in bilateral investment treaties. Most significantly, no Party asserts that the use of the phrase "in like circumstances" in NAFTA Chapter Twelve was intended to have a different meaning than it did in the United States–Canada Free Trade Agreement (FTA). Mexico notes that the "immediate source" of the "in like circumstances" language in Articles 1202 and 1203 of NAFTA was the FTA. The United States has referred to elaborating language in the FTA on the national treatment obligation to support the interpretation of the phrase used in NAFTA to permit differential treatment where appropriate to meet legitimate regulatory objectives. Again, the Parties do not differ on the general principle that differential treatment may be appropriate and consistent with a Party's national treatment obligations.

250. FTA Article 1402 is thus instructive. It provides a more detailed elaboration of the national treatment requirement for services than is found in NAFTA:

"1. Subject to paragraph 3, each Party shall accord to persons of the other Party treatment no less favourable [sic] than that accorded in like circumstances to its persons with respect to the measures covered by this Chapter [services, investment and temporary entry].

. . .

3. Notwithstanding paragraphs 1 and 2, the treatment a Party accords to persons of the other Party may be different from the treatment the Party accords its persons provided that:

a) the difference in treatment is no greater than that necessary for prudential, fiduciary, health and safety, or consumer protection reasons;

b) such different treatment is equivalent in effect to the treatment accorded by the Party to its persons for such reasons; and

c) prior notification of the proposed treatment has been given in accordance with Article 1803.''

The provision in the FTA also imposed the burden of establishing the consistency of the differential treatment with the above requirements on the party proposing or according different treatment.

* * *

254. It is not disputed that the United States prohibits consideration of applications from most Mexican service providers to supply truck transportation services from Mexico to points in the United States outside the border commercial zone. Yet, the obligation of NAFTA Article 1202 is to provide no less favorable treatment to service providers of Mexico. It appears from uncontested facts that the United States is not doing so. The United States has permitted roughly 150 Mexican-domiciled carriers who claim U.S. majority ownership, five Mexican-domiciled, Mexican owned carriers grand-fathered under U.S. law, and one Mexican-domiciled, Mexican owned carrier transiting the United States to reach Canada, to operate freely in the United States despite alleged deficiencies in the Mexican truck regulatory system. Similarly, until 1999, four years after restrictions on cross-border trucking were to be lifted under Annex I, the United States permitted U.S. motor carriers to lease Mexican trucks and drivers for operations in the United States.
* * *

255. However, in all other circumstances comprising Mexican trucking service providers-presumably hundreds or even thousands of firms-those Mexican service providers have been denied access to the U.S. border states since December 17, 1995, despite the requirements of Annex I and Articles 1202 and 1203.

* * *

257. Therefore, absent other justification, the moratorium imposed by the United States on the processing of applications since December 17, 1995, would constitute a de jure violation of the national treatment obligation in Article 1202. However, the United States asserts justification under the terms "like circumstances," and the proposed interpretation to include differential treatment for legitimate regulatory objectives related to safety.

258. The Panel has noted that the phrase "like circumstances" may properly include differential treatment under the conditions specified in the FTA Article 1402, as discussed earlier. However, the Panel is also aware of Chapter One, Article 102. Article 102(2) of NAFTA clearly states that "The Parties shall interpret and apply the provisions of this Agreement in the light of its objectives set out in paragraph 1 and in accordance with applicable rules of international law." The first of NAFTA's listed objectives is to "eliminate barriers to trade in, and

facilitate the cross-border movement of, goods and services between the territories of the Parties." These objectives are elaborated more specifically through the principles and rules in NAFTA, including national treatment. Further, the provisions of the Agreement are required to be interpreted in light of the objectives and applicable rules of international law. Given these requirements, and the use of the same term in the FTA, the Panel is of the view that the proper interpretation of Article 1202 requires that differential treatment should be no greater than necessary for legitimate regulatory reasons such as safety, and that such different treatment be equivalent to the treatment accorded to domestic service providers. With regard to objectives, it seems unlikely to the Panel that the "in like circumstances" language in Articles 1202 and 1203 could be expected to permit maintenance of a very significant barrier to NAFTA trade, namely a prohibition on cross-border trucking services.

259.   Similarly, the Panel is mindful that a broad interpretation of the "in like circumstances" language could render Articles 1202 and 1203 meaningless. If, for example, the regulatory systems in two NAFTA countries must be substantially identical before national treatment is granted, relatively few service industry providers could ultimately qualify. Accordingly, the Panel concludes that the U.S. position that the "in like circumstances" language permits continuation of the moratorium on accepting applications for operating authority in the United States from Mexican owned and domiciled carriers is an overly-broad reading of that clause.

260.   The United States also suggests that Article 2101 allows the United States to refuse to accept applications from Mexican trucking service providers because of safety concerns. The Panel's view that the "in like circumstances" language, as an exception, should be interpreted narrowly, applies equally to Article 2101. Here, the GATT/WTO history, liberally cited by the Parties, and the FTA language, noted earlier, are both instructive. Although there is no explicit language in Chapter Twelve that sets out limitations on the scope of the "in like circumstances" language, the general exception in Article 2101:2 invoked by the United States closely tracks the GATT Article XX language, and is similar to the FTA proviso limiting exceptions to national treatment to situations where "the difference in treatment is no greater than necessary for ... health and safety or consumer protection reasons."

261.   Thus, Article 2101:2 provides in pertinent part:

"Provided that such measures are not applied in a manner that would constitute a means of arbitrary or unjustifiable discrimination between countries where the same conditions prevail or a disguised restriction on [international] trade between the Parties, nothing in ... Chapter Twelve (Cross–Border Trade in Services) ... shall be construed to prevent the adoption of enforcement by any Party of measures necessary to secure compliance with laws or regulations that are not inconsistent with the provisions of this Agreement, including those relating to health and safety and consumer protection."

262. Under Article 2101, therefore, safety measures adopted by a Party—such as the moratorium on accepting applications for U.S. operating authority from Mexican trucking service providers—may be justified only to the extent they are "necessary to secure compliance" with laws or regulations that are otherwise consistent with NAFTA. Here again, the GATT/WTO jurisprudence proves helpful in determining what "necessary" means.

263. The "necessary to secure compliance" language in GATT Article XX has been interpreted strictly in numerous GATT/WTO decisions, including United States—Section 337 of the Tariff Act of 1930, Canada—Certain Measures Concerning Periodicals, United States—Standards for Reformulated and Conventional Gasoline, and United States—Import Prohibition on Certain Shrimp and Shrimp Products. * * *

264. In Periodicals, Canada had contended that its import ban on certain periodicals was justified under the GATT Article XX(d) "chapeau" (heading) as a measure "necessary to secure compliance with laws or regulations which are not inconsistent with the provisions of this Agreement." Canada had argued that this restriction was an important aspect of a government policy that sought to ensure that magazines with editorial content prepared for the Canadian market would be rewarded with an increase in their revenues from advertising. A parallel component of the policy was a tax deduction for advertising directed at the Canadian market, which would be defeated if periodicals could be imported. The WTO Panel rejected this interpretation and found for the United States. The Panel determined that the Canadian measure was not a measure that sought compliance with another law, and thus was not justified by GATT Article XX(d).

265. In Reformulated Gasoline, the WTO's Appellate Body determined that the chapeau of Article XX, prohibiting GATT-inconsistent measures from being unjustifiable discrimination or a disguised restriction on trade, required that a Party adopt measures reasonably available to it that were the least inconsistent with the GATT. Instead of imposing less favorable regulatory structures on foreign refiners exporting gasoline to the United States, the United States might have pursued cooperative agreements with the governments of Venezuela and Brazil.

266. This suggests, by analogy, that the United States did not, in the actions it took prior to December 17, 1995, make a sufficient effort to find a less trade-restrictive measure than continuation of the moratorium to address its safety concerns.

267. In Shrimp, the WTO Appellate Body rejected the rigid standard through which U.S. officials determined whether certain other countries would be certified as having sea turtle protective fishing methods, effectively granting or refusing other countries' right to export shrimp to the United States. According to the Appellate Body, "it is not

acceptable in international relations, for one WTO Member to use an economic embargo to require other Members to adopt essentially the same comprehensive regulatory program, to achieve a certain policy goal, as in force within that Member's territory, without taking into consideration different conditions which may occur in the territories of those other Members." The Appellate Body also rejected the idea that one member could attempt to dictate another member's regulatory policies by refusing access to the dictating member's market, where that access was otherwise required under the GATT. In the instant case, Mexico objects to the U.S. moratorium and legal position as implying that only adoption by Mexico of a truck regulatory regime fully compatible with that of the United States would require the United States to lift the moratorium.

268.   Here also, there is no evidence in the record that the United States considered more acceptable, less trade restrictive, alternatives, except to the extent that it does so for specific Mexican service providers exempted from the moratorium.

269.   The Panel is generally in agreement with Mexico that, consistent with the GATT/WTO history and the text of Article 2101, in order for the U.S. moratorium on processing of Mexican applications for operating authority to be NAFTA-legal, any moratorium must secure compliance with some other law or regulation that does not discriminate; be necessary to secure compliance; and must not be arbitrary or unjustifiable discrimination or a disguised restriction on trade.

270.   Also, if under the GATT/WTO jurisprudence a Party is "bound to use, among the measures reasonably available to it, that which entails the least degree of inconsistency with other ... provisions," in this NAFTA case, the United States has failed to demonstrate that there are no alternative means of achieving U.S. safety goals that are more consistent with NAFTA requirements than the moratorium. In fact, the application and use of exceptions would appear to demonstrate the existence of less-restrictive alternatives.

* * *

276.   With regard to most-favored-nation treatment under Article 1203, essentially the same considerations are relevant as with national treatment under Article 1202, discussed in detail above. If the "in like circumstances" language means that the foreign regulatory system must be equivalent or identical to the U.S. system, and the United States has concluded that the Canadian system meets this criterion, the United States would be justified in discriminating in favor of Canadian trucking firms. However, if "in like circumstances" does not permit this treatment, Article 1203 is violated as well as Article 1202, since U.S. and Canadian carriers are treated in the same manner (individually) while Mexican carriers are treated differently. This is true with regard to any

possible departures from most-favored-nation treatment based on other provisions of NAFTA, such as Article 2101, again as discussed earlier.

* * *

278. Based on these considerations, and noting the previously discussed objectives of NAFTA in facilitating increased trade in services, the Panel is of the view that the U.S. refusal to consider applications is not consistent with the obligation to provide national treatment. Thus, the continuation of the moratorium beyond December 18, 1995, was a violation of the national treatment and most-favored-nation provisions of Articles 1202 and 1203, respectively, in that there is no legally sufficient basis for interpreting "in like circumstances" as permitting a blanket moratorium on all Mexican trucking firms. Nor is the departure from national treatment and most-favored-nation treatment under these Articles justified under Article 2101.

Investment

279. The issue before this Panel with regard to investment is to determine whether the failure by the U.S. government to take appropriate regulatory actions to eliminate the moratorium on Mexican investments in companies providing international transportation by land constitutes a breach of Articles 1102, 1103 and 1104 of NAFTA, which provide:

ARTICLE 1102: NATIONAL TREATMENT

1. Each Party shall accord to investors of another Party treatment no less favorable than that it accords, in like circumstances, to its own investors with respect to the establishment, acquisition, expansion, management, conduct, operation, and sale or other disposition of investments.

2. Each Party shall accord to investments of investors of another Party treatment no less favorable than that it accords, in like circumstances, to investments of its own investors with respect to the establishment, acquisition, expansion, management, conduct, operation, and sale or other disposition of investments. . . .

ARTICLE 1103: MOST-FAVORED-NATION TREATMENT

1. Each Party shall accord to investors of another Party treatment no less favorable than that it accords, in like circumstances, to investors of any other Party or of a non-Party with respect to the establishment, acquisition, expansion, management, conduct, operation, and sale or other disposition of investments.

2. Each Party shall accord to investments of investors of another Party treatment no less favorable than that it accords, in like circumstances, to investments of investors of any other Party or of a non-Party with respect to the establishment, acquisition, expansion, management, conduct, operation, and sale or other disposition of investments.

ARTICLE 1104: STANDARD OF TREATMENT

Each Party shall accord to investors of another Party and to investments of investors of another Party the better of the treatment required by Articles 1102 and 1103.

* * *

286.   Here, Mexico has asserted and the United States has conceded that U.S. laws and regulations authorize the Department of Transportation to deny a newly created U.S.-domiciled carrier with Mexican investment the opportunity to obtain operating authority. Current U.S. regulatory policy also prohibits the acquisition of an existing U.S. carrier that already had operating authority, because of the requirement for the applicant to certify that the applicant is not a Mexican national, nor owned or controlled by Mexican nationals. Under these circumstances, an application filed by a Mexican carrier would be futile.

287.   The United States has made no significant effort to defend its position on investment on the merits. At the Oral Hearing, the representative of the United States stated the U.S. position as follows:

"On safety, the base defense goes to the services. We have a separate statement and position on the investments. What we said on investment is Mexico brought this case, [therefore] it's up to Mexico to prove its point.

This is not a safety case with that. The situation, I think, is quite forthright and clear enough. The investment restriction arose from the moratorium, it's part of the moratorium that is still in place.

When the safety issues are resolved, we would modify the moratorium to handle the investment issues. In our view, the investments has been a side show . . .

Mexican firms generally don't have capital investment in the United States. They haven't been pressing the United States on that. The services case is the core of this, and when the services case is resolved, the investment case will be resolved. What we said, is [that] our brief simply says Mexico has to prove its violation."

In essence, the United States has effectively conceded that the safety concerns, which are the claimed basis of the U.S. refusal to implement its cross-border service obligations, are not applicable to investment.

288.   When a Panelist asked, "But what you're saying is, that until a Mexican company requests the opportunity, say, to buy a U.S. carrier and is denied that opportunity, . . . there's no case, even if you have a rule that says if they apply they are going to be turned down?," the representative of the United States responded, "That's almost it. It's a little more subtle than that."

289.   Long-established doctrine under the GATT and WTO holds that where a measure is inconsistent with a Party's obligations, it is unnecessary to demonstrate that the measure has had an impact on trade. For example, GATT Article III (requiring national treatment of

goods) is interpreted to protect expectations regarding competitive opportunities between imported and domestic products and is applicable
even if there have been no imports. Moreover, it is well-established that
parties may challenge measures mandating action inconsistent with the
GATT regardless of whether the measures have actually taken effect.

290.   Furthermore, Article 2004 of NAFTA allows the Parties to
initiate the dispute settlement procedures with "respect to the avoidance
or settlement of all disputes between the Parties regarding the interpretation or application of [the treaty], or wherever a Party considers that
an actual or proposed measure of another Party is or would be inconsistent with the obligations of [the treaty]." The Panel is not faced with a
case brought in the context of NAFTA Annex 2004, which authorizes a
Party to have recourse to the dispute settlement procedure where it
considers that benefits one Party could reasonably have expected to
accrue to it have been nullified or impaired by a measure that is not
inconsistent with NAFTA . . .

292.   Because the United States expressly prohibits the above mentioned investment, this Panel finds such prohibitions as inconsistent
with NAFTA, even if Mexico cannot identify a particular Mexican
national or nationals that have been rejected. A blanket refusal to permit
a person of Mexico to establish an enterprise in the United States to
provide truck services for the transportation of international cargo
between points in the United States is, on its face, less favorable than
the treatment accorded to U.S. truck service providers in like circumstances, and is contrary to Article 1102. Where there have been direct
violations of NAFTA, as in this case, there is no requirement for the
Panel to make a finding that benefits have been nullified or impaired; it
is sufficient to find that the U.S. measures are inconsistent with NAFTA.

* * *

295.   On the basis of the analysis set out above, the Panel unanimously determines that the U.S. blanket refusal to review and consider
for approval any Mexican-owned carrier applications for authority to
provide cross-border trucking services was and remains a breach of the
U.S. obligations under Annex I (reservations for existing measures and
liberalization commitments), Article 1202 (national treatment for cross-
border services), and Article 1203 (most-favored-nation treatment for
cross-border services) of NAFTA. An exception to these obligations is not
authorized by the "in like circumstances" language in Articles 1202 and
1203, or by the exceptions set out in Chapter Nine or under Article 2101.

296.   The Panel unanimously determines that the inadequacies of
the Mexican regulatory system provide an insufficient legal basis for the
United States to maintain a moratorium on the consideration of applications for U.S. operating authority from Mexican-owned and/or domiciled
trucking service providers.

297.   The Panel further unanimously determines that the United
States was and remains in breach of its obligations under Annex I

(reservations for existing measures and liberalization commitments), Article 1102 (national treatment), and Article 1103 (most-favored-nation treatment) to permit Mexican nationals to invest in enterprises in the United States that provide transportation of international cargo within the United States.

298. It is important to note what the Panel is not determining. It is not making a determination that the Parties to NAFTA may not set the level of protection that they consider appropriate in pursuit of legitimate regulatory objectives. It is not disagreeing that the safety of trucking services is a legitimate regulatory objective. Nor is the Panel imposing a limitation on the application of safety standards properly established and applied pursuant to the applicable obligations of the Parties under NAFTA. Furthermore, since the issue before the Panel concerns the so-called "blanket" ban, the Panel expresses neither approval nor disapproval of past determinations by appropriate regulatory authorities relating to the safety of any individual truck operators, drivers or vehicles, as to which the Panel did not receive any submissions or evidence.

299. The Panel recommends that the United States take appropriate steps to bring its practices with respect to cross-border trucking services and investment into compliance with its obligations under the applicable provisions of NAFTA.

300. The Panel notes that compliance by the United States with its NAFTA obligations would not necessarily require providing favorable consideration to all or to any specific number of applications from Mexican-owned trucking firms, when it is evident that a particular applicant or applicants may be unable to comply with U.S. trucking regulations when operating in the United States. Nor does it require that all Mexican-domiciled firms currently providing trucking services in the United States be allowed to continue to do so, if and when they fail to comply with U.S. safety regulations. The United States may not be required to treat applications from Mexican trucking firms in exactly the same manner as applications from U.S. or Canadian firms, as long as they are reviewed on a case by case basis. U.S. authorities are responsible for the safe operation of trucks within U.S. territory, whether ownership is U.S., Canadian or Mexican.

301. Similarly, it may not be unreasonable for a NAFTA Party to conclude that to ensure compliance with its own local standards by service providers from another NAFTA country, it may be necessary to implement different procedures with respect to such service providers. Thus, to the extent that the inspection and licensing requirements for Mexican trucks and drivers wishing to operate in the United States may not be "like" those in place in the United States, different methods of ensuring compliance with the U.S. regulatory regime may be justifiable. However, if in order to satisfy its own legitimate safety concerns the United States decides, exceptionally, to impose requirements on Mexican carriers that differ from those imposed on U.S. or Canadian carriers,

then any such decision must (a) be made in good faith with respect to a legitimate safety concern and (b) implement differing requirements that fully conform with all relevant NAFTA provisions.

302.   These considerations are inapplicable with regard to the U.S. refusal to permit Mexican nationals to invest in enterprises in the United States that provide transportation of international cargo within the United States, since both Mexico and the United States have agreed that such investment does not raise issues of safety.

Notes and Questions

(1) At this writing, the United States has yet to comply with the panel ruling, although proposals to respond to it are pending.

(2) The panel seems to suggest that case-by-case evaluation of the applications of Mexican truckers to provide cross-border trucking services is required. Is it possible in such a process to address U.S. safety concerns adequately? Can the United States plausibly take the position that its licensing process for operators does little to ensure that their trucks are properly maintained and that their drivers are properly trained? That such matters are the province primarily of domestic drivers' licensing and safety inspection authorities, which are inadequate in Mexico? Thus, unless every truck crossing North at the border is to be given a thorough safety inspection and every driver a driver's examination by U.S. authorities, a denial of approval to operate is "reasonably necessary?"

(3) Might the case have turned out differently without the "grandfathering" of certain Mexican firms and the disparate treatment of Mexican firms with a majority U.S. ownership? Is there any defense for such policies?

(4) Suppose that the United States had made a better factual showing, based on a sizable sample of inspections at the border, that Mexican trucks are much less likely to meet U.S. safety standards than U.S. or Canadian trucks, or that a significant percentage of Mexican operators are unable to pass the road test given in the United States for commercial driver's licenses. Could it then justify a continued moratorium?

(5) What sort of "case-by-case" analysis will pass muster? Could the United States take the position that since the safety of Mexican trucks is in greater doubt due to the deficiencies of its domestic regulatory system, operating licenses will be granted only to those operators who post a million dollar bond or otherwise establish that they have substantial assets in the United States to satisfy civil liability judgments against them in the event of an accident?

(6) Suppose the United States responded to the panel ruling by approving most applications for operating licenses from Mexico, but put in place a system of safety inspection at the border that put every Mexican truck through a lengthy inspection process (not applicable to U.S. trucks returning from Mexico), and that required every entering Mexican driver to take a driving test or prove that they had passed the test previously. The result was huge lines at the border, delaying transit by many hours and placing Mexican truckers at a competitive disadvantage. Would NAFTA afford Mexican operators any relief? Would additional facts be relevant?

SECTION 19.3   GENERAL AGREEMENT ON TRADE IN SERVICES (GATS)

BERNARD HOEKMAN, THE GENERAL AGREEMENT ON TRADE IN SERVICES[1]

II.   The Framework

The GATS contains two sets of obligations: (1) a set of *general* concepts, principles and rules that create obligations that apply to *all* measures affecting trade in services; and (2) *specific* negotiated obligations that constitute commitments that apply to those service sectors and subsectors that are listed in a member country's schedule. The architecture of the GATS therefore differs significantly from that of the GATT. The Agreement also contains a set of attachments that include annexes that take into account sectoral specificities and various institutional decisions and understandings. Services are defined to include any service in any sector except those supplied in the exercise of governmental functions. The Agreement applies to four "modes of supply:" (1) cross-border supply of a service (that is, not requiring the physical movement of supplier or consumer); (2) provision of services implying movement of the consumer to the location of the supplier; (3) services sold in the territory of a Member by (legal) entities that have established a presence there but originate in the territory of another Member; and (4) provision of services requiring the *temporary* movement of *natural* persons (service suppliers or persons employed by a service supplier who is a national of a country that is a party to the agreement).

Article II on unconditional MFN is a core general obligation of the Agreement: each service or service supplier from a Member must be treated no less favorably than any other foreign service or service supplier. MFN applies to all trade in services as defined in Article I. Because the level of market openness varies among countries, a binding requirement to apply unconditional MFN was resisted by service industry representatives in a number of industrialized countries. They argued that unconditional MFN would allow countries with restrictive policies to main their *status quo* and "free ride" in the markets of more open countries. Financial service industries from G–7 countries and U.S. telecommunications providers successfully lobbied for MFN exemptions as a way to force sectoral reciprocity. An Annex allowing for MFN exemptions was included in the GATS. It specifies that MFN exemptions should in principle be time-bound (lasting no longer than ten years) and are subject to periodic review and negotiation in subsequent trade liberalizing rounds. Although the Annex does allow pressure to be exerted on countries with more restrictive regimes, invocation of MFN

---

1.   Paper prepared for presentation at an OECD Workshop on The New World Trading System, Paris, April 25–26, 1994. Reprinted with permission. See also Harry G. Broadman, GATS: The Uruguay Round Accord on International Trade and Investment in Services, 17 The World Economy, May 1994, at 281.

exemptions clearly will reduce the value of the GATS as a whole, especially as "domino effects" are likely to occur.

In the final days of the Uruguay Round it became clear that a number of participants were ready to invoke the Annex on Article II exceptions for financial services, basic telecommunications, maritime transport, and/or audio-visual services. Rather than allow a situation to develop where countries would withdraw conditional offers in these areas and exempt them from the MFN obligation, a compromise solution was reached under which negotiations on a number of these sectors could continue without endangering the establishment of the GATS. A second Annex on financial services was included, providing for negotiations on financial services to be concluded within six months of the entry into force of the agreement establishing the WTO. If negotiations are not successful—i.e., the market access offers made by a certain countries are not satisfactory to other, demandeur, countries—Members are free to withdraw conditional offers in this area (invoke an MFN exemption). During the six month period those countries that have listed exemptions conditional upon the level of commitments taken by other Members will not apply them. A Ministerial Decision was also taken to allow negotiations on basic telecommunications to start in early 1994. These are to be concluded by end-April 1996. Until then, both the MFN requirement and the possibility of invoking an exemption will not enter into force for these services, except to the extent that a Member has made a specific commitment for the sector. Maritime and audio-visual services were taken off the agenda altogether, with the agreement to initiate negotiations on these sectors within three years of the entry into force of the agreement establishing the WTO. Much depends therefore on ongoing or imminent negotiations.

There are three articles in Part III of the GATS on Specific Commitments, entitled Market Access, National Treatment, and Additional Commitments (Articles XVI, XVII and XVIII respectively). *Market access* is not defined in the GATS. Instead, agreement was reached on a list of six measures that in principle are prohibited. These consist of limitation on: (i) the number of service suppliers allowed, (ii) the value of transactions or assets, (iii) the total quantity of service output, (iv) the number of natural persons that may be employed, (v) the type of legal entity through which a service supplier is permitted to supply a service (e.g., branches vs. subsidiaries for banking), and (vi) participation of foreign capital in terms of a maximum percentage limit of foreign shareholding or the absolute value of foreign investment. *National treatment* for foreign services and service suppliers is defined as treatment no less favorable than that accorded to like domestic services and service suppliers. Such treatment may or may not be identical to that applying to domestic firms, in recognition of the fact that in some instances identical treatment may actually worsen the conditions of competition for foreign-based firms (e.g., a requirement for insurance firms that reserves be held locally). Although the measures that are prohibited under the market access article are mostly non-discriminatory, they also include discriminatory policies. The latter will also violate national treatment [e.g., number (vi)]].

Table 1

Format for Country Schedules of Specific Commitments

Sector or sub-sector	Mode of supply	Conditions and limitations on market access	Conditions and qualifications on national treatment	Additional commitments
	Cross-border			
	Commercial presence			
	Movement of consumer			
	Movement of personnel			

Specific commitments are scheduled by modes of supply and apply *only* to listed service sectors and subsectors (i.e., a positive list approach was taken towards sectoral coverage), subject to sector-specific qualifications, conditions and limitations that may continue to be maintained, either across all modes of supply or for a specific mode (i.e., a negative list approach for policies that violate national treatment or market access). Any or all of the six types of measures that are prohibited in the market access article may continue to be applied to a sector that is listed by a country as long as these measures are scheduled. Table 1 illustrates the rather confusing format of country schedules of specific commitments used in the GATS. A consequence of the decisions to distinguish between general and specific obligations, to schedule specific commitments by mode of supply, and to allow for MFN exemptions is that very much depends on the content of the country schedules and the extent to which MFN exemptions are invoked. In comparison to the GATT, general rules and principles are much less important (binding). As discussed further below, this can be expected to have consequences for the operation of the agreement, in particular dispute settlement.

Why did this structure emerge? An admittedly greatly oversimplified synopsis of initial negotiating stances is helpful in understanding the structure of the GATS. Before and during the 1986 Ministerial meeting at Punta del Este establishing the agenda of the Uruguay round, many developing countries defended the view that GATT negotiations should not address services. While these countries did not manage to block the inclusion of services on the round's agenda, they did succeed in putting services on a separate track in an attempt to establish the principle that no cross-issue linkages be possible between traditional GATT issues and services. Moreover, at their insistence economic development and growth were agreed to be an objective of any agreement. Many developing countries argued that the lack of comprehensive statistical information was a justification for excluding service transactions involving establishment by foreign providers from the coverage of an agreement. Great emphasis was put on the need for governments to be able to address restrictive business practices, impose conditions of inward FDI, and support infant industries. A consequence of this was that a generally applicable national treatment obligation was considered to be unacceptable.

The EU's initial negotiating position was that trade should be defined so as to include all types of transactions necessary in a sector in order to achieve "effective" market access. A "regulations committee" was proposed that would determine the "appropriateness" of regulation, criteria to determine this to be negotiated. Inappropriate measures were to be subject to liberalization over time, the goal being to achieve "comparable" market access on a sector-by-sector basis for all participating countries. Any framework agreement was to involve only limited obligations of a generally binding nature. In particular, national treatment was to be only an *objective*. The implication of this was that any binding commitments were to apply on a sector-specific level. The United States' initial proposal was the most liberal: MFN was to apply to all signatories and national treatment was to be a binding, general obligation. While the existence of national monopolies was accepted, the U.S. proposed that services should by such entities be provided to foreign-based users on a non-discriminatory basis. Trade was to be defined broadly, including FDI (commercial presence). All measures limiting market access for foreign service providers were to be put on the table.

Thus, both the EU and major developing countries expressed an early preference for an agreement with "soft" obligations—the EU arguing that national treatment should only apply to specific sectors, major developing countries opposing even that. Only the U.S. and certain small open economies—both OECD members and newly industrialized countries like Singapore—were in favor of a "hard" agreement along GATT lines from the start, with generally binding obligations and universal sectoral coverage. At the end of the day the original EU/developing country preference for a "soft" framework agreement prevailed. In return for acceptance that trade in services be defined to include the four possible "modes of supply," and agreement that certain non-discriminatory measures restricting market access were in principle negotiable, national treatment became a specific commitment, and it was agreed that scheduling of specific commitments would be on a sector-by-sector and modes-of-supply basis. The positive list approach to determining the sectoral coverage of specific commitments emerged in large part because many developing countries apparently felt they did not have the administrative resources required to determine all the measures that currently applied to each sector and decide which they would want to exempt. As many of these countries did not have the intention of making very substantial commitments to liberalize access to their service markets in any event, they much preferred a positive list approach. This then put the administrative burden on those countries that did intend to schedule the majority of their market services (i.e., mostly OECD countries and the NICs).

III. COUNTRY SCHEDULES OF SPECIFIC COMMITMENTS

The structure of the GATS implies that negotiations in the services area were (and will be) sectoral, and can be expected to be driven very much by the concerns and interests of the major players in each industry. Thus, although restrictions on inward FDI and non-discriminatory barriers to market access were agreed to be legitimate objects of negotiation, this is on a sector-by-sector basis. Two issues related to the specific commitments can be identified as having possible implications for the functioning of the GATS: (1) the design of the country schedules (see Table 1); and (2) the content of the country schedules. Several problems can be identified with respect to the design of the scheduling of specific commitments under the GATS, all of which may prove detrimental to the functioning of the agreement, and could affect the prospects for future multilateral liberalization by increasing the incentive to pursue regional options (more on the latter below). First, the *hybrid approach to scheduling* (i.e. a positive list of commitments requiring the negative listing of non-conforming measures to be maintained) yields a mostly unsatisfactory outcome from a transparency point of view. The GATS generates no information on sectors, sub-sectors and activities in which no commitments are scheduled—most often the sensitive ones where restrictions and discriminatory practices abound. This is a serious shortcoming when one considers the nature and origin of impediments to trade in the services area (i.e. regulatory barriers at both the national and subnational levels). The top-down "list it or lose it" approach used in the NAFTA or Australia–New Zealand agreement on trade in services would have significantly enhanced transparency. Second, the *à la carte approach to liberalization* foreseen under the GATS' hybrid approach to scheduling allows countries to schedule commitments whilst maintaining significant degrees of regulatory discretion (i.e. as potential departures from otherwise bound non-discriminatory undertakings). Thus, commitments relating to commercial presence may be subject to the right to maintain or impose authorization and/or screening procedures, and the criteria or specific measures that underpin such procedures may not necessarily be clearly defined or specified in the schedule. Third, the *scheduling of commitments according to modes of supply* creates incentives to offer fewer commitments on the cross-border movement of services and service providers (i.e. labor). Somewhat ironically, given the early resistance to discussing investment-related matters in the GNS, the bulk of commitments lodged under the GATS, especially by developing countries, relate to the commercial presence mode of supply. The decision to schedule by modes of supply has meant that commitments on commercial presence may be disguised trade-related investment measures (TRIMs) for services. That is, by only scheduling commercial presence as a mode of supply, foreign service providers may be compelled to establish as a prerequisite for market access, even if cross-border trade is feasible.

Nothing in the GATS compels Members to schedule commitments by mode of supply. What is useful from a definitional point of view may not be a good idea from an operational point of view. This appears to have been the conclusion drawn in the NAFTA context, where the concept of modes of supply was only used to define trade in services. The fact that the GATS itself does not mandate any particular scheduling methodology suggests that a more rational approach could be followed in future negotiations. Given that a sectoral approach has been chosen, the needs of service providers could be factored into specific commitments in any given sector (e.g. access to capital information, telecoms networks (public and private), or accompanying labor mobility). Much will depend in this connection on the experience that is obtained with the GATS in the coming years, and on the "case law" that will be developed through the functioning of the dispute settlement process.

As noted earlier, market access is not defined in the GATS, there being instead a closed list of in principle prohibited measures. The measures that are prohibited will frequently reflect a country's regulatory regime. For example, governments may impose limitations in the content of "natural monopolies" or public utilities. What matters then is not the limitation *per se*, but how contestable markets are. If a government periodically auctions licenses, are the limitations on the number of firms (licenses) a market access barrier? As it is worded that market access article gives a foreign firm the opportunity to use Article XVI as the justification for a complaint to the WTO independent of the degree of contestability of a regulated market. This is because the article focuses on the *form* of measures, not on their *effect*. The scope for disputes (i.e., need for interpretation by panels) appears great in this connection. The same applies with respect to allegations that national treatment commitments have been violated. Many sectors will continue to be subject to scheduled measures that violate national treatment but that may be worded somewhat ambiguously, again complicating dispute settlement. More generally, in the services context it is not possible to point to a bound tariff level, and argue that a policy nullifies or impairs an earlier concession. In comparison to the GATT, therefore, dispute settlement in the GATS will rely less on fundamental principles/concepts. Instead, interpretation of country schedules can be expected to form the main part of the panel process. This in itself will increase the number of cases as it reduces the scope for one panel finding to have a general impact in terms of interpreting the rules. Finally, the history of GATT dispute settlement cases relating to disciplines what were less than clearcut (e.g., subsidies) suggests that there is the potential for some controversy ...

IV. Disciplines on Preferential (Regional) Liberalization

The GATS is similar to GATT in permitting signatories to pursue preferential liberalization arrangement, subject to a number of conditions that are intended to minimize potential adverse effect on non-members as well as on the multilateral trading system as a whole. Two issues are of particular interest in this connection: (1) the rules that were negotiated in the GATS with respect to regional agreements; and (2) the effect that the GATS is likely to have on the incentive to pursue regional options.

Analogous to Article XXIV of the GATT, Article V of the GATS imposes three conditions on economic integration agreements involving GATS Members. First, they must have "substantial sectoral coverage" (Art. V:1(a)). An interpretive note states that this should be understood in terms of the number of sectors, volume of trade affected, and that no mode of supply should be excluded on an *a priori* basis. Substantial sectoral coverage is not the same as "substantially *all* trade" (the language of the GATT), suggesting that the intention of the drafters of GATS was perhaps to be less restrictive than those drafting Article XXIV of the GATT. This conclusion can also be drawn with respect to the other two conditions. Thus, the second requirement is that integration agreements are to eliminate substantially all discrimination between or among the parties to the agreement in sectors subject to multilateral commitments. More precisely, what is required is the elimination of existing discriminatory measures *and/or* the prohibition of new or more discriminatory measures (Art. V:1(b)). A mere *standstill* agreement may therefore be sufficient. Third, such agreements are not to raise the *overall* level of barriers to trade in services originating in other GATS member *within the respective sectors or subsectors* compared to the level applicable prior to such an agreement. As no distinction is made between customs unions and free trade areas in Article V, countries participating in a free trade area may be permitted to raise some barriers against non-members, as long as the overall level of barriers of all the members of the agreement vis-a-vis non-members, for each of the relevant sectors or sub-sectors, does not increase. This is a significant difference with the GATT, which prohibits such "rebalancing" for members of a free trade area, unless compensation is offered to affected GATT contracting parties.

Articles V:2 and V:3(a) of the GATS respectively allow for consideration to be given to the relationship between a particular regional agreement and the wider process of economic integration among member countries, and give developing countries flexibility regarding the realization of the internal liberalization requirements (i.e., Art. V:1). Given that a standstill may already be sufficient, presumably this flexibility applies to sectoral coverage. It is also worth noting that Article V:3(a) does not speak of agreements *between* developing countries, but of agreements that have developing countries as parties. Thus, in principle, this "flexibility" extends to agreements that have both developed and developing country signatories.

The conditions imposed by Article V are relatively weak. The requirements regarding the extent of internal liberalization that must occur under Article V imply only a limited constraint on "strategic" violations of the MFN obligation and the specific commitments on market access and national treatment made under the GATS. The absence of any requirement in Article V that integration agreements be "open" in principle (i.e., contain an accession clause) is an important shortcoming. Article V appears to have been worded primarily with a view to ensuring that existing regional agreements would be consistent with the GATS. Weak multilateral disciplines, in conjunction with the rather convoluted structure of the GATS and the resulting lack of transparency and significant scope for governments to determine the conditions of competition for foreign service suppliers, suggests that the net effect of the GATS may well be to increase the marginal incentive for Members to pursue regional options.

V.   GATS AND DEVELOPING COUNTRIES

A final issue is the helpfulness of the GATS to countries seeking to enhance the economic efficiency of their service industries. Participation in a multilateral agreement imposing certain disciplines and constraints on national policy formation key may help a government in pursuing or implementing desired changes in domestic policies. Membership in the GATS may increase both the credibility of initial reform and help governments resist demands from politically influential interest groups for altering policies in the future. The GATS imposes costs on "backsliding," reflected in Article XXI on Modification of Schedules. This provision allows parties to withdraw concessions subject to negotiation with—and compensation of—affected parties. In the event bilateral negotiations result in inadequate offers of compensation for affected parties, the GATS foresees an arbitration. If the Member state withdrawing a concession does not comply with the suggestions of the arbitration panel retaliation may be authorized. The existence of Article XXI will help governments to oppose attempts by domestic industries and other interest groups desiring to restrict market access at some point after liberalization has occurred.

But, this is all conditional upon significant liberalization taking place. Will membership of the GATS help governments pursue liberalization efforts? The standard rationale for the pursuit of multilateral (reciprocal) liberalization efforts is that increased access to foreign markets is likely to be of interest to domestic export-oriented industries, and that these are then given an incentive to oppose lobbying by import-competing industries against the opening of domestic markets. This political dynamic is arguably less strong in the GATS context because developing countries tend to have less of an interest in service exports (or, more accurately, many of the services where they are likely to have or develop a comparative advantage require movement of labor, and this is a mode of supply that has mostly been kept off the table). The main need for most developing countries is to liberalize access to their service markets, thereby reaping efficiency gains as firms and consumers obtain access to lower priced, higher quality services. The issue is what the GATS does to help a government liberalize in the face of opposition by powerful domestic lobbies. The non-generality of national treatment is an important negative factor in this connection, as is the sector-specificity of market access commitments. A government cannot tell its lobbies that it must join the GATS, and that this means it must automatically abide by the national treatment principle for all sectors to ensure that national treatment and market access obligations will apply. This clearly makes matters much more difficult for governments that "need" an external justification for resisting protectionist pressures. Another weakness of the GATS in this regard is Article XIX which allows for "appropriate flexibility for individual developing countries for opening fewer sectors, liberalizing fewer types of transactions, progressively extending market access in line with their development situation and, when making access to their markets available to foreign service suppliers, attaching to it conditions aimed at achieving the objectives" of increasing the participation of developing countries in world trade. This is a guideline for the conduct of future trade liberalizing rounds rather than "obligations" to be undertaken. But it does give developing countries substantial scope to limit the sectoral coverage of their offers.

More generally, GATS imposes few limitations on national policy, leaving a Member pretty much free to do as it likes in the policy domain, subject to the constraint that no discrimination across alternative sources of supply occurs. It allows parties to implement policies that are detrimental to—or inconsistent with—economic efficiency. A good example is the article specifying the conditions under which measures to safeguard the balance-of-payments may be taken, such measures rarely being efficient. It can also be noted that the GATS does not require a participating country to alter the regulatory structure of certain service sectors, or to pursue an active antitrust or competition policy. Liberalization of trade and investment may need to be augmented by regulatory change (frequently deregulation) and an effective competition policy in order to increase the efficiency of service sectors such as finance, transportation, and telecommunications. If liberalization is simply equated with increased market access for (certain) foreign suppliers, this may have little effect in markets that are characterized by a lack of competition. The main result will then simply be to redistribute rents across firms.

Notes and Questions

(1) Look at the definition of trade in services in the GATS. Does it encompass the sale of insurance by a U.S. company to a foreign national by mail? Does it encompass the opening of an insurance sales office abroad by a U.S. firm? Does it encompass the purchase of an insurance policy by a foreign national during a visit to the United States? Does it encompass the receipt of a television signal off a satellite? Does it encompass the acquisition of a foreign insurer by a U.S. company? Pay particular attention to Article I(2) of the GATS.

(2) Focus on Article II(2) of GATS, allowing reservations from the most-favored-nation obligation. Are there principled justifications for such reservations? To pressure another country to open its market? Other reasons?

(3) Suppose that an American bank desires to open an office in Japan. Assume that Japan has promised national treatment for banking in its national schedule. The American firm applies for permission to operate, much as would a Japanese firm. The response to the application takes a long time. Finally, the application is denied on the grounds that the American firm does not meet the solvency criteria that Japanese firms must meet. Is there any argument that Japan has violated the GATS? Focus on Article VI.

(4) Are preferences among NAFTA members consistent with the GATS? What must the NAFTA members show here in the event of a challenge?

(5) The details of the GATS remain to be worked out in a number of areas, as quick perusal of the agreement will suggest. Among the uncertainties are the standards for applying measures to guard against import surges and "unfair" trade. To what extent should the rules governing safeguards, subsidies and dumping differ for service sectors? For some thoughts on such issues, see the discussion in John H. Jackson, International Competition in Services: A Constitutional Framework (1988).

(6) Note that the GATS is in many ways an agreement respecting investment in services as well as trade in services. See, for example, Article XVI(2)(f).

(7) Some of the service sector restrictions in play in GATS involve arguable anticompetitive practices by professional and trade associations, especially when they are enforced by government regulation. How well will GATS perform when the issue is, say, whether a licensing restriction is a legitimate consumer protection measure or a mere restriction on competitive entry?

(8) GATS negotiations are ongoing and new, sector-specific disciplines may be expected. An example of recent progress, in this instance with respect to trade in accounting services, is the following.

DISCIPLINES ON DOMESTIC REGULATION IN THE ACCOUNTANCY SECTOR

S/WPPS/W/21

Adopted by WTO Council on Trade in Services, December 14, 2000

I. OBJECTIVES

1. Having regard to the Ministerial Decision on Professional Services, Members have agreed to the following disciplines elaborating upon the provisions of the GATS relating to domestic regulation of the sector. The purpose of these disciplines is to facilitate trade in accountancy services by ensuring that domestic regulations affecting trade in accountancy services meet the requirements of Article VI:4 of the GATS. The disciplines therefore do not address measures subject to scheduling under Articles XVI and XVII of the GATS, which restrict access to the domestic market or limit the application of national treatment to foreign suppliers. Such measures are addressed in the GATS through the negotiation and scheduling of specific commitments.

II. GENERAL PROVISIONS

2. Members shall ensure that measures not subject to scheduling under Articles XVI or XVII of the GATS,1 relating to licensing require-

ments and procedures, technical standards and qualification requirements and procedures are not prepared, adopted or applied with a view to or with the effect of creating unnecessary barriers to trade in accountancy services. For this purpose, Members shall ensure that such measures are not more trade-restrictive than necessary to fulfil a legitimate objective. Legitimate objectives are, inter alia, the protection of consumers (which includes all users of accounting services and the public generally), the quality of the service, professional competence, and the integrity of the profession.

III. Transparency

3.   Members shall make publicly available, including through the enquiry and contact points established under Articles III and IV of the GATS, the names and addresses of competent authorities (i.e. governmental or non-governmental entities responsible for the licensing of professionals or firms, or accounting regulations).

4.   Members shall make publicly available, or shall ensure that their competent authorities make publicly available, including through the enquiry and contact points:

(a) where applicable, information describing the activities and professional titles which are regulated or which must comply with specific technical standards;

(b) requirements and procedures to obtain, renew or retain any licences or professional qualifications and the competent authorities' monitoring arrangements for ensuring compliance;

(c) information on technical standards; and

(d) upon request, confirmation that a particular professional or firm is licensed to practise within their jurisdiction.

5.   Members shall inform another Member, upon request, of the rationale behind domestic regulatory measures in the accountancy sector, in relation to legitimate objectives as referred to in paragraph 2.

6.   When introducing measures which significantly affect trade in accountancy services, Members shall endeavour to provide opportunity for comment, and give consideration to such comments, before adoption.

7.   Details of procedures for the review of administrative decisions, as provided for by Article VI:2 of the GATS, shall be made public, including the prescribed time-limits, if any, for requesting such a review.

IV. Licensing Requirements

8.   Licensing requirements (i.e. the substantive requirements, other than qualification requirements, to be satisfied in order to obtain or renew an authorization to practice) shall be pre-established, publicly available and objective.

9.   Where residency requirements not subject to scheduling under Article XVII of the GATS exist, Members shall consider whether less trade restrictive means could be employed to achieve the purposes for

which these requirements were set, taking into account costs and local conditions.

10. Where membership of a professional organisation is required, in order to fulfil a legitimate objective in accordance with paragraph 2, Members shall ensure that the terms for membership are reasonable, and do not include conditions or pre-conditions unrelated to the fulfilment of such an objective. Where membership of a professional organization is required as a prior condition for application for a licence (i.e. an authorization to practice), the period of membership imposed before the application may be submitted shall be kept to a minimum.

11. Members shall ensure that the use of firm names is not restricted, save in fulfilment of a legitimate objective.

12. Members shall ensure that requirements regarding professional indemnity insurance for foreign applicants take into account any existing insurance coverage, in so far as it covers activities in its territory or the relevant jurisdiction in its territory and is consistent with the legislation of the host Member.

13. Fees charged by the competent authorities shall reflect the administrative costs involved, and shall not represent an impediment in themselves to practising the relevant activity. This shall not preclude the recovery of any additional costs of verification of information, processing and examinations. A concessional fee for applicants from developing countries may be considered.

V. Licensing Procedures

14. Licensing procedures (i.e. the procedures to be followed for the submission and processing of an application for an authorization to practise) shall be pre-established, publicly available and objective, and shall not in themselves constitute a restriction on the supply of the service.

15. Application procedures and the related documentation shall be not more burdensome than necessary to ensure that applicants fulfil qualification and licensing requirements. For example, competent authorities shall not require more documents than are strictly necessary for the purpose of licensing, and shall not impose unreasonable requirements regarding the format of documentation. Where minor errors are made in the completion of applications, applicants shall be given the opportunity to correct them. The establishment of the authenticity of documents shall be sought through the least burdensome procedure and, wherever possible, authenticated copies should be accepted in place of original documents.

16. Members shall ensure that the receipt of an application is acknowledged promptly by the competent authority, and that applicants are informed without undue delay in cases where the application is incomplete. The competent authority shall inform the applicant of the decision concerning the completed application within a reasonable time

after receipt, in principle within six months, separate from any periods in respect of qualification procedures referred to below.

17.   On request, an unsuccessful applicant shall be informed of the reasons for rejection of the application. An applicant shall be permitted, within reasonable limits, to resubmit applications for licensing.

18.   A licence, once granted, shall enter into effect immediately, in accordance with the terms and conditions specified therein.

VI.   QUALIFICATION REQUIREMENTS

19.   A Member shall ensure that its competent authorities take account of qualifications acquired in the territory of another Member, on the basis of equivalency of education, experience and/or examination requirements.

20.   The scope of examinations and of any other qualification requirements shall be limited to subjects relevant to the activities for which authorization is sought. Qualification requirements may include education, examinations, practical training, experience and language skills.

21.   Members note the role which mutual recognition agreements can play in facilitating the process of verification of qualifications and/or in establishing equivalency of education.

VII.   QUALIFICATION PROCEDURES

22.   Verification of an applicant's qualifications acquired in the territory of another Member shall take place within a reasonable time-frame, in principle within six months and, where applicants' qualifications fall short of requirements, shall result in a decision which identifies additional qualifications, if any, to be acquired by the applicant.

23.   Examinations shall be scheduled at reasonably frequent intervals, in principle at least once a year, and shall be open for all eligible applicants, including foreign and foreign-qualified applicants. Applicants shall be allowed a reasonable period for the submission of applications. Fees charged by the competent authorities shall reflect the administrative costs involved, and shall not represent an impediment in themselves to practising the relevant activity. This shall not preclude the recovery of any additional costs of verification of information, processing and examinations. A concessional fee for applicants from developing countries may be considered.

24.   Residency requirements not subject to scheduling under Article XVII of the GATS shall not be required for sitting examinations.

VIII.   TECHNICAL STANDARDS

25.   Members shall ensure that measures relating to technical standards are prepared, adopted and applied only to fulfil legitimate objectives.

26.   In determining whether a measure is in conformity with the obligations under paragraph 2, account shall be taken of internationally

recognized standards of relevant international organizations applied by that Member.

Notes and Questions

(1) Of particular interest to law students is international trade in legal services. To what extent should the rules applicable to accountants also be applied in the legal area? For comparison, the EC treatment of legal services is examined in George A. Bermann, Roger J. Goebel, Eleanor M. Fox & William J. Davey, European Community Law ch. 18 (2d ed. 2002).

(2) Do the disciplines contained in the accountancy measure go far enough? Again, perhaps it is useful to think about their application in the legal context. Nations have a reasonable basis for insisting that licensed attorneys possess a working knowledge of domestic law. They can also claim an interest in protecting the consumers of legal services, some of whom may be unable to judge the quality of their representation very well, against incompetence. Yet, Bar Associations are also effective interest groups in the political process, and may be expected to pursue protectionist measures disguised as rules for the protection of consumers. For example, is there any reason to prohibit the formation of partnerships between domestic and foreign lawyers that could give advice on both domestic and foreign law? Is there any reason to restrict the way that revenues are shared in such an arrangement? Is it acceptable to prohibit foreign law firms from entering the domestic market on the grounds that some of their partners are non-lawyers (e.g., accountants), violating domestic rules against multidisciplinary practice? Is it reasonable to require that applicants for licenses to practice domestic law must have a J.D. degree from a domestic institution, even if they have foreign law degrees from excellent schools and have no difficulty passing the domestic bar exam? If the accountancy rules above applied to legal services, what would they have to say about these issues?

(3) Legal services were on the agenda during the Uruguay Round negotiations, with the key issues relating to the commitments in the national schedules. The United States, in particular, had hoped to obtain substantially greater access to the Japanese market. But in the end, the Japanese offered only a "joint enterprise scheme." According to the *American Lawyer*, "under that arrangement, Japanese lawyers can only share revenue and profits that foreign firms generate from their Tokyo offices, not from the firm as a whole. Further * * * [t]he foreign firm and the Japanese lawyer can not even use the same office space without following strict cost accounting rules." The joint enterprise can give only limited advice on Japanese law, the Japanese lawyer cannot be a partner in the foreign firm, and the joint enterprise cannot employ Japanese lawyers as associates, offering them a guaranteed salary. The history of the negotiations, and their outcome, is recounted in Karen Dillon, Unfair Trade, The American Lawyer, April, 1994, at 53–56. For a discussion of the barriers to trade in legal services and how GATS might best address them, see the concluding section of Alan O. Sykes, "Efficient Protection" Through WTO Rulemaking, *in* Efficiency, Equity and Legitimacy: The Multilateral Trading System at the Millennium (Pierre Sauvé et. al. eds.) (Brookings Institution: 2001).

CANADA—CERTAIN MEASURES AFFECTING THE AUTOMOTIVE INDUSTRY

WT/DS139 & 142/R

Appellate Body Report adopted by the DSB on June 19, 2000

[In the materials on subsidies and countervailing measures, we considered an excerpt from this case raising the question whether certain import duty exemptions on motor vehicles, accorded to particular automobile manufacturers in Canada that met the requisite "ratio requirements" and value-added requirements, constituted prohibited subsidies. In another part of the case, it was urged that such measures discriminated among providers of wholesale selling services in violation of Article II of GATS.]

147.   Canada appeals the Panel's conclusion that the import duty exemption is inconsistent with Article II:1 of the GATS. Canada first appeals the Panel's finding that the measure is one "affecting trade in services" within the scope of Article I:1 of the GATS.

* * *

155.   With GATS, arts. I:1–2 & XXVIII(a), (b), (c), (d), (f) and (g)] in mind, we believe that at least two key legal issues must be examined to determine whether a measure is one "affecting trade in services": first, whether there is "trade in services" in the sense of Article I:2; and, second, whether the measure in issue "affects" such trade in services within the meaning of Article I:1.

156.   We look first at whether there is "trade in services" in this case. For the purposes of the GATS, "trade in services" is defined in Article I:2 as the "supply of a service" in any one of four listed modes of supply. At issue here is the supply of a service under mode (c) of Article I:2, that is, the supply of a service "by a service supplier of one Member, through *commercial presence* in the territory of any other Member". (emphasis added) "Commercial presence" is, in turn, defined in Article XXVIII(d) as "any type of business or professional establishment, including through (i) the constitution, acquisition or maintenance of a juridical person...".

157.   The complainants in this case allege that the "trade in services" here relevant is "wholesale trade services of motor vehicles", which is a category of services recognized in the Central Product Classification.[2] Canada does not dispute that there are service suppliers of the United States, the European Communities and Japan which are established in Canada and which provide wholesale trade services of motor vehicles. Accordingly, we hold that the "trade in services" here in

---

2.   [original note 157] Provisional Central Product Classification, United Nations Statistical Papers, Series M, No. 77, 1991, Subclass 61111, p. 189. This was replaced in 1997 by the Central Product Classification (CPC) Version 1.0 (United Nations Statistical Papers, Series M, No. 77, 1998, Subclass 61281, p. 363), which continues to recognize wholesale trade services of motor vehicles as a category of services.

issue is wholesale trade services of motor vehicles supplied by service suppliers of certain Members through commercial presence in Canada.

158. Having concluded that there is, in fact, "trade in services" in this case, we consider next whether the measure at issue "affects" trade in services. In *European Communities–Bananas*, we said:

> In our view, the use of the term "affecting" reflects the intent of the drafters to give a broad reach to the GATS. The ordinary meaning of the word "affecting" implies a measure that has "an effect on", which indicates a broad scope of application. This interpretation is further reinforced by the conclusions of previous panels that the term "affecting" in the context of Article III of the GATT is wider in scope than such terms as "regulating" or "governing".

159. We also found in that case that, although the subject matter of the GATT 1994 and that of the GATS are different, particular measures "could be found to fall within the scope of both the GATT 1994 and the GATS", and that such measures include those "that involve a service relating to a particular good or a service supplied in conjunction with a particular good." We further stated, in that case, that:

> Whether a certain measure affecting the supply of a service related to a particular good is scrutinized under the GATT 1994 or the GATS, or both, is a matter that can only be determined on a case-by-case basis.

160. In cases where the same measure can be scrutinized under *both* the GATT 1994 and the GATS, however, the focus of the inquiry, and the specific aspects of the measure to be scrutinized, under each agreement, will be different because the subjects of the two agreements are different. Under the GATS, as we stated in *European Communities–Bananas*, "the focus is on how the measure affects the supply of the service or the service suppliers involved."

161. We note that Canada argues that the import duty exemption is not a measure "affecting trade in services" within the meaning of Article I of the GATS, because it is a tariff measure that affects the *goods* themselves and not the supply of distribution services. As such, Canada maintains, the measure at issue does not "affect" a service supplier in its *capacity as a service supplier* and in its *supply of a service*. Canada relies on our report in *European Communities–Bananas* to support its argument that the import duty exemption falls exclusively within the scope of the GATT 1994, as it affects trade in goods as goods, and does *not* involve a service *relating to a particular good* or a service *supplied in conjunction with a particular good*.

162. The Panel, however, determined that:

> Like the measures at issue in the *EC–Bananas III* case, the import duty exemption granted only to manufacturer beneficiaries bears upon conditions of competition in the supply of distribution services, regardless of whether it directly governs or indirectly affects the

supply of such services. In our view, therefore, the import duty exemption falls in the third category of measures, identified by the Appellate Body in *EC–Bananas III*, as involving "a service relating to a particular good or a service supplied in conjunction with a particular good", which "could be scrutinized under both the GATT 1994 and the GATS".

163. In *European Communities–Bananas*, we agreed with the panel that "the operators as defined under the relevant regulations of the European Communities are, indeed, suppliers of 'wholesale trade services' within the definition set out in the Headnote to Section 6 of the CPC." Although the operators in that case were engaged in certain activities that were not, strictly speaking, within the definition of "distributive trade services" in the Headnote to Section 6 of the Central Product Classification, we concluded there that "there is no question that they are also engaged in other activities involving the wholesale distribution of bananas that are within that definition." With respect to the fact that the operators were vertically integrated with producers, ripeners and retailers, we stated, in that case, that "even if a company is vertically-integrated, and even if it performs other functions related to the production, importation, distribution and processing of a product, *to the extent that it is also engaged in providing 'wholesale trade services'* and is therefore *affected in that capacity* by a particular measure of a Member *in its supply of those 'wholesale trade services'*, that company *is a service supplier* within the scope of the GATS." (emphasis added)

164. In this case, the Panel did not examine any evidence relating to the provision of wholesale trade services of motor vehicles within the Canadian market and, as a result, did not make any factual findings as to the structure of the market for motor vehicles in Canada, nor as to which companies actually provide wholesale trade services of motor vehicles. As a result, the Panel also never examined whether or how the import duty exemption affects *wholesale trade service suppliers in their capacity as service suppliers*. Rather, the Panel simply stated:

> Like the measures at issue in the *EC–Bananas III* case, the import duty exemption granted only to *manufacturer beneficiaries* bears upon conditions of competition in the supply of distribution services, regardless of whether it directly governs or indirectly affects the supply of such services. (emphasis added)

165. We do not consider this statement of the Panel to be a sufficient basis for a legal finding that the import duty exemption "affects" wholesale trade services of motor vehicles *as services*, or wholesale trade service suppliers *in their capacity as service suppliers*. The Panel failed to analyze the evidence on the record relating to the provision of wholesale trade services of motor vehicles in the Canadian market. It also failed to articulate what it understood Article I:1 to require by the use of the term "affecting". Having interpreted Article I:1, the Panel should then have examined all the relevant facts, including *who* supplies wholesale trade services of motor vehicles through commer-

cial presence in Canada, and *how* such services are supplied. It is not enough to make assumptions. Finally, the Panel should have applied its interpretation of "affecting trade in services" to the facts it should have found.

166.   The European Communities and Japan may well be correct in their assertions that the availability of the import duty exemption to certain manufacturer beneficiaries of the United States established in Canada, and the corresponding unavailability of this exemption to manufacturer beneficiaries of Europe and of Japan established in Canada, has an effect on the operations in Canada of wholesale trade service suppliers of motor vehicles and, therefore, "affects" those wholesale trade service suppliers in their capacity as service suppliers. However, the Panel did not examine this issue. The Panel merely asserted its conclusion, without explaining how or why it came to its conclusion. This is not good enough.

167.   For these reasons, we believe that the Panel has failed to examine whether the measure is one "affecting trade in services" as required under Article I:1 of the GATS. The Panel did not show that the measure at issue affects wholesale trade services of motor vehicles, as services, or wholesale trade service suppliers of motor vehicles, in their *capacity as service suppliers*. [The Appellate Body went on to hold that the Panel had also done an inadequate job of examining whether discrimination among service suppliers existed in violation of Article II:1 of GATS.]

EUROPEAN COMMUNITIES—REGIME FOR THE IMPORTATION, SALE AND DISTRIBUTION OF BANANAS

WT/DS27/AB/R

Appellate Body Report adopted by the DSB on September 25, 1997

[Eds. note: The following description of the factual background to the dispute is taken from the Report of the Panel:

4.600   The Complaining parties claimed that the EC's banana regime went beyond WTO-inconsistent treatment of imported Latin American bananas. The regime's import licensing provisions directly targeted North and South American firms that distributed bananas. These licensing provisions provided definite competitive advantages to EC-and ACP-owned firms that wholesaled bananas vis-à-vis their competitors based in Latin America and the United States. [eds. note: The acronym ACP refers to Asian, Carribean and Pacific Countries, parties to the Lomé Convention and beneficiaries of European banana preferences.] * * *

4.601   The Complaining parties claimed further that the Latin American and US firms that imported and sold bananas in the EC market were in the wholesaling business. Wholesale and retail trade services made up the larger category of distributive trade services. Distribution of goods was a huge service sector, on which millions of service jobs depended worldwide. In the GATS, the EC had undertaken specific commitments that covered both cross-border wholesaling activities and wholesaling activities based on a commercial presence within the EC. The combination of cross-border and commercial presence activities encompassed the entire process of wholesaling products from abroad into and through the EC. All of the main Latin American and US companies supplied wholesale trade services to the EC on a cross-border and commercial presence basis. Each such company provided wholesale services by acting as a middleman, purchasing bananas from other companies and reselling them to other wholesalers or retailers. This was in addition to the activities these companies performed in marketing their own bananas to and in the EC.

4.602   The United States argued that the EC banana regime employed discrete but compounding measures to reconfigure the Latin American banana service market in favour of EC and ACP suppliers, including through the use of: (i) operator category allocations, which granted the right to import 30 per cent of the Latin American banana tariff quota predominantly to EC and ACP firms; ... and (iv) activity function allocations, which took the Latin American banana import rights that remained after the removal of 30 per cent under (i), and granted over 40 per cent of those remaining rights to predominantly EC firms that had ripened (but had not necessarily ever imported) bananas, or that had a role in importing bananas that was limited only to the administrative, frequently "paper-only" task of customs clearance. * * *

4.608   According to the Complaining parties, the EC thus manipulated these two features of the banana regime (the operator categories and activity functions) to strip opportunities for Latin American banana distribution business away from the firms that had traditionally supplied nearly all Latin American bananas into the EC market and award these opportunities to their competitors, which were EC or ACP-owned companies. By drastically altering competitive conditions in this manner, these aspects of the regime violated the principles of MFN and national treatment of Articles II and XVII of GATS. * * *

4.609   The EC noted that the measures contested under the GATS remained the same as those contested under the GATT, i.e. the licensing system and, in particular, the allocation. In the opinion of the EC, these were measures directed at goods and except for some broad allegations on competitive conditions, the Complainants concerned did not substantiate that these measures related to trade in services. * * *]

[Eds. note: In a section of the opinion that was referenced in our excerpt from the *Canada Autos* case, the Appellate Body rejected the argument of the European Communities that importers of bananas were not involved with trade in services. As it did in *Autos*, it found that a company involved with trade in goods could also be engaged in the service of wholesale or retail selling, and upheld the Panel's finding that some of the "operators" affected by the European banana import licensing scheme were indeed providing such services. It further noted "that the European Communities has made a full commitment for wholesale trade services (CPC 622), with no conditions or qualifications, in its Schedule of Specific Commitments under the GATS. Although these operators, as defined in the relevant EC regulations, are engaged in some activities that are not strictly within the definition of "distributive trade services" in the Headnote to Section 6 of the CPC, there is no question that they are also engaged in other activities involving the wholesale distribution of bananas that are within that definition."]

229. The European Communities appeals the Panel's finding:

... that the obligation contained in Article II:1 of GATS to extend "treatment no less favourable" should be interpreted *in casu* to require providing no less favourable conditions of competition.

The critical issue here is whether Article II:1 of the GATS applies only to *de jure*, or formal, discrimination or whether it applies also to *de facto* discrimination.

230. The Panel's approach to this question was to interpret the words "treatment no less favourable" in Article II:1 of the GATS by reference to paragraphs 2 and 3 of Article XVII of the GATS. The Panel said:

... we note that the standard of "no less favourable treatment" in paragraph 1 of Article XVII is meant to provide for no less favourable conditions of competition regardless of whether that is achieved through the application of formally identical or formally different measures. Paragraphs 2 and 3 of Article XVII serve the purpose of codifying this interpretation, and in our view, do not impose new obligations on Members additional to those contained in paragraph 1. In essence, the "treatment no less favourable" standard of Article XVII:1 is clarified and reinforced in the language of paragraphs 2 and 3. The absence of similar language in Article II is not, in our view, a justification for giving a different ordinary meaning in terms of Article 31(1) of the Vienna Convention to the words "treatment no less favourable", which are identical in both Articles II:1 and XVII:1.

231. We find the Panel's reasoning on this issue to be less than fully satisfactory. The Panel interpreted Article II of the GATS in the light of panel reports interpreting the national treatment obligation of Article III of the GATT. The Panel also referred to Article XVII of the GATS, which is also a national treatment obligation. But Article II of the GATS relates to MFN treatment, not to national treatment. Therefore, provisions elsewhere in the GATS relating to national treatment obligations, and previous GATT practice relating to the interpretation of the national treatment obligation of Article III of the GATT 1994 are not necessarily relevant to the interpretation of Article II of the GATS. The Panel would have been on safer ground had it compared the MFN obligation in Article II of the GATS with the MFN and MFN-type obligations in the GATT 1994.

232. Articles I and II of the GATT 1994 have been applied, in past practice, to measures involving *de facto* discrimination. We refer, in particular, to the panel report in *European Economic Community— Imports of Beef from Canada*, which examined the consistency of EEC regulations implementing a levy-free tariff quota for high quality grain-fed beef with Article I of the GATT 1947. Those regulations made suspension of the import levy for such beef conditional on production of a certificate of authenticity. The only certifying agency authorized to produce a certificate of authenticity was a United States agency. The panel, therefore, found that the EEC regulations were inconsistent with the MFN principle in Article I of the GATT 1947 as they had the effect of denying access to the EEC market to exports of products of any origin other than that of the United States.

233. The GATS negotiators chose to use different language in Article II and Article XVII of the GATS in expressing the obligation to provide "treatment no less favourable". The question naturally arises: if the GATS negotiators intended that "treatment no less favourable" should have exactly the same meaning in Articles II and XVII of the GATS, why did they not repeat paragraphs 2 and 3 of Article XVII in Article II? But that is not the question here. The question here is the meaning of "treatment no less favourable" with respect to the MFN obligation in Article II of the GATS. There is more than one way of writing a *de facto* non-discrimination provision. Article XVII of the GATS is merely one of many provisions in the *WTO Agreement* that require the obligation of providing "treatment no less favourable". The possibility that the two Articles may not have exactly the same meaning does *not* imply that the intention of the drafters of the GATS was that a *de jure*, or formal, standard should apply in Article II of the GATS. If that were the intention, why does Article II not say as much? The obligation imposed by Article II is unqualified. The ordinary meaning of this provision does not exclude *de facto* discrimination. Moreover, if Article II was not applicable to *de facto* discrimination, it would not be difficult—and, indeed, it would be a good deal easier in the case of trade in services, than in the case of trade in goods—to devise discriminatory measures aimed at circumventing the basic purpose of that Article.

234. For these reasons, we conclude that "treatment no less favourable" in Article II:1 of the GATS should be interpreted to include *de facto*, as well as *de jure*, discrimination. We should make it clear that we do not limit our conclusion to this case. We have some difficulty in understanding why the Panel stated that its interpretation of Article II of the GATS applied *"in casu"*.

* * *

WHETHER THE EC LICENSING PROCEDURES ARE DISCRIMINATORY UNDER ARTICLES II AND XVII OF THE GATS

240. The European Communities argues that the EC licensing system for bananas is not discriminatory under Articles II and XVII of

the GATS, because the various aspects of the system, including the operator category rules [and] the activity function rules ... "pursue entirely legitimate policies" and "are not inherently discriminatory in design or effect".

241.   We see no specific authority either in Article II or in Article XVII of the GATS for the proposition that the "aims and effects" of a measure are in any way relevant in determining whether that measure is inconsistent with those provisions. In the GATT context, the "aims and effects" theory had its origins in the principle of Article III:1 that internal taxes or charges or other regulations "should not be applied to imported or domestic products so as to afford protection to domestic production". There is no comparable provision in the GATS. Furthermore, in our Report in *Japan—Alcoholic Beverages*, the Appellate Body rejected the "aims and effects" theory with respect to Article III:2 of the GATT 1994 ...

Operator Category Rules

242.   The European Communities argues that the aim of the operator category system, in view of the objective of integrating the various national markets, and of the differing situations of banana traders in the various Member States, was not discriminatory but rather was to establish machinery for dividing the tariff quota among the different categories of traders concerned. In the view of the European Communities, the operator category system also serves the purpose of distributing quota rents among the various operators in the market. The European Communities emphasizes, furthermore, that the principle of transferability of licences is used in order to develop market structures without disrupting existing commercial links. The effect of the operator category rules, the European Communities argues, is to leave a commercial choice in the hands of the operators.

243.   We do not agree with the European Communities that the aims and effects of the operator category system are relevant in determining whether or not that system modifies the conditions of competition between service suppliers of EC origin and service suppliers of third-country origin. Based on the evidence before it, the Panel concluded "that most of the suppliers of Complainants' origin are classified in Category A for the vast majority of their past marketing of bananas, and that most of the suppliers of EC (or ACP) origin are classified in Category B for the vast majority of their past marketing of bananas". We see no reason to go behind these factual conclusions of the Panel.

244.   We concur, therefore, with the Panel's conclusion that "the allocation to Category B operators of 30 per cent of the licences allowing for the importation of third-country and non-traditional ACP bananas at in-quota tariff rates creates less favourable conditions of competition for like service suppliers of Complainants' origin and is therefore inconsistent with the requirement of Article XVII of GATS". We also concur with the Panel's conclusion that the allocation to Category B operators of 30 per cent of the licences for importing third-country and non-

traditional ACP bananas at in-quota tariff rates is inconsistent with the requirements of Article II of the GATS.

ACTIVITY FUNCTION RULES

245. The European Communities maintains that the aim of the activity function rules is to protect the banana ripeners against the concentration of economic bargaining power in the hands of the primary importers as a result of the tariff quota. The European Communities contends that the policy objective is to correct the position of all ripeners *vis-à-vis* all suppliers of bananas, without distinction as to nationality . . .

246. As indicated earlier, we do not accept the argument by the European Communities that the aims or effects of the activity function rules are relevant in determining whether they provide less favourable conditions of competition to services and service suppliers of foreign origin. In this respect, we note the Panel's factual conclusions that:

> . . . even the EC statistics suggest that 74 to 80 per cent of ripeners are EC controlled. Thus, we conclude that the vast majority of the ripening capacity in the EC is owned or controlled by natural or juridical persons of the EC and that most of the bananas produced in or imported to the EC are ripened in EC owned or controlled ripening facilities.

* * * Given these factual findings, we see no reason to reverse the Panel's legal conclusion that the allocation to ripeners of a certain proportion of the Category A and B licences allowing the importation of third-country and non-traditional ACP bananas at in-quota tariff rates creates less favourable conditions of competition for like service suppliers of Complainants' origin, and is therefore inconsistent with the requirements of Article XVII of GATS.

Notes and Questions

(1) Under what circumstances would importers of goods *not* also be involved in the supply of services?

(2) What information is required to determine whether trade in services is "affected" by the measures at issue? Contrast the *Bananas* case with the *Autos* case—why was it clear that the measures involved in *Bananas* were "affecting trade in services" but not the measures involved in *Autos?* With reference to the *Autos* case, assume that the automakers who benefited from the import duty exemption had integrated wholesale operations, and that those operations were engaged in selling the vehicles that had been imported duty free. Does that give those wholesaling operations a competitive edge over wholesaling operations that do not have access to duty free imports? Is that enough to establish that trade in services is "affected?" Is it enough to establish a violation of Article I:1 or II:1? What more information would you want to have, if any?

(3) Was the discrimination among operators in *Bananas* de juré or de facto, and why?

(4) Under any quota scheme, the rights to import under the quota must be allocated somehow. Consider the common situation in which importers are also wholesalers. What systems of allocating the quota rights will pass muster under national treatment and most-favored-nation principles of GATS (assuming they both apply under a Member's schedules)? Should a nation distribute quota rights in accordance with pre-quota market shares? Is it acceptable to let in the imports that show up first at the border, and exclude those that arrive later? Even if domestic importers seem to end up first in line with regularity? If the quota rights are allocated in a manner that complies with the requirements of GATT, can they still be challenged under GATS?

(5) The two preceding cases involved arguments by respondent countries to the effect that GATT governed the measures in question, but not GATS. The reverse situation may also arise.

CANADA—CERTAIN MEASURES CONCERNING PERIODICALS

WT/DS31/AB/R
Appellate Body Report adopted by the DSB on July 30, 1997

[Eds. note: The following description of the measure at issue in this excerpt is taken from the panel report in the case:

2.6 In 1995, Bill C–103, which added Part V.I—Tax on Split-run Periodicals to the Excise Tax Act, became law. The amendment calls for the imposition, levy and collection, in respect of each split-run edition of a periodical, a tax equal to 80 per cent of the value of all the advertisements contained in the split-run edition. The tax is levied on a per issue basis. The value of all advertisements in a split-run edition of a periodical is the total of all the gross fees for all the advertisements contained in the edition. The term "periodical" means printed material that is published in a series of issues that appear not less than twice a year and not more than once a week. Where an issue of a periodical is published in several versions, each version is an edition of the issue. Each edition of the issue must be considered separately when determining whether an edition is a split-run edition. The definition of "periodical" explicitly excludes a catalogue which is substantially made up of advertisements.

2.7 The amendment defines a split-run edition as an edition of an issue of a periodical that:

    (i) is distributed in Canada;

    (ii) in which more than 20 per cent of the editorial material is the same or substantially the same as editorial material that appears in one or more excluded editions of one or more issues of one or more periodicals; and

    (iii) contains an advertisement that does not appear in identical form in all the excluded editions.

There are two exclusionary provisions. Under the first, the particular edition is not a split-run edition if it is an edition that is primarily circulated outside Canada. In effect, this is an exemption for editions that are distributed in Canada, but are mainly distributed outside Canada. Under the second, a particular edition of an issue of a periodical that would otherwise be a split-run edition is not a split-run edition if all the advertisements in the particular edition appear in identical form in one or more editions of that issue that are primarily distributed outside Canada and that have a combined circulation outside Canada that is greater than the circulation in Canada of the particular edition. The purpose is to prevent a publisher from qualifying for this exemption by having all the advertisements in its Canadian split-run edition also appear in one of its excluded editions that has a very small circulation.]

The Panel Report * * * contains the following conclusions: * * * Part V.1 of the Excise Tax Act is inconsistent with Article III:2, first sentence, of GATT 1994 * * *

* * *

Canada submits that the Panel erred in law when it applied Article III:2, first sentence, of the GATT 1994 to a measure affecting advertising services. Canada asserts that the GATT 1994 applies, as the GATT 1947 had always applied previously, to measures affecting trade in goods, but it has never been a regime for dealing with services in their own right. In Canada's view, if the GATT 1994 applied to all aspects of services measures on the basis of incidental, secondary or indirect effects on goods, the GATT 1994 would effectively be converted into a services agreement. More precisely, the GATT 1994 should not apply merely on the ground that a service makes use of a good as a tangible medium of communication. Assuming that the measure at issue is designed essentially to restrict access to the services market, the mere fact that a service makes use of a good as a vehicle or a medium is an insufficient ground on which to base a challenge under the GATT 1994.

Canada asserts that the Panel's decision to consider Part V.1 of the Excise Tax Act as a measure subject to Article III of the GATT 1994 was based largely upon an unwarranted generalization of the terms of Article III:4, as well as a misconstruction of the word "indirectly" in Article III:2, first sentence. Canada argues that it is evident from its text that Article III:4 of the GATT 1994 governs only services measures that affect the ability of foreign goods to compete on an equal footing with domestic goods. Canada submits that advertising services are only subject to Article III:4 to the extent that they affect the "internal sale or offering for sale, purchase, transportation, distribution or use" of a product that is entitled to national treatment under Article III of the GATT 1994. The inference that advertising services in general are covered by Article III:2 of the GATT 1994 is without foundation.

Canada stresses that the concept of "indirectly" in Article III:2 of the GATT 1994 is intended to capture taxes which apply to "inputs" that contribute to the production or distribution of a good, such as raw materials, services inputs and intermediate inputs. It is important to distinguish services inputs that are directly involved in the production or marketing of a good from services that are "end-products" in their own right. In Canada's view, the advertising services of a publisher are not, like labour in the production of a car, an input into the production of a good. Canada asserts that services are often delivered by means of a good, and that the taxation of services that are associated with goods in this way does not "subject" those goods "indirectly" to the tax, because the tax does not affect the costs of the production, distribution and marketing of the goods. Canada argues that, although magazines serve as a tangible medium in which advertising is incorporated, this association, however close, does not meet the tests appropriate to the interpretation of Article III:2 of the GATT 1994. Canada maintains that advertising is not an input or a cost in the production, distribution or use of magazines as physical products. Therefore, the taxation of magazine advertising services is not indirect taxation of magazines as goods within the meaning of Article III:2.

Canada asserts that the Panel mischaracterized Part V.1 of the Excise Tax Act as a measure affecting trade in goods. It is a measure regulating access to the magazine advertising market. Most magazines represent two distinct economic outputs, that of a good and an advertising medium for providing a service, depending on the perspective of the purchaser. According to Canada, the tax is not applied to the consumer good because it is not based on, nor applied to, the price of a magazine. Instead, the tax is calculated using the value of advertising carried in a split-run edition of a magazine and is assessed against the publisher of each split-run magazine as the seller of the advertising service.

In Canada's view, since the provision of magazine advertising services falls within the scope of the General Agreement on Trade in Services (the "GATS"), and Canada has not undertaken any commitments in respect of the provision of advertising services in its Schedule of Specific Commitments, Canada is not bound to provide national treatment to Members of the WTO with respect to the provision of advertising services in the Canadian market.

* * *

We are unable to agree with Canada's proposition that the GATT 1994 is not applicable to Part V.1 of the Excise Tax Act. First of all, the measure is an excise tax imposed on split-run editions of periodicals. We note that the title to Part V.1 of the Excise Tax Act reads, "TAX ON SPLIT–RUN PERIODICALS", not "tax on advertising". Furthermore, the "Summary" of An Act to Amend the Excise Tax Act and the Income Tax Act, reads: "The Excise Tax Act is amended to impose an excise tax in respect of split-run editions of periodicals". Secondly, a periodical is a good comprised of two components: editorial content and advertising content. Both components can be viewed as having services attributes, but they combine to form a physical product—the periodical itself.

The measure in this appeal, Part V.1 of the Excise Tax Act, is a companion to Tariff Code 9958, which is a prohibition on imports of special edition periodicals, including split-run or regional editions that contain advertisements primarily directed to a market in Canada and that do not appear in identical form in all editions of an issue distributed in that periodical's country of origin. Canada agrees that Tariff Code 9958 is a measure affecting trade in goods, even though it applies to split-run editions of periodicals as does Part V.1 of the Excise Tax Act. As Canada stated in the oral hearing during this appeal:

> Tariff Code 9958 is basically an import prohibition of a physical good, i.e., the magazine itself. In that sense the entire debate was as to whether or not there was a possible defence against the application of Article XI of the GATT. In that case, therefore, there were direct effects and Canada recognized that there were effects on the physical good—the magazine as it crossed the border.

The Panel found that Tariff Code 9958 is an import prohibition, although it applies to split-run editions of periodicals which are distinguished by their advertising content directed at the Canadian market. Canada did not appeal this finding of the Panel. It is clear that Part V.1 of the Excise Tax Act is intended to complement and render effective the import ban of Tariff Code 9958. As a companion to the import ban, Part V.1 of the Excise Tax Act has the same objective and purpose as Tariff Code 9958 and, therefore, should be analyzed in the same manner.

An examination of Part V.1 of the Excise Tax Act demonstrates that it is an excise tax which is applied on a good, a split-run edition of a periodical, on a "per issue" basis. By its very structure and design, it is a tax on a periodical. It is the publisher, or in the absence of a publisher resident in Canada, the distributor, the printer or the wholesaler, who is liable to pay the tax, not the advertiser.

Based on the above analysis of the measure, which is essentially an excise tax imposed on split-run editions of periodicals, we cannot agree with Canada's argument that this internal tax does not "indirectly" affect imported products. It is a well-established principle that the trade effects of a difference in tax treatment between imported and domestic products do not have to be demonstrated for a measure to be found to be inconsistent with Article III. The fundamental purpose of Article III of the GATT 1994 is to ensure equality of competitive conditions between imported and like domestic products. We do not find it necessary to look to Article III:1 or Article III:4 of the GATT 1994 to give meaning to Article III:2, first sentence, in this respect. In *Japan—Alcoholic Beverages*, the Appellate Body stated that "Article III:1 articulates a general principle" which "informs the rest of Article III". However, we also said that it informs the different sentences in Article III:2 in different ways. With respect to Article III:2, second sentence, we held that "Article III:1 informs Article III:2, second sentence, through specific reference".

Article III:2, first sentence, uses the words "directly or indirectly" in two different contexts: one in relation to the application of a tax to imported products and the other in relation to the application of a tax to like domestic products. Any measure that indirectly affects the conditions of competition between imported and like domestic products would come within the provisions of Article III:2, first sentence, or by implication, second sentence, given the broader application of the latter.

The entry into force of the GATS, as Annex 1B of the *WTO Agreement*, does not diminish the scope of application of the GATT 1994. Indeed, Canada concedes that its position "with respect to the inapplicability of the GATT would have been exactly the same under the GATT 1947, before the GATS had ever been conceived".

We agree with the Panel's statement:

The ordinary meaning of the texts of GATT 1994 and GATS as well as Article II:2 of the WTO Agreement, taken together, indicates that obligations under GATT 1994 and GATS can co-exist and that one does not override the other.

We do not find it necessary to pronounce on the issue of whether there can be potential overlaps between the GATT 1994 and the GATS, as both participants agreed that it is not relevant in this appeal. Canada stated that its

... principal argument is not based ... on the need to avoid overlaps and potential conflicts. On the contrary it is based on a textual interpretation of the provision, on the plain meaning of the words in Article III:2—more precisely the word 'indirectly' interpreted in its legal context and in light of the object and purpose of the provision.

We conclude, therefore, that it is not necessary and, indeed, would not be appropriate, in this appeal to consider Canada's rights and obligations under the GATS. The measure at issue in this appeal, Part V.1 of the Excise Tax Act, is a measure which clearly applies to goods—it is an excise tax on split-run editions of periodicals ...

Notes and Questions

(1) Think through the pertinent comparisons under GATT Article III:2—which imported products are purportedly "like" which domestic products? Note that in a later part of the opinion, the Appellate Body determined that the excise tax was inconsistent with Article III:2, second sentence, but reversed the finding of inconsistency with Article III:2, first sentence.

(2) Suppose a nation wanted to encourage the development of its insurance industry. One type of insurance covers damage to goods in transit from abroad. The nation enacts a law providing that importers who buy their insurance coverage from foreign insurance carriers must pay a "foreign insurance tax" equal to 50% of the premiums paid to foreign insurers. Same case or different?

SECTION 19.4   DISCUSSION PROBLEM—
TRADE IN INSURANCE SERVICES

As the preceding materials make clear, the effects of both the NAFTA and the GATS on trade in services are quite sector specific. Just as the extent of liberalization under GATT for trade in goods depends heavily on the negotiated tariff bindings for each good entering each country, so do the services agreements treat various service sectors quite differently in the extent to which trade impediments are dismantled.

To understand the practical operation of the agreements, we find it instructive to consider an example. We have chosen insurance because of its importance. The following excerpt helps to define the scope of the issues.

U.S. NATIONAL STUDY ON TRADE IN SERVICES, A SUBMISSION BY THE UNITED STATES GOVERNMENT TO THE GENERAL AGREEMENT ON TARIFFS AND TRADE 141–46 (1982)

Insurance is one of the most important international service industries. It represents the acceptance of a relatively large risk by the insurer in return for relatively small payment. By insuring a large number of similar risks, the insurer can calculate the likely claims that will be paid, and the required premium for each risk that will be necessary to meet those claims. Risks come in many different sizes and forms. No individual country has the insurance capacity necessary to efficiently cover all of the risks present in that country. This is the fundamental basis for the internationalization of insurance. While these principles have always applied, the economic development of modern societies has resulted in a radical increase in individual risks which must utilize international insurance capacity. Nuclear power plants and large off-shore oil and gas drilling complexes are just two examples of risks that have emerged in recent years that require extraordinary insurance capacity to provide the necessary security.

Some classes of insurance are inherently "international": (1) transport insurance, including marine and aviation; (2) bonding and insurance related to the provision, installation and performance of goods in international trade; (3) insurance of large risks associated with natural catastrophes and large industrial facilities; and (4) reinsurance. The many other classes of insurance which are less directly "international" in nature offer, however, commercial opportunities which should be accessible to foreign insurers or intermediaries which desire to enter the market.

In addition to underwriting risks, the industry provides a wide range of services to help control these risks such as loss control, inspection and actuarial services and to minimize the cost of losses including loss control, rehabilitation, and recovery, salvage and subrogation services. The industry also provides a range of savings and investment programs. Brokerage and agency services serve insurance consumers by efficiently allocating risks among underwriters.

International insurance has grown and diversified as an essential part of the expansion of trade, worldwide industrialization, technological progress and economic development. Worldwide insurance premium value (excluding the Communist Bloc) totaled $450 billion in 1981, of which approximately 42 percent is attributable to life and 58 percent to nonlife business. This business was transacted by approximately 10,000 domestic companies and 3,000 branch offices abroad. About 95 percent of worldwide premium was produced by the OECD nations. The 5 percent of world premium attributable to nonindustrial countries has doubled since 1950. Overall, the growth of insurance has exceeded the pace of global economic development.

Insurers conduct business in foreign markets through branch offices, local subsidiaries, joint ventures, brokers and independent agents. In addition, insurers may conduct "home-foreign" insurance, i.e. insurance written in the home country of the company on risks located abroad. Each of the different forms of operations has advantages and disadvantages. Generally, insurance can be provided most efficiently when the insurer has the freedom to choose its method of operation based on its own assessment of how it can best serve the market rather than on government strictures on form of operation.

It is generally accepted that some control or regulation of insurance is necessary to protect against financially unsound operations and to ensure fairness of contract terms and performance. The degree and nature of such regulation varies among countries according to the composition, regional organization and operation of the market, differing perceptions of the need for protection of various types of insurers, and differing national attitudes toward governmental intervention in the economy and public administration in general.

The need for reasonable regulation and regulatory practices is not questioned. However, there are a wide variety of nontariff measures in law, regulation and administrative practice which discriminate against foreign insurance, insurers, reinsurers and intermediaries which have a protectionist or unnecessary "chilling" effect upon international trade in insurance. A wide variety of barriers exist which unreasonably restrict international commerce in insurance. Because of this, insurers find it increasingly difficult to gain access to foreign markets, to operate to full capacity in such markets or to enjoy competitive opportunity equivalent to that of domestic insurers. The discussion below examines the main types of obstacles to insurance services, the impact of these obstacles and suggests various means by which these problems can be pursued internationally.

Barriers to Trade in Insurance

Barriers may be grouped into three general categories as they relate to: (1) access to market and establishment; (2) transactions and financial operations; and (3) equivalent competitive position. (Restrictions on reinsurance and transportation insurance are described separately.)

a. *Restrictions on Access to Market and Establishment*

Denial of Market Access: Some governments do not allow any foreign participation in their insurance market, substantially restrict it, or are in the process of eliminating foreign participation. The most prevalent restriction on insurance placement requires that a particular line of insurance be purchased within the domestic market. In more severe cases, which are not uncommon, a prospective buyer must not only purchase locally, but with locally owned insurance firms or a state insurance agency (thereby excluding foreign admitted insurers). Regulations which restrict insurance placement involve many lines of general and life insurance.

Government Policies which Discourage Nationals from Purchasing Insurance From Foreign Entities: While "technically" permitting foreign insurers to compete, many governments carry out policies which effectively discourage nationals from placing insurance with foreign firms. A common restriction of this type is the assessment of a tax on insurance placed outside the local market (and in some cases with foreign-admitted insurers). Similarly, some governments discourage insurance placement with foreign entities by not allowing domestic policy-holders to charge premiums paid to foreign insurers as tax deductible business expenses (although such concessions exist for premiums paid to domestic insurers), or by treating claims received on insurance policies placed outside the local markets as income and thus subject to tax.

Another method is the prohibition or restriction on the placement of insurance through foreign intermediaries (brokers and agents). Such restrictions are commonly employed in markets which also limit the operations of foreign insurers. Typically in such a market, local companies operate only through paid staff agents. Accounts are coinsured or reinsured with other local companies. Thus foreign companies are effectively frozen out of participation in the market through local entities. By prohibiting or restricting foreign intermediaries, the market can be almost completely closed to foreign competition.

Arbitrary and Discriminatory Licensing Procedures: Licensing is the primary means used by governments to regulate insurers. Before an insurance company can operate within a market, it must obtain a license for each line of insurance it desires to sell. Arbitrary and discriminatory licensing procedures have been vigorously applied by some governments as a means of denying foreign participation (or additional foreign participation) in the market, either totally or with respect to certain lines of insurance. Such practices often discourage foreign firms from applying for licenses.

Characteristics of such discrimination vary but may include: (1) denial of a license to a qualified foreign branch or subsidiary; (2) grant of a license for only limited classes of business, in particular, classes deemed unprofitable or undesirable by local insurers; (3) absence of adequate written regulations or regulatory procedures, leaving extensive opportunity to use administrative discretion for protectionist purposes in considering licensing requests; (4) difficulty in obtaining an explanation as to the reasons an application to obtain a license has been denied; (5) lack of an administrative appeal process in cases of licensing requests being denied; (6) extensive delays in processing an application to obtain a license; and (7) failing to process an application to obtain a license.

Discrimination Against Foreign Branch Operations: Branch offices have traditionally been the predominant mode of operations for insurance companies in foreign markets. In recent years, some governments have moved to forbid and/or eliminate foreign branches by prohibiting any further establishment of branch operations and requiring the local incorporation of existing branches. Other forms of discrimination may include delays in granting licenses for branch operations, and blatantly discriminatory taxation of branches vis-a-vis local corporations, and arbitrary restrictions on the freedom of foreign branches to offer new products.

Forced Localization: In most instances, mandatory local incorporation is accompanied by national majority ownership requirements. Governments can also force localization through discriminatory regulatory policies (e.g., taxes, capital requirements) which make it impossible to stay in business in branch form. If a government has prohibited further foreign investment in insurance, it can, over the long run, force divestment of foreign holdings even without officially requiring it. One way is to raise capital requirements—requirements foreign insurers cannot comply with because additional investment is prohibited. To meet such capital requirements, a foreign investor must attract national investors and in the process dilute his percentage of ownership.

b.   Restrictions on Transactions and Financial Operations

Restrictions on Remittances: A common practice in a number of insurance markets is a system of exchange control which unreasonably restricts the remittance of funds by insurers, intermediaries or the insured. These practices may take the form of denial of foreign exchange needed; procedural and processing delays in obtaining permission from local authorities to carry out the transfer; or prohibition upon payments of component parts of an insurance transaction.

Discriminatory Deposit or Capital Requirements Placed on Foreign–Admitted Insurers: It is an accepted regulatory policy to require that insurance companies operating in a market meet and maintain a minimum deposit requirement. In a number of markets, however, the amount of the deposit, the form, or the manner in which it is held, is more stringent on the foreign company than on the domestic company. Foreign-admitted insurers may also be subject to higher requirements than domestic firms and more stringent solvency criteria.

Discriminatory Taxation of Foreign–Admitted Insurers: In a number of countries, various taxes, including income and premium taxes, fall more heavily on foreign-admitted insurers than on local insurance companies. In the case of income tax, foreign-admitted insurers may be required to pay a higher level of tax or have their taxes computed on a different, more costly, basis than local companies. Other discriminatory forms of taxation may include taxes on premiums paid to foreign insurers or taxation of indemnity payments as income from abroad. The higher taxes can have substantial impact on relative prices for insurance coverage, making the foreign insurer uncompetitive.

c. Restrictions on Competitive Equality

Discrimination in Government Procurement: A number of governments require that the insurance procured by government departments, local authorities, state corporations, other government related organizations and government contractors be placed only with local insurance companies owned by local citizens.

Exclusion of Foreign–Admitted Insurers: From Trade Associations: In many countries, trade associations provide a critical link to local regulators and market information. The exclusion of foreign companies from participation in such associations places them at a severe disadvantage vis-a-vis domestic firms. Membership in such associations also may give added prestige or credibility to the insurance company.

Restrictions on the Employment of Non–Nationals: To be competitive, it is necessary that a foreign insurance company have management, professional, and technical expertise adequate to relate local needs to its worldwide experience and accumulated insurance know-how. This is an important and often essential dimension of competition with local firms which often have superior personal contacts, market relationships, etc. Thus, it is often necessary to complement local management and technical personnel with personnel from elsewhere within a firm or from its home office. Restrictions or unreasonable delays in obtaining work permits often act as barriers to the provision of efficient insurance services.

d. Restrictions on Reinsurance and Transportation Insurance

Reinsurance: Restrictions on reinsurance placement may take many forms. Most common are compulsory internal cessions of reinsurance transactions. In some instances, governments require a fixed percentage of all reinsurance to be ceded to private companies within the local market. In other instances, reinsurance must first be offered to local companies before it can be placed outside. Some countries have established national or regional reinsurance institutions and require that all or part of reinsurance cessions made by companies be placed with the designated reinsurance entity. Other factors which may inhibit placement of reinsurance abroad include disallowance of credit for solvency computation purposes of reinsurance placed with a non-admitted insurer, and restrictions on the remittance of funds overseas.

Transportation Insurance: Some countries have applied restrictions specifically to transport insurance. These restrictive practices range from requiring that all imports, and, in some cases, all exports be insured within the domestic market, to financial incentives (usually tax or foreign exchange regulations) which benefit the domestic market.

* * *

POSSIBLE STRATEGIES FOR RESOLVING PROBLEMS

The proliferation of impediments to international insurance operations makes it essential to counter current protectionist trends and remove some of the uncertainty insurers face when seeking to expand overseas. A strategy for liberalizing insurance trade must recognize the special nature of insurance and the concomitant requirement for some level of government intervention. Insurance is essentially a contract for payment in the future. Generally, its fiduciary character makes it a legitimate subject of government regulation to guarantee performance. However, such regulation should be reasonable and not be used to protect domestic markets from foreign competition. Elements of specific concern to the insurance industry that should be considered in a multilateral understanding include the following:

MARKET ACCESS

The thrust of efforts internationally should be to obtain, perhaps through an agreement on insurance, acceptance of the principle of the right of access to domestic markets, subject to adherence to legitimate local regulatory requirements. "Access" would mean basically the right to sell policies within the guidelines established earlier in this study dealing with trade and investment. A multilateral arrangement might commit governments to establish guidelines that ensure fair and equitable access to local markets, taking into account the sovereignty of domestic regulatory procedures. Once access is gained, national treatment would be the operative principle.

REINSURANCE AND TRANSPORT INSURANCE

Although reinsurance and transport insurance could be included in a broader insurance code, it may be possible to negotiate some form of multilateral understanding in these sectors that would reflect their inherently international character. Transport insurance is, by nature, international business, covering the movement of imports and exports. The basic concept underlying reinsurance is the spread of large risks among companies and geographically. The objective of a multilateral understanding should be open competition and complete freedom of choice for the placement of reinsurance and the purchase of transport insurance. It might also be desirable to include special provisions to take into account the protection of "infant" insurance industries in certain countries, and to allow some method of graduation as local companies develop expertise and markets. In addition, provisions might be included that would subject state-owned or controlled insurance organizations to the same competitive pressures as market-oriented firms.

INVISIBLES AND ESTABLISHMENT

The insurance sector shares many of the same problems related to establishment in foreign countries as other business sectors. The objective for work in this area would be to allow the greatest freedom possible to respond to market forces without government-induced distortions. Although each government has the right to determine the conditions under which foreign firms will be permitted entry, national treatment would govern once establishment is attained. The current effort in the OECD to revise the insurance Annex of the Code of Current Invisibles Operations illustrates some of the establishment issues of particular concern to insurers:

- freedom of choice to operate in the form in which they wish to be established (subsidiary, branch or agency);

- transparency with respect to authorization procedures, market needs tests, and the cause for refusal of authorization; and

- deadlines for action on applications for authorization.

In addition, the OECD Code of Liberalization of Capital Movements, as it relates to right of establishment, may provide a basis for further work on that issue with respect to insurance and other services. Any discussion should consider the specific ideas being generated by the OECD Insurance Committee, which has examined difficulties in performing insurance business abroad in a thorough and systematic manner.

REGULATION

Another area where international efforts would be beneficial is the regulatory area. Government regulations on insurance have the purpose of affecting the quality, performance and safety of insurance services. These regulations are similar to government-mandated standards for the characteristics of a product. There already exists an international agreement concerning product standards, the GATT Standards Code, whose purpose is to ensure that signatory governments do not prepare, adopt or apply standards in a manner that would create obstacles to trade. It might be possible to build on this concept for insurance regulations and incorporate provisions for national treatment (or competitive equality), transparency, notification and surveillance, and dispute settlement.

The concept of national treatment, as employed in FCN treaties and the OECD Declaration on International Investment of 1976, means that foreign insurance companies, for example, are allowed to compete on essentially equal terms with domestic insurers in the host country, even if some specific regulations or requirements applied to foreign insurers differ from those affecting domestic insurers. National treatment in this sense is not necessarily the same as assuring competitive equality.

Equality of competitive opportunity focuses on the opportunity provided by rules and regulations, rather than the equality of the rules themselves. Sometimes laws and regulations applied equally to foreign and domestic companies may have a differentially adverse impact on foreign companies due to the nature of their operations. (For example, uniform controls on foreign exchange may be more burdensome for foreign insurers.) Government policy should seek de facto national treatment, not simply de jure national treatment.

A multilateral understanding should also require an adequate degree of transparency of regulations and their application. For example, insurers would be able to find out who applies insurance laws and regulations, and their criteria for making decisions. Officials would be available to answer the questions of foreign insurers and help them understand the domestic insurance regulatory system. Copies of relevant laws and regulations should be easily available.

With regard to notification and surveillance and dispute settlement, countries could set up an internal process for monitoring the complaints of foreign insurers. They might, for example, agree to notify other signatories before introducing new regulations or changing old ones, and give the other parties a chance to comment on the proposals. The dispute settlement mechanism of such an arrangement might begin with bilateral consultation between the parties involved. If bilateral discussions do not result in resolution of the dispute, discussions and appropriate actions might be taken by a broader group of countries that have accepted the provisions of the understanding.

Questions

To what extent do the NAFTA and GATS address the barriers to trade noted above through general obligations? To what extent through sector specific commitments?

Chapter 20

TRADE RELATED ASPECTS OF INTELLECTUAL PROPERTY RIGHTS

The growing importance and complexity of intellectual property law requires multiple courses for a thorough treatment, and it is not uncommon to find distinct curricular offerings on patents, copyrights and trademarks and related matters. In this brief survey, therefore, we can only scratch the surface of the issues that arise. Our emphasis will be on matters of special prominence in international trade, leaving the details of U.S. and other domestic laws to another forum.[1]

SECTION 20.1   INTRODUCTION

(A) INTELLECTUAL PROPERTY RIGHTS AND POLICIES

Traditional descriptions of intellectual property law often divide the subject into patent, copyright, trademark and trade dress, and trade secret law. These distinctions can blur at times (is a computer chip a proper subject of patent or should the blueprint for assembling it be copyrightable? what about a computer program?). But these categories provide a serviceable first cut at organizing the subject.

Patent law concerns "inventions," which can take many forms. They may constitute a new product, a new process for making an old product, a new molecule, or even a new organism. Typically, national patent laws require that inventions be "non-obvious," or some similar term, to be patentable, and that they have some actual or potential commercial application. The granting of a patent confers upon the inventor a number of rights, including the right to prevent others from copying and selling the invention for a specified period of years. The inventor may also prevent others from developing products that incorporate the invention without permission. Thus, the patent holder retains for a period of time the exclusive right to sell the invention, and may either produce it

------

1. Leading references on intellectual property law include Chisum, Chisum on Patents (looseleaf); McCarthy, Trademarks and Unfair Competition (4th ed. 1996); and Nimmer & Nimmer, Nimmer on Copyright (looseleaf).

for sale directly or permit others to produce and sell it after paying a fee for a "patent license." Patent holders may also receive a direct monetary reward for invention from the government that grants the patent.

The policy issues associated with patent law, even in a closed economy, are rich and fascinating. Patents are widely considered essential, at least under many circumstances, to provide appropriate incentives for innovation. Inventors typically bear the costs of research, and if others can appropriate the benefits by copying and selling the commercially valuable fruits of research, inventors may have no incentive to invent. But it is equally clear that patents have important social costs. Once an invention exists, it is desirable, other things being equal (such as the rate of inventive activity), that it be made available to all who are willing to pay the costs of reproducing it. Yet, a patent holder often enjoys a degree of monopoly power, and will tend to charge a monopoly price over the life of the patent, thus introducing the distortion of monopoly pricing into the economy. Further, because the returns to a patent can be large, the possibility arises that the patent system will induce excessive investment in research. The most widely studied example arises when a number of inventors all know that a patentable invention is just over the horizon, and each rushes to invent it first. The resources devoted to such a "patent race" can significantly exceed the resources that a careful social calculus would suggest appropriate. Additional issues arise when future innovators must build upon prior inventions to create others—how will the patent on an existing invention affect the incentive of another inventor to try and build upon it? The breadth of patent rights is also a matter of great importance. If minor changes to an invention suffice to create a new and different product that does not infringe the patent, then patent rights will have less value, perhaps too little. Yet, if patent rights are defined broadly so that similar but different products are infringing, the scope of monopoly power and the possible distortions associated with it and with patent races will grow.[1]

Taking these considerations together, one principle that emerges is that patent protection makes little sense where it is unnecessary to spur the innovation. This observation provides support for one of the most basic and oft-litigated principles of patent law—that patents may not be enforced if the invention is "obvious." But there are many more issues that must be resolved, and it is not at all clear what an ideal patent law should provide. Indeed, the contours of an ideal system are probably to a great degree unknowable and variable with circumstances, and it is not

1. The theoretical literature on patents is voluminous. Seminal papers include Arrow, Economic Welfare and the Allocation of Resources for Invention, in NBER, The Rate and Direction of Inventive Activity: Economic and Social Factors (1962); Kitch, The Nature and the Function of the Patent System, 20 J.L. & Econ. 265 (1977) and Machlup, An Economic Review of the Patent System, Study of the Subcomm. on Patents, Trademarks & Copyrights, Comm. on the Judiciary, 85th Cong., 2d Sess. (Study No. 15, 1958). More recent sources are noted in a symposium in 5 J.Econ. Perspectives 3 (1991). See particularly the papers by Besen & Raskind, Scotchmer and Ordover in that volume.

even clear that patents should exist at all in preference to government rewards for invention that provide innovators with incentive for research but do not introduce the distortions of monopoly after the fact. Nevertheless, the governments of developed countries have for many decades afforded their nationals—and to considerable degree the nationals of other countries—the opportunity to obtain patent rights, usually of significant duration (20 years from date of patent application after the Uruguay Round), and subject to a variety of restrictions on precisely what is patentable and what is not.

Copyright law concerns "literary and artistic expression," which again can take many forms. Books, films, songs and paintings are paradigm examples, but copyright can also extend to computer programs and operating systems, to a blueprint for making a computer chip, or to databases even though the individual bits of data are not themselves copyrightable. To a significant extent the policy issues with copyright are similar to those with patent—absent copyright protection, authors and other creators could not appropriate the returns to their work and would have little incentive to do it in many cases. But the policy concerns regarding the monopoly distortion from patents and patent races carry over to only a limited extent in the copyright context. As popular as Stephen King may be, his copyrights do not confer upon him nearly the degree of market power that, say, a patent on the internal combustion engine would confer, and we need not fear that the existence of copyright will induce someone else to race him to write "Carrie." These distinctions are easy to exaggerate, however, as brief reflection on the use of copyright to protect computer chip designs will suggest. Further, like patent, copyright confers upon creators some rights to control the use of their work by others who might build on it ("derivative uses"), and hence the incentives of other creators are to some extent in play. Indeed, one can imagine those incentives being profoundly affected depending upon what is copyrightable—imagine a world in which anyone who computed a definite integral owed a royalty to Newton's estate! Thus, copyright is conventionally limited to the "expression," and does not extend to the idea that underlies it; we can compute definite integrals at our pleasure and even sell our services for that purpose, but we cannot reproduce and sell our calculus texts to others if the copyright is still in force. Likewise, one cannot copyright a fact merely by writing it down.[2]

Because of these limitations, the grant of a copyright is *in most cases* less likely than a patent to raise concerns about monopoly and the incentives for subsequent creators. It is thus easier for creators to obtain copyright protection (for some purposes they need do nothing to obtain it

---

2. Again the literature is substantial. Many sources are collected in the Journal of Economic Perspectives symposium cited in note 2 supra. Well known papers include Breyer, The Uneasy Case for Copyright: A Study of Copyright in Books, Photocopies and Computer Programs, 84 Harv.L.Rev. 281 (1970) and Landes & Posner, An Economic Analysis of Copyright Law, 18 J. Legal Stud. 325 (1989).

but create), and it usually lasts longer (historically, the life of the author plus 50 years in the United States).

Trademark and trade dress law concern the rights of a seller to market a product or service in a distinctive manner, and to prevent others from passing their goods or services off in misleading fashion. Trademarks enable sellers to use a symbol or name to identify their wares, and in turn enable consumers quickly and readily to identify the good or service as that of a particular manufacturer, franchise system, or the like. They are useful to a seller when they come to symbolize a level of quality or value in existing goods or services or in the introduction of new goods and services. Absent legal restrictions, other sellers might then be tempted to mislead consumers by using the trademark established by another firm. And, even when the trademark itself is not used by another, similar packaging or other aspects of presentation (trade dress) may lead consumers to make mistaken purchases. Misstatements or misleading indications of geographic origin are another source of concern (imagine a beer brewed in Newark with the name "Beck" and a label entirely in German). Thus, the rationale for trademark and trade dress law is in large measure akin to the rationale for sanctioning fraud—misleading statements can cause individuals to enter transactions that are not valuable to them and that they would not enter but for the misinformation. In addition, if sellers can mislead buyers with impunity, buyers will no longer trust trademarks or trade dress as markers of quality. It will then become more difficult for sellers to reap the returns from efforts to produce high quality goods and services, and the incentive to provide quality in the marketplace will diminish.

The dangers of protection for trademarks and trade dress relate primarily to overbreadth. It would be most unfortunate if McDonald's could enjoin the use of an arch for any purpose, or if Levi Strauss & Co. could enjoin the sale by another of any trousers with two legs. Likewise, words that may have proprietary content at some point in time can become a part of ordinary language later, and restrictions on the use of such language can be costly. Thus, in one manner or another, trademark and trade dress law limit the rights of sellers to circumstances in which confusion is a serious risk (trademarks must be "distinctive"), and further limit the scope of words and symbols that may become protected as trademarks (for example, generic words cannot be trademarks). With such restrictions in place, trademark and trade dress law may be understood as promoting quality and lowering consumer search costs while simultaneously endeavoring to avoid undue restrictions on the use of language and symbols in ordinary communication and otherwise.[3]

Trade secret law is most closely related to patent law. Broadly speaking, a trade secret is information that has value to its holder, and that would have less value if generally known. Some trade secrets are the appropriate subject of patents, but their holder may elect not to

---

3. See Landes & Posner, Trademark Law: An Economic Perspective, 30 J.L. & Econ. 265 (1987); Besen & Raskind, supra note 1.

pursue a patent for various reasons, such as the fact that considerable information must be disclosed in the patent application process or that the application process and subsequent litigation may be costly. Other trade secrets are simply not patentable (such as customer lists). Protection for trade secrets is typically limited to a prohibition on the use of "improper means" to acquire them. Corporate espionage is actionable, as may be the disclosure of trade secrets by a former employee. But where a trade secret is discovered through proper means, such as reverse engineering or independent invention, there is usually no protection for it, in stark contrast to the situation with patent rights. These distinctions raise a number of puzzles that are not fully understood. One might wonder why protection for trade secrets is not broader on the one hand or, on the other, why it exists at all if the secret is not patentable.[4] We shall not purport to resolve these puzzles here, but simply note that some form of trade secret law seems to have evolved in most developed nations, although the details of that evolution and the extent of protection under the law has varied considerably.

(B) THE INTERNATIONAL DIMENSION

We are concerned in this chapter not so much with the details of national intellectual property policies, but with some of the ways that they relate to international commerce. Even with this limited focus, we can only touch briefly on the important questions, which roughly divide into two categories.

The first category concerns the extraterritorial reach of domestic law. Suppose that a domestic inventor with a valid patent observes its product being copied and sold in an overseas market, infringement that would clearly violate domestic law. Can the inventor bring an action in a domestic court, assuming that the infringer is subject to service of process and personal jurisdiction? The answer tends to be no, at least as long as the infringer is a foreign national. The remedy lies with an action, if any is available, under the patent law of the foreign nation in which the infringement occurs or the infringing good is sold. But what if the good is being imported from abroad into the domestic market? Or suppose that a good that is lawfully produced abroad subject to a patent or trademark license is imported into the territory of another country in a manner that infringes the exclusive license of another for that territory? Here, as we shall see, domestic law remedies are more widely available.

The second category concerns tensions among countries over their intellectual property policies, and resultant pressures for international cooperation. An obvious source of potential tension internationally is the temptation to discriminate against foreign nationals in the provision of intellectual property rights. Discrimination has been prohibited by a number of international agreements through the years, including to a

---

4. An interesting discussion of these issues is that of Friedman, Landes & Posner, Some Economics of Trade Secret Law, 5 J. Econ. Perspectives 61 (1991).

degree the national treatment obligation of GATT Article III, and now the Uruguay Round Agreement on Trade Related Aspects of Intellectual Property (hereafter the WTO TRIPS Agreement).

More difficult questions arise when nations do not pursue facially discriminatory policies, but disagree on the proper scope of intellectual property rights for domestic and foreign citizens alike. The United States has long been among the leading advocates for stronger intellectual property rights in the trading community, based on at least a perception that U.S. inventors and creators lose considerable sums due to lax protection overseas. A 1988 study by the U.S. International Trade Commission (relying mainly on industry-provided estimates) put the total loss to the U.S. economy due to "inadequate" intellectual property protection abroad at roughly $24 billion annually.[5] The accuracy of such estimates is open to some question, and indeed it is very difficult to know what the full costs and benefits of varying intellectual property regimes are to different nations. Nevertheless, there can be little doubt that the stakes are considerable.

Disputes have been commonplace through the years between developed and developing nations. Developing countries tend to have lower levels of human capital in the population at large than developed nations, and thus perhaps less capacity in relation to their size to generate commercially valuable innovations. Strict intellectual property laws in developing countries may thus facilitate profit-making by foreigners at the expense of domestic consumers. Weak laws, by contrast, which others may view as permitting "piracy," reduce domestic prices and may even facilitate export sales of the "pirated" items.[6] Hence, it is not unexpectable that developing countries may prefer less restrictive intellectual property regimes than developing nations.[7]

5. U.S. International Trade Commission, Foreign Protection of Intellectual Property Rights and the Effect on U.S. Industry and Trade, USITC Pub. No. 2065 (1988), at 4–2.

6. Weak intellectual property laws can be a double-edged sword, to be sure, as they stifle domestic innovation and may even have adverse effects on the rate of innovation abroad which will hurt consumers in the developed and developing nations alike. Likewise, if foreigners suspect that direct investment and technology transfer may facilitate piracy, developing nations with weak intellectual property laws may find it difficult to attract assistance that might be valuable for development. A notable effort to develop empirical information on such issues is that of Edwin Mansfield, Unauthorized Use of Intellectual Property: Effects on Investment, Technology Transfer and Innovation, *in* National Research Council, Global Dimensions of Intellectual Property Rights in Science and Technology 107

(1993). The other papers in that volume are also of considerable interest.

7. It does not follow that the policies preferred by developing nations will be worse for the world as a whole than the policies preferred by developed nations. Just as developing nations may prefer to be pirates, developed nations may delight in exploiting the monopoly power that strict intellectual property rights (particularly in the patent area) may facilitate. The globally "optimal" policy, therefore, might well lie in between, and in any case there can be no assurance that one side or the other is "right" from the global perspective. The literature on these issues has grown significantly in recent years, and includes Frederick Abbott, Protecting First World Assets in the Third World: Intellectual Property Negotiations in the GATT Multilateral Framework, 22 Vand.J.Transnatl.L. 689 (1989); Judith Chin & Gene Grossman, Intellectual Property Rights and North–South Trade, *in* The Political Economy of International

Important disputes have also arisen among developed nations. For example, a U.S. software manufacturers association recently alleged that Japan was the "worst country for software piracy," and further asserted that such piracy was costing the U.S. industry $3 billion a year. The same association estimated losses from piracy in Europe as a whole at $4.5 billion a year.[8] The President of the Motion Picture Association of America recently claimed that the industry's losses due to unauthorized showing of films were greatest in Italy, and put them at $225 million annually.[9]

These disputes have persisted and multiplied despite the existence of a number of long-standing international agreements on intellectual property, such as the Paris Convention for the Protection of Industrial Property (from 1883) and the Berne Convention for the Protection of Literary and Artistic Works (from 1886).[10] The most recent effort to resolve some of these matters of contention, and a most impressive one at that, is the Uruguay Round TRIPS agreement which we discuss in the latter part of this chapter.

SECTION 20.2   THE APPLICATION OF DOMESTIC LAW TO FOREIGN COMMERCE

(A) CONDUCT ABROAD

WELLS FARGO & COMPANY v. WELLS FARGO EXPRESS CO.

United States District Court, Nevada, 1973.
358 F.Supp. 1065.

FOLEY, C.J.: Plaintiff Wells Fargo & Company, a California corporation (the Bank), is engaged in business in the United States and various foreign countries. The Bank uses registered trade names, trade-marks and service marks comprising in whole or in part the name "Wells Fargo". The Bank is involved in banking services, trust services, toy manufacturing, restaurant services and the travel agency business and has registered trade-marks to cover these services.

Plaintiff Baker Industries, Inc., a Delaware corporation (Baker), owns and has registered the "Wells Fargo" trade-mark for the armored car business, i.e., the transportation of money and valuables.

Trade 90 (Ronald Jones & Anne Krueger eds., 1990); Alan Deardorff, Welfare Effects of Global Patent Protection, Economica, February 1992, at 35; Ishac Diwan & Dani Rodrik, Patents, Appropriate Technology and North–South Trade, 30 J.Intl.Econ. 27 (1991); and Arvind Subramanian, The International Economics of Intellectual Property Right Protection: A Welfare–Theoretic Trade Policy Analysis, 19 World Development 945 (1991).

8. 10 BNA ITR 960 (1993).

9. 10 BNA ITR 260 (1993).

10. These and other international agreements are collected in International Treaties on Intellectual Property (M. Leaffer ed., 1990).

The defendant Wells Fargo Express Company is a Nevada corporation, incorporated September 1, 1961.

The complaint was filed on September 18, 1970, alleging that the defendant is infringing on the Bank's and Baker's trade-marks, all of which have been registered under the Lanham Act, 15 U.S.C. secs. 1051–1127. * * * The plaintiffs allege that the defendant uses the name "Wells Fargo Express Co." in its American and foreign business activities and that the defendant has registered the plaintiffs' trade-mark and trade name in various foreign countries. Plaintiffs allege that the defendant has appropriated the trade-mark without their consent, that this use by the defendant confuses the public, that this use is likely to ultimately dilute their property rights in the registered trade-mark, that this use causes the plaintiffs irreparable harm and that the use unjustly enriches the defendant.

Both plaintiffs seek to enjoin the defendant from infringing their registered trade-marks and from using the words "Wells Fargo" in the United States or in foreign nations. Plaintiffs also seek an accounting for damages and profits * * *.

* * *

Jurisdiction Over Foreign Activities—Lanham Act

The plaintiffs have amassed numerous documents which show various foreign-based organizations using the name Wells Fargo for different activities throughout the world. The position of the plaintiffs appears to be that the use of the name Wells Fargo by numerous foreign organizations is causing the plaintiffs grave injury to their world-wide good will and will prevent the plaintiffs from expanding into international markets. The plaintiffs have registered trade-marks in the United States and do not approve of the foreign use of "their" trade-mark. Therefore, the plaintiffs seek to enjoin the defendant from using the name Wells Fargo in any foreign country and seek to have the existing foreign registrations allegedly belonging to the defendant removed as a violation of the Lanham Act. The plaintiffs' position is logical only if the Lanham Act of the United States is given world-wide effect. The plaintiffs can complain about the international injury to "their" good will only if their right in the Wells Fargo name is also international. That is hardly the posture of the law. Registration in the United States gives protection in the United States; if the plaintiffs seek international protection, they must register the mark in the foreign countries where the protection is needed.

The plaintiffs have shown that the Nevada defendant was owned by [A.G., a] Lichtenstein corporation. The plaintiffs have also alleged that the numerous organizations throughout the world which are using the name Wells Fargo are related in some way to the Lichtenstein corporation. Therefore, the plaintiffs reason, since the Nevada defendant is somehow remotely related to the foreign organizations using the name Wells Fargo in purely foreign activities, the Nevada defendant is liable for these foreign activities of the foreign relatives because the foreign relatives are infringing the plaintiffs' United States trade-mark. The plaintiffs have not explained how one domestic subsidiary could be responsible for the acts of other foreign subsidiaries, or even how the domestic subsidiary could be held responsible for the acts of the foreign parent corporation [A.G.]. A parent corporation may be liable for the acts of a subsidiary, but a subsidiary is not responsible for the acts of a parent, especially when the parent is a foreign parent and the acts being done by the foreign parent are legal in the foreign country where they are taking place.

But even if the plaintiffs could find a way to make the Nevada defendant liable for the acts of the numerous foreign organizations using the name Wells Fargo, the plaintiffs still would run into the problem of the extraterritorial application of the Lanham Act. If one were to assume arguendo that the Nevada defendant is the identical corporation that is making extensive foreign use of the name Wells Fargo, the Lanham Act would still not apply to the purely foreign activities of the defendant which are legal in those foreign countries. Under the above hypothesis, the plaintiffs would have personal jurisdiction over the defendant for the foreign activities, but that does not mean that the Lanham Act would apply to the foreign activities. * * *

* * * As stated in Callmann, Unfair Competition Trademarks and Monopolies, Third Edition (hereafter Callmann), Volume 4, page 865:

> Classically, the jurisdiction of each sovereign state is limited to its own boundaries. In the first instance, therefore, any challenge to the legality of an act will be determined by reference to the law of the sovereignty within which it was committed. It is an equally classical tradition that jurisdiction over the person can only be asserted if the defendant is subject to the judicial process of the sovereignty. Assuming personal jurisdiction, action normally lies for conduct which occurred in the sovereignty, although, in some instances, action will also lie for an act committed outside its boundaries, if the act would be illegal in both sovereignties or at least where it was effected.
>
> If the law of the place where the wrong was consummated, i.e., where it had its effect, recognizes no cause of action in tort, recovery should not be available in any other jurisdiction. If, on the other hand, a cause of action does lie at the place of the wrong, it should be recognized by the courts of other sovereignties—wherever jurisdiction can be obtained—even if the substantive law of the forum might be different. Thus, if the court has jurisdiction over the parties and the matter in controversy, it should apply the foreign law, unless, of course, such law is inherently offensive to the local public policy.

The three pertinent cases which deal with the question of whether a United States court may enjoin trade-mark infringement occurring in foreign countries are [discussed below].

In [Steele v. The Bulova Watch Co., Inc., 344 U.S. 280, 73 S.Ct. 252, 97 L.Ed. 319 (1952)], defendant Steele was an American citizen who registered the word "Bulova" as a trade-mark in Mexico in his name. Defendant Steele imported watch cases and faces from the United States into Mexico and affixed the name "Bulova" to the watches he assembled in Mexico. While defendant's sales were restricted to Mexico, nevertheless purchasers of defendant's watches brought the watches into the United States and caused injury to the reputation of the plaintiff Bulova Watch Company when these watches were presented for repair under the warranty. The District Court granted a motion to dismiss, the Fifth Circuit reversed, and the Supreme Court affirmed the Fifth Circuit and held that the complaint stated a claim upon which relief could be granted. In reaching this decision, the Supreme Court relied on the facts that defendant Steele was an American citizen and therefore amenable to the powers of the United States even for acts committed abroad, and that acts committed abroad by this United States citizen had a substantial effect on the commerce in the United States. The question of defendant Steele operating under a valid Mexican trade-mark was rendered moot by the cancellation of the Mexican trade-mark by the Bulova Watch Company after the decision of the Fifth Circuit and before the decision of the Supreme Court.

[Vanity Fair Mills Inc. v. T. Eaton Co., Inc., 234 F.2d 633 (2d Cir.1956), cert. den., 352 U.S. 871 (1956)], involved a suit brought in New York by a United States corporation that had registered the trade-mark "Vanity Fair" in the United States, and thereafter sought to enjoin a Canadian corporation from using in Canada the trade-mark "Vanity Fair". The Second Circuit affirmed the dismissal of the complaint by the District Court on the ground that the Court lacked jurisdiction as it related to the Canadian trade-mark. In an extensive discussion of the territoriality of trade-marks and conflict of law principles, the Second Circuit stated that trade-mark laws of one country have no extraterritorial effect, and that in actions for unfair competition the wrong occurs where the act of passing-off takes place.

In reviewing the Lanham Act to determine whether it should be given extraterritorial effect, the *Vanity Fair* court, interpreting *Bulova*, said it was quite obvious that "the rationale of the Court (in Bulova) was so thoroughly based on the power of the United States to govern 'the conduct of *its own citizens* ... in foreign countries *when the rights of other nations or their nationals are not infringed* ', that the absence of one of the above factors (that defendant was a foreigner and the legal owner of the mark in the foreign country) might well be determinative and that the absence of both is certainly fatal". 234 F.2d at 642. (Emphasis supplied.)

The plaintiff in *Vanity Fair*, just like the Bank and Baker in the instant case, also asserted that the International Convention for the protection of Industrial Property (Paris Union), 53 Stat. 1748 (1883, as revised 1934), provided for extraterritoriality of the trade-mark laws of each member nation. The Second Circuit concluded that "the Convention is not premised upon the idea that the trade-mark and related laws of each member nation shall be given extraterritorial application, but on exactly the converse principle that each nation's law shall have only territorial application". 234 F.2d at 640.

The third case, [Ramirez and Feraud Chili Co. v. Las Palmas Food Co., Inc., 146 F.Supp. 594 (S.D.Cal.1956), affirmed per curiam, 245 F.2d 874 (9th Cir.)], which was decided after *Vanity Fair*, involved a fact situation quite similar to the *Bulova* case. The defendant was an American citizen and an American corporation which counterfeited plaintiff's labels in America and shipped the labels to Mexico where they were affixed to canned goods of inferior quality to that of plaintiff's. These canned goods bearing the defendant's counterfeited label were then transported into the United States, thereby harming plaintiff and causing a substantial effect on commerce in the United States. The Ninth Circuit on appeal affirmed the decision of the District Court granting plaintiff's motion for preliminary injunction. The District Court commented that the jurisdictional base in the *Ramirez* case was greater than was evident in the *Bulova* case, since in *Ramirez* the defendants were American citizens and an American company and they carried out infringement of the plaintiff's trade-mark in the United States by counterfeiting the labels in the United States. The *Vanity Fair* case is mentioned in the *Ramirez* decision, and the *Ramirez* court does not reject the statement of the law in the *Vanity Fair* case.

One commentator, Oliver, in 51 Am.Jur.Intl.L. 380 (1957), studied the *Bulova* case and concluded that three factors must be present to justify the jurisdictional extension of that case: (1) Defendant's conduct must have had a substantial effect on United States commerce; (2) defendant must be a United States citizen, as the United States has broad power to regulate the conduct of its citizens in foreign countries; (3) there must be no conflict with trade-mark rights established under the foreign law.

Applying these principles to the present fact situation, the foreign activities of the foreign organizations are completely outside of the jurisdictional extension recognized as proper in the *Bulova* case. The plaintiffs have not shown (1) how the foregoing activities have a substantial effect on United States commerce; in fact, the plaintiffs allege that the injury is to their international good will. As discussed previously, the plaintiffs have not shown (2) that the foreign organizations and the Nevada defendant are in fact the same United States company, other than by the fact that the subsidiaries are of common parentage. Further, the plaintiffs have not shown (3) the requisite lack of conflict with trade-mark rights established under the foreign law; in fact, the plaintiffs admit that the foreign organizations have foreign trade-marks and seek to have this Court eradicate them.

WELLS FARGO & CO. v. WELLS FARGO EXPRESS CO.

United States Court of Appeals, Ninth Circuit, 1977.
556 F.2d 406.

CHOY, J.: A show-down over rights to the storied name "Wells Fargo" is the subject of this trademark infringement and unfair competition action. Two American corporations challenge the use of the name, in the United States and abroad, by two other corporations, one of which is foreign.

In a lengthy opinion, the district court held, among other things, that it lacked personal jurisdiction over the foreign defendant and that those portions of the suit concerning activities in foreign countries should be dismissed for want of subject matter jurisdiction. * * * We vacate the judgment of the district court on these issues and remand.

* * *

At the heart of plaintiffs' allegations is the claim that a group headed by Herman Heymann, a German national who resides in Gibraltar, has deliberately and wrongfully attempted to appropriate the "Wells Fargo" name both in Europe as well as in the United States. Defendant Wells Fargo Express Company, A.G. ("A.G."), a Liechtenstein corporation, was incorporated in 1967 by Heymann to engage in the business of loaning money and is the foreign defendant dismissed by the district court below. In the course of its activities, A.G. had acquired various European and American subsidiaries. While none of the European subsidiaries has been named in the instant action, an American subsidiary, Wells Fargo Express Company ("Express"), is a named defendant.

Express was originally incorporated in Nevada in 1961 for the purpose of providing traveler's checks under the name "Wells Fargo" by K.F. Wilkinson, Sr., a business associate of Heymann, but from that date until 1968 it lay dormant. In 1968, the only capital stock of Express was issued to A.G. for a consideration of $50,000. What business Express has done appears to be in the area of research and development, including the invention and marketing of electronic protective devices.

Express was the only defendant named when plaintiffs filed their original complaint on September 18, 1970, seeking damages as well as injunctive relief. Approximately three weeks later, its name was changed to Modern Research, Inc. On November 2, 1970, A.G. transferred all of its outstanding shares in Express to Albert L. Jacobs, Jr., Express' attorney in this case, for a consideration of $100. * * * A.G. was not named as a defendant until plaintiffs filed their amended complaint of December 22, 1971, seeking the same relief.

[The court discussed the requirements for personal jurisdiction to be secured over A.G. and remanded to the District Court for further proceedings on that issue.]

II.   SUBJECT MATTER JURISDICTION OVER A.G.'S ACTIVITIES

* * *

The district court ruled that the Lanham Act was generally limited to causes of action arising out of American activities. It held that foreign activities could be reached only if the following three factors were present:

> (1) Defendant's conduct must have had a substantial effect on United States commerce; (2) defendant must be a United States citizen, as the United States has broad powers to regulate the conduct of its citizens in foreign countries; (3) there must be no conflict with trademark rights established under the foreign law.

Although it is somewhat unclear, it appears that the district court's test required that all of the factors be present. This conclusion follows from the court's holding that, even if A.G. and Express be viewed as one corporation, the court would decline jurisdiction because A.G.'s "purely foreign activities have no substantial effect on commerce in the United States and there would exist a conflict between the trademark laws of the United States and the trademark laws of foreign countries."

In so holding, the district court carefully analyzed [Bulova, Vanity Fair, and Ramirez,] the three cases which have discussed whether foreign activities may be reached under the Lanham Act. It did not, however, have before it this court's recent decision in Timberlane Lumber Co. v. Bank of America, 549 F.2d 597 (9th Cir.1976, as modified 1977). In *Timberlane*, we set down a "jurisdictional rule of reason" to govern the extraterritorial reach of the Sherman Act which, like the Lanham Act, contains sweeping jurisdictional language.

Our review of the cases on which the district court relied, and the extensive analysis of extraterritoriality undertaken by us in *Timberlane*, lead us to the conclusion that the district court's denial of subject matter jurisdiction under the Lanham Act must be vacated. First, it seems clear that, just as in the interstate context, the extraterritorial coverage of the Lanham Act should be gauged not so much by the locus of the activity sought to be reached—as the district court below held—as by the nature of its effect on that commerce which Congress may regulate. See *Bulova*, 344 U.S. at 286, 73 S.Ct. 252.

Next, although foreign activities must of course have some effect on United States foreign commerce before they can be reached, we disagree with the district court's requirement that that effect must be "substantial." *Bulova* contains no such requirement. And, as we noted in *Timberlane*, since the origins of the "substantiality" test apparently lie in the effort to distinguish between intrastate commerce, which Congress may not regulate as such, and interstate commerce, which it can control, it may be unwise blindly to apply the factor in the area of foreign commerce over which Congress has exclusive authority. See *Timberlane*, 549 F.2d at 612.

Finally, while we agree with the district court that each of the three factors which it cited—degree of effect on United States commerce, the citizenship of defendants and the existence of a conflict with foreign trademark registrations—are indeed relevant to the resolution of the jurisdictional issue, contrary to the apparent view of the district court, the absence of one of the factors is not necessarily determinative of the issue. Rather, each factor is just one consideration to be balanced in the "jurisdictional rule of reason" of comity and fairness adopted by us in *Timberlane*:

> The elements to be weighed include the degree of conflict with foreign law or policy, the nationality or allegiance of the parties and the locations or principal places of business of corporations, the extent to which enforcement by either state can be expected to achieve compliance, the relative significance of effects on the United States as compared with those elsewhere, the extent to which there is explicit purpose to harm or affect American commerce, the foreseeability of such effect, and the relative importance to the violations charged of conduct within the United States as compared with conduct abroad. A court evaluating these factors should identify the potential degree of conflict if American authority is asserted. A difference in law or policy is one likely sore spot, though one which may not always be present. Nationality is another; though foreign governments may have some concern for the treatment of American citizens and businesses residing there, they primarily care about their own nationals. Having assessed the conflict, the court should then determine whether, in the face of it, the contacts and interests of the United States are sufficient to support the exercise of extraterritorial jurisdiction.

549 F.2d at 614–15 (footnotes omitted).

In the instant case, it appears that plaintiffs have been successful in securing the invalidation of some, but not all, foreign registrations held by A.G. and its European subsidiaries. While A.G. and its affiliates are alien corporations, they may indeed be conducting some commercial activity in the United States either themselves or through the Express entity. Moreover, A.G.'s activities may have some effect on both plaintiffs' domestic business and Wells Fargo Bank's heavily-advertised international affairs, and plaintiffs do maintain that A.G.'s scheme has all along been purposeful and deliberate.

We are, however, not prepared to say that some or all of A.G.'s foreign activities may be reached under the Lanham Act. Therefore, we vacate the dismissal of the district court and remand the issue to it for the opportunity to apply the *Timberlane* test to the jurisdictional facts which plaintiffs can establish.

Questions

(1) Assuming that A.G. conducts no activities of significance within the territory of the United States, either directly or through its U.S. subsidiary, how does the application of the *Timberlane* test come out?

(2) Assume, as may have been the case, that the activities of A.G. were carefully calculated to "free ride" on the worldwide reputation of Wells Fargo. Should that be enough for subject matter jurisdiction by itself? Or is it enough that Wells Fargo can, if it so chooses, undertake to register its trademark abroad?

(3) Suppose that in an effort to register abroad, a U.S. company discovers that a foreign firm has already registered the mark. Assume further that the registration does not appear to be coincidence, but rather an obvious effort by a firm providing similar goods or services to free ride on the worldwide reputation of the U.S. firm. Is that fact relevant to the exercise of subject matter jurisdiction under U.S. law? Should it be? Can U.S. domestic law hope to deal with such problems, or is international cooperation needed? What form should that cooperation take?

SUBAFILMS, LTD. v. MGM–PATHE COMMUNICATIONS CO.

United States Court of Appeals, Ninth Circuit, 1994.
24 F.3d 1088.

EN BANC: In this case, we consider the "vexing question" of whether a claim for infringement can be brought under the Copyright Act, 17 U.S.C. § 101 et seq. (1988), when the assertedly infringing conduct consists solely of the authorization within the territorial boundaries of the United States of acts that occur entirely abroad. We hold that such allegations do not state a claim for relief under the copyright laws of the United States.

In 1966, the musical group The Beatles, through Subafilms, Ltd., entered into a joint venture with the Hearst Corporation to produce the animated motion picture entitled "Yellow Submarine" (the "Picture"). Over the next year, Hearst, acting on behalf of the joint venture (the "Producer"), negotiated an agreement with United Artists Corporation ("UA") to distribute and finance the film. Separate distribution and financing agreements were entered into in May, 1967. Pursuant to these agreements, UA distributed the Picture in theaters beginning in 1968 and later on television.

In the early 1980s, with the advent of the home video market, UA entered into several licensing agreements to distribute a number of its films on videocassette. Although one company expressed interest in the Picture, UA refused to license "Yellow Submarine" because of uncertainty over whether home video rights had been granted by the 1967 agreements. Subsequently, in 1987, UA's successor company, MGM/UA Communications Co. ("MGM/UA"), over the Producer's objections, authorized its subsidiary MGM/UA Home Video, Inc. to distribute the Picture for the domestic home video market, and, pursuant to an earlier licensing agreement, notified Warner Bros., Inc. ("Warner") that the Picture had been cleared for international videocassette distribution. Warner, through its wholly owned subsidiary, Warner Home Video, Inc., in turn entered into agreements with third parties for distribution of the Picture on videocassette around the world.

In 1988, Subafilms and Hearst ("Appellees") brought suit against MGM/UA, Warner, and their respective subsidiaries (collectively the "Distributors" or "Appellants"), contending that the videocassette distribution of the Picture, both foreign and domestic, constituted copyright infringement and a breach of the 1967 agreements. The case was tried before a retired California Superior Court Judge acting as a special master. The special master found for Appellees on both claims, and against the Distributors on their counterclaim. * * * [T]he district court adopted all of the special master's factual findings and legal conclusions. Appellees were awarded $2,228,000.00 in compensatory damages, split evenly between the foreign and domestic home video distributions. In addition, Appellees received attorneys' fees and a permanent injunction that prohibited the Distributors from engaging in, or authorizing, any home video use of the Picture.

A panel of this circuit, in an unpublished disposition, affirmed the district court's judgment on the ground that both the domestic and foreign distribution of the Picture constituted infringement under the Copyright Act. * * * With respect to the foreign distribution of the Picture, the panel concluded that it was bound by this court's prior decision in Peter Starr Prod. Co. v. Twin Continental Films, 783 F.2d 1440 (9th Cir.1986), which it held to stand for the proposition that, although " 'infringing actions that take place entirely outside the United States are not actionable' [under the Copyright Act, an] 'act of infringement within the United States' [properly is] alleged where the illegal authorization of international exhibitions takes place in the United States." * * *

We granted Appellants' petition for rehearing en banc to consider whether the panel's interpretation of Peter Starr conflicted with our subsequent decision in Lewis Galoob Toys, Inc. v. Nintendo of Am., Inc., 964 F.2d 965 (9th Cir.1992), cert. denied, 113 S.Ct. 1582 (1993), which held that there could be no liability for authorizing a party to engage in an infringing act when the authorized "party's use of the work would not violate the Copyright Act," id. at 970. * * * Because we conclude that there can be no liability under the United States copyright laws for authorizing an act that itself could not constitute infringement of rights secured by those laws, and that wholly extraterritorial acts of infringement are not cognizable under the Copyright Act, we overrule Peter Starr insofar as it held that allegations of an authorization within the United States of infringing acts that take place entirely abroad state a claim for infringement under the Act. Accordingly, we vacate the panel's decision in part and return the case to the panel for further proceedings.

I. THE MERE AUTHORIZATION OF EXTRATERRITORIAL ACTS OF INFRINGEMENT DOES NOT STATE A CLAIM UNDER THE COPYRIGHT ACT

As the panel in this case correctly concluded, Peter Starr held that the authorization within the United States of entirely extraterritorial acts stated a cause of action under the "plain language" of the Copyright Act. Observing that the Copyright Act grants a copyright owner "the exclusive rights to do and to authorize" any of the activities listed in 17 U.S.C. sec. 106(1)-(5),[1] and that a violation of the "authorization" right constitutes infringement under section 501 of the Act, the *Peter Starr* court reasoned that allegations of an authorization within the United States of extraterritorial conduct that corresponded to the activities listed in section 106 "alleged an act of infringement within the United States," id. at 1442–43. Accordingly, the court determined that the district court erred "in concluding that 'Plaintiff alleged only infringing acts which took place outside of the United States,' " and reversed the district court's dismissal for lack of subject matter jurisdiction.

The *Peter Starr* court accepted, as does this court, that the acts authorized from within the United States themselves could not have constituted infringement under the Copyright Act because "in general, United States copyright laws do not have extraterritorial effect," and therefore, "infringing actions that take place entirely outside the United States are not actionable." * * * The central premise of the *Peter Starr* court, then, was that a party could be held liable as an "infringer" under section 501 of the Act merely for authorizing a third party to engage in acts that, had they been committed within the United States, would have violated the exclusive rights granted to a copyright holder by section 106.

Since *Peter Starr*, however, we have recognized that, when a party authorizes an activity not proscribed by one of the five section 106 clauses, the authorizing party cannot be held liable as an infringer. In *Lewis Galoob*, we rejected the argument that "a party can unlawfully authorize another party to use a copyrighted work even if that party's use of the work would not violate the Copyright Act," *Lewis Galoob*, 964 F.2d at 970, and approved of Professor Nimmer's statement that " 'to the extent that an activity does not violate one of the five enumerated rights [found in 17 U.S.C. sec. 106], authorizing such activity does not constitute copyright infringement.' " * * *

The apparent premise of *Lewis Galoob* was that the addition of the words "to authorize" in the Copyright Act was not meant to create a new form of liability for "authorization" that was divorced completely from the legal consequences of authorized conduct, but was intended to invoke the preexisting doctrine of contributory infringement. * * *

---

1. [original note 4] Section 106 of the Copyright Act provides:

Subject to sections 107 through 120, the owner of copyright under this title has the exclusive rights to do and to authorize any of the following:

(1) to reproduce the copyrighted work in copies or phonorecords;

(2) to prepare derivative works based upon the copyrighted work;

(3) to distribute copies or phonorecords of the copyrighted work to the public by sale or other transfer of ownership, or by rental, lease, or lending;

(4) in the case of literary, musical, dramatic, and choreographic works, pantomimes, and motion pictures and other audiovisual works, to perform the copyrighted work publicly; and

(5) in the case of literary, musical, dramatic, and choreographic works, pantomimes, and pictorial, graphic, or sculptural works ... to display the copyrighted work publicly.

Contributory infringement under the 1909 Act developed as a form of third party liability. Accordingly, there could be no liability for contributory infringement unless the authorized or otherwise encouraged activity itself could amount to infringement. See, e.g., Gershwin Publishing Corp. v. Columbia Artists Management, Inc., 443 F.2d 1159, 1162 (2d Cir.1971) ("One who, with knowledge of the infringing activity, induces, causes or materially contributes to the infringing conduct of another, may be held liable as a 'contributory' infringer."); cf. Deepsouth Packing Co. v. Laitram Corp., 406 U.S. 518 (1972) ("But it is established that there can be no contributory infringement without the fact or intention of a direct infringement. 'In a word, if there is no [direct] infringement of a patent there can be no contributory infringer.'" (quoting Mercoid Corp. v. Mid–Continent Inv. Co., 320 U.S. 661, 677, 88 L.Ed. 376, 64 S.Ct. 268 (1944) (Frankfurter, J., dissenting on other grounds))).

* * *

[T]he addition of the words "to authorize" in the 1976 Act appears best understood as merely clarifying that the Act contemplates liability for contributory infringement. * * * We believe that the *Peter Starr* court erred in not applying this principle to the authorization of acts that cannot themselves be infringing because they take place entirely abroad. As Professor Nimmer has observed:

> Accepting the proposition that a direct infringement is a prerequisite to third party liability, the further question arises whether the direct infringement on which liability is premised must take place within the United States. Given the undisputed axiom that United States copyright law has no extraterritorial application, it would seem to follow necessarily that a primary activity outside the boundaries of the United States, not constituting an infringement cognizable under the Copyright Act, cannot serve as the basis for holding liable under the Copyright Act one who is merely related to that activity within the United States.

3 Nimmer, sec. 12.04[A][3][b], at 12–86 (footnotes omitted).

Appellees resist the force of this logic, and argue that liability in this case is appropriate because, unlike in *Lewis Galoob*, in which the alleged primary infringement consisted of acts that were entirely outside the purview of 17 U.S.C. § 106(1)-(5) (and presumably lawful), the conduct authorized in this case was precisely that prohibited by section 106, and is only uncognizable because it occurred outside the United States. Moreover, they contend that the conduct authorized in this case would have been prohibited under the copyright laws of virtually every nation.

Even assuming arguendo that the acts authorized in this case would have been illegal abroad, we do not believe the distinction offered by Appellees is a relevant one. Because the copyright laws do not apply extraterritorially, each of the rights conferred under the five section 106 categories must be read as extending "no farther than the [United

States'] borders." In light of our above conclusion that the "authorization" right refers to the doctrine of contributory infringement, which requires that the authorized act itself could violate one of the exclusive rights listed in section 106(1)-(5), we believe that "it is simply not possible to draw a principled distinction" between an act that does not violate a copyright because it is not the type of conduct proscribed by section 106, and one that does not violate section 106 because the illicit act occurs overseas. In both cases, the authorized conduct could not violate the exclusive rights guaranteed by section 106. In both cases, therefore, there can be no liability for "authorizing" such conduct.

* * *

II. THE EXTRATERRITORIALITY OF THE COPYRIGHT ACT

Appellees additionally contend that, if liability for "authorizing" acts of infringement depends on finding that the authorized acts themselves are cognizable under the Copyright Act, this court should find that the United States copyright laws do extend to extraterritorial acts of infringement when such acts "result in adverse effects within the United States." Appellees buttress this argument with the contention that failure to apply the copyright laws extraterritorially in this case will have a disastrous effect on the American film industry, and that other remedies, such as suits in foreign jurisdictions or the application of foreign copyright laws by American courts, are not realistic alternatives.

We are not persuaded by Appellees' parade of horribles.[2] More fundamentally, however, we are unwilling to overturn over eighty years of consistent jurisprudence on the extraterritorial reach of the copyright laws without further guidance from Congress.

The Supreme Court recently reminded us that "it is a long-standing principle of American law 'that legislation of Congress, unless a contrary intent appears, is meant to apply only within the territorial jurisdiction of the United States.' " EEOC v. Arabian American Oil Co. (Aramco),

---

2. [original note 10] As Appellants note, breach of contract remedies (such as those pursued in this case) remain available. Moreover, at least one court has recognized that actions under the copyright laws of other nations may be brought in United States courts. See London Film Prods. Ltd. v. Intercontinental Communications, Inc., 580 F.Supp. 47, 48–50 (S.D.N.Y.1984). See generally 2 Goldstein, sec. 16.3, at 683 ("Subject to jurisdictional requirements, a copyright owner may sue an infringer in United States courts even though the only alleged infringement occurred in another country."). But see ITSI, 785 F.Supp. at 866 (discerning, despite *London Film*, "no clear authority for exercising such jurisdiction" (citing David R. Toraya, Note, Federal Jurisdiction Over Foreign Copyright Actions—An Unsolicited Reply to Professor Nimmer, 70 Cornell L.Rev. 1165 (1985)), and stating that "American courts should be reluctant to enter the bramble bush of ascertaining and applying foreign law without an urgent reason to do so"). Finally, although we note that the difficulty of protecting American films abroad is a significant international trade problem, see generally Jan D'Alessandro, Note, A Trade Based Response to Intellectual Property Piracy: A Comprehensive Plan to Aid the Motion Picture Industry, 76 Geo.L.J. 417 (1987), the United States Congress, in acceding to the Berne Convention, has expressed the view that it is through increasing the protection afforded by foreign copyright laws that domestic industries that depend on copyright can best secure adequate protection. See H.R.Rep.No. 609, 100th Cong., 2d Sess. 18–20; S.Rep. 352, 100th Cong., 2d Sess. 2–5, reprinted in 1988 U.S.C.C.A.N., 3706, 3707–10.

499 U.S. 244 (1991) (quoting Foley Bros., Inc. v. Filardo, 336 U.S. 281, 285, 93 L.Ed. 680, 69 S.Ct. 575 (1949)). Because courts must "assume that Congress legislates against the backdrop of the presumption against extraterritoriality," unless "there is 'the affirmative intention of the Congress clearly expressed'" congressional enactments must be presumed to be "'primarily concerned with domestic conditions.'" Id. at 1230.

* * *

Furthermore, we note that Congress chose in 1976 to expand one specific "extraterritorial" application of the Act by declaring that the unauthorized importation of copyrighted works constitutes infringement even when the copies lawfully were made abroad. See 17 U.S.C.A. § 602(a). Had Congress been inclined to overturn the preexisting doctrine that infringing acts that take place wholly outside the United States are not actionable under the Copyright Act, it knew how to do so.

Appellees, however, rely on dicta in a recent decision of the District of Columbia Circuit for the proposition that the presumption against extraterritorial application of U.S. laws may be "overcome" when denying such application would "result in adverse effects within the United States." Environmental Defense Fund, Inc. v. Massey, 300 U.S.App.D.C. 65, 986 F.2d 528, 531 (D.C.Cir.1993) (noting that the Sherman Act, Lanham Act, and securities laws have been applied to extraterritorial conduct). However, the *Massey* court did not state that extraterritoriality would be demanded in such circumstances, but that "the presumption is generally not applied where the failure to extend the scope of the statute to a foreign setting will result in adverse [domestic] effects." Id. at 531 (emphasis added). In each of the statutory schemes discussed by the *Massey* court, the ultimate touchstone of extraterritoriality consisted of an ascertainment of congressional intent; courts did not rest solely on the consequences of a failure to give a statutory scheme extraterritorial application. More importantly, as the *Massey* court conceded, see id. at 532–33, application of the presumption is particularly appropriate when "it serves to protect against unintended clashes between our laws and those of other nations which could result in international discord," *Aramco*, 111 S.Ct. at 1230.

We believe this latter factor is decisive in the case of the Copyright Act, and fully justifies application of the *Aramco* presumption even assuming arguendo that "adverse effects" within the United States "generally" would require a plenary inquiry into congressional intent. At the time that the international distribution of the videocassettes in this case took place, the United States was a member of the Universal Copyright Convention ("UCC"), and, in 1988, the United States acceded to the Berne Convention for the Protection of Literary and Artistic Works ("Berne Conv."). The central thrust of these multilateral treaties is the principle of "national treatment." A work of an American national first generated in America will receive the same protection in a foreign nation as that country accords to the works of its own nationals. See

UCC Art. II; Berne Conv. Art. V. Although the treaties do not expressly discuss choice-of-law rules,[3] it is commonly acknowledged that the national treatment principle implicates a rule of territoriality. See London Film Prods. Ltd. v. Intercontinental Communications, Inc., 580 F.Supp. 47, 50 n. 6 (S.D.N.Y.1984). Indeed, a recognition of this principle appears implicit in Congress's statements in acceding to Berne that "the primary mechanism for discouraging discriminatory treatment of foreign copyright claimants is the principle of national treatment," H.R.Rep.No. 609, 100th Cong., 2d Sess. 43, and that adherence to Berne will require "careful due regard for the [ ]values" of other member nations, id. at 20.

In light of the *Aramco* Court's concern with preventing international discord, we think it inappropriate for the courts to act in a manner that might disrupt Congress's efforts to secure a more stable international intellectual property regime unless Congress otherwise clearly has expressed its intent. The application of American copyright law to acts of infringement that occur entirely overseas clearly could have this effect. Extraterritorial application of American law would be contrary to the spirit of the Berne Convention, and might offend other member nations by effectively displacing their law in circumstances in which previously it was assumed to govern. Consequently, an extension of extraterritoriality might undermine Congress's objective of achieving " 'effective and harmonious' copyright laws among all nations." House Report, supra, at 20. Indeed, it might well send the signal that the United States does not believe that the protection accorded by the laws of other member nations is adequate, which would undermine two other objectives of Congress in joining the convention: "strengthening the credibility of the U.S. position in trade negotiations with countries where piracy is not uncommon" and "raising the likelihood that other nations will enter the Convention." S. Rep. 352, 100th Cong., 2d Sess. 4–5.

Notes and Questions

(1) A patent case analogous to *Subafilms*, cited therein, is Deepsouth Packing Co. v. Laitram Corp., 406 U.S. 518, 92 S.Ct. 1700, 32 L.Ed.2d 273 (1972). In *Deepsouth*, the plaintiff held a "combination patent," covering the assembly of components in a particular fashion. The defendant manufactured the components and exported them separately to be assembled abroad into the patented "combination" product. Because it is only infringement under 35 U.S.C. sec. 271 when one "makes, uses or sells any patented invention, within the United States" the Court found no infringement or contributory infringement. Assuming that the Court construed the statute properly, should it be amended to make clear that such behavior constitutes infringement?

(2) Consider an American firm that purchases copyrighted domestic videotapes and exports them to a parent corporation, which then redistributes them to subsidiaries around the world which copy them and sell them

---

3. [original note 15] The Berne Convention specifies that domestic law governs a work's protection in its country of origin. See Berne Conv. Art. V(3). For acts of infringement that occur in other nations, however, the treaty uses the ambiguous concept of the "law of the country where protection is claimed." Id. Art. V(2).

in foreign markets without paying any royalty. Assume further that it is not worth the time and expense for American copyright holders to pursue actions under foreign copyright law in each of these markets, even though in principle they have that opportunity. Is it clear that the domestic copyright holders have no action under U.S. copyright law? Is that the correct result? Does it matter if the same firm copies the tapes in the United States and direct markets them to foreign consumers? Should it?

(3) What do you think of the "*Aramco* presumption" in this context? Why not "presume" an aggressive construction of the law against acts that impose economic harm on American citizens in the absence of congressional expression to the contrary?

(4) Should the exercise of jurisdiction under U.S. copyright law turn at all on the adequacy of the remedies available abroad? Suppose, for example, that a particular nation does not recognize copyrights in films at all, and its nationals legally copy and export copies of films all over the world? If, by chance, they have assets in the United States that can be reached, should U.S. courts endeavor to reach them?

(B) INFRINGING IMPORTS: THE GRAY MARKET PROBLEM

It has long been settled that the holder of a valid U.S. patent can prevent the importation of infringing merchandise from abroad, even if it is lawfully produced and sold abroad. See Boesch v. Graff, 133 U.S. 697, 10 S.Ct. 378, 33 L.Ed. 787 (1890); Griffin v. Keystone Mushroom Co., 453 F.Supp. 1283 (E.D.Pa.1978). A issue that was much more controversial for many years, and remains so to an extent, concerns the importation of trademarked goods from a foreign country when they are sold abroad legally in accordance with a valid trademark registration or license. Such goods are commonly termed "gray market" imports.

K–MART CORP. v. CARTIER, INC.

Supreme Court of the United States, 1988.
486 U.S. 281, 108 S.Ct. 1811, 100 L.Ed.2d 313.

KENNEDY, J.: A gray-market good is a foreign-manufactured good, bearing a valid United States trademark, that is imported without the consent of the United States trademark holder. These cases present the issue whether the Secretary of the Treasury's regulation permitting the importation of certain gray-market goods, 19 CFR sec. 133.21 (1987), is a reasonable agency interpretation of sec. 526 of the Tariff Act of 1930 (1930 Tariff Act), 19 U.S.C. sec. 1526.

I

[Joined by REHNQUIST, C.J. & WHITE, BLACKMUN, O'CONNOR & SCALIA, JJ.]

A

The gray market arises in any of three general contexts. The prototypical gray-market victim (case 1) is a domestic firm that purchases from an independent foreign firm the rights to register and use the latter's trademark as a United States trademark and to sell its foreign-manufactured products here. Especially where the foreign firm has already registered the trademark in the United States or where the product has already earned a reputation for quality, the right to use that trademark can be very valuable. If the foreign manufacturer could import the trademarked goods and distribute them here, despite having sold the trademark to a domestic firm, the domestic firm would be forced into sharp intrabrand competition involving the very trademark it purchased. Similar intrabrand competition could arise if the foreign manufacturer markets its wares outside the United States, as is often the case, and a third party who purchases them abroad could legally import them. In either event, the parallel importation, if permitted to proceed, would create a gray market that could jeopardize the trademark holder's investment.

The second context (case 2) is a situation in which a domestic firm registers the United States trademark for goods that are manufactured abroad by an affiliated manufacturer. In its most common variation (case 2a), a foreign firm wishes to control distribution of its wares in this country by incorporating a subsidiary here. The subsidiary then registers under its own name (or the manufacturer assigns to the subsidiary's name) a United States trademark that is identical to its parent's foreign trademark. The parallel importation by a third party who buys the goods abroad (or conceivably even by the affiliated foreign manufacturer itself) creates a gray market. Two other variations on this theme occur when an American-based firm establishes abroad a manufacturing subsidiary corporation (case 2b) or its own unincorporated manufacturing division (case 2c) to produce its United States trademarked goods, and then imports them for domestic distribution. If the trademark holder or its foreign subsidiary sells the trademarked goods abroad, the parallel importation of the goods competes on the gray market with the holder's domestic sales.

In the third context (case 3), the domestic holder of a United States trademark authorizes an independent foreign manufacturer to use it. Usually the holder sells to the foreign manufacturer an exclusive right to use the trademark in a particular foreign location, but conditions the right on the foreign manufacturer's promise not to import its trademarked goods into the United States. Once again, if the foreign manufacturer or a third party imports into the United States, the foreign-manufactured goods will compete on the gray market with the holder's domestic goods.

B

* * * Section 526 of the 1930 Tariff Act, 19 U.S.C. sec. 1526, prohibits importing "into the United States any merchandise of foreign manufacture if such merchandise ... bears a trademark owned by a citizen of, or by a corporation or association created or organized within, the United States, and registered in the Patent and Trademark Office by a person domiciled in the United States ..., unless written consent of

the owner of such trademark is produced at the time of making entry." 19 U.S.C. sec. 1526(a).

The regulations implementing section 526 for the past 50 years have not applied the prohibition to all gray-market goods. The Customs Service regulation now in force provides generally that "[f]oreign-made articles bearing a trademark identical with one owned and recorded by a citizen of the United States or a corporation or association created or organized within the United States are subject to seizure and forfeiture as prohibited importations." But the regulation furnishes a "common-control" exception from the ban, permitting the entry of gray-market goods manufactured abroad by the trademark owner or its affiliate:

> (c) Restrictions not applicable. The restrictions ... do not apply to imported articles when:
>
>> (1) Both the foreign and the U.S. trademark or trade name are owned by the same person or business entity; [or]
>>
>> (2) The foreign and domestic trademark or trade name owners are parent and subsidiary companies or are otherwise subject to common ownership or control....

The Customs Service regulation further provides an "authorized-use" exception, which permits importation of gray-market goods where

> (3) [t]he articles of foreign manufacture bear a recorded trademark or trade name applied under authorization of the U.S. owner....

Respondents, an association of United States trademark holders and two of its members, brought suit in Federal District Court in February 1984, seeking both a declaration that the Customs Service regulation, 19 CFR secs. 133.21(c)(1)-(3) (1987), is invalid and an injunction against its enforcement. Coalition to Preserve the Integrity of American Trademarks v. United States, 598 F.Supp. 844 (DC 1984). They asserted that the common-control and authorized-use exceptions are inconsistent with section 526 of the 1930 Tariff Act. Petitioners K–Mart and 47th Street Photo intervened as defendants.

The District Court upheld the Customs Service regulation, but the Court of Appeals reversed, holding that the Customs Service regulation was an unreasonable administrative interpretation of section 526. We granted certiorari to resolve a conflict among the Courts of Appeals.

A majority of this Court now holds that the common-control exception of the Customs Service regulation, section 133.21(c)(1)-(2) is consistent with section 526. See opinion of Brennan, J., below. A different majority, however, holds that the authorized-use exception, section 133.21(c)(3), is inconsistent with section 526. See opinion of Scalia, J., infra. We therefore affirm the Court of Appeals in part and reverse in part.

II

* * *

B

[Joined by WHITE, J.]

I conclude that subsections (c)(1) and (c)(2) of the Customs Service regulation are permissible constructions designed to resolve statutory ambiguities. All Members of the Court are in agreement that the agency may interpret the statute to bar importation of gray-market goods in what we have denoted case 1 and to permit the imports under case 2a. See opinions of Brennan, J. and Scalia, J. As these writings state, "owned by" is sufficiently ambiguous, in the context of the statute, that it applies to situations involving a foreign parent, which is case 2a. This ambiguity arises from the inability to discern, from the statutory language, which of the two entities involved in case 2a can be said to "own" the United States trademark if, as in some instances, the domestic subsidiary is wholly owned by its foreign parent.

A further statutory ambiguity contained in the phrase "merchandise of foreign manufacture," suffices to sustain the regulations as they apply to cases 2b and 2c. This ambiguity parallels that of "owned by," which sustained case 2a, because it is possible to interpret "merchandise of foreign manufacture" to mean (1) goods manufactured in a foreign country, (2) goods manufactured by a foreign company, or (3) goods manufactured in a foreign country by a foreign company. Given the imprecision in the statute, the agency is entitled to choose any reasonable definition and to interpret the statute to say that goods manufactured by a foreign subsidiary or division of a domestic company are not goods "of foreign manufacture."

C

[Joined by REHNQUIST, C.J., & BLACKMUN, O'CONNOR & SCALIA, JJ.]

Subsection (c)(3) of the regulation, however, cannot stand. The ambiguous statutory phrases that we have already discussed, "owned by" and "merchandise of foreign manufacture," are irrelevant to the proscription contained in subsection (3) of the regulation. This subsection of the regulation denies a domestic trademark holder the power to prohibit the importation of goods made by an independent foreign manufacturer where the domestic trademark holder has authorized the foreign manufacturer to use the trademark. Under no reasonable construction of the statutory language can goods made in a foreign country by an independent foreign manufacturer be removed from the purview of the statute.

BRENNAN, J., dissenting, with whom MARSHALL and STEVENS, JJ., join, and with whom WHITE, J., joins as to Part IV, concurring in part and dissenting in part:

* * * There is no dispute that section 526 protects the trademark holder in the first of the three gray-market contexts identified by the Court—the prototypical gray-market situation in which a domestic firm purchases from an independent foreign firm the rights to register and use in the United States a foreign trademark (case 1). The dispute in

this litigation centers almost exclusively around the second context, involving a foreign manufacturer that is in some way affiliated with the United States trademark holder, whether the trademark holder is a subsidiary of (case 2a), the parent of (case 2b), or the same as (case 2c), the foreign manufacturer. The Customs Service's common-control exception denudes the trademark holder of section 526's protection in each of the foregoing cases. I concur in the Court's judgment that the common-control exception is consistent with section 526, [though I reach this conclusion for different reasons]. * * *

Also at issue, although the parties and amici give it short shrift, is the third context (case 3), in which the domestic firm authorizes an independent foreign manufacturer to use its trademark abroad. The Customs Service's authorized-use exception deprives the trademark holder of section 526's protection in such a situation. For reasons set forth in Part IV of this opinion, I dissent from the Court's judgment that the authorized-use exception is inconsistent with section 526.

I

* * *

The most blatant hint that Congress did not intend to extend section 526's protection to affiliates of foreign manufacturers (case 2) is the provision's protectionist, almost jingoist, flavor. Its structure bespeaks an intent, characteristic of the times, to protect only domestic interests. A foreign manufacturer that imports its trademarked products into the United States cannot invoke section 526 to prevent third parties from competing in the domestic market by buying the trademarked goods abroad and importing them here: The trademark is not "registered in the Patent and Trademark Office." The same manufacturer cannot protect itself against parallel importation merely by registering its trademark in the United States: It is not "a person domiciled in the United States." Nor can the manufacturer insulate itself by hiring a United States domiciliary to register the trademark: The owner is not "organized within ... the United States." For the same reason, it will not even suffice for the foreign manufacturer to incorporate a subsidiary here to register the trademark on the parent's behalf, if the foreign parent still owns the trademark.

The barriers that Congress erected seem calculated to serve no purpose other than to reserve exclusively to domestic, not foreign, interests the extraordinary protection that section 526 provides. But they are fragile barriers indeed if a foreign manufacturer might bypass them by the simple device of incorporating a shell domestic subsidiary and transferring to it a single asset—the United States trademark. Such a reading of section 526 seems entirely at odds with the protectionist sentiment that inspired the provision. If a foreign manufacturer could insulate itself so easily from the competition of parallel imports, much of § 526's limiting language would be pointless.

The language of section 526 can reasonably be read, as the Customs Service has, to avoid such an anomaly. Section 526 defines neither "owned by" nor "of foreign manufacture," and both phrases admit of considerable ambiguity when applied to affiliates of foreign manufacturers. More specifically, in each of the disputed gray-market cases involving a domestic affiliate of a foreign manufacturer (case 2), it cannot be confidently discerned either which entity owns the trademark or whether the goods in question are "of foreign manufacture."

* * *

IV

I turn now to my small area of disagreement with the Court's judgment—the Court's conclusion that the authorized-use exception is inconsistent with the plain language of section 526. In my view, section 526 does not unambiguously protect from gray-market competition a United States trademark owner who authorizes the use of its trademark abroad by an independent manufacturer (case 3).

Unlike the variations of corporate affiliation in case 2, the ambiguity in section 526, admittedly, is not immediately apparent in case 3. In that situation, the casual reader of the statute might suppose that the domestic firm still "own[s]" its trademark. Any such supposition as to the meaning of "owned by," however, bespeaks stolid anachronism not solid analysis. It follows only from an understanding of trademark law that established itself long after the 1922 enactment and 1930 reenactment of section 526. * * *

When section 526 was before Congress, the prevailing law held that a trademark's sole purpose was to identify for consumers the product's physical source or origin. See, E.G., Macmahan Pharmacal Co. v. Denver Chemical Mfg. Co., 113 F. 468, 475 (C.A.8 1901). "Under this early 'source theory' of protection, trademark licensing was viewed as philosophically impossible, since licensing meant that the mark was being used by persons not associated with the real manufacturing 'source' in a strict, physical sense of the word." 1 McCarthy, Trademarks and Unfair Competition, at 826. * * *

Nor was it at all obvious then that a trademark owner could authorize the use of its trademark in one geographic area by selling it along with business and goodwill, while retaining ownership of the trademark in another geographic area. * * *

Not until the 1930's did a trend develop approving of trademark licensing—so long as the licensor controlled the quality of the licensee's products—on the theory that a trademark might also serve the function of identifying product quality for consumers. 1 McCarthy, Trademarks and Unfair Competition, at 827–829. And not until the passage of the Lanham Trade–Mark Act in 1946 did that trend become the rule. Similarly, it was not until well after section 526's enactment that it became clear that a trademark owner could assign rights in a particular territory along with goodwill, while retaining ownership in another distinct territory.

Manifestly, the legislators who chose the term "owned by" viewed trademark ownership differently than we view it today. Any prescient legislator who could have contemplated that a trademark owner might license the use of its trademark would almost certainly have concluded that such a transaction would divest the licensor not only of the benefit of section 526's importation prohibition, but of all trademark protection; and anyone who gave thought to the possibility that a trademark holder might assign rights to use its trademark, along with business and goodwill, to an unrelated manufacturer in another territory had good reason to expect the same result. At the very least, it seems to me plain that Congress did not address case 3 any more clearly than it addressed case 2a, 2b, or 2c. To hold otherwise is to wrench statutory words out of their legislative and historical context and treat legislation as no more than a "collection of English words" rather than "a working instrument of government...." United States v. Dotterweich, 320 U.S. 277, 280 (1943).

Justice Scalia's assertion that the foregoing analysis of case 3 is not based on the "resolution of textual 'ambiguity,'" depends on the proposition that an ancient statute is not ambiguous—and judges can never inform their interpretation with reference to legislative purpose—merely because the scope of its language has, by some fortuitous development, expanded to embrace situations that its drafters never anticipated. The proposition is unexceptionable where the postenactment development does not implicate the purpose of the statute, [but] is fallacious, however, when the postenactment development does implicate the statute's purpose.

* * *

Particularly in light of that longstanding agency interpretation, I would uphold the authorized-use exception as reasonable.

SCALIA, J., concurring in part and dissenting in part (joined by REHNQUIST, C.J. & BLACKMUN and O'CONNOR, JJ.):

I agree with the Court's analytic approach to this matter, and with its conclusion that subsection (c)(3) of the regulation is not a permissible construction. I therefore join Parts I, II–A, and II–C of the Court's opinion. In my view, however, subsections (c)(1) and (c)(2) of the regulation are also in conflict with the clear language of section 526(a).

* * *

The Court observes that the statutory phrase "owned by" is ambiguous when applied to domestic subsidiaries of foreign corporations (case 2a). With this much I agree. It may be reasonable for some purposes to say that a trademark nominally owned by a domestic subsidiary is "owned by" its foreign parent corporation. This lawsuit would be different if the Customs Service regulation at issue here did no more than resolve this arguable ambiguity, by providing that a domestic subsidiary of a foreign parent could not claim the protection of section 526(a). In fact, however, that has never been asserted to be the theory of the regulation, and is assuredly not its only, or even its principal, effect. The authority to clarify an ambiguity in a statute is not the authority to alter even its unambiguous applications, and section 526(a) unambiguously encompasses most of the situations that the regulation purports to exclude.

Thus, the regulation excludes from section 526(a)'s import prohibition products bearing a domestic trademark that have been manufactured abroad by the trademark owner (case 2c), or by the trademark owner's subsidiary (case 2b). But the statutory requirement that the trademark be "owned by" a United States citizen or corporation is unambiguous with respect to these two cases. A parent corporation may or may not be said to "own" the assets owned by its subsidiary, but no matter how that ambiguity is resolved it is impossible to conclude that a trademark owned by a United States corporation and applied abroad either by the corporation or its foreign subsidiary is "owned by" anyone other than a United States corporation.

Five Members of the Court (hereinafter referred to as "the majority") assert, however, that the regulation's treatment of situations 2b and 2c is attributable to the resolution of yet another ambiguity in section 526(a). The statute excludes only merchandise "of foreign manufacture," which the majority says might mean "manufactured by a foreigner" rather than "manufactured in a foreign country." I think not. Words, like syllables, acquire meaning not in isolation but within their context. While looking up the separate word "foreign" in a dictionary might produce the reading the majority suggests, that approach would also interpret the phrase "I have a foreign object in my eye" as referring, perhaps, to something from Italy. The phrase "of foreign manufacture" is a common usage, well understood to mean "manufactured abroad." Hence, when statutes and regulations intend to describe the universe of manufactured goods, they do not refer to goods "of foreign or citizen manufacture," but to goods "of foreign or domestic manufacture." See, E.G., 19 CFR sec. 133.21(a)(1987). I know of no instance in which anyone, anywhere, has used the phrase with the meaning the majority suggests—and the majority provides no example.

In the particular context of the present statute, however, the majority's suggested interpretation is not merely unusual but inconceivable, since it would have the effect of eliminating section 526(a)'s protection for some trademark holders in case 1—which contains what the Court describes as the "proto-typical" gray-market victims. Not uncommonly a foreign trademark owner licenses an American firm to use its trademark in the United States and also licenses one or more other American firms to use the trademark in other countries. In this situation, the firm with the United States license could not keep out gray-market imports manufactured abroad by the other American firms, since, under the majority's interpretation, the goods would not be "of foreign manufacture." Thus, to save the regulation, the majority proposes an interpretation that undermines even the core of the statute.

* * *

If it were, as Justice Kennedy believes, "the current interpretation of the regulations we are sustaining," one would expect there to be in place some mechanism that enables the Customs Service to identify goods that are not only manufactured abroad but also (as the majority's interpretation requires) manufactured by foreigners. Acquiring this knowledge cannot be easy, since the importer of merchandise will often not know the manufacturer's identity, much less its corporate pedigree. International corporate ownership, not a matter of public record, is often a closely guarded secret. Yet although there is in place a regulation requiring the country of origin (i.e., whether "manufactured abroad") to be plainly indicated on all imports, see 19 CFR secs. 134.0–134.55 (1987), there is none requiring the nationality of the manufacturer to be stated. After today's decision, of course, the Customs Service, if it would not rather amend its regulations, will presumably have to devise means to enforce what we say it has been enforcing.

* * *

I find it extraordinary for this Court, on the theory of deferring to an agency's judgment, to burden that agency with an interpretation that it not only has never suggested, but that is contrary to ordinary usage, to the purposes of the statute, and to the interpretation the agency appears to have applied consistently for half a century.

Notes and Questions

(1) Are "gray market" imports good or bad in general? On the one hand, they increase competition and tend to lower prices to consumers. Some have argued, therefore, that restrictions on gray market imports are anti-competitive. On the other hand, they injure the holder of the domestic trademark, which may have an adverse effect on its incentives to maintain quality. Likewise, the imports may "free ride" on advertising and service networks of the domestic trademark holder, thus reducing the returns to such activities and discouraging them. How can one begin to decide which effects are more important? Might the remedy of exclusion be too severe? To what extent is it sufficient or insufficient to require the foreign-made product to disclose its foreign origin so that, for example, consumers will not mistakenly buy it if it is inferior and domestic service facilities can avoid providing uncompensated warranty service? This resolution of the problem is not unfamiliar—U.S. consumers can purchase cameras covered by a Nikon, U.S.A. warranty, for example, or can pay a slightly lower price for an ostensibly identical camera from Japan without the opportunity to obtain warranty service in the United States. Some of the issues are discussed in Michael Knoll, Gray–Market Imports: Causes, Consequences and Responses, 18 L. & Pol.Intl.Bus. 145 (1986).

(2) Reflect briefly on the question of why the gray market problem cannot be adequately addressed by contract. When gray market importation

occurs without the consent of the domestic trademark owner, it often occurs because the foreign trademark owner has sold goods to an unaffiliated third party, who then resells them in the domestic market. Thus, even if contractual solutions might be devised to govern the behavior of licensees, licensors and affiliates, resale by third-party purchasers is at issue as well. Yet, might not contractual solutions sometimes be viable there, at least when the third-party purchaser is buying in bulk quantities sufficient to resell substantial numbers of units abroad?

(3) Do not confuse gray market goods with unlicensed goods manufactured to copy or simulate a valid U.S. trademark. Here, exclusion has been held proper notwithstanding circumstances that fall within the common control exceptions discussed in *K-Mart*. See Lever Bros. Co. v. United States, 981 F.2d 1330 (D.C.Cir.1993).

(C) INFRINGING IMPORTS: THE ADMINISTRATIVE REMEDY

The cases above arose in federal court, which provides one forum for enforcing the rights of U.S. and foreign nationals that are cognizable under federal statutes. But U.S. law has long provided an additional, administrative forum in which domestic firms can seek relief from imports that infringe their intellectual property rights—Section 337 of the 1974 Trade Act.[4]

On its face, Section 337 applies to any form of "unfair competition," though in practice it is mainly employed in intellectual property disputes. Relief from imports that infringe valid and enforceable patents, copyrights, trademarks, or semiconductor mask works does not require a showing of injury under Section 337 after the 1988 Trade Act, merely a showing that a domestic industry relating to the imported articles "exists or is in the process of being established."[5] Other forms of "unfair competition," however, are only remediable under Section 337 if they are likely to destroy or "substantially injure" a domestic industry, prevent its establishment, or restrain or monopolize trade.[6]

A Section 337 proceeding begins with the filing of a complaint by an aggrieved party.[7] The ITC then decides whether to initiate an investigation, and if it does, the respondent must file a written answer. The case is assigned to an ITC administrative law judge (ALJ), who supervises discovery, rules on any motions and eventually issues a decision in the case. There are broad provisions for discovery, including the use of oral depositions, written interrogatories and inspection of documents. An ITC staff attorney is assigned to the case as well (the Investigating Attorney, or IA). Following discovery, a hearing is held before the ALJ, who then provides an initial determination to the ITC. The initial determination becomes the Commission's determination unless the Commission orders a review of it in its entirety or with respect to particular issues. The Commission is required to dispose of cases "at the earliest practicable

4. 19 U.S.C.A. sec. 1337.

5. 19 U.S.C.A. sec. 1337(a)(1)(B)-(D), (a)(2).

6. 19 U.S.C.A. sec. 1337(a)(1)(A).

7. The general procedures applicable to Section 337 cases are set out in 19 CFR pt. 210 (1993).

time." The President then has 60 days to exercise his right to override the Commission decision.[8]

A showing that Section 337 has been violated does not entitle the complainant to relief. The Commission may determine that relief is not in the national interest after examining the public health and welfare, competitive conditions, and effects on consumers.[9] The President also has broad discretion to overrule relief "for policy reasons."[10]

Subject to these constraints, the ITC is authorized to grant two types of relief. First, it may issue an order excluding from entry into the United States any article found to be imported in violation of Section 337, to be enforced by Customs.[11] It may also issue such an exclusion order on a preliminary basis during the course of the investigation, although importation will be permitted on payment of a bond.[12] Under ITC practice, exclusion orders may be "general," addressed to all importations that may violate Section 337, or may be "limited," addressed only to the products of the respondents in the investigation. Second, the Commission may order a person violating Section 337 to cease and desist.[13] Violations of such an order may be punished by a fine equal to the greater of $10,000 a day or the domestic value of the goods entered or sold on such day in violation of the order. Appeals of ITC decisions are made to the U.S. Court of Appeals for the Federal Circuit.[14]

As discussed in Section 12.2, prior procedures under Section 337 could afford considerable advantages to a plaintiff relative to a proceeding in Federal court, and these advantages were found by a GATT panel to deny national treatment. But the Uruguay Round implementing legislation made a number of changes designed to achieve GATT conformity. *Inter alia*, time limits for the completion of investigations were abolished; respondents were given the right to file counterclaims (removed to Federal court); parallel proceedings in Federal court could be stayed at the request of a respondent; and statutory limitations upon general exclusion orders were enacted. Whether these changes will suffice in the view of any future GATT panel remains to be seen.

The substantive issues that arise in Section 337 cases span the issues that arise in ordinary patent, trademark, copyright, and other unfair competition litigation. Hence, we make no effort to provide a survey here, but focus briefly on certain issues relating to remedy, to the "public interest," and to the "industry" requirement of Section 337 cases.

8. 19 U.S.C.A. sec. 1337(j)(2).
9. 19 U.S.C.A. sec. 1337(d).
10. 19 U.S.C.A. sec. 1337(j)(2).
11. 19 U.S.C.A. sec. 1337(d).

12. 19 U.S.C.A. sec. 1337(e).
13. 19 U.S.C.A. sec. 1337(f).
14. 19 U.S.C.A. sec. 1337(f)(2).

CERTAIN BATTERY–POWERED RIDE–ON TOY VEHICLES AND COMPONENTS THEREOF

United States International Trade Commission, 1991[15]

On May 15, 1990, Kransco filed a complaint with the Commission under section 337 of the Tariff Act of 1930. The complaint alleged that Chien Ti Enterprise Co., Ltd. ("Chien Ti"), a Taiwanese corporation that manufactures and exports children's toys, was violating section 337 by exporting to the United States rideable toy vehicles that infringe claims of five U.S. patents owned by Kransco.

* * *

On December 5, 1990, the presiding administrative law judge (ALJ) issued an initial determination (ID) granting the motion of complainant Kransco for summary determination. The ID concluded that a violation of section 337 had been established in the importation of certain battery-powered ride-on toy vehicles and components thereof by reason of infringement of the five patents at issue.

* * *

(1) We have determined that there has been a sale for importation of infringing battery-powered ride-on toy vehicles by respondent Chien Ti. Accordingly, we affirm the ID's conclusion that a violation of section 337 has been established.

(2) We have issued a general exclusion order directed to products that infringe the '666 or '009 design patents and a limited exclusion order directed to products that infringe the claims at issue of the '958,-'263, or '646 product patents.

(3) We have concluded that the public interest considerations articulated in section 337(d) do not preclude issuance of relief in this investigation.

* * *

Kransco's complaint is based on section 337(a)(1)(B)(i). That section proscribes:

> The importation into the United States, the sale for importation, or the sale within the United States after importation by the owner, importer, or consignee, of articles that infringe a valid and enforceable United States patent or a valid and enforceable United States copyright registered under Title 17, United States Code.

The sole issue under review is whether the "importation" requirement of the above provision has been satisfied. We conclude that importation has been demonstrated, because the record shows that Chien Ti made numerous shipments of infringing vehicles to the United States through a trading company, Qunsan Enterprise Co., Ltd. ("Qunsan").

The pertinent facts concerning the Qunsan shipments are not in dispute. Chien Ti itself admitted that it has sold its Jeep and Racer toy

15. Investigation No. 337–TA–314,
USITC Pub. No. 2420.

vehicle models to Qunsan and that Qunsan then exported these models to the United States. Chien Ti additionally sent a facsimile to J & L Meyer, Inc. on December 21, 1989, stating that it knew that its toys were being exported to Miami, San Francisco, and Long Beach, among other places.

The ALJ correctly found from this record that "Chien Ti knew that toy vehicles it sold to Qunsan were exported to the United States," but did not determine the legal significance of this finding. The statute itself, however, expressly states that section 337 proscribes "the sale for importation," as well as importation, by the "owner, importer or consignee" of infringing articles. Indeed, longstanding Commission precedent holds that a section 337 violation can be found when a foreign manufacturer sells infringing goods to a foreign trading company with the knowledge that the goods will subsequently be exported to the United States, even if the manufacturer does not itself export or deal directly with U.S. importers.

Consequently, the ALJ's finding that Chien Ti knew that Qunsan was exporting to the United States infringing Jeep and Racer model toy vehicles compels the legal conclusion that section 337's importation requirement has been satisfied with respect to all five Kransco patents at issue. In light of this conclusion and the ID's rulings on validity, infringement, and domestic industry which we determined not to review, we determine that a violation of section 337 has been established.

* * *

Complainant Kransco has requested issuance of a general exclusion order covering each of the five patents at issue. The [ITC investigating attorney] IA, by contrast, supports issuance of a general exclusion order with respect to the '666 and '009 patents and a limited exclusion order with respect to the three product patents.

In considering whether to issue a general exclusion order, we have traditionally balanced complainant's interest in obtaining complete relief against the public interest in avoiding the disruption of legitimate trade that such relief may cause. Thus we determined in Certain Airless Paint Spray Pumps, Inv. No. 337–TA–90, USITC Pub. 1199 at 18 (May 1981), that a complainant seeking a general exclusion order must prove "both a widespread pattern of unauthorized use of its patented invention and certain business conditions from which one might reasonably infer that foreign manufacturers other than the respondents to the investigation may attempt to enter the U.S. market with infringing articles." Factors relevant to demonstrating whether there is a "widespread pattern of unauthorized use" include:

(a) a Commission determination of unauthorized importation into the United States of infringing articles by numerous foreign manufacturers;

(b) the pendency of foreign infringement suits based upon foreign patents which correspond to the domestic patent at issue;

(c) other evidence which demonstrates a history of unauthorized foreign use of the patented invention.

Factors relevant to showing whether "certain business conditions" exist include:

(a) an established market for the patented product in the U.S. market and conditions of the world market;

(b) the availability of marketing and distribution networks in the United States for potential foreign manufacturers;

(c) the cost to foreign entrepreneurs of building a facility capable of producing the patented article;

(d) the number of foreign manufacturers whose facilities could be retooled to produce the patented article; or

(e) the cost to foreign manufacturers of retooling their facility to produce the patented article.

With respect to the criterion of "widespread pattern of unauthorized use," the record contains information suggesting that there is a pattern of use of the design patents at issue. Kransco has submitted documents purporting to show that five foreign manufacturers, in addition to Chien Ti, produce vehicles alleged to infringe the '666 patent, and that two foreign manufacturers, in addition to Chien Ti, produce vehicles that arguably infringe the '009 patent.

By contrast, Kransco has failed to submit evidence purporting to show even a pattern of use for any of the three product patents at issue. With respect to the '958 patent, Kransco has submitted evidence indicating merely that one non-respondent manufacturer produces a vehicle that allegedly infringes the patent.

The record contains considerable information indicating the existence of business conditions that would encourage new foreign entrants to enter the U.S. Market. Confidential information concerning sales revenue and volume furnished by Kransco indicates that there is an established market in the United States for the products utilizing the patents at issue. Additionally, marketing and distribution networks in the United States appear to be available for potential importers and foreign manufacturers of toy vehicles. Kransco has submitted deposition testimony of a toy distributor, who has no apparent pecuniary interest in the outcome of this investigation, indicating that foreign toy manufacturers have ready access to the U.S. market. Moreover, as previously discussed, numerous foreign manufacturers already produce allegedly infringing vehicles, and, according to Kransco, the plants of over ten additional foreign manufacturers could be retooled to produce such vehicles.

With respect to the two design patents at issue, complainant Kransco's strong showing with respect to the "business conditions" prong of the *Spray Pumps* test is not matched for the "widespread pattern of unauthorized use" prong. We have nonetheless determined to issue a general exclusion order with respect to the '666 and '009 design patents for four reasons. First, Kransco has shown that numerous manufacturers worldwide produce vehicles that appear to infringe the design patents, and that many others have the potential for manufacturing infringing vehicles. Second, Kransco's fears of imminent importation of infringing vehicles manufactured by entities other than respondent Chien Ti appear to be well-founded in light of the representations of TCV Industrial Co., Ltd., that its Jeep-like toy vehicles—which allegedly utilize the design of the '666 patent—will soon be marketed in the United States. Consequently, issuance of a limited exclusion order may be insufficient to accord Kransco complete relief against infringing imports. Third, issuing a general exclusion order in this investigation would not subvert the Commission's policy of "encourag[ing] complainants to include in an investigation all those foreign manufacturers which it believes have entered, or are on the verge of entering, the domestic market with infringing articles." There is nothing in the record to suggest that any manufacturer other than Chien Ti had entered or was about to enter the U.S. market with infringing vehicles at the time this investigation was instituted. Fourth, we do not believe that a general exclusion order limited to the design patents will be difficult for the Customs Service to administer, or will unduly restrain trade. Application of the standard for finding legal infringement of a design patent, which, as noted, concerns the similarity of designs in the eyes of an ordinary observer, does not require technical expertise or specialized equipment.

A number of the considerations militating in favor of issuance of a general exclusion order with respect to the design patents are not applicable to the three product patents at issue. Kransco has not made any showing of a "widespread pattern of unauthorized use" with respect to two of the product patents, and its showing with respect to the '958 patent is not strong. Consequently, we believe that the potential that a limited exclusion order will accord Kransco incomplete relief is much less significant with these patents. Buttressing this belief is testimony from Kransco's own official indicating that the vehicles' design, as opposed to their construction or mechanical systems, is a prime reason for their popularity with consumers. We consequently have issued a limited exclusion order with respect to the three product patents at issue.

* * *

Section 337 instructs the Commission to consider the effect of any remedy "upon the public health and welfare, competitive conditions in the United States economy, the production of like or directly competitive articles in the United States, and United States consumers." The legislative history of this provision, added to section 337 by the Trade Act of 1974, indicates that the Commission should decline to issue relief when the adverse effect on the public interest would be greater than the interest in protecting the patent holder.[16]

16. [original note 27] See S.Rep. 1298,   93d Cong., 2d Sess. 197 (1974). The Com-

We do not believe that either of these concerns is implicated in the instant investigation. We agree with Kransco and the IA that an adequate supply of ride-on toy vehicles is not necessary to ensure public health, safety, or welfare in the United States. In any event, the record indicates that an adequate supply of such vehicles will exist even upon issuance of an exclusion order. Consequently, we conclude that the public interest does not preclude granting relief.

CERTAIN PLASTIC ENCAPSULATED INTEGRATED CIRCUITS

United States International Trade Commission, 1992[17]

On July 9, 1990, Texas Instruments Incorporated (TI) filed a complaint under section 337 of the Tariff Act of 1930 (19 U.S.C. § 1337) alleging that respondents * * * had imported and sold within the United States certain plastic encapsulated integrated circuits manufactured by a [patented] process. * * *

On October 15, 1991, the presiding administrative law judge (ALJ) issued a final initial determination (ID) finding a violation of section 337 on the ground that certain of respondents' imported plastic encapsulated integrated circuits were manufactured by a process covered by [the] patent. * * *

After review, the Commission affirmed the ALJ's determination that all respondents had violated section 337. [In so doing, the ITC reversed an ALJ finding that "claim 17" of the patent had not been infringed, and issued a limited exclusion order and cease and desist orders.]

* * *

C. DOMESTIC INDUSTRY

The Omnibus Trade and Competitiveness Act of 1988 (OTCA) amended section 337 of the Tariff Act of 1930 to specify the types of unfair acts covered by that section.[18] As amended, section 337 explicitly prohibits the importation and sale of imported articles that—

(i) infringe a valid and enforceable United States patent . . . ; or

mission has declined to grant relief on public interest grounds in only three cases. See Certain Fluidized Supporting Apparatus, Inv. No. 337–TA–182/188, USITC Pub. 1667 (October 1984) (temporary relief denied when domestic industry could not provide adequate supply of medical product useful to public health); Certain Inclined–Field Acceleration Tubes, Inv. No. 337–TA–67, USITC Pub. 1119 (December 1980) (relief denied when exclusion order would have stifled nuclear structure research programs in public interest); Certain Automatic Crankpin Grinders, Inv. No. 337–TA–60, USITC Pub. 1022 (December 1979) (relief denied when domestic industry could not provide adequate supply of product needed for automobiles to satisfy federal energy efficiency requirements).

17. Investigation No. 337–TA–315, USITC Pub. No. 2574.

18. [original note 29] Under the amended statute, there is no requirement to show injury to the domestic industry in cases involving alleged infringement of patents (including process patents), copyrights, registered trademarks, or mask works. 19 U.S.C. sec. 1337(a)(1)(B).

(ii) are made, produced, processed, or mined under, or by means of, a process covered by the claims of a valid and enforceable United States patent.

In order to prove a violation of section 337 in a patent-based case, a complainant must show that an industry exists in the United States practicing the patent. Specifically, there can be a violation of section 337—

only if an industry in the United States, relating to the articles protected by the patent, . . . exists or is in the process of being established. 19 U.S.C. sec. 1337(a)(2).

In cases involving alleged infringement of statutory intellectual property rights, section 337(a)(3) defines domestic industry as follows:

(a)(3) . . . an industry in the United States shall be considered to exist if there is in the United States, with respect to the articles protected by the patent, copyright, [registered] trademark, or mask work concerned—

> (A) significant investment in plant and equipment;
>
> (B) significant employment of labor or capital; or
>
> (C) substantial investment in its exploitation, including engineering, research and development, or licensing.

19 U.S.C. sec. 1337(a)(3). Thus, this section 337 investigation requires a determination as to whether a domestic industry exists, that is, whether the complainant is exploiting or practicing the patent in controversy.

The ALJ applied the domestic industry criteria set out in section 337(a)(3) to find that TI's domestic activities are sufficient to demonstrate the existence of a domestic industry. He found that TI practices the patent at its domestic facility, and that TI is specifically practicing claims 12 and 14 of the * * * patent at its domestic facility. He based this finding on the agreement among witnesses that TI and the respondents use the same or similar processes, coupled with his finding that respondents use an encapsulation process covered by claims 12 and 14. Because the ALJ found no infringement of claim 17, he did not make a finding regarding TI's practice of claim 17.

As noted, the parties agree that the types of plastic encapsulated integrated circuits likely to have all conductors parallel to each other are those with low-pin counts. Respondents argue that because TI did not introduce into evidence any lead frames produced in the United States which include parallel leads and "because TI has never manufactured low-pin count integrated circuits (i.e. less than 8 leads) at its domestic facility," TI does not practice claim 17. TI admits that it is does not presently manufacture low-pin count package types at its domestic facility. * * *

In addressing domestic industry, we are mindful that the statute requires only that any one of the three criteria set out in section 337(a)(3) be met in order to satisfy the domestic industry requirement.

In this respect, we note that we have adopted, inter alia, the ALJ's factual findings and conclusions regarding the existence of a domestic industry as evidenced by TI's engineering and research and development efforts. As the ALJ found, "it is difficult in situations such as that presented in this investigation to draw a bright line dividing those projects which exploit the patent at issue from those which to not." Likewise, it is equally, if not more difficult to segregate those projects that exploit claims 12 and 14 of the patent, but not claim 17.

Given the close similarity and overlap among these three claims, there is no bright line separating the research and development efforts relating to one of these claims from those relating to the others.

We accordingly find that TI's research and development efforts represent a substantial investment in exploitation of all claims found infringed, including claim 17. By virtue of this finding, it is unnecessary to decide specifically whether the claims that are infringed must be the ones that are practiced by the domestic industry in order for there to be a violation of section 337.[19]

Notes and Questions

(1) A general exclusion order applies to all infringing products, even those of parties not before the ITC, and places in the hands of the Customs Service the task of determining whether a product is infringing. Should these orders be permitted?

(2) As noted, the ITC may grant a cease and desist order in addition to an exclusion order. These orders are typically directed at domestic importers or sellers, ordering them to cease and desist from selling the offending merchandise. Why is such an order needed if offending imports are excluded?

(3) When should the "public interest" counsel against relief? Given the statute's reference to "competitive conditions," is it right to say that the mere prospect of increased consumer prices will not preclude relief?

19. [original note 37] The IAs [staff investigating attorneys] argue that the language of section 337 and the legislative history of the 1988 amendments support the view that where the domestic industry practices some of the claims of a patent, a respondent's infringement of any of the claims of that patent provides a basis for finding a violation of section 337. The IAs note that the statute emphasizes infringement and practice of the patent, rather than infringement and practice of the individual claims of the patent. Specifically, the IAs quote the language of the statute referring to infringement of a U.S. patent (19 U.S.C. sec. 1337(a)(1)(B)(i)); the requirement that an industry exist in the United States "relating to the articles protected by the patent," (Id. at sec. 1337(a)(2)); and the domestic industry requirements "with respect to the articles protected by the patent" (Id. at sec. 1337(a)(3)).

In making this argument, the IAs question several IDs [initial determinations] or orders in which Commission ALJs have held that there must be "claim correspondence," i.e., that a violation of section 337 can be based on a particular claim only if the domestic industry practices that claim. * * * The claim correspondence requirement was not reviewed by the Commission and was not appealed to the Federal Circuit. The ID did, however, become the Commission's determination by virtue of the Commission's decision not to review it.

In light of our determination that there is a domestic industry meeting each claim at issue we need not determine whether claim correspondence is necessary to establish the existence of a domestic industry. The Commission notes, however, that, in a future investigation, it may be necessary to evaluate the propriety of a claim correspondence approach to the domestic industry analysis.

(4) What is the point of the "domestic industry" requirement? Suppose a U.S. citizen holds a valid U.S. patent for something not presently made in the United States, and not likely to be made here in the near future. Should foreign manufacturers nevertheless have to buy a license before exporting to this country a product that infringes the patent?

(5) Among the practices that the ITC has indicated could be unfair under Section 337, in addition to the infringement of patents, trademarks and copyrights, are price fixing, group boycotts, deceptive pricing, combination and conspiracy to restrain and monopolize trade, misrepresentation of the country of origin of the goods, an attempt to monopolize, a refusal to deal, predatory pricing, and trade secret misappropriation.[20] Thus, although most Section 337 cases seem to involve patents, the concept of unfair competition is broad enough to cover actions that violate other U.S. laws, including trade laws. For example, on occasion there have been complaints about an importer's use of predatory pricing, which by its very nature suggests the possibility of dumping. The 1974 Trade Act provided that if the ITC had reason to believe that an investigation might come under the antidumping or countervailing laws, it should notify the authorities administering those laws. In 1979, Section 337(b)(3) was clarified to indicate that the ITC investigation can proceed nevertheless under Section 337 unless it is based solely on alleged dumping or subsidization.

(6) Recall that where a U.S. registered trademark is involved, it is possible to register that trademark with the Customs Service. Entry will thereafter be denied to articles bearing that trademark, subject to the caveats discussed above in connection with gray market imports.

(7) After the GATT panel decision holding that Section 337 violated Article III, the use of Section 337 fell significantly, perhaps because complainants feared that relief obtained under it would not last. In the last few years, however, the number of new filings has increased. Between 1974 and the GATT panel decision in late 1988, about 275 Section 337 investigations were initiated. Since then (as of September 2001), about 200 cases have been initiated.

SECTION 20.3 INTERNATIONAL AGREEMENTS

The past few years have witnessed dramatic developments in the form of new international accords over intellectual property rights. First, the United States, Canada and Mexico reached agreement on the intellectual property provisions of NAFTA, especially significant for the commitment by a developing nation to afford intellectual property rights comparable to those prevalent in developed economies. Next, the Uruguay Round TRIPS Agreement created elaborate substantive and procedural obligations binding on all WTO signatories.

(A) HISTORY

International agreements on intellectual property date back over a

---

20. See U.S. Intl. Trade Commn., Office of the Administrative Law Judges, Compendium of Section 337 Decisions sec. 101, at 2 (1981).

century.[1] The Paris Convention for the Protection of Industrial Property was first concluded in 1883, though it has been revised a number of times since. It covers "industrial property" broadly, including patents, trademarks, marks of origin, and methods of unfair competition. The Berne Convention for the Protection of Literary and Artistic Works (focused on copyright) was first concluded in 1886. A number of other accords exist as well, though their membership tends to be considerably smaller. Both the Paris and Berne Conventions, as well as many of the other agreements, are administered by the World Intellectual Property Organization (WIPO), an arm of the United Nations.

The Paris and Berne Conventions (the latter joined only recently by the United States) include commitments to national treatment.[2] GATT Article III also required national treatment in matters affecting the importation of goods, as we saw in Chapter 11. The Conventions also include measures to prevent the appropriation of intellectual property by someone in another country who copies it and then registers, files, or produces it first in that country. For example, if company X files a patent application in country A, company X shall for a period of time be deemed to have filed on the same date in country B, quite important under a "first to file" system for granting patents.[3] Likewise, if company X has a trademark that is unregistered in country A but is widely recognized by consumers there, company X can for a period of time apply to cancel the registration of another company that registers the mark in country A.[4] To a limited extent, the Conventions also set minimum standards for the protection of intellectual property. The most important examples are perhaps those in the Berne Convention, which requires that most copyrights extend for the life of the author plus 50 years,[5] and that authors have the right to object to any "distortion, mutilation or other modification" of the work (the so-called "droit moral" or "moral rights.")[6]

Notwithstanding the variety of long-standing agreements in this area, many nations complained before the Uruguay Round that intellectual property protection was deficient in other nations. The weaknesses in the existing regime were numerous. Among other things, the membership of the various conventions and treaties was quite incomplete. Many of the newly industrialized and larger developing countries, in particular, were not parties to one or more of them. Also, especially in the area of patents, the substantive restrictions on domestic law were few. Signatories could exclude some categories of inventions from patentability altogether, and give minimal patent duration to others, as long as they did not discriminate against foreign nationals. Finally, as with many international agreements, there were concerns about the level of compli-

---

1. A compendium of the more important agreements is International Treaties on Intellectual Property (M. Leaffer ed. 1990).

2. See Article 2 of the Paris Convention and Article 5 of the Berne Convention, reprinted in International Treaties on Intellectual Property, supra.

3. See Article 4 of the Paris Convention.

4. See Article 6*bis* of the Paris Convention.

5. See Article 7.

6. See Article 6*bis*.

ance and the effectiveness of dispute resolution.[7] Attempts by the United States and other countries to address these issues in WIPO had proved unsuccessful, in large part because of the wide divergence of views on intellectual property rights in that organization. Moreover, in a single issue forum, such as WIPO, there was no possibility of securing changes in intellectual property laws in exchange for concessions on other trade issues, as there is in the GATT/WTO system.

(B) THE URUGUAY ROUND NEGOTIATIONS[8]

Because of U.S. dissatisfaction with the existing international intellectual property agreements, the United States was the prime mover to include the subject of intellectual property in the Uruguay Round. Inclusion of this subject was strongly opposed by a number of important developing countries. In the end, however, it was agreed to include intellectual property rights as a subject in the negotiations.

At about the same time as a new round of negotiations in GATT was under consideration, the United States began putting considerable pressure on certain of its trading partners to improve their enforcement of intellectual property rights. This pressure resulted in the adoption of new or revised intellectual property laws by a number of countries, including Brazil, Singapore, South Korea, Taiwan and Thailand. Initially this pressure was applied through initiation or threat of Section 301 actions, including actions under Special 301, a provision added to U.S. trade law in 1988. The U.S. has also pressured various developing countries to strengthen their intellectual property laws by threatening to withdraw their benefits under the Generalized System of preferences.

Because of the initial opposition of many developing countries to including intellectual property as a negotiating topic in the Uruguay Round, it was expected that the negotiations would center on North–South issues. In the end, however, there were many difficult disputes to resolve between developed countries as well. Once it became necessary to define exactly the terms of patent, copyright, trademark and other forms of intellectual property protection, the differences in industrialized country laws became more significant. In fact, developing country opposition to a TRIPS Agreement moderated significantly during the course of the negotiations. This was in part because as more of the advanced developing countries adopted or revised intellectual property laws, the amount of change required by an international agreement became less significant for many of them. Moreover, in a few of those countries, production of

---

7. A useful review of the pre-Uruguay Round institutions and negotiating positions may be found in Emmert, Intellectual Property in the Uruguay Round—Negotiating Strategies of the Western Industrialized Countries, 11 Mich.J.Intl.L. 1317 (1990), and in Benko, Protecting Intellectual Property Rights: Issues and Controversies (1987).

8. For a general description of the negotiations, see The GATT Uruguay Round: A Negotiating History (1986–1992), at 2241–2333 (T. Stewart ed., 1993); Reichman, The TRIPS Component of the GATT's Uruguay Round: Competitive Prospects for Intellectual Property Owners in an Integrated World Market, 4 Fordham Intellectual Prop., Media & Entertainment L.J. 171 (1993).

valuable intellectual property had started to occur and rules on protection of such property seemed likely to be more beneficial in the long run than they had in the past.

While we cannot trace all of the significant issues that the negotiators discussed, we will highlight some of the more important ones. Thereafter, in the next subsection, we describe the results of the negotiations. In reading the summary of the results, the student should consider how the following issues were resolved. We address the issues in the order they are treated in the TRIPS Agreement.

Copyright. As noted above, the Berne Convention provides for so-called moral rights. Article 6*bis* provides that an author has "the right * * * to object to any distortion, mutilation, or other modification of, or other derogatory action in relation to the work that would be prejudicial to his honor or reputation." Thus, an artist controls some aspects of the use of his or her work even after it is sold. Although the U.S. is a party to the Berne Convention, it does not generally provide copyright holders with such moral rights. Many other countries do. Should all countries be required to provide such rights, including the U.S? Why would you think that the U.S. does not provide such rights generally?

The extent to which computer software can be copyrighted (or patented) has been a controversial issue in a number of legal systems and specific statutes have sometimes been introduced to clarify the issue. Consequently, one of the issues faced by the Uruguay round negotiators was how to treat software. Consider whether distinctions should be made in the types of software that can be protected. And what about data bases? What policy issues do you see regarding whether they should be protected?

Third, there was the question of a copyright holder's right to control use of the work after it has been sold, in particular, the extent to which the holder should be able to prohibit rental of the work. To what extent does this right exist in the U.S.? Why would you expect the holder to want to control rental? Should the holder be able to? Should there be any conditions on exercising such control? Consider the position of libraries and video rental stores.

Finally, there was the question of what are called neighboring rights, so-called because they neighbor on copyright. These rights include the right of performers to control reproduction of their performances and the right of broadcasters to control rebroadcast of their programs. Such rights have been recognized at the international level only recently in a 1961 convention and are not as widely recognized as many other intellectual property rights. The issue was whether they should be more broadly recognized. What arguments can you see for and against such recognition?

Trademarks. One issue with respect to trademarks was whether the U.S. requirement of use as a condition of protection should be permitted. On the question of trademark enforcement, another issue concerned the extent to which countries had to take measures to prevent counterfeiting.

Industrial Designs. The principal dispute here concerned the scope of protection. What sort of products should be protected as industrial designs? Spare parts, for example? Would it be appropriate to let the maker of a product (such as automobiles) control the market for spare parts for its product through protection of industrial designs? What economic effects could be expected?

Patents. Among the important patent issues were whether the United States should be permitted to maintain its "first to invent" rule, which awards a patent to the first person to have invented a product, as opposed to the practice elsewhere in the world, where the first person to file a patent application for an invention is typically awarded the patent. The U.S. system also had a discriminatory element—the first to invent rule did not apply to noncitizens. Their priority was based on the date of their first filing. At issue was how, if at all, the U.S. system would be changed.

Another important issue was the subject matter that could be patented, and the extent to which certain products could be excluded from patent coverage, such as pharmaceutical products or the results of biotechnology research. Should different rules apply to such products?

Finally, there was the question of compulsory licensing. Many developing countries, and some developed ones, have rules requiring that a patent holder must license its patent in certain circumstances, particularly if the patent is not being utilized in the country where the patent exists. Multinational corporations obviously will want to patent a product throughout the world, but they may be less interested in establishing manufacturing facilities in every country where they have patent protection. Under what conditions, if any, should the use of the patent be allowed without the voluntary consent of the holder?

There are, of course, a multitude of other issues. But the foregoing discussion highlights some of the more important ones that were discussed in the TRIPS negotiations. In the next section, we describe the TRIPS Agreement, which is contained in the Documents Supplement. The reader should consider how, if at all, the foregoing issues were resolved.

(C) OVERVIEW OF THE TRIPS AGREEMENT

The Uruguay Round TRIPS Agreement is an extraordinary accomplishment that addresses many (though by no means all) of the concerns that existed prior to the Round. The agreement will include all WTO members, and thus is expected to incorporate virtually all of the major players in the international economy (China, Taiwan and certain former Eastern bloc countries being, at this writing, the major exceptions). It also goes well beyond what was in place previously regarding the requirements for substantive rights. Finally, dispute resolution under the TRIPs Agreement will be comparable to that elsewhere in the WTO/GATT system.

The Uruguay Round Agreement bears considerable similarity to the intellectual property provisions in NAFTA. The NAFTA provisions, aimed largely but not entirely at conforming the policies of Mexico to those of the United States and Canada, encompassed all forms of patent protection, compulsory licensing, copyright, trademark protection, trade secrets, semiconductor mask designs, domestic enforcement, and dispute resolution. Because of their overlap with and similarity to the Uruguay Round Agreement, we omit detailed discussion.[9] Likewise, amendments to U.S. law necessitated by TRIPs and NAFTA were generally modest, and at a level of detail that need not detain us here.

The following summary of TRIPs was prepared by the GATT Secretariat.

GATT FOCUS NEWSLETTER
December 1993, at 12–14

The agreement recognizes that widely varying standards in the protection and enforcement of intellectual property rights and the lack of a multilateral framework of principles, rules and disciplines dealing with international trade in counterfeit goods have been a growing source of tension in international economic relations. Rules and disciplines were needed to cope with these tensions. To that end, the agreement addresses the applicability of basic GATT principles and those of relevant international intellectual property agreements, the provision of adequate intellectual property rights; the provision of effective enforcement measures for those rights; multilateral dispute settlement; and transitional arrangements.

Part I of the agreement sets out general provisions and basic principles, notably a national-treatment commitment under which the nationals of other parties must be given treatment no less favourable than that accorded to a party's own nationals with regard to the protection of intellectual property. It also contains a most-favoured-nation clause, a novelty in an international intellectual property agreement, under which any advantage a party gives to the nationals of another country must be extended immediately and unconditionally to the nationals of all other parties, even if such treatment is more favourable than that which it gives to its own nationals.

Part II addresses each intellectual property right in succession. With respect to copyright, parties are required to comply with the substantive provisions of the Berne Convention for the protection of literary and artistic works, in its latest version (Paris 1971), though they will not be obliged to protect moral rights as stipulated in Article 6*bis* of that Convention. It ensures that computer programs will be protected as

---

9. A nice summary of the highlights may be found in Wineburg, NAFTA to   Break Down Barriers, Legal Times, October 26, 1992, at 21.

literary works under the Berne Convention and lays down on what basis data bases should be protected by copyright. Important additions to existing international rules in the area of copyright and related rights are the provisions on rental rights. The draft requires authors of computer programmes and producers of sound recordings to be given the right to authorize or prohibit the commercial rental of their works to the public. A similar exclusive right applies to films where commercial rental has led to widespread copying which is materially impairing the right of reproduction. The draft also requires performers to be given protection from unauthorized recording and broadcast of live performances (bootlegging). The protection for performers and producers of sound recordings would be for no less than 50 years. Broadcasting organizations would have control over the use that can be made of broadcast signals without their authorization. This right would last for at least 20 years.

With respect to trademarks and service marks, the agreement defines what types of signs must be eligible for protection as a trademark or service mark and what the minimum rights conferred on their owners must be. Marks that have become well-known in a particular country shall enjoy additional protection. In addition, the agreement lays down a number of obligations with regard to the use of trademarks and service marks, their term of protection, and their licensing or assignment. For example, requirements that foreign marks be used in conjunction with local marks would, as a general rule, be prohibited.

In respect of geographical indications, the agreement lays down that all parties must provide means to prevent the use of any indication which misleads the consumer as to the origin of goods, and any use which would constitute an act of unfair competition. A higher level of protection is provided for geographical indications for wines and spirits, which are protected even where there is no danger of the public's being misled as to the true origin. Exceptions are allowed for names that have already become generic terms, but any country using such an exception must be willing to negotiate with a view to protecting the geographical indications in question. Further more, provision is made for further negotiations to establish a multilateral system of notification and registration of geographical indications for wines.

Industrial designs are also protected under the agreement for a period of 10 years. Owners of protected designs would be able to prevent the manufacture, sale or importation of articles bearing or embodying a design which is a copy of the protected design.

As regards patents, there is a general obligation to comply with the substantive provisions of the Paris Convention (1967). In addition, the agreement requires that 20–year patent protection be available for all inventions, whether of products or processes, in almost all fields of technology. Inventions may be excluded from patentability if their commercial exploitation is prohibited for reasons of public order or morality; otherwise, the permitted exclusions are for diagnostic, therapeutic and surgical methods, and for plants and (other than microorganisms) animals and essentially biological processes for the production of plants or animals (other than microbiological processes). Plant varieties, however, must be protectable either by patents or by a *sui generis* system (such as the breeder's rights provided in a UPOV [International Convention for the Protection of New Varieties of Plants] Convention). Detailed conditions are laid down for compulsory licensing or governmental use of patents without the authorization of the patent owner. Rights conferred in respect of patents for processes must extend to the products directly obtained by the process; under certain conditions alleged infringers may be ordered by a court to prove that they have not used the patented process.

With respect to the protection of layout designs of integrated circuits, the agreement requires parties to provide protection on the basis of the Washington Treaty on Intellectual Property in Respect of Integrated Circuits which was opened for signature in May 1989, but with a number of additions: protection must be available for a minimum period of 10 years; the rights must extend to articles incorporating infringing layout designs; innocent infringers must be allowed to use or sell stock in hand or ordered before learning of the infringement against a suitable royalty; and compulsory licensing and government use is only allowed under a number of strict conditions.

Trade secrets and know-how which have commercial value must be protected against breach of confidence and other acts contrary to honest commercial practices. Test data submitted to government in order to obtain marketing approval for pharmaceutical or agricultural chemicals must also be protected against unfair commercial use.

The final section in this part of the agreement concerns anticompetitive practices in contractual licences. It provides for consultations between governments where there is reason to believe that licensing practices or conditions pertaining to intellectual property rights constitute an abuse of these rights and have an adverse effect on competition. Remedies against such abuses must be consistent with the other provisions of the agreement.

Part III of the agreement sets out the obligations of member governments to provide procedures and remedies under their domestic law to ensure that intellectual property rights can be effectively enforced, by foreign right holders as well as by their own nationals. Procedures should permit effective action against infringement of intellectual property rights but should be fair and equitable, not unnecessarily complicated or costly, and should not entail unreasonable time-limits or unwarranted delays. They should allow for judicial review of final administrative decisions. There is no obligation to put in place a judicial system distinct from that for the enforcement of laws in general, nor to give priority to the enforcement of intellectual property rights in the allocation of resources or staff.

The civil and administrative procedures and remedies spelled out in the text include provisions on evidence of proof, injunction, damages and other remedies which would include the right of judicial authorities to order the disposal or destruction of infringing goods. Judicial authorities must also have the authority to order prompt and effective provisional measures, in particular where any delay is likely to cause irreparable harm to the right holder, or where evidence is likely to be destroyed. Further provisions relate to measures to be taken at the border for the suspension by customs authorities of release, into domestic circulation, of counterfeit and pirated goods. Finally, parties should provide for criminal procedures and penalties at least in cases of wilful trademark counterfeiting or copyright piracy on a commercial scale. Remedies should include imprisonment and fines sufficient to act as a deterrent.

The agreement would establish a Council for Trade–Related Aspects of Intellectual Property Rights to monitor the operation of the agreement and governments' compliance with it. Dispute settlement would take place under the integrated GATT dispute-settlement procedures as revised in the Uruguay Round.

With respect to the implementation of the agreement, it envisages a one-year transition period for developed countries to bring their legislation and practices into conformity. Developing countries and countries in the process of transformation from a centrally-planned into a market economy would have a five-year transition period, and least-developed countries 11 years. Developing countries which do not at present provide product patent protection in an area of technology would have up to 10 years to introduce such protection. However, in the case of pharmaceutical and agricultural chemical products, they must accept the filing of patent applications from the beginning of the transitional period. Though the patent need not be granted until the end of this period, the novelty of the invention is preserved as of the date of filing the application. If authorization for the marketing of the relevant pharmaceutical or agricultural chemical is obtained during the transitional period, the developing country concerned must offer an exclusive marketing right for the product for five years, or until a product patent is granted, whichever is shorter.

Subject to certain exceptions, the general rule is that the obligations in the agreement would apply to existing intellectual property rights as well as to new ones.

———

The number of disputes under TRIPs thus far has been fairly modest. Some have involved essentially transitional issues. In Canada—Term of Patent Protection, WT/DS170/AB/R, Appellate Body Report adopted by the DSB on October 12, 2000, the issue was what to do about patents granted before TRIPs came into effect that do not conform to the length of patent requirement in TRIPs. In India—Patent Protection for Pharmaceutical and Agricultural Chemical Products, WT/DS50/AB/R, Appellate Body Report adopted by the DSB on January 16, 1998, the issue was whether India had provided an adequate administrative process to preserve the rights of patent applicants regarding subject matter that would not become patentable in India until 2005. Two disputes of more than transitional importance have involved the ability of nations to grant "limited exceptions" to the substantive requirements of TRIPs.

CANADA—PATENT PROTECTION OF PHARMACEUTICAL PRODUCTS
WT/DS114/R
Panel Report adopted by the DSB on April 7, 2000

7.1 At issue in this dispute is the [EC and its member states' challenge to the] conformity of two provisions of Canada's *Patent Act* with Canada's obligations under the *Agreement on Trade–Related Aspects of Intellectual Property Rights* ("the TRIPS Agreement"). The two provisions in dispute, Sections 55.2(1) and 55.2(2) of the Patent Act, create exceptions to the exclusive rights of patent owners. Under Article 28.1 of the TRIPS Agreement, patent owners shall have the right to exclude others from making, using, selling, offering for sale or importing the patented product during the term of the patent. According to Article 33 of the TRIPS Agreement, the term of protection available shall not end before the expiration of a period of 20 years counted from the filing date of the application against which the patent was granted. Sections 55.2(1) and 55.2(2) allow third parties to make, use or sell the patented product during the term of the patent without the consent of the patent owner in certain defined circumstances.

7.2 Section 55.2(1) provides as follows:

> "It is not an infringement of a patent for any person to make, construct, use or sell the patented invention solely for uses reasonably related to the development and submission of information required under any law of Canada, a province or a country other than Canada that regulates the manufacture, construction, use or sale of any product."

Section 55.2(1) is known as the "regulatory review exception". It applies to patented products such as pharmaceuticals whose marketing is subject to government regulation in order to assure their safety or effectiveness. The purpose of the regulatory review exception is to permit potential competitors of the patent owner to obtain government marketing approval during the term of the patent, so that they will have regulatory permission to sell in competition with the patent owner by the date on which the patent expires. Without the regulatory review exception, the patent owner might be able to prevent potential competitors from using the patented product during the term of the patent to comply with testing requirements, so that competitors would have to wait until the patent expires before they could begin the process of obtaining marketing approval. This, in turn, would prevent potential competitors from entering the market for the additional time required to complete the regulatory approval process, in effect extending the patent owner's period of market exclusivity beyond the end of the term of the patent.

* * *

7.7　Section 55.2(2) of the Patent Act, which is referred to as "the stockpiling exception", reads as follows:

> "It is not an infringement of a patent for any person who makes, constructs, uses or sells a patented invention in accordance with subsection (1) to make, construct or use the invention, during the applicable period provided for by the regulations, for the manufacture and storage of articles intended for sale after the date on which the term of the patent expires."

The provision allows competitors to manufacture and stockpile patented goods during a certain period before the patent expires, but the goods cannot be sold until the patent expires. Without this exception, the patent owner's right to exclude any person from "making" or "using" the patented good would enable the patent owner to prevent all such stockpiling.

7.8　The exception created by Section 55.2(2) does not become effective until implementing regulations are issued. The only regulations issued to date under the stockpiling exception have been regulations making the exception operative with regard to pharmaceutical products. The period during which pharmaceutical products can be made and stockpiled is six months immediately prior to the expiration of the patent.

7.9　The text of Section 55.2(2) gives permission only to "make, construct or use" the patented product for purposes of stockpiling. In answer to a question from the Panel, however, Canada has taken the position that the exception will be construed also to allow the "sale" of patented ingredients that have been ordered by a producer who is stockpiling the final patented product—for example, with regard to pharmaceuticals, sales by fine chemical producers of active ingredients ordered by the generic producer.

7.10　The stockpiling exception is available only to persons who have invoked the regulatory review exception in Section 55.2(1). This limitation has the effect of limiting the exception to products that are subject to the kind of government marketing regulations referred to in Section 55.2(1). As a practical matter, only persons who have actually obtained regulatory permission to market such regulated products would be able to benefit from the stockpiling exception, because there would be no commercial advantage in having a stock of goods on hand when the patent expires unless one also has regulatory permission to sell those goods as of that date. Conversely, the stockpiling exception does complement the competitive effects of the regulatory review exception. Without the additional permission to stockpile during the term of the patent, competitors who obtain regulatory permission to sell on the day the patent expires would still not be able to enter the market on that day, because they would first have to manufacture a sufficient stock of goods.

* * *

The Stockpiling Exception

7.17   The Panel began by considering the claims of violation concerning Section 55.2(2), the so-called stockpiling provision. It began by considering the EC claim that this measure was in violation of Article 28.1 of the TRIPS Agreement, and Canada's defence that the measure was an exception authorized by Article 30 of the Agreement.

7.18   Article 28.1 provides:

"Rights Conferred

1.   A patent shall confer on its owner the following exclusive rights:

(a) Where the subject-matter of a patent is a product, to prevent third parties not having the owner's consent from the acts of making, using, offering for sale, selling, or importing for these purposes that product;"

There was no dispute as to the meaning of Article 28.1 exclusive rights as they pertain to Section 55.2(2) of Canada's Patent Act. Canada acknowledged that the provisions of Section 55.2(2) permitting third parties to "make", "construct" or "use" the patented product during the term of the patent, without the patent owner's permission, would be a violation of Article 28.1 if not excused under Article 30 of the Agreement. The dispute on the claim of violation of Article 28.1 involved whether Section 55.2.(2) of the Patent Act complies with the conditions of Article 30.

7.19   The TRIPS Agreement contains two provisions authorizing exceptions to the exclusionary patent rights laid down in Article 28— Articles 30 and 31. Of these two, Article 30—the so-called limited exceptions provision–has been invoked by Canada in the present case. It reads as follows:

"Exceptions to Rights Conferred

Members may provide limited exceptions to the exclusive rights conferred by a patent, provided that such exceptions do not unreasonably conflict with the normal exploitation of the patent and do not unreasonably prejudice the legitimate interests of the patent owner, taking account of the legitimate interests of third parties."

7.20   Both parties agreed upon the basic structure of Article 30. Article 30 establishes three criteria that must be met in order to qualify for an exception: (1) the exception must be "limited"; (2) the exception must not "unreasonably conflict with normal exploitation of the patent"; (3) the exception must not "unreasonably prejudice the legitimate interests of the patent owner, taking account of the legitimate interests of third parties". The three conditions are cumulative, each being a separate and independent requirement that must be satisfied. Failure to comply with any one of the three conditions results in the Article 30 exception being disallowed.

7.21   The three conditions must, of course, be interpreted in relation to each other. Each of the three must be presumed to mean something different from the other two, or else there would be redundancy. Normally, the order of listing can be read to suggest that an exception that complies with the first condition can nevertheless violate the second or third, and that one which complies with the first and second can still violate the third. The syntax of Article 30 supports the conclusion that an exception may be "limited" and yet fail to satisfy one or both of the other two conditions. The ordering further suggests that an exception that does not "unreasonably conflict with normal exploitation" could nonetheless "unreasonably prejudice the legitimate interests of the patent owner".

* * *

"Limited Exceptions"

7.27   Canada asserted that the word "limited" should be interpreted according to the conventional dictionary definition, such as "confined within definite limits", or "restricted in scope, extent, amount". Canada argued that the stockpiling exception in Section 55.2(2) is restricted in scope because it has only a limited impact on a patent owner's rights. The stockpiling exception, Canada noted, does not affect the patent owner's right to an exclusive market for "commercial" sales during the patent term, since the product that is manufactured and stockpiled during the final six months of the term cannot be sold in competition with the patent owner until the patent expires. By "commercial sales", Canada clearly meant sales to the ultimate consumer, because it acknowledged that sales of patented ingredients to producers engaged in authorized stockpiling is permitted. Thus, Canada was arguing that an exception is "limited" as long as the exclusive right to sell to the ultimate consumer during the term of the patent is preserved. In addition, Canada also claimed that the exception is further limited by the six-month duration of the exception, and by the fact that it can be used only by persons that have made, constructed or used the invention under Section 55.2(1).

7.28   The EC interpreted the word "limited" to connote a narrow exception, one that could be described by words such as "narrow, small, minor, insignificant or restricted". The EC measured the "limited" quality of the proposed exception by reference to its impact on the exclusionary rights granted to the patent owner under Article 28.1. Applying that measure, the EC contended that the stockpiling exception is not "limited" because it takes away three of the five Article 28.1 rights—the rights to exclude "making", "using" and "importing". The EC argued that the impairment of three out of five basic rights is in itself extensive enough to be considered "not limited". The EC further contended that limitation of the exception to the last six months of the patent term does not constitute a limited impairment of rights when six months is taken as a percentage of the 20–year patent term, and especially not when taken as a percentage of the actual eight to 12–year period of effective market exclusivity enjoyed by most patented pharmaceuticals. In addition, the EC noted, there was no limitation on the quantities that could be produced during this period, nor any limitation on the markets in which such products could be sold. Finally, the EC pointed out that no royalty fees are due for such production, and that the patent holder does not even have a right to be informed of the use of the patent.

7.29   In considering how to approach the parties' conflicting positions regarding the meaning of the term "limited exceptions", the Panel was aware that the text of Article 30 has antecedents in the text of Article 9(2) of the Berne Convention. However, the words "limited exceptions" in Article 30 of the TRIPS Agreement are different from the corresponding words in Article 9(2) of the Berne Convention, which reads "in certain special cases". The Panel examined the documented negotiating history of TRIPS Article 30 with respect to the reasons why negotiators may have chosen to use the term "limited exceptions" in place of "in special circumstances". The negotiating records show only that the term "limited exceptions" was employed very early in the drafting process, well before the decision to adopt a text modelled on Berne Article 9(2), but do not indicate why it was retained in the later draft texts modelled on Berne Article 9(2).

7.30   The Panel agreed with the EC that, as used in this context, the word "limited" has a narrower connotation than the rather broad definitions cited by Canada. Although the word itself can have both broad and narrow definitions, the narrower being indicated by examples such as "a mail train taking only a limited number of passengers", the narrower definition is the more appropriate when the word "limited" is used as part of the phrase "limited exception". The word "exception" by itself connotes a limited derogation, one that does not undercut the body of rules from which it is made. When a treaty uses the term "limited exception", the word "limited" must be given a meaning separate from the limitation implicit in the word "exception" itself. The term "limited exception" must therefore be read to connote a narrow exception—one which makes only a small diminution of the rights in question.

7.31   The Panel agreed with the EC interpretation that "limited" is to be measured by the extent to which the exclusive rights of the patent owner have been curtailed. The full text of Article 30 refers to "limited exceptions to the exclusive rights conferred by a patent". In the absence of other indications, the Panel concluded that it would be justified in reading the text literally, focusing on the extent to which legal rights have been curtailed, rather than the size or extent of the economic impact. In support of this conclusion, the Panel noted that the following two conditions of Article 30 ask more particularly about the economic impact of the exception, and provide two sets of standards by which such impact may be judged. The term "limited exceptions" is the only one of the three conditions in Article 30 under which the extent of the curtailment of rights as such is dealt with.

7.32 The Panel does not agree, however, with the EC's position that the curtailment of legal rights can be measured by simply counting the number of legal rights impaired by an exception. A very small act could well violate all five rights provided by Article 28.1 and yet leave each of the patent owner's rights intact for all useful purposes. To determine whether a particular exception constitutes a limited exception, the extent to which the patent owner's rights have been curtailed must be measured.

7.33 The Panel could not accept Canada's argument that the curtailment of the patent owner's legal rights is "limited" just so long as the exception preserves the exclusive right to sell to the ultimate consumer during the patent term. Implicit in the Canadian argument is a notion that the right to exclude sales to consumers during the patent term is the essential right conveyed by a patent, and that the rights to exclude "making" and "using" the patented product during the term of the patent are in some way secondary. The Panel does not find any support for creating such a hierarchy of patent rights within the TRIPS Agreement. If the right to exclude sales were all that really mattered, there would be no reason to add other rights to exclude "making" and "using". The fact that such rights were included in the TRIPS Agreement, as they are in most national patent laws, is strong evidence that they are considered a meaningful and independent part of the patent owner's rights.

7.34 In the Panel's view, the question of whether the stockpiling exception is a "limited" exception turns on the extent to which the patent owner's rights to exclude "making" and "using" the patented product have been curtailed. The right to exclude "making" and "using" provides protection, additional to that provided by the right to exclude sale, during the entire term of the patent by cutting off the supply of competing goods at the source and by preventing use of such products however obtained. With no limitations at all upon the quantity of production, the stockpiling exception removes that protection entirely during the last six months of the patent term, without regard to what other, subsequent, consequences it might have. By this effect alone, the stockpiling exception can be said to abrogate such rights entirely during the time it is in effect.

7.35 In view of Canada's emphasis on preserving commercial benefits *before* the expiration of the patent, the Panel also considered whether the market advantage gained by the patent owner in the months after expiration of the patent could also be considered a purpose of the patent owner's rights to exclude "making" and "using" during the term of the patent. In both theory and practice, the Panel concluded that such additional market benefits were within the purpose of these rights. In theory, the rights of the patent owner are generally viewed as a right to prevent competitive commercial activity by others, and manufacturing for commercial sale is a quintessential competitive commercial activity, whose character is not altered by a mere delay in the commercial reward. In practical terms, it must be recognized that enforcement of the right to exclude "making" and "using" during the patent term will necessarily give all patent owners, for all products, a short period of extended market exclusivity after the patent expires. The repeated enactment of such exclusionary rights with knowledge of their universal market effects can only be understood as an affirmation of the purpose to produce those market effects.

7.36   For both these reasons, the Panel concluded that the stockpiling exception of Section 55.2(2) constitutes a substantial curtailment of the exclusionary rights required to be granted to patent owners under Article 28.1 of the TRIPS Agreement. Without seeking to define exactly what level of curtailment would be disqualifying, it was clear to the Panel that an exception which results in a substantial curtailment of this dimension cannot be considered a "limited exception" within the meaning of Article 30 of the Agreement.

7.37   Neither of the two "limitations" upon the scope of the measure are sufficient to alter this conclusion. First, the fact that the exception can only be used by those persons who have utilized the regulatory review exception of Section 55.2(1) does limit the scope of the exception both to those persons and to products requiring regulatory approval. In regard to the limitation to such persons, the Panel considered this was not a real limitation since only persons who satisfy regulatory requirements would be entitled to market the product. In regard to the limitation to such products, the Panel considered that the fact that an exception does not apply at all to other products in no way changes its effect with regard to the criteria of Article 30. Each exception must be evaluated with regard to its impact on each affected patent, independently. Second, the fact that the exception applied only to the last six months of the patent term obviously does reduce its impact on all affected patented products, but the Panel agreed with the EC that six months was a commercially significant period of time, especially since there were no limits at all on the volume of production allowed, or the market destination of such production.

7.38   Having concluded that the exception in Section 55.2(2) of the Canadian Patent Act does not satisfy the first condition of Article 30 of the TRIPS Agreement, the Panel therefore concluded that Section 55.2(2) is inconsistent with Canada's obligations under Article 28.1 of the Agreement. This conclusion, in turn, made it unnecessary to consider any of the other claims of inconsistency raised by the European Communities. Accordingly, the Panel did not consider the claims of inconsistency under the second and third conditions of Article 30, the claim of inconsistency with TRIPS Article 27.1, and the claim of inconsistency with Article 33.

The Regulatory Review Exception

"Limited Exceptions"

* * *

7.41   In the case of the regulatory review exception * * * Canada added two further arguments based on the negotiating history of Article 30 and on the subsequent practices of certain WTO Members. Canada pointed out that in 1984 the United States had enacted a regulatory review exception similar to Section 55.2(1) of Canada's Patent Act, known as the "Bolar exemption". Canada asserted that the United States "Bolar exemption" was well known during the negotiation of Article 30, and that governments were aware that the United States intended to secure an exception that would permit it to retain its "Bolar exemption". Canada further asserts that it was known that the United States agreed to the general language of Article 30 on the understanding that the provision would do so. Canada called attention to subsequent statements by United States officials stating that "[O]ur negotiators ensured that the TRIPS Agreement permits the Bolar exemption to be maintained."

7.42   With regard to subsequent practice, Canada pointed out that after the conclusion of the TRIPS Agreement four other WTO Members (Argentina, Australia, Hungary and Israel) adopted legislation containing similar regulatory review exceptions, and that both Japan and Portugal adopted interpretations of existing patent law which confirmed exemptions for regulatory review submissions. Canada argued that these actions are subsequent practices by parties to the agreement, within the meaning of Article 31(3)(b) of the Vienna Convention, that confirm its interpretation that regulatory review exceptions are authorized by TRIPS Article 30 . . .

7.44   In the previous part of this Report dealing with the stockpiling exception of Section 55.2(2), the Panel concluded that the words "limited exception" express a requirement that the exception make only a narrow curtailment of the legal rights which Article 28.1 requires to be granted to patent owners, and that the measure of that curtailment was the extent to which the affected legal rights themselves had been impaired. As was made clear by our conclusions regarding the stockpiling exception, the Panel could not accept Canada's contention that an exception can be regarded as "limited" just so long as it preserves the patent owner's exclusive right to sell to the ultimate consumer during the patent term.

7.45   In the Panel's view, however, Canada's regulatory review exception is a "limited exception" within the meaning of TRIPS Article 30. It is "limited" because of the narrow scope of its curtailment of Article 28.1 rights. As long as the exception is confined to conduct needed to comply with the requirements of the regulatory approval process, the extent of the acts unauthorized by the right holder that are permitted by it will be small and narrowly bounded. Even though regulatory approval processes may require substantial amounts of test production to demonstrate reliable manufacturing, the patent owner's rights themselves are not impaired any further by the size of such production runs, as long as they are solely for regulatory purposes and no commercial use is made of resulting final products.

7.46   The Panel found no basis for believing that activities seeking product approvals under foreign regulatory procedures would be any less subject to these limitations. There is no *a priori* basis to assume that the requirements of foreign regulatory procedures will require activities unrelated to legitimate objectives of product quality and safety, nor has the EC provided any evidence to that effect. Nor is there any reason to assume that Canadian law would apply the exception in cases where foreign requirements clearly had no regulatory purpose. Nor, finally, is there any reason to assume that it will be any more difficult to enforce the requirements of Canadian law when Canadian producers claim exceptions under foreign procedures. With regard to the latter point, the Panel concurred with Canada's point that the government is not normally expected to regulate the actual conduct of third parties in such cases. The enforcement of these conditions, as with other enforcement of patent rights, occurs by means of private infringement actions brought by the patent owner. The patent owner merely has to prove that the challenged conduct is inconsistent with the basic patent rights created by national law. Once that initial case is made, the burden will be on the party accused of infringement to prove its defence by establishing that its conduct with respect to foreign regulatory procedures was in compliance with the conditions of Section 55.2(1).

7.47   In reaching this conclusion, the Panel also considered Canada's additional arguments that both the negotiating history of Article 30 of the TRIPS Agreement and the subsequent practices of certain WTO Member governments supported the view that Article 30 was understood to permit regulatory review exceptions similar to Section 55.2(1). The Panel did not accord any weight to either of those arguments, however, because there was no documented evidence of the claimed negotiating understanding, and because the subsequent acts by individual countries did not constitute "practice in the application of the treaty which establishes the agreement of the parties regarding its interpretation" within the meaning of Article 31.3(b) of the Vienna Convention.

7.48   A final objection to the Panel's general conclusion remains to be addressed. Although the point was raised only briefly in the parties' legal arguments, the Panel was compelled to acknowledge that the economic impact of the regulatory review exception could be considerable. According to information supplied by Canada itself, in the case of patented pharmaceutical products approximately three to six-and-a-half years are required for generic drug producers to develop and obtain regulatory approval for their products. If there were no regulatory review exception allowing competitors to apply for regulatory approval during the term of the patent, therefore, the patent owner would be able to extend its period of market exclusivity, de facto, for some part of that three to six-and-half year period, depending on how much, if any, of the development process could be performed during the term of the patent under other exceptions, such as the scientific or experimental use exception. The Panel believed it was necessary to ask whether measures having such a significant impact on the economic interests of patent owners could be called a "limited" exception to patent rights.

7.49   After analysing all three conditions stated in Article 30 of the TRIPS Agreement, the Panel was satisfied that Article 30 does in fact address the issue of economic impact, but only in the other two conditions contained in that Article. As will be seen in the analysis of these other conditions below, the other two conditions deal with the issue of economic impact, according to criteria that relate specifically to that issue. Viewing all three conditions as a whole, it is apparent that the first condition ("limited exception") is neither designed nor intended to address the issue of economic impact directly.

* * *

"Normal Exploitation"

7.51   The second condition of Article 30 prohibits exceptions that "unreasonably conflict with a normal exploitation of the patent". Canada took the position that "exploitation" of the patent involves the extraction of commercial value from the patent by "working" the patent, either by selling the product in a market from which competitors are excluded, or by licensing others to do so, or by selling the patent rights outright. The European Communities also defined "exploitation" by referring to the same three ways of "working" a patent. The parties differed primarily on their interpretation of the term "normal".

* * *

7.54   The Panel considered that "exploitation" refers to the commercial activity by which patent owners employ their exclusive patent rights to extract economic value from their patent. The term "normal" defines the kind of commercial activity Article 30 seeks to protect. The ordinary meaning of the word "normal" is found in the dictionary definition: "regular, usual, typical, ordinary, conventional". As so defined, the term can be understood to refer either to an empirical conclusion about what is common within a relevant community, or to a normative standard of entitlement. The Panel concluded that the word "normal" was being used in Article 30 in a sense that combined the two meanings.

7.55   The normal practice of exploitation by patent owners, as with owners of any other intellectual property right, is to exclude all forms of competition that could detract significantly from the economic returns anticipated from a patent's grant of market exclusivity. The specific forms of patent exploitation are not static, of course, for to be effective exploitation must adapt to changing forms of competition due to technological development and the evolution of marketing practices. Protection of all normal exploitation practices is a key element of the policy reflected in all patent laws. Patent laws establish a carefully defined period of market exclusivity as an inducement to innovation, and the policy of those laws cannot be achieved unless patent owners are permitted to take effective advantage of that inducement once it has been defined.

7.56   Canada has raised the argument that market exclusivity occurring after the 20–year patent term expires should not be regarded as "normal". The Panel was unable to accept that as a categorical proposition. Some of the basic rights granted to all patent owners, and routinely exercised by all patent owners, will typically produce a certain period of market exclusivity after the expiration of a patent. For example, the separate right to prevent "making" the patented product during the term of the patent often prevents competitors from building an inventory needed to enter the market immediately upon expiration of a patent. There is nothing abnormal about that more or less brief period of market exclusivity after the patent has expired.

7.57   The Panel considered that Canada was on firmer ground, however, in arguing that the additional period of de facto market exclusivity created by using patent rights to preclude submissions for regulatory authorization should not be considered "normal". The additional period of market exclusivity in this situation is not a natural or normal consequence of enforcing patent rights. It is an unintended consequence of the conjunction of the patent laws with product regulatory laws, where the combination of patent rights with the time demands of the regulatory process gives a greater than normal period of market exclusivity to the enforcement of certain patent rights. It is likewise a form of exploitation that most patent owners do not in fact employ. For the vast majority of patented products, there is no marketing regulation of the kind covered by Section 55.2(1), and thus there is no possibility to extend patent exclusivity by delaying the marketing approval process for competitors.

7.58   The Panel could not agree with the EC's assertion that the mere existence of the patent owner's rights to exclude was a sufficient reason, by itself, for treating all gains derived from such rights as flowing from "normal exploitation". In the Panel's view, the EC's argument contained no evidence or analysis addressed to the various meanings of "normal"—neither a demonstration that most patent owners extract the value of their patents in the manner barred by Section 55.2(1), nor an argument that the prohibited manner of exploitation was "normal" in the sense of being essential to the achievement of the goals of patent policy. To the contrary, the EC's focus on the exclusionary rights themselves merely restated the concern to protect Article 28 exclusionary rights as such. This is a concern already dealt with by the first condition of Article 30 ("limited exception") and the Panel found the ultimate EC arguments here impossible to distinguish from the arguments it had made under that first condition.

7.59   In sum, the Panel found that the regulatory review exception of Section 55.2(1) does not conflict with a normal exploitation of patents, within the meaning of the second condition of Article 30 of the TRIPS Agreement. The fact that no conflict has been found makes it unnecessary to consider the question of whether, if a conflict were found, the conflict would be "unreasonable". Accordingly, it is also unnecessary to determine whether or not the final phrase of Article 30, calling for consideration of the legitimate interests of third parties, does or does not apply to the determination of "unreasonable conflict" under the second condition of Article 30.

"Legitimate Interests"

* * *

7.62   The European Communities argued that the regulatory review exception in Section 55.2(1) fails to satisfy the third condition of Article 30. The primary EC argument on this point rested on an interpretation that identified "legitimate interests" with legal interests. The EC asserted that the "legitimate interests" of the patent owner can only be the full enjoyment of his patent rights during the entire term of the patent. Given that starting point, it followed that any exception to Article 28.1 rights would constitute "prejudice" to the legitimate interests of a patent owner. Consequently, the remainder of the EC's argument concentrated on whether the prejudice was "unreasonable", an issue which in turn focused on whether the "legitimate interests of third parties" outweighed the patent owner's interests in full enjoyment of his legal rights. The EC first argued that the only relevant "third parties" for the purpose of Article 30 are the patent owner's competitors—in the case of pharmaceutical patents the generic drug producers, because they were the only parties with interests adverse to those of patent owners. According to the EC's view, the TRIPS Agreement constitutes a recognition that patent systems serve the interest of the society, including the multiple interests of its health policy. That being so, the patent rights granted by that Agreement, being a part of the balance of rights and obligations that governments have agreed to as beneficial, cannot be found to be adverse to, or in conflict with, the interests represented by general social welfare policy. And that, in turn, means that the only adverse third party interests to patent owners are the interests of those firms with whom they compete.

7.63   Then, following its position that "legitimate interests" are essentially legal interests, the EC went on to argue that the legitimate interests of competing producers are essentially the same as those of patent owners—that is, the full enjoyment of their legal rights. The legal rights of the patent owner's competitors, the EC argues, are the rights to make, use or sell the patented product on the day *after* the patent expires. Such competitors, therefore, could have no "legitimate" interest in the rights granted by the regulatory review exception of Section

55.2(1), because they could have no legal right to "make" or "use" (or "sell") the patented product during the term of the patent.

7.64   Given these interpretations of the third condition of Article 30, the EC concluded: (1) that the impairment of the patent owner's Article 28 legal rights by the regulatory review exception amounts to "prejudice" to the patent owner's legitimate interests; and (2) that in the absence of any legitimate third party interest to the contrary, the abrogation of rights authorized by Section 55.2(1) is substantial enough to be characterized as "unreasonable".

* * *

7.68   The word "legitimate" is commonly defined as follows:

(a) Conformable to, sanctioned or authorized by, law or principle: lawful; justifiable; proper;

(b) Normal, regular, conformable to a recognized standard type.

Although the European Communities' definition equating "legitimate interests" with a full respect of legal interests pursuant to Article 28.1 is within at least some of these definitions, the EC definition makes it difficult to make sense of the rest of the third condition of Article 30, in at least three respects. First, since by that definition every exception under Article 30 will be causing "prejudice" to some legal rights provided by Article 28 of the Agreement, that definition would reduce the first part of the third condition to a simple requirement that the proposed exception must not be "unreasonable". Such a requirement could certainly have been expressed more directly if that was what was meant. Second, a definition equating "legitimate interests" with legal interests makes no sense at all when applied to the final phrase of Article 30 referring to the "legitimate interests" of third parties. Third parties are by definition parties who have no legal right at all in being able to perform the tasks excluded by Article 28 patent rights. An exceptions clause permitting governments to take account of such third party legal interests would be permitting them to take account of nothing. And third, reading the third condition as a further protection of legal rights would render it essentially redundant in light of the very similar protection of legal rights in the first condition of Article 30 ("limited exception").

7.69   To make sense of the term "legitimate interests" in this context, that term must be defined in the way that it is often used in legal discourse—as a normative claim calling for protection of interests that are "justifiable" in the sense that they are supported by relevant public policies or other social norms. This is the sense of the word that often appears in statements such as "X has no legitimate interest in being able to do Y". We may take as an illustration one of the most widely adopted Article 30–type exceptions in national patent laws—the exception under which use of the patented product for scientific experimentation, during the term of the patent and without consent, is not an infringement. It is often argued that this exception is based on the notion that a key public policy purpose underlying patent laws is to facilitate the dissemination and advancement of technical knowledge and that allowing the patent owner to prevent experimental use during the term of the patent would frustrate part of the purpose of the requirement that the nature of the invention be disclosed to the public. To the contrary, the argument concludes, under the policy of the patent laws, both society and the scientist have a "legitimate interest" in using the patent disclosure to support the advance of science and technology. While the Panel draws no conclusion about the correctness of any such national exceptions in terms of Article 30 of the TRIPS Agreement, it does adopt the general meaning of the term "legitimate interests" contained in legal analysis of this type.

7.70   The negotiating history of the TRIPS Agreement itself casts no further illumination on the meaning of the term "legitimate interests", but the negotiating history of Article 9(2) of the Berne Convention, from which the text of the third condition was clearly drawn, does tend to affirm the Panel's interpretation of that term. With regard to the TRIPS negotiations themselves, the meaning of several important drafting changes turns out to be equivocal upon closer examination. The negotiating records of the TRIPS Agreement itself show that the first drafts of the provision that was to become Article 30 contemplated authorizing "limited exceptions" that would be defined by an illustrative list of exceptions—private use, scientific use, prior use, a traditional exception for pharmacists, and the like. Eventually, this illustrative list approach was abandoned in favour of a more general authorization following the outlines of the present Article 30. The negotiating records of the TRIPS Agreement give no explanation of the reason for this decision.

7.71   The text of the present, more general version of Article 30 of the TRIPS Agreement was obviously based on the text of Article 9(2) of the Berne Convention. Berne Article 9(2) deals with exceptions to the copyright holder's right to exclude reproduction of its copyrighted work without permission. The text of Article 9(2) is as follows:

> "It shall be a matter for legislation in the countries of the Union to permit the reproduction of [literary and artistic] works in certain special cases, provided that such reproduction does not conflict with a normal exploitation of the work and does not unreasonably prejudice the legitimate interests of the author."

The text of Berne Article 9(2) was not adopted into Article 30 of the TRIPS Agreement without change. Whereas the final condition in Berne Article 9(2) ("legitimate interests") simply refers to the legitimate interests of the author, the TRIPS negotiators added in Article 30 the instruction that account must be taken of "the legitimate interests of third parties". Absent further explanation in the records of the TRIPS negotiations, however, the Panel was not able to attach a substantive meaning to this change other than what is already obvious in the text itself, namely that the reference to the "legitimate interests of third parties" makes sense only if the term "legitimate interests" is construed as a concept broader than legal interests.

7.72   With regard to the meaning of Berne Article 9(2) itself, the Panel examined the drafting committee report that is usually cited as the most authoritative explanation of what Article 9(2) means. The drafting committee report states:

> "If it is considered that reproduction conflicts with the normal exploitation of the work, reproduction is not permitted at all. If it is considered that reproduction does not conflict with the normal exploitation of the work, the next step would be to consider whether it does not unreasonably prejudice the legitimate interests of the author. Only if such is not the case would it be possible in certain special cases to introduce a compulsory license, or to provide for use without payment. A practical example may be photocopying for various purposes. If it consists of producing a very large number of copies, it may not be permitted, as it conflicts with a normal exploitation of the work. If it implies a rather large number of copies for use in industrial undertakings, it may not unreasonably prejudice the legitimate interests of the author, provided that, according to national legislation, an equitable remuneration is paid. If a small number of copies is made, photocopying may be permitted without payment, particularly for individual or scientific use."

The Panel recognized that the drafting committee's examples concern the area of copyright as opposed to patents, and that, even further, they deal with the situation as it was in 1967, and accordingly the Panel was reluctant to read too much into these examples as guides to the meaning of Article 30. But the Panel did find that the concepts of "normal exploitation" and "legitimate interests" underlying the three examples used by the drafting committee were consistent with the Panel's definitions of these concepts and of the differences between them.

7.73   In sum, after consideration of the ordinary meaning of the term "legitimate interests", as it is used in Article 30, the Panel was unable to accept the EC's interpretation of that term as referring to legal interests pursuant to Article 28.1. Accordingly, the Panel was unable to accept the primary EC argument with regard to the third condition of Article 30. It found that the EC argument based solely on the patent owner's legal rights pursuant to Article 28.1, without reference to any more particular normative claims of interest, did not raise a relevant claim of non-compliance with the third condition of Article 30.

7.74   After reaching the previous conclusion concerning the EC's primary argument under the "legitimate interests" condition of Article 30, the Panel then directed its attention to another line of argument raised in statements made by the EC and by one third party. This second line of argument called attention to the fact that patent owners whose innovative products are subject to marketing approval requirements suffer a loss of economic benefits to the extent that delays in obtaining government approval prevent them from marketing their product during a substantial part of the patent term. According to information supplied by Canada, regulatory approval of new pharmaceuticals usually does not occur until approximately eight to 12 years after the patent application has been filed, due to the time needed to complete development of the product and the time needed to comply with the regulatory procedure itself. The result in the case of pharmaceuticals, therefore, is that the innovative producer is in fact able to market its patented product in only the remaining eight to 12 years of the 20–year patent term, thus receiving an effective period of market exclusivity that is only 40–60 per cent of the period of exclusivity normally envisaged in a 20–year patent term. The EC argued that patent owners who suffer a reduction of effective market exclusivity from such delays should be entitled to impose the same type of delay in connection with corresponding regulatory requirements upon the market entry of competing products. According to the EC,

> "[T]here exists no reason why the research based pharmaceutical enterprise is obliged to accept the economic consequence of patent term erosion because of marketing approval requirements which reduce their effective term of protection to 12–8 years while the copy producer should be entirely compensated for the economic consequence of the need of marketing approval for his generic product, and at the expense of the inventor and patent holder".

Applied to the regulatory review exception, this argument called for the removal of such exceptions so that patent owners may use their exclusionary patent rights to prevent competitors from engaging in product development and initiating the regulatory review process until the patent has expired. The result of removing the exception would be to allow patent owners to create a period of further, de facto market exclusivity after the expiration of the patent, for the length of time it would take competing producers to complete product development and obtain marketing approval.

7.75 The normative claim being made in this second argument ultimately rested on a claim of equal treatment for all patent owners. The policy of the patent laws, the argument would run, is to give innovative producers the advantage of market exclusivity during the 20–year term of the patent. Although patent laws do not guarantee that patent owners will obtain economic benefits from this opportunity, most patent owners have at least the legal opportunity to market the patented product during all or virtually all this 20–year period of market exclusivity. Producers whose products are subject to regulatory approval requirements may be deprived of this opportunity for a substantial part of the 20–year period.

7.76 Under the Panel's interpretation of Article 30, this argument could be characterized as a claim of "legitimate interest" under the third condition of Article 30. It was distinct from the claim made under the second condition of Article 30 ("normal exploitation"), because it did not rest on a claim of interest in the "normal" means of extracting commercial benefits from a patent. Instead, it was a distinctive claim of interest, resting on a distinctive situation applicable only to patent owners affected by marketing approval requirements, asking for an additional means of exploitation, above and beyond "normal exploitation," to compensate for the distinctive disadvantage claimed to be suffered by this particular group of claimants.

7.77 The Panel therefore examined whether the claimed interest should be considered a "legitimate interest" within the meaning of Article 30. The primary issue was whether the normative basis of that claim rested on a widely recognized policy norm.

7.78 The type of normative claim put forward by the EC has been affirmed by a number of governments that have enacted *de jure* extensions of the patent term, primarily in the case of pharmaceutical products, to compensate for the de facto diminution of the normal period of market exclusivity due to delays in obtaining marketing approval. According to the information submitted to the Panel, such extensions have been enacted by the European Communities, Switzerland, the United States, Japan, Australia and Israel. The EC and Switzerland have done so while at the same time allowing patent owners to continue to use their exclusionary rights to gain an additional, de facto extension of market exclusivity by preventing competitors from applying for regulatory approval during the term of the patent. The other countries that have enacted *de jure* patent term extensions have also, either by legislation or by judicial decision, created a regulatory review exception similar to Section 55.2(1), thereby eliminating the possibility of an additional de facto extension of market exclusivity.

7.79 This positive response to the claim for compensatory adjustment has not been universal, however. In addition to Canada, several countries have adopted, or are in the process of adopting, regulatory review exceptions similar to Section 55.2(1) of the Canadian Patent Act, thereby removing the de facto extension of market exclusivity, but these countries have not enacted, and are not planning to enact, any *de jure* extensions of the patent term for producers adversely affected by delayed marketing approval. When regulatory review exceptions are enacted in this manner, they represent a decision not to restore any of the period of market exclusivity due to lost delays in obtaining marketing approval. Taken as a whole, these government decisions may represent either disagreement with the normative claim made by the EC in this proceeding, or they may simply represent a conclusion that such claims are outweighed by other equally legitimate interests.

7.80 In the present proceeding, Canada explicitly disputed the legitimacy of the claimed interest. As noted above, Canada appeared to interpret the term "legitimate interests" in accordance with the Panel's view of that term as a widely recognized normative standard. Canada asserted:

> "[N]otwithstanding the private economic advantage that would be obtained by doing so, a patentee can have no legitimate interest

deriving from patent law in exercising its exclusive use and enforcement rights within the term of protection to achieve, through exploitation of regulatory review laws, a *de facto* extension of that term of protection beyond the prescribed period, thereby unilaterally altering the bargain between the patentee and society. In this respect, the interests of a patentee of a pharmaceutical invention can be no different from those of patentees in other fields of technology.''

7.81 Canada's argument that all fields of technology must be treated the same implicitly rejected the EC's argument that those fields of technology affected by marketing approval requirements should be given certain additional marketing advantages in compensation. Canada was asked by the Panel to explain the distinction between its decision in Section 55.2(1) to remove the delay in obtaining marketing approval for competitive producers seeking to enter the market after the patent expires and its decision not to correct or compensate for the similar delay encountered by the patent owner himself. Canada responded that the de facto diminution of the market exclusivity for patent owners was an unavoidable consequence of the time required to ensure and to demonstrate the safety and efficacy of the product, whereas the delay imposed on competitors by use of the patent rights to block product development and initiation of the regulatory review process during the term of the patent was neither necessary to product safety nor otherwise an appropriate use of patent rights. Canada's answer implied a further question as to the extent to which the marketing delays experienced by patent owners were in fact the result of government regulatory action, as opposed to the normal consequence of the necessary course of product development for products of this kind.

7.82 On balance, the Panel concluded that the interest claimed on behalf of patent owners whose effective period of market exclusivity had been reduced by delays in marketing approval was neither so compelling nor so widely recognized that it could be regarded as a "legitimate interest" within the meaning of Article 30 of the TRIPS Agreement. Notwithstanding the number of governments that had responded positively to that claimed interest by granting compensatory patent term extensions, the issue itself was of relatively recent standing, and the community of governments was obviously still divided over the merits of such claims. Moreover, the Panel believed that it was significant that concerns about regulatory review exceptions in general, although well known at the time of the TRIPS negotiations, were apparently not clear enough, or compelling enough, to make their way explicitly into the recorded agenda of the TRIPS negotiations. The Panel believed that Article 30's "legitimate interests" concept should not be used to decide, through adjudication, a normative policy issue that is still obviously a matter of unresolved political debate.

7.83 Consequently, having considered the two claims of "legitimate interest" put forward by the EC, and having found that neither of these claimed interests can be considered "legitimate interests" within the meaning of the third condition of Article 30 of the TRIPS Agreement, the Panel concluded that Canada had demonstrated to the Panel's satisfaction that Section 55.2(1) of Canada's Patent Act did not prejudice "legitimate interests" of affected patent owners within the meaning of Article 30.

7.84   Having reviewed the conformity of Section 55.2(1) with each of the three conditions for an exception under Article 30 of the TRIPS Agreement, the Panel concluded that Section 55.2(1) does satisfy all three conditions of Article 30, and thus is not inconsistent with Canada's obligations under Article 28.1 of the TRIPS Agreement.

Article 27.1 of the TRIPS Agreement

7.85   The EC claimed that Section 55.2(1) of the Canada Patent Act is also in conflict with the obligations under Article 27.1 of the TRIPS Agreement. Article 27.1 provides:

"Article 27

Patentable Subject Matter

1.   Subject to the provisions of paragraphs 2 and 3, patents shall be available for any inventions, whether products or processes, in all fields of technology, provided that they are new, involve an inventive step and are capable of industrial application. Subject to paragraph 4 of Article 65, paragraph 8 of Article 70 and paragraph 3 of this Article, *patents shall be available and patent rights enjoyable without discrimination as to the place of invention, the field of technology and whether products are imported or locally produced.*" (emphasis added)

7.86   The EC argued that the anti-discrimination rule stated in the italicized language in the text of Article 27.1 above not only requires that the core patent rights made available under Article 28 be non-discriminatory, but also requires that any exceptions to those basic rights made under Articles 30 and 31 must be non-discriminatory as well. Thus, the EC concluded, Article 27.1 requires that the exception made by Section 55.2(1) must be non-discriminatory. The EC contended that Section 55.2(1) does not comply with the obligations of Article 27.1, because it is limited, both *de jure* and de facto, to pharmaceutical products alone, and thus discriminates by field of technology.

7.87   Canada advanced two defences to the EC's claim of an Article 27.1 violation. First, Canada argued that the non-discrimination rule of Article 27.1 does not apply to exceptions taken under Article 30. Second, Canada argued that Section 55.2(1) does not discriminate against pharmaceutical products. The Panel examined these two defences in order.

7.88   Canada took the position that Article 27.1's reference to "patent rights" that must be enjoyable without discrimination as to field of technology refers to the basic rights enumerated in Article 28.1 subject to any exceptions that might be made under Article 30. In other words, governments may discriminate when making the "limited" exceptions allowed under Article 30, but they may not discriminate as to patent rights as modified by such exceptions.

7.89 In support of this position, Canada argued that the scope of Article 30 would be reduced to insignificance if governments were required to treat all fields of technology the same, for if all exceptions had to apply to every product it would be far more difficult to meet the requirement that Article 30 exceptions be "limited". It would also be more difficult to target particular social problems, as are anticipated, according to Canada, by Articles 7 and 8 of the TRIPS Agreement. Conversely, Canada argued, requiring that exceptions be applied to all products would cause needless deprivation of patent rights for those products as to which full enforcement of patent rights causes no problem.

7.90 Canada acknowledged that there are certain textual difficulties with this position. It acknowledged that two of the primary purposes of Article 27.1 were to eliminate two types of discrimination that had been practised against pharmaceuticals and certain other products—either a denial of patentability for such products, or, if patents were granted, automatic compulsory licences permitting others to manufacture such products for a fee. Canada acknowledged that, in order to preclude discrimination as to compulsory licences, the non-discrimination rule of Article 27 was made applicable to Article 31 of the TRIPS Agreement, which grants a limited exception for compulsory licences under specified conditions. To defend its position, therefore, Canada was required to explain how Article 27.1 could apply to exceptions made under Article 31, but not to exceptions made under its neighbouring exception provision in Article 30. Canada argued that Article 31 was "mandatory" in character while Article 30 was "permissive," and that this distinction made it appropriate to apply the non-discrimination provision to the former but not the latter.

7.91 The Panel was unable to agree with Canada's contention that Article 27.1 did not apply to exceptions granted under Article 30. The text of the TRIPS Agreement offers no support for such an interpretation. Article 27.1 prohibits discrimination as to enjoyment of "patent rights" without qualifying that term. Article 30 exceptions are explicitly described as "exceptions to the exclusive rights conferred by a patent" and contain no indication that any exemption from non-discrimination rules is intended. A discriminatory exception that takes away enjoyment of a patent right is discrimination as much as is discrimination in the basic rights themselves. The acknowledged fact that the Article 31 exception for compulsory licences and government use is understood to be subject to the non-discrimination rule of Article 27.1, without the need for any textual provision so providing, further strengthens the case for treating the non-discrimination rules as applicable to Article 30. Articles 30 and 31 are linked together by the opening words of Article 31 which define the scope of Article 31 in terms of exceptions not covered by Article 30. Finally, the Panel could not agree with Canada's attempt to distinguish between Articles 30 and 31 on the basis of their mandatory/permissive character; both provisions permit exceptions to patent rights subject to certain mandatory conditions. Nor could the Panel understand how such a "mandatory/permissive" distinction, even if present, would logically support making the kind of distinction Canada was arguing. In the Panel's view, what was important was that in the rights available under national law, that is to say those resulting from the basic rights and any permissible exceptions to them, the forms of discrimination referred to in Article 27.1 should not be present.

7.92 Nor was the Panel able to agree with the policy arguments in support of Canada's interpretation of Article 27. To begin with, it is not true that being able to discriminate against particular patents will make it possible to meet Article 30's requirement that the exception be "limited". An Article 30 exception cannot be made "limited" by limiting it to one field of technology, because the effects of each exception must be found to be "limited" when measured against each affected patent. Beyond that, it is not true that Article 27 requires all Article 30 exceptions to be applied to all products. Article 27 prohibits only discrimination as to the place of invention, the field of technology, and whether products are imported or produced locally. Article 27 does not prohibit bona fide exceptions to deal with problems that may exist only in certain product areas. Moreover, to the extent the prohibition of discrimination does limit the ability to target certain products in dealing with certain of the important national policies referred to in Articles 7 and 8.1, that fact may well constitute a deliberate limitation rather than a frustration of purpose. It is quite plausible, as the EC argued, that the TRIPS Agreement would want to require governments to apply exceptions in a non-discriminatory manner, in order to ensure that governments do not succumb to domestic pressures to limit exceptions to areas where right holders tend to be foreign producers.

7.93 The Panel concluded, therefore, that the anti-discrimination rule of Article 27.1 does apply to exceptions of the kind authorized by Article 30. We turn, accordingly, to the question of whether Section 55.2(1) of the Canadian Patent Act discriminates as to fields of technology.

7.94 The primary TRIPS provisions that deal with discrimination, such as the national treatment and most-favoured-nation provisions of Articles 3 and 4, do not use the term "discrimination". They speak in more precise terms. The ordinary meaning of the word "discriminate" is potentially broader than these more specific definitions. It certainly extends beyond the concept of differential treatment. It is a normative term, pejorative in connotation, referring to results of the unjustified imposition of differentially disadvantageous treatment. Discrimination may arise from explicitly different treatment, sometimes called "*de jure* discrimination", but it may also arise from ostensibly identical treatment which, due to differences in circumstances, produces differentially disadvantageous effects, sometimes called "de facto discrimination". The standards by which the justification for differential treatment is measured are a subject of infinite complexity. "Discrimination" is a term to be avoided whenever more precise standards are available, and, when employed, it is a term to be interpreted with caution, and with care to add no more precision than the concept contains . . .

7.99   With regard to the issue of *de jure* discrimination, the Panel concluded that the European Communities had not presented sufficient evidence to raise the issue in the face of Canada's formal declaration that the exception of Section 55.2(1) was not limited to pharmaceutical products. Absent other evidence, the words of the statute compelled the Panel to accept Canada's assurance that the exception was legally available to every product that was subject to marketing approval requirements. In reaching this conclusion, the Panel took note that its legal finding of conformity on this point was based on a finding as to the meaning of the Canadian law that was in turn based on Canada's representations as to the meaning of that law, and that this finding of conformity would no longer be warranted if, and to the extent that, Canada's representations as to the meaning of that law were to prove wrong.

7.100   The Panel then turned to the question of de facto discrimination. Although the EC's response to the Panel's questions indicated that it did intend to raise the issue of de facto discrimination, the EC did not propose a formal definition of de facto discrimination, nor did it submit a systematic exposition of the evidence satisfying the elements of such a concept. Australia and the United States, third parties in the proceedings, referred to previous GATT and WTO legal rulings treating de facto discrimination, but primarily for the purpose of suggesting the mirror image principle—that not all differential treatment is "discrimination". Canada did not associate itself with the Australian and United States positions. Notwithstanding the limited development of the arguments on the issue of de facto discrimination, the Panel concluded that its terms of reference required it to pursue that issue once raised, and accordingly the Panel proceeded to examine the claim of a de facto discrimination violation on the basis of its own examination of the record in the light of the concepts usually associated with claims of de facto discrimination.

7.101   As noted above, de facto discrimination is a general term describing the legal conclusion that an ostensibly neutral measure transgresses a non-discrimination norm because its actual effect is to impose differentially disadvantageous consequences on certain parties, and because those differential effects are found to be wrong or unjustifiable. Two main issues figure in the application of that general concept in most legal systems. One is the question of de facto discriminatory effect—whether the actual effect of the measure is to impose differentially disadvantageous consequences on certain parties. The other, related to the justification for the disadvantageous effects, is the issue of purpose—not an inquiry into the subjective purposes of the officials responsible for the measure, but an inquiry into the objective characteristics of the measure from which one can infer the existence or non-existence of discriminatory objectives.

7.102   With regard to the first issue—the actual effects of the measure, the EC had argued that, despite its potentially broad coverage of many industries, the exception created by Section 55.2(1) had "in effect" applied only to pharmaceutical patents. The Panel received no systematic information on the range of industries that have actually made use of Section 55.2(1). In the absence of such information, the critical question was whether there was some practical reason why the regulatory review exception would in reality work only to the disadvantage of producers of patented pharmaceutical products. The Panel asked the parties for an explanation of any practical considerations that would limit the scope of application of Section 55.2(1) to pharmaceutical products, but no such explanation was provided. Nor was the Panel able to find such a practical reason from the information before it. The Panel concluded that the EC had not demonstrated that Section 55.2(1) had had a discriminatory effect limited to patented pharmaceutical products.

7.103   On the issue of discriminatory purpose, the EC had stressed on several occasions that, in the public discussion of Section 55.2(1), all relevant participants had been exclusively concerned with the impact of the measure on pharmaceutical products, with both support and opposition to the measure being argued in terms of that one dimension. Canada did not contest this characterization of the public debates.

7.104   The Panel did not find this evidence from the debates on Section 55.2(1) to be persuasive evidence of a discriminatory purpose. To be sure, such evidence makes it clear that the primary reason for passing the measure was its effect on promoting competition in the pharmaceutical sector. This is also evident from Canada's justification for the measure presented in this dispute settlement proceeding. But preoccupation with the effects of a statute in one area does not necessarily mean that the provisions applicable to other areas are a sham, or of no actual or potential importance. Individual problems are frequently the driving force behind legislative actions of broader scope. The broader scope of the measure usually reflects an important legal principle that rules being applied in the area of primary interest should also be applied to other areas where the same problem occurs. Indeed, it is a common desideratum in many legal systems that legislation apply its underlying principles as broadly as possible. So long as the broader application is not a sham, the legislation cannot be considered discriminatory. In the absence of any proof that the broader scope was a sham, it must be found that the evident concentration of public attention upon the effects of Section 55.2(1) on the pharmaceutical industry is not, by itself, evidence of a discriminatory purpose.

7.105   In sum, the Panel found that the evidence in record before it did not raise a plausible claim of discrimination under Article 27.1 of the TRIPS Agreement. It was not proved that the legal scope of Section 55.2(1) was limited to pharmaceutical products, as would normally be required to raise a claim of *de jure* discrimination. Likewise, it was not proved that the adverse effects of Section 55.2(1) were limited to the pharmaceutical industry, or that the objective indications of purpose demonstrated a purpose to impose disadvantages on pharmaceutical patents in particular, as is often required to raise a claim of de facto discrimination. Having found that the record did not raise any of these basic elements of a discrimination claim, the Panel was able to find that Section 55.2(1) is not inconsistent with Canada's obligations under Article 27.1 of the TRIPS Agreement. Because the record did not present issues requiring any more precise interpretation of the term "discrimination" in Article 27.1, none was made.

Notes and Questions

(1) Canada did not appeal the decision. It has since amended its patent law to comply with the ruling.

(2) The regulatory review exception allows the manufacturers of generic drugs to enter the market quickly after the patent on the competing drug expires (by securing regulatory approval in advance of the expiration date). Without it, a period of several years might be needed after the expiration of the patent to secure approval of the generic product. By contrast, the stockpiling exception simply allows manufacturing of the generic product starting six months before the expiration of the patent, and thus facilitates generic entry a few months earlier than otherwise at most (assuming that regulatory approval has been secured). As a practical matter, therefore, the regulatory review exception appears far more important to the facilitation of quick generic entry than the stockpiling exception, and can be expected to impose far greater economic costs on the holders of pharmaceutical patents. In light of these facts about their relative economic impact, has the Panel given a coherent explanation of why the regulatory review exception is "limited" but the stockpiling exception is not? What reading of "limited" is to be given if it is uncorrelated with the economic impact of the exception on the patent holder? Would it make more sense to treat the negotiating history presented by Canada, and the proliferation of regulatory review exceptions in national legislation, as the key to the finding on this issue?

(3) Is it not "normal" for patent holders to enforce their rights so as to delay competition as long as possible? Why is it not "legitimate" for pharmaceutical patent holders to enforce their rights to delay generic competition, especially when much of the life of their patent is consumed by the clinical trials and regulatory hurdles that they must surmount before they can obtain regulatory approval and begin to sell the drug?

(4) Were you satisfied with the Panel's response to the claim that the regulatory review exception is de *facto* discriminatory?

(5) An issue of considerable political importance at this writing involves claims that the TRIPs Agreement imprudently requires developing nations to enforce pharmaceutical patent rights that raise the prices of vital medicines in poor nations facing medical crises (such as the nations affected by the Sub–Saharan AIDS pandemic). Consider the pertinent provisions of TRIPS—can any exceptions be invoked to deal with this problem? Could a developing nation exempt particular drugs from its patent regime? Require compulsory licensing of pharmaceutical patent rights for a nominal fee? Consider in particular Article 31 of the TRIPS Agreement and the Doha Declaration on TRIPS and Public Health (Section 27.2 infra.)

(6) A similar dispute, involving the "limited exceptions" permitted to copyright protection under Article 13, was the following.

UNITED STATES—SECTION 110(5) OF THE US COPYRIGHT ACT

WT/DS160/R
Panel Report adopted by the DSB on July 27, 2000

2.1   The dispute concerns Section 110(5) of the US Copyright Act of 1976, as amended * * *. The provisions of Section 110(5) place limitations on the exclusive rights provided to owners of copyright in Section 106 of the Copyright Act in respect of certain performances and displays.

* * *

2.9   The 1998 Amendment has added a new subparagraph (B) to Section 110(5), to which we, for the sake of brevity, hereinafter refer to as a "business" exemption. It exempts, under certain conditions, communication by an establishment of a transmission or retransmission embodying a performance or display of a nondramatic musical work intended to be received by the general public, originated by a radio or television broadcast station licensed as such by the Federal Communications Commission, or, if an audiovisual transmission, by a cable system or satellite carrier.

2.10   The beneficiaries of the business exemption are divided into two categories: establishments other than food service or drinking establishments ("retail establishments"), and food service and drinking establishments. In each category, establishments under a certain size limit are exempted, regardless of the type of equipment they use. The size limits are 2,000 gross square feet (186 m2) for retail establishments and 3,750 gross square feet (348 m2) for restaurants.

* * *

2.12   In 1999, Dun & Bradstreet, Inc. * * * estimated that 70 per cent of eating establishments and 73 per cent of drinking establishments fell under the 3,750 square feet limit, and that 45 per cent of retail establishments fell under the 2,000 square feet limit.

* * *

2.14   If the size of an establishment is above the limits referred to in paragraph 2.10 above (there is no maximum size), the exemption applies provided that the establishment does not exceed the limits set for the equipment used. The limits on equipment are different as regards, on the one hand, audio performances, and, on the other hand, audiovisual performances and displays. The rules concerning equipment limitations are the same for both retail establishments and restaurants above the respective size limits.

* * *

6.30   A major issue in this dispute is the interpretation and application to the facts of this case of Article 13 of the TRIPS Agreement. The US defense is firmly based upon it. The United States submits that the Article clarifies and articulates the "minor exceptions" doctrine applicable under certain provisions of the Berne Convention (1971) and incorporated into the TRIPS Agreement. * * *

[Eds. note: The panel next proceeds through a lengthy discussion of the Berne Convention and its relationship to the TRIPS Agreement, after which it finds:]

6.94   We conclude that Article 13 of the TRIPS Agreement applies to Articles 11*bis*(1)(iii) and 11(1)(ii) of the Berne Convention (1971) as incorporated into the TRIPS Agreement, given that neither the express wording nor the context of Article 13 or any other provision of the TRIPS Agreement supports the interpretation that the scope of application of Article 13 is limited to the exclusive rights newly introduced under the TRIPS Agreement.

* * *

6.97   Article 13 of the TRIPS Agreement requires that limitations and exceptions to exclusive rights (1) be confined to certain special cases, (2) do not conflict with a normal exploitation of the work, and (3) do not unreasonably prejudice the legitimate interests of the right holder. * * *

* * *

6.103   The United States submits that the fact that the TRIPS Agreement does not elaborate on the criteria for a case to be considered "special" provides Members flexibility to determine for themselves whether a particular case represents an appropriate basis for an exception. But it acknowledges that the essence of the first condition is that the exceptions be well-defined and of limited application.

* * *

6.107   We start our analysis of the first condition of Article 13 by referring to the ordinary meaning of the terms in their context and in the light of its object and purpose. It appears that the notions of "exceptions" and "limitations" in the introductory words of Article 13 overlap in part in the sense that an "exception" refers to a derogation from an exclusive right provided under national legislation in some respect, while a "limitation" refers to a reduction of such right to a certain extent.

6.108   The ordinary meaning of "certain" is "known and particularised, but not explicitly identified", "determined, fixed, not variable; definitive, precise, exact". In other words, this term means that, under the first condition, an exception or limitation in national legislation must be clearly defined. However, there is no need to identify explicitly each and every possible situation to which the exception could apply, provided that the scope of the exception is known and particularised. This guarantees a sufficient degree of legal certainty.

6.109   We also have to give full effect to the ordinary meaning of the second word of the first condition. The term "special" connotes "having an individual or limited application or purpose", "containing details; precise, specific", "exceptional in quality or degree; unusual; out of the ordinary" or "distinctive in some way". This term means that more is needed than a clear definition in order to meet the standard of the first condition. In addition, an exception or limitation must be limited in its field of application or exceptional in its scope. In other words, an exception or limitation should be narrow in quantitative as well as a qualitative sense. This suggests a narrow scope as well as an exceptional or distinctive objective. To put this aspect of the first condition into the context of the second condition ("no conflict with a normal exploitation"), an exception or limitation should be the opposite of a non-special, i.e., a normal case.

* * *

6.113   In the case at hand, in order to determine whether subparagraph (B) * * * Section 110(5) [is] confined to "certain special cases", we first examine whether the exceptions have been clearly defined. Second, we ascertain whether the exemptions are narrow in scope, *inter alia*, with respect to their reach. In that respect, we take into account what percentage of eating and drinking establishments and retail establishments may benefit from the business exemption under subparagraph (B) * * *. On a subsidiary basis, we consider whether it is possible to draw inferences about the reach of the business ... exemption from the stated policy purposes underlying these exemptions according to the statements made during the US legislative process.

6.114   As noted above, the United States argues that the essence of the first condition of Article 13 of the TRIPS Agreement is that exceptions be well-defined and of limited application. It claims that the business exemption of subparagraph (B) meets the requirements of the first condition of Article 13, because it is clearly defined in Section 110(5) of the US Copyright Act by square footage and equipment limitations.

* * *

6.116   The European Communities contends that the business exemption is too broad in its scope to pass as a "certain special case", given the large number of establishments which potentially may benefit from it. For the European Communities, it is irrelevant that the size of establishments and the type of equipment are clearly defined, when the broad scope of the business exemption turns an exception into the rule.

6.117   It appears that the European Communities does not dispute the fact that subparagraph (B) is clearly defined in respect of the size limits of establishments and the type of equipment that may be used by establishments above the applicable limits. The primary bone of contention between the parties is whether the business exemption, given its scope and reach, can be considered as a "special" case within the meaning of the first condition of Article 13.

* * *

6.133 The factual information presented to us indicates that a substantial majority of eating and drinking establishments and close to half of retail establishments are covered by the exemption contained in subparagraph (B) of Section 110(5) of the US Copyright Act. Therefore, we conclude that the exemption does not qualify as a "certain special case" in the meaning of the first condition of Article 13.

Notes and Questions

(1) The brief excerpt above omits discussion of the other limitations contained in Article 13. The panel found that the business exception also "conflict[s] with a normal exploitation" of the rights of copyright holders, and that it "unreasonably prejudice[s] the legitimate interests of the right holder[s]." By contrast, the "homestyle exemption" under U.S. copyright law, which provides that smaller establishments may expose their customers to certain broadcasts over "homestyle" receiving equipment without having to obtain a license from the copyright holder, was found by the Panel to be permissible under Article 13. The United States did not appeal the decision, but at this writing conforming changes in U.S. copyright law are still pending.

(2) Compare the Canadian pharmaceutical patent case to the U.S. Copyright Act case. Is the difference in the language of Articles 13 and 30 critical to the difference in outcomes (regarding the regulatory review exception and the business exception)? Are they consistent as a policy matter in your view?

Chapter 21

LINKAGES BETWEEN INTER-NATIONAL TRADE POLICY AND THE ENVIRONMENT, HUMAN RIGHTS, LABOR STANDARDS AND NATIONAL SECURITY

SECTION 21.1 INTRODUCTION

(A) OVERVIEW

The linkages between trade policies and non-economic policy objectives pose some of the most perplexing conceptual questions that exist in the subject of international relations. On the one hand, what is the relationship between expanded international trade and the environment, human rights and labor standards? How do they interact? On the other hand, when a nation (like the United States) has considerable economic power, there is a temptation to use that power to pursue a wide variety of national objectives. Should trade measures be used to pressure other nations to protect the environment? To protect human rights? To promote minimum labor standards? To inhibit trafficking in illegal drugs? To discourage or punish assistance to terrorism or weapons sales (especially of missiles or nuclear arms)? To deter or punish aggression? To engage generally in economic warfare against nations viewed as unfriendly?

We cannot here resolve the issue of what is the exact relationship between expanded international trade and the environment, human rights and labor standards. Nor can we answer the questions of whether nations should use trade measures to promote the environment, human rights and labor standards. We can, however, explore the debates over the relationships and consider what nations have done in the past in such circumstances and attempt to assess the effectiveness of their actions.

We start in this introductory section with an historical overview of the use of trade and other economic sanctions and some reflections on their effectiveness. In Section 21.2, we consider the relationship of expanded trade and the environment and the extent to which existing trade rules allow for the promotion of environmental goals. In Section 21.3, we turn to an examination of human rights generally and how trade controls have been used to promote them. In Section 21.4 we look more closely at one specific aspect of individual rights—worker rights—and consider U.S. attempts to use the threat of revoking trade preferences to promote such rights. Finally, in Section 21.5, we consider foreign policy and national security goals and their relationship to trade.

(B) HISTORICAL USE OF ECONOMIC SANCTIONS

GARY CLYDE HUFBAUER, JEFFREY J. SCHOTT & KIMBERLY ANN ELLIOT, ECONOMIC SANCTIONS RECONSIDERED 5–7 (2d ed. 1990)[1]

In the period following World War II, other foreign policy motives became increasingly common, but sanctions were still deployed to force a target country to withdraw its troops from border skirmishes, to abandon plans of territorial acquisition, or to desist from other military adventures. In most instances in the postwar period where economic pressure was brought to bear against the exercise of military power, the United States played the role of international policeman. For example, in 1948–49 the United States was able to coerce the Netherlands into backing away from its military efforts to forestall Indonesian independence; in 1956, the United States pressed the French and British into withdrawing their troops from the Suez region; and in the early 1960s, the United States persuaded Egypt to withdraw from Yemen and the Congo by withholding development and PL 480 food aid.

More recent attempts have not been as successful. Turkish troops continue to be stationed in Cyprus more than 15 years after their invasion and in spite of US economic pressure in the mid–1970s. The Carter grain embargo and boycott of the 1980 Moscow Olympics did not discourage the Soviet occupation of Afghanistan. Indeed, aside from the 1956 Suez incident, major powers have never been able to deter the military adventures of other major powers simply through the use of economic sanctions.

Closely related to military adventure cases are those episodes where sanctions are imposed to impair the economic capability of the target country, thereby limiting its potential for military activity. This was an important rationale for the broad-based multilateral controls on strategic trade that the United States instituted against the Soviet Union and China in the late 1940s, and the same rationale was cited by US officials in defense of recent sanctions against the Soviet Union following the invasion of Afghanistan and the crisis in Poland in the early 1980s. It is doubtful whether these cases have yielded positive results, not least because it is difficult to hamper the military capabilities of a major power with marginal degrees of economic deprivation.

* * *

Sanctions have also been deployed in pursuit of a number of foreign policy goals other than those related to warfare and national security. Especially noteworthy is the frequent resort to sanctions in an effort to destabilize foreign governments, usually in the context of a foreign policy dispute involving other issues. Destabilization episodes have often found a superpower pitted against a smaller country. By our count the United States has engaged in destabilization efforts 15 times, often against other countries in the Western Hemisphere such as Cuba, the Dominican Republic, Nicaragua, Brazil, Chile, and Panama. Sanctions contributed at least modestly to the overthrow of Trujillo in 1961, of Brazilian dictator João Goulart in 1964, and of Chilean President Salvador Allende in 1973; sanctions played a minor role in the electoral defeat of the Sandinistas in Nicaragua in 1990. On the other hand, Cuba under Fidel Castro has not succumbed to three decades of US economic pressure, in large measure because Castro received compensating aid from the Soviet Union. Likewise, despite intense US economic sanctions, Noriega was able to retain power in Panama; it finally took US military intervention to dislodge him.

The Soviet Union has also picked on its neighbors, though less successfully. Every time the Soviets have used sanctions in an effort to topple a rebellious government within the socialist bloc—Yugoslavia in 1948, China in 1960, and Albania in 1961—the effort failed; the only Soviet success came in the "Nightfrost Crisis" of 1958, when Finland was coerced into adopting a more pliant attitude toward Soviet policies. Finally, the United Kingdom also has participated in the destabilization game through the use of economic sanctions to topple hostile or repressive regimes in areas where Britain once exercised colonial influence—Iran in 1951–53, Rhodesia in 1965–79, and Uganda in 1972–79.

Since the early 1960s, sanctions have been deployed in support of numerous other foreign policy goals, most of them relatively modest compared to the pursuit of war, peace, and political destabilization. For example, sanctions have been used on behalf of efforts to protect human rights, to halt nuclear proliferation, to settle expropriation claims, and to combat international terrorism. Here again, the United States has played the dominant role as guardian of its version of global morality. Following a series of congressionally inspired initiatives beginning in 1973, human rights became a *cause célèbre* of the Carter administration. In the early phase, country-specific riders were attached to military aid bills requiring the Nixon and Ford administrations to deny or reduce assistance to countries found abusing human rights. Later, President Carter adopted the congressional mandate as his own guiding light. Eventually, many countries in Latin America and elsewhere became targets of US sanctions. In a more limited way, Presidents Reagan and

Bush also used sanctions to defend human rights and support democracy in Suriname, Haiti, Burma, Somalia, and the Sudan.

Sanctions were also frequently used, by both the United States and Canada in the 1970s and 1980s, to enforce compliance with nuclear nonproliferation safeguards. In 1974, Canada acted to prevent Pakistan from acquiring a nuclear explosive capability, and tried to control the reprocessing of spent fuel in both India and Pakistan to guard against weapons production. The United States joined the Canadians in applying financial pressure on South Korea to forestall its purchase of a nuclear reprocessing plant. Subsequently, the United States imposed sanctions on shipments of nuclear fuel and technology to South Africa, Taiwan, Brazil, Argentina, India, and Pakistan in similar attempts to secure adequate multilateral surveillance of nuclear facilities. Australia used sanctions in an effort to deter French testing in the South Pacific. These assorted efforts were highly successful with respect to Korea and Taiwan (at least initially) but had little impact on India, Pakistan, or France.

Since World War II the United States has used sanctions nine times in its efforts to negotiate compensation for property expropriated by foreign governments. However, expropriation claims have become less urgent in recent years; the last recorded use of sanctions in an expropriation dispute was against Ethiopia (commencing in 1976). In almost all the expropriation cases, the United States hoped to go beyond the claims issue and resolve conflicting political philosophies. This was true the first time the United States (in conjunction with the United Kingdom) pressured Iran with economic sanctions—seeking the overthrow of the regime of Prime Minister Mohammed Mussadiq in the early 1950s—and was behind US efforts to undermine Castro in Cuba, Goulart in Brazil, and Allende in Chile.

Antiterrorism has been another of the modest—but increasingly important—policy goals sought by the United States through the imposition of economic sanctions. A wave of international plane hijackings in the 1960s and 1970s, together with the massacre of Israeli athletes at the Munich Olympics in 1972, focused world attention on terrorism. The hijacking problem was greatly reduced through international hijacking agreements, including one signed in 1973 by the United States and Cuba. Lethal terrorist raids, often funded by oil-rich radical, Islamic countries, have proven much harder to control. In 1980, following a congressional directive, the US State Department branded four countries—Libya, Syria, Iraq, and South Yemen—as international outlaws because of their support of terrorist activities. The United States soon thereafter imposed sanctions on Libya and Iraq in an attempt to limit their ability as suppliers of military equipment to terrorist groups. Iraq was removed from the terrorism list in 1982, despite congressional opposition, whereas sanctions against Libya were expanded to cover all trade and finance in early 1986. Since then, Cuba, North Korea, and Iran have been added to the list of target countries on account of their support for terrorism.

This brief historical review illustrates the important role that economic sanctions have played since World War I in the conduct of US foreign policy. Of the 116 cases documented in table 1.1, the United States, either alone or in concert with its allies, has deployed sanctions 77 times. Other significant users have been the United Kingdom (22 instances, often in cooperation with the League of Nations and later the United Nations); the Soviet Union (10 uses, usually against recalcitrant satellites); and the Arab League and its members (4 uses of its oil muscle).

This overview demonstrates that sanctions have been deployed quite frequently in the post-World War II era. Table 1.3 summarizes the record, presenting, first, the number of sanctions episodes initiated in each five-year period beginning with 1911–15; the second, the total cost imposed on target countries every fifth year beginning with 1915 (expressed as an annualized figure in current US dollars); and third, for comparison, the value of total world exports (expressed in current US dollars). The table indicates that the incidence of new episodes has increased from less than 5 in the pre–1945 period to approximately 10 to 15 in the post–1960 period. The annual cost imposed on target countries was quite high in 1915, on account of World War I; it fell markedly thereafter, and has since risen from very low levels in the 1920s and 1930s to some $1.5 billion and higher in the post–1965 period. The aggregate cost of sanctions peaked in 1980, when costs totaling some $5.9 billion were imposed on target countries.

————

Since the above excerpt was written, the U.S. has imposed (or threatened to impose) trade sanctions for national security or political purposes on many countries, including China, Haiti, Libya, India, Iran, Iraq, Panama, Pakistan, South Africa, Sudan and the former Yugoslavia (Serbia and Montenegro).

(C) ANALYZING THE EFFECTIVENESS OF ECONOMIC SANCTIONS

The foregoing historical discussion suggests that economic sanctions are often not successful in achieving their goals. One interesting question is what types of circumstances, if any, make it more likely that sanctions will succeed. Consider the following:

GARY CLYDE HUFBAUER ET AL., ECONOMIC SANCTIONS RECONSIDERED 92–105 (2d ed. 1990)

A number of lessons can be abstracted from the sanctions episodes of the past 75 years. In this concluding chapter, we first assess the overall effectiveness of sanctions as a tool of foreign policy, based on the experience of 115 cases, and group the lessons learned into a list of suggestions for increasing the prospects for success. We then explore the implications of recent US experience, and of the end of the Cold War, for the future use of economic sanctions. We conclude with a list of do's and don'ts—nine commandments—to guide governments in the use of economic sanctions.

* * *

* * * [A] word of caution. Forecasting the outcome of statecraft, like forecasting the stock market, is hazardous business. As one might expect from a diverse collection of 115 cases, the statistical results are not always clear-cut. Idiosyncratic influences are often at play. Human personalities and plain luck may well determine the outcome of a sanctions episode. Much depends on the kaleidoscope of contemporaneous world events and other factors which are not captured by our variables. Hence our summary assessments and nine commandments must be read as general indicators, not infallible guideposts, in the fine art of statecraft.

Are Sanctions Effective?

In designing foreign policy strategy, policy makers need to take a close look at the cost and effectiveness of sanctions. Although it is not true that sanctions "never work," they are of limited utility in achieving foreign policy goals that depend upon compelling the target country to take actions it stoutly resists. Still, in some instances, particularly situations involving small target countries and modest policy goals, sanctions have helped alter foreign behavior. * * *

* * *

Table 5.1 Success by type of policy goal

Policy goal	Success cases	Failure cases	Success ratio (percentage of total)
Modest policy changes	17	34	33
Destabilization	11	10	52
Disruption of military adventures	6	12	33
Military impairment	2	8	20
Other major policy changes	5	15	20
Totals [a]	41	79	34

a. Five cases are classified under two different policy goals. * * * Since all but one of these cases are failures, double counting them adds a small negative bias to the success ratio.

Sanctions have been successful—by our definition—in 34 percent of the cases overall. However, the success rate depends importantly on the type of policy or governmental change sought. Episodes involving destabilization succeeded in half the cases, usually against target countries that were small and shaky. Cases involving modest goals and attempts to disrupt minor military adventures were successful about a third of the time. Efforts to impair a foreign adversary's military potential, or otherwise to change its policies in a major way, succeeded only infrequently.

Of course, some sanctions fail because they were never intended to succeed, in the sense of producing a real change in the target's behavior. As one analyst has noted, when sanctions have been used primarily for domestic political or other rhetorical purposes, " 'effective' sanctions were not a primary policy goal." * * *

* * *

NINE COMMANDMENTS

It is clear that sanctions sometimes bear fruit, but only when planted in the right soil and nurtured in the proper way. We therefore offer nine propositions for the statesman who would act as a careful gardener. * * *

I. *"Don't Bite Off More Than You Can Chew."*

Policymakers often have inflated expectations of what sanctions can accomplish. This is especially true of the United States today and was true of the United Kingdom in an earlier era. At most, there is a weak correlation between economic deprivation and political willingness to change. The *economic* impact of sanctions may be pronounced, both on the sender and the target country, but other factors in the situation often overshadow the impact of sanctions in determining the *political* outcome.

* * * Excluding the two world wars and the two civil wars (India–Hyderabad and Nigeria–Biafra), we have found only three cases in which economic coercion was effective in changing a major domestic policy of the target country.

In [Arab League v. US and Netherlands], the Arab oil embargo helped accomplish two of its four objectives: it caused a significant shift, namely a more pro-Arab slant, in European and Japanese policies toward the Palestinian question; and it supported OPEC's decision to boost the world price of oil, to its members' enormous economic benefit. But the embargo failed to get Israel to retreat behind its pre–1967 frontiers, and it failed to persuade the US to abandon its pro-Israel policy stance. * * * In [U.S. v. Poland], sanctions exacerbated a deteriorating economic situation and encouraged the gradual softening of the Communist government's crackdown on the Solidarity union movement. In the third case, India's trade embargo against land-locked Nepal contributed to the political unrest that forced King Birenda to recognize long-banned opposition parties and ultimately allowed a more pro-Indian government to take power. In other cases where impairment was sought and attempts were made to change major policies of target countries, sanctions have been ineffective.

To justify even a remote hope for success in military impairment and major change cases, sender countries should form a near monopoly over trading relations with the target country. This obvious precept, learned in the first and second world wars, was forgotten in the case of UN sanctions against South Africa and turned on its head in the case of US sanctions to block construction of the Soviet–European gas pipeline. * * *

II.   *"More Is Not Necessarily Merrier."*

In general, the greater the number of countries needed to implement sanctions, the less likely it is that they will be effective. The 1990 UN embargo against Iraq, which is unprecedented in its comprehensive coverage and almost universal participation, is the exception that proves the rule. * * * In most instances, multilateral sanctions are not associated with success.

The idea that international cooperation is a necessary ingredient in all sanctions cases is misplaced. A country looks to its allies for help because its goals are ambitious; in cases involving more modest goals, such cooperation is not needed. * * *

* * *

To be sure, international cooperation may serve three useful functions: to increase the moral suasion of the sanction, to help isolate the target country from the global community psychologically as well as economically, and to preempt foreign backlash, thus minimizing corrosive friction within the alliance. * * *

* * *

III.   *"The Weakest Go to The Wall."*

For our case sample as a whole, there seems to be a direct correlation between the political and economic health of the target country and its susceptibility to economic pressure. * * * The table clearly indicates that countries in distress or experiencing significant problems are far more likely to succumb to coercion by the sender country.

* * *

IV.   *"Attack Your Allies, Not Your Adversaries."*

Economic sanctions seem most effective when aimed against erstwhile friends and close trading partners. By contrast, sanctions directed against target countries that have long been adversaries of the sender country, or against targets that have little trade with the sender country, are generally less successful.

* * *

The higher compliance with sanctions by allies and trading partners reflects their willingness to bend on specific issues in deference to an overall relationship with the sender country. Such considerations may not be decisive in the calculus of an antagonistic target country, or a target country that has little economic contact with the sender. * * *

* * *

V. *"If It Were Done, When 'Tis Done, Then 'Twere Well It Were Done Quickly."*

A heavy, slow hand invites both evasion and the mobilization of domestic opinion in the target country. Sanctions imposed slowly or incrementally may simply strengthen the target government at home as it marshals the forces of nationalism. Moreover, such measures are likely to be undercut over time either by the sender's own firms or by foreign competitors. Sanctions generally are regarded as a short-term policy, with the anticipation that normal commercial relations will be reestablished after the resolution of the crisis. Thus, even though popular opinion in the sender country may welcome the introduction of sanctions, the longer an episode drags on, the more public support for sanctions dissipates.

* * *

VI. *"In For a Penny, In For a Pound."*

Cases that inflict heavy costs on the target country are generally successful. [Our analysis indicates that] the average cost to the target for all successful cases was over 2.4 percent of GNP; by contrast, failed episodes barely dented the economy of the target country, with costs averaging only 1 percent of GNP. * * *

* * *

VII. *"If You Need to Ask the Price, You Can't Afford the Yacht."*

The more it costs a sender country to impose sanctions, the less likely it is that the sanctions will succeed. * * *

* * *

These results suggest that sender governments should design sanctions so as not to inflict unduly concentrated costs on particular domestic groups. One example of actions to avoid, in all but extreme situations, is the retroactive application of sanctions to cancel existing contracts. Such actions not only leave the affected firms high and dry, with unsold inventories and excess capacity, but they also sour those firms' chances of competing for future business. If the sender government believes that retroactive application is essential to the success of an episode, then it should compensate the affected domestic firms at least for the loss on unsold inventories.

The sanctions episodes that are least costly to the sender are often those that make use of financial leverage—manipulating aid flows, denying official credits, or, at the extreme, freezing assets—rather than trade controls. [Our analysis] shows that financial sanctions have been used alone more often and more effectively than trade controls alone.

* * *

VIII. *"Choose the Right Tool for the Job."*

Economic sanctions are often deployed in conjunction with other measures directed against the target: covert action, quasi-military measures, or regular military operations. * * *

* * *

* * * Rather than buttressing a sanctions campaign, companion measures are frequently used when sanctions are perceived to be either wholly inadequate or simply too slow.

IX. *"Look Before You Leap."*

Sender governments should think through their means and objectives *before* taking a final decision to deploy sanctions. Leaders in the sender country should be confident that their goals are within their reach; that they can impose sufficient economic pain to command the attention of the target country, that their efforts will not prompt offsetting policies by other powers, and that the sanctions chosen will not impose insupportable costs on their domestic constituents and foreign allies. These conditions will arise only infrequently, and even then the odds of success are slim.

Notes and Questions

(1) Is it sensible to place great stress on the question of effectiveness? If a government wishes to show its support of certain principles, such as basic human rights, why should it not use trade controls to do so? Does the fact that imposing trade controls is by itself unlikely to change a foreign government's policies mean that it should not be done?

(2) In light of the fact that economic sanctions often do not work, should the U.S. government be required to make public its determination of the likely effect on the U.S. economy and the likely effectiveness of the sanctions before implementing them?

SECTION 21.2   ENVIRONMENT AND INTERNATIONAL TRADE: CON-FLICT OR CO–EXISTENCE?[1]

Protecting the environment was not a major concern when the General Agreement on Tariffs and Trade was drafted in 1947. In recent years, however, it has become an issue of great importance to many countries. The result has been no little tension between trade treaty

1. There have been numerous books and articles written on the general theme of trade and the environment. See, e.g., Daniel C. Esty, Greening the GATT (1994); The Greening of World Trade Issues (Kym Anderson & Richard Blackhurst eds., 1992).

negotiators and environmentalists, each of whom sees the other as threatening principles they hold dear. The conflict was brought to the forefront in dramatic fashion in September 1991 by the GATT panel decision in the so-called *Tuna-Dolphin* case, which ruled that a U.S. embargo on tuna from countries that did not follow U.S. rules on protecting dolphins during tuna fishing violated GATT rules and could not be justified under Article XX. The panel report was never adopted by the Contracting Parties, and the panel's reasoning is only of historical interest given the Appellate Body's decisions in the so-called *Shrimp-Turtle* case (see Section 13.4 supra). Nonetheless for almost a decade after its announcement, the case received much attention and at the time was the subject of very critical full-page newspaper advertisements in the United States, taken out by environmental and other public interest groups.[2]

The *Tuna-Dolphin* case was decided at a time of heightened international interest in the environment. In the summer of 1992, the United Nations Conference on the Environment and Development (UNCED) met in Rio de Janeiro, Brazil, and was attended by 178 nations. The conference adopted a number of instruments, including a declaration of environmental principles known as the Rio Principles, treaties on global warming and biological diversity, a nonbinding declaration on forest conservation principles and a document known as Agenda 21, which addressed many aspects of the environment and development.[3] UNCED had been preceded by the 1972 Stockholm Conference on the Human Environment, which was sponsored by the United Nations and led to the creation of the United Nations Environment Programme. The OECD has also been active in the past in discussing environmental issues.

A number of the Rio Principles are important for our consideration of trade and the environment. The basic theme of the Rio conference was sustainable development and a number of the Rio Principles are concerned with that theme. In order to allow states to achieve sustainable development, Principle 8 provides that "states should reduce and eliminate unsustainable patterns of production and consumption." While Principle 2 recognized that "[s]tates have, in accordance with the Charter of the United Nations and the principles of international law, the sovereign right to exploit their own resources pursuant to their own environmental and developmental policies," Principle 3 noted that the "right to development must be fulfilled so as to equitably meet developmental and environmental needs of present and future generations." Two other important principles found in the Rio Principles are the "polluter pays" principle, which holds that those responsible for pollution should pay for its consequences and elimination (Principle 16), and the precautionary principle, which provides that "[w]here there are threats of serious or irreversible damage, lack of full scientific certainty

2.   See, e.g., N.Y.Times, Apr. 20, 1992, at A9 (natl. ed.).

3.   31 Int'l Legal Matls. 818 et seq. (1992). The Rio Principles are set out following page 874.

shall not be used as a reason for postponing cost-effective measures to prevent environmental degradation." (Principle 15)

Against this background, we start this section with a consideration of the extent to which expanded international trade is inconsistent with improved environmental quality.

(A) THE EFFECT OF EXPANDED INTERNATIONAL TRADE ON ENVIRONMENTAL QUALITY

HAKAN NORDSTROM & SCOTT VAUGHAN
WTO SECRETARIAT SPECIAL STUDIES NO. 4
TRADE AND ENVIRONMENT 1–7 (1999)*

* * * Slow progress in introducing adequate environmental taxes and regulations has in part been blamed on the multilateral trading system. There are essentially two sides to the argument, one legal and the other involving political economy considerations. * * * The *political economy* argument is that competitive pressure from the world market sometimes makes it impossible to forge the necessary political support at home to upgrade environmental standards. The perceived costs of acting alone in terms of lost investments and jobs often take the steam out of regulatory initiatives. In the worst case scenario, environmental regulations may even be bid down in the relentless competition for market share, investments, and jobs. In addition, the environmental community is fearful that international trade will magnify the effects of poor environmental polices in the world. For example, demand from the world market may magnify the tendency of over-fishing. Or more generally, economic growth driven by trade may speed up the process of environmental degradation unless sufficient environmental safeguards are put in place. * * *

One of the unfortunate features of the trade and environment debate is that at times it has generated more heat than light. Sweeping generalizations are too often heard from both the trade and the environmental communities. This study attempts to make a constructive contribution to the debate by taking stock of economic research on the subject, which has developed in the shadows of the public debate, and seemingly without much influence. * * *

Several key questions are addressed in this study. First, is economic integration through trade and investment a threat to the environment? Second, does trade undermine the regulatory efforts of governments to control pollution and resource degradation? Third, will economic growth driven by trade help us to move towards a sustainable use of the world's environmental resources?

* * *

* Reprinted with permission.

To appreciate why and where trade enters into the sustainable development debate, it is important to understand the root causes of environmental degradation. These can often be traced back to various market and policy failures. "Market failures" refer to situations in which the market forces of supply and demand fail to deliver an optimal outcome for society as a whole. Market failures commonly occur when producers and consumers do not have to bear the full cost of their actions, such as pollution inflicted on third parties (environmental externalities). In such cases, too many resources are invested in polluting activities and too few in pollution abatement. Undefined property rights over natural resources are another cause. If anyone, without restriction, can harvest the riches of the seas, extract the resources of forests, graze animals or collect firewood on common land, or tap water freely from municipal wells, the result is often overexploitation, a phenomenon known as the "tragedy of the commons". In some cases, the people that depend on a given resource may be able to work out between themselves a conservation-cum-distribution scheme, which may include quotas and sanctions for overuse. However, age-old common property systems sometimes crumble under the pressure of rapid population growth, social changes, and increased mobility. Equally, polluters and victims of pollution may be able to reach a mutually satisfactory solution in cases where the source of pollution is indisputable and the cost of organizing collective action among victims is low. However, if the sources of pollution are diffuse and difficult to identify or the victims many and difficult to organize, a "market solution" may be difficult to find. Ultimately, therefore, it is up to governments to arbitrate conflicting claims over natural resources and to strike a balance between polluters and victims of pollution. In many cases, however, governments not only omit to correct market failures by appropriate taxes and regulations, but they may add a few distortions of their own. Well-known examples include the subsidization of energy, agriculture, and fishing, which aggravates pollution problems and resource degradation rather than solving them. Such instances can be described as "policy failures".

In the best of all worlds, governments would use proper environmental polices to "internalize" the full environmental costs of production and consumption—the "Polluter Pays Principle." Specifically, market failures would be corrected directly at the source by appropriate taxes and regulations, and policy failures would promptly be removed, including subsidization of polluting and resource degrading activities. In this idealized world, trade liberalization would unambiguously raise welfare. However, as this is not always the case, trade liberalization could potentially exacerbate the consequences of poor environmental polices. For example, demand from the world market may encourage unsustainable logging, when no proper management scheme is in place. Indeed, such concerns are often voiced by the environmental community which opposes further trade liberalization until proper environmental polices have been put in place. In other instances, removal of trade-distorting policy measures may mitigate the underlying distortions. For example, a reduction in trade-distorting fishing subsidies, currently amounting to some $54 billion annually, would reduce overcapitalization in the industry and lessen over-fishing.

* * *

One conclusion that arises from [the] case studies is that environmental problems are best addressed at the source, whether they involve polluting production processes or undefined property rights over natural resources. What is more, tackling the problems by targeting some indirect linkage, such as imports or exports, may divert attention from the underlying problems. In some cases, putative trade remedies may even aggravate the problems. This may be the case, for example, with tropical deforestation, where trade barriers on forest products may increase deforestation pressure by forcing people to convert land into alternative sources for employment, such as agriculture and ranching.

As a general rule, whenever we sidestep the first-best principles of environmental policy, i.e., policies directed at the source of the problem—the benefits do not only become difficult to predict, but we also impose unnecessary costs on the society. This would not just be poor economics, but potentially bad for the environment as well, by making the costs of environmental polices look higher than they actually are were we to use the most efficient instruments available. It must be recognized, however, that while trade measures are rarely, if ever, the first-best policy for addressing environmental problems, governments have found trade measures a useful mechanism for encouraging participation in and enforcement of multilateral environmental agreements in some instances, and for attempting to modify the behavior of foreign governments in others. * * *

* * * [E]nvironmental repercussions of economic integration depend on three interacting elements: a composition effect, a scale effect, and a technique effect.

The *composition effect* refers to the industrial restructuring that takes place when a country exposes itself to the world market. The repercussions on the local environment will be positive if expanding export sectors are less polluting than contracting import-competing sectors, and vice versa. Since one country's exportables are another country's importables, all countries cannot specialize in clean industries. Trade is therefore associated with a relocation of pollution problems in the world. The *scale effect* arises from the boost of economic activity stimulated by trade. Economic growth is harmful for the environment unless production becomes cleaner and less resource consuming at the same time, and consumers become more willing to recycle waste instead of merely jettisoning it. The silver lining of the scale effect is the associated income growth that drives a countervailing demand for a cleaner environment. Provided that governments respond to public demands, environmental policies will be upgraded as income grows, thereby offsetting or perhaps more than offsetting the scale effect. This effect is called the *technique effect*. The net outcome of these interacting elements is theoretically ambiguous, and is therefore ultimately an empirical question.

To some extent, the answer depends on which countries will attract the polluting industry when trade is liberalized. In the public debate it is often assumed that polluting industries are likely to migrate from developed to developing countries to take advantage of lax regulations, thereby shifting the pollution problems from richer to poorer countries, and also increasing overall emissions in the world. However, this assertion does not seem to be supported by standard trade theory, nor by empirical evidence. Polluting industries tend to be capital intensive, including such industries as chemical industries, ferrous and non-ferrous metals, pulp and paper, and oil refining. According to classical trade theory based on differences in factor endowments, these industries are more likely to conglomerate in capital-abundant developed countries, and to a lesser extent, in economies in transition and newly industrialized countries. What complicates the analysis is that the pattern of trade is determined not just by "natural" comparative advantage, but also by government policies, including environmental regulations. However, pollution abatement costs in developed countries are no more than 1 per cent of production costs for the average industry, rising to perhaps 5 per cent for the worst polluters. It is questionable, although ultimately an empirical issue, if a regulatory cost-disadvantage of a few percentage points can turn comparative advantage around. If not, trade liberalization would tend to shift capital-intensive polluting industries towards developed countries in spite of tougher environmental regulations, and not the other way round.

Indeed, data seem to reject the assertion that polluting industries are migrating from developed to developing countries, although there are of course exceptions. Developed countries' share of polluting industries has remained more or less constant (at around 75–80 per cent) in recent decades, and has even increased marginally in the 1990s. * * *

What is more interesting, perhaps, is that the income gain associated with trade could *in principle* pay for the necessary abatement costs and still leave an economic surplus. This has been shown in various economic simulations. In other words, by combining trade and environmental reforms one can find ways to raise consumption without compromising the natural environment. At least in this sense, there is no inherent conflict between trade and environment. Rather, the conflict arises as a result of the failure of political institutions to address environmental problems, especially those of a global nature which require a concerted effort to solve.

DOES ECONOMIC INTEGRATION UNDERMINE ENVIRONMENTAL POLICIES?

Some have argued that regulatory shortcomings are related to the globalization of the world economy, which has made industries more foot-loose and therefore more difficult to regulate. This is an argument that we shall turn to now.

* * *

* * * In our substantive review of this line of argument, we have divided the issue into four parts: Do stringent environmental regulations undermine the competitiveness of developed countries? Do polluting industries relocate from developed to developing countries to take advantage of lax environmental standards? Are environmental standards being bid down in accordance with the "race-to-the-bottom" hypothesis? Or, if not, has the globalization of the world economy been followed by increased political reluctance to address environmental problems, as suggested by the "regulatory chill" hypothesis?

As far as the consequences of competition under regulatory diversity are concerned, we conclude that these have been somewhat overstated in the public debate. As noted above, the direct cost of pollution control is minor, just a few percentage points of production costs for most industries. No corresponding estimates are available for developing countries, but unless the regulatory cost is zero, the cost savings of moving offshore are less than suggested above. Moreover, some observers have noted that these numbers are in any event exaggerated. The "Porter hypothesis" holds that regulatory pressure, just like competitive pressure, encourages industrial innovations that make production both leaner (less energy and resource demanding) and cleaner at the same time, thereby offsetting the direct compliance costs. The empirical evidence partly supports this hypothesis, although it would be wrong to conclude that environmental regulations do not cost anything. They *do* cost, but they also bring significant benefit to society and the quality of life. How much they cost depends also on the kind of instruments used to regulate an industry. Command-and-control regulations are considerably more costly than modern market-based instruments that allow producers greater flexibility in meeting the targets, for example, through clean reengineering of the production process as an alternative to retrofitting end-of-pipe abatement equipment. What is more, while the public debate has focused on the cost side, studies that have compared the profitability of firms in the same industry have not found much evidence that environmental leaders pay a price in terms of reduced profitability. For several reasons, environmental leaders can often recoup costs in the marketplace. Firstly, a growing number of consumers are willing to pay a premium for "green labels." Secondly, firms that accord with the environmental management standards promulgated by the International Organization for Standardization (ISO 14000) seem to enjoy certain competitive advantages, including lower liability insurance, less regulatory oversight, and increased access to customers (including the public sector) that care about their own environmental reputation. Nor is there much evidence that polluting industries are migrating from developed to developing countries to reduce environmental compliance costs, although there are of course exceptions. While it is certainly true that developing countries are net recipients of foreign direct investment, the composition of investments they receive is *not* biased towards polluting industries, but rather to labor-intensive industries that are less polluting on average. What the data tell us is that, to the extent developed countries are exporting their dirty industries, they are exporting them to each other, not to less developed economies. This suggests that environmental regulations are at most of secondary importance for international investment decisions.

It should also be noted that many multinational firms are moving towards a policy of standardized technologies for all their production plants in the world. The reason is simple. It is less costly to duplicate the home technology than to modify the process in each country. What is more, the choice of technology is not just based on current standards, but on what is expected in the future. It makes commercial sense to install state-of-the-art technology at the time an investment is made rather than retrofitting abatement equipment at a later stage at a much greater expense. Finally, multinationals are becoming more sensitive to the reputation they earn in the market place, at least those multinational firms that are based in countries with an active environmental community. Market forces often reward good environmental performance rather than cost savings at any price, including financial markets that react negatively to environmental mishaps. It has not always been this way, but the tide has changed in recent years. Much of this advance is thanks to the relentless efforts of non-governmental organizations around the world that have made consumers sensitive to the environmental profile of products and producers. In short, when consumers care, producers care.

This is not to say that market forces can be entrusted to solve all problems themselves. Governments must do their part by regulating polluting and resource degrading activities appropriately. And here we seem to have a difficult political dilemma. If policy makers and voters *think* that domestic industry is crumbling under environmental regulations at the expense of domestic investments and jobs, it may be difficult to forge the necessary political support for new regulatory initiatives. And this problem may become worse still when trade and investment barriers are removed, since industries then become more mobile and more difficult to regulate.

Indeed, some evidence suggests that industries often appeal to competitiveness concerns when lobbying against environmental regulations, and on occasion with some success. How serious is this problem? It would clearly be a serious problem if competitiveness concerns prevented environmental standards from being raised to appropriate levels, or if governments were compelled to build in protectionist elements in environmental regulations to "compensate" industry for alleged adverse competitive effects. However, competitiveness concerns could potentially be a positive force if governments that find it difficult to act individually for political reasons seek cooperative solutions to environmental problems. The growing number of multilateral environmental agreements (currently some 216) may be one indication of the trend in that direction. The lasting effect of the "regulatory chill" may then be more procedural than substantial. That is, initiative may have to shift from the national to the supranational level, just as we saw a shift from the local to the central level in federal states in the 1970s to overcome environmental policy foot-dragging at the local level. Admittedly, however, international cooperation in these matters is not easy to achieve unless governments are convinced of its urgency.

Turning now to the issue of economic growth, numerous reports in the last decades have questioned the sustainability of economic growth. The most influential report was perhaps the *Limits to Growth*, authored by the Club of Rome, forecasting that key natural resources—in particular non-renewable resources such as fossil fuels would become increasingly scarce over time and eventually exhausted if economic growth, as we know it, were to continue. The same report also warned that the earth's environmental carrying capacities would become overburdened by different pollutants, and possibly collapse, unless human activities were held at bay. In short, economic growth and environmental quality were viewed as being on a collision course where one would eventually have to surrender.

Three decades later, some of the earlier warnings—in particular those related to fossil fuel exhaustion—have been found to be somewhat premature. The discovery of new deposits of fossil fuel in combination with less energy demanding technologies have kept pace with demand, and the current issue is rather whether we can afford to burn these plentiful reserves because of the potential consequences on the global climate. On the positive side, relatively simple abatement technologies, such as catalytic converters on cars and scrubbers on smokestacks, have proven effective in bringing down air pollution in countries were such equipment has become mandatory. Yet the early warning signals were not misguided or unhelpful even if they may have turned out to be exaggerated. They served as a catalyst for governments to pass environmental legislation without which the gloomy scenarios may have proven more accurate. Moreover, the adoption of adequate environmental standards is still lagging behind in many places, and it is still true that economic growth without the necessary sensitivity to environmental quality is not sustainable over the longer run. One reason why environmental protection is lagging in many countries is low incomes. Countries that live on the margin may simply not be able to afford to set aside resources for pollution abatement, nor may they think that they should sacrifice their growth prospects to help solve global pollution problems that in large part have been caused by the consuming lifestyle of richer countries.

In any event, if poverty is at the core of the problem, economic growth will be part of the solution, to the extent that it allows countries to shift gear from more immediate concerns to long run sustainability issues. Indeed, at least *some* empirical evidence (see further below) suggests that pollution increases at the early stages of development but decreases after a certain income level has been reached, an observation that has become known in academic circles as the environmental Kuznets curve (EKC).

* * *

The empirical evidence in support of the EKC hypothesis is mixed. The evidence suggests that the EKC hypothesis may be valid for some types of environmental indicators, but equally untrue for other important indicators. Those indicators that appear to demonstrate some characteristics of an inverted U-shape pollution path are certain types of local, primarily urban air pollution, and to a lesser extent some types of freshwater pollutants. In contrast, pollutants of a more global nature do not seem to accord with the EKC hypothesis, notably emissions of carbon dioxide. In essence, countries seem more prone to act on pollutants that affect their own backyard than pollutants that degrade the global environment, although there are also some encouraging developments for the latter, such as the reductions in ozone-depleting substances rendered possible by international cooperation under the Montreal Protocol.

It should also be emphasized that nothing in the EKC literature suggests that environmental degradation will turn around with increasing income by compelling necessity. If economic incentives facing producers and consumers do not change with higher incomes, pollution will continue to grow unabated with the growing scale of economic activity. In other words, income growth, while perhaps a necessary condition for allowing countries to shift gear from more immediate economic and social concerns to more long term sustainability issues, is not sufficient to reverse environmental degradation. Environmental polices must be brought to bear. The importance of a democratic political process cannot be underestimated in this regard. Governments that are not held accountable for their actions, or rather inaction in this case, may fail to deliver the necessary upgrading of environmental polices. A recent study by Torras and Boyce (1998) makes this case convincingly. Comparing countries at the same income level, pollution tends to be worse in countries with skewed income distribution, a high degree of illiteracy, and few political and civil liberties. Moreover, these "political access" variables considerably weaken the relationship between per capita income and environmental quality. This suggests that the EKC relationship is not so much dependent on income levels *per se*, but rather on institutional and democratic reforms that tend to go hand in hand with increased income, and which are necessary for allowing ordinary citizens to articulate their preferences for environmental quality and influence the political decision-making process.

* * *

The political obstacles to sound environmental policy should not be exaggerated. The turning points that have been estimated for different kinds of pollutants have a tendency to fall within the income range of leading countries at the time the specific problems became an issue of intense public debate. For example, there may be nothing special about a turning point for CFC emissions at some $12,000 to $18,000—it just happened to be the income range of the leading countries (which have also assumed the fastest phase-out commitments) at the time the Montreal Protocol was signed in 1987. And although we find estimates of a turning point of CO_2 emissions of up to several hundred thousand dollars in per capita income, reflecting the almost linear historical relationship between consumption of energy and income, the fact that global warming has now risen to the forefront of public attention may result in a curbing of emissions at an earlier date.

* * * In the end, the environmental Kuznets curve may not have a "natural" turning point—it will turn whenever political conditions are ripe for delivering the necessary policies to address environmental degradation effectively, including through transfers of resources and technologies to allow developing countries to modernize their production.

It should also be kept in mind that not all kinds of growth are equally benign for the environment. Economic growth requiring ever more inputs of natural resources is obviously not as benign for the environment as economic growth driven by technological progress that saves inputs and reduces emissions per unit of output. This kind of growth will not necessarily emerge spontaneously, but may require economic incentives that steer development in a sustainable direction.

Trade could play a positive role in this process by facilitating the diffusion of environment-friendly technologies around the world. Of course, this would require that countries be ready to scrap trade barriers on modern technologies and suppliers of environmental services. A new round of trade liberalization negotiations could make a contribution here. Another potential contribution of such a round would be to address subsidies that harm the environment, including energy, agricultural and fishing subsides. This would yield a double dividend by benefiting the environment and the world economy at the same time.

HERMAN E. DALY, FROM ADJUSTMENT TO SUSTAINABLE DEVELOPMENT: THE OBSTACLE OF FREE TRADE[4]

III. WHY FREE TRADE CONFLICTS WITH SUSTAINABLE DEVELOPMENT

International free trade conflicts sharply with the national policies of:

(a) getting prices right,

(b) moving toward a more just distribution,

(c) fostering community,

(d) controlling the macroeconomy, and

---

4. Symposium: Free Trade and the Environment in Latin America, 15 Loy. L.A.Intl. & Comp.L.J. 33, 36–42 (1992). Re-printed with the permission of the Loyola Los Angeles International and Comparative Law Journal.

(e) keeping scale within ecological limits.

Each conflict will be discussed in turn.

(a) If one nation internalizes environmental and social costs to a high degree, following the dictates of adjustment, and then enters into free trade with a country that does not force its producers to internalize those costs, then the result will be that the firms in the second country will have lower prices and will drive the competing firms in the first country out of business.

If the trading entities were nations rather than individual firms trading across national boundaries, then the cost-internalizing nation could limit its volume and composition of trade to an amount that did not ruin its domestic producers, and thereby actually take advantage of the opportunity to acquire goods at prices that were below full cost. The country that sells at less than full-cost prices only hurts itself as long as other countries restrict their trade with that country to a volume that does not ruin their own producers. That of course would not be free trade. There is clearly a conflict between free trade and a national policy of internalization of external costs. External costs are now so important that the latter goal should take precedence. In this case there is a clear argument for tariffs to protect, not an inefficient industry, but an efficient national policy of internalizing external costs into prices.

Of course, if all trading nations agreed to common rules for defining, evaluating, and internalizing external costs, then this objection would disappear and the standard arguments for free trade could again be made in the new context. But how likely is such agreement? Even the small expert technical fraternity of national income accountants cannot agree on how to measure environmental costs in the system of national accounts, let alone on rules for internalizing these costs into prices at the firm level. Politicians are not likely to do better. Some economists will argue against uniform cost internalization on the grounds that different countries have different tastes for environmental services and amenities, and that these differences should be reflected in prices as legitimate reasons for profitable trade. Certainly agreement on uniform principles, and the proper extent of departure from uniformity in their application, will not be easy. Nevertheless, suppose that this difficulty is overcome so that all countries internalize external costs by the same rules applied in each case to the appropriate degree in the light of differing tastes and levels of income. There are two further problems arising from capital mobility and wage differentials.

(b) Wage levels vary enormously between countries and are largely determined by the supply of labor, which in turn depends on population size and growth rates. Overpopulated countries are naturally low-wage countries, and if population growth is rapid they will remain low-wage countries. This is especially so because the demographic rate of increase of the lower class (labor) is frequently twice or more that of the upper class (capital). For most traded goods labor is still the largest item of cost and consequently the major determinant of price. Cheap labor means low prices and a competitive advantage in trade. (The theoretical possibility that low wages reflect a taste for poverty and therefore a legitimate reason for cost differences is not taken seriously here.) But adjustment economists do not worry about that because economists have proved that free trade between high-wage and low-wage countries can be mutually advantageous thanks to comparative advantage.

The doctrine of comparative advantage is quite correct given the assumptions on which it rests, but unfortunately one of these assumptions is that capital is immobile internationally. The theory is supposed to work as follows. When in international competition the relatively inefficient activities lose out and jobs are eliminated, at the same time the relatively efficient activities (those with the comparative advantage) expand, absorbing both the labor and capital that were disemployed in activities with a comparative disadvantage. Capital and labor are reallocated within the country, specializing according to that country's comparative advantage. However, when both capital and goods are internationally mobile, then capital will follow absolute advantage to the low-wage country rather than reallocate itself according to comparative advantage within its home country. It will follow the highest absolute profit, which is usually determined by the lowest absolute wage.

Of course, further inducements to absolute profits such as low social insurance charges or a low degree of internalization of environmental costs also attract capital, usually toward the very same low-wage countries. But we have assumed that all countries have internalized costs to the same degree, in order to focus on the wage issue. Once capital is mobile then the entire doctrine of comparative advantage and all its comforting demonstrations become irrelevant. The consequence of capital mobility would be similar to that of international labor mobility—a strong tendency to equalize wages throughout the world. Given the existing overpopulation and high demographic growth of the Third World it is clear that the equalization will be downward, as it has indeed been during the last decade in the United States. Of course, returns to capital will also be equalized by free trade and capital mobility, but the level at which equalization will occur will be higher than at present. United States capital will benefit from cheap labor abroad followed by cheap labor at home, at least until checked by a crisis of insufficient demand due to a lack of worker purchasing power resulting from low wages. But that can be forestalled by efficient reallocation to serve the new pattern of effective demand resulting from the greater concentration of income. More luxury goods will be produced and fewer basic wage goods. Efficiency is attained, but distributive equity is sacrificed.

The standard neoclassical adjustment view argues that wages will eventually be equalized worldwide at high levels, thanks to the enormous increase in production made possible by free trade. This increase in production presumably will trigger the automatic demographic transition to lower birth rates—a doctrine that might be considered a part of the adjustment package in so far as any attention at all is paid to population. Such a thought can only be entertained by those who ignore the issue of scale, as of course neoclassicals traditionally do. For all 5.4 billion people presently alive to consume resources and absorptive capacities at the same per capita rate as Americans or Europeans is ecologically impossible. Much less is it possible to extend that level of consumption to future generations. Development as it currently is understood on the United States model, is only possible for a minority of the world's population over a few generations—i.e., it is neither just nor sustainable. The goal of sustainable development is, by changes in allocation, distribution and scale, to move the world toward a state in which "development," whatever it concretely comes to mean, will be for all people in all generations. This is certainly not achievable by a more finely tuned adjustment to the standard growth model which is largely responsible for having created the present impasse in the first place.

Of course if somehow all countries decided to control their populations and adopt distributive and scale limiting measures such that wages could be equalized world wide at an acceptably high level, then this problem would disappear and the standard arguments for free trade could again be evoked in the new context. Although the likelihood of that context seems infinitesimal, we might for purposes of a fortiori argument consider a major problem with free trade that would still remain.

(c) Even with uniformly high wages made possible by universal population control and redistribution, and with uniform internalization of external costs, free trade and free capital mobility still increase the separation of ownership and control and the forced mobility of labor which are so inimical to community. Community economic life can be disrupted not only by your fellow citizen who, though living in another part of your country, might at least share some tenuous bonds of community with you, but by someone on the other side of the world with whom you have no community of language, history, culture, law, etc. These foreigners may be wonderful people—that is not the point. The point is that they are very far removed from the life of the community that is affected significantly by their decisions. Your life and your community can be disrupted by decisions and events over which you have no control, no vote, no voice.

Specialization and integration of a local community into the world economy does offer a quick fix to problems of local unemployment, and one must admit that carrying community self sufficiency to extremes can certainly be impoverishing. But short supply lines and relatively local control over the livelihood of the community remain obvious prudential measures which require some restraint on free trade if they are to be effective. Libertarian economists look at Homo economicus as a self-contained individual who is infinitely mobile and equally at home anywhere. But real people live in communities, and in communities of communities. Their very individual identity is constituted by their relations in community. To regard community as a disposable aggregate of individuals in temporary proximity only for as long as it serves the interests of mobile capital is bad enough when capital stays within the nation. But when capital moves internationally it becomes much worse.

When the capitalist class in the United States in effect tells the laboring class, "sorry, you have to compete with the poor of the world for jobs and wages—the fact that we are fellow citizens of the same country creates no obligations on our part" then admittedly not much community remains, and it is not hard to understand why a United States worker would be indifferent to the nationality of his or her employer. Indeed, if local community is more respected by the foreign company than by the displaced American counterpart, then the interests of community could conceivably be furthered by foreign ownership in some specific cases. But this could not be counted as the rule, and serves only to show that the extent of pathological disregard for community in our own country has not yet been equalled by others. In any event the further undercutting of local and national communities (which are real) in the name of a cosmopolitan world community which does not exist, is a poor trade, even if we call it free trade. The true road to international community is that of a federation of communities and communities of communities— not the destruction of local and national communities in the service of a single cosmopolitan world of footloose money managers who constitute, not a community, but merely an interdependent, mutually vulnerable, unstable coalition of short-term interests.

(d) Free trade and free capital mobility have interfered with macroeconomic stability by permitting huge international payment imbalances and capital transfers resulting in debts that are unrepayable in many cases and excessive in others. Efforts to service these debts can lead to unsustainable rates of exploitation of exportable resources; and to an eagerness to make new loans to get the foreign exchange with which to pay old loans, with a consequent disincentive to take a hard look at the real productivity of the project for which the new loan is being made. Efforts to pay back loans and still meet domestic obligations lead to government budget deficits and monetary creation with resulting inflation. Inflation, plus the need to export to pay off loans, leads to currency devaluations, giving rise to foreign exchange speculation, capital flight, and hot money movements, disrupting the macroeconomic stability that adjustment was supposed to foster.

To summarize so far: Free trade sins against allocative efficiency by making it difficult for nations to internalize external costs; it sins against distributive justice by widening the disparity between labor and capital in high wage countries; it sins against community by demanding more mobility and by further separating ownership and control; it sins against macroeconomic stability. Finally, it sins against the criterion of sustainable scale in a more subtle manner that will now be considered.

(e) As previously mentioned, part of the free trade dogma of adjustment thinking is based on the assumption that the whole world, and all future generations, can consume resources at the levels current in today's high-wage countries without inducing ecological collapse. So, in this way, free trade sins against the criterion of sustainable scale. But, in its physical dimensions the economy really is an open subsystem of a materially closed, non-growing, and finite ecosystem with a limited throughput of solar energy. The proper scale of the economic subsystem relative to the finite total system is a very important question. Free trade has obscured the scale limit in the following way.

Sustainable development means living within environmental constraints of absorptive and regenerative capacities. These constraints are both global (greenhouse effect, ozone shield), and local (soil erosion, deforestation). Trade between nations or regions offers a way to loosen local constraints by importing environmental services (including waste absorption (from elsewhere). Within limits this can be quite reasonable and justifiable. But carried to extremes in the name of free trade it becomes destructive. It leads to a situation in which each country is trying to live beyond its own absorptive and regenerative capacities by importing these capacities from elsewhere. Of course they pay for these capacities and all is well as long as other countries have made the complementary decision—namely to keep their own scale well below their own national carrying capacity in order to export some of its services. In other words, the apparent escape from scale constraints enjoyed by some countries via trade depends on other countries' willingness and ability to adopt the very discipline of limiting scale that the importing country is seeking to avoid.

What nations have actually made this complementary choice? All countries now aim to grow in scale, and it is merely the fact that some have not yet reached their limits that allows other nations to import carrying capacity. Free trade does not remove carrying capacity constraints—it just guarantees that nations will hit that constraint more or less simultaneously rather than sequentially. It converts differing local constraints into an aggregated global constraint. It converts a set of problems, some of which are manageable, into one big unmanageable problem. Evidence that this is not understood is provided by the countless occasions when someone who really should know better points to The Netherlands or Hong Kong as both an example to be emulated, and as evidence that all countries could become as densely populated as these two. How it would be possible for all countries to be net exporters of goods and net importers of carrying capacity is not explained.

Of course the drive to grow beyond carrying capacity has roots other and deeper than the free trade dogma. The point is that free trade makes it very hard to deal with these root causes at a national level, which is the only level at which effective social controls over the economy exist. The adjustment theorist will argue that free trade is just a natural extension of price adjustment across international boundaries, and that right prices must reflect global scarcities and preferences. But if the unit of community is the nation—the unit in which there are institutions and traditions of collective action, responsibility, and mutual help—the unit in which government tries to carry out policy for the good of its citizens, then right prices should not reflect the preferences and scarcities of other nations. Right prices should differ between national communities. Such differences traditionally have provided the whole reason for international trade in goods.

Notes and Questions

(1) If the prescription offered by Mr. Daly is no or only very limited trade between the developed world and countries with low wages or low environmental standards (and no loans to them either), what effect would that have on economic development in the developing world? We will see in Chapter 25 that developing countries have become largely disenchanted with economic development strategies based on going it alone. The more economically successful developing countries (the newly industrialized and industrializing countries of East Asia) have been active participants in the world trading system, particularly as exporters to the developed world.

(2) Tensions between the developed and developing world were evident at the Rio summit. The developing world is not at all happy with the view that the world cannot support its development to levels reached in industrialized countries. Assuming that the industrialized countries are not going to lower their living standards, even if that would be "just," does this view imply the developing world must remain permanently behind (in economic terms)?

(3) What about Mr. Daly's prescription that countries should focus internally? Is that in the world's interest? The western countries tightly controlled trade with the Soviet bloc until the end of the Cold War. Was that in the environmental interest of the planet? We know now that the Soviet bloc generally placed environmental considerations very low in economic decisionmaking. With an internal focus, will the U.S. lose power to influence events (including environmental policy) that ultimately will affect it?

(4) But if Mr. Daly is right that the world cannot provide a U.S./EU style lifestyle to the whole world, what should be done? If he is right, does the WTO Secretariat's report have any response?

(5) If the WTO report is correct that people will demand better environmental standards as development occurs, do you think that the WTO/GATT system should push for increased trade and development, which will ultimately lead to better use of scarce resources, and hope for the best? What are the alternatives? Is it realistic to expect the adoption of policies that will restrict trade and development and lower living standards?

(B) TENSIONS BETWEEN INTERNATIONAL TRADE RULES AND ENVIRONMENTAL MEASURES

Following the *Tuna-Dolphin* case, there was considerable concern among environmentalists that GATT and now WTO rules were inconsistent with environmental protection. Much has happened, however, in the last few years that may have reduced those fears. In considering the following problems,[5] the reader should review the cases in Chapters 12 to 14, and in particular, the four cases with an environmental aspect. Those cases were *U.S. Gasoline* (blatantly discriminatory U.S. regulation found to violate Article III, without Article XX justification, Section 13.3 supra); *U.S. Shrimp* (U.S. embargo on shrimp imports from countries

---

5. Some of the following problems have been adapted from John H. Jackson, World Trade and Environmental Policies: Congruence or Conflict?, 49 Wash. & Lee L. Rev. 1227 (1992).

not adopting U.S. rules on turtle protection found to violate Article XI, without Article XX justification; but slightly revised U.S. rules upheld on compliance review under Article XX, section 13.4 supra); *EC Hormones* (EC hormone rules found not to be based on risk assessment in case where EC refused to argue application of SPS Agreement precautionary principle; EC implementation now pending and based in large part on precautionary principle, Section 14.2 supra); and *EC Asbestos* (French asbestos ban found justified under Article XX(b), Section 13.1 supra).

(1) Suppose that a country (ENV) wants to regulate the sale of a polluting or unsafe product. Do WTO rules limit its ability to do so? Generally, the rules permit product-based standards as long as they are not discriminatory or disguised restrictions on trade.

(2) ENV prohibits the importation of tropical hardwoods on the ground that imports of tropical hardwood products tend to induce deforestation in important tropical forest areas, and that such deforestation damages the world environment. ENV is a temperate zone nation with temperate forests, but does not apply any rule against temperate forest products, domestic or imported. Should ENV's actions be permitted by WTO rules? Are they?

(3) ENV bans the use of a certain polluting production process in ENV. May it, consistently with WTO rules, also ban imported goods made using the polluting process? How is the like-product issue relevant to this? See Sections 12.4, 13.3 and 13.4 supra.

(4) ENV imposes a countervailing duty on any product that is imported from a country that does not have environmental rules as strict as those imposed by ENV. ENV argues that the lack of such a rule is in effect a subsidy and that the subsidy should be off-set by a countervailing duty. Do current WTO rules on subsidies and countervailing duties permit such action? See Chapter 18.

The NAFTA environmental side agreement (see Documents Supplement) permits imposition of fines in the event that a party fails to enforce its own environmental rules. This provision was designed to discourage U.S. companies from moving to Mexico to take advantage of Mexico's lax enforcement of environmental rules, thereby retaining access to the U.S. market, but avoiding U.S. environmental controls. How does the NAFTA provision differ from using countervailing duties as described in the preceding paragraph? Is the situation of a country that has agreed to follow a standard, but failed to, fundamentally different from that of a country that fails to meet standards unilaterally determined by someone else? Suppose that "someone else" is an international organization with broad membership?

(5) Suppose ENV subsidizes the purchase of environmental protection devices, such as smoke stack cleaners. When products from plants benefiting from the subsidy are exported, may an importing country impose a countervailing duty on ENV's exports to offset the benefits of the subsidy? Is it, or should it be, a defense that the subsidy was for a good purpose? What is the relevance of the "polluter pays" principle,

which is generally recognized internationally and is one of the Rio Principles? See Chapter 18 supra.

(6) ENV establishes a rule that requires any business firm which sells a product in the ENV market to establish a center that will recycle, or appropriately dispose of, the product when the ENV consumer is finished with it or at the end of the product's useful life. Such centers are relatively easy for domestic producers to establish, but by their very nature are inherently much more difficult for importers or exporters, and particularly difficult for exporters of small quantities to establish. Should this requirement be permitted by WTO rules? Is it?

(7) ENV bans importation of a product, justifying its action by reference to an multilateral environmental agreement authorizing such action. How would such an action be judged under WTO rules? What if the agreement required the ban? Consider the relevance of the Vienna Convention on the Law of Treaties, excerpted in Chapter 5 supra.

The North American Free Trade Agreement specifies in Article 104 that the trade obligations of certain specified international environmental agreements prevail over NAFTA, "provided that where a Party has a choice among equally effective and reasonably available means of complying with such obligations, the Party chooses the alternative that is least inconsistent with the other provisions of [NAFTA]." The agreements initially specified were (i) the Convention on International Trade in Endangered Species of Wild Fauna and Flora; (ii) the Montreal Protocol on Substances that Deplete the Ozone Layer; (iii) the Basel Convention on the Control of Transboundary Movements of Hazardous Wastes and Their Disposal; (iv) the U.S.-Canada Agreement Concerning the Transboundary Movement of Hazardous Waste; and (v) the U.S.-Mexico Agreement on Cooperation for the Protection and Improvement of the Environment in the Border Area. Should WTO members agree on a similar list? Is the "least-inconsistent" test a workable one?

(8) ENV establishes a rule against the importation of products from any producer in a foreign country that employs women in its factories. ENV argues that it is culturally offensive to employ women in factories and its industries do not do so. Should this be permitted by WTO rules? Is it? Should this culture-based rule be deserving of less protection than a rule against products of prison labor (see Article XX(e))? Of less protection than environmental rules? This question foreshadows issues raised in the next section of this Chapter.

In light of your answers to the foregoing problems, what measures should be adopted by the WTO system to deal with environmental issues? The preamble of the WTO Agreement provides that its economic goals should "allow for the optimal use of the world's resources in accordance with the objective of sustainable development, seeking both to protect and preserve the environment and to enhance the means for doing so in a manner consistent with [the parties'] respective needs and concerns at different levels of economic development." At the April 1994 Marrakesh signing of the WTO Agreement, a WTO committee on trade and environment was established. Although the committee has not proposed specific changes in WTO rules, over the past seven years it has considered a number of areas, including some where new rules may be proposed. Among the topics considered:

— the relationship between the provisions of the multilateral trading system and trade measures for environmental purposes, including those pursuant to multilateral environmental agreements;

— the relationship between environmental policies relevant to trade and environmental measures with significant trade effects and the provisions of the multilateral trading system;

— the relationship between the provisions of the multilateral trading system and:

   (a) charges and taxes for environmental purposes

   (b) requirements for environmental purposes relating to products, including standards and technical regulations, packaging, labeling and recycling;

— the provisions of the multilateral trading system with respect to the transparency of trade measures used for environmental purposes and environmental measures and requirements which have significant trade effects;

— the relationship between the dispute settlement mechanisms in the multilateral trading system and those found in multilateral environmental agreements;

— the effect of environmental measures on market access, especially in relation to developing countries, in particular to the least developed among them, and environmental benefits of removing trade restrictions and distortions;

— the issue of exports of domestically prohibited goods.

Notes and Questions

(1) Who represents environmental concerns in the WTO committee? Is there an international organization that could serve that function? After all, few would argue that the WTO ought to set environmental rules. Rather, it is necessary that it deal some other body to determine the interrelationship between WTO rules and environmental rules.

(2) Would it be appropriate for the representative of environmental concerns to be a nongovernmental organization?

(3) For the environment-related results of the Doha Ministerial, see section 27.1 supra.

SECTION 21.3 HUMAN RIGHTS AND INTERNATIONAL TRADE POLICY: TENSION OF CONFLICTING GOALS

One of the more controversial issues involving linkages has been the question of whether trade sanctions should be used to promote human rights. In the United States, the issue has been most controversial in the case of the People's Republic of China and whether the U.S. should continue to grant China MFN treatment or whether it should deny MFN treatment to Chinese goods in an effort to promote human rights in China. In this section, we first consider the question of defining international human rights—what does that concept embrace and who decides what are international human rights? We then consider whether trade sanctions should be used to promote them. Finally, we look at a U.S. law—known as the Jackson–Vanik Amendment—that conditions MFN treatment for some countries in some circumstances to human rights.

(A) INTERNATIONAL HUMAN RIGHTS DEFINED

Different people and different organizations have defined human rights in different ways. Indeed, most of international human rights law developed after World War II, in large part in response to Nazi atrocities. Nonetheless, there are some common threads in what are generally considered to be basic human rights.[1]

Probably the most important expression of the concept of human rights is contained in the United Nation's Universal Declaration of Human Rights.[2] The declaration includes a long list of rights, some of which will be mentioned below, and it provides in its preamble that governments and individuals should "strive by teaching and education to promote respect for these rights and freedoms and by progressive measures, national and international, to secure their universal and effective recognition and observance."

The declaration proclaims that all people are born free and equal in dignity and rights and that everyone has the right to life, liberty and the security of person. It bans slavery, torture, and inhuman or degrading punishment. It holds that all are equal before the law. It contains provisions providing rights to accused criminals, as well as establishing rights to found families and own property. It also includes rights to participate in governance and to assemble. It encompasses such rights as the right to work, to education and to an adequate standard of living.

Compared to the U.S. Constitution (including the Bill of Rights), the U.N. Declaration contains provisions dealing with most of what is in the

---

1. See generally Lori F. Damrosch, Louis Henkin, Richard C. Pugh, Oscar Schachter & Hans Smit, International Law: Cases and Materials 586–683 (4th ed. 2001); Barry E. Carter & Phillip R. Trimble, International Law 844–925 (3rd ed. 1999).

2. Dec. 10, 1948, U.N.G.A. Res. 217A(III), U.N. Doc. A/810 (1948).

U.S. Constitution (in general terms), but goes beyond it in several areas, such as the family, education and economic rights mentioned above.

There are other significant, multilateral instruments that establish human rights. In its annual report to Congress, the State Department listed the following "International Human Rights Conventions," the substance of which is often apparent from the title.[3] As of February 2001, the United States was a party to those conventions marked with an asterisk and a signatory to those marked with two asterisks.

— Convention to Suppress the Slave Trade and Slavery (1926)*

— Convention Concerning Forced Labor (ILO, 1930)

— Convention Concerning Freedom of Association and Protection of the Right to Organize (ILO, 1948)

— Convention on the Prevention and Punishment of the Crime of Genocide (1948)*

— Convention Concerning the Application of the Principles of the Right to Organize and Bargain Collectively (ILO, 1949)

— Geneva Convention Relative to Treatment of Prisoners of War (1949)*

— Geneva Convention Relative to the Protection of Civilian Persons in Time of War (1949)*

— Convention for the Suppression of the Traffic in Persons and of the Exploitation of the Prostitution of Others (1950)

— European Convention for the Protection of Human Rights and Fundamental Freedoms (1950)

— Convention on the Political Rights of Women (1953)*

— Supplementary Convention on the Abolition of Slavery, the Slave Trade, and Institutions and Practices Similar to Slavery (1956)*

— Convention Concerning the Abolition of Forced Labor (ILO, 1957)*

— International Convention on the Elimination of All Forms of Racial Discrimination (1965)*

— International Covenant on Civil and Political Rights (1966)*

— International Covenant on Economic, Social and Cultural Rights (1966)**

— United Nations Convention Relating to the Status of Refugees (1951)

— Protocol Relating to the Status of Refugees (1967)*

— American Convention on Human Rights (1969)**

3. U.S. Dept. of State, 2000 Country Reports on Human Rights Practices, Appendix C (Feb. 2001).

— Convention Concerning Minimum Age for Admission to Employment (ILO, 1973)

— Protocol Additional to the Geneva Conventions of August 12, 1949, and Relating to the Protection of Victims of International Armed Conflicts (Protocol I) (1977)**

— Protocol Additional to the Geneva Conventions of August 12, 1949, and Relating to the Protection of Victims of Non–International Armed Conflicts (Protocol II) (1977)**

— Convention on the Elimination of All Forms of Discrimination Against Women (1979)**

— Convention Against Torture and Other Cruel, Inhuman or Degrading Treatment or Punishment (1984)*

— Convention on the Rights of the Child (1989)**

Notes and Questions

(1) Some scholars question whether the rights listed in the U.N. Declaration and the above conventions are really universal. They suggest that they are derived from Western concepts of government and social structure and that they are not necessarily accepted or appropriately applied in other cultures. For example, there is great stress on individual rights as opposed to group (family, community or state) rights and on freedom of action as opposed to societal order. How would you respond to such arguments? Who should decide such issues?

(2) These issues were presented in a Spring 1994 debate over the question of whether applying several strokes of a cane, which inflicts considerable pain and may lead to scarring, is an appropriate punishment for vandalism (or any other offense). Singapore imposes such a punishment for a number of offenses, including vandalism. The U.S. government urged Singapore not to cane a U.S. youth living in Singapore who had been convicted of vandalism, arguing that his confession may have been coerced and that caning was too severe a punishment.[4] Singapore rejected the U.S. request, although the number of strokes was reduced from six to four. Singapore Senior Minister Lee Kuan Yew, who was prime minister for the three decades prior to 1990, was quoted in the U.S. press as stressing the need for a well-ordered society, "arguing that the Western concept of individual rights had been taken to extremes and left the United States in a crisis." He cited a "list of social ills that plague the United States but scarcely exist in Singapore—street violence, homelessness, unemployment."[5] Is caning an inappropriate punishment? Is it a violation of human rights (the UN declaration bans "inhuman or degrading treatment or punishment")? Who should decide the answer to that question?

(B) LINKING TRADE AND HUMAN RIGHTS: THE JACKSON–VANIK AMENDMENT

The most important link between international human rights and U.S. trade law is found in title IV of the Trade Act of 1974 (the so-called

4. See 30 Weekly Compilation of Presidential Documents 838 (1994).

5. Philip Shenon, To Justify Flogging, Singapore Cites "Chaos" on U.S. Streets, N.Y.Times, Apr. 13, 1994, at A2, col. 3.

Jackson–Vanik provision). This provision establishes a complicated scheme for determining when Communist countries may be given most-favored-nation (now called in U.S. law "normal trade relations") treatment under U.S. trade law and requires annual consideration of whether to renew such treatment. Its most controversial application occurred in the 1990's in connection with China. While the importance of Jackson–Vanik continues to shrink as more and more former Communist countries are removed from its coverage,[6] the controversy over China remains of interest as an example of the various issues that may present themselves when a country considers imposing trade sanctions to promote human rights.

The United States began giving MFN treatment to Chinese goods in 1980 and such treatment was relatively non-controversial until 1989 when the Chinese government suppressed pro-democracy demonstrators in Tiananmen Square. This led to calls for non-renewal of MFN treatment. President Bush, however, continued to renew such treatment. In 1993, President Clinton, who had criticized the Bush Administration policy, renewed MFN treatment, subject to specific conditions in respect of granting exit visas to certain individuals, Chinese compliance with the 1992 U.S.-China agreement on prison labor and overall significant progress by China in respect of (i) taking steps to begin adhering to the Universal Declaration of Human Rights, (ii) releasing and providing an acceptable accounting of those imprisoned for the nonviolent expression of their political and religious beliefs, (iii) ensuring humane treatment of prisoners, (iv) protecting Tibet's distinctive religious and cultural heritage and (v) permitting international radio and television broadcasts into China.[7]

In 1994, President Clinton extended MFN treatment despite only limited progress on these issues and announced his intention to break the link between MFN treatment and human rights issues. He did, however, impose restrictions on Chinese munitions exports to the U.S. to record continuing U.S. dissatisfaction with Chinese human rights policies. In his statement announcing his decision, he noted that "serious human rights abuses continue in China." He concluded, however, that[8]

> [t]he question for us now is, given the fact that there has been some progress but that not all of the requirements of the executive order were met, how can we best advance the cause of human rights and other profound interests the United States has in our relationship with China.
>
> I have decided that the United States should renew Most Favored Nation trading status toward China. This decision, I believe, offers us the best opportunity to lay the basis for long-term sustainable progress in human rights and for the advancement of

6. In 2000, Congress provided for permanent normal trade relations with China, conditional on its entry into the WTO, which occurred in December 2001. See Section 6.6 supra.

7. 58 Fed.Reg. 31327, 31329 (1993).

8. 1994 Westlaw 209851, #1 (White House).

our other interests with China. Extending M.F.N. will avoid isolating China and instead will permit us to engage the Chinese with not only economic contacts but with cultural, educational and other contacts, and with a continuing aggressive effort in human rights—an approach that I believe will make it more likely that China will play a responsible role, both at home and abroad.

I am moving, therefore, to delink human rights from the annual extension of Most Favored Nation trading status for China. That linkage has been constructive during the past year, but I believe, based on our aggressive contacts with China in the past several months, that we have reached the end of the usefulness of that policy, and it is time to take a new path toward the achievement of our constant objectives. We need to place our relationship into a larger and more productive framework.

* * * I am also pursuing a new and vigorous American program to support those in China working to advance the cause of human rights and democracy. This program will include increased broadcasts for Radio Free Asia and the Voice of America, increased support for nongovernmental organizations working on human rights in China, and development, with American business leaders, of a voluntary set of principles for business activity in China.

* * *

* * * [T]he question, therefore, is not whether we continue to support human rights in China but how can we best support human rights in China and advance our other very significant issues and interests. I believe we can do it by engaging the Chinese.

At the time of this announcement, there were at least two other issues between the U.S. and China that were of particular concern. First, the U.S. wanted Chinese assistance in persuading North Korea not to develop nuclear weapons and to permit inspections of its nuclear facilities by the International Atomic Energy Agency. Second, the U.S. did not want to lose large orders placed in the U.S. by the Chinese government and corporations, particularly those for aircraft.

Notes and Questions

(1) The China MFN issue had become more controversial in part because of the large increase in U.S. imports from China in recent years. In 1993, U.S. imports from China were valued at $31.5 billion, making China the fourth largest supplier of goods to the U.S. (trailing only Canada, Japan and Mexico). U.S. exports to China in 1993 totaled only $8.8 billion, which meant a trade deficit in 1993 of $22.8 billion (second only to the U.S. deficit with Japan).[9] In 1988, in contrast, the deficit was only $3.5 billion.[10] The volume of Chinese exports, many of which would probably not have been viable if subjected to the non-MFN (Smoot–Hawley) tariff rates, meant that

9. U.S. Dept. of Commerce, Business America, Apr. 1994, at 39.

10. 1994 Economic Report of the President & Annual Report of the Council of Economic Advisors 216 (1994).

general denial of MFN would have been quite disruptive for U.S. businesses selling Chinese products in the U.S., as well as for the Chinese exporters themselves. Making such a large volume of trade dependent on an all-or-nothing, subjective annual evaluation of Chinese human rights practices may not have made good policy sense. But did the decision have to be all-or-nothing? What about withdrawal of MFN treatment for only some products or some (e.g., state-or army-controlled) enterprises? Would such an approach be workable? It was urged by opponents of MFN renewal, who seemed to concede that a complete withdrawal of MFN treatment was too draconian.

(2) Review the nine factors that Hufbauer et al. list as the requirements for effective use of sanctions in Section 21.1 supra. In light of those factors, do you think that suspension of MFN treatment of Chinese goods would have likely caused the Chinese government to respect human rights? Is effectiveness an important consideration if the goal is to express strongly held beliefs about the inappropriateness of another country's actions?

(3) The proponents of continuing MFN treatment for China argued that expanding trade with China strengthened its private sector, which would ultimately weaken the authority of the central Communist government and over time lead to more freedom in China. It is, of course, impossible to know if they are right, but what do you think?

(4) Another response that is sometimes made to complaints about a country's failure to respect basic political rights is that in developing countries it is more meaningful for the government to improve living standards than it is to worry about political rights. The suggestion is that over time adequate political rights will develop. Do you agree? Some would argue that an equitable income distribution, not overall GDP levels, is the key factor. Should that be taken into account?

(5) Is it ever appropriate to use trade sanctions to enforce human rights? If so, which human rights should be selected as candidates for such enforcement? Are the concerns listed in President Clinton's memorandum the type of rights that deserve to be so protected? He listed concerns with emigration rights, prison labor, implementation of the UN Declaration, release of nonviolent political and religious prisoners, prisoner rights, treatment of Tibet and allowing radio and TV broadcasts into China. Are all of these human rights? Are they of same importance? Should there have to be a connection with international trade (e.g., exports of prison labor) before it is appropriate to use trade sanctions to promote human rights?

(6) One of GATT's biggest concerns historically was to control discrimination in international trade. Should there be WTO/GATT review of trade sanctions imposed for human rights purposes to ensure that similarly situated countries (in terms of human rights) are treated the same? Should there be WTO/GATT review to ensure that trade sanctions ostensibly for human rights purposes are not really for protectionist purposes? How could such a review be undertaken?

(7) In Section 21.5, we will see that the WTO does not effectively oversee trade actions taken under the GATT Article XXI for national security or political reasons. Should a similar rule apply for human rights?

(8) One of the issues raised by U.S. complaints about human rights practices in other countries is whether it is appropriate for the U.S. to "intervene" in the internal affairs of another country. Needless to say, countries that are the targets of U.S. complaints are quick to raise this argument. What gives the United States the right to tell other sovereign nations how to structure their governments and treat their citizens? At the time that President Clinton was considering the China MFN issue, the Prime Minister of Singapore, Goh Chok Tong, was quoted as suggesting "that the Chinese may one day threaten to withhold most-favored-nation status from the U.S. unless it does more to improve living conditions in Detroit, Harlem and South Central Los Angeles."[11] Suppose such action was taken by an advanced industrialized country having a more equal income distribution than the U.S. does. How, if at all, would sanctions imposed by that country against the U.S. be fundamentally different than the U.S. taking such action to promote democracy? Again we are led to the question: Who should decide what the important human rights are, whether they are satisfactorily met and what sanctions are appropriate?

Note on the Jackson–Vanik Amendment

The United States began to deny MFN treatment to Communist countries in the 1950's. As of 1972, most Communist countries did not receive MFN treatment, with Poland and Yugoslavia being the two exceptions. Then, in 1972, as part of his efforts to establish better relations with the former Soviet Union, President Nixon announced plans to negotiate a U.S.-U.S.S.R. trade agreement, and such an agreement was negotiated in 1973. That agreement was considered by Congress as part of its debate over the 1974 Trade Act. During this time, there was some controversy in the United States over Soviet limits on Jewish emigration, as well as some concern over the wisdom of normalizing relations with the Soviet Union. In one way or another, these concerns resulted in title IV of the 1974 Trade Act, which contains the so-called Jackson–Vanik procedures.

Under title IV, section 402, in order for a country, not receiving MFN treatment as of the effective date of the 1974 Act, to receive such treatment and to benefit from certain other U.S. credit and guarantee programs, it must comply with the freedom of emigration requirements of section 402 and enter into a trade agreement with the U.S. under section 405 of the Act. Section 402 requires that a country not deny its citizens the right or opportunity to emigrate and not impose more than a nominal tax on emigration, or on visas or other documents required for emigration. Section 402 permits the waiver of these strict requirements by the President in certain specified circumstances, subject to disapproval by a joint resolution by Congress, which would itself be subject to presidential veto.

Although section 402 is concerned specifically with emigration, the introductory sentence to Section 402(a) refers to "the continued dedication of the United States to fundamental human rights." In those cases where the withdrawal of MFN through non-renewal of the waiver has been an

---

11. Quoted in Karen Elliott House,   Wall St.J., May 27, 1994, at A–10.
" ... But Asia Holds Us in Contempt,"

issue—Romania in 1988 and China in the 1990's, U.S. concerns seem to have been based on broader issues of respect for fundamental human rights generally, and not simply emigration practices.

As of mid–2001, of the countries subject to title IV of the 1974 Trade Act, Armenia, Azerbaijan, Belarus, China, Kazakhstan, Moldova, Russia, Tajikistan, Turkmenistan, Ukraine and Uzbekistan benefited from waivers; while Cuba, North Korea and Vietnam did not, although President Bush submitted a proposed trade agreement with Vietnam to Congress in 2001.[12]

SECTION 21.4   LABOR STANDARDS AND INTERNATIONAL TRADE POLICY[1]

(A) LABOR STANDARDS AND THE WTO

At the end of the Uruguay Round, the United States and France proposed that the WTO agenda include consideration of the relationship of trade, on the one hand, and labor standards and social justice, on the other. This proposal was opposed by many developing countries, who saw it as an attempt to restrict their exports to the developed world. In their view, any attempt to label exports from low-wage countries as unfair was an attempt to repeal comparative advantage—the driving force behind international trade. While nothing became of the specific proposal, the issue of labor standards arose again and was probably the most controversial subject at the WTO's first ministerial meeting in Singapore in December 1996.

In paragraph 4 of the Singapore ministerial declaration, WTO Members included the following statement on core labor standards:

> We renew our commitment to the observance of internationally recognized core labour standards. The International Labour Organization (ILO) is the competent body to set and deal with these standards, and we affirm our support for its work in promoting them. We believe that economic growth and development fostered by increased trade and further trade liberalization contribute to the promotion of these standards. We reject the use of labour standards for protectionist purposes, and agree that the comparative advantage of countries, particularly low-wage developing countries, must in no way be put into question. In this regard, we note that the WTO and ILO Secretariats will continue their existing collaboration.

The internationally recognized core labor standards referred to are (i) the right of association, (ii) the right to organize and bargain collectively, (iii) the prohibition of forced labor, (iv) the prohibition of exploitive child labor and (v) nondiscrimination in employment. The rights are specified

---

12. To the extent that Cambodia and Laos were communist controlled as of January 3, 1975, they would be subject to Jackson–Vanik as well.

1. See generally Lance Compa, Labor Rights and Labor Standards in Internation-

al Trade, 25 L. & Pol.Intl.Bus. 165 (1993); Steve Charnovitz, The Influence of International Labour Standards on the World Trading Regime: A Historical Overview, 126 Intl. Labor Rev. 565 (1987).

in more detail in the eight fundamental conventions of the ILO, two conventions on each of the right of association, forced labor, child labor and discrimination. The United States is a party to only two of the conventions (one on forced labor and one on child labor).

The issue of trade and labor standards arose again in the course of the WTO's failed 1999 Seattle ministerial. Initially, the United States had proposed the creation of a WTO working party on labor rights with focus on a range of areas such as social protections and core labor standards, while the EU had proposed the creation of a standing forum on labor involving the WTO and the ILO. While the U.S. and the EU were apparently willing to scale back their proposals, ultimately nothing was agreed at Seattle. According to some observers, the efforts to obtain agreement on some type of discussion of labor issues in the WTO were seriously set back following an interview given by U.S. President Clinton in which he said ultimately he wanted the WTO system to be able to enforce labor standards with sanctions (a position that had been denied by U.S. negotiators).[2] It was not a major issue at Doha (section 27.1).

Notes and Questions

(1) Although the subject of labor standards or worker rights is thought of as a new issue, it is not. There were discussions of the need to have some sort of international trade/minimum labor standard connection in the 1920's.[3] Indeed, Article 7:1 of the ITO Charter provided:

> The Members recognize that measures relating to employment must take into account the rights of workers under inter-governmental declarations, conventions and agreements. They recognize that all countries have a common interest in the achievement and maintenance of fair labour standards related to productivity, and thus in the improvement of wages and working conditions as productivity may permit. The Members recognize that unfair labor conditions, particularly in production for export, create difficulties in international trade, and, accordingly, each Member shall take whatever action may be appropriate and feasible to eliminate such conditions within its territory.

Could this serve as a basis for an addition to the WTO agreements?

(2) GATT Article XX(e) allows a country to ban imports of prison labor. A review of the conventions listed in Section 21.3 supra shows that the only human rights conventions existing in 1947 were those on slavery and forced labor. Thus, the General Agreement arguably reflected the international consensus on worker rights at the time it was drafted. Since that time, however, there have been other conventions recognizing certain worker rights. Is that an argument for "updating" the WTO view of what measures should be possible under Article XX?

(3) Section 307 of the Tariff Act of 1930, 19 U.S.C.A. sec. 1307, bars the entry into the United States of goods "mined, produced, or manufactured wholly or in part in any foreign country by convict labor or/and forced labor

---

2. "U.S., EU Back Off From Modest Proposals for Labor Rights–Trade Link, Inside U.S. Trade," December 10, 1999.

3. See generally Charnovitz, supra note 1.

or/and indentured labor under penal sanctions." "Forced labor" is defined as "all work or service which is extracted from any person under the menace of any penalty for its nonperformance and for which the worker does not offer himself voluntarily." See generally 19 CFR secs. 12.42–.45 (2001). As of April 1, 2001, several Mexican products were subject to exclusion under this provision. 19 CFR sec. 12.42(h). In recent years, there has been considerable controversy over the extent to which Chinese exports to the United States include products of forced or prison labor. The U.S. and China entered into an agreement in 1992 dealing with this subject and improved implementation of the agreement was a condition for U.S. renewal of Chinese MFN status.

(4) During the NAFTA negotiations, there were concerns that U.S. industry would move to Mexico to take advantage of low Mexican wages and lax labor laws generally and that Mexican exporters (whether transplanted U.S. companies or others in Mexico) would be able to expand their exports to the United States. In deciding to support NAFTA, President Clinton announced that he would negotiate side agreements on the environment, labor and import surges. In the labor field, the result was the North American Agreement on Labor Cooperation, which is reproduced in the Documents Supplement. Under this agreement, each party recognized the right of the others to establish their own labor standards, but the agreement obligated each party to "promote compliance with and effectively enforce its labor law through appropriate government action." Agreement, art. 3. The parties are also obligated to ensure that "persons with a legally recognized interest under [their] law in a particular matter have appropriate access to administrative, judicial or labor tribunals for the enforcement of [their] labor law." Agreement, art. 4. The agreement also requires certain procedural guarantees be afforded. Agreement, art. 5. In addition, it establishes a procedure under which an Evaluation Committee of Experts (ECE) may analyze patterns of practice by a party in the enforcement of its occupational safety and health or other technical labor standards, which would seem to include child labor and minimum wage laws. Agreement, art. 23. On basis of the ECE's report, one party may claim that "there has been a persistent pattern of failure by [another] to effectively enforce such standards." Agreement, art. 27. If consultations between the parties fail and the NAFTA Labor Council (i.e., the Canadian, Mexican and U.S. labor ministers) cannot agree, then an arbitral panel may be appointed, which will consist of independent experts, to consider whether the persistent pattern of failure is trade-related and covered by mutually recognized labor laws. Agreement, art. 29. If the panel concludes that there has been such a failure, it may ultimately impose a monetary fine if a party fails to adopt and implement an action plan to correct the failure. Agreement, art. 39 and annex 39. If the fine is not paid, NAFTA benefits otherwise owed to the nonpaying party may be suspended. Agreement, art. 41. How would you evaluate this procedure as a means of enforcing labor standards? The GAO indicated in 2001 that no labor disputes under NAFTA had reached the dispute settlement phase. See Section 11.3(B) supra.

(5) The NAFTA Labor Agreement does not specify any minimum labor standards, but in Annex 1 it lists guiding principles that the parties are committed to promote, each in its own way. The eleven principles are:

— Freedom of association and protection of the right to organize

— The right to bargain collectively

— The right to strike

— Prohibition of forced labor

— Labor protections for children and young persons

— Minimum employment standards (e.g., minimum wages and overtime pay)

— Elimination of employment discrimination

— Equal pay for men and women

— Prevention of occupational injuries and illnesses

— Compensation for occupational injuries and illnesses

— Protection of migrant workers

How do these compare to the worker rights listed in the U.S. GSP statute?

(6) In an effort to defuse opposition to ratification of NAFTA in the United States, President Salinas of Mexico committed Mexico to raise its minimum wage in line with Mexican productivity increases.[4] How could such a commitment be enforced? Note that a similar commitment was contained in the ITO Charter, as quoted above in Note 1.

(B) LABOR STANDARDS AND THE U.S. GSP SCHEME

The concept of "internationally recognized worker rights," is defined in Title V of the Trade Act of 1974, which establishes the U.S. Generalized System of Preferences for developing countries. That program is discussed more generally in Section 25.3(B) infra. Here we will examine the procedure that may lead to the withdrawal of GSP benefits if a beneficiary developing country (BDC) fails to afford such worker rights. Under the regulations implementing the GSP program, interested parties may ask that a BDC be investigated to determine if it meets the criteria for continued inclusion in the GSP program. The following case highlights the rights at issue and the approach taken by U.S. authorities.

GENERALIZED SYSTEM OF PREFERENCES SUBCOM-
MITTEE OF THE TRADE POLICY STAFF COMMIT-
TEE, 1992 GSP ANNUAL REVIEW—WORKER
RIGHTS REVIEW SUMMARY—INDONESIA (CASE
007–CP–92, JULY 1993)

Introduction

In response to petitions filed in June 1992 by Asia Watch and the International Labor Rights Education and Research Fund, the interagency Subcommittee on the Generalized System of Preferences (GSP) conducted a review of worker rights laws and practices in Indonesia. The

---

4. Keith Bradsher, The Free–Trade Accord: 3 Nations Resolve Issues Holding Up Trade Pact Vote, N.Y.Times, Aug. 14, 1993, sec. 1, at 1, col. 6; Anthony DePalma, Mexico Raises Minimum Wages as Pledged, id., Dec. 12, 1993, sec. 1, at 6, col. 1.

purpose of the review was to determine whether Indonesia is complying with the worker rights provision of Section 502(b) of the U.S. GSP law, which requires beneficiary countries to have taken or be taking steps to afford internationally recognized worker rights.

The GSP program, originally enacted in 1974, provides duty-free entry to eligible products from beneficiary developing countries. [It] defines internationally recognized worker rights as follows:

a) the right of association;

b) the right to organize and bargain collectively;

c) a prohibition against any form of forced or compulsory labor;

d) a minimum age for the employment of children;

e) acceptable conditions of work with respect to minimum wages, hours of work and occupational safety and health.

The legislative history * * * indicates that Congress intended for level of development to be taken into account in assessing whether GSP beneficiary countries meet the "taking steps" standard. The 1984 report of the Committee on Ways and Means on the renewal act states that:

> It is not the expectation of the Committee that developing countries come up to the prevailing labor standards of the U.S. and other highly-industrialized countries. It is recognized that acceptable minimum standards may vary from country to country.

The Subcommittee noted that it is established United States policy that basic human rights are universal and that all governments are required to respect basic human rights, which include the first three cited worker rights, irrespective of social systems or state of economic development.

In the course of its review, the Subcommittee examined several submissions from the petitioners and the Government of Indonesia, the Department of State's Country Reports on Human Rights Practices, documents from the International Labor Organization (ILO), and a number of reports from the U.S. Embassy in Jakarta, Indonesia.

PRINCIPAL ISSUES

The GSP Subcommittee identified possible worker rights problems in all five worker rights categories listed in the GSP statute: right of association, the right to organize and bargain collectively, the minimum age for the employment of children, acceptable conditions of work, and forced labor.

Right of Association

The right of association includes the right of workers to establish and join organizations of their own choosing. The right of association also includes the right to strike.

Principal problems identified were 1) a union registration requirement which severely inhibits the formation of worker organizations; 2) a requirement that all unions be members of a single nationwide union structure (the All Indonesian Workers Union (SPSI)) over which the government has a great deal of influence; 3) a prohibition on union formation by civil servants; 4) government harassment of groups and individuals attempting to form new labor unions; 5) harassment of those who risk work action; and 6) police and military intervention between management and workers.

Under the Indonesian labor regulations in force when the review began, a worker organization could register as a "worker union" only if it consisted of a minimum of 1000 workplace level units. These units in turn had to be located in at least 100 districts in at least 20 different provinces. This numerical requirement operated as a significant barrier to union formation, thus impinging on workers' right to establish organizations of their own choosing. In its February 26 submission, the Government of Indonesia provided a draft of a union registration regulation which lowers the registration requirements to 100 workplace level units in 25 districts in 5 provinces. The regulation also requires that a "worker union" have at least 10,000 members.

While lowering the numerical requirements for establishing a "worker union" could result in workers enjoying a greater degree of freedom in establishing organizations of their own choosing, there is a concern that even these new limits may operate as a barrier to union formation. The Subcommittee noted that the 10,000 member requirement is not in conformity with the ILO's standards for freedom of association. On the question of numerical requirements for union formation, the ILO's Freedom of Association Committee has stated:

> Restrictions concerning race, minimum number of members, supervisors and the structure of trade unions

> Para. 256. The establishment of a trade union may be considerably hindered, or even rendered impossible, when legislation fixes the minimum number of members of a trade union at obviously too high a figure, as is the case, for example, where legislation requires that a union must have at least 50 founder members.

> Para. 257. The legal requirement that there be a minimum number of 20 members to form a union does not seem excessive and, therefore, does not in itself constitute an obstacle to the formation of a trade union.

> *Freedom of Association*
> Digest of Decisions and Principles
> of the Freedom of Association
> Committee (3d Ed.)

Indonesian law and practice effectively prohibits the formation of organizations as alternatives to the SPSI. By law, all worker organizations wishing to engage in traditional labor union activity (e.g., negotiating collective bargaining agreements) must be part of the SPSI, thus preventing workers from establishing and joining alternative unions. For example, the Government of Indonesia recently promulgated a regulation requiring that when a group of workers in a company wishes to form a union, they must first register with an existing union, of which there is only one—the SPSI. Further, during the review the Subcommittee obtained credible reports of harassment of individuals who attempt to form alternatives to the SPSI. Harassment has taken many forms, including the disruption of meetings and the detainment of individuals involved in efforts to create alternative worker organizations.

This infringement of workers' right of association is exacerbated by the fact that the SPSI is not a truly independent workers' organization. The extent to which it is controlled by the Government of Indonesia was noted in the State Department's 1992 Human Rights Report:

> [T]he government has a great deal of influence over the SPSI, the head of the SPSI is a senior member of GOLKAR [a government-sponsored political organization], two senior SPSI officials are Members of Parliament representing GOLKAR, and the Minister of Manpower is a member of the SPSI's Consultative Council. According to credible reports, the Government interferes in the selection of SPSI officers, especially the placing of retired military officers in mid-level positions.

* * *

In addition, Indonesian law does not allow civil servants to join labor unions. Civil servants must join the civil servants corps (KORPRI), a nonunion association whose leadership council is chaired by the Minister of Home Affairs. Indeed, KORPRI's charter states that its "main duty" is to implement policy as set forth by its central trustees (all of whom are government ministers) as opposed to representing the labor interests of civil servants. Further, KORPRI does not fit the definition of a truly independent labor union because its leadership is dominated by government ministers. The subcommittee noted that workers in some state owned enterprises are covered by collective labor agreements negotiated by SPSI units, but these are rare. The overwhelming majority of civil servants do not enjoy true freedom of association and, as a result, are denied the right to bargain collectively.

The Subcommittee viewed seriously these obstructions to the free formation of independent trade unions. The requirement that union formation is dependent upon participation in an organization heavily influenced by the government not only infringes the workers' right to join organizations of their own choosing, but is contrary to the ILO's standard that workers should be able to create and join unions that are free of government domination and control. Mandatory membership in organizations which do not engage in union activities is not a substitute for true freedom of association. In addition, the ILO has specifically criticized the prohibition on the formation of independent unions by civil servants as incompatible with the principles of freedom of association. The Subcommittee did note, however, that the Government of Indonesia has recently requested input from the ILO as to how to bring its union registration regulation into closer compliance with international norms. Such input could prove to be a valuable asset in any effort to improve the rights of Indonesian workers in this important area.

With respect to the right to strike, the Subcommittee noted several shortcomings when it compared Indonesian law and practice with international norms. One of the more serious concerns regarded the involvement and interference by the police and/or military in strikes, often when there is no threat to property and public order. When this involvement has occurred, it has taken various forms such a significant police or military presence during strikes, or presence during negotiations between workers and management when there is no apparent threat to public order. Plant level union officials have stated that this presence during negotiations is intimidating. In addition, workers assert that the military and police have beaten strike leaders.

Another concern in this area involves the obstacles to workers who wish to conduct a legal strike. In order to comply with the law, disaffected workers must go through a cumbersome and time-consuming dispute settlement process, including intensive mediation by the Ministry of Manpower, before legally being able to engage in strike activity. The process has little credibility with the workers and is therefore mostly ignored. As a result, most strikes are illegal. While leaders of illegal strikes are not usually arrested, they often lose their jobs because of their activities.

The Government of Indonesia is considering amendments to its strike law, and provided the subcommittee with a draft of the new law. The Subcommittee was concerned because the draft law contains inadequate procedures for protecting workers' right to strike. The new law would allow either party to an industrial dispute to request compulsory arbitration. While the matter is being arbitrated, workers would be prohibited from engaging in strike activity. However, the new law does not set forth any deadline for resolution of the dispute. As a result, for an indefinite length of time workers could be effectively denied their right to strike.

The Subcommittee was especially concerned to learn that on February 5, 1993, the Ministry of Manpower issued a directive which constitutes a serious infringement upon workers' right to strike. The directive provides that in the event of "any strike," the local office of the Ministry of Manpower is to invite labor and management to engage in settlement negotiations and that workers are to return to work during the negotiations. The directive further provides that if workers do not return to work, they are to be considered having resigned. By providing advance authorization for employers to retaliate against workers who engage in strike activity, the directive is contrary to the ILO's principles on freedom of association.

A final issue of concern in the area of the right of association is military and police interference in routine labor activities. As noted in the [1992 State Department] Human Rights Report, the Government of

Indonesia interferes in the selection of SPSI officers by placing retired military officers in mid-level positions. In addition, the police require any organization to obtain a permit before holding a meeting. While permits are routinely issued to the SPSI, there is concern that other organizations have difficulty obtaining the necessary permits.

Right to Organize and Bargain Collectively

With respect to the right to organize and bargain collectively, the principal problem is the legal requirement that a group of workers can negotiate a collective labor agreement (CLA) only if it is a chapter of a government-recognized union. The only government-recognized union is the SPSI. Therefore, this law effectively limits the right to organize and bargain collectively to SPSI members (who constitute less than 2% of Indonesia's total work force and approximately 6% of the industrial work force). Further, only about one half of the SPSI units have CLAs. Thus, the collective labor agreements in force cover only a small percentage of Indonesian workers.

Workers who are members of organizations that are unable to obtain union status (primarily because of the numerical requirements) are prohibited from negotiating the terms of a CLA with management. These workers can be covered by "company regulations" which define generally the terms and conditions of employment. Company regulations are subject to review by the Ministry of Manpower and are good for a period of two years. However, there are several key respects in which company regulations differ from CLAs:

— CLAs are negotiated between labor and management and signed by representatives of both parties. Company regulations are promulgated by management, albeit after receiving input from labor.

— CLAs set forth the wage scales for the employees. Company regulations do not establish employee's base wages beyond stating that the company will agree to pay the legally mandated minimum wage.

— When an employer violates the provisions of a CLA, an employee can seek redress through the industrial dispute settlement system. It appears that violations of company regulations can only be addressed through an individual breach of contract action in court.

While CLAs cover only a very small percentage of Indonesian workers, the Subcommittee noted that the number of CLAs in force has increased over the past several years.

Prohibition of any form of forced labor

The petitioner alleged that the Government of Indonesia condones the practice of forced labor by logging companies among the Asmat tribe in Irian Jaya, and there were credible reports of forced labor in 1990. There were also reports of girls being sold as domestic workers and men being sold as agricultural workers. In the course of several years, the

Government of Indonesia has stated on numerous occasions that it intends to investigate these allegations, but has not provided the results of any investigation.

The petitioners also alleged that forced labor exists with respect to certain East Timorese workers. According to the petition, these workers were lured to Java with the promise of vocational training and high-paying jobs, promises which did not materialize. It remains unclear as to whether these East Timorese workers were the victims of fraud. Regardless, it did not appear to the Subcommittee that the condition of these workers constitutes forced labor as defined by international standards.

Minimum age for employment of children

Child labor is a serious problem in both the formal and informal sectors in Indonesia. A 1987 regulation on child labor legalizes the employment of children under the age of 14, but only under certain circumstances. Because the regulation does not set a minimum age for the employment of children, it has effectively superseded a 1925 government ordinance which set a minimum employment age of 12. The Government of Indonesia has never promulgated implementing regulations for its 1951 labor act which included provisions on child labor. Further, there is no evidence that the Government of Indonesia enforces the existing restrictions on the employment of children. Since the promulgation of the current regulation in 1987, no employers have been taken to court for violating it. The government rarely conducts inspections of workplaces, choosing instead to rely primarily on Ministry of Manpower supervisors who learn of irregularities through other means. In the two inspections which the Government of Indonesia described in its November 16 submission, it claims to have found "very few child workers under 14 years old" in one instance and "no child labor" in another.

Acceptable conditions of work

The regional minimum wage rates in Indonesia are consistently less than the figure needed to enable a single worker or family to meet basic needs of nutrition, clothing and shelter. In addition to being inadequate, the legally-mandated minimum wage is widely ignored by employers. Failure to provide the minimum wage is most common grounds for strikes on the part of Indonesian workers.

Proactive enforcement of the minimum wage law is virtually nonexistent. There are few instances of ministry personnel conducting inspections of workplaces. The supervisors in each provincial office of the Ministry of Manpower instead rely upon reports of violations submitted by others. When the supervisor learns of a violation, he is supposed to issue a warning; only after three warnings can the employer be penalized for failing to comply with the law. When an employer is punished, the most common sanction is a nominal fine. The ineffectiveness of this system appears to contribute to the widespread disregard of the minimum wage laws by employers.

Occupational safety and health laws are likewise ineffectual. The 1992 Human Rights Report describes government enforcement and supervision of these laws are generally "weak." The government's efforts in this area are hampered by a scarcity of trained inspectors. Further, while employees who report unsafe working conditions are protected by law against employer retaliation, ineffective enforcement of this law allows retaliation to occur without sanction.

POSITIVE ACTIONS NOTED

The Subcommittee noted favorably that the Government of Indonesia has indicated an interest in amending certain of its laws and practices to bring them into closer compliance with international norms. In particular, the Government of Indonesia has requested input from the International Labor Organization (ILO) on how to bring its regulation on the registration of unions into closer compliance with international standards. The Subcommittee hopes that the Government of Indonesia will, in the near future, act to bring its law and practice into conformity with international standards regarding this fundamental worker right.

The Government of Indonesia has also indicated an interest in reviewing its laws and regulations governing the right to strike. While the draft law presented by the Government of Indonesia in its submission is flawed, the Subcommittee appreciated the fact that Government of Indonesia was reviewing its strike law. The Subcommittee hopes that the Government of Indonesia, with further input regarding international standards in this area, will promulgate a law which will constitute a concrete step towards providing this important worker right. Equally important, the Subcommittee hopes that the Government of Indonesia will show evidence of respecting the exercise of this right in practice. Such an advance could obviate workers' need to engage in illegal strikes.

The Subcommittee also noted that the SPSI is planning a restructuring through which it will decentralize into autonomous sectoral organizations. This restructuring will not be formalized before the next SPSI convention in 1995. The Subcommittee welcomes this move as decentralization may serve to improve the SPSI's efficiency at representing the concerns of its members. It should be noted, however, that decentralization is not a substitute for freedom of association.

RECOMMENDATION

The Subcommittee viewed the Government of Indonesia's positive actions as indicative of interest in bringing its worker rights laws and practices into closer compliance with international norms. Accordingly, the Subcommittee recommended that the review of Indonesian worker rights laws and practices be extended until February 5, 1994 in order to monitor developments in all the areas of concern, and to provide the Government of Indonesia with an opportunity to incorporate ILO advice regarding its labor laws and practices.

While noting the above positive actions, the Subcommittee determined that there were numerous significant deficiencies in Indonesia's labor laws and practices. The Subcommittee's most serious concerns had to do with the right of association, particularly with respect to the right to freely form independent unions and the right to strike. Additional concerns were in the areas of the right to organize and bargain collectively, child labor, and acceptable conditions of work. Questions about the use of forced labor remain unanswered.

The Subcommittee's concerns made it unable to recommend that Indonesia is taking steps to provide internationally recognized worker rights. The Subcommittee particularly noted that there has been little progress to date with respect to the areas of major concern. The Subcommittee believed it important to underline the central importance of the right of association, a basic human right and fundamental right of workers. In the absence of substantial concrete progress in the key issue areas in the future, Indonesia's continued GSP eligibility will be in serious jeopardy.

Notes and Questions

(1) Ultimately, GSP benefits were not withdrawn from Indonesia, presumably because of political concerns. Indonesia is the fourth largest country in the world in terms of population. It is strategically located, and it was to be the 1994 host of the Asia–Pacific Economic Cooperation meeting. As such, it is a country with whom the U.S. wants to maintain good relations.

(2) Other U.S. trade laws also make reference to the same worker rights criteria that are contained in the GSP statute. For example, benefits under the Caribbean Basin Economic Recovery Act and the Andean Trade Preferences Act, both discussed in Section 25.3(B) infra, are also subject to a beneficiary country meeting the worker rights standard. A similar condition is imposed for beneficiaries of the Overseas Private Investment Corporation (OPIC), which insures, reinsures, guarantees and finances projects in developing countries.[5] Section 301 of the 1974 Trade Act, which is described in Chapter 7 supra, includes in its definition of "unreasonable" acts, a "persistent pattern of conduct" that denies the same worker rights outlined in the GSP statute. Section 301(d)(3)(B)(iii), 19 U.S.C.A. sec. 2411(d)(3)(B)(iii).

(3) Although many investigations are made of BDC labor practices, relatively few countries lose GSP benefits. Indeed, an examination of the pattern of suspensions and withdrawals, suggests that countries tend to lose benefits only when they have other political problems in their relationship with the United States. It appears to be true, however, that the investigations do give the United States an opportunity to put some pressure on countries to modify their labor practices. How successful does it appear from the above extract that the United States has been in this regard in the case of Indonesia?

(4) Look again at the five specified worker rights, as listed in the above decision. What does "(e) acceptable conditions of work with respect to minimum wages, hours of work and occupational safety and health" mean?

5.   22 U.S.C.A. sec. 2191a(a)(1)(incorporating GSP statute definition of worker rights).

Does the Indonesian decision clarify this standard sufficiently? Would it be possible, or appropriate, under this standard to require a BDC to meet U.S. standards for wages and working conditions?

SECTION 21.5   TRADE CONTROLS FOR NATIONAL SECURITY AND POLITICAL PURPOSES

(A) INTRODUCTION

A classic exception to liberal trade policies and rules is the so-called national security exception. It is generally accepted that the benefits normally associated with free markets, such as efficient allocation of resources, do not outweigh the imperative need to ensure national survival. Thus, if a nation's defense and security depend, or are believed to depend, on the existence of industries such as shipbuilding or steel-making, those industries are likely to be maintained regardless of cost or any other economic considerations. The issue of national security being so important, it has always seemed inevitable that a national security exception would apply to international trade rules. The problem with a national security exception in international agreements, however, is that it is virtually impossible to define its limits. Almost every sector of economic endeavor can and does argue that it is necessary for national security, from shoes to watches, radios to beef production.

The basic justification for the national security exception is that it is necessary to provide for national defense by ensuring production of goods essential for defense. That is not, however, the only reason that the exception exists. Nations often wish to use trade controls for political purposes that may have only a tangential relationship to national security. For example, a country may dislike the discriminatory racial policies of another government and therefore exercise controls over trade with that government. Countries may choose to refrain from granting MFN status to other countries, because those countries are viewed as unfriendly or because to grant such status would be politically unpopular and therefore risk the survival of elected officials in their positions. For whatever the reasons, the facts of international economic life are that nations will pursue political goals with economic means.

The materials in this section review the GATT rules applicable to the use of trade controls for national security and political purposes. In subdivision D, we summarize some U.S. laws related to such purposes.

(B) THE GATT EXCEPTION FOR NATIONAL SECURITY TRADE CONTROLS

GATT Article XXI contains a general exception to all GATT obligations for certain measures taken by a member "necessary for the protection of its essential security interests." Although in principle limited to the three specified situations listed in Article XXI(b), the exception is broad enough to be subject to abuse.[1] Essentially the same language appears in GATS Article XIV*bis* and TRIPS Article 73. In addition, at the time a country becomes a WTO member, WTO Article XIII permits that country or any other member to refuse to apply the WTO Agreement as between themselves (a similar provision was contained in GATT Article XXXV). This authority can be used to prevent WTO rules applying for any reason—political, national security or otherwise.[2]

The question of the scope of Article XXI has only infrequently arisen in GATT. Czechoslovakia complained against the United States in 1949, arguing that the U.S. export controls preventing certain exports to Czechoslovakia were a violation of U.S. GATT obligations. The Czechoslovakian complaint was rejected by the GATT Contracting Parties. During the discussion it was contended that:

> every country must have the last resort on questions relating to its own security. On the other hand, the CONTRACTING PARTIES should be cautious not to take any step which might have the effect of undermining the General Agreement.[3]

As a result of congressional action, the United States suspended MFN treatment in 1951 towards Communist countries, including Czechoslovakia.[4] Again, the United States–Czechoslovakia relationship was brought to GATT, and the GATT Contracting Parties finally ruled that these two governments "shall be free to suspend, each with respect to the other, the obligations of the General Agreement on Tariffs and Trade."[5] No explicit reference was made in this declaration to any clause of the General Agreement that authorized this action, although it might be termed a "waiver." Other comparably ambiguous cases have included a Peruvian prohibition of Czechoslovakian imports, ultimately lifted after consultation, and a Ghanaian ban on Portuguese products, exercising Article XXXV of GATT.[6] Article XXXV has been invoked in a number of other situations, of course.[7]

More recently, the issue of the scope of the national security exception came before GATT as a result of Nicaragua's protest of U.S. controls on trade between the United States and Nicaragua. In 1983, when the United States cut Nicaragua's sugar import quota from 58,000 to 6,000 short tons, the GATT Council adopted a panel report concluding that the U.S. action violated Article XIII:2 because the United States did not hold negotiations with Nicaragua.[8] The United States did not press

1. See generally John H. Jackson, World Trade and the Law of GATT 748–752 (1969).

2. Id. at 100–102.

3. Id. at 749; GATT Doc. CP.3/SR. 22, at 7 (1949).

4. 65 Stat. 73, sec. 5 (1951).

5. Jackson, supra note 1, at 749–750; GATT, II BISD 36 (1952).

6. Jackson, supra note 1, at 750–751; see GATT Doc. SR. 9/27, at 10 (1955), but see also GATT Doc. L/2844 (1967), wherein Peru announced that it had abrogated, as of August 1, 1967, its decree of March 11, 1953, which restricted trade with countries having centrally planned economies. GATT Doc. SR. 19/12, at 196 (1961).

7. See Section 6.6(C) supra.

8. United States—Imports of Sugar from Nicaragua, GATT, 31st Supp. BISD 67 (1985) (Panel report adopted Mar. 13, 1984).

an argument that its actions were justified under Article XXI, and it did not attempt to block a decision by the Council on the Nicaraguan complaint. Nonetheless, the United States did not change its policy as a result of the GATT decision.

In 1985, President Reagan prohibited all trade between the United States and Nicaragua.[9] Nicaragua again raised objections in GATT. This time the United States explicitly took the position that its actions were imposed for national security reasons pursuant to Article XXI and that, in the reported words of the U.S. ambassador to GATT, "The GATT is not an appropriate forum for debating political and security issues." According to the U.S. ambassador, the United States "sees no basis for GATT Contracting Parties to question, approve, or disapprove the judgment of each Contracting Party as to what is necessary to protect its national security interests." Reportedly, the U.S. position was supported by Australia, Canada and most European countries, as well as the EU, whose ambassador stated, "while we do not wish to pass judgment before the Council, it is not the role of GATT to resolve disputes in the field of national security." Nicaragua argued that the United States could not credibly claim that Nicaragua was a threat to U.S. security.[10]

In the end, the United States did not block the creation of a panel to consider Nicaragua's complaint. In its report, the panel ultimately concluded that[11]

"as it was not authorized to examine the justification for the U.S. invocation of a general exception to the obligations under the General Agreement, it could find the United States neither to be complying with its obligations under the General Agreement nor to be failing to carry out its obligations under that Agreement."

On the wider task of assisting the Contracting Parties in further action on this matter, the panel noted that "embargoes such as the one imposed by the United States, independent of whether or not they were justified under Article XXI, ran counter to the basic aims of the GATT." The panel also recommended that the Council, in any further consideration of the matter, take into account the following general questions:

If it were accepted that the interpretation of Article XXI was reserved entirely to the contracting party invoking it, how could the Contracting Parties ensure that this general exception to all obligations under the General Agreement is not invoked excessively or for purposes other than those set out in this provision? If the Contracting Parties give a panel the task of examining a case involving in Article XXI invocation without authorizing it to examine the justification of that invocation, do they limit the adversely affected contracting party's right to have its com-

9. Executive Order No. 12513, 50 Fed. Reg. 18629 (1985).

10. 2 BNA Intl. Trade Rptr. 765 (1985); 3 BNA Intl. Trade Rptr. 380 (1986).

11. GATT, GATT Activities 1986, at 58–59 (1987).

plaint investigated in accordance with Article XXIII:2? Are the powers of the Contracting Parties under Article XXIII:2 sufficient to provide redress to contracting parties subjected to a two-way embargo?

Nicaragua said it was unfortunate that the panel did not answer the fundamental questions raised in the report, and that it had failed to consider the International Court of Justice's ruling that the US embargo was in violation of international law. It then asked the Council to recommend the following: first, the immediate removal of the embargo; second, the authorization of special support measures to that countries could grant trade preferences aimed at re-establishing a balance in Nicaragua's pre-embargo global trade relations and at compensating Nicaragua for the damage caused by the embargo; and finally, to prepare an interpretative note on Article XXI which would reflect the elements in this case.

In the US view, the panel had reached sound conclusions in a difficult situation. It therefore believed that the Council should adopt the report, decline to consider the panel's questions, and remove the matter from its agenda. It added that there had been many instances of trade sanctions imposed by various contracting parties for reasons of national security. Rarely had those been raised in the GATT and never before had a party insisted on establishing a panel. It reiterated the view that GATT was not the proper forum for examining or judging national security disputes. In May 1987, the panel report was still under consideration by the Council.

The U.S. supported adoption of the panel report, but Nicaragua opposed adoption. Consequently, the report was never adopted. U.S.-Nicaragua trade relations were normalized following the electoral defeat of the Sandinista party in 1990.

Notes and Questions

(1) Suppose that imports of watches increase to the point that they threaten to eliminate all U.S. watch production. Could the United States impose import restrictions on watch imports under GATT Article XXI? What if a similar situation existed for bicycles? Shoes? Cotton? Computers? Steel? Foodstuffs? Is there any limiting principle to the national security exception? After all, don't armies need watches and shoes and food and just about everything imaginable at one time or another?

(2) Review GATT Article XXI(b). Can you formulate more precisely defined and limited rules as to when the national security exception may be used? What assumptions must be made for such a formulation?

(C) THE USE OF ECONOMIC SANCTIONS FOR POLITICAL PURPOSES UNDER INTERNATIONAL LAW

The General Agreement does not specifically authorize the use of trade controls for political purposes, except that in Article XXI(c) there is an exemption from GATT obligations in respect of actions taken by a

Contracting Party "in pursuance of its obligations under the United Nations Charter for the maintenance of international peace and security."

The United Nations Charter empowers the Security Council to impose economic and military sanctions upon nations which threaten world peace. A prerequisite to the imposition of such sanctions is a Security Council determination of the existence of "any threat to the peace, breach of the peace, or act of aggression."[12] Once such a determination is made, recourse may be had to either Article 41 or Article 42 of the Charter.

Article 41 provides in a general way for taking measures "not involving the use of armed force." Economic and diplomatic sanctions are suggested, along with interruption of communications. Article 42 permits military action should the Council "consider that measures provided for in Article 41 would be inadequate or have proved to be inadequate." Once the Security Council has made an Article 39 determination and has decided upon sanctions, it may invoke Article 25 of the Charter, which binds member nations "to accept and carry out the decisions of the Security Council."

In the first 40 years of the U.N.'s existence, the Security Council only once called for broad-based economic sanctions to be applied against a country. In that instance, it asked member nations to impose economic sanctions on Rhodesia, after it unilaterally declared independence from the United Kingdom in 1965.[13] The sanctions were lifted after Rhodesia returned to its prior colonial status in 1979. The following year it became independent as Zimbabwe. During this period, the Security Council also adopted resolutions calling for limited sanctions to be applied to the Republic of South Africa to protest its policy of apartheid. For example, in 1977 it called for an arms embargo to be imposed on

---

12. United Nations Charter arts. 25, 39, 41, 42:

Art. 25. The Members of the United Nations agree to accept and carry out the decisions of the Security Council in accordance with the present Charter.

* * *

Art. 39. The Security Council shall determine the existence of any threat to the peace, breach of the peace, or act of aggression and shall make recommendations, or decide what measures shall be taken in accordance with Articles 41 and 42, to maintain or restore international peace and security.

* * *

Art. 41. The Security Council may decide what measures not involving the use of armed force are to be employed to give effect to its decisions, and it may call upon the Members of the United Nations to ap-

ply such measures. These may include complete or partial interruption of economic relations and of rail, sea, air, postal, telegraphic, radio, and other means of communication, and the severance of diplomatic relations.

Art. 42. Should the Security Council consider that measures provided for in Article 41 would be inadequate or have proved to be inadequate, it may take such action by air, sea, or land forces as may be necessary to maintain or restore international peace and security. Such action may include demonstrations, blockade, and other operations by air, sea, or land forces of Members of the United Nations.

13. S.C.Res. 232, U.N.Doc. S/Res/232 (1966); 30 U.N. SCOR, Spec.Supp. No. 2, Vol. II, at 100; U.N.Doc. S/11594/Rev. 1 (1975). See also Myres S. McDougall & W. Michael Riesman, Rhodesia and the United Nations: The Lawfulness of International Concern, 62 Am.J.Intl.L. 1 (1968).

South Africa and in 1985 it called for the adoption of such measures as suspension of new investment, prohibition of the sale of South African gold coins, suspension of guaranteed export loans, prohibition of new contracts in the nuclear field and prohibition of all sales of computer equipment that might be used by South African army or police units.[14] The U.N. General Assembly had called upon the Security Council to impose broader economic sanctions on South Africa, but the Security Council did not do so.[15] The apartheid system was later abolished and South Africa had free elections in 1994.

In the late 1980's and 1990's, the Security Council has been more active in calling for economic sanctions. In the last decade, sanctions have been imposed against Iraq, the former Yugoslavia, Libya, Haiti, Liberia, Rwanda, Somalia, UNITA forces in Angola, Sudan, Sierra Leone, FRY (including Kosovo), Afghanistan and Eritrea and Ethiopia. The range of sanctions has included comprehensive economic and trade sanctions and/or more specific measures such as arms embargoes, travel bans, financial or diplomatic restrictions.

Notes and Questions

(1) Should the WTO Charter contain an explicit "political escape clause" to allow any country to "opt out" of trading relationships with any other country on political grounds (much as WTO Article XIII now allows at the time a country becomes a member)?

(2) Do the GATT responses to the U.S.-Czechoslovakia and U.S.-Nicaragua cases essentially create a political purposes exception to the General Agreement and, by implication, the WTO Charter?

(D) U.S. NATIONAL SECURITY AND FOREIGN POLICY CONTROLS

As noted in Section 9.1 supra, the United States imposes export controls for national security and foreign policy purposes under the Export Administration Act. Here we look at several other U.S. statutes related to trade and other controls for national security and foreign policy purposes.

(1) National Security Controls Under Section 232

Section 232 of the Trade Expansion Act of 1962 authorizes the imposition of import controls for national security purposes. It provides in the first instance that the President shall not reduce duties or eliminate other import restrictions if such action would threaten to impair national security. In addition, it establishes a procedure by which any interested party can ask that an investigation be conducted to determine if imports of any article into the United States are threatening to impair the national security. Although the wording of Section 232

---

14. S.C.Res. 569, U.N.Doc. S/Res/569 (1985); S.C.Res. 418, U.N.Doc. S/Res/417 (1977).

15. See, e.g., G.A.Res. 35/227, U.N.Doc. A/Res/35/227 (1981).

suggests that it could have broad application, it has not often been applied, particularly in recent years.

(2) *Trade and Other Controls Under IEEPA*[16]

When the United States wants to impose economic sanctions for national security or foreign policy purposes, it typically acts to control more than just import or export flows. It may ban a range of financial transactions with the target country. Accordingly, it typically acts under the International Emergency Economic Powers Act (IEEPA), which was described in Section 3.3(C)(1) supra and which grants the President very broad discretionary powers to regulate international economic relations with other countries, once he declares a national emergency exists. IEEPA is set out in the Documents Supplement.[17] Formerly, wide-ranging economic sanctions were imposed under the Trading with the Enemy Act and some continue to be applied under that act. Section 3.3(C)(1) supra.

(3) *Foreign Use of Trade Controls: U.S. Antiboycott Rules*[18]

Section 8 of the Export Administration Act (EAA) regulates compliance by U.S. persons with a boycott by foreign countries against a country that is friendly to the United States and that is not the object of a boycott pursuant to U.S. law or regulation.[19] Essentially, the purpose of the provision, which was first adopted in 1977, is to make it unlawful for U.S. companies to participate in the Arab boycott of Israel. That boycott, which is followed to varying degrees by the various Arab countries, calls for a ban on imports from and exports to Israel. In addition, it provides for a so-called secondary boycott of Israel, pursuant to which firms that do business with Israel or have certain other relations with it are blacklisted and unable to do business in the Arab world. The U.S. antiboycott rules usually do not, as a practical matter, prevent U.S. businesses from doing business with Arab countries or complying with the terms of the primary Arab boycott, i.e. that part of the boycott prohibiting the importation into Arab countries of Israeli origin goods. They do serve, however, to discourage U.S. businesses from complying too readily with the secondary boycott. As such, the rules seem to have been largely accepted by all concerned, although U.S. business interests cite them as an impediment that costs them business vis-à-vis European and Japanese competitors who do not have to worry about such rules. Moreover, the complexity of the rules creates a trap for the unwary, as the distinction between what is permitted and what is prohibited by the EAA may often seem virtually indistinguishable to the untrained eye.[20] For example, it is permissible to agree to certify that the goods to be

---

16. See generally Michael P. Malloy, United States Economic Sanctions: Theory and Practice (2001).

17. Executive orders issued under IEEPA appear in the notes to 50 U.S.C.A. sec. 1701.

18. See generally Kennan L. Teslik, Congress, the Executive Branch, and Special Interests: The American Response to the Arab Boycott of Israel (1982).

19. 50 U.S.C.A.App. sec. 2407.

20. The regulations are set out at 15 CFR pt. 760 (2001).

supplied to an Arab country are of U.S., Canadian or whatever origin, but not that the goods are not of Israeli origin.[21]

Section 8 of the EAA applies only to U.S. persons (broadly defined to include controlled foreign subsidiaries) and only with respect to activities in the interstate or foreign commerce of the United States. Obviously, many activities of U.S. controlled subsidiaries would not involve the foreign commerce of the United States. The EAA provides that U.S. persons should not engage in any boycott-related activities listed in Section 8(a)(1), except to the extent permitted by Section 8(a)(2). In addition, the law requires extensive reporting of requests to support boycotts.

Different antiboycott rules are found in the Internal Revenue Code. These provisions, added by the Tax Reform Act of 1976, require U.S. taxpayers to report operations in, with or related to a boycotting country or national thereof and participation in the boycott, including receipt of requests to participate. Participation may lead to a loss of tax benefits.[22]

---

21. 50 U.S.C.A.App. sec. 2407(a)(2)(B).

22. Tax Reform Act of 1976, Pub.L. No. 94–455, sec. 1061–64, 90 Stat. 1520 (adding 26 U.S.C.A. secs. 908, 952(a), 995(b)(1)(F)(ii) and 999). The Treasury Department issued Guidelines explaining the scope of the statute on several occasions between 1976 and 1978. See 1976–2 C.B. 628, 1977–1 C.B. 529, 1977–2 C.B. 505, 1978–1 C.B. 521. See generally Richard L. Kaplan, Income Taxes and the Arab Boycott, 32 Tax Lawyer 313 (1979).

Chapter 22

MONETARY AFFAIRS AND TRADE POLICY

SECTION 22.1   INTRODUCTION

Although the focus of this book is on the regulation of international trade, some attention to international monetary issues is valuable. Exchange rate fluctuations can have profound effects upon trade flows, as may direct intervention in trade to address balance of payments "problems." Thus, in this chapter, we consider several topics relating to international monetary policy and its interface with trade.

We begin with a brief look at trade finance and foreign exchange transactions, their effect on the balance of payments, and the effects of exchange rate determination on trade. In Section 22.2, we sketch the operations of the IMF, in particular its lending activities. Section 22.3 considers national and international regulation of government intervention into foreign exchange markets. Section 22.4 examines trade intervention for balance of payments purposes and the international rules applicable to countries with balance of payments problems.

(A) THE ROLE OF FOREIGN EXCHANGE IN TRADE

Suppose that a U.S. company wants to export its widgets to a buyer in country X. How will the buyer pay for them? One possibility is that the buyer will export some other good in exchange for the widgets—"barter" in traditional parlance, a form of "countertrade" in modern parlance. Or perhaps a trading house will orchestrate a multiparty barter transaction. But barter is often infeasible or at least quite costly to coordinate, and it is much more convenient if the parties to the transaction can employ money (to see its advantages, you need only reflect briefly on how difficult it would be to go about your own day-to-day transactions on a barter basis).

In domestic transactions, the use of money is routine. The buyer gives domestic currency or its equivalent to the seller, who can then use it to pay workers, buy more raw materials, and so on. But in the typical international transaction, the buyer does not have a store of the seller's home currency, and the seller may not have much desire for the buyer's currency because all of the seller's expenses are payable in its own currency. Thus, in our hypothetical example, the need arises for a transaction whereby the buyer's home currency is exchanged for dollars, which can then be used to pay the U.S. widget exporter. Such transactions are viable as long as there are other parties who desire to exchange dollars for the buyer's home currency. A foreign exchange market brings these parties together directly or indirectly through the intermediation of exchange traders.

The need to purchase foreign exchange can introduce another concern for the parties, termed "exchange risk." Perhaps the buyer obtains a price quote of $100/widget, but knows that the widgets will not be shipped for awhile and thus payment will not be due until later. The exchange rate between the buyer's home currency and dollars may change in the interim. If the buyer waits until payment is due to buy dollars, therefore, the effective price may be higher or lower in terms of the buyer's home currency. To a "risk averse" buyer, this uncertainty can be an added cost of the transaction. The buyer can reduce or avoid it in most cases by entering the exchange market to buy dollars when the order is placed, probably under a forward contract. The desire to avoid exchange risk thus explains in part the existence of forward markets for foreign exchange in addition to the spot market.[1]

The foreign exchange market serves as a perfectly satisfactory mechanism with respect to many international transactions, but in some instances the demand for a particular currency is too thin to support an active market. With the currencies of smaller developing nations or former Communist countries, for example, the number of entities wishing to buy the currency at a point in time may be quite small, and exchange traders may be unwilling to hold onto the currency very long because of economic and political risks affecting its value. Potential buyers in those countries may thus have difficulty obtaining dollars, marks, yen and the like to make their purchases, because no one wants the home currency that they can offer in exchange. Here, old-fashioned barter and its more sophisticated modern incarnations may take over again.[2] Currencies that are readily traded for others are sometimes termed "hard" currencies, while those that are not are sometimes termed "soft" currencies.

(B) EXCHANGE RATE DETERMINATION

Presently, the prices of the dollar and many other major currencies on foreign exchange markets are determined primarily by private market forces—so-called "floating" rates. Thus, roughly speaking, if the demand by U.S. firms for Japanese yen exceeds the demand of Japanese firms for U.S. dollars, the yen will appreciate relative to the dollar. Arbitrage

---

1. On the importance of exchange risk to trade volumes generally, a leading paper is Peter Hooper and Stephen Kohlhagen, The Effects of Exchange Rate Uncertainty on the Prices and Volumes of International Trade, 8 J.Intl.Econ. 483 (1978) (concluding that effect is minimal).

2. See Jean–Francois Hennart, The Transaction Cost Rationale for Countertrade, 5 J.L.Econ. & Org. 127 (1989).

among currencies ensures that other effects will be seen as well (see the excerpt to follow). Anything priced in yen becomes more expensive to U.S. buyers, and anything priced in dollars becomes cheaper for Japanese buyers. This tends to increase the Japanese demand for dollars and to reduce the U.S. demand for yen, thereby restoring the balance between supply and demand.

The result of floating rates can be considerable volatility. A small change in relative interest rates, for example, may cause a large shift in the demand for a particular currency to buy financial assets. Exchange rate volatility, in turn, can create considerable variability in the extent to which a nation's exports are competitive on world markets. For political and perhaps economic reasons as well, such variability is sometimes seen as harmful, and central banks may intervene in the exchange markets to try and suppress it, with different degrees of success.

Various alternatives to floating rates are imaginable, and indeed for many years the governments of the major trading nations endeavored to maintain "fixed" exchange rates. They did so essentially by having their central banks offer to buy or sell currency as needed to balance supply and demand at the fixed exchange rate, or by offering (at least to other governments) to exchange their currency for gold at a fixed price (a "gold standard"). Such a policy required that central banks hold substantial reserves of foreign currencies or of specie. The United States pegged the dollar to gold, and backed up its commitment by promising to trade dollars for gold with foreign central banks, until 1971.

As Section 22.2 will indicate, the International Monetary Fund was originally conceived to help support this system of fixed rates by lending monetary reserves to nations that ran short. In the end, however, the availability of IMF lending was not enough to persuade all of the major trading nations that efforts to maintain fixed rates were worthwhile. Periodic "devaluations" put the lie to the notion that rates were really fixed anyway. The global fixed rate system came to an end when, in 1971, the United States indicated that it would no longer exchange dollars for gold and closed the "gold window."[3]

Under the current provisions of the International Monetary Fund Agreement, a country has considerable flexibility in deciding how to manage its exchange rates—from allowing the rate to float freely to tying it to some other rate or to a formula. As noted, the United States has generally elected to let its exchange rate float freely. Most of the members of the European Union have agreed to eliminate exchange fluctuations between them altogether by creating a common currency, the Euro, a development discussed briefly below.

Whether the future will see a general movement back toward "fixed" or "stabilized" exchange rates, with greater central bank inter-

---

3. A nice history of the gold standard years and its connection to the international monetary situation is provided by Kenneth Dam, From the Gold Clause Cases to the Gold Commission: A Half Century of American Monetary Law, 50 U.Chi.L.Rev. 504 (1983).

vention to support all of the major currencies, remains uncertain at this writing. It is also unclear to what extent central bank intervention in the exchange markets has the capacity to influence exchange rates in the modern era given the growth of international commerce and the sheer magnitude of exchange markets. The following excerpt provides some additional background and detail on their operation.

K. ALEC CHRYSTAL, A GUIDE TO FOREIGN EXCHANGE MARKETS[4]

How Does "the" Foreign Exchange Market Operate?

It is generally not possible to go to a specific building and "see" the market where prices of foreign exchange are determined. With few exceptions, the vast bulk of foreign exchange business is done over the telephone between specialist divisions of major banks. Foreign exchange dealers in each bank usually operate from one room; each dealer has several telephones and is surrounded by video screens and news tapes. Typically, each dealer specializes in one or a small number of markets (such as sterling/dollar or deutschemark/dollar). Trades are conducted with other dealers who represent banks around the world. These dealers typically deal regularly with one another and are thus able to make firm commitments by word of mouth.

Only the head or regional offices of the larger banks actively deal in foreign exchange. The largest of these banks are known as "market makers" since they stand ready to buy or sell any of the major currencies on a more or less continuous basis. Unusually large transactions, however, will only be accommodated by market makers on more favorable terms. In such cases, foreign exchange brokers may be used as middlemen to find a taker or takers for the deal. Brokers (of which there are four major firms and a handful of smaller ones) do not trade on their own account, but specialize in setting up large foreign exchange transactions in return for a commission (typically 0.03 cents or less on the sterling spread). In April 1983, 56 percent of spot transactions by value involving banks in the United States were channeled through brokers. If all interbank transactions are included, the figure rises to 59 percent.

Most small banks and local offices of major banks do not deal directly in the interbank foreign exchange market. Rather they typically will have a credit line with a large bank or their head office. Transactions will thus involve an extra step. The customer deals with a local bank, which in turn deals with a major bank or head office. The interbank foreign exchange market exists between the major banks either directly or indirectly via a broker.

* * *

Foreign Exchange Market Activities

Much foreign exchange market trading does not appear to be related to the simple basic purpose of allowing businesses to buy or sell foreign

---

4. 66 The Federal Reserve Bank of St.   Louis Review, No. 3, at 5 (Mar. 1984).

currency in order, say, to sell or purchase goods overseas. It is certainly easy to see the usefulness of the large range of foreign exchange transactions available through the interbank and organized markets (spot, forward, futures, options) to facilitate trade between nations. It is also clear that there is a useful role for foreign exchange brokers in helping to "make" the interbank market. There are several other activities, however, in foreign exchange markets that are less well understood and whose relevance is less obvious to people interested in understanding what these markets accomplish.

Two major classes of activity will be discussed. First, the existence of a large number of foreign exchange markets in many locations creates opportunities to profit from "arbitrage." Second, there is implicitly a market in (foreign exchange) risk bearing. Those who wish to avoid foreign exchange risk (at a price) may do so. Those who accept the risk in expectation of profits are known as "speculators."

Triangular Arbitrage

Triangular arbitrage is the process that ensures that all exchange rates are mutually consistent. If, for example, one U.S. dollar exchanges for one Canadian dollar, and one Canadian dollar exchanges for one British pound, then the U.S. dollar-pound exchange rate should be one pound for one dollar. If it differs, then there is an opportunity for profit making. To see why this is so, suppose that you could purchase two U.S. dollars with one British pound. By first buying C$1 with U.S. $1, then purchasing £1 with C$1, and finally buying U.S. $2 with £1, you could double your money immediately. Clearly this opportunity will not last for long since it involves making large profits with certainty. The process of triangular arbitrage is exactly that of finding and exploiting profitable opportunities in such exchange rate inconsistencies. As a result of triangular arbitrage, such inconsistencies will be eliminated rapidly. Cross rates, however, will only be roughly consistent given the bid-ask spread associated with transaction costs.

In the past, the possibility of making profits from triangular arbitrage was greater as a result of the practice of expressing exchange rates in American terms in the United States and in European terms elsewhere. The adoption of standard practice has reduced the likelihood of inconsistencies. Also, in recent years, such opportunities for profit making have been greatly reduced by high-speed, computerized information systems and the increased sophistication of the banks operating in the market.

* * *

Interest Arbitrage

Interest arbitrage is slightly different in nature from triangular or space arbitrage; however, the basic motive of finding and exploiting profitable opportunities still applies. There is no reason why interest rates denominated in different currencies should be equal. Interest rates are the cost of borrowing or the return to lending for a specific period of time. The relative price (exchange rate) of money may change over time so that the comparison of, say, a U.S. and a British interest rate requires some allowance for expected exchange rate changes. Thus, it will be not at all unusual to find interest rates denominated in dollars and interest rates denominated in, say, pounds being somewhat different. However, real returns on assets of similar quality should be the same if the exchange rate risk is covered or hedged in the forward market. Were this not true, it would be possible to borrow in one currency and lend in another at a profit with no exchange risk.

Suppose we lend one dollar for a year in the United States at an interest rate of r_{us}. The amount accumulated at the end of the year per dollar lent will be $1 + r_{us}$ (capital plus interest). If, instead of making dollar loans, we converted them into pounds and lent them in the United Kingdom at the rate r_{uk}, the amount of pounds we would have for each original dollar at the end of the year would be $S(1 + r_{uk})$, where S is the spot exchange rate (in pounds per dollar) at the beginning of the period. At the outset, it is not known if $1 + r_{us}$ dollars is going to be worth more than $S(1 + r_{uk})$ pounds in a year's time because the spot exchange rate in a year's time is unknown. This uncertainty can be avoided by selling the pounds forward into dollars. Then the relative value of the two loans would no longer depend on what subsequently happens to the spot exchange rate. By doing this, we end up with $S/F(1 + r_{uk})$ dollars per original dollar invested. [F is the price of a dollar at the end of the period, in pounds, purchased forward at the beginning of the period.] This is known as the "covered," or hedged, return on pounds.

Since the covered return in our example is denominated in dollars, it can reasonably be compared with the U.S. interest rate. If these returns are very different, investors will move funds where the return is highest on a covered basis. This process is interest arbitrage. It is assumed that the assets involved are equally safe and, because the returns are covered, all exchange risk is avoided. Of course, if funds do move in large volume between assets or between financial centers, then interest rates and the exchange rates (spot and forward) will change in predictable ways. Funds will continue to flow between countries until there is no extra profit to be made from interest arbitrage. This will occur when the returns on both dollar-and sterling-denominated assets are equal, that is, when

$$(1) \quad (1 + r_{us}) = \frac{S}{F} (1 + r_{uk}).$$

This result is known as covered interest parity. It holds more or less exactly, subject only to a margin due to transaction costs, so long as the appropriate dollar and sterling interest rates are compared.

Speculation

Arbitrage in the foreign exchange markets involves little or no risk since transactions can be completed rapidly. An alternative source of profit is available from outguessing other market participants as to what future exchange rates will be. This is called speculation.

* * *

Speculation is important for the efficient working of foreign exchange markets. It is a form of arbitrage that occurs across time rather than across space or between markets at the same time. Just as arbitrage increases the efficiency of markets by keeping prices consistent, so speculation increases the efficiency of forward, futures and options markets by keeping those markets liquid. Those who wish to avoid foreign exchange risk may thereby do so in a well-developed market. Without speculators, risk avoidance in foreign exchange markets would be more difficult and, in many cases, impossible.

(C) BALANCE OF PAYMENTS MEASUREMENT AND AC-COUNTING

The balance of payments is always in balance (save for a "statistical discrepancy"), an accounting identity. Thus, when we hear of a "balance of payments deficit," what the speaker means (if the speaker understands what he or she is saying at all) is that when one or more entries on the balance of payments ledger is ignored, payments outflows exceed inflows.

Why might it be useful to exclude certain items from the accounts to create the possibility of "surplus" or "deficit"? The following excerpt, dated in its figures but not in the lucidity of its explanation, introduces some of the issues.

CHARLES PIGOTT, WHICH TRADE BALANCE?[5]

In February, newspapers across the nation reported that the U.S. "trade" deficit for 1983 was $60.6 billion. A month later they reported a 1983 "trade" deficit of $40.8 billion. But the national income account data given in the recent *Survey of Current Business* lists still another version of the "trade" deficit—$7.1 billion. Will the real trade deficit please stand up?

Neither media inaccuracy nor government revisions can be blamed for these discrepancies. Rather, what is commonly referred to as "the trade balance" is actually measured and reported in several different ways. Anyone wanting to know this balance has the following choices: the merchandise trade balance, itself measured in several ways; "GNP net exports", which gives the balance of trade in merchandise *and* services; or the current account balance. While these balances generally move closely together over time, their levels are typically very different. For example, it was the merchandise balance that was $60.6 billion in

5. Research Department, Federal Reserve Bank of San Francisco, FRB SF   Weekly Letter (April 20, 1984).

deficit last year, while the current account and GNP net export deficits were $40.8 and $7.1 billion, respectively. For those who still want to know what the deficit really was, this *Letter* provides a short "guide to the perplexed", explaining the various balances, their relation to one another, and their economic significance.

CURRENT ACCOUNT

The most comprehensive summary of U.S. trade with the rest of the world is given by the current account balance. Indeed, the current account contains the other balances mentioned above and all the transactions in them.

The current account includes all transactions that are "current" in an accounting sense, that is, all payments and receipts for goods and services exchanged with foreigners, as well as transfers. Excluded from the current account are U.S. purchases from or sales to foreigners of financial or real assets. These items, which represent U.S. entities' lending to or borrowing from foreigners, comprise the capital account of the U.S. balance of payments.

If, in any year, total U.S. payments to foreigners on a current basis exceed our receipts from them (that is, we run a current account deficit), our country must borrow from abroad to make up the difference. Conversely, we must lend to foreigners any difference between our sales to them on a current basis and our payments. The current account surplus or deficit therefore also measures the *net* amount the U.S. as a whole is lending to or borrowing from abroad during a given year. Last year, we ran a current account deficit of $40.8 billion; this means that we borrowed a net amount of $40.8 billion from abroad.

The current account itself, though, contains three distinct types of transactions: *merchandise trade, productive services* provided by land, labor, and capital; and *transfers,* which include foreign aid and private remittances as well as payments to foreigners of interest on their holdings of U.S. government debt. These, in turn, are "arranged" into the three basic balances—merchandise trade, GNP net exports of goods and services, and, finally, the current account balance itself.

MERCHANDISE TRADE BALANCE

The merchandise trade account contains all exports and imports of *tangible commodities,* e.g., agricultural products, industrial materials such as steel, consumer manufactures, and capital goods. Actual merchandise trade figures are reported several different ways depending on the extent to which various services involved in transporting them are included.

Imports and exports on a "free-along-side" (f.a.s.) basis are valued as delivered to their point of embarkation for or departure from the U.S. The f.a.s. figures are thus the purest measures of the values of the commodities themselves. Other export/import figures refer to their value "free-on-board" (f.o.b.), that is, inclusive of loading and related costs.

Still other figures include the "cost of insurance and freight" (c.i.f.) in addition to the loading costs and the actual (f.a.s.) commodity value.

The first merchandise trade balance figures reported each month by the Commerce Department, and the ones most frequently quoted in the media, are the "census" figures based on the export and import invoices recorded at various U.S. customs stations. These figures value imports at their *point of entry* into the U.S., that is on a c.i.f. basis, while they value exports on an f.a.s. basis. (Commerce reports the balance on an f.a.s. basis for both exports and imports several days following the release of the census data.) The census balance thus includes the transport and other service costs of bringing imports to the U.S. but excludes the service costs involved in getting our exports abroad. Not surprisingly then, last year's census-based deficit of $69 billion was substantially larger than the f.a.s. merchandise deficit of $60.6 billion.

SERVICES

Services provided by factors of production—land, labor and capital—are the second major category of transactions in the current account. Included in such "factor" services are personal travel and tourism, royalties and other fees from professional services, as well as all services associated with transporting and insuring U.S. merchandise trade.

However, the largest and most rapidly growing component of factor services represents payments for services provided by physical capital. These include recorded earnings from U.S. investments abroad as well as payments to foreigners on their investments in the U.S., *except* for the interest they earn on their holdings of U.S. government (federal, state and local) debt. Interest payments to foreigners on government debt are not included in these services (although they are included in the current account) because, according to U.S. national income accounting conventions, they represent a transfer rather than a payment for a current factor service.

Overall, the service balance typically records a large surplus, nearly $54 billion in 1983. This mainly reflects the fact that the U.S. earns considerably more on its investments abroad than it pays to foreigners on their investments here. Indeed, our reported investment receipts totaled $85 billion last year (nearly two-thirds of all service exports), exceeding payments to foreigners on their investments in the U.S. by nearly $47 billion.

The sum of the (f.a.s.) merchandise trade and service balances yields what is known as "GNP net exports." This is the net export figure given in the U.S. national income statistics and it is one of the four major components of U.S. GNP.

TRANSFERS AND THE REMAINDER

The remainder of the current account consists of unilateral transfers such as private contributions, pension payments, official foreign aid, as well as interest payments to foreigners on their holdings of U.S. government debt. The U.S. always runs a large deficit overall in these items, amounting to nearly $33 billion in 1983, $18 billion of which represented U.S. government interest paid to foreigners.

MEANING

On this basis, last year's $41 billion current account deficit was the sum of our $61 billion merchandise trade *deficit,* the $54 billion *surplus* on factor services (together making up the $7 billion deficit on GNP net exports), and our $33 billion *deficit* in transfers and U.S. government interest payments to foreigners (Chart 1).

Chart 1

Components of the Current Account: 1983

(Billions of Dollars)

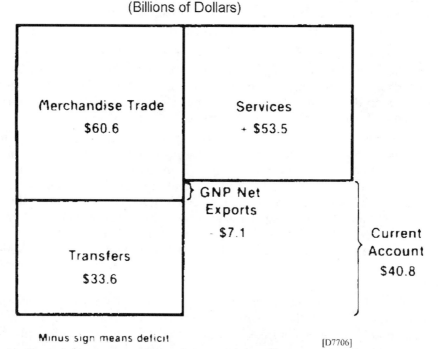

Minus sign means deficit   [D7706]

Our merchandise trade balance has been in deficit in all but two of the last fourteen years, while the current account and GNP net exports have more often been in surplus. This pattern is due to the large U.S. surplus in factor services—a surplus that has grown very quickly in recent years mainly because of the rapid increase in receipts from our investments abroad. The services surplus means that the U.S. can have a substantial trade deficit even in years when our total current international payments and receipts (the current account) are in balance. Interestingly, the situation is the opposite for several of our trading partners. Japan, for example, typically runs a substantial deficit in services. Its merchandise trade therefore may be in surplus, as is usually the case, even when its current account is in deficit.

Although the merchandise trade balance gets the most media attention, the GNP net export and current account balances are more economically significant. In particular, GNP net exports provide the best summary measure of the foreign sector's impact on U.S. output and employment, while the current account balance measures the impact of the foreign sector on U.S. financial markets, including the value of the dollar on the foreign exchange markets.

GNP net exports comprise one of the four major components of U.S. GNP (along with private consumption and investment, and government expenditures), measuring the difference between foreign purchases of U.S. goods and services and U.S. purchases of foreign goods and services. As such, variations in GNP net exports have a direct and potentially substantial impact on the growth of our national output. As the foreign sector has grown in importance to the U.S. economy over the last decade, forecasts of U.S. growth have become increasingly sensitive to assessments of GNP net exports.

Finally, the current account's significance lies mainly in the fact that it measures the net flow of U.S. lending to or borrowing from abroad, and hence, the change over time in net U.S. indebtedness to foreigners. (The U.S. is still a net claimant on abroad, but this could change if our present deficits persist.) This flow, in turn, has potentially very important implications for financial conditions in the U.S. and for the value of the dollar on the foreign exchanges. In particular, the nearly $41 billion in funds the U.S. "imported" from abroad last year helped to meet the credit needs of our private sector and the growing demand for credit by the federal government. Upward pressures on U.S. interest rates would probably have been greater had these foreign funds not been available.

(D) TRADE IN A SYSTEM OF FLOATING RATES

When exchange rates are fixed by governments, it comes as no surprise that they may fail to balance the forces of supply and demand and prove unsustainable in the end. Yet, it has also been suggested at times that market-determined or "floating" rates reflect "misalignment." The claim was heard frequently in the 1980's, for example, that the dollar was "overvalued," contributing to the large U.S. trade deficit.

C. FRED BERGSTEN & JOHN WILLIAMSON, EXCHANGE RATES AND TRADE POLICY[6]

Trade policy has traditionally been associated with tariffs, quotas, export subsidies, and other nontariff distortions. Relatively little attention has been paid to the impact of exchange rates on trade policy, despite widespread analyses by international monetary economists of

6. © 1983, Institute for International Economics. Reproduced by permission from   W. Cline (ed.), Trade Policy in the 1980s, at 99–103, 107–09 (1983).

their impact on trade flows. This paper argues that the continued failure to link the trade and monetary aspects of international economic exchange is a major mistake, in terms both of diagnosing the policy problems which now confront the trading system and of dealing with those problems in the foreseeable future.

MISALIGNED CURRENCIES AND TRADE PROTECTION

The bifurcation between money and trade, at both the analytical and policy levels, is understandable yet strange. It is understandable for three reasons. First, different officials and, usually, different ministries are responsible for monetary and trade matters in most countries. * * *

Second, there is a legitimate difference between the focus of trade policy on the *level* of trade flows and the focus of exchange rates (and international monetary policy, more broadly) on trade *balances*. As long as trade negotiations are reciprocal in practice as well as in principle, trade policy has a neutral impact on the trade balance. Similarly, the balance of payments adjustment process addresses the problem of the trade balance rather than the trade level. * * *

But the main reason why the money-trade relationship has been so ignored is probably the widespread assumption that the international monetary system will not permit the existence of substantial exchange rate misalignments for prolonged periods. * * *

This bifurcation is strange, however, because exchange rates demonstrably do deviate substantially from their equilibrium paths for substantial periods of time, and because the basic case for liberal trade rests upon the assumption inter alia of balance of payments equilibrium, hence equilibrium exchange rates. If the exchange rate conveys price signals to producers and consumers which are incorrect reflections of the underlying economic relationships, significant distortions can result for production, hence trade.

Persistent overvaluation of a country's exchange rate will, of course, adversely affect the country's price competitiveness in international trade (in both goods and services). Exports will be discouraged and imports will be encouraged. The tradable goods sector of the economy, as a whole, will be disadvantaged with resulting distortions in the distribution of domestic output. The current account will shift adversely, financed via private capital inflows or a decline in the country's external reserves. The amounts of money involved can be quite sizable; for the United States, the typical analysis suggests that the merchandise trade balance declines by about $3 billion for every percentage point decline in US international price competitiveness.

From the standpoint of trade policy, the chief implication is the (additional?) pressure that is generated for protectionist measures. Export- and import-competing firms and workers will tend to seek help from their governments to offset these distortions, which undermine their ability to compete, with some degree of legitimacy since the distortions are accepted—in some cases, even fostered—by those governments. Coalitions in support of trade restrictions will be much easier to form, and much broader in their political clout, because no longer will only the most vulnerable firms and workers be seeking help—and no longer will the countervailing pressures from successful exporters be as effective. As we shall see below, overvaluation of the dollar has proved to be an accurate "leading indicator" of trade policy in the United States—perhaps the most accurate of all such indicators—in the postwar period.

The protectionist impact of an overvalued currency, moreover, may persist beyond the duration of the overvaluation itself. Once adopted, protection is frequently maintained long after its initial cause (or justification) has passed. A return to currency equilibrium, or even "reverse overshooting" to undervalued levels, may not produce elimination of restrictions implemented to offset a previous overvaluation. Exchange rate oscillations may thus produce a ratchet effect on protection, raising it during (the inevitably reversible) periods of overvaluation but failing to undo it when equilibrium is restored.

* * *

THE IMPACT OF MISALIGNMENTS ON TRADE FLOWS

* * *

During the 1960s a number of studies attempted to estimate separately "exchange-rate elasticities" and "tariff elasticities," the former representing the impact on trade flows of exchange rate changes and the latter the impact of tariff changes. The stylized fact emerged that tariff elasticities were substantially larger, by a factor of two or three, than exchange rate elasticities. The usual explanation of this empirical regularity was the greater confidence presumably felt by traders that tariff changes would result in "permanent" changes in competitiveness.

In comparing the relative importance of tariff and exchange rate changes, however, it must be recognized that there has been a much greater degree of fluctuation in exchange rates than in tariffs during the postwar period. The celebrated trade liberalization of the Kennedy Round, for example, which is widely referred to as a 35 percent reduction, cut tariffs by an average of only 4–5 percentage points for the United States and European Economic Community (EEC) and about 7 percentage points for Japan and the United Kingdom. By contrast, real effective exchange rates frequently change by such amounts within very short periods of time—and remain further away from their underlying equilibrium paths (by as much as 10–20 percent) for extended episodes, as noted below. Hence the economic impact of exchange rate changes may at times substantially exceed the impact of tariff changes, even if tariff elasticities are in fact a good bit higher than exchange rate elasticities.

As to the future, tariffs remaining after the Multilateral Trade Negotiations (MTN) cuts will average about 4–6 percent in each of the major industrialized trading areas. Their complete elimination would then be overshadowed by the fluctuations which frequently occur, and the misalignments which periodically persist, in exchange rates. This is not to say that further trade liberalization would not be significant, of course, but that shifts in trade balances are likely to be more influenced by changes in exchange rates than in tariffs (although changes in other forms of protection may well be more important in certain sectors).

The evidence therefore indicates that changes in real effective exchange rates have significant effects on international trade flows—and, through trade, on key domestic economic variables such as output, employment and prices. Deardorff and Stern have made the following estimates of the effects of each percentage point of exchange rate change for the major trading areas (between the second quarters of 1980 and 1981):

Table 3.1   Effects of Exchange Rate Change, Major Trading Areas

	Price level (percentage)	Unemployment	Trade balance (dollars)
United States	0.3	70,000	3 billion
European Community	0.4	100,000	3 billion
Japan	0.5	40,000	1 billion

These estimates suggest that a 20 percent overvaluation could raise unemployment by 1.4 million in the United States or 2 million in Europe, while a similar undervaluation could add 6 percent to the price level in the United States, 8 percent in Europe and 10 percent in Japan.

Notes and Questions

(1) What sense can one make of the notion of "misalignment" when rates are market-determined? What causes "misalignment?" Economist John Williamson, one of the co-authors of the foregoing excerpt, ascribes most misalignment to market inefficiencies and macroeconomic policies, such as those pursued by the United States in the early 1980s, when he claims the use of monetary restraint to reduce inflation led to abnormally high interest rates and an overvalued dollar. See John Williamson, The Exchange Rate System (1983). Do you understand why high interest rates in the United States cause the dollar to appreciate? How is "misalignment" as a result of high interest rates to be distinguished from "equilibrium?"

(2) The authors suggest some effects of misalignment. If a firm's home currency is overvalued, for example, the firm may contract its operations undesirably because its export sales are slow or its import competition is intense, and later have to re-expand them when the exchange rates are properly aligned. This will lead to considerable and unnecessary adjustment costs, it might be argued. But what is to be

made of this observation? *Given* the purported misalignment of currencies, is it not better for such adjustments to occur than not? And, if the fear is of an excessive adjustment to a transitory phenomenon, why do private actors not figure out that the phenomenon is transitory before deciding how much to adjust?

(E) EUROPEAN MONETARY UNIFICATION

The Treaty of Rome, which established the EEC in 1957, contained significant provisions on the use of controls on foreign exchange. The Treaty called for the elimination of restrictions on capital movements and related payments between member states (Article 67). The member states further committed themselves to try to avoid imposing any new restrictions (Article 71). The liberalization of current payments was provided for in Article 106. The Treaty also had provisions on coordination of economic policies so as to avoid balance of payments disequilibria (Articles 104 and 105).

Subsequently, EEC members created the "European Monetary System," under which central banks undertook to stabilize exchange rates between European currencies within an agreed band of permissible fluctuation. The system did not work perfectly, and there were some crisis-like revaluations during its history (most notably the Fall of 1992).

In the Maastricht Treaty, effective in 1993, the European Union agreed upon eventual monetary unification through the creation of a single European currency, which is to be implemented for most EU members on January 1, 2002. Academics have argued over the merits of this policy. The benefits of monetary unification relate to a reduction in the transaction costs of doing business (no need for a foreign exchange transaction) and to the elimination of exchange risk. A single currency also disables national governments from pursuing independent monetary policies, a virtue if some of them would otherwise pursue foolish policies. But this aspect of currency unification can also be a vice. If one believes that monetary policy can be employed usefully to address business cycle problems, and if one further believes that such problems vary significantly across Europe at a point in time, then the ability to pursue different monetary policies in different regions can be important, particularly if other macroeconomic policies are quite imperfect substitutes. Such matters have been the focus of a lively debate for some time, with many economists expressing doubt that monetary unification is worth its costs and others defending it.[7]

7. See, e.g., Neils Thygesen, Why is Economic and Monetary Union an Important Objective for Europe?, 14 Intl.Rev.L. & Econ. 133 (1994); Robert Inman & Daniel Rubinfeld, The EMU and Fiscal Policy in the New European Community: An Issue for Economic Federalism, 14 Intl.Rev.L. & Econ. 147 (1994); Barry Eichengreen, European Monetary Unification, 31 J.Econ.Lit. 1321 (1993).

SECTION 22.2 OPERATIONS OF THE INTERNATIONAL MONETARY FUND: INTERNATIONAL LIQUIDITY

The concept of "international liquidity" is important for the regulation of the international monetary system. To illustrate the problem of liquidity, suppose you own thousands of acres of land, but have no money in the bank. When the bills for your purchases of seed and fertilizer are received, you will find it difficult to pay those bills, even though you may be very rich. You are said to be "illiquid." One of the ways you could make yourself more "liquid" would be to mortgage some of the land, borrowing cash which you would then keep in the bank to pay bills as they become due, replenishing this fund with receipts from the harvest. Of course, if the land (including the value of the future harvest) is not worth enough to pay your bills, you are not merely "illiquid" but "insolvent."

Governments and their economies may encounter such difficulties as well. In the 1970's and 1980's, for example, many developing countries had obligations to repay loans from abroad, denominated in hard currencies. The stocks of foreign currency held by those nations, its foreign currency "reserves", in many cases proved inadequate. The problem has resurfaced again over the past several years.

More generally, nations often wish to support the value of their currencies on exchange markets. To do this, a government uses its foreign exchange reserves to buy its own currency, propping up demand for it. If it runs out of its own reserves, it may want to borrow reserves from other nations or international organizations.

One of the principal functions of the IMF is to provide reserves to countries with liquidity or balance of payments problems. The purposes of the IMF are set out in its Articles of Agreement in Article I and Article IV (1) (see Documents Supplement). The resources of the IMF are derived from the subscriptions (quotas) that the members are required to pay, and to a lesser degree from its borrowings. The IMF uses its resources in accordance with various programs, which are described briefly below. One of the more controversial issues surrounding the IMF is the extent to which it should attach conditions to its assistance.

(A) IMF FACILITIES

HOW DOES THE IMF LEND?
A FACTSHEET[1]

A main function of the IMF is to provide loans to countries experiencing balance-of-payments problems so that they can restore conditions for sustainable economic growth. The financial assistance provided by the IMF enables countries to rebuild their international reserves, stabilize their currencies, and continue paying for imports without having to impose trade restrictions or capital controls. Unlike development banks, the IMF does not lend for specific projects.

---

1. IMF Website, September 2001 (www.imf.org, visited October 10, 2001.)

IMF loans are usually provided under an "arrangement", which stipulates the conditions the country must meet in order to gain access to the loan. All arrangements must be approved by the Executive Board, whose 24 directors represent the IMF's 183 member countries. Arrangements are based on economic programs formulated by countries in consultation with the IMF, and presented to the Executive Board in a "letter of intent". Loans are then released in phased installments as the program is carried out.

* * *

Over the years, the IMF has developed a number of loan instruments, or "facilities", that are tailored to address the specific circumstances of its diverse membership. Low-income countries may borrow at a concessional interest rate through the Poverty Reduction and Growth Facility (PRGF). Non-concessional loans are provided through five main facilities: Stand–By Arrangements (SBA), the Extended Fund Facility (EFF), the Supplemental Reserve Facility (SRF), the Contingent Credit Lines (CCL), and the Compensatory Financing Facility (CFF).

Except for the PRGF, all facilities are subject to the IMF's market-related interest rate, known as the "rate of charge", and some carry an interest rate premium, a "surcharge". The rate of charge is based on the SDR interest rate, which is revised weekly to take account of changes in short-term interest rates in the major international money markets. The rate of charge is currently about 4 percent. The IMF discourages excessive use of its resources by imposing a surcharge on large loans, and countries are expected to repay loans early if their external position allows them to do so.

Poverty Reduction and Growth Facility (PRGF). The IMF for many years provided assistance to low-income countries through the Enhanced Structural Adjustment Facility (ESAF). In 1999, however, a decision was made to strengthen the focus on poverty, and the ESAF was replaced by the PRGF. Loans under the PRGF are based on a Poverty Reduction Strategy Paper (PRSP), which is prepared by the country in cooperation with civil society and other development partners, in particular the World Bank. The interest rate levied on PRGF loans is only 0.5 percent, and loans may be repaid over a maximum period of 10 years.

Stand-By Arrangements (SBA). The SBA is designed to address short-term balance-of-payments problems and is the most widely used facility of the IMF. The length of a SBA is typically 12–18 months. Repayment must take place within a maximum of 5 years, but countries are expected to repay within 2–4 years.

Extended Fund Facility (EFF). This facility was established in 1974 to help countries address more protracted balance-of-payments problems with roots in the structure of the economy. Arrangements under the EFF are thus longer (3 years) and the repayment period can extend to 10 years, although repayment is expected within 4½–7 years.

Supplemental Reserve Facility (SRF). The SRF was introduced in 1997 to meet a need for very short-term financing on a large scale. The sudden loss of market confidence experienced by emerging market economies in the 1990s led to massive outflows of capital, which required loans on a much larger scale than anything the IMF had previously been asked to provide. Countries must repay the loan after a maximum of 2.5 years, but are expected to repay one year earlier. All SRF loans carry a substantial surcharge of 3–5 percentage points.

Contingent Credit Lines (CCL). The CCL differs from other IMF facilities in that it aims to help members prevent crises. Established in 1997, it is designed for countries implementing sound economic policies, which may find themselves threatened by a crisis elsewhere in the world economy-a phenomenon known as "financial contagion". The CCL is subject to the same repayment conditions as the SRF, but carries a smaller surcharge.

Compensatory Financing Facility. The CFF was established in the 1960s to assist countries experiencing either a sudden shortfall in export earnings or an increase in the cost of food imports caused by fluctuating world commodity prices. The financial terms are the same as those applying to the SBA, except that CFF loans carry no surcharge.

The IMF also provides emergency assistance to countries that have experienced a natural disaster or are emerging from conflict. Emergency loans are subject to the basic rate of charge and must be repaid within 5 years.

Note

The special drawing right (SDR) is an international reserve asset created by the International Monetary Fund to supplement existing reserves of its members. It is valued on the basis of a basket of four currencies (US dollar, Euro, Yen and UK pound) and can be used in a wide variety of transactions and operations among official holders. On October 10, 2001, its value was US$1.28. There are 21.4 billion SDRs outstanding and a 1997 proposed amendment to the IMF Agreement would double cumulative SDR allocations to SDR 42.87 billion.

(B) CONDITIONALITY

ACCESS TO RESOURCES FROM FUND AND USE OF STAND–BY ARRANGEMENTS

Decision of IMF Executive Board, March 2, 1979[2]

1. Members should be encouraged to adopt corrective measures, which could be supported by use of the Fund's general resources in accordance with the Fund's policies, at an early stage of their balance of payments difficulties or as a precaution against the emergence of such

---

2. The text of the Decision is set out and each paragraph is commented upon in J. Gold, Conditionality (1979). See also Pir-zio–Biroli, Making Sense of the IMF Conditionality Debate, 17 J. World Trade L. 115 (1983).

difficulties. The Article IV consultations are among the occasions on which the Fund would be able to discuss with members adjustment programs, including corrective measures, that would enable the Fund to approve a stand-by arrangement.

2. The normal period for a stand-by arrangement will be one year. If, however, a longer period is requested by a member and considered necessary by the Fund to enable the member to implement its adjustment program successfully, the stand-by arrangement may extend beyond the period of one year. This period in appropriate cases may extend up to but not beyond three years.

3. Stand-by arrangements are not international agreements and therefore language having a contractual connotation will be avoided in stand-by arrangements and letters of intent.

4. In helping members to devise adjustment programs, the Fund will pay due regard to the domestic social and political objectives, the economic priorities, and the circumstances of members, including the causes of their balance of payments problems.

5. Appropriate consultation clauses will be incorporated in all stand-by arrangements. Such clauses will include provision for consultation from time to time during the whole period in which the member has outstanding purchases in the upper credit tranches. This provision will apply whether the outstanding purchases were made under a stand-by arrangement or in other transactions in the upper credit tranches.

6. Phasing and performance clauses will be omitted in stand-by arrangements that do not go beyond the first credit tranche. They will be included in all other stand-by arrangements but these clauses will be applicable only to purchases beyond the first credit tranche.

7. The Managing Director will recommend that the Executive Board approve a member's request for the use of the Fund's general resources in the credit tranches when it is his judgment that the program is consistent with the Fund's provisions and policies and that it will be carried out. A member may be expected to adopt some corrective measures before a stand-by arrangement is approved by the Fund, but only if necessary to enable the member to adopt and carry out a program consistent with the Fund's provisions and policies. In these cases the Managing Director will keep Executive Directors informed in an appropriate manner of the progress of discussions with the member.

8. The Managing Director will ensure adequate coordination in the application of policies relating to the use of the Fund's general resources with a view to maintaining the nondiscriminatory treatment of members.

9. The number and content of performance criteria may vary because of the diversity of problems and institutional arrangements of members. Performance criteria will be limited to those that are necessary to evaluate implementation of the program with a view to ensuring the achievement of its objectives. Performance criteria will normally be

confined to (i) macroeconomic variables, and (ii) those necessary to implement specific provisions of the Articles or policies adopted under them. Performance criteria may relate to other variables only in exceptional cases when they are essential for the effectiveness of the member's program because of their macroeconomic impact.

10. In programs extending beyond one year, or in circumstances where a member is unable to establish in advance one or more performance criteria for all or part of the program period, provision will be made for a review in order to reach the necessary understandings with the member for the remaining period. In addition, in those exceptional cases in which an essential feature of a program cannot be formulated as a performance criterion at the beginning of a program year because of substantial uncertainties concerning major economic trends, provision will be made for a review by the Fund to evaluate the current macroeconomic policies of the member, and to reach new understandings if necessary. In these exceptional cases the Managing Director will inform Executive Directors in an appropriate manner of the subject matter of a review.

11. The staff will prepare an analysis and assessment of the performance under programs supported by use of the Fund's general resources in the credit tranches in connection with Article IV consultations and as appropriate in connection with further requests for use of the Fund's resources.

12. The staff will from time to time prepare, for review by the Executive Board, studies of programs supported by stand-by arrangements in order to evaluate and compare the appropriateness of the programs, the effectiveness of the policy instruments, the observance of the programs, and the results achieved. Such reviews will enable the Executive Board to determine when it may be appropriate to have the next comprehensive review of conditionality.

SIR JOSEPH GOLD, FINANCIAL ASSISTANCE BY THE INTERNATIONAL MONETARY FUND: LAW AND PRACTICE 13–23 (2d ed. 1980)

* * * The Fund formulates the stand-by arrangement by reference to certain aspects of the letter of intent. The main purpose of this reference is to select those aspects of the program that are to be performance criteria and to ensure that the member will have access to the Fund's resources under the arrangement only if the performance criteria are being observed.

* * *

Performance criteria are as few as are necessary to provide both the Fund and a member reasonable evidence that the program is on course, but the observance of performance criteria is not irrefutable proof that the aims of the program are being achieved or that policies stated in the letter of intent but not incorporated in performance criteria are being followed. If a performance criterion is not being observed, the member will know without having to be told, and the Fund will know because of the periodic reporting of essential data by the member. In these circumstances, the right to make further purchases under the stand-by arrangement will be interrupted. Sometimes the right will revive if the member resumes observance of the performance criterion, but sometimes the right will revive only after a consultation is held between the Fund and the member in which understandings are reached on the advisability of maintaining the original performance criteria or of adapting them or other aspects of the program.

There is no single code of performance criteria for all cases. One performance criterion that is always used is a ceiling on the expansion of credit by the central bank or the banking system, supported in most cases by a ceiling on the expansion of bank credit to the government or the public sector. Balance of payments problems often arise from national overspending, so that it becomes necessary to ensure that aggregate demand for goods and services is brought into line with output. Ceilings on the expansion of domestic credit help to regulate aggregate demand and to enhance the effectiveness of financial policies, including the channeling of sufficient credit to meet the needs of the private sector. If the policies on credit could have detrimental effects on employment and growth, policies must be devised to encourage savings and investment as well as a proper direction of investment.

Almost all stand-by arrangements include performance criteria that deal with the avoidance of all restrictions on payments and transfers for current international transactions as well as restrictions on imports for balance of payments reasons. If existing restrictions have resulted in substantial arrears in payments for current international transactions, a schedule for the aggregate reduction of them may be established as a performance criterion. If external debt service is a present or prospective burden on the balance of payments of undue proportions, limits on the amount and maturity of new short-and medium-term debt may be made a performance criterion. If the exchange rate for the member's currency is not consistent with underlying economic conditions, a performance criterion may take the form of minimum levels of net foreign exchange reserves, the effect of which is to restrain the use of reserves in intervention in the exchange market to support the exchange rate.

The performance criteria that have been cited are not exhaustive. There are others that may be suitable to a member's circumstances. Flexibility is maintained not only to do what is most suitable in the circumstances of each member but also to gain experience in order to broaden the instruments of policy that can be recommended to members.

* * *

The stand-by arrangement and its offshoot, the extended arrangement, are unique legal instruments. * * * They are analogous to the movement away from the classical concept of a relationship between parties governed by a contract that is considered the complete and immutable law of the parties to a concept of a continuing and adaptable relationship, of which "hardship clauses," particularly in long-term contracts, are a symptom. The member's letter of intent and the Fund's decision (the stand-by arrangement) are parallel declarations, and although, unlike parallel lines, they meet this side of infinity, they do not constitute a contract between the member and the Fund. If the member departs from its policies and intentions as stated in its letter of intent, the Fund does not regard the departure as a violation of obligation even if, when a performance criterion is not being observed, the member cannot make further purchases until observance of the performance criterion has been resumed or the outcome of a consultation is known.

* * *

CONDITIONALITY

The fundamental and distinctive characteristic of the Fund's financial assistance is the Fund's doctrine of conditionality. Four strands are woven into it. First, to qualify for the use of the Fund's resources in order to deal with a balance of payments problem, a member must be prepared to pursue policies that are designed to overcome its problem. The policies are often referred to as policies of adjustment of the balance of payments or as a stabilization program. The objective of the program is a balance of payments position that can be sustained over a medium term such as five to eight years ahead. A member's willingness to undertake a program is not a concession to the Fund. Adjustment is inevitable for any member that does not have the means to neglect adjustment. The conditionality of the Fund helps a member to achieve adjustment with the financial, technical, and moral support of the Fund. Second, the policies must be consistent with the purposes of the Fund. For example, the policies should enable the member to avoid the introduction of restrictions on trade and payments for balance of payments purposes and if possible eliminate existing restrictions, because restrictions are likely to intensify and not correct the distortions that give rise to the need for adjustment, and are likely to be harmful to other members. Third, the policies must be designed to overcome the member's problem within a moderate ("temporary") period. Fourth, the policies must be likely to result in augmenting the member's monetary reserves so that it will be able to repurchase its currency from the Fund in accordance with the principle that use of the Fund's resources must be temporary in order that they can revolve for the benefit of all members.

* * *

The purpose of conditionality is not to change the basic character or the organization of a member's economy. For example, the degree to which the economy is under government ownership or control is accepted as part of the framework within which a program of adjustment must be made to fit. Similarly, the social objectives or priorities of a member are accepted as beyond negotiation, subject to the proviso that the policies to promote them will permit the member to achieve a sustainable balance of payments position. In short, the Fund does not seek to modify the political or social policies of a member. The character of the Fund is determined by its technical tasks, the principle of universal membership, and the uniform treatment of all members.

* * *

It is sometimes said that conditionality is progressively more severe as the amounts made available ascend through the upper credit tranches. This proposition is doubtful because conditionality always has the same objective, the conquest of a member's balance of payments difficulty. It could even be argued that in many instances conditionality is less severe when more resources are made available. It may be easier for a government to give effect to a program over a longer period. Stand-by or extended arrangements for the longer periods that have become a feature of the Fund's practice in recent years tend to be associated with substantial amounts in terms of quota. The apparent truism that more time means more ease is not always true, however, because a program for a longer period may require a perseverance that is politically difficult to maintain.

The word "harsh" is sometimes attached to particular operations involving conditionality. The inevitable determinant of the severity of a program, however it may be measured, is the intensity of a member's problem. Conditionality should be regarded as harsh only if it were to go beyond what was necessary to overcome a problem within the period that was reasonable in the circumstances, but this view does not mean that what is necessary in accordance with this criterion is always beyond controversy.

CONDITIONALITY IN FUND–SUPPORTED PROGRAMS—OVERVIEW

Prepared by the IMF Policy Development and Review Department
February 20, 2001[3]

2.   Conditionality—the link between the approval or continuation of the Fund's financing and the implementation of specified elements of economic policy by the country receiving this financing—is a salient aspect of the Fund's involvement with its member countries. This link arises from the fact that the Fund's financing and policy adjustments by the country are intended to be two sides of a common response to external imbalances. Conditionality is intended to ensure that these two components are provided together: it provides safeguards to the Fund to ensure that successive tranches of financing are delivered only if key policies are on track, and assurances to the country that it will continue

---

3.   From the IMF website (www.imf.org,   visited October 10, 2001).

to receive the Fund's financing provided that it continues to implement the policies envisaged.

* * *

4.   The period since the [1979] Guidelines—and especially the past decade—has seen a major expansion of conditionality, particularly in the structural area. While structural measures were rarely an element in Fund-supported programs until the 1980s, by the 1990s almost all programs included some element of structural conditionality. The expansion of structural conditionality was also reflected in increasing numbers of performance criteria, structural benchmarks, and prior actions.

5.   These changes were the result of several forces. First, the Fund has over time placed increasing emphasis on economic growth as a policy objective, with the recognition that raising growth on a sustainable basis requires strengthening the supply side through structural reforms. * * * Growth became increasingly prominent as an objective in the 1980s, against the background of the poor growth record of the heavily indebted countries and mounting criticisms that Fund programs had focused excessively on austerity.

6.   Second, the Fund became increasingly involved with different groups of countries in which structural reforms were viewed as a particularly important part of an overall policy package. * * *

7.   A third factor behind the expansion of structural conditionality was an increasing awareness that the monetary and fiscal policy objectives that are key to macroeconomic adjustment often themselves depend critically on structural conditions—including the removal of extensive market distortions and the establishment of the institutional underpinnings for effective policy making in a market economy. * * *

8.   * * * The 1979 Conditionality Guidelines envisaged that program monitoring would be mainly through performance criteria: a performance criterion is a condition that must be met for the Fund's financing to continue, unless the Board grants a waiver. The other main tool of conditionality, program reviews, was seen mainly as an occasion to set performance criteria beyond the first year of a program * * *. In recent years, however, program reviews have increased in importance as an opportunity for both backward- and forward-looking assessments of program implementation.

9.   The increasing importance of reviews reflects, in part, greater uncertainty about key macroeconomic relationships in a world of high capital mobility; these circumstances exacerbate the difficulty of specifying a path of performance criteria a year ahead. * * *

10.   Along with this shift in monitoring techniques has come an increasing lack of clarity with regard to the boundaries of conditionality. * * *

* * *

12. Both the increasing structural content of Fund-supported pro-grams and the changing approach to program monitoring has taken place, at least in part, for good reasons. Nevertheless, it has prompted legitimate concerns: in particular, that the Fund is overstepping its mandate and core area of expertise, using its financial leverage to promote an extensive policy agenda and short-circuiting national deci-sion-making processes. * * *

13. Concerns have also been voiced about whether recent Fund-supported programs have taken adequate account of the authorities' ability to muster political support for a multitude of policy changes at one time, as well as their capacity to implement these reforms.* * *

* * *

15. The issues highlighted in the previous section set the stage for consideration of how to streamline the Fund's conditionality. Streamlin-ing requires:

— reassessing the scope of conditionality—i.e. *what* policies are to be covered by the Fund's conditionality—particularly in the structural areas;

— choosing the appropriate degree of detail of conditionality—i.e. *how* these policies are to be monitored; and

— clarifying the boundaries between what is covered by conditional-ity and what is not, as well as between the Fund's conditionality and that of other institutions.

16. There are two main approaches to curtailing the scope of structural conditionality. First, a higher threshold of relevance could be applied in deciding whether a particular policy action should be covered by conditionality in a particular instance. The existing Guidelines on Conditionality prescribe that performance criteria should be limited to those needed to ensure the achievement of program objectives. * * * Accordingly, the Interim Guidance Note on Streamlining Structural Conditionality stresses the need to limit conditionality to those measures that are critical for the achievement of the program's macroeconomic objectives. * * *

17. A second aspect of streamlining is establishing a better division of labor with the World Bank and other involved multilateral and bilateral institutions and agencies. In the past, the Fund's cooperation with these institutions has not generally contributed to streamlining: on the contrary, in many cases policy measures important to these institu-tions' objectives have been included in the authorities' Letters of Intent and sometimes established as structural benchmarks or even perfor-mance criteria. Steps are now underway to establish a more efficient division of labor. * * *

18. Another important aspect of streamlining is with regard to the degree of detail with which policies are monitored. * * *

19.   One solution to the perception of micromanagement would be to rely to an increasing degree on results-based conditionality: making the Fund's financing conditional on the achievement of specified outcomes—such as bank recapitalization, or improved tax enforcement, or foreign exchange market liberalization—rather than on the steps toward those outcomes. The main argument for this approach is that it would give the authorities greater flexibility in choosing the appropriate method of achieving agreed objectives. * * *

Notes and Questions

The IMF's conditionality policy is quite controversial in the developing world, for reasons that area alluded to in the foregoing excerpt. How do the proposed policy changes attempt to address those concerns?

Problems

Consider the following problems in the light of the materials above, and the IMF Articles of Agreement in the Documents Supplement.

(1) You have been retained by the Ministry of Development and Finance and the Ministry of Foreign Affairs of a small developing nation named Vanzia, a member of the IMF, with a quota of 36 million United States dollars. IMF now holds 30 million dollars' worth of Vanzia currency. Vanzia has been running a deficit on its balance of payments for the last four quarters, amounting to an annual deficit of 50 million United States dollars, because of a drastic decline in the world market price of cocoa, one of Vanzia's principal exports. Vanzia's reserves are now dangerously low and it must take drastic action if its imports of vitally needed machinery are to continue. The Ministry of Development and Finance has put forth a series of proposals, and asks you to evaluate these proposals in the light of the international legal obligations of Vanzia and its trading partners.

(a) Vanzia desires to draw 40 million United States dollars from the IMF. Can it do so? How much can it draw? How does it obtain this right? Suppose some of the dollars were intended to be used by the Ministry for the purchase of machinery for a candy factory? (IMF Article V.)

(b) Vanzia desires to borrow 50 million dollars to obtain foreign exchange to import the necessary foreign machinery for a new candy factory. A bank in the United States was willing to loan the money, but declined on the grounds that the United States Government forbade it. If this were true, has the United States violated any international obligation towards Vanzia? (IMF Article VI.)

(c) Vanzia's currency, the "bobble," now has a value of 20 to the dollar. Can Vanzia act to reduce its value? (IMF Article IV.)

(2) One of the essential machines needed in Vanzia for its development plan is widgets. The Trans–Vanzia Preparation Company has approached the Golddust Mfg. Co. to place a large order of widgets, and plans to buy more. This approach, and United States tax considerations, have led Golddust to consider setting up a branch or corporate subsidiary in Vanzia, and possibly even attempting to manufacture widgets there. Golddust asks your opinion

as to the probability of being able to repatriate such profits as it might earn in Vanzia during the next few years.

(3) Suppose Vanzia entered into a stand-by agreement with the Fund. How would that agreement be enforced?

SECTION 22.3   INTERNATIONAL REGULATION OF FOREIGN EXCHANGE RESTRICTIONS

(A) OBLIGATIONS UNDER THE IMF AGREEMENT

Article VIII of the Articles of Agreement of the International Monetary Fund contains a series of obligations regarding what a national government may do in restricting foreign exchange transactions. It contains obligations requiring member countries to avoid the use of discriminatory currency practices and to avoid restrictions on "current payments." On the other hand, restrictions on capital payments are not prohibited.

IMF members are also obligated by Article IV of the IMF Agreement to collaborate with the Fund and with other members to assure orderly exchange arrangements and to promote a stable system of exchange rates. To oversee compliance with those obligations, the IMF exercises surveillance over the exchange rate policies of members and adopts specific principles for their guidance.[1]

Problem

Consider the following hypothetical cases:

(1) Vanzia would like to require all payments to persons outside the country to be subject to prior permission of the Ministry of Development and Finance, under a licensing law. Can it do so? (IMF Article VIII.)

(2) Vanzia contemplates entering into a bilateral trade and payments arrangement with Xonia, envisaging the setting up of an account in Vanzia through which payments for specified trade items between the two countries must be made, and prohibiting the payment for specified goods except through that account. What international obligations of Vanzia would be involved? (IMF Article VIII.)

(3) Vanzia has considered selling foreign currency (or foreign exchange) at a favored rate equivalent to $1 United States dollar for only 10 bobbles, to those importers importing goods designated as "vital to the 7–year development plan." Can it do so? (IMF Article VIII.)

(4) In addition, Vanzia is considering several restrictions on imports, including: i) raising tariffs; ii) placing import quotas on non-essential goods; iii) placing an internal sales tax on certain goods if they have been imported. Do any of these measures involve the IMF? (See Section 22.4 infra.)

---

1. The IMF's current surveillance practices are described in IMF Survey: Supplement on the Fund, Oct. 1993, at 8–9.

(B) THE OECD LIBERALISATION CODES

The IMF Agreement only limits national restrictions on payments and transfers for current international transactions. Given the diversity of the IMF membership, the IMF Agreement could not reasonably be expected to do more. The advanced industrialized countries, however, have tried to agree among themselves on more stringent limitations on national foreign exchange restrictions.

These efforts have been sponsored by the Organization for Economic Cooperation and Development (OECD), one of the goals of which is to "reduce or abolish obstacles to the exchange of goods and services and current payments and maintain and extend the liberalisation of capital movements." To this end, the OECD has adopted a Code of Liberalisation of Capital Movements and a Code of Liberalisation of Current Invisible Operations.[2] Adherents commit themselves to authorize certain specified transactions and to work to liberalize any remaining restrictions. There are broad exceptions to the Codes, allowing derogations if the economic and financial situation of the country justifies them. In addition, many countries adhere to the Codes with reservations. Nonetheless, the fact that the adherents are committed to liberalization and that national restrictions receive international scrutiny on a regular basis has probably played an important role in the gradual liberalization of exchange controls that has occurred in recent years.

(C) PRIVATE RELIANCE ON THE IMF AGREEMENT

Article VIII, section 2, of the IMF Agreement reads as follows:

Section 2. *Avoidance of Restrictions on Current Payments*

(a) Subject to the provisions of Article VII, Section 3(b), and Article XIV, Section 2, no member shall, without the approval of the Fund, impose restrictions on the making of payments and transfers for current international transactions.

(b) Exchange contracts which involve the currency of any member and which are contrary to the exchange control regulations of that member maintained or imposed consistently with this Agreement shall be unenforceable in the territories of any member. In addition, members may, by mutual accord, cooperate in measures for the purpose of making the exchange control regulations of either member more effective, provided that such measures and regulations are consistent with this Agreement.

This provision has been at issue with some regularity in private litigation, as the cases below illustrate.

---

2. The current versions of each Code are published and updated regularly by the OECD.

BANCO DO BRASIL v. A.C. ISRAEL COMMODITY CO., INC.

Court of Appeals of New York, 1963.
12 N.Y.2d 371, 239 N.Y.S.2d 872, 190 N.E.2d 235, cert. denied,
376 U.S. 906, 84 S.Ct. 657, 11 L.Ed.2d 605.

BURKE, JUDGE.

The action upon which the attachment here challenged is based is brought by appellant as an instrumentality of the Government of Brazil to recover damages for a conspiracy to defraud the Government of Brazil of American dollars by illegally circumventing the foreign exchange regulations of Brazil.

Defendant-respondent, Israel Commodity, a Delaware corporation having its principal place of business in New York, is an importer of Brazilian coffee. The gist of plaintiff's complaint is that Israel conspired with a Brazilian exporter of coffee to pay the exporter American dollars which the exporter could sell in the Brazilian free market for 220 Brazilian cruzeiros each instead of complying with Brazil's foreign exchange regulations which in effect required a forced sale of the dollars paid to the exporter to the Government of Brazil for only 90 cruzeiros. Through this conspiracy, the Brazilian exporter profited by the difference between the amount (in cruzeiros) it would have received for the dollars from the Government of Brazil and the amount it received in the open market in violation of Brazilian law, Israel profited by being able to pay less dollars for the coffee (because the dollars were worth so much more to the seller), and the plaintiff suffered a loss measured by the difference in amount it would have to pay for the same number of dollars in the open market and what it could have paid for them through the "forced sale" had its foreign exchange regulations been obeyed. The evasion was allegedly accomplished through the exporter's forgery of the documents evidencing receipt of the dollars by plaintiff Banco Do Brasil, S.A., and without which the coffee could not have left Brazil.

Plaintiff argues that respondent's participation in the violation of Brazilian exchange control laws affords a ground of recovery because of article VIII (§ 2, subd. [b])of the Bretton Woods Agreement, a multilateral treaty to which both this country and Brazil are signatories. The section provides: "Exchange contracts which involve the currency of any member and which are contrary to the exchange control regulations of that member maintained or imposed consistently with this Agreement shall be unenforceable in the territories of any member." (60 U.S.Stat. 1411.) It is far from clear whether this sale of coffee is covered by subdivision (b) of section 2. The section deals with "exchange contracts" which "involve" the "currency" of any member of the International Monetary Fund, "and * * * are contrary to the exchange control regulations of that member maintained or imposed consistently with" the agreement. Subdivision (b) of section 2 has been construed as reaching only "transactions which have as their immediate object 'exchange,' that is, international media of payment" (Nussbaum, Exchange Control and the International Monetary Fund, 59 Yale L.J. 421, 426), or a contract where the consideration is payable in the currency of the country whose exchange controls are violated (Mann, The Exchange Control Act, 1947, 10 Mod.L.Rev. 411, 418). More recently, however, it has been suggested that it applies to "contracts which in any way affect a country's exchange resources" (Mann, The Private International Law of Exchange Control Under the International Monetary Fund Agreement, 2 International and Comp.L.Q. 97, 102; Gold and Lachman, The Articles of Agreement of the International Monetary Fund and the Exchange Control Regulations of Member States, Journal du Droit International, Paris (July–Sept., 1962). A similar view has been advanced to explain the further textual difficulty existing with respect to whether a sale of coffee in New York for American dollars "involves the currency" of Brazil, the member whose exchange controls were allegedly violated. Again it is suggested that adverse effect on the exchange resources of a member *ipso facto* "involves" the "currency" of that member (Gold and Lachman, op. cit.). We are inclined to view an interpretation of subdivision (b) of section 2 that sweeps in all contracts affecting any members' exchange resources as doing considerable violence to the text of the section. It says "involve the currency" of the country whose exchange controls are violated; not "involve the exchange resources". While noting these doubts, we nevertheless prefer to rest this decision on other and clearer grounds.

The sanction provided in subdivision (b) of section 2 is that contracts covered thereby are to be "unenforceable" in the territory of any member. The clear import of this provision is to insure the avoidance of the affront inherent in any attempt by the courts of one member to render a judgment that would put the losing party in the position of either complying with the judgment and violating the exchange controls of another member or complying with such controls and refusing obedience to the judgment. A further reasonable inference to be drawn from the provision is that the courts of no member should award any recovery for breach of an agreement in violation of the exchange controls of another member. Indeed, the International Monetary Fund itself, in an official interpretation of subdivision (b) of section 2 issued by the Fund's Executive Directors, construes the section as meaning that "the obligations of such contracts will not be implemented by the judicial or administrative authorities of member countries, for example, by decreeing performance of the contracts or by awarding damages for their non-performance". (International Monetary Fund Ann.Rep. 82–83 [1949], 14 Fed.Reg. 5208, 5209 [1949].) An obligation to withhold judicial assistance to secure the benefits of such contracts does not imply an obligation to impose tort penalties on those who have fully executed them.

From the viewpoint of the individuals involved, it must be remembered that the Bretton Woods Agreement relates to international law. It imposes obligations among and between States, not individuals. The fact that by virtue of the agreement New York must not "enforce" a contract between individuals which is contrary to the exchange controls of any member, imposes no obligation (under the law of the transaction—New

York law*) on such individuals not to enter into such contracts. While it does mean that they so agree at their peril inasmuch as they may not look to our courts for enforcement, this again is far from implying that one who so agrees commits a tort in New York for which he must respond in damages. It is significant that a proposal to make such an agreement an "offense" was defeated at Bretton Woods. (1 Proceedings and Documents of the United Nations Monetary and Financial Conference 334, 341, 502, 543, 546—referred to in Nussbaum, Exchange Control and the International Monetary Fund, 59 Yale L.J. 421, 426, 429, supra.)

Lastly, and inseparable from the foregoing, there is a remedial consideration which bars recovery in this case. Plaintiff is an instrumentality of the Government of Brazil and is seeking, by use of an action for conspiracy to defraud, to enforce what is clearly a revenue law. Whatever may be the effect of the Bretton Woods Agreement in an action on "A contract made in a foreign country between citizens thereof and intended by them to be there performed" (see Perutz v. Bohemian Discount Bank in Liquidation, 304 N.Y. 533, 537, 110 N.E.2d 6, 7), it is well established since the day of Lord Mansfield (Holman v. Johnson, 1 Cowp. 341, 98 E.R. 1120 [1775])that one State does not enforce the revenue laws of another. (Government of India v. Taylor, 1 All.E.R. 292 [1955]; City of Philadelphia v. Cohen, 11 N.Y.2d 401, 230 N.Y.S.2d 188, 184 N.E.2d 167; 1 Oppenheim, International Law, § 144*b* [Lauterpacht ed., 1947].) Nothing in the Bretton Woods Agreement is to the contrary. In fact its use of the unenforcibility device for effectuation of its purposes impliedly concedes the unavailability of the more direct method of enforcement at the suit of the aggrieved government. By the second sentence of subdivision (b) of section 2, further measures to make exchange controls more effective may be agreed upon by the member States. This is a matter for the Federal Government which not only has not entered into such further accords but has not even enacted the enabling provision into law (U.S.Code, tit. 22, § 286h).

Therefore, the order should be affirmed and the certified questions answered no and yes respectively.

CHIEF JUDGE DESMOND (dissenting).

The order should be reversed and the warrant of attachment reinstated since the complaint alleges a cause of action within the jurisdiction of the New York State courts.

If there had never been a Bretton Woods Agreement and if this were a suit to enforce in this State the revenue laws of Brazil it would have to be dismissed under the ancient rule most recently restated in City of Philadelphia v. Cohen, 11 N.Y.2d 401, 230 N.Y.S.2d 188, 184 N.E.2d 167. But *Cohen* and its predecessor cases express a public policy which lacks applicability here because of the adherence of the United States to the

---

* All of respondent's acts allegedly in furtherance of the conspiracy took place in New York where it regularly did business.

Bretton Woods Agreement. As we noted in Perutz v. Bohemian Discount Bank in Liquidation, 304 N.Y. 533, 537, 110 N.E.2d 6, 7, the membership of our Federal Government in the International Monetary Fund and other Bretton Woods enterprises makes it impossible to say that the currency control laws of other member States are offensive to our public policy. Furthermore, the argument from City of Philadelphia v. Cohen (supra) and similar decisions assumes erroneously that this is a suit to collect internal taxes assessed by the Brazilian Government. In truth, it is not even an effort to enforce Brazil's currency regulations. This complaint and other papers charge a tortious fraud and conspiracy to deprive plaintiff, an instrumentality of the Brazilian Government, of the dollar proceeds of coffee exports to which proceeds the bank and its government were entitled. This fraud, it is alleged, was accomplished by inserting in coffee shipping permits references to nonexistent exchange contracts and to nonexistent assignments to plaintiff of the foreign exchange proceeds of the coffee exports and by forging the signatures of banking officials and Brazilian officials, all with the purpose of making it appear that there had been compliance with the Brazilian statutes or regulations. The alleged scheme and effect of the conspiracy as charged was to obtain for defendant-respondent coffee in New York at a reduced price, to enable the Brazilian defendants to get more "cruzeiros" per dollar in violation of law and to deprive Brazil of the cruzeiros which it would have received from these coffee sales had the fraud not been committed. According to the complaint and affidavits defendant Israel not only knew of and intended to benefit by the perpetration of this fraud but participated in it in New York by making its purchase agreements here and by here receiving the shipping documents and making payments. The Israel corporation is alleged to have been one of the consignees of some 36,000 bags of coffee exported from Brazil to New York in 1961 without compliance with the Brazilian law and thus to have fraudulently and conspiratorially caused to Brazil damage of nearly $2,000,000. Refusal to entertain this suit does violence to our national policy of co-operation with other Bretton Woods signatories and is not required by anything in our own State policy.

Van Voorhis, Foster and Scileppi, JJ., concur with Burke, J.

Desmond, C.J., dissents in an opinion in which Dye and Fuld, JJ., concur.

BANCO FRANCES E BRASILEIRO S.A. v. DOE

Court of Appeals of New York, 1975.
36 N.Y.2d 592, 370 N.Y.S.2d 534, 331 N.E.2d 502, cert.
denied, 423 U.S. 867, 96 S.Ct. 129, 46 L.Ed.2d 96.

Jasen, Judge.

The principal question before us is whether a private foreign bank may avail itself of the New York courts in an action for damages for tortious fraud and deceit and for rescission of currency exchange contracts arising from alleged violations of foreign currency exchange regulations.

Plaintiff, a private Brazilian bank, brings this action for fraud and deceit, and conspiracy to defraud and deceive, against 20 "John Doe" defendants whose identities are unknown to it. The gravamen of plaintiff's complaint is that these defendants over a period of approximately six weeks participated, in violation of Brazilian currency regulations, in the submission of false applications to Banco–Brasileiro of Brazil, which the plaintiff relied upon, resulting in the improper exchange by the bank of Brazilian cruzeiros into travelers checks in United States dollars totaling $1,024,000. A large amount of the fraudulently obtained travelers checks were deposited by defendant "John Doe No. 1" in an account having a code name of "Alberta" at Bankers Trust Company, New York. Other of such travelers checks were deposited by defendant "John Doe No. 2" in an account having the code name of "Samso" at Manfra Tordella & Brookes, Inc., New York. An order of attachment was granted at Special Term against the property of defendants John Doe No. 1 and John Doe No. 2 held by Bankers Trust and Manfra Tordella & Brookes, Inc. Service of summons by publication was authorized by Special Term.

Subsequent to the granting of the order of attachment and the service of the summons by publication, motions were made by the plaintiff for disclosure from Bankers Trust Co. and Manfra Tordella & Brookes of the true names and addresses of John Doe Nos. 1 and 2 and to direct the attorney for defendant John Doe No. 1 to disclose the true name(s) and address(es) of defendant(s) and the basis of the attorney's authority to act, or, in the alternative, to vacate his appearance in the action. The defendant John Doe No. 1, by way of order to show cause, moved to vacate the order of attachment, to dismiss plaintiff's complaint and to intervene in the motion of plaintiff for disclosure from Bankers Trust Co. so as to defend against the disclosure.

Special Term, *inter alia,* denied the motion to vacate the order of attachment and to dismiss the complaint except as to the third cause of action for damages which was dismissed for failure to plead actual damages. Motions for ancillary relief—for discovery and inspection and for disclosure from the attorney for defendant "John Doe No. 1" of the name and address of his client—were granted.

On cross appeals, the Appellate Division, by a unanimous court (44 A.D.2d 353, 355 N.Y.S.2d 145), relying on Banco do Brasil v. Israel Commodity Co., 12 N.Y.2d 371, 239 N.Y.S.2d 872, 190 N.E.2d 235, cert. den. 376 U.S. 906, 84 S.Ct. 657, 11 L.Ed.2d 605, modified by granting defendants' motion to dismiss the complaint and denying all applications for ancillary relief on the ground that the New York courts were not open to an action arising from a tortious violation of foreign currency regulations.

Plaintiff bank appeals as of right to this court. (CPLR 5601, subd. [a].) We are unable to assent to the decision of the Appellate Division and, accordingly, modify the order appealed from by reinstating the order of attachment and the first two causes of action, with leave to plaintiff, if so advised, to apply to Special Term for permission to serve a supplemental pleading alleging special damages in its third cause of action for damages, and by granting the ancillary relief requested to the extent hereafter specified.

It is an old chestnut in conflict of laws that one State does not enforce the revenue laws of another. * * * But the modern analog of the revenue law rule is justifiable neither precedentially nor analytically.

* * *

In the international sphere, cases involving foreign currency exchange regulations represent perhaps the most important aspect of the revenue law rule. This assumes, of course, that a currency exchange regulation, normally not designed for revenue purposes as such, but rather, to prevent the loss of foreign currency which in turn increases the country's foreign exchange reserves, is properly characterizable as a revenue law. * * *

But even assuming the continuing validity of the revenue law rule and the correctness of the characterization of a currency exchange regulation thereunder, United States membership in the International Monetary Fund (IMF) makes inappropriate the refusal to entertain the instant claim. The view that nothing in article VIII (§ 2, subd. [b])of the Bretton Woods Agreement Act (60 U.S.Stat. 1401, 1411) requires an American court to provide a forum for a private tort remedy, while correct in a literal sense (see Banco do Brasil v. Israel Commodity Co., supra, p. 376, 239 N.Y.S.2d p. 874, 190 N.E.2d p. 236), does not represent the only perspective. Nothing in the agreement prevents an IMF member from aiding, directly or indirectly, a fellow member in making its exchange regulations effective. And United States membership in the IMF makes it impossible to conclude that the currency control laws of other member States are offensive to this State's public policy so as to preclude suit in tort by a private party. Indeed, conduct reasonably necessary to protect the foreign exchange resources of a country does not offend against international law. (Restatement, Second, Foreign Relations Law of the United States, § 198, comment b.) Moreover, where a true governmental interest of a friendly nation is involved—and foreign currency reserves are of vital importance to a country plagued by balance of payments difficulties—the national policy of co-operation with Bretton Woods signatories is furthered by providing a State forum for suit.

The *Banco do Brasil* case relied upon by the Appellate Division is quite distinguishable.

* * *

There the Government of Brazil, through Banco do Brasil, a government bank, sought redress for violations of its currency exchange regulations incident to a fraudulent coffee export transaction. Here, the plaintiff is a private bank seeking rescission of the fraudulent currency exchange transactions and damages. And no case has come to our attention where a private tort remedy arising from foreign currency regulations has been denied by the forum as an application of the revenue law rule and we decline so to extend the *Banco do Brasil* rationale. Thus, in the instant case we find no basis for reliance upon the revenue law rule to deny a forum for suit. Moreover, where the parties are private, the "jealous sovereign" rationale is inapposite (cf. Loucks v. Standard Oil Co., 224 N.Y. 99, 102–103, 120 N.E. 198, 199 [Cardozo, J.]) even as it might seem inapposite in the *Banco do Brasil* situation where the sovereign itself, or its instrumentality, asks redress and damages in a foreign forum for violation of the sovereign's currency laws. (But cf. Moore v. Mitchell, 2 Cir., 30 F.2d 600, 603 [L. Hand, J., concurring].)

Accordingly, the order of the Appellate Division should be modified in accordance with the views here expressed and the action remitted to the Supreme Court, New York County.

WACHTLER, JUDGE (dissenting).

We are asked to determine when claims between private parties which spring from jural relationships created by the laws of a foreign country, here Brazil, may be enforced in our courts. The issue turns on the essential nature of the rights and obligations sought to be enforced as the forum court characterizes them. As stated by the United States Supreme Court: "The test is not by what name the statute is called by the legislature or the courts of the State in which it was passed, but whether it appears, to the tribunal which is called upon to enforce it, to be, in its essential character and effect, a punishment of an offense against the public, or a grant of a civil right to a private person."

* * *

It has long been recognized that the courts of one jurisdiction will not enforce the tax laws, penal laws, or statutory penalties and forfeitures of another jurisdiction. * * *

In previous cases our court held that governmental foreign exchange regulation may present an aspect of the exercise of sovereign power by a foreign State to implement its national fiscal policy. Thus, in Banco do Brasil v. Israel Commodity Co. (supra), we decided that our courts were not open to enforce a Brazilian foreign currency exchange regulation. Although the regulation in that case was characterized as a revenue measure, the essence of the matter was that we declined to enforce what we considered to be an exercise of Brazil's sovereign power. Whether a regulation denominated "currency exchange regulation" has or does not have a revenue-producing effect, it must be presumed to have been adopted to accomplish fiscal regulation and ultimate economic objectives significantly similar to, if not identical with, the objectives which underlie what would be characterized as revenue measures—namely, governmental management of its economy by a foreign country. Accordingly, the result is not determined by the threshold appearance of the particular law sought to be enforced or whether such law be denominated by the foreign government as a penal law or a revenue law or otherwise. The bottom line is that the courts of one country will not enforce the laws adopted by another country in the exercise of its sovereign capacity for the purpose of fiscal regulation and management.

* * *

Nothing in the Bretton Woods Agreements Act or in any other agreement between the United States and Brazil of which we are aware, however, mandates a complete abrogation of the normal conflicts rule or requires our courts *affirmatively* to enforce foreign currency regulation, as we are invited to do in the present case. This distinction was expressly recognized and held to be dispositive in Banco do Brasil (supra), in which we said (12 N.Y.2d p. 376, 239 N.Y.S.2d p. 874, 190 N.E.2d p. 237): "An obligation to withhold judicial assistance to secure the benefits of such contracts [i.e., those violative of the foreign currency control regulation] does not imply an obligation to impose tort penalties on those who have fully executed them." (See Dicey & Morris, Conflict of Laws [8th ed.], op. cit., p. 161, n. 19; pp. 898–900.)

The appellant seeks to distinguish our decision in *Banco do Brasil* on the ground that the plaintiff in that case was recognized as an instrumentality of the Brazilian Government. I find this unpersuasive.

* * *

The majority, however, argues that the time may have come for a change in what historically has been the applicable rule. I recognize that strong arguments can be mounted for a change in view of the increased frequency and importance of international commerce and the significantly different perspective in today's world in which one nation views another nation and its interests. In my opinion, however, the responsibility for any change lies with our Federal Government rather than with the highest court of any single State. Change, if at all, in my view, would better come at the hands of the State Department and the Congress, through the negotiation of international agreement or otherwise in the discharge of the constitutional responsibility of the Federal Government "to regulate commerce with foreign nations" (cf. Bretton Woods Agreements Act). A fitting sense of judicial restraint would dictate that the courts of no single State should enunciate a change, however large that State's relative proportion of foreign commerce may be, particularly since the authoritative effect thereof would necessarily be confined to the borders of that State.

Accordingly, I believe the order of the Appellate Division should be affirmed.

BREITEL, C.J., and GABRIELLI, JONES, FUCHSBERG and COOKE, JJ., concur with JASEN, J.; WACHTLER, J., dissents and votes to affirm in a separate opinion.

CALLEJO v. BANCOMER, S.A.

United States Court of Appeals, Fifth Circuit, 1985.
764 F.2d 1101.

GOLDBERG, J.: This suit is one of several arising from the promulgation by Mexico of exchange control regulations on August 13, 1982, and from the subsequent nationalization of privately-owned Mexican banks on September 1, 1982. The exchange control regulations mandated that all deposits in Mexican banks, however denominated, be repaid in Mexican pesos at specified rates of change. Because the dollar rate of exchange was well below the market rate, the regulations constituted a Montezuma's revenge on American investors who had dollar deposits in Mexican banks. A number of these indisposed investors, including the plaintiffs in the present suit, have brought claims against Mexican banks for breach of contract.

Thus far, the courts that have passed on these cases have been unanimous in dismissing the plaintiffs' claims, either on the ground that the banks are immune from suit under the doctrine of sovereign immunity (citations omitted).

* * *

[The Court held that suit was not barred by the Foreign Sovereign Immunities Act because of the commercial activity exception, and proceeded to consider the Act of State doctrine.]

The act of state doctrine received its classic expression in Underhill v. Hernandez, 168 U.S. 250, 18 S.Ct. 83, 42 L.Ed. 456 (1897): "Every sovereign state is bound to respect the independence of every other sovereign state, and the courts of one country will not sit in judgment on the acts of the government of another, done within its own territory. Redress of grievances by reason of such acts must be obtained through the means open to be availed of by sovereign powers as between themselves." 168 U.S. at 252 . * * *

In the present case, Bancomer claims that Mexico's promulgation of exchange control regulations constituted an act of state, and that consideration of the Callejos' claims would require us to inquire into the validity of those regulations. The Callejos argue, in response, that the act of state doctrine is inapplicable [because] * * * the "treaty exception" to the act of state doctrine applies, since the exchange control regulations violate Mexico's obligations under the Articles of Agreement of the International Monetary Fund.

* * *

The act of state doctrine is premised not only on an unwillingness to apply American public policy to invalidate foreign laws but also on a pessimism about the competence of the judiciary to ascertain norms of international law. Potentially, international law as well as American public policy could serve as a touchstone for evaluating foreign acts of state: if an act of state were contrary to international law we could treat the act as invalid and adjudicate the plaintiff's claim. This approach would allow us to review foreign acts of state without engaging in the dubious practice of evaluating these acts against the potentially parochial norms of American public policy.

The Court, however, in large part foreclosed this avenue of review in Banco Nacional de Cuba v. Sabbatino, 376 U.S. 398, 84 S.Ct. 923, 11 L.Ed.2d 804 (1964). There the Court was asked to review the validity of Cuba's expropriation of a Cuban sugar company owned by United States residents. The Court declined to do so, holding that the country's response to Cuba's acts should be fashioned and implemented by the executive, not the judiciary. Id. at 431–32. Although the Court admitted that Cuba's acts might have violated international law, it held that international opinion was sufficiently divided that international law did not provide a firm basis for adjudicating the validity of Cuba's acts. Id. at 428–31. In essence, the Court held that international law generally does not provide "judicially discoverable and manageable standards for resolving" cases.

In *Sabbatino*, however, the Court recognized that "the greater the degree of codification or consensus concerning a particular area of international law, the more appropriate it is for the judiciary to render decisions regarding it, since the courts can then focus on the application of an agreed upon principle to circumstances of fact rather than on the sensitive task of establishing a principle not inconsistent with national interest or with international justice." *Sabbatino*, 376 U.S. at 428. On this basis, the Court elaborated an exception to the act of state doctrine under which the doctrine may not apply if there is "a treaty or other unambiguous agreement regarding controlling legal principles." Id.

Here, the Callejos claim that the Mexican exchange control regulations violate the Articles of Agreement of the International Monetary Fund ("Fund Agreement"), Dec. 27, 1945, 60 Stat. 1401, T.I.A.S. 1501, 2 U.N.T.S. 39, as amended April 30, 1976, 29 U.S.T. 2203, T.I.A.S. No. 8937, U.N.T.S. (amendments effective April 1, 1978), to which Mexico is a party.

In particular, they claim that the regulations violate Article VIII, Section 2(a), which forbids members for imposing exchange control regulations on "current international transactions"[3] without the prior approval of the International Monetary Fund ("IMF" or "Fund"). The

---

3. [original note 19] The term "current international transactions" is defined in Article XXX(d) of the Fund Agreement, which states in pertinent part:

(d) Payments for current transactions means payments which are not for the purpose of transferring capital, and includes, without limitation:

(1) all payments due in connection with foreign trade, other current business, including services, and normal short-term banking and credit facilities;

(2) payments due as interest on loans and as net income from other investments;

The Fund may, after consultation with the members concerned, determine whether specific transactions are to be considered current transactions or capital transactions.

Callejos argue that because the Fund Agreement is "a treaty or other unambiguous agreement," the act of state doctrine does not apply."

In the twenty years that have elapsed since its inception in *Sabbatino*, the treaty exception to the act of state doctrine has been applied sparingly. * * * Although *Sabbatino* refers merely to "treat[ies] or other unambiguous agreements," treaties are not all of a piece; they come in different sizes and shapes, ranging from the Convention for the Unification of Certain Rules relating to International Transportation by Air ("Warsaw Convention"), Oct. 12, 1929, 49 Stat. 3000, T.S. No. 876, which sets forth unambiguous rules governing the air carriage of passengers, baggage, and cargo, to the United Nations Charter, June 26, 1945, 59 Stat. 1031, T.S. No. 993, whose broad but vague pronouncement are more similar to those of the United States Bill of Rights. For this reason, the treaty exception was not stated in *Sabbatino* as "an inflexible and all-encompassing rule," 376 U.S. at 428; instead, its application depends on pragmatic considerations, including both the clarity of the relevant principles of international law and the potential implications of a decision on our foreign policy.

In determining whether the Fund Agreement—and Article VIII, Section 2(a) in particular—warrant application of the treaty exception, we tread upon uncharted ground. Thus far, no court has passed on this issue, and commentators have made, at best, ambiguous pronouncements. See, e.g., 2 J. Gold, The Fund Agreement in the Courts 138–39 (1982) ("The Articles of Agreement [of the IMF] could come within" the treaty exception.); Paradise, Cuban Refugee Insureds and the Articles of Agreement of the International Monetary Fund, 18 U.Fla.L.Rev. 29, 67 (1965). Initially, we note that it is unclear to what extent the Fund Agreement is unclear. Article VIII, Section 2(a) applies by its terms only to exchange control regulations governing "current international transactions" (as opposed to "capital transfers"). Under Article VI, Section 3 of the Fund Agreement, members may validly impose restrictions on international capital movements. Thus, determining whether a set of exchange control regulations requires approval by the Fund pursuant to Article VIII, Section 2(a) depends in part on determining whether they apply to "current" or "capital" transactions. Given the substantial uncertainty regarding the meanings of these terms, we are doubtful that Article VIII, Section 2(a) is the type of "unambiguous agreement" referred to in *Sabbatino*.

In the context of the present case, however, we need not pass on this question in the abstract, since the IMF has itself clarified the meaning of the Fund Agreement as it applies to the Mexican regulations by indicating that they are consistent with the Agreement. On May 3, 1983, in response to an inquiry from Bancomer's counsel, the Director of the Legal Department of the Fund specifically stated that "the 'provisions of Mexico's Currency Regulations (enacted in August and continuing in effect today) which require repayment of deposits in Mexican banks to be made in Mexican pesos regardless of the currency in which the deposits are denominated' ... do not violate and are not inconsistent with the

Articles of the Agreement of the International Monetary Fund." This determination at once renders the Fund Agreement unambiguous in its application to the present case, but also defeats, on the merits, the Callejos' Article VIII, Section 2(a) claim.

We consider the Fund's interpretations to be persuasive authority on the meaning of the Fund Agreement. The Fund Agreement is a complex regulatory document whose sense is often obscure. In interpreting it, we defer to the greater expertise of the Fund. This difference is akin to the deference that we accord to an administrative agency's interpretations of its own statutory scheme. See Chevron, U.S.A., Inc. v. Natural Resources Defense Council, 467 U.S. 837 (1984). * * *

The exact basis for the Fund's conclusion that the Mexican regulations are consistent with the Fund Agreement is somewhat unclear. The Fund's conclusion could be based (1) on its view that the Mexican regulations govern capital rather than current transactions, in which case Article VIII, Section 2(a) approval was not required, and/or (2) on its granting approval of the regulations pursuant to Article VIII, Section 2(a). If the Fund's conclusion is based on the first ground, then, at most, we can only review the Fund's interpretation to determine whether it is reasonable, since we consider the Fund's interpretation to be highly persuasive authority. Here this standard is clearly met, particularly given the uncertainty that exists regarding the dividing line between current and capital transactions. If, however, the Fund's conclusion rests on the latter ground, then we are precluded from exercising even this limited level of review. Article VIII, Section 2(a) only requires that exchange control regulations receive the approval of the Fund; once such approval is given, the regulations are by definition valid. The decision whether to approve exchange control regulations is committed to the discretion of the Fund. We have no power to review the Fund's exercise of this discretion.

Thus, even if we did not accept the Fund's interpretation of the Fund Agreement as persuasive authority, its decision to approve exchange control regulations pursuant to Article VIII, Section 2(a) would be final.

The Callejos attempt to avoid this result by arguing that even if the Fund did approve the Mexican regulations, it failed to do so prior to their promulgation. While such prior approval is technically required by Article VIII, Section 2(a), we do not believe that the violation of this requirement is of a magnitude sufficient to justify disregarding the act of state doctrine, particularly where approval is later given by the Fund. The treaty exception to the act of state doctrine does not penalize a foreign country for every failure to "go by the book." The same prudential considerations that underlie the act of state doctrine apply to the treaty exception as well.

Note

Other useful cases on this general set of issues include Libra Bank Ltd. v. Banco Nacional de Costa Rica, 570 F.Supp. 870 (S.D.N.Y.1983), and J.

Zeevi & Sons v. Grindlays Bank (Uganda), 37 N.Y.2d 220, 371 N.Y.S.2d 892, 333 N.E.2d 168 (1975), cert. denied, 423 U.S. 866, 96 S.Ct. 126, 46 L.Ed.2d 95. For a rare more recent case, see Lehman Bros. Commercial Corp. v. Minmetals Intern. Non–Ferrous Metals Trading Co., 2000 WL 1702039 (S.D.N.Y.2000) (held Article VIII did not apply to the People's Republic of China prior to its acceptance thereof in 1996).

Problem

Vanzia has a law on its books entitled "Foreign Exchange and Trade Control Law," one part of which reads:

Vanzia Exchange Control Act of 1963

Article 26: Any exchange of the bobble for any other currency at a rate less than the value set by the Vanzian Central Bank shall be illegal, and participants in such exchange shall be liable to fine and imprisonment.

* * *

Article 32: An "exchange" within the meaning of this statute shall include any exchange between any two persons, no matter where they are.

On the date in question, the Vanzian Central Bank has set the exchange rate of the bobble at 10 bobbles to the United States dollar. The IMF has "approved" this law under Article VIII, section 2 as part of a stand-by arrangement between Vanzian and the IMF for Vanzian drawings.

Golddust Widget Mfg. Co. succeeded in penetrating the Vanzia market, but in order to make some of its initial sales, it had to take some payments in bobbles. As a consequence, Golddust now has a deposit in the Bank of America, San Francisco, of 20,000 bobbles, another deposit in a private bank in Vanzia ("V Bank") of 50,000 bobbles, and a deposit in a Swiss Bank of 100,000 bobbles. In seeking to convert these deposits into dollars, it has entered into the following contracts:

(a) with Joe Moneybags, United States citizen of San Jose, California to sell 10,000 bobbles on deposit in California for 900 United States dollars;

(b) with Mr. Z, citizen and resident of Vanzia, now in Los Angeles doing business, to sell 10,000 bobbles on deposit in California for 850 United States dollars;

(c) with Mr. G, of Cologne, Germany, to sell 50,000 bobbles on deposit in Switzerland for 15,000 Deutsch Marks;

(d) with Joe Moneybags, United States citizen of San Jose, to sell 20,000 bobbles on deposit in Switzerland for 6,000 Swiss Francs;

(e) with Ms. X, citizen and resident of Vanzia, to sell 20,000 bobbles on deposit in Vanzia in exchange for 700 United States dollars.

In addition, Golddust has shipped widgets to Vanzia buyers under the following circumstances:

(f) 1000 tin widgets to UU Inc. for 1000 United States dollars, plus freight and insurance on open line of credit. UU Inc. has a bank deposit in California sufficient to cover this purchase. Extrinsic evidence would show that these widgets would sell on the United States market for 50 cents each.

Golddust asks your advice on the probability of success of court proceedings anywhere in the world to realize upon these various contracts. Outline your response.

SECTION 22.4 TRADE MEASURES FOR BALANCE OF PAYMENTS REASONS

Nations with balance of payments difficulties may intervene in the exchange market, as we have seen. They may also intervene to discourage or prevent the expenditure of scarce foreign exchange on imports, using the familiar instruments of trade protection. The wisdom of such measures is often in doubt, but their use has been extensive and the WTO/GATT system expressly permits them under certain conditions.

The jurisdiction of WTO/GATT here overlaps with that of the IMF, which has been a source of some tension and confusion through the years. The IMF has general jurisdiction over payments matters and considerable competence regarding balance of payments problems. The WTO has general jurisdiction over trade matters. The GATT articles dealing with the use of trade restrictions for balance of payments reasons require, among other things, a determination whether balance of payments measures are justified by balance of payments difficulties— information bearing upon that determination is often available only in the IMF. The case involving India below gives some indication of the interplay of the two organizations.[1]

(A) GATT AND TRADE RESTRICTIONS FOR BALANCE OF PAYMENTS REASONS

(1) *Legal Background: The Original GATT Agreement*

Some of the most elaborate and complex provisions of the General Agreement on Tariffs and Trade are concerned with the use of trade restrictions for balance of payments reasons. (See Articles XII through XV.) These provisions were the result of extensive debates during the preparatory work.[2] In addition, GATT contains obligations relating to exchange rate and currency controls which can operate to restrict imports.

It will be recalled that Article XI of GATT prohibits the use of quotas generally. The principal exceptions to this prohibition are Article XII and XVIII (applying to developing countries), which both contain

---

1. See John H. Jackson, World Trade and the Law of GATT ch. 18 (1969). Concerning some of the institutional aspects of the IMF, see American Society of International Law, Report of Panel on International Monetary Policy: Long–Term International Monetary Reform: A Proposal for an Improved International Adjustment Process, (1972); see also UNCTAD, Money, Finance and Development: Papers on International Monetary Reform, U.N.Doc. TD/B/479 (1974).

2. Jackson, supra note 1, at chs. 18 and 26.

provisions that authorize the use of quantitative restrictions or quotas against imports in case of balance of payments difficulties. (There is no explicit authorization in the General Agreement for the use of higher tariffs or tariff surcharges for balance of payments reasons.) It will also be recalled that the most-favored-nation obligation is one of the most important features of GATT, contained in Article I. When quotas or quantitative restrictions are utilized, however, the Article I non-discrimination language may not adequately support the MFN principle, and consequently Article XIII of GATT sets forth a "non-discrimination principle" tailored to the use of quotas. It speaks of the need to administer quotas so as not to damage or reduce imports from countries in a way that would change the historical shares of the importing market. But departures from this principle are permitted in certain more difficult balance of payments situations, and Article XIV sets forth this exception. Finally, Article XV of GATT tries to establish a satisfactory relationship between GATT and the IMF, requiring the existence of certain facts to be determined by the IMF. Article XVIII, section B, deals with the special balance of payments problems of developing countries.

The provisions of Article XVIII differ somewhat, but not drastically, from those of Article XII.[3]

(2) The Use of Payments Measures Under GATT: Policy and Practice

At one time, particularly during the period of "fixed" exchange rates prior to 1971, even developed nations invoked the GATT balance of payment provisions with some regularity. The United States imposed a temporary import surcharge[4] in August of 1971, signaling the crisis that led in September of that year to the closing of the "gold window" and the collapse of the fixed exchange rate system. The President's authority to take that action was questioned but withstood court challenge. Later, Section 122 of the Trade Act of 1974, 19 U.S.C.A. sec. 2132, made clear that the President may impose temporary import surcharges for balance of payments purposes, though it has not been invoked since its enactment. The GATT legality of the tariff surcharge is discussed briefly below.

Other major trading nations that have at one time resorted to surcharges include France in 1955, Canada in 1962, the United Kingdom in 1968, and Denmark in 1971. As for other measures, the Treaty of Rome allowed certain "protective measures" for balance of payments reasons (see Articles 108 and 109), and authority to utilize them has been given at times. See Commission Decision 76/446/EEC of 5 May 1976 Authorizing the Italian Republic to Take Certain Protective Measures Under Article 108(3) of the Treaty, [1976] Eur.Comm.O.J. No. L 120/30.

3. See a chart of these differences in Jackson, supra note 1, at 689.

4. An import or tariff surcharge refers to a uniform ad valorem tariff in addition to any tariff already imposed.

In recent years, however, most of the use (and abuse) of the balance of payments provisions in GATT has been by developing nations. The legitimacy of these actions has at times been challenged, both on economic and legal grounds.

ISAIAH FRANK, IMPORT QUOTAS, THE BALANCE OF PAYMENTS AND THE GATT[5]

The exception for dealing with balance-of-payments problems consists of a set of lengthy, complex and rather opaque provisions scattered over several GATT articles (Articles XII to XV and XVIII). The provisions are of three types: (i) the criteria for invoking the exception, (ii) the obligations applying to the use of quantitative restrictions under the exception and (iii) procedural rules relating to review and consultation.

No useful purpose would be served by attempting to recount the detailed articles, but a brief summary is essential. The basic provision is that quantitative restrictions may be used to safeguard a country's "external financial position and its balance of payments", but only to the extent necessary "(i) to forestall the imminent threat of, or to stop, a serious decline in its monetary reserves or (ii), in the case of a contracting party with very low monetary reserves, to achieve a reasonable rate of increase in its reserves" (Article XII [1 and 2]). Determinations as to the adequacy of reserves are left to the IMF.

But the right to impose quantitative restrictions for balance-of-payments reasons is not unlimited. Countries are obliged to relax the restrictions as conditions permit. Moreover, the restrictions must be applied on a non-discriminatory basis. Since quantitative restrictions are readily open to discrimination in their administration, Article XIII(2) of the GATT calls on countries, in applying such restrictions on any product, to "aim at a distribution of trade in such product approaching as closely as possible the shares which the various contracting parties might be expected to obtain in the absence of such restrictions".

* * *

The focus of the balance-of-payments exception on the adequacy of a country's monetary reserves suggests that the provision is predicated on the existence of a par-value system. Under such a system, an adequate level of reserves is needed to defend the fixed parity without resorting to severe deflationary measures that could result in an abrupt contraction of employment and economic activity. If, however, the level of reserves is low or falling, a second line of defence of the exchange rate is the reduction of imports through trade restrictions. The idea that a less expansionary macro-economic policy might render unnecessary the resort to trade restrictions is specifically rejected in Article XII of the GATT.

5. 10 World Economy 307 (1987), reprinted with permission of the author. See also Richard Eglin, Surveillance of Balance of Payments Measures in the GATT, 10 World Economy 1 (1987).

It is true that the need for reserves may not have been greatly reduced with the adoption of a system of floating rates of exchange. Under a managed float, countries continue to hold reserves for intervention in foreign-exchange markets, as a precaution against unanticipated disturbances and as a demonstration of creditworthiness. As a means of defending reserve positions, however, countries possess today an alternative to import restrictions in their freedom to let the exchange rate move.

Even if a temporary reduction of imports is deemed necessary to deal with a balance-of-payments problem, it remains something of a mystery as to why it should take the form of quantitative restrictions rather than tariffs. One possible justification under the Bretton Woods system of fixed rates of exchange might be the need for speed in a situation where a country was rapidly losing reserves. But this was precisely the explanation given by the United Kingdom in 1964 for *avoiding* the use of quantitative restrictions and adopting instead an import surcharge to defend its payments position, even though the surcharge was unauthorized by the GATT. In its notification to the GATT, the United Kingdom stated that reduction in its balance-of-payments deficit "required urgent action which would only have been delayed while the elaborate administrative machinery of import licensing was re-established and licences were allocated to importers".

Similarly, when the United States adopted an import surcharge in 1971, it stressed the need "to provide relatively quick benefits to its trade balance" until the problem could be adequately dealt with in other ways. Thus the need for speed in defending the balance of payments through trade measures would appear to argue in favour of the imposition of a uniform tariff rather than inherently selective and discriminatory quantitative restrictions that inevitably carry a heavy administrative load.

An alternative justification for import quotas in cases of balance-of-payments difficulties is the desire to concentrate the import restriction on luxury goods so that scarce foreign exchange would be conserved for imports of more essential products. But the effect of such a restriction is to encourage the domestic production of non-competitive luxury goods and the increased importation of raw materials and intermediate products to support that production. If the intention is to reduce the consumption of luxury goods without diverting fungible domestic resources to their production at home, the preferred method would be a tax on the consumption of luxury goods regardless of whether they are produced at home or abroad. In short, it is difficult to find a defensible rationale for the specification of quantitative restrictions as the preferred trade measure to counter temporary balance-of-payments problems.

Resort to Balance-of-Payments Exception

So far as can be ascertained, no industrial country has invoked balance-of-payments reasons for quantitative restrictions imposed in recent years. When a balance-of-payments justification has been given for trade restrictions, the action has generally taken the form of tariffs which, in turn, have been in the form of across-the-board surcharges rather than selective tariffs that protect particular categories of goods.

Developing countries, however, have resorted extensively to quantitative restrictions for balance-of-payments reasons. For example, in 1983 Brazil notified the GATT that she had in effect 361 quantitative restrictions, the justification for which, according to the IMF, was "balance of payments reasons related to the process of development". The same justification was given for 442 quantitative restrictions by Ghana, 122 by India, 253 by the Republic of Korea, 330 by Nigeria, 434 by Pakistan, 492 by Tunisia and lesser numbers by other developing countries.

In fact the use by developing countries of quantitative restrictions for balance-of-payments reasons may be presumed to be far more extensive than indicated by those self-notifications to the GATT. The table in the IMF report from which the above data were taken showed no notifications for many developing countries—including, for example, Argentina and Colombia, countries which are known to have had wide-ranging systems of import controls.

* * *

Neither the principle nor the practice of the use of quantitative restrictions for balance-of-payments reasons has been seriously examined in the almost forty years of the GATT's existence. But experience over that period has unequivocally demonstrated the essentially protective nature of such restrictions. The most telling evidence is that in the vast majority of cases the quantitative restrictions have been applied to highly selective groups of products rather than across the board. Quantitative restrictions should therefore be recognized for what they are, namely a subterfuge for protection. The best way to deal with the problem would be to eliminate from the GATT the right to impose quantitative restrictions for balance-of-payments reasons.

INDIA—QUANTITATIVE RESTRICTIONS ON IMPORTS OF AGRICULTURAL, TEXTILE AND INDUSTRIAL PRODUCTS
WT/DS90/AB/R
Appellate Body Report adopted by the DSB on September 22, 1999

2. India maintains quantitative restrictions on the importation of agricultural, textile and industrial products falling in 2,714 tariff lines. India invoked balance-of-payments justification in accordance with Article XVIII:B of the GATT 1994, and notified these quantitative restrictions to the Committee on Balance-of-Payments Restrictions (the "BOP Committee"). On 30 June 1997, following consultations in the BOP Committee, India proposed eliminating its quantitative restrictions over a seven-year period. Some of the Members of the BOP Committee, including the United States, were of the view that India's balance-of-

payments restrictions could be phased out over a shorter period than that proposed by India . . .

110.   India appeals the Panel's interpretation of the Note *Ad* Article XVIII:11 of the GATT 1994 and, in particular, the word "thereupon". India claims that the Panel erred in law in interpreting the word "thereupon" to mean "immediately". According to India, "thereupon":

> . . . indicates that there must be a *direct* causal link between the removal of measures imposed [for] balance-of-payments reasons and the recurrence of the conditions defined in Article XVIII:9. (emphasis added)

111.   The Note *Ad* Article XVIII:11 provides:

> The second sentence in paragraph 11 shall not be interpreted to mean that a contracting party is required to relax or remove restrictions if such relaxation or removal *would thereupon produce* conditions justifying the intensification or institution, respectively, of restrictions under paragraph 9 of Article XVIII. (emphasis added)

112.   The conditions which justify the intensification or institution of balance-of-payments restrictions under Article XVIII:9 (a) and (b) are a threat of a serious decline in monetary reserves, a serious decline in monetary reserves, or inadequate monetary reserves.

113.   The Panel found that to maintain balance-of-payments restrictions under the Ad Note:

> . . . it must be determined that one of the conditions contemplated in sub-paragraphs (a) and (b) of Article XVIII:9 would appear immediately after the removal of the measures, and a causal link must be established between the anticipated reoccurrence of the conditions of Article XVIII:9 and the removal. It should be noted that the text requires more than a mere possibility of reoccurrence of the conditions ("would produce"). The Ad Note therefore allows for the maintenance of measures on the basis only of clearly identified circumstances, and not on the basis of a general possibility of worsening of balance-of-payments conditions after the measures have been removed. (underlining added)

114.   We agree with the Panel that the Ad Note, and, in particular, the words "would thereupon produce", require a *causal link of a certain directness* between the removal of the balance-of-payments restrictions and the recurrence of one of the three conditions referred to in Article XVIII:9. As pointed out by the Panel, the Ad Note demands more than a mere possibility of recurrence of one of these three conditions and allows for the maintenance of balance-of-payments restrictions on the basis only of clearly identified circumstances. In order to meet the requirements of the Ad Note, the probability of occurrence of one of the conditions would have to be clear.

115.   We also agree with the Panel that the Ad Note and, in particular, the word "thereupon", expresses a *notion of temporal sequence* between the removal of the balance-of-payments restrictions and

the recurrence of one of the conditions of Article XVIII:9. We share the Panel's view that the purpose of the word "thereupon" is to ensure that measures are not maintained because of some distant possibility that a balance-of-payments difficulty may occur.

116.   The Panel considered the various dictionary definitions of the word "thereupon" and came to the conclusion that "the most appropriate meaning should be 'immediately'." The Panel found support for this interpretation in the context in which the word "thereupon" is used , the objective of paragraphs 4 and 9 of Article XVIII and the Ad Note, and the object and purpose of the *WTO Agreement.*

117.   We recall that balance-of-payments restrictions may be maintained under the Ad Note if their removal or relaxation would thereupon produce: (i) a threat of a serious decline in monetary reserves; (ii) a serious decline in monetary reserves; *or* (iii) inadequate monetary reserves. With regard to the first of these conditions, we agree with the Panel that the word "thereupon" means "immediately".

118.   As to the two other conditions, i.e., a serious decline in monetary reserves or inadequate monetary reserves, we note that the Panel, in paragraph 5.198 of its Report, qualified its understanding of the word "thereupon" as follows:

> We do not mean that the term "thereupon" should necessarily mean within the days or weeks following the relaxation or removal of the measures; this would be unrealistic even though instances of very rapid deterioration of balance-of-payments conditions could occur.

119.   We agree with the Panel that it would be unrealistic to require that a serious decline or inadequacy in monetary reserves should actually occur within days or weeks following the relaxation or removal of the balance-of-payments restrictions. The Panel was, therefore, correct to qualify its understanding of the word "thereupon" with regard to these two conditions. While not explicitly stating so, the Panel in fact interpreted the word "thereupon" for these two conditions as meaning "soon after". This is also one of the possible dictionary meanings of the word "thereupon". We are of the view that instead of using the word "immediately", the Panel should have used the words "soon after" to express the temporal sequence required by the word "thereupon". However, in view of the Panel's own qualification of the word "thereupon", the use of "immediately" with respect to these two conditions does not amount to a legal error.

120.   We, therefore, uphold the Panel's interpretation of the Ad Note and, in particular, the word "thereupon".

121.   India claims that the Panel erred in law:

> ... by requiring India to use macro-economic and other development policy instruments to meet balance-of-payments problems caused by the immediate removal of its import restrictions.

India argues that such a requirement amounts to a change in its development policy, and is, therefore, inconsistent with the proviso to Article XVIII:11 of the GATT 1994.

122.   The second sentence of Article XVIII:11 provides that Members:

> ... shall progressively relax any restrictions applied under this Section as conditions improve, maintaining them only to the extent necessary under the terms of paragraph 9 of this Article and shall eliminate them when conditions no longer justify such maintenance;

and adds the following proviso:

> *Provided* that no contracting party shall be required to withdraw or modify restrictions on the ground that a change in its development policy would render unnecessary the restrictions which it is applying under this Section.

123.   In reply to a question by the Panel, the IMF stated:

> The Fund's view remains ... that the external situation can be managed using macro-economic policy instruments alone. Quantitative restrictions (QRs) are not needed for balance-of-payments adjustments and should be removed over a relatively short period of time. ...

124.   In reaching its conclusion that the removal of India's balance-of-payments restrictions will not "immediately" produce the recurrence of any of the conditions of Article XVIII:9 and that the maintenance of these measures is, therefore, not justified under the Note *Ad* Article XVIII:11, the Panel took this statement of the IMF into account.

125.   India argues that the Panel required India to change its development policy in order that the removal of the balance-of-payments restrictions would not produce a recurrence of any of the conditions of Article XVIII:9. We disagree. Nothing in the Panel Report suggests that the Panel imposed this requirement. On the contrary, in paragraph 5.220 of its Report, the Panel stated:

> India had in the past used macroeconomic policy instruments to defend the rupee, suggesting that the use of macroeconomic policy instruments as mentioned by the IMF would not necessarily constitute a change in India's development policy.

126.   Furthermore, we are of the opinion that the use of macroeconomic policy instruments is not related to any particular development policy, but is resorted to by all Members regardless of the type of development policy they pursue. The IMF statement that India can manage its balance-of-payments situation using macroeconomic policy instruments alone does not, therefore, imply a change in India's development policy.

127.   In paragraph 5.209 of the Panel Report, the Panel referred to the following IMF statement:

The macroeconomic policy instruments would need to be complemented by structural measures such as scaling back reservations on certain products for small-scale units and pushing ahead with agricultural reforms.

128.   We believe structural measures are different from macroeconomic instruments with respect to their relationship to development policy. If India were asked to implement agricultural reform or to scale back reservations on certain products for small-scale units as indispensable policy changes in order to overcome its balance-of-payments difficulties, such a requirement would probably have involved a change in India's development policy.

129.   We note that the Panel did not take a position on the question whether the adoption of the structural measures of the type mentioned by the IMF would entail a change in India's development policy. The Panel concluded in paragraph 5.211 of its Report as follows:

> The IMF's suggestions on "structural measures" should not be taken in isolation from the context in which they are made. We recall that the IMF began its reply to Question 3 by stating that India's "external situation can be managed by using macroeconomic policy instruments alone". Its comments on structural measures appear only at the end of its answer after it has suggested other liberalization measures, such as tariff reductions. The adoption by India of "structural measures" is not suggested as a condition for preserving India's reserve position. Thus, we cannot conclude that the removal of India's balance-of-payment measures would thereupon lead to conditions justifying their reinstitution that could be avoided only by a change in India's development policy.

Clearly, the Panel interpreted the IMF statement to the effect that the implementation of structural measures is not a condition for the preservation of India's external financial position. We consider this interpretation to be reasonable.

130.   We conclude that the Panel did not require India to change its development policy and, therefore, did not err in law with regard to the proviso to Article XVIII:11.

Notes and Questions

(1) A major issue in the *India QR* case was whether the dispute settlement system should consider the U.S. claim at all, or whether it was more appropriately handled in the WTO Balance-of-Payments Committee. Of course, in the committee, India or the United States could have blocked any outcome they did not like under the WTO practice of consensus decision-making. The panel, upheld by the Appellate Body, concluded that it could consider the case on the basis of the Uruguay Round Understanding on the Balance-of-Payments Provisions of GATT 1994, the first footnote of which provides: "The provisions of Articles XXII and XXIII of GATT 1994, as elaborated and applied by the [DSU] may be invoked with respect to any matters arising from the application of restrictive import measures taken for

balance-of-payments purposes." India argued that this language did not allow consideration of the justification of balance-of-payments measures.

(2) Is there any plausible justification, even in a country experiencing severe balance of payments difficulties, for import measures that are more restrictive with respect to particular imported goods than others? Should the WTO ban such selective measures outright?

(3) The United States has also resorted to unilateral initiatives to attack import restrictions justified by purported balance of payments concerns. A 1989 "Super 301" case against Brazil resulted in the elimination of a number of quantitative restrictions by the Brazilian government. See Brazil Import Licensing, Inv. No. 301–73, 55 Fed.Reg. 22876 (1990).

(4) Various proposals have been introduced in the U.S. Congress from time to time to require import surcharges to deal with the trade deficit generally or with particular nations (read, Japan). Putting aside their legality under GATT, can such measures work when exchange rates float? Or will reduced demand for imports cause the price of foreign currencies to fall, reducing the price of imports, increasing the price of U.S. exports abroad, and thus accomplishing little or nothing?

(3) Tariff Surcharges and The Uruguay Round Agreement

Most of the tariffs of industrialized countries (particularly those on non-agricultural goods) are "bound" in their GATT schedules as a result of negotiated "concessions." There is no general exception in GATT to these "bindings" for balance of payments reasons. Thus, while the original GATT authorized the use of quantitative restrictions for balance of payments reasons, it did not allow tariff increases to be so used. As Isaiah Frank indicated in the excerpt above, however, a case can be made that "tariff surcharges" are preferable to quantitative restrictions if any trade intervention is to occur at all.[6]

6. A paper by the GATT secretariat written in 1965 elaborates some of the reasons:

2. (i) Surcharges were preferred to quantitative restrictions because they were administratively less cumbersome and were less likely to freeze the pattern of trade.

(ii) The substantial revenues obtained from use of surcharges were essential to the success of the country's stabilization programme.

(iii) The surcharges were placed both on bound and unbound items to avoid unfair discrimination between exporters.

3. (i) The conversion of surcharges to internal measures could aggravate industrial conditions, especially in situations where there are accumulation of stocks. The use of such internal measures in place of surcharges could also cause serious internal political difficulties.

(ii) Internal measures alone were not sufficient to restore equilibrium and balance-of-payments and additional measures to restrict imports were necessary.

(iii) In urgent situations, surcharges could be quickly imposed. Otherwise, there could be disastrous delays in bringing a new law before parliament.

Contracting parties have in various instances noted the following considerations in authorizing the use of surcharges:

(i) In one or two instances, the use of surcharges represented a significant simplification over the system of restrictions previously enforced.

(ii) The effect of the surcharges would be less restrictive than quantitative restrictions permitted under Articles XII or XVIII.

(iii) In addition to its direct effect on the level of reserves, the use of sur-

Not surprisingly, import surcharges were used with some regularity despite the absence of legal authorization for them, even to the point that some would argue that GATT had been "amended de facto." The legal force of such arguments need not be tested here, however, in light of the results of the Uruguay Round.

The "Understanding on the Balance of Payments Provisions of the General Agreement on Tariffs and Trade 1994" [Understanding], contained in the Documents Supplement, provides in paragraph 2 that "notwithstanding the provisions of Article II, price-based measures taken for balance of payments purposes may be applied in excess of the duties inscribed in the schedule of a Member." Indeed, in paragraph 3, the Understanding strongly encourages price-based measures (such as import surcharges and import deposit requirements) in preference to new quantitative restrictions unless the price-based measures would prove inadequate. It further indicates in paragraph 4 that measures may only be applied to control the "general level of imports." An exception exists for "essential products," but trade measures that burden particular products greatly relative to others appear to be prohibited.

Other provisions of the Understanding encourage announced time schedules for the removal of balance of payments measures and require notification of all new measures to the WTO/GATT. They also provide for consultations under the auspices of a Committee on Balance of Payments Restrictions, which will make recommendations to the General Council regarding the conformity of measures under review with GATT obligations.

(B) GATT OBLIGATIONS RELATING TO CURRENCY PAR VALUES AND EXCHANGE CONTROLS

Regardless of the balance of payments condition of a nation, currency par values and exchange controls can be manipulated to defeat the effect of other trade obligations of GATT. The drafters of GATT thus included several obligations relating to these practices. For example, it was well known that a requirement of a license, in order to make a payment in foreign exchange, could effectively prevent the importation of goods or control them through the control exercised in the granting of licenses. In some cases, the obligations of the International Monetary Fund suffice to prevent the abusive practices which would affect trade, and Article XV of GATT recognizes this fact. Some of the parties to GATT are not members of the IMF, however, and consequently it was necessary to include in GATT some substitute for the IMF obligations in these cases. Article XV, paragraph 4, contains such substitutes, and paragraph 6 of that Article provides that a non-Fund member should establish a "special exchange agreement" with the Contracting Parties of GATT, presumably to provide some of the IMF-type obligations.[7]

charges was in certain instances, necessary to insure success of the government stabilization program.

See GATT Doc.Com.TD/F/W.3, at 1–2.

7. See generally Jackson, supra note 1, at ch. 18.

Scattered throughout GATT are various other commitments relating to similar problems.[8] For example, MFN under Article 1 imposes the obligation of nondiscrimination with respect to international transfer of payments; and Article II, paragraphs 3 and 6, limit the possibility of using devaluation or other currency exchange techniques to "impair the value of any of the concessions" under GATT.[9]

SECTION 22.5   COHERENCE: THE PROBLEM OF COORDINATING TRADE AND MONETARY POLICY

JOHN H. JACKSON, MANAGING THE TRADING SYSTEM: THE WTO AND POST URUGUAY ROUND GATT AGENDA[1]

An important defect of the previous system (a Bretton Woods without an international trade organization) was perceived by many to be the lack of "coherence". This meant the lack of appropriate coordination and discussion between national government officials and international organizational officials who concentrated on monetary and lending questions on the one hand; and those involved in the somewhat "messier" problems of trade in goods (involving many different interest groups and political/economic forces on the other hand.) One of the purposes of a new WTO is clearly to assist in providing this coherence, partly by establishing a higher profile, understandability, and prestige for the WTO and its organization officials and national government officials accredited to it. If managed appropriately, there should be a considerably greater interchange and among the three Bretton Woods institutions, possibly with certain joint committees, or at least more attention to some issues such as how trade matters affect balance of payments or other monetary questions; and vice versa, how monetary affairs, including exchange rate changes, can have great effects on trade policy.

Indeed, in recent years and even recent weeks (as of this writing—June 1994), there has been a number of circumstances which have poignantly demonstrated the importance of the connection between monetary and trade policy. The bilateral trade tensions between United States and Japan and the ensuing dramatic exchange rate shifts are one such example. The desire and advantage of some of the newly privatiz-

---

8. See Jackson, supra note 1, at 492; commitments relating to exchange controls and currency practices occur in Articles I, para. 1; II, paras. 3 and 6; VI, pars. 2 and 3; VII, para. 4(a) and (c); VIII, paras. 1 and 4, and, of course, the elaborate BOP exceptions in Articles XI through XIV and Article XVIII, Section B.

9. The floating exchange rate system has posed some new problems for GATT rules. If a currency increases in value in relation to other currencies, can that be the basis for an adjustment in the tariff under bindings, pursuant to Article II of GATT? See Frieder Roessler, Selective Balance-of-Payment Adjustment Measures Affecting Trade: The Roles of the GATT and the IMF, 9 J.World Trade L. 622 (1975).

1. From a chapter in a volume based on a conference sponsored by the Institute for International Economics, Washington, D.C. on the subject "Managing the World Economy: 50 Years after Bretton Woods (1994). Reprinted with permission.

ing, or "marketizing" economies (Russia and other Republics, China, etc.) also amply demonstrate this link, as economists and policy makers stress the need for floating exchange rates in order for trade relations to be successful.

Even in the GATT there was recognition of the monetary-trade link in several articles. Countries who were GATT Contracting Parties but not Members of the IMF had an obligation under GATT to enter into some sort of monetary framework agreement. Likewise, the GATT had provisions for trade measures linked to balance of payment difficulties.

A number of issues that are left over for future work will have important implications for the work of the World Bank and possibly the Fund. For example, antidumping and subsidy rules have often been contentious. Apparently there have occasionally been recommendations to developing countries to use these rules in a way that would seem less than optimal by trade specialists. Hopefully the new institutional structure will create an environment of better coordination and mutual understanding between trade specialists and monetary specialists.

Likewise agriculture and food policy deserve much more attention, and so also do policies relating to commodities and commodity agreements. All of these can be substantially affected by monetary movements, particularly for some smaller countries.

Dispute resolution procedures are an important attribute of an international treaty "regime", and looked upon as an essential component of effectively implementing treaty obligations so as to produce the degree of credibility for those obligations that makes them operate successfully in international economic relations. It is inevitable that some monetary issues will find their way into some disputes brought into these procedures.

Other monetary and financial links to trade policy include:

— effects of exchange rate shifts on trade rules regarding financial services

— methods of financial adjustment costs caused by liberalizing new trade rules

— questions whether and when trade barriers and other distorting measures (such as subsidies) affect exchange rates or inhibit the ability of the monetary system to adjust

— the question of the responsibility of a balance of payments global surplus country to contribute to "re-balancing"

— the question of use of trade measures to offset BOP difficulties

— calculations of anti-dumping margins and subsidy impacts in the context of exchange rate shifts

— effects of debt on trade and monetary imbalances (and vice versa).

Chapter 23

COMPETITION RULES
AND THE WTO

SECTION 23.1 INTRODUCTION

With the passage of the Sherman Act in 1890, the United States became the first country to attempt general statutory control of the power wielded by large business enterprises. Since World War II, most of the world's developed countries and many developing nations have enacted laws of one sort or another to control restrictive or anticompetitive business practices. In addition to these national laws, the EU has its own competition rules effective in its member states. The growing interdependence of national economies, the increase in the size and reach of multinational enterprises (MNEs) and the developing nations' concern with the power that MNEs have over their economies, all have raised doubts as to whether existing national or regional controls adequately regulate restrictive business practices and as to whether such practices are appropriately the subject of control only by uncoordinated national laws. Particularly in respect of international transactions affecting more than one country, it has been argued that it may be necessary to establish international standards and, as a consequence, various international organizations have examined these problems and in some cases have acted to establish standards. Of particular interest is the 1996 decision by WTO ministers to establish a Working Group on the Interaction Between Trade and Competition Policy and subsequent proposals (particularly by the EU) that competition rules be a subject in the next general round of WTO negotiations.

After a brief description in this introduction of the types of behavior typically regulated by competition rules, we consider first the close relationship between trade and competition policies. Indeed, in reviewing the material in Section 23.2, the reader should ask whether the interrelationship is so great that the rules applicable to trade should be required to be taken into account in applying competition rules and vice versa. Then in Section 23.3, we trace the history and prospects of efforts to establish international rules on restrictive business practices, with particular reference to the work ongoing in the WTO.

In this brief introductory overview of the interrelationship of competition policies and international economic relations, we cannot hope to sketch the substance of national antitrust laws except with a broad brush.[1] National antitrust and competition laws vary considerably in their treatment of various business behavior. Moreover, even similar laws may be enforced quite differently.

Most national antitrust laws prohibit cartels—groups of competing firms that agree to fix their prices, divide markets or rig bids–although enforcement varies from country to country. In the United States, for example, section 1 of the Sherman Act makes illegal "[e]very contract, combination * * * or conspiracy, in restraint of commerce or trade among the several States, or with foreign nations."[2] Certain types of agreements are regarded as illegal per se—including, most notably, agreements among competitors to fix prices at which their offerings are sold, or to allocate territories or customers in order to avoid competing with each other. Many other restraints are tested by a full factual inquiry as to whether they will have any significantly adverse effect on competition, what the justification for them is, and whether that justification could be achieved in a less anticompetitive way. This test is the so-called "rule of reason" first enunciated by the Supreme Court in 1911.[3]

In the EU, Article 81(1) of the EC Treaty prohibits all agreements and concerted practices "which may affect trade between Member States and which have as their object or effect the prevention, restriction or distortion of competition within the common market." Among the examples given of such agreements are those that fix prices, limit production and share markets. Article 81(3) provides, however, that the EC Commission may exempt agreements and practices from Article 81(1) in certain circumstances where they are found to be beneficial overall.

Of particular significance for international trade is the fact that export and import cartels are often exempted, explicitly or by practice, from cartel prohibition. For example, although the U.S. antitrust laws apply to foreign commerce, there are two statutes—the Webb–Pomerene Act and the Export Trading Company Act—that explicitly permit conduct in connection with exportation that would otherwise violate U.S. law.[4] In the EU, export cartels may be viewed as outside the prohibitions

---

1. The OECD and WTO committees charged with studying competition policy issues have produced a wealth of material on the interaction of trade and competition policies, the competition policies followed by individual countries and related issues, which is available in their publications (in the case of the OECD) and on their respective websites. For a concise summary of U.S. antitrust law, see Stephen F. Ross, Principles of Antitrust Law (1993). See also American Bar Association, Section of Antitrust Law, Antitrust Law Developments (Fourth) (1997). For materials on EU com-

petition rules, see George A. Bermann, Roger J. Goebel, William J. Davey & Eleanor M. Fox, European Community Law part III (2d ed. 2002).

2. 15 U.S.C.A. sec. 1.

3. Standard Oil Co. v. United States, 221 U.S. 1, 31 S.Ct. 502, 55 L.Ed. 619 (1911).

4. The Webb–Pomerene Act, 15 U.S.C.A. secs. 61–65, provides an antitrust exemption for the formation and operation of associations of otherwise competing businesses to engage in collective export sales.

of Article 81 if they do not have effect on the common market and do not affect trade between member states.

The Sherman Act, in section 2, prohibits monopolization and attempts to monopolize.[5] The analogous provision in the EC Treaty is Article 82, which prohibits abuses of a dominant position insofar as they affect trade between Member States. Examples of such abuses are imposing unfair prices or trading conditions, limiting production to the prejudice of consumers, applying dissimilar conditions to equivalent transactions to the disadvantage of others and making contracts subject to unrelated supplementary obligations.

Another typical subject of antitrust laws is merger control. A merger of two companies may lead to a violation of the rules already described. In particular, the merger of two companies in the same market eliminates a competitor and arguably decreases competition in that market. In order to determine whether a merger should be blocked, antitrust laws have in recent years begun to provide for pre-clearance review. Essentially this means that the proposed merger partners must submit detailed information to the antitrust authorities so that they may determine whether the merger is likely to have an adverse affect on competition. If they conclude that it will, the merger may be prohibited.[6] Merger control rules are a particular problem internationally since any merger involving a large business enterprise is likely to involve operations in many markets, raising the question of which merger control authorities should have primary responsibility for examining the merger. If more than one authority is going to examine it, should there be a way of resolving conflicts? Or should each authority be able to make its own decision, independently of the views and decisions of the others?

In addition, various other types of anticompetitive conduct are sometimes regulated by national antitrust laws. For example, in the United States, there is an explicit statutory framework for dealing with price discrimination, which we considered briefly in Chapter 16 in connection with our examination of antidumping laws, which deal with international price discrimination.[7]

Associations seeking the exemption under the Act must file certain material with the Federal Trade Commission, but approval is not required. The Export Trading Company Act of 1982, 15 U.S.C.A. secs. 4011–4021, enables any person engaged in U.S. export trade to obtain an export trade certificate, issued by the Commerce Department, with Justice Department concurrence, which confers immunity from suit under the antitrust laws for activities that are specified in and comply with the certificate. An applicant must show, inter alia, that the proposed export conduct will not substantially lessen competition within the United States nor substantially restrain the export trade of any competitor of the applicant. It was apparently intended to help small-and medium-sized businesses enter export markets. See U.S. Dept. of Commerce, Intl. Trade Admin., Guidelines for the Issuance of Export Trade Certificates of Review.

5. 15 U.S.C.A. sec. 2.

6. In the U.S., the principal merger regulation statute is section 7 of the Clayton Act, 15 U.S.C.A. sec. 18. Pre-clearance was implemented by the Hart–Scott–Rodino Act, 15 U.S.C.A. sec. 18a. Pre-clearance in the EC was provided for in the EC Merger Regulation, Council Regulation 4064/89, Eur. Comm. O.J. L 395/1 (Dec. 12, 1989), as amended.

7. Robinson-Patman Act, 15 U.S.C.A. sec. 13.

SECTION 23.2   THE RELATIONSHIP OF COMPETITION AND TRADE POLICIES

The Sherman Act is the cornerstone of U.S. antitrust laws. In discussing the principles underlying the Act, the Supreme Court has said:[1]

> The Sherman Act was designed to be a comprehensive charter of economic liberty aimed at preserving free and unfettered competition as the rule of trade. It rests on the premise that the unrestrained interaction of competitive forces will yield the best allocation of our economic resources, the lowest prices, the highest quality and the greatest material progress, while at the same time providing an environment conducive to the preservation of our democratic political and social institutions. But even were that premise open to question, the policy unequivocally laid down by the Act is competition.

The fact that antitrust laws are aimed at promoting free competition suggests their importance to international trade. If private parties are permitted to interfere with free market forces and to restrain trade between countries, e.g., by entering into anticompetitive price-fixing or market-sharing agreements, they may effectively replace the government-imposed barriers to trade that the WTO/GATT system is supposed to limit. Indeed, a major purpose of the competition rules of the EC Treaty was to prevent business enterprises from reconstructing barriers to trade between Member States that the treaty had abolished.[2] Conversely, to the extent WTO rules allow departures from the free trade norm, e.g., by allowing inefficient producers to be protected from the rigors of competition, it may thwart the policies of antitrust laws.

OECD, COMPETITION AND TRADE POLICIES: THEIR INTERACTION 87, 112–13 (1984)[3]

* * * [R]estrictive business practices can have significant effects on the competitive functioning of international markets and are thus of concern to trade policy. It is similarly the case that trade policy measures that result in barriers to international trade can have important detrimental effects on domestic market structures by diminishing competition. For example, a trade policy that permits domestic firms to co-ordinate their exports in a cartel-like manner may weaken competition to the extent that export co-ordination also facilitates co-ordination of domestic sales. On the other hand, trade policy that permits a free flow of imports is likely to cause domestic markets to behave more competi-

---

1. Northern Pacific Railway Co. v. United States, 356 U.S. 1, 4, 78 S.Ct. 514, 517, 2 L.Ed.2d 545, 549 (1958).

2. Consten & Grundig v. Commission, Cases 56 & 58/64, [1966] ECR 299.

3. Reprinted by permission of the Organization for Economic Cooperation and Development.

tively. Thus, trade policy can either significantly promote or substantially impede the economic goals of competition policy. With national economies being increasingly linked and interdependent, trade liberalisation policies maintain a climate conducive to the effective functioning of competition in national and international markets.

* * *

* * * [T]rade policy measures exercise a significant impact on competition and on markets. This is also the case with the enforcement of laws relating to unfair trade practices. While designed to adjust competitive disequilibria brought about by unfair and injurious import pricing practices, the enforcement of these laws can, in certain circumstances, restrict competition in domestic markets by raising entry barriers to foreign competitors. In this respect, two fundamental concerns arise for competition policy. The first is whether private firms abuse unfair trade laws by bringing actions to gain leverage over foreign competitors and either control or exclude their presence in domestic markets. Second, the question arises whether the effects on competition of proceedings under laws relating to unfair trade practices are adequately considered, in particular in the measurement of injury to domestic industry and in the level of relief granted. * * *

There are certain common elements in competition policy and laws relating to unfair trade practices. Both share the common objective of seeking to remove artificial distortions in markets. But differences emerge in the nature of the interests they seek to protect and in the ways in which standards are applied. The principal goal in competition policy is to preserve and maintain competitive domestic market structures and the efficient allocation of resources by prohibiting practices that restrain competition or impose barriers to new entrants. Emphasis is placed on market performance, costs and scale economies. The principal concern is to protect competition, and not competitors. Competition policy does not seek to protect inefficient competitors against lower prices that are achieved through efficiency, economies of scale, cheap labor or technological expertise, so long as the advantage is fairly attained. Nor, in most countries, does competition policy allow a departure from competitive principles for firms buffeted by recessionary conditions, shrinking markets or technological obsolescence.

Laws relating to unfair trade practices, in contrast, aim to protect domestic industry from unfair import pressures causing injury to domestic competitors. Thus, the basic issue in the application of these trade laws is generally the legitimacy or illegitimacy of various competitive advantages which foreign producers enjoy over domestic firms and the resultant harm to domestic industry. Under these laws, the effect of the practices on competition in the market and the ultimate effect on consumers are not at issue, nor are they elements of the offence, except insofar as they relate to the causation of harm to the domestic industry. These differences in comparison with competition policy can be partly explained by the divergent concepts upon which rules of international trade are based and the different interests considered in formulating and applying trade policies.

Notes and Questions

(1) The economic analysis of tariffs in Chapter 1 demonstrates that government interference in the marketplace through artificially raising a price by imposing a tariff is inefficient. The same analysis applies in the case of private parties raising a price by agreement between themselves. The incentive for such agreements can easily be seen. As the analysis of Chapter 1 showed, the increased prices resulting from interference with market prices may mean increased profits for the sellers of the particular product. Thus, those sellers, absent legal constraints, may be eager to obtain those increased profits. Antitrust laws exist to prevent them from doing so.

(2) As noted in the introduction, national antitrust laws sometimes do not concern themselves with, or often even explicitly permit, anticompetitive behavior in international markets. Among the competition policies noted by the OECD study that affect international trade are (A) laws authorizing export cartels, which may restrict international trade by causing excessively high export prices or trade-inhibiting market allocation, (B) laws authorizing import cartels, which may allow private parties to control prices and quantities as if they had the power to impose tariffs and quotas, (C) policies that fail to control the practices of trading companies, which means the prices and quantities of significant numbers of imported and exported products in some countries are determined by a small number of private companies and (D) policies that allow multinational enterprises to allocate functions among various components and to set transfer prices that do not reflect market prices. Should the WTO/GATT system concern itself with such practices? Are there meaningful differences between the effects on international trade of a state-owned trading company with exclusive trading rights (the activities of which would be subject to some controls under the General Agreement, see Section 9.3 supra) and a private firm or group of firms that enjoys an effective monopoly? We will consider the desirability of international antitrust rules in the next section.

(3) As stated in the OECD study, exceptions to general free trade policies that are designed to prevent unfair trade practices often operate not to protect competition per se, but rather to protect individual competitors. An example is the protection afforded by antidumping or countervailing duty proceedings, such as those discussed in Chapters 16–18 supra. Should more consideration be given by competition authorities to trade policy issues and vice versa? The OECD study suggests that the answer is clearly yes. The difficult question then becomes how much consideration should be given? For example, should escape clause relief, or imposition of antidumping or countervailing duties, be conditioned upon a finding that there will be no adverse competitive effects? Would such a requirement preclude relief in most cases and thereby effectively repeal those statutes? Is there a more acceptable intermediate position?

(4) To the extent that imports represent a competitive threat to domestic producers, those producers may attempt to have the government limit imports through escape clause, antidumping or countervailing duty actions.

Even if it is accepted that such actions ought to be permitted, without consideration of the anticompetitive effects that such relief may have, there remains the question of whether the antitrust laws ought to be concerned with potential abuse of those actions. For example, if domestic industry is clearly not entitled to relief, should the antitrust authorities be concerned with an attempt to obtain relief, particularly where the attempt may disrupt the market for the imports? In its 1988 Guidelines for International Operations, the Justice Department analyzed this problem as follows:[4]

> The individual or joint conduct of U.S. firms in petitioning the U.S. Government for protection from foreign competition generally is immune from prosecution under the U.S. antitrust laws. Under the Noerr–Pennington doctrine, the courts have construed the Sherman Act not to apply to individual or collective petitioning of the U.S. federal or state governments, even when the government action sought would have an anticompetitive effect.

> * * *

> Ostensible petitioning conduct is not immune, however, when it is in fact a mere sham concealing a direct restraint by the parties. Examples of petitioning that is not protected by Noerr–Pennington immunity include the meritless invocation of administrative procedures to delay a competitor's entry or to deny its access to governmental processes and the deliberate misleading of the government during such administrative proceedings. The threat to consumer welfare from such abuse may be substantial. Although most litigated findings of sham petitioning have involved a pattern of abuse, a single anticompetitive abuse of governmental processes may suffice in appropriate circumstances. * * *

Do you agree with this policy? The authors are unaware of any case where U.S. parties have been subject of a government enforcement action as a result of invoking U.S. trade laws. The discussion does not appear in the 1995 Guidelines.

(5) A related issue arises when exporters to the U.S. market who are subject of trade actions attempt to settle them by raising their prices or limiting their exports. To what extent should the antitrust authorities concern themselves with the potential anticompetitive effects of such settlements. In its 1995 Guidelines, the Justice Department and FTC provided the following example:[5]

> Six U.S. producers of product Q have initiated an antidumping action alleging that imports of Q from country Sigma at less than fair value are causing material injury to the U.S. Q industry. The ITC has made a preliminary decision that there is a reasonable indication that the U.S. industry is suffering material injury from Q imported from Sigma. The Department of Commerce has preliminarily concluded that the foreign

---

4. U.S. Dept. of Justice, Antitrust Enforcement Guidelines for International Operations sec. 7 (Nov. 10, 1988), reprinted in 4 CCH Trade Reg. Rptr. para. 13109; BNA Antitrust & Trade Reg. Rep., vol. 55, no. 1391 (Spec. Supp. Nov. 17, 1988).

5. U.S. Department of Justice & Federal Trade Commission, Antitrust Enforcement Guidelines for International Operations, April, 1995, sec. 3.4, Illustrative Example M.

market value of Q imported into the United States by Sigma's Q
producers exceeds the price at which they are selling Q in this country
by margins of 10 to 40 percent. Sigma's Q producers jointly initiate
discussions with the Department of Commerce that lead to suspension
of the investigation in accordance with Section 734 of the Tariff Act of
1930, 19 U.S.C. 1673c. The suspension agreement provides that each of
Sigma's Q producers will sell product Q in the United States at no less
than its individual foreign market value, as determined periodically by
the Department of Commerce in accordance with the Tariff Act. Before
determining to suspend the investigation, the Department of Commerce
provides copies of the proposed agreement to the U.S. Q producers, who
jointly advise the Department that they do not object to the suspension
of the investigation on the terms proposed. The Department also determines that suspension of the investigation would be in the public
interest. As a result of the suspension agreement, prices in the United
States of Q imported from Sigma rise by an average of 25 percent from
the prices that prevailed before the antidumping action was initiated.

Discussion:

While an unsupervised agreement among foreign firms to raise their
U.S. sales prices ordinarily would violate the Sherman Act, the suspension agreement outlined above qualifies for an implied immunity from
the antitrust laws. As demonstrated here, the parties have engaged only
in conduct contemplated by the Tariff Act and none of the participants
have engaged in conduct beyond what is necessary to implement that
statutory scheme.

(6) Antitrust authorities typically try to discourage mergers that significantly increase market concentration, i.e., the extent to which a few firms
have a large share of the market. One difficult issue in analyzing market
concentration and the effect of mergers is the extent to which the possibility
or existence of international trade flows should be considered. In its 1992
Merger Guidelines, revised in 1997, the U.S. Department of Justice explained its treatment of import competition in analyzing the competitive
impacts of mergers as follows:[6]

> Market shares will be assigned to foreign companies in the same
> way in which they are assigned to domestic competitors. * * *

> If shipments from a particular country to the United States are
> subject to a quota, the market shares assigned to firms in that country
> will not exceed the amount of shipments by such firms allowed under
> the quota. In the case of restraints that limit imports to some percent-
> age of the total amount of the product sold in the United States (i.e.,
> percentage quotas), a domestic price increase that reduced domestic
> consumption would reduce the volume of imports into the United States.
> Accordingly, actual import sales and capacity data will be reduced for
> purposes of calculating market shares. * * *

6. U.S. Dept. of Justice, Merger Guidelines, para. 1.43 (1992), reprinted in 4 CCH
Trade Reg. Rptr. para. 13,104. This language was not affected by the 1997 revisions.

Given the various U.S. laws that allow domestic industry to seek protection from imports, how much should foreign competition be considered in merger analysis? Do the Guidelines give too little or too much consideration?

In 1984, the Justice Department initially announced that it would oppose the merger of LTV Corporation and Republic Steel Corporation, the third largest and fourth largest U.S. steelmakers, a position that in part led United States Steel Corporation, the largest U.S. steelmaker, and National Steel Corporation to call off merger plans. Because of the precarious state of the U.S. steel industry, largely blamed upon import competition, there was considerable criticism of this position, including that of other government agencies.[7] The Justice Department did not oppose a subsequent merger proposal between Republic and LTV that provided for divestment of certain mills.[8] Should merger restrictions be relaxed in the case of industries injured by imports, as determined, for example, in an escape clause proceeding?

If potential or actual import competition is given prominent consideration in analyzing mergers, what does that imply for the degree of concentration among national firms in national economies? Are these effects desirable or not? Given that a domestic industry may succeed in obtaining political support to reduce imports, is it unrealistic to rely upon imports as a restraining force on the behavior of domestic firms? Or will a failure to consider imports lead to disallowance of mergers necessary to maintain the competitiveness of domestic industry?

SECTION 23.3 INTERNATIONAL EFFORTS TO CONTROL RESTRICTIVE BUSINESS PRACTICES

Throughout the period since the end of World War II, efforts have been made to achieve an international agreement on the control of restrictive business practices—a sort of international law of antitrust or competition. In this section, after an overview of the relationship of antitrust and trade policies, we will examine a number of rules that have already been adopted and a variety of proposals. In examining the current rules and proposals, you should consider whether they would provide a reasonable basis for an international agreement. We conclude with an overview of the activities of the WTO Working Group on the Interaction between Trade and Competition Policy.

(A) OVERVIEW

JOHN H. JACKSON, ALTERNATIVE APPROACHES FOR IMPLEMENTING COMPETITION RULES: IN INTERNATIONAL ECONOMIC RELATIONS[1]

* * *

7. 9 BNA ITIM 673, 756, 757 (1984).

8. 9 BNA ITIM 812 (1984).

1. Aussenwirtschaft, 49.Jahrgang (1994), Heft II, Zurich: Rüeggers S.XX–XX. Reprinted by permission.

2. Competition Policy and the Policies of International Trade Regulation

* * * [I]nternational trade policy cannot be completely separated from competition policy. Indeed, there are many examples of how trade policy issues touch upon, or overlap with competition policy, or certainly are influenced by failures of the market due to monopolistic or cartel-like behavior. A suggestive list would include:

— Various "buy-national" policies, whether in connection with government procurement or government encouragement of private purchases ("buy American", "buy Japanese").

— Antidumping laws and the question of dumping raise a number of competition policy issues. Writers and policy makers have for many decades commented on the question of "predatory" price discrimination behavior as a basis for antidumping responses, but it is now clear that antidumping actions go well beyond this. In addition controversy exists about the issues (and likely existence) of "predatory" pricing behavior.

— Intellectual property issues have a number of questions relating to fair competition policies. The world trading system, particularly in the GATT Uruguay Round is now giving considerable attention to these issues.

— The formulation and application of product standards, sometimes designed to promote the free flow of products among nations, can nevertheless be utilized to inhibit fair competition. Standards can be designed to it easier for particular groupings of nations to trade among themselves, while inhibiting the flow of trade from third parties.

— Private firms have a number of cross border arrangements, such as the development of agencies, subsidiaries, franchisees, and sales with tying arrangements, which can undermine the free operation of the market. So-called "gray area" imports are part of this problem.

— Trade in a variety of primary commodities, such as metals or coffee, have long been the subject of special international arrangements and indeed many treaty provisions, directly bear on questions of whether market principles should or can apply to trade in these products. Likewise, service sectors such as maritime shipping, or air transport and tourism, are affected by many international, national, and private arrangements that raise important questions of competition policy.

— Many governments have "state trading enterprises," or "state trading monopolies" which in certain circumstances may be justified for specific and valid governmental purposes, but in other circumstances may undermine international trade flows and market principles.

— Subsidies can be sued to restrain trade, as can quantitative restrictions.

— Product liability rules have also been cited as affecting competition.

— Within nations, there is a variety of different approaches to what we in the U.S. call "antitrust policy". Some of these have been generating sources of tension between nations, such as the Japanese Keiretsu system and worries in the United States about how that system affects potential U.S. exports to Japan.

Thus there is thus no dearth of illustrations that suggests that a problem exists.

In exploring the question of competition policy, however, it is useful to try to focus some attention on just what policies or approaches are being suggested in the area of regulation of competition. The following come to mind, (but this is not an exhaustive list):

First, the notion is often expressed that anti-competitive practices can, if not regulated, greatly inhibit market access for foreign producers. This can undermine the policies of comparative advantage and the general policies behind liberal trade. Indeed, the policies of liberal trade include the notion that competition will increase efficiencies among different producers, even when (or especially when) the producers are located in different countries. Yet it is not always clear how anti-competitive actions would inhibit import access. The anti-competitive activities which tend to provide collusive hesitations to buy foreign goods would be one such example. Sometimes these activities are identified with vertical integration in a society, and particularly attention is focused on the Keiretsu in Japan as having a major protectionist effect. Yet different economies have different approaches to vertical integration, and arguments can be made that vertical integration of certain types may be efficient and thus welfare enhancing.

Another objective sometimes expressed is that of harmonization of competition policies and procedures. Sometimes harmonization focuses on procedures, resulting in agreements for cooperation in specific procedures such as assisting with evidence, and providing sufficient harmonization so that there will not be procedural clashes between countries that are more vigorously enforcing anti-trust or anti-monopoly policies.

Other times, however, there are attempts to harmonize the substance or negotiations. Then objections are raised against intrusion on sovereignty, or too much centralization of authority ("don't regulate my sausages in Geneva or Brussels"), reflections of concepts of subsidiarity.

Another dimension of the policies relating to competition is that of "competitiveness." It is sometimes suggested that lax enforcement of anti-monopoly practices provides an unfair advantage in the society where laxness occurs. It has even been suggested that the lax enforcement of an economic regulatory matter should be designated a "subsidy," for countervailing duty purposes. Again, harmonization might be one way to partially cure this, except that when societies differ so much in their approaches to these regulatory issues, it is often very difficult to achieve much in the way of harmonization. The tendency is towards a set of international rules that converge on the least common denominator of differing national views.

Other policies that are related include the so-called "strategic trade theories." If countries wish to pursue a policy of enhancing their own welfare (sometimes at the expense of the welfare of other countries, or of world welfare) then there may be certain kinds of approaches suggested which would appear "anti-competitive."

(B) THE ITO AND RESTRICTIVE BUSINESS PRACTICES[2]

The proposed International Trade Organization's charter contained nine articles dealing with restrictive business practices, but none of them were carried over into the General Agreement. The ITO provisions would have required members to prevent business practices affecting international trade which restrained competition, limited access to markets or fostered monopolistic control, whenever such practices had harmful effects on the expansion of production or trade.[3] The kind of practices that would have been subject to ITO investigations were:[4]

   (a) fixing prices, terms or conditions to be observed in dealing with others in the purchase sale or lease of any product;

   (b) excluding enterprises from, or allocating or dividing, any territorial market or field of business activity, or allocating customers, or fixing sales quotas or purchase quotas;

   (c) discriminating against particular enterprises;

   (d) limiting production or fixing production quotas;

   (e) preventing by agreement the development or application of technology or invention whether patented or unpatented; and

   (f) extending the use of rights under patents, trade marks or copyrights granted by an Member to matters which, according to its laws and regulations, are not within the scope of such grants, or to products or conditions of production, use or sale which are likewise not the subject of such grants.

The ITO Charter would have established a consultation procedure in the event that one party believed that another was permitting a restrictive business practice, and it also would have established a procedure by which the ITO would investigate complaints brought by one party.[5] At the ITO hearing to determine whether such a practice existed, the private parties involved were to be heard. If the ITO determined that one of the above-mentioned practices had caused harmful effects on the

---

2. See generally John H. Jackson, World Trade and the Law of GATT 522–29 (1969).

3. ITO Charter, art. 46(1).

4. Id., art. 46(3).

5. Id., arts. 47–48.

expansion of production or trade, then it would request the party to take every possible remedial action.

Despite the fact that the ITO provisions were not incorporated in the General Agreement, interest in reaching some sort of agreement in GATT on restrictive business practices did not die. Proposals were made for GATT action in both 1954 and in 1956. In 1956, the matter was referred to the GATT Intersessional Committee, which commissioned a study of existing intergovernmental agreements in this area. Later, in 1959 the Contracting Parties appointed a group of experts to recommend whether, to what extent and how GATT should undertake to deal with restrictive business practices. In the end, however, no agreement could be reached on how GATT could regulate such practices, without structural change. The group concluded:[6]

> it would be unrealistic to recommend at present a multilateral agreement for the control of international restrictive business practices. The necessary consensus among countries upon which such an agreement could be based did not yet exist, and countries did not yet have sufficient experience of action in this field to devise an effective control procedure.

As noted in the introduction, however, there is renewed interest in having the WTO/GATT system tackle this problem.

(C) 2000 OECD GUIDELINES FOR MULTINATIONAL ENTERPRISES

The OECD Guidelines for Multinational Enterprises, issued in 1976 and revised in June 2000, contain several provisions dealing with competition practices:

IX. *Competition*

Enterprises should, within the framework of applicable laws and regulations, conduct their activities in a competitive manner. In particular, enterprises should:

1. Refrain from entering into or carrying out anti-competitive agreements among competitors:

    a) To fix prices;

    b) To make rigged bids (collusive tenders);

    c) To establish output restrictions or quotas; or

    d) To share or divide markets by allocating customers, suppliers, territories or lines of commerce.

2. Conduct all of their activities in a manner consistent with all applicable competition laws, taking into account the applicability

6. GATT, 9th Supp. BISD 171 (1961). tices (1959).
See also GATT, Restrictive Business Prac-

of the competition laws of jurisdictions whose economies would be likely to be harmed by anti-competitive activity on their part.

3. Co-operate with the competition authorities of such jurisdictions by, among other things and subject to applicable law and appropriate safeguards, providing as prompt and complete responses as practicable to requests for information.

4. Promote employee awareness of the importance of compliance with all applicable competition laws and policies.

Notes and Questions

(1) Among the issues that many antitrust laws address are (i) cartel behavior, such as agreements between firms that fix prices or allocate markets, (ii) abuses of dominant positions or monopolization, (iii) merger control and (iv) the relationship of antitrust laws to intellectual property rights. The U.S. and EC rules on the first two issues were described in the introduction to this chapter. How do the OECD Guidelines on competition practices compare to those in the ITO Charter in these four categories?

(2) The preface to the 2000 Guidelines provides that they are "recommendations addressed by governments to multinational enterprises." They go on to state that "They provide voluntary principles and standards for responsible business conduct consistent with applicable laws." At the time the Guidelines were first issued in 1976, the OECD set up a Committee on International Investment and Multinational Enterprise. The Committee is to exchange views on the application of the Guidelines and to be responsible for their "clarification." Although the Committee is not authorized to reach conclusions on the conduct of an individual company, it does consider interpretative issues arising out of concrete factual situations. Indeed, in the 1977 Badger case involving the closing of a bankrupt Belgian subsidiary by a U.S. corporation, the guidelines seemed to be discussed in the Committee as if they were binding. One author has concluded that the Guidelines were used successfully in that case to pressure the U.S. parent to modify its refusal to cover obligations of the subsidiary. "The assertion [was] made in the closed-door intergovernmental discussion of the Badger case that the Guidelines, while not legally binding, may become *de facto* part of customary international law." Thus, "[w]hile there is no question of the OECD governments constituting a court to sit in judgment over individual multinationals, the Guidelines themselves can clearly be used as a strong basis for high-level political and economic leverage outside the formal context of the [OECD] Committee."[7] It seems less likely, however, that the OECD committee would be as active in the competition area.

(D) UNITED NATIONS SET OF MULTILATERALLY AGREED EQUITABLE PRINCIPLES AND RULES FOR THE CONTROL OF RESTRICTIVE BUSINESS PRACTICES

The most detailed internationally agreed statement on restrictive business practices has been that adopted by the United Nations.[8] The

7. John Robinson, Multinationals and Political Control 125–28 (1983).

8. Phillipe Brusick, UN Control of Restrictive Business Practices, 17 J. World initial consideration of the issue occurred under the auspices of UNC-TAD in the 1970's. In 1979 and 1980 the United Nations Conference on Restrictive Business Practices met and adopted a code of conduct that was later adopted by the United Nations General Assembly as a resolution.[9]

The Set of Multilaterally Agreed Equitable Principles and Rules for the Control of Restrictive Business Practices provide that independent enterprises should refrain from certain practices when they would limit access to markets or otherwise unduly restrain competition:

(a) agreements fixing prices, including as to exports and imports;

(b) collusive tendering;

(c) market or customer allocation arrangements;

(d) allocation by quota as to sales and production;

(e) collective action to enforce arrangements, e.g. by concerted refusals to deal;

(f) concerted refusal of supplies to potential importers; and

(g) collective denial of access to an arrangement, or association, which is crucial to competition.[10]

In addition, they provide that enterprises should refrain from abusing a dominant position by limiting access to the market or otherwise unduly restraining competition by the following acts:

(a) predatory behavior towards competitors, such as using below-cost pricing to eliminate competitors;

(b) discriminatory (i.e. unjustifiably differentiated) pricing or terms or conditions in the supply or purchase of goods or services, including by means of the use of pricing policies in transactions between affiliated enterprises which overcharge or undercharge for goods or services purchased or supplied as compared with prices for similar or comparable transactions outside the affiliated enterprises;

(c) mergers, takeovers, joint ventures or other acquisitions of control, whether of a horizontal, vertical or a conglomerate nature;

(d) fixing the prices at which goods exported can be resold in importing countries;

(e) restrictions on the importation of goods which have been legitimately marked abroad with a trademark identical with or similar to the trademark protected as to identical or similar goods in the importing country where the trademarks in question are of the same origin, i.e. belong to the same owner or are used by enterprises between which

Trade L. 337 (1983); Debra L. Miller & Joel Davidow, Antitrust at the U.N.: A Tale of Two Codes, 18 Stan.J.Intl.L. 347 (1982); Recent Development, The Set of Multilaterally Agreed Equitable Principles and Rules for the Control of Restrictive Business Practices, 13 Law & Poly.Intl.Bus. 313 (1981).

9. Set of Multilaterally Agreed Equitable Principles and Rules, U.N.Doc. TD/RBP/10 (1980).

10. Id., para. D.3.

there is economic, organizational, managerial or legal interdependence and where the purpose of such restrictions is to maintain artificially high prices; and

(f) when not for ensuring the achievement of legitimate business purposes, such as quality, safety, adequate distribution or service: (i) partial or complete refusals to deal on the enterprise's customary commercial terms; (ii) making the supply of particular goods or services dependent upon the acceptance of restrictions on the distribution or manufacture of competing or other goods; (iii) imposing restrictions concerning where, or to whom, or in what form or quantities, goods supplied or other goods may be resold or exported; (iv) making the supply of particular goods or services dependent upon the purchase of other goods or services from the supplier or his designee.[11]

Notes and Questions

(1) How do the coverage and substance of the Principles and Rules compare to the ITO Charter and the OECD Guidelines? What differences in emphasis do you see?

(2) The Principles and Rules do not seem to have had much effect to date. They have been reviewed from time to time, most recently in 2000. The review conference reaffirmed their validity and called for better implementation.

(3) The Principles and Rules also included a provision requiring states to "take into account in their control of restrictive business practices the development, financial and trade needs of developing countries, in particular of the least developed countries, for the purposes especially of developing countries in: (a) promoting the establishment or development of domestic industries and the economic development of other sectors of the economy, and (b) encouraging their economic development through regional or global arrangements among developing countries."[12]

(E) FUTURE INTERNATIONAL NEGOTIATIONS

(1) The WTO Working Group on the Interaction of Trade and Competition Policy

The WTO website described the activities of its Working Group on the Interaction of Trade and Competition Policies as follows (Sept. 21, 2001):

Approximately 80 WTO Member countries, including some 50 developing and transition countries, have adopted competition laws, also known as "antitrust" or "anti-monopoly" laws. Typically, these laws provide remedies to deal with a range of anti-competitive practices, including price fixing and other cartel arrangements, abuses of a dominant position or monopolization, mergers that limit competition, and agreements between suppliers and distributors ("vertical agreements") that foreclose markets to new competitors. The concept of competition

---

11. Id., para. D.4. **12.** Id., para. C.7.

"policy" includes competition laws in addition to other measures aimed at promoting competition in the national economy, such as sectoral regulations and privatization policies.

The WTO Working Group on the Interaction between Trade and Competition Policy (WGTCP) was established at the Singapore Ministerial Conference in December 1996 to consider issues raised by Members relating to the interaction of these two policy fields. Since its initial meeting in July 1997, the Group has examined a wide range of such issues. The approximately 125 submissions received by the Working Group from Members thus far attest to the keen interest that has been shown by Members in the subject.

In 1997 and 1998, the work of the WTO Working Group was organized around a Checklist of Issues Suggested For Study which was developed at the first meeting of the Group. In particular, the work focused on the following main elements of the Checklist:

— The relationship between the objectives, principles, concepts, scope and instruments of trade and competition policy; and their relationship to development and economic growth.

— Stocktaking and analysis of existing instruments, standards and activities regarding trade and competition policy, including of experience with their application.

— The interaction between trade and competition policy, including consideration of the following sub-elements:

— the impact of anti-competitive practices of enterprises and associations on international trade;

— the impact of state monopolies, exclusive rights and regulatory policies on competition and international trade;

— the relationship between the trade-related aspects of intellectual property rights and competition policy;

— the relationship between investment and competition policy;

— the impact of trade policy on competition.

A detailed Report on the Group's deliberations on the above matters was issued in December 1998. The Report documents views expressed by Members regarding matters such as the mutually supportive relationship between trade liberalization and competition policy, the categories of anti-competitive practices that can impact adversely on international trade and investment and the potential contributions of competition policies to economic development. In addition, since 1997 the WTO has organized, in cooperation with UNCTAD and the World Bank, four Symposia on issues related to the work of the Working Group.

Pursuant to a decision by the General Council of the WTO, the Working Group examined in 1999 three further topics:

— the relevance of the fundamental WTO principles of national treatment, transparency, and most-favored-nation treatment to competition policy and vice versa;

— approaches to promoting cooperation and communication among Members, including in the field of technical cooperation; and

— the contribution of competition policy to achieving the objectives of the WTO, including the promotion of international trade.

While the relevance of WTO principles to competition policy and the need for enhanced cooperation among Members in addressing anti-competitive practices were affirmed by a number of Members, views differed as to the need for action at the level of the WTO to enhance the relevance of competition policy to the multilateral trading system. In particular, while a number of Members expressed support for the development of a multilateral framework on competition policy in the WTO, to support the implementation of effective competition policies by Member countries and reduce the potential for conflicts in this area, others questioned the desirability of such a framework and favored bilateral and/or regional approaches to cooperation in this field.

Notes and Questions

(1) The WTO process has produced a wealth of information and expression of diverse viewpoints on many competition policy subjects. For the most part the materials are available at the WTO website.

(2) As of mid–2001, the EU was particularly anxious to have competition policy included in any new WTO round of trade negotiations. The United States was decidedly less interested in including that topic, in particular because of a desire to avoid any possibility of antidumping rules becoming a subject in such negotiations. Given the joint EU–U.S. interest in having such a round, a compromise of some sorts may well be reached if it appears in the near future that launching a new, broad-based round of trade negotiations is feasible at all. That raises the following issue:

(2) *The Desirability of International Negotiations on Competition Rules*

DIANE P. WOOD, INTERNATIONAL COMPETITION POLICY IN A DIVERSE WORLD: CAN ONE SIZE FIT ALL?[13]

The question I should like to explore in this paper is to what extent the same set of competition rules do apply and can apply across such diverse local conditions. * * *

In no country in the world, no matter how committed to Adam Smith's free market it may be, does the market operate without governmental distortions. Industries everywhere receive subsidies; government

13. EC and U.S. Competitive Law and Policy (Barry Hawk ed.), 1991 Fordham   Corp. L. Inst. 71–85 (1992). Reprinted by permission.

contracts distribute largess according to political rather than economic criteria; social pressures resulting from unemployment lead to selective bailouts; and, perhaps most troubling, national industries never tire of pleading for special consideration so that they can become more successful internationally.

This diversity of perspective and priorities leads naturally to a number of different antitrust regimes at work across the globe. Some countries both define competition policy in the same way as the United States does, and place it at the forefront of their economic policy. Other countries, while agreeing in principle with the content of competition policy, regard it as only part of an overall industrial policy, and a part that can be overcome by other considerations. Still other countries regard U.S. style antitrust law as inappropriate for their circumstances, whether because of underdevelopment, fears of dependency on foreigners, the harsh inflationary or unemployment consequences that the free market may bring, or a lack of understanding of the interaction between high prices, consumer demand, and entrepreneurial responses.

The system that has characterized U.S. competition policy—at time more aspirationally than actually—can be described in a few words. First, private decision-making should be left free to dictate the direction of the economy to the greatest extent possible. That means that government regulation should exist only in situations where predictable distortions prevent the market from operating properly (for example, when one finds natural monopoly, public goods, or externalities), or, somewhat more problematically, situations in which society deliberately decides to shift allocations of resources through various methods of public assistance. The consequence of this first point ought to be to minimize public subsidies to failing industries, to accept the hardships of bankruptcy and unemployment, to allow the painful shifts in production induced by competition from foreign producers (whether or not they are subsidized in turn by their own governments, and whether or not they are selling at lower prices in the United States than at home)—in short, to accept the difficult side of the market system—and in return, to enjoy the prosperity that constant innovation, constant searches for ways to make a better widget, and constant re-evaluation can bring.

Second, an in some tension with the first point, U.S. doctrine recognizes that a purist *laissez faire* system will not bring about the competitive market that we desire, because of another familiar conundrum: the free rider problem. Even though society as a whole is better off with free and unfettered competition, individual firms will always be tempted to "cheat" on the system, enjoying the benefits others create through competition without contributing their share. This happens, of course, when groups of firms attempt to form cartels and to pursue and exploit monopoly power. Thus, the competition process needs a guardian, and the antitrust laws for more than a century have fulfilled that function.

There is an old saying that the devil is in the details, and antitrust law illustrates this as well as anything. At the level of general principle just described, antitrust law is an indispensable part of the legal apparatus supporting every free market system in the world. To the extent that these principles are missing, the success of the market will suffer. The trick, however, is to go further and to specify exactly which particular antitrust rules will lead to this desirable result. Although differences at the policy level certainly still exist, and are not insignificant, I submit that the differences in the details account for far more of the diversity among competition laws that we observe today. Moreover, although some of those differences result from a failure to understand just how far a competition law should extend (bluntly speaking, in other words, some of the differences represent mistakes on the part of legal drafters), other differences are better explained by local variations in economic development, institutional infrastructures, and the like. To the extent that the latter explanation applies, the fact that particular antitrust rules are perceived as unimportant or even undesirable in a developed country like the United States does not imply that they are inappropriate for these other countries.

III. THE DETAILS: CONSENSUS AND DIVERGENCE

A. *Consensus*

Virtually all national and multilateral efforts to articulate antitrust principles have included a small number of basic points in their lists of prohibitions: First, cartel behavior (such as price-fixing market allocations, and output restrictions among competitors undertaken without any efficiency justification) is anti-competitive; second, a firm with a monopoly or a dominant position must not abuse its power in an exclusionary way, nor should it take actions that have the effect of strengthening its dominance in the market; and third, mergers and acquisitions can be anticompetitive when they have the effect of facilitating express or tacit collusion, or when they lead to the creation or extension of a monopoly or dominant position. * * *

This degree of consensus is no accident, given the effects on consumer welfare and the allocation of society's resources that predictably flow from cartels, monopolies, and anticompetitive mergers. In each of these cases, the existence of significant market power enables the firm or firms to reduce output below the socially optimal level (and thus to cause a misallocation of resources to inferior products), and it also leads to a transfer of wealth from consumers to the cartel members or the monopolist (which may regard as an evil in itself, and which also tends to induce powerful firms to invest resources in acquiring or retaining a monopoly.) * * *

Only a few would argue that these three elements are not necessary to assure the successful functioning of a competitive, market-based economy. Disagreements abound about how aggressively they should be enforced, what the optimal penalties for violations should be, and in whose hands enforcement powers should lie, but these disagreements relate to the risks of error in detecting violations, not to the notion that the conduct correctly identified is anticompetitive. The consensus, both within the United States and more generally world-wide, breaks down in two different ways. First, some argue that the list of anticompetitive practices given above is too limited, and that items such as exclusionary conduct, predation, and vertical restrictions should appear there as well precisely because these other practices threaten consumer welfare just as much as the first three do. Second, debate has always raged over the question of purposes: if antitrust law is not *just* a set of rules designed to achieve economic allocative efficiency, then it ought to include additional elements as well. What elements must be added depend entirely on what those additional purposes are.

B. Divergences: What Threatens Consumer Welfare?

It is no secret that American antitrust law has changed, and changed again, over its century of existence, in the way that it approaches business practices and the precise practices that it condemns. * * *

I do not wish to argue here whether or not these developments [more tolerance of group boycotts, tying arrangements and vertical restraints; less concern with monopolistic distortions] were appropriate for the U.S. economy as it stands in the late 20th century. Most of them are based on the often plausible assumption that cartels and monopolistic positions are difficult to maintain for any length of time, because anticompetitive agreements are inherently unstable, because entry and entrepreneurial activity will defeat market powers, and because competition from both domestic and foreign competitors is generally vigorous. Furthermore, the risks of deterring potentially procompetitive behavior are not trivial. One person's group boycott may be another person's efficiency-enhancing selective joint venture; one person's tying arrangement may be another person's effort to assure quality control in the marketing of related products. If U.S. doctrine is approximately where it ought to be, then the question is whether that is also the appropriate place for other countries as well. If U.S. doctrine has eliminated too many antitrust rules, then the question changes only slightly, in that it deals with whether those rules are needed to the same degree in the United States as they are elsewhere. Put differently, it is important either way to decide to what extent the doctrinal developments we have observed in the United States derive their force from universal economic truisms, and to what extent they are correct because of culturally dependent factors.

The example of other countries suggests to me that factors peculiar to the United States make possible the adoption of a more narrow antitrust policy than has been the case at other times in our own history, and than ought to prevail in some other countries. The evidence for this proposition can be found both by examining the characteristics and competition policy of other countries (including for this purpose the EC) that are similar in most respects to the United States, and by contrasting the competition policy needs of countries with significantly different economic problems and cultural traditions.

The best examples of countries and regions that are functionally the same as the United States are (not surprisingly) the European Community, both taken as a whole and at the Member State level, and Canada. Like the United States, the EC countries and Canada have sophisticated, highly developed economies; like the United States, they have a long tradition of free markets within a democratic tradition; like the United States, they follow (with the exception of the few sensitive sectors mentioned above) a more or less free international trade policy. Workforces are well trained and highly mobile; capital, services, and goods flow freely within their borders and from one region to another.

In these types of societies it is safe to assume that the market will correct imperfections relatively well. If high prices appear in a certain sector, ambitious potential entrants are likely to be watching, and are likely to enter either by gathering together new capital and other inputs, or by expanding capacity that serves other markets. For the same reason, exclusionary behavior is not likely to succeed for very long. Even if a firm invests in a predatory course of action, hoping to recoup its investment and to collect supracompetitive profits in a later period, it will often be true that the same entrepreneurial instincts will cause others to enter before recoupment can succeed. Finally, where entry is relatively easy at every stage of the vertical production and distribution process—from suppliers, through manufacturers, to distributors, wholesalers, and retailers—one can feel relatively confident that the combination of vertical integration and contractual arrangements selected by firms in any given industry is efficient. In such a setting, one might assume that there is nothing inherently anticompetitive with a manufacturer's decision to dictate resale price terms in a contract with a retailer (the classic distributional restraint) since the manufacturer certainly could have accomplished the same goal by expanding the firm to include the distribution function.

In these circumstances, even if the antitrust laws theoretically include the wider range of prohibitions described above, some kinds of suits would occur rarely as an empirical matter, and succeed even more rarely, precisely because the market is healthy. However, in places where the market is not so strong, for whatever reason, adequate antitrust enforcement would require more aggressive action. Both Japan and the Eastern European countries offer examples of this problem.

Although Japan clearly has just as highly developed and technologically sophisticated an economy as the United States, Canada, or Europe, with many of the characteristics noted above for the latter countries, there is one important difference between the Japanese economy and the North Atlantic economies: the principle of consumer welfare has not attained the same importance in Japanese anti-monopoly law. Thus, it is a well known fact that consumer prices for many goods and services are considerably higher in Japan than they are in the North American and European countries, for reasons that evidently go beyond factors like transportation costs, input costs, or other neutral economic elements. In fact, during the bilateral Structural Impediments Initiative talks that took place between the United States government and the Japanese government, which were designed to address deep structural reasons for the persistent Japanese trade surpluses and U.S. deficits, the representatives of the United States government strongly indicated that lax Anti–Monopoly Act enforcement was creating one of those structural problems. Because the Japanese were in effect voluntarily taxing their consumers with monopolistic prices, manufacturers in Japan were allowed to earn high profits, which in turn eventually caused distortions in patterns of international trade (in the sense that trade followed different patterns than it would have under a perfectly functioning international market). Several flaws in Anti–Monopoly Act enforcement were identified, including the low level of cartel fines and the impediments to entry into the distributional sector resulting from laws like the Large Scale Retail Stores Act.

* * *

The point about the need for different rules and different priorities holds even more strongly in the Eastern European case. Antitrust doctrines long placed in subordinate positions in North America and the EC have an active and important role to play in countries just beginning to make the transition to a free market economy. The best example occurs in the law of monopolization. It has been commonplace for years for academic critics of section 2 of the Sherman Act to note that monopolization cases are difficult to try, and that the search for appropriate remedies is so elusive that it may not be worth the effort. Cases like *Alcoa*, which were brought before external events fundamentally changed the industry, or *United Shoe*, which attempted to use structural remedies with questionable success, led commentators to argue that Section 2 was something better left alone.

In the Eastern European countries, that suggestion makes little sense. Industry after industry was under the sole control of the state, and was physically and legally incapable of division. Even if these industries are privatized, they will continue to be monopolies. With inflation running at high levels, and strong social biases against excessive profits, the control of such monopolies will be a matter of high priority. Control may take a variety of forms, of course. It may consist of conduct regulation, such as injunctions against courses of conduct that have the effect of excluding actual or potential new entrants into the business. Theories like predatory pricing, tying arrangements and refusals to deal may need to be dusted off and put back into use in these extraordinary circumstances. Control may also mean efforts at restructuring, if conduct regulation is not enough. Ideally, control would also mean a coordination of the competition laws and the trade laws, such that effective competition could come from outside the countries to discipline local monopolies. Even trade, however, will be a minor deterrent until the scarcity of hard currency becomes less acute.

Finally, just as use of antitrust theories for vertical arrangements that have fallen out of favor in the United States will be important in Japan, it should also be a central part of the antitrust regime in Eastern Europe. The risk that vertical arrangements there will lead to manufacturer market power, and a reduction in ultimate consumer choice of distributional service and price options, is great. A manufacturer and a high-priced distributor using such an arrangement to preclude parallel imports, or to prevent low-priced discount competition, should bear the burden of justifying the restriction on efficiency grounds.

C. Divergence: Difference Policy Goals

The divergences I have discussed thus far do not call into question the primary consumer welfare/allocative efficiency orientation of antitrust laws. Even with a consensus on this point, differences should arise, and do arise, among countries due to differences in cultural background and economic development. Therefore, the final point to consider is whether one can acknowledge the value of competition laws whose basic goals differ from the consumer welfare model, or if, in the alternative, such laws in the final analysis hamper economic performance.

To a certain degree, every country articulates different reasons for having competition laws. In Europe, Articles 85 and 86 were passed as an integral part of the Treaty creating the European Economic Community because it was believed that private distortions of competition would impede the creation and maintenance of the market just as surely as governmental distortions did. The French law has traditionally included elements of so-called industrial policy, whereby the government may take broader macroeconomic effects into account (such as unemployment or balance of payments) when it applied the law. Some countries may wish to emphasize the unfair trade practices aspect of the laws, much of which falls in the United States within the Federal Trade Commission's deceptive trade practices jurisdiction. Some may wish to put the interests of small businesses above those of the consumer, to preserve a certain way of life or for other political reasons. And some countries may, and do, use their competition laws to favor local businesses over foreigners.

No one doubts that a sovereign state may make any of the choices suggested above; the only question is whether it makes any difference whether the rule is included in a "competition," or "anti-monopoly," or "antitrust" law. The answer is no, with one critical qualification. As long as the country is aware of the effect that the additional policy will have on consumer welfare and it is making a conscious choice, it accomplishes little to tell it not to group the several topics together. Indeed, it would be hard to argue that any of the additional policies mentioned above is fundamentally inconsistent with a market economy country, since so many healthy market economies have laws that accomplish precisely those goals.

IV. CONCLUSION

I began by asking the question whether, in today's diverse world, one competition policy either could or should apply to all countries. Like some of the one-size-fits all gloves you may have bought from time to time, I think the answer is that you might be able to squash a unitary, American-style policy into each country, but the fit might not be very comfortable. Both because local conditions demand differential application of traditional antitrust rules, including in my view some that have fallen into disuse in the United States, and because different countries may simply wish to pursue additional policy goals, we are likely for some time to come to live with diversity of competition policy. The challenge in years to come will be to find the common elements and to build on them, without losing sight of the differences in perspective and culture that inevitably exist.

ELEANOR M. FOX, COMPETITION LAW AND THE MILLENNIUM ROUND[14]

Competition policy problems of an international dimension are as vast as the world. They include not only international cartels and international mergers but export cartels, anti-dumping laws, distribution agreements imposing territorial restraints, and various practices and acts by firms with market power, including tie-ins and refusals to deal. Some nations allow what other nations proscribe. One nation's efficient competition policy is another nation's abuse of dominance. Moreover, one nation's preference for competition among systems contrasts with another nation's desire for a "level playing field" (i.e. uniform law) for the world.

The trade/competition dialogues at the [WTO] Working Group have led to much fruitful discussion among the varied nations of the WTO. Not least among the benefits has been greater understanding of facts, issues, and concerns of nations at different levels of wealth and development and with different traditions of political economy. There is consensus that discussions should continue; but discussions must normally either move forward or dissipate. Moving forward may mean building upon nations' mutual interests in a more nearly integrated world, with sympathy and hospitality towards openness and the linking of nations and systems. Terminating discussions may augur nationalistic stances and conflicting policies.

Even against this complex background, there is a way forward for competition and the Millennium Round. Progress may be made on discrete issues tightly related to trade where the interests within and among nations converge. Market access is such an issue. Under the principle of market access, nations would prohibit their citizen/residents from impairing access to markets by artificial private, as well as public,

14. 2   J.Intl.Econ.L.   665,   670–678
(1999). © Oxford University Press 1999.
Reprinted with permission.

restraints. At this point, liberal trade policy and liberal (market-freeing) competition policy converge.

Access to markets may be impaired by conduct in one of three categories: (1) abuse of dominance: exclusions by monopoly or dominant firms, (2) cartels with boycotts, and (3) vertical restraints such as exclusive dealing by the few leading firms in high barrier, concentrated markets wherein entry by outsiders is difficult. The laws of virtually all nations that have competition laws cover such restraints.

A new competence on market access could not only require prohibition of private and other commercial restraints, but also it could bolster states' obligations not to tolerate commercial restraints, and it could usefully craft an integrated treatment of hybrid (public/private) restraints. The following is a possible blueprint.

1. Nations should have and enforce laws prohibiting commercial conduct that unreasonably impairs market access.

2. Nations should enforce their law without discrimination as to nationality.

3. In order to assure transparency, admissibility of non-competition criteria (e.g. environment, national security) should be clearly stated, and conduct or transactions challenged as anticompetitive should be analyzed first and separately under competition criteria.

4. As in TRIPs, and as in the bilateral positive comity agreements between the United States and the European Community, there should be opportunity for harmed nations and persons to complain of violations to domestic authorities; and protocols should be established for co-operation in discovery and enforcement.

5. The importing nation should be obliged to provide an accessible litigation system accompanied by the safeguards of due process, as recourse for harmed nations and persons (as in TRIPs). If this rule is violated, the harmed nation or person should be free to contest the restraints in the courts of its own country.

6. For the purpose of market access disputes, the law of the importing nation should apply—no matter where suit is brought—as long as the importing nation has adopted the required law and that law is nonparochial.

7. As a counterpart to GATT Article XXIII, and to make the prohibition against unreasonable restraints of market access more nearly seamless and complete: Nations should be obliged not to take action that nullifies or impairs the benefits designed to be obtained from the above rules and principles. Nations should not be permitted to impair the benefits by, among other things, facilitation of prohibited restraints, or non-enforcement of the law against restraints on market access.

8. Dispute resolution should be limited to provable breaches of these obligations (again, as in TRIPs).

A set of arguments is commonly made against a world trade-and-competition initiative. None is applicable to this proposal. The arguments are as follows:

1. Such an initiative will put competition rules into the hands of trade lawyers and policy-makers; and trade experts tend to fashion rules to protect producers rather than consumers, thus degrading competition law.

2. An international initiative implies bargaining with the trading nations of the world to reach a common rule or standard. Bargaining will lead to the lowest common denominator.

3. An international initiative will spawn bureaucracy, including excessive regulation far from the pulse of the people. Bureaucracies tend to produce more and more law, and to be less and less accountable. "Faceless bureaucrats", not likely to understand competition law nor value impartial application of law, will be charged with resolving disputes. Sovereignty and autonomy will be lost. So, too, will we lose the benefits of regulatory competition among nations.

4. Competition law is fact-specific, and the competition laws of nations differ. Dispute resolution panels will not know what the law is; nor will they be capable of developing rules of law; nor will they be able to handle the necessary fact-finding; nor can they be trusted to handle confidential documents, while if deprived of the documents, they will be unable to find the necessary facts.

None of these arguments, even if otherwise valid, is applicable to the proposal. The proposal contains a choice-of-law rule: the law of the excluding nation applies. If the forum's domestic competition rules are consumer-oriented, they will continue to be so in the international arena. If the forum's domestic competition rules also protect sellers' rights of access, they will continue to do so.

As for dispute resolution and confidentiality, the only issue subject to dispute resolution would be the alleged violation of the terms of the agreement itself; for example, not adopting the agreed substantive law or procedural safeguards. A dispute resolution panel would not act as a trial court to resolve facts. It could determine, on the basis of the record and with deference to the national court, whether the national law was credibly (nondiscriminatorily) applied—the standard of review under NAFTA Article 19. The main remedies would be self-empowering remedies: the requirements that each nation has a hospitable, accessible procedural system so that victims can enforce their own rights (as in TRIPs); and the acknowledgment that, if rights cannot feasibly be exonerated in the excluding nation, the victim (nation or firm) may sue in its home courts—thus solving by agreement the problem of extraterritorial legitimacy.

Transparency regarding and accountability of the dispute resolution process should be assured by requirements of reasoned decisions and publication of decisions.

The effort then is to provide a minimal but meaningful, largely self-executing, system that exemplifies the spirit of the EU principle of subsidiarity, and that also, and thereby, allows the continued interplay of regulatory competition among nations and regulatory choices by nations.

It may be argued that the proposal is too unambitious. Strikingly, it does not cover cartels as such, although cartels are—at least to Americans—the most heinous antitrust restraint. It does not cover even export cartels, which are the most obvious sort of anticompetitive beggar-thy-neighbor conduct. It does not cover anti-dumping law reform, although it is possible that repeal of anti-dumping laws would produce more wealth and consumer welfare for the world than does antitrust enforcement itself. It does not cover the multitudinous, redundant merger control laws that impose high avoidable costs on global mergers. It does not provide for common world substantive standards, which would grease the wheels of trade and provide a helpful referent for the competition competences that are tucked into existing trade agreements, such as the GATS and the Telecoms annex. Each of these problems deserves attention.

Two of the excluded issues outlined above are tightly trade-related: anti-dumping laws and export cartels. Both deserve to be included in a WTO agreement. Both are excluded from the modest proposal for reasons of pragmatism.

The anti-dumping law controversy is so politically charged that its inclusion in a competition agenda at this time will sound the death knell of the agenda. Moreover, the anti-dumping law issue is not a competition *law* issue. Antitrust predatory pricing law is not a credible substitute for anti-dumping law; low-priced exports are almost never a part of exporters' strategy to monopolize foreign markets. The anti-dumping law issue must be dealt with on its own terms.

The export cartel problem is of a different order. Nations (at least now) seem to resist an initiative to ban export cartels on grounds of "sovereignty" (Why should we—nations ask—protect the foreigners?) The resistance is short-sighted. It is in everyone's interest to be free of export cartels in an integrated world. The resisters add: Inbound extraterritoriality is now widely accepted, and nations can protect themselves from off-shore cartels that harm their markets by applying their own laws and, if necessary, seeking co-operation from the cartelists' home country under principles of positive comity. Therefore national law works. At least, pressure is removed from the pressure point. The effort to eliminate export cartels at their source remains significant both substantively and symbolically; but politically and pragmatically the issue is not likely to advance the current competition agenda.

Each of the other problems is not tightly trade-related. Some are urgent. As to them, my point is not that pragmatism requires reticence but that these issues are at the heart of *competition* law, not trade law, and they deserve to be placed on "competition" ground. In some cases, continued conversations may produce more convergence of law and analysis, common understandings, and common culture. As to some issues, nations may and probably should reach agreement, much as environmental, labor, and intellectual property concerns have produced agreements outside of the trade arena to control externalities and to solve prisoners' dilemmas.

A free standing World Competition Forum should be created. * * *

* * *

In any event, an expanded competence for the WTO in relation to market access issues only would not be a trivial addition. The anticompetitive closing of foreign markets is a major perturbation in the world trading system, and conversely, the opening of closed markets promises major improvements in the trading system. A market access protocol promises not only to regularize and institutionalize the means to eliminate improper private restraints but also to narrow the occasions both for extraterritorial antitrust and for the use of anti-dumping laws.

As we move into the next century, and if and as countries such as China join the WTO, the problems of market access will surely deepen, and the line between public and private restraints will be increasingly opaque.

As expanded market access initiative will not be a panacea; and the market access proposal contained in this paper will probably catch only the clearest and simplest of consensus antitrust market-blocking wrongs; but at least we will have taken an important step forward to fill a gap.

Notes and Questions

(1) In light of the foregoing excerpts and the other materials in this chapter, would you say that there is enough consensus on competition issues to make international negotiations on competition rules meaningful and likely to succeed?

(2) In 1991, a Special Committee on International Antitrust of the American Bar Association's Section on Antitrust issued a working draft report, in which it concluded that no initiative on a world code should be pursued at present.[15]

15. American Bar Association Section on Antitrust, Special Committee on International Antitrust, Report 29 (Working draft, Sept. 1, 1991).

Chapter 24

TRADE AND INVESTMENT

SECTION 24.1   INTRODUCTION

The emphasis of this book is on international trade, but we would be remiss to ignore investment. Trade and foreign investment may be substitutes to a degree—if barriers to trade impede the export of finished products, manufacturers may elect instead to invest in a manufacturing facility in the target market. And as we further noted in the materials on trade in services, investment and services trade are often inextricably intertwined, especially where services exports require the establishment of a foreign presence in a target market. Barriers to investment, therefore, may have consequences akin to those of trade barriers. The political economy of investment barriers may thus track the political economy of trade policy to a considerable degree.

Many of the economic treaties that we have considered directly or indirectly create international rules that bear on investment. We touched briefly in Chapter 5 on the history of Friendship, Commerce and Navigation treaties, and the subsequent Bilateral Investment Treaties (BITs). Among other things, these agreements sought to secure opportunities for foreign investors and to protect prior investments against expropriation. GATT had something to say about investment rules as well—when restrictions on foreign investors had the effect of discouraging the importation of foreign goods, they had the potential to violate the GATT national treatment obligation or other GATT provisions. This principle was embodied formally in the Uruguay Round Agreement on Trade–Related Investment Measures (TRIMs), considered below. The Uruguay Round GATS has profound implications for investment in service sectors, as we noted in our chapter on trade in services.

Nevertheless, broad multilateral disciplines on investment restrictions remain lacking in the trading community. In response to this situation, and on the premise that considerable economic gains would attend a reduction in international barriers to investment, the OECD undertook during the 1990's to promote the concept of a Multilateral Agreement on Investment (MAI). The proposed MAI would have included general non-discrimination obligations, transparency provisions, provisions governing the migration of investors, provisions affecting state

1136

monopolies, and various sector specific disciplines, among other things.[1] The timing of the MAI initiative proved unfortunate from the perspective of its proponents. It ran squarely into the anti-globalization sentiment of the late 1990's, fueled in large measure by environmental and labor groups. The OECD has for now abandoned the initiative, although there is at this writing some discussion of taking up broader investment issues within the WTO. See Doha Declaration (Section 27.1 infra).

If global progress on investment issues has been slow, more dramatic developments are visible at the regional level. NAFTA incorporates broad rules on investment within the region, including general obligations to afford MFN and national treatment to NAFTA investors. The "investor rights" provisions of NAFTA are particularly remarkable in that they create private rights of action to enforce their terms (unlike most of the provisions of NAFTA, which can only be enforced by member nations), including a private right of action for damages in the event of "expropriation," a concept that has proved elusive.

The remainder of this chapter is divided into two sections. Section 24.2 considers the limited WTO rules on investment, with particular emphasis on the TRIMs agreement. Section 24.3 then considers some important recent developments under NAFTA.

SECTION 24.2 WTO AND TRIMS

Although GATT contains no direct restrictions on the ability of members to regulate foreign investment, it was settled before the Uruguay Round that restrictions on investors might impermissibly encourage the purchase of domestic over imported goods. In Canada—Administration of the Foreign Investment Review Act (FIRA),[1] Canada was accused of conditioning the approval of applications for foreign investment in Canada on commitments by the investor/applicant to use a certain amount of Canadian goods in their manufacturing operations. Such "domestic content" requirements were found to conflict with GATT Article III:4 (the panel did not reach the question whether Article III:5 had also been violated).

The TRIMs agreement, negotiated during the Uruguay Round, built on the Canadian FIRA case to prohibit trade-related investment measures that conflict with Article III or Article XI of GATT. Domestic content restrictions are offered as an illustration of such measures in the annex to TRIMs, as are certain other restrictions on the ability of investors to import or export. The TRIMs agreement was one of many provisions of WTO law at issue in a dispute between Indonesia and major automobile exporters (Japan, the European Union and the United States) over Indonesia's programs to encourage the development of its domestic auto industry.

---

1. The 1998 negotiating text for the MAI may be found in the ASIL basic documents of international economic law, 1998 BDIEL AD LEXIS 33.

1. GATT, 30th Supp. BISD 140 (panel report adopted Feb. 7, 1984).

INDONESIA—CERTAIN MEASURES AFFECTING THE AUTOMOBILE INDUSTRY

WT/DS44/R

Panel Report adopted by the DSB on July 23, 1998

CLAIMS OF LOCAL CONTENT REQUIREMENTS

14.58 The European Communities and the United States claim that the 1993 car programme, by providing for local content requirements linked to tax benefits for finished cars incorporating a certain percentage value of domestic products, and to customs duty benefits for imported parts and components used in cars incorporating a certain percentage value of domestic products, violates the provisions of Article 2 of the TRIMs Agreement, and Article III:4 of the GATT.

14.59 Japan, the European Communities and the United States also claim that the 1996 car programme, by providing for local content requirements linked to tax benefits for National Cars (which by definition incorporate a certain percentage value of domestic products), and to customs duty benefits for imported parts and components used in National Cars, violates the provisions of Article 2 of the TRIMs Agreement and Article III:4 of the GATT.

* * *

14.63 As to which claims, those under Article III:4 of GATT or Article 2 of the TRIMs Agreement, to examine first, we consider that we should first examine the claims under the TRIMs Agreement since the TRIMs Agreement is more specific than Article III:4 as far as the claims under consideration are concerned. * * *

THE APPLICATION OF THE TRIMS AGREEMENT

14.64 Article 2.1 of the TRIMs Agreement provides that

"... no Member shall apply any TRIM that is inconsistent with the provisions of Article III or Article XI of GATT 1994."

By its terms, Article 2.1 requires two elements to be shown to establish a violation thereof: first, the existence of a TRIM; second, that TRIM is inconsistent with Article III or Article XI of GATT. No claims have been raised with reference to a violation of Article XI of GATT.

* * *

14.66 We note also that Article 2.2 of the TRIMs Agreement provides:

"2.2 An Illustrative List of TRIMs that are inconsistent with the obligations of national treatment provided for in paragraph 4 of Article III of GATT 1994 ... is contained in the Annex to this Agreement."

* * *

ARE THE INDONESIAN MEASURES "INVESTMENT MEASURES"?

14.73 We note that the use of the broad term "investment measures" indicates that the TRIMs Agreement is not limited to measures taken specifically in regard to *foreign* investment. Contrary to India's argument, we find that nothing in the TRIMs Agreement suggests that the nationality of the ownership of enterprises subject to a particular measure is an element in deciding whether that measure is covered by the Agreement. We therefore find without textual support in the TRIMs Agreement the argument that since the TRIMs Agreement is basically designed to govern and provide a level playing field for foreign investment, measures relating to internal taxes or subsidies cannot be construed to be a trade-related investment measure. We recall in this context that internal tax advantages or subsidies are only one of many types of advantages which may be tied to a local content requirement which is a principal focus of the TRIMs Agreement. The TRIMs Agreement is not concerned with subsidies and internal taxes as such but rather with local content requirements, compliance with which may be encouraged through providing any type of advantage. Nor, in any case, do we see why an internal measure would necessarily not govern the treatment of foreign investment.

14.74 We next consider whether the Indonesian measures are investment measures. In this regard, we consider the following extracts (emphases added) from the official Indonesian legislation relevant and instructive.

14.75 With regard to the 1993 car programme, we note:

— The "considerations section" of the Decree of the Ministry of Industry announcing the 1993 car programme states:

> "a. that within the framework of *supporting and promoting the development of the automotive industry and/or the component industry* in the future, it is deemed necessary to regulate the local content levels of domestically produced motor vehicles or components in connection with the grant of incentives in the imposition of import duty rates;
>
> b. that in order to *further strengthen domestic industrial development* by taking into account the trend of technological advance and the increase of the capability and mastering of industrial design and engineering, it is necessary to improve the relevant existing regulations already laid down;"

— The "considerations section" of the 1995 amendment to the 1993 car programme states:

> "That *in the framework of further promoting of the development of the motor vehicles industry and/or domestically produced components*, it is considered necessary to amend . . ."

14.76 With regard to the February 1996 car programme, we note the following:

— The title of the Presidential Instruction for the National Car programme (No. 2) is "The *Development* of the National Automobile Industry".

— Paragraph a) of the "Considering" section of the Government Regulation No. 20 states:

"that in the effort *to promote the growth of the domestic automotive industry*, it is deemed necessary to enact regulations concerning the Sales Tax on Luxury Goods upon the delivery of domestically produced motor vehicles".

— In addition, the State Minister for Mobilization of Investment Funds/Chairman of the Investment Coordinating Board issued a decree entitled "Investment Regulations within the Framework of the Realisation of the Establishment of the National Automobile Industry" which emphasized that the new measures were intended to promote investment, stating in its fifth considering:

"5. that it is therefore necessary to issue *a decree for the regulation of investment* in the national automobile industry."

— Article 2 of that same Investment Regulation by the Minister of State for Mobilization of Investment Funds/Chairman of the Investment Coordinating Board provides:

"In order *to realise the development of the national automobile industry* as meant in Article 1:

1.   . . .

2.   *In the endeavour to realise the development of such national car industry, the investment approval will be issued to the automobile industry sector with tax facilities in accordance with legal provisions enacted specifically for such purpose.*"

— The Decision relating to the investment facilities regarding the Determination of PT. Timor Putra National to Establish and Produce a National Car, entitled "Decision of the State Minister for the Mobilization of Investment Funds/Chairman of the Capital Investment Co-ordinating Board" states:

"1.   That *in implementing a national car industry it is deemed necessary to determine investment approval* for a car industry which will build and produce a national car.

2.   That in the framework of investment for the car industry, PT.Timor Putra National has submitted an application and working program to build a national car industry and *has obtained domestic investment approval* (PMDN) NO.607/PMDN/ 1995, dated 9 November 1995".

14.77   With regard to the June 1996 car programme, we note that the "Considering" section of the Decree of the President of the Republic No. 4267 on the Extension (June) to the February 1996 car programme provides:

"a. that the *development of the national car is aimed at improving the nation's self-reliance* ... and to achieve this solid preparations and continuous support are necessary;

b. that the preparation for domestic production of national cars require the *availability of huge financing* and therefore will be carried out in stages;

c. that in connection with the preparations, it is considered necessary to establish a policy on the implementation stage of the production of national cars."

— The "Considering" section of the Government Regulation No. 3667 states:

"That within the *framework of promoting the development of the automotive industry in the increased use of domestically produced automotive components*, it is deemed necessary to grant Sales Tax on Luxury Goods facilities to the group of luxury goods upon delivery of certain motor vehicles"

— The Elucidation to the Government Regulation No. 36 states:

"Within the *framework of speeding up the realisation of production of national motor vehicles using domestically made automotive components, it is necessary to promote the domestic automotive industry* in order to further its growth particularly in the face of global competition. *One of the endeavours which can be exerted is the provision of a tax incentive in the form of exemption* from the assessment of Sales Tax on Luxury Goods on the delivery of certain motor vehicles which have achieved certain levels of local content."

14.78 We note also that Indonesia indicates that the objectives of the National Car programme include the following:

— To improve the competitiveness of local companies and strengthen overall industrial development;

— To develop the capacity of multiple-source auto parts and components;

— To encourage the development of the automotive industry and the automotive component industry;

— To bring about major structural changes in the Indonesian automobile industry;

— To encourage the transfer of technology and contribute to large-scale job creation;

— To encourage car companies to increase their local content, resulting in a rapid growth of investment in the automobile industry.

14.79 Indonesia has also stated that PT TPN is a "domestic capital investment company".

14.80   On the basis of our reading of these measures applied by Indonesia under the 1993 and the 1996 car programmes, which have investment objectives and investment features and which refer to investment programmes, we find that these measures are aimed at encouraging the development of a local manufacturing capability for finished motor vehicles and parts and components in Indonesia. Inherent to this objective is that these measures necessarily have a significant impact on investment in these sectors. For this reason, we consider that these measures fall within any reasonable interpretation of the term "investment measures". We do not intend to provide an overall definition of what constitutes an investment measure. We emphasize that our characterization of the measures as "investment measures" is based on an examination of the manner in which the measures at issue in this case relate to investment. There may be other measures which qualify as investment measures within the meaning of the TRIMs Agreement because they relate to investment in a different manner.

14.81   With respect to the arguments of Indonesia that the measures at issue are not investment measures because the Indonesian Government does not regard the programmes as investment programmes and because the measures have not been adopted by the authorities responsible for investment policy, we believe that there is nothing in the text of the TRIMs Agreement to suggest that a measure is not an investment measure simply on the grounds that a Member does not characterize the measure as such, or on the grounds that the measure is not explicitly adopted as an investment regulation. In any event, we note that some of the regulations and decisions adopted pursuant to these car programmes were adopted by investment bodies.

Are the Indonesian measures "trade-related"?

14.82   We now have to determine whether these investment measures are "trade-related". We consider that, if these measures are local content requirements, they would necessarily be "trade-related" because such requirements, by definition, always favour the use of domestic products over imported products, and therefore affect trade.

Illustrative List of the TRIMs Agreement

14.83   An examination of whether these measures are covered by Item (1) of the Illustrative List of TRIMs annexed to the TRIMs Agreement, which refers amongst other situations to measures with local content requirements, will not only indicate whether they are trade-related but also whether they are inconsistent with Article III:4 and thus in violation of Article 2.1 of the TRIMs Agreement.

14.84   The Annex to the TRIMs Agreement reads as follows:

"ANNEX: ILLUSTRATIVE LIST

1.   TRIMs that are inconsistent with the obligation of national treatment provided for in paragraph 4 of Article III of GATT 1994 include those which are mandatory or enforceable under domestic

law or under administrative rulings, or compliance with which is necessary to obtain an advantage, and which require:

(a) the purchase or use by an enterprise of products of domestic origin or from any domestic source, whether specified in terms of particular products, in terms of volume or value of products, or in terms of a proportion of volume or value of its local production;"

14.85 We note that all the various decrees and regulations implementing the Indonesian car programmes operate in the same manner. They provide for tax advantages on finished motor vehicles using a certain percentage value of local content and additional customs duty advantages on imports of parts and components to be used in finished motor vehicles using a certain percentage value of local content. We also note that under the June 1996 car programme, the local content envisaged in the February 1996 car programme could be performed through an undertaking by the foreign producer of National Cars to counterpurchase Indonesian parts and components.

14.86 For instance, the Decision to issue the Decree of the Minister of Industry Concerning The Determination of Local Content Levels of Domestically Made Motor Vehicles or Components attached to the Decree of the Ministry of Industry announcing the 1993 car programme states in its Article 2:

"(1) The Automotive Industry and/or the Components Industry *may obtain certain Incentives* within the framework of importing needed Components, Sub–Components, basic materials and semi-Finished Goods, originating in one source as well as various sources (multi sourcing), *if the production has reached/can achieve certain Local Content levels.* (. . .)

(3) The *Local Content levels* of domestically made Motor Vehicles and/or Components which are *eligible for Incentives* including their Incentive rates shall be those listed in Attachment I to this decree." (emphasis added)

The Instruction of the President of the Republic of Indonesia No.2 of 1996 of the National Car programme (dated 19 February 1998) states in its "INSTRUCT . . . SECONDLY:

"WITHIN the framework of establishment of the National Car Industry:

1. The Minister of Industry and Trade will foster, guide and grant facilities in accordance with provisions of laws in effect such that the national car industry:

a. uses a brand name of its own;

b. *uses components produced domestically as much as possible*;

c. is able to export its products." (emphasis added)

More specifically Regulation No. 20/1996 established the following sales tax structure where passenger cars of more than 1600cc and jeeps with local content of less than 60% would pay 35% tax; passenger cars of less than 1600cc, jeeps with local content of more than 60%, and light commercial vehicles (other than jeeps using gas) would pay 20% tax; and National Cars would pay 0% tax. We recall that one of the requirements for designation as a "National Car" is that the local content rate must be 20% at the end of the first year, 40% at the end of the second year and 60% at the end of the third year.

14.87 We also note with reference to the June 1996 car programme, that the Decree of the President of the Republic of Indonesia Number 42 of 1996 on the production of National Cars provides in Article 1:

"National Cars which are made overseas by Indonesian workers and fulfil the local content stipulated by the Minister of Industry and Trade will be treated equally to those made in Indonesia."

The Decree of the Minister of Industry and Trade adopted pursuant to this Presidential Decree 42 states in Articles 1, 2 and 3:

"ARTICLE 1

Within the framework of preparations, the production of national cars can be carried out overseas for a one-time maximum period of 1 (one) year on the condition that Indonesian made parts and components are used.

ARTICLE 2

The procurement of Indonesian made parts and components shall be performed through a system of counter purchase of parts and components of motor vehicles by the overseas company carrying out the production and reexporting of national cars to Indonesia.

ARTICLE 3

The value of the Counter purchase referred to in Article 2 shall be fixed at the minimum of 25% (twenty-five percent) of the import value of the national cars assembled abroad (C & F value)".

14.88 We believe that under these measures compliance with the provisions for the purchase and use of particular products of domestic origin is necessary to obtain the tax and customs duty benefits on these car programmes, as referred to in Item 1(a) of the Illustrative List of TRIMs.

14.89 We need now to decide whether these tax and customs duty benefits are "advantages" in the meaning of the chapeau of paragraph 1 of that Illustrative List. In the context of the claims under Article III:4 of GATT, Indonesia has argued that the reduced customs duties are not internal regulations and as such cannot be covered by the wording of Article III:4. We do not consider that the matter before us in connection with Indonesia's obligations under the TRIMs Agreement is the customs duty relief as such but rather the internal regulations, i.e. the provisions on purchase and use of domestic products, compliance with which is necessary to obtain an advantage, which advantage here is the customs duty relief. The lower duty rates are clearly "advantages" in the meaning of the chapeau of the Illustrative List to the TRIMs Agreement and as such, we find that the Indonesian measures fall within the scope of the Item 1 of the Illustrative List of TRIMs.

14.90   Indonesia also argues that the local content requirements of its car programmes do not constitute classic local content requirements within the meaning of the *FIRA* panel (which involved a binding contract between the investor and the Government of Canada) because they leave companies free to decide from which source to purchase parts and components. We note that the Indonesian producers or assemblers of motor vehicles (or motor vehicle parts) must satisfy the local content targets of the relevant measures in order to take advantage of the customs duty and tax benefits offered by the Government. The wording of the Illustrative List of the TRIMs Agreement makes it clear that a simple advantage conditional on the use of domestic goods is considered to be a violation of Article 2 of the TRIMs Agreement even if the local content requirement is not binding as such. We note in addition that this argument has also been rejected in the Panel Report on *Parts and Components*.

14.91   We thus find that the tax and tariff benefits contingent on meeting local requirements under these car programmes constitute "advantages". Given this and our earlier analysis of whether these local content requirements are TRIMs and covered by the Illustrative List annexed to the TRIMs Agreement, we further find that they are in violation of Article 2.1 of the TRIMs Agreement.

14.92   We note that a violation of Article 2.1 of the TRIMs Agreement may be justified under Articles 3, 4 or 5 of the TRIMs Agreement. However, Indonesia has not invoked any of the general exceptions of GATT as referred to in Article 3 of the TRIMs Agreement, nor the provisions available to developing countries referred to in Article 4. In addition, Indonesia does not claim that the measures in dispute benefit from the transitional period under Article 5 of the TRIMs Agreement.

Notes and Questions

(1) Numerous other provisions of WTO law were at issue in the case, resulting in several findings of violations by Indonesia. The case was not appealed.

(2) Consider the illustrative list of TRIMs in the annex to the agreement—are you clear on the distinction between TRIMs that conflict with GATT Article III and TRIMs that conflict with GATT Article XI?

(3) Pay attention to the relationship between the TRIMs Agreement and GATS. Suppose Indonesia required that foreign-owned banks must hire 90% of their workforce from the domestic labor force at some minimum wage or above—requirements that do not apply to domestically-owned banks. Does

the TRIMs Agreement have any bearing on the permissibility of such policies?

(4) Reflect on the scope of the TRIMs Agreement. Suppose that a government enacts discriminatory corporate tax rates that are higher on corporations whose shareholders are predominantly foreign. Is that measure a TRIM? What about a rule that prohibits foreign investors from bidding on the rights to harvest timber from government lands, where most of the lumber produced therefrom will eventually be exported?

(5) The Canadian *FIRA* case, noted in the introduction to this section, involved a further challenge to Canada's so-called "export performance requirements," whereby commitments were extracted from investors to export some proportion of the output from their manufacturing facilities. The *FIRA* panel determined that such requirements did not violate GATT. Was the panel correct (see GATT Article XVII:1(c))? Does the TRIMs Agreement do anything to condemn export performance requirements?

SECTION 24.3   INVESTOR RIGHTS UNDER NAFTA

Before proceeding, the reader should review the investment provisions contained in NAFTA Chapter 11. Section A contains the substantive obligations. In addition to general non-discrimination principles, note the elaboration of the issues addressed by the TRIMs Agreement in Article 1106 on "Performance Requirements." (In what ways does NAFTA go farther than the TRIMs Agreement in constraining such measures?) Note also Article 1110, which affords investors a right to compensation for "expropriation."

Section B pertains to the settlement of disputes between investors and NAFTA members. It permits investors to submit claims involving the violation of provisions in Section A to arbitration through the International Center for the Settlement of Investment Disputes (ICSID, affiliated with the World Bank) or under UNCITRAL arbitration rules. It thus creates a "private right of action" that is quite unusual in the world of trade agreements (the European Union affords private rights of action on "trade issues" to its citizens, however, as do typical BITs.) In addition to the private action, Section B allows the arbitrators to award monetary damages.

These investor rights provisions were perhaps expected to be of little moment when NAFTA was negotiated, in part because private rights of action had not been perceived as problematic during the history of BITs. Inspired by modern thinking about "regulatory takings," however, investor plaintiffs under NAFTA have advanced some unexpected claims of "expropriation," which have made the investor rights provisions highly controversial and has led NAFTA members to consider the possibility of changing them. In the materials that follow, we afford a flavor of the developments to date.

AZINIAN v. UNITED MEXICAN STATES

International Centre for the Settlement of Investment
Disputes (Additional Facility)
Case No. ARB(AF)/97/2

AWARD, NOVEMBER 1, 1999[1]

Before the Arbitral Tribunal constituted under Chapter Eleven of the North American Free Trade Agreement

[The claimants were American citizens and shareholders of DESONA, a Mexican corporation formed for the purpose of providing solid waste disposal services to the city of Naucalpan de Juarez pursuant to a "concession contract" entered in 1993.]

9. On 15 November, the Concession Contract was signed. Two days later DESONA commenced its commercial and industrial waste collection * * *.

* * *

12. In January and February, there were a number of meetings between the personnel of DESONA and the Ayuntamiento [the City Council] concerning implementation of the Concession Contract. * * *

13. In mid-February, the Ayuntamiento sought independent legal advice about the Concession Contract. It was advised that there were 27 "irregularities" in connection with the conclusion and performance of the Concession Contract.

* * *

17. On 21 March, despite a protest from DESONA on 16 March, the Ayuntamiento decided to annul the Concession Contract. * * *

* * *

21. On 13 July, DESONA appealed to the Superior Chamber of the Administrative Tribunal, which upheld the Ayuntamiento's annulment of the Concession Contract by a judgment dated 17 November. The Superior Chamber held that of the 27 alleged irregularities, nine had been demonstrated. Of these, seven related to various perceived misrepresentations by the Claimants in connection with the conclusion of the Concession Contract.

22. On 10 December, DESONA lodged a further appeal, in the form of a so-called amparo petition, to the Federal Circuit Court.

23. On 18 May 1995, the Federal Circuit Court ruled in favour of the Naucalpan Ayuntamiento, specifically upholding the Superior Chamber's judgment as to the legality of the nine bases accepted for the annulment.

1. 39 Intl. Legal Materials 537 (2000).

24. On 17 March 1997, the Claimant shareholders of DESONA initiated the present arbitral proceedings against the Government of Mexico under Chapter Eleven of the North American Free Trade Agreement (hereinafter "NAFTA"), by submitting a claim to arbitration pursuant to Article 1137(1)(b) thereof.

* * *

75. The Claimants contend that "the City's wrongful repudiation of the Concession Contract violates Articles 1110 ("Expropriation and Compensation") and 1105 ("Minimum Standard of Treatment") of NAFTA" and accordingly seek the following relief, as articulated in their Prayer for Relief dated 23 June 1999:

"A. With respect to the enterprise, as follows:

1. The value of the concession as an ongoing enterprise on March 21, 1994, the date of the taking based upon the values obtained: * * *

2. Interest on the amount awarded as the value of the concession as set forth in section A above from the date of the taking at the rate of 10% per annum to the date of the award.

3. Cost of the proceedings, including but not limited to attorneys fees, experts and accounting fees and administrative fees. * * *

* * *

79. As this is the first dispute brought by an investor under NAFTA to be resolved by an award on the merits, it is appropriate to consider first principles.

80. NAFTA is a treaty among three sovereign States which deals with a vast range of matters relating to the liberalisation of trade. Part Five deals with "Investment, Services and Related Matters." Chapter Eleven thereunder deals specifically with "Investment."

81. Section A of Chapter Eleven establishes a number of substantive obligations with respect to investments. Section B concerns jurisdiction and procedure; it defines the method by which an investor claiming a violation of the obligations established in Section A may seek redress.

82. Arbitral jurisdiction under Section B is limited not only as to the persons who may invoke it (they must be nationals of a State signatory to NAFTA), but also as to subject matter: claims may not be submitted to investor-state arbitration under Chapter Eleven unless they are founded upon the violation of an obligation established in Section A.

83. To put it another way, a foreign investor entitled in principle to protection under NAFTA may enter into contractual relations with a public authority, and may suffer a breach by that authority, and still not be in a position to state a claim under NAFTA. It is a fact of life everywhere that individuals may be disappointed in their dealings with public authorities, and disappointed yet again when national courts reject their complaints. It may safely be assumed that many Mexican

parties can be found who had business dealings with governmental entities which were not to their satisfaction; Mexico is unlikely to be different from other countries in this respect. NAFTA was not intended to provide foreign investors with blanket protection from this kind of disappointment, and nothing in its terms so provides.

84.   It therefore would not be sufficient for the Claimants to convince the present Arbitral Tribunal that the actions or motivations of the Naucalpan Ayuntamiento are to be disapproved, or that the reasons given by the Mexican courts in their three judgements are unpersuasive. Such considerations are unavailing unless the Claimants can point to a violation of an obligation established in Section A of Chapter Eleven attributable to the Government of Mexico.

85.   The Claimants have alleged violations of the following two provisions of NAFTA:

Article 1110(1)

"No party may directly or indirectly nationalize or expropriate an investment of an investor of another Party in its territory or take a measure tantamount to nationalization or expropriation of such investment ("expropriation") except:

(a) for a public purpose;

(b) on a non-discriminatory basis;

(c) in accordance with due process of law and Article 1105(1); and

(d) on payment of compensation in accordance with paragraphs 2 through 6."

Article 1105(1)

"Each Party shall accord to investments of investors of another Party treatment in accordance with international law, including fair and equitable treatment and full protection and security."

86.   Although the parties to the Concession Contract accepted the jurisdiction of the Mexican courts, the Claimants correctly point out that they did not exclude recourse to other courts or arbitral tribunals—such as this one—having jurisdiction on another foundation. Nor is the fact that the Claimants took the initiative before the Mexican courts fatal to the jurisdiction of the present Arbitral Tribunal. The Claimants have cited a number of cases where international arbitral tribunals did not consider themselves bound by decisions of national courts. Professor Dodge, in his oral argument, stressed the following sentence from the well-known ICSID case of Amco v. Indonesia: "An international tribunal is not bound to follow the result of a national court." As the Claimants argue persuasively, it would be unfortunate if potential claimants under NAFTA were dissuaded from seeking relief under domestic law from national courts, because such actions might have the salutary effect of resolving the dispute without resorting to investor-state arbitration under NAFTA. Nor finally has the Respondent argued that it cannot be

held responsible for the actions of a local governmental authority like the Ayuntamiento of Naucalpan.

87.   The problem is that the Claimants' fundamental complaint is that they are the victims of a breach of the Concession Contract. NAFTA does not, however, allow investors to seek international arbitration for mere contractual breaches. Indeed, NAFTA cannot possibly be read to create such a regime, which would have elevated a multitude of ordinary transactions with public authorities into potential international disputes. The Claimants simply could not prevail merely by persuading the Arbitral Tribunal that the Ayuntamiento of Naucalpan breached the Concession Contract.

88.   Understanding this proposition perfectly well, Professor Dodge insisted that the claims are not simply for breach of contract, but involve "the direct expropriation of DESONA's contractual rights" and "the indirect expropriation of DESONA itself."

89.   Professor Dodge then argued that a breach of contract constitutes an expropriation "if it is confiscatory," or, quoting Professor Brownlie, Principles of Public International Law, 5th edition at 550, if "the state exercises its executive or legislative authority to destroy the contractual rights as an asset." Specifically, he invoked a "wealth of authority treating the repudiation of concession agreements as an expropriation of contractual rights."

90.   Labelling is, however, no substitute for analysis. The words "confiscatory," "destroy contractual rights as an asset," or "repudiation" may serve as a way to describe breaches which are to be treated as extraordinary, and therefore as acts of expropriation, but they certainly do not indicate on what basis the critical distinction between expropriation and an ordinary breach of contract is to be made. The egregiousness of any breach is in the eye of the beholder—and that is not satisfactory for present purposes.

91.   It is therefore necessary to examine whether the annulment of the Concession Contract may be considered to be an act of expropriation violating NAFTA Article 1110. If not, the claim must fail. The question cannot be more central.

92.   Before examining this crucial issue, it should be recalled that the Claimants originally grounded their claim on an alleged violation of Article 1105 as well as one of Article 1110. While they have never abandoned the ground of Article 1105, it figured very fleetingly in their later pleadings, and not at all in Professor Dodge's final arguments. This is hardly surprising. The only conceivably relevant substantive principle of Article 1105 is that a NAFTA investor should not be dealt with in a manner that contravenes international law. There has not been a claim of such a violation of international law other than the one more specifically covered by Article 1110. In a feeble attempt to maintain Article 1105, the Claimants' Reply Memorial affirms that the breach of the Concession Contract violated international law because it was "motivated by noncommercial considerations, and compensatory damages

were not paid." This is but a paraphrase of a complaint more specifically covered by Article 1110. For the avoidance of doubt, the Arbitral Tribunal therefore holds that under the circumstances of this case if there was no violation of Article 1110, there was none of Article 1105 either.

93. The Respondent argues that the Concession Contract came to an end on two independently justified grounds: invalidity and rescission.

94. The second is the more complex. It postulates that the Ayuntamiento was entitled to rescind the Concession Contract due to DESONA's failure of performance. If the Ayuntamiento was not so entitled, its termination of the Concession Contract was itself a breach. Most of the evidence and debate in these proceedings have focused on this issue: was DESONA in substantial non-compliance with the Concession Contract? The subject is complicated by the fact that DESONA was apparently not given the benefit of the 30–day cure period defined in Article 31 of the Concession Contract.

95. The logical starting point is to examine the asserted original invalidity of the Concession Contract. If this assertion was founded, there is no need to make findings with respect to performance; nor can there be a question of curing original invalidity.

96. From this perspective, the problem may be put quite simply. The Ayuntamiento believed it had grounds for holding the Concession Contract to be invalid under Mexican law governing public service concessions. At DESONA's initiative, these grounds were tested by three levels of Mexican courts, and in each case were found to be extant. How can it be said that Mexico breached NAFTA when the Ayuntamiento of Naucalpan purported to declare the invalidity of a Concession Contract which by its terms was subject to Mexican law, and to the jurisdiction of the Mexican courts, and the courts of Mexico then agreed with the Ayuntamiento's determination? Further, the Claimants have neither contended nor proved that the Mexican legal standards for the annulment of concessions violate Mexico's Chapter Eleven obligations; nor that the Mexican law governing such annulments is expropriatory.

97. With the question thus framed, it becomes evident that for the Claimants to prevail it is not enough that the Arbitral Tribunal disagree with the determination of the Ayuntamiento. A governmental authority surely cannot be faulted for acting in a manner validated by its courts unless the courts themselves are disavowed at the international level. As the Mexican courts found that the Ayuntamiento's decision to nullify the Concession Contract was consistent with the Mexican law governing the validity of public service concessions, the question is whether the Mexican court decisions themselves breached Mexico's obligations under Chapter Eleven.

98. True enough, an international tribunal called upon to rule on a Government's compliance with an international treaty is not paralysed by the fact that the national courts have approved the relevant conduct of public officials. As a former President of the International Court of Justice put it: "The principles of the separation and independence of the

judiciary in municipal law and of respect for the finality of judicial decisions have exerted an important influence on the form in which the general principle of State responsibility has been applied to acts or omissions of judicial organs. These basic tenets of judicial organization explain the reluctance to be found in some arbitral awards of the last century to admit the extension to the judiciary of the rule that a State is responsible for the acts of all its organs. However, in the present century State responsibility for acts of judicial organs came to be recognized. Although independent of the Government, the judiciary is not independent of the State: the judgment given by a judicial authority emanates from an organ of the State in just the same way as a law promulgated by the legislature or a decision taken by the executive. The responsibility of the State for acts of judicial authorities may result from three different types of judicial decision. The first is a decision of a municipal court clearly incompatible with a rule of international law. The second is what it known traditionally as a 'denial of justice.' The third occurs when, in certain exceptional and well-defined circumstances, a State is responsible for a judicial decision contrary to municipal law." Eduardo Jimenez de Arechaga, "International Law in the Past Third of a Century," 159–1 Recueil des cours (General Course in Public International Law, The Hague, 1978). (Emphasis added.)

99.   The possibility of holding a State internationally liable for judicial decisions does not, however, entitle a claimant to seek international review of the national court decisions as though the international jurisdiction seised has plenary appellate jurisdiction. This is not true generally, and it is not true for NAFTA. What must be shown is that the court decision itself constitutes a violation of the treaty. Even if the Claimants were to convince this Arbitral Tribunal that the Mexican courts were wrong with respect to the invalidity of the Concession Contract, this would not per se be conclusive as to a violation of NAFTA. More is required; the Claimants must show either a denial of justice, or a pretence of form to achieve an internationally unlawful end.

100.   But the Claimants have raised no complaints against the Mexican courts; they do not allege a denial of justice. Without exception, they have directed their many complaints against the Ayuntamiento of Naucalpan. The Arbitral Tribunal finds that this circumstance is fatal to the claim, and makes it unnecessary to consider issues relating to performance of the Concession Contract. For if there is no complaint against a determination by a competent court that a contract governed by Mexican law was invalid under Mexican law, there is by definition no contract to be expropriated.

101.   The Arbitral Tribunal does not, however, wish to create the impression that the Claimants fail on account of an improperly pleaded case. The Arbitral Tribunal thus deems it appropriate, ex abundante cautela, to demonstrate that the Claimants were well advised not to seek to have the Mexican court decisions characterised as violations of NAFTA.

102.   A denial of justice could be pleaded if the relevant courts refuse to entertain a suit, if they subject it to undue delay, or if they administer justice in a seriously inadequate way. There is no evidence, or even argument, that any such defects can be ascribed to the Mexican proceedings in this case.

103.   There is a fourth type of denial of justice, namely the clear and malicious misapplication of the law. This type of wrong doubtless overlaps with the notion of "pretence of form" to mask a violation of international law. In the present case, not only has no such wrongdoing been pleaded, but the Arbitral Tribunal wishes to record that it views the evidence as sufficient to dispel any shadow over the bona fides of the Mexican judgments. Their findings cannot possibly be said to have been arbitrary, let alone malicious.

Notes and Questions

(1) Suppose an "investor" loses a breach of contract action against a private party in the national courts of a member state. Might that conceivably constitute "expropriation?" Should such a claim be possible?

(2) Must a potential claimant exhaust its remedies under national law before proceeding to NAFTA arbitration? Sensible? As a strategic matter, how should a potential complainant proceed in deciding when to initiate NAFTA arbitration? How should arbitrators approach a case in which no authoritative judicial decision has been rendered in a national court?

(3) What behavior would constitute a "clear and malicious" misapplication of the law? How might a court "administer justice in a seriously inadequate way?" Do these principles mean that the arbitrators should apply a highly deferential standard of review, but may hold for the complainant in cases where the arbitrators find clear legal error? Or must the complainant show that national courts exhibited personal animosity, corruption, or some other impropriety?

METALCLAD CORP. v. UNITED MEXICAN STATES

40 I.L.M. 36 (2001).
Before the Arbitral Tribunal constituted under Chapter Eleven
of the North American Free Trade Agreement

1.   This dispute arises out of the activities of the Claimant, Metalclad Corporation (hereinafter "Metalclad"), in the Mexican Municipality of Guadalcazar (hereinafter "Guadalcazar"), located in the Mexican State of San Luis Potosi (hereinafter "SLP"). Metalclad alleges that Respondent, the United Mexican States (hereinafter "Mexico"), through its local governments of SLP and Guadalcazar, interfered with its development and operation of a hazardous waste landfill. Metalclad claims that this interference is a violation of the Chapter Eleven investment provisions of the North American Free Trade Agreement (hereinafter "NAFTA"). * * *

2.   Metalclad is an enterprise of the United States of America, incorporated under the laws of Delaware. EcoMetalclad Corporation

(hereinafter "ECO") is an enterprise of the United States of America, incorporated under the laws of Utah. Eco is wholly-owned by Metalclad, and owns 100% of the shares in Ecosistemas Nacionales, S.A. de C.V. (hereinafter "ECONSA), a Mexican corporation. In 1993, ECONSA purchased the Mexican company Confinamiento Tecnico de Residuos Industriales, S.A. de C.V. (hereinafter "COTERIN") with a view to the acquisition, development and operation of the latter's hazardous waste transfer station and landfill in the valley of La Pedrera, located in Guadalcazar. COTERIN is the owner of record of the landfill property as well as the permits and licenses which are at the base of this dispute.

* * *

28. In 1990 the federal government of Mexico authorized COTERIN to construct and operate a transfer station for hazardous waste in La Pedrera, a valley located in Guadalcazar in SLP. * * *

29. On January 23, 1993, the National Ecological Institute (hereinafter "INE"), an independent sub-agency of the federal Secretariat of the Mexican Environment, National Resources and Fishing (hereinafter "SEMARNAP"), granted COTERIN a federal permit to construct a hazardous waste landfill in La Pedrera (hereinafter "the landfill").

* * *

31. Shortly thereafter, on May 11, 1993, the government of SLP granted COTERIN a state land use permit to construct the landfill. * * *

32. One month later, on June 11 1993, Metalclad met with Governor of SLP to discuss the project. Metalclad asserts that at this meeting it obtained the Governor's support for the project. In fact, the Governor acknowledged at the hearing that a reasonable person might expect that the Governor would support the project if studies confirmed the site as suitable or feasible and if the environmental impact was consistent with Mexican standards.

33. Metalclad further asserts that it was told by the President of the INE and the General Director of the Mexican Secretariat of Urban Development and Ecology (hereinafter "SEDUE" [the predecessor organization to SEMARNAP]) that all necessary permits for the landfill had been issued with the exception of the federal permit for operation of the landfill. A witness statement submitted by the President of the INE suggests that a hazardous waste landfill could be built if all permits required by the corresponding federal and state laws have been acquired.

34. Metalclad also asserts that the General Director of SEDUE told Metalclad that the responsibility for obtaining project support in the state and local community lay with the federal government.

35. On August 10, 1993, the INE granted COTERIN the federal permit for operation of the landfill. On September 10, 1993, Metalclad * * * purchased COTERIN, the landfill site and the associated permits.

* * *

37.   Metalclad asserts that shortly after its purchase of COTERIN, the Governor of SLP embarked on a public campaign to denounce and prevent the operation of the landfill.

38.   Metalclad further asserts, however, that in April 1994, after months of negotiation, Metalclad believed that it had secured SLP's agreement to support the project. Consequently, in May 1994, after receiving an eighteen-month extension of the previously issued federal construction permit from the INE, Metalclad began construction of the landfill. Mexico denies the SLP's agreement or support had ever been obtained.

* * *

45.   Metalclad completed construction of the landfill in March 1995. On March 10, 1995, Metalclad held an "open house," or "inauguration," of the landfill which was attended by a number of dignitaries from the United State and from Mexico's federal, state and local governments.

46.   Demonstrators impeded the "inauguration," blocked the exit and entry of buses carrying guests and workers, and employed tactics of intimidation against Metalclad. Metalclad asserts that the demonstration was organized at least in part by the Mexican state and local governments, and that state troopers assisted in blocking traffic into and out of the site. Metalclad was thenceforth effectively prevented from opening the landfill.

* * *

50.   On December 5, 1995, thirteen months after Metalclad's application for the municipal construction permit was filed, the application was denied. * * *

* * *

52.   Metaclad has pointed out that there was no evidence of inadequacy of performance by Metaclad of any legal obligation, nor any showing that Metalclad violated the terms of any federal or state permit; that there was no evidence that the Municipality gave any consideration to the recently completed environmental reports indicating that the site was in fact suitable for a hazardous waste landfill; that there was no evidence that the site, as constructed, failed to meet specific construction requirements; that there was no evidence that the Municipality ever required or issued a municipal construction permit for any other construction project in Guadalcazar; and that there was no evidence that there was an established administrative process with respect to municipal construction permits in the Municipality of Guadalcazar.

53.   Mexico asserts that Metaclad was aware through due diligence that a municipal permit might be necessary on the basis of the case of COTERIN (1991, 1992), and other past precedents for various projects in SLP.

* * *

58. From May 1996 through December 1996, Metaclad and the State of SLP attempted to resolve their issues with respect to the operation of the landfill. These efforts failed and, on January 2, 1997, Metaclad initiated the present arbitral proceeding against the Government of Mexico under Chapter Eleven of the NAFTA.

59. On September 23, 1997, three days before the expiry of his term, the Governor issued an Ecological Decree declaring a Natural Area for the protection of rare cactus. The Natural Area encompasses the area of the landfill. Metaclad relies in part on this Ecological Decree as an additional element in its claim of expropriation, maintaining that the decree effectively and permanently precluded the operation of landfill.

* * *

72. Metalclad contends that Mexico, through its local governments of SLP and Guadalcazar, interfered with and precluded its operation of the landfill. Metalclad alleges that this interference is a violation of Articles 1105 and 1110 of Chapter Eleven of the investment provisions of NAFTA.

73. A threshold question is whether Mexico is internationally responsible for the acts of SLP and Guadalcazar. The issue was largely disposed of by Mexico in paragraph 233 of its post-hearing submission, which stated that "[Mexico] did not plead that the acts of the Municipality were not covered by NAFTA. [Mexico] was, and remains, prepared to proceed on the assumption that the normal rule of state responsibility applies; that is, that the Respondent can be internationally responsible for the acts of state organs at all three levels of government." Parties to that Agreement must ensure that all necessary measures are taken in order to give effect to the provisions of the Agreement, including their observance, except as otherwise provided in this Agreement, by state and provincial governments." (NAFTA Article 105) A reference to a state or province includes local governments of that state or province. (NAFTA Article 201(2)) The exemptions from the requirements of Articles 1105 and 1110 laid down in Article 1108(1) do not extend to states or local governments. This approach accords fully with the established position in customary international law. * * *

74. NAFTA Article 1105(1) provides that "each Party shall accord to investments of investors of another Party treatment in accordance with international law, including fair and equitable treatment and full protection and security." For the reasons set out below, the Tribunal finds that Metalclad's investment was not accorded fair and equitable treatment in accordance with international law, and that Mexico has violated NAFTA Article 1105(1).

75. An underlying objective of NAFTA is to promote and increase cross-border investment opportunities and ensure the successful implementation of investment initiatives. (NAFTA Article 102(1)).

76. Prominent in the statement of principles and rules that introduces the Agreement is the reference to "transparency" (NAFTA Article

102(1)). The Tribunal understands this to include the idea that all relevant legal requirements for the purpose of initiating, completing and successfully operating investments made, or intended to be made, under the Agreement should be capable of being readily known to all affected investors of another Party. There should be no room for doubt or uncertainty on such matters. Once the authorities of the central government of any Party (whose international responsibility in such matters has been identified in the preceding section) become aware of any scope for misunderstanding or confusion in this connection, it is their duty to ensure that the correct position is promptly determined and clearly stated so that investors can proceed with all appropriate expedition in the confident belief that they are acting in accordance with all relevant laws.

77. Metalclad acquired COTERIN for the sole purpose of developing and operating a hazardous waste landfill in the valley of La Pedrera, in Guadalcazar, SLP.

78. The Government of Mexico issued a federal construction and operating permits for the landfill prior to Metalclad's purchase of COTERIN, and the Government of SLP likewise issued a state operating permit which implied its political support for the landfill project.

79. A central point in this case has been whether, in addition to the above-mentioned permits, a municipal permit for the construction of a hazardous waste landfill was required.

80. When Metalclad inquired, prior to its purchase of COTERIN, as to the necessity for municipal permits, federal officials assured it that it had all that was needed to undertake the landfill project. Indeed, following Metalclad's acquisition of COTERIN, the federal government extended the federal construction permit for eighteen months.

81. As presented and confirmed by Metalclad's expert on Mexican law, the authority of the municipality extends only to the administration of the construction permit, "... to grant licenses and permits for constructions and to participate in the creation and administration of ecological reserve zones ...". (Mexican Const. Art. 115, Fraction V). However, Mexico's experts on constitutional law expressed a different view.

82. Mexico's General Ecology Law of 1988 (hereinafter "LGEEPA") expressly grants to the Federation the power to authorize construction and operation of hazardous waste landfills. Article 5 of the LGEEPA provides that the powers of the Federation extend to:

> V. the regulation and control of activities considered to be highly hazardous, and of the generation, handling and final disposal of hazardous materials and wastes for the environments of ecosystems, as well as for the preservation of natural resources, in accordance with [the] Law, other applicable ordinances and their regulatory provisions.

83.   LGEEPA also limits the environmental powers of the municipality to issues relating to non-hazardous waste. Specifically, Article 8 of the LGEEPA grants municipalities the power in accordance with the provisions of the law and local laws to apply:

legal provisions in matters of prevention and control of the effects on the environment caused by generation, transportation, storage, handling treatment and final disposal of solid industrial wastes which are not considered to be hazardous in accordance with the provisions of Article 137 of [the 1988] law.

84.   The same law also limits state environmental powers to those not expressly attributed to the federal government. Id., Article 7.

85.   Metalclad was led to believe, and did believe, that the federal and state permits allowed for the construction and operation of the landfill. Metalclad argues that in all hazardous waste matters, the Municipality has no authority. However, Mexico argues that constitutionally and lawfully the Municipality has the authority to issue construction permits.

86.   Even if Mexico is correct that a municipal construction permit was required, the evidence also shows that, as to hazardous waste evaluations and assessments, the federal authority's jurisdiction was controlling and the authority of the municipality only extended to appropriate construction considerations. Consequently, the denial of the permit by the Municipality by reference to environmental impact considerations in the case of what was basically a hazardous waste disposal landfill, was improper, as was the municipality's denial of the permit for any reason other than those related to the physical construction or defects in the site.

87.   Relying on the representations of the federal government, Metalclad started constructing the landfill, and did this openly and continuously, and with the full knowledge of the federal, state, and municipal governments, until the municipal "Stop Work Order" on October 26, 1994. The basis of this order was said to have been Metalclad's failure to obtain a municipal construction permit.

88.   In addition, Metalclad asserted that federal officials told it that if it submitted an application for a municipal construction permit, the Municipality would have no legal basis for denying the permit and that it would be issued as a matter of course. The absence of a clear rule as to the requirement or not of a municipal construction permit, as well as the absence of any established practice or procedure as to the manner of handling applications for a municipal construction permit, amounts to a failure on the part of Mexico to ensure the transparency required by NAFTA.

89.   Metalclad was entitled to rely on the representations of federal officials and to believe that it was entitled to continue its construction of the landfill. In following the advice of these officials, and filing the municipal permit application on November 15, 1994, Metalclad was

merely acting prudently and in the full expectation that the permit would be granted.

90. On December 5, 1995, thirteen months after the submission of Metalclad's application—during which time Metalclad continued its open and obvious investment activity—the Municipality denied Metalclad's application for a construction permit . . .

91. Moreover, the permit was denied at a meeting of the Municipal Town Council of which Metalclad received no notice, to which it received no invitation, and at which it was given no opportunity to appear.

92. The Town Council denied the permit for reasons which included, but may not have been limited to, the opposition of the local population, the fact that construction had already begun when the application was submitted, the denial of the permit to COTERIN in December 1991 and January 1992, and the ecological concerns regarding the environmental effect and impact on the site and surrounding communities. None of the reasons included a reference to any problems associated with the physical construction of the landfill or to any physical defects therein.

93. The Tribunal therefore finds that the construction permit was denied without any consideration of, or specific reference to, construction aspects or flaws of the physical facility.

* * *

96. In 1997 SLP re-entered the scene and issued an Ecological Decree in 1997 which effectively and permanently prevented the use by Metalclad of its investment.

97. The actions of the Municipality following its denial of the municipal construction permit, coupled with the procedural and substantive deficiencies of the denial, support the Tribunal's finding, for the reasons stated above, that the Municipality's insistence upon and denial of the construction permit in this instance was improper.

98. This conclusion is not affected by NAFTA Article 1114, which permits a Party to ensure that investment activity is undertaken in a manner sensitive to environmental concerns. The . . . issuance of the federal permits show clearly that Mexico was satisfied that this project was consistent with, and sensitive to, its environmental concerns.

99. Mexico failed to ensure a transparent and predictable framework for Metalclad's business planning and investment. The totality of these circumstances demonstrates a lack of orderly process and timely disposition in relation to an investor of a party acting in the expectation that it would be treated fairly and justly in accordance with the NAFTA.

100. Moreover, the acts of the State and the Municipality—and therefore the acts of Mexico—fail to comply with or adhere to the requirements of NAFTA, Article 1105(1) that each Party accord to investments of investors of another Party treatment in accordance with the international law, including fair and equitable treatment. This is so

particularly in light of the governing principle that internal law (such as the Municipality's stated permit requirements) does not justify failure to perform a treaty. (Vienna Convention on the Law of Treaties, Arts. 26, 27.)

101.   The Tribunal therefore holds that Metalclad was not treated fairly or equitably under the NAFTA and succeeds on its claim under Article 1105.

102.   NAFTA Article 1110 provides that "no party shall directly or indirectly ... expropriate an investment ... or take a measure tantamount to ... expropriation ... except: (a) for a public purpose; (b) on a non-discriminatory basis; (c) in accordance with due process of law and Article 1105(1); and (d) on payment of compensation.... " "A measure" is defined in Article 201(1) as including "any law, regulation, procedure, requirement or practice."

103.   Thus, expropriation under NAFTA includes not only open, deliberate and acknowledged takings of property, such as outright seizure or formal or obligatory transfer of title in favour of the host State, but also covert or incidental interference with the use of property which has the effect of depriving the owner, in whole or in significant part, of the use or reasonably-to-be-expected economic benefit of property even if not necessarily to the obvious benefit of the host State.

104.   By permitting or tolerating the conduct of Guadalcazar in relation to Metalclad which the Tribunal has already held amounts to unfair and inequitable treatment breaching Article 1105 and by thus participating or acquiescing in the denial to Metalclad of the right to operate the landfill, notwithstanding the fact that the project was fully approved and endorsed by the federal government, Mexico must be held to have taken a measure tantamount to expropriation in violation of NAFTA Article 1110(1).

105.   The Tribunal holds that the exclusive authority for siting and permitting a hazardous waste landfill resides with the Mexican federal government. This finding is consistent with the testimony of the Secretary of SEMARNAP and, as stated above, is consistent with the express language of the LGEEPA.

106.   As determined earlier (see above, para. 92), the Municipality denied the local construction permit in part because of the Municipality's perception of the adverse environmental effects of the hazardous waste landfill and the geological unsuitability of the landfill site. In so doing, the Municipality acted outside its authority. As stated above, the Municipality's denial of the construction permit without any basis in the proposed physical construction or any defect in the site ... effectively and unlawfully prevented the Claimant's operation of the landfill.

107.   These measures, taken together with the representations of the Mexican federal government, on which Metalclad relied, and the absence of a timely, orderly or substantive basis for the denial by the

Municipality of the local construction permit, amount to an indirect expropriation.

108. The present case resembles in a number of pertinent respects that of Biloune, et al. v. Ghana Investment Centre, et al., *95 I.L.R. 183, 207–10 (1993)* (Judge Schwebel, President; Wallace and Leigh, Arbitrators). In that case, a private investor was renovating and expanding a resort restaurant in Ghana. As with Metalclad, the investor, basing itself on the representations of a government affiliated entity, began construction before applying for a building permit. As with Metalclad, a stop work order was issued after a substantial amount of work had been completed. The order was based on the absence of a building permit. An application was submitted, but although it was not expressly denied, a permit was never issued. The Tribunal found that an indirect expropriation had taken place because the totality of the circumstances had the effect of causing the irreparable cessation of work on the project. The Tribunal paid particular regard to the investor's justified reliance on the government's representations regarding the permit, the fact that government authorities knew of the construction for more than one year before issuing the stop work order, the fact that permits had not been required for other projects and the fact that no procedure was in place for dealing with building permit applications. Although the decision in Biloune does not bind this Tribunal, it is a persuasive authority and the Tribunal is in agreement with its analysis and its conclusion.

109. Although not strictly necessary for its conclusion, the Tribunal also identifies as a further ground for a finding of expropriation the Ecological Decree issued by the Governor of SLP on September 20, 1997. The Decree covers an area of 188,758 hectares within the "Real de Guadalcazar" that includes the landfill site, and created therein an ecological preserve. This Decree had the effect of barring forever the operation of the landfill.

* * *

111. The Tribunal need not decide or consider the motivation or intent of the adoption of the Ecological Decree. Indeed, a finding of expropriation on the basis of the Ecological Decree is not essential to the Tribunal's finding of a violation of NAFTA Article 1110. However, the Tribunal considers that the implementation of the Ecological Decree would, in and of itself, constitute an act tantamount to expropriation.

112. In conclusion, the Tribunal holds that Mexico has indirectly expropriated Metalclad's investment without providing compensation to Metalclad for the expropriation. Mexico has violated Article 1110 of the NAFTA.

113. In this instance, the damages arising under NAFTA, Article 1105 and the compensation due under NAFTA, Article 1110 would be the same since both situations involve the complete frustration of the operation of the landfill and negate the possibility of any meaningful

return on Metalclad's investment. In other words, Metalclad has completely lost its investment.

114. Metalclad has proposed two alternative methods for calculating damages: the first is to use a discounted cash flow analysis of future profits to establish the fair market value of the investment (approximately $90 million); the second is to value Metalclad's actual investment in the landfill (approximately $20–25 million).

115. Metalclad also seeks an additional $20–25 million for the negative impact the circumstances are alleged to have had on its other business operations. The Tribunal disallows this additional claim because a variety of factors, not necessarily related to the La Pedrera development, have affected Metalclad's share price. The causal relationship between Mexico's actions and the reduction in value of Metalclad's other business operations are too remote and uncertain to support this claim. This element of damage is, therefore, left aside.

* * *

118. NAFTA, Article 1135(1)(a), provides for the award of monetary damages and applicable interest where a Party is found to have violated a Chapter Eleven provision. With respect to expropriation, NAFTA, Article 1110(2), specifically requires compensation to be equivalent to the fair market value of the expropriated investment immediately before the expropriation took place. This paragraph further states that "the valuation criteria shall include going concern value, asset value including declared tax value of tangible property, and other criteria, as appropriate, to determine fair market value."

119. Normally, the fair market value of a going concern which has a history of profitable operation may be based on an estimate of future profits subject to a discounted cash flow analysis. Benvenuti and Bonfant Srl v. The Government of the People's Republic of Congo, 1 ICSID Reports 330; *21 I.L.M. 758;* AGIP SPA v. The Government of the People's Republic of Congo, 1 ICSID Reports 306; *21 I.L.M. 737.*

120. However, where the enterprise has not operated for a sufficiently long time to establish a performance record or where it has failed to make a profit, future profits cannot be used to determine going concern or fair market value. In Sola Tiles, Inc. v. Iran (1987) (14 Iran–U.S.C.T.R. 224, 240–42; *83 I.L.R. 460, 480–81),* the Iran–U.S. Claims Tribunal pointed to the importance in relation to a company's value of "its business reputation and the relationship it has established with its suppliers and customers." Similarly, in Asian Agricultural Products v. Sri Lanka (4 ICSID Reports 246 (1990) at 292), another ICSID Tribunal observed, in dealing with the comparable problem of the assessment of the value of goodwill, that its ascertainment "requires the prior presence on the market for at least two or three years, which is the minimum period needed in order to establish continuing business connections."

121. The Tribunal agrees with Mexico that a discounted cash flow analysis is inappropriate in the present case because the landfill was

never operative and any award based on future profits would be wholly speculative.

122.   Rather, the Tribunal agrees with the parties that fair market value is best arrived at in this case by reference to Metalclad's actual investment in the project. Thus, in Phelps Dodge Corp. v. Iran (10 Iran–U.S. C.T.R. 121 (1986)), the Iran–U.S. Claims Tribunal concluded that the value of the expropriated property was the value of claimant's investment in that property. In reaching this conclusion, the Tribunal considered that the property's future profits were so dependent on as yet unobtained preferential treatment from the government that any prediction of them would be entirely speculative. (Id. at 132–33.) Similarly, in the Biloune case (see above), the Tribunal concluded that the value of the expropriated property was the value of the claimant's investment in that property. While the Tribunal recognized the validity of the principle that lost profits should be considered in the valuation of expropriated property, the Tribunal did not award lost profits because the claimants could not provide any realistic estimate of them. In that case, as in the present one, the expropriation occurred when the project was not in operation and had yet to generate revenue. (Biloune, *95 I.L.R. at 228–229).* The award to Metalclad of the cost of its investment in the landfill is consistent with the principles set forth in Chorzow Factory (Claim for Indemnity) (Merits), Germany v. Poland, P.C.I.J. Series A., No. 17 (1928) at p. 47, namely, that where the state has acted contrary to its obligations, any award to the claimant should, as far as is possible, wipe out all the consequences of the illegal act and reestablish the situation which would in all probability have existed if that act had not been committed (the status quo ante).

123.   Metalclad asserts that it invested $20,474,528.00 in the landfill project, basing its value on its United States Federal Income Tax Returns and Auditors' Workpapers of Capitalized Costs for the Landfill reflected in a table marked Schedule A and produced by Metalclad as response 7(a) in the course of document discovery. The calculations include landfill costs Metalclad claims to have incurred from 1991 through 1996 for expenses categorized as the COTERIN acquisition, personnel, insurance, travel and living, telephone, accounting and legal, consulting, interest, office, property, plant and equipment, including $328,167.00 for "other."

* * *

125.   The Tribunal agrees, however, with Mexico's position that costs incurred prior to the year in which Metalclad purchased COTERIN are too far removed from the investment for which damages are claimed. The Tribunal will reduce the Award by the amount of the costs claimed for 1991 and 1992.

* * *

127.   The question remains of the future status of the landfill site, legal title to which at present rests with COTERIN. Clearly, COTERIN's

substantive interest in the property will come to an end when it receives payment under this award. COTERIN must, therefore, relinquish as from that moment all claim, title and interest in the site. The fact that the site may require remediation has been borne in mind by the Tribunal and allowance has been made for this in the calculation of the sum payable by the Government of Mexico.

128. The question arises whether any interest is payable on the amount of the compensation. In providing in Article 1135(1) that a Tribunal may award "monetary damages and any applicable interest," NAFTA clearly contemplates the inclusion of interest in an award. On the basis of a review of the authorities, the tribunal in Asian Agricultural Products v. Sri Lanka (4 ICSID Reports 245) held that "interest becomes an integral part of the compensation itself, and should run consequently from the date when the State's international responsibility became engaged (ibid., p. 294, para. 114). The Tribunal sees no reason to depart from this view. As has been shown above, Mexico's international responsibility is founded upon an accumulation of a number of factors. In the circumstances, the Tribunal considers that of the various possible dates at which it might be possible to fix the engagement of Mexico's responsibility, it is reasonable to select the date on which the Municipality of Guadalcazar wrongly denied Metalclad's application for a construction permit. The Tribunal therefore concludes that interest should be awarded from that date until the date 45 days from that on which this Award is made. So as to restore the Claimant to a reasonable approximation of the position in which it would have been if the wrongful act had not taken place, interest has been calculated at 6% p.a., compounded annually.

* * *

130. Both parties seek an award of costs and fees. However, the Tribunal finds that it is equitable in this matter for each party to bear its own costs and fees, as well as half the advance payments made to ICSID.

131. For the reasons stated above, the Tribunal hereby decides that, reflecting the amount of Metalclad's investment in the project, less the disallowance of expenses claimed for 1991 and 1992 ... and less the estimated amount allowed for remediation, plus interest at the rate of 6% compounded annually, the Respondent shall, within 45 days from the date on which this Award is rendered, pay to Metalclad the amount of $16,685,000.00. Following such period, interest shall accrue on the unpaid award or any unpaid part thereof at the rate of 6% compounded monthly.

Notes and Questions

(1) With reference to NAFTA Article 1105, precisely how did Mexico fail to afford to Metalclad "treatment in accordance with international law, including fair and equitable treatment ...?" Is the arbitral tribunal saying that the lack of transparency in its system constitutes a violation of Article

1105? Are there any transparency obligations in Chapter 11? Does the reference to transparency in Article 102 create those obligations? Are they simply an inherent part of "international law?" If Mexico has violated its own law, is that a basis for finding a violation of Article 1105?

(2) To what extent does the decision rest on the conclusion that, as a matter of Mexican law, the municipality lacked authority to deny a construction permit, at least on the grounds apparently relied on by the municipality? Mexico disputed this proposition in the arbitration—what standard do the arbitrators apply to resolve the conflict? What standard should they apply? If indeed "the exclusive authority for siting and permitting a hazardous waste landfill resides with the Mexican federal government," (para. 105), why not require Metalclad to pursue its remedy in the Mexican legal system?

(3) Suppose that a proper interpretation of Mexican law would afford the municipality some latitude to deny a permit, notwithstanding the representations of certain Mexican federal officials to the contrary. Would "expropriation" nevertheless exist on grounds akin to promissory estoppel or a lack of "transparency?" Why not put the burden on the investor to obtain authoritative legal guidance before it can "rely?" Suppose that after a landfill is constructed following the issuance of all necessary permits, new information comes to light about its environmental consequences, leading the government to shut it down. Expropriation?

(4) With regard to damages, is Metalclad's investment expense a good measure of the "fair market value" of the expropriated investment? Why disallow its expenses relating to the purchase of COTERIN?

(5) NAFTA foresees the possibility of court review of an arbitral award made pursuant to Chapter 11 (see article 1136(3)) and Mexico challenged the award in the Supreme Court of British Columbia (Vancouver being the designated place of arbitration). The relevant BC statute provides for an award to be set aside if the arbitral tribunal makes a decision on matters beyond the scope of the submissions to arbitration. In *The United Mexican States v. Metalclad Corp.*, 2001 BCSC 664 (May 2, 2001), the BC court took a broad view of the scope of review permitted by the statute and ruled that in two instances the arbitral tribunal had decided on matters beyond the scope of the submission to arbitration by relying on ostensible "transparency" obligations. However, the basic finding of the tribunal was not overruled. Thus, the effect of the BC court ruling was limited and only led to a reduction in the period for which interest was due.

(6) A number of other claims under Chapter 11 have been brought, but at this writing the Metalclad case is the only one to have resulted in a final arbitral award of damages. Ethyl Corp. of the United States brought a claim against Canada alleging that federal regulations banning a particular gasoline additive had effectively "expropriated" the value of its investment in a processing plant that produced the additive in Ontario, and that Canada had violated its national treatment obligation as well. While the Ethyl case was pending, a case brought against the Canadian federal government by some provinces held that the additive regulation was "arbitrary." At that point, the government of Canada settled the case with Ethyl for a reported $20 million.

A claim by Waste Management, Inc. against Mexico, similar in some respects to the Metalclad case, was dismissed by the arbitrators for lack of jurisdiction—they concluded that Waste Management had failed to execute a proper waiver of its rights to pursue other remedial options, a prerequisite for NAFTA arbitration under Chapter 11.

Pope & Talbot, Inc., an American wood products company, brought a claim against Canada claiming that Canada's implementation of the Softwood Lumber Agreement (an agreement that for a time settled a long running subsidy dispute between the United States and Canada) had allocated export quotas to Pope & Talbot's Canadian operations in a way that, among other things, was discriminatory and amounted to expropriation. The arbitral tribunal rejected all but one of the claims, but the case is not yet concluded. See 13 World Trade & Arbitration Materials 19 (2001).

These cases are discussed in Jason Gudofsky, Shedding Light on Article 1110 of the North American Free Trade Agreement (NAFTA) Concerning Expropriations: An Environmental Case Study, 21 J. Intl. L. Bus. 243 (2000).

More recently, United Parcel Service has brought a claim against Canada asserting that its postal service uses revenue from its ordinary mail monopoly to cross-subsidize courier and express mail service, to the detriment of UPS. Methanex, a Canadian company, has brought a claim against the United States relating to a California ban on a gasoline additive called MBTE. Loewen Group, a Canadian funeral home chain, has brought a claim against the United States based on the notion that an appellate bond requirement in Mississippi courts was excessive and coerced it into settling a lawsuit for less than it could have obtained otherwise.

S.D. Myers, an American company, brought a claim against Canada relating to a ban on the exportation of PCB chemicals. Canada has also initiated a proceeding similar to that brought by Mexico in British Columbia in respect of an interim award in which the arbitral tribunal found Canada to be liable (without yet setting damages in a final award). Attorney General of Canada v. S.D. Myers, Inc., 2001 FCT 317 (Federal Court of Canada, Trial Division).

(7) The flurry of investor rights litigation under Chapter 11 has led the NAFTA parties to consider modifying Chapter 11. For now, they have settled on some "clarifications," adopted by the NAFTA Free Trade Commission. Some of them relate to procedural matters involving access to confidential information. The others relate to the interpretation of Article 1105:

"Minimum Standard of Treatment in Accordance with International Law

1.   Article 1105(1) prescribes the customary international law minimum standard of treatment of aliens as the minimum standard of treatment to be afforded to investments of investors of another Party.

2.   The concepts of 'fair and equitable treatment' and 'full protection and security' do not require treatment in addition to or beyond that which is required by the customary international law minimum standard of treatment of aliens.

3.   A determination that there has been a breach of another provision of NAFTA, or of a separate international agreement, does not establish that there has been a breach of Article 1105(1)."

How would this "clarification" have affected the Metalclad case?

Chapter 25

DEVELOPING COUNTRIES AND THE WTO SYSTEM

SECTION 25.1   INTRODUCTION

One of the more difficult problems that has faced the WTO/GATT system is how developing countries should be integrated into that system. Of course, there are great differences among the countries commonly referred to as developing countries—they include the poorest of the poor nations as well as the so-called newly industrialized countries, they include dictatorships and democracies, state-run economies and free-market economies, and they vary politically from one end of the spectrum to the other. There are nonetheless many issues on which the developing countries seem to take a common position and they often refer to themselves as part of the same group, so despite the differences it is useful to treat them together in this chapter.

Historically, the developing world was dissatisfied with GATT. It felt that it had little influence in GATT decisions, that the dispute settlement system was not particularly useful for its purposes and that some fundamental GATT principles were unsuited for trade involving developing countries. As a consequence, for many years, developing countries pressed for special treatment in GATT and attempted in the United Nations (and related organizations such as UNCTAD) to create new rules, not based on GATT, to embody their concept of how the world economy should operate. In this chapter, we examine the special provisions of the WTO Agreement that provide for special treatment for developing countries and the results of the Tokyo and Uruguay Rounds from the perspective of the developing countries. In doing so, we will see that there has been sea change in developing country attitudes towards the WTO/GATT system in recent years. We then turn to the most ambitious scheme adopted by the developed countries to promote trade with developing countries—the Generalized System of Preferences, with particular attention to U.S. implementation of that system. We conclude by considering the efforts of the developing countries to reorder legal thinking in respect of the international economic system by pressing for the acceptance of a new international economic order.

SECTION 25.2 GATT RULES AND DEVELOPING COUNTRIES

The debate over whether developing countries should receive special treatment in the WTO/GATT system is not new. In the negotiations on the ITO, the developing countries tried to obtain rules more favorable to them. However, as Professor Jackson has concluded:[1]

> The issues at Geneva in 1947 did not, viewed from the perspective of the present day, seem to be free trade versus protectionism, or internationalism versus national sovereignty. Each of the groups in the debate desired international control of some things and not of others. Both sides desired to use certain types of trade protective measures but wanted to limit or restrict others. The controversy seemed to be over *which* trade restrictions would be subjected to international control and which not. From the point of view of the less-developed country, the wealthy countries wanted freedom to use those restrictions that only they were most able to use effectively while banning those restrictions that less-developed countries felt they were most able to use.

Although the developing countries were largely unsuccessful in their early efforts to obtain special treatment, they continued to press their case.

GATT was not oblivious to developing country complaints, and they have been studied by GATT committees of experts on more than one occasion. For example, in 1958, the so-called Haberler Report concluded that the developed countries should lower their barriers to exports of primary products from developing countries.[2] In 1984, a GATT-sponsored group of experts noted the adverse effect that nontariff barriers were having on developing country exports and called for their reduction.[3]

In this section, we examine the rules of the General Agreement that explicitly provide for differential treatment of developing countries as opposed to other WTO members.[4] We then consider how developing country concerns were treated in the Tokyo and Uruguay Rounds. We conclude with an examination of how the WTO has dealt with developing country issues since its formation in 1995.

In overview, it is worth noting that in practice developing countries in GATT were often able in to maintain many trade restrictions, particularly high tariffs and quotas. While GATT Article II requires WTO members to limit tariffs to bound levels, many developing countries

1. John H. Jackson, World Trade and the Law of GATT 637–38 (1969).

2. GATT, Trends in International Trade (1958).

3. GATT, Trade Policies for A Better Future (1985) (Report of Eminent Persons on Problems Facing the International Trading System).

4. See generally J. Jackson, supra note 1, ch. 25.

historically bound very few tariffs. While they were required to bind tariffs in the Uruguay Round as a condition of WTO membership, many did so at a relatively high level. As to quotas, under GATT rules, they may be imposed to counter balance-of-payments difficulties, a problem of many developing countries. In addition, it is probably true that there was a tendency in GATT to overlook trade policy actions of developing countries which were "technically" inconsistent with GATT obligations. In the WTO, however, there have been many more dispute settlement cases brought to enforce WTO rules against the more advanced developing countries.

(A) GATT ARTICLE XVIII

Article XVIII was the original article of GATT designed to grant certain privileges to developing countries. Although amended in 1955, it has not often been formally invoked. The reader will note, in examining Article XVIII, that it first establishes criteria describing those nations entitled to utilize its provisions, and then basically grants four privileges:

> Part A: The right to renegotiate tariff bindings so as to raise tariffs on products a developing country desires to produce, thus enabling protection of so-called infant industries;

> Part B: The privilege to use quantitative restrictions when in balance-of-payments difficulties (with criteria and actions permitted being slightly different from the general balance-of-payment clause of GATT Article XII);

> Part C: A privilege to use any measure necessary to promote a *particular* industry;

> Part D: Under this part, certain countries with economies in process of development, but not falling within the criteria of low living standards, can apply for permission to deviate from GATT rules so as to establish a particular industry.

What nations are eligible to invoke Article XVIII? By its terms, Article XVIII refers to "contracting parties the economies of which can only support low standards of living and are in the early stages of development." Article XVIII:1. Interpretative notes to this provision specify:[5]

1. When they consider whether the economy of a contracting party "can only support low standards of living," the CONTRACTING PARTIES shall take into consideration the normal position of that economy and shall not base their determination on exceptional circumstances such as those which may result from the temporary existence of exceptionally favourable conditions for the staple export product or products of such contracting party.

2. The phrase "in the early stages of development" is not meant to apply only to contracting parties which have just started their economic development, but also to contracting parties the economies

---

5. GATT, Annex I, Note Ad Article XVI-II, paras. 1 and 4.

of which are undergoing a process of industrialization to correct an excessive dependence on primary production.

A 1958 panel report, which judged Ceylon (now Sri Lanka) qualified to invoke Article XVIII, noted:[6]

(1) Its economy could support only low standards of living:

The gross national product *per caput* for Ceylon in 1955 is estimated at $128; although this figure is higher than the gross national product *per caput* of countries such as Burma and India, it is lower than the corresponding figure for Greece, Cuba and the Dominican Republic and very substantially below the figure of industrialized countries in Western Europe.

(2) It was in the early stages of development:

[T]he Panel has taken as a general indication the share of manufacturing, mining and construction in the gross national product; in the case of Ceylon, this share (including mining which is a primary industry) is about 10 per cent, a figure lower than that of Burma and Greece and very substantially smaller than that of industrial countries.

Notes and Questions

(1) Would an oil exporting country such as Saudi Arabia, if it were a WTO member, be entitled to the Article XVIII exceptions?

(2) Could a WTO member eligible for Article XVIII treatment prohibit all imports of a luxury good (perfume from Paris or VCRs from Japan) on the grounds that such imports were a low priority use of scarce foreign exchange?

(3) Could a WTO member which was accumulating reserves of foreign exchange through excellent export sales of one primary product (e.g., bauxite or coffee beans) invoke Article XVIII to prohibit imports of processed products depending on that primary good (e.g., aluminum products or powdered instant coffee) so as to develop an indigenous processing industry for such goods?

(4) As in (3), could such a country limit or prohibit *exports* under Article XVIII so as to favor its domestic processing industry?

(5) Article XVIII is seldom invoked, except for its balance-of-payments provisions.

(B) PART IV OF GATT

Following the 1958 Haberler Report referred to above, and as a result of developing country initiatives in the early and mid–1960's, Articles XXXVI, XXXVII and XXXVIII were added to GATT as Part IV.[7]

---

6. See Report of the Panel on Article XVIII Applications by Ceylon (Sri Lanka), GATT, 6th Supp. BISD 14, 112 (1958); Notifications by Ceylon (Sri Lanka) under Article XVIII(C), GATT, 7th Supp. BISD 25, 75 (1959). See also the Bangkok Agreement, Report of Working Party, 25th Supp. BISD 109 (1979).

7. GATT, 13th Supp. BISD 1–11 (1965); J. Jackson, supra note 1, ch. 25.

These articles are devoted solely to the problems of developing countries. Although it has been suggested that they are primarily "hortatory" in wording, and so without direct legal implications, Article XXXVII, paragraphs 1(b) and 1(c), arguably may have direct legal impact:

> 1. The developed contracting parties shall to the fullest extent possible—that is, except when compelling reasons, which may include legal reasons, make it impossible—give effect to the following provisions:
>
> * * *
>
> (b) refrain from introducing, or increasing the incidence of, customs duties or non-tariff import barriers on products currently or potentially of particular export interest to less-developed contracting parties; and
>
> (c)(i) refrain from imposing new fiscal measures, and (ii) in any adjustments of fiscal policy accord high priority to the reduction and elimination of fiscal measures, which would hamper, or which hamper, significantly the growth of consumption of primary products [produced in less-developed contracting parties].

In addition, some procedural obligations are spelled out in Part IV.

Notes and Questions

(1) Is section 106 of the United States Trade Act of 1974 (U.S. negotiating objective vis à vis developing countries is mutual growth and expansion of market opportunities) compatible with U.S. obligations under Article XXXVI, paragraph 8 (developed countries do not expect reciprocity of commitments from developing countries)?

(2) Does Article XXXVII, paragraph 1(b), amount to a "standstill" pledge by developed countries against new trade barriers? For example, could the EU or the United States consistently with Article XXXVII, paragraph 1(b):

> (a) Raise a tariff on a particular developing country product pursuant to an escape clause action?
>
> (b) Introduce an antidumping or countervailing duty against a product from a developing country?
>
> (c) Negotiate a voluntary restraint agreement on a product which a developing country exports?
>
> (d) Establish a tariff surcharge for balance of payments reasons without exempting developing countries from its operation?

In fact, the EU, the U.S. and other developed countries often have taken such actions, especially of types (b) and (c).

(C) DEVELOPING COUNTRIES IN THE TOKYO ROUND

Only a few years after the addition of Part IV, the Kennedy Round of tariff negotiations was concluded. The developing countries were generally very dissatisfied with the results of that negotiation. Little was done with respect to nontariff barriers that they had complained about and the tariff cuts were mainly on goods that held little interest for them. Although the Generalized System of Preferences, described in the next section, was implemented in the period between the Kennedy and Tokyo Rounds, the developing countries entered the Tokyo Round with the hope that at last their concerns would receive serious attention and that the Round would result in significantly improved access for their exports to developed countries through the liberalization of tariff and non-tariff barriers.

According to the Tokyo Declaration, which launched the Tokyo Round, the aim of the with respect to developing countries was to

> secure additional benefits for the international trade of developing countries so as to achieve a substantial increase in their foreign exchange earnings, the diversification of their exports, the acceleration of the rate of growth of their trade, taking into account their development needs, an improvement in the possibilities for these countries to participate in the expansion of world trade and a better balance as between developed and developing countries in the sharing of the advantages resulting from this expansion, through, in the largest possible measure, a substantial improvement in the conditions of access for the products of interest to the developing countries and, wherever appropriate, measures designed to attain stable, equitable and remunerative prices for primary products.[8]

An UNCTAD analysis of the Tokyo Round Results concluded that in considering:

> the extent to which the aims and objectives of the MTN for the developing countries have been achieved, the overall results of the trade negotiations would appear to be modest and wanting in many specific respects. * * * The proposals by developing countries for the application in concrete terms of differential and more favorable treatment in the various codes or agreements have not been fully realized. While general provisions are included in many of these instruments, concrete and specific measures for their application are somewhat vague, lacking or inadequate. The tariff reductions resulting from the MTN will erode the preference margins that developing countries currently enjoy in many products of export interest to these countries, thus reducing whatever tariff advantages they now have. Also, many products of export interest to developing countries not enjoying preferences have been excepted from the tariff cuts. The failure to reach agreement on safeguards, an area of crucial importance for the developing countries, leaves an element of uncertainty hanging over the results of the negotiations. The institutionalization of the concept of conditionality and graduation have far-reaching consequences for these countries and could lead to arbitrary discriminatory treatment of developing countries.

8.   20th Supp. BISD 19, 20 (1974).

It cannot be said, however, that the developing countries obtained nothing of significance in the Tokyo Round. In particular, they obtained the adoption by the GATT Contracting Parties of an explicit recognition of the principle that developing countries should receive differential and more favorable treatment in GATT, at least under certain circumstances.

GATT CONTRACTING PARTIES, DECISION OF NOVEMBER 28, 1979 ON DIFFERENTIAL AND MORE FAVORABLE TREATMENT, RECIPROCITY AND FULLER PARTICIPATION OF DEVELOPING COUNTRIES[9]

Following negotiations within the framework of the Multilateral Trade Negotiations, the Contracting Parties *decide* as follows:

1. Notwithstanding the provisions of Article I of the General Agreement, contracting parties may accord differential and more favorable treatment to developing countries, without according such treatment to other contracting parties.

2. The provisions of paragraph 1 apply to the following:

(*a*) Preferential tariff treatment accorded by developed contracting parties to products originating in developing countries in accordance with the Generalized System of Preferences,

(*b*) Differential and more favorable treatment with respect to the provisions of the General Agreement concerning non-tariff measures governed by the provisions of instruments multilaterally negotiated under the auspices of the GATT;

(*c*) Regional or global arrangements entered into amongst less-developed contracting parties for the mutual reduction or elimination of tariffs and, in accordance with criteria or conditions which may be prescribed by the Contracting Parties, for the mutual reduction or elimination of non-tariff measures, on products imported from one another;

(*d*) Special treatment of the least developed among the developing countries in the context of any general or specific measures in favor of developing countries.

3. Any differential and more favorable treatment provided under this clause:

(*a*) shall be designed to facilitate and promote the trade of developing countries and not to raise barriers to or create undue difficulties for the trade of any other contracting parties;

---

9. GATT, 26th Supp. BISD 203 (1980). See generally Abdulqawi A. Yusuf, "Differential and More Favorable Treatment": The GATT Enabling Clause, 14 J. World Trade L. 488 (1980); Bela Balassa, The Tokyo Round and the Developing Countries, 14 J. World Trade L. 93 (1980); Gerald M. Meier, The Tokyo Round of Multilateral Trade Negotiations and the Developing Countries, 13 Cornell Intl.L.J. 249 (1980).

(*b*) shall not constitute an impediment to the reduction or elimination of tariffs and other restrictions to trade on a most-favored-nation basis;

(*c*) shall in the case of such treatment accorded by developed contracting parties to developing countries be designed and, if necessary, modified, to respond positively to the development, financial and trade needs of developing countries.

4. Any contracting party taking action to introduce an arrangement pursuant to paragraphs 1, 2 and 3 above or subsequently taking action to introduce modification or withdrawal of the differential and more favorable treatment so provided shall:

(*a*) notify the Contracting Parties and furnish them with all the information they may deem appropriate relating to such action;

(*b*) afford adequate opportunity for prompt consultations at the request of any interested contracting party with respect to any difficulty or matter that may arise. The Contracting Parties shall, if requested to do so by such contracting party, consult with all contracting parties concerned with respect to the matter with a view to reaching solutions satisfactory to all such contracting parties.

5. The developed countries do not expect reciprocity for commitments made by them in trade negotiations to reduce or remove tariffs and other barriers to the trade of developing countries, i.e., the developed countries do not expect the developing countries, in the course of trade negotiations, to make contributions which are inconsistent with their individual development, financial and trade needs. Developed contracting parties shall therefore not seek, neither shall less-developed contracting parties be required to make, concessions that are inconsistent with the latters' development, financial and trade needs.

6. Having regard to the special economic difficulties and the particular development, financial and trade needs of the least-developed countries, the developed countries shall exercise the utmost restraint in seeking any concessions or contributions for commitments made by them to reduce or remove tariffs and other barriers to the trade of such countries, and the least-developed countries shall not be expected to make concessions or contributions that are inconsistent with the recognition of their particular situation and problems.

7. The concessions and contributions made and the obligations assumed by developed and less-developed contracting parties under the provisions of the General Agreement should promote the basic objectives of the Agreement, including those embodied in the Preamble and in Article XXXVI. Less-developed contracting parties expect that their capacity to make contributions or negotiated concessions or take other mutually agreed action under the provisions and procedures of the General Agreement would improve with the progressive development of their economies and improvement in their trade situation and they

would accordingly expect to participate more fully in the framework of rights and obligations under the General Agreement.

8. Particular account shall be taken of the serious difficulty of the least-developed countries in making concessions and contributions in view of their special economic situation and their development, financial and trade needs.

9. The contracting parties will collaborate in arrangements for review of the operation of these provisions, bearing in mind the need for individual and joint efforts by contracting parties to meet the development needs of developing countries and the objectives of the General Agreement.

1982 REPORT BY THE SECRETARY–GENERAL OF UNCTAD, ASSESSMENT OF THE RESULTS OF THE MULTILATERAL TRADE NEGOTIATIONS[10]

176. * * * The key provisions of the clause allow countries parties to the General Agreement to accord differential and more favorable treatment to developing countries without according such treatment to other countries, notwithstanding the MFN provisions of article I of the General Agreement. The enabling clause imposes no obligation on developed countries to accord differential treatment to developing countries. As its name implies, it merely "enables" Contracting Parties to accord differential and more favorable treatment to developing countries. * * *

178. The "enabling clause" is counterbalanced by the "graduation" clause in paragraph 7 of the decision. The graduation clause restates the non-reciprocity principle of article XXXVI, paragraph 8, of the General Agreement, but goes on to provide that the developing countries would accept greater obligations under the GATT as their economic situation improves, i.e. "that their capacity to make contributions or negotiated concessions ... would improve with the progressive development of their economies ... and they would accordingly expect to participate more fully in the framework of rights and obligations under the General Agreement." It is also stated that differential treatment should be modified as the development, financial and trade needs of developing countries change.

179. It may be noted that the results achieved in this area of the negotiations are more a matter of form than of substance. On the one hand, the enabling clause introduces in the GATT legal system differential treatment in four areas where the developing countries already enjoyed it on a *de facto* basis (and to some extent on a legal basis). On the other hand, the clause limits any further enlargement of the scope of differential treatment within the GATT structure by making it subject to approval by the Contracting Parties to the General Agreement. Furthermore, the decision introduces the graduation principle, which, although vaguely worded, establishes a legal precedent within the GATT system

10. UNCTAD Doc. T/B/778/Rev.1, at 29.

by requiring the developing countries to accept greater obligations as their economic situation improves. This concept could have far-reaching consequences for the future world trading system if its implementation were to allow developed countries to discriminate among developing countries in a unilateral and arbitrary manner.

Notes and Questions

(1) To what extent does the granting of special treatment to developing countries undermine the basic WTO/GATT principle of most-favored-nation treatment? In considering your answer, you should review the materials in Chapter 10 above.

(2) Do you agree with the UNCTAD Report's criticisms, which suggest that developing countries should be disappointed with the results of the Tokyo Round? Is it realistic to complain that falling tariffs harm those with special tariff preferences?

(3) Should there be a graduation principle applied to developing countries, such as that contained in paragraph 7 of the Decision? How can it be applied? Given the diversity of economic development in the developing countries, should those countries be subdivided according to their level of development, with the more advanced countries being entitled to fewer special privileges than the least developed developing countries? How many subdivisions should there be? What becomes of the most-favored-nation principle if this is done? If it is not done, consider whether the whole GSP scheme may be jeopardized? In this connection, the way in which the U.S. GSP scheme handles the problem of graduation is described in the next section of this chapter.

(4) Would the Enabling Clause permit a developing country to give tariff preferences exclusively to least developed countries? In 1999, the WTO General Council granted a general ten-year waiver for such preferences. WT/L/304 (June 17, 1999). As is the practice in the WTO, the waiver incorporates the UN definition of least developed countries. Developing-country status in the WTO, including for the purposes of the waiver, is self-determined by each member.

(D) DEVELOPING COUNTRIES IN THE URUGUAY ROUND

In the 15 years between the conclusion of the Tokyo Round in 1979 and the conclusion of the Uruguay Round in 1994, far reaching changes occurred in the world economy. One result was a change in the thinking of many developing countries about GATT.

THE URUGUAY ROUND AND BEYOND: THE FINAL RE-PORT FROM THE FORD FOUNDATION SUPPORTED PROJECT ON DEVELOPING COUNTRIES AND THE GLOBAL TRADING SYSTEM 11–14, 17, 21, 28–29, 31–34 & 36–37 (COORDINATED BY JOHN WHALLEY, 1989)[11]

THE DEVELOPING COUNTRIES' INTEREST IN THE SYSTEM

The overriding interest that developing countries have traditionally seen themselves as having in the trading system is to use it to speed their growth and development. Their interest in the present-day trading system is a reflection of how important or unimportant they see it in helping to achieve their overriding objective of development.

For most countries, their approach to the trading system involves a computation of benefits and costs. The benefits developing countries can get from a multilateral trading system depend upon what they can gain from an effective rules-based multilateral system of discipline. The main benefit is to set limits on the trade policy behavior of other countries, particularly more powerful developed countries. Effective discipline provides better assurance of access for developing country exports to developed country markets, and, in addition, limits their ability to distort third-country markets by means of export subsidies. The smaller and weaker the country, the more value there is in multilateral discipline. For it is only through such disciplines that small countries can restrain the behavior of larger and more powerful governments. As a group, therefore, and since they are small, developing countries stand to benefit from multilateral sources of discipline.

The costs to developing countries are somewhat less obvious. There are differences of opinion among developing countries as to whether and to what extent multilateral disciplines may actually help developing countries by assisting governments in eliminating unwanted protection where domestic political support for liberalization is diffuse and weak. There is, however, fairly broad agreement in the developing world that extra freedom from trade policy disciplines for developing countries, over that applying to developed countries, is necessary in order to achieve their growth and development objectives, and beyond a certain point restrictions on their use of trade policy are undesirable.

In understanding what the growth and development objective of developing countries implies for the global trading system, it is important to emphasize how different the circumstances of developed and developing countries typically are. Developing countries are economically small compared to developed countries, and their leverage in global negotiations is correspondingly limited. In addition, exports by individual countries are often concentrated on a few product lines, so that there is typically substantially more volatility in developing country terms of

---

11. Reprinted with the permission of John Whalley.

trade compared to developed countries. In general, developing countries see themselves as more susceptible to external shocks than developed countries.

* * *

The need for special treatment under the rules of the system is however, accepted as being different across countries. Those that have largely achieved their developmental objectives, such as Korea, accept that they have less need to be able to preserve a chosen developmental strategy in the face of trade shocks (and, indeed, will typically face less extreme trade shocks) than would be true for a lower income African country such as Tanzania. Special and Differential treatment does not imply equally special rules in the trading system for all developing countries at all times. Developing countries accept that different rules should apply to different countries at various stages of development. While their aim is to use the system to allow for development to proceed according to the strategies which countries see as in their best interest, it is accepted that the most latitude should be given to the least developed countries.

Given these potential benefits and costs, the interest of the developing countries in any actual or proposed trading system depends on their calculation as to how benefits and costs balance. On the benefit side, they need to know how well the rules of the system protect their particular trading interests, and how effective the enforcement of those rules will be in practice. On the cost side, they have to determine how much freedom from rules they need, and how much freedom the system will give them.

As we indicate in our introduction, until recently developing countries appear to have made a fairly negative calculation about the GATT system, and thus about their interest in participating in it. While one of the benefits of the GATT was supposed to be discipline over trade partners' policies, they noted that the rules of GATT did not cover some of their key trade interests, such as agriculture, and that ad hoc exceptions had been made for other key export interests such as textiles and clothing. They believed, further, that developed countries had not observed the rules that did exist, and that the developing countries had little or no power to achieve better enforcement. With regard to costs, developing countries seem to have concluded that they needed substantial freedom from international disciplines in order to pursue development policies. This view, coupled with a pessimistic view of the benefits offered by the GATT system, had led them to seek a fairly broad interpretation of the principle of Special and Differential treatment. The net result was that developing countries were relatively disinterested in GATT negotiations. There was a willingness to make demands of developed countries but a reluctance to offer participation of their own which would satisfy the requests of the developed countries.

[R]elatively little trade liberalization occurred in developing countries after the formation of GATT in 1947 up to the early to mid–1980s.

Over these years, many developing countries considered it to be acceptable and desirable to use high tariffs and quotas to restrain imports, to maintain fixed exchange rates, and to use foreign exchange rationing as a further trade-restricting device. While there are a range of views on import substitution, one view persuasively argued in the 1950s and 1960s and widely associated with Prebisch, held that protection (and induced import substitution) allowed developing countries to achieve more rapid industrialization, which was, in turn, seen as development promoting. As a result, countries following import substitution development strategies argued that they should be free from internationally negotiated disciplines limiting their trade policy actions. Others argued that import substitution was less of a long term strategy and more a consequence of recurrent and chronic balance-of-payments problems and the potentially large adjustment costs that exchange rate adjustments would imply. Poor export prospects were created, to some degree, by external factors such as commodity price instability and developed country macropolicies. Protectionism in developed country markets worsened the problem.

In short, multilaterally-negotiated trade liberalization was widely viewed in the developing world as both infeasible and undesirable. Reciprocity should not and could not be expected from developing countries in trade negotiations. They were small and had no bargaining leverage; the onus was on developed countries unilaterally to impalement trade policies which would speed the developmental process.

It also followed from this line of argument that, in addition to protection in the home market, developing country producers also needed preferential access to developed country markets to offset their poor export prospects. This pressure for preferential access was to lead to the establishment of the Generalized System of Preferences (GSP), and became a central element in the call for Special and Differential treatment for developing countries in the GATT.

Besides the pressures for protection which have restrained liberalization in the developing world, negotiated liberalization has also been made progressively more difficult by the failure of successive negotiating efforts. As this has happened, each group of countries has accused the other of either violating earlier commitments, or refusing to take on any new obligations, and mistrust has grown.

A strongly-held view in the developing world, for instance, is that developed countries simply have not lived up to their commitments. Developing countries point to a number of unresolved trade issues in the GATT which have resulted in an erosion of multilateral discipline.[12] Even though the GATT inconsistency of some of these measures has yet

---

12. [original note 40] These backlog issues are generally accepted to include the failure of various standstill and rollback undertakings by developed countries, restrictions covering trade in textiles and clothing, promised liberalization in tropical products, the failure to agree to a strengthened safeguards code, the absence of GATT discipline in agriculture, the absence of special action to ease tariff escalation, and VERs.

to be proven, from a developing country perspective they so clearly violate the principles underlying the GATT system that they demand action.

* * *

THE CLIMATE ON THE EVE OF THE URUGUAY ROUND

Prior to the launch of the Uruguay Round, then, the various tensions described above led most observers to view multilaterally-negotiated trade liberalization involving developed and developing countries as more and more of an impossibility. Developing countries were, generally speaking, opposed to any major trade liberalization in which their trade barriers would fall, either unilaterally or multilaterally, since this was seen as inconsistent with their chosen development strategies. They also felt betrayed by a trading system in which larger developed countries seemed to be allowed to take actions against them with impunity. And they viewed the system as yielding little or no positive benefits for them. Developed countries had not lived up to their promises to help them develop through trade, and they believed themselves to be too small to exercise much leverage to make developed countries change their position.

Developed countries, on the other hand, tended to see disciplines within the system as largely one-sided. They had taken on GATT discipline and liberalized, while developing countries had not. Until developing countries indicated their willingness to participate more fully by taking on further multilateral disciplines, developed countries offered little hope that negotiations could advance.

RECENT CHANGES IN THE TRADING SYSTEM AND THE OPPORTUNITIES THEY CREATE IN THE URUGUAY ROUND

One of the main arguments of this report is that despite the accumulation of tensions in the trading system documented in the preceding section, thinking on trade matters involving developed and developing countries may be undergoing more change than at any time in the post-war years. Ongoing re-evaluation seems to be present on many fronts in the developing world, including the role that trade plays in development, and how developing countries should participate in global trade negotiations. While perhaps less apparent, a re-evaluation of options also seems to be underway in the developed world.

These developments suggest that what developed countries have been seeking all these years—namely fuller participation by developing countries in the system, including developing countries taking on more disciplines through multilateral negotiations—may be coming within reach. At the same time, what developing countries have been seeking—namely, that developed countries live up to their GATT commitments—may also be something that developing countries can now begin to pursue using their growing leverage within the system.

The factors which limited trade liberalization by developing countries in the post-war years, both multilaterally and unilaterally, have not, by any means, been removed. Neither have developing countries suddenly obtained sufficient leverage in multilateral negotiations to force developed countries to remedy all past grievances. Nor is this the first time that developing countries have attempted to liberalize. Also, even though change is evident in a large number of developing countries, it is certainly not evident in all.

These developments find their reflection in the surprisingly large number of developing countries which, over the last few years, have made concrete strides towards both unilateral liberalization and fuller involvement in the negotiating process in the GATT.

What these changes reflect is, in large part, new thinking on trade matters in developing countries. This is, of course, hard to quantify. But as we see the intellectual process now underway, it involves a re-evaluation of the merits of import substitution development strategies in a number of countries, and a growing appreciation of the importance of maintaining as open a trading system as possible. The latter factor has been accentuated by the fear from the early to mid–1980s that developed countries would turn increasingly protectionist.

Recent re-evaluation of the desirability of import substitution strategies in developing countries can be traced to many factors. One has been the perception that import substitution strategies have not worked as well as was hoped; rather than promoting growth, they are now seen in some circles in the developing world as having spawned domestic inefficiency and a bureaucracy administering import controls. Importantly, such policies are also seen as inhibiting export performance. Another has been the increased leverage of multilateral agencies resulting from widespread balance-of-payments problems in developing countries. They usually condition financial assistance on, among other things, greater liberalization of countries' trade and payments regimes.

The allegedly stronger performance of those developing countries which have been more outward-oriented in their trade strategies has been central to debate on these matters. The performance of the Asian NICs, and particularly Korea, has frequently been held up as a prime example of how import substitution trade strategies have failed, while outward-oriented trade strategies have succeeded.

This is somewhat of an oversimplification of, especially, the earlier period of high Korean growth. The statement that growth in exports was crucial to Korean growth seems to us incontrovertible, even though free trade was not the chosen route in the early years. During the period that Korea dramatically increased its growth rate (from the early 1960s through to the late 1970s), it maintained most of its existing protection, using import duty remissions for export industries instead. It was major export promotion programs which moved the economy towards trade neutrality and substantially changed Korea's trade dependency. Only subsequently did reductions in tariffs occur. A pattern of high export growth following a move from trade repressing import substitution towards a more neutral system of incentives also occurred in other developing countries in the 1960s, such as Brazil, which still maintains relatively high levels of protection today.

The crucial issue is whether import substitution helps domestic manufacturing industries grow so they can later become important in world markets, or whether it simply generates inefficient protected domestic industries and the economy is ultimately prevented from obtaining the benefits from access to more efficient foreign products. The comparison between economies in Asia, and Africa and Latin America where growth rates have been low if not negative has been part of the debate. Our sense is that a perception is growing in the developing world that widespread import substitution has not worked as well as was hoped; rather than growth, it is now frequently seen as having spawned domestic inefficiency and a bureaucracy administering import controls.

This feeling is especially strong in the large number of developing countries with major balance-of-payments problems, and which have made high export growth and economic diversification a top policy priority. In these countries, achieving efficient domestic production, as opposed to reducing imports, has become the essential element in industrial policy. Increasingly the view is heard that the solution to their problems lies in more trade involvement rather than less. This represents a fundamental change in the stance of policy towards industrialization and trade policies in the developing world as compared to the views which prevailed previously.

* * *

In short, in all of the eleven developing countries [studied], there are clear and unmistakable signs of recent movement towards unilateral liberalization. These range from the dramatic (Mexico, Nigeria, Korea) to the small but discernible with potentially major re-evaluations of policy underway (Argentina, Brazil and India). The concern everywhere seems to be the same; improving growth performance by making the domestic economy more efficient, and achieving better export performance through a more open trade policy for imports. The circumstances may differ by country, especially the weight attached to IMF/World Bank conditionality, but the direction of both thinking and implementation of policy is common.

Notes and Questions

(1) The issues of what is the best approach for developing countries to take vis à vis GATT and what is the optimal trade policy for them remain controversial. On the first issue, see Robert E. Hudec, Developing Countries in the GATT Legal System (1987), who recommends that developing countries (i) support strengthening the most-favored nation rule, which means accepting the gradual dilution of GSP, but working for nonselectivity in safeguards and (ii) accept the basic legal disciplines of GATT. For extensive comparative statistics on the results of different trade policies on develop-

ment prior to the Uruguay Round, see Poor Man's Burden: A Survey of the Third World, The Economist, Sept. 23, 1989.

(2) In addition to the increased interest of developing countries in the GATT system, the developed countries in the Uruguay Round had their own reasons for encouraging increased developing country participation in the GATT system. The developed world wanted the developing world to make commitments to respect intellectual property rights, open their markets to services trade and limit trade-related investment measures. Consequently, the developed world seemed more willing than in the past to address seriously issues of concern to the developing countries, and the results of the Round reflect that.

(3) The foregoing excerpt, in footnote 40, listed several "backlog issues" of concern to the developing world: standstill and rollback measures; textile/clothing trade; tropical products; safeguards code and VERs; agriculture and tariff escalation. Significant reforms were introduced in the Uruguay Round agreements on all of these issues. Deep cuts in tariffs on tropical products were implemented as a result of the Uruguay Round midterm review process. (The GATT Secretariat estimated the final cuts at 42% in November 1993.) Much more significantly, there was an agreement on the phasing out over ten years of the Multifiber Arrangement (see Section 9.2(B) infra); a Safeguards Agreement was negotiated (see Chapter 15 supra), which requires the phase out of existing VERs; barriers to agricultural trade were reduced (see Section 9.2(A) infra); and some (albeit limited) new disciplines were applied to the application of antidumping and countervailing duties. See Chapters 16–18 supra. In addition, there were significant tariff cuts agreed to. All of these measures should provide greater market access for developing country products in developed countries.

(4) One major result of the Uruguay Round was the new Dispute Settlement Understanding, which was analyzed in Chapter 7 supra. As emphasized in the foregoing report, developing countries have a considerable interest in "multilateral discipline" in trade matters. Put another way, they want a rule-based system with effective methods to enforce the rules against developed countries. In light of the materials in Chapter 7, how would you evaluate the new Dispute Settlement Understanding insofar as the needs and interests of developing countries are concerned? What additional reforms might be introduced to make WTO/GATT dispute settlement more useful for developing countries?

(5) As in the case of the Tokyo Round, most Uruguay Round agreements have special provisions applicable to developing countries. While it is not possible to detail all of these provisions, a number can be cited: Agriculture Agreement, arts. 15 (longer phase-in of reduction commitments for developing countries, no commitments required of least developed) & 16 (consideration of effect of agreement on least developed and net-food-importing developing countries); SPS Agreement, arts. 10 (general) & 14 (longer transitional period); Textiles Agreement, art. 6(6) (least developed countries to be treated more favorably in application of transitional safeguards); Antidumping Agreement, art. 15 (other "constructive remedies" to be explored before imposition of antidumping duties); Valuation Agreement, art. 20 (expanded transitional period); TBT Agreement, art. 12 (general); TRIMS

Agreement, arts. 4 (exemption for balance-of-payment measures of developing countries) & 5 (expanded transitional period); Subsidies Agreement, art. 27 (least developed developing countries exempted from export subsidy ban; others given longer time to phase-out export subsidies); Safeguards Agreement, art. 9 (special exemption from safeguards in cases of low market share; more freedom to use safeguards); GATS, art. IV (increased participation of developing countries); and TRIPS Agreement, arts. 65 (implementation normally required within one year, but developing countries given up to five years generally and ten years in some cases in respect of patent protection) & 66 (least developed developing countries given 11 years to implement, with possible extensions). There was also a decision taken on measures in favor of least-developed countries, which provides that they will only be required to comply with WTO/GATT obligations "to the extent consistent with their individual development, financial and trade needs, or their administrative and institutional capabilities." In light of the comments of the UNCTAD report on the Tokyo Round, how would you expect developing countries to evaluate these Uruguay Round provisions? Do developing countries get more or less "differential and more favorable" treatment on paper in the Uruguay Round than they did in the Tokyo Round? To what extent does the favorable treatment consist of different rules compared to longer transition periods?

(6) The results of the Uruguay Round were not viewed by all as uniformly favorable to the developing world. In addition to accepting WTO discipline over intellectual property, services and some investment measures, the developing countries also agreed to bind many of their tariffs (even if at high levels), to a tightening of the balance-of-payments exceptions and to a continuing erosion of GSP preferences. Moreover, the Safeguards Agreement allows selective safeguards in some instances, something that the developing countries have strongly opposed. In addition, it remains to be seen how significant the market openings in agriculture will prove to be.

(E) DEVELOPING COUNTRIES IN THE WTO

Developing countries have played an active and vocal role in the WTO. Given space constraints, it is difficult to describe in detail the many issues of particular concern to developing countries. Nonetheless, a number of issues may be highlighted. As summarized in paragraph 10 of the Bangkok Declaration: Global Dialogue and Dynamic Engagement, adopted at UNCTAD X, held in Bangkok Thailand, February 12–19, 2000:

> The Conference emphasizes commitment to a multilateral trading system that is fair, equitable and rules-based and that operates in a non-discriminatory and transparent manner and in a way that provides benefits for all countries, especially developing countries. This will involve, among other things, improving market access for goods and services of particular interest to developing countries, resolving issues relating to the implementation of World Trade Organization (WTO) agreements, fully implementing special and differential treatment, facilitating accession to the WTO, and providing technical assistance. The Conference reiterates that all countries

and international organizations should do their utmost to ensure that the multilateral trading system fulfils its potential in terms of promoting the integration of all countries, in particular the least developed countries, into the global economy. A new round of multilateral trade negotiations should take account of the development dimension. Securing early progress on all these issues remains a matter of urgency for the international community. The Conference emphasizes the role and contribution of regional integration in this process.

More specifically, some of the foregoing concerns and others can be elaborated as follows:

First, as developing countries have become more active in the WTO/GATT system, they have expressed dissatisfaction with the decision-making mechanisms. Often in the WTO, important decisions are first reached by a small group of countries, who then convince the rest of the membership to accept them. While the major developing countries have long been involved in this process, newer and smaller developing country members have felt excluded and that their views are not given adequate consideration. In theory, the small groups are representative and include those with particular concerns about an issue, but there is no doubt that the process of internal decision-making needs to become more inclusive and open.

Second, developing countries undertook very extensive obligations by joining the WTO. In many cases, they need to reform or adopt new laws and administrative practices. Given their limited resources, they have strongly supported a significant increase in assistance from relevant international organizations and developed countries. Their difficulties in this regard have made some of them reluctant to start a new round of negotiations that will inevitably lead to even more obligations that they must meet. This reluctance has perhaps made developed countries more interested in providing the necessary technical assistance. The existence of these implementation problems for developing countries has also led to requests for extended transitional periods beyond those provided in the Uruguay Round (e.g., under the TRIMs Agreement) and for more specific and useful special and differential treatment to be provided to developing countries.

Third, developing countries have been concerned that they have yet to receive substantial market access benefits from the Uruguay Round. This is viewed as a particular problem in agriculture, where market access commitments in the Uruguay Round were rather limited, and in textiles, where the major textile importing countries have been slow to phase out quotas. In respect of textiles, the quotas are supposed to end as of 2005, but so far relatively few significant quotas have been liberalized. The developing countries want improved market access in developed-country markets for goods and services (e.g., low-wage services) that are of interest to them.

Fourth, they want stricter controls on various import restrictions that they perceive are used by developed countries to keep out developing-country exports. These restrictions include those imposed in the form of antidumping or countervailing duties and those that impose unnecessary SPS standards to keep out developing country agricultural exports.

Fifth, some developing countries are concerned that the TRIPS Agreement not be interpreted so strictly that they are hampered in combating serious health problems (e.g., AIDS) or in protecting traditional knowledge.

Finally, some developing countries have also expressed concern that some of the new "new" issues for the WTO/GATT system—environment, human rights, labor standards—may lead to disguised protectionism. See Chapter 21 supra.

It is likely that any future round of trade negotiations will not be successful (and perhaps not even launched) unless these problems are addressed to some degree.

SECTION 25.3   THE GENERALIZED SYSTEM OF PREFERENCES (GSP)

(A) HISTORY

The GATT contracting parties authorized the creation of the generalized system of preferences (GSP) by a waiver adopted in 1971.[1] The waiver was for ten years, but the need to extend it was eliminated by the 1979 GATT decision on differential and more favorable treatment for developing countries, which was reproduced in the preceding section. The history and rationale for GSP schemes is described in the following report.

REPORT BY THE SECRETARY–GENERAL OF THE OECD, THE GENERALIZED SYSTEM OF PREFERENCES: REVIEW OF THE FIRST DECADE 9–12, 90–91 (1983)[2]

At the first session of the United Nations Conference on Trade and Development (UNCTAD I) in 1964, a report was presented by Raul Prebisch, first Secretary–General of UNCTAD, which brought international attention to focus on the idea that preferential tariff rates in the markets of developed countries could provide impetus for the industrial development of the Third World. The thesis of Prebisch was that the promotion of developing countries' exports of manufactured products could help free those countries from heavy dependence on trade in

---

1. Generalized System of Preferences, Decision of the Contracting Parties, June 25, 1971, in GATT, 18th Supp. BISD 24 (1972).

2. Reprinted by permission of the OECD.

primary products, whose slow long-term growth and marked price instability contributed to chronic trade deficits. By adopting a deliberate policy of export-oriented industrialization, developing countries could benefit not only from employment and production creation but also from greater export earning potential, based on products for which demand was strong. To attain these goals, however, only the markets of the industrialized countries appeared large enough to provide the desired growth stimulus.

The solution proposed was the creation of a system of generalized, non-reciprocal preferences, under which the developed countries would lower the customs duties they assessed on goods imported from developing countries. Through this approach, producers in the latter countries would benefit from a price advantage over other foreign producers, whose goods would continue to attract duty at the normal rates. At the same time, developing country producers would be able to compete on more equal terms with domestic producers in importing countries. The basic economic justification for such a system of tariff preferences was seen as an extension of the infant industry argument, assisting developing countries to overcome difficulties in export markets arising from high initial costs.

Some experience already existed in operating more limited preferential systems between developed and developing regions. These had been created in the past principally between certain industrial countries and their colonies, for example in the framework of the [British] Commonwealth or between France and her colonies. The principle of these preferential regimes was continued in the Yaoundé Convention, first signed in 1963 by the European Economic Community and a group of 18 former colonies in Africa.

It was not possible to reach agreement at UNCTAD I on the creation of a new system of generalized tariff preferences for all developing countries and with the participation of all industrialized countries. Some OECD countries had difficulty accepting the principle of such action; at the very least, it would raise a number of new technical problems. It was therefore agreed to continue to study the issue in appropriate international bodies.

During the next few years discussions continued in bodies set up under UNCTAD. At the same time a detailed consideration of the issue was undertaken in OECD, in the course of which there emerged a broad measure of agreement among developed countries on general principles and elements for a system of preferences in favor of developing countries. This work provided the basis for the adoption of Resolution 21(II) at the second session of UNCTAD in 1968, which recognized "the unanimous agreement in favor of the early establishment of a mutually acceptable system of generalized, non-reciprocal and non-discriminatory preferences". The objectives of the system would be: (a) to increase developing countries' export earnings; (b) to promote their industrialization; and (c) to accelerate their rates of economic growth.

Following the adoption of this resolution, intensive work continued in OECD and in the newly created Special Committee on Preferences of UNCTAD. It became increasingly apparent that it would be very difficult to create one unified system under which identical concessions would be granted across-the-board by all developed countries, because of the differences in these countries' economic structures and systems of tariff protection. The GSP thus came to be understood as a system composed of individual national schemes each based on common goals and principles and aiming to provide developing countries with broadly equivalent opportunities for expanded export growth. At the same time, each developed country would be free to determine the exact nature of the preferential concessions it would include in its national scheme.

The legal basis for the system was laid in June 1971 when the Contracting Parties to the General Agreement on Tariffs and Trade (GATT) approved a waiver to Article I of the General Agreement, which requires that trade policy measures be applied without discrimination to all contracting parties ("most-favored-nation treatment"). Under the waiver, developed contracting parties were permitted to accord more favorable tariff treatment to products imported from developing countries than to similar products imported from developed countries, for a period of 10 years.

Following the approval of this waiver, the GSP fell quickly into place, with the first scheme of generalized preferences being implemented by the European Economic Community on 1st July, 1971. Over the following months most of the other developed countries put their own schemes into effect. Australia had established a system of tariff preferences for developing countries as early as 1966, which it expanded and brought under the GATT GSP waiver at the beginning of 1974. The GSP itself became complete on 1st January, 1976, when the scheme of the United States became operational. Since the accession of Greece to the European Communities in 1981, twenty OECD countries accord preferences under the GSP to developing countries (Australia, Austria, Canada, Finland, Japan, New Zealand, Norway, Sweden, Switzerland, the United States and the EEC: Belgium, Denmark, France, Federal Republic of Germany, Greece, Ireland, Italy, Luxembourg, the Netherlands and the United Kingdom).

* * *

From the beginning, the OECD preference schemes represented a delicate compromise between the developing countries' desire to have the fewest possible obstacles to market access and the fear in the industrialized countries that a general tariff "disarmament" would create serious disruptions. Initially, the developed countries considered that their preference schemes represented the maximum concession they could give in this field and they consequently looked forward to a period of stability in the operation of the system. Most of the schemes were established for a period of 10 years, although a few schemes had no time-limit. However, the beneficiary developing countries continued to press for a broader system corresponding more to their original demands, in terms of product and country coverage and depth of preferential tariff reduction. As time passed, the preference-giving countries came to accept that the system should evolve and be improved. As a result, the GSP has in fact continued to change and develop throughout its first decade of operation, despite the domestic economic difficulties experienced in the preference-giving countries during this period and the political pressures which these difficulties have on occasion aroused.

As each of the schemes originally implemented by OECD countries had distinct characteristics, the improvements and changes made to each scheme have been neither the same nor systematically coordinated. Some schemes have been reviewed and modified annually, while others have been modified as the occasion arose. In some cases these changes have added to the apparent complexity of the schemes, even though their aim was generally to expand the benefits accorded. The numerous changes to the schemes, accompanied by the strong growth of preferential imports from developing countries, underscore the dynamic nature of the GSP. These two broad aspects of the operation of the system have been the subject of continuing consultations and discussions in UNCTAD and in OECD since the implementation of the schemes.

It has proved difficult to assess the actual effects of the GSP, due to the unavailability of relevant statistics in certain cases and the problem of isolating the GSP from other factors influencing the rapid overall growth of developing countries' exports since the early 1970s. Some of these growth factors are outside the realm of trade policy; others are directly related to the elements of such policy. In this latter category, some measures are *relatively favorable* for developing countries: for example, the duty-free treatment which is already applicable at MFN levels to a fairly high proportion of developing countries' exports to OECD countries (about 42 per cent in 1980). This reflects the fact that primary commodities, which continue to make up a large part of developing countries' exports, are often exempt from duty in developed countries. In addition, the latter countries are committed under Part IV of the GATT to give special attention to the interests of developing countries in the formulation of trade policy. On the other hand, some aspects of the industrialized countries' trade policies may seem *relatively disadvantageous* for many developing countries, such as the trade restrictions which exist in the field of textiles and clothing and the tariff escalation which may still be observed in some cases, particularly with respect to more processed goods not covered by preferential arrangements. It is against the background of such policy factors, both favorable and unfavorable for developing countries, that the GSP must be seen. (The same is true for preferential arrangements other than the GSP which are available for some developing countries, as discussed at the end of this report.)

In the context of the developed countries' overall trade policies toward developing countries it appears nevertheless that the GSP has been playing an important role in contributing to freer market access and to trade expansion. During the 1970s the developing countries as a group were the most dynamic participants in world trade, increasing their shares in both world exports and world imports. From 1976 to 1980 OECD imports from developing countries grew at an average annual rate of 21 per cent, compared with 19.6 per cent growth for OECD imports from all sources. The positive influence of the GSP on the evolution of imports from developing countries can be seen from the fact that imports benefiting from GSP treatment grew over the period at an average rate of nearly 27 per cent per year.

This is not to say, however, that the system has completely fulfilled its original goals. In 1980 UNCTAD undertook a general review of the GSP, as had been foreseen, to determine whether the system should be continued, modified or ended after the initial period of operation. At the conclusion of this exercise the Special Committee on Preferences agreed in its Resolution 6(IX) that the objectives of the GSP as set out in Conference Resolution 21(II) had not been fully achieved and that the system should be continued beyond its initial period. Accordingly, in 1981 as the schemes originally limited in time began to expire, they have been renewed for a second period of 10 years.

Notes and Questions

(1) UNCTAD maintains extensive, up-to-date information concerning GSP systems in various countries on its website.

(2) Some countries grant preferential treatment under non-GSP schemes as well. The largest such program is the EU's Lomé Convention, which benefits many African, Caribbean and Pacific countries (the so-called ACP countries). The Lomé Convention expired in 2000, but its trade provisions are carried forward by the replacement agreement, the Cotonou Agreement. The Lomé preferences are broader than those granted under the EU's GSP scheme.

(3) The U.S. has special preference programs for Caribbean Basin, Andean and African countries, which afford more generous treatment to their imports than is given under the U.S. GSP program described below.[3]

(B) THE U.S. GSP SCHEME

The U.S. GSP scheme was authorized for ten years by Title V of the Trade Act of 1974.[4] It has been revised and renewed several times, most recently through September 2001. The provisions of Title V are very detailed, reflecting congressional desires to exclude certain categories of countries and products from the scheme and to afford protection to U.S.

---

3. These programs were implemented pursuant to the Caribbean Basin Economic Recovery Act (as amended and extended by the Caribbean Basin Economic Recovery Expansion Act of 1990 and the Caribbean Basin Trade Partnership Act of 2000), codified in 19 U.S.C.A. secs. 2701–2707; the Andean Trade Preferences Act, codified in 19 U.S.C.A. secs. 3201–3206; and the Afri-

can Growth and Opportunity Act, codified in 19 U.S.C.A. secs. 3701–3741. The Caribbean and African preferences are provided on an open-ended basis; the Andean preferences are scheduled to expire on December 4, 2001, but will likely be renewed.

4. Title V is codified at 19 U.S.C.A. secs. 2461–2467.

industry in certain cases. The key issues under Title V are the criteria (i) that a country must initially meet to be designated as a beneficiary developing country, (ii) for including products in the scheme, (iii) for removing products from the scheme and (iv) for removing countries from the scheme.

(1) Criteria for Inclusion of Countries

The U.S. GSP scheme is potentially applicable to most developing countries. The statutory scheme grants broad discretionary authority to the President to designate countries as beneficiaries. It does, however, direct the President to take a number of factors into account.[5] Some of these factors are simple enough: Has the country in question expressed a desire to be a GSP beneficiary? Is it truly a developing country? Do other major developed countries grant it GSP status? Other factors focus on whether the country follows policies promoted by the United States: Has the country assured the United States of equitable and reasonable access to its markets and commodity resources? Has it assured the United States that it will refrain from engaging in unreasonable export practices? Does the country provide adequate and effective protection of intellectual property rights? Has the country taken action to reduce trade distorting investment policies and to reduce or eliminate barriers to trade in services? Has it taken steps or is it taking steps to afford workers internationally recognized worker rights?

Even if the President is disposed to grant GSP status, there are certain countries that Congress has excluded from receiving GSP status: Communist countries (except in certain instances), certain export cartel members, countries that expropriate U.S. property without compensation, countries that fail to recognize arbitral awards in favor of U.S. citizens, countries that aid and abet international terrorism, and countries that do not afford internationally recognized worker rights to workers in the country.[6] In respect of the last four categories, the President has the power to designate a country as a GSP beneficiary despite the exclusion provisions if he determines that to do so would be in the national economic interest of the United States.

(2) Criteria for Product Coverage

Section 503(b) provides that certain articles are not eligible for GSP treatment: certain textiles and apparel articles; certain watches; import-sensitive electronic articles; import-sensitive steel articles; import-sensi-

5. Section 502(c); 19 U.S.C.A. sec. 2462(c).

6. Section 502(b); 19 U.S.C.A. sec. 2462(b). The statute also excludes by name the following countries: Australia, Canada, EU member states, Iceland, Japan, Monaco, New Zealand, Norway and Switzerland. Countries that give preferences to products from developed countries other than the United States are also excluded. In addition, the Narcotics Control Trade Act, codified at 19 U.S.C.A. sec. 2492, provides that the President shall deny GSP treatment to products from major drug producing countries and major drug-transit countries to achieve the purposes of that act if the President considers it necessary to do so. The President has the discretion not to take such action on the grounds that the country is cooperating with the U.S. or because the vital interests of the U.S. require that such action not be taken.

tive glass products; and certain articles of footwear, handbags, luggage, flat goods, work gloves and leather wearing apparel. As to articles that are not automatically excluded, the President has fairly broad discretion in selecting articles to receive GSP treatment.[7]

(3) *Criteria for Excluding Products from Coverage*

There are two provisions in the Act that may result in an otherwise eligible product being denied GSP treatment because it comes from a beneficiary country that is deemed to be sufficiently competitive in the U.S. market such that it does not need preferential treatment any more with respect to that particular product. If these so-called "competitive need" exclusions are applied, a specific product from a specific beneficiary is denied GSP treatment. Imports of the product in question from other not-so-competitive beneficiary countries continue to receive GSP treatment. Moreover, other not-so-competitive products from the beneficiary country subject to the competitive need exclusion remain eligible for GSP treatment.

Section 503(c)(2), which establishes the basic competitive need exclusion, dates from the 1974 Act. It provides that if a GSP beneficiary becomes a significant supplier, in percentage or dollar terms, of a particular product to the U.S. market, it may lose its GSP status in respect of that product. The theory is that if the specified thresholds are exceeded, the country in question has demonstrated its ability to compete in the United States without special treatment and that its GSP benefits should be restricted so as to allow other GSP beneficiaries to have a better chance to compete for the market in question. For 1996, the thresholds were set at 50% or more of the total import value, or $75 million, to be increased annually by $5 million. Section 503(c)(2)(E)-(F) authorizes the President to disregard the 50% threshold if imports from a country are less than a de minimis amount—$13 million as of 1996, to be increased annually by $500,000, or if the product was not produced in the United States as of January 1, 1995. Section 503(d) authorizes the President to waive a competitive need exclusion, subject to a number of conditions such as that the waiver is in the U.S. national economic interest. Section 503(c)(2)(D) provides an exemption from the competitive need rules for the least-developed developing countries.

(4) *Criteria for Excluding or Graduating Countries*

Section 502(d)(2) requires the President to withdraw or suspend a country's beneficiary status under the U.S. GSP scheme if he determines that, as a result of changed circumstances, the country would be barred by Section 502(b)(2) from designation as a beneficiary country. The U.S. Trade Representative annually accepts petitions to reconsider the beneficiary status of countries for these reasons.[8] The President has very broad

---

7. Section 503(a); 19 U.S.C.A. sec. 2463(a).

8. The procedures, which are found in 15 C.F.R., part 2007 (2001), are described in Office of the U.S. Trade Representative, discretion in deciding whether to withdraw GSP benefits from a country on these grounds.[9] The most common reason for a review of GSP beneficiary country status is based on a claim that a country has not taken steps to afford internationally recognized rights to their work forces. We discuss that issue in detail in Section 21.4 supra.

If the President determines that a beneficiary of the U.S. GSP scheme has become a "high income" country, as defined by the World Bank ($9,636 per capita GNP in 1996) then that country is graduated from the U.S. GSP scheme under Section 502(e).

Notes and Questions

(1) Congress has taken a substantial interest in the operation of the GSP system and has placed many limitations on its use. In particular, the statute indicates Congress' penchant for using trade legislation in an attempt to accomplish other U.S. foreign policy goals such as discouraging export cartels, expropriation and terrorism and encouraging protection of worker rights. Is this appropriate, especially given the foreign assistance aspect of GSP legislation? What about those provisions of the U.S. statute that suggest GSP status may be affected by a country's position on protection of intellectual property rights or trade in services? We explore the desirability of linkages between trade and other policies in Chapter 21 supra.

(2) The EU's GSP scheme uses a different approach for promoting EU policy objectives in that it offers additional benefits to those beneficiary countries that meet certain labor or environmental standards. While this approach has thus far had limited success (see Commission document COM (2001) 293 final), is it a better approach than suspending the benefits of countries that fail to meet standards?

(3) The purpose of the GSP statute is to further the economic development of developing countries through expansion of their exports (see Section 501(1)). In this connection, recall the concern expressed by the UNCTAD Special Committee on Preferences on measures that limit the stability and predictability of GSP benefits. Is the annual review process described above consistent with the statutory purpose? Does it adequately consider the need for stability and predictability noted by the Special Committee? If you were advising a client about an investment in a GSP beneficiary, what would tell the client about the permanence of GSP benefits?

(4) The General Accounting Office reported in 2001 that 13% ($133 billion) of total U.S. imports for 1999 came from beneficiaries of non-reciprocal preference programs (e.g., the GSP, Caribbean and Andean programs), but that only 2% ($18 billion) of such imports received preferential treatment. GAO, U.S. and European Union Preference Programs, GAO-01-647, p. 7. If the purpose of the GSP statute is to assist developing countries

Generalized System of Preferences Guidebook, March 1999.

9. International Labor Rights Educ. & Research Fund v. Bush, 752 F.Supp. 495 (D.D.C.1990)(Presidential discretion so broad that challenge is not justiciable), aff'd, 954 F.2d 745 (D.C.Cir.1992)(two judges voted to affirm—one found that only the Court of International Trade could have jurisdiction of such a claim and the other that plaintiffs lacked standing; one judge dissented and found standing and justiciability in respect of one portion of plaintiff's complaint).

by helping them to help themselves through the provision of trading opportunities as opposed to foreign aid, should the U.S. expand the relatively limited scope of the program?

(5) A key issue in GSP schemes is how to define the origin of goods. If strict definitions are not used, the goal of promoting development may be undermined by exporters performing only minor finishing activities in the developing country. The basic U.S. rule is that for a product to qualify for GSP treatment, (i) the cost or value of materials incorporated in the product that were produced in the beneficiary country, plus (ii) the direct costs of processing operations performed on the product in that country, must amount to at least 35% of the customs value of the product on import into the United States. Preferential and other rules of origin are analyzed in Section 8.3(D) supra.

SECTION 25.4 THE NEW INTERNATIONAL ECONOMIC ORDER AND THE CHARTER OF ECONOMIC RIGHTS AND DUTIES OF STATES[1]

The developing countries have attempted in the past to move global negotiations on trade issues into the United Nations and away from the so-called Bretton Woods institutions–the World Bank, the International Monetary Fund and GATT. One aspect of this effort was the creation of UNCTAD—the United Nations Conference on Trade and Employment. Their efforts in this regard have not had great success. In particular, in the area of international trade, UNCTAD's role has been primarily limited to the commodities area. In the 1970's, as part of this effort, UNCTAD promoted the so-called New International Economic Order (NIEO). Although some observers have concluded that the NIEO "no longer exists," having fallen with communism, the problems that gave rise to it and some of the ideas associated with it are still present.[2] For example, some of the ideas found in the Charter can also be found in the Rio Principles adopted in 1992 by the United Nations Conference on Environment and Development. Accordingly, we briefly describe its history and content.

On April 19, 1972, President Echeverria of Mexico proposed to the Third United Nations Conference on Trade and Development that a Charter of Economic Rights and Duties of States should be drafted in order to protect the economic rights of all countries, especially the developing countries. The original intent was to create a document that

1. The text of the charter is found in Report of the Second Committee, U.N. Doc. A/9946, 28 (Dec. 9, 1974) and U.N. Doc. A/RES/3281 (XXIX) (Jan. 15, 1975); see also 14 Intl.Leg. Matls. 251; Charles N. Brower & John B. Tepe, Jr., The Charter of Economic Rights and Duties of States: A Reflection or Rejection of International Law?, 9 Intl.Law. 295 (1975); American Society of

International Law, Proceedings of the 68th Annual Meeting 209, 302 (1975).

2. See Maurice Flory, New GATT and New International Economic Order, in Thomas Oppermann & Josef Molsberger (eds.), A New GATT for the Nineties and Europe '92, at 387 (1991).

would be binding upon the signatories and become a part of international law. Given the lukewarm reception the proposal received from most developed countries, however, political reality eventually dictated that this would not be possible.

Many of the countries that refused to accept the Charter did so partly because of its failure to contain either a commitment to follow international law or an acknowledgement of the relevance of international law.[3] With regard to expropriation, the Charter calls for questions of compensation to be "settled under the domestic law of the nationalizing state and its tribunals," unless otherwise agreed by the states concerned. While the Charter affirms that "[n]o State shall be compelled to grant preferential treatment to foreign investment," it fails to disavow discriminatory treatment of aliens. The Charter proclaims "full, permanent sovereignty," without any suggestion of the inviolability of contracts. An amendment to Article 2, which would have required States to exercise good faith in fulfillment of their international obligations, was defeated.[4]

A second contested area concerned the legitimacy of cartels. The Charter states that all States have the right to associate in organizations of primary commodity procedures to further their national interests. "Correspondingly all States have the duty to respect that right by refraining from applying economic and political measures that would limit it."[5]

The developed countries also unsuccessfully opposed Article 28 which imposes a duty on all States to adjust the prices of the exports of developing countries in relation to those of their imports.

Article 16 calls for restitution to be made for the economic and social costs of "colonialism, *apartheid*, racial discrimination, neocolonialism and all forms of foreign aggression, occupation and domination." It also provides that States shall not encourage investments that inhibit "the liberation of a territory occupied by force." This Article was opposed by the developed countries as irrelevant and not in accord with international law. An attempt to delete Article 15 calling for disarmament, on grounds of irrelevance, also failed.[6] The United Nations General Assembly adopted the resolution incorporating the Charter on December 12, 1974, by a roll-call vote of 120 to 6, with 10 abstentions. The United States, Belgium, Denmark, the Federal Republic of Germany, Luxembourg, and the United Kingdom voted against. Austria, Canada, France,

3. Eighteen different amendments were offered by various combinations of a total of fourteen developed countries in an effort to conform the Charter to their understanding of international law. All failed adoption. See Brower & Tepe, supra note 1, at 303–04. For the amendments, see U.N. Doc. A/9946, 14–19 (1974). Votes on the amendments are shown at 22–23.

4. See Brower & Tepe, supra note 1, at 305–06; Art. 2(1) of U.N. Doc. A/9946 (1974) at 16 and 22.

5. Art. 5 of the Charter.

6. For an analysis of the Charter provisions and proposed amendments, see generally Brower & Tepe, supra note 1, at 303–18, and U.N. Doc. A/9946 (1974).

Ireland, Israel, Italy, Japan, the Netherlands, Norway, and Spain abstained.[7]

7. U.N. Doc. A/RES/3281 (XXIX).

Chapter 26

PERSPECTIVES AND CONCLU-SIONS: WHERE TO NEXT?

SECTION 26.1 INTRODUCTION

There is no dearth of perplexing issues presented in this book. The underlying economic policies involved are themselves intricate, subject to challenge, and often undergoing reappraisal. In a world of dramatically reduced transportation and communication costs, coupled with government tendencies to influence market structures and mechanisms, do the traditional economic theories of comparative advantage really work? To what extent can political leaders and practitioners afford to ignore these economic policies? Why do governments seem to opt often for third or even fourth best measures?

But our concern, as law professionals or prospective lawyers, must also be directed to the jurisprudential and governmental questions of how to make the world system work so as to promote the appropriate economic, political, and social policies. In this book we have faced dozens of difficult conceptual problems related to this broad theme. Is a rule system really appropriate for this endeavor? Are the international institutions adequate to cope with the problems of the next decades or the next century? Are national institutions adequate? Does the U.S. Constitutional system penalize the United States in the context of today's interdependent world and the many international negotiations which occur in it? Do the constitutional and other legal constraints on policy makers nudge them into inferior policy choices? Or do these choices merely reflect compromises which attempt to balance alternative and competing policy goals?

Is the asymmetry of economic power an advantage for the world or does it prevent necessary progress? How can developing countries, non-market economies, or the giant combination of both, be integrated into the system so as to complement the underlying policies of that system? A further detailed inventory of the many problems and issues would take considerably more space.

In this final chapter of this book, we look at a pervasive theme of considerable interest to thoughtful legal practitioners: the role of rules

(Section 26.2). Then in later sections we discuss some fundamental perspectives and offer some tentative conclusions, while attempting a brief look at future prospects.

SECTION 26.2   LEGAL RULES OR GOVERNMENT DISCRETION? WHICH IS BEST?

(A) INTRODUCTION

One of the recurring themes of international trade diplomacy and policy is the question of the role of "rule" or "law." To greatly oversimplify the issue, one can observe a sort of dichotomy between a goal of developing and implementing rules of national economic behavior, and a goal of keeping as much freedom or discretion for national political leaders as possible. A great deal has been written on this theme in the broader context of international affairs. Much has also been written on this theme in the particular context of international trade and economic relations. In many of the chapters of this book we have had occasion to refer both to writings of this type, and to particular problems or issues which concern this issue. In some of the published writings about trade policy generally, one can sometimes observe ambivalence and indeed even contradiction within the same work!

In this section we would like explicitly to address this issue of "rule" versus "government discretion." In doing this we will avoid repeating materials on this subject found elsewhere in this book, but we will refer to them as needed.

There are several dimensions to this issue, three of which we will take up in separate parts of this section. First, we turn to the question of the "legalistic" U.S. system, sometimes alleged to be itself a nontariff barrier because of its costs. Second, we briefly examine some issues of judicial review in the U.S. system. The key question here, addressed also in Chapter 3, is what is the appropriate role of the courts in reviewing and supervising administrative agencies in the United States? Third, and finally, we turn to the international dimension of this problem. To what extent should the international economic regulatory system—the Bretton Woods System—rely on a rule structure with implementing mechanisms such as dispute settlement procedures and retaliation?

(B) THE UNITED STATES AND LEGAL PROCEDURES: COSTS AND BENEFITS APPRAISED

JOHN H. JACKSON, PERSPECTIVES ON THE JURISPRUDENCE OF INTERNATIONAL TRADE: COSTS AND BENEFITS OF LEGAL PROCEDURES IN THE UNITED STATES[1]

Both in the United States and abroad the U.S. legal system has been strongly criticized for its handling of international trade regulation. Some of this criticism parallels general statements made about the United States as a litigious society, with too many lawyers and too much attention to "legalism." Despite their serious data faults and some serious misconceptions about comparing the role of a lawyer in the United States to false counterparts in other countries, I feel that it is worthwhile to examine these criticisms more systematically.

* * *

Having given due obeisance to substantive policy, most of the remaining policies that I will mention could be categorized as "procedural." These are the policies that underlie the way that institutions and procedures have been shaped within the United States. Unfortunately, many of these policies are overlooked by important critics of the system. Perhaps it will be easiest for the reader if I enumerate them briefly:

(1) The procedure should maximize the opportunity of government officials to receive all relevant information, arguments, and perspectives. Thus, a procedure that allows all interested parties to present evidence and arguments would enhance the realization of this goal.

(2) The procedure should prevent corruption and ethical *mala fides*, even when the latter fall short of corruption and illegal activity. Another way to express this is that an important policy goal of the procedure is to prevent "back room political deals" that favor special or particular interests while defeating broader policy objectives of the U.S. government.

(3) The procedure should enhance the perception of all parties who will be affected by a decision that they have had their chance to present information and arguments, i.e., that they have had their "day in court." This is an important policy objective, particularly for democratic societies; affected parties must have some confidence in the decision-making process, even when the decision goes against them.

(4) The procedure should be perceived by the citizens at large as fair and tending to maximize the chances for a correct decision. A sense of fairness will include a desire that even weaker interests in a society be treated fairly, i.e., that the ability to get a favorable decision will not

1. 82 Mich.L.Rev. 1570, 1570, 1574–76, 1578–82, 1587 (1984). Reprinted by permission of the Michigan Law Review Association.

depend only on money, political power, status, or other elements deemed unfair.

(5) The procedure should be reasonably efficient, that is, it should allow reasonably quick government decisions and minimize the cost both to government and to private parties of arriving at those decisions. It is this policy goal that is most questioned by the criticisms of the American "legalistic" procedures.

(6) The procedure should tend to maximize the likelihood that a decision will be made on a general national basis (or international basis), not catering particularly to special interests. In other words, the procedure should be designed so that government officials can realistically be assisted in "fending off" special interests that conflict with the general good of the nation.

(7) The procedure must fit into the overall constitutional system of the society concerned and be consistent with policy goals underpinning that constitutional system. For the United States, as stated above, an important policy underpinning the Constitution is the prevention of power monopolies within our society. The system of checks and balances thus creates a constant tension between various branches of the government, which may often appear messy, costly, and inefficient, but which is based on fundamental constitutional principles.

(8) Predictability and stability of decisions are important values. Predictability of decisions, whether based on precedent, statutory formulas, or something else, enables private parties and their counselors (lawyers, economists, and politicians) to calculate generally the potential or lack of potential for a favorable decision under each of a variety of different regulatory schemes. The greater the predictability, the more likely that cases will be brought only if they have a good chance to succeed. The private lawyer often experiences the situation wherein he counsels clients in the privacy of his office in such a way that the client will use her best judgment to decide not to bring a case.

I make no claim that the list of policy objectives enumerated above is exhaustive; I am certain that others can be considered. Likewise, as stated earlier, the policy goals mentioned tend to be related to national procedures rather than to international procedures. However, many of these goals also apply, sometimes with modified weight, to international institutions and procedures.

IV. COSTS OF THE U.S. SYSTEM? QUANTIFIABLE AND NONQUANTIFIABLE

I want to turn now to an attempt to appraise the costs to U.S. society of the U.S. government system of regulating imports. Again, I am only looking at the import side (export regulations could be taken up separately). Furthermore, I am attempting to evaluate the costs of the "legalistic system." There are certain costs that would be incurred no matter what type of import regulation system a government operated, whether it was a system of broad government discretion or a more legalistic system with hearings, statutory criteria, and judicial review.

[The original article then presented a chart, based on crude empirical data for the years 1982 and 1983 and thus substantially out of date, estimating the governmental costs of the U.S. trade laws (escape clause, anti-dumping, countervailing duty, Section 337, Section 301, etc.), as well as the private costs (extra-firm, such as lawyers and consultants, and intra-firm such as in-house corporate personnel.]

* * *

4. Combining the Various Figures

The figures under the three parts above would total approximately $238 million for 1983. To give due allowance to the imprecision of the estimates, we can expand that figure and say that the probability is very high that the total is less than $250 million.

With what can we compare this figure? One obvious comparison is the total value of imports during the year, which for 1983 is estimated to be $254 billion. The result is that the cost of the U.S. import regulation system is 0.0009, or approximately 1/10th of 1 percent of the total annual value of imports. One could conclude that this figure is reasonably insignificant, if it were considered as a sort of "transaction cost" for a regulatory system that had other benefits. It is perhaps not entirely fair, however, to measure or evaluate the cost of the system by dividing those quantifiable costs by the total value of imports. A better cost-benefit approach would be to look at the regulatory system's welfare benefit to society, and I return to that question in the next section of this article. It should also be recognized that this aggregate approach does not answer all relevant questions. For example, the distribution of costs can vary enormously, and may in fact be very unfair (imposing, for example, substantial burdens on certain sectors of the economy, and few burdens on other sectors). Finally, we must remember that there are a number of nonquantifiable costs that need to be weighed in the balance.

B. Nonquantifiable Costs of the Import Regulatory System

To focus only on the quantifiable dollar costs of the system would be a major mistake. Some of the most important costs may in fact be non-quantifiable. A few of these should be mentioned.

1. Foreign Policy Rigidity

A system that depends on statutory criteria and procedures, allows citizen access, and establishes predictability will inherently diminish the discretion and flexibility of government officials. Indeed, that is exactly what it is designed to do. However, certain types of foreign policy activities may be inhibited by such a system. Secret negotiations are much more difficult and quick decisions are sometimes almost impossible under a "legalistic" system. Indeed, as was demonstrated in the recent countervailing duty case concerning Chinese textiles, as well as in certain portions of the 1982 carbon steel countervailing duty cases, a "legalistic system" tends to give citizen complainants a considerable amount of control over their cases, which in turn risks giving those particular citizens undue advantage to the detriment of broader U.S. foreign policy considerations.

2. *Manipulation or Harassment*

The legalistic type of system that exists in the United States also lends itself to some abuse by special interests that manipulate the system for their own advantage in ways not necessarily contemplated by the Congress when it enacted the relevant statutes. For example, a complainant may be tempted to initiate a proceeding knowing that the procedure will present considerable opportunity to create mischief and difficulty for U.S. foreign policy while the real motive for using the procedure is to negotiate with the government towards some solution that is not contemplated within the statutory or regulatory procedure set up by Congress. A complainant may really desire certain tax benefits or cartel-like quotas dividing up the U.S. market and ensuring domestic interests of a certain portion of that market. It may bring a trade proceeding that contemplates relief through imposition of a certain amount of tariff-like duties at the border solely to try to get the U.S. government to negotiate in a way that would achieve the complainant's true objective of quota-like restraints. In addition, it has been alleged in some commentary and by some foreign observers that the U.S. system tends to result in "multiple harassment," by which domestic industry complainants can bring one procedure after another even though they know that they probably will not succeed in such procedures. The running battle of domestic television interests against imported television sets is often cited as one instance of multiple harassment. The mere institution of such procedures creates considerable uncertainty in the market for the imports and creates costs for the importing firms concerned. Both factors tend to reduce the importation of such challenged goods initially and to increase importers' general costs of penetrating the U.S. market, with attendant effects upon their later price structure and competitiveness in the U.S. market. Although appraisal of the "multiple harassment" charge is not easy, there appear to be few instances in which it can actually be established that such action has occurred. Even the threat of such activity, however, may itself be somewhat inhibiting to foreign exporters who are eyeing the potential of the U.S. market.

3. *Wrong Law Rigidity*

One of the results of the U.S. "legalistic" system of regulating imports is that criteria tend to be embodied in statutes enacted by Congress and then become very hard to change. Because Congress distrusts executive discretion, it tends to establish rather elaborate detail in statutory criteria. But on some occasions the statutory formulas prove later to be inappropriate from a policy or economic point of view. Or an international proceeding will find that the U.S. law violates U.S. international obligations. In these cases it has proved very difficult to get the Congress to change the law, because a variety of special interests tend to be able to block such change. Consequently, the result is that the system has a certain amount of "wrong law rigidity" built into it.

4.   Special Interest Influence on the Formulation of the Statutory Criteria

The processes by which the Congress writes the statutory criteria and formulates the law are reasonably well known. The system sometimes lends itself to manipulation by special economic interests in the United States that can foresee the results of certain statutory wordings on their potential cases in the future. Thus, an important economic sector can sometimes influence the Congress in developing criteria that will later prove to be very beneficial to it in particular cases, even though such criteria may not be in the overall best interests of the United States. In this respect, however, the process is no different from that of any domestic subject matter. It is perhaps a price one pays for an open democratic system.

5.   Big Cases Mishandled

One of the allegations often made is that the United States' elaborate legalistic system of import regulation may operate with reasonable satisfaction only as to the little cases that are generally unimportant in themselves. But when it comes to very big cases that have a broad influence in major sectors of the economy (such as autos, textiles, agriculture, and steel), it is said that the system breaks down and in fact returns, by one subterfuge or another, to a "non-rule system" of extensive executive discretion and "back-room bargaining."

6.   The Dilemma of a Legalistic System

As one can begin to surmise from analyzing these various costs, both quantifiable and nonquantifiable, there is to a certain extent a dilemma involved in designing any institutional system for regulating imports. The dilemma is not unique to this subject and is involved in a number of other areas of governmental endeavor also. This dilemma is that the more one maximizes the goals of a legalistic system (predictability, transparency and elimination of corruption and political back-room deals), the more one sacrifices other desirable goals such as flexibility and the ability of government officials to make determinations in the broad national interest as opposed to catering to specific special interests.

V.   The Benefits of the System

The benefits of the legalistic system may be considerable, but they are perhaps harder to appraise. I will discuss them under two categories.

A.   Procedural Benefits of the System

Apart from costs and delays, the legalistic system responds well to many of the goals and objectives set out in section III above. Clearly, the more extensive and detailed are the statutory criteria, the public proceedings, the opportunity for judicial review and the like, the more likely that the system will be predictable, corruption-proof and devoid of back-room political deals. An exception to this might be the "big case" question: If the system becomes too rigid, the big cases—those involving considerable political power—will tend to make "end runs" around the system, and thus will not be channeled by the rules and will perhaps be even more vulnerable to flexible executive official discretion than would be the case if the formal procedures were less rigid and could better accommodate the big cases.

B. *Substantive Benefits*

One of the critical questions, and perhaps the most critical question, is whether this legalistic system, given its costs, in fact provides a substantial measure of benefits (benefits that exceed the costs) to the general welfare of the United States. Here it is necessary to indulge in some assumptions, and to recognize that conclusions are only tentative, in the form of hypotheses that need further testing.

The basic assumption that may be required to justify the legalistic system is that it in fact allows a higher degree of liberal trade access for imports into the U.S. economy. This assumption itself is premised on the assumption that such trade liberalization provides a benefit to the U.S. economy. Most economists believe that trade liberalization does provide such a benefit.

If we can believe (and although it is essentially a "judgment call" many people do believe it) that the U.S. legalistic system?cumbersome, rigid, and costly as it is?in fact provides for an economy more open to imports than virtually any other major industrial economy in the world, then we could count this as a benefit. But measuring that benefit is obviously very difficult. We are measuring it against an unknown— namely, what would be the degree of import restraint in the U.S. economy if the U.S. system were not so legalistic and were more "discretion prone."

One must not forget, however, that there are also a number of non-quantifiable benefits to the system? greater confidence of the citizenry in the operation of its government in this subject matter, the business planning advantage of a higher degree of stability in governmental actions, reduction of corruption, etc.

SECTION 26.3   THE WTO'S "CONSTITUTION" AND ITS WEAKNESSES

JOHN H. JACKSON, THE WTO "CONSTITUTION" AND PROPOSED REFORMS: SEVEN "MANTRAS" REVISITED[2]

II. THE INTERNAL CONSTITUTION OF THE WTO

A. *Mantras*

My second subject is the internal constitution. Some of the ideas expressed here can be attributed to ambassadors, governments, or academics. I have not tried to identify authorship for each piece of this

2. First published as: John H. Jackson, "The WTO 'Constitution' and Proposed Re- forms: Seven 'Mantras' Revisited." 4 J.Intl.Econ.L. 67–78 (March 2001).

puzzle, because usually there have been a number of parallel suggestions. In this part, I will first introduce a series of what I call "mantras." These are phrases that are used commonly, particularly in Geneva and among those who are well experienced as well as some of those who are less experienced. Quite often, these phrases are used in a context in which they do not easily suggest that the content of the phrase should be examined in depth. In other words, the phrases are used to *avoid thinking* certain issues through. Here, I provide a brief overview of seven of these mantras.

(1) The first mantra is that "consensus is great or even sacred." It is said that we must maintain the consensus system of decision making. Often, this is in the context of thinking that there are only two approaches to decision making, that this is a binary choice—one choice is consensus, and the other is voting—and you have to choose between them. However, we do not have to choose between those two. There are a lot of things in between, and there are some real pitfalls about the consensus rule that at least should make us think more about where in between we might focus attention.

(2) Another mantra is that the WTO is an organization that is "government to government." This implies that non-governmental entities have no role here. Once again, we should think this through.

(3) The third mantra is: we must be sure to preserve national or nation-state sovereignty. This mantra is used not only in Geneva, but also in Washington and other capitals. This "mantra" overlooks a good many things. Again, it is not a binary question; it is not a question of all or nothing. The word "sovereignty" has overtones that are totally out of date, but nevertheless the concept of sovereignty probably has some policy merit that we should think about. The policy question really involved in the sovereignty question is: How do you want to allocate power?[1] What decisions do you want made in Geneva, Washington, Sacramento, California, or a neighborhood in Berkeley? By viewing it as a decision about how to *allocate power,* we can disaggregate the question of sovereignty and make people think about how to correctly design that allocation. Some of the policies discussed in Part I suggest directions in this regard. In other words, some of the reasons for going to a higher level of decision making are to solve such questions as the prisoner's dilemma or the race to the bottom.

(4) Another mantra often used is that the organization is "member driven." Member driven means that the members want to keep the WTO Secretariat out of their hair. They do not want to give the Secretariat or the officials or the Director–General any power whatsoever. A totally member driven organization is, in many cases, counterproductive, and most certainly inefficient. Furthermore, if this mantra is used to ques-

---

1. *See* John H. Jackson, The Great 1994 Sovereignty Debate: United States Acceptance and Implementation of the Uruguay Round Results, *in* The Jurisprudence of GATT and the WTO: Insights on Treaty Law and Economic Relations 367 (2000).

tion the independence of the dispute settlement organs, it undermines the integrity of the adjudicative process of the system.

There are three additional points, which I will call mantras just to put them in sequence, although they are more targeted to current negotiating atmospheres and ideas of structure. Yet, like the other mantras mentioned, these may not have been fully understood or examined.

(5) One is the notion of "single undertaking," a single package idea. I have great concerns and doubts about the single undertaking concept, although I can see its advantages. (Indeed, I can discern the advantages of all these mantras. I do not mean to suggest that they are totally useless.) But I can also perceive certain circumstances where it might be wise to experiment with an approach that would not be part of a single package. There might be different subjects that would require a different time line or a different composition of participants.

(6) Similarly, another concept is "MFN" or the most-favored-nation-clause. MFN has enormous strength and advantages in the system, but we should not view it as sacrosanct in its purity, because it has major problems, such as the free-rider problem and the tendency towards the lowest-common-denominator.

(7) Finally, there has been talk about the need for so-called "deliverables". At the outset of discussions regarding a new trade negotiating round, diplomats have worried about the length of time a round often takes (ten years or more) and have spoken of the need to conclude some parts of the round early and have those implemented so that the benefits are "delivered" early.

Indeed, deliverables have advantages, as do these other items. On the other hand, deliverables tend to push policymakers towards sacrificing longer-term institutional strengths for short-term political advantages.

I have raised each of these mantras, and my suggestion is that they can bear examination and should not be off limits from more careful examination.

* * *

B. The Implications of Seattle

One of the things that the failure of the Seattle ministerial meeting seems to show us is that even the world as recent as 1980 or 1990 is no longer the landscape that we have to deal with today. Part of this change is due to the very fast-moving technology that is influencing trade and everything else. There are two dimensions of this for the internal constitution of the WTO, and there are similar dimensions for external relations of the WTO, which will be discussed in Part III. These two dimensions are: (1) the dispute settlement process and (2) the rest of the decision-making or negotiating process, in other words, the non-dispute settlement process. To some extent, we could think of these dimensions as analogous to political structures at the national level, namely, the relationship of the judiciary to the legislature. One of the questions is: Do we have an effectively working legislature? Do we have an effectively working decision-making or rule-making process? These issues are of considerable importance. Why? Currently, we have a very effective judicial process, certainly more effective than before. It has received lots of credit, and although it is not without some problems, it is well worthwhile. It is a big improvement in things that help to underpin some of the policies mentioned in Part I above. For instance, the rule orientation of the institutions is enhanced by the predictability and stability that the dispute settlement system adds to the implementation of the rules.

However, if the decision-making and rule-making processes fail to produce results, there is a tendency to throw their issues at the dispute settlement process. Therefore, there could be a tendency to ask the dispute settlement process to take on issues that it ought not to. For instance, there could be temptations to put in the hands of the dispute settlement process, issues that are really "rule making" instead of "rule applying."

There are real concerns about the current decision-making structure. This structure developed in the Uruguay Round negotiations, when negotiations focused on a WTO, a World Trade Organization, particularly in the fall of 1993 when major players worked hard to alter some of the previous drafts. While alterations were appropriate in many ways, one of the things that the negotiators did was to constrain and put checks and balances on the decision-making process. They did this by requiring decision by consensus and by super-majorities and through certain other kinds of procedures. Today we realize that those constraints can lead to a lack of effectiveness of the decision-making process. This is one of the issues and one of the dilemmas that we have before us and that requires more examination.

C. Decision Making

There are advantages and disadvantages to a consensus-based decision-making process. One downside of requiring full consensus is that it may be a recipe for impasse, stalemate, and paralysis. In other words, the result may be that things do not get done. We have seen some very interesting examples of that in the last year. There are also examples that often are not easily visible.

For example, there are situations where the participants in this constitution would like to see some evolution and change. These changes may be rather detailed and technical, such as modifying elements of the Dispute Settlement Understanding. Yet, proponents of change may abandon such an effort even before trying, because of their perception that the consensus process makes it impossible to do what they want to do.

What are some alternate methods for decisions? One possibility is to figure out a way to distinguish the more detailed procedural aspects from things that have real substance. There is already a distinction in the amending clause of the WTO between the non-substantive and the more substantive issues. There might be ways to develop a similar distinction in the consensus process. Of course, one of the problems with the consensus process is that in order to change it you must have consensus. Therefore, any country can block a proposed change. This leads us to a search for alternative ways to make changes without amending either the DSU or the WTO as a whole. Often this is a delicate question, and I am not sure the alternatives are workable. If they are not workable, and the parties are without recourse to make changes, we are likely to be in very great trouble.

There are, however, some other possibilities. One possibility is a so-called "critical mass" idea, which has been experimented with. The basic idea is to develop a practice where countries refrain from blocking consensus when a critical mass of countries support a proposed change. This critical mass of countries could be expressed as an overwhelming majority of countries and an overwhelming amount of the trade weight in the world, such as 90 percent of both of these factors. In addition, there could be other factors. Of course, the proposed change would need to be consistent with the existing treaty obligations, including MFN. One could try to develop a practice, maybe through something called "peer pressure," by encouraging states to refrain from blocking a consensus in certain kinds of decision-making, if these other attributes existed. One parallel or analog to this approach is roughly (but not precisely) the so-called Luxembourg Compromise in the history of the European Communities development.

Another possibility is to use expert or smaller groups attached to a particular committee, such as the Dispute Settlement Body. Such a group would meet with diplomats and perhaps outside experts to draft a proposal that coincided with criteria, such as those mentioned above. Then, when a proposed change is put forward to the final decision makers, the parties could argue that governments should refrain from blocking the consensus in that particular circumstance because of the critical mass argument, the percentage of trade, and so forth.

A third approach is to use a "tariff scheduling" approach. This approach was used in the telecommunications agreement and, to some extent, the financial services agreement. Under this approach, commitments resulting from further negotiations were put in the schedules, which are annexed to the services agreement of those governments that were willing to go along with the measure. Of course, these commitments are usually subject to MFN, depending on some of the aspects of the services agreement. This approach addresses both the difficulties with the consensus rule and the single package. It is analogous to something that was built into the WTO, namely, the Annex 4 Plurilateral Trade Agreements, which are optional.

Unfortunately, it takes a full consensus to add an agreement to Annex 4, so there could well be blocking against that approach. But if there were not blocking, this might also be an approach where certain innovation could occur with smaller groupings than the whole.

Another problem is whether there needs to be some kind of a "steering group," some kind of a small group in the organization, which can help the Director–General and others. Without going into detail, something like this is going to be required. There has been a fair amount of writing, both academic and diplomatic, about how to constitute such a group. There are a number of different proposals, and I would hope that maybe some of them might work. In each of these cases, it is possible to try them for a limited period of time, such as two years. At the end of the two-year period, the provisions could expire. This approach allows the parties to renew negotiations and reach agreement, based on their view of how the provisions played out. If these provisions appear to have been effective, the parties could renew them for an additional period of time.

III.   EXTERNAL RELATIONS IN THE WTO CONSTITUTION

A.   *The Role of Non–Governmental*
Organizations

About Seattle, many of us talked about the "inside problem" and the "outside problem." The "inside problem" is what was really going on in the negotiations and the various half a dozen or more factors that prevented success there. The "outside problem" includes the demonstrations, the tensions involved with that, and the organization of NGO and public participation. These are analogous to the structure of this article, with attention to internal problems compared to external. You can look at these problems under both dispute settlement and decision-making dimensions. There are really two parts under each of those, and it may be helpful to view it as a two-by-two matrix. One is the subject or "transparency" and the other is the subject of "participation." Please note that I separate these terms rather dramatically because quite often the word transparency is used in an ambiguous way to cover both. Transparency, as I and others see it, really means information for the public, but it can also mean internal flow of information. Ways of making information available to the public include available documentation, open hearings, and open meetings, at least for the press. Participation, on the other hand, is somewhat more of a problem and is a more delicate issue. Participation by civil society or non-governmental entities means that they have an opportunity to be heard and present their views.

The basic question, and the one most vital here, is the role of NGOs. There are arguments both for and against NGO participation. We should thus recognize both the advantages and disadvantages of NGO participation. The governments are the authorized legitimate representative in the WTO structure. The NGOs sometimes forget that, as we see that in some of their arguments and how they go about their business. In some cases, an NGO may have no legitimate role and no true constituency.

Sometimes it is said that some NGOs are part of the so-called "uncivil" society. They are abusive and destructive and can cause various problems, including safety problems. Generally NGOs, even the good ones, can create resource problems. For example, it will involve some resources to open hearings and provide additional documentation, space, and time. On the other hand, there are advantages to NGO participation. First, they can be quite useful. Sometimes they have resources for study and analysis that governments lack. They can bring to the table information that can be very useful in the proceedings. They can also transmit information to concerned and important constituencies in the various countries. They can come to an understanding and then explain the issues to a broader constituency that has not had the time or the information to try to grasp them. In addition, they have real power, as demonstrated by the MAI (Multilateral Agreement on Investment) exercise and the impact of the Internet, and in Seattle, to some extent.

What to do? It is surprising how far behind the WTO is, compared to most of the international organizations in Geneva and other cities, with respect to how it handles NGOs. Other organizations have very elaborate methodologies of accreditation of NGOs based on a variety of criteria, which vary from organization to organization. For example, the United Nations has been doing this for forty or fifty years.[2] In addition, the International Labor Organization (ILO) has fairly elaborate measures, as does the World Intellectual Property Organization (WIPO). WIPO integrates key NGOs that have expertise in some of the technical aspects, such as its "domain name" exercise. UNCTAD also has measures. Why not the WTO? At a minimum, there should be a study, which could be done by a committee reporting to the General Council chairman or one under the supervision of the Director–General.

B. Transparency and Participation

With respect to transparency, there is a problem of documents. To some extent, the very ingenious program of computer documentation in the WTO is quite advanced and can be a real help as part of the outreach, not only to the delegates themselves, but also to civil society and NGOs. There is also a question of whether meetings should be open. I was surprised recently at how willing some experienced diplomats were to see such things as WTO committee meetings made open for public attendance. Even if one is not willing to go that far, because of the negotiating function of at least some of those committee meetings, maybe the Council meetings could be open, or maybe there could be a press gallery for the various Councils, not just the General Council.

Likewise, in the dispute settlement system, some of the same questions arise. For example, there is a problem of the documentation,

2. United Nations Non–Governmental Liaison Service, The NGLS Handbook of UN Agencies, Programmes and Funds Working for Economic and Social Development (2d ed. 1997).

particularly the panel reports and the delay that is caused in part by translation resource problems, which surely can be overcome.

"Participation" is a different and more difficult question in the context of decision making. There may be grounds to call upon some of the NGOs for assistance as experts, and there certainly is authority to do so. Indeed, the WTO Charter, Article IX, paragraph 2, suggests certain relationships for NGOs. In the dispute settlement system, we have already seen the "amicus curiae" brief as one way to transmit information to the panels. That can be constructive, but it needs to be thought through so as not to cause certain kinds of problems.

IV. Conclusion

This article examines the world trading system in its historical context and in light of recent developments. Looking ahead, it is useful to consider how to move forward. By providing leadership, the trade superpowers—the United States, the European Union, and Japan—can play a major role. There are other groups of countries that could get together and try to thrash out ideas, and discuss the pros and cons of some of these measures, and then see if there is some in-between measure that tends to maximize the advantages and minimize the disadvantages. Such measures could then be introduced for limited periods of time.

Already suggested by the European Community and the Director–General and others, is an idea of forming a group of parliamentarians to meet at the WTO on a regular basis to exchange information, ideas, and attitudes. Other ideas that have been set forth include the formation of a steering group[3] and an NGO consultative group. There may be a parallel here in the European Community, which has something like an economic and cultural consultation committee that works with it on various subjects. Suggestions for increasing transparency include public sessions and increased access to reports and other documents. Short of amending the agreements, there are many steps that can be taken to strengthen the institution and its agreements. It is worthwhile to focus our efforts on these steps. Clearly, this brief article only touches the surface, so let us hope much further analysis and discussion on these and other WTO "constitutional issues" will occur in the near future.

---

3. *See* Jeffrey J. Schott & Jayashree Watal, Decision-making in the WTO (Institute of International Economics Policy Brief No. 00–2, March 2000) <http://www. iie.com/NEWSLETR/news002.htm> (suggesting that "the WTO needs to establish a small, informal steering committee (20 or so in number) that can be delegated responsi-

SECTION 26.4 MUSINGS ON THE FUTURE: GLOBALIZATION AND ITS PERILS

JOHN H. JACKSON, INTERNATIONAL ECONOMIC LAW IN TIMES THAT ARE INTERESTING[1]

I. The World Financial Crisis and Its Implications

Both the many causes of the 1997–98 world financial crisis and the various remedies tried or proposed for it have been very controversial. It does appear that we witnessed an extreme case of "market failure", or to put it more strongly, the events of those years not unreasonably suggested to some that markets are not working and that, indeed, market economics is not the solution to the world's problems. The major clamor of that period, including that of many market-oriented advocates, was for government to do something, i.e., "to act." And the markets themselves seemed at one point to watch for signals that governments would cope with the problems, whether using interest rate adjustments, bailout programs, ad hoc bankruptcy measures, lending of last resort, changes in international institutions, or what have you. Perhaps a decade's perspective would suggest that with the fall of the Berlin wall as the symbol of the diminished popularity of socialist or state-controlled economic structures and viewpoints, there arose an aura of overconfidence in market-oriented approaches to solve major human problems, and maybe this hubris itself is one source of fault in the crisis. Here we cannot do more than ask the question, but clearly this thought in various forms of articulation is not deemed irrelevant by many.

But from the legal scholar/practitioner's perspective, it appears that a very important feature of this crisis is what it says about the institutions of the global market. Economists in recent decades have been focusing more attention on the "human institutions" which are a necessary condition for markets to function successfully.[2] In many ways this is also lawyers' territory. Since the crisis, much has been written and discussed about the Bretton Woods system and its architecture, for example.

The context of these and other reactions to the crisis mingles deeply into the broad subject of the philosophy of government, or maybe what today we would describe as the philosophy of governance. And this, it seems clear, will necessarily be colored by many of the great ideas of civilization, such as what is human nature (about which market economics is generally pessimistic and skeptical); what form of government works best in some situations (referring sometimes to democratic forms compared with representative forms); how in a democracy can the elite and those with high levels of expertise operate effectively and appropri-

bility for developing consensus on trade issues among the member countries").

1. First published as: John H. Jackson, International Economic Law in Times that are Interesting. 3 J.Intl.Econ.L. 3–14 (2000).

2. Yet even when stressing the benefits of market economics, important thinkers note the importance of human institutions which guide and shape markets. Many economists, particularly in recent decades, have stressed this. Nobel Prize winners Ronald Coase and Douglas North have each made this point in their writings. See Ronald Coase, The Firm, the Market and the Law (reprint of 1960 article) ch. 5; Douglas C. North, Institutions, Institutional Change and Economic Performance (1990).

ately while avoiding abuse of power (the general dangers of concentration of power which the United States approaches through checks and balances or separation of powers, as well as its antitrust laws); what is the role and perhaps the crucial importance of human liberties or human rights, etc.? That is too big a terrain for a brief editorial, so I won't try to play too much with some of these ideas here.

As government leaders attempt to deal with the international economic crisis, which has been described by some to be the worst crisis since the beginning of the Bretton Woods system, clearly what they are addressing is the institutional framework for needed government intervention, and generally this means international government intervention with nation-state participation. Lessons from the history of many international institutions, but especially those of the Bretton Woods system including the GATT/WTO history, are obviously crucial parts of the necessary learning and expertise which will be needed for these measures.

The legal structures of the institutions impose constraints as well as suggest potentials for change. The very structure of international law and particularly the normal rigidities of treaties and their formation, as well as the intricate links of treaty developments to many national constitutional structures, will often create barriers to what some policy makers perceive to be the optimum solutions to problems. Yet sometimes these constraints have important longer range policy underpinnings and, dare I say it, derive from fundamental "constitutional" considerations.

For example, the IMF and World Bank have an interesting structure of weighted voting which has been highly criticized in some quarters, but very prized in others. The political realities of world economic institutions today are very strongly opposed to weighted voting or even certain other constructions that might be considered for new institutions so as to more realistically recognize the actual power relations in the world, for better or worse. To a great extent the WTO Charter has been heavily shaped by some of these considerations, as a result tilting toward consensus decision making for even detailed procedural rules. As to the IMF and World Bank, it seems very unlikely that the major economic powers will lightly abandon these considerations, and thus it appears very unlikely that those institutions will be discarded or put aside in favor of totally new institutions. If this is the case, solutions are most likely to be arranged within the constitutional parameters of those existing institutions.

Yet existing institutions tend understandably to have inherited characteristics that may be difficult to overcome. Some of the current WTO discourse suggests this in relation to the very large shift in the dispute settlement process. Nevertheless there are strong suggestions for similar large shifts of attitudes and practices in the financial institutions of the IMF and World Bank, with proposals for greater transparency, more checks and balances on discretionary exercise of power and decision making, and more inputs from what is currently termed the "civil society," generally meaning non-government active citizen or private group participation.

Another aspect of the approaches regarding reform of the world financial system, whether it be called constitutional reform or reconstructing the architecture, is the relationship of the financial institutions with that of trade, namely, the WTO. The financial institutions are now more than before realizing the microeconomic sources of important defects in the macroeconomic world structure as they digest the failures within nation-state economic systems that are linked to such defects as lack of transparency and lack of important economic information, arbitrary and capricious and therefore often unpredictable governmental decisions, and decisions discriminating against those from outside the society (which in today's global market are often the most significant source of capital inputs which can drive economic development). Virtually all the solutions suggested involve a degree of intrusiveness into domestic governance that will be unprecedented and several decades ago would have been deemed impossible.

A key question in these directions will be whether the international and other non-domestic pressures (whether multilateral, bilateral, or non-governmental) will always be in the best interests of the target countries and world prosperity, or whether they will be tilted to favor certain special interests which have the ability to strongly influence the direction of reforms being hatched.

II. THE EVOLVING WORLD TRADE ORGANIZATION IN ITS FORMATION YEARS

The new WTO is now just over five-years old, hardly yet an adolescent, but it clearly is having a profound impact on world economic relations. As one observer writing in the *New York Times* said recently, noting the huge protests planned for the Seattle WTO Ministerial, "The trade group has become such a target of ire in part because it has proved one of the most powerful world bodies of any kind." [3] And the U.N. Secretary General Kofi Annan said recently "globalization should not be made a scapegoat for domestic policy failures ... the WTO must not be distracted from its own vital task: extending the benefits of free trade fully to the developing world." [4]

The 1994 Uruguay Round treaty which created the WTO has enormous implications for almost every topic of nation-state economic regulation. Already it is being invoked for a variety of different economic problems including some relating to the current financial crisis. The development of treaty norms did not stop with the Uruguay Round either. Negotiators continued after 1994 to pursue agreements in various

---

3. Joseph Kahn, "Global Trade Forum Reflects a Burst of Conflict and Hope," *New York Times*, November 28, 1999, p. 1, 14. He added: "Unlike the trade and tariffs group, its predecessor, this trade group has the power to decide disputes on its own and impose penalties on countries that do not abide by its conclusions. To avoid pressure from lobby groups and possible adverse effects on international financial markets, three-judge panels decide cases in closed chambers without having to reveal much about the process. Most of the appointee judges are trade lawyers."

4. Kofi Annan, *New York Times*, November 29, 1999, p. A28.

other subjects, notably financial services and telecommunications. Financial services obviously relates to the current financial crisis, and telecommunications is in reality replacing ports as the new infrastructure for international trade. Negotiators for both of these subjects were basically trying to catch up with the fast moving developments of globalizing markets. These agreements would truly astonish sovereigns of several decades ago, as the agreements penetrate deep into national regulation and government. The launching of a new round of negotiation could take the WTO system further in these directions.

Probably the most significant characteristic and evolution of the WTO is the nature of its dispute settlement system. Building on the GATT (General Agreement on Tariffs and Trade, the WTO predecessor) and its remarkable dispute settlement procedures shaped by over 40 years of practice and experimentation, the WTO has corrected some of the GATT defects and created a stronger, more rule-oriented, dispute settlement process, including automatic adoption of reports that have binding international law force, and an appellate process that has increased the rigor and careful reasoning of panel, and appeal reports that are grappling with very sophisticated systemic "governing questions" of the international trade system. These tough questions include reconciling interests competing with international trade policies, such as national "sovereignty" and "subsidiarity", environmental considerations, and risk levels appropriate for human health impacts of food. Profoundly important and elaborately reasoned decisions such as those in the Shrimp Turtle[5] and the Beef Hormones[6] cases are clearly landmark tribunal opinions for international law generally.

With treaty clauses as profound as those mentioned above, and with dispute settlement cases facing deep philosophical questions of national versus international governance, come some important constitutional problems. It is not surprising that the Uruguay Round treaty has many gaps and ambiguities, since it was negotiated with over 120 national participants and diplomatic needs to come to closure often dictates papering over differences. A key question facing the dispute settlement system is whether it is appropriate or feasible to pass to it the responsibility of correcting these gaps and problems. In many of these cases it would demand that the panels and appellate body undertake tasks that would appear to be law making rather than law applying arguably more appropriate for a legislature which does not exist, or negotiations which substitute for legislation. Yet the WTO rules regarding decision making and negotiation were purposely designed by the Uruguay round negoti-

5. *US—Import Prohibition of Certain Shrimp and Shrimp Products,* WT/DS58/AB/R, adopted on 6 November 1998. See Arthur E. Appleton, Shrimp Turtle: Untangling the Nets, 2 J.Intl.Econ.L. 477 (1999).

6. *EC—Measures Affecting Meat and Meat Products (Hormones)* WT/DS26 & 48/AB/R, adopted 13 February 1998. See Rein-

hard Quick/Andreas Bluethner, Has the Appellate Body erred? An appraisal and criticism of the ruling in the WTO Hormones case, 2 J.Intl.Econ.L. 603 (1998); Donna Roberts, Preliminary assessment of the effects of the WTO Agreement on Sanitary and Phytosanitary trade regulations, 3 J.Intl.Econ.L. 377 (1998).

ators to preserve so-called "sovereignty" for the nation-states, and thus impose a number of constraints on the exercise of power. These restraints could result in stalemate or impasse. In such cases the temptation will be stronger to overburden the dispute settlement process, despite treaty clauses also aimed at constraining the authority of that process. The GATT/WTO history thus stimulates many generalizations. To mention only a few:

— Treaties are often an awkward albeit necessary method of designing institutions needed in today's interdependent world, but they do not solve many problems. The human institutions established, like those in other contexts including that of the U.S. constitution, have a way of evolving and indeed surprising the participants including the creators. Probably no nation that accepted the Uruguay round really knew quite what it was getting into.

— Such institutions need constant on-going attention to help them evolve in appropriate directions, because they certainly will evolve, like it or not.

— The GATT history shows a strong tendency, at least for economic matters, for international institutions to develop in the direction of rule orientation.

— These processes must be understood in the context, not only of international law and practice but also of the very great influence of national constitutions and diverse legal systems. The nation-state is still very important. There is continuing tension between the role of the nation-state and the needs for international institutions to facilitate cooperative mechanisms to enhance the efficient and just operation of markets, especially as the markets become more and more globalized.

* * *

China's membership in the WTO will also be a major event for the WTO. Few people doubt that the China membership will have a deep and serious impact on the world trading system and the WTO. Such a serious impact is likely inevitable, even without Chinese formal WTO membership. Worries are expressed about the suitability of the Chinese economic structure for the disciplines and rules of the WTO,[7] however even those with worries seem to feel that Chinese membership is better than alternatives. Indeed perceptive journalists have commented on the significance of the potential impact of the WTO and its rules structure, on the further evolution of the Chinese economic structure.[8]

7. James V. Feinerman, "Free Trade, To a Point", *New York Times,* November 27, 1999, p. A31; Robert Herzstein, "Is China Ready for the WTO's Rigors?", *Wall Street Journal,* November 16, 1999, p. A30.

8. David E. Sanger, "At the Last Hour, Down to the Last Trick, and It Worked",

New York Times, November 17, 1999, p. A 14; John Pomfret, "China's Bold Leap Into World Markets", *The Washington Post,* November 16, 1999, p. 1; Thomas Friedman, *New York Times,* December 1, 1999, p. A31.

III. Perspectives for the Future: Challenges of Globalization

It seems clear to this observer and to many others, that the current period is a time of fundamental change in economic structures and these changes will influence lifestyles of billions. Some of this may be a result of the electronic technical revolution, the communication revolution, the transportation revolution (including freight and passengers), the shifting attitudes towards roles of governments, and the stress and thus change these factors impose on individual human beings and families and on human institutions including national and international institutions. Part of this fundamental change can be characterized by reference to "globalization", but not all. One observer recently analogized this change to that of mid–19th century, which spawned the writings of Marx and Engels[9] and the changed institutions they stimulated. That observer predicts that writers will similarly emerge by the end of the new century to challenge ideas of free-market, private-property capitalism.

Some challenge much earlier than that could be welcome, if it forces world leaders and their constituents to face up to the dilemmas posed for old thinking and institutions by the forces of globalization and technology. Indeed maybe that will be a benefit derived from the Seattle failure. Will the safety net for individuals need repairing? Are governments neglecting their appropriate functions to keep institutions working to preserve markets? Are older ideas of the "social market economy" or newer articulations of the "third way", with their great ambiguities, now ripe for more serious development and consideration? How will we balance deeply held "non-economic" personal goals and lifestyles? How can the international institutions cope with the enormous diversity of the many world cultures and economic/political systems? How will they tame the threat of weapons of mass destruction? It is important to remember that the most important policy objective of the post-World War II Bretton Woods institutions and the economic structure it implied was the prevention of war and military strife (overall quite a success story for the political leaders at the end of World War II).

At the very least, minds must open to new styles of international decision making. This can push thoughts in different directions. We must, for example, reflect on a deeper meaning for international structures that is a common thread in the landscape painted above, namely, challenge to "sovereignty".

This word is so constantly misused that many argue we should abolish it. Certainly many of the centuries old concepts of sovereignty are no longer part of today's world of international law and international relations. Almost no one thinks sovereigns have unfettered power to treat their own citizens as they like, to arbitrarily chop off heads or hands or violate virgins, and the like. A massive structure of treaty law already evidences virtual unanimity among nations that at least certain

9. Kurt Andersen, "The Next Big Dialectic," (Op Ed), *New York Times*, November 28, 1999, p. 11.

human rights are subject to international legal controls, which are sometimes but not always effective but almost always respected by word if not deed. Likewise, we now see a growing body of economic regulatory principles imposed by international treaty, and between these two subjects we see the system edging towards international legal principles of "good governance", as I noted before.

But there remains an important sub-topic of the concept of sovereignty, namely the question of appropriate allocation of power. This refers to allocation of power between nation-states and international bodies; but, in my view, this is really part of a broader matrix or roadmap of power allocation that can apply vertically from the multilateral international institutions, through regional and specialized international organizations, to the nation-state and to sub-units of nation-states such as federal sub-entities and even to the local neighborhood. The term "subsidiarity" is sometimes used to refer to this problem of allocation.[10]

Some (but not all) of these thoughts can be carried out in the context of traditional economic analysis of market failure and the need for various types of government intervention. A central question, for example, is what is the impact of globalization on a decision whether market failure exists; a follow-up question then is whether the government intervention should be at the nation-state level, or at another level of government. Those close to current debates about competition or antitrust policy, as well as a number of other regulatory subjects, will instantly see some of the implications of these issues.[11]

The question of allocation of power has a horizontal as well as a vertical dimension, however. Allocations can occur between institutions within a nation-state as well as between nation-states, and within international organizations as well as between international organizations. For example, an important allocation is often confronted between judicial-type institutions and legislatures or executives. At the international level and particularly the WTO, the question is raised as to the appropriate role of the dispute settlement processes compared to negotiations, as was mentioned above in Part II.

In this context it is also useful to consider the role of the United States in world affairs today, where it is viewed as the most dominant and powerful of the nation-states. It is remarkable (although predictable) how much resentment there is in the world against U.S. power and "hegemony", and how this plays in various spheres of diplomacy, not just in military spheres but also in economic ones, such as in the corridors of the WTO. Among things troubling other parts of the world about U.S. "leadership" is the perception that U.S. democratic governmental institutions are deeply flawed, with emphasis on election finance

10. John H. Jackson, The Great 1994 Sovereignty Debate: United States Acceptance and Implementation of the Uruguay Round Results, 36 Colum.J.Transnatl.L. 157 (1997); John H. Jackson, Status of Treaties in Domestic Legal Systems: A Policy Analysis, 86 Am.J.Intl.L. 310 (1992).

11. See John H. Jackson, Global Economics and International Economic Law, 1 J.Intl.Econ.L. 1, 12 ff (1998).

scandals and a catering to "well-paying" constituent groups. Thus, we hear the allegation that the U.S. leadership and power is exercised in its trade policy so as to promote the interests of corporate America or special interests such as affluent environmentalists or insecure labor union leaders, while poorer nations of the world suffer when U.S. borders are closed to their products. These perceptions color (at least) the reactions of many developing countries to certain proposals for improving the trade and financial systems made by the U.S. (or sometimes by other industrial nations.)

* * *

Some major industrial trading nations want linkage of labor standards to the WTO structure. The vast majority of WTO members adamantly oppose that, fearing the misuse of such linkage to repel their exports. This fear is justified by unfortunate experience and empirical evidence. Then if a country like the United States wants the linkage, but proclaims its motives (and that of its citizens pushing for this end) are pure, why does not it have the responsibility for coming up with a proposal that will largely alleviate this fear of the poor countries? Why have not we seen some serious thought like that? What could be considered? Again thinking "foolishly", why not play with special burdens for a country that is found by impartial panels to have abused the link? For example, a payment of money to be used to enhance investment in the abused societies, or the utilization of provisional interim measures against the abusive trade import limits?

* * *

Environmental linkage to the WTO is a much more complex issue, since there are so many different environmental problems and measures which have different effects. A stronger case can be made for linkage, but again there is potential for abuse to use environmental policies to keep out imports for protectionist reasons. Indeed, some of the environmental groups' strident criticisms of the WTO panel and appellate reports on environmental measures studiously ignore the role such abuse can and sometimes does play. Could remedies for such abuse be similar to those suggested above for labor standards linkage abuses? Could structure be set up to have an environmental advisory expert panel comment on each case in the WTO which must balance environmental policies with trade policies? Is this an added role for the WTO Committee on Trade and Environment? Or the Trade Policy Review Mechanism?

* * *

Finally, this leads us to notice that one of the major structural problems of the WTO is clearly its constitutional constraints on decision making, including the awkward "consensus" rules. The constraints, designed to protect "sovereignty" but bluntly applied, have resulted in major impasse situations such as that experienced in the selection of a new Director General, and in the attempt to achieve some reforms of the dispute settlement process, including reforms to promote greater transparency and participation. Some rethinking of the decision-making procedures seems in order.[12]

The crucial question, therefore, is whether the existing international economic institutions can evolve through intelligent discourse, some trial and error, and a sense of conservative need to preserve what is good about them. The alternatives could be much worse.

12. See John H. Jackson, Dispute Settlement and the WTO: Emerging Problems, 1 J.Intl.Econ.L. 329 (1998).

Chapter 27

THE DOHA MINISTERIAL CONFERENCE

As this volume went to press, ministers of WTO members met at Doha, Qatar, and took several important decisions. Most significantly, the Doha Ministerial Declaration established a broad work program for the WTO. In addition, several other important actions were taken: (i) the adoption of a declaration on the relationship of the TRIPS Agreement and public health; (ii) the admission of the People's Republic of China and Chinese Taipei as members of the WTO; and (iii) a waiver for the EC–ACP Cotonou Agreement, which should ultimately result in a solution to the longstanding *Bananas* dispute involving the EC and many other countries. There was also a decision on implementation issues and concerns of developing countries, which is related to the work program mentioned above.

Following the failure of the Seattle ministerial in late 1999, it was felt by many knowledgeable observers that the WTO badly needed a successful ministerial at Doha, so as to avoid trade policy negotiating activity becoming more and more the preserve of regional arrangements. From that standpoint, the Doha ministerial was a success. The actions at Doha lay out a work program including negotiations on a broad range of subjects. Ultimately, of course, success will be judged in light of the results of the negotiations, but for the moment, it seems clear that the WTO will remain the main locus of trade negotiations for the foreseeable future.

SECTION 27.1 THE MINISTERIAL DECLARATION

(A) GENERAL

The Doha Ministerial Declaration, adopted on November 14, 2001 (WTO Document WT/MIN(01)/DEC/1, dated Nov. 20, 2001), consisted of several general statements, followed by a detailed work program. In the declaration's general statements, WTO members reiterated themes found in the preamble to the WTO Agreement and in prior ministerial declarations at Singapore and Geneva. In particular, they stressed the importance of ensuring that developing countries, and especially the least developed countries among them, secure a share in the growth of world trade commensurate with the needs of their economic development (paras. 2–3, see also paras. 38–44, 50). See generally Chapter 25 supra.

In respect of the environment, the ministers noted their conviction "that the aims of upholding and safeguarding an open and non-discriminatory multilateral trading system, and acting for the protection of the environment and the promotion of sustainable development can and must be mutually supportive." In this regard, they stated that "under WTO rules no country should be prevented from taking [WTO consistent] measures for the protection of human, animal or plant life or health, or of the environment at the levels it considers appropriate, subject to the requirement that they are not applied in a manner which would constitute a means of arbitrary or unjustifiable discrimination between countries where the same conditions prevail or a disguised restriction on international trade" (para. 6; see also paras. 31–33, 51). See generally Chapters 12, 13 and 21.2 supra.

In respect of labor standards, they reaffirmed their Singapore Declaration regarding internationally recognized core labor standards (see Section 21.4 supra) and took note of work underway in the International Labor Organization on the social dimension of globalization. Proposals for additional work in the WTO on labor standards were not adopted (para. 8).

(B) THE WORK PROGRAM (DOHA DEVELOPMENT AGENDA)

The Doha Ministerial Declaration lays out a broad and ambitious "work program" for the WTO. Interestingly, the term "round", which figured so prominently in GATT times was not used in Doha to describe the forthcoming negotiations. Instead, Director–General Moore has referred to the negotiations as the "Doha Development Agenda" (which others have shortened that to the "DDA"), reflecting the strong emphasis in the Declaration on the importance of promoting development. It would not be surprising, however, if past usage prevails and references to the Doha Round become common.

The negotiations called for in the work program are to be completed by January 1, 2005, and are to be supervised by a Trade Negotiations Committee (TNC) operating under the authority of the General Council. With the exception of improvements and clarifications to be made to the Dispute Settlement Understanding (to be agreed by May 2003), the outcome of the negotiations shall be treated as a single undertaking (paras. 30, 45–47). Among the topics for negotiations are a continuation of the services market access negotiations started in 2000; the reduction of industrial tariffs (including tariff peaks, high tariffs and tariff escalation); WTO rules on dumping, subsidies and regional trade agreements; and the continuation of the work program on electronic commerce.

Reaching agreement on the treatment of a number of topics proved difficult. Among those topics were (i) implementation issues; (ii) agriculture; (iii) intellectual property; (iv) the so-called Singapore issues and (v) the environment. These topics are dealt with in the following paragraphs.

The so-called implementation-related issues and concerns are listed in a separate ministerial decision and consist of matters that developing countries wish to be discussed. These matters range from concerns over WTO dispute settlement decisions (e.g., in the balance of payments area) to desires for longer transitional periods. To the extent that these matters do not fall within any of the more specific negotiating mandates, they will be considered in the regular WTO committees, which are to report to the TNC by the end of 2002 for appropriate action.

One of the more difficult areas for reaching agreement was agriculture. Negotiations on agriculture started, as required by the Agreement on Agriculture, at the beginning of 2000. The question was what sort of commitment would members make at Doha as to the ultimate aim of the negotiations. The Cairns Group of agricultural exporting countries wanted a commitment to the phasing out of export subsidies, something difficult for the EC (and particularly France) to agree to in advance. Ultimately, the work program called for "reductions of, with a view to phasing out, all forms of export subsidies" (para. 13).

In respect of intellectual property, the key issue was the relationship of the TRIPS Agreement to public health, which was addressed in a separate declaration discussed in Section 27.2 infra. In addition, it was agreed to negotiate the establishment of a registration system for geographical indications of wines and spirits. A number of other topics are supposed to be examined by the TRIPS Council, including the relationship of the TRIPS Agreement to the Convention on Biodiversity, the protection of traditional knowledge and folklore; a review of TRIPS article 27.3(b); and the review of the TRIPS Agreement under TRIPS article 71.

The so-called Singapore issues principally concern competition, investment and transparency in government procurement. The EC was particularly desirous of having negotiations on competition and investment rules in the WTO. The US was willing to go along with the EC, but such negotiations were opposed by a number of developing countries, particularly India. In the end, the declaration provides that with respect to these three topics and the general issue of trade facilitation "negotiations will take place after the Fifth Session of the Ministerial Conference on the basis of a decision to be taken, by explicit consensus, at that Session on modalities of negotiation" (paras. 20, 23, 26 and 27). India's view is that such negotiations are still subject to an agreement on modalities that may or may not be reached at the next ministerial conference.

In that regard, the Chairman of the Ministerial Conference stated, immediately prior to the adoption of the Declaration:

"I would like to note that some delegations have requested clarification concerning Paragraphs 20, 23, 26 and 27 of the draft declaration. Let me say that with respect to the reference to an 'explicit consensus' being needed, in these paragraphs, for a decision to be taken at the Fifth Session of the Ministerial Conference, *my understanding* is that, at that session, a decision would indeed need to be taken by explicit consensus, before negotiations on trade and investment and trade and competition policy, transparency in government procurement, and trade facilitation could proceed.

In my view, this would also give each member the right to take a position on modalities that would prevent negotiations from proceeding after the Fifth Session of the Ministerial Conference until that member is prepared to join in an explicit consensus." (emphasis added)

It may be noteworthy that the Chairman only expressed personal views; there was no statement that the declaration was being adopted on the basis of those views or that there was an understanding that those views were shared by the conference. Nonetheless, it seems clear that an additional consensus decision, albeit in theory only on the modalities of the negotiations, must be taken before the negotiations will proceed.

In respect of the environment, it was agreed to have negotiations (without prejudging their outcome) on (i) the relationship between WTO rules and specific trade obligations set out in multilateral environmental agreements (MEAs) to which WTO members belong; (ii) information exchanges between MEA secretariats and the relevant WTO committees; and (iii) reductions on tariffs and non-tariffs barriers to environmental goods and services. The Committee on Trade and Environment was directed to give particular attention to (i) the effect of environmental measures on market access; (ii) the relevant provisions of the TRIPS Agreement; and (iii) labeling requirements for environmental purposes.

Although the issues dealt with in the declaration have, for the most part, been under consideration in WTO bodies since the 1998–1999 preparations for the failed Seattle ministerial, it took great effort to reach agreement on the text of the declaration. For the most part, the final text follows a text proposed shortly in advance of the meeting by the chair of the General Council and the Director–General (referred to as the "Harbinson" text, as Stuart Harbinson of Hong Kong was the chair of the General Council). Given that the declaration is for the most part only an agenda for negotiations, it may be expected that the actual negotiations will be even more difficult.

It is probably not all that useful to speculate on the winners and losers at Doha, particularly since little of substance was agreed. Nonetheless, it may be worth mentioning that the EC achieved at least in part its desire to have a broad round of negotiations. While only the negotiations on the environment will start immediately, there is at least a commitment by the ministers to start negotiations on competition and investment in a couple of years. To achieve that, the EC had to agree to the stated goal of phasing out agricultural export subsidies, but it committed to no date in that respect.

For the United States, it had hoped to avoid any negotiations on antidumping rules, but the existence of such negotiations does not mean that the rules will be changed significantly, especially given the support that the current rules have in the U.S. Congress.

SECTION 27.2   TRIPS AND PUBLIC HEALTH

One of the more controversial issues in the preparations for the Doha conference was what, if anything, should the ministers say about the relationship of the TRIPS Agreement to public health. This has become a major issue in the developing world, where there are concerns that pharmaceutical companies are exercising their patent rights on drugs in a way that effectively makes those drugs unavailable to any significant degree in developing countries. In particular, there has been concern about the availability of drugs to fight AIDS, particularly in Africa.

The declaration adopted by ministers provides:

1.   We recognize the gravity of the public health problems afflicting many developing and least-developed countries, especially those resulting from HIV/AIDS, tuberculosis, malaria and other epidemics.

2.   We stress the need for the WTO Agreement on Trade–Related Aspects of Intellectual Property Rights (TRIPS Agreement) to be part of the wider national and international action to address these problems.

3.   We recognize that intellectual property protection is important for the development of new medicines. We also recognize the concerns about its effects on prices.

4.   We agree that the TRIPS Agreement does not and should not prevent Members from taking measures to protect public health. Accordingly, while reiterating our commitment to the TRIPS Agreement, we affirm that the Agreement can and should be interpreted and implemented in a manner supportive of WTO Members' right to protect public health and, in particular, to promote access to medicines for all.

In this connection, we reaffirm the right of WTO Members to use, to the full, the provisions in the TRIPS Agreement, which provide flexibility for this purpose.

5.   Accordingly and in the light of paragraph 4 above, while maintaining our commitments in the TRIPS Agreement, we recognize that these flexibilities include:

— In applying the customary rules of interpretation of public international law, each provision of the TRIPS Agreement shall be read in the light of the object and purpose of the Agreement as expressed, in particular, in its objectives and principles.

— Each Member has the right to grant compulsory licences and the freedom to determine the grounds upon which such licences are granted.

— Each Member has the right to determine what constitutes a national emergency or other circumstances of extreme urgency, it being understood that public health crises, including those relating to HIV/AIDS, tuberculosis, malaria and other epidemics, can represent a national emergency or other circumstances of extreme urgency.

— The effect of the provisions in the TRIPS Agreement that are relevant to the exhaustion of intellectual property rights is to leave each Member free to establish its own regime for such exhaustion without challenge, subject to the MFN and national treatment provisions of Articles 3 and 4.

6.   We recognize that WTO Members with insufficient or no manufacturing capacities in the pharmaceutical sector could face difficulties in making effective use of compulsory licensing under the TRIPS Agreement. We instruct the Council for TRIPS to find an expeditious solution to this problem and to report to the General Council before the end of 2002.

7.   We reaffirm the commitment of developed-country Members to provide incentives to their enterprises and institutions to promote and encourage technology transfer to least-developed country Members pursuant to Article 66.2. We also agree that the least-developed country Members will not be obliged, with respect to pharmaceutical products, to implement or apply Sections 5 and 7 of Part II of the TRIPS Agreement or to enforce rights provided for under these Sections until 1 January 2016, without prejudice to the right of least-developed country Members to seek other extensions of the transition periods as provided for in Article 66.1 of the TRIPS Agreement. We instruct the Council for TRIPS to take the necessary action to give effect to this pursuant to Article 66.1 of the TRIPS Agreement.

Notes and Questions

(1) In adopting this declaration, the ministers made no reference to the basis for their action. In those circumstances, is it possible to argue that the declaration is, at least in part, an "interpretation" of the TRIPS Agreement pursuant to Article IX of the WTO Agreement? If not, then to what extent is the declaration relevant in the interpretation of the TRIPS Agreement in dispute settlement proceedings? Is the Vienna Convention on the Law of Treaties (VCLT) helpful in answering this question? See Section 5.2 supra. In particular, could this be viewed as a "subsequent agreement between the parties regarding the interpretation of the treaty or application of its provisions" (see VCLT, art. 31(3)(a))? Or is Article IX the exclusive means of

interpretation of the WTO Agreement by WTO members? What is the relevance of VCLT, art. 31(3)(b), on "subsequent practice"? In *Japan— Alcohol Taxes*, the Appellate Body said that a decision adopting a panel report does not create "subsequent practice", but what about a consensus decision by the WTO's highest governing body?

(2) Note that the DSU applies only to "disputes brought pursuant to the consultation and dispute settlement provisions of the [covered] agreements," as defined in DSU, art. 1(1). Is this relevant to whether the declaration can be used in interpretation of the TRIPS Agreement? Would it be relevant if a ministerial declaration purported to establish an obligation on the part of WTO members?

(3) Under the terms of the declaration, could a developing country X invoke its right to use compulsory licensing and appoint a manufacturer in another country Y to produce drugs for sale in X. What does paragraph 6 of the declaration suggest?

(4) Overall, would you say that developing countries have adequate discretion under the TRIPS Agreement, in light of this declaration, to address serious health problems such as AIDS? What about other diseases?

SECTION 27.3   ACCESSION OF CHINA AND CHINESE TAIPEI

During the Doha ministerial, the admission of the People's Republic of China to the WTO was approved, and one day later, so was the admission of the Separate Customs Territory of Taiwan, Penghu, Kinmen and Matsu (to be known in the WTO as Chinese Taipei). The signing ceremony for China occurred immediately after the approval of the admission of Chinese Taipei, and at that ceremony China announced that it would immediately deposit its formal acceptance of the WTO Agreement. As such, Chinese membership became effective on December 11, 2001. Chinese Taipei's membership became effective on January 1, 2002. The WTO will then have 144 members.

The United States did not invoke the non-application provisions of Article XIII of the WTO Agreement prior to approval of the Chinese accession; only El Salvador did so.

SECTION 27.4   WAIVER FOR EC– ACP COTONOU AGREEMENT

The ministers also two waivers requested by the EC with respect to its relationship with the so-called ACP [African, Caribbean, Pacific] countries. The first one waives the application of GATT Article I:1 to the extent necessary to permit the EC to provide preferential tariff treatment to ACP countries as required by specified provisions of the ACP–EC Partnership Agreement (known as the Cotonou Agreement). WT/MIN(01)/15 (November 14, 2001). The waiver extends until December 31, 2007, at which point the EC and the ACP countries are expected to start the implementation of a free trade area. The waiver includes an annex dealing with bananas and the process (including possible arbitration) pursuant to which the EC will rebind its banana tariffs in implementing a tariff-only regime for bananas.

The second waiver waives the application of GATT Article XIII:1 & 2 with respect to the EC's imports of bananas from ACP countries (up to 750,000 tons annually) until December 31, 2005, at which time the EC's tariff-only regime for bananas is expected to come into effect. WT/MIN(01)/16 (November 14, 2001).

These actions will hopefully put an end to the dispute over the EC's bananas regime, which has been the subject of five GATT/WTO panel reports (three unadopted) and two "retaliation" arbitrations under DSU article 22.6.

Index

References are to Pages

INDUSTRIAL POLICY, 24–31

INDUSTRY
Definition of Domestic (Escape Clause, etc.), 611–616, 730–736
Infant Industry Argument, 22

INHERENT POWERS
See President (U.S.) and Presidency

INJURY, 616–623, 724–766
See also Countervailing Duties, Dumping; Escape Clause; Market Disruption; Section 301; Section 337 Procedure; Subsidies
Analysis of, 746–766
Commercial Policy Analysis System (COMPAS), 754
Industry Definition, 730–736
Like Products, 730–736
Material Injury, 737–766
Interpretation of, 737–746
Multiple Producers, 748–749
"Serious Injury", 616–623
U.S. Law, Injury in, 724–729
WTO and, 727–729

INSURANCE
C.I.F., 49–50
Trade in Services, Example of, 912–920

INTELLECTUAL PROPERTY, 921–996
Berne Convention, 961, 963, 965–966
Copyright, 923–924, 935–942, 963
Gray–Market Goods, 942–951
International Agreements on, 960–996
History of, 960–962
International Dimension, 925–927
Paris Convention, 961, 966
Patents, 921–923, 941, 964
Policies, 921–925
Rights, Types of, 921–925
Section 337, 485–494, 951–960
Trademarks, 924, 927–935, 942–951, 963–964
Trade–Related Aspects of Intellectual Property (TRIPS), Uruguay Round Agreement on, 210, 964–996
Dispute Settlement, 968–996
Exceptions to, 968–996
NAFTA, Similarity to, 965
Uruguay Round Negotiations, 962–963
Trade Secrets, 924–925
U.S. Law, Extraterritorial Application of, 927–942
Uruguay Round Negotiations, 962–964

INTERDEPENDENCE, ECONOMIC, 1–2, 724–726

INTERFACE, 402–403, 678–680

INTERGOVERNMENTAL POLICY ADVISORY COMMITTEE (IGPAC), 137–139

INTERNAL CHARGES
See Taxes

INTERNAL REVENUE CODE
See Taxes

INTERNAL SALE, MEASURES AFFECTING
See National Treatment Obligation

INTERNAL TAXES
See Taxes

INTERNATIONAL AGREEMENTS, 181–184
In EC Law, 162–165
In Japanese Law, 169
In United States Domestic Law, 90–105, 238–245

INTERNATIONAL BANK FOR RECONSTRUCTION AND DEVELOPMENT (IBRD or WORLD BANK), 200

INTERNATIONAL CHAMBER OF COMMERCE (ICC), 52

INTERNATIONAL COURT OF JUSTICE (ICJ), 178, 189

INTERNATIONAL ECONOMIC LAW & RELATIONS, 193–199
Policies of Int'l Economic Relations, 7–39

INTERNATIONAL ECONOMIC POLICY, 7–37
Political Goals of, 37–39
Role of U.S., EU, and Quad in Formulation of, 140–141
See also General Agreement on Tariffs and Trade (GATT); Quotas; Tariff and Trade Negotiations and Conferences

INTERNATIONAL INSTITUTE FOR THE UNIFICATION OF PRIVATE LAW (UNIDROIT), 46 n.2

INTERNATIONAL INSTITUTIONS, 199–200
See also Dispute Settlement; also named International Organizations

INTERNATIONAL LABOR ORGANIZATION (ILO), 1027–1028, 1033–1034, 1036–1040, 1043

INTERNATIONAL LIQUIDITY
See International Monetary Fund

INTERNATIONAL MONETARY FUND (IMF), 199–207, 1067–1094
See also Exchange Rates; Monetary Affairs and Trade Policy
Compensatory Financing Facility (CFF), 1070
Conditionality, 1070–1079
Contingent Credit Lines (CCL), 1070
Coordination with WTO/GATT, 1105–1106
Council, 202–203
Executive Directors, 203–205

†